International Management

Culture, Strategy, and Behavior

Ninth Edition

Fred Luthans
University of Nebraska–Lincoln

Jonathan P. Doh
Villanova University

Mc
Graw
Hill
Education

INTERNATIONAL MANAGEMENT: CULTURE, STRATEGY, AND BEHAVIOR,
NINTH EDITION
International Edition 2015

10 09 08 07 06 05 04 03
20 19 18 17 16
CTP   MPM

When ordering this title, use ISBN 978-981-4577-29-8 or MHID 978-981-4577-29-4

The Internet addresses listed in the text were accurate at the time of publication. The inclusion of a
website does not indicate an endorsement by the authors or McGraw-Hill Education, and McGraw-Hill
Education does not guarantee the accuracy of the information presented at these sites.

Printed in Singapore

www.mhhe.com

Dedicated in Memory of

Richard M. Hodgetts
A Pioneer in International Management Education

Preface

Changes in the global business environment continue at a rapid and often unpredictable pace. The global financial crisis and economic recession of 2008–2010 have given way to destabilizing political changes in many regions of the world, especially North Africa and the Middle East (see Chapter 2 opening article). In addition, rapid advances in social media have not only accelerated globalization but also provided a means for those who seek political and economic changes to organize and influence their leaders for more responsible governance (see Chapter 1 opening article). In addition, concerns about the exhaustion of finite resources and the need to pursue more sustainable growth have prompted governments, companies, and NGOs to consider alternate approaches to business and governance (see Chapter 3 opening article).

Some of these developments have challenged assumptions about globalization and economic integration, but they also underscore the inexorably interconnected nature of global economies. Although many countries and regions around the world are closely and inextricably linked, important differences in institutional and cultural environments persist, and some of these differences have become even starker in recent years. The challenges for international management reflect this dynamism and the increasing unpredictability of global economic and political events. Continued growth of the emerging markets is reshaping the global balance of economic power, even though differences exist between and among regions and countries. Although many emerging markets continued to experience growth during a period when developed countries' economies stagnated or declined, some developed economies bucked this trend and some developing countries did not share in what was otherwise a dynamic period for the emerging world.

The global political and security environment remains unpredictable and volatile, with ongoing conflicts in the Middle East and Africa and continuing tensions in Iran, North Korea, Iraq, and Afghanistan. On the economic front, although little progress was made in the efforts to conclude a global multilateral agreement under the World Trade Organization (WTO), regional and bilateral agreements have proliferated, including the Trans-Pacific Partnership (TPP), a proposed free-trade agreement that would involve more than a dozen countries in the Americas and Asia. In addition, the tragic fire, building collapse, and other industrial accidents in India, Bangladesh, and China have renewed calls for corporations to do more to protect workers and for governments to get tougher with companies in terms of oversight and accountability. (See Chapter 3 for additional discussion.)

As noted above, the advent of social networking has transformed the way citizens interact, how businesses market, promote, and distribute their products globally, and how civil society expresses its concerns that governments provide greater freedoms and accountability. Concurrently, companies, individuals, and even students can now engage in broad "mass" collaboration through digital, online technology for the development of new and innovative systems, products, and ideas. Both social networking and mass collaboration bring new power and influence to individuals across borders and transform the nature of their relationships with global organizations. Although globalization and technology continue to link nations, businesses, and individuals, these connections also highlight the importance of understanding different cultures, national systems, and corporate management practices around the world. The world is now interconnected geographically, but also electronically and psychologically; as such, nearly all businesses have been touched in some way by globalization. Yet, as cultural, political, and economic differences persist, astute international managers must be in a position to adapt and adjust to the vagaries of different contexts and environments.

v

In this new ninth edition of International Management, we have retained the strong and effective foundations gained from research and practice over the past decades while incorporating the important latest research and contemporary insights that have changed the context and environment for international management. Several trends have emerged that pose both challenges and opportunities for international managers.

First, emerging markets continue to rise in importance, with dynamic growth and development in many emerging regions and countries. This includes the emergence of multinationals from emerging markets that are becoming globally competitive. Second, pressure for greater social and environmental responsibility among multinational organizations has increased, especially in light of rising pollution and the exposure of poor working conditions in many factories around the world. Third, the importance of cultural differences continues to be an omnipresent reality for international managers. And social media and other forms of electronic connectivity continue to facilitate international business of all sorts.

Although we have extensive new, evidence-based material in this edition, we continue to strive to make the book even more user-friendly and applicable to practice. We continue to take a balanced approach in the ninth edition of *International Management: Culture, Strategy, and Behavior*. Whereas other texts stress culture, strategy, or behavior, our emphasis on all three critical dimensions—and the interactions among them—has been a primary reason why the previous editions have been the market-leading international management text. Specifically, this edition has the following chapter distribution: environment (three chapters), culture (four chapters), strategy (four chapters), and organizational behavior/human resource management (three chapters). Because the context of international management changes rapidly, all the chapters have been updated and improved. New real-world examples and research results are integrated throughout the book, accentuating the experiential relevance of the straightforward content. As always, we emphasize a balance of research and application.

For the new ninth edition we have incorporated important new content in the areas of sustainability and sustainable management practices, the emergence and role of social media as a means of transacting business around the world, the rise of emerging market multinationals and the challenges they pose for developed country MNCs, and other important developments in the international management field. Many of these topics—such as social media—are integrated throughout the book, as they touch on—and influence—many aspects of international management. We have incorporated the latest research and practical insights on pressure for MNCs to adopt more sustainable practices, and the strategies many companies are using to differentiate their products through such "green" management practices. We have updated discussion of a range of contemporary topics, including continued exploration of the role of the comprehensive GLOBE study on cross-cultural leadership.

A continuing and relevant end-of-chapter feature in this edition is the "Internet Exercise." The purpose of each exercise is to encourage students to use the Internet to find information from the websites of prominent MNCs to answer relevant questions about the chapter topic. An end-of-book feature is a series of Skill-Building and Experiential Exercises for aspiring international managers. These in-class exercises represent the various parts of the text (culture, strategy, and behavior) and provide hands-on experience.

We have extended from the eighth edition of International Management the chapter-opening discussions called "The World of International Management" (WIM) based on very recent, relevant news stories to grab readers' interest and attention. Many of these opening articles are new to this edition and all have been updated. These timely opening discussions transition the reader into the chapter topic. At the end of each chapter, there is a pedagogical feature that recapitulates the chapter's subject matter: "The World of International Management—Revisited." Here we pose several discussion questions based on the topic of the opening feature in light of the student's entire reading of the chapter. Answering these questions requires readers to reconsider and to draw from the chapter material. Suggested answers to these "WIM—Revisited" discussion questions appear in the completely updated Instructor's Manual, where we also provide some multiple-choice and true-false questions that draw directly from the chapters' World of International Management topic matter for instructors who want to include this material in their tests.

The use and application of cases is further enhanced in this edition. All cases have been updated and several new ones have been added. The short within-chapter country case illustrations—"In the International Spotlight"—can be read and discussed in class. These have all been revised and two have been added—Turkey and Indonesia. The revised or newly added "Integrative Cases" positioned at the end of each main part of the text were created exclusively for this edition and provide opportunities for reading and analysis outside of class. Review questions provided for each case are intended to facilitate lively and productive written analysis or in-class discussion. Our "Brief Integrative Cases" typically explore a specific situation or challenge facing an individual or team. Our longer and more detailed "In-Depth Integrative Cases" provide a broader discussion of the challenges facing a company. These two formats allow maximum flexibility so that instructors can use the cases in a tailored and customized fashion. Accompanying many of the in-depth cases are short exercises that can be used in class to reinforce both the substantive topic and students' skills in negotiation, presentation, and analysis. The cases have been extensively updated and several are new to this edition. Cases concerning the global AIDS epidemic, Dansko, Russell Athletics/Fruit of the Loom, Euro Disneyland and Disney Asia, Google in China, IKEA, HSBC, Nike, Walmart, Tata, AirAsia, Sony, Danone, Chiquita, Coca-Cola, and others are unique to this book and specific to this edition. Of course, instructors also have access to Create (www.mcgraw-hillcreate.com), McGraw-Hill's extensive content database, which includes thousands of cases from major sources such as Harvard Business School, Ivey, Darden, and NACRA case databases.

Along with the new or updated "International Management in Action" boxed application examples within each chapter and other pedagogical features at the end of each chapter (i.e., "Key Terms," "Review and Discussion Questions," "The World of International Management—Revisited," and "Internet Exercise"), the end-of-part brief and in-depth cases and the end-of-book skill-building exercises and simulations on the Online Learning Center complete the package.

To help instructors teach international management, this text is accompanied by a revised and expanded Instructor's Resource Manual, Test Bank, and PowerPoint Slides, all of which are available password protected on the Online Learning Center at www. mhhe.com/luthans9e.

Another important innovation is carried over and updated from the 8th edition: we have provided instructors with a guide to online publicly available videos, many available on YouTube, that link directly to chapter themes. These short clips give instructors an opportunity to use online visual media in conjunction with traditional lecture, discussion, and PowerPoint presentations. Our guide includes the name, short description, and link for the videos, which we will keep updated on the book website.

International Management is generally recognized to be the first "mainstream" text of its kind. Strategy casebooks and specialized books in organizational behavior, human resources, and, of course, international business, finance, marketing, and economics preceded it, but there were no international management texts before this one, and it remains the market leader. We have had sustainability because of the effort and care put into the revisions. We hope you agree that this ninth edition continues the tradition and remains the "world-class" text for the study of international management.

like to give special recognition to two international management scholars: Henry H. Albers, former Chair of the Management Department at the University of Nebraska and former Dean at the University of Petroleum and Minerals, Saudi Arabia, to whom previous editions of this book were dedicated; and Sang M. Lee, former Chair of the Management Department at Nebraska, founding and current President of the Pan Pacific Business Association, and close colleague on many ventures around the world over the past 30 years. Jonathan Doh would like to thank the Villanova School of Business and its leadership, especially Dean Pat Maggitti, Vice Dean Daniel Wright, and Herb Rammrath who generously endowed the Chair in International Business Jonathan now holds. Also, for this new ninth edition we would like to thank Ben Littell, who did much of the research and drafting of the chapter opening World of International Management features and provided extensive research assistance for other revisions to the book.

In addition, we would like to acknowledge the help that we received from the many reviewers from around the globe, whose feedback guided us in preparing the ninth edition of the text. These include:

Thomas M. Abbott, Post University
David Elloy, Gonzaga University
James Gran, Buena Vista University
Julie Huang, Rio Hondo College

Jae C. Jung, University of Missouri–Kansas City
Emeric Solymossy, Western Illinois University.

Our thanks, too, to the reviewers of previous editions of the text:

Yohannan T. Abraham, Southwest Missouri State University
Janet S. Adams, Kennesaw State University
Irfan Ahmed, Sam Houston State University
Chi Anyansi-Archibong, North Carolina A&T State University
Kibok Baik, James Madison University
R. B. Barton, Murray State University
Lawrence A. Beer, Arizona State University
Koren Borges, University of North Florida
Tope A. Bello, East Carolina University
Mauritz Blonder, Hofstra University
Gunther S. Boroschek, University of Massachusetts–Boston
Charles M. Byles, Virginia Commonwealth University
Constance Campbell, Georgia Southern University
Scott Kenneth Campbell, Georgia College & State University
M. Suzanne Clinton, University of Central Oklahoma
Helen Deresky, SUNY Plattsburgh
Dr. Dharma deSilva, Center for International Business Advancement (CIBA)
Val Finnigan, Leeds Metropolitan University
David M. Flynn, Hofstra University
Jan Flynn, Georgia College and State University

Joseph Richard Goldman, University of Minnesota
Robert T. Green, University of Texas at Austin
Annette Gunter, University of Central Oklahoma
Jerry Haar, Florida International University–Miami
Jean M. Hanebury, Salisbury State University
Richard C. Hoffman, Salisbury State University
Johan Hough, University of South Africa
Steve Jenner, California State University–Dominguez Hills
James P. Johnson, Rollins College
Marjorie Jones, Nova Southeastern University
Ann Langlois, Palm Beach Atlantic University
Curtis Matherne III, East Tennessee State University
Alan N. Miller, University of Nevada, Las Vegas
Mohd Nazari Ismail, University of Malaya
Robert Kuhne, Hofstra University
Christine Lentz, Rider University
Ben Lever III, College of Charleston
Robert C. Maddox, University of Tennessee

Douglas M. McCabe, Georgetown University

Jeanne M. McNett, Assumption College

Lauryn Migenes, University of Central Florida

Ray Montagno, Ball State University

Rebecca J. Morris, University of Nebraska–Omaha

Ernst W. Neuland, University of Pretoria

William Newburry, Rutgers Business School

Yongsun Paik, Loyola Marymount University

Valerie S. Perotti, Rochester Institute of Technology

Richard B. Peterson, University of Washington

Suzanne J. Peterson, University of Nebraska–Lincoln

Joseph A. Petrick, Wright State University

Juan F. Ramirez, Nova Southeastern University

Richard David Ramsey, Southeastern Louisiana University

Mansour Sharif-Zadeh, California State Polytechnic University–Pomona

Owen Sevier, University of Central Oklahoma

Jane H. Standford, Texas A&M University–Kingsville

Dale V. Steinmann, San Francisco State University

Randall Stross, San Jose State University

George Sutija, Florida International University

Deanna Teel, Houston Community College

David Turnipseed, University of South Alabama–Mobile

Katheryn H. Ward, Chicago State University

Li Weixing, University of Nebraska–Lincoln

Aimee Wheaton, Regis College

Timothy Wilkinson, University of Akron

Marion M. White, James Madison University

George Yacus, Old Dominion University

Corinne Young, University of Tampa

Zhe Zhang, University of Central Florida–Orlando

Anatoly Zhuplev, Loyola Marymount University

Finally, thanks to the team at McGraw-Hill who worked on this book: Paul Ducham, Managing Director; Anke Weekes, Senior Brand Manager; Kelly Delso, Senior Developmental Editor; Lori Bradshaw, Managing Developmental Editor; Michael Gedatus, Marketing Manager; and Jessica Portz, Project Manager. Last but by no means least, we greatly appreciate the love and support provided by our families.

Fred Luthans and Jonathan P. Doh

LUTHANS   DOH

The ninth edition of *International Management: Culture, Strategy, and Behavior* is still setting the standard. Current authors Fred Luthans and Jonathan P. Doh have taken care to retain the effective foundation gained from research and practice over the past decades. At the same time, they have fully incorporated important new and emerging developments that have changed what international managers are currently facing and likely to face in the coming years.

x

New and Enhanced Themes

- Thoroughly revised and updated chapters to reflect the most critical issues for international managers.
- Greater attention to and focus on global sustainability and sustainable management practices and their impact on international management.
- New or revised opening World of International Management features written by the authors on current international management challenges; these mini-cases were prepared expressly for this edition and are not available elsewhere.
- Discussions of the impact of the global economic recession on international management in the opening chapter and throughout the book, and the aftermath and ongoing challenges associated with the "Arab Spring" (in Chapter 2).
- New and updated discussions of project GLOBE and its importance for international management.
- Greater emphasis on emerging markets and developing countries, and the increasing influence of emerging markets multinationals on global competition.

Thoroughly Revised and Updated Chapter Content

- New or revised opening WIM discussions on topics including the global influences of social media, the role of social networking in the Arab Spring, sustainability as a global competitive advantage, Apple vs. Samsung, Amazon vs. Alibaba, global trends in the automotive and pharmaceutical industries, managing global teams, offshoring and culture, and many other subjects. These features were written expressly for this edition and are not available elsewhere.
- Updated and strengthened emphasis on ethics, social responsibility, and sustainability.
- Extensive coverage of Project GLOBE, its relationship to other cultural frameworks, and its application to international management practice (Chapters 4, 13).
- Revised or new "In the International Spotlight" inserts which profile the key economic and political issues relevant to managers in specific countries, including new spotlights on Turkey and Indonesia.
- Greater coverage of the challenges and opportunities for international strategy targeted to the developing "base of the pyramid" economies (Chapter 8, and Tata cases).

Thoroughly Updated and/or New Cases, Inserts, and Exercises

- New and/or updated country spotlights, "International Management in Action" features.
- Thoroughly updated cases (not available elsewhere): *Pharmaceutical Companies, Intellectual Property, and the Global AIDS Epidemic; Advertising or Free Speech? The Case of Nike and Human Rights; Beyond Tokyo: Disney's Expansion In Asia; HSBC in China; Coca Cola in India; Walmart's Global Strategies; Can Sony Regain its Innovative Edge? The OLED Project; Tata "Nano": The People's Car; The Ascendance of AirAsia: Building a Successful Budget Airline;* and *Chiquita's Global Turnaround.*
- Brand new end-of-part cases developed exclusively for this edition (not available elsewhere): *Dansko puts its Right Foot Forward, Google in China: Protecting Property and Rights; IKEA's Global Renovations.*

Totally Revised Instructor and Student Support

The following instructor and student support materials can be found on the Online Learning Center (OLC) for the Ninth Edition. You can access the OLC at www.mhhe.com/luthans9e.

- The Instructor's Manual offers a summary of Learning Objectives and teaching outline with lecture notes and teaching tips, as well as suggested answers to questions found throughout and at the conclusion of each chapter. Suggested answers are also provided for all the cases found in the book.
- The TestBank is offered in both Word and EZ Test formats and offers over 1,000 test items consisting of true/false, multiple choice, and essay. Answers are provided for all testbank questions.
- PowerPoint Presentations consisting of 30 slides per chapter give instructors talking points, feature exhibits from the text, and are summarized with a review and discussion slide.
- Student Quizzes are provided for each chapter and give students feedback to help them understand where additional study is required.
- A guide to videos available online, with title, short description, and url.
- **Create:** Instructors can now tailor their teaching resources to match the way they teach! With McGraw-Hill Create, **www.mcgrawhillcreate. com**, instructors can easily rearrange chapters, combine material from other content sources, and quickly upload and integrate their own content, like course syllabi or teaching notes. Find the right content in Create by searching through thousands of leading McGraw-Hill textbooks. Arrange the material to fit your teaching style. Order a Create book and receive a complimentary print review copy in 3–5 business

days or a complimentary electronic review copy (echo) via e-mail within one hour. Go to **www.mcgrawhillcreate.com** today and register.

McGraw-Hill Campus™

McGraw-Hill Campus is a new one-stop teaching and learning experience available to users of any learning management system.

This institutional service allows faculty and students to enjoy single sign-on (SSO) access to all McGraw-Hill Higher Education materials, including the award-winning McGraw-Hill *Connect* platform, from directly within the institution's website. With McGraw-Hill Campus, faculty receive instant access to teaching materials (e.g., eText-books, test banks, PowerPoint slides, learning objectives, etc.), allowing them to browse, search, and use any instructor ancillary content in our vast library at no additional cost to instructor or students. In addition, students enjoy SSO access to a variety of free content and subscription-based products (e.g., McGraw-Hill *Connect*). With McGraw-Hill Campus enabled, faculty and students will never need to create another account to access McGraw-Hill products and services. Learn more at **www.mhcampus.com.**

Assurance of Learning Ready

Many educational institutions today focus on the notion of *assurance of learning,* an important element of some accreditation standards. *International Business* is designed specifically to support instructors' assurance of learning initiatives with a simple yet powerful solution. Each test bank question for *International Business* maps to a specific chapter learning objective listed in the text. Instructors can use our test bank software, EZ Test and EZ Test Online, to easily query for learning objectives that directly relate to the learning outcomes for their course. Instructors can then use the reporting features of EZ Test to aggregate student results in similar fashion, making the collection and presentation of assurance of learning data simple and easy.

AACSB Tagging

McGraw-Hill Education is a proud corporate member of AACSB International. Under-standing the importance and value of AACSB accreditation, *International Business* rec-ognizes the curricula guidelines detailed in the AACSB standards for business accredita-tion by connecting selected questions in the text and the test bank to the six general knowledge and skill guidelines in the AACSB standards. The statements contained in *International Business* are provided only as a guide for the users of this textbook. The AACSB leaves content coverage and assessment within the purview of individual schools, the mission of the school, and the faculty. While the *International Business* teaching package makes no claim of any specific AACSB qualification or evaluation, we have within *International Business* labeled selected questions according to the six general knowledge and skills areas.

About the Authors

FRED LUTHANS is University and the George Holmes Distinguished Professor of Management at the University of Nebraska–Lincoln. He is also Chair of the Master Research Council for HUMANeX, Inc. He received his BA, MBA, and PhD from the University of Iowa, where he received the Distinguished Alumni Award in 2002. While serving as an officer in the U.S. Army from 1965–1967, he taught leadership at the U.S. Military Academy at West Point. He has been a visiting scholar at a number of colleges and universities and has lectured in most European and Pacific Rim countries. He has taught international management as a visiting faculty member at the universities of Bangkok, Hawaii, Henley in England, Norwegian Management School, Monash in Australia, Macau, Chemnitz in the former East Germany, and Tirana in Albania. A past president of the Academy of Management, in 1997 he received the Academy's Distinguished Educator Award. In 2000 he became an inaugural member of the Academy's Hall of Fame for being one of the "Top Five" all-time published authors in the prestigious Academy journals. Currently, he is co-editor-in-chief of the *Journal of World Business,* editor of *Organizational Dynamics,* co-editor of *Journal of Leadership and Organization Studies,* and the author of numerous books. His book *Organizational Behavior* (Irwin/McGraw-Hill) is now in its 12th edition and the groundbreaking book *Psychological Capital* (Oxford University Press) with Carolyn Youssef and Bruce Avolio will be out in its second edition in 2014. He is one of very few management scholars who is a Fellow of the Academy of Management, the Decision Sciences Institute, and the Pan Pacific Business Association, and he has been a member of the Executive Committee for the Pan Pacific Conference since its beginning 30 years ago. This committee helps to organize the annual meeting held in Pacific Rim countries. He has been involved with some of the first empirical studies on motivation and behavioral management techniques and the analysis of managerial activities in Russia; these articles have been published in the *Academy of Management Journal*, *Journal of International Business Studies, Journal of World Business,* and *European Management Journal.* Since the very beginning of the transition to market economies after the fall of communism in Eastern Europe, he has been actively involved in management education programs sponsored by the U.S. Agency for International Development in Albania and Macedonia, and in U.S. Information Agency programs involving the Central Asian countries of Kazakhstan, Kyrgyzstan, and Tajikistan. For example, Professor Luthans' recent international research involves his construct of positive psychological capital (PsyCap). He and colleagues have published their research demonstrating the impact of Chinese workers' PsyCap on their performance in the *International Journal of Human Resource Management* and *Management and Organization Review.* He is applying his positive approach to positive organizational behavior (POB), PsyCap, and authentic leadership to effective global management and has recently been the keynote at programs in China (several times), Malaysia, Korea, Indonesia, England, Norway, Finland, South Africa, and soon Italy.

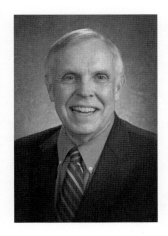

JONATHAN P. DOH is the Herbert G. Rammrath Chair in International Business, founding Director of the Center for Global Leadership, and Professor of Management at the Villanova School of Business. Jonathan teaches, does research, and serves as an executive instructor and consultant in the areas of international strategy and corporate responsibility and serves as an occasional executive educator for the Aresty Institute of Executive Education at the Wharton Business School. Previously, he was on the faculty of American and Georgetown Universities and a senior trade official with the U.S. government. Jonathan is author or co-author of more than 75 refereed articles published in the top international

business and management journals, 30 chapters in scholarly edited volumes, and more than 75 conference papers. Recent articles have appeared in journals such as *Academy of Management Review, California Management Review, Journal of International Business Studies, Journal of World Business, Organization Science, Sloan Management Review,* and *Strategic Management Journal.* He is co-editor and contributing author of *Globalization and NGOs* (Praeger, 2003) and Handbook on Responsible Leadership and *Governance in Global Business* (Elgar, 2005) and co-author of the previous edition of *International Management: Culture, Strategy, and Behavior* (8th ed., McGraw-Hill/Irwin, 2012), the best-selling international management text. His current research focus is on strategy for emerging markets, global corporate responsibility, and offshore outsourcing of services. His most recent scholarly books are *Multinationals and Development* (with Alan Rugman, Yale University Press, 2008), *NGOs and Corporations: Conflict and Collaboration* (with Michael Yaziji, Cambridge University Press, 2009) and *Aligning for Advantage: Competitive Strategy for the Social and Political Arenas* (with Tom Lawton and Tazeeb Rajwani, Oxford University Press, 2014). He is co-Editor-in-Chief of *MRN International Environment of Global Business* (SSRN Journal), Senior Editor of *Journal of World Business,* Associate Editor of *Business & Society,* and *Consulting Editor of Long Range Planning.* Beginning in January of 2015 he will assume the position of Editor-in-Chief of *Journal of World Business.* Jonathan has also developed more than a dozen original cases and simulations published in books, journals, and case databases and used at many leading global universities. He has been a consultant or executive instructor for ABB, Anglo American, Bodycote, Bosch, China Minsheng Bank, Hana Financial, HSBC, Ingersoll Rand, Medtronic, Shanghai Municipal Government, Siam Cement, the World Economic Forum, and Deloitte Touche, where he served as senior external adviser to the Global Energy Resource Group. Jonathan is part of the Executive Committee of the Academy of Management Organizations and Natural Environment Division with increasing responsibilities culminating in the chair of the division in 2016. He was ranked among the top 15 most prolific international business scholars in the world for the period 2001–2009 (Lahiri and Kumar, 2012). He holds a PhD in strategic and international management from George Washington University.

Brief Contents

Part Four   **Organizational Behavior and Human Resource Management**

Skill-Building and Experiential Exercises

Table of Contents

International Strategic Management   Part Three

Skill-Building and Experiential Exercises

In-Class Simulations (available on the Online Learning Center at www.mhhe.com/luthans9e)

PART ONE

ENVIRONMENTAL
FOUNDATION

Chapter 1

GLOBALIZATION AND INTERNATIONAL LINKAGES

Globalization is one of the most profound forces in our contemporary economic environment. And its practical impact on international management is substantial. In nearly every country, increasing numbers of large, medium, and even small corporations are going international, and a growing percentage of company revenue is derived from overseas markets. This is even true for U.S.-based companies that historically have relied on the large domestic market. Yet, the reverberations of the financial crisis and global economic recession, and continued economic and political uncertainties in many world regions present challenges for governments, corporations, and communities around the world, causing some to question the current system for regulating and overseeing international trade, investments, and global financial flows. Nonetheless, international management—the process of applying management concepts and techniques in a multinational environment—continues to retain importance.

Although globalization and international linkages have been part of history for centuries (see the International Management in Action box later in the chapter, "Tracing the Roots of Modern Globalization"), the principal focus of this opening chapter is to examine the process of globalization in the contemporary world. The rapid integration of countries, advances in information technology, and the explosion in electronic communication have created a new, more integrated world and true global competition. Yet, the complexities of doing business in distinct markets persist. These developments both create and influence the opportunities, challenges, and problems that managers in the international arena will face during the years ahead. Since the environment of international management is all-encompassing, this chapter is mostly concerned with the economic dimensions, while the following two chapters are focused on the political, legal, and technological dimensions and ethical and social dimensions, respectively. The specific objectives of this chapter are:

1. **ASSESS** the implications of globalization for countries, industries, firms, and communities.

2. **REVIEW** the major trends in global and regional integration.

3. **EXAMINE** the changing balance of global economic power and trade and investment flows among countries.

4. **ANALYZE** the major economic systems and recent developments among countries that reflect those systems.

The World of *International Management*

An Interconnected World

May 18, 2012, marked one of the most highly-anticipated initial public offerings (IPOs) in history. Facebook, which had grown from a college dorm room to a 900-million-member social network in just eight years, was set to offer shares to the public for the first time. As May 18 approached, founder Mark Zuckerberg, wearing his characteristic "hoodie" sweatshirt, embarked on a roadshow to promote the company. Facebook programmers celebrated with all-night "hackathons," and huge demand for the IPO prompted Facebook to release 25 percent more shares than initially planned. The IPO price was set to $38 per share, valuing Facebook at $104 billion. Many analysts predicted the price would soar as high as $60 on the first day alone. On the morning of May 18, Mark Zuckerberg ceremoniously rang a bell from Facebook's California campus to celebrate the opening of the market at 9:30 A.M. As Wall Street's closing bell rang just a few hours later, however, the original optimism that started the day had all but faded. The shares were trading only $0.23 above the IPO price—and down $3.82 from the opening bell price. In the following weeks, Facebook's stock continued its downward trajectory. By mid-August, Facebook stock had decreased to nearly half its original offering price, leaving many to wonder, "Is social networking really here to stay?"

Social Media Has Changed How We Connect

Though some have second-guessed the longevity of online networks, one thing is certain: We currently live in a world interconnected by social media. Through online networking, the way we connect with others has drastically changed. Virtually anyone on the globe is only a few clicks away. In fact, the average number of links separating any two random people on Facebook is now only 4.74.[1] Facebook's statistics underscore how social media has connected people across the globe:

- More than one billion people have active accounts on Facebook.
- More than 50 percent of these active users log onto Facebook in any given day.[2]
- The average user has 190 friends.[3]
- 3.2 billion comments and likes are uploaded per day.
- 18 percent of time spent online is dedicated to social media.[4]
- Over 80 percent of Facebook users are outside the United States.
- More than 70 translations are available on Facebook.
- Over 200 million people from the emerging nations of Brazil, India, Indonesia, and Mexico are now active Facebook users.[5]

Certainly, social networks are a part of many people's lives. Yet, has the virtual world of social media networks made a permanent impact in the world of international business?

Social Media Has Changed Business Strategy

Procter & Gamble (P&G), which owns several of the most recognizable brands on the planet, has strategically leveraged social media to improve its long-term brand image. In 2010, P&G unveiled a Billion Acts of Green™ Facebook application which allows people to "make a pledge to lessen their environmental impact and promote environmentally beneficial habits to friends and family via social media channels." This social media application enables users to share their "act of green" pledges with their Facebook network. As of 2013, there were over one billion acts of green pledged.[6]

P&G has also utilized social networking to increase revenue. After stagnant sales in 2010, P&G decided to refocus the advertising of Pepto-Bismol online. By monitoring Facebook activity, P&G discovered that the most social media buzz regarding Pepto-Bismol was occurring on weekend mornings, likely after customers had overindulged the night before. To tap into this market, P&G created a Facebook initiative called "Celebrate Life." Within one year, Pepto-Bismol gained 11 percent market share.[7]

The following year, in 2011, Secret deodorant sales began to drop. In an effort to shift its advertising toward teenage females, P&G created a Facebook marketing campaign that addressed the issue of bullying. Titled "Mean Stinks," the campaign encouraged users to "like" the Facebook page and share stories and videos. This campaign increased activity on Secret's Facebook page by 25 times, and sales spiked by 9 percent over a six-month period.[8]

Through its use of Facebook, P&G has connected with millions of people around the world at little cost to increase sales and enhance its brand. Businesses have gained huge competitive edges by seizing the opportunities inherent in this new global society of online social networks.

Social Media Has Changed How We Do Business

In his book *Socialnomics: How Social Media Transforms the Way We Live and Do Business*, Erik Qualman writes, "Social media platforms like Facebook, YouTube, and Twitter are fundamentally changing the way businesses and consumers behave, connecting hundreds of millions of people to each other via instant communication." In essence, social media is reshaping how "consumers and companies communicate and interact with each other."[9]

Social media has changed how consumers search for products and services. Qualman gives the example of a woman who wants to take a vacation to South America, but she is not sure which country she wants to visit. In the past, she would have typed in "South American vacation" to Google, which would have brought her to travel websites such as TripAdvisor. After hours of research, she would have picked a destination. Then, after more research, she would pick a place to stay. With social media, this woman's vacation planning becomes streamlined. When she types "South American vacation" into a social network, she finds that five of her friends have taken a trip to South America in the last year. She notices that two of her friends highly recommended their vacations to Chile with GoAhead Tours. She clicks on a link to GoAhead Tours and books her vacation. In a social network, online word of mouth among friends carries great weight for consumers. With the data available from their friends about products and services, consumers know what they want without traditional marketing campaigns.[10]

This trend means that marketers must be responsive to social networks. For example, an organization that gives travel tours has a group on Facebook. A marketer at that organization could create a Facebook application that allows its group members to select "places I'd like to visit." Let's say that 25 percent of group members who use the application choose Victoria Falls as a place they would like to visit. The organization could develop a tour to Victoria Falls, and then could send a message to all of its Facebook group members to notify them about this new tour. In this way, a social network serves as an inexpensive, effective means of marketing directly to a business's target audience.

Social Media Has Impacted Diplomacy

In February 2010, Washington sent an unconventional delegation to Moscow, which included the creator of Twitter, the chief executive of eBay, and the actor Ashton Kutcher. One of the delegation's goals was "to persuade Russia's thriving online social networks to take up social causes like fighting corruption or human trafficking," according to Jared Cohen who serves on Secretary of State Hillary Clinton's policy planning staff. In Russia, the average adult spends 10.4 hours a month on social networking sites, based on comScore market research. This act of diplomacy by Washington underscores how important social networks have become in our world today, a world in which Twitter has helped mobilize people to fight for freedom from corruption.

Social media networks have accelerated technological integration among the nations of the world. People across the globe are now linked more closely than ever before. This social phenomenon has implications for businesses as corporations can now leverage networks such as Facebook to achieve greater success. Understanding the global impact of social media is key to understanding our global society today.

Social networks have rapidly diffused from the United States and Europe to every region of the world, underscoring the inexorable nature of globalization. As individuals who share interests and preferences link up, they are afforded opportunities to connect in ways that were unimaginable just a decade ago. Facebook, Twitter, Linkedin, and others are all providing communication platforms for individuals and groups in disparate—and even isolated—locations around the world. Such networks also offer myriad business opportunities for companies large and small to identify and target discrete groups of consumers or other business partners. These networks are revolutionizing the nature of management—including international management—by allowing producers and consumers to interact directly without the usual intermediaries. Networks and the individuals who make them up are bringing populations of the world closer together and further accelerating the already rapid pace of globalization and integration.

Though the disappointing Facebook IPO left many to initially question the value and longevity of social media, the pace of interconnectivity across the globe has not slowed. Social media has altered the way that we interact with each other, and businesses, like P&G, have gained real advantages by leveraging online networks. In this chapter, we examine the globalization phenomenon, the growing integration among countries and regions, the changing balance of global economic power, and examples of different economic systems. As you read this chapter, keep in mind that although there are periodic setbacks, such as the recession of 2008–2009, globalization is moving at a rapid pace and that all nations, including the United States, as well as individual companies and their managers, are going to have to keep a close watch on the current environment if they hope to be competitive in the years ahead.

management
Process of completing activities efficiently and effectively with and through other people.

international management
Process of applying management concepts and techniques in a multinational environment and adapting management practices to different economic, political, and cultural contexts.

■ Introduction

Management is the process of completing activities with and through other people. **International management** is the process of applying management concepts and techniques in a multinational environment and adapting management practices to different economic, political, and cultural contexts. Many managers practice some level of international management in today's increasingly diverse organizations. International management is distinct from other forms of management in that knowledge and insights about global issues and specific cultures are a requisite for success. Today more firms than ever are earning some of their revenue from international operations, even nascent organizations as illustrated in The World of International Management chapter opening.

Table 1–1
The World's Top Nonfinancial TNCs, Ranked by Foreign Assets, 2012
(in millions of dollars)

Rank	Company Name	Home Economy	Foreign Assets	Total Assets	Foreign Sales	Total Sales
1	General Electric	United States	$338,157	$685,328	$75,640	$144,796
2	Royal Dutch/ Shell plc	Netherlands/ United Kingdom	307,938	360,325	282,930	467,153
3	British Petroleum Company Plc	United Kingdom	270,247	300,193	300,216	375,580
4	Toyota Motor Corporation	Japan	233,193	376,841	170,486	265,770
5	Total SA	France	214,507	227,107	180,440	234,287
6	Exxon Mobil Corporation	United States	214,349	333,795	301,840	420,714
7	Vodafone Group Plc	United Kingdom	199,003	217,031	62,065	70,224
8	GDF Suez	France	175,057	271,607	78,555	124,711
9	Chevron Corporation	United States	158,865	232,982	132,743	222,580
10	Volkswagen Group	Germany	158,046	409,257	199,129	247,624

Source: UNCTAD *World Investment Report 2013,* Web Table 28.

Many of these companies are multinational corporations (MNCs). An **MNC** is a firm that has operations in more than one country, international sales, and a mix of nationalities among managers and owners. In recent years such well-known American MNCs as Avon Products, Chevron, Citicorp, Coca-Cola, Colgate Palmolive, Du Pont, ExxonMobil, Eastman Kodak, Gillette, Hewlett-Packard, McDonald's, Motorola, Ralston Purina, Texaco, the 3M Company, and Xerox have all earned more annual revenue in the international arena than they have stateside. GE, one of the world's largest companies, with 2012 revenue of more than $147 billion, earned 57 percent of its industrial revenue from overseas that year. Table 1–1 lists the world's top nonfinancial companies ranked by foreign assets in 2012.

In addition, companies from developing economies, such as India, Brazil, and China, are providing formidable competition to their North American, European, and Japanese counterparts. Names like Cemex, Embraer, Haier, Lenovo, LG Electronics, Ping An, Rambaxy, Telefonica, Santander, Reliance, Samsung, Grupo Televisa, Tata, and Infosys are becoming well-known global brands. Globalization and the rise of emerging markets' MNCs have brought prosperity to many previously underdeveloped parts of the world, notably the emerging markets of Asia. Since 2009, sales of automobiles in China have exceeded those in the United States. Vehicle sales in China reached a record 19.3 million units in 2012, according to the China Association of Automobile Manufacturers, far ahead of the 14.5 million cars and light trucks sold in the U.S.[11] Moreover, a number of Chinese auto companies are becoming global players through their exporting, foreign investment, and international acquisitions, including the purchase by Geely of ailing Ford unit Volvo, Fiat's investment in Chrysler, and Tata's purchase of Jaguar-Land Rover.

In a striking move, Cisco Systems, one of the world's largest producers of network equipment, such as routers, announced it would establish a "Globalization Center East" in Bangalore, India. This center includes all the corporate and operational functions of U.S. headquarters, which have been mirrored in India. Under this plan, which includes an investment of over $1.1 billion, one-fifth of Cisco's senior management will move to Bangalore.[12,13]

In September 2012, Procter and Gamble relocated their skin care, cosmetics, and personal care headquarters from Cincinnati to Singapore. According to P&G, Asia accounts for roughly half of the skin care market globally, and, with the growing prosperity in Asia, is expected to continue to expand.[14] Similarly, citing the massive growth in the healthcare market in Asia, General Electric moved its X-ray business headquarters to China in 2011, and vice chairman John Rice relocated to Hong Kong.[15,16]

MNC
A firm having operations in more than one country, international sales, and a nationality mix among managers and owners.

Table 1–2
The World's Top Nonfinancial TNCs from Developing and Transitioning Economies, Ranked by Foreign Assets, 2011
(in millions of dollars)

Rank	Company Name	Home Economy	Foreign Assets	Total Assets	Foreign Sales	Total Sales
1	Hutchison Whampoa Limited	Hong Kong/ China	$77,291	$92,788	$23,477	$30,023
2	CITIC Group	China	71,512	514,847	9,923	51,659
3	Hon Hai Precision Industries	Taiwan	52,198	57,451	114,285	117,992
4	Vale SA	Brazil	48,045	128,728	49,475	60,389
5	China Ocean Shipping (Group) Company	China	40,435	52,230	19,454	29,579
6	Petronas – Petroliam Nasional BhD	Malaysia	38,907	150,435	43,228	72,853
7	Cemex S.A.B. de C.V.	Mexico	34,601	39,191	11,792	15,208
8	America Movil SAB De CV	Mexico	32,694	67,590	38,315	53,553
9	VimpelCom Ltd	Russian Federation	29,829	54,039	11,280	20,262
10	China National Offshore Oil Group	China	29,802	112,887	19,786	75,518

Source: UNCTAD *World Investment Report 2013,* Web Table 29.

IBM, another American archetype, had about 433,000 employees globally in 2012, with only about 95,000 in the U.S. This is fewer than in India, which has about 130,000 IBM employees. In 2011, IBM drew 64 percent of its $100 billion in revenue from overseas.[17] With a focus on large-scale projects in emerging markets, such as building a wireless phone network across Africa, IBM plans to receive 30 percent of its revenue from emerging markets by 2015.[18,19] As of 2012, IBM had operations in over 20 African nations, and, in August 2012, IBM announced the opening of a research lab in Kenya.[20] More than half of IBM's research staff are currently located outside of the United States.

These trends reflect the reality that firms are finding they must develop international management expertise, especially expertise relevant to the increasingly important developing and emerging markets of the world. Managers from today's MNCs must learn to work effectively with those from many different countries. Moreover, more and more small and medium-sized businesses will find that they are being affected by internationalization. Many of these companies will be doing business abroad, and those that do not will find themselves doing business with MNCs operating locally. Table 1–2 lists the world's top nonfinancial companies from developing countries ranked by foreign assets in 2011.

■ Globalization and Internationalization

International business is not a new phenomenon; however, the volume of international trade has increased dramatically over the last decade. Today, every nation and an increasing number of companies buy and sell goods in the international marketplace. A number of developments around the world have helped fuel this activity.

Globalization, Antiglobalization, and Global Pressures

globalization
The process of social, political, economic, cultural, and technological integration among countries around the world.

Globalization can be defined as the process of social, political, economic, cultural, and technological integration among countries around the world. Globalization is distinct

Tracing the Roots of Modern Globalization

Globalization is often presented as a new phenomenon associated with the post–World War II period. In fact, globalization is not new. Rather, its roots extend back to ancient times. Globalization emerged from long-standing patterns of transcontinental trade that developed over many centuries. The act of barter is the forerunner of modern international trade. During different periods of time, nearly every civilization contributed to the expansion of trade.

Middle Eastern Intercontinental Trade

In ancient Egypt, the King's Highway or Royal Road stretched across the Sinai into Jordan and Syria and into the Euphrates Valley. These early merchants practiced their trade following one of the earliest codes of commercial integrity: *Do not move the scales, do not change the weights, and do not diminish parts of the bushel.* Land bridges later extended to the Phoenicians, the first middlemen of global trade. Over 2,000 years ago, traders in silk and other rare valued goods moved east out of the Nile basin to Baghdad and Kashmir and linked the ancient empires of China, India, Persia, and Rome. At its height, the Silk Road extended over 4,000 miles, providing a transcontinental conduit for the dissemination of art, religion, technology, ideas, and culture. Commercial caravans crossing land routes in Arabian areas were forced to pay tribute—a forerunner of custom duties—to those who controlled such territories. In his youth, the Prophet Muhammad traveled with traders, and prior to his religious enlightenment the founder of Islam himself was a trader. Accordingly, the Qur'an instructs followers to respect private property, business agreements, and trade.

Trans-Saharan Cross-Continental Trade

Early tribes inhabiting the triad cities of Mauritania, in ancient West Africa below the Sahara, embraced caravan trade with the Berbers of North Africa. Gold from the sub-Saharan area was exchanged for something even more prized—salt, a precious substance needed for retaining body moisture, preserving meat, and flavoring food. Single caravans, stretching five miles and including nearly 2,500 camels, earned their reputation as ships of the desert as they ferried gold powder, slaves, ivory, animal hides, and ostrich feathers to the northeast and returned with salt, wool, gunpowder, porcelain pottery, silk, dates, millet, wheat, and barley from the East.

China as an Ancient Global Trading Initiator

In 1421, a fleet of over 3,750 vessels set sail from China to cultivate trade around the world for the emperor. The voyage reflected the emperor's desire to collect tribute in exchange for trading privileges with China and China's protection. The Chinese, like modern-day multinationals, sought to extend their economic reach while recognizing principles of economic equity and fair trade. In the course of their global trading, the Chinese introduced uniform container measurements to enable merchants to transact business using common weight and dimension measurement systems. Like the early Egyptians and later the Romans, they used coinage as an intermediary form of value exchange or specie, thus eliminating complicated barter transactions.

European Trade Imperative

The concept of the alphabet came to the Greeks via trade with the Phoenicians. During the time of Alexander the Great, transcontinental trade was extended into Afghanistan and India. With the rise of the Roman Empire, global trade routes stretched from the Middle East through central Europe, Gaul, and across the English Channel. In 1215 King John of England signed the Magna Carta, which stressed the importance of cross-border trade. By the time of Marco Polo's writing of *The Description of the World,* at the end of the 13th century, the Silk Road from China to the city-states of Italy was a well-traveled commercial highway. His tales, chronicled journeys with his merchant uncles, gave Europeans a taste for the exotic, further stimulating the consumer appetite that propelled trade and globalization. Around 1340, Francisco Balducci Pegolotti, a Florentine mercantile agent, authored *Practica Della Mercatura (Practice of Marketing),* the first widely distributed reference on international business and a precursor to today's textbooks. The search for trading routes contributed to the Age of Discovery and encouraged Christopher Columbus to sail west in 1492.

Globalization in U.S. History

The Declaration of Independence, which set out grievances against the English crown upon which a new nation was founded, cites the desire to "establish Commerce" as a chief rationale for establishing an independent state. The king of England was admonished "for cutting off our trade with all parts of the world" in one of the earliest antiprotectionist free-trade statements from the New World.

Globalization, begun as trade between and across territorial borders in ancient times, was historically and is even today the key driver of world economic development. The first paths in the creation of civilization were made in the footsteps of trade. In fact the word meaning "footsteps" in the old Anglo-Saxon language is *trada,* from which the modern English word *trade* is derived. Contemporary globalization is a new branch of a very old tree whose roots were planted in antiquity.

offshoring
The process by which companies undertake some activities at offshore locations instead of in their countries of origin.

outsourcing
The subcontracting or contracting out of activities to external organizations that had previously been performed by the firm.

from internationalization in that internationalization is the process of a business crossing national and cultural borders, while globalization is the vision of creating one world unit, a single market entity. Evidence of globalization can be seen in increased levels of trade, capital flows, and migration. Globalization has been facilitated by technological advances in transnational communications, transport, and travel. Thomas Friedman, in his book *The World Is Flat,* identified 10 "flatteners" that have hastened the globalization trend, including the fall of the Berlin Wall, **offshoring**, and **outsourcing**, which have combined to dramatically intensify the effects of increasing global linkages.[21] Hence, in recent years, globalization has accelerated, creating both opportunities and challenges to global business and international management.

On the plus side, global trade and investment continue to grow, bringing wealth, jobs, and technology to many regions around the world. While some emerging countries have not benefited from globalization and integration, the emergence of MNCs from developing countries reflects the increasing inclusion of all regions of the world in the benefits of globalization. Yet, as the pace of global integration quickens, so have the cries against globalization and the emergence of new concerns over mounting global pressures.[22] These pressures can be seen in protests at the meetings of the World Trade Organization (WTO), International Monetary Fund (IMF), and other global bodies and in the growing calls by developing countries to make the global trading system more responsive to their economic and social needs. These groups are especially concerned about rising inequities between incomes, and nongovernmental organizations (NGOs) have become more active in expressing concerns about the potential shortcomings of economic globalization.[23]

Who benefits from globalization? Proponents believe that everyone benefits from globalization, as evidenced in lower prices, greater availability of goods, better jobs, and access to technology. Theoretically, individuals in established markets will strive for better education and training to be prepared for future positions, while citizens in emerging markets and underdeveloped countries will reap the benefits of large amounts of capital flowing into those countries which will stimulate growth and development. Critics disagree, noting that the high number of jobs moving abroad as a result of the offshoring of business services jobs to lower-wage countries does not inherently create greater opportunities at home and that the main winners of globalization are the company executives. Proponents claim that job losses are a natural consequence of economic and technological change and that offshoring actually improves the competitiveness of American companies and increases the size of the overall economic pie.[24] Critics point out that growing trade deficits and slow wage growth are damaging economies and that globalization may be moving too fast for some emerging markets, which could result in economic collapse. Moreover, critics argue that when production moves to countries to take advantage of lower labor costs or less regulated environments, it creates a "race to the bottom" in which companies and countries place downward pressure on wages and working conditions.[25]

India is one country at the center of the globalization debate. As noted above, India has been the beneficiary of significant foreign investment, especially in services such as software and IT. Limited clean water, power, paved roadways, and modern bridges, however, are making it increasingly difficult for companies to expand. There have even been instances of substantial losses for companies using India as an offshore base, such as occurred when Nokia Corp. experienced the destruction of thousands of cellular phones due to a lack of storage space at an airport during a rainstorm. With India's public debt at around 70 percent of GDP, the country now stands where China did a decade ago. It is possible that India will follow in China's footsteps and continue rapid growth in incomes and wealth; however, it is also possible that the challenges India faces are greater than the country's capacity to respond to them.[26]

This example illustrates just one of the ways in which globalization has raised particular concerns over environmental and social impacts. According to antiglobalization activists, if corporations are free to locate anywhere in the world, the world's poorest

Outsourcing and Offshoring

The concepts of outsourcing and offshoring are not new, but these practices are growing at an extreme rate. *Offshoring* refers to the process by which companies undertake some activities at offshore locations instead of in their countries of origin. *Outsourcing* is the subcontracting or contracting out of activities to external organizations that had previously been performed within the firm and is a wholly different phenomenon. Often the two combine to create "offshore outsourcing." Offshoring began with manufacturing operations. Globalization jump-started the extension of offshore outsourcing of services, including call centers, R&D, information services, and even legal work. During 2006, Du Pont hired attorneys in Manila to oversee documentation in preparation for legal cases. The company hopes to save an estimated $6 million in legal spending by moving offshore and cutting documentation by 40 to 60 percent once everything is scanned and digitally saved. This is a risky venture as legal practices are not the same across countries, and the documents may be too sensi-

tive to rely on assembly-line lawyers. It also raises the question as to whether or not there are limitations to offshore outsourcing. Many companies, including Deutsche Bank, spread offshore outsourcing opportunities across multiple countries such as India and Russia for economic or political reasons. The advantages, concerns, and issues with offshoring span a variety of subjects. Throughout the text we will revisit the idea of offshore outsourcing as it is relevant. Here in Chapter 1 we see how skeptics of globalization wonder if there are benefits to offshore outsourcing, while in Chapter 2 we see how these are related to technology, and finally in Chapter 14 we see how offshore practices affect human resource management and the global distribution of work.

Source: Pete Engardio and Assif Shameen, "Let's Offshore the Lawyers," *BusinessWeek,* September 18, 2006, p. 42; and Tony Hallett and Andy McCue, "Why Deutsche Bank Spreads Its Outsourcing," *BusinessWeek,* March 15, 2007.

countries will relax or eliminate environmental standards and social services in order to attract first-world investment and the jobs and wealth that come with it. Proponents of globalization contend that even within the developing world, it is protectionist policies, not trade and investment liberalization, that result in environmental and social damage. They believe globalization will force higher-polluting countries such as China and Russia into an integrated global community that takes responsible measures to protect the environment. However, given the significant changes required in many developing nations to support globalization, such as better infrastructure, greater educational opportunities, and other improvements, most supporters concede that there may be some short-term disruptions. Over the long term, globalization supporters believe industrialization will create wealth that will enable new industries to employ more modern, environmentally friendly technology. We discuss the social and environmental aspects of globalization in more detail in Chapter 3.

These contending perspectives are unlikely to be resolved anytime soon. Instead, a vigorous debate among countries, MNCs, and civil society will likely continue and affect the context in which firms do business internationally. Business firms operating around the world must be sensitive to different perspectives on the costs and benefits of globalization and adapt and adjust their strategies and approaches to these differences.

Global and Regional Integration

One important dimension of globalization is the increasing economic integration among countries brought about by the negotiation and implementation of trade and investment agreements. Here we provide a brief overview of some of the major developments in global and regional integration.

Over the past six decades, succeeding rounds of global trade negotiations have resulted in dramatically reduced tariff and nontariff barriers among countries. Table 1–3 shows the history of these negotiation rounds, their primary focus, and the number of countries involved. These efforts reached their crest in 1994 with the conclusion of the Uruguay Round of multilateral trade negotiations under the General Agreement on Tariffs and Trade (GATT) and the creation of the **World Trade Organization (WTO)** to

World Trade Organization (WTO) The global organization of countries that oversees rules and regulations for international trade and investment.

Table 1–3
Completed Rounds of the Negotiations under the GATT and WTO

Year	Place (name)	Subjects Covered	Countries
1947	Geneva	Tariffs	23
1949	Annecy	Tariffs	13
1951	Torquay	Tariffs	38
1956	Geneva	Tariffs	26
1960–1961	Geneva (Dillon Round)	Tariffs	26
1964–1967	Geneva (Kennedy Round)	Tariffs and antidumping measures	62
1973–1979	Geneva (Tokyo Round)	Tariffs, nontariff measures, "framework" agreements	102
1986–1994	Geneva (Uruguay Round)	Tariffs, nontariff measures, services, intellectual property, dispute settlement, textiles, agriculture, creation of WTO	123

Source: Understanding the WTO (Geneva: World Trade Organization, 2008), http://www.wto.org/english/thewto_e/whatis_e/tif_e/understanding_e.pdf. Reprinted with permission.

oversee the conduct of trade around the world. The WTO is the global organization of countries that oversees rules and regulations for international trade and investment, including agriculture, intellectual property, services, competition, and subsidies. Recently, however, the momentum of global trade agreements has slowed. In December 1999, trade ministers from around the world met in Seattle to launch a new round of global trade talks. In what later became known as the "Battle in Seattle," protesters disrupted the meeting, and representatives of developing countries who felt their views were being left out of the discussion succeeded in ending the discussions early and postponing a new round of trade talks. Two years later, in November 2001, the members of the WTO met again and successfully launched a new round of negotiations at Doha, Qatar, to be known as the "Development Round," reflecting the recognition by members that trade agreements needed to explicitly consider the needs of and impact on developing countries.[27] However, after a lack of consensus among WTO members regarding agricultural subsidies and the issues of competition and government procurement, progress slowed. At a meeting in Cancún in September 2003, a group of 20-plus developing nations, led by Brazil and India, united to press developed countries such as the United States, the European Union (EU), and Japan to reduce barriers to agricultural imports. Failure to reach agreement resulted in another setback, and although there have been attempts to restart the negotiations, they have remained stalled, especially in light of rising protectionism in the wake of the global economic crisis.[28]

Partly as a result of the slow progress in multilateral trade negotiations, the United States and many other countries have pursued bilateral and regional trade agreements. The United States, Canada, and Mexico make up the **North American Free Trade Agreement (NAFTA)**, which in essence has removed all barriers to trade among these countries and created a huge North American market. A number of economic developments have occurred because of this agreement which are designed to promote commerce in the region. Some of the more important developments include (1) the elimination of tariffs as well as import and export quotas; (2) the opening of government procurement markets to companies in the other two nations; (3) an increase in the opportunity to make investments in each other's country; (4) an increase in the ease of travel between countries; and (5) the removal of restrictions on agricultural products, auto parts, and energy

North American Free Trade Agreement (NAFTA)
A free-trade agreement between the United States, Canada, and Mexico that has removed most barriers to trade and investment.

goods. Many of these provisions were implemented gradually. For example, in the case of Mexico, quotas on Mexican products in the textile and apparel sectors were phased out over time, and customs duties on all textile products were eliminated over 10 years. Negotiations between NAFTA members and many Latin American countries, such as Chile, have concluded, and others are ongoing. Moreover, other regional and bilateral trade agreements, including the U.S.–Singapore Free Trade Agreement, concluded in May 2003, and the U.S.–Central American Free Trade Agreement (CAFTA), later renamed CAFTA-DR to reflect the inclusion of the Dominican Republic in the agreement and concluded in May 2004, were negotiated in the same spirit as NAFTA. The U.S. Congress approved the CAFTA-DR in July 2005, and the president signed it into law on August 2, 2005. The export zone created will be the United States' second largest free-trade zone in Latin America after Mexico. The United States is implementing the CAFTA-DR on a rolling basis as countries make sufficient progress to complete their commitments under the agreement. The agreement first entered into force between the United States and El Salvador on March 1, 2006, followed by Honduras and Nicaragua on April 1, 2006, Guatemala on July 1, 2006, and the Dominican Republic on March 1, 2007. Implementation by Costa Rica was delayed by concerns over the impact of the opening of Costa Rica's energy and telecommunications monopoly, and a subsequent election and referendum; however, the agreement finally entered into force for Costa Rica on January 1, 2009.[29]

Agreements like NAFTA and CAFTA not only reduce barriers to trade but also require additional domestic legal and business reforms in developing nations to protect property rights. Most of these agreements now include supplemental commitments on labor and the environment to encourage countries to upgrade their working conditions and environmental protections, although some critics believe the agreements do not go far enough in ensuring worker rights and environmental standards. Partly due to the stalled progress with the WTO and FTAA, the United States has pursued bilateral trade agreements with a range of countries, including Australia, Bahrain, Chile, Colombia, Israel, Jordan, Malaysia, Morocco, Oman, Panama, Peru, and Singapore.[30]

Economic activity in Latin America continues to be volatile. Despite the continuing political and economic setbacks these countries periodically experience, economic and export growth continue in Brazil, Chile, and Mexico. In addition, while outside MNCs continually target this geographic area, there also is a great deal of cross-border investment between Latin American countries. Regional trade agreements are helping in this cross-border process, including NAFTA, which ties the Mexican economy more closely to the United States. The CAFTA agreement, signed August 5, 2006, between the United States and Central American countries presents new opportunities for bolstering trade, investment, services, and working conditions in the region. Within South America there are Mercosur, a common market created by Argentina, Brazil, Paraguay, Uruguay, and Venezuela, and the Andean Common Market, a subregional free-trade compact that is designed to promote economic and social integration and cooperation between Bolivia, Colombia, Ecuador, and Peru.

The **European Union** (EU) has made significant progress over the past decade in becoming a unified market. In 2003 it consisted of 15 nations: Austria, Belgium, Denmark, Finland, France, Germany, Great Britain, Greece, the Netherlands, Ireland, Italy, Luxembourg, Portugal, Spain, and Sweden. In May 2004, 10 additional countries joined the EU: Cyprus, the Czech Republic, Estonia, Hungary, Latvia, Lithuania, Malta, Poland, Slovakia, and Slovenia. On January 1, 2007, Romania and Bulgaria acceded to the EU, and on July 1, 2013, Croatia officially became the newest and 28th member of the EU. Not only have most trade barriers between the members been removed, but a subset of European countries have adopted a unified currency called the euro. As a result, it is now possible for customers to compare prices between most countries and for business firms to lower their costs by conducting business in one, uniform currency. With access to the entire pan-European market, large MNCs can now achieve the operational scale and scope necessary to reduce costs and increase efficiencies. Even though long-standing

European Union
A political and economic community consisting of 28 member states.

cultural differences remain, and the EU has recently experienced some substantial challenges, the EU is more integrated as a single market than NAFTA, CAFTA, or the allied Asian countries. With many additional countries poised to join the EU, the resulting pan-European market will be one that no major MNC can afford to ignore.

Although Japan has experienced economic problems since the early 1990s, it continues to be one of the primary economic forces in the Pacific Rim. Japanese MNCs want to take advantage of the huge, underdeveloped Asian markets. At the same time, China continues to be a major economic force, with many predictions that it will surpass the United States as the largest economy in the world by 2027.[31] Although all the economies in Asia are now feeling the impact of the economic uncertainty of the post-9/11 era and the Asian economic crisis of the late 1990s, Hong Kong, Taiwan, South Korea, and Singapore have been doing relatively well, and the Southeast Asia countries of Malaysia, Thailand, Indonesia, and even Vietnam are bouncing back to become major export-driven economies. The Association of Southeast Asian Nations (ASEAN), made up of Indonesia, Malaysia, the Philippines, Singapore, Brunei, Thailand, and in recent years Cambodia, Myanmar, and Vietnam, is advancing trade and economic integration and now poses challenges to China as a region of relatively low cost production and export. In addition, under the Trans-Pacific Partnership (TPP), Asian facing countries have initiated negotiations to conclude an ambitious, next-generation, Asia-Pacific trade agreement. The TPP group currently includes Australia, Brunei Darussalam, Canada, Chile, Malaysia, Mexico, New Zealand, Peru, Singapore, the United States, and Vietnam. On April 24, 2013, the U.S. trade representative notified Congress of its intent to include Japan, the world's third largest economy, in the TPP negotiations, pending the successful conclusion of the domestic procedures of each of the current members. Japan's entry further distinguishes TPP as the most credible pathway to broader Asia-Pacific regional economic integration.[32]

Central and Eastern Europe, Russia, and the other republics of the former Soviet Union currently are still trying to make stable transitions to market economies. Although the Czech Republic, Slovenia, Poland, and Hungary have accelerated this process through their accession to the EU, others (the Balkan countries, Russia, and the other republics of the former Soviet Union) still have a long way to go. However, all remain a target for MNCs looking for expansion opportunities. For example, after the fall of the Berlin Wall in 1989, Coca-Cola quickly began to sever its relations with most of the state-run bottling companies in the former communist-bloc countries. The soft drink giant began investing heavily to import its own manufacturing, distribution, and marketing techniques. To date, Coca-Cola has pumped billions into Central and Eastern Europe—and this investment is beginning to pay off. Its business in Central and Eastern Europe has been expanding at twice the rate of its other foreign operations.

These are specific, geographic examples of emerging internationalism. Equally important to this new climate of globalization, however, are broader trends that reflect the emergence of developing countries as major players in global economic power and influence.

The Shifting Balance of Economic Power in the Global Economy

Economic integration and the rapid growth of emerging markets are creating a shifting international economic landscape. Specifically, the developing and emerging countries of the world are now predicted to occupy increasingly dominant roles in the global economic system. In a 2004 report, the Goldman Sachs global economics team released a follow-up report to its initial 2001 BRIC study, taking the analysis a step further by focusing on the impact that the growth of these four economies will have on global markets. In this report, they estimated that the BRIC economies' share of world growth could rise from 20 percent in 2003 to more than 40 percent in 2025. Also, their total weight in the world economy would rise from approximately 10 percent in 2004 to more than 20 percent in 2025. Furthermore, between 2005 and 2015 over 800 million people in these countries will have crossed the annual income threshold of $3,000. In 2025, it is calculated that approximately 200 million people in these economies will have annual incomes above $15,000. Therefore, the huge pickup in demand will not be restricted to basic goods but will impact higher-priced branded goods as well.[33] In 2011, Goldman Sachs further argued that the economic potential of Brazil, Russia, India, and China (the "BRIC" economies) is growing at an even faster pace such that they may constitute four of the top five most dominant economies by the year 2050, with China surpassing the United States in output by 2027. Additionally, the report estimated that the economies of the four BRIC nations will surpass the collective economies of the G7 nations by 2032.[34] It is notable that the group of BRIC countries has met for an annual summit since 2009 and in 2010, the leaders of the founding members agreed to admit South Africa to the group, making it the BRICS.

Using data from the World Bank, PricewaterhouseCoopers has made estimates about the future growth of emerging versus developed economies, the result of which appear in summary form in Tables 1–4 and 1–5. Table 1–4 shows the world's largest economies in 2009 and 2050 (projected) using (current) market exchange rates. By this calculation, China would surge past the United States and Japan by 2050, and India would move from eleventh to third. Viewing the data on a purchasing power parity (PPP) basis, a method which adjusts GDP to account for different prices in countries, a more dramatic picture is presented. Using this method, both China and India would surpass the United States as the largest world economic power by 2050. In both the Goldman Sachs and PricewaterhouseCoopers scenarios, global growth over the next decade, and next 40 years, is heavily supported by Asia, as seen in Table 1–6. In addition, China and India will remain the most populous countries in the world in 2050, although India will surpass China as the most populous (Table 1–7).

Some analysts, including Goldman Sachs, are beginning to turn their attention to a new group of emerging markets. The N-11 (N stands for "next") are a group of economies that may constitute the next wave of emerging markets growth. These countries, which include Bangladesh, Egypt, Indonesia, Iran, Mexico, Nigeria, Pakistan, Philippines, Turkey, South Korea, and Vietnam, represent a diverse global set, with

Table 1–4
The World's Largest Economies 2009 and 2050 (Projected) Measured by GDP at Market Exchange Rates
(in millions of dollars)

	2009 GDP	2009 Rank	2050 GDP	2050 Rank
United States	14,256	1	37,876	2
Japan	5,068	2	7,664	5
China	4,909	3	51,180	1
Germany	3,347	4	5,707	8
France	2,649	5	5,344	11
United Kingdom	2,175	6	5,628	9
Italy	2,113	7	3,798	13
Brazil	1,572	8	9,235	4
Spain	1,460	9	3,195	16
Canada	1,336	10	3,322	15
India	1,296	11	31,313	3
Russia	1,231	12	6,112	6
Australia	925	13	2,486	20
Mexico	875	14	5,800	7

Source: From *The World in 2050: The accelerating shift of global economic power: challenges and opportunities.* Copyright © 2009 PricewaterhouseCoopers LLP.

Table 1–5
The World's Largest Economies 2009 and 2050 (Projected) Measured by GDP at Purchasing Power Parity
(in millions of dollars)

	2009		2050	
	GDP	Rank	GDP	Rank
United States	14,256	1	37,876	3
China	8,888	2	59,475	1
Japan	4,138	3	7,664	5
India	3,752	4	43,180	2
Germany	2,984	5	5,707	9
Russia	2,687	6	7,559	6
United Kingdom	2,257	7	5,628	10
France	2,172	8	5,344	11
Brazil	2,020	9	9,762	4
Italy	1,922	10	3,798	15
Mexico	1,540	11	6,682	7
Spain	1,496	12	3,195	18
South Korea	1,324	13	3,258	17
Canada	1,280	14	3,322	16

Source: From *The World in 2050: The accelerating shift of global economic power: challenges and opportunities.* Copyright © 2009 PricewaterhouseCoopers LLP.

relative strengths (and weaknesses) in terms of their future potential. The MIST countries (Mexico, Indonesia, South Korea, and Turkey), a subset of the N-11, are sometimes grouped as a particularly attractive subset of the N-11. Goldman views the MIST countries as the most promising and advanced of the N-11, all of which have young, growing populations and other positive good conditions for economic growth. Other groupings of fast-growing developing countries include the CEVITS (Colombia, Indonesia, Vietnam, Egypt, Turkey and South Africa), EAGLES (which stands for emerging and growth-leading economies) and includes the original BRIC and MIST plus Egypt and Taiwan.[35] Table 1–8 compares the G-7 (advanced countries), BRIC and N-11 by population, GDP, and GDP per capita in 2000, 2010, and 2016.

Table 1–6
Countries Expected to Contribute Most to Global Growth 2006–2020
(percent contribution)

China	26.7
United States	15.9
India	12.2
Brazil	2.4
Russia	2.3
Indonesia	2.3
South Korea	2.1
United Kingdom	1.9

Source: From *Foresight 2020: Economic, Industry and Corporate Trends.* Copyright © 2006 The Economist Intelligence Unit. Reprinted with permission of The Economist Intelligence Unit.

Table 1–7
Changing Global Demographics: Developing Countries on the Rise (ranked by size)

	1950	2014	2050
1	China	China	India
2	Soviet Union	India	China
3	India	United States	United States
4	United States	Indonesia	Indonesia
5	Japan	Brazil	Pakistan
6	Indonesia	Pakistan	Ethiopia
7	Germany	Bangladesh	Nigeria
8	Brazil	Nigeria	Brazil
9	United Kingdom	Russia	Bangladesh
10	Italy	Japan	Philippines
11	France	Mexico	Mexico
12	Bangladesh	Philippines	Congo

Source: U.S. Census Bureau (IDB). Retrieved September 18, 2012.

Most African countries have not, to date, fully benefited from globalization. However, recent increases in the price of commodities, such as oil and gas, agricultural products, and mineral and mining products, have helped boost incomes and wealth in the African continent. Moreover, rapid population growth in many African countries, similar to growth in India and China in earlier periods, may suggest that African countries could constitute the next wave of dynamic emerging markets.

Although the emerging nations have experienced unprecedented GDP growth since the global recession, it is important to note that the growth rates of the developing world are beginning to show signs of a slowdown. In 2013, developed nations contributed more to global GDP growth than emerging nations for the first time in almost a decade.[36] Perhaps the most striking evidence of a pending slowdown is in China, where GDP grew just 7.5 percent—significantly less than its 14.5 percent growth in 2007. Russia, India, and Brazil experienced slower growth rates in 2013 as well.[37] While emerging markets still hold the most potential for growth in the coming years, the rapid rate of expansion that was experienced over the last decade may prove difficult to match.[38]

Despite the global recession of 2009, in which merchandise exports fell 23 percent to $12.15 trillion and commercial services exports declined 13 percent to $3.31 trillion in 2009, global trade and investment continues to grow at a healthy rate, outpacing domestic growth in most countries. According to the World Trade Organization, in 2011 merchandise exports reached a record high $18.2 trillion, and commercial services exports have rebounded to $4.2 trillion.[39] **Foreign direct investment (FDI)**—the term used to indicate the amount invested in property, plant, and equipment in another country—also has been growing at a healthy rate. Despite dropping almost 50 percent in the wake of the global recession to $896 billion in 2009, global FDI has rebounded to $1.5 trillion in 2011. By 2014, FDI is estimated to reach $1.9 trillion, surpassing the all-time high set in 2007.[40] Interestingly, according to data from the World Bank, in 2010 Hong Kong received more FDI than Germany, and China received eight times as much as Canada, showing the shifting balance of economic influence among developed and developing countries. Table 1–9 shows trade flows among major world regions in both absolute and percentage terms. Tables 1–10 and 1–11 show FDI inflows and outflows by leading developed and emerging economies.

foreign direct investment (FDI)
Investment in property, plant, or equipment in another country.

Table 1–8
Population, GDP, and GDP per Capita of G-7, BRIC, and N-11 Countries, 2000, 2010, and 2016 (projection)

Country	2000			2010			2016		
	Population (millions)	GDP (billions)	GDP (per cap.)	Population (millions)	GDP (billions)	GDP (per cap.)	Population (millions)	GDP (billions)	GDP (per cap.)
Canada	30	$725.0	$23,653	34	$1,577.0	$46,303	36	$2,106.0	$58,674
France	59	1,332.0	22,550	63	2,563.0	40,704	65	3,268.0	50,497
Germany	82	1,892.0	23,051	82	3,286.0	40,274	81	3,929.0	48,731
Italy	57	1,101.0	19,334	60	2,055.0	34,059	62	2,476.0	40,100
Japan	127	4,667.0	36,800	128	5,459.0	42,783	127	6,783.0	53,615
United Kingdom	59	1,481.0	25,142	62	2,250.0	36,164	65	3,224.0	49,777
United States	282	9,951.0	35,252	310	14,527.0	46,860	328	18,251.0	55,622
Total/Average	**697**	**$21,149.0**	**30,343**	**739**	**$31,717.0**	**42,919**	**764**	**$40,037.0**	**52,404**
BRICs									
Brazil	171	$642.0	$3,751	193	$2,090.0	$10,816	203	$3,373.0	$16,635
China	1,267	1,198.0	946	1,341	5,878.0	4,382	1,382	11,780.0	8,523
India	1,024	476.0	465	1,191	1,632.0	1,371	1,289	3,027.0	2,349
Russia	146	260.0	1,775	143	1,480.0	10,356	140	3,088.0	22,066
Total/Average	**2,608**	**$2,576.0**	**$988**	**2,868**	**$11,080.0**	**$3,863**	**3,014**	**$21,268.0**	**$7,056**
Next-11									
Bangladesh	141	$47.0	$334	164	$106.0	$642	179	$174.0	$973
Egypt	63	99.0	1,566	78	218.0	2,808	88	342.0	3,901
Indonesia	205	166.0	807	238	707.0	2,974	255	1,382.0	5,429
Iran	55	85.0	1,559	75	407.0	5,449	82	630.0	7,702
S. Korea	47	533.0	11,317	49	1,014.0	20,756	50	1,686.0	33,948
Mexico	98	672.0	6,859	109	1,034.0	9,522	115	1,505.0	13,052
Nigeria	119	46.0	390	156	203.0	1,298	184	359.0	1,957
Pakistan	138	74.0	539	172	177.0	1,030	194	303.0	1,566
Philippines	77	81.0	1,053	94	200.0	2,123	106	307.0	2,907
Turkey	66	266.0	4,026	71	735.0	10,309	76	1,133.0	14,839
Vietnam	78	31.0	402	88	104.0	1,174	95	210.0	2,217
Total/Average	**1,087**	**$2,100.0**	**$2,626**	**1,294**	**$4,905.0**	**5,280**	**1,424**	**$8,031.0**	**$7,056**
TOTALS	**4,392**	**$25,825.0**	**$5,880**	**4,901**	**$47,702.0**	**$9,734**	**5,202**	**$69,336.0**	**$13,329**
World	**6,115**	**$32,216.0**	**$5,268**	**6,909**	**$62,911.0**	**$9,106**	**7,302**	**$91,575.0**	**$12,541**

Source: IMF, "World Economic Outlook Database." September 2011. http://www.imf.org/.

Table 1–9
World Merchandise Trade by Region and Selected Country, 2012
(in US$ billions and percentages)

	Exports					Imports				
	Value	Annual Percentage Change				Value	Annual Percentage Change			
	2012	2005–12	2010	2011	2012	2012	2005–12	2010	2011	2012
World	17,850	8	22	20	0	18,155	8	21	19	0
North America	2,373	7	23	16	4	3,192	5	23	15	3
United States	1,547	8	21	16	5	2,335	4	23	15	3
Canada	455	3	23	17	1	475	6	22	15	2
Mexico	371	8	30	17	6	380	8	28	16	5
South and Central America	749	11	26	27	0	753	14	30	25	3
Brazil	243	11	32	27	−5	233	17	43	24	−2
Other South and Central America	506	11	22	28	2	520	13	24	25	5
Europe	6,373	5	12	18	−4	6,519	5	13	17	−6
European Union (27)	5,792	5	12	18	−5	5,927	5	13	17	−6
Germany	1,407	5	12	17	−5	1,167	6	14	19	−7
France	569	3	8	14	−5	674	4	9	18	−6
Netherlands	656	7	15	15	−2	591	7	17	16	−1
United Kingdom	468	3	15	17	−7	680	4	14	14	1
Italy	500	4	10	17	−4	486	3	17	15	−13
Commonwealth of Independent States (CIS)	804	13	31	34	2	568	15	25	30	5
Russian Federation	529	12	32	30	1	335	15	30	30	4
Africa	626	11	30	17	5	604	13	16	18	8
South Africa	87	8	31	21	−11	123	10	27	29	1
Africa less South Africa	539	11	30	16	8	481	14	13	15	9
Oil exporters	370	11	34	15	12	179	14	10	10	8
Non oil exporters	169	11	22	20	−1	303	14	15	18	10
Middle East	1,287	13	28	37	3	721	12	13	17	6
Asia	5,640	11	31	18	2	5,795	12	33	23	4
China	2,049	15	31	20	8	1,818	16	39	25	4
Japan	799	4	33	7	−3	886	8	26	23	4
India	293	17	37	34	−3	489	19	36	33	5
Newly industrialized economies (4)	1,280	8	30	16	−1	1,310	9	32	19	0
Memorandum items:										
MERCOSUR	340	11	29	26	−4	325	16	43	25	−3
ASEAN	1,254	10	29	18	1	1,221	11	31	21	6
EU (27) extra-trade	2,166	7	17	21	0	2,301	7	18	18	−4
Least developed countries (LDCs)	204	14	27	25	1	223	14	11	22	8

Source: WTO Press Release 688, April 10, 2013, Appendix Table 1. Reprinted with permission.

Table 1–10
Foreign Direct Investment Inflows, by Region
(in US$ billions)

	2012	2011	2010
Developed economies	$560.7	$820.0	$696.4
Developing economies	702.8	735.2	637.1
Africa	50.0	47.6	43.6
East and Southeast Asia	326.1	342.9	312.5
South Asia	33.5	44.2	28.7
West Asia	47.1	49.1	59.5
Latin America and the Caribbean	243.9	249.4	189.9
Transition economies	87.4	96.3	87.4

Source: UNCTAD, World Investment Report 2013, Web Table 1.

As nations become more affluent, they begin looking for countries with economic growth potential where they can invest. Over the last two decades, for example, Japanese MNCs have invested not only in their Asian neighbors but also in the United States and the EU. European MNCs, meanwhile, have made large financial commitments in Japan and more recently in China and India, because they see Asia as having continued growth potential. American multinationals have followed a similar approach in regard to both Europe and Asia.

The following quiz illustrates how transnational today's MNCs have become. This trend is not restricted to firms in North America, Europe, or Asia. An emerging global community is becoming increasingly interdependent economically. Take the quiz and see how well you do by checking the answers given at the end of the chapter. However, although there may be a totally integrated global market in the near future, at present, regionalization, as represented by North America, Europe, Asia, and the less developed countries, is most descriptive of the world economy.

1. Where is the parent company of Braun household appliances (electric shavers, coffee makers, etc.) located?

   a. Italy   *b.* Germany   *c.* the United States   *d.* Japan

2. The BIC pen company is

   a. Japanese   *b.* British   *c.* U.S.–based   *d.* French

Table 1–11
Foreign Direct Investment Outflows, by Region
(in US$ billions)

	2012	2011	2010
Developed economies	$909.4	$1,183.1	$1,029.8
Developing economies	426.1	422.1	413.2
Africa	14.3	5.4	9.3
East and Southeast Asia	275.0	271.5	254.2
South Asia	9.2	13.0	16.4
West Asia	23.9	26.2	13.4
Latin America and the Caribbean	103.0	105.2	119.2
Transition economies	55.5	72.9	61.8

Source: UNCTAD, World Investment Report 2013, Web Table 2.

3. The company that owns Jaguar is based in
   a. Germany   *b.* the United States   *c.* the United   *d.* India
                                                            Kingdom

4. RCA television sets are produced by a company based in
   a. France   *b.* the United States   *c.* Malaysia   *d.* Taiwan

5. The firm that owns Green Giant vegetables is
   a. U.S.-based   *b.* Canadian   *c.* British   *d.* Italian

6. The owners of Godiva chocolate are
   a. U.S.-based   *b.* Swiss   *c.* Dutch   *d.* Turkish

7. The company that produces Vaseline is
   a. French   *b.* Anglo-Dutch   *c.* German   *d.* U.S.-based

8. Wrangler jeans are made by a company that is
   a. Japanese   *b.* Taiwanese   *c.* British   *d.* U.S.-based

9. The company that owns Holiday Inn is headquartered in
   a. Saudi Arabia   *b.* France   *c.* the United States   *d.* Britain

10. Tropicana orange juice is owned by a company that is headquartered in
    a. Mexico   *b.* Canada   *c.* the United States   *d.* Japan

■ Global Economic Systems

The evolution of global economies has resulted in three main systems: market economies, command economies, and mixed economies. Recognizing opportunities in global expansion includes understanding the differences in these systems, as they affect issues such as consumer choice and managerial behavior.

Market Economy

A *market economy* exists when private enterprise reserves the right to own property and monitor the production and distribution of goods and services while the state simply supports competition and efficient practices. Management is particularly effective here since private ownership provides local evaluation and understanding, opposed to a nationally standardized archetype. This model contains the least restriction as the allocation of resources is roughly determined by the law of demand. Individuals within the community disclose wants, needs, and desires to which businesses may appropriately respond. A general balance between supply and demand sustains prices, while an imbalance creates a price fluctuation. In other words, if demand for a good or service exceeds supply, the price will inevitably rise, while an excess supply over consumer demand will result in a price decrease.

Since the interaction of the community and firms guides the system, organizations must be as versatile as the individual consumer. Competition is fervently encouraged to promote innovation, economic growth, high quality, and efficiency. The focus on how to best serve the customer is necessary for optimal growth as it ensures a greater penetration of niche markets.[41] The government may prohibit such things as monopolies or restrictive business practices in order to maintain the integrity of the economy. Monopolies are a danger to this system because they tend to stifle economic growth and consumer choice with their power to determine supply. Factors such as efficiency of production and quality and pricing of goods can be chosen arbitrarily by monopolies, leaving consumers without a choice and at the mercy of big business.

Command Economy

A *command economy* is comparable to a monopoly in the sense that the organization, in this case the government, has explicit control over the price and supply of a good or service. The particular goods and services offered are not necessarily in response to consumers' stated needs but are determined by the theoretical advancement of society. Businesses in this model are owned by the state to ensure that investments and other business practices are done in the best interest of the nation despite the often contradictory outcomes. Management within this model ignores demographic information. Government subsidies provide firms with enough security so they cannot go out of business, which simply encourages a lack of efficiency or incentive to monitor costs. Devoid of private ownership, a command economy creates an environment where little motivation exists to improve customer service or introduce innovative ideas.[42]

History confirms the inefficiency and economic stagnation of this system with the dramatic decline of communism in the 1980s. Communist countries believe that the goals of the so-called "people" take precedence over individualism. While the communist model once dominated countries such as Ethiopia, Bulgaria, Hungary, Poland, and the former U.S.S.R., among others, it survives only in North Korea, Cuba, Laos, Vietnam, and China today, in various degrees or forms. A desire to effectively compete in the global economy has resulted in the attempt to move away from the communist model, especially in China, which will be considered in greater depth later in the chapter.

Mixed Economy

A *mixed economy* is a combination of a market and a command economy. While some sectors of this system reflect private ownership and the freedom and flexibility of the law of demand, other sectors are subject to government planning. The balance allows competition to thrive while the government can extend assistance to individuals or companies. Regulations concerning minimum wage standards, social security, environmental protection, and the advancement of civil rights may raise the standard of living and ensure that those who are elderly, sick, or have limited skills are taken care of. Ownership of organizations seen as critical to the nation may be transferred to the state to subsidize costs and allow the firms to flourish.[43]

Below we discuss general developments in key world regions reflective of these economic systems and the impact of these developments on international management.

■ Economic Performance and Issues of Major Regions

From a vantage point of development, performance, and growth, the world's economies can be evaluated as established economies, emerging economies, and developing economies (some of which may soon become emerging).

Established Economies

North America As noted earlier, North America constitutes one of the four largest trading blocs in the world. The combined purchasing power of the United States, Canada, and Mexico is more than $12 trillion. Even though there will be more and more integration both globally and regionally as time goes on, effective international management still requires knowledge of individual countries.

The free-market-based economy of this region allows considerable freedom in decision-making processes of private firms. This allows for greater flexibility and low barriers for other countries to establish business. Despite factors such as the Iraq War beginning in 2003, Hurricane Katrina in 2005, high oil prices through 2005 and 2006, and the global recession in 2009, the U.S. economy continues to grow. U.S. MNCs have holdings throughout the world, and foreign firms are welcomed as investors in the U.S. market. U.S. firms maintain particularly dominant global positions in technology-intensive industries, including computing (hardware and services), telecommunications, media, and biotechnology. At the same time, foreign MNCs are finding the United States to be a lucrative market for expansion. Many foreign automobile producers, such as BMW, Honda, Hyundai, Nissan, and Toyota, have established a major manufacturing presence in the United States. Given the near collapse of the "domestic" automotive industries, North American automotive production will come increasingly from these foreign "transplants."

Canada is the United States' largest trading partner, a position it has held for many years. The United States also has considerable foreign direct investment in Canada, more than in any other country except the United Kingdom. This helps explain why most of the largest foreign-owned companies in Canada are totally or heavily U.S.-owned. The legal and business environment in Canada is similar to that in the United States, and the similarity helps promote trade between the two countries. Geography, language, and culture also help, as does NAFTA, which will assist Canadian firms in becoming more competitive worldwide. They will have to be able to go head to head with their U.S. and Mexican competitors as trade barriers are removed, which should result in greater efficiency and market prowess on the part of the Canadian firms, which must compete successfully or go out of business. In recent years, Canadian firms have begun investing heavily in the United States while gaining international investment from both the United States and elsewhere. Canadian firms also do business in many other countries, including Mexico, Great Britain, Germany, and Japan, where they find ready markets for Canada's vast natural resources, including lumber, natural gas, crude petroleum, and agriproducts.

By the early 1990s Mexico had recovered from its economic problems of the previous decade and had become the strongest economy in Latin America. In 1994, Mexico became part of NAFTA, and it appeared to be on the verge of becoming the major economic power in Latin America. Yet, an assassination that year and related economic crisis underscored that Mexico was still a developing country with considerable economic volatility. Mexico now has free-trade agreements with over 50 countries, including Guatemala, Honduras, El Salvador, the EU, the European Free Trade Area, and Japan.[44] In 2000 the 71-year hold of the Institutional Revolutionary Party on the presidency of the country came to an end, and many investors believe that the administration of Vicente Fox and his successor, Felipe Calderon, have been especially pro-business. Calderon battled Mexico's narcotics gangs which, unfortunately, have been responsible for an ongoing epidemic of violence and casualties, including those of innocent civilians. In 2012, the Institutional Revolutionary Party returned to power with the election of Peña Nieto as president, who, despite uncertainty from some, promises to continue to advance pro-business initiatives, such as opening the oil industry to the private sector and forcing greater competition in telecommunications, an industry long-dominated by Carlos Slim Helú, the world's richest inidividual.[45].

Because of NAFTA, Mexican businesses are finding themselves able to take advantage of the U.S. market by producing goods for that market that were previously purchased by the U.S. from Asia. Mexican firms are now able to produce products at highly competitive prices thanks to lower-cost labor and proximity to the American market. Location has helped hold down transportation costs and allows for fast delivery. This development has been facilitated by the **maquiladora** system, under which materials and equipment can be imported on a duty- and tariff-free basis for assembly or manufacturing and re-export mostly in Mexican border towns. Mexican firms, taking advantage of a new arrangement that the government has negotiated with the EU, can also now export goods into the European community without having to pay a tariff. The country's trade with both the EU and Asia is on the rise, which is important to Mexico as it wants to reduce its overreliance on the U.S. market.

maquiladora
Factory, mostly located in Mexican border towns, that imports materials and equipment on a duty- and tariff-free basis for assembly or manufacturing and re-export.

The EU   The ultimate objective of the EU is to eliminate all trade barriers among member countries (like between the states in the United States). This economic community eventually will have common custom duties as well as unified industrial and commercial policies regarding countries outside the union. Another goal that has finally largely become a reality is a single currency and a regional central bank. With the addition of Croatia in 2013, 28 countries now comprise the EU, with 17 having adopted the euro. Another 9 countries, having joined the EU in either 2004, 2007, or 2013, are legally bound to adopt the euro upon meeting the monetary convergence criteria.[46]

Such developments will allow companies based in EU nations that are able to manufacture high-quality, low-cost goods to ship them anywhere within the EU without paying duties or being subjected to quotas. This helps explain why many North American and Pacific Rim firms have established operations in Europe; however, all these outside firms are finding their success tempered by the necessity to address local cultural differences.

The challenge for the future of the EU is to absorb its eastern neighbors, the former communist-bloc countries. This could result in a giant, single European market. In fact, a unified Europe could become the largest economic market in terms of purchasing power in the world. Between 2004 and 2007, Poland, the Czech Republic, Hungary, Bulgaria, and Romania all joined the EU, improving economic growth, inflation, and employment rates throughout. Such a development is not lost on Asian and U.S. firms, which are working to gain a stronger foothold in Eastern European countries as well as the existing EU. In recent years, foreign governments have been very active in helping to stimulate and develop the market economies of Central and Eastern Europe to enhance their economic growth as well as world peace.

Since 2009, the EU has faced one of the most severe challenges of its short tenure. Several European governments, including Greece, Portugal, Spain, and Ireland, have found themselves with dangerously large deficits that resulted from both structural conditions (stagnant population growth, overly generous pension systems, early retirements) and shorter-term economic pressures. These conditions have placed pressure on the euro, the currency adopted by most EU countries, and have forced substantial rescue packages led by Germany and France.[47]

Japan   During the 1970s and 1980s, Japan's economic success had been without precedent. The country had a huge positive trade balance, the yen was strong, and the Japanese became recognized as the world leaders in manufacturing and consumer goods.

Analysts ascribe Japan's phenomenal success to a number of factors. Some areas that have received a lot of attention are the Japanese cultural values supporting a strong work ethic and group/team effort, consensus decision making, the motivational effects of guaranteed lifetime employment, and the overall commitment that Japanese workers have to their organizations. However, at least some of these assumptions about the Japanese workforce have turned out to be more myth than reality, and some of the former strengths have become weaknesses in the new economy. For example, consensus decision making turns out to be too time-consuming in the new speed-based economy. Also, there has been a steady decline in Japan's overseas investments since the 1990s due to a slowing Japanese economy, poor management decisions, and competition from emerging economies, such as China.

Ministry of International Trade and Industry (MITI)
A Japanese government agency that identifies and ranks national commercial pursuits and guides the distribution of national resources to meet these goals.

keiretsu
An organizational arrangement in Japan in which a large group of vertically integrated companies bound together by cross-ownership, interlocking directorates, and social ties provide goods and services to end users.

Some of the early success of the Japanese economy can be attributed to the **Ministry of International Trade and Industry (MITI)**. This is a governmental agency that identifies and ranks national commercial pursuits and guides the distribution of national resources to meet these goals. In recent years, MITI has given primary attention to the so-called ABCD industries: automation, biotechnology, computers, and data processing.

Another major reason for Japanese success may be the use of **keiretsus**. This Japanese term stands for the large, vertically integrated corporations whose holdings supply much of the assistance needed in providing goods and services to end users. Being able to draw from the resources of the other parts of the keiretsu, a Japanese MNC often can get things done more quickly and profitably than its international competitors.

Despite setbacks, Japan remains a formidable international competitor and is well poised in all three major economic regions: the Pacific Rim, North America, and Europe.

Emerging Economies

In contrast to the fully developed countries of North America, Europe, and Asia are the less developed countries (LDCs) around the world. An LDC typically is characterized by two or more of the following: low GDP, slow (or negative) GDP growth per capita, high unemployment, high international debt, a large population, and a workforce that is

Recognizing Cultural Differences

One objective of multicultural research is to learn more about the customs, cultures, and work habits of people in other countries. After all, a business can hardly expect to capture an overseas market without knowledge of the types of goods and services the people there want to buy. Equally important is the need to know the management styles that will be effective in running a foreign operation. Sometimes this information can change quite rapidly. For example, as Russia continues to move from a central to a market economy, management is constantly changing as the country attempts to adjust to increased exposure in the global environment. Russia entered into a strategic partnership with the United States in 2002. However, while U.S. perspectives of "partnerships" are flexible they are generally seen as inherently having some hierarchical structure. Russia, on the other hand, sees "partnerships" as entailing equality, especially in the decision-making process. This may be a part of the reason Russia formed a strategic partnership with China in 2005, since both countries emerged from a communist regime and can understand similar struggles. Regardless, as Russia moves to privatize its organizations, the new partnership may pose a threat to the Americas and the West if efforts to understand each other and work together are abandoned.

It is evident that the United States and Russia differ on many horizons. Russian management is still based on authoritarian styles, where the managerial role is to pass orders down the chain of command, and there is little sense of responsibility, open communication, or voice in the decision-making process. Furthermore, while 64 percent of U.S. employees see retirement as an opportunity for a new chapter in life, only 15 percent of Russian employees feel that way, and another 23 percent see retirement as "the beginning of the end." Despite such differences, there are points of similarity that a U.S. firm can use as leverage when considering opening a business in Russia. About 46 percent of employees in both the United States and Russia would prefer a work schedule that fluctuates between work and leisure, mirroring a pattern of recurring sabbaticals. Also, Russia currently has a post–Cold War mentality, much like the United States experienced after the Great Depression of the 1930s. Looking back at history and incorporating the evolutionary knowledge can assist in understanding emerging economies.

These examples show the importance of studying international management and learning via systematic analysis of culture and history and firsthand information how managers in other countries really do behave toward their employees and their work. Such analysis is critical in a firm's ensuring a strong foothold in effective international management.

either unskilled or semiskilled. In some cases, such as in the Middle East, there also is considerable government intervention in economic affairs. Emerging markets are developing economies that exhibit sustained economic reform and growth.

Central and Eastern Europe In 1991, the Soviet Union ceased to exist. Each of the individual republics that made up the U.S.S.R. in turn declared their independence and now are attempting to shift from a centrally planned to a market-based economy. The Russian Republic has the largest population, territory, and influence, but others, such as Ukraine, also are industrialized and potentially important in the global economy. Of most importance to the study of international management are the Russian economic reforms, the dismantling of Russian price controls (allowing supply and demand to determine prices), and privatization (converting the old communist-style public enterprises to private ownership).

Russia's economy continues to grow as poverty declines and the middle class expands. Direct investment in Russia, along with its membership in the International Monetary Fund (IMF), is helping to raise GDP and decrease inflation, offsetting the hyperinflation created from the initial attempt at transitioning to a market-based economy. In addition, the Group of Seven (the United States, Germany, France, England, Canada, Japan, and Italy) has pledged billions of dollars for humanitarian and other types of assistance. So while the Russian economy likely will have a number of years of painfully slow economic recovery and many recurrent problems, most economic experts predict that, if the Russians can hold things together politically and maintain social order, the situation could improve in the long run.

Although these economic reforms are being implemented slowly, there are significant problems in Russia associated with growing crime of all kinds as well as political uncertainty.

Many foreign investors feel that the risk is still too high. Russia is such a large market, however, and has so much potential for the future that many MNCs feel they must get involved, especially with a promising rise in GDP. There also has been a movement toward teaching Western-style business courses, as well as MBA programs, in all the Central European countries, creating a greater preparation for trends in globalization.

In Hungary, state-owned hotels have been privatized, and Western firms, attracted by the low cost of highly skilled, professional labor, have been entering into joint ventures with local companies. MNCs also have been making direct investments, as in the case of General Electric's purchase of Tungsram, the giant Hungarian electric company. Another example is Britain's Telfos Holdings, which paid $19 million for 51 percent of Ganz, a Hungarian locomotive and rolling stock manufacturer. Still others include Suzuki's investment of $110 million in a partnership arrangement to produce cars with local manufacturer Autokonzern, Ford Motor's construction of a new $80 million car component plant, and Italy's Ilwa's $25 million purchase of the Salgotarjau Iron Works.

Poland had a head start on the other former communist-bloc countries. General political elections were held in June 1989, and the first noncommunist government was established well before the fall of the Berlin Wall. In 1990, the Communist Polish United Workers Party dissolved, and Lech Walesa was elected president. Earlier than its neighbors, Poland instituted radical economic reforms (characterized as "shock therapy"). Although the relatively swift transition to a market economy has been very difficult for the Polish people, with very high inflation initially, continuing unemployment, and the decline of public services, Poland's economy has done relatively well. In fact, Poland's economy was the only economy in the EU to continue to grow during the global recession of 2008-2009. In 2011, Poland's GDP grew by over 4 percent. However, political instability and risk, large external debts, a deteriorating infrastructure, and only modest education levels have led to continuing economic problems.

Although Russia, the Czech Republic, Hungary, and Poland receive the most media coverage and are among the largest of the former communist countries, others also are struggling to right their economic ships. A small but particularly interesting example is Albania. Ruled ruthlessly by the Stalinist-style dictator Enver Hoxha for over four decades following World War II, Albania was the last, but most devastated, Eastern European country to abandon communism and institute radical economic reforms. At the beginning of the 1990s, Albania started from zero. Industrial output initially fell over 60 percent, and inflation reached 40 percent monthly. Today, Albania still struggles but is slowly making progress.

The key for Albania and the other Eastern European countries is to maintain the social order, establish the rule of law, rebuild the collapsed infrastructure, and get factories and other value-added, job-producing firms up and running. Foreign investment must be forthcoming for these countries to join the global economy. A key challenge for Albania and the other "have-not" Eastern European countries will be to make themselves less risky and more attractive for international business.

China   China's GDP has remained strong, growing at 9.1 percent in 2009, 10.4 percent in 2010, 9.3 percent in 2011, and 8.0 percent in 2012, despite the global economic crisis.[48] China faces other formidable challenges, including a massive savings glut in the corporate sector, the globalization of manufacturing networks, vast developmental needs, and the requirement for 15–20 million new jobs annually to avoid joblessness and social unrest.

China also remains a major risk for investors. The one country, two systems (communism and capitalism) balance is a delicate one to maintain, and foreign businesses are often caught in the middle. Most MNCs find it very difficult to do business in and with China. Concerns about undervaluation of China's currency, the remnimbi (also know as the yuan), and continued policies that favor domestic companies over foreign ones, make China a complicated and high-risk venture.[49] Even so, MNCs know that China with its 1.3 billion people will be a major world market and that they must have a presence there.

Trade relations between China and developed countries and regions, such as the United States and the EU, remain tense. Many in the United States argue that the value of the Chinese currency is kept artificially low, giving China an unfair advantage in selling its exports. In early 2012, the Chinese premier Wen Jiabao insisted that the yuan's exchange rate was close to an equilibrium level, despite estimates released by the Peterson Institute that suggest that the currency is still undervalued by at least 24 percent.[50,51] In addition, China's policy toward foreign investors continues to be fluid and sometimes unpredictable. Both Walmart and Yum Brands found themselves accused of improper business practices and each had to close stores and issues public apologies. Walmart stores in southwest China's Chongqing have been forced to close following allegations that they have been labeling non organic pork as organic. Yum Brands suffered a 29 percent drop in same store sales in China in April of 2013 after concerns about the safety of some chicken and the spread of Avian flu caused customers to stay away from the outlets.[52,53]

Other Emerging Markets of Asia

In addition to Japan and China, there are a number of other important economies in the region, including South Korea, Hong Kong, Singapore, and Taiwan. Together, the countries of the ASEAN bloc are also fueling growth and development in the region.

In South Korea, the major conglomerates, called **chaebols**, include such internationally known firms as Samsung, Daewoo, Hyundai, and the LG Group. Many key managers in these huge firms have attended universities in the West, where in addition to their academic programs they learned western culture, customs, and language. Now they are able to use this information to help formulate competitive international strategies for their firms. This will be very helpful for South Korea, which has shifted to privatizing a wide range of industries and withdrawing some of the restrictions on overall foreign ownership. Like other Asian economies, Korea fared reasonably well throughout the recession of 2008–2009, with a solid economy with moderate growth, moderate inflation, low unemployment, an export surplus, and fairly equal distribution of income.

chaebols
Very large, family-held Korean conglomerates that have considerable political and economic power.

Bordering southeast China and now part of the People's Republic of China (PRC), Hong Kong has been the headquarters for some of the most successful multinational operations in Asia. Although it can rely heavily on southeast China for manufacturing, there is still uncertainty about the future and the role that the Chinese government intends to play in local governance.

Singapore is a major success story. Its solid foundation leaves only the question of how to continue expanding in the face of increasing international competition. To date, however, Singapore has emerged as an urban planner's ideal model and the leader and financial center of Southeast Asia.

Taiwan has progressed from a labor-intensive economy to one that is dominated by more technologically sophisticated industries, including banking, electricity generation, petroleum refining, and computers. Although its economy has also been hit by the downturn in Asia, it continues to steadily grow.

Besides South Korea, Singapore, and Taiwan, other countries of Southeast Asia are also becoming dynamic platforms for growth and development. Thailand, Malaysia, Indonesia, and now Vietnam (see In the International Spotlight at the end of Chapter 2) have developed economically with a relatively large population base and inexpensive labor despite the lack of considerable natural resources. These countries have been known to have social stability, but in the aftermath of the recent economic crisis there has been considerable turmoil in this part of the world. This instability first occurred in Indonesia, the fourth most populous country in the world, and more recently in Thailand, where supporters of exiled former Prime Minister Thaksin, who left the country in the face of corruption charges, engaged in sometimes violent protests that have caused real concern over the stability of the country. After the Thaksin's party returned to power in a landslide victory in 2011, with Thaksin's sister winning the presidency, the country appeared to return to a more stable environment and outlook.[54] On balance, these export-driven Southeast Asian countries remain attractive to outside investors.

India

With a population of about 1 billion and growing, India has traditionally had more than its share of political and economic problems. The recent trend of locating software and other higher-value-added services has helped to bolster a large middle- and upper-class market for goods and services and a GDP that is quickly reaching the level of China. India may soon be viewed as a fully developed country if it can withstand the intense growth period.

For a number of reasons, India is attractive to multinationals, especially U.S. and British firms. Many Indian people speak English, are very well educated, and are known for advanced information technology expertise. Also, the Indian government is providing funds for economic development. For example, India is expanding its telecommunication systems and increasing the number of phone lines fivefold, a market that AT&T is vigorously pursuing. Many frustrations remain in doing business in India (see In the International Spotlight at the end of this chapter), but there is little question that the country will receive increased attention in the years ahead.

Developing Economies on the Verge

Around the world there are many economies that can be considered developing (what might formally have been termed "less developed" or in some cases "least developed") that are worthy of attention and understanding. Some of these economies are on the verge of emerging as impressive contributors to global growth and development.

South America   Over the years, countries in South America have had difficult economic problems. They have accumulated heavy foreign debt obligations and experienced severe inflation. Although most have tried to implement economic reforms reducing their debt, periodic economic instability and the emergence of populist leaders have had an impact on the attractiveness of countries in this region.

Brazil's economy has evolved into a flourishing system. Though Brazil's GDP has slowed somewhat since 2011, its growth continues to outpace most developed nations. This economy outweighs that of any other South American country and is quickly becoming a worldwide presence. Brazil continues to attract outside investors, partly drawn to opportunities created by Brazil's privatization of power, telecommunications, and other infrastructure sectors. (See the International Management in Action box: Brazilian Economic Reform.) Power companies such as AES and General Electric have constructed more than $20 billion worth of electricity plants throughout the country. At the same time, many other well-known companies have set up operations in Brazil, including Arby's, JCPenney, Kentucky Fried Chicken, McDonald's, and Walmart. All this international business activity should spell success. Brazil has benefited from one of the most stable governments throughout Latin America, which has helped secure the country's place today as the undisputed economic leader of South America.

Chile's market-based economic growth has fluctuated between 3 and 6 percent over the last decade, one of the best performances in Latin America. Chile attracts a lot of foreign direct investment, mainly dealing with gas, water, electricity, and mining. It continues to participate in globalization by engaging in further trade agreements, including those with Mercosur, China, India, the EU, South Korea, and Mexico.

Argentina has one of the strongest economies overall with abundant natural resources, a highly literate population, an export-oriented agricultural sector, and a diversified industrial base; however, it has suffered the recurring economic problems of inflation, external debt, capital flight, and budget deficits. While Argentina's GDP slowed to .09 percent in 2009 due to the global recession, growth has since rebounded, with GDP growth at 8.9 percent in 2011.

Despite the ups and downs, a major development in South America is the growth of intercountry trade, spurred on by the progress toward free-market policies. For example, beginning in 1995, 90 percent of trade among Mercosur members was duty-free. At the same time, South American countries are increasingly looking to do business with the United States. In fact, a survey of businesspeople from Argentina, Brazil, Chile, Colombia, and Venezuela found that the U.S. market, on average, was more important for them than any other. Some of these countries, however, also are looking outside the Americas for growth opportunities. Mercosur continues talks with the EU to create free trade between

Brazilian Economic Reform

Over the past two decades, Brazil's economic reform and progress have been nothing short of spectacular. Beginning with a comprehensive privatization program in the early and mid-1990s under which dozens of state-owned enterprises were sold to commercial interests, Brazil has transformed itself from a relatively closed and frequently unstable economy to one of the global leading "BRIC" countries and the anchor of South American economic development. Brazil's reform, which has included macroeconomic stabilization, liberalization of import and export restrictions, and improved fiscal and monetary management, reflects a definitive break from past inward-looking policies that characterized much of Latin America in the 1960s and 1970s. A critical milestone was the introduction of the Plano Real ("Real Plan"), instituted in the spring of 1994, which sought to break inflationary expectations by pegging the real to the U.S. dollar. Inflation was brought down to single digit annual figures, but not fast enough to avoid substantial real exchange rate appreciation during the transition phase of the Plano Real. This appreciation meant that Brazilian goods were now more expensive relative to goods from other countries, which contributed to large current account deficits. However, no shortage of foreign currency ensued because of the financial community's renewed interest in Brazilian markets as inflation rates stabilized and memories of the debt crisis of the 1980s faded.

The Real Plan successfully eliminated inflation, after many failed attempts to control it. Almost 25 million people turned into consumers. The maintenance of large current account deficits via capital account surpluses became problematic as investors became more risk averse to emerging market exposure as a consequence of the Asian financial crisis in 1997 and the Russian bond default in August 1998. After crafting a fiscal adjustment program and pledging progress on structural reform, Brazil received a $41.5 billion IMF-led international support program in November 1998. In January 1999, the Brazilian Central Bank announced that the real would no longer be pegged to the U.S. dollar. This devaluation helped moderate the downturn in economic growth in 1999 that investors had expressed concerns about over the summer of 1998. Brazil's debt to GDP ratio of 48 percent for 1999 beat the IMF target and helped reassure investors that Brazil will maintain tight fiscal and monetary policy even with a floating currency.

The economy grew 4.4 percent in 2000, but problems in Argentina in 2001, and growing concerns that the presidential candidate considered most likely to win, leftist Luis Inácio Lula da Silva, would default on the debt, triggered a confidence crisis that caused the economy to decelerate. Poverty was down to near 16 percent.

In 2002, Luis Inácio Lula da Silva won the presidential elections, and he was re-elected in 2006. During his government, the economy began to grow more rapidly. In 2004 Brazil saw promising growth of 5.7 percent in GDP; following in 2005 with 3.2 percent growth; in 2006, 4.0 percent; in 2007, 6.1 percent; and in 2008, 5.1 percent growth. Although the financial crisis caused some slowdown in Brazil's economy, it has weathered the period much better than nearly every other economy in the Western Hemisphere. Indeed, confidence in Brazil's economic performance, and the relatively smooth presidential election and transition in 2010, have resulted in an appreciation of the real in relation to other global currencies, a dramatic turnaround from an earlier era when currency concerns were almost always on the side of depreciation.

Although Brazil remains the world's largest exporter of several agricultural products including beef, chicken, coffee, orange juice, and sugar, the country's international trade and investment relationships have diversified considerably to include manufacturing and services.

Brazil has become the second-biggest destination for foreign direct investment into developing countries after China. For the past two years, Brazil has been the world's fastest-growing car market. Vale (VALE) has become one of the world's biggest mining companies and exports virtually all of its iron ore production to China. Embraer (ERJ) jet, the global leader in small and medium-sized airplanes, is now the world's third-largest manufacturer of passenger jets after Boeing and Airbus. Petrobras is one of the world's largest oil and gas companies and has recently discovered major deposits of both oil and gas off the Brazilian coast. Odebrecht is a Brazilian business conglomerate in the fields of Engineering and Construction and Chemicals and Petrochemicals and is responsible for building a number of large infrastructure projects around the world, including roads, bridges, mass transit systems, more than 30 airports, and sports stadiums such as Florida International University's FIU stadium.

the two blocs, and Chile has joined the Asia-Pacific Economic Cooperation group and the TPP negotiations described above. These developments help illustrate the economic dynamism of South America and, especially in light of Asia's recent economic problems, explain why so many multinationals are interested in doing business with this part of the world.

Middle East and Central Asia Israel, the Arab countries, Iran, Turkey, and the Central Asian countries of the former Soviet Union are a special group of emerging countries.

Because of their oil, however, some of these countries are considered to be economically rich. Recently, this region has been in the world news because of the wars and terrorism concerns in the aftermath of the September 11, 2001, terrorist attack on the United States. However, these countries continue to try to balance geopolitical/religious forces with economic viability and activity in the international business arena. Students of international management should have a working knowledge of these countries' customs, culture, and management practices since most industrial nations rely, at least to some degree, on imported oil and since many people around the world work for international, and specifically Arab, employers.

The Arab and Central Asian countries rely almost exclusively on oil production. The price of oil greatly fluctuates, and the Organization of Petroleum Exporting Countries (OPEC) has trouble holding together its cartel. In recent years the price has been relatively high, and world demand is likely to keep it there. Arab countries have invested billions of dollars in U.S. property and businesses. Many people around the world, including those in the West, work for Arab employers. For example, the bankrupt United Press International was purchased by the Middle East Broadcasting Centre, a London-based MNC owned by the Saudis.

The "Arab Spring," described in the next chapter, has had a profound impact on the political and economic environment of many countries in this region.

Africa   Even though they have considerable natural resources, many African nations remain very poor and undeveloped, and international trade is only beginning to serve as a major source of income. One major problem of doing business in the African continent is the overwhelming diversity of approximately one-billion people, divided into 3,000 tribes, that speak 1,000 languages and dialects. Also, political instability is pervasive, and this instability generates substantial risks for foreign investors.

In recent years, Africa, especially sub-Saharan Africa, has had a number of severe problems. In addition to tragic tribal wars, there has been the spread of terrible diseases such as AIDS and Ebola. In 2002–2003, the WTO agreed to relax intellectual property rights (IPR) rules to allow for greater and less costly access by African countries to anti-viral AIDS medications (see the In-Depth Integrative Case at the end of Part One of this text). While globalization has opened up new markets for developed countries, developing nations in Africa lack the institutions, infrastructure, and economic capacity to take full advantage of globalization. Other big problems include poverty, malnutrition, illiteracy, corruption, social breakdown, vanishing resources, overcrowded cities, drought, and homeless refugees. There is still hope in the future for Africa despite this bleak situation, because the potential of African countries remains virtually untapped. Not only are there considerable natural resources, but the diversity itself can also be used to advantage. For example, many African people are familiar with the European cultures and languages of the former colonial powers (e.g., English, French, Dutch, and Portuguese), and this can serve them well in international business as they strive for continued growth. Uncertain times are ahead, but a growing number of MNCs are attempting to make headway in this vast continent. Also, the spirit of these emerging countries has not been broken. There are continuing efforts to stimulate economic growth. Examples of what can be done include Togo, which has sold off many of its state-owned operations and leased a steel-rolling mill to a U.S. investor, and Guinea, which has sold off some of its state-owned enterprises and cut its civil service force by 30 percent. A special case is South Africa, where apartheid, the former white government's policies of racial segregation and oppression, has been dismantled and the healing process is progressing. Long-jailed former black president Nelson Mandela is recognized as a world leader. These significant developments have led to an increasing number of the world's MNCs returning to South Africa; however, there continue to be both social and economic problems that, despite Mandela's and his successors' best efforts, signal uncertain times for the years ahead. One major initiative is the country's Black Economic Empowerment (BEE) program, designed to reintegrate the disenfranchised majority into business and economic life.

Africa's economic growth and dynamism have accelerated in recent years. Real GDP rose by 4.9 percent a year from 2000 through 2008, more than twice its pace in the 1980s and 90s. Telecommunications, banking, and retailing are all flourishing. Many African economies saw their growth accelerate in 2006–2008 due in part to higher commodity prices. While growth in sub-Saharan Africa slowed to 2.1 percent in 2009, growth rebounded to about 5 percent in 2011 and 2012, and the World Bank predicts that output will continue to grow at a similar pace in 2013 and 2014 (see Table 1–12). McKinsey, the global consultancy,

Table 1–12
Overview of the World Economic Outlook; Projections
(percentage change, unless otherwise noted)

	Year over Year				Q4 over Q4		
			Projections		Estimates	Projections	
	2011	2012	2013	2014	2012	2013	2014
World Output	3.9	3.2	3.5	4.1	2.9	3.8	4.0
Advanced Economies	1.6	1.3	1.4	2.2	0.9	2.0	2.1
United States	1.8	2.3	2.0	3.0	1.9	2.4	3.2
Euro Area	1.4	−0.4	−0.2	1.0	−0.7	0.5	1.0
Germany	3.1	0.9	0.6	1.4	0.6	1.3	1.1
France	1.7	0.2	0.3	0.9	0.3	0.3	1.2
Italy	0.4	−2.1	−1.0	0.5	−2.4	0.1	0.4
Spain	0.4	−1.4	−1.5	0.8	−1.9	−0.3	0.8
Japan	−0.6	2.0	1.2	0.7	0.2	2.6	−0.1
United Kingdom	0.9	−0.2	1.0	1.9	0.0	1.4	2.0
Canada	2.6	2.0	1.8	2.3	1.3	2.2	2.3
Other Advanced Economies	3.3	1.9	2.7	3.3	2.0	3.5	3.2
Newly Industrialized Asian Economies	4.0	1.8	3.2	3.9	2.4	3.9	3.8
Emerging and Developing Economies	6.3	5.1	5.5	5.9	5.5	5.9	6.2
Central and Eastern Europe	5.3	1.8	2.4	3.1	1.6	3.2	3.1
Commonwealth of Independent States	4.9	3.6	3.8	4.1	2.4	4.3	3.4
Russia	4.3	3.6	3.7	3.8	2.4	4.4	3.4
Excluding Russia	6.2	3.9	4.3	4.7	...	...	...
Developing Asia	8.0	6.6	7.1	7.5	7.3	7.1	7.8
China	9.3	7.8	8.2	8.5	8.1	7.9	8.8
India	7.9	4.5	5.9	6.4	5.4	6.0	6.4
ASEAN–5	4.5	5.7	5.5	5.7	7.7	5.8	5.5
Latin America and the Caribbean	4.5	3.0	3.6	3.9	3.1	4.2	3.6
Brazil	2.7	1.0	3.5	4.0	2.1	4.0	4.1
Mexico	3.9	3.8	3.5	3.5	2.8	4.9	2.5
Middle East and North Africa (MENA)	3.5	5.2	3.4	3.8	...	...	...
Sub-Saharan Africa	5.3	4.8	5.8	5.7	...	...	...
South Africa	3.5	2.3	2.8	4.1	1.5	4.2	4.1
Memorandum							
European Union	1.6	−0.2	0.2	1.4	−0.3	1.0	1.2
World Growth Based on Market Exchange Rates	2.9	2.5	2.7	3.4	2.1	3.1	3.3
World Trade Volume (goods and services)	5.9	2.8	3.8	5.5	...	...	...
Imports							
Advanced Economies	4.6	1.2	2.2	4.1	...	...	...
Emerging and Developing Economies	8.4	6.1	6.5	7.8	...	...	...
Exports							
Advanced Economies	5.6	2.1	2.8	4.5	...	...	...
Emerging and Developing Economies	6.6	3.6	5.5	6.9	...	...	...

Source: IMF World Economic Outlook, January 2013.

Table 1–13
World's Most Competitive Nations, 2013

Country	Rank
USA	1
Switzerland	2
Hong Kong	3
Sweden	4
Singapore	5
Norway	6
Canada	7
UAE	8
Germany	9
Qatar	10

Source: World Competitive Scoreboard, 2013. PDF-IMD.org

has found that the rate of return on foreign investment in Africa is actually higher than any other region, offering positive prospects for this historically struggling region.[55]

Table 1–12 shows economic growth rates and projections for major world regions and countries from 2011 to 2014. Of note is the fact that a number of emerging regions and countries are growing faster than developed countries; notably, China, India, and other Asian economies. Table 1–13 ranks the top 10 countries globally on their "competitiveness" as reported by the World Economic Forum. For 2013, Hong Kong and Singapore were ranked third and fifth, respectively. Table 1–14 ranks emerging markets according to several key indicators.

■ The World of International Management—Revisited

In the World of International Management at the start of the chapter you read about how social media is changing how we connect, shaping business strategy and operations, and even affecting diplomacy. Social media and social networks are revolutionizing the nature of international management by allowing producers and consumers to interact directly and bringing populations of the world closer together. Having read this chapter, you should now be more cognizant of the impacts of globalization and many international linkages among countries, firms, and societies on international management. Although controversial, globalization appears unstoppable. The creation of free-trade agreements worldwide has helped to trigger economic gains in many developing nations. The consolidation and expansion of the EU will continue to open up borders and make it easier and more cost-effective for exporters from less developed countries to do business there. In Asia, formerly closed economies such as India and China have opened up, and other emerging Asian countries such as Indonesia, Malaysia, the Philippines, and Thailand are becoming important emerging economies in their own right. Continued efforts to privatize, deregulate, and liberalize many industries will increase consumer choice and lower prices as competition increases. The rapid growth of social media networks around the world is but one reflection of the interconnected nature of global economies and individuals. In some ways, social media are transcending traditional barriers and impediments to global integration; however, differences in economic systems and approaches persist, making international management an ongoing challenge.

In light of these developments, answer the following questions: (1) What are some of the pros and cons of globalization and free trade? (2) How might the rise of social media result in closer connections (and fewer conflicts) among nations? (3) Which regions of the world are most likely to benefit from globalization and integration in the years to come, and which may experience dislocations or setbacks?

Table 1–14
Market Potential Indicators Ranking for Emerging Markets, 2013

Country	Market Size	Market Growth Rate	Market Intensity	Market Consumption Capacity	Commercial Infra-Structure	Economic Freedom	Market Receptivity	Country Risk	Overall Score
Singapore	1	86	74	66	80	83	97	100	62
Hong Kong	1	44	100	58	100	90	100	92	61
China	100	100	1	70	39	8	4	54	56
South Korea	9	40	56	100	87	82	18	65	49
Israel	1	39	65	79	70	78	22	66	43
Czech Republic	1	11	45	95	88	88	16	71	43
Poland	3	33	55	82	72	81	8	63	41
Turkey	6	73	65	79	52	53	5	49	41
India	37	74	28	78	22	52	3	42	41
Chile	1	40	48	35	60	100	15	79	38
Hungary	1	1	58	88	77	78	20	37	37
Malaysia	3	60	29	58	63	52	21	61	37
Russia	19	45	36	68	73	17	4	43	36
Peru	2	76	40	56	40	70	6	50	35
Mexico	9	31	53	49	47	63	21	53	35
Indonesia	10	68	28	77	32	54	3	39	34
Brazil	18	36	42	37	56	60	1	55	34
Argentina	4	68	49	67	60	45	4	11	33
Saudi Arabia	4	68	15	0	56	15	14	67	32
Thailand	3	19	31	66	47	49	17	48	30
Egypt	4	33	58	83	47	27	4	10	30
Colombia	3	44	42	31	45	62	4	52	29
Philippines	4	24	52	58	31	51	5	37	28
Pakistan	5	37	66	83	1	32	1	1	25
Venezuela	3	40	36	67	44	1	8	10	24
South Africa	5	29	40	1	25	66	5	50	22

Source: GlobalEdge Market Potential Index for Emerging Markets 2013, http://globaledge.msu.edu/Knowledge-Tools/MPI. Reprinted with permission.

SUMMARY OF KEY POINTS

1. Globalization—the process of increased integration among countries—continues at an accelerated pace. More and more companies—including those from developing countries—are going global, creating opportunities and challenges for the global economy and international management. Globalization has become controversial in some quarters due to perceptions that the distributions of its benefits are uneven and due to the questions raised by offshoring. There have emerged sharp critics of globalization among academics, NGOs, and the developing world, yet the pace of globalization and integration continues unabated.

2. Economic integration is most pronounced in the triad of North America, Europe, and the Pacific Rim. The North American Free Trade Agreement (NAFTA) is turning the region into one giant market. In South America, there is an increasing amount of intercountry trade, sparked by Mercosur. Additionally, trade agreements such as the Central American Free Trade Agreement (CAFTA) are linking countries of the Western Hemisphere together. In Europe, the expansion of the original countries of the European Union (EU) is creating a larger and more diverse union, with dramatic transformation of Central and Eastern European countries such as the Czech Republic, Poland, and Hungary. Asia is another major regional power, as reflected in the rapid growth shown not only by Japan but also the economies of China, India, and other emerging

markets. Countries in Africa and the Middle East continue to face complex problems but still hold economic promise for the future. Emerging markets in all regions present both opportunities and challenges for international managers.

3. Different growth rates and shifting demographics are dramatically altering the distribution of economic power around the world. Notably, China's rapid growth will make it the largest economic power in the world by midcentury, if not before. India will be the most populous country in the world, and other emerging markets will also become important players. International trade and investment have been increasing dramatically over the years. Major multinational corporations (MNCs) have holdings throughout the world, from North America to Europe to the Pacific Rim to Africa. Some of these holdings are a result of direct investment; others are partnership arrangements with local firms. Small firms also are finding that they must seek out international markets to survive in the future. MNCs from emerging markets are growing rapidly and expanding their global reach. The internationalization of nearly all business has arrived.

4. Different economic systems characterize different countries and regions. These systems, which include market, command, and mixed economies, are represented in different nations and have changed as economic conditions have evolved.

KEY TERMS

chaebols, *25*

European Union, *11*

foreign direct investment (FDI), *15*

globalization, *6*

international management, *4*

keiretsu, *22*

management, *4*

maquiladora, *21*

Ministry of International Trade and Industry (MITI), *22*

MNC, *5*

North American Free Trade Agreement (NAFTA), *10*

offshoring, *8*

outsourcing, *8*

World Trade Organization (WTO), *9*

REVIEW AND DISCUSSION QUESTIONS

1. How has globalization affected different world regions? What are some of the benefits and costs of globalization for different sectors of society (companies, workers, communities)?

2. How has NAFTA affected the economies of North America and the EU affected Europe? What

importance do these economic pacts have for international managers in North America, Europe, and Asia?

3. Why are Russia and Eastern Europe of interest to international managers? Identify and describe some reasons for such interest.

4. Many MNCs have secured a foothold in Asia, and many more are looking to develop business relations there. Why does this region of the world hold such interest for international management? Identify and describe some reasons for such interest.

5. Why would MNCs be interested in South America, India, the Middle East and Central Asia, and Africa, the less developed and emerging countries of the world? Would MNCs be better off focusing their efforts on more industrialized regions? Explain.

6. MNCs from emerging markets (India, China, Brazil) are beginning to challenge the dominance of developed country MNCs. What are some advantages that firms from emerging markets bring to their global business? How might MNCs from North America, Europe, and Japan respond to these challenges?

ANSWERS TO THE IN-CHAPTER QUIZ

1. **a.** De'Longhi, an Italy.-based MNC, bought the Braun company from Proctor & Gamble in 2012.

2. **d.** BIC SA is a French company.

3. **d.** Tata Motors, a division of the Indian conglomerate the Tata Group, purchased Jaguar, Land Rover, and related brands from Ford in 2008.

4. **a.** Technicolor SA of France produces RCA televisions.

5. **a.** General Mills, of the United States, acquired the Green Giant product line (together with the Pillsbury company) in 2001 from Britain's Diageo PLC.

6. **d.** Godiva chocolate is owned by Yildiz Holding, a Turkish conglomerate.

7. **b.** Vaseline is manufactured by the Anglo-Dutch MNC Unilever PLC.

8. **d.** Wrangler jeans are made by the VF Corporation based in the United States.

9. **d.** Holiday Inn is owned by Britain's InterContinental Hotels Group PLC.

10. **c.** Tropicana orange juice was purchased by U.S.-based PepsiCo.

INTERNET EXERCISE: GLOBAL COMPETITION IN FAST FOOD

One of the best-known franchise operations in the world is McDonald's, and in recent years, the company has been working to expand its international presence. But emerging market fast food companies have succeeded in slowing McDonald's global expansion by catering to local and regional tastes. Philippines based Jollibee is one such success story. Jollibee has 780 outlets in the Philippines and more than 90 around the world, including in the United States. Visit the McDonald's and Jollibee websites, and find out what each has planned in terms of their global expansion. Compare their presence in Asia to each other and to Yum! Brands' KFC and Pizza Hut presence in Asia.

Then, based on this assignment and the chapter material, answer these last three questions: (1) Which of these companies seems best positioned in Southeast Asia? (2) What advantages might a "local" brand like Jollibee have over the global companies? What advantages to the global MNCs have? (3) What is your prediction in terms of future growth potential?

India

India is located in southern Asia, with the Bay of Bengal on the east and the Arabian Sea on the west. One-sixth of the world's population (approximately 1.205 billion people) lives within the country's 1.27 million square miles. Though Hindi is the dominant language in terms of number of speakers (it is the mother tongue to over 40 percent of Indians), India is essentially a multilingual nation with more than 10 other languages spoken by 20 million people or more. Most states are divided along linguistic lines, with different states accepting different "official" languages (one each). English serves as the national language among the educated Indians. The Indian economy derives only 19 percent of its output from agriculture, with services contributing almost 55 percent. However, more than 70 percent of Indians are directly or indirectly dependent on agriculture. Three-quarters of Indians live in over 600,000 villages. Many of these communities lack infrastructure such as roads, power, and telecommunications. Hence, India's rural population presents a huge untapped potential for many marketers. The country has operated as a democratic republic since its independence in 1947. At that time, India was born of the partition of the former British Indian empire into the new countries of India and Pakistan. This division has been a source of many problems through the years. For example, much to the dismay of the world community, both countries have had nuclear tests in a cold war atmosphere. Also, many millions of Indians still live at the lowest level of subsistence, and per capita income is very low. India's misaligned central and local public finances have contributed to an overall fiscal deficit of more than 37 percent of GDP.

In the past, doing business in India has been quite difficult. For example, it took PepsiCo three years just to set up a soft drink concentrate factory, and Gillette, the U.S. razor blade company, had to wait eight years for its application to enter the market to be accepted.

In recent years, the government has been relaxing its bureaucratic rules, particularly those relating to foreign investments. In 2000, foreign direct investment exceeded $3 billion and by 2011 had reached $50.8 billion, making India the third highest recipient of FDI in the world. Although much of this investment has historically come from the United Kingdom and the United States, many Asian investors are also viewing India as an attractive location for new business investment. One reason for this change is that the government realizes many MNCs are making a critical choice: India or China? Additionally, foreign investments are having a very positive effect on the Indian economy. Despite slowing to 5.7 percent in 2009 during the global recession, GDP increased by 7.2 percent in 2011 but fell again to 5.3 percent in 2012. As of 2011, per capita GDP stood at US$3,900 on a purchasing power parity basis.

With the disbandment of the "License Raj," a socialist-inspired system that made government permits mandatory for almost every aspect of business, the climate for foreign investment has improved markedly. Coca-Cola was able to get permission for a 100-percent-owned unit in India in eight weeks, and Motorola received clearance in two days to add a new product line. Other companies that have reported rapid progress include DaimlerChrysler, Procter & Gamble, and Whirlpool.

In addition, there are other attractions: (1) a large number of highly educated people, especially in areas such as medicine, engineering, and computer science; (2) widespread use of English, long accepted as the international language of business; and (3) low wages and salaries, which often are 10 to 30 percent of those in the world's economic superpowers. While these factors will continue to have a positive impact, the growing debate over jobs outsourced from the United States could dampen some of the impressive growth prospect for India. Also, the election upset of May 2004, in which the opposition National Congress Party defeated the ruling BJP Party, suggests Indians are concerned about attention to social needs, not just economic growth. However, the Congress-led coalition under Prime Minister Manmohan Singh has continued economic reforms as well. When terrorists who perpetrated violent attacks in Mumbai in November 2008, were traced to a Pakistani organization, there was concern that India's already delicate relationship with its northern neighbor would unravel. To date, the two countries appear to be committed to working toward stability across their long border and broader cooperation. Elections in May 2009 further solidified the Congress Party's coalition as the solid leader of the government.

www.infoplease.com, data.worldbank.org/indicator/

Questions

1. What is the climate for doing business in India? Is it supportive of foreign investment?
2. How important is a highly educated human resource pool for MNCs wanting to invest in India? Is it more important for some businesses than for others?
3. Given the low per capita income of the country, why would you still argue for India to be an excellent place to do business in the coming years?

Chapter 2

THE POLITICAL, LEGAL, AND TECHNOLOGICAL ENVIRONMENT

The World of *International Management*

Social Media and the Pace of Change

The struggle for government reform has traditionally been a long, painful process. In the past, uprisings in the Middle East were violently repressed, lasted for many months, and rarely resulted in any real changes. The Bahrain protests of the 1990s, for example, lasted for five years. More recently, the 2009 Iranian protests lasted for close to a year and achieved no reforms. The pace of change, however, appears to be rapidly increasing.

Between 2010 and 2012, a series of spontaneous, loosely-related uprisings broke out in over a dozen countries throughout Northern Africa and the Middle East. Referred to as the "Arab Spring," these independent protests arose primarily as a reaction to high unemployment, exposed human rights violations, government corruption, and general dissatisfaction with the unelected dictatorships. Unlike previous rebellions in the region, which were quashed, the Arab Spring led to real reforms at a pace never before seen in the region. In Tunisia, the first country to experience protests, the government collapsed in less than a month. Egypt followed shortly after, and the Yemeni and Libyan governments were completely overthrown in late 2011. Major reforms were rapidly enacted in close to a dozen other countries, and Syria descended into a civil war.

The Egyptian government, in particular, was overthrown at an unprecedented speed. After just 18 days of citizen protests, Egyptian President Hosni Mubarak's 30-year hold on power came to a jolting end on February 11, 2011. Similar to Tunisian President Ben Ali, who was overthrown one month earlier, Mubarak was forced to resign and flee the country in less than one month. The second Arab-League government overthrown in the region in a period of just a few weeks sent shockwaves across the Middle East. How could Mubarak, one of the most powerful leaders in the region for 30 years, be removed from power in less than three weeks?

Social Media as an Organizing Tool

Evidence suggests that the ability to communicate instantaneously with fellow protestors was a critical factor in the rapid success of the Arab Spring rebellions. Unlike previous revolutions, which lacked any widespread, immediate communication tools, the Arab Spring protestors were equipped with smartphones and social media. Twitter and Facebook morphed from informal, friendly networking sites to powerful weapons. Evidence shows that the initial "Day of Revolt" in Egypt on January 25, 2011, was coordinated online through a Facebook group.[1] Because Facebook groups allow users to see how many other people are planning to take part in the event, and because of the mass showing of support online, a greater number of people were likely more comfortable and confident showing up to protest on the initial day.[2] Over 80,000 social media users stated that they would participate in the "Day of Revolt."[3]

During the protests, social media activity in Arab countries more than doubled. This was especially true in Egypt. Roughly 9 out of 10 Egyptian protestors stated that they used Facebook to communicate and organize. Furthermore, during the protests, 88 percent of Egyptians stated that they received their information over social media, as opposed to just 63 percent from the local media.[4] Using social networking, Egyptian protestors effectively coordinated their actions on a massive scale that would have been impossible just a few years ago. When situations arose that disrupted their plans, such as spontaneous clashes with security officials, Egyptian protestors were able to adapt and instantly communicate new plans through Twitter postings. Dispersing the crowd, with the attempt to confuse the protestors' preplanned actions, was no longer effective for the government officials.

Social media provided such a powerful tool that, on January 28, 2011, the Egyptian government attempted to disrupt Internet service completely.[5] During this blackout, a third of the Egyptian protestors stated that their communication was impacted. However, over half of those surveyed agreed that the blackout only further motivated their cause.[6]

Social Media as a Journalism Tool

The creation of "protestors-as-journalists," through the use of social media, was another contributing factor in the rapid regime change in Egypt. For the first time in history, citizens could instantly record video from within the heart of the riots and, using smartphones, transmit that footage to the Internet in real-time. Rather than relying on news reporters located outside of the actual protests to gather and send information, news organizations gathered the uploaded information to build their reports. Because the footage was first-hand, the accuracy of the information and speed of delivery improved. "Protestors-as-journalists" gave international validity to their cause overnight.[7]

More importantly, smartphones and social networks ensured that every retaliatory action that the government forces took was certain to be transmitted to a worldwide audience within minutes. In Egypt, in particular, this complicated the government's strategy to combating the protestors. Whereas previous uprisings had been violently dissolved by the fist of government, Mubarak's administration was literally under the watch of the world. The Egyptian government's reactions against those in Tahir Square could not be controversial; any human rights violations would be broadcast online, likely eroding the little outside support his regime had left.[8]

Social Media as a Support-Building Tool

International support for the protests heavily benefited the rebels, and social media served as a catalyst for that support. On Twitter, the hashtags "Egypt" and "Jan25" were tweeted 1.4 million and 1.2 million times, respectively, between January and March of 2011.[9] The details from within Egypt, leaked primarily over Twitter, heavily favored the protestors and gave legitimacy to the revolution abroad. Rather than continuing its hands-off approach, the U.S. government was forced to address the revolution directly. The Obama administration shifted its tone and began to speak of the "transition" due to occur in Egypt.[10]

When news of widespread looting was rumored, many outsiders were quick to rethink their opinion of the previously peaceful protestors. Almost instantly, however, neighborhood watch groups spread information over Twitter that police officers, dressed as protestors, were actually the ones looting and destroying property. Rather than seeing protestors as a reckless mob, outsiders saw the Egyptian government as attempting to paint an inaccurate picture of the protestors, likely as an excuse to use greater force.[11] Whether or not the protestors were participating in the vandalism, social media set the narrative in favor of the revolution.

Social Media's Impact on International Business

The sudden uncertainty in Egypt and the Middle East rapidly impacted international business dealings in the region. Production and GDP were negatively affected almost overnight, and fuel prices spiked globally. Supply chain routes were disrupted for months, increasing the shipping and logistical costs of goods passing through the region.[12]

According to a Geopolicity study from 2011, the Arab Spring cost the region roughly US$56 billion in lost productivity.[13] In Egypt, the GDP growth rate dropped to just 1.22 percent.[14] Developing economies appear to be shying away from the region, at least in the short-term. Seventeen percent of the companies surveyed in the BRIC nations stating that they were less likely to do business in the region.[15] The economic effects have not been limited to just the countries that experienced uprisings. According to a Grant Thornton study released in late 2011, 22 percent of businesses worldwide reported negative effects as a direct result of the Arab Spring uprisings. In the United States, which is heavily dependent on fossil fuels from the region, the number affected swelled to over a quarter.[16]

Perhaps one silver lining from the rapid regime changes is the potential for equally as fast transitions to more open trade and business dealings. New governments, with control over the vast resources of the region, could welcome outside investment and the opportunity to join the international economic arena.

The Arab Spring uprisings highlight how the pace of change, aided by social media, is ever increasing. The experience in Egypt highlights how long-established governments can collapse suddenly and how these changes can have serious ramifications for international management. It is important for international managers to think through these complex political, legal, and technological issues that arise in a world that embraces rapid change so that they are prepared for potential challenges. MNCs must collaboratively work with new governments as laws, policies, and regulations are introduced and altered. Managing the political and legal environment will continue to be an important challenge for international managers, as will the rapid changes in the technological environment of global business.

■ Political Environment

Both domestic and international political environments have a major impact on MNCs. As government policies change, MNCs must adjust their strategies and practices to accommodate the new perspectives and actual requirements. Moreover, in a growing number of regions and countries, governments appear to be less stable; therefore, these areas carry more risk than they have in the past. The assessment of political risk and strategies to cope with it will be given specific attention in Chapter 10, but in this chapter we focus on general political systems with selected areas used as illustrations relevant to today's international managers.

The political system or system of government in a country greatly influences how its people manage and conduct business. We discussed in Chapter 1 how the government regulates business practices via economic systems. Here we review the general systems currently in place throughout the world. Political systems vary greatly between nation-states across the world. The issue with understanding how to conduct international management extends beyond general knowledge of the governmental practices to the specifics of the legal and regulatory frameworks in place. Underlying the actions of a government is the ideology informing the beliefs, values, behavior, and culture of the nation and its political system. We discussed ideologies and the philosophies underpinning them above. Effective management occurs when these different ideologies and philosophies are recognized and understood.

A political system can be evaluated along two dimensions. The first dimension focuses on the rights of citizens under governments ranging from fully democratic to totalitarian. The other dimension measures whether the focus of the political system is on individuals or the broader collective. The first dimension is the ideology of the system, while the second measures the degree of individualism or collectivism. No pure form of government exists in any category, so we can assume that there are many gradations along the two extremes. The observed correlation suggests that democratic societies emphasize individualism, while totalitarian societies lean toward collectivism.[17]

Ideologies

Individualism   Adopters of **individualism** adhere to the philosophy that people should be free to pursue economic and political endeavors without constraint. This means that government interest should not solely influence individual behavior. In a business context, this is synonymous with capitalism and is connected to a free-market society, as discussed in Chapter 1, which encourages diversity and competition, compounded with private ownership, to stimulate productivity. It has been argued that private property is more successful, progressive, and productive than communal property due to increased incentives for maintenance and focus on care for individually owned property. The idea is that working in a group requires less energy per person to achieve the same goal, but an individual will work as hard as he or she has to in order to survive in a competitive environment. Simply following the status quo will stunt progress, while competing will increase creativity and progress. Modern managers may witness this when dealing with those who adopt an individualist philosophy and then must work in a team situation. Research has shown that team performance is negatively influenced by those who consider themselves individualistic; however competition stimulates motivation and encourages increased efforts to achieve goals.[18]

> **individualism**
> The political philosophy that people should be free to pursue economic and political endeavors without constraint.

The groundwork for this ideology was founded long ago. Philosophers such as David Hume (1711–1776), Adam Smith (1723–1790), and even Aristotle (384–322 BC) contributed to these principles. While philosophers created the foundation for this belief system long ago, it can be witnessed playing out through modern practice. Eastern Europe, the former Soviet Union, areas of Latin America, Great Britain, and Sweden all have moved toward the idea that the betterment of society is related to the level of freedom individuals have in pursuing economic goals, along with general individual freedoms and self-expression without governmental constraint. The well-known movement in Britain toward privatization was led by Prime Minister Margaret Thatcher during her 11 years in office (1979–1990), when she successfully transferred ownership of many companies from the state to individuals and reduced the government-owned portion of gross national product from 10 to 3.9 percent. She was truly a pioneer in the movement toward a capitalistic society, which has since spread across Europe.

International managers must remain alert as to how political changes may impact their business, as a continuous struggle for a foothold in government power often affects leaders in office. For example, Britain's economy improved under the leadership of Tony Blair; however, his support of the Iraq War severely weakened his position. Conservative David Cameron, elected prime minister in 2010, has sought to integrate traditional conservative principles without ignoring social development policies, something the Labour Party has traditionally focused on. Government policy, in its attempt to control the economic environment, waxes and wanes, something the international manager must be keenly sensitive to.

Europe has added complexity to the political environment with the unification of the EU, which celebrated its 50th "birthday" in 2007. Notwithstanding the increasing integration of the EU, MNCs still need to be responsive to the political environment of individual countries, some due to the persistence of cultural differences, which will be discussed in Chapter 5. Yet, there are also significant interdependencies. For example, the recent economic crises in Greece, Spain, Portugal, and Ireland have prompted Germany and France to mobilize public and private financial support, even though the two largest economies in the euro zone have residual distrust from earlier eras of conflict and disagreement.[19] Europe is no longer a group of fragmented countries; it is a giant and expanding interwoven region in which international managers must be aware of what is happening politically, not only in the immediate area of operations but also throughout the continent. The EU consists of countries that adhere to individualistic orientations as well as those that follow collectivist ideals.

collectivism
The political philosophy that views the needs or goals of society as a whole as more important than individual desires.

Collectivism

Collectivism views the needs and goals of society at large as more important than individual desires.[20] The reason there is no one rigid form of collectivism is because societal goals and the decision of how to keep people focused on them differ greatly among national cultures. The Greek philosopher Plato (427–347 BC) believed that individual rights should be sacrificed and property should be commonly owned. While on the surface one may assume that this would lead to a classless society, Plato believed that classes should still exist and that the best suited should rule over the people. Many forms of collectivism do not adhere to that idea.

Collectivism emerged in Germany and Italy as "national socialism," or fascism. Fascism is an authoritarian political ideology (generally tied to a mass movement) that considers individual and other societal interests inferior to the needs of the state and seeks to forge a type of national unity, usually based on ethnic, religious, cultural, or racial attributes. Various scholars attribute different characteristics to fascism, but the following elements are usually seen as its integral parts: nationalism, authoritarianism, militarism, corporatism, collectivism, totalitarianism, anticommunism, and opposition to economic and political liberalism.

We will explore individualism and collectivism again in Chapter 4 in the context of national cultural characteristics.

socialism
A moderate form of collectivism in which there is government ownership of institutions, and profit is not the ultimate goal.

Socialism

Socialism directly refers to a society in which there is government ownership of institutions but profit is not the ultimate goal. In addition to historically communist states such as China, North Korea, and Cuba, socialism has been practiced to varying degrees in recent years in a more moderate form—"democratic socialism"—by Great Britain's Labour Party, Germany's Social Democrats, as well as in France, Spain, and Greece.[21]

Modern socialism draws on the philosophies of Karl Marx (1818–1883), Friedrich Engels (1820–1895), and Vladimir Ilyich Lenin (1870–1924). Marx believed that governments should own businesses because in a capitalistic society only a few would benefit, and it would probably be at the expense of others in the form of not paying wages due to laborers. He advocated a classless society where everything was essentially communal. Socialism is a broad political movement and forms of it are unstable. In modern times it branched off into two extremes: communism and social democracy.

Communism is an extreme form of socialism which was realized through violent revolution and was committed to the idea of a worldwide communist state. During the 1970s, most of the world's population lived in communist states. The communist party encompassed the former Soviet Union, China, and nations in Eastern Europe, Southeast Asia, Africa, and Latin America. Cuba, Nicaragua, Cambodia, Laos, and Vietnam headed a notorious list. Today much of the communist collective has disintegrated. China still exhibits communism in the form of limiting individual political freedom. China has begun to move away from communism in the economic and business realms because it has discovered the failure of communism as an economic system due to the tendency of common goals to stunt economic progress and individual creativity.

Some transition countries, such as Russia, are postcommunist, but still retain aspects of an authoritarian government. Russia presents one of the most extreme examples of how the political environment affects international management. Poorly managed approaches to the economic and political transition resulted in neglect, corruption, and confusing changes in economic policy.[22] Devoid of funds and experiencing regular gas pipeline leaks, toxic drinking water, pitted roads, and electricity shutoffs, Russia did not present attractive investment opportunities as it moved away from communism. Yet more companies are taking the risk of investing in Russia because of increasing ease of entry, the new attempt at dividing and privatizing the Unified Energy System, and the movement by the Kremlin to begin government funding for the good of society including education, housing, and health care.[23] Actions by the Russian government over the past few years, however, continue to call into question the transparency and reliability of the Russian government. BP, Shell, and Ikea have each encountered de facto expropriation, corruption, and state-directed industrialization.

One of the biggest problems in Russia and in other transition economies is corruption, which we will discuss in greater depth in Chapter 3. The 2012 Corruption Perception Index from Transparency International ranked Russia 133rd out of 176 countries, falling behind Egypt and Uganda.[24] Brazil, China, and India, part of the BRIC emerging markets block, consistently score higher than Russia. In the 2013 Heritage Foundation's Index of Economic Freedom, Russia's overall rating in the measurement of economic openness, regulatory efficiency, the rule of law, and competitiveness remained at 51.1 this year, ranking it only 1.1 points away from being a repressive economic business environment.[25] As more MNCs invest in Russia, these unethical practices will face increasing scrutiny if political forces can be contained. To date, some multinationals feel that the risk is too great, especially with corruption continuing to spread throughout the country. Despite the Kremlin's support of citizens, Russia is in danger of becoming a unified corrupt system. Still most view Russia as they do China: Both are markets that are too large and potentially too lucrative to ignore.

Social democracy refers to a socialist movement that achieved its goals through nonviolent revolution. This system was pervasive in such Western nations as Australia, France, Germany, Great Britain, Norway, Spain, and Sweden, as well as in India and Brazil. While social democracy was a great influence on these nations at one time or another, in practice it was not as viable as anticipated. Businesses that were nationalized were quite inefficient due to the guarantee of funding and the monopolistic structure. Citizens suffered a hike in both taxes and prices, which was contrary to the public interest and the good of the people. The 1970s and 1980s witnessed a response to this unfair structure with the success of Britain's Conservative Party and Germany's Christian Democratic Party, both of which adopted free-market ideals. Margaret Thatcher, as mentioned previously, was a great leader in this movement toward privatization. Although many businesses have been privatized, Britain still has a central government that adheres to the ideal of social democracy. With Britain facing severe budget shortfalls, Prime Minister David Cameron, elected in 2010, has proposed a comprehensive restructuring of public services which could further alter the country's longstanding commitment to a broad social support program.[26]

It is important to note here the difference between the nationalization of businesses and nationalism. The nationalization of businesses is the transference of ownership of a business from individuals or groups of individuals to the government. This may be done for several reasons: The ideologies of the country encourage the government to extract more money from the firm, the government believes the firm is hiding money, the government has a large investment in the company, or the government wants to secure wages and employment status because jobs would otherwise be lost. Nationalism, on the other hand, is an ideal in and of itself whereby an individual is completely loyal to his or her nation. People who are a part of this mindset gather under a common flag for such reasons as language or culture. The confusing thing for the international businessperson is that it can be associated with both individualism and collectivism. Nationalism exists in the United States, where there is a national anthem and all citizens gather under a common flag, even though individualism is practiced in the midst of a myriad of cultures and extensive diversity. Nationalism also exists in China, exemplified in the movement against Japan in the mid-1930s and the communist victory in 1949 when communist leader Mao Tse-tung gathered communists and peasants to fight for a common goal. This ultimately led to the People's Republic of China. In the case of modern China nationalism presupposes collectivism.

Political Systems

There are two basic anchors to political systems, each of which represents an "ideal type" that may not exist in pure form.

Democracy **Democracy**, with its European roots and strong presence in Northern and Western Europe, refers to the system in which the government is controlled by the citizens either directly or through elections. Essentially, every citizen should be involved in

democracy
A political system in which the government is controlled by the citizens either directly or through elections.

decision-making processes. The representative government ensures individual freedom since anyone who is eligible may have a voice in the choices made.

A democratic society cannot exist without at least a two-party system. Once elected, the representative is held accountable to the electorate for his or her actions, and this ultimately limits governmental power. Individual freedoms, such as freedom of expression and assembly, are secured. Further protections of citizens include impartial public service, such as a police force and court systems which also serve the government and, in turn, the electorate, though they are not directly affiliated with any political party. Finally, while representatives may be re-elected, the number of terms is often limited, and the elected representative may be voted out during the next election if he or she does not sufficiently adhere to the goals of the majority ruling. As mentioned above, a social democracy combines a socialist ideology with a democratic political system, a situation that has characterized many modern European states as well as some in Latin America and other regions.

totalitarianism
A political system in which there is only one representative party which exhibits control over every facet of political and human life.

Totalitarianism   **Totalitarianism** refers to a political system in which there is only one representative party which exhibits control over every facet of political and human life. Power is often maintained by suppression of opposition, which can be violent. Media censorship, political repression, and denial of rights and civil liberties are dominant ideals. If there is opposition to government, the response is imprisonment or even worse tactics, often torture. This may be used as a form of rehabilitation or simply a warning to others who may question the government.

Since only one party within each entity exists, there are many forms of totalitarian government. The most common is communist totalitarianism. Most dictatorships under the communist party disintegrated by 1989, but as noted above, aspects and degrees of this form of government are still found in Cuba, North Korea, Laos, Vietnam, and China. The evolution of modern global business has substantially altered the political systems in Vietnam, Laos, and China, each of which has moved toward a more market-based and pluralistic environment. However, each still exhibits some oppression of citizens through denial of civil liberties. The political environment in China is very complex because of the government's desire to balance national, immediate needs with the challenge of a free-market economy and globalization. Since joining the WTO in 2001, China has made trade liberalization a top priority. However, MNCs still face a host of major obstacles when doing business with and in China. For example, government regulations severely hamper multinational activity and favor domestic companies, which results in questionable treatment such as longer document processing times for foreign firms.[27] This makes it increasingly difficult for MNCs to gain the proper legal footing. The biggest problem may well be that the government does not know what it wants from multinational investors, and this is what accounts for the mixed signals and changes in direction that it continually sends. All this obviously increases the importance of knowledgeable international managers.

China may be moving further away from its communist tendencies as it begins supporting a more open, democratic society, at least in the economic sphere. China continues to monitor what it considers antigovernment actions and practices, but there is a discernible shift toward greater tolerance of individual freedoms.[28] For now, China continues to challenge the capabilities of current international business theory as it transitions through a unique system favoring high governmental control yet striving to unleash a more dynamic market economy.[29]

Though the most common, the totalitarian form of government exhibited in China is not the only one. Other forms of totalitarianism exhibit other forms of oppression as well. Parties or governments that govern an entity based on religious principles will ultimately oppress religious and political expression of its citizens. Examples are Iran or Saudi Arabia, where the laws and government are based on Islamic principles. Conducting business in the Middle East is, in many ways, similar to operating a business in the Western world. The Arab countries have been a generally positive place to do business, as many of these nations are seeking modern technology and most have the financial ability to pay for quality services. Worldwide fallout from the war on terrorism, the Afghanistan and Iraq wars, and the ongoing Israel–Arab conflicts, however, have raised tensions in the Middle East considerably, making the business environment there risky and potentially dangerous.

As discussed in the opening case, the 2011 Arab Spring uprisings have affected business dealings in the authoritarian and/or totalitarian countries across northern Africa and the Middle East. Reasons for the political unrest varied, but most commonly included factors such as oppressive government rule, economic decline, high unemployment, and human rights violations. As discussed above, protestors successfully overthrew four government regimes and forced reforms in almost a dozen others. The fallout from the Arab Spring has left the business environment with much uncertainty. Supply chain disruptions in the region have resulted in longer shipping times, and, in May, 2011, oil prices spiked to over $125 a barrel, a three-year high.[30] According to a late 2011 study by Grant Thornton, 26 percent of businesses in North America, and 22 percent of businesses globally, reported negative effects from the uprisings.[31] A map of the countries that were impacted by the Arab Spring can be seen in Figure 2–1. Though the region has somewhat stabilized, long-term business impacts of these revolutions have yet to be seen.

One final form of totalitarianism, sometimes referred to as "right-wing," allows for some economic (but not political) freedoms. While it directly opposes socialist and communist ideas, this form may gain power and support from the military, often in the form of a military leader imposing a government "for the good of the people." This results in military officers filling most government positions. Such military regimes ruled in Germany and Italy from the 1930s to 1940s and persisted in Latin America and Asia until the 1980s when the latter moved toward democratic forms. Recent examples include Myanmar, where the military has ruled since the suspension of democracy in 1962.

Figure 2–1	**Summary of Arab Spring Uprisings**

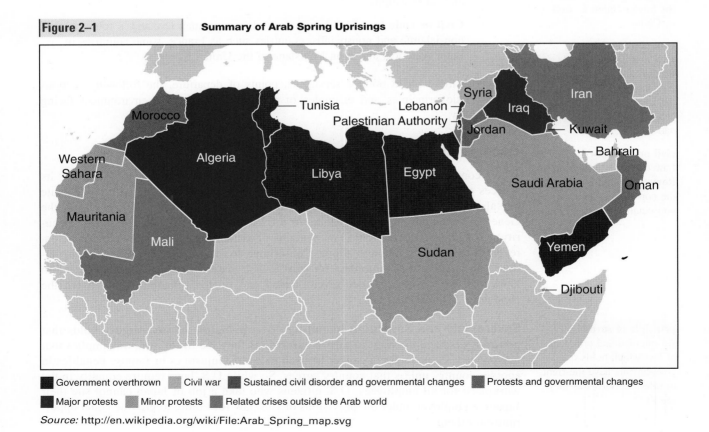

■ Government overthrown ■ Civil war ■ Sustained civil disorder and governmental changes ■ Protests and governmental changes

■ Major protests ■ Minor protests ■ Related crises outside the Arab world

Source: http://en.wikipedia.org/wiki/File:Arab_Spring_map.svg

■ Legal and Regulatory Environment

One reason why today's international environment is so confusing and challenging for MNCs is that they face so many different laws and regulations in their global business operations. These factors affect the way businesses are developed and managed within host nations, so special consideration must be paid to the subtle differences in the legal codes from one country to another. Adhering to disparate legal frameworks sometimes prevents large MNCs from capitalizing on manufacturing economies of scale and scope within these regions. In addition, the sheer complexity and magnitude of bureaucracies require special attention. This, in turn, results in slower time to market and greater costs. MNCs must take time to carefully evaluate the legal framework in each market in which they do business before launching products or services in those markets.

There are four foundations on which laws are based around the world. Briefly summarized, these are:

Islamic law
Law that is derived from interpretation of the Qur'an and the teachings of the Prophet Muhammad and is found in most Islamic countries.

socialist law
Law that comes from the Marxist socialist system and continues to influence regulations in countries formerly associated with the Soviet Union as well as China.

common law
Law that derives from English law and is the foundation of legislation in the United States, Canada, and England, among other nations.

civil or code law
Law that is derived from Roman law and is found in the non-Islamic and nonsocialist countries.

1. **Islamic law.** This is law derived from interpretation of the Qur'an and the teachings of the Prophet Muhammad. It is found in most Islamic countries in the Middle East and Central Asia.

2. **Socialist law.** This law comes from the Marxist socialist system and continues to influence regulations in former communist countries, especially those from the former Soviet Union, as well as present-day China, Vietnam, North Korea, and Cuba. Since socialist law requires most property to be owned by the state or state-owned enterprises, MNCs have traditionally shied away from these countries.

3. **Common law.** This comes from English law, and it is the foundation of the legal system in the United States, Canada, England, Australia, New Zealand, and other nations.

4. **Civil or code law.** This law is derived from Roman law and is found in the non-Islamic and nonsocialist countries such as France, some countries in Latin America, and even Louisiana in the United States.

With these broad notions serving as points of departure, the following sections discuss basic principles and examples of the international legal environment facing MNCs today.

Basic Principles of International Law

When compared with domestic law, international law is less coherent because its sources embody not only the laws of individual countries concerned with any dispute but also treaties (universal, multilateral, or bilateral) and conventions (such as the Geneva Convention on Human Rights or the Vienna Convention of Diplomatic Security). In addition, international law contains unwritten understandings that arise from repeated interactions among nations. Conforming to all the different rules and regulations can create a major problem for MNCs. Fortunately, much of what they need to know can be subsumed under several broad and related principles that govern the conduct of international law.

principle of sovereignty
An international principle of law which holds that governments have the right to rule themselves as they see fit.

Sovereignty and Sovereign Immunity   The **principle of sovereignty** holds that governments have the right to rule themselves as they see fit. In turn, this implies that one country's court system cannot be used to rectify injustices or impose penalties in another country unless that country agrees. So while U.S. laws require equality in the workplace for all employees, U.S. citizens who take a job in Japan cannot sue their Japanese employer under the provisions of U.S. law for failure to provide equal opportunity for them.

International Jurisdiction   International law provides for three types of jurisdictional principles. The first is the **nationality principle**, which holds that every country has jurisdiction (authority or power) over its citizens no matter where they are located. Therefore, a U.S. manager who violates the American Foreign Corrupt Practices Act while traveling abroad can be found guilty in the United States. The second is the **territoriality principle**, which holds that every nation has the right of jurisdiction within its legal territory. Therefore, a German firm that sells a defective product in England can be sued under English law even though the company is headquartered outside England. The third is the **protective principle**, which holds that every country has jurisdiction over behavior that adversely affects its national security, even if that conduct occurred outside the country. Therefore, a French firm that sells secret U.S. government blueprints for a satellite system can be subjected to U.S. laws.

Doctrine of Comity   The **doctrine of comity** holds that there must be mutual respect for the laws, institutions, and governments of other countries in the matter of jurisdiction over their own citizens. Although this doctrine is not part of international law, it is part of international custom and tradition.

Act of State Doctrine   Under the **act of state doctrine**, all acts of other governments are considered to be valid by U.S. courts, even if such acts are inappropriate in the United States. As a result, for example, foreign governments have the right to set limits on the repatriation of MNC profits and to forbid companies from sending more than this amount out of the host country back to the United States.

Treatment and Rights of Aliens   Countries have the legal right to refuse admission of foreign citizens and to impose special restrictions on their conduct, their right of travel, where they can stay, and what business they may conduct. Nations also can deport aliens. For example, the United States has the right to limit the travel of foreign scientists coming into the United States to attend a scientific convention and can insist they remain within five miles of their hotel. After the horrific events of 9/11, the U.S. government began greater enforcement of laws related to illegal aliens. As a consequence, closer scrutiny of visitors and temporary workers, including expatriate workers from India and elsewhere who have migrated to the United States for high-tech positions, may result in worker shortages.[32]

Forum for Hearing and Settling Disputes   This is a principle of U.S. justice as it applies to international law. At their discretion, U.S. courts can dismiss cases brought before them by foreigners; however, they are bound to examine issues including where the plaintiffs are located, where the evidence must be gathered, and where the property to be used in restitution is located. One of the best examples of this principle is the Union Carbide pesticide plant disaster in Bhopal, India. Over 2,000 people were killed and thousands left permanently injured when a toxic gas enveloped 40 square kilometers around the plant. The New York Court of Appeals sent the case back to India for resolution.

Examples of Legal and Regulatory Issues

The principles described above help form the international legal and regulatory framework within which MNCs must operate. In the following we examine some examples of specific laws and situations that can have a direct impact on international business.

Financial Services Regulation   The global financial crisis of 2008–2010 underscored the integrated nature of financial markets around the world and the reality that regulatory failure in one jurisdiction can have severe and immediate impacts on others.[33] The global contagion that enveloped the world was exacerbated, in part, by the availability of global derivatives trading and clearing and the relatively lightly regulated private equity and hedge fund industries. The crisis and its broad economic effects have prompted regulators around the world to consider tightening aspects of financial services regulation,

---

nationality principle
A jurisdictional principle of international law which holds that every country has jurisdiction over its citizens no matter where they are located.

territoriality principle
A jurisdictional principle of international law which holds that every nation has the right of jurisdiction within its legal territory.

protective principle
A jurisdictional principle of international law which holds that every country has jurisdiction over behavior that adversely affects its national security, even if the conduct occurred outside that country.

doctrine of comity
A jurisdictional principle of international law which holds that there must be mutual respect for the laws, institutions, and governments of other countries in the matter of jurisdiction over their own citizens.

act of state doctrine
A jurisdictional principle of international law which holds that all acts of other governments are considered to be valid by U.S. courts, even if such acts are illegal or inappropriate under U.S. law.

especially those related to the risks associated with the derivatives activities of banks and their involvement in trading for their own account. In the United States, financial reform legislation was approved in July of 2010, although the degree to which that legislation would prevent another crisis remained hotly debated.[34] The nearby Closer Look box provides a comparison of proposed and implemented financial reform approaches in the EU and United States.

Foreign Corrupt Practices Act (FCPA)
An act that makes it illegal to influence foreign officials through personal payment or political contributions; became U.S. law in 1977 because of concerns over bribes in the international business arena.

Foreign Corrupt Practices Act   During the special prosecutor's investigation of the Watergate scandal in the early 1970s, a number of questionable payments made by U.S. corporations to public officials abroad were uncovered. These bribes became the focal point of investigations by the U.S. Internal Revenue Service, Securities and Exchange Commission (SEC), and Justice Department. This concern over bribes in the international arena eventually culminated in the 1977 passage of the **Foreign Corrupt Practices Act (FCPA)**, which makes it illegal to influence foreign officials through personal payment or political contributions. The objectives of the FCPA were to stop U.S. MNCs from initiating or perpetuating corruption in foreign governments and to upgrade the image of both the United States and its businesses abroad.

Critics of the FCPA feared the loss of sales to foreign competitors, especially in those countries where bribery is an accepted way of doing business. Nevertheless, the U.S. government pushed ahead and attempted to enforce the act. Some of the countries that were named in early bribery cases under the law included Algeria, Kuwait, Saudi Arabia, and Turkey. The U.S. State Department tried to convince the SEC and Justice Department not to reveal countries or foreign officials who were involved in its investigations for fear of creating internal political problems for U.S. allies. Although this political sensitivity was justified for the most part, several interesting developments occurred: (1) MNCs found that they could live within the guidelines set down by the FCPA and (2) many foreign governments actually applauded these investigations under the FCPA, because it helped them crack down on corruption in their own country.

One analysis reported that since passage of the FCPA, U.S. exports to "bribe prone" countries actually increased.[35] Investigations reveal that once bribes were removed as a key competitive tool, more MNCs were willing to do business in that country. This proved to be true even in the Middle East, where many U.S. MNCs always assumed that bribes were required to ensure contracts. Evidence shows that this is no longer true in most cases; and in cases where it is true, those companies that engage in bribery face a strengthened FCPA that now allows the courts to both fine and imprison guilty parties. In addition, stepped up enforcement appears to be having a real impact. A report from the law firm Jones Day found that FCPA actions are increasingly targeting individual executives, not just corporations, and that penalties imposed under the FCPA have skyrocketed, and violations have spurred a number of collateral civil actions.[36]

Bureaucratization   Very restrictive foreign bureaucracies are one of the biggest problems facing MNCs. This is particularly true when bureaucratic government controls are inefficient and left uncorrected. A good example is Japan, whose political parties feel more beholden to their local interests than to those in the rest of the country. As a result, it is extremely difficult to reorganize the Japanese bureaucracy and streamline the ways things are done, because so many politicians are more interested in the well-being of their own districts than in the long-term well-being of the nation as a whole. In turn, parochial actions create problems for MNCs trying to do business there. The administration of Prime Minister Junichiro Koizumi of Japan tried to reduce some of this bureaucracy, although the fact that Japan has had six different prime ministers from 2006 to 2012 has not helped these efforts. Certainly the long-running recessionary economy of the country is inspiring reforms in the nation's antiquated banking system, opening up the Japanese market to more competition.[37]

Comparing European Union (EU) and U.S. Financial Reform

Preventing More Tax-Funded Bailouts

The G20 wants to end the belief among banks that they are "too big to fail" by requiring resolution mechanisms and "living wills" for speedy windups that don't destabilize markets. The U.S. Senate has set up an "orderly liquidation" process. The EU, a collection of 28 states with no common insolvency laws, faces a much harder task of thrashing out a pan-EU mechanism even though cross-border banks dominate the sector. EU executive European Commission published a policy outline on resolution funds so that banks pay for future bailouts with legislation adopted in June 2012. Internal splits exist over what to do with money raised.

Winners/Losers: Banks face an extra levy on top of higher capital and liquidity requirements. Taxpayers should be better shielded. Messy patchwork for global banks which will come under pressure to "subsidiarize" operations in different countries.

Over-the-Counter Derivatives

The G20 agreed that derivatives should be standardized where possible so they can be centrally cleared and traded on an exchange by the end of 2012. The U.S. Senate adopted legislation (Dodd-Frank Act) that went further by requiring banks to spin off their swaps desk to isolate risks from depositors.

The EU adopted legislation in December 2012, that focused on mandatory clearing of contracts. It is less fixated on mandatory exchange trading and won't look at the issue until much later in the year. It has no appetite so far to force structural changes on bank swap desks. The EU and the United States are likely to agree to exemptions for companies who hedge but there could be differences in scope.

Winners/Losers: Global banks could shift some trading from the United States to the EU. Corporates face costlier hedging as there will be heavier capital charges on uncleared trades but differences in exemption scope could be exploited.

Bonuses

The G20 has introduced principles to curb excessive pay and bonuses, such as requiring a big chunk of a bonus to be deferred over several years with a clawback mechanism. The United States and the EU are applying these principles and taking their own actions, such as a one-off tax in Britain.

Winners/Losers: Harder to justify big bonuses in the future.

Credit Ratings Agencies

The G20 agreed that ratings agencies should be required to register, report to supervisors, and show how they manage internal conflicts of interest. In 2012, the EU adopted even stricter laws, increasing the liability of ratings agencies and improving transparency. Under the EU law, ratings agencies can be sued for errors and must justify the release date of countries' ratings. U.S. reform plans are similar so no real differences are expected.

Winners/Losers: Ratings agencies will have to justify what they do much more in the future. The "Big Three"—Fitch, S&P, and Moody's—may face more competition in the EU. The sector faces more efforts to dilute their role in determining bank capital requirements.

Hedge Funds/Private Equity

The United States and the EU are working in parallel to introduce a G20 pledge to require hedge fund managers to register and report a range of data on their positions. U.S. law is in line with G20 but exempts private equity and venture capital. The EU wants to go much further by including private equity and requiring third-country funds and managers to abide by strict requirements if they want to solicit European investors, a step the United States says is discriminatory. Managers of alternative funds in the EU would also have curbs on remuneration, an element absent from U.S. reform.

Winners/Losers: U.S. hedge fund managers may find it harder to do business in the EU. European investors may end up with less choice. Regulators will have better data on funds. EU managers may decamp to Switzerland, though also for tax reasons.

Banks Trading

The U.S. Senate has adopted the "Volcker rule" which would ban risky trading unrelated to customers' needs at deposit-insured banks. Key EU states are against the rule as they want to preserve their universal banking model.

Winners/Losers: Some trading could switch to the EU from the United States inside global banks.

Systemic Risk

The G20 wants mechanisms in place to spot and tackle systemwide risks better, a core lesson from the crisis. The U.S. Senate bill sets up a council of regulators that includes the Federal Reserve but the U.S. House wants a bigger role for the Fed. The EU is approving a reform that will make the European Central Bank the hub of a pan-EU systemic risk board.

Winners/Losers: ECB is a big winner with an enhanced role that many see as a platform for a more pervasive role in the future. Banks will have yet another pair of eyes staring down at them.

Bank Capital Requirements

The push to beef up bank capital and liquidity requirements is being led by the global Basel Committee of central bankers and supervisors, which is toughening up its global accord as requested by the G20. It took at the end of 2012. The U.S. bill directs regulators to increase capital requirements on large financial firms as they grow in size or engage in riskier activities.

The EU is approving new rules to beef up capital on trading books and allow supervisors to slap extra capital requirements if remuneration is encouraging excessively risky behavior. It will debate a further set of rules at the turn of the year to toughen up definitions of capital and introduce leverage caps.

Winners/Losers: Bank return on equity is set to be squeezed. Regulators will have many more tools to control the sector. Higher costs are likely to be passed on to consumer investors. There could be timing issues

as the EU has been more willing than the United States in the past to adopt Basel rules.

Fixing Securitization

The U.S. Senate bill forces securitizers to keep a baseline 5 percent of credit risk on securitized assets. The EU has already approved a law to this effect.

Winners/Losers: Banks say privately the 5 percent level is low enough not to make much difference and that the key problem is restoring investor confidence into the tarnished sector.

Source: "Factbox: Comparing EU and U.S. Financial Reform," Reuters, May 19, 2010. Additional research by authors.

Japanese businesses are also becoming more aware of the fact that they are dependent on the world market for many goods and services and that when bureaucratic red tape drives up the costs of these purchases, local consumers pay the price. These businesses are also beginning to realize that government bureaucracy can create a false sense of security and leave them unprepared to face the harsh competitive realities of the international marketplace.

In many developing and emerging markets, bureaucratic red tape impedes business growth and innovation. The World Bank conducts an annual survey to determine the ease of doing business in a variety of countries around the world. The survey includes individual items related to starting a business, dealing with construction permits, employing workers, registering property, getting credit, protecting investors, paying taxes, trading across borders, enforcing contracts, and closing a business. A composite ranking, as shown in Table 2–1, ranks the overall ease of doing business in these countries. Although developed countries generally rank better (higher), there are some developing countries (Georgia, Malaysia) that do well, and some developed economies (Greece) that do poorly.

In Table 2–1 economies are ranked on their ease of doing business, from 1 to 185, with first place being the best. A high ranking on the ease-of-doing-business index means the regulatory environment is conducive to the operation of business. This index averages the country's percentile rankings on 10 topics, made up of a variety of indicators, giving equal weight to each topic. The rankings are benchmarked to June, 2012.

Privatization

Another example of the changing international regulatory environment is the current move toward privatization by an increasing number of countries. The German government, for example, has sped up privatization and deregulation of its telecommunications market. This has opened a host of opportunities for MNCs looking to create joint ventures with local German firms. Additionally, the French government has put some of its businesses on the sale block. Meanwhile, in China the government has ordered the military to close or sell off between 10,000 and 20,000 companies that earn an estimated $9.5 billion annually. Known collectively as PLA Inc., the Chinese Army's business interests stretch from Hong Kong to the United States and include five-star hotels, paging services, golf courses, and Baskin-Robbins ice cream franchises. When the government cut the military budget during the early 1990s, it allowed

Table 2–1
Ease-of-Doing-Business Ranking among Select Countries (2013)

Economy	Ease of Doing Business (Overall) Rank	Starting a Business	Dealing with Construction Permits	Getting Electricity	Registering Property	Getting Credit	Protecting Investors	Paying Taxes	Trading Across Borders	Enforcing Contracts	Closing a Business
Singapore	1	4	2	5	36	12	2	5	1	12	2
United States	4	13	17	19	25	4	6	69	22	6	16
United Kingdom	7	19	20	62	73	1	10	16	14	21	8
Korea, Rep.	8	24	26	3	75	12	49	30	3	2	14
Georgia	9	7	3	50	1	4	19	33	38	30	81
Finland	11	49	34	21	24	40	70	23	6	9	5
Malaysia	12	54	96	28	33	1	4	15	11	33	49
Sweden	13	54	25	9	35	40	32	38	8	27	22
Mauritius	19	14	62	44	60	53	13	12	15	58	64
Germany	20	106	14	2	81	23	100	72	13	5	19
Japan	24	114	72	27	64	23	19	127	19	35	1
United Arab Emirates	26	22	13	7	12	83	128	1	5	104	101
Switzerland	28	97	50	8	15	23	169	18	35	20	45
South Africa	39	53	39	150	79	1	10	32	115	82	84
Bahrain	42	88	7	48	29	129	82	7	54	113	27
Poland	55	124	161	137	62	4	49	114	50	56	37
Turkey	71	72	142	68	42	83	70	80	78	40	124
Greece	78	146	31	59	150	83	117	56	62	87	50
Vietnam	99	108	28	155	48	40	169	138	74	44	149
Pakistan	107	98	105	171	126	70	32	162	85	155	78
Russian Federation	112	101	178	184	46	104	117	64	162	11	53
Kenya	121	126	45	162	161	12	100	164	148	149	100
Argentina	124	154	171	74	135	70	117	149	139	48	94
Brazil	130	121	131	60	109	104	82	156	123	116	143
India	132	173	182	105	94	23	49	152	127	184	116
Philippines	138	161	100	57	122	129	128	143	53	111	165
Ecuador	139	169	104	146	101	83	139	84	128	99	137
Iran, Islamic Rep.	145	87	166	163	165	83	150	129	143	53	126
Gambia, the	147	123	90	119	120	159	177	179	87	65	108
Algeria	152	156	138	165	172	129	82	170	129	126	62
Uzbekistan	154	90	152	167	138	154	139	161	185	46	73
Afghanistan	168	28	164	110	174	154	185	94	178	164	115
Zimbabwe	172	143	170	157	85	129	128	134	167	111	169
Venezuela, R.B.	180	152	109	160	90	159	181	185	166	80	163
Central African Republic	185	170	147	173	132	104	139	181	182	177	185

Source: "Table 1.1: Rankings on the Ease of Doing Business," *Doing Business 2013,* The World Bank, p. 6, http://www.doingbusiness.org/rankings. Copyright © 2013. Reprinted with permission.

Many suggest that the trade relationship between the United States and China is "unbalanced." In 2012, the United States accumulated a $319 billion deficit with China, with U.S. politicians and trade officials claiming that an undervalued yuan and government subsidies and regulations that favor Chinese MNCs were the main sources of the problem. This is not the first time the United States has voiced complaints. For a number of years, the United States has negotiated with China in an attempt to open its markets. The United States holds some leverage in these exchanges, since about 60 percent of China's exports are produced from companies that are in whole or part owned by foreign investors; however, the emerging economy still does not operate on a purely market-based economy. In recent years, China has built up its alternative energy export industries, including photovoltaic cells and panels and wind energy equipment.

U.S. administrations have pushed hard to level the playing field for trading with China. The main strategy has been threats to impose tariffs on Chinese imports. In response to petitions by U.S. producers, including Broadwind, Fergus Falls, Otter Tail Corp. (OTTR)'s DMI Industries, Katana Summit LLC, headquartered in Ephrata, Washington, and a unit of Dallas-based Trinity Industries (TRN) Inc., in 2011, the U.S. Commerce Department began investigating imports of wind energy equipment from China. Specifically, U.S. producers alleged that imports benefited from Chinese government subsidies and therefore should be subject to countervailing duties, and that imported products were being sold at below home, market, or full value process and should be subjected to antidumping duties. In

December of 2012, the department issued final punitive tariffs on the products from China and Vietnam. Chinese and Vietnamese imports of wind towers account for about 25 percent of the total U.S. market. The decision coincided with the start of two days of trade and economic talks between U.S. and Chinese officials. Tensions between the world's two largest economies have risen within the past year over government support for clean-energy products, including solar cells and wind towers. Final duties imposed ranged from 47.59 percent to more than 58 percent.

The future of these claims and disagreements is uncertain. The United States believes that continued undervaluation of the yuan and subsidies or regulations that favor domestic Chinese companies and protect them from foreign competition maintain a very unlevel playing field. There is evidence of monopolies in aviation, steel, and telecommunications, but the United States has begun chipping away at other, more manageable fields. The United States also recognizes that China is an economic powerhouse and that an excess of tariffs could result in a trade war. It is evident that the EU and the United States would like to break down trade walls and be a part of the lucrative Chinese market, but they may need the added support of the WTO for effective negotiations.

The steps being taken by the U.S. government and the EU are important in opening up the Chinese market. Much needs to be done, however, and the U.S. government believes that success in this area will require it to "go to the mat" with China. The outcome promises to be interesting and vital to the success of world trade.

the army to make up the shortfall by earning commercial revenue. However, now the government has decided that the army must exit this end of the business and let the free market take over.[38]

According to one source, in 2010, Poland intensified its efforts to privatize more than 300 state-owned enterprises by the end of 2011; Turkey had issued various privatization tenders in the energy and electricity sectors; Nigeria finalized the privatization of three of the Power Holding Company of Nigeria successor companies in 2012; and Pakistan had privatized 167 state-owned enterprises since its inception, yielding US$9 billion in proceeds to the government.[39] As described in the International Management in Action box in Chapter 1, "Brazilian Economic Reform," many developing countries are privatizing their state-owned companies to provide greater competition and access to service.

Regulation of Trade and Investment

The regulation of international trade and investment is another area in which individual countries use their legal and regulatory policies to affect the international management environment. The rapid increase in trade and investment has raised concerns among countries that others are not engaging in fair trade, based on the fundamental principles of international trade as specified in the WTO and other trade and investment agreements. Specifically, international trade rules require countries to provide "national treatment," which means that they will not discriminate against others in their trade relations. Unfortunately, many countries engage in government support (subsidies) and other types of practices that distort trade. For example, many developing countries require that foreign MNCs take on local partners in order to do business. Others mandate that MNCs employ a certain percentage of local workers or produce a specific amount in their country. These practices are not limited to developing countries. Japan, the United States, and many European countries use product standards, "buy local" regulations, and other policies to protect domestic industries and restrict trade.

In addition, most trade agreements require that countries extend most-favored-nation status such that trade benefits accorded one country (such as tariff reductions under the WTO) are accorded all other countries that are parties to that agreement. The emergence of regional trade arrangements has called into question this commitment because, by definition, agreements among a few countries (NAFTA, EU) give preference to those specific members over those who are not part of these trading "blocs." As discussed in Chapter 1, many countries engage in antidumping actions intended to offset the practice of trading partners "dumping" products at below cost or home market price, as well as countervailing duty actions intended to offset foreign government subsidization. In each case, there is evidence that many countries abuse these laws to protect domestic industries, something the WTO has been more vigilant in monitoring in recent years.

■ Technological Environment and Global Shifts in Production

Technological advancements not only connect the world at incredible speed but also aid in the increased quality of products, information gathering, and R&D. Manufacturing, information processing, and transportation are just a few examples of where technology improves organizational and personal business. The need for instant communication increases exponentially as global markets expand. MNCs need to keep their businesses connected; this is becoming increasingly easier as technology contributes to "flattening the world." Thomas Friedman, in his book *The World Is Flat,* writes that such events as the introduction of the Internet or the World Wide Web, along with mobile technologies, open sourcing, and work flow software distribution, not only enable businesses and individuals to access vast amounts of information at their fingertips in real time but are also resulting in the world flattening into a more level playing field.[40]

Trends in Technology, Communication, and Innovation

The innovation of the microprocessor could be considered the foundation of much of the technological and computing advancements seen today.[41] The creation of a digital framework allowed high-power computer performance at low cost. This then gave birth to such breakthroughs as the development of enhanced telecommunication systems, which will be explored in greater depth later in the chapter. Now, computers, telephones, televisions, and wireless forms of communication have merged to create multimedia products and allow users anywhere in the world to communicate with one another. The Internet allows one to obtain information from literally billions of sources.

Global connections do not necessarily level the playing field, however. The challenge of integrating telecom standards has become an issue for MNCs in China. Qualcomm Corporation had wanted to sell China narrowband CDMA (code division multiple access) technology; however, Qualcomm was initially unsuccessful in convincing the government that it could build enough products locally. Instead, China's current network, the world's largest mobile network, uses primarily GSM technology that is popular in Europe.[42] Since 2009, however, CDMA had gained a foothold in China. In 2013 alone, China Telecom expects to sell 80 million CDMA handsets in China and 80 percent of those are expected to be smartphones.[43] China will become the world's largest CDMA smartphone market in 2013, with expected sales of 240 million smartphones.[44]

Furthermore, concepts like the open-source model allow for free and legal sharing of software and code, which may be utilized by underdeveloped countries in an attempt to gain competitive advantage while minimizing costs. India exemplifies this practice as it continues to increase its adoption of the Linux operating system (OS) in place of the global standard Microsoft Windows. The state of Kerala is shifting the software of its 2,600 high schools to the Linux system, which will enable a user to configure it to his or her needs with the goal of creating a new generation of adept programmers. In 2008, Microsoft unveiled DreamSpark, a software giveaway for an estimated 10 million-plus qualified students in the country. DreamSpark will provide students access to the latest Microsoft developer and designer tools at no charge to unlock their creative potential and set them on the path to academic and career success. The program is aligned to Microsoft Unlimited Potential, the company's global effort to creating sustained social and economic opportunity for everyone.[45] More broadly, a number of for profit and nonprofit firms have been aggressively working to bring low-cost computers into the hands of the hundreds of millions of children in the developing world who have not benefited from the information and computing revolution.

One initiative—One Laptop Per Child (OLPC)—is a U.S. nonprofit organization set up to oversee the creation of an affordable educational device for use in the developing world. Its mission is "to create educational opportunities for the world's poorest children by providing each child with a rugged, low-cost, low-power, connected laptop with content and software designed for collaborative, joyful, self-empowered learning." Its current focus is on the development, construction, and deployment of the XO-1 laptop and its successors, notably the release of the so-called XO-3, the long-awaited upgrade to the nonprofit's XO, the so-called "hundred-dollar laptop" launched in 2007. The organization is led by chairman Nicholas Negroponte and Charles Kane, president and chief operating officer. OLPC is a nonprofit organization funded by member organizations such as AMD, eBay, Google, News Corporation, Red Hat, and Marvell. As of March 2010, there are 2 million free books available for OLPC computers. Most recently, the One Laptop Per Child foundation's aim is to create the world's most innovative tablet computer for the developing world, priced at less than $100. The new device is modeled in part on the education-focused Moby tablet Marvell introduced earlier in 2010, with modifications to keep the price low ($100 or less) and make the device usable in challenging environmental conditions.[46]

There also exists a great potential for disappointment as the world relies more and more on digital communication and imaging. The world is connected by a vast network of cables which we do not see because they are either buried underground or under water. One disruption occurred off the shores of Asia on December 26, 2006, when undersea cables were destroyed by rock slides, cutting phone and Internet connections in Taiwan, China, South Korea, Japan, and India. The fact that so many were reliant on a mere 4-inch-thick cable shows the potential risks associated with greater global connectivity. Restoration of some services to most of the affected areas was accomplished within 12 hours of the earthquake by rerouting digital traffic through Europe to the United States with other network cables.[47]

We have reviewed general influences of technology here, but what are some of the specific dimensions of technology and what other ways does technology affect international management? Here, we explore some of the dimensions of the technological environment currently facing international management, with a closer look at biotechnology, e-business, telecommunications, and the connection between technology, outsourcing, and offshoring.

In addition to the trends discussed above, other specific ways in which technology will affect international management in the next decade include:

1. Rapid advances in biotechnology that are built on the precise manipulation of organisms, which will revolutionize the fields of agriculture, medicine, and industry.

2. The emergence of nanotechnology, in which nanomachines will possess the ability to remake the whole physical universe.

3. Satellites that will play a role in learning. For example, communication firms will place tiny satellites into low orbit, making it possible for millions of people, even in remote or sparsely populated regions such as Siberia, the Chinese desert, and the African interior, to send and receive voice, data, and digitized images through handheld telephones.

4. Automatic translation telephones, which will allow people to communicate naturally in their own language with anyone in the world who has access to a telephone.

5. Artificial intelligence and embedded learning technology, which will allow thinking that formerly was felt to be only the domain of humans to occur in machines.

6. Silicon chips containing up to 100 million transistors, allowing computing power that now rests only in the hands of supercomputer users to be available on every desktop.

7. Supercomputers that are capable of 1 trillion calculations per second, which will allow advances such as simulations of the human body for testing new drugs and computers that respond easily to spoken commands.[48]

The development and subsequent use of these technologies have greatly benefited the most developed countries in which they were first deployed. However, the most positive effects should be seen in developing countries where inefficiencies in labor and production impede growth. Although all these technological innovations will affect international management, specific technologies will have especially pronounced effects in transforming economies and business practices. The following discussion highlights some specific dimensions of the technological environment currently facing international management.

Biotechnology

The digital age has given rise to such innovations as computers, cellular phones, and wireless technology. Advancements within this realm allow for more efficient communication and productivity to the point where the digital world has extended its effect from information systems to biology. Biotechnology is the integration of science and technology, but more specifically it is the creation of agricultural or medical products through industrial use and manipulation of living organisms. At first glance, it appears that the fusion of these two disciplines could breed a modern bionic man immune to disease, especially with movements toward technologically advanced prosthetics, cell regeneration through stem cell research, or laboratory-engineered drugs to help prevent or cure diseases such as HIV or cancer.

Pharmaceutical competition is also prevalent on the global scale with China's raw material reserve and the emergence of biotech companies such as Genentech and the new Merck, after its acquisition of Swiss biotech company Serono. India is emerging as a major player, with its largest, mostly generic, pharmaceutical company Ranbaxy's ability to produce effective and affordable drugs.[49] While pharmaceutical companies mainly manufacture drugs through a process similar to that of organic chemistry, biotech companies attempt to discover genetic abnormalities or medicinal solutions through exploring organisms at the molecular level or by formulating compounds from inorganic materials that mirror organic substances. DNA manipulation in the laboratory extends beyond human research. As mentioned above, another aspect of biotech research is geared toward agriculture. Demand for ethanol in the United States is on the rise due to uncertain future oil supplies, making corn-derived ethanol a viable alternative. Yet, using corn as a fuel alternative will not only increase the cost of fuel but also create an imbalance between consumable corn and stock used for biofuel.[50] For this and many other reasons, global companies like Monsanto are collaborating with others such as BASF AG to work toward creating genetically modified seeds such as drought-tolerant corn and herbicide-tolerant soybeans.[51] Advancements in this industry include nutritionally advanced crops that may help alleviate world hunger.[52]

Aside from crops, the meat industry can also benefit from this process. The outbreak of mad cow disease in Great Britain sparked concern when evidence of the disease spread throughout Western Europe; however, the collaborative work of researchers in the United States and Japan may have engineered a solution to the problem by eliminating the gene which is the predecessor to making the animal susceptible to this ailment.[53] Furthermore, animal cloning, which simply makes a copy of pre-existing DNA, could boost food production by producing more meat or dairy-producing animals. The first evidence of a successful animal clone was Dolly, born in Scotland in 1996. Complications arose, and Dolly aged at an accelerated rate, indicating that while she provided hope, there still existed many flaws in the process. While the United States is the only country that allows cloned animal products to be incorporated in the food supply, other countries actively cloning animals include Australia, Italy, China, South Korea, Japan, and New Zealand.[54] The world is certainly changing, and the trend toward technological integration is far from over. Whether one desires laser surgery to correct eyesight, a vaccine for emerging viruses, or more nutritious food, there is a biotechnology firm competing to be the first to achieve these goals. Hunger and poor health care are worldwide issues, and advancement in global biotechnology is working to raise the standards.

E-Business

As the Internet becomes increasingly widespread, it is having a dramatic effect on international commerce. Table 2–2 shows Internet penetration rates for major world regions, illustrating the dramatic increase from 2000 to 2012 and the accompanying growth in penetration rates, with Asia exhibiting the highest rate at more than 40 percent.

Tens of millions of people around the world have now purchased books from Amazon.com, and the company has now expanded its operations around the world. So have a host of other electronic retailers (e-tailers) which are discovering that their home-grown retailing expertise can be easily transferred and adapted for the international market.[55] Dell Computer has been offering B2C (electronic business-to-consumer) goods and services in Europe for a number of years, and the automakers are now beginning to move in this direction. Most automotive firms sell custom cars online.[56] Other firms are looking to use e-business to improve their current operations. For example, Deutsche Bank has overhauled its entire retail network with the goal of winning affluent customers across the continent.[57] Yet the most popular form of e-business is for business-to-business (B2B) dealings, such as placing orders and interacting with suppliers worldwide. Business-to-consumer (B2C) transactions will not be as large, but this is an area where many MNCs are trying to improve their operations.

The area of e-business that will most affect global customers is e-retailing and financial services. For example, customers can now use their keyboard to pay by credit card,

Table 2–2
World Internet Usage and Population Statistics

World Regions	Population (2012 Est.)	Internet Users 2000	Internet Users 2012	Penetration (% Population)	Growth 2000–2009	Users % of Total
Africa	1,073,380,925	4,514,400	167,335,676	15.6%	3,606.7%	7.0%
Asia	3,922,066,987	114,304,000	1,076,681,059	27.5	841.9	44.8
Europe	820,918,446	105,096,093	518,512,109	63.2	393.4	21.5
Middle East	223,608,203	3,284,800	90,000,455	40.2	2,639.9	3.7
North America	348,280,154	108,096,800	273,785,413	78.6	153.3	11.4
Latin America/ Caribbean	593,688,638	18,068,919	254,915,745	42.9	1,310.8	10.6
Oceania/Australia	35,903,569	7,620,480	24,279,579	67.8	218.6	1.0
WORLD TOTAL	7,017,846,922	360,985,492	2,405,510,036	34.3	566.4	100.0

Source: Internet World Stats—www.internetworldstats.com/stats.htm. Estimated Internet users are 2,405,510,036 for June 30, 2012. Copyright © 2010, Miniwatts Marketing Group.

although security remains a problem. However, the day is fast approaching when electronic cash (e-cash) will become common. This scenario already occurs in a number of forms. A good example is prepaid smart cards, which are being used mostly for telephone calls and public transportation. An individual can purchase one of these cards and use it in lieu of cash. This idea is blending with the Internet, allowing individuals to buy and sell merchandise and transfer funds electronically. The result will be global digital cash, which will take advantage of existing worldwide markets that allow buying and selling on a 24-hour basis.

Some companies, such as ING DIRECT, the U.S.'s largest direct bank, are completely "disintermediating" banking by eliminating the branches and other "bricks and mortar" facilities altogether. ING has more than 7.6 million savings customers and $89.7 billion in assets. ING DIRECT has developed a comprehensive social media "Savers Community," including Twitter, Facebook, and its "We, the Savers" blog. And so far, not one of the 275-plus bank failures in the U.S., since the financial crisis began in 2008, has been online banks.[58] HSBC and other global banks are learning from ING's success and growing their Internet banking globally. AirAsia, a growing regional airline in Southeast Asia, has distributed tickets electronically since its inception, demonstrating that even in regions where Internet penetration had not been extensive, electronic distribution is possible and profitable (see the In-Depth Integrative Case after Part Three).

Telecommunications

One of the most important dimensions of the technological environment facing international management today is telecommunications. To begin with, it no longer is necessary to hardwire a city to provide residents with telephone service. This can be done wirelessly, thus allowing people to use cellular phones, pagers, and other telecommunications services. As a result, a form of technologic leapfrogging is occurring, in which regions of the world are moving from a situation where phones were unavailable to one where cellular is available everywhere, including rural areas, due to the quick and relatively inexpensive installation of cellular infrastructure. In addition, technology is merging the telephone and the computer. As a result, growing numbers of people in Europe and Asia are now accessing the Web through their cell phones. Over the next decade, the merging of the Internet and wireless technology will radically change the ways people communicate.[59]

Wireless technology is also proving to be a boon for less developed countries, such as in South America and Eastern Europe where customers once waited years to get a telephone installed.

One reason for this rapid increase in telecommunications services is many countries believe that without an efficient communications system their economic growth may stall. Additionally, governments are accepting the belief that the only way to attract foreign investment and know-how in telecommunications is to cede control to private industry. As a result, while most telecommunications operations in the Asia-Pacific region were state-run a decade ago, a growing number are now in private hands. Singapore Telecommunications, Pakistan Telecom, Thailand's Telecom Asia, Korea Telecom, and Globe Telecom in the Philippines all have been privatized, and MNCs have helped in this process by providing investment funds. Today, NYNEX holds a stake in Telecom Asia; Bell Atlantic and Ameritech each own 25 percent of Telecom New Zealand; and Bell South has an ownership position in Australia's Optus. At the same time, Australia's Telestra is moving into Vietnam, Japan's NTT is investing in Thailand, and Korea Telecom is in the Philippines and Indonesia.

Many governments are reluctant to allow so much private and foreign ownership of such a vital industry; however, they also are aware that foreign investors will go elsewhere if the deal is not satisfactory. The Hong Kong office of Salomon Brothers, a U.S. investment bank, estimates that to meet the expanding demand for telecommunication service in Asia, companies will need to considerably increase the investment, most of which will have to come from overseas. MNCs are unwilling to put up this much money unless they are assured of operating control and a sufficiently high return on their investment.

Developing countries are eager to attract telecommunication firms and offer liberal terms. This liberalization has resulted in rapid increases in wireless penetration, with more than 550 million wireless devices in circulation in China and 360 million in India. Between 2000 and 2005 the total number of mobile subscribers in developing countries grew more than fivefold—to nearly 1.4 billion. Growth was rapid in all regions, but fastest in sub-Saharan Africa—Nigeria's subscriber base grew from 370,000 to 16.8 million in just four years.[60] And mobile users are increasingly relying on their devices for e-mail and data communications. According to the International Telecommunications Union, in 2008, the number of users accessing the Internet from mobile devices exceeded those accessing the Internet via PCs. Nokia, one of the world's largest telecommunications providers, has been aggressive in penetrating the emerging markets of China and India, and these two countries are now the two largest markets for the provider of mobile devices and other communications technologies. Unfortunately, counterfeit products continue to erode markets for authentic products in China and other developing and emerging markets.[61]

Technological Advancements, Outsourcing, and Offshoring

As MNCs use advanced technology to help them communicate, produce, and deliver their goods and services internationally, they face a new challenge: how technology will affect the nature and number of their employees. Some informed observers note that technology already has eliminated much and in the future will eliminate even more of the work being done by middle management and white-collar staff. Mounting cost pressures resulting from increased globalization of competition and profit expectations exerted by investors have placed pressure on MNCs to outsource or offshore production to take advantage of lower labor and other costs.[62] In the past century, machines replaced millions of manual laborers, but those who worked with their minds were able to thrive and survive. During the past three decades in particular, employees in blue-collar, smokestack industries such as steel and autos have been downsized by technology, and the result has been a permanent restructuring of the number of employees needed to run factories efficiently. In the 1990s, a similar trend unfolded in the white-collar service industries (insurance, banks, and even government). Most recently, this trend has affected high-tech companies in the late 1990s and early 2000s, when after the dot-com bubble burst, hundreds of thousands of jobs were lost, and again in 2008–2010, when many jobs were lost in finance and related industries as a result of the financial crisis and global recession. According to the U.S. Bureau of Labor Statistics, on a net basis, more than 400,000 finance jobs were lost in the U.S. from July 2008 to June 2009, and nearly 1.5 million jobs were lost in professional and business services.[63]

Some experts predict that in the future technology has the potential to displace employees in all industries, from those doing low-skilled jobs to those holding positions traditionally associated with knowledge work. For example, voice recognition is helping to replace telephone operators; the demand for postal workers has been reduced substantially by address-reading devices; and cash-dispensing machines can do 10 times more transactions in a day than bank tellers, so tellers can be reduced in number or even eliminated entirely in the future. Also, expert (sometimes called "smart") systems can eliminate human thinking completely. For example, American Express has an expert system that performs the credit analysis formerly done by college-graduate financial analysts. In the medical field, expert systems can diagnose some illnesses as well as doctors can, and robots capable of performing certain operations are starting to be used.

Emerging information technology also makes work more portable. As a result, MNCs have been able to move certain production activities overseas to capitalize on cheap labor resources. This is especially true for work that can be easily contracted with overseas locations. For example, low-paid workers in India and Asian countries now are being given subcontracted work such as labor-intensive software development and code-writing jobs. A restructuring of the nature of work and of employment is a result of such information technology; Table 2–3 identifies some winners and losers in the workforce in recent years.

The new technological environment has both positives and negatives for MNCs and societies as a whole. On the positive side, the cost of doing business worldwide should decline thanks to the opportunities that technology offers in substituting lower-cost machines for higher-priced labor. Over time, productivity should go up, and prices should go down. On the negative side, many employees will find either their jobs eliminated or their wages and salaries reduced because they have been replaced by machines and their skills are no longer in high demand. This job loss from technology can be especially devastating in developing countries. However, it doesn't have to be this way. A case in point is South Africa's showcase for automotive productivity as represented by the Delta Motor Corporation's Opel Corsa plant in Port Elizabeth. To provide as many jobs as possible, this world-class operation automated only 23 percent, compared to more than 85 percent auto assembly in Europe and North America.[64] Also, some industries can add jobs. For example, the positive has outweighed the negative in the computer and information technology industry, despite its ups and downs. Specifically, employment in the U.S. computer software industry has increased over the last decade. In less developed countries such as India, a high-tech boom in recent years has created jobs and opportunities for a growing number of people.[65] Additionally, even though developed countries such as Japan and the United States are most affected by technological displacement of workers, both nations still lead the world in creating new jobs and shifting their traditional industrial structure toward a high-tech, knowledge-based economy.

The precise impact that the advanced technological environment will have on international management over the next decade is difficult to forecast. One thing is certain, however; there is no turning back the technological clock. MNCs and nations alike must evaluate the impact of these changes carefully and realize that their economic performance is closely tied to keeping up with, or ahead of, rapidly advancing technology.

Table 2–3
Winners and Losers in Selected Occupations: Percentage Change Forecasts for 2010–2020

The 10 occupations with the largest projected employment growth 2010–20

| Occupation | Employment in millions | | Difference | Percent change |
	2010	2020		
Registered nurses	2737.4	3449.3	711.9	26.0%
Retail salespersons	4261.6	4968.4	706.8	16.6
Home health aides	1017.7	1723.9	706.3	69.4
Personal care aides	861.0	1468.0	607.0	70.5
Office clerks, general	2950.7	3440.2	489.5	17.0
Combined food preparation and serving workers, including fast food	2682.1	3080.1	398.0	14.8
Customer service representatives	2187.3	2525.6	338.4	15.5
Heavy and tractor-trailer truck drivers	1604.8	1934.9	330.1	20.6
Laborers and freight, stock, and material movers, hand	2068.2	2387.3	319.1	15.4
Postsecondary teachers	1756.0	2061.7	305.7	17.4

The 10 occupations with the largest projected employment declines, 2010–20

| Occupation | Employment in millions | | Difference | Percent change |
	2010	2020		
Farmers, ranchers, and other agricultural managers	1202.5	1106.4	−96.1	−8.0%
Postal Service mail sorters, processors, and processing machine operators	142.0	73.0	−68.9	−48.5
Sewing machine operators	163.2	121.1	−42.1	−25.8
Postal Service mail carriers	316.7	278.5	−38.1	−12.0
Switchboard operators, including answering service	142.5	109.3	−33.2	−23.3
Postal Service clerks	65.6	34.0	−31.6	−48.2
Cooks, fast food	530.4	511.4	−19.1	−3.6
Miscellaneous agricultural workers	746.4	727.3	−19.1	−2.6
Data entry keyers	234.7	218.8	−15.9	−6.8
Word processors and typists	115.3	102.1	−13.2	−11.5

Source: Bureau of Labor Statistics, Economic News Release, Tables 6 & 8. February 1, 2012. http://www.bls.gov/news.release/.

■ The World of International Management—Revisited

Political, legal, and technological environments can alter the landscape for global companies. The chapter opening The World of International Management described how rapid political change, fueled by social media, transformed the political landscape of the North African and Middle East region, with significant consequences for international business. This situation underscores the increasing uncertainty in the global business environment and the rapidity and extent of political and legal change. It also highlights how technology is contributing to accelerating change, and how traditional legal systems have difficulty keeping pace with these changes. International managers need to be aware of how differing political, legal, and technological environments are affecting their business and how globalization, security concerns, and other developments influence these environments. Changes in political, legal, and environmental conditions also open up new business opportunities but close some old ones.

In light of the information you have learned from reading this chapter, you should have a good understanding of these environments and some of the ways in which they will affect companies doing business abroad. Drawing on this knowledge, answer the following questions: (1) How will changes in the political and legal environment in the Middle East and North Africa affect U.S. MNCs conducting business there? (2) How might evolving political interests and legal systems affect future investment in the region? (3) How does technology result in greater integration and dependencies among economies, political systems, and financial markets, but also greater fragility?

SUMMARY OF KEY POINTS

1. The global political environment can be understood via an appreciation of ideologies and political systems. Ideologies, including individualism and collectivism, reflect underlying tendencies in society. Political systems, including democracy and totalitarianism, incorporate ideologies into political structures. There are fewer and fewer purely collectivist or socialist societies, although totalitarianism still exists in several countries and regions. Many countries are experiencing transitions from more socialist to democratic systems, reflecting related trends discussed in Chapter 1 toward more market-oriented economic systems.

2. The current legal and regulatory environment is both complex and confusing. There are many different laws and regulations to which MNCs doing business internationally must conform, and each nation is unique. Also, MNCs must abide by the laws of their own country. For example, U.S. MNCs must obey the rules set down by the Foreign

Corrupt Practices Act. Privatization and regulation of trade also affect the legal and regulatory environment in specific countries.

3. The technological environment is changing quickly and is having a major impact on international business. This will continue in the future with, for example, digitization, higher-speed telecommunication, and advancements in biotechnology as they offer developing countries new opportunities to leapfrog into the 21st century. New markets are being created for high-tech MNCs that are eager to provide telecommunications service. Technological developments also impact both the nature and the structure of employment, shifting the industrial structure toward a more high-tech, knowledge-based economy. MNCs that understand and take advantage of this high-tech environment should prosper, but they also must keep up, or go ahead, to survive.

KEY TERMS

act of state doctrine, *45*

civil or code law, *44*

collectivism, *40*

common law, *44*

democracy, *41*

doctrine of comity, *45*

Foreign Corrupt Practices Act (FCPA), *46*

individualism, *39*

Islamic law, *44*

nationality principle, *45*

principle of sovereignty, *44*

protective principle, *45*

socialism, *40*

socialist law, *44*

territoriality principle, *45*

totalitarianism, *42*

REVIEW AND DISCUSSION QUESTIONS

1. In what ways do different ideologies and political systems influence the environment in which MNCs operate? Would these challenges be less for those

operating in the EU than for those in Russia or China? Why or why not?

2. How do the following legal principles impact MNC operations: the principle of sovereignty, the nationality principle, the territoriality principle, the protective principle, and principle of comity?

3. How will advances in technology and telecommunications affect developing countries? Give some specific examples.

4. Why are developing countries interested in privatizing their state-owned industries? What opportunities does privatization have for MNCs?

INTERNET EXERCISE: HITACHI GOES WORLDWIDE

Hitachi products are well known in the United States, as well as in Europe and Asia. However, in an effort to maintain its international momentum, the Japanese MNC is continuing to push forward into new markets, especially emerging markets, while also developing new products. Visit the MNC at its website www.hitachi.com and examine some of the latest developments that are taking place. Begin by reviewing the firm's current activities in Asia, specifically Hong Kong and Singapore. Then look at how it is doing business in North America.

Finally, read about its European operations. Then answer these three questions: (1) What kinds of products and systems does the firm offer? What are its primary areas of emphasis? (2) In what types of environments does it operate? Is Hitachi primarily interested in developed markets, or is it also pushing into newly emerging markets? (3) Based on what it has been doing over the last two to three years, what do you think Hitachi's future strategy will be in competing in the environment of international business?

Vietnam

Located in Southeast Asia, the Socialist Republic of Vietnam is bordered to the north by the People's Republic of China, to the west by Laos and Cambodia, and to the east and south by the South China Sea. The country is a mere 127,000 square miles but has a population of almost 90 million. The language is Vietnamese, and the principal religion Buddhism, although there are a number of small minorities, including Confucian, Christian (mainly Catholic), Caodist, Daoist, and Hoa Hao. In recent years, the country's economy has been up and down, but average annual per capita income remains around $1,200, as the peasants remain very poor.

One of the reasons that Vietnam has lagged behind its fast-developing neighbors in Southeast Asia, such as Thailand and Malaysia, is its isolation from the industrial West, and the United States in particular, because of the Vietnam War. From the mid-1970s, the country had close relations with the U.S.S.R., but the collapse of communism there forced the still-communist Vietnamese government to work on establishing stronger economic ties with other countries. The nation recently has worked out many of its problems with China, and today, the Chinese have become a useful economic ally. And Vietnam is well on its way in establishing a vigorous trading relationship with the United States. Efforts toward this end began over a decade ago, but because of lack of information concerning the many U.S. soldiers still unaccounted for after the war, it was not until 1993 that the United States permitted U.S. companies to take part in ventures in Vietnam that were financed by international aid agencies. Then, in 1994, the U.S. trade embargo was lifted, and a growing number of American firms began doing business in Vietnam.

Caterpillar began supplying equipment for a $2 billion highway project. Mobil teamed with three Japanese partners to begin drilling offshore. Exxon, Amoco, Conoco, Unocal, and Arco negotiated production-sharing contracts with Petro Vietnam. General Electric opened a trade office and developed plans to use electric products throughout the country. AT&T began working to provide long-distance service both in and out of the country. Coca-Cola began bottling operations. Within the first 12 months, 70 U.S. companies obtained licenses to do business in Vietnam. Besides the United States, the largest investors have been Singapore, Taiwan, Japan, South Korea, and Hong Kong, which collectively have put over $22 billion into the country. In 2012, Nokia broke ground on a $302 million manufacturing facility. The plant is expected to employ 10,000 and produce 45 million mobile devices per quarter. Over the past couple of years, Vietnamese authorities have acted swiftly to implement the structural reforms needed to modernize the national economy and to produce more competitive exports for sale in the global economy. In July 2000 the United States and Vietnam signed a bilateral trade agreement that opens up trade and foreign investment in Vietnam and gives Vietnamese exporters access to the vast U.S. market. The treaty, which entered into force near the end of 2001, resulted in dramatic increases in foreign direct investment from the United States.

As in China, many U.S. firms have found doing business in Vietnam frustrating because of the numerous and ever-changing bureaucratic rules enacted by the communist government officials; but these concerns are beginning to subside with the induction of Vietnam into the World Trade Organization on January 11, 2007. After 11 years of preparation, with eight years of negotiation, Vietnam finally became the 150th member of the WTO. As a result, Vietnam is experiencing continued economic stimulus through its liberalizing reforms. Overall, this opportunity may open the market to foreign investors who were unsure of the risks involved in entering Vietnam. Vietnam's accession to the WTO provides a context of greater certainty and predictability in the business and broader economic environment. As one measure, foreign direct investment grew dramatically after 2007. Peaking in 2008 at US$71 billion, Vietnam averaged around US$15 billion in foreign direct investment from 2009 to 2012. In 2011, foreign direct investment accounted for 6.0 percent of Vietnam's total GDP. U.S.-based AES Corporation, a builder of power plants, invested US$2.147 billion in the Mong Duong thermal power plant project in Quang Ninh province, one of many FDI projects across Vietnam in a range of industries and sectors. **vietnambusiness.asia, www.vietnam-report.com, www.vir.com.vn, data.worldbank.org**

Questions

1. In what way does the political environment in Vietnam pose both an opportunity and a threat for American MNCs seeking to do business there?
2. Why are U.S. multinationals so interested in going into Vietnam? How much potential does the country offer? How might Vietnam compare to China as a place to do business?
3. Will there be any opportunities in Vietnam for high-tech American firms? Why or why not?

Chapter 3

ETHICS, SOCIAL RESPONSIBILITY, AND SUSTAINABILITY

OBJECTIVES OF THE CHAPTER

Recent concerns about ethics, social responsibility, and sustainability transcend national borders. In this era of globalization MNCs must be concerned with how they carry out their business and their social role in foreign countries. This chapter examines business ethics and social responsibility in the international arena, and it looks at some of the critical social issues that will be confronting MNCs in the years ahead. The discussion includes ethical decision making in various countries, regulation of foreign investment, the growing trends toward environmental sustainability, and current responses to social responsibility by today's multinationals. The specific objectives of this chapter are:

1. **EXAMINE** ethics in international management and some of the major ethical issues and problems confronting MNCs.

2. **DISCUSS** some of the pressures on and actions being taken by selected industrialized countries and companies to be more socially and environmentally responsive to world problems.

3. **EXPLAIN** some of the initiatives to bring greater accountability to corporate conduct and limit the impact of corruption around the world.

The World of *International Management*

Sustaining Sustainable Companies

With a more environmentally-aware public, becoming a "sustainable" business has become an important part of the business model for many MNCs. Three of these companies—Patagonia, Philips, and Tesla—have in different ways transformed their corporate strategy to emphasize "doing good" socially and environmentally while "doing well" economically.

Sustainability in the Supply Chain—Patagonia

Founded by Yvon Chouinard in 1972, Patagonia is a private, outdoor-clothing company. Patagonia's transition to a sustainability-focused company started in 1988 after several employees in one of their Boston retail stores suddenly fell ill. After a thorough investigation, it was discovered that formaldehyde, emitted from Patagonia's cotton-based merchandise, was cycling into the air. In response, Patagonia committed in 1994 to use only formaldehyde-free, 100 percent organic cotton in the manufacture of its clothing; within just 18 months, they achieved that goal.[1] Since then, Patagonia has examined and modified its entire supply chain from both a corporate social responsibility and environmental viewpoint. Its revised mission statement reflects that ideal: "Build the best product, cause no unnecessary harm, and use business to inspire and implement solutions to the environmental crisis."[2]

Internally, recycled products constitute a large percentage of the material used in Patagonia's products. Recycled polyester and nylon, made of postconsumer soda bottles and waste fabric, are used in the production of fleece and linings.[3] This reuse cuts down on oil usage and CO_2 emissions. All of Patagonia's wool products are now chlorine-free, preventing the contamination of wastewater in the developing countries where the products are manufactured. Furthermore,

Patagonia's finished products are fully recyclable, and the company has encouraged its customers to properly dispose of their products. Any Patagonia product can be dropped off at a retail store for guaranteed recycling.[4]

Social sustainability, with an emphasis on employee welfare, has also become a key tenet of Patagonia's strategy. Beginning in 1990, Patagonia instituted a policy of visiting every factory that manufactured its goods to evaluate and score working conditions.[5] Patagonia refuses to do business with any factory that does not allow full access or breaks local labor laws. Additionally, third-party audits of factories were established to provide nonbiased assessments of the factories. Every factory along its supply chain is listed on its website. In 1999, Patagonia became one of the founding members of the Fair Labor Association.[6] Since 1985, Patagonia has donated one percent of its sales to environmental nonprofits.[7] In 2002, Chouinard expanded on his vision for corporate sustainability by cofounding "One Percent for the Planet," an international nonprofit dedicated to philanthropy for environmental organizations. The program encourages companies to follow Patagonia's lead and donate one percent of sales to worthwhile, environmentally-focused causes. As of 2013, over 1,300 companies have joined the organization. Over 1,500 different nonprofits have received funding from the over US$100 million donated by the member companies.[8]

The decision to invest in sustainable products has not been without repercussions. Chlorine-free wool has been more costly to manufacture, cutting down on profits. Following the shift to 10 percent organic cotton, Patagonia's profits dropped.[9] Furthermore, the high priority that Patagonia puts on only using factories that follow its strict standards means higher labor costs than the competition. However, Patagonia has gained a competitive advantage by doing good. The company has developed a loyal customer base that is willing to pay a premium for the sustainability that Patagonia provides.

Sustainability in Operations and Products—Philips

Founded in 1891, Koninklijke Philips Electronics N.V., a Dutch MNC, is best known for its lighting and electronic products. Divided into Healthcare, Lighting, and Consumer Lifestyle divisions, the company employs over 120,000 people across 60 countries.[10] For Philips, sustainability means improving people's lives across the globe.

In 1998, Philips launched its EcoVision program. With a focus on company-wide sustainable initiatives, EcoVision divides Philips' approach to sustainability into three key innovation areas: care, energy efficiency, and materials. Sustainability goals are then set within each of these areas. The latest iteration, EcoVision5, was introduced in 2010, with goals set for 2015. By 2015, Philips aims to improve the lives of 2 billion, achieving a 50 percent improvement in the energy efficiency of its products, and doubling the amount of recycled content in its products compared to 2009.[11]

Continual environmental-friendly innovation is a priority for Philips. In 2012, Philips committed US$569 million in green technology. As a direct result of these investments, Philips developed over a dozen new health care products that improve patient care while simultaneously reducing environmental impact.[12] Philips retrofitted the Empire State Building with LED lighting, cutting down on energy consumption by 73 percent.[13] And PVC, which requires oil for manufacture, has been eliminated from all new coffee machines. To cut its carbon footprint, Philips altered its shipping methods and reworked its supply chain. Renewable energy investments have increased efficiency while eliminating CO_2 emissions.[14] Between 2007 and 2012, Philips' operational carbon footprint was reduced by 25 percent. Furthermore, arsenic use has been reduced by 99 percent, and lead emissions have dropped by 96 percent.[15] Over 10,000 tons of recycled material went into Philips products in 2012 alone.[16]

As with Patagonia, customers seem eager to purchase products that are sustainable, giving Philips a competitive advantage over the competition. In 2012, Philips' green product sales reached US$11.3 billion, increasing by 45 percent over 2011's figures.[17] Green products now constitute 39 percent of all company product sales.[18] In 2013, Philips reached number 7 on the Corporate Knights list of "Global 100 Most Sustainable Corporations in the World"[19].

Sustainability as a Competitive Advantage—Tesla Motors

Tesla Motors, an independent Silicon Valley-based auto manufacturer, focuses on creating and mass-producing reliable electric automobiles. Using technology descended from 19th-century physicist Nikola Tesla, Tesla Motors has developed the longest-range electric car battery on the market. Visionary billionaire Elon Musk, who is also behind SpaceX, cofounded the company in 2003.[20]

Unlike previously developed electric cars, which were clunky and unattractive, Tesla aimed to design automobiles that were attractive and high-quality. Tesla's first vehicle, the Roadster, was designed to be a high-performance sports car. Released in 2008, the Roadster can accelerate from zero to sixty in less than four seconds, reaching top speeds of over 125 miles per hour.[21] The Model S, released in 2012, was designed to be a luxury sedan for the masses. Starting at US$57,400, the Model S was introduced for less than half of the cost of the Roadster. The car won multiple awards upon its release, including Motor Trend's "Car of the Year" award for 2013. Tesla shipped approximately 20,000 Model S cars in 2013.[22]

Inspiring sustainability across the entire automobile industry is a secondary goal for the company. To achieve that goal, Tesla has collaborated with several other car manufacturers to produce greener automobiles. In its partnerships with Smart and Toyota, Tesla is producing batteries and chargers.[23,24] In its partnership with Mercedes, Tesla is designing efficient powertrain equipment.[25]

As an innovator, Tesla has faced some major obstacles. Tesla's first automobile, the Roadster, faced two high-profile recalls, one of which dealt with the potential loss of control of the car.[26,27] In a highly-publicized February 2013 article, a New York Times reporter took the Model S on an infamous test drive along the East Coast. Not only did the car fall short of the estimated 200-mile range per charge, but the battery actually ran completely out of power and the car ended up having to be towed.[28] Musk estimated that the negative *New York Times* review resulted in several hundred vehicle cancellations and cost Tesla US$100 million in valuation.[29] Financially, Tesla has invested hundreds of millions of dollars into its operations. Tesla posted a US$200 million loss in 2012 (US$90 million in the fourth quarter of 2012 alone).[30]

Tesla, despite its setbacks, still maintains a competitive advantage from its dedicated investor and customer bases. Customers seem willing to deal with minor issues and recalls for the sake of the overall sustainability goal of the company. By targeting high-income customers with the Roadster, Tesla was able to spend the funds necessary to develop and fine-tune its technology. Investors have also been willing to bet on the idea of Tesla Motors. The IPO on June 29, 2010, raised US$226 million for the company.[31]

Our opening discussion of Patagonia, Tesla, and Philips demonstrates how corporations are shifting their focus from traditional market-responsive strategies to broader approaches that incorporate both business and social or environmental goals. Patagonia has radically transformed its business to focus on what it expects to be increasing demand for "green" products as well as those that contribute to improved working conditions in developing countries. EcoVision called attention to Philip's commitment to contributing to a more sustainable economy via its development of recycled materials and other environmentally sensitive technologies. Tesla Motors' Model S is focused on developing and deploying a reasonably priced all-electric car to the masses. By combining their commitment to social and environmental sustainability, aligned with their business and commercial objectives, these three companies appear to be setting an example for a new approach to integrating social and business goals among global corporations, tapping into consumers' desire for products and services that are consistent with their values. This "triple bottom line" approach, which simultaneously considers social, environmental, and economic sustainability ("people, planet, profits") could make a real and lasting impact on the world's human and environmental conditions by harnessing business and managerial skills and techniques.

More broadly, recent scandals have called attention to the perceived lack of ethical values and corporate governance standards in business. In addition, assisting impoverished countries by helping them gain a new level of independence is both responsible and potentially profitable. Indeed, corporate social responsibility is becoming more than just good moral behavior. It can assist in avoiding future economic and environmental setbacks and may be the key to keeping companies afloat.

■ Ethics and Social Responsibility

The ethical behavior of business and the broader social responsibilities of corporations have become major issues in the United States and all countries around the world. Ethical scandals and questionable business practices have received considerable media attention, aroused the public's concern about ethics in international business, and brought attention to the social impact of business operations.

Ethics and Social Responsibility in International Management

Unbiased ethical decision-making processes are imperative to modern international business practices. It is difficult to determine a universal ethical standard when the views and norms in one country can vary substantially from others. **Ethics**, the study of morality and standards of conduct, is often the victim of subjectivity as it yields to the will of cultural relativism, or the belief that the ethical standard of a country is based on the culture that created it and that moral concepts lack universal application.[32]

The adage "When in Rome, do as the Romans do" is derived from the idea of cultural relativism and suggests that businesses and the managers should behave in accordance with the ethical standards of the country they are active in, regardless of MNC headquarter location. It is necessary, to some extent, to rely on local teams to execute under local rule; however, this can be taken to extremes. While a business whose only objective is to make a profit may opt to take advantage of these differences in norms and standards in order to legally gain leverage over the competition, it may find that negative consumer opinion about unethical business practices, not to mention potential legal action, could affect the bottom line. Dilemmas that arise from conflicts between ethical standards of a country and business ethics, or the moral code guiding business behavior, are most evident in employment and business practices, recognition of human rights, including women in the workplace, and corruption. The newer area of **corporate social responsibility (CSR)** is closely related to ethics. However, we discuss CSR issues separately. Ethics is the study of or the learning process involved in understanding morality, while CSR involves taking action. Furthermore, the area of ethics has a lawful component and implies right and wrong in a legal sense, while CSR is based more on voluntary actions. Business ethics and CSR may be therefore viewed as two complementary dimensions of a company's overall social profile and position.

ethics
The study of morality and standards of conduct.

corporate social responsibility (CSR)
The actions of a firm to benefit society beyond the requirements of the law and the direct interests of the firm.

Ethics Theories and Philosophy

There are a range of ethical theories and approaches around the world, many emanating from religious and cultural traditions. We focus on the cultural factors in Part Two of the book. Here we review three tenets from Western philosophy, and briefly describe Eastern philosophy, which can be used to evaluate and inform international management decisions. The International Management in Action feature on page 67 explores how these perspectives might be used to inform the ethics of a specific international business decision.

Kantian philosophical traditions argue that individuals (and organizations) have responsibilities based on a core set of moral principles that go beyond those of narrow self-interest. In fact, a Kantian moral analysis rejects consequences (either conceivable or likely) as morally irrelevant when evaluating the choice of an agent: "The moral worth of an action does not lie in the effect expected from it, nor in any principle of action which requires to borrow its motive from this expected effect."[33] Rather, a Kantian approach asks us to consider our choices as implying a general rule, or maxim, that must be evaluated for its consistency as a universal law. For Kant, what is distinctive about rational behavior is not that it is self-interested or even purpose driven, though all actions do include some purpose as part of their explanation. Instead, rational beings, in addition to having purposes and being able to reason practically in their pursuit, are also capable of evaluating their choices through the lens of a universal law, what Kant calls the moral law, or the "categorical imperative" (Kant 1949). From this perspective, we ought always to act under a maxim that we can will consistently as a universal law for all rational beings similarly situated.

Aristotelian virtue ethics focus on core, individual behaviors and actions, and how they express and form individual character. They also consider social and institutional arrangements and practices in terms of their contribution to the formation of good character in individuals. A good, or virtuous, individual does what is right for the right reasons and derives satisfaction from such actions because his or her character is rightly formed.

For Aristotle, moral success and failure largely come down to a matter of right desire, or appetite: "In matters of action, the principles of initiating motives are the ends at which our actions are aimed. But as soon as people become corrupted by pleasure or pain, the goal no longer appears as a motivating principle: he no longer sees that he should choose and act in every case for the sake of and because of this end. For vice tends to destroy the principle or initiating motive of action."[34] It is important to have an understanding of what is truly good and practical wisdom to enable one to form an effective plan of action toward realizing what is good; however, absent a fixed and habitual desire for the good, there is little incentive for good actions. There is also an important social component to virtue theory insofar as one's formation is a social process. The exemplars and practices one finds in one's cultural context guide one's moral development. Virtue theory relies heavily on existing practices to provide an account of what is good and what character traits contribute to pursuing and realizing the good in concrete ways.

Utilitarianism—a form of consequentialism—favors the greatest good for the greatest number of people under a given set of constraints.[35] A given act is morally correct if it maximizes utility, that is, if the ratio of benefit to harm (calculated by taking everyone affected by the act into consideration) is greater than the ratio resulting from an alternative act. This theory was given its most famous modern expression in the works of Jeremy Bentham (1988) and John Stuart Mill (1957), two English utilitarians writing in the 18th and 19th centuries, both of whom emphasized the greatest happiness principle as their moral standard.[36] Utilitarianism is an attractive perspective for business decision making, especially in Western countries, because its logic is similar to an economic calculation of utility or cost-benefit, something many Western managers are accustomed to doing.

Eastern philosophy, which broadly can include various philosophies of Asia, including Indian philosophy, Chinese philosophy, Iranian philosophy, Japanese philosophy, and Korean philosophy tend to view the individual as part of, rather than separate from, nature. Many Western philosophers generally assume as a given that the individual is something distinct from the entire universe, and many Western philosophers attempt to describe and categorize the universe from a detached, objective viewpoint. Eastern perspectives, on the other hand, typically hold that people are an intrinsic and inseparable part of the universe, and that attempts to discuss the universe from an objective viewpoint, as though the individual speaking were something separate and detached from the whole, are inherently absurd.

In international management, executives may rely upon one or more of these perspectives when confronted with decisions that involve ethics or morality. While they may not invoke the specific philosophical tradition by name, they likely are drawing from these fundamental moral and ethical beliefs when advancing a specific agenda or decision. The International Management in Action box regarding an offshoring decision shows how a given action could be informed by each of these perspectives.

■ Human Rights

Human rights issues present challenges for MNCs as there is currently no universally adopted standard of what constitutes acceptable behavior. It is difficult to list all rights inherent to humanity since there is considerable subjectivity involved, and cultural differences exist among societies. Some basic rights include life, freedom from slavery or torture, freedom of opinion and expression, and a general ambiance of nondiscriminatory practices.[37] One violation of human rights that resonated with MNCs and made them question whether to move operations into China was the violent June 1989 crackdown on student protesters in Beijing's Tiananmen Square. Despite this horrific event, most MNCs continued their involvement in China, although friction still exists between countries with high and low human rights standards. Even South Africa is beginning to experience the healing process of transitioning to higher human rights standards after the 1994 dismantling of apartheid, the former white government's policy of racial segregation. Unfortunately,

The Ethics of an Offshoring Decision

The financial services industry has been especially active in offshoring. Western investment banks including Citigroup, Deutsche Bank, Goldman Sachs, Credit Suisse, and UBS have established back-office functions in India. JP Morgan was the first to offshore staff to the country in 2001 and has more than 8,000 staff in Mumbai, nearly 5 percent of its 170,000 employees worldwide. In October 2007, Credit Suisse announced the expansion of its center of excellence in Pune, India, with 300 new jobs, bringing staff numbers to 1,000 by December. Deutsche Bank has 3,500 staff in Bangalore and Mumbai. UBS began outsourcing work to third-party information technology vendors in 2003 and has 1,220 employees in Hyderabad and Mumbai. Goldman Sachs started offshoring to India three years ago and has about 2,500 employees there. On October 17, 2007, JP Morgan announced plans to build a back-office workforce of 5,000 in the Philippines over the next two years. Its traditional offshoring center of Mumbai in India has become overcrowded by investment banks that have set up similar operations. The bank will develop credit card and treasury services in the Philippines. A source close to the bank said the move was to diversify its back-office locations and because JP Morgan has strong links with a human resources network in the country. Mark Kobayashi-Hillary, an outsourcing specialist, said: "Because India's finance center is almost wholly based in Mumbai, the resources are finite and there is a supply and demand problem. It's no surprise people are looking elsewhere. But banks are not just after keeping costs down; these moves are also strategic." He said he was surprised that banks had not opened more offices in the Philippines, considering its strong links with the U.S., cheap rent and wealth of resources. "In Manila there is a high density of people who have worked in the financial sector with the skills that investment banks look for. We should see more banks setting up shop there soon."

Ethical philosophy and reasoning could be used to inform offshoring decisions such as these. A *Kantian* approach to offshoring would require us to consider a set of principles in accord with which offshoring choices were made such that decisions were measured against these core tenets, such as a corporate code of conduct. A *virtue theory* perspective would suggest that the decision should consider the impact on communities and a goal of humans flourishing more generally; such an analysis could include economic as well as social impacts. A *utilitarian* perspective would urge that benefits and costs be measured; e.g., who is losing jobs, who is gaining, and do the gains (either measured in jobs, income, utility, quality of life) outweigh the losses. An *Eastern* philosophical approach would suggest a broader, more integrative and longer term view, considering impacts not just on humans but also on the broader natural environment in which they operate.

Taken together, an understanding of these ethical perspectives could help managers to decide how to make their own ethical decisions in the international business environment.

human rights violations are still rampant worldwide. For several decades, for example, Russia has experienced widespread human trafficking, but this practice has accelerated in recent years.[38] Here, we take a closer look at women in the workplace.

Women's rights and gender equity can be considered a subset of human rights. While the number of women in the workforce has increased substantially worldwide, most are still experiencing the effects of a "glass ceiling," meaning that it is difficult, if not impossible, to reach the upper management positions. Japan is a good example, since both harassment and a glass ceiling have existed in the workplace. Sexual harassment also remains a major social issue in Japan. Many women college graduates in Japan are still offered only secretarial or low-level jobs. Japanese management still believes that women will quit and get married within a few years of employment, leading to a two-track recruiting process: one for men and one for women.[39] Japan ranked 101st in the "gender gap index" study by the World Economic Forum, an international nonprofit organization, which measured the economic opportunities and political empowerment of women by nation in 2012. Iceland ranked no. 1, and the U.S. was no. 22. Japanese women make up 9 percent of senior executives and managers, a tiny share compared with 43 percent in the U.S., 17 percent in China, and 38 percent in France, according to data from the International Labor Office compiled by Catalyst Inc., a New York–based nonprofit that pushes for business opportunities for women. There is some evidence that women are beginning to assume managerial positions in some industries, but Japan has a long way to go in this regard.[40]

Equal employment opportunities may be more troubled in Japan than other countries, but the glass ceiling is pervasive throughout the world. Today, women earn less than men for the same job in the United States, although progress has been made in this regard. France, Germany, and Great Britain have seen an increase in the number of women not only in the workforce but also in management positions. Unfortunately, women in management tend to represent only the lower level and do not seem to have the resources to move up in the company. This is partially due to social factors and perceived levels of opportunity or lack thereof. The United States, France, Germany, and Great Britain all have equal opportunity initiatives, whether they are guaranteed by law or are represented by growing social groups. Despite the existence of equal opportunity in French and German law, the National Organization for Women in the United States, and British legislation, there is no guarantee that initiatives will be implemented. It is a difficult journey as women attempt to make their mark in the workplace, but soon it may be possible for them to break through the glass ceiling.

Labor, Employment, and Business Practices

Labor policies vary widely among countries around the world. Issues of freedom to work, freedom to organize and engage in collective action, and policies regarding notification and compensation for layoffs are treated differently in different countries. Political, economic, and cultural differences make it difficult to agree on a universal foundation of employment practices. It does not make much sense to standardize compensation packages within an MNC that spans both developed and underdeveloped nations. Elements such as working conditions, expected consecutive work hours, and labor regulations also create challenges in deciding which employment practice is the most appropriate. For example, the low cost of labor entices businesses to look to China; however, workers in China are not well paid, and to meet the demand for output, they often are forced to work 12-hour days, seven days a week. In some cases, children are used for this work. Child labor initially invokes negative associations and is considered an unethical employment practice. The reality is that of the 215 million children age 5–17 working globally in 2012, most are engaged in work to help support their families.[41] In certain countries it is necessary for children to work due to low wages. UNICEF and the World Bank recognize that in some instances family survival depends on all members working; and that intervention is necessary only when the child's developmental welfare is compromised. There has been some progress in the reduction of child labor. It continues to decline, especially among girls, but only modestly. Child labor was reduced by 10 percent from 2000 to 2004 and an additional 3 percent from 2004 to 2008, although it has stagnated since 2009. There has also been considerable progress in the ratification of ILO standards concerning child labor, namely of Conventions 182 (on the worst forms of child labor) and 138 (on minimum age). However, roughly one-quarter of the children in the world live in countries that have not ratified these conventions.[42]

In early 2010, the issue of relatively low wages paid by Chinese subcontractors made the headlines after a number of suicides by workers at factories run by Foxconn, one of the largest contractors for electronics firms such as Apple, and a strike by workers at a Honda plant. A year later, in May 2011, an explosion at a Foxconn iPad factory killed two employees. In a survey of Foxconn employees, over 43 percent of workers stated that they have seen or been part of a workplace accident.[43] As a result of these controversies, Foxconn, which employs more than 800,000 workers in China making products for companies such as Dell, Hewlett-Packard, and Apple, agreed to raise its base wage by more than 30 percent. Earlier, Honda had raised wages at some of its factories by 24 percent.[44] Additional pressure from Apple in 2012 further improved employee safety and reduced working hours at Foxconn. By July 2013, weekly work hours were limited to just 49 per employee; this reduced overtime hours from 80 per month to just 36. Apple also partnered with the Fair Labor Association to independently audit the safety of the Foxconn plants.[45] Some analysts believe these higher wages, combined with the longstanding shortage of and high turnover of factory workers in China, will eventually result in the lowest wage manufacturing moving to other countries, such as Vietnam, while higher value-added production will remain in China.

Ensuring that all contractors along the global supply chain are compliant with company standards is an ongoing issue and one that is not without challenges. This issue came to a head once again when a Bangalore factory that produced products for Walmart caught fire in November 2012, killing 112 workers. Walmart immediately responded by severing all ties with suppliers who use subcontractors without Walmart's knowledge and began requiring all overseas factories to pass audits before they could be used to produce Walmart products.[46] Yet, a subsequent collapse of a garment factory in Bangladesh in April of 2013 that killed more than 1,000, and a fire not two weeks later, also in Bangladesh, killing eight, underscored the challenges companies face in trying to develop and implement policies for production that is largely outsourced. After a number of NGOs pressed companies to take responsibility for the conditions that allowed for these tragedies, several global apparel firms, including Swedish-based retailer H&M, Inditex, owner of the Zara chain, the Dutch retailer C&A, and British companies Primark and Tesco, agreed to a plan to help pay for fire safety and building improvements in Bangladesh. The Bangladesh government announced that it would improve its labor laws and raise wages, and ease restrictions on forming trade unions.[47] Walmart and Gap chose not to sign on to the European-led agreement out of concerns that they could be subject to litigation. Instead, they initiated a separate agreement with U.S. retail trade groups and a bipartisan think tank. These challenges, and the reforms they bring, should contribute to improved workers' conditions and help prevent similar tragedies.

Environmental Protection and Development

Conservation of natural resources is another area of ethics and social responsibility in which countries around the world differ widely in their values and approach. Many poor, developing countries are more concerned with improving the basic quality of life for their citizens than worrying about endangered species or the quality of air or water. There are several hypotheses regarding the relationship between economic development, as measured by per capita income, and the quality of the natural environment. The most widely accepted thesis is represented in the Environmental Kuznets Curve (EKC), which hypothesizes that the relationship between per capita income and the use of natural resources and/or the emission of wastes has an inverted U-shape. (See Figure 3–1.) According to this specification, at relatively low levels of income the use of natural resources and/or the emission of wastes increase with income. Beyond some turning point, the use of the natural resources and/or the emission of wastes decline with income. Reasons for this inverted U-shaped relationship are hypothesized to include income-driven changes in (1) the composition of

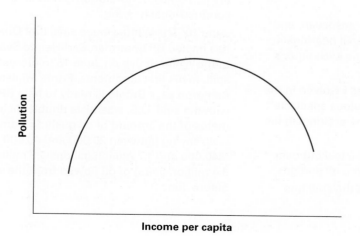

Figure 3–1

The Environmental Kuznets Curve

Anatomy of a Disaster: Key Events in 2010 BP Oil Spill, the Largest in History

Below is a timeline of the BP oil spill in the Gulf of Mexico and its impact.

April 20, 2010: Explosion and fire on Transocean Ltd's drilling rig Deepwater Horizon licensed to BP; 11 workers are killed. The rig was drilling in BP's Macondo project 42 miles southeast of Venice, Louisiana, beneath about 5,000 feet of water and 13,000 feet under the seabed.

April 22: The Deepwater Horizon rig, valued at more than $560 million, sinks and a 5-mile-long oil slick forms.

April 25: Efforts to activate the well's blowout preventer fail.

April 29: U.S. President Barack Obama pledges "every single available resource," including the U.S. military, to contain the spreading spill and says BP is responsible for the cleanup.

April 30: An Obama aide says no drilling will be allowed in new areas, as the president had recently proposed, until the cause of the Deepwater Horizon accident is known. BP Chief Executive Tony Hayward says the company takes full responsibility and will pay all legitimate claims and the cost of the cleanup.

May 2: Obama visits the Gulf Coast. U.S. officials close areas affected by the spill to fishing for 10 days. BP starts drilling a relief well alongside the failed well, a process that may take two to three months to complete.

May 7: An attempt to place a containment dome over the spewing well fails when the device is rendered useless by frozen hydrocarbons that clogged it.

May 9: BP says it might try to plug the undersea leak by pumping materials, such as shredded tires and golf balls, into the well at high pressure, a method called a "junk shot."

May 11/12: Executives from BP, Transocean, and Halliburton appear at congressional hearings in Washington. The executives blame each other's companies.

May 14: Obama slams companies involved in the spill, criticizing them for a "ridiculous spectacle" of publicly trading blame over the accident in his sternest comments yet.

May 16: BP inserts a tube into the leaking riser pile of the well and captures some oil and gas.

May 19: The first heavy oil from the spill hits fragile Louisiana marshlands. Part of the slick enters a powerful current that could carry it to the Florida Keys and beyond.

May 26: A "top kill" maneuver starts, involving pumping drilling mud and other material into the well shaft to try to stifle the flow.

May 28: Obama tours the Louisiana coast, saying, "I am the president and the buck stops with me." BP CEO Tony Hayward flies over the Gulf.

May 29: BP says the complex "top kill" maneuver to plug the well has failed, crushing hopes for a quick end to the largest oil spill in U.S. history on its 40th day.

June 1: BP shares plunge 17 percent in London trading, wiping $23 billion off its market value, on news the latest attempt to plug the well has failed. U.S. Attorney General Eric Holder says the Justice Department has launched a criminal and civil investigation into the rig explosion and the spill.

June 2: BP tries another capping strategy but has difficulty cutting off a leaking riser pipe. U.S. authorities expand fishing restrictions to cover 37 percent of U.S. federal waters in the Gulf.

June 4: Obama, on his third trip to the region, warns BP against skimping on compensation to residents and businesses.

June 7: BP, which says it has now spent $1.25 billion on the spill, sees shares gain on news of the progress in containing the leak.

June 8: Obama says he wants to know "whose ass to kick" over the spill, adding to the pressure on BP. U.S. weather forecasters give their first confirmation that some of the oil leaking has lingered beneath the surface rather than rising to the top.

June 9: U.S. Interior Secretary Ken Salazar says BP must pay the salaries of thousands of workers laid off by a moratorium on drilling, at a congressional hearing.

June 10: The White House says that Obama has invited BP Chairman Carl-Henric Svanberg to the White House on June 16 to discuss the spill. In his first comments, Prime Minister David Cameron says Britain is ready to help BP deal with the spill. U.S. scientists double their estimates of the amount of oil gushing from the well, saying between 20,000 and 40,000 barrels (840,000 and 1.7 million gallons/3.2 million and 6.4 million liters) of oil flowed from the well before June 3.

August 4: After several unsuccessful efforts BP is able to stop the leak by injecting mud and in so doing, pushing crude back to the source.

June 11: Supportive comments from Britain lift BP's shares in London gaining 6.4 percent. However, the rise does not mend damage done to BP shares—the company is worth 70 billion pounds ($102 billion) against over 120 billion pounds in April.

June 14: Obama, on his fourth trip to the Gulf, says he will press BP executives at a White House meeting on June 16 to deal "justly, fairly and promptly" with damage claims. Under intense pressure, BP unveils a new plan to vastly boost the amount of oil it is siphoning off. Two U.S. lawmakers release a letter to BP CEO Hayward saying: "It appears that BP repeatedly chose risky procedures in order to reduce costs and save time and made minimal efforts to contain the added risk."

June 15: Lawmakers summon top executives from Exxon Mobil, Chevron, ConocoPhillips, Royal Dutch Shell, and BP in what is likely to be a heated showdown on the safety of drilling in the deep waters off America's coasts. Obama says in his first televised speech from the Oval Office in the White House: "But make no mistake: we will fight this spill with everything we've got for as long it takes. We will make BP pay for the damage their company has caused. And we will do whatever's necessary to help the Gulf Coast and its people recover from this tragedy."

June 16: The White House and BP announce agreement on the establishment of a $20 billion compensation fund for victims of the Gulf oil spill to be headed by Kenneth Feinberg.

production and/or consumption; (2) the preference for environmental quality; (3) institutions that are needed to internalize externalities; and/or (4) increasing returns to scale associated with pollution abatement. The term EKC is based on its similarity to the time-series pattern of income inequality described by Simon Kuznets in 1955. A 1992 World Bank Development Report made the notion of an EKC popular by suggesting that environmental degradation can be slowed by policies that protect the environment and promote economic development. Subsequent statistical analysis, however, showed that while the relationship might hold in a few cases, it could not be generalized across a wide range of resources and pollutants.[48]

Despite improvements in environmental protection and ethical business practices, many companies continue to violate laws and/or jeopardize safety and environmental concerns in their operations. The tragic 2010 Gulf of Mexico oil rig explosion and leak has underscored the importance of continued vigilance when it comes to the environment, health, and safety as well as the disastrous consequences for companies such as BP, which appears to have cut corners when it came to these considerations. The A Closer Look feature provides a timeline of the devastating BP Gulf of Mexico oil rig explosion and leak and its impact.

■ Globalization and Ethical Obligations of MNCs

All this conjures the question, How much responsibility do MNCs have in changing these practices? Should they adopt the regulations in the country of origin or yield to those in the country of operation? One remedy could be to instill a business code of ethics that extends to all countries, or to create contracts for situations that may arise. The following International Management in Action box regarding Johnson & Johnson underscores how, despite a strong commitment to ethics and social responsibility in its "credo," J&J found itself the subject of numerous safety and quality problems which resulted in lawsuits and severely tarnished its reputation.

The corporate credo of Johnson & Johnson follows:

We believe our first responsibility is to the doctors, nurses and patients, to mothers and fathers and all others who use our products and services. In meeting their needs everything we do must be of high quality. We must constantly strive to reduce our costs in order to maintain reasonable prices. Customers' orders must be serviced promptly and accurately. Our suppliers and distributors must have an opportunity to make a fair profit.

We are responsible to our employees, the men and women who work with us throughout the world. Every one must be considered as an individual. We must respect their dignity and recognize their merit. They must have a sense of security in their jobs. Compensation must be fair and adequate, and working conditions clean, orderly and safe. We must be mindful of ways to help our employees fulfill their family responsibilities. Employees must feel free to make suggestions and complaints. There must be equal opportunity for employment, development and advancement for those qualified. We must provide competent management, and their actions must be just and ethical.

We are responsible to the communities in which we will live and work and to the world community as well. We must be good citizens—support good works and charities and bear our fair share of taxes. We must encourage civic improvements and better health and education. We must maintain, in good order, the property we are privileged to use, protecting the environment and natural resources.

Johnson & Johnson (J&J) has experienced its fair share of ethical dilemmas over the past 25 years. The first occurred in 1982 in Chicago, Illinois, when bottles of extra-strength Tylenol capsules were found to be laced with cyanide. J&J looked to its credo of "the customer always comes first," and quickly responded to the tragedy only three days after the second tainted bottle was discovered. A recall of an estimated 31 million bottles swept the nation and lightened J&J's wallet as it experienced losses of about $100 million and an almost 30 percent drop, bringing it to single digits, in market share for pain relievers. By 1986 an almost full recovery showed J&J with a 33 percent market share for pain relievers when another unfortunate poisoning occurred. At this point, J&J recalled all Tylenol capsules and still maintained 96 percent of sales despite the setback. J&J is often cited for its impressive response to this crisis. More recently, J&J disclosed that "improper payments in connection with the sale of medical devices" were made in some units. Adding insult to injury, Janssen, a J&J subsidiary, inappropriately marketed a psychiatric product targeted for use in children, resulting in a combined $117 million in costs to the Texas Medicaid program. More recently, J&J has faced several scandals. In January 2010, the U.S. Justice Department charged J&J with paying millions of dollars in kickbacks to Omnicare, the nation's largest pharmacy that specializes in dispensing drugs to nursing home patients so its Risperdal antipsychotic would be widely prescribed. In April 2010, J&J's Ortho-McNeil Pharmaceutical and Ortho-McNeil-Janssen Pharmaceuticals subsidiaries agreed to pay $81 million in order to resolve criminal and civil lawsuits charging the units with illegally promoting the Topamax epilepsy drug for so-called off-label use. The government alleged that the company promoted Topamax for off-label psychiatric uses through a program called "Doctor-for-a-Day" in which the J&J unit hired outside physicians to join sales reps in visiting other doctors and to speak at meetings and dinners about prescribing Topamax for unapproved uses and doses. In January 2013, J&J faced questions over the withholding of internal information regarding the failure rate of its metal hip replacement. Despite downplaying the recall of the hip implant in 2011, J&J's internal study estimated that the product was failing at a rate of 37 percent within 5 years. Over 10,000 lawsuits have been filed against the company. Why is Johnson & Johnson facing continued problems of this sort? Is the credo helping J&J to resolve these issues?

Source: Johnson & Johnson website, http://www.jnj.com.

"Doing the right thing" is not always as simple as it appears. Levi Strauss experienced this issue in the early 1990s with its suppliers from Bangladesh. Children under the age of 14 were working at two locations, which did not violate the law in Bangladesh, but did go against the policy of Levi Strauss. Ultimately, Levi Strauss decided to continue paying the wages of the children and secured a position for them once they reached the age of 14, after their return from schooling.[49] While the level of involvement is hard to standardize, having a basic set of business ethics and appropriately applying it to the culture in which one is managing is a step in the right direction. Managers need to be cautious not to blur the lines of culture in these situations. The Prince of Wales was once quoted as saying, "Business can only succeed in a sustainable environment. Illiterate, poorly trained, poorly housed, resentful communities, deprived of a sense of belonging or of roots, provide a poor workforce and an uncertain market."[50] Businesses face much difficulty in attempting to balance organizational and cultural roots with the advancement of globalization.

One recent phenomenon in response to globalization has been not just to offshore low-cost labor-intensive practices, as described in Chapter 1, but to transfer a large percentage of current employees of all types to foreign locations. The inexpensive labor available through offshore outsourcing in India has aided many institutions, but has also put a strain on some industries, particularly home-based technology services. Accenture, a company specializing in management consulting, technology services, and outsourcing, moved almost 22 percent of its employees to India by August 2007 in hopes of avoiding dwindling revenues and stock prices due to the continuous investment in India. With labor costs in India at less than half of those in the United States, Accenture is already gaining the competitive advantage by offering similar low-cost services, but with consulting expertise that is not yet matched by Indian cohorts. Accenture recognized the rising competition early, and careful strategies have enabled it to maintain, if not gain, a foothold in India.[51]

The transfer of the labor force overseas creates an interesting dynamic in the scope of ethics and corporate responsibility. While most international managers concern themselves with understanding the social culture in which the corporation is enveloped and how that can mesh with the corporate culture, this recent wave involves the extension of an established corporate culture into a new social environment. The difference here is that the individuals being moved offshore are part of a corporate citizenship, meaning that they will identify with the corporation and not necessarily the outside environment; the opposite occurs when the firm moves to another country and seeks to employ local citizens. Accenture proves that it is possible to succeed with such an effort, but as more and more companies follow suit, other questions and concerns may arise. How will the two cultures work together? Will employees adhere to the work schedule of the home or the host country? Will the host country be open or reluctant to an influx of new citizens? The latter may not be a current concern due to the infrequency of offshoring, but MNCs may face a time when they have to consider more than just survival of the company. One must also bear in mind the effects these choices will have on both cultures.

Reconciling Ethical Differences across Cultures

As noted in the introduction to this section, ethical dilemmas arise from conflicts between ethical standards of a country and business ethics, or the moral code guiding business behavior. Most MNCs seek to adhere to a code of ethical conduct while doing business around the world, yet must make some adjustments to respond to local norms and values. Navigating this natural tension can be challenging. One approach advocated by two prominent business ethicists suggests that there exist implied social contracts that generally govern behavior around the world, some of which are universal or near universal. These "hyper" norms include fundamental principles like respect for human life, or abstention from cheating, lying, and violence. Local community norms are respected within the context of such hyper norms, when they deviate from one society to another.

This approach, called "Integrative Social Contracts Theory" (ISCT), attempts to navigate a moral position that does not force decision makers to engage exclusively in relativism versus absolutism. It allows substantial latitude for nations and economic communities to develop their unique concepts of fairness, but draws the line at flagrant neglect of core human values. It is designed to provide international managers with a framework when confronted with a substantial gap between the apparent moral and ethical values in the country in which the MNC is headquartered and the many countries in which it does business. Although ISCT has been criticized for its inability to provide precise guidance for managers under specific conditions, it nonetheless offers one approach to helping reconcile a fundamental contradiction in international business ethics.[52]

Corporate Social Responsibility and Sustainability

In addition to expectations that they adhere to specific ethical codes and principles, corporations are under increasing pressure to contribute to the societies and communities in which they operate and to adopt more socially responsible business practices throughout their entire range of operations. Corporate social responsibility (CSR) can be defined as the actions of a firm to benefit society beyond the requirements of the law and the direct interests of the firm.[53] It is difficult to provide a list of obligations since the social, economic, and environmental expectations of each company will be based on the desires of the stakeholders. Pressure for greater attention to CSR has emanated from a range of stakeholders, including civil society (the broad societal interests in a given region or country) and from **nongovernmental organizations (NGOs)**. These groups have urged MNCs to be more responsive to the range of social needs in developing countries, including concerns about working conditions in factories or service centers and the environmental impacts of their activities.[54] As a result of recent ethics scandals and concerns about the lack of corporate responsibility, trust in business and government declined sharply in 2012, but began to recover a bit in 2013 (see Figure 3–2).[55]

Many MNCs such as Intel, HSBC, Lenovo, and others take their CSR commitment seriously. These firms have integrated their response to CSR pressures into their core business strategies and operating principles around the world (see the section "Response to Social and Organizational Obligations" on the following page and the Internet Exercise later in this chapter).

Civil Society, NGOs, MNCs, and Ethical Balance
The emergence of organized civil society and NGOs has dramatically altered the business environment globally and the role of MNCs within it. Although social movements have been part of the political and economic landscape for centuries, the emergence of NGO activism in the United States during the modern era can be traced to mid-1984, when a range of NGOs, including church and community groups, human rights organizations, and other antiapartheid activists, built strong networks and pressed U.S. cities and states to divest their public pension funds of companies doing business in South Africa. This effort, combined with domestic unrest, international governmental pressures, and capital flight, posed a direct, sustained, and ultimately successful challenge to the white minority rule, resulting in the collapse of apartheid.

nongovernmental organizations (NGOs) Private, not-for-profit organizations that seek to serve society's interests by focusing on social, political, and economic issues such as poverty, social justice, education, health, and the environment.

Figure 3–2

Most Institutions See Return to 2011 Highs; Gap Between Business and Government Nearly as Wide as in 2007

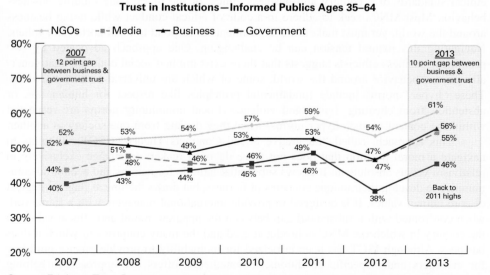

Trust in Institutions—Informed Publics Ages 35–64

Source: Edelman Trust Barometer 2013 (www.edelman.com/trust/). Reprinted by permission.

Since then, NGOs generally have grown in number, power, and influence. Large global NGOs such as Save the Children, Oxfam, CARE, Amnesty International, World Wildlife Fund, and Conservation International are active in all parts of the world. Their force has been felt in a range of major public policy debates, and NGO activism has been responsible for major changes in corporate behavior and governance. Some observers now regard NGOs as a counterweight to business and global capitalism. NGO criticisms have been especially sharp in relation to the activities of MNCs, such as Nike, Levi's, Chiquita, and others whose sourcing practices in developing countries have been alleged to exploit low-wage workers, take advantage of lax environmental and workplace standards, and otherwise contribute to social and economic problems. Three recent examples illustrate the complex and increasingly important impact of NGOs on MNCs.

In January 2004, Citigroup announced it would no longer finance certain projects in emerging markets identified by the Rainforest Action Network (RAN) as damaging to the environment. This announcement came after several years of aggressive pressure and lobbying by RAN, including full-page advertising in daily newspapers showing barren landscapes and blackened trees, lobbying by film and television personalities urging consumers to cut up their credit cards, blockades of Citigroup branches, and campaigns involving schoolchildren who sent cards to Citigroup's chairman, Sanford Weil, asking him to stop contributing to the extinction of endangered species.[56] After heavy lobbying from NGOs, in August 2003, the U.S. pharmaceutical industry dropped its opposition to relaxation of intellectual property provisions under the WTO to make generic, low-cost antiviral drugs available to developing countries facing epidemics or other health emergencies.[57] In November 2009, after nearly two years of student campaigning in coordination with the apparel workers, a Honduran workers' union concluded an agreement with Russell Athletics, the apparel manufacturer owned by Fruit of the Loom, that puts all of the workers back to work, provides compensation for lost wages, recognizes the union and agrees to collective bargaining, and provides access for the union to all other Russell apparel plants in Honduras for union organizing drives in which the company will remain neutral. According to a November 18, 2009, press release of United Students Against Sweatshops, this has been an "unprecedented victory for labor rights."[58]

Many NGOs recognize that MNCs can have positive impacts on the countries in which they do business, often adhering to higher standards of social and environmental responsibility than local firms. In fact, MNCs may be in a position to transfer "best practices" in social or environmental actions from their home to host countries' markets. In some instances, MNCs and NGOs collaborate on social and environmental projects and in so doing contribute both to the well-being of communities and to the reputation of the MNC. The emergence of NGOs that seek to promote ethical and socially responsible business practices is beginning to generate substantial changes in corporate management, strategy, and governance.

Response to Social and Organizational Obligations   MNCs are increasingly engaged in a range of responses to growing pressures to contribute positively to the social and environmental progress of the communities in which they do business. One response is the agreements and codes of conduct in which MNCs commit to maintain certain standards in their domestic and global operations. These agreements, which include the U.N. Global Compact (see Table 3–1), the Global Reporting Initiative, the social accountability "SA8000" standards, and the ISO 14000 environmental quality standards, provide some assurances that when MNCs do business around the world, they will maintain a minimum level of social and environmental standards in the workplaces and communities in which they operate.[59] These codes help offset the real or perceived concern that companies move jobs to avoid higher labor or environmental standards in their home markets. They may also contribute to the raising of standards in the developing world by "exporting" higher standards to local firms in those countries.

Table 3–1
Principles of the Global Compact

Human Rights

Principle 1: Support and respect the protection of international human rights within their sphere of influence.

Principle 2: Make sure their own corporations are not complicit in human rights abuses.

Labor

Principle 3: Freedom of association and the effective recognition of the right to collective bargaining.

Principle 4: The elimination of all forms of forced and compulsory labor.

Principle 5: The effective abolition of child labor.

Principle 6: The elimination of discrimination with respect to employment and occupation.

Environment

Principle 7: Support a precautionary approach to environmental challenges.

Principle 8: Undertake initiatives to promote greater environmental responsibility.

Principle 9: Encourage the development and diffusion of environmentally friendly technologies.

Anticorruption

Principle 10: Business should work against all forms of corruption, including extortion and bribery.

Source: Reprinted by permission of the United Nations Global Compact.

---

fair trade
An organized social movement and market-based approach that aims to help producers in developing countries obtain better trading conditions and promote sustainability.

Another interesting trend among businesses and NGOs is the movement toward increasing the availability of "fairly traded" products. Beginning with coffee and moving to chocolate, fruits, and other agricultural products, **fair trade** is an organized social movement and market-based approach that aims to help producers in developing countries obtain better trading conditions and promote sustainability. See A Closer Look box for a discussion of fair trade systems and products.

Sustainability   In the boardroom, the term **sustainability** may first be associated with financial investments or the hope of steadily increasing profits, but for a growing number of companies, this term means the same to them as it does to an environmental conservationist. Partially this is due to corporations recognizing that dwindling resources will eventually halt productivity, but the World Economic Forum in Davos, Switzerland, has also played a part in bringing awareness to this timely subject. In a report published in 2012, the World Economic Forum discussed the challenges created by the speed of business growth. With half as many people living in poverty as just 30 years ago, the consumer class is growing rapidly in emerging markets. The report focused on how sustainable consumption of energy and resources can be used to ease the problems brought about from this need for rapid business scaling.[60]

sustainability
Development that meets current needs without harming the future.

While the United States has the Environmental Protection Agency to provide information about and enforce environmental laws,[61] the United Nations also has a division dedicated to the education, promotion, facilitation, and advocacy of sustainable practices and environmentally sound concerns called the United Nations Environment Programme (UNEP).[62] The degree to which global awareness and concern are rising extends beyond laws and regulations, as corporations are now taking strides to be leaders in this "green" movement.

Fair Trade in the U.S.: Transfair USA

Fair Trade helps farming families across Latin America, Africa, and Asia to improve the quality of life in their communities. Fair Trade Certification empowers farmers and farm workers to lift themselves out of poverty by investing in their farms and communities, protecting the environment, and developing the business skills necessary to compete in the global marketplace. Fair Trade is much more than a fair price. Fair Trade principles include:

- **Fair price:** Democratically organized farmer groups receive a guaranteed minimum floor price and an additional premium for certified organic products. Farmer organizations are also eligible for preharvest credit.

- **Fair labor conditions:** Workers on Fair Trade farms enjoy freedom of association, safe working conditions, and living wages. Forced child labor is strictly prohibited.

- **Direct trade:** With Fair Trade, importers purchase from Fair Trade producer groups as directly as possible, eliminating unnecessary middlemen and empowering farmers to develop the business capacity necessary to compete in the global marketplace.

- **Democratic and transparent organizations:** Fair Trade farmers and farm workers decide democratically how to invest Fair Trade revenues.

- **Community development:** Fair Trade farmers and farm workers invest Fair Trade premiums in social and business development projects like scholarship programs, quality improvement trainings, and organic certification.

- **Environmental sustainability:** Harmful agro-chemicals and GMOs are strictly prohibited in favor of environmentally sustainable farming methods that protect farmers' health and preserve valuable ecosystems for future generations.

TransFair USA, a nonprofit organization, is the only independent, third-party certifier of Fair Trade products in the U.S. and one of 20 members of Fairtrade Labeling Organizations International (FLO). TransFair's rigorous audit system, which tracks products from farm to finished product, verifies industry compliance with Fair Trade criteria. TransFair allows U.S. companies to display the Fair Trade Certified label on products that meet strict Fair Trade standards. Fair Trade Certification is currently available in the U.S. for coffee, tea and herbs, cocoa and chocolate, fresh fruit, sugar, rice, and vanilla.

Walmart, one of the most well-known and pervasive global retailers, has begun to recognize the numerous benefits of the adage, "Think globally, act locally." Walmart has set three broad corporate goals in regards to sustainability: to use 100 percent renewable energy, to achieve zero-waste, and to sell products that are sustainable for the environment and people.[63] Working with environmentalists, it discovered that many changes in production and supply chain practices could reduce waste and pollution and therefore reduce costs. By cutting back on packaging, Walmart saves an estimated $2.4 million a year, 3,800 trees, and 1 million barrels of oil. Over 80,000 suppliers compete to put their products on Walmart shelves, which means that this company has a strong influence on how manufacturers do business.[64] To encourage sustainability from these suppliers, Walmart created a "Sustainability Hub" website to share standards and encourage innovation.[65] And Walmart's efforts are truly global. In line with the three corporate goals, the company is buying solar and wind power in Mexico, sourcing local food in China and India, and analyzing the life cycle impact of consumer products in Brazil. Alleviating hunger has become a goal of Walmart's charitable efforts, and so with CARE it is backing education, job-training, and entrepreneurial programs for women in Peru, Bangladesh, and India. Walmart is attempting to change global standards as it offers higher prices to coffee growers in Brazil and increases pressures on the factory owners in China to reduce energy and fuel costs.[66] Although Walmart has faced some setbacks in its global CSR efforts, it continues to respond to pressures for social responsibility and sustainability.

GE has pursued an aggressive initiative to integrate environmental sustainability with its business goals through the "ecomagination" program. Management styles again are changing as agendas are refocused on not only seeing the present but also looking to the future of human needs and the environment. Ecomagination is a GE strategic initiative to use innovation to improve energy efficiency across the globe. By meeting the demand for "green" products and services, GE is generating value for shareholders as well as promoting environmental sustainability. At a GE Hitachi Nuclear Energy power plant in North Carolina, a new wastewater system "has reduced water usage by 25 million gallons annually, avoiding nearly 80 tons per year of CO_2 emissions and realizing annual savings of \$160,000 in water and energy costs." GE's ecomagination ZeeWeed® membrane bioreactor (MBR) technology transforms up to 65,000 gallons per day of wastewater into treated water that can be used in the facility's cooling towers. GE Jenbacher engines capture gas from various fuel sources, even garbage, to create power. Jenbacher engines are at the core of a Mexican landfill gas-to-energy project, which President Felipe Calderón called "a model renewable energy project" for Latin America. This project's power supports "Monterrey's light-rail system during the day and city street lights at night."

In addition, GE's Flight Management System (FMS) for Boeing 737 planes has enabled airlines to lower fuel costs and reduce emissions. According to a GE Ecomagination Annual Report, "The FMS enables pilots to determine, while maintaining a highly efficient cruise altitude, the exact point where the throttle can be reduced to flight idle while allowing the aircraft to arrive precisely at the required runway approach point without the need for throttle increases." SAS Scandinavian Airlines estimates that FMS will save the airline \$10 million annually. According to CEO Jeffrey R. Immelt and vice president of Ecomagination Steven M. Fludder, "Ecomagination is playing a role in boosting economic recovery, supporting the jobs of the future, improving the environmental impact of our customers' (and our own) operations, furthering energy independence, and fostering innovation and growth in profitable environmental solutions."[67]

Corporate Governance

The recent global, ethical, and governance scandals have placed corporations under intense scrutiny regarding their oversight and accountability. Adelphia, Arthur Andersen, Enron, Olympus, HSBC, Tyco, and Barclays are just a few of the dozens of companies that have been found to engage in inappropriate and often illegal activities related to governance. In addition, a number of financial services firms, including Credit Suisse, Deutsche Bank, Lehman Brothers, Citigroup, and many others have been found to have engaged in inappropriate trading or other activities. Corporate governance is increasingly high on the agenda for directors, investors, and governments alike in the wake of financial collapses and corporate scandals in recent years. The collapses and scandals have not been limited to a single country, or even a single continent, but have been a global phenomenon.

corporate governance
The system by which business corporations are directed and controlled.

Corporate governance can be defined as the system by which business corporations are directed and controlled.[68] The corporate governance structure specifies the distribution of rights and responsibilities among different participants in the corporation—such as the board, managers, shareholders, and other stakeholders—and spells out the rules and procedures for making decisions on corporate affairs. By doing this, it also provides the structure through which the company objectives are set and the means of attaining those objectives and monitoring performance.

Governance rules and regulations differ among countries and regions around the world. For example, the UK and U.S. systems have been termed "outsider" systems because of dispersed ownership of corporate equity among a large number of outside investors. Historically, although institutional investor ownership was predominant, institutions generally did not hold large shares in any given company; hence they had limited direct control.[69] In contrast, in an insider system, such as that in many continental European countries, ownership tends to be much more concentrated, with shares often being owned by holding companies, families, or banks. In addition, differences in legal systems, as described in Chapter 2, also affect shareholders' and other stake-holders' rights and, in turn, the responsiveness and accountability of corporate managers to these constituencies. Notwithstanding recent scandals, in general, North American and European systems are considered comparatively responsive to shareholders and other stakeholders. In regions with less well-developed legal and institutional protections and poor property rights, such as some countries in Asia, Latin America, and Africa, forms of "crony capitalism" may emerge in which weak corporate governance and government interference can lead to poor performance, risky financing patterns, and macroeconomic crises.

Corporate governance will undoubtedly remain high on the agenda of governments, investors, NGOs, and corporations in the coming years, as pressure for accountability and responsiveness continues to increase.

Corruption

As noted in Chapter 2, government corruption is a pervasive element in the international business environment. Recently publicized scandals in Russia, China, Brazil, Pakistan, South Africa, Costa Rica, Egypt, and elsewhere underscore the extent of corruption globally, especially in the developing world. However, a number of initiatives have been taken by governments and companies to begin to stem the tide of corruption.[70]

The Foreign Corrupt Practices Act (FCPA) makes it illegal for U.S. companies and their managers to attempt to influence foreign officials through personal payments or political contributions. Prior to passage of the FCPA, some American multinationals had engaged in this practice, but realizing that their stockholders were unlikely to approve of these tactics, the firms typically disguised the payments as entertainment expenses, consulting fees, and so on. Not only does the FCPA prohibit these activities, but the U.S. Internal Revenue Service also continually audits the books of MNCs. Those firms that take deductions for such illegal activities are subject to high financial penalties, and individuals who are involved can even end up going to prison. Strict enforcement of the FCPA has been applauded by many people, but some critics wonder if such a strong stance has hurt the competitive ability of American MNCs. On the positive side, many U.S. multinationals have now increased the amount of business in countries where they used to pay bribes. Additionally, many institutional investors in the United States have made it clear that they will not buy stock in companies that engage in unethical practices and will sell their holdings in such firms. Given that these institutions have hundreds of billions of dollars invested, senior-level management must be responsive to their needs.

Looking at the effect of the FCPA on U.S. multinationals, it appears that the law has had far more of a positive effect than a negative one. Given the growth of American MNCs in recent years, it seems fair to conclude that bribes are not a basic part of business in many countries, for when multinationals stopped this activity, they were still able to sell in that particular market. On the other hand, this does not mean that bribery and corruption are a thing of the past.

Indeed bribery continues to be a problem for MNCs around the world. In fact, recent scandals at ALSTOM, BAE, Daimler, Halliburton, Siemens, Walmart, and many other multinationals underscore the reality that executives continue to participate in bribery and corruption. Although Siemens paid a record fine, U.S. authorities are still concerned about enforcement of corruption laws in other countries.[71] Figure 3–3 gives the latest corruption index of countries around the world. Notice that the United States ranks 19th in this independent analysis. These rankings fluctuate somewhat from year to year. Factors that appear to contribute to these fluctuations include changes in government or political party in power, economic crises, and crackdowns in individual countries.

In complying with the provisions of the FCPA, U.S. firms must be aware of changes in the law that make FCPA violators subject to Federal Sentencing Guidelines.

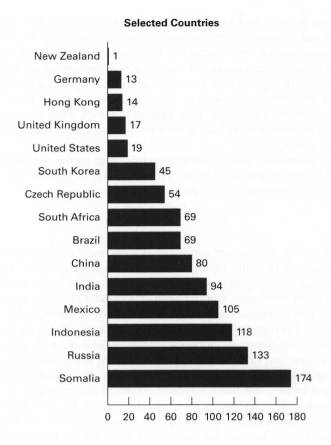

The origin of this law and the guidelines that followed can be traced to two Lockheed Corporation executives who were found guilty of paying a $1 million bribe to a member of the Egyptian parliament in order to secure the sale of aircraft to the Egyptian military. One of the executives was sentenced to probation and fined $20,000 and the other, who initially fled prosecution, was fined $125,000 and sentenced to 18 months in prison.[72]

Another development that promises to give teeth to "antibribing" legislation is the recent formal agreement by a host of industrialized nations to outlaw the practice of bribing foreign government officials. The treaty, which initially included 29 nations that belong to the Organization for Economic Cooperation and Development (OECD), marked a victory for the United States, which outlawed foreign bribery two decades previously but had not been able to persuade other countries to follow its lead. As a result, American firms had long complained that they lost billions of dollars in contracts each year to rivals that bribed their way to success.[73]

This treaty does not outlaw most payments to political party leaders. In fact, the treaty provisions are much narrower than U.S. negotiators wanted, and there undoubtedly will be ongoing pressure from the American government to expand the scope and coverage of the agreement. For the moment, however, it is a step in the direction of a more ethical and level playing field in global business. Additionally, in summing up the impact and value of the treaty, one observer noted: "For their part, business executives say the treaty . . . reflects growing support for antibribery initiatives among corporations in Europe and Japan that have openly opposed the idea. Some of Europe's leading industrial corporations, including a few that have been embroiled in recent allegations of bribery, have spoken out in favor of tougher measures and on the increasingly corrosive effect of corruption."[74]

In addition to the 34 members of the OECD, a number of developing countries, including Argentina, Brazil, Bulgaria, and South Africa, have signed on to the OECD agreement.

Latin American countries have established the Organization of American States (OAS) Inter-American Convention Against Corruption, which entered into force in March 1997, and more than 25 Western Hemisphere countries are signatories to the convention, including Argentina, Brazil, Chile, Mexico, and the United States. As a way to prevent the shifting of corrupt practices to suppliers and intermediaries, the Transparent Agents Against Contracting Entities (TRACE) standard was developed after a review of the practices of 34 companies. It applies to business intermediaries, including sales agents, consultants, suppliers, distributors, resellers, subcontractors, franchisees, and joint-venture partners, so that final producers, distributors, and customers can be confident that no party within a supply chain has participated in corruption.

Both governments and companies have made important steps in their efforts to stem the spread of corruption, but much more needs to be done in order to reduce the impact of corruption on companies and the broader societies in which they operate.[75]

International Assistance

In addition to government- and corporate-sponsored ethics and social responsibility practices, governments and corporations are increasingly collaborating to provide assistance to communities around the world through global partnerships. This assistance is particularly important for those parts of the world that have not fully benefited from globalization and economic integration. Using a cost-benefit analysis of where investments would have the greatest impact, a recent study identified the top priorities around the world for development assistance. The results of this analysis are presented in Table 3–2. Controlling and preventing AIDS, fighting malnutrition, reducing subsidies and trade restrictions, and controlling malaria are shown to be the best investments. Governments, international institutions, and corporations are involved in several ongoing efforts to address some of these problems.[76]

Table 3–2
Copenhagen Consensus Development Priorities

Project Rating		Challenge	Opportunity
Very good	1	Diseases	Control of HIV/AIDS
	2	Malnutrition	Providing micronutrients
	3	Subsidies and trade	Trade liberalization
	4	Diseases	Control of malaria
Good	5	Malnutrition	Development of new agricultural technologies
	6	Sanitation and water	Small-scale water technology for livelihoods
	7	Sanitation and water	Community-managed water supply and sanitation
	8	Sanitation and water	Research on water productivity in food production
	9	Government	Lowering the cost of starting a new business
Fair	10	Migration	Lowering barriers to migration for skilled workers
	11	Malnutrition	Improving infant and child nutrition
	12	Malnutrition	Reducing the prevalence of low birth weight
	13	Diseases	Scaled-up basic health services
Bad	14	Migration	Guest-worker programs for the unskilled
	15	Climate	"Optimal" carbon tax
	16	Climate	The Kyoto protocol
	17	Climate	Value-at-risk carbon tax

Source: Copenhagen Consensus.
Note: Some of the proposals were not ranked.

| Figure 3–4 | | Millennium Development Goals: 2012 Progress Chart |

Goals and Targets	Africa		Asia				Oceania	Latin America & Caribbean	Caucasus & Central Asia
	Northern	Sub-Saharan	Eastern	South-Eastern	Southern	Western			

GOAL 1 | Eradicate extreme poverty and hunger

Reduce extreme poverty by half	low poverty	very high poverty	moderate poverty	high poverty	very high poverty	low poverty	very high poverty	moderate poverty	low poverty
Productive and decent employment	large deficit in decent work	very large deficit in decent work	large deficit in decent work	large deficit in decent work	very large deficit in decent work	large deficit in decent work	very large deficit in decent work	moderate deficit in decent work	moderate deficit in decent work
Reduce hunger by half	low hunger	very high hunger	moderate hunger	moderate hunger	high hunger	moderate hunger	moderate hunger	moderate hunger	moderate hunger

GOAL 2 | Achieve universal primary education

Universal primary schooling	high enrollment	moderate enrollment	high enrollment	high enrollment	high enrollment	high enrollment	–	high enrollment	high enrollment

GOAL 3 | Promote gender equality and empower women

Equal girls' enrollment in primary school	close to parity	close to parity	parity	parity	parity	close to parity	close to parity	parity	parity
Women's share of paid employment	low share	medium share	high share	medium share	low share	low share	medium share	high share	high share
Women's equal representation in national parliaments	low representation	moderate representation	moderate representation	low representation	low representation	low representation	very low representation	moderate representation	low representation

GOAL 4 | Reduce child mortality

Reduce mortality of under-five-year-olds by two thirds	low mortality	high mortality	low mortality	low mortality	moderate mortality	low mortality	moderate mortality	low mortality	moderate mortality

GOAL 5 | Improve maternal health

Reduce maternal mortality by three quarters	low mortality	very high mortality	low mortality	moderate mortality	high mortality	low mortality	high mortality	low mortality	low mortality
Access to reproductive health	moderate access	low access	high access	moderate access	moderate access	moderate access	low access	high access	moderate access

GOAL 6 | Combat HIV/AIDS, malaria and other diseases

Halt and begin to reverse the spread of HIV/AIDS	low incidence	high incidence	low incidence	low incidence	low incidence	low incidence	low incidence	low incidence	low incidence
Halt and reverse the spread of tuberculosis	low mortality	high mortality	low mortality	moderate mortality	moderate mortality	low mortality	high mortality	low mortality	moderate mortality

GOAL 7 | Ensure environmental sustainability

Halve proportion of population without improved drinking water	high coverage	low coverage	high coverage	moderate coverage	high coverage	moderate coverage	low coverage	high coverage	moderate coverage
Halve proportion of population without sanitation	high coverage	very low coverage	low coverage	low coverage	very low coverage	moderate coverage	low coverage	moderate coverage	high coverage
Improve the lives of slum-dwellers	moderate proportion of slum-dwellers	very high proportion of slum-dwellers	moderate proportion of slum-dwellers	high proportion of slum-dwellers	high proportion of slum-dwellers	moderate proportion of slum-dwellers	moderate proportion of slum-dwellers	moderate proportion of slum-dwellers	–

GOAL 8 | Develop a global partnership for development

Internet users	high usage	moderate usage	high usage	moderate usage	low usage	high usage	low usage	high usage	high usage

The progress chart operates on two levels. The words in each box indicate the present degree of compliance with the target. The colors show progress towards the target according to the legend below:

▪ Target already met or expected to be met by 2015.   ▪ No progress or deterioration

▪ Progress insufficient to reach the target if prevailing trends persist.   ▪ Missing or insufficient data.

For the regional groupings and country data, see mdgs.un.org. Country experiences in each region may differ significantly from the regional average. Due to new data and revised methodologies, this Progress Chart is not comparable with previous versions.

Sources: United Nations, based on data and estimates provided by: Food and Agriculture Organization of the United Nations; Inter-Parliamentary Union; International Labour Organization; International Telecommunication Union; UNAIDS; UNESCO; UN-Habitat; UNICEF; UN Population Division; World Bank; World Health Organization–based on statistics available as of June 2012.

Table 3–3
The U.N. Millennium Development Goals

Goal 1: Eradicate extreme poverty and hunger.

Goal 2: Achieve universal primary education.

Goal 3: Promote gender equality and empower women.

Goal 4: Reduce child mortality.

Goal 5: Improve maternal health.

Goal 6: Combat HIV/AIDS, malaria, and other diseases.

Goal 7: Ensure environmental sustainability.

Goal 8: Develop a Global Partnership for Development.

Source: www.unmillenniumproject.org.

At the United Nations Millennium Summit in September 2000, world leaders placed development at the heart of the global agenda by adopting the Millennium Development Goals (see Table 3–3). The eight Millennium Development Goals constitute an ambitious agenda to significantly improve the human condition by 2015. The goals set clear targets for reducing poverty, hunger, disease, illiteracy, environmental degradation, and discrimination against women.[77] For each goal, a set of targets and indicators have been defined and are used to track the progress in meeting the goals. Figure 3–4 shows the progress in meeting the goals as of 2012. The UN is currently developing a similar plan to continue the progress post-2015.[78]

A more specific initiative is the Global Fund to Fight AIDS, Tuberculosis and Malaria, which was established in 2001. Through the end of 2011, the Global Fund had committed over US$22.9 billion in grants to over 151 countries.[79]

Through these and other efforts, MNCs, governments, and international organizations are providing a range of resources to communities around the world to assist them as they respond to the challenges of globalization and development. International managers will increasingly be called upon to support and contribute to these initiatives.

■ The World of International Management—Revisited

The World of International Management feature that opened this chapter outlines how three companies have sought to incorporate social responsibility and sustainability in their business strategy and operations. In each case, the companies have responded to changes in the external environment, and sought to capitalize on increasing interest in and support of sustainability in business. This interest has spread around the globe such that both developed and developing countries and their companies are increasingly committed to a sustainable future.

In this chapter we focused on ethics and social responsibility in global business activities, including the role of governments, MNCs, and NGOs in advancing greater ethical and socially responsible behavior. MNCs' new focus on environmental sustainability and "doing well by doing good" is an important dimension of this broad trend.

Global ethical and governance scandals have rocked the financial markets and implicated dozens of individual companies. New corporate ethics guidelines passed in the United States have forced many MNCs to take a look at their own internal ethical practices and make changes accordingly. Lawmakers in Europe and Asia have also made adjustments in rules over corporate financial disclosure. The continuing trend toward globalization and free trade appears to be encouraging development of a set of global ethical, social responsibility, and anticorruption standards. This may actually help firms cut compliance costs as they realize that economies have common global frameworks.

Having read the chapter, answer the following questions: (1) Do governments and companies in developed countries have an ethical responsibility to contribute to economic growth and social development in developing countries? (2) Are governments, companies, or NGOs best equipped to provide this assistance? (3) Do corporations have a responsibility to use their "best" ethics and social responsibility practices when they do business in other countries, even if those countries' practices are different? (4) How can companies leverage their ethical reputation and social and environmental responsibility to improve business performance?

SUMMARY OF KEY POINTS

1. Ethics is the study of morality and standards of conduct. It is important in the study of international management because ethical behavior often varies from one country to another. Ethics manifests itself in the ways societies and companies address issues such as employment conditions, human rights, and corruption. A danger in international management is the ethical relativism trap—"When in Rome, do as the Romans do."

2. During the years ahead, multinationals likely will become more concerned about being socially responsible. NGOs are forcing the issue. Countries are passing laws to regulate ethical practices and

governance rules for MNCs. MNCs are being more proactive (often because they realize it makes good business sense) in making social contributions in the regions in which they operate and in developing codes of conduct to govern ethics and social responsibility. One area in which companies have been especially active is in pursuing strategies that blend environmental sustainability and business objectives.

3. MNCs—in conjunction with governments and NGOs—are also contributing to international development assistance and working to ensure that corporate governance practices are sound and effective.

KEY TERMS

corporate governance, 78

corporate social responsibility (CSR), 65

ethics, 65

fair trade, 76

nongovernmental organizations (NGOs), 74

sustainability, 76

REVIEW AND DISCUSSION QUESTIONS

1. How might different ethical philosophies influence how managers make decisions when it comes to offshoring of jobs?

2. What lessons can U.S. multinationals learn from the political and bribery scandals in recent years, such as those affecting contractors doing business in Iraq (Halliburton), as well as large MNCs such as Siemens, HP, and others? Discuss two.

3. In recent years, rules have tightened such that those who work for the U.S. government in trade negotiations are now restricted from working for

lobbyists for foreign firms. Is this a good idea? Why or why not?

4. What are some strategies for overcoming the impact of counterfeiting? Which strategies work best for discretionary (for instance, movies) versus nondiscretionary (pharmaceutical) goods?

5. Why are MNCs getting involved in corporate social responsibility and sustainable business practice? Are they displaying a sense of social responsibility, or is this merely a matter of good business, or both? Defend your answer.

INTERNET EXERCISE: SOCIAL RESPONSIBILITY AT JOHNSON & JOHNSON AND HP

In this chapter, the social responsibility actions of companies such Hewlett-Packard (HP) were discussed.

At Hewlett-Packard, "global citizenship" means engaging in public-private partnerships and demonstrating model behavior and activities in governance, environmental policy and practices, community engagement models, and "e-inclusion initiatives." Go to the HP website, www.hp.com, to the sections on global citizenship and e-inclusion. Then answer these questions: (1) What does it mean to be a global citizen at HP? (2) How does HP measure and evaluate its success in global citizenship? (3) What is e-inclusion, and what are some specific examples of projects that advance HP's e-inclusion goals?

Saudi Arabia

Saudi Arabia is a large Middle Eastern country covering 865,000 square miles. Part of its east coast rests on the Persian Gulf, and much of the west coast rests along the Red Sea. One of the countries on its border is Iraq. After Iraq's military takeover of Kuwait in August 1990, Iraq threatened to invade Saudi Arabia. This, of course, did not happen, and Saudi Arabia was not an Iraqi target during the U.S.-led war in Iraq during 2003–2004. However, accusations stemming from rumors of terrorists financing activities have made Saudi Arabia a focus in the global war on terrorism, and Saudi Arabia itself was the target of terrorist attacks in 2003–2004.

As of 2012, there were approximately 27 million people in Saudi Arabia, and the annual per capita GDP was around $24,000. This apparent prosperity is misleading because most Saudis are poor farmers and herders who tend their camels, goats, and sheep. In recent years, however, more and more have moved to the cities and have jobs connected to the oil industry. Nearly all are Arab Muslims. The country has the two holiest cities of Islam: Mecca and Medina. The country depends almost exclusively on the sale of oil (it is the largest exporter of oil in the world) and has no public debt. The government is a monarchy, and the king makes all important decisions but is advised by ministers and other government officials. Royal and ministerial decrees account for most of the promulgated legislation. In 2011, King Abdullah granted women the right to vote and run for seats on the Shura council, which advises the King on policy issues. The ruling will not go into effect until the next election cycle in 2015. Still, the decision is a significant victory for women in a country where they are not allowed to drive and must have a male chaperone with them in public at all times. There are no political parties.

Recently, Robert Auger, the executive vice president of Skyblue, a commercial aircraft manufacturing firm based in Kansas City, had a visit with a Saudi minister. The Saudi official explained to Auger that the government planned to purchase 10 aircraft over the next two years. A number of competitive firms were bidding for the job. The minister went on to explain that despite the competitiveness of the situation, several members of the royal family were impressed with Auger's company. The firm's reputation for high-quality performance aircraft and state-of-the-art technology gave it the inside track. A number of people are involved in the decision, however, and in the minister's words, "Anything can happen when a committee decision is being made."

The Saudi official went on to explain that some people who would be involved in the decision had recently suffered large losses in some stock market speculations on the London Stock Exchange. "One relative of the King, who will be a key person in the decision regarding the purchase of the aircraft, I have heard, lost over $200,000 last week alone. Some of the competitive firms have decided to put together a pool of money to help ease his burden. Three of them have given me $100,000 each. If you were to do the same, I know that it would put you on a par with them, and I believe it would be in your best interests when the decision is made." Auger was stunned by the suggestion and told the minister that he would check with his people and get back to the minister as soon as possible.

As soon as he returned to his temporary office, Auger sent a coded message to headquarters asking management what he should do. He expects to have an answer within the next 48 hours. In the interim, he has had a call from the minister's office, but Auger's secretary told the caller that Auger had been called away from the office and would not be returning for at least two days. The individual said he would place the call again at the beginning of this coming week. Meanwhile, Auger has talked to a Saudi friend whom he had known back in the United States and who is currently an insider in the Saudi government. Over dinner, Auger hinted at what he had been told by the minister. The friend seemed somewhat puzzled about what Auger was saying and indicated that he had heard nothing about any stock market losses by the royal family or pool of money being put together for certain members of the decision-making committee. He asked Auger, "Are you sure you got the story straight, or as you Americans say, is someone pulling your leg?"

Questions

1. What are some current issues facing Saudi Arabia? What is the climate for doing business in Saudi Arabia today?

2. Is it legal for Auger's firm to make a payment of $100,000 to help ensure this contract?

3. Do you think other firms are making these payments, or is Auger's firm being singled out? What conclusion can you draw from your answer?

4. What would you recommend that Skyblue do?

Brief Integrative Case 1.1

Advertising or Free Speech? The Case of Nike and Human Rights

Nike Inc., the global leader in the production and marketing of sports and athletic merchandise including shoes, clothing, and equipment, has enjoyed unparalleled worldwide growth for many years. Consumers around the world recognize Nike's brand name and logo. As a supplier to and sponsor of professional sports figures and organizations, and as a large advertiser to the general public, Nike is widely known. Nike was a pioneer in offshore manufacturing, establishing company-owned assembly plants and engaging third-party contractors in developing countries.

In 1996, Life magazine published a landmark article about the labor conditions of Nike's overseas subcontractors, entitled, "On the Playgrounds of America, Every Kid's Goal Is to Score: In Pakistan, Where Children Stitch Soccer Balls for Six Cents an Hour, Their Goal Is to Survive." Accompanying the article was a photo of a 12-year-old Pakistani boy stitching a Nike embossed soccer ball. The photo caption noted that the job took a whole day, and the child was paid US$.60 for his effort. Up until this time, the general public was neither aware of the wide use of foreign labor nor familiar with the working arrangements and treatment of laborers in developing countries. Since then, Nike has become a poster child for the questionable unethical use of offshore workers in poorer regions of the world. This label has continued to plague the corporation as many global human interest and labor rights organizations have monitored and often condemned Nike for its labor practices around the world.

Nike executives have been frequent targets at public events, especially at universities where students have pressed administrators and athletic directors to ban products that have been made under "sweatshop" conditions. Indeed, at the University of Oregon, a major gift from Phil Knight, Nike's CEO, was held up in part because of student criticism and activism against Nike on campus.[1]

In 2003, the company employed 86 compliance officers (up from just three in 1996) to monitor its plant operations and working conditions and ensure compliance with its published corporate code of conduct. Even so, the stigma of past practices—whether perceived or real—remains emblazoned on its image and brand name. Nike found itself constantly defending its activities, striving to shake this reputation and perception.

In 2002, Marc Kasky sued Nike, alleging that the company knowingly made false and misleading statements in its denial of direct participation in abusive labor conditions abroad. Through corporate news releases, full-page ads in major newspapers, and letters to editors, Nike defended its conduct and sought to show that allegations of misconduct were unwarranted. The action by the plaintiff, a local citizen, was predicated on a California state law prohibiting unlawful business practices. He alleged that Nike's public statements were motivated by marketing and public relations and were simply false. According to the allegation, Nike's statements misled the public and thus violated the California statute. Nike countered by claiming its statements fell under and within the protection of the First Amendment, which protects free speech. The state court concluded that a firm's public statements about its operations have the effect of persuading consumers to buy its products and therefore are, in effect, advertising. Therefore, the suit could be adjudicated on the basis of whether Nike's pronouncements were false and misleading. The court stated that promoting a company's reputation was equivalent to sales solicitation, a practice clearly within the purview of state law. The majority of justices summarized their decision by declaring, "because messages in question were directed by a commercial speaker to a commercial audience, and because they made representations of fact about the speaker's own business operations for the purpose of promoting sales of its products, we conclude that these messages are commercial speech for purposes of applying state laws barring false and misleading commercial messages" (Kasky v. Nike Inc., 2002). The conclusion reached by the court was that statements by a business enterprise to promote its reputation must, like advertising, be factual representations and that companies have a clear duty to speak truthfully about such issues.[2]

In January 2003, the U.S. Supreme Court agreed to hear Nike's appeal of the decision in Kasky v. Nike Inc. from the California Supreme Court. In particular, the U.S. Supreme Court agreed to rule on whether Nike's previous statements about the working conditions at its subcontracted, overseas plants were in fact "commercial speech" and, separately, whether a private individual (such as Kasky) has the right to sue on those grounds. Numerous amici briefs were filed on both sides. Supporters of Kasky included California, as well as 17 other states, Ralph Nader's Public Citizen Organization, California's AFL/CIO, and California's attorney general. Nike's friends of the court included the American Civil

Liberties Union, the Business Roundtable, the U.S. Chamber of Commerce, other MNCs including Exxon/Mobil and Microsoft, and the Bush administration (particularly on the grounds that it does not support private individuals acting as public censors).[3]

Despite the novelty of this First Amendment debate and the potentially wide-reaching effects for big business (particularly MNCs), the U.S. Supreme Court dismissed the case (6 to 3) in June 2003 as "improvidently granted" due to procedural issues surrounding the case. In their dissenting opinion, Justices Stephen G. Breyer and Sandra Day O'Connor suggested that Nike would likely win the appeal at the U.S. Supreme Court level. In both the concurring and dissenting opinions, Nike's statements were described as a mix of "commercial" and "noncommercial" speech.[4] This suggested to Nike, as well as other MNCs, that if the Court were to have ruled on the substantive issue, Nike would have prevailed.

Although this case has set no nationwide precedent for corporate advertising about business practices or corporate social responsibility (CSR) in general, given the sensitivity of the issue, Nike has allowed its actions to speak louder than words in recent years. As part of its international CSR profile, Nike has assisted relief efforts (donating $1 million to tsunami relief in 2004) and advocated fair wages and employment practices in its outsourced operations. Nike claims that it has not abandoned production in certain countries in favor of lower-wage labor in others and that its factory wages abroad are actually in accordance with local regulations, once one accounts for purchasing power and cost-of-living differences.[5] The Nike Foundation, a nonprofit organization supported by Nike, is also an active supporter of the Millennium Development Goals, particularly those directed at improving the lives of adolescent girls in developing countries (specifically Bangladesh, Brazil, China, Ethiopia, and Zambia) through better health, education, and economic opportunities.[6]

As part of its domestic CSR profile, Nike is primarily concerned with keeping youth active, presumably for health, safety, educational, and psychological/esteem reasons. Nike has worked with Head Start (2005) and Special Olympics Oregon (2007), as well as created its own community program, NikeGO, to advocate physical activity among youth. Furthermore, Nike is committed to domestic efforts such as Hurricane Katrina relief and education, the latter through grants made by the Nike School Innovation Fund in support of the Primary Years Literacy Initiative.[7]

Despite Nike's impressive CSR profile, if the California State Supreme Court decision is sustained and sets a global precedent, Nike's promotion or "advertisement" of its global CSR initiatives could still be subjected to legal challenge. This could create a minefield for multinational firms. It would effectively elevate statements on human rights treatment by companies to the level of corporate marketing and advertising. Under these conditions, it might be difficult for MNCs to defend themselves against allegations of human rights abuses. In fact, action such as the issuance and dissemination of a written company code of conduct could fall into the category of advertising declarations. Although Kasky v. Nike was never fully resolved in court, the issues that it raised remain to be addressed by global companies.

Also to be seen is what effect a court decision would have on Nike's financial success. Despite the publicity of the case, at both the state and Supreme Court levels, and the lingering criticism about its labor practices overseas, Nike has maintained strong and growing sales and profits. The company has expanded its operations into different types of clothing and sports equipment and has continued to choose successful athletes to advertise its gear. Nike has shown no signs of slowing down, suggesting that its name and logo have not been substantially tarnished in the global market.

Questions for Review

1. What ethical issues faced by MNCs in their treatment of foreign workers could bring allegations of misconduct in their operations?

2. Would the use of third-party independent contractors insulate MNCs from being attacked? Would that practice offer MNCs a good defensive shield against charges of abuse of "their employees"?

3. Do you think that statements by companies that describe good social and moral conduct in the treatment of their workers are part of the image those companies create and therefore are part of their advertising message? Do consumers judge companies and base their buying decision on their perceptions of corporate behavior and values? Is the historic "made in" question (e.g., "Made in the USA") now being replaced by a "made by" inquiry (e.g., "Made by Company X" or "Made for Company X by Company Y")?

4. Given the principles noted in the case, how can companies comment on their positive actions to promote human rights so that consumers will think well of them? Would you propose that a company (a) do nothing, (b) construct a corporate code of ethics, or (c) align itself with some of the universal covenants or compacts prepared by international agencies?

5. What does Nike's continued financial success, in spite of the lawsuit, suggest about consumers' reactions to negative publicity? Have American media and NGOs exaggerated the impact of a firm's labor practices and corporate social responsibility on its sales? How should managers of an MNC respond to such negative publicity?

Source: This case was prepared by Lawrence Beer, W. P. Carey School of Business, Arizona State University as the basis for class discussion.

Dansko Puts its Right Foot Forward

In 1990, a unique footwear company was born when wife and husband team Mandy Cabot and Peter Kjellerup discovered their perfect "barn shoes" in a tiny shop in Denmark. Since that time, Cabot and Kjellerup have not only transformed footwear tastes and styles among a discerning U.S. customer base, but they have also transformed their company into one of the most socially responsible, sustainable, and well-known consumer brands.[1]

Along the way, Dansko, which means "Danish shoe," has been recognized more than any shoe company by the American Podiatric Medical Association, has developed its own, highly sophisticated R&D lab, and in 2011 sold more than 2.5 million heels, boots, sandals, flats, sneakers, socks, and health care apparel. In addition, Dansko has committed to supporting employee volunteerism and hosted its township's only Community Recycling Station, providing a place for local residents to recycle. Dansko recycled an impressive 86 percent of its waste and supported more than 80 nonprofit organizations through its community foundation. It has also been recognized for its ecologically friendly construction. In 2012, Dansko became a 100 percent employee-owned business and the first footwear company to be a founding member of B Corporation, a group of for-profit businesses who take care of their employees, community, and environment.[2]

Dansko's success results, in part, from a combination of authentic Danish practicality, extreme comfort, and a sort of alternative, offbeat fashion sense that appeals to key demographics in the U.S. and around the world. Dansko's line has expanded to include dress shoes, slip-ons, sandals, sneakers, boots, and even clothing for medical professionals, but all with the emphasis on comfort and practicality.

Dansko has benefited from a number of trends and fashion waves, including a return to simplicity and comfort, as well as "FanDansko" devotees who are passionate and vocal about their love of the shoes. In addition, a number of celebrities, including Kim Basinger, Mathew Broderick, Edie Falco, Tina Fey, Jennifer Garner, Melanie Griffith, Felicity Huffman, Sean Hayes, Heidi Klum, Jane Lynch, Juliana Moore, and Julia Roberts, have embraced Dansko and called attention to the brand in public appearances. The shoes have also been featured in major magazines and periodicals, and were named in the New York Times as among the best shoes for travel.[3]

The Early Years

Like many successful businesses, Dansko's start could be characterized by a combination of entrepreneurial penchant and good timing. The first milestone was Cabot and Kjellerup discovering stapled clogs on a trip to his native Denmark. Thinking they were perfect for farm use, they brought them back and sold them one pair at a time.[4]

According to Mandy Cabot,

> Peter and I had no idea that we would ever start a shoe company. We simply found ourselves in the path of an unexpected opportunity, and we seized it. We were professional horse trainers and we literally stumbled upon what we thought would be the perfect barn shoe, both for ourselves and for our clients.
>
> A large part of our business was about importing, training and selling horses and horse-related gear that wasn't readily available in the United States. Another part of our business was service-related—training Olympic hopefuls and making dreams come true. Those were the "business" elements that we carried forward into Dansko. We knew about importing, had some perspective on retailing, and had a lot of experience in making customers happy.[5]

And so Mandy and Peter embarked on a journey that had many ups and downs, but their resilience, commitment, vision, and values served them well through their more than two-decade journey.

After commissioning production from a Danish manufacturer, they moved assembly to Maine, importing the outsoles from Italy, using leather from the U.S., and leveraging technical expertise of Danish technicians. Later, they moved production to Italy and China, taking advantage of both costs and competencies in those two regions.[6]

Table 1 shows the milestones of the company as it grew and expanded, including the key developments related to its social responsibility and sustainability commitments.

Social Responsibility and Sustainability

Dansko's commitment to social responsibility runs deep. In a publication issued in 2010 to commemorate the company's 20th anniversary, Dansko founder Mandy Cabot outlined its overarching philosophy and approach to sustainability and social responsibility as follows:

Table 1   Company Milestones[7]

1990   Dansko is incorporated and a comfort generation is born.
1992   The American Podiatric Medical Association (APMA) awards Dansko its first Seal of Acceptance for the Stapled Collection.
1998   Dansko constructs a new 26,000-square-foot office and warehouse in West Grove, Pennsylvania, to house the growing business.
1999   Dansko is included in the Inc 500: *Inc Magazine's* list of America's fastest-growing privately-held companies.
2002   Dansko soars by the one million pairs mark with a staggering 46 percent growth rate.
2004   *Footwear Plus Magazine* honors Dansko with its first Award for Excellence in Design in the Women's Comfort Category.
2004   Dansko hires 100th employee.
2005   Dansko launches the Employee Stock Ownership Program (ESOP) to celebrate its 15th anniversary.
2007   Dansko constructs an environmentally-friendly 80,000-square-foot office complex to supplement the current office space and warehouse facilities.
2007   Dansko becomes the first footwear company to be a founding member of B Corporation, a group of like-minded for-profit businesses who take care of their employees, community, and environment.
2008   Dansko's newly constructed office complex is LEED© Gold certified. LEED certification is administered by the US Green Building Council and recognizes leadership in energy and environmental design.
2009   Dansko opened an onsite SATRA-accredited R&D lab.
2010   Dansko is voted one of the best companies to work for in Philadelphia. The company will repeat in 2011.
2010   Dansko relaunches its kids' collection to great esteem.
2010   Dansko launches its health care apparel collection.
2011   Dansko introduces Sanibel its first ever sneaker-clog.
2011   Dansko wins its sixth *Footwear Plus Magazine* Award for Excellence in Design in Women's Comfort Category.
2012   Dansko becomes a 100 percent employee-owned company.

How would we want to be treated, both as retailers and as consumers? At the end of the day, all successful businesses have to be grounded in that. As a Dane, Peter has always been sensitive to the impact we make on the planet. Denmark is a tiny country with very limited resources, and kids are taught from an early age how to care for them responsibly with an eye toward future generations. In that sense, Denmark—and, by extension, Dansko—has an incredibly strong heritage of "sustainability." I, too, was taught from an early age to give back and pay it forward. I grew up believing what we stand for and how we behave matters more than anything else. Legacy is important. And that played out in Dansko's business model: If you've got something great to share (in this case, our shoes), you share it. If, in the sharing, you can reinvest in more to share, you do that, too. And the gift keeps on giving. Dansko is our baby. We didn't plan for her, but, once conceived, we taught her everything we knew and shared all our values with her. Like all parents, we want Dansko not only to prosper and flourish, but to outlive us, outgrow us, and accomplish things we might only dream of. For Dansko to be around for the long haul, we need to take the long view. We need to be agile, adaptive, attuned to the world around us, and cognizant of how the decisions we make today affect the ability of future generations to meet their own needs. For us, that's the essence of sustainability. We would no more squander resources, treat our stakeholders unfairly or dishonestly, or be tight-fisted or irresponsible with our profits, than we would throw trash from a moving car. There are a lot of challenges in doing the right thing, but we wouldn't have it any other way. We do what we do because we're hardwired that way. Speaking as a parent, I am beyond thrilled to watch our baby blossom into a responsible global citizen. It gives me tremendous comfort to know that everyone here at Dansko has her best interests at heart; we are all her stewards and we are all aligned in her continued development and long term success.[8]

Dansko's CSR and sustainability commitment can be divided into four basic elements: Mindful Governance, which reflects the company's vision and commitment to its various stakeholders and overall purpose, Sustainable Business Ethics, which reflects its overall ethics and values, including the use of independent thirdparties to evaluate and validate whether it is meeting its own commitments, Corporate Philanthropy, which represents its commitment to the community and other nonprofits, and finally Responsible Environmentalism, which manifests in a policy of "doing no harm" and leaving the planet in better shape.[9]

The commitment to sustainability and social responsibility manifests in a number of specific initiatives. The Employee Stock Ownership Program (ESOP) transfers a share of the company's profits and ownership to its employees. Dansko's responsibility and sustainability commitments are validated by SATRA (Shoe and Allied Trade Research Association), ASTM (American Society for Testing and Materials), and APMA (American Podiatric Medical Association). But according to Cabot, the most important of all of the CSR initiatives is the B Corp. In 2007, Dansko became one of 80 founding members of B Corp, an innovative designation that allows companies to alter their stakeholder obligations to favor employees and other stakeholders as strongly as share owners (in the case of Dansko, the employees are the shareholders, so this traditional conflict is not nearly as problematic). In terms of Corporate Philanthropy, Dansko has established the Dansko Foundation and the volunteer program.

The Foundation is funded by profits and run entirely by employees. While the Foundation donates considerable sums (more than $500,000 as of 2011), it is also designed to help train employees in the "art" of philanthropy. Under the volunteer program, Dansko compensates employees up to two full days a year, resulting in hundreds of hours of volunteer action. And its commitment to Responsible Environmentalism, Dansko has supported environmental organizations but has also committed to lessen its own environmental footprint through energy consumption and the construction of its LEED® Gold certified headquarters.[10]

The Challenge of Foreign versus Domestic Production

Notwithstanding this impressive record of commercial and socially responsible growth, most Dansko shoes are made in China and Italy. This reality reflects the changing global distribution of specific industries, sectors, and workers, as well as the relative cost differentials in production in various geographic locations. So, "like countless footwear companies in the past two decades as the nation hemorrhaged its shoe-manufacturing footprint overseas, Dansko has failed to achieve perhaps the most symbolic goal of a company attuned to its place in the economic ecosystem. It has not found a way to make in America the shoes it sells to Americans."[11]

But the issue is more than cost. Rather, it stems from changing global concentrations of skilled workers and production capacity. "Being made in the U.S. was a really great thing, and we would have loved to continue there," Cabot said. "But after about 18 months of manufacturing in Maine, there was so much attrition in the workers and workforce up there that we simply couldn't continue."[12]

Dansko told the Philadelphia Inquirer that its move to China and continued production in Italy was not due to cost concerns, but rather the production capabilities and skilled workers that ensure that its shoes are long lasting. Dansko's products sell for $120–$250, so quality and reliability are more important than low-cost production and price.[13]

Nonetheless, in 2012, Dansko indicated it was developing a new line of shoes that will be manufactured from molds in the U.S. It hopes to manufacture this new clog from recycled material in Arkansas; the nonrecycled version called Avalon Pippa is already being produced in China. If it goes ahead, Dansko will have a chance to test whether global production chains that include manufacturing in the U.S. can succeed in an industry that mostly left North America long ago.[14]

Questions for Review

1. How did Dansko's founder Peter Kjellerup's Danish heritage affect the development of Dansko's shoe line and its commitment to ethics and social responsibility?

2. Why might employee ownership be a positive thing for a company's growth and development? What might be some downsides?

3. Is Dansko's production in China a concern from an ethics and social responsibility perspective? Should its decision to return some production to the U.S. be viewed positively by its customers and stakeholders?

Source: This case was prepared by Professor Jonathan Doh of Villanova University as the basis for class discussion.

In-Depth Integrative Case 1.1

Student Advocacy and "Sweatshop" Labor: The Case of Russell Athletic

Introduction

In November 2009, after nearly two years of student campaigning in coordination with the apparel workers, the Honduran workers' union concluded an agreement with Russell Athletic, a major supplier of clothing and sportswear to college campuses around the country. The agreement included a commitment by Russell to put all of the workers back to work, to provide compensation for lost wages, to recognize the union and agree to collective bargaining, and to allow access for the union to all other Russell apparel plants in Honduras for union organizing drives in which the company will remain neutral. According to a November 18, 2009, press release of United Students Against Sweatshops (USAS), this has been an "unprecedented victory for labor rights."[1]

Outsourcing of production facilities and labor to developing countries has been one of the important business strategies of large U.S. corporations. While in the United States, a typical corporation is subject to various regulations and laws such as minimum wage law, labor laws, safety and sanitation requirements, and trade union organizing provisions, in some developing countries these laws are soft and rudimentary, allowing a large corporation to derive significant cost benefits from outsourcing. Moreover, many developing countries like India, China, Vietnam, Pakistan, Bangladesh, and Honduras encourage the outsourcing of work from the developed world to factories within their borders as a source of employment for their citizens, who otherwise would suffer from lack of jobs in their country.

However, in spite of the obvious positive fact of creating new jobs in the hosting country, large multinational corporations very often have been criticized for violating the rights of the workers, creating unbearable working conditions, and increasing workloads while cutting compensation. They have been attacked for creating a so-called "sweatshop" environment for their employees. A few of the recent targets of the criticism have been Walmart,[2] Disney,[3] JCPenney, Target, Sears,[4] Toys R Us,[5] Nike,[6] Reebok,[7] Adidas,[8] Gap,[9] IBM, Dell, HP,[10] Apple and Microsoft,[11] etc.

This case addresses advocacy by students and other stakeholders toward one of these companies and documents the evolution and outcome of the dispute.

What Is a Sweatshop?

By common agreement, a sweatshop is a workplace that provides low or subsistence wages under harsh working conditions, such as long hours, unhealthy conditions, and/or an oppressive environment. Some observers see these work environments as essentially acceptable if the laborers freely contract to work in such conditions. For others, to call a workplace a sweatshop implies that the working conditions are illegitimate and immoral. The U.S. General Accounting Office would hone this definition for U.S. workplaces to include those environments where an employer violates more than one federal or state labor, industrial homework, occupational safety and health, workers' compensation, or industry registration laws. The AFL-CIO Union of Needletrades, Industrial and Textile Employees would expand on that to include workplaces with systematic violations of global fundamental workers' rights. The Interfaith Center on Corporate Responsibility (ICCR) defines sweatshops much more broadly than either of these; even where a factory is clean, well organized, and harassment free, the ICCR considers it a sweatshop if its workers are not paid a sustainable living wage. The purpose of reviewing these varied definitions is to acknowledge that, by definition, sweatshops are oppressive, unethical, and patently unfair to workers.[12]

History of Sweatshops

Sweatshop labor systems were most often associated with garment and cigar manufacturing of the period 1880–1920. Sweated labor can also be seen in laundry work, green grocers, and most recently in the "day laborers," often legal or illegal immigrants, who landscape suburban lawns.[13] Now, sweatshops are often found in the clothing industry because it is easy to separate higher and lower skilled jobs and contract out the lower skilled ones. Clothing companies can do their own designing, marketing, and cutting, and contract out sewing and finishing work. New contractors can start up easily; all they need are a few sewing machines in a rented apartment or factory loft located in a neighborhood where workers can be recruited.[14] Sweatshops make the most fashion-oriented clothing—women's and girls'—because production has to be flexible, change quickly, and be done in small batches. In less style-sensitive sectors—men's and boys' wear, hosiery, and knit products—there is less change and longer production runs, and clothing can be made competitively in large factories using advanced technology.[15] Since their earliest days, sweatshops have relied on immigrant labor, usually women, who were desperate for work under any pay and conditions. Sweatshops in New York City, for example, opened in Chinatown, the mostly Jewish Lower East Side, and Hispanic neighborhoods in the boroughs. Sweatshops in Seattle are near neighborhoods of Asian immigrants. The evolution of sweatshops in London and Paris—two early and major centers of the garment industry—followed the pattern in New York City. First, garment manufacturing was localized in a few districts: the Sentier of Paris and the Hackney, Haringey, Islington, the Tower Hamlets, and Westminster boroughs of London. Second, the sweatshops employed mostly immigrants, at first men but then primarily women, who had few job alternatives.[16]

In developing countries, clothing sweatshops tend to be widely dispersed geographically rather than concentrated in a few districts of major cities, and they often operate alongside sweatshops, some of which are very large, that produce toys, shoes (primarily athletic shoes), carpets, and athletic equipment (particularly baseballs and soccer balls), among other goods. Sweatshops of all types tend to have child labor, forced unpaid overtime, and widespread violations of workers' freedom of association (i.e., the right to unionize). The underlying cause of sweatshops in developing nations—whether in China, Southeast Asia, the Caribbean or India and Bangladesh—is intense cost-cutting done by contractors who compete among themselves for orders from larger contractors, major manufacturers, and retailers.[17] Sweatshops became visible through the public exposure given to them by reformers in the late 19th and early 20th centuries in both England and the United States. In 1889–1890, an investigation by the House of Lords Select Committee on the Sweating System brought attention in Britain. In the United States the first public investigations came as a result of efforts to curb tobacco homework, which led to the outlawing of the production of cigars in living quarters in New York State in 1884.[18]

The spread of sweatshops was reversed in the United States in the years following a horrific fire in 1911 that destroyed the Triangle Shirtwaist Company, a women's blouse manufacturer near Washington Square in New York City. The company employed 500 workers in notoriously poor conditions. One hundred and forty-six workers perished in the fire; many jumped out windows to their deaths because the building's emergency exits were locked. The Triangle fire made the public acutely aware of conditions in the clothing industry and led to pressure for closer regulation. The number of sweatshops gradually declined as unions organized and negotiated improved wages and conditions and as government regulations were stiffened (particularly under the 1938 Fair Labor Standards Act, which imposed a minimum wage and required overtime pay for work of more than 40 hours per week).[19] Unionization and government regulation never completely eliminated clothing sweatshops, and many continued on the edges of the industry; small sweatshops were difficult to locate and could easily close and move to avoid union organizers and government inspectors. In the 1960s, sweatshops began to reappear in large numbers among the growing labor force of immigrants, and by the 1980s sweatshops were again "business as usual." In the 1990s, atrocious conditions at a sweatshop once again shocked the public.[20] A 1994 U.S. Department of Labor spot check of garment operations in California found that 93 percent had health and safety violations, 73 percent of the garment makers had improper payroll records, 68 percent did not pay appropriate overtime wages, and 51 percent paid less than the minimum wage.[21]

Sweatshop Dilemma

The fight against sweatshops is never a simple matter; there are mixed motives and unexpected outcomes. For example, unions object to sweatshops because they are genuinely concerned about the welfare of sweated labor, but they also want to protect their own members' jobs from low-wage competition even if this means ending the jobs of the working poor in other countries.[22] Also, sweatshops can be evaluated from moral and economic perspectives. Morally, it is easy to declare sweatshops unacceptable because they exploit and endanger workers. But from an economic perspective, many now argue that, without sweatshops, developing countries might not be able to compete with industrialized countries and achieve export growth. Working in a sweatshop may be the only alternative to subsistence farming, casual labor, prostitution, and unemployment. At least most sweatshops in other countries, it is argued, pay their workers above the poverty level and provide jobs for women who are otherwise shut out of manufacturing. And American consumers have greater purchasing power and a higher standard of living because of the availability of inexpensive imports.[23]

NGOs Anti-Sweatshop Involvement

International nongovernmental organizations (NGOs) have attempted to step into the sweatshop conflict to suggest voluntary standards to which possible signatory countries or organizations could commit. For instance, the International Labour Office has promulgated its Tripartite Declaration of Principles Concerning Multinational Enterprises and Social Policy, which offers guidelines for employment, training, conditions of work and life, and industrial relations. The "Tripartite" nature refers to the critical cooperation necessary from governments, employers' and workers' organizations, and the multinational enterprises involved.[24]

On December 10, 1948, the General Assembly of the United Nations adopted its Universal Declaration of

Human Rights, calling on all member countries to publicize the text of the Declaration and to cause it to be disseminated, displayed, and read. The Declaration recognizes that all humans have an inherent dignity and specific equal and inalienable rights. These rights are based on the foundation of freedom, justice, and peace. The UN stated that the rights should be guaranteed without distinction of any kind, such as race, color, sex, language, religion, political or other opinion, national or social origin, property, birth, or other status. Furthermore, no distinction shall be made on the basis of the political, jurisdictional, or international status of the country or territory to which a person belongs. The foundational rights also include the right to life, liberty, and security of person and protection from slavery or servitude, torture, or cruel, inhuman, or degrading treatment or punishment.[25] Articles 23, 24, and 25 discuss issues with immediate implications for sweatshops. By extrapolation, they provide recognition of the fundamental human right to nondiscrimination, personal autonomy or liberty, equal pay, reasonable working hours and the ability to attain an appropriate standard of living, and other humane working conditions. All these rights were reinforced by the United Nations in its 1966 International Covenant on Economic, Social, and Cultural Rights.[26]

These are but two examples of standards promulgated by the international labor community, though the enforcement of these and other norms is spotty. In the apparel industry in particular, the process of internal and external monitoring has matured such that it has become the norm at least to self-monitor, if not to allow external third-party monitors to assess compliance of a supplier factory with the code of conduct of a multinational corporation or with that of NGOs. Though a number of factors affected this evolution, one such factor involved pressure by American universities on their apparel suppliers, which resulted in two multistakeholder efforts—the Fair Labor Association, primarily comprising and funded by the multinational retailers, and the Worker Rights Consortium, originally perceived as university driven. Through a cooperative effort of these two organizations, large retailers such as Nike and Adidas have not only allowed external monitoring but Nike has now published a complete list of each of its suppliers.[27]

The Case of Russell Athletic

While some argue that sweatshop scandals cause little or no impact on the corporate giants because people care more for the ability to buy cheap and affordable products rather than for working conditions of those who make these products,[28] the recent scandal around Russell Athletic brand has proved that it may no longer be as easy for a corporation to avoid the social responsibility for its outsourcing activities as it has been for a long time. November 2009 became a tipping point in the many years of struggle between the student anti-sweatshop movement

and the corporate world. An unprecedented victory was won by United Students Against Sweatshops (USAS) coalition against Russell Athletic, a corporate giant owned by Fruit of the Loom, a Berkshire-Hathaway portfolio company. USAS pressure tactics persuaded one of the nation's leading sportswear companies, Russell Athletic, to agree to rehire 1,200 workers in Honduras who lost their jobs when Russell closed their factory soon after the workers had unionized.[29]

Russell Corporation, founded by Benjamin Russell in 1902, is a manufacturer of athletic shoes, apparel, and sports equipment. Russell products are marketed under many brands, including Russell Athletic, Spalding, Brooks, Jerzees, Dudley Sports, etc. This company with more than 100 years of history has been a leading supplier of team uniforms at the high school, college, and professional level. Russell Athletic™ active wear and college licensed products are broadly distributed and marketed through department stores, sports specialty stores, retail chains, and college bookstores.[30] After an acquisition in August 2006, Russell's brands joined Fruit of the Loom in the Berkshire-Hathaway family of products.

Russell/Fruit of the Loom is the largest private employer in Honduras. Unlike other major apparel brands, Russell/Fruit of the Loom owns all eight of its factories in Honduras rather than subcontracting to outside manufacturers.[31] The incident related to Russell Athletic's business in Honduras that led to a major scandal in 2009 was the company's decision to fire 145 workers in 2007 for supporting a union. This ignited the anti-sweatshop campaign against the company. Russell later admitted its wrongdoing and was forced to reverse its decision. However, the company continued violating worker rights in 2008 by constantly harassing the union activists and making threats to close the Jerzees de Honduras factory. It finally closed the factory on January 30, 2009, after months of battling with a factory union.[32]

NGOs Anti-Sweatshop Pressure

The Worker Rights Consortium (WRC) has conducted a thorough investigation of Russell's activities, and ultimately released a 36-page report on November 7, 2008, documenting the facts of worker rights violations by Russell in its factory Jerzees de Honduras, including the instances of death threats received by the union leaders.[33] The union's vice president, Norma Mejia, publicly confessed at a Berkshire-Hathaway shareholders' meeting in May 2009 that she had received death threats for helping lead the union.[34] The Worker Rights Consortium continued monitoring the flow of the Russell Athletic scandal, and issued new reports and updates on this matter throughout 2009 including its recommendation for Russell's management on how to mediate the situation and resolve the conflict.

As stated in its mission statement, the Worker Rights Consortium is an independent labor rights monitoring organization, whose purpose is to combat sweatshops and protect the rights of workers who sew apparel and make other products sold in the United States. The WRC conducts independent, in-depth investigations, issues public reports on factories producing for major U.S. brands, and aids workers at these factories in their efforts to end labor abuses and defend their workplace rights. The WRC is supported by over 175 college and university affiliates and is primarily focused on the labor practices of factories that make apparel and other goods bearing university logos.[35]

Worker Rights Consortium assessed that Russell's decision to close the plant represented one of the most serious challenges yet faced to the enforcement of university codes of conduct. If allowed to stand, the closure would not only unlawfully deprive workers of their livelihoods, it would also send an unmistakable message to workers in Honduras and elsewhere in Central America that there is no practical point in standing up for their rights under domestic or international law and university codes of conduct and that any effort to do so will result in the loss of one's job. This would have a substantial chilling effect on the exercise of worker rights throughout the region.[36]

The results of the WRC investigation of Russell Athletic unfair labor practices in Honduras spurred the nationwide student campaign led by United Students Against Sweatshops (USAS) who persuaded the administrations of Boston College, Columbia, Harvard, NYU, Stanford, Michigan, North Carolina, and 89 other colleges and universities to sever or suspend their licensing agreements with Russell. The agreements—some yielding more than $1 million in sales—allowed Russell to put university logos on T-shirts, sweatshirts, and fleeces.[37]

As written in its mission statement, United Students Against Sweatshops (USAS) is a grassroots organization run entirely by youth and students. USAS strives to develop youth leadership and run strategic student-labor solidarity campaigns with the goal of building sustainable power for working people. It defines "sweatshop" broadly and considers all struggles against the daily abuses of the global economic system to be a struggle against sweatshops. The core of its vision is a world in which society and human relationships are organized cooperatively, not competitively. USAS struggles toward a world in which all people live in freedom from oppression, in which people are valued as whole human beings rather than exploited in a quest for productivity and profits.[38]

The role of the USAS in advocating for the rights of the Honduran workers in the Russell Athletic scandal is hard to overestimate. One can only envy the enthusiasm and effort contributed by students fighting the problem that did not seem to have any direct relationship to their own lives. They did not just passively sit on campus, but went out to the public with creative tactical actions such as picketing the NBA finals in Orlando and Los Angeles

to protest the league's licensing agreement with Russell, distributing fliers inside Sports Authority sporting goods stores and sending Twitter messages to customers of Dick's Sporting Goods urging them to boycott Russell products. The students even sent activists to knock on Warren Buffett's door in Omaha because his company, Berkshire-Hathaway, owns Fruit of the Loom, Russell's parent company.[39]

United Students Against Sweatshops involved students from more than 100 campuses where it did not have chapters in the anti-Russell campaign. It also contacted students at Western Kentucky University in Bowling Green, where Fruit of the Loom has its headquarters.[40] The USAS activists even reached Congress trying to gain more support and inflict more political and public pressure on Russell Athletic. On May 13, 2009, 65 congressmen signed the letter addressed to Russell CEO John Holland expressing their grave concern over the labor violations.[41]

In addition, the Fair Labor Association (FLA), a nonprofit organization dedicated to ending sweatshop conditions in factories worldwide, issued a statement on June 25, 2009, putting Russell Athletic on probation for noncompliance with FLA standards.[42] The Fair Labor Association, one of the powerful authorities that oversees the labor practices in the industry, represents a powerful coalition of industry and nonprofit sectors. The FLA brings together colleges and universities, civil society organizations, and socially responsible companies in a unique multistakeholder initiative to end sweatshop labor and improve working conditions in factories worldwide. The FLA holds its participants, those involved in the manufacturing and marketing processes, accountable to the FLA Workplace Code of Conduct.[43] The 19-member Board of Directors, the FLA's policy-making body, comprises equal representation from each of its three constituent groups: companies, colleges and universities, and civil society organizations.[44]

Victory for USAS and WRC

As mentioned at the start of this case, on November 2009, after nearly two years of student campaigning in coordination with the apparel workers, the Honduran workers' union concluded an agreement with Russell that put all of the workers back to work, provided compensation for lost wages, recognized the union and agreed to collective bargaining, and provided access for the union to all other Russell apparel plants in Honduras for union organizing drives in which the company will remain neutral. According to the November 18, 2009, press release of USAS, this has been an "unprecedented victory for labor rights."[45]

"This is the first time we know of where a factory that was shut down to eliminate a union was later reopened after a worker-activist campaign. This is also the first company-wide neutrality agreement in the history of the Central American apparel export industry, and it has been entered into by the largest private employer in Honduras, the largest exporter of T-shirts to the U.S. market in the world. This is a breakthrough of enormous significance for the right to organize—and worker rights in general—in one of the harshest labor rights environments in the world," said Rod Palmquist, USAS International Campaign Coordinator and University of Washington alumnus.[46]

This was not an overnight victory for the student movement and the coalition of NGOs such as USAS, WCR, and FLA. It took over 10 years of building a movement that persuaded scores of universities to adopt detailed codes of conduct for the factories used by licensees like Russell.[47] It is another important lesson for the corporate world in the era of globalization, which can no longer expect to conduct business activities in isolation from the rest of the world. The global corporations such as Russell Athletic, Nike, Gap, Walmart, and others will have to assess the impact of their business decisions on all the variety of stakeholders and take higher social responsibility for what they do in any part of the world.

More recently, a fire at a Bangalore textile factory in late 2012, and two horrific accidents at garment factories in Bangladesh in 2013, have placed renewed pressure on U.S. and European clothing brands to take greater responsibility for the working conditions of the factories from which they source products. On April 24, 2013, more than 1,000 workers were killed when an eight-story building collapsed while thousands of people were working inside. Less then two weeks later, eight people were killed in a fire at a factory in Dhaka that was producing clothes for western retailers. After a number of investor, religious, labor, and human rights groups voiced concerns about the lack of oversight and accountability by the major companies, several of the world's largest apparel firms agreed to a plan to help pay for fire safety and building improvements. Companies agreeing to the plan included the Swedish-based retailer H&M, Inditex, owner of the Zara chain, the Dutch retailer C&A, and British companies Primark and Tesco. At the same time, the Bangladesh government announced that it would improve its labor laws and raise wages, and ease restrictions on forming trade unions. U.S. retailers Walmart and Gap did not commit to the agreement, expressing concerns about legal liability in U.S. courts. Instead, with the help of a U.S.-based think tank, they announced they would pursue a separate accord to improve factory conditions in Bangladesh.[48]

Questions for Review

1. Assume that you are an executive of a large U.S. multinational corporation planning to open new manufacturing plants in China and India to save on labor costs. What factors should you consider when making your decision? Is labor outsourcing to developing countries a legitimate business strategy that can be handled without risk of running into a sweatshop scandal?

2. Do you think that sweatshops can be completely eliminated throughout the world in the near future? Provide an argument as to why you think this can or cannot be achieved.

3. Would you agree that in order to eliminate sweatshop conflicts large corporations such as Russell Athletic should retain the same high labor standards and regulations that they have in the home country (for example, in the U.S.) when they conduct business in developing countries? How hard or easy can this be to implement?

4. Do you think that the public and NGOs like USAS should care about labor practices in other countries? Isn't this a responsibility of the government of each particular country to regulate the labor practice within the borders of its country? Who do you think provides a better mechanism of regulating and improving the labor practices: NGOs or country governments?

5. Would you agree that Russell Athletic made the right decision by conceding to USAS and union demands? Isn't a less expensive way to handle this sort of situation simply to ignore the scandal? Please state your pros and cons regarding Russell's decision to compromise with the workers' union and NGOs as opposed to ignoring this scandal.

Source: This case was prepared by Jonathan Doh and Tetyana Azarova of Villanova University as the basis for class discussion. Ben Littell provided research assistance.

In-Depth Integrative Case 1.2

Pharmaceutical Companies, Intellectual Property, and the Global AIDS Epidemic

In August 2003, after heavy lobbying from nongovernmental organizations (NGOs) such as Doctors Without Borders, the U.S. pharmaceutical industry finally dropped its opposition to relaxation of the intellectual property rights (IPR) provisions under World Trade Organization (WTO) regulations to make generic, low-cost antiviral drugs available to developing countries like South Africa facing epidemics or other health emergencies.[1] Although this announcement appeared to end a three-year dispute between multinational pharmaceutical companies, governments, and NGOs over the most appropriate and effective response to viral pandemics in the developing world, the specific procedures for determining what constitutes a health emergency had yet to be worked out. Nonetheless, the day after the agreement was announced, the government of Brazil said it would publish a decree authorizing imports of generic versions of patented AIDS drugs that the country said it could no longer afford to buy from multinational pharmaceutical companies. Although the tentative WTO agreement would appear to allow such production under limited circumstances, former U.S. trade official Jon Huenemann remarked, "They're playing with fire. . . . The sensitivities of this are obvious and we're right on the edge here."[2]

Despite the role of developed and developing country governments, NGOs, large pharmaceutical companies, and their generic competitors in crafting this agreement, it was unclear how it would be implemented and whether action would be swift enough to stem the HIV/AIDS epidemic ravaging South Africa and many other countries.

The AIDS Epidemic and Potential Treatment

In 2008, after over two decades of fighting the AIDS epidemic and raising the public awareness, HIV/AIDS still remained one of the leading causes of death in the world, occupying the 6th position on the WHO Top 10 Causes of Death list.[3] According to the World Health Organization (WHO), in 2008 there were approximately 33.4 million people living with AIDS, with 2.7 million newly infected, and 2 million deaths (see Table 1). Since 1980, AIDS has killed more than 25 million people. HIV is especially deadly because it often remains dormant in an infected person for years without showing symptoms and is transmitted to others often without the knowledge of either person. HIV leads to AIDS when the virus attacks the immune system and cripples it, making the person vulnerable to diseases.[4]

Table 1   Regional HIV/AIDS Statistics, 2008

	Adults and Children Living with HIV/AIDS	Adults and Children Newly Infected with HIV	Adult Prevalence Rate [%]*	Adult and Child Deaths Due to AIDS
Sub-Saharan Africa	20.8–24.1 million	1.6–2.2 million	4.9–5.4	1.1–1.7 million
North Africa and Middle East	250,000–380,000	24,000–46,000	0.2–0.3	15,000–25,000
South and Southeast Asia	3.4–4.3 million	240,000–320,000	0.2–0.3	220,000–310,000
East Asia	700,000–1.0 million	58,000–88,000	<0.1	46,000–71,000
Latin America	1.8–2.2 million	150,000–200,000	0.5–0.6	66,000–89,000
Caribbean	220,000–260,000	16,000–24,000	0.9–1.1	9,300–14,000
Eastern Europe and Central Asia	1.4–1.7 million	100,000–130,000	0.6–0.8	72,000–110,000
Western & Central Europe	710,000–970,000	23,000–35,000	0.2–0.3	10,000–15,000
North America	1.2–1.6 million	36,000–61,000	0.5–0.7	9,100–55,000
Oceania	51,000–68,000	2,900–5,100	<0.3–0.4	1,100–3,100
TOTAL	33.4 million [31.1–35.8 million]	2.7 million [2.4–3 million]	0.8% [<0.8–0.8]	2 million [1.7–2.4 million]

*The proportion of adults [15 to 49 years of age] living with HIV/AIDS in 2008, using 2008 population numbers. The ranges around the estimates in this table define the boundaries within which the actual numbers lie, based on the best available information. These ranges are more precise than those of previous years, and work is under way to increase even further the precision of the estimates.

Source: World Health Organization, UNAIDS, December 2009.

Table 2 **Prices (in $) of Daily Dosage of ARV, April 2000**

Drug	U.S.A.	Côte d'Ivoire	Uganda	Brazil	Thailand
Zidovudine	10.12	2.43	4.34	1.08	1.74
Didanosine	7.25	3.48	5.26	2.04	2.73
Stavudine	9.07	4.10	6.19	0.56	0.84
Indinavir	14.93	9.07	12.79	10.32	NA
Saquinavir	6.5	4.82	7.37	6.24	NA
Efavirenz	13.13	6.41	NA	6.96	NA

Source: UNAIDS, *2000 Report on the Global HIV/AIDS Epidemic.*

The health of a nation's population is closely correlated with its economic wealth. Poor countries lack resources for health care generally, and for vaccination in particular. They are unable to provide sanitation and to buy drugs for those who cannot afford them. They also have lower levels of education, and therefore people are less aware of measures needed to prevent the spread of disease.[5] There is no cure or vaccine for AIDS. Therefore, public health experts place a high priority on prevention. However, only a small percentage of the funds targeted to prevent AIDS was deployed in developing countries.

Drugs help combat AIDS by prolonging the lives of those infected and by slowing the spread of the disease. These drugs significantly reduce deaths in developed countries. Treatment, however, is very expensive. As with most medicines, manufacturers hold patents for drugs, thereby limiting competition from generic products and allowing firms to price well above manufacturing costs in order to recoup R&D investment and make a fair profit.

In 2000–2001, a year's supply of a "cocktail" of antiretroviral (ARV) drugs used to fight AIDS cost between $10,000 and $12,000 in developed countries, putting it beyond the reach of those in most developing countries, where per capita income is a fraction of this cost (see Tables 2 and 3).[6] This discrepancy provokes strong reactions. Dr. James Orbinski, president of Doctors Without Borders (Médecins Sans Frontières), an international humanitarian nongovernmental organization (NGO) that won the 1999 Nobel Peace Prize, lamented, "The poor have no consumer power, so the market has failed them. I'm tired of the logic that says: 'He who can't pay dies.'"[7]

AIDS in Southern and Western Africa

In sub-Saharan Africa, approximately 22.4 million people are living with AIDS. Of the 2 million AIDS deaths globally in 2003, approximately three-quarters or 1.6 million were in sub-Saharan Africa (see Table 1).[8] The disease took a heavy toll on women and children. In 2008, more than 1.8 million children were infected in the region and a disproportionate percentage of infected adults were women.

Most HIV transmission among southern Africans occurred through sexual activity rather than blood transfusion or use of infected needles. As a result of historic and economic factors, there are large numbers of single migrant male communities in southern Africa. These communities, many of whom served the mining industry, are at great risk of AIDS transmission, especially with easy access to alcohol and commercial sex workers (prostitutes).[9]

There is great stigma attached to AIDS in southern Africa. On International AIDS Day in 1998, Gugu Dlamini, a South African AIDS activist, declared on television that she was HIV-positive and was subsequently stoned to death for having shamed her community. Dr. Peter Piot, head of UNAIDS (the AIDS program of the United Nations), pointed out the tragic irony in the situation: Some of those who murdered Dlamini probably had AIDS but didn't know it—25 percent of her community was infected.[10]

In the nation of South Africa, one out of every nine residents has HIV/AIDS. The disease had slashed South African life expectancy from 66 years to below 50, a level not seen since the late 1950s. Large pharmaceutical companies and the U.S. government resisted calls to relax intellectual property laws that were thought to limit the provision of low-cost AIDS treatments. South African president Thabo Mbeki himself had been accused of engaging in "denial" as he had disputed established wisdom regarding the source of and treatment for AIDS. Meanwhile, South Africans continued to die from the disease, and the South African economy also suffered direct and indirect costs from the disease's ravaging effects.[11]

Table 3 **Estimated Number of People in 2002 Who Needed "Triple Therapy" AIDS Treatment, Compared with the Number Who Received Treatment (in thousands)**

	In Need of Treatment	Received Treatment
Latin America and the Caribbean	370	196
North Africa and Middle East	7	3
Eastern Europe and Central Asia	80	7
Asia Pacific	1,000	43
Sub-Saharan Africa	**4,100**	**50**

Source: UNAIDS, *2002 Report on the Global HIV/AIDS Epidemic.*

Table 4   **2003 Global Pharmaceutical Sales by Region**

World Audited Market	2003 Sales ($bn)	% Global Sales ($)	% Growth (constant $)
North America	229.5	49%	111%
European Union	115.4	25	8
Rest of Europe	14.3	3	14
Japan	52.4	11	3
Asia, Africa, and Australasia	37.3	8	12
Latin America	17.4	4	6
Total	$466.3bn	100%	19%

Source: IMS World Review (2004).

The HIV crisis stretches beyond southern Africa, affecting most of the African continent. As of 2012, UNAIDS estimates that only 630,000, or roughly 30 percent, of those living with HIV in western Africa currently receive antiretroviral medicines. UNAIDS also estimates that African countries, as a whole, only control roughly 1 percent (US$10 billion) of the global market for antiretroviral medicine, despite representing approximately 25 percent of the global health burden.[12]

The Global Pharmaceutical Industry, R&D, and Drug Pricing

Most of the global $466 billion of pharmaceutical sales in 2003 were in the developed countries of North America, Japan, and Western Europe (see Table 4). Leading pharmaceutical companies were large and profitable (see Table 5), although all of them have come under pressure from a range of factors—most notably, calls for lower health care costs in most major industrialized countries. Drug discovery is a long, expensive, and uncertain process. In recent years, the development of a new drug, starting with laboratory research and culminating in FDA approval, was estimated to take 10 to 15 years and cost around $800 million on average. Only 30 percent of drugs marketed were reported to earn revenues that matched average R&D costs.[13]

Like most for-profit firms, pharmaceutical companies pursue opportunities with high profit potential. A spokesman for Aventis, a French-German pharmaceutical company, said, "We can't deny that we try to focus on top markets—cardiovascular, metabolism, anti-infection, etc. But we're an industry in a competitive environment—we have a commitment to deliver performance for shareholders."[14] The industry tends to focus on diseases prevalent in its major markets. Drug patents enable companies to charge prices several times the variable manufacturing costs and generate hefty margins to help recover R&D costs and deliver profits. Drugs tend to be relatively price insensitive during the period of patent protection.

Prices vary considerably across markets, as illustrated by the price of fluconazole, an antifungal agent as well as a cure for cryptococcal meningitis, which attacked 9 percent of people with AIDS and killed them within a month. According to a study by Doctors Without Borders, in 2000, wholesale prices for fluconazole averaged $10 per pill and ranged from $3.60 in Thailand to $27 in Guatemala. Pfizer, which reportedly earned $1 billion annually on fluconazole, claimed the range was narrower ($6). Prices were considerably lower in countries that did not uphold foreign patents for pharmaceuticals. In India, Bangladesh, and Thailand it was sold by generic manufacturers for prices ranging from 30 to 70 cents.[15] (Some of the countries that didn't recognize patents for pharmaceuticals did have laws for patent protection of other products.)

The pharmaceutical industry was criticized for spending large sums on sales, marketing, and lobbying. Pfizer's spokesman, Brian McGlynn, countered, "Yes, we spend a lot of money on advertising and marketing. But we don't sell soda pop. It's an enormous transfer of knowledge from our lab scientists to doctors, through those sales reps."[16] Companies also spent heavily on lobbying governments on issues such as government-managed prescription drug plans for the elderly, which could create pressure to cap drug prices, and on strengthening and enforcing intellectual property protections.

Table 5   **2001 Financials for Selected Pharmaceutical Companies ($bn)**

	Merck	Pfizer	GlaxoSmithKline
Country	U.S.	U.S.	U.K.
Revenue	47.7	32.3	29.7
COGS	29.0	5.0	6.9
SG&A	6.2	11.3	12.2
R&D	2.5	4.8	3.8
Net income	7.3	7.8	4.4

Source: Sushil Vachani, "South Africa and the AIDS Epidemic," *Vilkapala* 29, no. 1 (January–March 2004), p. 104; and company annual reports.

WTO and Intellectual Property Rights[17]

Intellectual property rights (IPR) grant investors rights for original creations. The goal of IPR protection is to stimulate creativity and innovation, and to provide incentives and funding for R&D. Intellectual property rights, such as patents, prevent people from using inventors' creations without permission.

The WTO's Agreement on Trade-Related Aspects of Intellectual Property Rights (TRIPS), which was agreed to under the Uruguay Round of the GATT (1986–1994), attempted to bring conformity among different nations' protection of IPR. TRIPS covered five basic areas (see Exhibit 1). Patent protection extended a minimum of 20 years. Governments could deny patent protection on certain grounds (e.g., public order or morality) or for certain classes of inventions (e.g., surgical methods, plants, and so on). If the patent holder abused the rights granted by the patent (e.g., by refusing to supply the product to the market), the government could, under prescribed conditions, issue compulsory licenses that allowed competitors to produce the product.[18]

Also under TRIPS, a country that is in a state of medical emergency could resort to two actions: compulsory licensing, under which it could have generic products manufactured while paying a royalty to the patent holder, and parallel importing, which meant importing legally produced copies of a product that were cheaper in a foreign country than in the importing country. However, the WTO guidelines did not define a medical emergency. Developing countries' view of what constituted a medical emergency was substantially different from that held by drug companies and the U.S. government.

Despite being a country with 85,000 AIDS patients[19] Brazil responded to international pressures and passed a

law recognizing patents in 1996. This law specified that products commercialized anywhere before May 15, 1997, would forever remain unpatented in Brazil. The Brazilian government encouraged local companies to produce unlicensed copies of several AIDS drugs, which it bought from them to distribute to its patients free of charge in a policy of universal access. AIDS deaths were halved between 1996 and 1999. Between 1996 and 2000, local production, together with bulk imports, reduced annual treatment costs by 80 percent for double therapy (a cocktail of two AIDS drugs, both nucleosides) and by about 35 percent for triple therapies (two nucleosides and a protease inhibitor or non-nucleoside).[20]

For drugs that had valid patents in Brazil, the government attempted to negotiate lower prices. When negotiations between Merck and the Brazilian government over prices of the drug Stocrin initially stalled, the government threatened to license the drug compulsorily under the provisions of Brazilian law. When Merck learned a copy was being developed in a government lab, it threatened to file a lawsuit. The U.S. government filed a complaint with the WTO, but Brazil refused to budge.[21] President Fernando Cardoso defended the patent-breaking practice, suggesting that this approach was not one of commercial interest, but rather a moral issue that could not be solved by the market alone. The pharmaceutical industry association's position on intellectual property rights was summarized as follows:

> Strong intellectual property protection is the key to scientific, technological and economic progress. Such protection is the *sine qua non* of a vibrant and innovative pharmaceutical industry—and thus to patients—in the United States and around the world. Without such protection, far fewer drugs would be developed, fewer generic copies would be manufactured, and the flow of medicines to the public would be greatly slowed—to the detriment of patients, public health, and economic development throughout the world.[22]

Pharmaceutical companies were worried about more than losing contributions from sales of a drug faced with a knockoff in a specific country. They feared a domino effect—compulsory licensing spreading across developing countries and sharply hurting profits in multiple markets. Even more alarming was the prospect that prices in developed countries might sink either because of a gray market in generics or because of pressure to cap prices as information on the significant price differential between countries became widely available and developed-country consumers clamored for lower prices.

Drug Pricing in Developing Countries: Government, Industry, and NGO Perspectives[23]

Dr. Christopher Ouma, who cared for AIDS patients in a Kenyan public hospital, pointed out that half his patients couldn't pay the $2.60 daily bed charge. He usually didn't

Exhibit 1   Broad Areas Covered by the WTO Agreement on Trade-Related Aspects of Intellectual Property Rights (TRIPS)

1. Basic principles
   a. National treatment. Equal treatment of foreign and domestic nationals.
   b. Most-favored-nation treatment. Equal treatment of nationals of all WTO members.
   c. Technological progress. Intellectual property rights had to strike a balance between technological innovation and technology transfer. The objective was to enhance economic and social welfare by making both producers and users benefit.
2. How to provide adequate protection.
3. Enforcement.
4. Dispute settlement.
5. Special transitional arrangements. WTO agreements took effect January 1, 1995. Developed countries were given one year to bring their laws and practices in line with TRIPS. Developing countries were given five years and least developed countries 11 years.

Source: WTO, www.wto.org/english/tratop_e/trips_e/trips _e.htm.

tell patients' families about the existence of drugs to treat AIDS. "This is where the doctor's role goes from care-giver to undertaker," he added. "You talk to them about the cheapest method of burial. Telling them about the drugs is always kind of a cruel joke."[24]

Drug companies had been reluctant to provide AIDS drugs to developing countries at prices much lower than those charged in developed countries. They expressed concern that distributing drugs in unregulated and unreliable environments could risk creating new strains of drug-resistant HIV. In 1997, South Africa passed a law to permit compulsory licensing of essential drugs. Pharmaceutical companies, including Bristol-Myers Squibb and Merck, sued the South African government in an attempt to delay implementation of the law.

The Clinton administration lobbied the South African government to reverse its decision. U.S. Trade Representative Charlene Barshefsky placed South Africa on the "301 watch list," which puts a nation on notice that U.S. trade sanctions will be imposed if it doesn't change its policies.[25]

The Washington Post reported, "Critics have accused U.S. trade policy of placing the profits of drug companies above public health, moving to block poor countries from manufacturing the drugs themselves, despite international laws that permit countries to do so when facing a public health emergency."[26] British newspaper The Guardian referred to the U.S. government's actions as "trade terrorism" and called for efforts to "defend developing countries against U.S. aggression."[27] The World Bank official who oversaw the Bank's African health investments and its annual $800 million drug procurement said the drug-price structure "shows an increasing disconnect with the needs of the majority of the people in the world."[28]

As the U.S. government began to exert pressure on developing countries through the WTO and unilaterally, AIDS activists and NGOs, such as Doctors Without Borders, Act-Up, Health Action International, and the Consumer Project on Technology, swung into action. They targeted the public appearances of Vice President Al Gore during his presidential campaign. In September 1999, the administration backed off from the threats of placing trade sanctions against South Africa. The administration informed the South African government it would not object to issuance of compulsory licenses for essential drugs provided this was done within WTO guidelines.

In December 1999, President Bill Clinton told members of the WTO that the U.S. government would show "flexibility" and allow countries to obtain cheaper drugs during health emergencies on a case-by-case basis.[29] NGOs immediately called on the U.S. government to end trade pressure on poor countries in health care industry disputes.[30] Over the following year, the U.S. government declared it would not block compulsory licenses in the rest of sub-Saharan Africa and Thailand and elsewhere on a selected basis.

In the summer of 2000, at the 13th International AIDS Conference in Durban, South Africa, Boehringer Ingelheim, a German pharmaceutical company, offered to make its AIDS drug, Viramune, available for free. Bristol-Myers Squibb, Merck, and Glaxo Wellcome made similar offers. NGOs and developing governments, however, criticized the companies for making the announcements without consulting and working with the concerned governments, and for placing restrictions on distribution.[31] Jack Watters, Pfizer's medical director for Africa, defended the conditions of the company's pilot free-drug program in South Africa: "We want to evaluate how much impact the program has on survival." The company was also concerned about corruption and diversion of supplies. He added, "There's no guarantee that the drug will find its way to the people who need it most."[32] NGO activists continued to press the U.S. government, the WTO, and the pharmaceutical industry to make it easier for developing countries to produce or import generics. Some felt that if the pharmaceutical industry really wanted to make its products available it should drop its lawsuit against the South African government.[33]

In spring 2001, three U.S. pharmaceutical companies—Merck, Bristol-Myers Squibb, and Abbott—announced they would sell HIV drugs to developing countries at cost. GlaxoSmithKline offered 90 percent discounts.[34] Merck planned to use the United Nations Human Development Index and offer the lowest prices to countries that received "low" rankings or had an AIDS infection rate of 1 percent or higher. It offered Brazil, which didn't fall in that category, prices about 75 percent higher. Still, this was a steep discount compared to U.S. prices. Merck would sell efavirenz in Brazil for $920 per year per patient (compared to $4,700 in the United States) and Crixivan for $1,029 ($6,000 in the United States).[35] In October 2002, Merck announced further cuts in the price for Stocrin from the (already reduced) price of $1.37 per patient per day to $0.95 per patient per day in the poorest, hardest-hit countries. The price for middle-development countries with less than 1 percent HIV prevalence would be $2.10 per patient per day, down from $2.52.

On September 5, 2002, GlaxoSmithKline announced an additional price cut for antiretroviral drugs and malaria drugs for poor countries. The British company said it would cut the prices of its HIV/AIDS drugs by as much as 33 percent and the prices of its antimalarial drugs by as much as 38 percent in developing countries to help health workers fight two of the deadliest diseases that afflict the developing world. Under the new pricing plan, GlaxoSmithKline said it would supply its AIDS and antimalarial drugs at not-for-profit prices to the public sector, nongovernmental organizations, aid agencies, the United Nations, and the Global Fund to Fight AIDS, Tuberculosis and Malaria. To prevent cut-price drugs from being reimported into the West, Glaxo said it would seek regulatory approval to provide special packaging for the cut-price drugs.

Indian generic manufacturers, such as Cipla, offered among the lowest prices in the world. Over the years Cipla had developed a range of pharmaceuticals. In 1985 the U.S. FDA approved Cipla's bulk drug manufacturing facilities. Cipla's net income in 2001–2002 was $48 million on sales of $292 million. Its major export markets were the Americas (41%), Europe (24%), and the Middle East and Africa (12% each). In late 2001 Cipla agreed to supply a three-drug antiretroviral combination to Nigeria for $350 per person per year.[36] The Nigerian government initiated a $4 million pilot program covering 10,000 adults and 5,000 children in which it planned to charge patients $120 per year and cover the remaining cost from government funds.[37]

In March 2002 the WHO released its first list of companies that are regarded as manufacturers of safe AIDS drugs. Of the 41 drugs listed, 26 were sold by multinationals and 10 by Cipla.

The Global Fund

In April 2001, while addressing an African summit in Nigeria, UN Secretary General, Kofi Annan, proposed creation of a global fund to combat AIDS. He stressed the need to ratchet up spending on fighting AIDS in developing countries from the current $1 billion level to $7–10 billion. He noted that pharmaceutical companies were beginning to accept that "generic medication can be produced where it can save lives." The previous week pharmaceutical companies had dropped their lawsuit against the South African government over patent laws.[38]

The proposal attracted significant support from world leaders. In May 2001, President George W. Bush announced $200 million in seed money for the fund. The following month, addressing delegates from 180 nations at a UN conference, U.S. Secretary of State Colin Powell declared, "No war on the face of the world is more destructive than the AIDS pandemic. I was a soldier. I know of no enemy in war more insidious or vicious than AIDS, an enemy that poses a clear and present danger to the world." He added, "We hope this seed money will generate billions more from donors all over the world, and more will come from the United States as we learn where our support can be most effective."

The Global Fund, set up as an independent corporation, was broadened to address not just AIDS but tuberculosis and malaria as well. By July 2003, more than $2 billion had been paid in by developed countries (see Table 6). In addition to leading country donors that included the United States, the EU, individual European countries, and Japan, the Gates Foundation contributed $100 million. In April 2002, the Global Fund made its first awards, totaling $616 million, to programs in 40 countries. Slightly more than half was designated for Africa. Experts predicted that the

Table 6   Leading Donors to the Global Fund, July 2004

Country	$m
U.S.A.	623
EU	401
France	304
Japan	230
Italy	215
U.K.	173
Gates Foundation	100

Source: theglobalfundatm.org.

Fund's success hinged on how effective it proved to be as a "hard-nosed judge of its grantees' performance."

In October 2003, the Fund announced it would slow the pace of its awards to one round per year because it had fallen short of its fund-raising goals and was concerned about running out of money. The Fund announced it had received pledges through 2008 of about $5.2 billion, well short of its $8–$10 billion goal.[39] The decision came as the Fund announced $623 million in grants to 71 disease prevention and treatment programs in about 50 countries. This round of grants, the third, was substantially smaller than the $884 million awarded in January 2003.

By May of 2008 the Global Fund had distributed a total of US$5.67 billion. Around 58 percent of funding in November 2007 was spent on HIV and AIDS.[40] Since the inception of the Global Fund, 50 donor governments have pledged US$20.3 billion up to 2015 and paid in US$14.5 billion. In 2007 and 2008 those 16 member countries of OECD/DAC that are the largest supporters of the Global Fund contributed 96 percent of the contributions of the public donors. Some additional 20 donor governments collectively provided the remaining 4 percent of such resources for the two-year period.[41]

Other Funding Sources

A very large proportion of foreign funding for responses to the AIDS epidemic is provided by donor governments. The American government donates a substantial amount of money for the AIDS epidemic. In 2008 the United States was the largest donor in the world, accounting for more than half of disbursements by governments. It was followed by the United Kingdom, the Netherlands, France, Germany, Norway, and Sweden.[42]

In his State of the Union address in January 2003, President Bush announced the creation of PEPFAR, the President's Emergency Plan for AIDS Relief, a commitment to significantly increase U.S. spending on HIV/AIDS initiatives around the world. PEPFAR was a five-year program which was to direct US$15 billion to countries most in need. PEPFAR was renewed in July 2008 with the intention of spending $48 billion from 2009 to 2013 on programs to tackle HIV and AIDS as well as tuberculosis and malaria. The U.K.'s Department for International Development (DFID), the world's second biggest bilateral donor for HIV/AIDS, spent about $850 million in 2005/06, and is also a major donor to the Global Fund, committing up to £1 billion of funds for the years leading up to 2015.[43]

The World Bank is the second largest multilateral donor to the HIV/AIDS response in developing countries besides the Global Fund and is one of eight co-sponsors of UNAIDS. By the end of 2006, it had dispersed US$879.22 million to 75 projects to prevent, treat, and reduce the impact of HIV and AIDS. There are also a very large number of private sector organizations involved in the response to AIDS, including corporate donors, individual philanthropists, religious groups, charities, and nongovernmental organizations (NGOs). These organizations vary in size, from small groups such as local churches, to large contributors such as the Bill and Melinda Gates Foundation and corporate donors. Overall, the private sector is by far the smallest of the four main sources of funding for the global AIDS response, accounting for around 4 percent of spending.[44]

Pressure Mounts

In June 2002, two weeks before the 14th International AIDS Conference in Barcelona, the WTO council responsible for intellectual property extended until 2016 the transition period during which least-developed countries (LDCs) did not have to provide patent protection for pharmaceuticals.[45] Previously they'd been expected to comply by 2006. (See Exhibit 2 for a list of least-developed countries.)

The delegates from the 194 countries left the July 2002 International AIDS Conference in Barcelona with cautious optimism. Joep Lange, president of the International AIDS Society, said, "If we can get Coca-Cola and cold beer to every remote corner of Africa, it should not be impossible to do the same with drugs." However the conference wasn't without protests. Activists tore down the European Union exhibition stand, demanding larger contributions to the Global Fund. The World Health Organization estimated that given the public health infrastructure in developing countries, the maximum that could be spent productively each year by 2005 was about $9 billion. This assumed $4.8 billion for prevention and $4.2 billion for treatment. It also estimated that with a commitment of

$4.8 billion per year to prevention, 29 million infections could probably be avoided by 2010.

Several challenges remained. Drug prices had fallen significantly, but not low enough for everyone. While the large pharmaceutical companies were selling antiretroviral combinations for about $1,200 per person per year in some developing countries, the lowest generic prices out of India were $209. Health economists estimated that prices needed to fall as low as $30–$40 per person per year for drugs to reach the poorest recipients. Such low prices were unlikely to materialize anytime soon. NGOs, such as Doctors Without Borders, were expected to push for optimizing use of scarce funds by deploying Global Fund allocations for purchase of generics only. Tough decisions needed to be made about the allocation of resources between AIDS and other diseases, and between prevention and treatment of AIDS.

In early August 2003, the South African government reversed its policy on AIDS, signed the Global Fund, and announced production of its first generic AIDS drug. Aspen Pharmacare, a South African firm, announced it would be the initial provider of generic treatments. Backed by many activist groups, including the influential Treatment Action Campaign, revisions to the $41 million deal detailed an operational plan to make the drugs available by the end of September 2003. South African president Thabo Mbeki finally agreed to the long-standing proposal after a recent World Bank report predicted "a complete economic collapse" within four generations if the government didn't act swiftly.

The 2003 WTO Agreement and Its Aftermath

In August 2003, the United States and other WTO members announced that they had finalized a solution to streamline the supply of disease-fighting medications to poor countries. As part of the compromise deal, the United States agreed to language that would allow compulsory licensing only for "genuine health reasons" and not for commercial advantage. This appeared to prompt action.

On December 10, 2003, Britain's GlaxoSmithKline and Germany's Boehringer Ingelheim agreed to expand the licensing of their patented AIDS drugs to three generic manufacturers in South Africa and other African countries as part of an out-of-court settlement with South Africa's

Exhibit 2   Countries Classified as Least-Developed by WTO

Angola	Djibouti	Maldives	Sierra Leone
Bangladesh	Gambia	Mali	Solomon Islands
Benin	Guinea	Mauritania	Tanzania
Burkina Faso	Guinea Bissau	Mozambique	Togo
Burundi	Haiti	Myanmar	Uganda
Central African Republic	Lesotho	Niger	Zambia
Chad	Madagascar	Rwanda	
Congo	Malawi	Senegal	

Treatment Action Campaign. In return, the South African Competition Commission, a government body that monitors free-market practices, agreed to drop a yearlong probe into whether the companies had overcharged for their AIDS drugs. Glaxo and Boehringer Ingelheim already had existing agreements with a fourth generic manufacturer, South Africa's Aspen Pharmacare. Under the settlement pact in South Africa, Glaxo also agreed to cap royalty fees at no more than 5 percent of net sales and to extend the generic licenses to the private and public sectors. It said it would allow the generic licensees to export AIDS drugs manufactured in South Africa to 47 sub-Saharan African countries. The Competition Commission said it had not asked for a fine or administrative penalty against Glaxo, which is the world's largest maker of AIDS medicines.[46]

Shareholder activists have also begun to put pressure on companies to provide more comprehensive reporting about their potential to support efforts to fight AIDS. In March 2004, a consortium of religious investors forwarded shareholder resolutions at four top drug makers, asking the companies to assess how much charity work they are doing for HIV and AIDS in developing countries and to estimate how much the epidemic could affect their businesses. The Interfaith Center on Corporate Responsibility (ICCR) and roughly 30 religious groups requested that pharmaceutical companies offer shareholders a report of their conclusions six months after the annual meetings. Although the boards of directors at Pfizer, Merck, and Abbott said they opposed the measure, Coca-Cola's board said it supported a similar shareholder proposal to assess the business risks associated with the HIV/AIDS epidemic.[47]

2005: Making the WTO Agreement Official and Its Aftermath

At the end of 2005, members of the WTO approved changes to the intellectual property agreement making permanent the August 2003 "waiver" which facilitated access for developing countries to cheaper, generic versions of patented medications.[48] Director-General Pascal Lamy said, "This is of particular personal satisfaction to me, since I have been involved for years in working to ensure that the TRIPS Agreement is part of the solution to the question of ensuring the poor have access to medicines."[49]

According to Doctors Without Borders, prices of first-line treatments have dropped from more than $10,000 to as little as $150 a year since 2000 largely due to competition from generics.[50] Brazil and Thailand have been able to launch successful national AIDS programs because key pharmaceuticals were not patent protected and could be locally produced for very low costs. Still, the method of implementation at the national or regional trade level of TRIPS can cause problems.[51]

In early 2006, Bristol-Myers Squibb (BMY) announced an agreement for technology transfer and voluntary license with generic manufacturers Aspen Pharmacare and Emcure Pharmaceuticals for atazanavir, first approved for combination therapy in the United States in June 2003. Peter R. Dolan, Bristol-Myers Squibb's CEO, highlighted his company's commitment to the global fight against AIDS: Under the deal, the generic company will set prices in Africa and India.

Generic drug manufacturers have lowered the costs of some much-needed drugs to developing countries, but often new drugs were still priced much higher than old treatments, and are hence unavailable in many of the countries with the most need. Doctors Without Borders spoke out in March 2006 against what it calls the standard practice of drug companies marketing less adapted drugs to African, Asian, and Latin American countries, while reserving new and improved drugs for more wealthy countries.[52] The NGO specifically criticized Abbot Laboratories' lopinavir/ritonavir, which was only available in the United States at a cost of US$9,687 per patient per year. Doctors Without Borders worker Dr. Helen Bygrave commented, "It's a cruel irony that although this drug—with no need for refrigeration—seems to have been designed for places like Nigeria, it is not available here."[53]

In December 2005, the WHO released a statement urging countries to adopt a policy of free access at the point of service delivery to HIV care and treatment, including antiretroviral therapy.[54] This recommendation came in the wake of a 2005 endorsement by G8 leaders and UN member states to provide universal access to HIV treatment and care by 2010. After a similar effort, the "3 by 5" program, which aimed to provide treatment for 3 million patients in 50 developing countries by the conclusion of 2005, it had become apparent that charging users at the point of service undermines efforts to provide universal care.

The number of people receiving antiretroviral aid has increased under the 3 by 5 program, but not to desired levels. More than 1 million people in developing countries received antiretroviral treatment in 2005, and expanded treatment helped to prevent 250,000–350,000 deaths.[55]

Pressure Mounts Again

The increasing severity of the AIDS epidemic, compounded by the constant lack of access to drugs, has recently prompted more drastic action among some developing countries. In January 2007, Thailand, a nation with nearly half a million residents infected with HIV, announced its intentions to break the patent on an important AIDS drug (Kaletra) produced by Abbott Laboratories,[56] setting a precedent for other nations such as Brazil, Indonesia, and the Philippines. Abbott retaliated by revoking the introduction of seven new drugs in Thailand. Doctors Without Borders called Abbott's reaction "callous," and Abbott has since backed down.

The UN and World Bank have openly supported Thailand's landmark patent-breaking decision as part of its serious treatment of AIDS within its new health program.[57] The global impact of Thailand's decision is likely to be magnified by subsequent policy changes by other countries; for instance, Brazil renounced the patent on a Merck AIDS drug in May 2007 (after years of threatening to do so).[58] Although the U.S.-Brazil Business Council warns that this IPR violation might deter future business investment from Brazil, the government still went through with the decision, likely prompted by Thailand's precedent as well as Merck's inability to offer what Brazil viewed as a satisfactory discount on patented drug purchases.[59]

The increased global effort to fight HIV/AIDS has been supported by other organizations. Among others, the Clinton Foundation has recently stepped up its work with drug companies to lower prices of AIDS medications. In October 2003, former president Bill Clinton first announced a landmark program to attack two of the toughest obstacles to treating AIDS in the developing world: high drug prices and low-quality health infrastructures. The Clinton Foundation HIV/AIDS Initiative reached a deal with four generic-drug companies, including one in South Africa, to slash the price of antiretroviral AIDS medicine. In April 2004, Clinton's foundation announced that these special drug prices were being extended from the initial 16 countries in the Caribbean and Africa to any country supported by UNICEF, the World Bank, and the UN-administered Global Fund to Fight AIDS, Tuberculosis, and Malaria. "With these agreements, we are one step closer to making sure future generations can live without the scourge of AIDS," Clinton said in a statement released by his U.S.-based foundation.

In May 2007 the Foundation struck a deal with Cipla and Matrix Laboratories to lower prices on "second-line" AIDS drugs.[60] The Clinton Foundation, which is financed by UNITAID (an organization of 20 nations that donate a portion of airline tax revenues for HIV/AIDS programs in developing countries), provides access to lower-priced AIDS drugs for approximately 65,000 people in 65 countries worldwide.[61]

Under the Clinton Foundation agreement, five generic-drug manufacturers—Pharmacare Holdings of South Africa and the Indian companies Cipla, Hetero Drugs, Ranbaxy Laboratories, and Matrix Laboratories—provide basic HIV treatment for as little as $140 per person per year, one-third to one-half of the lowest price available elsewhere. Diagnostic tests are supplied by five different companies and include machines, training, chemicals, and maintenance at a price that is up to 80 percent cheaper than the normal market price. "This new partnership works to break down some of the barriers—such as price, supply and demand—that are impeding access to lifesaving AIDS medicines and diagnostics in developing countries," said UNICEF Executive Director Carol Bellamy.[62]

AIDS Medicine Development

As reported by Pharmaceutical Research and Manufacturers of America (PhRMA) at the end of 2008, U.S. pharmaceutical research companies were testing 109 medicines and vaccines to treat or prevent HIV/AIDS and related conditions.[63] This showed a substantial effort by the pharmaceutical community to combat the disease, although only 31 medicines to treat HIV/AIDS have been approved so far since the virus that causes AIDS was first identified more than 20 years ago.[64] As noted in PhRMA 2008 Report, an effective HIV vaccine could prevent almost 30 million of the 150 million new infections projected in the coming decades. A highly effective vaccine could prevent more than 70 million infections in 15 years. In 2008, 29 vaccines were in development. In addition to the vaccines, there were 57 antivirals, 4 cancer treatments, 6 immunomodulators, 2 gene therapies, and 12 other medicines in human clinical trials or before the Food and Drug Administration awaiting approval.[65]

Opportunistic infections are a particular problem for patients infected with the HIV virus. Opportunistic infections include candidiasis of the mouth (thrush), the most common opportunistic infection in people with HIV; Mycobacterium avium complex (MAC), a bacterial infection that up to 50 percent of people with AIDS may develop; and Pneumocystis carinii pneumonia (PCP), the most common AIDS-defining infection in the United States. Examples of HIV medicines and vaccines in the pipeline for HIV-related opportunistic infections include antisense gene therapy that uses two novel technologies to boost immune responsiveness against HIV; and a vaccine that is designed to protect against the three most common types of HIV-1 virus found around the world.[66]

From 2000 to 2007, pharmaceutical research companies contributed more than $9.2 billion to improve health care in the developing world, according to the International Federation of Pharmaceutical Manufacturers & Associations.[67] Despite that progress, AIDS remains a devastating and growing worldwide health problem in developing countries, particularly in sub-Saharan Africa, China, India, and the Russian Federation.

Pharmaceutical Companies and UN Joint Efforts to Combat AIDS

United Nations Secretary-General Ban Ki-moon and other UN officials met in September 2008 with senior executives from 17 companies, including Abbott, Boehringer Ingelheim, Glaxo, Pfizer, Roche, Merck, Becton-Dickinson, Johnson & Johnson, Gilead Sciences, and Ranbaxy, among others. Companies agreed to invest further in research and development of new HIV-related medicines adapted to resource-limited settings. All participants agreed that increasing access to vaccines, diagnostics, and medicines is essential in scaling up prevention and treatment efforts.[68]

Some progress was noted by UN officials in 2008: As many as 3 million people were on treatment by the end of 2007, up from 1.3 million in 2006. There have been significant price reductions for first-line and pediatric antiretroviral drugs, and some second-line products. Two new classes of drugs have been introduced and new heat-stable formulations and fixed-dose combinations have been developed. There has also been further investment and development of technologies for prevention and diagnosis of HIV and for monitoring the efficacy of antiretroviral therapy in adults and children.[69]

The parties agreed to continuing to hold periodic high-level meetings, under the leadership of UNAIDS, to take stock of progress and to identify new collaborative measures.[70]

Recent Initiatives

In April of 2009 two pharmaceutical rivals, GlaxoSmithKline and Pfizer, announced that they intend to create a new company, headquartered in London, to manage their HIV operations with initial working capital of £250m. The lion's share of the business will be owned by GSK, which will take 85 percent to reflect its portfolio of big-selling HIV drugs such as Combivir and Kivexa. The other 15 percent will go to Pfizer, which will contribute potentially promising new treatments. The new company will have 11 drugs on the market and a further six in clinical development. It will have a market share of 19 percent and annual sales of £1.6bn.[71]

GSK's chief executive, Andrew Witty, said the "clear focus" of the joint venture would be in delivering new drugs to build on what he described as the drug industry's remarkable success in tackling HIV over the last two decades. Witty recalled that as recently as 1990, it was extremely difficult to conduct clinical trials in HIV because patients rarely lived long enough to complete studies. He said: "I think it's one of the finest performances of the pharmaceuticals industry to have transformed an incredibly frightening infectious disease into something more manageable."[72]

Speaking in Kenya in July of 2009, Andrew Witty, GSK's chief executive, said the treatment of the conditions in children remains a "significant unmet medical need." Therefore, GSK will create a new Positive Action for Children Fund that will have access to £50m over the next 10 years, and has also granted Aspen Pharmacare, of which it acquired a 16 percent stake in May, a royalty-free license to develop a cheaper, generic version of its HIV treatment abacavir. The company could make more drugs "appropriate for use in an African setting" available for a license, added Mr. Witty. GSK's new fund is designed to work alongside health organizations and pregnant mothers to prevent mother-to-child transmission of HIV in the developing world, especially sub-Saharan Africa. The company will also make £10m available to support a new public-private partnership which will research and develop new drugs.[73]

In September 2009, after a yearlong study of the actions of nine major pharmaceutical companies to address the contagion in the United States, a group of AIDS treatment activists issued a report with the grades for the pharma efforts to fight HIV/AIDS. The report card graded the drug makers overall with a below-average C-minus and recommended improvements. The report gave its highest grade, a B, to Merck, for producing Isentress, the first of a new class of AIDS drugs called integrase inhibitors. It also praised Merck for freezing prices for lower income users. Isentress, approved in 2007, is already used by 11 percent of the more than 550,000 people treated in the United States. The group gave an F to Abbott for raising the wholesale price of Norvir, the first drug proved to increase survival in AIDS patients, by 400 percent in 2003. Norvir is a key ingredient in most AIDS treatment cocktails. The price increase provoked an outcry by many patients and others.[74]

In 2010, ViiV Healthcare reported that they awarded £3.6 million in grant money to support twelve projects. These projects focused on preventing the transmission of HIV from mother to child and on improving the health of families. The £3.6 million was part of the £50 million from the Positive Action for Children Fund established in 2009.[75] In October of 2011, ViiV Healthcare announced that it awarded another £3.9 million of the £50 million from Positive Action for Children Fund to sixteen different organizations—the majority of which were located in Africa.[76] The organizations that received funding in 2010 and 2011 are listed in Tables 7 and 8.

Thanks to collaboration between the Clinton Health Access Initiative and UNITAID, among other companies, cost and access to antiretrovirals used to combat AIDS have greatly improved. Through the use of "pooled procurement" across 40 countries, price reductions for the antiretroviral of up to 80 percent have been achieved, as of 2012. In addition, roughly 75 percent of the world's total children living with HIV (400,000) are currently being treated under this program. UNITAID has also helped achieve price reductions of up to 60 percent for second-line antiretrovirals. This benefits adults in poorer countries suffering from HIV who could not previously afford these treatments. It has led to more than 100,000 people being able to shift to a stronger HIV treatment. The key source of UNITAID's funding is the introduction of a small levy on air tickets which has made up roughly 65 percent of their revenue. The small levy, ranging from US$1-US$40, has raised US$1.3 billion through its initiation in the following nine countries: Cameroon, Chile, Congo, France, Madagascar, Mali, Mauritius, Niger, and the Republic of Korea. Needing more money to continue the fight against AIDS, UNITAID is lobbying for a financial transaction tax on stocks, bonds, and derivatives.[77]

Table 7   2010 Recipients of Positive Action for Children Fund Grant Funding

1) Ntankah Village Women Common Initiative Group, Republic of Cameroon
2) Public Health Research Institute of India
3) Partners in Health, Lesotho
4) Women Friendly Initiative (WFI), Nigeria
5) International Medical Foundation (IMF) and the National Community of Women Living With HIV/AIDS in Uganda (NACWOLA), Uganda
6) Wakiso Integrated Rural Development Association (WIRDA), Uganda
7) Miroi Growers Cooperative Society, Uganda
8) Hodi, Zambia
9) Rajasthan Network for People Living with HIV/AIDS (RNP+), India
10) Save the Children, Democratic Republic of Congo
11) Kenya AIDS Intervention Prevention Project Group (KAIPPG)
12) IPPF and Family Health Options Kenya

Source: ViiV Healthcare. (30 June 2010). http://www.viivhealthcare.com. In ViiV Healthcare Awards Grants from the Positive Action for Children Fund of £3.6m. Retrieved 7/31/12, from http://www.viivhealthcare.com/media/press-releases/2010/june/viiv-healthcare-awards-grants-from-the-positive-action-for-children-fund-of-%C2%A336m.aspx

Table 8   2011 Recipients of Positive Action for Children Fund Grant Funding

1) Action Plus: "Community HIV Prevention Project," Sierra Leone
2) African Union of the BLIND (AFUB): Equalize It: Making HIV/AIDS and SRH Programs Accessible to Blind Adolescents and Youth, Kenya
3) AMREF: Community-based PMTCT, Ethiopia
4) Cameroon Baptist Health Convention Health Board: Cameroon Baptist Convention Health Board, Cameroon
5) Community of People Living with HIV: Rehabilitation Centres for HIV+ Women and Mothers, Russia
6) Elizabeth Glaser Pediatric AIDS Foundation: NAKINAE AKIYAR, Kenya
7) Human Rights Awareness and Promotion Forum – Uganda (HRAPF): Human Rights Advocacy Project for Strengthening the Legal, Human Rights & Policy Response to the HIV/AIDS Epidemic
8) ICHANGE CI' 'I CHANGE CI: Mother to Child project / M2C, Cote d'Ivoire
9) Infectious Diseases Institute: Building and maintaining the capacity of Community-Based Organisations to contribute to the Prevention of Mother to Child Transmission of HIV, Uganda
10) Interact Worldwide: Interventions to address PMTCT issues, Ethiopia
11) Intl HIV AIDS Alliance: Expanding the Role of PLHIV and Communities to PMTCT services, Uganda
12) Kenya Council of Imams and Ulamaa: Strengthening Muslim Community Linkages to Health Facilities, Kenya
13) Kuwangisana: Hope and a Future Maternal Child Health (HFMCH), Mozambique
14) Population Council: Kalkidan ("Keeping the Promise"): Addressing Marital Transmission of HIV, Ethiopia
15) Tilla Association of HIV Positive Women: Scaling up the demand for PMTCT service & for the provision & improvement of better services to HIV positive pregnant women & their children, Ethiopia
16) Vanderbilt University for Global Health: Increase male participation in maternal health care services by raising awareness in Inhassunge District communities, about the important role men play in their partner's and children's health, Mozambique

Source: ViiV Healthcare. (13 October 2011). http://www.viivhealthcare.com. In Media Alert: ViiV Healthcare's Positive Action for Children Fund announces 16 new grantees for the year 2011/2012. Retrieved 7/31/12, from http://www.viivhealthcare.com/media/press-releases/2011/october/media-alert-viiv-healthcare%E2%80%99s-positive-action-for-children-fund-announces-16-new-grantees-for-the-year-20112012.aspx

Questions for Review

1. Do pharmaceutical companies have a responsibility to distribute drugs for free or at low cost in developing countries? What are the main arguments for and against such an approach? What are the advantages and disadvantages of giving drugs for free versus offering them at low no-profit prices?

2. What are the principal arguments of pharmaceutical companies that oppose making exceptions to IPR laws for developing countries? What are the arguments by NGOs and others for relaxing IPR laws?

3. What impact would you expect South Africa's decision to levy duties on drug imports from Western nations to have on the international distribution of drugs to South Africa?

4. In June 2002, the WTO extended the transition period during which least-developed countries (LDCs) had to provide patent protection for pharmaceuticals. In your opinion, was this an appropriate change in policy or a dangerous precedent? What could be some of the negative ramifications of this resolution? What about the effects for other industries?

5. Given the initiatives announced by global development and aid organizations and among pharmaceutical companies themselves, was it necessary to relax IPR rules in order to ensure that adequate supplies of AIDS medications would be available for distribution in the developing world?

6. What role do MNCs have in providing funding or other assistance to international organizations such as the Global Fund, UN, and WHO?

Exercise

Although the WTO has now agreed to relax intellectual property rules in order to facilitate the production and distribution of inexpensive generic antivirals, the conditions under which this provision allows for production or importation of generics ("genuine health reasons") are not entirely clear. The WTO is to hold a hearing for interested parties to provide input about how these rules should be implemented. Your group represents the interests of one of the key stakeholders (see table) and will be responsible for arguing that stakeholder's position.

Team	Stakeholder
1	The WTO
2	Doctors Without Borders (NGO)
3	CIPLA (Indian generic manufacturer)
4	GlaxoSmithKline (representing pharma companies)
5	Government of Brazil (representing developing countries)
6	The Clinton Foundation HIV/AIDS Initiatives

Discuss with your group the major points to make to advance your perspectives. Come prepared to make a five-minute presentation summarizing how you would like the WTO to implement the new rules. The WTO group should ask questions during the hearing. It should then take 10 minutes to deliberate and come up with a proposed plan incorporating the interests of all of the stakeholders.

Source: This case was prepared by Jonathan Doh and Erik Holt of Villanova University with research assistance by Courtney Asher, Tetyana Azarova, and Ben Littell as the basis for class discussion. The authors thank Sushil Vachani for comments, suggestions, and input.

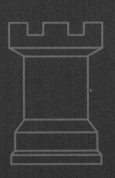

PART TWO

THE ROLE
OF CULTURE

THE MEANINGS AND DIMENSIONS OF CULTURE

A major challenge of doing business internationally is to respond and adapt effectively to different cultures. Such adaptation requires an understanding of cultural diversity, perceptions, stereotypes, and values. In recent years, a great deal of research has been conducted on cultural dimensions and attitudes, and the findings have proved useful in providing integrative profiles of international cultures. However, a word of caution must be given when discussing these country profiles. It must be remembered that stereotypes and overgeneralizations should be avoided; there are always individual differences and even subcultures within every country.

This chapter examines the meaning of culture as it applies to international management, reviews some of the value differences and similarities of various national groups, studies important dimensions of culture and their impact on behavior, and examines country clusters. The specific objectives of this chapter are:

1. DEFINE the term *culture,* and discuss some of the comparative ways of differentiating cultures.

2. DESCRIBE the concept of cultural values, and relate some of the international differences, similarities, and changes occurring in terms of both work and managerial values.

3. IDENTIFY the major dimensions of culture relevant to work settings, and discuss their effects on behavior in an international environment.

4. DISCUSS the value of country cluster analysis and relational orientations in developing effective international management practices.

The World of *International Management*

The Cultural Roots of Toyota's Quality Crisis

Worldwide, the Toyota brand name has been a symbol of quality. Toyota's focus on Kaizen (the Japanese term meaning "continuous improvement") helped Toyota become the number one seller of automobiles in the world.

In light of Toyota's commitment to quality, it was shocking when Toyota announced multiple massive recalls of many of its vehicles between 2010 and 2013. In early 2010, Toyota stated that it would recall approximately 2.3 million vehicles to correct sticking accelerator pedals, and, on top of that, approximately 5.2 million vehicles would have an ongoing recall for a floor mat pedal entrapment issue. Later that year, another 1.5 million vehicles were recalled over concerns of leaking brake fluid and electrical problems. In October 2012, 7.4 million vehicles were recalled to repair faulty power window switches, and in early 2013, another 1 million automobiles were recalled due to airbag issues.[1]

In addition to a $1.1 billion class-action settlement, Jeff Kingston of Temple University Japan estimated that the 2010 recall cost Toyota $2 billion.[2] Moreover, the way Toyota managed the crises has been even worse than the financial consequences. The president of the company, Akio Toyoda, the grandson of Toyota's founder, did not appear publicly for two weeks after the 2010 recall announcement. When he did appear, Toyoda took the path of minimizing the problem, citing a software issue, rather than a defect, as the source of the pedal problems. Toyota also failed to disclose the malfunctions to the Department of Transportation within the legal 5-day window, resulting in fines of $48.8 million in 2010 and $17.35 million in 2012.[3] Some uncertainty remains as to whether the problems originated in Toyota plants in America or whether the problems can be traced to designers in Japan. Kingston asserted that Toyota's failure to be forthcoming on critical safety issues has put "the trust of its customers worldwide" in jeopardy.

Where did Toyota go wrong? How did the symbol of quality become tarnished? Some contend that cultural factors contributed to Toyota's current crisis.

How Japanese Culture Influenced Toyota

In his *Wall Street Journal* article, Kingston explained the cultural roots of Toyota's woes. He indicated that "a culture of deference" in Japanese firms "makes it hard for those lower in the hierarchy to question their superiors or inform them about problems." In addition, the Japanese tend to focus on the consensus, which can make it difficult "to challenge what has been decided or designed." In Japan, Kingston noted, "employees' identities are closely tied to their company's image and loyalty to the firm overrides concerns about consumers."[4]

One can deduce how Toyota's problems arose in this cultural environment. If subordinates noticed a problem in vehicular accelerators, they would likely be hesitant to

- Report the problem to their superiors (culture of deference)
- Criticize their team members who designed the accelerators (focus on consensus)
- Request the firm spend extra money to redesign the accelerators for greater consumer safety (loyalty to the firm over concern for consumers)

Moreover, Kingston noted that Japanese corporations have a poor record when responding to consumer safety issues. He described the typical Japanese corporation's response in the following way:

- Minimization of the problem
- Reluctance to recall the product
- Poor communication with the public about the problem
- Too little compassion and concern for customers adversely affected by the product[5]

Toyota has not been the only high-profile Japanese company to face scrutiny based on its corporate culture. When the earthquake and resulting tsunami caused a meltdown at the Fukushima nuclear power plant in 2011, outsiders questioned the delayed response by both the Tokyo Electric Power Company and the government. In 2012, an independent report, drafted by a Japanese commission, found that the meltdown was likely preventable.

Communication broke down on multiple levels, and employees failed to question authority. The cultural tendency to favor the collective group delayed the implementation of emergency measures, according to the report. In the case of Fukushima, this led to disastrous consequences.[6,7]

Why do Japanese firms usually respond this way to consumer safety issues? Kingston gave three reasons. First, "compensation for product liability claims is mostly derisory or nonexistent" in Japan. In other words, Japanese corporations have little to lose by their minimal response. Second, Kingston describes Japan as "a nation obsessed with craftsmanship and quality." In such an environment, there is significant "shame and embarrassment of owning up to product defects." Corporations may seek to deny their products have safety concerns in order to "save face," i.e., to protect their companies' reputations. Third, Kingston told CNN that "Japanese companies are oddly disconnected with their consumers."[8] In an article printed in *The Wall Street Journal,* Toyota President Akio Toyada wrote: "[I]t is clear to me that in recent years we didn't listen as carefully as we should—or respond as quickly as we must—to our customers' concerns."[9]

Cultural factors can explain another aspect of Toyota's problems—public relations. Toyota has received much less negative attention in the Japanese media as compared with the American media. Professors Johnson, Lim, and Padmanabhan of St. Mary's University offer insight on why this may be: "The American culture demands transparency and action, whereas the Japanese culture assumes that taking ownership of problems and apologies will suffice."[10] Akio Toyoda publicly apologized at press conferences for the inconvenience caused by the Toyota recall and took personal responsibility for the consumer safety issues. For the Japanese media, that was enough. But not for the American media.

Johnson, Lim, and Padmanabhan explained that, while American corporations are expected to be transparent about their problems, Japanese firms have adopted the business practice of keeping problems "in-house." Americans have interpreted Toyota's reticent attitude to mean that Toyota is trying to cover up its problems. Johnson, Lim, and Padmanabhan pointed out, "Since Toyota is firmly established in the U.S., it needs to be meticulously transparent."[11]

Toyota's Global Strategy Challenge

In contrast to the cultural explanation of Toyota's issues, Bill Fischer on Management Issues.com offered a different perspective, suggesting that Toyota's obsession with growth was the cause of the problems. In his view, companies "can expand by either opening new markets or offering new competencies, but not by doing both at the same time!" Fischer emphasized that companies lack a "head-start" based on using their existing "know-how" by "moving into new product areas, in new geographic markets with new factory settings." Transmitting "know-how" requires personal interaction which is difficult over long distances. Fischer concluded that "successful globalization is much too difficult a journey without the assurance of having some knowledge that gives your organization a basis for advantage. . . . To do otherwise is to risk following on the wrong Toyota path to success."[12] In other words, Toyota made a strategic error in its global expansion.

Johnson, Lim, and Padmanabhan offered further explanation on this idea: "When Toyota focused on the Kaizen culture, it was able to maintain closer links with its suppliers, and ensure the quality of its components primarily because they were located in close proximity to Toyota's plants. However, when their expansion and growth strategies required them to build production facilities overseas, and given intense competition in the auto industry, Toyota had to resort to a strategy where they forced suppliers to compete on price. Since it is difficult to pursue Kaizen because of geographic distance, Toyota may have inadvertently sacrificed quality for cost considerations. Mr. Toyoda admitted as much himself when he recently told Congress that his company's focus on growth replaced its traditional priorities of improvements in safety and quality."[13]

Going Forward

With an understanding of what caused Toyota's crisis, what steps should Toyota take going forward? Kingston recommended that Toyota become more focused on the customer and improve corporate governance by appointing independent outside directors. Johnson, Lim, and Padmanabhan suggest that Toyota use this crisis as an opportunity "to adapt its management style to become more decentralized and responsive." Toyota managers need to keep their key cultural strength (Kaizen) while mitigating the negative aspects of their culture which have contributed to the company's present problems. With good managerial oversight, Toyota may once again regain its status as a worldwide symbol of quality.

Our opening discussion in The World of International Management about Toyota shows how culture can have a great impact on business practices. National cultural characteristics can strengthen, empower, and enrich management effectiveness and success. Some cultural qualities, however, may interfere with or constrain managerial decision making and efficacy. Japan's culture has often been credited with creating high-quality products that are the envy of the world. Canon, SONY, Toyota, and others are cited as exemplars in their respective industries, partly because they have leveraged some of the most productive aspects of Japanese culture. At the same time, these same cultural characteristics may retard communication and openness, which may be critical in times of crisis. MNCs that are aware of the potential positives and negatives of different cultural characteristics will be better equipped to manage under both smooth and trying times and environments.

■ The Nature of Culture

culture
Acquired knowledge that people use to interpret experience and generate social behavior. This knowledge forms values, creates attitudes, and influences behavior.

The word *culture* comes from the Latin *cultura*, which is related to cult or worship. In its broadest sense, the term refers to the result of human interaction.[14] For the purposes of the study of international management, **culture** is acquired knowledge that people use to interpret experience and generate social behavior.[15] This knowledge forms values, creates attitudes, and influences behavior. Most scholars of culture would agree on the following characteristics of culture:

1. *Learned.* Culture is not inherited or biologically based; it is acquired by learning and experience.

2. *Shared.* People as members of a group, organization, or society share culture; it is not specific to single individuals.

3. *Transgenerational.* Culture is cumulative, passed down from one generation to the next.

4. *Symbolic.* Culture is based on the human capacity to symbolize or use one thing to represent another.

5. *Patterned.* Culture has structure and is integrated; a change in one part will bring changes in another.

6. *Adaptive.* Culture is based on the human capacity to change or adapt, as opposed to the more genetically driven adaptive process of animals.[16]

Because different cultures exist in the world, an understanding of the impact of culture on behavior is critical to the study of international management.[17] If international managers do not know something about the cultures of the countries they deal with, the results can be quite disastrous. For example, a partner in one of New York's leading private banking firms tells the following story:

> I traveled nine thousand miles to meet a client and arrived with my foot in my mouth. Determined to do things right, I'd memorized the names of the key men I was to see in Singapore. No easy job, inasmuch as the names all came in threes. So, of course, I couldn't resist showing off that I'd done my homework. I began by addressing top man Lo Win Hao with plenty of well-placed Mr. Hao's—sprinkled the rest of my remarks with a Mr. Chee this and a Mr. Woon that. Great show. Until a note was passed to me from one man I'd met before, in New York. Bad news. "Too friendly too soon, Mr. Long," it said. Where diffidence is next to godliness, there I was, calling a room of VIPs, in effect, Mr. Ed and Mr. Charlie. I'd remembered everybody's name—but forgot that in Chinese the surname comes first and the given name last.[18]

■ Cultural Diversity

There are many ways of examining cultural differences and their impact on international management. Culture can affect technology transfer, managerial attitudes, managerial ideology, and even business-government relations. Perhaps most important, culture affects how people think and behave. Table 4–1, for example, compares the most important cultural values of the United States, Japan, and Arab countries. A close look at this table shows a great deal of difference among these three cultures. Culture affects a host of business-related activities, even including the common handshake. Here are some contrasting examples:

Culture	Type of Handshake
United States	Firm
Asian	Gentle (shaking hands is unfamiliar and uncomfortable for some; the exception is the Korean, who usually has a firm handshake)
British	Soft
French	Light and quick (not offered to superiors); repeated on arrival and departure
German	Brusque and firm; repeated on arrival and departure
Latin American	Moderate grasp; repeated frequently
Middle Eastern	Gentle; repeated frequently
South Africa	Light/soft; long and involved[19]

Table 4–1
Priorities of Cultural Values: United States, Japan, and Arab Countries

United States	Japan	Arab Countries
1. Freedom	1. Belonging	1. Family security
2. Independence	2. Group harmony	2. Family harmony
3. Self-reliance	3. Collectiveness	3. Parental guidance
4. Equality	4. Age/seniority	4. Age
5. Individualism	5. Group consensus	5. Authority
6. Competition	6. Cooperation	6. Compromise
7. Efficiency	7. Quality	7. Devotion
8. Time	8. Patience	8. Patience
9. Directness	9. Indirectness	9. Indirectness
10. Openness	10. Go-between	10. Hospitality

Note: "1" represents the most important cultural value. "10" the least.

Source: Adapted from information found in F. Elashmawi and Philip R. Harris, *Multicultural Management* (Houston: Gulf Publishing, 1993), p. 63.

In overall terms, the cultural impact on international management is reflected by basic beliefs and behaviors. Here are some specific examples where the culture of a society can directly affect management approaches:

- *Centralized vs. decentralized decision making.* In some societies, top managers make all important organizational decisions. In others, these decisions are diffused throughout the enterprise, and middle- and lower-level managers actively participate in, and make, key decisions.
- *Safety vs. risk.* In some societies, organizational decision makers are risk-averse and have great difficulty with conditions of uncertainty. In others, risk taking is encouraged, and decision making under uncertainty is common.
- *Individual vs. group rewards.* In some countries, personnel who do outstanding work are given individual rewards in the form of bonuses and commissions. In others, cultural norms require group rewards, and individual rewards are frowned on.
- *Informal vs. formal procedures.* In some societies, much is accomplished through informal means. In others, formal procedures are set forth and followed rigidly.
- *High vs. low organizational loyalty.* In some societies, people identify very strongly with their organization or employer. In others, people identify with their occupational group, such as engineer or mechanic.
- *Cooperation vs. competition.* Some societies encourage cooperation between their people. Others encourage competition between their people.
- *Short-term vs. long-term horizons.* Some cultures focus most heavily on short-term horizons, such as short-range goals of profit and efficiency. Others are more interested in long-range goals, such as market share and technological development.
- *Stability vs. innovation.* The culture of some countries encourages stability and resistance to change. The culture of others puts high value on innovation and change.

These cultural differences influence the way that international management should be conducted. The International Management in Action, "Business Customs in South Africa," provides some examples from a country where many international managers are unfamiliar with day-to-day business protocol.

Another way of depicting cultural diversity is through visually separating its components. Figure 4–1 provides an example by using concentric circles. The outer ring consists

Figure 4–1

A Model of Culture

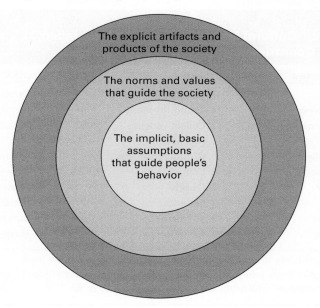

The explicit artifacts and products of the society

The norms and values that guide the society

The implicit, basic assumptions that guide people's behavior

Business Customs in South Africa

The proper methods for conducting business in Africa can vary greatly depending on the region. As mentioned in Chapter 2, Africa consists of many traditions often within the same area. Adding further complication is the propensity for northern regions of Africa to mirror Islamic fundamentals. For simplicity, we will focus on some suggestions with regard to business customs in one country, South Africa:

1. Arrange a meeting before discussing business over the phone. Most South Africans prefer face-to-face interactions. Be prepared for informal small talk before and during the meeting to be better acquainted. In most cases, first meetings are less about business and more about establishing a relationship. Sincere inquiries about family or discussion of topics such as sports (e.g., rugby, cricket, or soccer) are encouraged to avoid talking about racial politics as it is viewed as taboo.

2. Appointments should be made as far in advance as possible. There is a chance that senior-level managers may be unavailable on short notice, but last-minute arrangements occur often. South Africans are early risers, so breakfast and lunch meetings are quite common. If you have a few meetings scheduled, be sure to allow ample time between them as the view of time is more lax in this area and meetings are prone to being postponed.

3. When introduced, maintain eye contact, shake hands, and provide business cards to everyone. Do not sit until invited to do so. Men and women do not shake hands as often in South Africa, so wait for women to initiate handshakes. Women visiting the country who extend their hand may not have it taken by a South African male, so do not take this as a rude response.

4. Since women are not yet in senior level positions in South Africa, female representatives may encounter condescending behavior or "tests" that would not be extended to male counterparts. Men are expected to leave a room before the women as a "protective" measure, and when a woman or elder enters the room, men are expected to stand.

5. After establishing a trustworthy relationship, make business plans clear, including deadlines, since these are seen as more fluid than contractual. Be sure to keep a tone of negotiation while keeping figures manageable. Negotiation is not their strong point, and an aggressive approach will not prove to be successful. Maintain a win-win strategy.

6. Patience is very important when dealing with business. Never interrupt a South African. Be prepared for a long lag-time between business proposition and acceptance or rejection. Decision-making procedures include a lot of discussion between top managers and subordinates, resulting in slow processes.

7. Keep presentations short, and do away with flashy visuals. Follow up and be clear that you intend to continue relations with the business or individual; a long-term business relationship is valued with South Africans.

Source: www.kwintessential.co.uk/resources/global-etiquette/south-africa-country-profile.html; Going Global Inc., "Cultural Advice," *South Africa Career Guide, 2006,* content.epnet.com.ps2.villanova.edu/pdf18_21/pdf/2006/ONI/01Jan06/22291722.pdf; Fons Trompenaars and Charles Hampden-Turner, *Riding the Waves of Culture: Understanding Diversity in Global Business,* 2nd ed. (New York: McGraw-Hill, 1998), p. 25.

of the explicit artifacts and products of the culture. This level is observable and consists of such things as language, food, buildings, and art. The middle ring contains the norms and values of the society. These can be both formal and informal, and they are designed to help people understand how they should behave. The inner circle contains the implicit, basic assumptions that govern behavior. By understanding these assumptions, members of a culture are able to organize themselves in a way that helps them increase the effectiveness of their problem-solving processes and interact well with each other. In explaining the nature of the inner circle, Trompenaars and Hampden-Turner have noted that:

> The best way to test if something is a basic assumption is when the [situation] provokes confusion or irritation. You might, for example, observe that some Japanese bow deeper than others. . . . If you ask why they do it the answer might be that they don't know but that the other person

Figure 4–2

Comparing Cultures as Overlapping Normal Distributions

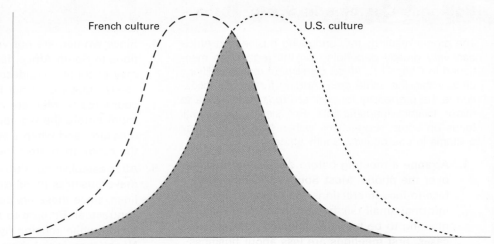

Source: Adapted from Fons Trompenaars and Charles Hampden-Turner, *Riding the Waves of Culture: Understanding Diversity in Global Business,* 2nd ed. (New York: McGraw-Hill, 1998), p. 25.

does it too (norm) or that they want to show respect for authority (value). A typical Dutch question that might follow is: "Why do you respect authority?" The most likely Japanese reaction would be either puzzlement or a smile (which might be hiding their irritation). When you question basic assumptions you are asking questions that have never been asked before. It might lead others to deeper insights, but it also might provoke annoyance. Try in the USA or the Netherlands to raise the question of why people are equal and you will see what we mean.[20]

A supplemental way of understanding cultural differences is to compare culture as a normal distribution, as in Figure 4–2, and then to examine it in terms of stereotyping, as in Figure 4–3. French culture and American culture, for example, have quite different norms and values. So the normal distribution curves for the two cultures have only limited overlap. However, when one looks at the tail-ends of the two curves, it is possible to identify stereotypical views held by members of one culture about the other. The stereotypes

Figure 4–3

Stereotyping from the Cultural Extremes

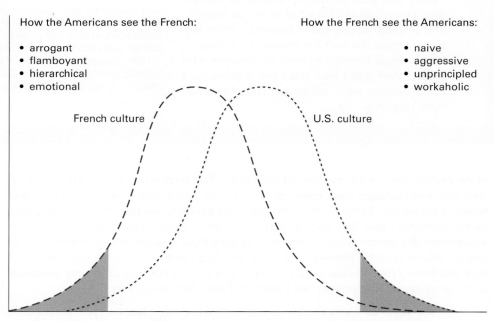

How the Americans see the French:

- arrogant
- flamboyant
- hierarchical
- emotional

How the French see the Americans:

- naive
- aggressive
- unprincipled
- workaholic

Source: Adapted from Fons Trompenaars and Charles Hampden-Turner, *Riding the Waves of Culture: Understanding Diversity in Global Business,* 2nd ed. (New York: McGraw-Hill, 1998), p. 23.

are often exaggerated and used by members of one culture in describing the other, thus helping reinforce the differences between the two while reducing the likelihood of achieving cooperation and communication. This is one reason why an understanding of national culture is so important in the study of international management.

■ Values in Culture

A major dimension in the study of culture is values. **Values** are basic convictions that people have regarding what is right and wrong, good and bad, and important and unimportant. These values are learned from the culture in which the individual is reared, and they help direct the person's behavior. Differences in cultural values often result in varying management practices. Table 4–2 provides an example. Note that U.S. values can result in one set of business responses and that alternative values can bring about different responses.

values
Basic convictions that people have regarding what is right and wrong, good and bad, and important and unimportant.

Value Differences and Similarities across Cultures

Personal values have been the focus of numerous intercultural studies. In general, the findings show both differences and similarities between the work values and managerial values of different cultural groups. For example, one study found differences in work values between Western-oriented and tribal-oriented black employees in South Africa.[21] The Western-oriented group accepted most of the tenets of the Protestant work ethic, but the tribal-oriented group did not. The results were explained in terms of the differences of the cultural backgrounds of the two groups.

Differences in work values also have been found to reflect culture and industrialization. Researchers gave a personal-values questionnaire (PVQ) to over 2,000 managers in five countries: Australia ($n = 281$), India ($n = 485$), Japan ($n = 301$), South Korea

Table 4–2
U.S. Values and Possible Alternatives

U.S. Cultural Values	Alternative Values	Examples of Management Function Affected
Individuals can influence the future (where there is a will there is a way).	Life follows a preordained course, and human action is determined by the will of God.	Planning and scheduling.
Individuals should be realistic in their aspirations.	Ideals are to be pursued regardless of what is "reasonable."	Goal setting and career development.
We must work hard to accomplish our objectives (Puritan ethic).	Hard work is not the only prerequisite for success. Wisdom, luck, and time are also required.	Motivation and reward system.
A primary obligation of an employee is to the organization.	Individual employees have a primary obligation to their family and friends.	Loyalty, commitment, and motivation.
Employees can be removed if they do not perform well.	The removal of an employee from a position involves a great loss of prestige and will rarely be done.	Promotion.
Company information should be available to anyone who needs it within the organization.	Withholding information to gain or maintain power is acceptable.	Organization, communication, and managerial style.
Competition stimulates high performance.	Competition leads to imbalances and disharmony.	Career development and marketing.
What works is important.	Symbols and the process are more important than the end point.	Communication, planning, and quality control.

Source: Adapted from information found in Philip R. Harris and Robert T. Moran, *Managing Cultural Differences* (Houston: Gulf Publishing, 1991), pp. 79–80.

(n = 161), and the United States (n = 833).[22] The PVQ consisted of 66 concepts related to business goals, personal goals, ideas associated with people and groups of people, and ideas about general topics. Ideologic and philosophic concepts were included to represent major value systems of all groups. The results showed some significant differences between the managers in each group. U.S. managers placed high value on the tactful acquisition of influence and on regard for others. Japanese managers placed high value on deference to superiors, company commitment, and the cautious use of aggressiveness and control. Korean managers placed high value on personal forcefulness and aggressiveness and low value on recognition of others. Indian managers put high value on the nonaggressive pursuit of objectives. Australian managers placed major importance on values reflecting a low-key approach to management and a high concern for others.[23] In short, value systems across national boundaries often are different.

At the same time, value similarities exist between cultures. In fact, research shows that managers from different countries often have similar personal values that relate to success. England and Lee examined the managerial values of a diverse sample of U.S. (n = 878), Japanese (n = 312), Australian (n = 301), and Indian (n = 500) managers. They found that:

1. There is a reasonably strong relationship between the level of success achieved by managers and their personal values.

2. It is evident that value patterns predict managerial success and could be used in selection and placement decisions.

3. Although there are country differences in the relationships between values and success, findings across the four countries are quite similar.

4. The general pattern indicates that more successful managers appear to favor pragmatic, dynamic, achievement-oriented values, while less successful managers prefer more static and passive values. More successful managers favor an achievement orientation and prefer an active role in interaction with other individuals who are instrumental to achieving the managers' organizational goals. Less successful managers have values associated with a static and protected environment in which they take relatively passive roles.[24]

The International Management in Action box, "Common Personal Values," on page 119 discusses these findings in more depth.

Values in Transition

Do values change over time? George England found that personal value systems are relatively stable and do not change rapidly.[25] However, changes are taking place in managerial values as a result of both culture and technology. A good example is the Japanese. Reichel and Flynn examined the effects of the U.S. environment on the cultural values of Japanese managers working for Japanese firms in the United States. In particular, they focused attention on such key organizational values as lifetime employment, formal authority, group orientation, seniority, and paternalism. Here is what they found:

1. Lifetime employment is widely accepted in Japanese culture, but the stateside Japanese managers did not believe that unconditional tenure in one organization was of major importance. They did believe, however, that job security was important.

2. Formal authority, obedience, and conformance to hierarchic position are very important in Japan, but the stateside managers did not perceive obedience and conformity to be very important and rejected the idea that one should not question a superior. However, they did support the concept of formal authority.

3. Group orientation, cooperation, conformity, and compromise are important organizational values in Japan. The stateside managers supported these values but also believed it was important to be an individual, thus maintaining a balance between a group and a personal orientation.

Common Personal Values

One of the most interesting findings about successful managers around the world is that while they come from different cultures, many have similar personal values. Of course, there are large differences in values within each national group. For example, some managers are very pragmatic and judge ideas in terms of whether they will work; others are highly ethical and moral and view ideas in terms of right or wrong; still others have a "feeling" orientation and judge ideas in terms of whether they are pleasant. Some managers have a very small set of values; others have a large set. Some have values that are related heavily to organization life; others include a wide range of personal values; others have highly group-oriented values. There are many different value patterns; however, overall value profiles have been found within successful managers in each group. Here are some of the most significant:

U.S. managers
- Highly pragmatic
- High achievement and competence orientation
- Emphasis on profit maximization, organizational efficiency, and high productivity

Japanese managers
- Highly pragmatic
- Strong emphasis on size and growth
- High value on competence and achievement

Korean managers
- Highly pragmatic
- Highly individualistic
- Strong achievement and competence orientation

Australian managers
- High moral orientation
- High humanistic orientation
- Low value on achievement, success, competition, and risk

Indian managers
- High moral orientation
- Highly individualistic
- Strong focus on organization compliance and competence

The findings listed here show important similarities and differences. Most of the profiles are similar in nature; however, note that successful Indian and Australian managers have values that are distinctly different. In short, although values of successful managers within countries often are similar, there are intercountry differences. This is why the successful managerial value systems of one country often are not ideal in another country.

4. In Japan, organizational personnel often are rewarded based on seniority, not merit. Support for this value was directly influenced by the length of time the Japanese managers had been in the United States. The longer they had been there, the lower their support for this value.

5. Paternalism, often measured by a manager's involvement in both personal and off-the-job problems of subordinates, is very important in Japan. Stateside Japanese managers disagreed, and this resistance was positively associated with the number of years they had been in the United States.[26]

There is increasing evidence that individualism in Japan is on the rise, indicating that Japanese values are changing—and not just among managers outside the country. The country's long economic slump has convinced many Japanese that they cannot rely on the large corporations or the government to ensure their future. They have to do it for themselves. As a result, today a growing number of Japanese are starting to embrace what is being called the "era of personal responsibility." Instead of denouncing individualism as a threat to society, they are proposing it as a necessary solution to many of the country's economic ills. A vice chairman of the nation's largest business lobby summed up this thinking at the opening of a recent conference on economic change when he said, "By establishing personal responsibility, we must return dynamism to the economy and revitalize society."[27] This thinking is supported by Lee and Peterson's research which reveals that a culture with a strong entrepreneurial orientation is important to global competitiveness, especially in the small business sector of an economy. So this current trend may well be helpful to the Japanese economy in helping it meet foreign competition at home.[28]

The focus here has been on Japan due to the concrete experiential and experimental evidence. While Japanese cultures and values continue to evolve, other countries such as China are just beginning to undergo a new era. We discussed in Chapter 2 how China is moving away from a collectivist culture, and it appears as though even China is not sure what cultural values it will adhere to. Confucianism was worshipped for over 2,000 years, but the powerful messages through Confucius's teachings were overshadowed in a world where profit became a priority. Now, Confucianism is slowly gaining popularity once again, emphasizing respect for authority, concern for others, balance, harmony, and overall order. While this may provide sanctuary for some, it poses problems within the government, since it will have to prove its worthiness to remain in power. As long as China continues to prosper, hope for a unified culture may be on the horizon. Many are still concerned with the lack of an alternative if China's growth is stunted, creating even more confusion in the journey to maintain cultural values.[29]

Cultural Dimensions

Understanding the cultural context of a society, and being able to respond and react appropriately to cultural differences, is becoming increasingly important as the global environment becomes more interconnected. Over the past several decades, researchers have attempted to provide a composite picture of culture by examining its subparts, or dimensions.

Hofstede

In 1980, Dutch researcher Geert Hofstede identified four original, and later two additional, dimensions of culture that help explain how and why people from various cultures behave as they do.[30] His initial data were gathered from two questionnaire surveys with over 116,000 respondents from over 70 different countries around the world—making it the largest organizationally based study ever conducted. The individuals in these studies all worked in the local subsidiaries of IBM. As a result, Hofstede's research has been criticized because of its focus on just one company; however, he has countered this criticism. Hofstede is well aware of the amazement of some people about how employees of a very specific corporation like IBM can serve as a sample for discovering something about the culture of their countries at large. "We know IBMers," they say. "They are very special people, always in a white shirt and tie, and not at all representative of our country." The people who say this are quite right. IBMers do not form representative samples from national populations. However, samples for cross-national comparison need not be representative, as long as they are functionally equivalent. IBM employees are a narrow sample, but very well matched. Employees of multinational companies in general and of IBM in particular form attractive sources of information for comparing national traits, because they are so similar in respects other than nationality: their employers, their kind of work, and—for matched occupations—their level of education. The only thing that can account for systematic and consistent differences between national groups within such a homogenous multinational population is nationality itself; the national environment in which people were brought up before they joined this employer. Comparing IBM subsidiaries therefore shows national culture differences with unusual clarity.[31] Hofstede's massive study continues to be a focal point for additional research, including the most recent GLOBE project, discussed at the end of this chapter.

The original four dimensions that Hofstede examined were (1) power distance, (2) uncertainty avoidance, (3) individualism, and (4) masculinity.[32]

power distance
The extent to which less powerful members of institutions and organizations accept that power is distributed unequally.

Power Distance   **Power distance** is "the extent to which less powerful members of institutions and organizations accept that power is distributed unequally."[33] Countries in which people blindly obey the orders of their superiors have high power distance. In many societies, lower-level employees tend to follow orders as a matter of procedure. In societies with high power distance, however, strict obedience is found even at the upper levels; examples include Mexico, South Korea, and India. For example, a senior Indian executive with a PhD from a prestigious U.S. university related the following story:

> What is most important for me and my department is not what I do or achieve for the company, but whether the [owner's] favor is bestowed on me. . . . This I have achieved by saying "yes" to everything [the owner] says or does. . . . To contradict him is to look for another job. . . . I left my freedom of thought in Boston.[34]

The effect of this dimension can be measured in a number of ways. For example, organizations in low-power-distance countries generally will be decentralized and have flatter organization structures. These organizations also will have a smaller proportion of supervisory personnel, and the lower strata of the workforce often will consist of highly qualified people. By contrast, organizations in high-power-distance countries will tend to be centralized and have tall organization structures. Organizations in high-power-distance countries will have a large proportion of supervisory personnel, and the people at the lower levels of the structure often will have low job qualifications. This latter structure encourages and promotes inequality between people at different levels.[35]

Uncertainty Avoidance　**Uncertainty avoidance** is "the extent to which people feel threatened by ambiguous situations and have created beliefs and institutions that try to avoid these."[36] Countries populated with people who do not like uncertainty tend to have a high need for security and a strong belief in experts and their knowledge; examples include Germany, Japan, and Spain. Cultures with low uncertainty avoidance have people who are more willing to accept that risks are associated with the unknown, and that life must go on in spite of this. Examples include Denmark and Great Britain.

uncertainty avoidance
The extent to which people feel threatened by ambiguous situations and have created beliefs and institutions that try to avoid these.

The effect of this dimension can be measured in a number of ways. Countries with high-uncertainty-avoidance cultures have a great deal of structuring of organizational activities, more written rules, less risk taking by managers, lower labor turnover, and less ambitious employees.

Low-uncertainty-avoidance societies have organization settings with less structuring of activities, fewer written rules, more risk taking by managers, higher labor turnover, and more ambitious employees. The organization encourages personnel to use their own initiative and assume responsibility for their actions.

Individualism　We discussed individualism and collectivism in Chapter 2 in reference to political systems. **Individualism** is the tendency of people to look after themselves and their immediate family only.[37] Hofstede measured this cultural difference on a bipolar continuum with individualism at one end and collectivism at the other. **Collectivism** is the tendency of people to belong to groups or collectives and to look after each other in exchange for loyalty.[38]

individualism
The tendency of people to look after themselves and their immediate family only.

collectivism
The tendency of people to belong to groups or collectives and to look after each other in exchange for loyalty.

Like the effects of the other cultural dimensions, the effects of individualism and collectivism can be measured in a number of different ways.[39] Hofstede found that wealthy countries have higher individualism scores and poorer countries higher collectivism scores (see Table 4–3 for the 74 countries used in Figure 4–4 and subsequent figures). Note that in Figure 4–4, shown on page 123, the United States, Canada, Australia, Denmark, and Sweden, among others, have high individualism and high GNP. Conversely, Indonesia, Pakistan, and a number of South American countries have low individualism (high collectivism) and low GNP. Countries with high individualism also tend to have greater support for the Protestant work ethic, greater individual initiative, and promotions based on market value. Countries with low individualism tend to have less support for the Protestant work ethic, less individual initiative, and promotions based on seniority.

Table 4–3
Countries and Regions Used in Hofstede's Research

Arabic-speaking countries (Egypt, Iraq, Kuwait, Lebanon, Libya, Saudi Arabia, United Arab Emirates)	Ecuador	Panama
	Estonia	Peru
	Finland	Philippines
	France	Poland
	Germany	Portugal
	Great Britain	Romania
	Greece	Russia
Argentina	Guatemala	Salvador
Australia	Hong Kong (China)	Serbia
Austria		Singapore
Bangladesh	Hungary	Slovakia
Belgium Flemish (Dutch speaking)	India	Slovenia
	Indonesia	South Africa
Belgium Walloon (French speaking)	Iran	Spain
	Ireland	Suriname
Brazil	Israel	Sweden
Bulgaria	Italy	Switzerland French
Canada Quebec	Jamaica	Switzerland German
Canada total	Japan	Taiwan
Chile	Korea (South)	Thailand
China	Luxembourg	Trinidad
Colombia	Malaysia	Turkey
Costa Rica	Malta	United States
Croatia	Mexico	Uruguay
Czech Republic	Morocco	Venezuela
Denmark	Netherlands	Vietnam
East Africa (Ethiopia, Kenya, Tanzania, Zambia)	New Zealand	West Africa (Ghana, Nigeria, Sierra Leone)
	Norway	
	Pakistan	

Source: From Hofstede and Hofstede, *Cultures and Organizations: Software of the Mind.* Copyright © 2005 The McGraw-Hill Companies, Inc. Reprinted with permission.

masculinity
A cultural characteristic in which the dominant values in society are success, money, and things.

femininity
A cultural characteristic in which the dominant values in society are caring for others and the quality of life.

Masculinity **Masculinity** is defined by Hofstede as "a situation in which the dominant values in society are success, money, and things."[40] Hofstede measured this dimension on a continuum ranging from masculinity to femininity. Contrary to some stereotypes and connotations, **femininity** is the term used by Hofstede to describe "a situation in which the dominant values in society are caring for others and the quality of life."[41]

Countries with a high masculinity index, such as the Germanic countries, place great importance on earnings, recognition, advancement, and challenge. Individuals are encouraged to be independent decision makers, and achievement is defined in terms of recognition and wealth. The workplace is often characterized by high job stress, and many managers believe that their employees dislike work and must be kept under some degree of control. The school system is geared toward encouraging high performance. Young men expect to have careers, and those who do not often view themselves as failures. Historically, fewer women hold higher-level jobs, although this is changing. The school system is geared toward encouraging high performance.

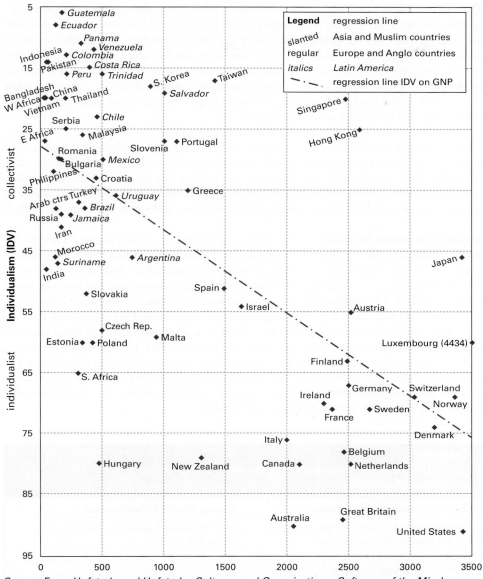

Figure 4–4

GNP per Capita in 2000 versus Individualism

Source: From Hofstede and Hofstede, *Cultures and Organizations: Software of the Mind.*
Copyright © 2005 The McGraw-Hill Companies, Inc. Reprinted with permission.

Countries with a low masculinity index (Hofstede's femininity dimension), such as Norway, tend to place great importance on cooperation, a friendly atmosphere, and employment security. Individuals are encouraged to be group decision makers, and achievement is defined in terms of layman contacts and the living environment. The workplace tends to be characterized by low stress, and managers give their employees more credit for being responsible and allow them more freedom. Culturally, this group prefers small-scale enterprises, and they place greater importance on conservation of the environment. The school system is designed to teach social adaptation. Some young men and women want careers; others do not. Many women hold higher-level jobs, and they do not find it necessary to be assertive.

Further research by Hofstede led to the recent identification of the fifth and sixth cultural dimensions: (5) time orientation, identified in 1988, and (6) indulgence versus restraint, identified in 2010.[42]

Time Orientation   Originally called Confucian Work Dynamism, time orientation is defined by Hofstede as "dealing with society's search for virtue." Long-term oriented societies tend to focus on the future. They have the ability to adapt their traditions when conditions change, have a tendency to save and invest for the future, and focus on achieving long-term results. Short-term oriented cultures focus more on the past and present than on the future. These societies have a deep respect for tradition, focus on achieving quick results, and do not tend to save for the future.[43] Table 4–4 highlights ten differences between long- and short-term oriented cultures.

Asian cultures primarily exhibit long-term orientation. Countries with a high long-term orientation index include China, Japan, and Brazil. In these cultures, individuals are persistent, thrifty with their money, and highly adaptable to unexpected circumstances. Spain, the USA, and the UK were identified as having a low long-term orientation index (Hofstede's short-term orientation). Individuals in short-term oriented societies believe in absolutes (good and evil), value stability and leisure time, and spend money more freely.[44]

Indulgence versus Restraint   Based on research related to relative happiness around the world, Hofstede's most recent dimension measures the freedom to satisfy one's natural needs and desires within a society. Indulgent societies encourage instant gratification of natural human needs, while restrained cultures regulate and control behavior based on social norms.[45] Table 4–5 highlights ten differences between indulgent and restrained cultures.

Countries that show a high indulgence index include the USA, Australia, the UK, and Chile. Freely able to satisfy their basic human desires, individuals in these societies tend to live in the moment. They participate in more activities, express happiness freely, and view themselves as being in control of their own destiny. Countries that show a low indulgence index (Hofstede's dimension of restraint) include Egypt, Romania, and China. In these societies, individuals participate in fewer activities, express less happiness, and believe that their own destiny is not in their control.[46]

Table 4–4
Ten Differences between Short- and Long-Term Oriented Societies

Short-Term Orientation	Long-Term Orientation
Most important events in life occurred in the past or take place now	Most important events in life will occur in the future
Personal steadiness and stability: a good person is always the same	A good person adapts to the circumstances
There are universal guidelines about what is good and evil	What is good and evil depends on the circumstances
Traditions are sacrosanct	Traditions are adaptable to changed circumstances
Family life guided by imperatives	Family life guided by shared tasks
Supposed to proud of one's country	Trying to learn from other countries
Service to others is an important goal	Thrift and perseverance are important goals
Social spending and consumption	Large savings quote, funds available for investment
Students attribute success and failure to luck	Students attribute success to effort and failure to lack of effort
Slow or no economic growth of poor countries	Fast economic growth of countries up till a level of prosperity

Source: From Hofstede, G. (2011). "Dimensionalizing Cultures: The Hofstede Model in Context," *Online readings in Psychology and Culture, Unit 2.* http://scholarworks.gvsu.edu/orpc/vol2/iss1/8. © 2011 IACCP.

Table 4–5
Ten Differences between Indulgent and Restrained Societies

Indulgent	Restrained
Higher percentage of people declaring themselves very happy	Fewer very happy people
A perception of personal life control	A perception of helplessness: what happens to me is not my own doing
Freedom of speech seen as important	Freedom of speech is not a primary concern
Higher importance of leisure	Lower importance of leisure
More likely to remember positive emotions	Less likely to remember positive emotions
In countries with educated populations, higher birthrates	In countries with educated populations, lower birthrates
More people actively involved in sports	Fewer people actively involved in sports
In countries with enough food, higher percentages of obese people	In countries with enough food, fewer obese people
In wealthy countries, lenient sexual norms	In wealthy countries, stricter sexual norms
Maintaining order in the nation is not given a high priority	Higher number of police officers per 100,000 population

Source: From Hofstede, G. (2011). "Dimensionalizing Cultures: The Hofstede Model in Context," *Online readings in Psychology and Culture, Unit 2. http://scholarworks.gvsu. edu/orpc/vol2/iss1/8.* © 2011 IACCP.

Integrating the Dimensions   A description of the four original and two additional dimensions of culture is useful in helping to explain the differences between various countries, and Hofstede's research has extended beyond this focus and shown how countries can be described in terms of pairs of dimensions. In Hofstede's and later research, pairings and clusters can provide useful summaries for international managers. It is always best to have an in-depth understanding of the multicultural environment, but the general groupings outline common ground that one can use as a starting point. Figure 4–5, which incorporates power distance and individualism, provides an example.

Upon first examination of the cluster distribution, the data may appear confusing. However, they are very useful in depicting what countries appear similar in values, and to what extent they differ with other country clusters. The same countries are not always clustered together in subsequent dimension comparisons. This indicates that while some beliefs overlap between cultures, it is where they diverge that makes groups unique to manage.

In Figure 4–5, the United States, Australia, Canada, Britain, Denmark, and New Zealand are located in the lower-left-hand quadrant. Americans, for example, have very high individualism and relatively low power distance. They prefer to do things for themselves and are not upset when others have more power than they do. The other countries, while they may not be a part of the same cluster, share similar values. Conversely, many of the underdeveloped or newly industrialized countries, such as Colombia, Hong Kong, Portugal, and Singapore, are characterized by large power distance and low individualism. These nations tend to be collectivist in their approach.

Similarly, Figure 4–6 plots the uncertainty-avoidance index against the power-distance index. Once again, there are clusters of countries. Many of the Anglo nations tend to be in the upper-left-hand quadrant, which is characterized by small power distance and weak uncertainty avoidance, while, in contrast, many Latin, Mediterranean, and Asian nations are characterized by high power distance and strong uncertainty avoidance.

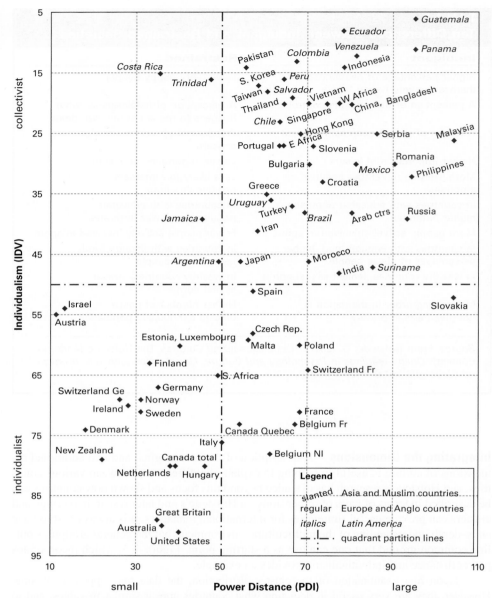

Source: From Hofstede and Hofstede, *Cultures and Organizations: Software of the Mind.* Copyright © 2005 The McGraw-Hill Companies, Inc. Reprinted with permission.

The integration of these cultural factors into two-dimensional plots helps illustrate the complexity of understanding culture's effect on behavior. A number of dimensions are at work, and sometimes they do not all move in the anticipated direction. For example, at first glance, a nation with high power distance would appear to be low in individualism, and vice versa, and Hofstede found exactly that (see Figure 4–5). However, low uncertainty avoidance does not always go hand in hand with high masculinity, even though those who are willing to live with uncertainty will want rewards such as money and power and accord low value to the quality of work life and caring for others (see Figure 4–7). Simply put, empirical evidence on the impact of cultural dimensions may differ from commonly held beliefs or stereotypes. Research-based data are needed to determine the full impact of differing cultures.

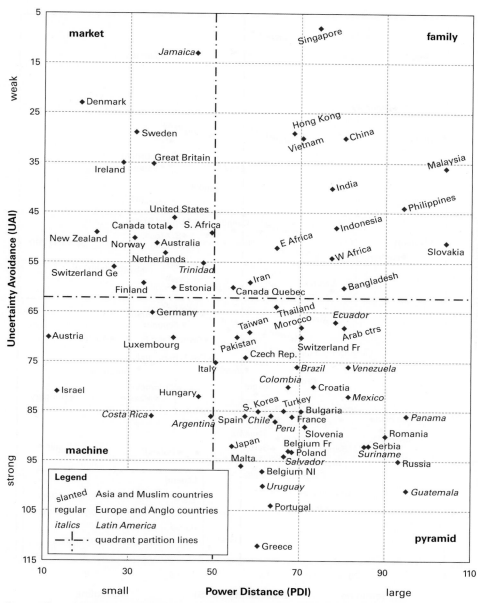

Source: From Hofstede and Hofstede, *Cultures and Organizations: Software of the Mind.*
Copyright © 2005 The McGraw-Hill Companies, Inc. Reprinted with permission.

The Hofstede cultural dimensions and country clusters are widely recognized and accepted in the study of international management. His work has served as a springboard to numerous recent cultural studies and research projects.

Trompenaars

In 1994, another Dutch researcher, Fons Trompenaars, expanded on the research of Hofstede and published the results of his own 10-year study on cultural dimensions.[47] He administered research questionnaires to over 15,000 managers from 28 countries and received usable responses from at least 500 in each nation; the 23 countries in his

Figure 4–7

Masculinity versus Uncertainty Avoidance

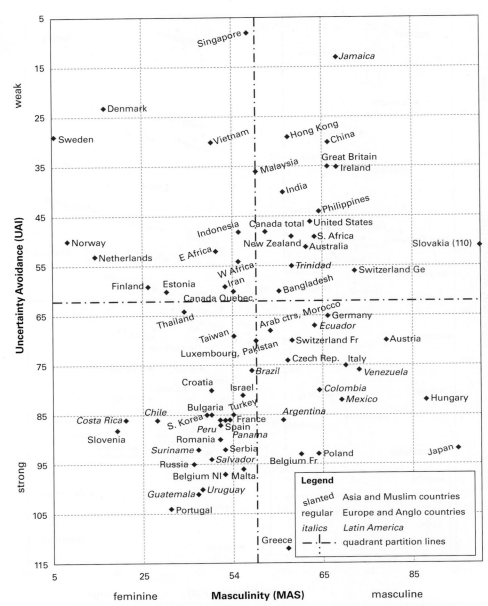

Source: From Hofstede and Hofstede, *Cultures and Organizations: Software of the Mind.*
Copyright © 2005 The McGraw-Hill Companies, Inc. Reprinted with permission.

research are presented in Table 4–6. Building heavily on value orientations and the relational orientations of well-known sociologist Talcott Parsons,[48] Trompenaars derived five relationship orientations that address the ways in which people deal with each other; these can be considered to be cultural dimensions that are analogous to Hofstede's dimensions. Trompenaars also looked at attitudes toward both time and the environment, and the result of his research is a wealth of information helping explain how cultures differ and offering practical ways in which MNCs can do business in various countries. The following discussion examines each of the five relationship orientations as well as attitudes toward time and the environment.[49]

Table 4–6
Trompenaars's Country Abbreviations

Abbreviation	Country
ARG	Argentina
AUS	Austria
BEL	Belgium
BRZ	Brazil
CHI	China
CIS	Former Soviet Union
CZH	Former Czechoslovakia
FRA	France
GER	Germany (excluding former East Germany)
HK	Hong Kong
IDO	Indonesia
ITA	Italy
JPN	Japan
MEX	Mexico
NL	Netherlands
SIN	Singapore
SPA	Spain
SWE	Sweden
SWI	Switzerland
THA	Thailand
UK	United Kingdom
USA	United States
VEN	Venezuela

Universalism vs. Particularism **Universalism** is the belief that ideas and practices can be applied everywhere without modification. **Particularism** is the belief that circumstances dictate how ideas and practices should be applied. In cultures with high universalism, the focus is more on formal rules than on relationships, business contracts are adhered to very closely, and people believe that "a deal is a deal." In cultures with high particularism, the focus is more on relationships and trust than on formal rules. In a particularist culture, legal contracts often are modified, and as people get to know each other better, they often change the way in which deals are executed. In his early research, Trompenaars found that in countries such as the United States, Australia, Germany, Sweden, and the United Kingdom, there was high universalism, while countries such as Venezuela, the former Soviet Union, Indonesia, and China were high on particularism. Figure 4–8 shows the continuum.

In follow-up research, Trompenaars and Hampden-Turner presented the respondents with a dilemma and asked them to make a decision. Here is one of these dilemmas along with the national scores of the respondents:[50]

> You are riding in a car driven by a close friend. He hits a pedestrian. You know he was going at least 35 miles per hour in an area of the city where the maximum allowed speed is 20 miles per hour. There are no witnesses. His lawyer says that if you testify under oath that he was driving 20 miles per hour it may save him from serious consequences. What right has your friend to expect you to protect him?
>
> (*a*) My friend has a definite right as a friend to expect me to testify to the lower figure.
> (*b*) He has some right as a friend to expect me to testify to the lower figure.
> (*c*) He has no right as a friend to expect me to testify to the lower figure.

universalism
The belief that ideas and practices can be applied everywhere in the world without modification.

particularism
The belief that circumstances dictate how ideas and practices should be applied and that something cannot be done the same everywhere.

| **Figure 4–8** |
| **Trompenaars's Relationship Orientations on Cultural Dimensions** |

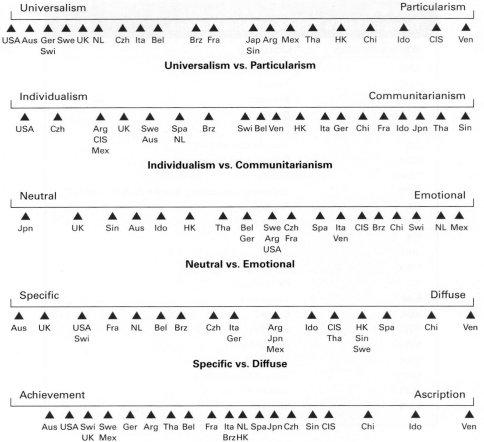

Source: Adapted from information found in Fons Trompenaars, *Riding the Waves of Culture* (New York: Irwin, 1994); Charles M. Hampden-Turner and Fons Trompenaars, "A World Turned Upside Down: Doing Business in Asia," in *Managing Across Cultures: Issues and Perspectives,* ed. Pat Joynt and Malcolm Warner (London: International Thomson Business Press, 1996), pp. 275–305.

With a high score indicating strong universalism (choice c) and a low score indicating strong particularism (choice a), here is how the different nations scored:

Universalism (no right)	
Canada	96
United States	95
Germany	90
United Kingdom	90
Netherlands	88
France	68
Japan	67
Singapore	67
Thailand	63
Hong Kong	56
Particularism (some or definite right)	
China	48
South Korea	26

As noted earlier, respondents from universalist cultures (e.g., North America and Western Europe) felt that the rules applied regardless of the situation, while respondents from particularist cultures were much more willing to bend the rules and help their friend.

Based on these types of findings, Trompenaars recommends that when individuals from particularist cultures do business in a universalistic culture, they should be prepared for rational, professional arguments and a "let's get down to business" attitude. Conversely, when individuals from universalist cultures do business in a particularist environment, they should be prepared for personal meandering or irrelevancies that seem to go nowhere and should not regard personal, get-to-know-you attitudes as mere small talk.

Individualism vs. Communitarianism Individualism and communitarianism are key dimensions in Hofstede's earlier research. Although Trompenaars derived these two relationships differently than Hofstede does, they still have the same basic meaning, although in his more recent work Trompenaars has used the word **communitarianism** rather than collectivism. For him, individualism refers to people regarding themselves as individuals, while communitarianism refers to people regarding themselves as part of a group, similar to the political groupings discussed in Chapter 2. As shown in Figure 4–8, the United States, former Czechoslovakia, Argentina, the former Soviet Union (CIS), and Mexico have high individualism.

communitarianism
Refers to people regarding themselves as part of a group.

In his most recent research, Trompenaars posed the following situation. If you were to be promoted, which of the two following issues would you emphasize most: (a) the new group of people with whom you will be working or (b) the greater responsibility of the work you are undertaking and the higher income you will be earning? The following reports the scores associated with the individualism of option b—greater responsibility and more money.[51]

Individualism (emphasis on larger responsibilities and more income)	
Canada	77
Thailand	71
United Kingdom	69
United States	67
Netherlands	64
France	61
Japan	61
China	54
Singapore	50
Hong Kong	47
Communitarianism (emphasis on the new group of people)	
Malaysia	38
Korea	32

These findings are somewhat different from those presented in Figure 4–8 and show that cultural changes may be occurring more rapidly than many people realize. For example, findings show Thailand very high on individualism (possibly indicating an increasing entrepreneurial spirit/cultural value), whereas the Thais were found to be low on individualism a few years before, as shown in Figure 4–8. At the same time, it is important to remember that there are major differences between people in high-individualism societies and those in high-communitarianism societies. The former stress personal and individual matters; the latter value group-related issues. Negotiations in cultures with high individualism typically are made on the spot by a representative, people ideally achieve things alone, and they assume a great deal of personal responsibility. In cultures with high communitarianism, decisions typically are referred to committees, people ideally achieve things in groups, and they jointly assume responsibility.

Trompenaars recommends that when people from cultures with high individualism deal with those from communitarianistic cultures, they should have patience for the time taken to consent and to consult, and they should aim to build lasting relationships. When people from cultures with high communitarianism deal with those from individualistic cultures, they should be prepared to make quick decisions and commit their organization to these decisions. Also, communitarianists dealing with individualists should realize that the reason they are dealing with only one negotiator (as opposed to a group) is that this person is respected by his or her organization and has its authority and esteem.

Neutral vs. Emotional   A **neutral culture** is one in which emotions are held in check. As seen in Figure 4–8, both Japan and the United Kingdom are high-neutral cultures. People in these countries try not to show their feelings; they act stoically and maintain their composure. An **emotional culture** is one in which emotions are openly and naturally expressed. People in emotional cultures often smile a great deal, talk loudly when they are excited, and greet each other with a great deal of enthusiasm. Mexico, the Netherlands, and Switzerland are examples of high emotional cultures.

Trompenaars recommends that when individuals from emotional cultures do business in neutral cultures, they should put as much as they can on paper and submit it to the other side. They should realize that lack of emotion does not mean a lack of interest or boredom, but rather that people from neutral cultures do not like to show their hand. Conversely, when those from neutral cultures do business in emotional cultures, they should not be put off stride when the other side creates scenes or grows animated and boisterous, and they should try to respond warmly to the emotional affections of the other group.

Specific vs. Diffuse   A **specific culture** is one in which individuals have a large public space they readily let others enter and share and a small private space they guard closely and share with only close friends and associates. A **diffuse culture** is one in which public space and private space are similar in size and individuals guard their public space carefully, because entry into public space affords entry into private space as well. As shown in Figure 4–8, Austria, the United Kingdom, the United States, and Switzerland all are specific cultures, while Venezuela, China, and Spain are diffuse cultures. In specific cultures, people often are invited into a person's open, public space; individuals in these cultures often are open and extroverted; and there is a strong separation of work and private life. In diffuse cultures, people are not quickly invited into a person's open, public space, because once they are in, there is easy entry into the private space as well. Individuals in these cultures often appear to be indirect and introverted, and work and private life often are closely linked.

An example of these specific and diffuse cultural dimensions is provided by the United States and Germany. A U.S. professor, such as Robert Smith, PhD, generally would be called "Doctor Smith" by students when at his U.S. university. When shopping, however, he might be referred to by the store clerk as "Bob," and when golfing, Bob might just be one of the guys, even to a golf partner who happens to be a graduate student in his department. The reason for these changes in status is that, with the specific U.S. cultural values, people have large public spaces and often conduct themselves differently depending on their public role. In high-diffuse cultures, on the other hand, a person's public life and private life often are similar. Therefore, in Germany, Herr Professor Doktor Schmidt would be referred to that way at the university, local market, and bowling alley—and even his wife might address him formally in public. A great deal of formality is maintained, often giving the impression that Germans are stuffy or aloof.

Trompenaars recommends that when those from specific cultures do business in diffuse cultures, they should respect a person's title, age, and background connections, and they should not get impatient when people are being indirect or circuitous. Conversely,

neutral culture
A culture in which emotions are held in check.

emotional culture
A culture in which emotions are expressed openly and naturally.

specific culture
A culture in which individuals have a large public space they readily share with others and a small private space they guard closely and share with only close friends and associates.

diffuse culture
A culture in which public space and private space are similar in size and individuals guard their public space carefully, because entry into public space affords entry into private space as well.

when individuals from diffuse cultures do business in specific cultures, they should try to get to the point and be efficient, learn to structure meetings with the judicious use of agendas, and not use their titles or acknowledge achievements or skills that are irrelevant to the issues being discussed.

Achievement vs. Ascription   An **achievement culture** is one in which people are accorded status based on how well they perform their functions. An **ascription culture** is one in which status is attributed based on who or what a person is. Achievement cultures give high status to high achievers, such as the company's number-one salesperson or the medical researcher who has found a cure for a rare form of bone cancer. Ascription cultures accord status based on age, gender, or social connections. For example, in an ascription culture, a person who has been with the company for 40 years may be listened to carefully because of the respect that others have for the individual's age and longevity with the firm, and an individual who has friends in high places may be afforded status because of whom she knows. As shown in Figure 4–8, Austria, the United States, Switzerland, and the United Kingdom are achievement cultures, while Venezuela, Indonesia, and China are ascription cultures.

Trompenaars recommends that when individuals from achievement cultures do business in ascription cultures, they should make sure that their group has older, senior, and formal position holders who can impress the other side, and they should respect the status and influence of their counterparts in the other group. Conversely, he recommends that when individuals from ascription cultures do business in achievement cultures, they should make sure that their group has sufficient data, technical advisers, and knowledgeable people to convince the other group that they are proficient, and they should respect the knowledge and information of their counterparts on the other team.

Time   Aside from the five relationship orientations, another major cultural difference is the way in which people deal with the concept of time. Trompenaars has identified two different approaches: sequential and synchronous. In cultures where sequential approaches are prevalent, people tend to do only one activity at a time, keep appointments strictly, and show a strong preference for following plans as they are laid out and not deviating from them. In cultures where synchronous approaches are common, people tend to do more than one activity at a time, appointments are approximate and may be changed at a moment's notice, and schedules generally are subordinate to relationships. People in synchronous-time cultures often will stop what they are doing to meet and greet individuals coming into their office.

A good contrast is provided by the United States, Mexico, and France. In the United States, people tend to be guided by sequential-time orientation and thus set a schedule and stick to it. Mexicans operate under more of a synchronous-time orientation and thus tend to be much more flexible, often building slack into their schedules to allow for interruptions. The French are similar to the Mexicans and, when making plans, often determine the objectives they want to accomplish but leave open the timing and other factors that are beyond their control; this way, they can adjust and modify their approach as they go along. As Trompenaars noted, "For the French and Mexicans, what was important was that they get to the end, not the particular path or sequence by which that end was reached."[52]

Another interesting time-related contrast is the degree to which cultures are past- or present-oriented as opposed to future-oriented. In countries such as the United States, Italy, and Germany, the future is more important than the past or the present. In countries such as Venezuela, Indonesia, and Spain, the present is most important. In France and Belgium, all three time periods are of approximately equal importance. Because different emphases are given to different time periods, adjusting to these cultural differences can create challenges.

Trompenaars recommends that when doing business with future-oriented cultures, effective international managers should emphasize the opportunities and limitless scope that any agreement can have, agree to specific deadlines for getting things done, and be aware of the core competence or continuity that the other party intends to carry with it

achievement culture
A culture in which people are accorded status based on how well they perform their functions.

ascription culture
A culture in which status is attributed based on who or what a person is.

into the future. When doing business with past- or present-oriented cultures, he recommends that managers emphasize the history and tradition of the culture, find out whether internal relationships will sanction the types of changes that need to be made, and agree to future meetings in principle but fix no deadlines for completions.

The Environment   Trompenaars also examined the ways in which people deal with their environment. Specific attention should be given to whether they believe in controlling outcomes (inner-directed) or letting things take their own course (outer-directed). One of the things he asked managers to do was choose between the following statements:

1. What happens to me is my own doing.
2. Sometimes I feel that I do not have enough control over the directions my life is taking.

Managers who believe in controlling their own environment would opt for the first choice; those who believe that they are controlled by their environment and cannot do much about it would opt for the second.

Here is an`example by country of the sample respondents who believe that what happens to them is their own doing:[53]

United States	89%
Switzerland	84%
Australia	81%
Belgium	76%
Indonesia	73%
Hong Kong	69%
Greece	63%
Singapore	58%
Japan	56%
China	35%

In the United States, managers feel strongly that they are masters of their own fate. This helps account for their dominant attitude (sometimes bordering on aggressiveness) toward the environment and discomfort when things seem to get out of control. Many Asian cultures do not share these views. They believe that things move in waves or natural shifts and one must "go with the flow," so a flexible attitude, characterized by a willingness to compromise and maintain harmony with nature, is important.

Trompenaars recommends that when dealing with those from cultures that believe in dominating the environment, it is important to play hardball, test the resilience of the opponent, win some objectives, and always lose from time to time. For example, representatives of the U.S. government have repeatedly urged Japanese automobile companies to purchase more component parts from U.S. suppliers to partially offset the large volume of U.S. imports of finished autos from Japan. Instead of enacting trade barriers, the United States was asking for a quid pro quo. When dealing with those from cultures that believe in letting things take their natural course, it is important to be persistent and polite, maintain good relationships with the other party, and try to win together and lose apart.

Cultural Patterns or Clusters   Like Hofstede's work, Trompenaars's research lends itself to cultural patterns or clusters. Table 4–7 relates his findings to the five relational orientations. It is useful to compare Hofstede and Trompenaars, because of the overlapping information. For example, Hofstede's country assessments included India but not China. Trompenaars, conversely, shows results for China but not India. Today, international managers must become familiar with beliefs and traditions in both areas, since they play a significant role in the new

Table 4–7
Cultural Groups Based on Trompenaars's Research

	Anglo Cluster	
Relationship	**United States**	**United Kingdom**
Individualism (I)	I	I
Communitarianism (C)		
Specific relationship (S)	S	S
Diffuse relationship (D)		
Universalism (U)	U	U
Particularism (P)		
Neutral relationship (N)	E	N
Emotional relationship (E)		
Achievement (Ach)	Ach	Ach
Ascription (As)		

	Asian Cluster				
Relationship	**Japan**	**China**	**Indonesia**	**Hong Kong**	**Singapore**
Individualism (I)	C	C	C	C	C
Communitarianism (C)					
Specific relationship (S)	D	D	D	D	D
Diffuse relationship (D)					
Universalism (U)	P	P	P	P	P
Particularism (P)					
Neutral relationship (N)	N	E	N	N	N
Emotional relationship (E)					
Achievement (Ach)	As	As	As	As	As
Ascription (As)					

	Latin American Cluster			
Relationship	**Argentina**	**Mexico**	**Venezuela**	**Brazil**
Individualism (I)	I	I	C	I
Communitarianism (C)				
Specific relationship (S)	D	D	D	S
Diffuse relationship (D)				
Universalism (U)	P	P	P	U
Particularism (P)				
Neutral relationship (N)	N	N	N	E
Emotional relationship (E)				
Achievement (Ach)	Ach	Ach	As	As
Ascription (As)				

	Latin European Cluster			
Relationship	**France**	**Belgium**	**Spain**	**Italy**
Individualism (I)	C	C	I	C
Communitarianism (C)				
Specific relationship (S)	S	S	D	S
Diffuse relationship (D)				
Universalism (U)	U	U	P	U
Particularism (P)				
Neutral relationship (N)	E	E	N	E
Emotional relationship (E)				
Achievement (Ach)	As	As	Ach	As
Ascription (As)				

(continued)

Table 4–7 (continued)
Cultural Groups Based on Trompenaars's Research

Relationship	Germanic Cluster			
	Austria	Germany	Switzerland	Czechoslovakia
Individualism (I) Communitarianism (C)	I	C	C	C
Specific relationship (S) Diffuse relationship (D)	S	D	S	S
Universalism (U) Particularism (P)	U	U	U	U
Neutral relationship (N) Emotional relationship (E)	N	E	E	N
Achievement (Ach) Ascription (As)	Ach	Ach	As	Ach

Source: Fons Trompenaars, *Riding the Waves of Culture*. Copyright © 1994 McGraw-Hill Education. Reprinted by permission of McGraw-Hill Education.

world economy (see Chapter 1). Further examination of Table 4–7 shows that while general clusters can be formed, there still exist inherent, significant differences within. For example, Brazil is considered to be a part of the Latin American cluster, though some of the unique findings suggest that Brazil is more independent than strictly "Latin American." The Latin European grouping mirrors similar results, with Italy showing some preferences that are different from both France and Belgium, and with Spain displaying distinguishing characteristics as compared to the other three in the cluster.

Overall, Table 4–7 shows that a case can be made for cultural similarities between clusters of countries. With only small differences, Trompenaars's research helps support and, more importantly, extend the work of Hofstede. Such research provides a useful point of departure for recognizing cultural differences, and it provides guidelines for doing business effectively around the world.

■ Integrating Culture and Management: The GLOBE Project

GLOBE
A multicountry study and evaluation of cultural attributes and leadership behaviors among more than 17,000 managers from 951 organizations in 62 countries.

Most recently, the **GLOBE** (Global Leadership and Organizational Behavior Effectiveness) research program reflects an additional approach to measuring cultural differences. Conceived in 1991, the GLOBE project is an ongoing research project, currently consisting of three major interrelated phases. GLOBE extends and integrates the previous analyses of cultural attributes and variables published by Hofstede and Trompenaars. The three completed GLOBE phases explore the various elements of the dynamic relationship between the culture and organizational behavior.[54]

At the heart of phases one and two, first published in 2004 and 2007, is the study and evaluation of nine different cultural attributes using middle managers from 951 organizations in 62 countries.[55,56] A team of 170 scholars worked together to survey over 17,000 managers in three industries: financial services, food processing, and telecommunications. When developing the measures and conducting the analysis, they also used archival measures of country economic prosperity and of the physical and psychological well-being of the cultures studied. Countries were selected so that every major geographic location in the world was represented. Additional countries, including those with unique types of political and economic systems, were selected to create a complete and comprehensive database upon which to build the analysis.[57] This research has been considered among the most sophisticated in the field to date, and a collaboration of the work of Hofstede and GLOBE researchers could provide an influential outlook on the major factors characterizing global cultures.[58]

While phases one and two focus on middle management, phase three, first published in 2012, examines the interactions of culture and leadership in upper-level management positions. More than 1,000 CEOs, and more than 5,000 of their direct reports, were surveyed by 40 researchers across 24 countries. To provide compatibility across all phases of the GLOBE project, 17 of the 24 countries surveyed in phase 3 were also included in the initial study performed for phases one and two.[59] A further explanation of phase three, which deals primarily with leadership, occurs in Chapter 13. Table 4–8 also provides an overview of the purposes and results of the different phases.

The GLOBE study is interesting because its nine constructs were defined, conceptualized, and operationalized by a multicultural team of over 100 researchers. In addition, the data in each country were collected by investigators who were either natives of the cultures studied or had extensive knowledge and experience in those cultures.

Culture and Management

GLOBE researchers adhere to the belief that certain attributes that distinguish one culture from others can be used to predict the most suitable, effective, and acceptable organizational and leader practices within that culture. In addition, they contend that societal culture has a direct impact on organizational culture and that leader acceptance stems from tying leader attributes and behaviors to subordinate norms.[60]

The GLOBE project set out to answer many fundamental questions about cultural variables shaping leadership and organizational processes. The meta-goal of GLOBE was to develop an empirically based theory to describe, understand, and predict the impact of specific cultural variables on leadership and organizational processes and the effectiveness of these processes. Overall, GLOBE hopes to provide a global standard guideline that allows managers to focus on local specialization. Specific objectives include answering these fundamental questions:[61]

- Are there leader behaviors, attributes, and organizational practices that are universally accepted and effective across cultures?
- Are there leader behaviors, attributes, and organizational practices that are accepted and effective in only some cultures?
- How do attributes of societal and organizational cultures affect the kinds of leader behaviors and organizational practices that are accepted and effective?

Table 4–8
GLOBE Cultural Variable Results

Variable	Highest Ranking	Medium Ranking	Lowest Ranking
Assertiveness	Spain, U.S.	Egypt, Ireland	Sweden, New Zealand
Future orientation	Denmark, Canada	Slovenia, Egypt	Russia, Argentina
Gender differentiation	South Korea, Egypt	Italy, Brazil	Sweden, Denmark
Uncertainty avoidance	Austria, Denmark	Israel, U.S.	Russia, Hungary
Power distance	Russia, Spain	England, France	Denmark, Netherlands
Collectivism/societal	Denmark, Singapore	Hong Kong, U.S.	Greece, Hungary
In-group collectivism	Egypt, China	England, France	Denmark, Netherlands
Performance orientation	U.S., Taiwan	Sweden, Israel	Russia, Argentina
Humane orientation	Indonesia, Egypt	Hong Kong, Sweden	Germany, Spain

Source: From Mansour Javidan, Peter W. Dorfman et al., "In the Eye of the Beholder: Cross Cultural Lessons in Leadership from Project GLOBE," *Perspectives—Academy of Management* 20, no. 1 (2006), p. 76. Reproduced with permission of Academy of Management via Copyright Clearance Center.

- What is the effect of violating cultural norms that are relevant to leadership and organizational practices?
- What is the relative standing of each of the cultures studied on each of the nine core dimensions of culture?
- Can the universal and culture-specific aspects of leader behaviors, attributes, and organizational practices be explained in terms of an underlying theory that accounts for systematic differences across cultures?

GLOBE's Cultural Dimensions

Phase one of the GLOBE project identified the nine cultural dimensions:[62]

1. *Uncertainty avoidance* is defined as the extent to which members of an organization or society strive to avoid uncertainty by reliance on social norms, rituals, and bureaucratic practices to alleviate the unpredictability of future events.

2. *Power distance* is defined as the degree to which members of an organization or society expect and agree that power should be unequally shared.

3. *Collectivism I: Societal collectivism* refers to the degree to which organizational and societal institutional practices encourage and reward collective distribution of resources and collective action.

4. *Collectivism II: In-group collectivism* refers to the degree to which individuals express pride, loyalty, and cohesiveness in their organizations or families.

5. *Gender egalitarianism* is defined as the extent to which an organization or a society minimizes gender role differences and gender discrimination.

6. *Assertiveness* is defined as the degree to which individuals in organizations or societies are assertive, confrontational, and aggressive in social relationships.

7. *Future orientation* is defined as the degree to which individuals in organizations or societies engage in future-oriented behaviors such as planning, investing in the future, and delaying gratification.

8. *Performance orientation* refers to the extent to which an organization or society encourages and rewards group members for performance improvement and excellence.

9. *Humane orientation* is defined as the degree to which individuals in organizations or societies encourage and reward individuals for being fair, altruistic, friendly, generous, caring, and kind to others.

The first six dimensions have their origins in Hofstede's cultural dimensions. The collectivism I dimension measures societal emphasis on collectivism; low scores reflect individualistic emphasis, and high scores reflect collectivistic emphasis by means of laws, social programs, or institutional practices. The collectivism II scale measures in-group (family or organization) collectivism such as pride in and loyalty to family or organization and family or organizational cohesiveness. In lieu of Hofstede's masculinity dimension, the GLOBE researchers developed the two dimensions they labeled gender egalitarianism and assertiveness. Likewise, the future orientation, performance orientation, and humane orientation measures have their origin in past research.[63] These measures are therefore integrative and combine a number of insights from previous studies. Recently, further analysis has been conducted with regard to corporate social responsibility (CSR), a topic discussed in detail in Chapter 3.[64]

GLOBE Country Analysis

The initial results of the GLOBE analysis are presented in Table 4–9. The GLOBE analysis corresponds generally with those of Hofstede and Trompenaars, although with some

Table 4–9
Globe Phases 1, 2, & 3

Purpose	Method	Design strategy	Major results
GLOBE phases 1 & 2 • Design and implement multi-phase and multi-method program to examine the relationship between national culture, leadership effectiveness and societal phenomena • Identify leadership attributes critical for outstanding leadership • Develop societal culture questionnaire • Develop leadership questionnaire	• Involve a total of over 160 researchers from 62 national societies were involved in the research project • Conduct individual and focus group interviews with mid-level managers in domestic organizations • Check items for relevance and understandability • Survey over 17,000 managers representing 951 organizations in 62 cultures	• Employ rigorous psychometric assessment procedures for scale items • Translate and back translate survey instruments in each country • Conduct pilot tests in several countries • Control for common source error in research design • Use rigorous statistical procedures to ensure scales can be aggregated and reliable • Assess cultures and organizations on practices (i.e., as is) and values (should be) • HLM used to test hypotheses (culture to leadership at organizational and societal level)	• Validation of culture and leadership scales • Ranking of 62 societal cultures on 9 culture dimensions • Grouping of 62 cultures into 10 culture clusters • Creation of 21 primary leadership and 6 global leadership scales • Determining relationships between culture dimensions and leadership dimensions • Determination of universally desirable and culturally specific leadership qualities (i.e., CLTs)
GLOBE phase 3 • Determine the manner in which national culture influences executive leadership processes • Examine the relationship between leadership expectations (CLTs) and CEO behavior • Examine the relationship between CEO leadership behavior and effectiveness • Determine which CEO leadership behaviors are most effective	• Involvement of more than 40 researchers in 24 countries • 17 of the 24 countries completed phases 1 and 2 in addition to phase 3 • Interviews and surveys were conducted for 40 CEOs within each country • A total of more than 1000 CEOs and 5000 of their direct reports were respondents in the project • Previously defined leadership qualities from phases 1 and 2 (i.e., CLTs) were converted into behavioral leadership items and combined into scales for phase 3	• Between 6 and 9 direct reports of each CEO assessed the CEOs leadership behaviors, their personal reactions, and firm performance • Common method and response variance eliminated through research design • Internally oriented top management team (TMT) outcomes included commitment, effort, and team solidarity • Externally oriented firm outcomes included competitive sales performance, competitive ROI and competitive domination of the industry	• Leaders tend to behave in a manner expected within their country • Cultural values do NOT have a direct effect on CEO behavior, rather the effect is indirect through CLTs (culturally endorsed theory – i.e., leadership expectations) • Both the fit of CEO behaviors (to expectations) and degree of leadership behavior predict effectiveness • Superior and inferior CEOs exhibit different patterns of behavior within their country

Source: From Peter Dorfman, Mansour Javidan, Paul Hanges, Ali Dastmalchian, and Robert House, "GLOBE: A twenty year journey into the intriguing world of culture and leadership," *Journal of World Business 47*, (2012), p. 505.

variations resulting from the variable definitions and methodology. Hofstede critiqued the GLOBE analysis, pointing out key differences between the research methods; Hofstede was the sole researcher and writer of his findings, while GLOBE consisted of a team of perspectives; Hofstede focused on one institution and surveyed employees, while GLOBE interviewed managers across many corporations, and so on. The disparity of the terminology between these two, coupled with the complex research, makes it challenging to compare and fully reconcile these two approches.[65] Other assessments have pointed out that Hofstede may have provided an introduction into the psychology of culture, but further research is necessary in this changing world. The GLOBE analysis is sometimes seen as complicated, but so are cultures and perceptions. An in-depth understanding of all facets of culture is difficult, if not impossible, to attain, but GLOBE provides a current comprehensive overview of general stereotypes that can be further analyzed for greater insight.[66]

Examination of the GLOBE project has resulted in an extensive breakdown of how managers behave and how different cultures can yield managers with similar perspectives in some realms, with quite divergent opinions in other sectors. One example, as illustrated in Figure 4–9, shows how managers in Brazil compare to managers in the United States in a web structure, based on factors such as individualism, consciousness of social and professional status, and risky behaviors. Brazilian managers are typically class and status conscious, rarely conversing with subordinates on a personal level within or outside of work. They are known for avoiding conflict within groups and risky endeavors and tend to exhibit group dynamics with regard to decision-making processes. Managers in the United States, on the other hand, do not focus intensely on different class or status levels. They are more likely to take risks, and while it appears as though they are more individualistic, the graph

Figure 4–9

GLOBE Analysis: Managerial Perspectives in the United States and Brazil

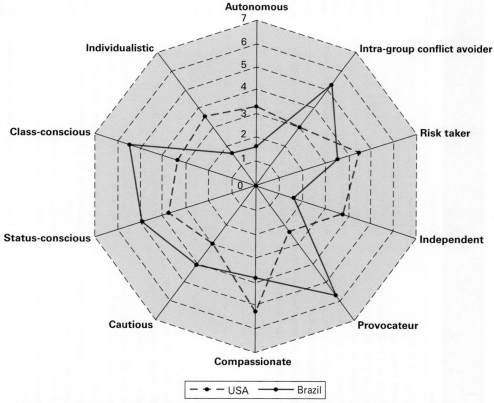

Source: From Mansour Javidan, Peter W. Dorfman et al., "In the Eye of the Beholder: Cross Cultural Lessons in Leadership from Project GLOBE," *Perspectives—Academy of Management 20*, no. 1 (2006), p. 76. Reproduced with permission of Academy of Management via Copyright Clearance Center.

implies a more tolerant attitude than direct single-person-decision-making structure. Here, both Brazil and the United States show how it is important to have group communication on some level. While Americans value mutual respect and open dialogue, Brazilians may see this behavior as unacceptable, even aggressive, if discussion discloses a large amount of information and includes members from different groups; subordinate and managerial positions.[67]

It has been suggested that if Americans are preparing to do business in Brazil, the representatives should spend an ample amount of time getting to know the Brazilian executives. Be sure to show respect for top managers, and inform subordinates of any plans or changes, encouraging feedback. Managers still make the final decisions, and it is very unlikely that workers will provide any suggestions, but they also do not appreciate simply being told what to do. In other words, family structures, including in-group structures, are very important to Brazilians, but the head of the household still has the last word. Finally, stress short-term, risk-aversive goals to maintain vision and interest in business proposals.[68]

We will explore additional implications of the GLOBE findings as they relate to managerial leadership in Chapter 13.

■ The World of International Management—Revisited

The discussion of Toyota's problems in the World of International Management that opened this chapter illustrates the importance of culture and how cultural differences may contribute to global management challenges. Cultural distance can influence both positively and negatively how decisions are made, reported, and resolved. Having read this chapter, you should understand the impact culture has on the actions of MNCs, including general management practices and relations with employees and customers, and on maintaining overall reputation.

Recall the chapter opening discussion about Toyota and then draw on your understanding of Hofstede's and Trompenaars's cultural dimensions to answer the following questions: (1) What dimensions contribute to the differences between how Americans and Japanese workers address management problems, including operational or product flaws? (2) What are some ways that Japanese culture may affect operational excellence in a positive way? How might it hurt quality, especially when things go wrong? (3) How could managers from Japan or other Asian cultures adopt practices from U.S. and European cultures when investing in those regions?

SUMMARY OF KEY POINTS

1. Culture is acquired knowledge that people use to interpret experience and generate social behavior. Culture also has the characteristics of being learned, shared, transgenerational, symbolic, patterned, and adaptive. There are many dimensions of cultural diversity, including centralized vs. decentralized decision making, safety vs. risk, individual vs. group rewards, informal vs. formal procedures, high vs. low organizational loyalty, cooperation vs. competition, short-term vs. long-term horizons, and stability vs. innovation.

2. Values are basic convictions that people have regarding what is right and wrong, good and bad, important and unimportant. Research shows that

there are both differences and similarities between the work values and managerial values of different cultural groups. Work values often reflect culture and industrialization, and managerial values are highly related to success. Research shows that values tend to change over time and often reflect age and experience.

3. Hofstede has identified and researched four major dimensions of culture: power distance, uncertainty avoidance, individualism, and masculinity. Recently, he has added a fifth dimension, time orientation and more recently yet, a sixth dimension indulgence vs. restraint: Each will affect a country's political and social system. The integration of these factors into

two-dimensional figures can illustrate the complexity of culture's effect on behavior.

4. In recent years, researchers have attempted to cluster countries into similar cultural groupings to study similarities and differences. Through analyzing the relationship between two dimensions, as Hofstede illustrated, two-dimensional maps can be created to show how countries differ and where they overlap.

5. Research by Trompenaars has examined five relationship orientations: universalism vs. particularism, individualism vs. communitarianism, affective vs. neutral, specific vs. diffuse, and achievement vs. ascription. Trompenaars also looked at attitudes toward time and toward the environment. The result

is a wealth of information helping to explain how cultures differ as well as practical ways in which MNCs can do business effectively in these environments. In particular, his findings update those of Hofstede while helping support the previous work by Hofstede on clustering countries.

6. Recent research undertaken by the GLOBE project has attempted to extend and integrate cultural attributes and variables as they relate to managerial leadership and practice. These analyses confirm much of the Hofstede and Trompenaars research, with greater emphasis on differences in managerial leadership styles.

KEY TERMS

achievement culture, *133*

ascription culture, *133*

collectivism, *121*

communitarianism, *131*

culture, *112*

diffuse culture, *132*

emotional culture, *132*

femininity, *122*

GLOBE, *136*

individualism, *121*

masculinity, *122*

neutral culture, *132*

particularism, *129*

power distance, *120*

specific culture, *132*

uncertainty avoidance, *121*

universalism, *129*

values, *117*

REVIEW AND DISCUSSION QUESTIONS

1. What is meant by the term *culture?* In what way can measuring attitudes about the following help differentiate between cultures: centralized or decentralized decision making, safety or risk, individual or group rewards, high or low organizational loyalty, cooperation or competition? Use these attitudes to compare the United States, Germany, and Japan. Based on your comparisons, what conclusions can you draw regarding the impact of culture on behavior?

2. What is meant by the term *value?* Are cultural values the same worldwide, or are there marked differences? Are these values changing over time, or are they fairly constant? How does your answer relate to the role of values in a culture?

3. What are the four major dimensions of culture studied by Geert Hofstede? Identify and describe each. What is the cultural profile of the United States? Of Asian countries? Of Latin American countries? Of Latin European countries? Based on your comparisons of these four profiles, what conclusions can you draw regarding cultural challenges facing individuals

in one group when they interact with individuals in one of the other groups? Why do you think Hofstede added the fifth dimension of time orientation and the sixth dimension related to indulgence versus restraint?

4. As people engage in more international travel and become more familiar with other countries, will cultural differences decline as a roadblock to international understanding, or will they continue to be a major barrier? Defend your answer.

5. What are the characteristics of each of the following pairs of cultural characteristics derived from Trompenaars's research: universalism vs. particularism, neutral vs. emotional, specific vs. diffuse, achievement vs. ascription? Compare and contrast each pair.

6. How did project GLOBE build on and extend Hofstede's analysis? What unique contributions are associated with project GLOBE?

7. In what way is time a cultural factor? In what way is the need to control the environment a cultural factor? Give an example for each.

INTERNET EXERCISE: RENAULT-NISSAN IN SOUTH AFRICA

The Renault-Nissan alliance, established in March 1999, is the first industrial and commercial partnership of its kind involving a French company and a Japanese company. The Alliance invested more than 1 billion rand in upgrading Nissan's manufacturing plant in Rosslyn, outside Pretoria, to increase output and produce the Nissan NP200 pickup and the Renault Sandero for the South African market. Visit the Renault-Nissan website at http://www.renault.com to see where factories reside for each car group. Compare and contrast the similarities and differences in these markets. Then answer these three questions: (1) How do you think cultural differences affect the way the firm operates in South Africa versus France versus Japan? (2) In what way is culture a factor in auto sales? (3) Is it possible for a car company to transcend national culture and produce a global automobile that is accepted by people in every culture? Why or why not?

In the
International
Spotlight

South Africa

South Africa, as the name reflects, is located on the far southern tip of the African continent. It is surrounded by water on three sides: in the south and in the west by the Atlantic Ocean, and in the east by the Indian Ocean. Neighboring countries are Zimbabwe, Swaziland, Botswana, Namibia, and Lesotho. The form of government is a presidential democracy. South Africa has three capitals: Pretoria, Cape Town, and Bloemfontein. The country is 1,219,080 square kilometers. The population (in 2011) was 50.6 million people. GDP in 2011 was $408.2 billion, with per capita income at $8,070.

South Africa is known as the "Rainbow Nation," a title that reflects its cultural diversity and the fact that the country's population is one of the most diverse and complex in the world. Of the total population, about 31 million are Black, 5 million White, 3 million Coloured, and 1 million Indian. The Black population covers four major ethnic groups consisting of Nguni, Sotho, Shangaan-Tsonga, and Venda. There are a number of subgroups; the Zulu and Xhosa are the largest subgroups of the Nguni. The majority of the White population has Afrikaans roots, and 40 percent are of British descent. In South Africa eleven official languages are spoken.

The most significant characteristic of South Africa's modern history was apartheid, a system of legal racial segregation enforced by the Nationalist Party between 1948 and 1994, under which the rights of the majority nonwhite population were curtailed in all avenues of life. Apartheid sparked significant tension and violence internally as well as a UN trade embargo against South Africa. A series of popular uprisings and protests were met with the banning of opposition and imprisonment of anti-apartheid leaders, including Nobel Peace Prize winner Nelson Mandela. Reforms to apartheid in the 1980s failed to quell the mounting opposition, and in 1990 President Frederik Willem de Klerk began negotiations to end apartheid, culminating in multiracial democratic elections in 1994, which were won by the African National Congress under Nelson Mandela.

One feature of post-apartheid South Africa was the program Black Economic Empowerment (BEE) designed to redress the inequalities of apartheid by giving previously disadvantaged groups (Black Africans, Coloureds, Indians, and Chinese) economic opportunities previously not available to them. It has included measures such as employment equity; skills development; ownership, management, and socioeconomic development; and preferential procurement.

The BEE is not free of criticism; many claim the program has caused qualified white expertise to leave for areas where they would not be discriminated against. Inkatha Freedom Party leader Mangosu-thu Buthelezi has stated that "the government's reckless implementation of the affirmative action policy is forcing many white people to leave the country in search of work, creating a skills shortage crisis." Archbishop Desmond Tutu has warned that South Africa is sitting on a "powder keg" because millions are living in "dehumanising poverty" stating that Black Economic Empowerment only serves an elite few.

The 2010 World Cup Soccer tournament put South Africa on the international stage and provided significant economic stimulus, with more than 160,000 new jobs created. An economist of the German Standard Bank said: "The World Championship 2010 is an important impulse for the South African people. Many people doubted that South Africa would be able to host an event of such international attention, but its stable political situation under the government of the African National Congress, which Nelson Mandela was a member of, is a good sign for potential investors and the finance market." In advance of the games, South Africa invested heavily in transportation infrastructure. South Africa finished most of the first section of their new high-speed Gautrain passenger railway and installed new bus lines. Highways have been upgraded, and the city of Durban managed to complete South Africa's first new greenfield airport in 50 years. The infrastructure projects are creating employment opportunities and are providing workers long-term skills and training. One of many challenges in building the infrastructure for the World Championship was generating power without an unduly adverse environmental impact. Environmentally friendly features such as natural ventilation and rain water capture systems were used in the new stadium facilities.

Despite these developments and improvements, South Africa is still plagued by severe social problems such as pervasive poverty, lack of infrastructure in Black African areas, AIDS, crime, and corruption.

Although South Africa is a transactional culture, meaning they do not require a history with people in order to do business, they are a personable people that have deeply rooted traditions. This means it is a good idea to build a rapport with them before doing business as well as furnish counterparts with some background information about oneself or company. South Africans follow the European approach to personal space, meaning people keep their distance when speaking and interacting in the public space.

www.southafrica.info, www.kwintessential.co.uk, www. infoplease.com, data.worldbank.org

Questions

1. In what way could the huge cultural diversity in South Africa pose challenges for MNCs seeking to set up a business there?

2. How is South African culture different from or similar to U.S. culture?

3. In what ways could South Africa benefit from hosting the World Cup in the long term?

4. What do you think are the most pressing social issues in South Africa and how is the country doing in resolving them?

Chapter 5

MANAGING ACROSS CULTURES

Traditionally, both scholars and practitioners assumed the universality of management. There was a tendency to take the management concepts and techniques that worked at home into other countries and cultures. It is now clear, from both practice and cross-cultural research, that this universality assumption, at least across cultures, does not hold up. Although there is a tendency in a borderless economy to promote a universalist approach, there is enough evidence from many cross-cultural researchers to conclude that the universalist assumption that may have held for U.S. organizations and employees is not generally true in other cultures.[1]

The overriding purpose of this chapter is to examine how MNCs can and should manage across cultures. This chapter puts into practice Chapter 4's discussion on the meaning and dimensions of culture and serves as a foundation and point of departure for Chapters 8 and 9 on strategic management. The first part of this chapter addresses the traditional tendency to attempt to replicate successful home-country operations overseas without taking into account cultural differences. Next, attention is given to cross-cultural challenges, focusing on how differences can impact multinational management strategies. Finally, the cultures in specific countries and geographic regions are examined. The specific objectives of this chapter are:

1. **EXAMINE** the strategic dispositions that characterize responses to different cultures.

2. **DISCUSS** cross-cultural differences and similarities.

3. **REVIEW** cultural differences in select countries and regions, and note some of the important strategic guidelines for doing business in each.

The World of *International Management*

Apple v. Samsung: Comparing Corporate Culture

Constituting 50 percent of the global market share, Samsung and Apple have achieved unmatched success in the smartphone industry. Culturally, however, these two companies could not be more different. Their approach to innovation, the supply chain, product lines, and even their ideas about intellectual property rights are diametrically opposed. How have these two incredibly different companies achieved such similar levels of success, and which corporate culture will ultimately win the smartphone battle?

Individual versus the Collective

At Apple, individual achievement is highly regarded. Innovating for the company, as an individual, is expected and required. In fact, according to an urban legend, Steve Jobs once fired an employee in the elevator for not having an answer to the question, "So what have you done for Apple lately?" Personal excellence is required by every employee, with an overall focus on end results and exceeding corporate goals.[2] Internal competition, and challenging others, is strongly encouraged. Hierarchy exists, but individuals are encouraged to speak up if it means achieving a better, more innovative product. According to a former employee, "There's a mentality that it's okay to shred somebody in the spirit of making the best products."[3]

Collectivism and group achievement, on the other hand, permeate Samsung's corporate culture. At Samsung, employees are expected "to fall in line."[4] Working together to achieve the corporate goals is valued above individual innovation. With a strong hierarchy that sets the direction of the company, product innovation is often overruled by managers. Creativity is secondary to achieving the preset corporate goals. This focus on group achievement has enabled Samsung to quickly respond to new Apple products and counter with changes to its product line. With the collective group working together, new products can be designed and produced within months.[5] For many at Samsung, the "group" identity has even spread beyond the work environment. The personal and professional lives of employees often blend together, with some employees choosing to live in dormitories right on the factory campuses.[6]

Supply Chain Management

The approach to the supply chain and manufacturing processes at Samsung and Apple could not be more different. Apple has been able to maximize profits through its complex, yet carefully doctored, supply chain. To minimize costs, Apple outsources the majority of its production processes. Nearly a thousand factories produce components for Apple across the globe, with over 600 in Southeast Asia alone.[7] As a result of its low manufacturing costs, Apple is able to sell the majority of its products with a 70 percent gross profit margin. Relinquishing its control over the manufacturing process, however, has led to some major negative consequences for Apple. In 2012, Apple was unable to meet customer demand for the iPad Mini due to supply chain issues that resulted in lower-than-expected production numbers.[8] Furthermore, the lack of control over its suppliers' actions has exposed Apple to criticism over human rights violations. Highly publicized worker suicides and alleged underage labor have tarnished Apple's image, even though the abuses occurred at the suppliers' facilities.

Samsung, on the contrary, maintains direct control over most of its supply chain processes. Over 90 percent of its products are manufactured within its own factories across South Korea and China. As a result, Samsung's workforce has swelled to over 200,000 employees. This internal manufacturing system results in smaller profit margins and higher overhead costs. However, organizationally, Samsung is able to retain some key advantages by maintaining control over manufacturing. For example, the company can quickly adapt production to meet demand, cutting some costs and avoiding time-sensitive errors. Manufacturing internally has also given Samsung the ability to maintain oversight of its employee's wages and hours, allowing the company to largely avoid the public relations nightmares

and accusations of human rights violations that have plagued Apple's supply chain. Additionally, when Samsung has excess capacity, the company has the ability to manufacture for its competition—including Apple.[9]

Product Focus

Apple is dedicated to maintaining first-mover advantage. As a result, Apple focuses narrowly on a few key products, with little variation in features and price. The iPhone, for example, is the only phone offered by Apple. When purchasing the latest Apple product, customers know that they are buying the most current technology on the market. By continually being the first to market with new technology, Apple is able to maintain a loyal customer base that is willing to put up with minor defects and flaws in design. This narrow product focus has created a trendy "brand" image for the company. However, by only offering one product line, Apple sacrifices sales to potential customers who are less concerned with the latest technology.

Unlike Apple, Samsung offers a wide array of products at multiple price points. With over a dozen different phone products, for example, customers can sacrifice features and the most current technology for a phone within their budget. Samsung is willing to quickly try multiple products, altering production as customers trend toward specific phones.[10] Knowing that it cannot compete for the first-mover customers who want the newest technology fastest, Samsung focuses on being "first to follow" Apple, rather than first to market. For example, Samsung's Galaxy offers many of the same features as the Apple iPhone. Though released several months after the iPhone, Samsung's Galaxy was able to sell to customers who valued technology but were not as brand focused or time-sensitive as the typical Apple customer.

Intellectual Property

Differences in product development have led directly to recent legal conflicts between the two companies. Cultural differences regarding intellectual property rights have perhaps been the most publicized. Apple, having spent millions in research and development for new technology and improved designs, has accused Samsung of essentially stealing patent-protected technology. Samsung claims that it is developing its own technology, and that Apple has infringed its technology as well.

As a component manufacturer for Apple products, Samsung has benefited from getting a direct look at Apple's newest innovations before they hit the market. Furthermore, by knowing what technology Apple is launching in its latest round of products, Samsung has basically been given Apple's strategic roadmap. This has undoubtedly given Samsung the ability to respond more rapidly to Apple's innovation.[11]

In 2012 alone, Apple and Samsung launched over a dozen lawsuits against each other, primarily over patent infringements. Contested issues range from component technology to software design. The South Korean and Japanese rulings largely favored Samsung, while the U.S. lawsuits ended in wins for Apple. According to Apple, protecting its patents allows it to provide "distinctive products that stand apart from the masses," while Samsung claims that these patents result in "fewer choices, less innovation, and potentially higher prices" for customers.[12]

Looking Forward—Which Strategy Is Working?

Whether Apple or Samsung ultimately wins the smartphone battle is yet to be seen. The first-mover advantage that Apple has leveraged since 2007 has all but disappeared. In 2011, Samsung surpassed Apple in smartphone sales for the first time.[13] Samsung achieved 21.8 percent of the global smartphone market share in 2012, while Apple took 15.1 percent. Samsung's growth rate is also escalating; shipments of new smartphones grew by 97.5 percent in 2012, far eclipsing the 38.3 percent growth of Apple. And in 2013, Samsung ranked first for smartphone brand loyalty, knocking Apple off of the number one position for the first time.[14]

Despite Samsung's gains, Apple maintains one huge advantage—profits. In 2012, despite selling 20 million fewer phones than Samsung, Apple posted profits that were 43 percent greater.[15] Whether or not Apple will be able to maintain its finely-tuned supply chain and high profit margin is yet to be seen.

The cultural differences of Samsung and Apple highlight how, within the same industry, two companies can achieve similar levels of success despite opposing strategies. This chapter provides insight into uncovering similarities and differences across cultures and using those insights to develop international management approaches that are effective and responsive to local cultures.

■ The Strategy for Managing across Cultures

As MNCs become more transnational, their strategies must address the cultural similarities and differences in their varied markets. A good example is provided by Renault, the French auto giant. For years Renault manufactured a narrow product line that it sold primarily in France. Because of this limited geographic market and the fact that its cars continued to have quality-related problems, the company's performance was at best mediocre. Several years ago, however, Renault made a number of strategic decisions that dramatically changed the way it did business. Among other things, it bought controlling stakes in Nissan Motors of Japan, Samsung Motors of South Korea, and Dacia, the Romanian automaker. The company also built a $1 billion factory in Brazil to produce its successful Mégane sedan and acquired an idle factory near Moscow to manufacture Renaults for the Eastern European market.

Today, Renault is a multinational automaker with operations on four continents. The challenge the company now faces is to make all these operations profitable. This has not been easy. Nissan's profits are unpredictable, and while it has had a good run since 1999, profits plummeted in 2007. Experiencing a net income loss of 234 billion yen in 2009, Nissan has since rebounded with net incomes of 42 billion yen in 2010, 319 billion yen in 2011, and 341 billion yen in 2012. Similarly, Renault, experiencing a net loss of 3.13 billion euros in 2009, has rebounded to net incomes of 3.55 billion euros and 2.65 billion euros in 2010 and 2011, respectively.[16] In a world market that contracted 4.7 percent in 2009, the Renault Group was down just 3.1 percent, with sales of 2.309 million vehicles. Renault's quest for greater global market share continues to progress, with world market share up to 3.6 percent in 2011. In the passenger car market, the Renault Group reported market share of 4.0 percent.[17] The Renault brand reclaimed the position of third-ranked brand in Western Europe mainly owing to the success of the Mégane family and Twingo. In the light commercial vehicle (LCV) market, the Renault brand has been the number-one brand in Western Europe since 1998.

Dacia has manufactured what some call a genuine world car, known as the Logan. Now sold in 36 countries, this simple, compact vehicle is sold at an affordable price in European markets and has recently been introduced in India. Renault maintains innovative strategies by offering the Logan under either the Dacia, Renault, or Nissan name, depending on the market. Constituting 17 percent of Renault's total sales volume in Western Europe in 2012, Dacia's healthy 9.0 percent operating margin far exceeded the 0.4 percent operating margin of Renault as a whole. The decision to integrate its sales organizations with those of Nissan in Europe, thus creating one well-integrated, efficient sales force on the continent, and the decision to start producing Nissan models in its Brazilian plant, so that it can expand its South American offerings by more efficiently using current facilities, have led to continual growth year-over-year.[18]

In 2012, Renault announced plans for an ultra-low-cost compact car for India. Scheduled to enter production in 2014, the new low-cost car will be priced to compete directly with Hyundai's Eon, currently priced at US$5,500.[19] On the 10th year of the Renault-Nissan alliance, the Group called attention to a number of milestones achieved over that period:

- Growth in sales from 4,989,709 units in 1999 to 6,090,304 in 2008.
- Common platforms and common parts: sales of cars using common platforms among the two firms represented more than 50 percent of the vehicles sold by Renault and Nissan globally in 2008.
- Achievement of the Renault-Nissan Purchasing Organization (RNPO); RNPO is the Alliance's largest common organization, negotiating with parts suppliers on behalf of Renault and Nissan.
- Exchanges of powertrains and common powertrains; in total, eight engines are commonly used.
- Expansion of the portfolio of advanced technologies.
- Manufacturing standardization.
- Cross production.
- Global footprint—Renault and Nissan cover key markets on all continents.
- Expansion of product line-ups.
- Cross-cultural management.[20]

Regarding this last issue (cross-cultural management), the Renault-Nissan Alliance has sought to foster multicultural management at all levels. Each year, more than 30 teams with Renault and Nissan employees from all regions and functions work together to identify synergies and best practices. Thousands of people with cross-cultural experience have been in collaboration since the beginning of the Alliance. Renault's chief Carlos Ghoshen, who also serves as CEO of Nissan Motor Co., is widely credited with both the operational and strategic improvements at both Renault and Nissan. His multicultural and multinational upbringing and career have convinced him of the value of cultural diversity and the creativity they generate.

Renault's recent experiences underscore the need to carefully consider different national cultures and practices when developing international strategies.

Strategic Predispositions

Most MNCs have a cultural strategic predisposition toward doing things in a particular way. Four distinct predispositions have been identified: ethnocentric, polycentric, regiocentric, and geocentric.

A company with an **ethnocentric predisposition** allows the values and interests of the parent company to guide strategic decisions. Firms with a **polycentric predisposition** make strategic decisions tailored to suit the cultures of the countries where the MNC operates. A **regiocentric predisposition** leads a firm to try to blend its own interests with those of its subsidiaries on a regional basis. A company with a **geocentric predisposition**

ethnocentric predisposition
A nationalistic philosophy of management whereby the values and interests of the parent company guide strategic decisions.

polycentric predisposition
A philosophy of management whereby strategic decisions are tailored to suit the cultures of the countries where the MNC operates.

regiocentric predisposition
A philosophy of management whereby the firm tries to blend its own interests with those of its subsidiaries on a regional basis.

most common

geocentric predisposition
A philosophy of management whereby the company tries to integrate a global systems approach to decision making.

Table 5–1
Orientation of an MNC Under Different Profiles

	Orientation of the Firm			
	Ethnocentric	**Polycentric**	**Regiocentric**	**Geocentric**
Mission	Profitability (viability)	Public acceptance (legitimacy)	Both profitability and public acceptance (viability and legitimacy)	Same as regiocentric
Governance	Top-down	Bottom-up (each subsidiary decides on local objectives)	Mutually negotiated between region and its subsidiaries	Mutually negotiated at all levels of the corporation
Strategy	Global integration	National responsiveness	Regional integration and national responsiveness	Global integration and national responsiveness
Structure	Hierarchical product divisions	Hierarchical area divisions, with autonomous national units	Product and regional organization tied through a matrix	A network of organizations (including some stakeholders and competitor organizations)
Culture	Home country	Host country	Regional	Global
Technology	Mass production	Batch production	Flexible manufacturing	Flexible manufacturing
Marketing	Product development determined primarily by the needs of home country customers	Local product development based on local needs	Standardize within region, but not across regions	Global product, with local variations
Finance	Repatriation of profits to home country	Retention of profits in host country	Redistribution within region	Redistribution globally
Personnel practices	People of home country developed for key positions everywhere in the world	People of local nationality developed for key positions in their own country	Regional people developed for key positions anywhere in the region	Best people everywhere in the world developed for key positions everywhere in the world

Source: From Balaji S. Chakravarthy and Howard V. Perlmutter, "Strategic Planning for a Global Business," *Columbia Journal of World Business,* Summer 1985, pp. 5–6. Copyright © 1985 Elsevier. Reprinted with permission.

tries to integrate a global systems approach to decision making. Table 5–1 provides details of each of these orientations.

If an MNC relies on one of these profiles over an extended time, the approach may become institutionalized and greatly influence strategic planning. By the same token, a predisposition toward any of these profiles can provide problems for a firm if it is out of step with the economic or political environment. For example, a firm with an ethnocentric predisposition may find it difficult to implement a geocentric strategy, because it is unaccustomed to using global integration. Commonly, successful MNCs use a mix of these predispositions based on the demands of the current environment described in the chapters in Part One.

Meeting the Challenge

globalization imperative
A belief that one worldwide approach to doing business is the key to both efficiency and effectiveness.

Despite the need for and, in general, the tendency of MNCs to address regional differentiation issues, many MNCs remain committed to a **globalization imperative**, which is a belief that one worldwide approach to doing business is the key to both efficiency and effectiveness. However, despite this predilection to use home strategies, effective MNCs are continuing their efforts to address local needs. A number of factors are moving companies to facilitate the development of unique strategies for different cultures, including:

1. The diversity of worldwide industry standards such as those in broadcasting, where television sets must be manufactured on a country-by-country basis.

2. A continual demand by local customers for differentiated products, as in the case of consumer goods that must meet local tastes.

3. The importance of being an insider, as in the case of customers who prefer to "buy local."

4. The difficulty of managing global organizations, as in the case of some local subsidiaries that want more decentralization and others that want less.

5. The need to allow subsidiaries to use their own abilities and talents and not be restrained by headquarters, as in the case of local units that know how to customize products for their market and generate high returns on investment with limited production output.

Responding to the cultural needs of local operations and customers, MNCs find that regional strategies can be used effectively in capturing and maintaining worldwide market niches. One example is Haier, which you may become more familiar with after completing the Internet Exercise at the end of the chapter. One of the best examples is Warner-Lambert, which has manufacturing facilities in Belgium, France, Germany, Italy, Ireland, Spain, and the United Kingdom. Each plant is specialized and produces a small number of products for the entire European market; in this way, each can focus on tailoring products for the unique demands of the various markets.

The globalization versus national responsiveness challenge is even more acute when marketing cosmetics and other products that vary greatly in consumer use. For example, marketers sell toothpaste as a cosmetic product in Spain and Greece but as a cavity fighter in the Netherlands and United States. Soap manufacturers market their product as a cosmetic item in Spain but as a functional commodity in Germany. Moreover, the way in which the marketing message is delivered also is important. For example:

- Germans want advertising that is factual and rational; they fear being manipulated by "the hidden persuader." The typical German spot features the standard family of two parents, two children, and grandmother.

- The French avoid reasoning or logic. Their advertising is predominantly emotional, dramatic, and symbolic. Spots are viewed as cultural events—art for the sake of money—and are reviewed as if they were literature or films.

- The British value laughter above all else. The typical broad, self-deprecating British commercial amuses by mocking both the advertiser and consumer.[21]

In some cases, however, both the product and the marketing message are similar worldwide. This is particularly true for high-end products, where the lifestyles and expectations of the market niche are similar regardless of the country. Heineken beer, Hennessey brandy, Porsche cars, and the Financial Times all appeal to consumer niches that are fairly homogeneous, regardless of geographic locale. The same is true at the lower end of the market for goods that are impulse purchases, novel products, or fast foods, such as Coca-Cola's soft drinks, Levi's jeans, pop music, and ice-cream bars. In most cases, however, it is necessary to modify products as well as the market approach for the regional or local market. One analysis noted that the more marketers understand about the way in which a particular culture tends to view emotion, enjoyment, friendship, humor, rules, status, and other culturally based behaviors, the more control they have over creating marketing messages that will be interpreted in the desired way.

Figure 5–1 provides an example of the role that culture should play in advertising by recapping the five relationship orientations identified through Trompenaars's research (see Chapter 4). Figure 5–1 shows how value can be added to the marketing approach by carefully tailoring the advertising message to the particular culture. For example, advertising in the United States should target individual achievement, be expressive and direct, and appeal to U.S. values of success through personal hard work. On the other hand, the focus in China and other Asian countries should be much more indirect and subtle, emphasizing group references, shared responsibility, and interpersonal trust.

Figure 5–1

Trompenaar's Cultural Dimensions and Advertising: Adjusting the Message for Local Meaning

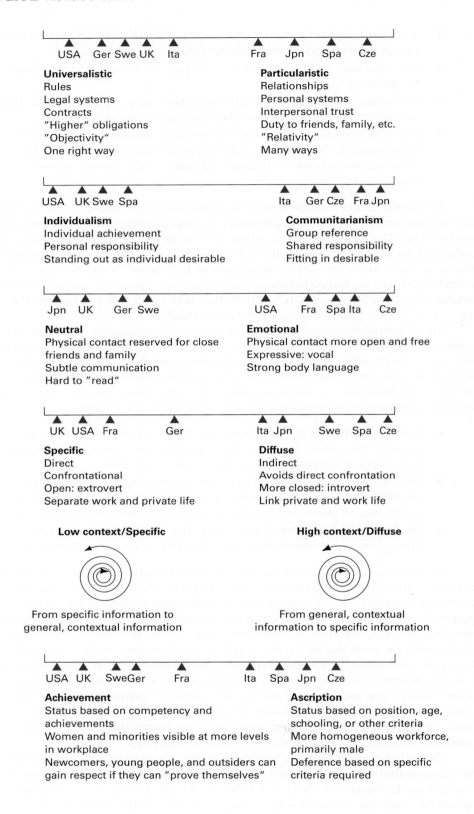

Universalistic
Rules
Legal systems
Contracts
"Higher" obligations
"Objectivity"
One right way

Particularistic
Relationships
Personal systems
Interpersonal trust
Duty to friends, family, etc.
"Relativity"
Many ways

Individualism
Individual achievement
Personal responsibility
Standing out as individual desirable

Communitarianism
Group reference
Shared responsibility
Fitting in desirable

Neutral
Physical contact reserved for close friends and family
Subtle communication
Hard to "read"

Emotional
Physical contact more open and free
Expressive: vocal
Strong body language

Specific
Direct
Confrontational
Open: extrovert
Separate work and private life

Diffuse
Indirect
Avoids direct confrontation
More closed: introvert
Link private and work life

Low context/Specific

From specific information to general, contextual information

High context/Diffuse

From general, contextual information to specific information

Achievement
Status based on competency and achievements
Women and minorities visible at more levels in workplace
Newcomers, young people, and outsiders can gain respect if they can "prove themselves"

Ascription
Status based on position, age, schooling, or other criteria
More homogeneous workforce, primarily male
Deference based on specific criteria required

Source: Lisa Hoecklin, *Managing Cultural Differences: Strategies for Competitive Advantage* (Workingham, England: Addison-Wesley, 1995), p. 107, which is drawn from information found in Fons Trompenaars, *Riding the Waves of Culture.* Copyright © 1994 McGraw-Hill Education. Reprinted by permission of McGraw-Hill Education.

Ten Key Factors for MNC Success

Why are some international firms successful while others are not? Some of the main reasons are that successful multinational firms take a worldwide view of operations, support their overseas activities, pay close attention to political winds, and use local nationals whenever possible. These are the overall findings of a report that looked into the development of customized executive education programs. Specifically, there are 10 factors or guidelines that successful global firms seem to employ. Successful global competitors:

1. See themselves as multinational enterprises and are led by a management team that is comfortable in the world arena.

2. Develop integrated and innovative strategies that make it difficult and costly for other firms to compete.

3. Aggressively and effectively implement their worldwide strategy and back it with large investments.

4. Understand that innovation no longer is confined to the United States and develop systems for tapping innovation abroad.

5. Operate as if the world were one large market rather than a series of individual, small markets.

6. Have organization structures that are designed to handle their unique problems and challenges and thus provide them the greatest efficiency.

7. Develop a system that keeps them informed about political changes around the world and the implications of these changes on the firm.

8. Have management teams that are international in composition and thus better able to respond to the various demands of their respective markets.

9. Allow their outside directors to play an active role in the operation of the enterprise.

10. Are well managed and tend to follow such important guidelines as sticking close to the customer, having lean organization structures, and encouraging autonomy and entrepreneurial activity among the personnel.

The need to adjust global strategies for regional markets presents three major challenges for most MNCs. First, the MNC must stay abreast of local market conditions and sidestep the temptation to assume that all markets are basically the same. Second, the MNC must know the strengths and weaknesses of its subsidiaries so that it can provide these units with the assistance needed in addressing local demands. Third, the multinational must give the subsidiary more autonomy so that it can respond to changes in local demands. The International Management in Action, "Ten Key Factors for MNC Success," provides additional insights into the ways that successful MNCs address these challenges.

■ Cross-Cultural Differences and Similarities

As you saw in Chapter 4, cultures can be similar or quite different across countries. The challenge for MNCs is to recognize and effectively manage the similarities and differences. Generally, the way in which MNCs manage their home businesses often should be different from the way they manage their overseas operations.[22] After recognizing the danger for MNCs of drifting toward parochialism and simplification in spite of cultural differences, the discussion in this section shifts to some examples of cultural similarities and differences and how to effectively manage across cultures by a *contingency approach.*

Parochialism and Simplification

Parochialism is the tendency to view the world through one's own eyes and perspectives. This can be a strong temptation for many international managers, who often come from advanced economies and believe that their state-of-the-art knowledge is more than adequate to handle the challenges of doing business in less developed countries. In addition,

parochialism
The tendency to view the world through one's own eyes and perspectives.

many of these managers have a parochial point of view fostered by their background.[23] A good example is provided by Randall and Coakley, who studied the impact of culture on successful partnerships in the former Soviet Union. Initially after the breakup of the Soviet Union, the republics called themselves the Commonwealth of Independent States (CIS). Randall and Coakley found that while outside MNC managers typically entered into partnerships with CIS enterprises with a view toward making them efficient and profitable, the CIS managers often brought a different set of priorities to the table.

Commenting on their research, Randall and Coakley noted that the way CIS managers do business is sharply different from that of their American counterparts. CIS managers are still emerging from socially focused cultural norms embedded in their history, past training, and work experiences which emphasize strategic values unlike those that exist in an international market-driven environment. For example, while an excess of unproductive workers may lead American managers to lay off some individuals for the good of the company, CIS managers would focus on the good of the working community and allow the company to accept significant profit losses as a consequence. This led the researchers to conclude:

> As behavioral change continues to lag behind structural change, it becomes imperative to understand that this inconsistency between what economic demands and cultural norms require manifests problems and complexities far beyond mere structural change. In short, the implications of the different perspectives on technology, labor, and production . . . for potential partnerships between U.S. and CIS companies need to be fully grasped by all parties entering into any form of relationship.[24]

simplification
The process of exhibiting the same orientation toward different cultural groups.

Simplification is the process of exhibiting the same orientation toward different cultural groups. For example, the way in which a U.S. manager interacts with a British manager is the same way in which he or she behaves when doing business with an Asian executive. Moreover, this orientation reflects one's basic culture. Table 5–2 provides an example, showing several widely agreed-on, basic cultural orientations and the range of variations for each. Asterisks indicate the dominant U.S. orientation. Quite obviously, U.S. cultural values are not the same as those of managers from other cultures; as a result, a U.S. manager's attempt to simplify things can result in erroneous behavior. Here is an example of a member of the purchasing department of a large European oil company who was negotiating an order with a Korean supplier:

> At the first meeting, the Korean partner offered a silver pen to the European manager. The latter, however, politely refused the present for fear of being bribed (even though he knew about the Korean custom of giving presents). Much to our manager's surprise, the second meeting began with the offer of a stereo system. Again the manager refused, his fear of being bribed probably heightened. When he gazed at a piece of Korean china on the third meeting, he finally realized what was going on. His refusal had not been taken to mean "let's get on with business right away," but rather "If you want to get into business with me, you had better come up with something bigger."[25]

Understanding the culture in which they do business can make international managers more effective.[26] Unfortunately, when placed in a culture with which they are unfamiliar, most international managers are not culturally knowledgeable, so they often misinterpret what is happening. This is particularly true when the environment is markedly different from the one from which they come. Consider, for example, the difference between the cultures in Malaysia and the United States. Malaysia has what could be called a high-context culture, which possesses characteristics such as:

1. Relationships between people are relatively long lasting, and individuals feel deep personal involvement with each other.
2. Communication often is implicit, and individuals are taught from an early age to interpret these messages accurately.
3. People in authority are personally responsible for the actions of their subordinates, and this places a premium on loyalty to both superiors and subordinates.

Table 5–2
Six Basic Cultural Variations

Orientations	Range of Variations
What is the nature of people?	Good (changeable/unchangeable)
	A mixture of good and evil*
	Evil (changeable/unchangeable)
What is the person's relationship to nature?	Dominant*
	In harmony with nature
	Subjugation
What is the person's relationship to other people?	Lineal (hierarchic)
	Collateral (collectivist)
	Individualist*
What is the modality of human activity?	Doing*
	Being and becoming
	Being
What is the temporal focus of human activity?	Future*
	Present
	Past
What is the conception of space?	Private*
	Mixed
	Public

Note: *Indicates the dominant U.S. orientation.
Source: Adapted from the work of Florence Rockwood Kluckhohn and Fred L. Stodtbeck.

4. Agreements tend to be spoken rather than written.
5. Insiders and outsiders are easily distinguishable, and outsiders typically do not gain entrance to the inner group.

These Malaysian cultural characteristics are markedly different from those of low-context cultures such as the United States, which possess the following characteristics:

1. Relationships between individuals are relatively short in duration, and in general, deep personal involvement with others is not valued greatly.
2. Messages are explicit, and individuals are taught from a very early age to say exactly what they mean.
3. Authority is diffused throughout the bureaucratic system, and personal responsibility is hard to pin down.
4. Agreements tend to be in writing rather than spoken.
5. Insiders and outsiders are not readily distinguished, and the latter are encouraged to join the inner circle.[27]

These differences are exacerbated by the fact that Malaysian culture is based on an amalgamation of diverse religions, including Hinduism, Buddhism, and Islam. The belief is pervasive that success and failure are the will of God, which may create issues with American managers attempting to make deals, as Malaysians will focus less on facts and more on intuitive feelings.[28]

At the same time, it is important to realize that while there are cultural differences, there also are similarities. Therefore, in managing across cultures, not everything is totally different. Some approaches that work at home also work well in other cultural settings.

Similarities across Cultures

When internationalization began to take off in the 1970s, many companies quickly admitted that it would not be possible to do business in the same way in every corner of the globe. There was a secret hope, however, that many of the procedures and strategies that worked so well at home could be adopted overseas without modification. This has proved to be a false hope. At the same time, some similarities across cultures have been uncovered by researchers. For example, a co-author of this text (Luthans) and his associates studied through direct observation a sample of managers in the largest textile factory in Russia to determine their activities. Like U.S. managers studied earlier, Russian managers carried out traditional management, communication, human resources, and networking activities. The study also found that, as in the United States, the relative attention given to the networking activity increased the Russian managers' opportunities for promotion, and that communication activity was a significant predictor of effective performance in both Russia and the United States.[29]

Besides the similarities of managerial activities, another study at the same Russian factory tested whether organizational behavior modification (O.B.Mod.) interventions that led to performance improvements in U.S. organizations would do so in Russia.[30] As with the applications of O.B.Mod. in the United States, Russian supervisors were trained to administer social rewards (attention and recognition) and positive feedback when they observed workers engaging in behaviors that contributed to the production of quality fabric. In addition, Russian supervisors were taught to give corrective feedback for behaviors that reduced product quality. The researchers found that this O.B.Mod. approach, which had worked so well in the United States, produced positive results in the Russian factory. They concluded that the hypothesis that "the class of interventions associated with organizational behavior modification are likely to be useful in meeting the challenges faced by Russian workers and managers [is] given initial support by the results of this study."[31]

In another cross-cultural study, this time using a large Korean sample, Luthans and colleagues analyzed whether demographic and situational factors identified in the U.S.-based literature had the same antecedent influence on the commitment of Korean employees.[32] As in the U.S. studies, Korean employees' position in the hierarchy, tenure in their current position, and age all related to organizational commitment. Other similarities with U.S. firms included (1) as organizational size increased, commitment declined; (2) as structure became more employee-focused, commitment increased; and (3) the more positive the perceptions of organizational climate, the greater the employee commitment. The following conclusion was drawn:

> This study provides beginning evidence that popular constructs in the U.S. management and organizational behavior literature should not be automatically dismissed as culture bound. Whereas some organizational behavior concepts and techniques do indeed seem to be culture specific . . . a growing body of literature is demonstrating the ability to cross-culturally validate other concepts and techniques, such as behavior management. . . . This study contributed to this cross-cultural evidence for the antecedents to organizational commitment. The antecedents for Korean employees' organizational commitment were found to be similar to their American counterparts.[33]

Many Differences across Cultures

We have stressed throughout the text how different cultures can be from one another and how important it is for MNCs to understand the points of disparity. Here, we look at some differences from a human resources perspective, a topic which will be covered in depth in Chapter 14. We introduce human resource management (HRM) here as a way to illustrate that the cultural foundations utilized in the selection of employees can further form the culture that international managers will oversee. In other words, understanding the HRM strategies before becoming a manager in the industry can aid in effective performance. The focus here is more from a socially cultural perspective; the organizational perspective will be discussed further in Chapter 14.

Despite similarities between cultures in some studies, far more differences than similarities have been found. MNCs are discovering that they must carefully investigate and understand the culture where they intend to do business and modify their approaches appropriately. Sometimes these cultures are quite different from the United States—as well as from each other! One human resource management example has been offered by Trompenaars, who examined the ways in which personnel in international subsidiaries were appraised by their managers. The head office had established the criteria to be used in these evaluations but left the prioritization of the criteria to the national operating company. As a result, the outcome of the evaluations could be quite different from country to country because what was regarded as the most important criterion in one subsidiary might be ranked much lower on the evaluation list of another subsidiary. In the case of Shell Oil, for example, Trompenaars found that the firm was using a HAIRL system of appraisal. The five criteria in this acronym stood for (a) helicopter—the capacity to take a broad view from above; (b) analysis—the ability to evaluate situations logically and completely; (c) imagination—the ability to be creative and think outside the box; (d) reality—the ability to use information realistically; and (e) leadership—the ability to effectively galvanize and inspire personnel. When staff in Shell's operating companies in four countries were asked to prioritize these five criteria from top to bottom, the results were as follows:

Netherlands	France	Germany	Britain
Reality	Imagination	Leadership	Helicopter
Analysis	Analysis	Analysis	Imagination
Helicopter	Leadership	Reality	Reality
Leadership	Helicopter	Imagination	Analysis
Imagination	Reality	Helicopter	Leadership

Quite obviously, personnel in different operating companies were being evaluated differently. In fact, no two of the operating companies in the four countries had the same criterion at the top of their lists. Moreover, the criterion at the top of the list for operating companies in the Netherlands—reality—was at the bottom of the list for those in France; and the one at the top of the list in French operating companies—imagination—was at the bottom of the list of the Dutch firms. Similarly, the German operating companies put leadership at the top of the list and helicopter at the bottom, while the British companies did the opposite! In fact, the whole list for the Germans is in the exact reverse order of the British list.[34]

Other HRM differences can be found in areas such as wages, compensation, pay equity, and maternity leave. Here are some representative examples.

1. The concept of an hourly wage plays a minor role in Mexico. Labor law requires that employees receive full pay 365 days a year.

2. In Austria and Brazil, employees with one year of service are automatically given 30 days of paid vacation.

3. Some jurisdictions in Canada have legislated pay equity—known in the United States as comparable worth—between male- and female-intensive jobs.

4. In Japan, compensation levels are determined by using the objective factors of age, length of service, and educational background rather than skill, ability, and performance. Performance does not count until after an employee reaches age 45.

5. In the United Kingdom, employees are allowed up to 40 weeks of maternity leave, and employers must provide a government-mandated amount of pay for 18 of those weeks.

6. In 87 percent of large Swedish companies, the head of human resources is on the board of directors.[35]

These HRM practices certainly are quite different from those in the United States, and U.S. MNCs need to modify their approaches when they go into these countries if they hope to be successful. Compensation plans, in particular, provide an interesting area of contrast across different cultures.

Drawing on the work of Hofstede (see Chapter 4), it is possible to link cultural clusters and compensation strategies. Table 5–3 shows a host of different cultural groupings, including some in Asia, the EU, and Anglo countries. Each cluster requires a different approach to formulating an effective compensation strategy, and after analyzing each such cluster, we suggest that:

1. In Pacific Rim countries, incentive plans should be group-based. In high-masculinity cultures (Japan, Hong Kong, Malaysia, the Philippines, Singapore), high salaries should be paid to senior-level managers.

2. In EU nations such as France, Spain, Italy, and Belgium, compensation strategies should be similar. In the latter two nations, however, significantly higher salaries should be paid to local senior-level managers because of the high masculinity index. In Portugal and Greece, both of which have a low individualism index, profit-sharing plans would be more effective than individual incentive plans, while in Denmark, the Netherlands, and Germany, personal-incentive plans would be highly useful because of the high individualism in these cultures.

3. In Great Britain, Ireland, and the United States, managers value their individualism and are motivated by the opportunity for earnings, recognition, advancement, and challenge. Compensation plans should reflect these needs.[36]

Figure 5–2 shows how specific HRM areas can be analyzed contingently on a country-by-country basis. Take, for example, the information on Japan. When it is contrasted with U.S. approaches, a significant number of differences are found. Recruitment

---

Table 5–3
Cultural Clusters in the Pacific Rim, EU, and United States

	Power Distance	Individualism	Masculinity	Uncertainty Avoidance
Pacific Rim				
Hong Kong, Malaysia, Philippines, Singapore	+	−	+	−
Japan	+	−	+	+
South Korea, Taiwan	+	−	−	+
EU and United States				
France, Spain	+	+	−	+
Italy, Belgium	+	+	+	+
Portugal	+	−	−	+
Greece	+	−	+	+
Denmark, Netherlands	−	+	+	−
Germany	−	+	+	+
Great Britain, Ireland, United States	−	−	+	+

Note: + indicates high or strong; − indicates low or weak.

Source: Based on research by Hofstede and presented in Richard M. Hodgetts and Fred Luthans, "U.S. Multinationals' Compensation Strategies for Local Management: Cross-Cultural Implications," *Compensation and Benefits Review,* March–April 1993, p. 47. Reproduced with permission of Sage Publications, Inc. via Copyright Clearance Center.

| Figure 5–2 | | A Partially Completed Contingency Matrix for International Human Resource Management | | |

	Japan	Germany	Mexico	China
Recruitment and selection	• Prepare for long process • Ensure that your firm is "here to stay" • Develop trusting relationship with recruit	• Obtain skilled labor from government subsidized apprenticeship program	• Use expatriates sparingly • Recruit Mexican nationals at U.S. colleges	• Recent public policy shifts encourage use of sophisticated selection procedures
Training	• Make substantial investment in training • Use general training and cross-training • Training is everyone's responsibility	• Reorganize and utilize apprenticeship programs • Be aware of government regulations on training	• Use bilingual trainers	• Careful observations of existing training programs • Utilize team training
Compensation	• Use recognition and praise as motivator • Avoid pay for performance	• Note high labor costs for manufacturing	• Consider all aspects of labor cost	• Use technical training as reward • Recognize egalitarian values • Use "more work more pay" with caution
Labor relations	• Treat unions as partners • Allow time for negotiations	• Be prepared for high wages and short work week • Expect high productivity from unionized workers	• Understand changing Mexican labor law • Prepare for increasing unionization of labor	• Tap large pool of labor cities • Lax labor laws may become more stringent
Job design	• Include participation • Incorporate group goal setting • Use autonomous work teams • Use uniform, formal approaches • Encourage co-worker input • Empower teams to make decision	• Utilize works councils to enhance worker participation	• Approach participation cautiously	• Determine employee's motives before implementing participation

Source: From Fred Luthans, Paul A. Marsnik, and Kyle W. Luthans, "A Contingency Matrix Approach to IHRM," *Human Resource Management Journal* 36, no. 2, 1997. Reprinted with permission of John Wiley & Sons, Inc.

and selection in Japanese firms often are designed to help identify those individuals who will do the best job over the long run. In the United States, people often are hired based on what they can do for the firm in the short run, because many of them eventually will quit or be downsized. Similarly, the Japanese use a great deal of cross-training, while the Americans tend to favor specialized training. The Japanese use group performance appraisal and reward people as a group; at least traditionally, Americans use manager-subordinate performance appraisal and reward people as individuals. In Japan, unions are regarded as partners; in the United States, management and unions view each other in a much more adversarial way. Only in the area of job design, where the Japanese use a great deal of participative management and autonomous work teams, are the Americans beginning to employ a similar approach. The same types of differences can be seen in the matrix of Figure 5–2 among Japan, Germany, Mexico, and China.

These differences should not be interpreted to mean that one set of HRM practices is superior to another. In fact, recent research from Japan and Europe shows these firms often have a higher incidence of personnel-related problems than do U.S. companies. Figure 5–2 clearly indicates the importance of MNCs' using a contingency approach to HRM across cultures. Not only are there different HRM practices in different cultures, but there also are different practices within the same cultures. For instance, one study involving 249 U.S. affiliates of foreign-based MNCs found that in general, affiliate HRM practices closely follow local practices when dealing with the rank and file but even more closely approximate parent-company practices when dealing with upper-level management.[37] In other words, this study found that a hybrid approach to HRM was being used by these MNCs.

Aside from the different approaches used in different countries, it is becoming clear that common assumptions and conventional wisdom about HRM practices in certain countries no longer are valid. For example, for many years, it has been assumed that Japanese employees do not leave their jobs for work with other firms, that they are loyal to their first employer, and that it would be virtually impossible for MNCs operating in Japan to recruit talent from Japanese firms. Recent evidence, however, reveals that job-hopping among Japanese employees is increasingly common. One report concluded:

> While American workers, both the laid-off and the survivors, grapple with cutbacks, one in three Japanese workers willingly walks away from his job within the first 10 years of his career, according to the Japanese Institute of Labor, a private research organization. And many more are thinking about it. More than half of salaried Japanese workers say they would switch jobs or start their own business if a favorable opportunity arose, according to a survey by the Recruit Research Corporation.[38]

These findings clearly illustrate one important point: Managing across cultures requires careful understanding of the local environment, because common assumptions and stereotypes may not be valid. Cultural differences must be addressed, and this is why cross-cultural research will continue to be critical in helping firms learn how to manage across cultures.[39]

■ Cultural Differences in Selected Countries and Regions

As noted in Part One and in Chapter 4, MNCs are increasingly active in all parts of the world, including the developing and emerging regions because of their recent growth and future potential. Chapter 4 introduced the concept of country clusters, which is the idea that certain regions of the world have similar cultures. For example, the way that Americans do business in the United States is very similar to the way that British do business in England. Even in this Anglo culture, however, there are pronounced differences, and in other clusters, such as in Asia, these differences become even more pronounced. The International Management in Action, "Managing in Hong Kong," depicts such differences. The next sections focus on cultural highlights and differences in selected countries and regions that provide the necessary understanding and perspective for effective management across cultures.

One interesting development is the increasing frequency of managers and executives from one part of the world assuming leadership roles in another. For example, in 2008 Aozora Bank hired Brian Prince as their new CEO, becoming one of only a few—but an increasing number—of foreign heads of Japanese firms who now include Eva Chen of Trend Micro and Carlos Ghoshen of Nissan Motor Co. Foreign CEOs still face cultural difficulties, however. At Nippon Sheet Glass, for example, American Craig Naylor resigned suddenly in 2012 after just two years as CEO. Naylor cited "fundamental disagreements

Managing across cultures has long been recognized as a potential problem for multinationals. To help expatriates who are posted overseas deal with a new culture, many MNCs offer special training and coaching. Often, however, little is done to change expatriates' basic cultural values or specific managerial behaviors. Simply put, this traditional approach could be called the *practical school of management thought,* which holds that effective managerial behavior is universal and a good manager in the United States also will be effective in Hong Kong or any other location around the world. In recent years, it generally has been recognized that such an approach no longer is sufficient, and there is growing support for what is called the *cross-cultural school of management thought,* which holds that effective managerial behavior is a function of the specific culture. As Black and Porter pointed out, successful managerial action in Los Angeles may not be effective in Hong Kong.

Black and Porter investigated the validity of these two schools of thought by surveying U.S. managers working in Hong Kong, U.S. managers working in the United States, and Hong Kong managers working in Hong Kong. Their findings revealed some interesting differences. The U.S. managers in Hong Kong exhibited managerial behaviors similar to those of their counterparts back in the United States; however, Hong Kong managers had managerial behaviors different from either group of U.S. managers. Commenting on these results, the researchers noted:

This study . . . points to some important practical implications. It suggests that American firms and the practical school of thought may be mistaken in the assumption that a good manager in Los Angeles will necessarily do fine in Hong Kong or some other foreign country. It may be that because firms do not include in their selection criteria individual characteristics such as cognitive flexibility, cultural flexibility, degree of ethnocentricity, etc., they end up sending a number of individuals on international assignments who have a tendency to keep the same set of managerial behaviors they used in the U.S. and not adjust or adapt to the local norms and practices. Including the measurement of these characteristics in the selection process, as well as providing cross-cultural training before departure, may be a means of obtaining more effective adaptation of managerial behaviors and more effective performance in overseas assignments.

Certainly the study shows that simplistic assumptions about culture are erroneous and that what works in one country will not necessarily produce the desired results in another. If MNCs are going to manage effectively throughout the world, they are going to have to give more attention to training their people about intercultural differences.

with the board on company strategy" as the key reason for his departure.[40] Chapters 13 and 14 provide an in-depth discussion of leadership and human resource management across cultures, respectively. Because of the increasing importance of developing and emerging regions and countries in the global economy, knowledge of these contexts is more and more important for global managers. In a study by the China Europe International Business School's Leadership Behavioral Laboratory and the Center for Creative Leadership, executives identified critical characteristics in their careers that contributed to their development as managers in emerging markets settings. These included setting an example for junior employees and learning to thrive in unstable environments.[41] In addition, managers emphasized the importance of learning about their business and the emerging markets environment, through formal classes, mentoring, and direct experience.

Doing Business in China

The People's Republic of China (PRC or China, for short) has had a long tradition of isolation. In 1979, Deng Xiaoping opened this country to the world. Although his bloody 1989 put-down of protesters in Tiananmen Square was a definite setback for progress, China is rapidly trying to close the gap between itself and economically advanced nations and to establish itself as a power in the world economy. As noted in Chapter 1, China is actively trading in world markets, is a member of the WTO, and is a major trading partner of the United States. Despite this global presence, many U.S. and European multinationals still find that doing business in the PRC can be a long, grueling process.[42] Very few outside firms have yet to make a profit in China. One primary reason is that Western-based MNCs do not appreciate the important role and impact of Chinese culture.

Experienced executives report that the primary criterion for doing business in China is technical competence. For example, in the case of MNCs selling machinery, the Chinese want to know exactly how the machine works, what its capabilities are, and how repairs and maintenance must be handled. Sellers must be prepared to answer these questions in precise detail. This is why successful multinationals send only seasoned engineers and technical people to the PRC. They know that the questions to be answered will require both knowledge and experience, and young, fresh-out-of-school engineers will not be able to answer them.

A major cultural difference between the PRC and many Western countries is the issue of time. The Chinese tend to be punctual, so it is important that those who do business with them arrive on time, as discussed in Chapter 4. During meetings, such as those held when negotiating a contract, the Chinese may ask many questions and nod their assent at the answers. This nodding usually means that they understand or are being polite; it seldom means that they like what they are hearing and want to enter into a contract. For this reason, when dealing with the Chinese, one must keep in mind that patience is critically important. The Chinese will make a decision in their own good time, and it is common for outside businesspeople to make several trips to China before a deal is finally concluded. Moreover, not only are there numerous meetings, but sometimes these are unilaterally cancelled at the last minute and rescheduled. This often tries the patience of outsiders and is inconvenient in terms of rearranging travel plans and other problems.

guanxi
Chinese for "good connections."

Another important dimension of Chinese culture is **guanxi**, which means "good connections."[43] In turn, these connections can result in such things as lower costs for doing business.[44] Yet guanxi goes beyond just lower costs. Yi and Ellis surveyed Hong Kong and PRC Chinese managers and found that both groups agreed that guanxi networking offered a number of potential benefits, including increased business, higher sales revenue, more sources of information, greater prospecting opportunities, and the facilitation of future transactions.[45] In practice, guanxi resembles nepotism, where individuals in authority make decisions on the basis of family ties or social connections rather than objective indices. Tung has reported:

> In a survey of 2,000 Chinese from Shanghai and its surrounding rural community, 92 percent of the respondents confirmed that guanxi played a significant role in their daily lives. Furthermore, the younger generation tended to place greater emphasis on guanxi. In fact, guanxi has become more widespread in the recent past. . . . Most business practitioners who have experience in doing business with East Asians will readily agree that in order to succeed in these countries "who you know is more important than what you know." In other words, having connections with the appropriate individuals and authorities is often more crucial than having the right product and/or price.[46]

Additionally, outsiders doing business in China must be aware that Chinese people will typically argue that they have the guanxi to get a job done, when in reality they may or may not have the necessary connections.

In China, it is important to be a good listener. This may mean having to listen to the same stories about the great progress that has been made by the PRC over the past decade. The Chinese are very proud of their economic accomplishments and want to share these feelings with outsiders.

When dealing with the Chinese, one must realize they are a collective society in which people pride themselves on being members of a group. This is in sharp contrast to the situation in the United States and other Western countries, where individualism is highly prized. For this reason, one must never single out a Chinese and praise him or her for a particular quality, such as intelligence or kindness, because doing so may embarrass the individual in the presence of his or her peers. It is equally important to avoid using self-centered conversation, such as excessive use of the word "I," because it appears that the speaker is trying to single him- or herself out for special consideration.

The Chinese also are much less animated than Westerners. They avoid open displays of affection, do not slap each other on the back, and are more reticent, retiring, and reserved than North or South Americans. They do not appreciate loud, boisterous behavior, and when speaking to each other, they maintain a greater physical distance than is typical in the West.

Cultural highlights that affect doing business in China can be summarized and put into some specific guidelines as follows:

1. The Chinese place values and principles above money and expediency.[47]

2. Business meetings typically start with pleasantries such as tea and general conversation about the guest's trip to the country, local accommodations, and family. In most cases, the host already has been briefed on the background of the visitor.

3. When a meeting is ready to begin, the Chinese host will give the appropriate indication. Similarly, when the meeting is over, the host will indicate that it is time for the guest to leave.

4. Once the Chinese decide who and what are best, they tend to stick with these decisions. Therefore, they may be slow in formulating a plan of action, but once they get started, they make fairly good progress.

5. In negotiations, reciprocity is important. If the Chinese give concessions, they expect some in return. Additionally, it is common to find them slowing down negotiations to take advantage of Westerners' desire to conclude arrangements as quickly as possible. The objective of this tactic is to extract further concessions. Another common ploy used by the Chinese is to pressure the other party during final arrangements by suggesting that this counterpart has broken the spirit of friendship in which the business relationship originally was established. Again, through this ploy, the Chinese are trying to gain additional concessions.

6. Because negotiating can involve a loss of face, it is common to find Chinese carrying out the whole process through intermediaries. This allows them to convey their ideas without fear of embarrassment.[48]

7. During negotiations, it is important not to show excessive emotion of any kind. Anger or frustration, for example, is viewed as antisocial and unseemly.

8. Negotiations should be viewed with a long-term perspective. Those who will do best are the ones who realize they are investing in a long-term relationship.[49]

While these are the traditional behaviors of Chinese businesspeople, the transitioning economy (see Chapter 1) has also caused a shift in business culture, which has affected working professionals' private lives. Performance, which was once based on effort, is now being evaluated from the angle of results as the country continues to maintain its flourishing profits. While traditional Chinese culture focused on family first, financial and material well-being has become a top priority. This performance orientation has increased stress and contributed to growing incidence of burnout, depression, substance abuse, and other ailments. Some U.S. companies have attempted to curb these psychological ailments by offering counseling; however, this service is not as readily accepted by the Chinese. Instead of bringing attention to the "counseling" aspect, firms instead promote "workplace harmony" and "personal well-being services."[50] This suggests that while some aspects of Chinese culture are changing, international managers must recognize the foundational culture of the country and try to deal with such issues according to local beliefs.

Doing Business in Russia

As pointed out in Chapter 1, the Russian economy has experienced severe problems, and the risks of doing business there cannot be overstated. At the same time, however, by following certain guidelines, MNCs can begin to tap the potential opportunities. Here are some suggestions for being successful in Russia:

1. Build personal relationships with partners. Business laws and contracts do not mean as much in Russia as they do in the West. When there are

contract disputes, there is little protection for the aggrieved party because of the time and effort needed to legally enforce the agreement. Detailed contracts can be hammered out later on; in the beginning, all that counts is friendship.

2. Use local consultants. Because the rules of business have changed so much in recent years, it pays to have a local Russian consultant working with the company. Russian expatriates often are not up to date on what is going on and, quite often, are not trusted by local businesspeople who have stayed in the country. So the consultant should be someone who has been in Russia all the time and understands the local business climate.

3. Consider business ethics. Ethical behavior in the United States is not always the same as in Russia. For example, it is traditional in Russia to give gifts to those with whom one wants to transact business, an approach that may be regarded as bribery in the United States.

4. Be patient. In order to get something done in Russia, it often takes months of waiting. Those who are in a hurry to make a quick deal are often sorely disappointed.

5. Stress exclusivity. Russians like exclusive arrangements and often negotiate with just one firm at a time. This is in contrast to Western businesspeople who often "shop" their deals and may negotiate with a half-dozen firms at the same time before settling on one.

6. Remember that personal relations are important. Russians like to do business face to face. So when they receive letters or faxes, they often put them on their desk but do not respond to them. They are waiting for the businessperson to contact them and set up a personal meeting.

7. Keep financial information personal. When Westerners enter into business dealings with partners, it is common for them to share financial information with these individuals and to expect the same from the latter. However, Russians wait until they know their partner well enough to feel comfortable before sharing financial data. Once trust is established, then this information is provided.

8. Research the company. In dealing effectively with Russian partners, it is helpful to get information about this company, its management hierarchy, and how it typically does business. This information helps ensure the chances for good relations because it gives the Western partner a basis for establishing a meaningful relationship.

9. Stress mutual gain. The Western idea of "win-win" in negotiations also works well in Russia. Potential partners want to know what they stand to gain from entering into the venture.

10. Clarify terminology. For-profit business deals are new in Russia, so the language of business is just getting transplanted there. As a result, it is important to double-check and make sure that the other party clearly understands the proposal, knows what is expected and when, and is agreeable to the deal.[51]

11. Be careful about compromising or settling things too quickly, because this is often seen as a sign of weakness. During the Soviet Union days, everything was complex, and so Russians are suspicious of anything that is conceded easily. If agreements are not reached after a while, a preferred tactic on their part is to display patience and then wait it out. However, they will abandon this approach if the other side shows great patience because they will realize that their negotiating tactic is useless.

12. Written contracts are not as binding to Russians as they are to Westerners. Like Asians, Russians view contracts as binding only if they continue to be mutually beneficial. One of the best ways of dealing with this is to be able to continually show them the benefits associated with sticking to the deal.[52]

These 12 steps can be critical to the success of a business venture in Russia. They require careful consideration of cultural factors, and it often takes a lot longer than initially anticipated. However, the benefits may be worth the wait. And when everything is completed, there is a final cultural tradition that should be observed: Fix and reinforce the final agreements with a nice dinner together and an invitation to the Russians to visit your country and see your facilities.[53]

Doing Business in India

In recent years, India has begun to attract the attention of large MNCs. Unsaturated consumer markets, coupled with cheap labor and production locations, have helped make India a desirable market for global firms. The government continues to play an important role in this process, although recently many of the bureaucratic restrictions have been lifted as India works to attract foreign investment and raise its economic growth rate.[54] In addition, although most Indian businesspeople speak English, many of their values and beliefs are markedly different from those in the West. Thus, understanding Indian culture is critical to successfully doing business in India.

Shaking hands with male business associates is almost always an acceptable practice. U.S. businesspeople in India are considered equals, however, and the universal method of greeting an equal is to press one's palms together in front of the chest and say namaste, which means "greetings to you." Therefore, if a handshake appears to be improper, it always is safe to use namaste.

Western food typically is available in all good hotels. Most Indians do not drink alcoholic beverages, or if they do, they tend to prefer liquor and avoid the popular Western choice of beer, and many are vegetarians or eat chicken but not beef. Therefore, when foreign businesspeople entertain in India, the menu often is quite different from that back home. Moreover, when a local businessperson invites an expatriate for dinner at home, it is not necessary to bring a gift, although it is acceptable to do so. The host's wife and children usually will provide help from the kitchen to ensure that the guest is well treated, but they will not be at the table. If they are, it is common to wait until everyone has been seated and the host begins to eat or asks everyone to begin. During the meal, the host will ask the guest to have more food. This is done to ensure that the person does not go away hungry; however, once one has eaten enough, it is acceptable to politely refuse more food.

For Western businesspeople in India, shirt, trousers, tie, and suit are proper attire. In the southern part of India, where the climate is very hot, a light suit is preferable. In the north during the winter, a light sweater and jacket are a good choice. Indian businesspeople, on the other hand, often will wear local dress. In many cases, this includes a dhoti, which is a single piece of white cloth (about five yards long and three feet wide) that is passed around the waist up to half its length and then the other half is drawn between the legs and tucked at the waist. Long shirts are worn on the upper part of the body. In some locales, such as Punjab, Sikhs will wear turbans, and well-to-do Hindus sometimes will wear long coats like the Rajahs. This coat, known as a sherwani, is the dress recognized by the government for official and ceremonial wear. Foreign businesspeople are not expected to dress like locals, and in fact, many Indian businesspeople will dress like Europeans. Therefore, it is unnecessary to adopt local dress codes.

When doing business in India, one will find a number of other customs useful to know, such as:

1. It is important to be on time for meetings.

2. Personal questions should not be asked unless the other individual is a friend or close associate.

3. Titles are important, so people who are doctors or professors should be addressed accordingly.

4. Public displays of affection are considered to be inappropriate, so one should refrain from backslapping or touching others.

5. Beckoning is done with the palm turned down; pointing often is done with the chin.

6. When eating or accepting things, use the right hand because the left is considered to be unclean.

7. The namaste gesture can be used to greet people; it also is used to convey other messages, including a signal that one has had enough food.

8. Bargaining for goods and services is common; this contrasts with Western traditions, where bargaining might be considered rude or abrasive.[55]

Finally, it is important to remember that Indians are very tolerant of outsiders and understand that many are unfamiliar with local customs and procedures. Therefore, there is no need to make a phony attempt to conform to Indian cultural traditions. Making an effort to be polite and courteous is sufficient.[56]

Doing Business in France

Many in the United States believe that it is more difficult to get along with the French than with other Europeans. This feeling probably reflects the French culture, which is markedly different from that in the United States. In France, one's social class is very important, and these classes include the aristocracy, the upper bourgeoisie, the upper-middle bourgeoisie, the middle, the lower middle, and the lower. Social interactions are affected by class stereotypes, and during their lifetime, most French people do not encounter much change in social status. Unlike an American, who through hard work and success can move from the lowest economic strata to the highest, a successful French person might, at best, climb one or two rungs of the social ladder. Additionally, the French are very status conscious, and they like to provide signs of their status, such as knowledge of literature and the arts; a well-designed, tastefully decorated house; and a high level of education.

The French also tend to be friendly, humorous, and sardonic (sarcastic), in contrast to Americans, for example, who seldom are sardonic. The French may admire or be fascinated with people who disagree with them; in contrast, Americans are more attracted to those who agree with them. As a result, the French are accustomed to conflict and during negotiations accept that some positions are irreconcilable and must be accepted as such. Americans, on the other hand, believe that conflicts can be resolved and that if both parties make an extra effort and have a spirit of compromise, there will be no irreconcilable differences. Moreover, the French often determine a person's trustworthiness based on his or her firsthand evaluation of the individual's character. This is in marked contrast to Americans, who tend to evaluate a person's trustworthiness based on past achievements and other people's evaluations of this person.

In the workplace, many French people are not motivated by competition or the desire to emulate fellow workers. They often are accused of not having as intense a work ethic as, for example, Americans or Asians. Many French workers frown on overtime, and statistics show that on average, they have the longest vacations in the world (four to five weeks annually). On the other hand, few would disagree that they work extremely hard in their regularly scheduled time and have a reputation for high productivity. Part of this reputation results from the French tradition of craftsmanship. Part of it also is accounted for by a large percentage of the workforce being employed in small, independent businesses, where there is widespread respect for a job well done.

Most French organizations tend to be highly centralized and have rigid structures. As a result, it usually takes longer to carry out decisions. Because this arrangement is quite different from the more decentralized, flattened organizations in the United States, both middle- and lower-level U.S. expatriate managers who work in French subsidiaries often find bureaucratic red tape a source of considerable frustration. There also are marked differences at the upper levels of management. In French companies, top managers have far more authority than their U.S. counterparts, and they are less accountable for their actions. While top-level U.S. executives must continually defend their decisions to the CEO or board of directors, French executives are challenged only if the company has poor performance. As a result, those who have studied French management find that they take a more autocratic approach.[57]

In countries such as the United States, a great deal of motivation is derived from professional accomplishment. Americans realize there is limited job and social security in their country, so it is up to them to work hard and ensure their future. The French do not have the same view. While they admire Americans' industriousness and devotion to work, they believe that quality of life is what really matters. As a result, they attach a great deal of importance to leisure time, and many are unwilling to sacrifice the enjoyment of life for dedication to work.

The values and beliefs discussed here help to explain why French culture is so different from that in other countries. Some of the sharp contrasts with the United States, for example, provide insights regarding the difficulties of doing business in France. Additional cultural characteristics, such as the following, may act as guides in situations outsiders may encounter in France:

1. When shaking hands with a French person, use a quick shake with some pressure in the grip. A firm, pumping handshake, which is so common in the United States, is considered to be uncultured.

2. It is extremely important to be on time for meetings and social occasions. Being "fashionably late" is frowned on.

3. During a meal, it is acceptable to engage in pleasant conversation, but personal questions and the subject of money are never brought up.

4. Great importance is placed on neatness and taste. Therefore, visiting businesspeople should try very hard to be cultured and sophisticated.[58]

5. The French tend to be suspicious of early friendliness in the discussion and dislike first names, taking off jackets, or disclosure of personal or family details.

6. In negotiations the French try to find out what all of the other side's aims and demands are at the beginning, but they reveal their own hand only late in the negotiations.

7. The French do not like being rushed into making a decision, and they rarely make important decisions inside the meeting. In fact, the person who is ultimately responsible for making the decision is often not present.

8. The French tend to be very precise and logical in their approach to things, and will often not make concessions in negotiations unless their logic has been defeated. If a deadlock results, unlike Americans, who will try to break the impasse by suggesting a series of compromises by both sides, the French tend to remain firm and simply restate their position.[59]

Doing Business in Brazil

Brazil is considered a Latin American country, but it is important to highlight this nation since some characteristics make it markedly different to manage as compared to other Latin American countries.[60] Brazil was originally colonized by Portugal, and remained affiliated with its parent country until 1865. Even though today Brazil is extremely multicultural, the country still demonstrates many attributes derived from its Portuguese heritage, including its official language. For example, the Brazilian economy was once completely centrally controlled like many other Latin American countries, yet was motivated by such Portuguese influences as flexibility, tolerance, and commercialism.[61] This may be a significant reason behind its successful economic emergence.

Brazilians have a relaxed work ethic, often respecting those who inherit wealth and have strong familial roots over those seeking entrepreneurial opportunities. They view time in a very relaxed manner, so punctuality is not a strong suit in this country. Overall, the people are very good-natured and tend to avoid confrontation, yet they seek out risky endeavors.

Here are some factors to consider when pursuing business in Brazil:

1. Physical contact is acceptable as a form of communication. Brazilians tend to stand very close to others when having a conversation, and will touch the person's back, arm, or elbow as a greeting or sign of respect.

2. Face-to-face interaction is preferred as a way to communicate, so avoid simply e-mailing or calling. Do not be surprised if meetings begin anywhere from 10 to 30 minutes after the scheduled time, since Brazilians are not governed by the clock. Greet with a pleasant demeanor, and accept any offering of cafezinho, or small cups of Brazilian coffee, as it is one indication of a relaxed, social setting.

3. Brazilians tend not to trust others, so be sure to form a strong relationship before bringing up business issues. Be yourself, and be honest, since rigid exteriors or putting on a show is not revered. Close relationships are extremely important, since they will do anything for friends, hence the expression, "For friends, everything. For enemies, the law." Showing interest in their personal and professional life is greatly appreciated, especially if international representatives speak some Portuguese.

4. Appearance is very important, as it will reflect both you and your company. Be sure to have polished shoes. Men should wear conservative dark suits, shirts, and ties. Women should dress nicely, but avoid too conservative or formal attire. Think fashion. Brazilian managers often wonder, for example, if Americans make so much money, why do they dress like they are poor?

5. Patience is key. Many processes are long and drawn out, including negotiations. Expressing frustration or impatience and attempting to speed up procedures may lose the deal. It is worth waiting out, as Brazilians will be very committed and loyal once an agreement is reached.

6. The slow processes and relaxed atmosphere do not imply that it is acceptable to be ill-prepared. Presentations should be informative and expressive, as Brazilians respond to such emotional cues. Consistency is important. Be prepared to state your case multiple times. It is common for Brazilians to bring a lot of people to attend negotiations, mostly to observe and learn. Subsequent meetings may include members of higher management, requiring a rehashing of information.[62]

Doing Business in Arab Countries

The intense media attention given to the Iraq War, terrorist actions, and continuing conflicts in the Middle East have perhaps revealed to everyone that Arab cultures are distinctly different from Anglo cultures.[63] Americans often find it extremely hard to do business in Arab countries, and a number of Arab cultural characteristics can be cited for this difficulty.

One is the Arab view of time. In the United States, it is common to use the cliché, "Time is money." In Arab countries, a favorite expression is *Bukra insha Allah,* which means "Tomorrow if God wills," an expression that explains the Arabs' fatalistic approach to time. Arabs believe that Allah controls time, in contrast to Westerners, who believe that they control their own time. As a result, if Arabs commit themselves to a date in the future and fail to show up, they feel no guilt or concern because they believe they have no control over time in the first place.

(This is perhaps a good point in our discussion to provide a word of caution on overgeneralizing about cultures, which is needed here and in all the examples in this chapter's discussion of cultural characteristics. There are many Arabs who are very particular about promises and appointments. There are also many Arabs who are very proactive and not fatalistic. The point is that there are always exceptions, and stereotyping in cross-cultural dealings is unwarranted. In this chapter we reviewed general cultural characteristics, but from your own experience you know the importance of an understanding of the particular individuals or situations you are dealing with.)

An Arab cultural belief that generally holds is that destiny depends more on the will of a supreme being than on the behavior of individuals. A higher power dictates the outcome of important events, so individual action is of little consequence. This thinking affects not only Arabs' aspirations but also their motivation. Also of importance is that the status of Arabs largely is determined by family position and social contact and connections, not necessarily by their own accomplishments. This view helps to explain why some Middle Easterners take great satisfaction in appearing to be helpless. In fact, helplessness can be used as a source of power, for in this area of the world, the strong are resented and the weak compensated. Here is an example:

> In one Arab country, several public administrators of equal rank would take turns meeting in each other's offices for their weekly conferences, and the host would serve as chairman. After several months, one of these men had a mild heart attack. Upon his recovery, it was decided to hold the meetings only in his office, in order not to inconvenience him. From then on, the man who had the heart attack became the permanent chairman of the conference. This individual appeared more helpless than the others, and his helplessness enabled him to increase his power.[64]

This approach is quite different from that in the United States, where the strong tend to be compensated and rewarded. If a person was ill, such as in this example, the individual would be relieved of his responsibility until he or she had regained full health. In the interim, the rest of the group would go on without the sick person, and he or she might lose power.

Another important cultural contrast between Arabs and Americans is that of emotion and logic. Arabs often act based on emotion; in contrast, those in an Anglo culture are taught to act on logic. Many Arabs live in unstable environments where things change constantly, so they do not develop trusting relationships with others. Americans, on the other hand, live in a much more predictable environment and develop trusting relationships with others.

Arabs also make wide use of elaborate and ritualized forms of greetings and leave-takings. A businessperson may wait past the assigned meeting time before being admitted to an Arab's office. Once there, the individual may find many others present; this situation is unlike the typical one-on-one meetings that are so common in the United States. Moreover, during the meeting, there may be continuous interruptions, visitors may arrive and begin talking to the host, and messengers may come in and go out on a regular basis. The businessperson is expected to take all this activity as perfectly normal and remain composed and ready to continue discussions as soon as the host is prepared to do so.

Business meetings typically conclude with an offer of coffee or tea. This is a sign that the meeting is over and that future meetings, if there are to be any, should now be arranged.

Unlike the case in many other countries, titles are not in general use on the Arabian Peninsula, except in the case of royal families, ministers, and high-level military officers. Additionally, initial meetings typically are used to get to know the other party. Business-related discussions may not occur until the third or fourth meeting. Also, in contrast to the common perception among many Western businesspeople who have never been to an Arab country, it is not necessary to bring the other party a gift. If this is done, however, it should be a modest gift. A good example is a novelty or souvenir item from the visitor's home country.

Arabs attach a great deal of importance to status and rank. When meeting with them, one should pay deference to the senior person first. It also is important never to criticize or berate anyone publicly. This causes the individual to lose face, and the same is true for the person who makes these comments. Mutual respect is required at all times.

Other useful guidelines for doing business in Arab cultures include:

1. It is important never to display feelings of superiority, because this makes the other party feel inferior. No matter how well someone does something, the individual should let the action speak for itself and not brag or put on a show of self-importance.

2. One should not take credit for joint efforts. A great deal of what is accomplished is a result of group work, and to indicate that one accomplished something alone is a mistake.

3. Much of what gets done is a result of going through administrative channels in the country. It often is difficult to sidestep a lot of this red tape, and efforts to do so can be regarded as disrespect for legal and governmental institutions.

4. Connections are extremely important in conducting business. Well-connected businesspeople can get things done much faster than their counterparts who do not know the ins and outs of the system.

5. Patience is critical to the success of business transactions. This time consideration should be built into all negotiations, thus preventing one from giving away too much in an effort to reach a quick settlement.

6. Important decisions usually are made in person, not by correspondence or telephone. This is why an MNC's representative's personal presence often is a prerequisite for success in the Arab world. Additionally, while there may be many people who provide input on the final decision, the ultimate power rests with the person at the top, and this individual will rely heavily on personal impressions, trust, and rapport.[65]

The World of International Management—Revisited

Management at many companies and in many countries is becoming more and more multicultural, yet individual corporate cultures persist. Apple and Samsung are both examples of highly successful companies with radically different approaches to strategy and management. Apple prides itself on groundbreaking innovation, individual achievement, and excellence. At Samsung, the emphasis is on extending innovations and applications and on group achievement and collective responsibility, all geared toward company-wide success. The two companies even take a very different approach to their supply chains, with Apple outsourcing the entirety of its production, while Samsung manufactures more than 90 percent of its products in company-owned factories. In terms of products, Apple is a first-mover, while Samsung is a "fast follower." In some ways, these two companies epitomize the cultures from which they emanate, but both are now global players.

Cross-border investments by Chinese, Indian, and other developing-country firms have prompted investing firms especially in Europe and North America to more thoughtfully consider cultural issues as they seek to integrate local companies and employees into their global organizations. As we saw in Chapter 4, East Asian, U.S., and Western European cultures differ on many dimensions, which may pose challenges for companies seeking to operate across these geographical/cultural boundaries.

Now that you have read this chapter, you should have a good understanding of the importance and the difficulties of managing across cultures. Using this knowledge as a platform, answer the following questions: (1) Which aspects of Apple's culture have helped it succeed in its global growth and which may have impeded it? (2) Which aspects of Samsung's culture have helped it succeed in its global growth and which may have impeded it? (3) How would you characterize Apple and Samsung in terms of the four basic strategic predispositions? (4) What might Apple learn from Samsung and Samsung learn from Apple?

SUMMARY OF KEY POINTS

1. One major problem facing MNCs is that they sometimes attempt to manage across cultures in ways similar to those of their home country. MNC dispositions toward managing across cultures can be characterized as (1) ethnocentric, (2) polycentric, (3) regiocentric, and (4) geocentric. These different approaches shape how companies adapt and adjust to cultural pressures around the world.

2. One major challenge when dealing with cross-cultural problems is that of overcoming parochialism and simplification. Parochialism is the tendency to view the world through one's own eyes and perspectives. Simplification is the process of exhibiting the same orientation toward different cultural groups. Another problem is that of doing things the same way in foreign markets as they are done in domestic markets. Research shows that in some cases, this approach can be effective; however, effective cross-cultural

management more commonly requires approaches different than those used at home. One area where this is particularly evident is human resource management. Recruitment, selection, training, and compensation often are carried out in different ways in different countries, and what works in the United States may have limited value in other countries and geographic regions.

3. Doing business in various parts of the world requires the recognition and understanding of cultural differences. Some of these differences revolve around the importance the society assigns to time, status, control of decision making, personal accomplishment, and work itself. These types of cultural differences help to explain why effective managers in China or Russia often are quite different from those in France, and why a successful style in the United States will not be ideal in Arab countries.

KEY TERMS

ethnocentric predisposition, *149*

geocentric predisposition, *149*

globalization imperative, *150*

guanxi, *162*

parochialism, *153*

polycentric predisposition, *149*

regiocentric predisposition, *149*

simplification, *154*

REVIEW AND DISCUSSION QUESTIONS

1. Define the four basic predispositions MNCs have toward their international operations.

2. If a locally based manufacturing firm with sales of $350 million decided to enter the EU market by setting up operations in France, which orientation would be the most effective: ethnocentric, polycentric, regiocentric, or geocentric? Why? Explain your choice.

3. In what way are parochialism and simplification barriers to effective cross-cultural management? In each case, give an example.

4. Many MNCs would like to do business overseas in the same way that they do business domestically. Do research findings show that any approaches that

work well in the United States also work well in other cultures? If so, identify and describe two.

5. In most cases, local managerial approaches must be modified for doing business overseas. What are three specific examples that support this statement? Be complete in your answer.

6. What are some categories of cultural differences that help make one country or region of the world different from another? In each case, describe the value or norm and explain how it would result in different behavior in two or more countries. If you like, use the countries discussed in this chapter as your point of reference.

INTERNET EXERCISE: HAIER'S APPROACH

Haier is a China-based multinational corporation that sells a wide variety of commercial and household appliances in the international marketplace. These range from washers, dryers, refrigerators, and industrial heating and ventilations systems. Visit Haier.com and read about some of the latest developments in which the company is engaged: (1) What type of cultural challenges does Haier face when it attempts to market its products worldwide? Is demand

universal for all these offerings, or is there a "national responsiveness" challenge, as discussed in the chapter, that must be addressed? (2) Investigate the way in which Haier has adapted its products in different countries and regions, especially emerging markets. What are some examples? (3) In managing its far-flung enterprise, what are two cultural challenges that the company is likely to face and what will it need to do to respond to these?

Mexico

Located directly south of the United States, Mexico covers an area of 756,000 square miles. The most recent estimates place the population at around 114 million, and this number is increasing at a rate of about 1.4 percent annually. As a result, with a median age of just 27.4, today Mexico is one of the "youngest" countries in the world. Approximately 25 percent of the population is under the age of 14, while a mere 6.6 percent is 65 years of age or older. Mexico's GDP in 2011 was US$1.2 trillion, or approximately US$10,064 per capita.

Although global economic uncertainty persists, Mexico has made itself attractive for foreign investment. Trade agreements with the United States and Canada (NAFTA), the EU, Japan, and dozens of Latin American countries have begun to fully integrate the Mexican economy into the global trading system. Multinationals in a wide variety of industries, from computers to electronics and from pharmaceuticals to manufacturing, have invested billions of dollars in the country. Telefonica, the giant Spanish telecommunications firm, is putting together a wireless network across Latin America, and Mexico is one of the countries that it has targeted for investment. Meanwhile, manufacturers not only from the United States but also from Asia to Europe have helped sustain Mexico's booming maquiladora assembly industry. In 2005 over 1.15 million people were employed in this industry.

Thomson SA, the French consumer electronics firm, has three plants in the border states that make export TVs and digital decoder boxes. And like a growing number of MNCs located in Mexico, the firm is now moving away from importing parts and materials from outside and producing everything within the country. One reason for this move is that under the terms of the North American Free Trade Agreement only parts and materials originating in one of the three NAFTA trading partners are now allowed to enter the processing zones duty-free. Anything originating outside these three countries is subject to tariffs of as much as 25 percent. So the French MNC Thomson is building a picture-tube factory in Baja California so that it will no longer have to import dutiable tubes from Italy. In many cases, imported items from the European Union, however, are allowed to enter duty-free because in 1999 Mexico signed a free-trade agreement with the EU. Over 90 percent of trade is under free trade agreements. As a result, a host of firms, including Philips Electronics and Siemens, have poured large amounts of investment into the country. At the same time Mexico also has begun negotiating another free-trade pact with the four Nordic countries. As a result firms such as Nokia, Ericsson, and Saab-Scania to this point invest heavily in the country.

While many European MNCs are now investing in Mexico, the United States still remains the largest investor and trading partner. Over 50 percent of all outside investment is by U.S. firms. Asian companies, in particular Japanese MNCs, also have large holdings in the country, although these firms have been scaling back in recent years because of the import duties and the fact that Mexican labor costs are rising, thus making it more cost-effective to produce some types of goods in Asia and export them to North America. The largest investments in Mexico are in the industrial sector (around 60 percent of the total) and services (around 30 percent).

One of the major benefits of locating in Mexico is the highly skilled labor force that can be hired at fairly low wages when compared with those paid elsewhere, especially in the United States. Additionally, manufacturing firms that have located there report high productivity growth rates and quality performance. A study by the Massachusetts Institute of Technology on auto assembly plants in Canada, the United States, and Mexico reported that Mexican plants performed well. Another by J. D. Power and Associates noted that Ford Motor's Hermosillo plant was the best in all of North America. In January of 2012, Renault-Nissan announced it would be investing more than $2 billion to build a new manufacturing plant in Aguascalientes to serve the entire Americas region. Computer and electronics firms are also finding Mexico to be an excellent choice for new expansion plants. Intel, for example, has invested more than $200 million in its Mexican plant. The technology industry must be very innovative to stay competitive. Intel operates out of many countries, but an investment of this size shows that Mexico is extremely valuable, and operations here will continue for years to come.

www.mexicool.com, www.state.gov/r/pa/prs/ps/2010/05/142020.htm, data.worldbank.org/country/mexico

Questions

1. Why would multinationals be interested in setting up operations in Mexico? Give two reasons.

2. Would cultural differences be a major stumbling block for U.S. MNCs doing business in Mexico? For European firms? For Japanese firms? Explain your answer.

3. Why might MNCs be interested in studying the organizational culture in Mexican firms before deciding whether to locate there? Explain your logic.

Chapter 6

ORGANIZATIONAL CULTURES AND DIVERSITY

OBJECTIVES OF THE CHAPTER

The previous two chapters focused on national cultures. The overriding objective of this chapter is to examine the interaction of national culture (diversity) and organizational cultures and to discuss ways in which MNCs can manage the often inherent conflicts between national and organizational cultures. Many times, the cultural values and resulting behaviors that are common in a particular country are not the same as those in another. To be successful, MNCs must balance and integrate the national cultures of the countries in which they do business with their own organizational culture. Employee relations, which includes how organizational culture responds to national culture or diversity, deals with internal structures and defines how the company manages. Customer relations, associated with how national culture reacts to organizational cultures, reflects how the local community views the company from a customer service and employee satisfaction perspective.

Although the field of international management has long recognized the impact of national cultures, only recently has attention been given to the importance of managing organizational cultures and diversity. This chapter first examines common organizational cultures that exist in MNCs, and then presents and analyzes ways in which multiculturalism and diversity are being addressed by the best, world-class multinationals. The specific objectives of this chapter are:

1. DEFINE exactly what is meant by *organizational culture*, and discuss the interaction of national and MNC cultures.

2. IDENTIFY the four most common categories of organizational culture that have been found through research, and discuss the characteristics of each.

3. PROVIDE an overview of the nature and degree of multiculturalism and diversity in today's MNCs.

4. DISCUSS common guidelines and principles that are used in building multicultural effectiveness at the team and the organizational levels.

The World of *International Management*

Managing Culture and Diversity in Global Teams

According to many international consultants and managers, diverse and global teams are one of the most consistent sources of competitive advantage for any organization. Applied Materials, a global multinational manufacturer of nanotechnology, has a corporate culture that regards diversity as a competitive advantage. Its employees are located in Belgium, Canada, China, France, Germany, India, Ireland, Israel, Italy, Japan, Korea, Malaysia, the Netherlands, Singapore, Spain, Switzerland, Taiwan, the United Kingdom, and the United States. According to the company, "understanding different perspectives, taking advantage of varied approaches and working together in cross-cultural teams are intrinsic to the company and have been integral to our success."[1]

Most global teams are also virtual teams. According to a study by Kirkman, Rosen, Gibson, and Tesluk, virtual teams are "groups of people who work interdependently with shared purpose across space, time, and organization boundaries using technology to communicate and collaborate."[2] These teams are often cross-cultural and cross-functional. Furthermore, Kirkman and colleagues explain that virtual teams allow "organizations to combine the best expertise regardless of geographic location."[3] To manage a global team, international managers must take into consideration three factors: culture, communication, and trust.

Culture

A leader's management approach may vary based on his or her employees' culture. In his article "Culture Matters in Virtual Teams," Surinder Kahai explains how a manager's approach may differ based on whether the employees are part of an individualist or collectivist national culture. He first identifies four different possible management approaches:

- Outcome control—measure and regulate outcomes sought
- Behavior control—specify the procedures to be followed by employees
- Clan control—implement a set of values where employees are rewarded or punished according to their conformity with these values
- Self-control—allow individuals to set their own goals and then monitor their performance in achieving their goals[4]

Kahai cites the research of Ravi Narayanaswamy, who found that managers are most effective in using self-control and outcome control in virtual teams whose members come from a "high individualism culture, i.e., a culture in which ties between individuals are loose and people tend to achieve things individually and assume personal responsibility."[5] This culture is found in places such as the U.S., the U.K., and Australia. These individuals perform better when given freedom to do their work as they see fit. Outcome controls are needed to ensure that individuals' goals are aligned with the overall project's goals. In contrast, managers are most effective in using clan control and behavior control in virtual teams whose members come from a "high collectivistic culture, i.e., a culture characterized by strong interpersonal ties and by collective achievement and responsibility."[6] This culture is found in places such as China, the Philippines, and South Korea. These individuals perform better when their values are in harmony with their managers. Clan control can help create that harmony. Also, workers in these cultures tend to be motivated to follow procedures, so behavior control is recommended.[7]

Communication

Communicating without face-to-face interaction can have its drawbacks. Specifically, it is more likely that a message is misinterpreted. (See the figure below.) In her article, "Tips for Working in Global Teams," Melanie Doulton provides helpful suggestions for good communication in a global team:

- When starting a project with a new team, hold an initial meeting in which all members introduce themselves and describe the job each one is going to do.
- Hold regular meetings throughout the project to ensure everyone is "on the same page." Follow up conference calls with written minutes to reinforce what was discussed and what individual team members are responsible for.
- Put details of the project in writing, especially for a new team in which everyone speaks in different accents and uses different idioms and colloquialisms.
- Communicate using the most effective technology. For example, decide when e-mail is preferable to a phone call or instant messaging is preferable to a videoconference. In addition, try to understand everyone's communication style. For example, for a high-context culture such as India's, people tend to speak in the passive voice, whereas in North America, people use the active voice.[8]

Moreover, while acknowledging the challenges of communication in virtual teams, Steven R. Rayner also points out that written communication can have an advantage. He states, "The process of writing—where the sender must carefully examine how to communicate his/her message—provides the sender with the opportunity to create a more refined response than an 'off-the-cuff' verbal comment."[9]

Likelihood of Message Getting Interpreted Correctly

LOW				**HIGH**
Fax/Letter	E-mail	Telephone	Video Conferencing	Face-to-Face Interaction

←————————————————————————————→

Source: Adapted from Steven R. Rayner, "The Virtual Team Challenge," Rayner & Associates, Inc., 1997.

Trust

Kirkman and colleagues emphasize that "a specific challenge for virtual teams, compared to face-to-face teams, is the difficulty of building trust between team members who rarely, or never, see each other."[10] Rayner notes that "by some estimates, as much as 30 percent of senior management time is spent in 'chance' encounters (such as unplanned hallway, parking lot, and lunch room conversations). . . . In a virtual team setting, these opportunities for relationship building and idea sharing are far more limited."[11]

How can managers build trust among virtual team members? From their research, Kirkman and colleagues discovered that "building trust requires rapid responses to electronic communications from team members, reliable performance, and consistent follow-through. Accordingly, team leaders should coach virtual team members to avoid long lags in responding, unilateral priority shifts, and failure to follow up on commitments."[12] In addition, Doulton recommends that virtual team members "exchange feedback early" and allow an extra day or two for responses due to time zone differences.[13]

Team building activities also build trust. According to Kirkman, as part of the virtual team launch, it is recommended that all members meet face-to-face to "set objectives, clarify roles, build personal relationships, develop team norms, and establish group identity."[14] Picking the right team members can help the teams become more cohesive as well. When Kirkman and colleagues interviewed 75 team leaders and members in virtual teams, people responded that skills in communication, teamwork, thinking outside the box, and taking

initiative were more important than technical skills. This finding was surprising, considering most managers select virtual team members based on technical skills. Having people with the right skills is essential to bring together a successful virtual team.[15]

Advantages of Global Virtual Teams

In addition to its challenges of overcoming cultural and communication barriers, global virtual teams have certain advantages over face-to-face teams.

First, Kirkman concluded that "working virtually can reduce team process losses associated with stereotyping, personality conflicts, power politics, and cliques commonly experienced by face-to-face teams. Virtual team members may be unaffected by potentially divisive demographic differences when there is minimal face-to-face contact." Managers may even give fairer assessments of team members' work because managers are compelled to rely on objective data rather than being influenced by their perceptual biases.[16]

Second, Rayner observes that "having members span many different time zones can literally keep a project moving around the clock. . . . Work doesn't stop—it merely shifts to a different time zone."[17]

Third, according to Rayner, "The ability for an organization to bring people together from remote geography and form a cohesive team that is capable of quickly solving complex problems and making effective decisions is an enormous competitive advantage."[18]

For an international manager, this competitive advantage makes overcoming challenges of managing global teams worth the effort.

Clearly, there are both benefits and challenges inherent in multinational, multicultural teams. These teams, which almost always include a diverse group of members with varying functional, geographic, ethnic, and cultural backgrounds, can be an efficient and effective vehicle for tackling increasingly multidimensional business problems. At the same time, this very diversity brings challenges which are often exacerbated when the teams are primarily "virtual." Research has demonstrated the benefits of diversity and has also offered insight on how best to overcome the inherent challenges of global teams, including those that are "virtual."

In this chapter we will explore the nature and characteristics of organizational culture as it relates to doing business in today's global context. In addition, strategies and guidelines for establishing a strong organizational culture in the presence of diversity are presented.

■ The Nature of Organizational Culture

The chapters in Part One provided the background on the external environment, and the chapters so far in Part Two have been concerned with the external culture. Regardless of whether this environment or cultural context affects the MNC, when individuals join an MNC, not only do they bring their national culture, which greatly affects their learned beliefs, attitudes, values, and behaviors, but they also enter into an organizational culture. Employees of MNCs are expected to "fit in." For example, at PepsiCo, personnel are expected to be cheerful, positive, enthusiastic, and have committed optimism; at Ford, they are expected to show self-confidence, assertiveness, and machismo.[19] Regardless of the external environment or their national culture, managers and employees must understand and follow their organization's culture to be successful. In this section, after first defining organizational culture, we analyze the interaction between national and organizational cultures. An understanding of this interaction has become recognized as vital to effective international management.

Definition and Characteristics

Organizational culture has been defined in several different ways. In its most basic form, organizational culture can be defined as the shared values and beliefs that enable members to understand their roles in and the norms of the organization. A more detailed definition is offered by organizational cultural theorist Edgar Schein, who defines it as a pattern of shared basic assumptions that the group learned as it solved its problems of external adaptation and internal integration, and that has worked well enough to be considered valid and, therefore, to be taught to new members as the correct way to perceive, think, and feel in relation to those problems.[20]

> **organizational culture**
> Shared values and beliefs that enable members to understand their roles in and the norms of the organization.

Regardless of how the term is defined, a number of important characteristics are associated with an organization's culture. These have been summarized as:

1. Observed behavioral regularities, as typified by common language, terminology, and rituals.
2. Norms, as reflected by things such as the amount of work to be done and the degree of cooperation between management and employees.
3. Dominant values that the organization advocates and expects participants to share, such as high product and service quality, low absenteeism, and high efficiency.
4. A philosophy that is set forth in the MNC's beliefs regarding how employees and customers should be treated.
5. Rules that dictate the dos and don'ts of employee behavior relating to areas such as productivity, customer relations, and intergroup cooperation.
6. Organizational climate, or the overall atmosphere of the enterprise, as reflected by the way that participants interact with each other, conduct themselves with customers, and feel about the way they are treated by higher-level management.[21]

This list is not intended to be all-inclusive, but it does help illustrate the nature of organizational culture.[22] The major problem is that sometimes an MNC's organizational culture in one country's facility differs sharply from organizational cultures in other countries. For example, managers who do well in England may be ineffective in Germany, despite the fact that they work for the same MNC. In addition, the cultures of the English and German subsidiaries may differ sharply from those of the home U.S. location. Effectively dealing with multiculturalism within the various locations of an MNC is a major challenge for international management.

A good example is provided by the British-Swedish MNC AstraZeneca PLC, the fifth-largest pharmaceutical company in the world. With operations in over 100 countries on six continents, AstraZeneca's twelve-member senior executive team includes leaders from the United Kingdom, Sweden, France, the United States, and the Netherlands. Over 24 percent of the company's employees work in North America, and about 21 percent are employed in Asia.[23] To unite such a diverse set of employees under a common corporate culture, AstraZeneca's Global Steering Group has focused on three universal cultural pillars: "Leadership and Management Capability," "Transparency in Talent Management and Career Progression," and "Work/Life Challenges."[24] Furthermore, in 2012, the company introduced a new cross-cultural mentorship program, called Insight Exchange. By pairing senior- and junior-level employees from different cultural and professional backgrounds, AstraZeneca hopes to create a "more open culture."[25]

In some cases companies have deliberately maintained two different business cultures because they do not want one culture influencing the other. A good example is JCPenney, the giant department store chain. When this well-known retailer bought control of Renner, a Brazilian retail chain with 20 stores, it used a strategy that is not very common when one company controls another. Rather than impose its own culture on the chain, Penney's management took a back seat. Recognizing Renner's reputation for value and service among its middle-class customers, Penney let the Brazilian managers continue to run the stores while it provided assistance in the form of backroom operations, merchandise presentation, logistics, branding, and expansion funds. In a country where fashion is constantly evolving, Renner is able to keep up with the market by changing fashion lines seven to eight times a year. The company also provides rapid checkout service, credit cards to individuals who earn as little as $150 a month, and interest-free installment plans that allow people to pay as little as $5 a month toward their purchases. Thanks to Penney's infusion of capital, in the first two years Renner opened 30 more stores and sales jumped from $150 million to over $300 million. The company proved to be profitable for a while; however, the run did not last forever, and JCPenney sold its controlling interest in the company in 2005.

■ Interaction between National and Organizational Cultures

There is a widely held belief that organizational culture tends to moderate or erase the impact of national culture. The logic of such conventional wisdom is that if a U.S. MNC set up operations in, say, France, it would not be long before the French employees began to "think like Americans." In fact, evidence is accumulating that just the opposite may be true. Hofstede's research found that the national cultural values of employees have a significant impact on their organizational performance, and that the cultural values employees bring to the workplace with them are not easily changed by the organization. So, for example, while some French employees would have a higher power distance than Swedes and some a lower power distance, chances are "that if a company hired locals in Paris, they would, on the whole, be less likely to challenge hierarchical power than would the same number of locals hired in Stockholm."[26]

Andre Laurent's research supports Hofstede's conclusions.[27] He found that cultural differences are actually more pronounced among foreign employees working within the same multinational organization than among personnel working for firms in their native lands. Nancy Adler summarized these research findings as follows:

> When they work for a multinational corporation, it appears that Germans become more German, Americans become more American, Swedes become more Swedish, and so on. Surprised by these results, Laurent replicated the research in two other multinational corporations, each with subsidiaries in the same nine Western European countries and the United States. Similar to the first company, corporate culture did not reduce or eliminate national differences in the second and third corporations. Far from reducing national differences, organization culture maintains and enhances them.[28]

There often are substantial differences between the organizational cultures of different subsidiaries, and of course, this can cause coordination problems. For example, when the Upjohn Company of Kalamazoo, Michigan, merged with Pharmacia AB of Sweden, which also has operations in Italy, the Americans failed to realize some of the cultural differences between themselves and their new European partners. As was reported in The Wall Street Journal, "Swedes take off the entire month of July for vacation, virtually en masse, and Italians take off August. Everyone in Europe knows, that is, but apparently hardly anyone in Kalamazoo, Michigan, does."[29] As a result, a linkup that was supposed to give a quick boost to the two companies, solving problems such as aging product lines and pressure from giant competitors, never got off the ground. Things had to be rescheduled, and both partners ended up having to meet and talk about their cultural differences, so that each side better understood the "dos and don'ts" of doing business with the other.

When the two firms first got together, they never expected these types of problems. Upjohn, with household names such as Rogaine and Motrin, had no likely breakthroughs in its product pipeline, so it was happy to merge with Pharmacia. The latter had developed a solid roster of allergy medicines, human-growth hormone, and other drugs, but its distribution in the United States was weak and its product line was aging. So a merger seemed ideal for both firms. The big question was how to bring the two companies together. Given that Pharmacia had recently acquired an Italian firm, there was a proposal by the European group that there be three major centers—Kalamazoo, Stockholm, and Milan—as well as a new headquarters in London. However, this arrangement had a number of built-in problems. For one, the executives in Italy and Sweden were accustomed to reporting to local bosses. Second, the people in London did not know a great deal about how to coordinate operations in Sweden and Italy. American cultural values added even more problems in that at Upjohn workers were tested for drug and alcohol abuse, but in Italy waiters pour wine freely every afternoon in the company dining room, and Pharmacia's boardrooms were stocked with humidors for executives who liked to light a cigar during long meetings. Quite obviously, there were cultural differences that had to be resolved by the companies. In the end, Pharmacia and Upjohn said they would meld the different cultures and attitudes and get on with their growth plans. However, one thing is certain: The different cultures of the merged firms created a major challenge.

In examining and addressing the differences between organizational cultures, Hofstede provided the early database of a set of proprietary cultural-analysis techniques and programs known as DOCSA (Diagnosing Organizational Culture for Strategic Application). This approach identifies the dimensions of organizational culture summarized in Table 6–1. It was found that when cultural comparisons were made between different subsidiaries of an MNC, different cultures often existed in each one. Such cultural differences within an MNC could reduce the ability of units to work well together. An example is provided in Figure 6–1, which shows the cultural dimensions of a California-based MNC and its European subsidiary as perceived by the Europeans. A close comparison of these perceptions reveals some startling differences.

The Europeans viewed the culture in the U.S. facilities as only slightly activities oriented (see Table 6–1 for a description of these dimensions), but they saw their own European operations as much more heavily activities oriented. The U.S. operation was viewed as moderately people oriented, but their own relationships were viewed as very job oriented. The Americans were seen as having a slight identification with their own organization, while the Europeans had a much stronger identification. The Americans were perceived as being very open in their communications; the Europeans saw themselves as moderately closed. The Americans were viewed as preferring very loose control, while the Europeans felt they preferred somewhat tight control. The Americans were seen as somewhat conventional in their conduct, while the Europeans saw themselves as somewhat pragmatic. If these perceptions are accurate, then it obviously would be necessary for both groups to discuss their cultural differences and carefully coordinate their activities to work well together.

This analysis is relevant to multinational alliances. It shows that even though an alliance may exist, the partners will bring different organizational cultures with them. Lessem and Neubauer, who have portrayed Europe as offering four distinct ways of dealing with multiculturalism (based on the United Kingdom, French, German, and Italian characteristics), provide an example in Table 6–2, which briefly describes each of these sets of cultural characteristics. A close examination of the differences highlights how difficult it can be to do business with two or more of these groups, because each

---

Table 6–1
Dimensions of Corporate Culture

Motivation	
Activities	**Outputs**
To be consistent and precise. To strive for accuracy and attention to detail. To refine and perfect. Get it right.	To be pioneers. To pursue clear aims and objectives. To innovate and progress. Go for it.

Relationship	
Job	**Person**
To put the demands of the job before the needs of the individual.	To put the needs of the individual before the needs of the job.

Identity	
Corporate	**Professional**
To identify with and uphold the expectations of the employing organizations.	To pursue the aims and ideals of each professional practice.

Communication	
Open	**Closed**
To stimulate and encourage a full and free exchange of information and opinion.	To monitor and control the exchange and accessibility of information and opinion.

Control	
Tight	**Loose**
To comply with clear and definite systems and procedures.	To work flexibly and adaptively according to the needs of the situation.

Conduct	
Conventional	**Pragmatic**
To put the expertise and standards of the employing organization first. To do what we know is right.	To put the demands and expectations of customers first. To do what they ask.

Source: Adapted from a study by the Diagnosing Organizational Culture for Strategic Application (DOCSA) group and reported in Lisa Hoecklin, *Managing Cultural Differences: Strategies for Competitive Advantage* (Workingham, England: Addison-Wesley), 1995, p. 146.

---

group perceives things differently from the others. Another example is the way in which negotiations occur between groups; here are some contrasts between French and Spanish negotiators:[30]

French	Spanish
Look for a meeting of minds.	Look for a meeting of people.
Intellectual competence is very important.	Social competence is very important.
Persuasion through carefully prepared and skilled rhetoric is employed.	Persuasion through emotional appeal is employed.
Strong emphasis is given to a logical presentation of one's position coupled with well-reasoned, detailed solutions.	Socialization always precedes negotiations, which are characterized by an exchange of grand ideas and general principles.
A contract is viewed as a well-reasoned transaction.	A contract is viewed as a long-lasting relationship.
Trust emerges slowly and is based on the evaluation of perceived status and intellect.	Trust is developed on the basis of frequent and warm interpersonal contact and transaction.

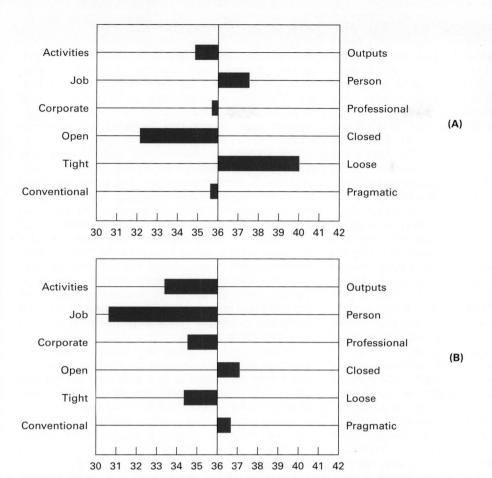

Figure 6–1

Europeans' Perception of the Cultural Dimensions of U.S. Operations (A) and European Operations (B) of the Same MNC

Source: Adapted from a study by the Diagnosing Organizational Culture for Strategic Application (DOCSA) group and reported in Lisa Hoecklin, *Managing Cultural Differences: Strategies for Competitive Advantage* (Workingham, England: Addison-Wesley), 1995, pp. 147–148.

Table 6–2
European Management Characteristics

	Characteristic			
Dimension	**Western (United Kingdom)**	**Northern (France)**	**Eastern (Germany)**	**Southern (Italy)**
Corporate	Commercial	Administrative	Industrial	Familial
Management attributes				
Behavior	Experiential	Professional	Developmental	Convivial
Attitude	Sensation	Thought	Intuition	Feeling
Institutional models				
Function	Salesmanship	Control	Production	Personnel
Structure	Transaction	Hierarchy	System	Network
Societal ideas				
Economics	Free market	Dirigiste	Social market	Communal
Philosophy	Pragmatic	Rational	Holistic	Humanistic
Cultural images				
Art	Theatre	Architecture	Music	Dance
Culture	(Anglo-Saxon)	(Gallic)	(Germanic)	(Latin)

Source: Adapted from Ronald Lessen and Fred Neubauer, European Management Systems (McGraw-Hill, London), 1994 and reported in Lisa Hoecklin, *Managing Cultural Differences: Strategies for Competitive Advantage* (Workingham, England: Addison-Wesley), 1995, p. 149.

Doing Things the Walmart Way; Germans Say, "Nein, vielen Dank"

Across the globe, Walmart employees engage in the "Walmart cheer" to start their day. It is a way to show inclusivity and express their pride in the company, and can be heard in many different languages. Walmart not only operates in 27 countries but is also a leader in diversity in the workplace. In June 2007, Walmart was named one of the top 50 companies for diversity by *DiversityInc* magazine, and, in 2012, CEO Mike Duke was inducted into the CPG/Retail Diversity Hall of Fame. However, despite Walmart's multinational presence and representation, its internal culture proved to be less than satisfactory to the German market.

Walmart has experienced a fair share of negative PR over the years, so it is no surprise that some may have adverse reactions to news of Walmart moving into the neighborhood. Before the unflattering buzz, Walmart sometimes discovers that even the best intentions can fall flat. Walmart entered the German market in 1997 and stressed the idea of friendly service with a smile, where the customers always come first. Even before the employees walked onto the sales room floor, employee dissatisfaction became clear.

The pamphlet which outlined the workplace code of ethics was simply translated from English to German, but the message was not expressed the way Walmart had intended. It warned employees of potential supervisor-employee relationships, implying sexual harassment, and encouraged reports of "improper behavior," which spoke more to legal matters. The Germans interpreted this to mean that there was a ban on any romantic relationships in the workplace and saw the reporting methods as more of a way to rat out co-workers than benefit the company. As we saw in Chapter 3, ethical values in one country may not be the same as in another, and Walmart experienced this firsthand. Another employee relations issue that arose dealt with local practices. Walmart has never been open to unionized employees,

so when the German operations began dealing with workers' councils and adhering to co-determination rules, a common practice there, Walmart was less than willing to listen to suggestions as to how to improve employee working conditions. As if this was not enough, Walmart soon experienced problems with customer relations as well.

Doing things the Walmart way included smiling at customers and assisting them by bagging their groceries at the Supercenter locations. This policy presented problems in the German environment. Male employees who were ordered to smile at customers were often seen as flirtatious to male customers, and Germans do not like strangers handling their groceries. These are just a few reasons that customers did not enjoy their shopping experience. This does not mean that everything Walmart attempted was wrong. Products which are popular in Germany were available on the shelves in place of products that would be common in other countries. Enhanced distribution processes guaranteed availability of most requested items, and efficiency was pervasive.

Despite some successes and good intentions and numerous attempts to improve the German stores, the Walmart culture proved to be a poor fit for the German market, and Walmart vacated Germany in 2006. Unfortunately, Walmart learned the hard way that in the retail or service industry, local customs are often more important than a strong, unyielding organizational culture. The challenge to incorporate everyone into the Walmart family certainly fell short of expectations. If the Walmart culture does not become more flexible, or locally relevant, it may be chastised from numerous global markets, and the company could hear, "no, thank you" in even more languages than German as it continues to expand. (See the In-Depth Integrative Case at the end of Part Two for more detail on Walmart's experiences around the world.)

Such comparisons also help explain why it can be difficult for an MNC with a strong organizational culture to break into foreign markets where it is not completely familiar with divergent national cultures. The International Management in Action, "Doing Things the Walmart Way," provides an illustration. When dealing with these challenges, MNCs must work hard to understand the nature of the country and institutional practices to both moderate and adapt their operations in a way that accommodates the company and customer base.

■ Organizational Cultures in MNCs

Organizational cultures of MNCs are shaped by a number of factors, including the cultural preferences of the leaders and employees. In the international arena, some MNCs have subsidiaries that, except for the company logo and reporting procedures, would not be easily recognizable as belonging to the same multinational.[31]

Given that many recent international expansions are a result of mergers or acquisition, the integration of these organizational cultures is a critical concern in international management. Numeroff and Abrahams have suggested that there are four steps that are critical in this process: (1) The two groups have to establish the purpose, goal, and focus of their merger. (2) Then they have to develop mechanisms to identify the most important organizational structures and management roles. (3) They have to determine who has authority over the resources needed for getting things done. (4) They have to identify the expectations of all involved parties and facilitate communication between both departments and individuals in the structure.

Companies all over the world are finding out firsthand that there is more to an international merger or acquisition than just sharing resources and capturing greater market share. Differences in workplace cultures sometimes temporarily overshadow the overall goal of long-term success of the newly formed entity. With the proper management framework and execution, successful integration of cultures is not only possible, but also the most preferable paradigm in which to operate. It is the role of the sponsors and managers to keep sight of the necessity to create, maintain, and support the notion of a united front. It is only when this assimilation has occurred that an international merger or acquisition can truly be labeled a success.[32]

In addition, there are three aspects of organizational functioning that seem to be especially important in determining MNC organizational culture: (1) the general relationship between the employees and their organization; (2) the hierarchical system of authority that defines the roles of managers and subordinates; and (3) the general views that employees hold about the MNC's purpose, destiny, goals, and their place in them.[33]

When examining these dimensions of organizational culture, Trompenaars suggested the use of two continua. One distinguishes between equity and hierarchy; the other examines orientation to the person and the task. Along these continua, which are shown in Figure 6–2, he identifies and describes four different types of organizational cultures: family, Eiffel Tower, guided missile, and incubator.[34]

In practice, of course, organizational cultures do not fit neatly into any of these four, but the groupings can be useful in helping examine the bases of how individuals relate to each other, think, learn, change, are motivated, and resolve conflict. The following discussion examines each of these cultural types.

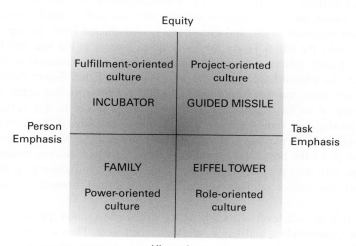

Figure 6–2

Organizational Cultures

Source: Adapted from Fons Trompenaars, *Riding the Waves of Culture: Understanding Diversity in Global Business* (Burr Ridge, IL: Irwin, 1994), p. 154.

Family Culture

Family culture is characterized by a strong emphasis on hierarchy and orientation to the person. The result is a family-type environment that is power-oriented and headed by a leader who is regarded as a caring parent and one who knows what is best for the personnel. Trompenaars found that this organizational culture is common in countries such as Turkey, Pakistan, Venezuela, China, Hong Kong, and Singapore.[35]

In this culture, personnel not only respect the individuals who are in charge but look to them for both guidance and approval as well. In turn, management assumes a paternal relationship with personnel, looks after employees, and tries to ensure that they are treated well and have continued employment. Family culture also is characterized by traditions, customs, and associations that bind together the personnel and make it difficult for outsiders to become members. When it works well, family culture can catalyze and multiply the energies of the personnel and appeal to their deepest feelings and aspirations. When it works poorly, members of the organization end up supporting a leader who is ineffective and drains their energies and loyalties.

This type of culture is foreign to most managers in the United States, who believe in valuing people based on their abilities and achievements, not on their age or position in the hierarchy. As a result, many managers in U.S.-based MNCs fail to understand why senior-level managers in overseas subsidiaries might appoint a relative to a high-level, sensitive position even though that individual might not appear to be the best qualified for the job. They fail to realize that family ties are so strong that the appointed relative would never do anything to embarrass or let down the family member who made the appointment. Here is an example:

> A Dutch delegation was shocked and surprised when the Brazilian owner of a large manufacturing company introduced his relatively junior accountant as the key coordinator of a $15 million joint venture. The Dutch were puzzled as to why a recently qualified accountant had been given such weighty responsibilities, including the receipt of their own money. The Brazilians pointed out that the young man was the best possible choice among 1,200 employees since he was the nephew of the owner. Who could be more trustworthy than that? Instead of complaining, the Dutch should consider themselves lucky that he was available.[36]

Eiffel Tower Culture

Eiffel Tower culture is characterized by strong emphasis on hierarchy and orientation to the task. Under this organizational culture, jobs are well defined, employees know what they are supposed to do, and everything is coordinated from the top. As a result, this culture—like the Eiffel Tower itself—is steep, narrow at the top, and broad at the base. Unlike family culture, where the leader is revered and considered to be the source of all power, the person holding the top position in the Eiffel Tower culture could be replaced at any time, and this would have no effect on the work that organization members are doing or on the organization's reasons for existence. In this culture, relationships are specific, and status remains with the job. Therefore, if the boss of an Eiffel Tower subsidiary were playing golf with a subordinate, the subordinate would not feel any pressure to let the boss win. In addition, these managers seldom create off-the-job relationships with their people, because they believe this could affect their rational judgment. In fact, this culture operates very much like a formal hierarchy—impersonal and efficient.

Each role at each level of the hierarchy is described, rated for its difficulty, complexity, and responsibility, and has a salary attached to it. Then follows a search for a person to fill it. In considering applicants for the role, the personnel department will treat everyone equally and neutrally, match the person's skills and aptitudes with the job requirements, and award the job to the best fit between role and person. The same procedure is followed in evaluations and promotions.[37]

Eiffel Tower culture most commonly is found in northwestern European countries. Examples include Denmark, Germany, and the Netherlands. The way that people in this culture learn and change differs sharply from that in the family culture. Learning involves the accumulation of skills necessary to fit a role, and organizations will use qualifications in deciding how to schedule, deploy, and reshuffle personnel to meet their needs. The organization also will employ such rational procedures as assessment centers, appraisal systems, training and development programs, and job rotation in managing its human resources. All these procedures help ensure that a formal hierarchic or bureaucracy-like approach works well. When changes need to be made, however, the Eiffel Tower culture often is ill-equipped to handle things. Manuals must be rewritten, procedures changed, job descriptions altered, promotions reconsidered, and qualifications reassessed.

Because the Eiffel Tower culture does not rely on values that are similar to those in most U.S. MNCs, U.S. expatriate managers often have difficulty initiating change in this culture. As Trompenaars notes:

> An American manager responsible for initiating change in a German company described to me the difficulties he had in making progress, although the German managers had discussed the new strategy in depth and made significant contributions to its formulation. Through informal channels, he had eventually discovered that his mistake was not having formalized the changes to structure or job descriptions. In the absence of a new organization chart, this Eiffel Tower company was unable to change.[38]

Guided Missile Culture

Guided missile culture is characterized by strong emphasis on equality in the workplace and orientation to the task. This organizational culture is oriented to work, which typically is undertaken by teams or project groups. Unlike the Eiffel Tower culture, where job assignments are fixed and limited, personnel in the guided missile culture do whatever it takes to get the job done. This culture gets its name from high-tech organizations such as the National Aeronautics and Space Administration (NASA), which pioneered the use of project groups working on space probes that resembled guided missiles. In these large project teams, more than a hundred different types of engineers often were responsible for building, say, a lunar landing module. The team member whose contribution would be crucial at any given time in the project typically could not be known in advance. Therefore, all types of engineers had to work in close harmony and cooperate with everyone on the team.

To be successful, the best form of synthesis must be used in the course of working on the project. For example, in a guided missile project, formal hierarchical considerations are given low priority, and individual expertise is of greatest importance. Additionally, all team members are equal (or at least potentially equal), because their relative contributions to the project are not yet known. All teams treat each other with respect, because they may need the other for assistance. This egalitarian and task-driven organizational culture fits well with the national cultures of the United States and United Kingdom, which helps explain why high-tech MNCs commonly locate their operations in these countries.

Unlike family and Eiffel Tower cultures, change in guided missile culture comes quickly. Goals are accomplished, and teams are reconfigured and assigned new objectives. People move from group to group, and loyalties to one's profession and project often are greater than loyalties to the organization itself.

Trompenaars found that the motivation of those in guided missile cultures tends to be more intrinsic than just concern for money and benefits. Team members become enthusiastic about, and identify with, the struggle toward attaining their goal. For example, a project team that is designing and building a new computer for the Asian market may be highly motivated to create a machine that is at the leading edge of

guided missile culture
A culture that is characterized by strong emphasis on equality in the workplace and orientation to the task.

technology, user-friendly, and likely to sweep the market. Everything else is secondary to this overriding objective. Thus, both intragroup and intergroup conflicts are minimized and petty problems between team members set aside; everyone is so committed to the project's main goal that no one has time for petty disagreements. As Trompenaars notes:

> This culture tends to be individualistic since it allows for a wide variety of differently specialized persons to work with each other on a temporary basis. The scenery of faces keeps changing. Only the pursuit of chosen lines of personal development is constant. The team is a vehicle for the shared enthusiasm of its members, but is itself disposable and will be discarded when the project ends. Members are garrulous, idiosyncratic, and intelligent, but their mutuality is a means, not an end. It is a way of enjoying the journey. They do not need to know each other intimately, and may avoid doing so. Management by objectives is the language spoken, and people are paid for performance.[39]

Incubator Culture

incubator culture
A culture that is characterized by strong emphasis on equality and orientation to the person.

Incubator culture is the fourth major type of organizational culture that Trompenaars identified, and it is characterized by strong emphasis on equality and personal orientation. This culture is based heavily on the existential idea that organizations per se are secondary to the fulfillment of the individuals within them. This culture is based on the premise that the role of organizations is to serve as incubators for the self-expression and self-fulfillment of their members; as a result, this culture often has little formal structure. Participants in an incubator culture are there primarily to perform roles such as confirming, criticizing, developing, finding resources for, or helping complete the development of an innovative product or service. These cultures often are found among start-up firms in Silicon Valley, California, or Silicon Glen, Scotland. These incubator-type organizations typically are entrepreneurial and often founded and made up by a creative team who left larger, Eiffel Tower–type employers. They want to be part of an organization where their creative talents will not be stifled.

Incubator cultures often create environments where participants thrive on an intense, emotional commitment to the nature of the work. For example, the group may be in the process of gene splitting that could lead to radical medical breakthroughs and extend life. Often, personnel in such cultures are overworked, and the enterprise typically is underfunded. As breakthroughs occur and the company gains stability, however, it starts moving down the road toward commercialization and profit. In turn, this engenders the need to hire more people and develop formalized procedures for ensuring the smooth flow of operations. In this process of growth and maturity, the unique characteristics of the incubator culture begin to wane and disappear, and the culture is replaced by one of the other types (family, Eiffel Tower, or guided missile).

As noted, change in the incubator culture often is fast and spontaneous. All participants are working toward the same objective. Because there may not yet be a customer who is using the final output, however, the problem itself often is open to redefinition, and the solution typically is generic, aimed at a universe of applications. Meanwhile, motivation of the personnel remains highly intrinsic and intense, and it is common to find employees working 70 hours a week—and loving it. The participants are more concerned with the unfolding creative process than they are in gathering power or ensuring personal monetary gain. In sharp contrast to the family culture, leadership in this incubator culture is achieved, not gained by position.

The four organizational cultures described by Trompenaars are "pure" types and seldom exist in practice. Rather the types are mixed and, as shown in Table 6–3, overlaid with one of the four major types of culture dominating the corporate scene. Recently, Trompenaars and his associates have created a questionnaire designed to identify national patterns of corporate culture as shown in Figure 6–3.

Table 6–3
Summary Characteristics of the Four Corporate Cultures

Characteristic	Corporate Culture			
	Family	**Eiffel Tower**	**Guided Missile**	**Incubator**
Relationships between employees	Diffuse relationships to organic whole to which one is bonded.	Specific role in mechanical system of required interaction.	Specific tasks in cybernetic system targeted on shared objectives.	Diffuse, spontaneous relationships growing out of shared creative process.
Attitude toward authority	Status is ascribed to parent figures who are close and powerful.	Status is ascribed to superior roles that are distant yet powerful.	Status is achieved by project group members who contribute to targeted goal.	Status is achieved by individuals exemplifying creativity and growth.
Ways of thinking and learning	Intuitive, holistic, lateral, and error correcting.	Logical, analytical, vertical, and rationally efficient.	Problem centered, professional, practical, cross-disciplinary.	Process oriented, creative, ad hoc, inspirational.
Attitudes toward people	Family members.	Human resources.	Specialists and experts.	Co-creators.
Ways of changing	"Father" changes course.	Change rules and procedures.	Shift aim as target moves.	Improvise and attune.
Ways of motivating and rewarding	Intrinsic satisfaction in being loved and respected.	Promotion to greater position, larger role.	Pay or credit for performance and problems solved.	Participation in the process of creating new realities.
	Management by subjectives.	Management by job description.	Management by objectives.	Management by enthusiasm.
Criticism and conflict resolution	Turn other cheek, save other's face, do not lose power game.	Criticism is accusation of irrationalism unless there are procedures to arbitrate conflicts.	Constructive task-related only, then admit error and correct fast.	Improve creative idea, not negate it.

Source: Adapted from Fons Trompenaars and Charles Hampden-Turner, *Riding the Waves of Culture: Understanding Diversity in Global Business,* 2nd ed. (New York: McGraw-Hill, 1998), p. 183.

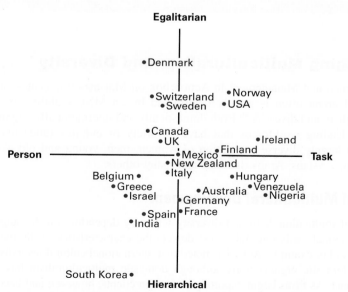

Figure 6–3

National Patterns of Corporate Culture

Source: Adapted from Fons Trompenaars and Charles Hampden-Turner, *Riding the Waves of Culture: Understanding Diversity in Global Business,* 2nd ed. (New York: McGraw-Hill, 1998), p. 184.

Matsushita Goes Global

In recent years, growing numbers of multinationals have begun to expand their operations, realizing that if they do not increase their worldwide presence now, they likely will be left behind in the near future. In turn, this has created a number of different challenges for these MNCs, including making a fit between their home organizational culture and the organizational cultures at local levels in the different countries where the MNC operates. Matsushita provides an excellent example of how to handle this challenge with its macromicro approach. This huge, Japanese MNC has developed a number of guidelines that it uses in setting up and operating its more than 150 industrial units. At the same time, the company complements these macro guidelines with on-site micro techniques that help create the most appropriate organizational culture in the subsidiary.

At the macro level, Matsushita employs six overall guidelines that are followed in all locales: (1) Be a good corporate citizen in every country by, among other things, respecting cultures, customs, and languages. (2) Give overseas operations the best manufacturing technology the company has available. (3) Keep the expatriate head count down, and groom local management to take over. (4) Let operating plants set their own rules, fine-tuning manufacturing processes to match the skills of the workers. (5) Create local research and development to tailor products to markets. (6) Encourage competition between overseas outposts and plants back home. Working within these macro guidelines, Matsushita then allows each local unit to create its own culture. The Malaysian operations are a good example. Matsushita has erected 23 subsidiaries in Malaysia which collectively consist of about 30,000 employees. Less than 1 percent of the employee population, however, is

Japanese. From these Malaysian operations, Matsushita has been producing more than 1.3 million televisions and 1.8 million air conditioners annually, and 75 percent of these units are shipped overseas. To produce this output, local plants reflect Malaysia's cultural mosaic of Muslim Malays, ethnic Chinese, and Indians. To accommodate this diversity, Matsushita cafeterias offer Malaysian, Chinese, and Indian food, and to accommodate Muslim religious customs, Matsushita provides special prayer rooms at each plant and allows two prayer sessions per shift.

How well does this Malaysian workforce perform for the Japanese MNC? In the past, the Malaysian plants' slogan was "Let's catch up with Japan." Today, however, these plants frequently outperform their Japanese counterparts in both quality and efficiency. The comparison with Japan no longer is used. Additionally, Matsushita has found that the Malaysian culture is very flexible, and the locals are able to work well with almost any employer. Commenting on Malaysia's multiculturalism, Matsushita's managing director notes, "They are used to accommodating other cultures, and so they think of us Japanese as just another culture. That makes it much easier for us to manage them than some other nationalities."

Today, Matsushita faces a number of important challenges, including remaining profitable in a slow-growth, high-cost Japanese economy. Fortunately, this MNC is doing extremely well overseas, which is buying it time to get its house in order back home. A great amount of this success results from the MNC's ability to nurture and manage overseas organizational cultures (such as in Malaysia) that are both diverse and highly productive.

■ Managing Multiculturalism and Diversity

As the International Management in Action box on Matsushita indicates, success in the international arena often is greatly determined by an MNC's ability to manage both multiculturalism and diversity.[40] Both domestically and internationally, organizations find themselves leading workforces that have a variety of cultures (and subcultures) and consist of a largely diverse population of women, men, young and old people, blacks, whites, Latins, Asians, Arabs, Indians, and many others.

Phases of Multicultural Development

The effect of multiculturalism and diversity will vary depending on the stage of the firm in its international evolution. Table 6–4 depicts the characteristics of the major phases in this evolution. For example, Adler has noted that international cultural diversity has minimal impact on domestic organizations, although domestic multiculturalism has a highly significant impact. As firms begin exporting to foreign clients, however, and become what she calls "international corporations" (Phase II in Table 6–4), they must adapt their approach and products to those of the local market. For these international firms, the impact of

Table 6–4
The Evolution of International Corporations

Characteristics/ Activities	Phase I (Domestic Corporations)	Phase II (International Corporations)	Phase III (Multinational Corporations)	Phase IV (Global Corporations)
Primary orientation	Product/service	Market	Price	Strategy
Competitive strategy	Domestic	Multidomestic	Multinational	Global
Importance of world business	Marginal	Important	Extremely important	Dominant
Product/service	New, unique	More standardized	Completely standardized (commodity)	Mass-customized
	Product engineering emphasized	Process engineering emphasized	Engineering not emphasized	Product and process engineering
Technology	Proprietary	Shared	Widely shared	Instantly and extensively shared
R&D/sales	High	Decreasing	Very low	Very high
Profit margin	High	Decreasing	Very low	High, yet immediately decreasing
Competitors	None	Few	Many	Significant (few or many)
Market	Small, domestic	Large, multidomestic	Larger, multinational	Largest, global
Production location	Domestic	Domestic and primary markets	Multinational, least cost	Imports and exports
Exports	None	Growing, high potential	Large, saturated	Imports and exports
Structure	Functional divisions	Functional with international division	Multinational lines of business	Global alliances, hierarchy
	Centralized	Decentralized	Centralized	Coordinated, decentralized
Primary orientation	Product/service	Market	Price	Strategy
Strategy	Domestic	Multidomestic	Multinational	Global
Perspective	Ethnocentric	Polycentric/ regiocentric	Multinational	Global/multicentric
Cultural sensitivity	Marginally important	Very important	Somewhat important	Critically important
With whom	No one	Clients	Employees	Employees and clients
Level	No one	Workers and clients	Managers	Executives
Strategic assumption	"One way"/ one best way	"Many good ways," equifinality	"One least-cost way" simultaneously	"Many good ways"

Source: From Adler. *International Dimensions of Organizational Behavior,* 5th ed. © 2008 South-Western, a part of Cengage Learning, Inc. Reproduced by permission. www.cengage.com/permissions.

multiculturalism is highly significant. As companies become what she calls "multinational corporations" (Phase III), they often find that price tends to dominate all other considerations, and the direct impact of culture may lessen slightly. For those who continue this international evolution and become full-blown "global corporations" (Phase IV), the impact of culture again becomes extremely important. Notes Adler:

> Global firms need an understanding of cultural dynamics to plan their strategy, to locate production facilities and suppliers worldwide, to design and market culturally appropriate products and services, as well as to manage cross-cultural interaction throughout the organization—from senior executive committees to the shop floor. As more firms today move from domestic, international, and multinational organizations to operating as truly global organizations and alliances, the importance of cultural diversity increases markedly. What once was "nice to understand" becomes imperative for survival, let alone success.[41]

Figure 6–4

Locations of International Cross-Cultural Interaction

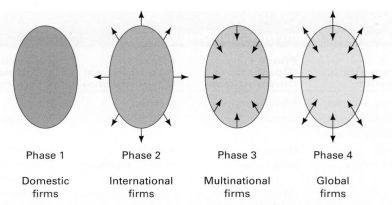

Phase 1 Phase 2 Phase 3 Phase 4

Domestic firms | International firms | Multinational firms | Global firms

Source: From Adler. *International Dimensions of Organizational Behavior,* 5th ed. © 2008 South-Western, a part of Cengage Learning, Inc. Reproduced by permission. www.cengage .com/permissions.

As shown in Figure 6–4, international cultural diversity traditionally affects neither the domestic firm's organizational culture nor its relationship with its customers or clients. These firms work domestically, and only domestic multiculturalism has a direct impact on their dynamics as well as on their relationship to the external environment.

Conversely, among international firms, which focus on exporting and producing abroad, cultural diversity has a strong impact on their external relationships with potential buyers and foreign employees. In particular, these firms rely heavily on expatriate managers to help manage operations; as a result, the diversity focus is from the inside out. This is the reverse of what happens in multinational firms, where there is less emphasis on managing cultural differences outside the firm and more on managing cultural diversity within the company. This is because multinational firms hire personnel from all over the world. Adler notes that these multinational firms need to develop cross-cultural management skills up the levels of the hierarchy. As shown in Figure 6–4, this results in a diversity focus that is primarily internal.

Global firms need both an internal and an external diversity focus (again see Figure 6–4). To be effective, everyone in the global organization needs to develop cross-cultural skills that allow them to work effectively with internal personnel as well as external customers, clients, and suppliers.

Types of Multiculturalism

For the international management arena, there are several ways of examining multiculturalism and diversity. One is to focus on the domestic multicultural and diverse workforce that operates in the MNC's home country. In addition to domestic multiculturalism, there is the diverse workforce in other geographic locales, and increasingly common are the mix of domestic and overseas personnel found in today's MNCs. The following discussion examines both domestic and group multiculturalism and the potential problems and strengths.

Domestic Multiculturalism It is not necessary for today's organizations to do business in another country to encounter people with diverse cultural backgrounds. Culturally distinct populations can be found within organizations almost everywhere in the world. In Singapore, for example, there are four distinct cultural and linguistic groups: Chinese, Eurasian, Indian, and Malay. In Switzerland, there are four distinct ethnic communities: French, German, Italian, and Romansch. In Belgium, there are two linguistic groups: French and Flemish. In the United States, millions of first-generation immigrants have brought both their languages and their cultures. In Los Angeles, for example, there are more Samoans than on the island of Samoa, more Israelis than in any other city outside Israel, and more first- and second-generation Mexicans than in any other city except Mexico City. In Miami, over one-half the population is Latin, and most residents speak Spanish fluently. More Puerto Ricans live in New York City than in Puerto Rico.

It is even possible to examine domestic multiculturalism within the same ethnic groups. For example, Lee, after conducting research in Singapore among small Chinese family businesses, found that the viewpoints of the older generation differ sharply from those of the younger generation.[42] Older generations tend to stress hierarchies, ethics, group dynamics and the status quo, while the younger generations focus on worker responsibility, strategy, individual performance, and striving for new horizons. These differences can slow organizational processes as one generation considers the other to be ineffective in its methods. Managers, therefore, need to consider employees on an individual basis and try to compile techniques that convey a common message, ultimately maximizing productivity while satisfying everyone across the ages. In short, there is considerable multicultural diversity domestically in organizations throughout the world, and this trend will continue. For example, the U.S. civilian labor force of the next decade will change dramatically in ethnic composition. In particular, there will be a significantly lower percentage of white males in the workforce and a growing percentage of women, African Americans, Hispanics, and Asians.

Group Multiculturalism There are a number of ways that diverse groups can be categorized. Four of the most common include:

1. **Homogeneous groups,** in which members have similar backgrounds and generally perceive, interpret, and evaluate events in similar ways. An example would be a group of male German bankers who are forecasting the economic outlook for a foreign investment.

2. **Token groups,** in which all members but one have the same background. An example would be a group of Japanese retailers and a British attorney who are looking into the benefits and shortcomings of setting up operations in Bermuda.

3. **Bicultural groups,** in which two or more members represent each of two distinct cultures. An example would be a group of four Mexicans and four Canadians who have formed a team to investigate the possibility of investing in Russia.

4. **Multicultural groups,** in which there are individuals from three or more different ethnic backgrounds. An example is a group of three American, three German, three Uruguayan, and three Chinese managers who are looking into mining operations in Chile.

As the diversity of a group increases, the likelihood of all members perceiving things in the same way decreases sharply. Attitudes, perceptions, and communication in general may be a problem. On the other hand, there also are significant advantages associated with the effective use of multicultural, diverse groups. Sometimes, local laws require a certain level of diversity in the workplace. More and more, people are moving to other countries to find the jobs that match their skills. International managers need to be cognizant of the likelihood that they will oversee a group that represents many cultures, not just the pervasive culture associated with that country. The following sections examine the potential problems and the advantages of workplace diversity.

homogeneous group
A group in which members have similar backgrounds and generally perceive, interpret, and evaluate events in similar ways.

token group
A group in which all members but one have the same background, such as a group of Japanese retailers and a British attorney.

bicultural group
A group in which two or more members represent each of two distinct cultures, such as four Mexicans and four Taiwanese who have formed a team to investigate the possibility of investing in a venture.

multicultural group
A group in which there are individuals from three or more different ethnic backgrounds, such as three U.S., three German, three Uruguayan, and three Chinese managers who are looking into mining operations in South Africa.

Potential Problems Associated with Diversity

Overall, diversity may cause a lack of cohesion that results in the unit's inability to take concerted action, be productive, and create a work environment that is conducive to both efficiency and effectiveness. These potential problems are rooted in people's attitudes. An example of an attitudinal problem in a diverse group may be the mistrust of others. For example, many U.S. managers who work for Japanese operations in the United States complain that Japanese managers often huddle together and discuss matters in their native language. The U.S. managers wonder aloud why the Japanese do not speak English. What are they talking about that they do not want anyone else to hear? In fact, the Japanese often find it easier to communicate among themselves in their native language, and because no Americans are present, the Japanese managers ask why they should speak English. If there is no reason for anyone else to be privy to our conversation, why should we not opt for our own language? Nevertheless, such practices do tend to promote an atmosphere of mistrust.

Another potential problem may be perceptual. Unfortunately, when culturally diverse groups come together, they often bring preconceived stereotypes with them. In initial meetings, for example, engineers from economically advanced countries often are perceived as more knowledgeable than those from less advanced countries. In turn, this perception can result in status-related problems, because some of the group initially are regarded as more competent than others and likely are accorded status on this basis. As the diverse group works together, erroneous perceptions often are corrected, but this takes time. In one diverse group consisting of engineers from a major Japanese firm and a world-class U.S. firm, a Japanese engineer was assigned a technical task because of his stereotyped technical educational background. The group soon realized that this particular Japanese engineer was not capable of doing this job, because for the last four years, he had been responsible for coordinating routine quality and no longer was on the technological cutting edge. His engineering degree from the University of Tokyo had resulted in the other members perceiving him as technically competent and able to carry out the task; this perception proved to be incorrect.

A related problem is inaccurate biases. For example, it is well known that Japanese companies depend on groups to make decisions. Entrepreneurial behavior, individualism, and originality are typically downplayed.[43] However, in a growing number of Japanese firms this stereotype is proving to be incorrect.[44] Here is an example.

> Mr. Uchida, a 28-year-old executive in a small software company, dyes his hair brown, keeps a sleeping bag by his desk for late nights in the office and occasionally takes the day off to go windsurfing. "Sometimes I listen to soft music to soothe my feelings, and sometimes I listen to hard music to build my energy," said Mr. Uchida, who manages the technology development division of the Rimnet Corporation, an Internet access provider. "It's important that we always keep in touch with our sensibilities when we want to generate ideas." The creative whiz kid, a business personality often prized by corporate America, has come to Japan Inc. Unlikely as it might seem in a country renowned for its deference to authority and its devotion to group solidarity, freethinkers like Mr. Uchida are popping up all over the workplace. Nonconformity is suddenly in.[45]

Still another potential problem with diverse groups is miscommunication or inaccurate communication, which can occur for a number of reasons. Misunderstandings can be caused by a speaker using words that are not clear to other members. For example, in a diverse group in which one of the authors was working, a British manager told her U.S. colleagues, "I will fax you this report in a fortnight." When the author asked the Americans when they would be getting the report, most of them believed it would be arriving in four days. They did not know that the common British word fortnight (14 nights) means two weeks.

Another contribution to miscommunication may be the way in which situations are interpreted. Many Japanese nod their heads when others talk, but this does not mean that they agree with what is being said. They are merely being polite and attentive. In many societies, it is impolite to say no, and if the listener believes that the other person wants a positive answer, the listener will say yes even though this is incorrect. As a result, many U.S. managers find out that promises made by individuals from other cultures cannot be taken at face value—and in many instances, the other individual assumes that the American realizes this!

Diversity also may lead to communication problems because of different perceptions of time. For example, many Japanese will not agree to a course of action on the spot. They will not act until they have discussed the matter with their own people, because they do not feel empowered to act alone. Many Latin managers refuse to be held to a strict timetable, because they do not have the same time urgency that U.S. managers do. Here is another example, as described by a European manager:

> In attempting to plan a new project, a three-person team composed of managers from Britain, France, and Switzerland failed to reach agreement. To the others, the British representative appeared unable to accept any systematic approach; he wanted to discuss all potential problems before making a decision. The French and Swiss representatives agreed to examine everything before making a decision, but then disagreed on the sequence and scheduling of operations. The Swiss, being more pessimistic in their planning, allocated more time for each suboperation than did the French. As a result, although everybody agreed on its validity, we never started the project. If the project had been discussed by three Frenchmen, three Swiss, or three Britons, a decision, good or bad, would have been made. The project would not have been stalled for lack of agreement.[46]

Advantages of Diversity

While there are some potential problems to overcome when using culturally diverse groups in today's MNCs, there are also very many benefits to be gained.[47] In particular, there is growing evidence that culturally diverse groups can enhance creativity, lead to better decisions, and result in more effective and productive performance.[48]

One main benefit of diversity is the generation of more and better ideas. Because group members come from a variety of cultures, they often are able to create a greater number of unique (and thus creative) solutions and recommendations. For example, a U.S. MNC recently was preparing to launch a new software package aimed at the mass consumer market. The company hoped to capitalize on the upcoming Christmas season with a strong advertising campaign in each of its international markets. A meeting of the sales managers from these markets in Spain, the Middle East, and Japan helped the company revise and better target its marketing effort. The Spanish manager suggested that the company focus its campaign around the coming of the Magi (January 6) and not Christmas (December 25), because in Latin cultures, gifts typically are exchanged on the date that the Magi brought their gifts. The Middle Eastern manager pointed out that most of his customers were not Christians, so a Christmas campaign would not have much meaning in his area. Instead, he suggested the company focus its sales campaign around the value of the software and how it could be useful to customers and not worry about getting the product shipped by early December at all. The Japanese manager concurred with his Middle Eastern colleague but further suggested that some of the colors being proposed for the sales brochure be changed to better fit with Japanese culture. Thanks to these diverse ideas, the sales campaign proved to be one of the most effective in the company's history.

A second major benefit is that culturally diverse groups can prevent **groupthink**, which is caused by social conformity and pressures on individual members of a group

groupthink
Consensus reached because of social conformity and pressures on individual members of a group to conform to group norms.

to conform and reach consensus. When groupthink occurs, group participants come to believe that their ideas and actions are correct and that those who disagree with them are either uninformed or deliberately trying to sabotage their efforts. Multicultural diverse groups often are able to avoid this problem, because the members do not think similarly or feel pressure to conform. As a result, they typically question each other, offer opinions and suggestions that are contrary to those held by others, and must be persuaded to change their minds. Therefore, unanimity is achieved only through a careful process of deliberation. Unlike homogeneous groups, where everyone can be "of one mind," diverse groups may be slower to reach a general consensus, but the decision may be more effective and free of "groupthink."

Diversity in the workplace enhances more than the internal operations but relationships to customers as well. It is commonly held that anyone will have insight into and connect better with others of the same nationality or cultural background, resulting in more quickly building trust and understanding of one another's preferences. Therefore, if the customer base is composed of many cultures, it may benefit the company to have representatives from corresponding nationalities. The U.S. multinational cosmetic firm Avon adopted this philosophy over a decade ago. When Avon observed an increase in the number of Korean shoppers at one of its U.S. locations, it quickly employed Korean sales staff.[49] The external environment, even in the MNC home country, can encompass many cultures that managers should bear in mind. Expanding diversity in the workplace to better serve the customer means that even local managers have an international exposure, further emphasizing the importance of learning about the multicultural surroundings.

Building Multicultural Team Effectiveness

Multiculturally diverse teams have a great deal of potential, depending on how they are managed. As shown in Figure 6–5, Dr. Carol Kovach, who conducted research on the importance of leadership in managing cross-cultural groups, reports that if cross-cultural groups are led properly, they can indeed be highly effective; unfortunately, she also found that if they are not managed properly, they can be highly ineffective. In other words, diverse groups are more powerful than single-culture groups. They can hurt the organization, but if managed effectively, they can be the best.[50] The following sections provide the conditions and guidelines for managing diverse groups in today's organizations effectively.

Figure 6–5

Group Effectiveness and Culture

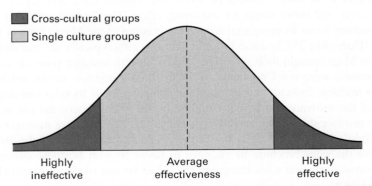

Cross-cultural groups

Single culture groups

Highly ineffective   Average effectiveness   Highly effective

Source: From Adler. *International Dimensions of Organizational Behavior,* 5th ed. © 2008 South-Western, a part of Cengage Learning, Inc. Reproduced by permission. www.cengage.com/permissions.

Understanding the Conditions for Effectiveness Multicultural teams are most effective when they face tasks requiring innovativeness. They are far less effective when they are assigned to routine tasks. As Adler explains:

> Cultural diversity provides the biggest asset for teams with difficult, discretionary tasks requiring innovation. Diversity becomes less helpful when employees are working on simple tasks involving repetitive or routine procedures. Therefore, diversity generally becomes more valuable during the planning and development of projects (the "work" stage) and less helpful during their implementation (the "action" stage). The more senior the team members, the more likely they are to be working on projects that can benefit from diversity. Diversity is therefore extremely valuable to senior executive teams, both within and across countries.[51]

To achieve the greatest effectiveness from diverse teams, the focus of attention must be determined by the stage of team development (e.g., entry, working, and action stages). In the entry stage, the focus should be on building trust and developing team cohesion, as we saw in The World of International Management at the opening of the chapter. This can be difficult for diverse teams, whose members are accustomed to working in different ways. For example, Americans, Germans, and Swiss typically spend little time getting to know each other; they find out the nature of the task and set about pursuing it on their own without first building trust and cohesion. This contrasts sharply with individuals from Latin America, Southern Europe, and the Middle East, where team members spend a great deal of initial time getting to know each other. This contrast between task-oriented and relationship-oriented members of a diverse team may slow progress due to communication and strategic barriers. To counteract this problem, it is common in the entry stage of development to find experienced multicultural managers focusing attention on the team members' equivalent professional qualifications and status. Once this professional similarity and respect are established, the group can begin forming a collective unit. In the work stage of development, attention may be directed more toward describing and analyzing the problem or task that has been assigned. This stage often is fairly easy for managers of multicultural teams, because they can draw on the diversity of the members in generating ideas. As noted earlier, diverse groups tend to be most effective when dealing with situations that require innovative approaches.

In the action stage, the focus shifts to decision making and implementation. This can be a difficult phase, because it often requires consensus building among the members. In achieving this objective, experienced managers work to help the diverse group recognize and facilitate the creation of ideas with which everyone can agree. In doing so, it is common to find strong emphasis on problem-solving techniques such as the nominal group technique (NGT), where the group members individually make contributions before group interaction takes place and consensus is reached.

Using the Proper Guidelines Some specific guidelines have proved to be helpful as a quick reference for managers when setting out to manage a culturally diverse team. Here are some of the most useful ideas:

1. Team members must be selected for their task-related abilities and not solely based on ethnicity. If the task is routine, homogeneous membership often is preferable; if the task is innovative, multicultural membership typically is best.

2. Team members must recognize and be prepared to deal with their differences. The goal is to facilitate a better understanding of cross-cultural differences and generate a higher level of performance and rapport. In doing so, members need to become aware of their own stereotypes, as well as those of the others, and use this information to better understand the real differences that exist between them. This can then serve as a basis for determining how each individual member can contribute to the overall effectiveness of the team.

3. Because members of diverse teams tend to have more difficulty agreeing on their purpose and task than members of homogeneous groups, the team leader

must help the group to identify and define its overall goal. This goal is most useful when it requires members to cooperate and develop mutual respect in carrying out their tasks.

4. Members must have equal power so that everyone can participate in the process; cultural dominance always is counterproductive. As a result, managers of culturally diverse teams distribute power according to each person's ability to contribute to the task, not according to ethnicity.

5. It is important that all members have mutual respect for each other. This is often accomplished by managers' choosing members of equal ability, making prior accomplishments and task-related skills known to the group, and minimizing early judgments based on ethnic stereotypes.

6. Because teams often have difficulty determining what is a good or a bad idea or decision, managers must give teams positive feedback on their process and output. This feedback helps the members see themselves as a team, and it teaches them to value and celebrate their diversity, recognize contributions made by the individual members, and trust the collective judgment of the group.

The World of International Management—Revisited

Our discussion in The World of International Management at the outset of the chapter introduced the challenges and the benefits of diverse, multicultural teams. These teams have become commonplace in organizations around the world as work becomes more flexible and less geographically bound. In addition, companies are looking to such teams to solve intractable problems and bring creativity and fresh thinking to their organizations. Using what you have learned from this chapter, answer the following: (1) What steps should organizations take to get the most out of their global virtual teams? (2) What types of organizational culture (family, Eiffel Tower, guided missile, incubator) would be best for leveraging global teams? (3) What advantages and problems associated with diversity have been experienced by global teams? How might they be overcome? (4) What features of multicultural teams are most critical for successful global team collaboration?

SUMMARY OF KEY POINTS

1. Organizational culture is a pattern of basic assumptions developed by a group as it learns to cope with its problems of external adaptation and internal integration and taught to new members as the correct way to perceive, think, and feel in relation to these problems. Some important characteristics of organizational culture include observed behavioral regularities, norms, dominant values, philosophy, rules, and organizational climate.

2. Organizational cultures are shaped by a number of factors. These include the general relationship between employees and their organization, the hierarchic system of authority that defines the roles of managers and subordinates, and the general views that employees hold about the organization's

purpose, destiny, and goals and their place in the organization. When examining these differences, Trompenaars suggested the use of two continua: equity-hierarchy and person-task orientation, resulting in four basic types of organizational cultures: family, Eiffel Tower, guided missile, and incubator.

3. Family culture is characterized by strong emphasis on hierarchic authority and orientation to the person. Eiffel Tower culture is characterized by strong emphasis on hierarchy and orientation to the task. Guided missile culture is characterized by strong emphasis on equality in the workplace and orientation to the task. Incubator culture is characterized by strong emphasis on equality and orientation to the person.

4. Success in the international arena often is heavily determined by a company's ability to manage multiculturalism and diversity. Firms progress through four phases in their international evolution: (1) domestic corporation, (2) international corporation, (3) multinational corporation, and (4) global corporation.

5. There are a number of ways to examine multiculturalism and diversity. One is by looking at the domestic multicultural and diverse workforce that operates in the MNC's home country. Another is by examining the variety of diverse groups that exist in MNCs, including homogeneous groups, token groups, bicultural groups, and multicultural groups. Several potential problems as well as advantages are associated with multicultural, diverse teams. Diverse teams are not only helpful to internal operations but can enhance sales to customers as well, as shown at Avon.

6. A number of guidelines have proved to be particularly effective in managing culturally diverse groups. These include careful selection of the members, identification of the group's goals, establishment of equal power and mutual respect among the participants, and delivering positive feedback on performance.

KEY TERMS

bicultural group, *191*

Eiffel Tower culture, *184*

family culture, *184*

groupthink, *193*

guided missile culture, *185*

homogeneous group, *191*

incubator culture, *186*

multicultural group, *191*

organizational culture, *177*

token group, *191*

REVIEW AND DISCUSSION QUESTIONS

1. Some researchers have found that when Germans work for a U.S. MNC, they become even more German, and when Americans work for a German MNC, they become even more American. Why would this knowledge be important to these MNCs?

2. When comparing the negotiating styles and strategies of French versus Spanish negotiators, a number of sharp contrasts are evident. What are three of these, and what could MNCs do to improve their position when negotiating with either group?

3. In which of the four types of organizational cultures—family, Eiffel Tower, guided missile, incubator—would most people in the United States feel comfortable? In which would most Japanese feel comfortable? Based on your answers, what conclusions could you draw regarding the importance of understanding organizational culture for international management?

4. Most MNCs need not enter foreign markets to face the challenge of dealing with multiculturalism. Do you agree or disagree with this statement? Explain your answer.

5. What are some potential problems that must be overcome when using multicultural, diverse teams in today's organizations? What are some recognized advantages? Identify and discuss two of each.

6. A number of guidelines can be valuable in helping MNCs to make diverse teams more effective. What are five of these? How do these relate to the guidelines established by Matsushita, as discussed in the International Management in Action box?

INTERNET EXERCISE: LENOVO'S INTERNATIONAL FOCUS

Based in China, Lenovo is one of the largest computer brands in the world. Several years ago Lenovo purchased IBM's PC business and now sells more computers to retail customers and businesses than any company in the world. From its base in China, it is moving aggressively into global markets, especially emerging countries like India.

Visit Lenovo's website at lenovo.com, and review some of the latest developments. In particular, pay close attention to its product line and international expansion. Using the country/language tab in the upper center of the screen, choose three different countries where the firm is doing business: one from the Americas, one from Europe, and one from Southeast Asia or India. (The sites are all presented in the local language, so you might want to make India your choice because this site is in English.) Compare and contrast the product offerings and ways in which HP goes about marketing itself over the Web in these locations. What do you see as some of the major differences? Second, using Figure 6–2 and Table 6–3 as your guide, in what way are differences in organizational cultures internationally likely to present significant challenges to Lenovo efforts to create a smooth-running international enterprise? Look at the web page showing Lenovo's leadership team. What do you notice? What would you see as two of the critical issues with which management will have to deal? Third, what are two steps that you think Lenovo will have to take in order to build multicultural team effectiveness? What are two guidelines that can help it do this?

Japan

Japan is located in eastern Asia, and it comprises a curved chain of more than 3,000 islands. Four of these—Hokkaido, Honshu, Shikoku, and Kyushi—account for 89 percent of the country's land area. The population of Japan is approximately 128 million, with over 35 million people living in the metro of the nation's capital, Tokyo. According to the WorldBank, the country's gross domestic product in 2011 was approximately US$5.9 trillion, or US$45,900 per capita. Japan has faced a long period of stagnant economic growth. Japan's economy was especially hard hit by the global economic financial crisis, with GDP shrinking by 5.2 percent in 2009. The economy was still contracting in 2012 by about 1 percent.

Surprisingly, Japan has become a fashion mecca. Spanish clothing company Zara, Swedish brand H&M, French designer Louis Vuitton, and American jeweler Tiffany & Co. are very popular and prosperous throughout Japan. The new generation of fashion aficionados also makes Japan a country to watch. Japan is usually associated with a minimalist nature, not owning more than is necessary. In Tokyo, however, younger people are beginning to express themselves by quickly purchasing any item that appears to be part of a new trend, only to abandon it for the next craze in the blink of an eye. Investment in Japan has been supported by this phenomenon, since many fashion companies use Japan as their new testing ground before launching expensive lines in other markets. While New York City in the United States was once considered the primary region to try out new styles, experience has shown that what catches on in Japan often works across the globe as well and that the Japanese are much faster to respond to new products. This does not imply that everything that is tested in Japan will work worldwide. For example, bags with bubbly, cartoon printing containing the likes of Hello Kitty or indistinguishable characteristics that thrive in the kawaii, or "cute," market segment may not make a profit elsewhere. Essentially, there are times when Japan is distinctly ahead of the crowd, and it may take quite some time for the rest of the world to catch up.

Considering workplace ethics and customs in the home, most would not immediately think of Japan as such a vogue region. For instance, in business, employees often dress conservatively, are well groomed, and do not leave the work space until after the boss has left, which can be many hours after the office has officially closed. In fact, it is usually embarrassing for a worker to leave the moment the office closes, since that is seen as leaving "early," and it singles out the employee. Homes can be small, with little extra room for extravagant purchases, though with gift giving so prevalent in the country, it is unpredictable what someone else may procure for your household. These reasons and many more would imply that the Japanese would not want to call more attention to themselves. However, as Japan continues to move toward individualistic tendencies, citizens may be scrambling to find a way to express their own unique voice.

www.japanlink.com, www.businessweek.com, www.infoplease.com/ipa/A0107666.html, data.worldbank.org/country/japan

Questions

1. Based on their home country, how might the organizational cultures of the four fashion companies mentioned be distinct from one another, and in what ways could they be the same?

2. If the first two companies and the last two companies want to form joint ventures (Zara with H&M, and Louis Vuitton with Tiffany & Co.), what could be some potential ways the organizational cultures interact?

3. What types of problems might a culturally diverse top management team at headquarters create for the two joint ventures? Give some specific examples. How could these problems be overcome?

4. How could work structures and schedules of these companies at their respective headquarters affect operations in Japan? In what ways are they different or similar?

Chapter 7

CROSS-CULTURAL COMMUNICATION AND NEGOTIATION

Communication takes on special importance in international management because of the difficulties in conveying meanings between parties from different cultures. The problems of misinterpretation and error are compounded in the international context. Chapter 7 examines how the communication process in general works, and it looks at the downward and upward communication flows that commonly are used in international communication. Then the chapter examines the major barriers to effective international communication and reviews ways of dealing with these communication problems. Finally, one important dimension of international communication, international negotiation, is examined, with particular attention to how negotiation approaches and strategies must be adapted to different cultural environments. The specific objectives of this chapter are:

1. DEFINE the term *communication,* examine some examples of verbal communication styles, and explain the importance of message interpretation.

2. ANALYZE the common downward and upward communication flows used in international communication.

3. EXAMINE the language, perception, and culture of communication and nonverbal barriers to effective international communications.

4. PRESENT the steps that can be taken to overcome international communication problems.

5. DEVELOP approaches to international negotiations that respond to differences in culture.

6. REVIEW different negotiating and bargaining behaviors that may improve negotiations and outcomes.

The World of *International Management*

Offshoring Culture and Communication

Offshore call-center agents for a North American airline had difficulty relating to customers stranded at airports because of a snowstorm. The reason? These agents had never seen snow or been to an airport. The solution? The airline set up TVs broadcasting CNN in the break rooms so that agents could be exposed to snow, airports, and flight delays.

Offshoring, or the practice of a company moving certain services overseas, has highlighted cultural differences between employees around the world. Yet, if offshoring is managed correctly, companies can save money and increase productivity. By offshoring, Mamas and Papas, a U.K.-based baby stroller company, has benefited from the decreased labor and material costs and the ability to send work to places in the world best equipped to complete each piece of the manufacturing process. An employee of the company, Gill Kingston-Warren, told the Financial Times: "The U.K. is known for design and intellectual property and other countries have skills we are not known for any more. Some countries have strong traditions of craftsmanship, while others are focused on technology."[1] Offshoring enables companies to capitalize on other countries' cultural advantages. By the same token, however, these cultural differences can create challenges for firms that engage in offshoring.

Cultural Challenges

According to the global management consultants A.T. Kearney, when companies offshore certain operations, they face four main cultural challenges: communication, context, relationships, and working norms.

First, employees may encounter communication difficulties. In "The Offshore Cultural Clash," A.T. Kearney consultants wrote:

An American financial services manager e-mailed a counterpart in India laying out a project and asking for a work plan. Her counterpart's reply: "I will do the needful." The meaning, clear to people in India, is "I will do what's necessary to accomplish what we've been talking about." Most Westerners in Europe and North America have probably never heard the phrase and don't understand it. They prefer to convey their views directly and clarify the details of their contracts and intentions. In India, where e-mails are far less specific, such detail seems not only unnecessary, but also distrustful. The two cultures hold different expectations of what is said, what needs to be said, and what can remain unsaid but understood.[2]

Understanding the communication style of different cultures is key to managing employees in different regions of the world. In addition, it is essential to prevent communication lapses. For instance, an American bank had offshore service providers that it had worked with for the past five years, yet their relationships remained strained. The bank eventually discovered that U.S.-based IT teams received important updates for changing business requirements, but the offshore partners never received these updates. As a result, the bank had to re-do much of its work at significant cost. Companies can avoid this problem by having a dedicated liaison between the "home country" and offshore employees to verify that every team has clear information and work expectations.[3]

Second, managers must be aware of offshore workers' "context." Do these workers possess a cultural context necessary to understand the product or service? One credit card company executive told A.T. Kearney that his employees in India struggled to apply their accounting knowledge to credit card payment processing because "Consumer credit markets are not as pervasive in India as they are in the United States, where it's hard to find anyone who doesn't have an intuitive understanding of credit-card transactions. For our offshore agents, we had to develop that foundation."[4]

Third, companies need to understand how offshore agents perceive relationships. According to A.T. Kearney, one manager noticed that offshore agents are very deferential to their superiors. He said that if a manager is in the room, offshore agents "will not answer questions or make comments without specific invitations to do so."[5]

Fourth, managers must be aware of different cultural working norms. Indeed, by fostering collaboration between employees with cultural strengths, managers can increase productivity. One executive told A.T. Kearney that his company was very consensus-driven, but it lacked discipline. He found an offshore service provider that had a culture of discipline. Offshoring can be an opportunity for a company to find employees with different strengths to handle work that is best suited for them.[6]

Tips for Managing Offshoring

The following are a few tips for managing the cultural challenges of offshore operations.

Avoid an "us vs. them" mentality. Instead, insist on mutual respect. Companies that have a strong hierarchical and "clan" culture often resent their offshore colleagues. One manager compared this situation to a transplant patient rejecting a new organ. To prevent this problem, A.T. Kearney recommended: "All parties to the offshoring arrangement should understand that mutual respect for cultures, both national and corporate, is not negotiable. One way to demonstrate mutual respect is to send a healthy mix of rote and 'intelligent' activities to the offshore location. Delegating complex activities to the offshore team also requires a close working relationship, which can build trust."[7] Also, personal face-to-face interactions can help managers work through cultural differences so that offshore counterparts can be true partners.

Provide training to managers to meet new expectations. When companies move certain operations offshore, managers are often expected to be able to manage offshore employees without any additional training. Companies need to provide training opportunities to managers to fulfill their new roles, such as teaching them to use metrics to manage people rather than supervising by line of sight.[8]

Foster collaboration between "home country" and offshore employees. Based on their study of 130 offshore operations in India, Kannan Srikanth and

Phanish Puranam found that the operations that "paid close attention to managing coordination performed almost four times as well as their less-successful counterparts."[9] Furthermore, Srikanth and Puranam indicated that by focusing on teamwork between offshore and "home country" employees, companies could expand their offshore operations beyond merely call-centers and IT support. They noted that "if Western companies focused more on fostering collaboration between workers separated by geography and culture, and less on forcing offshore workers to perform tasks in very specific ways, the range of work they could source offshore would be significantly expanded."[10] How do managers achieve this collaboration? Srikanth and Puranam suggested that managers concentrate on "building common ground—essentially, shared knowledge—across locations, so that employees working offshore

can anticipate the actions and decisions of their onshore counterparts without the need for extensive discussion."[11] Companies can develop common ground in two ways. Managers can train employees together so they become familiar with others' work habits and adopt the same business vocabulary. Also, firms can utilize technology that allows employees to see work across locations as it is being performed.[12]

As A.T. Kearney consultants point out, "Cultural issues are not insurmountable, but they must be purposely and diligently addressed."[13] In A.T. Kearney's 2007 study of offshoring performance, A.T. Kearney found that cross-border culture and communications issues were a significant problem for companies engaging in offshoring. By understanding cultural differences ahead of time, managers increase their chances that they can make offshoring operations a success for their companies.[14]

Offshoring problems

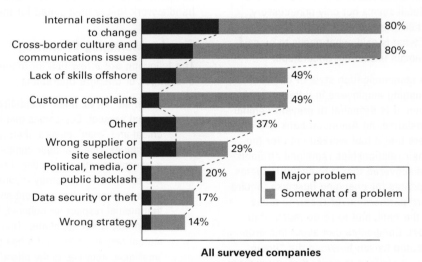

All surveyed companies

Source: Execution Is Everything: The Keys to Offshoring Success, copyright A. T. Kearney, 2007. All rights reserved. Reprinted with permission.

The opening World of International Management illustrates how cross-border communication is affected by cultural differences—both national and organizational—and how the increased offshoring of service tasks has exacerbated those challenges. Many firms offshore tasks in order to save costs without considering the implications for service and managerial oversight, issues that can quickly erode the cost benefits. The stark differences in culture, some emanating from basic variation in political, geographic, and even climatic realities (as in the example of the call-center staff who had never seen snow or been in an airport) can frustrate the coordination of global operations. Yet, there are some simple approaches that can alleviate some of these challenges and begin to bridge cultural divides. These center around anticipating, or at least responding quickly to, cultural gaps, and also creating an environment of continuous information exchange and communication. They also depend on deeper understanding of cultural differences and willingness to adapt and adjust to those differences when appropriate.

In this chapter, we explore communication and negotiation styles across cultures, emphasizing the importance of understanding different approaches to the development of effective international communication and negotiation strategies.

■ The Overall Communication Process

Communication is the process of transferring meanings from sender to receiver. On the surface, this appears to be a fairly straightforward process. On analysis, however, there are a great many problems in the international arena that can result in the failure to transfer meanings correctly.

In addition, as suggested in the opening World of International Management, the means and modes of communication have changed dramatically in recent decades. For example, the advent of the telephone, then Internet, and most recently personal communication devices ("smartphones") has influenced how, when, and why people communicate. These trends have both benefits and disadvantages. On the plus side, we have many more opportunities to communicate rapidly, without delays or filters, and often can incorporate rich content, such as photos, videos, and links to other information, in our exchanges. On the other hand, some are concerned that these devices are rendering our communication less meaningful and personal. In a recent book, Nicholas Carr argues that when we go online, "we enter an environment that promotes cursory reading, hurried and distracted thinking, and superficial learning." Mr. Carr calls the Web "a technology of forgetfulness." Web pages draw us into a myriad of embedded links while we are assaulted by other messages via e-mail, RSS, and Twitter and Facebook accounts. He suggests that greater access to knowledge is not the same as greater knowledge and that an ever-increasing plethora of facts and data is not the same as wisdom.[15]

Despite these concerns, communication—verbal and otherwise—remains an important dimension of international management. In this chapter, we survey different communication styles, how communication is processed and interpreted, and how culture and language influence communication (and miscommunication).

Verbal Communication Styles

One way of examining the ways in which individuals convey information is by looking at their communication styles. In particular, as has been noted by Hall, context plays a key role in explaining many communication differences.[16] **Context** is information that surrounds a communication and helps convey the message. In high-context societies, such as Japan and many Arab countries, messages are often highly coded and implicit. As a result, the receiver's job is to interpret what the message means by correctly filtering through what is being said and the way in which the message is being conveyed. This approach is in sharp contrast to low-context societies such as the United States and Canada, where the message is explicit and the speaker says precisely what he or she means. These contextual factors must be considered when marketing messages are being developed in disparate societies. For example, promotions in Japan should be subtle and convey a sense of community (high context). Similar segments in the United States, a low-context environment, should be responsive to expectations for more explicit messages. Figure 7–1 provides an international comparison of high-context/implicit and low-context/explicit societies. In addition, Table 7–1 presents some of the major characteristics of communication styles.

Indirect and Direct Styles In high-context cultures, messages are implicit and indirect. One reason is that those who are communicating—family, friends, co-workers, clients— tend to have both close personal relationships and large information networks. As a result, each knows a lot about others in the communication network; they do not have to rely on language alone to communicate. Voice intonation, timing, and facial expressions can all play roles in conveying information.

communication
The process of transferring meanings from sender to receiver.

context
Information that surrounds a communication and helps convey the message.

Figure 7–1

Explicit-Implicit Communication: An International Comparison

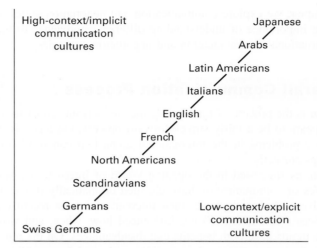

High-context/implicit communication cultures

Japanese
Arabs
Latin Americans
Italians
English
French
North Americans
Scandinavians
Germans
Swiss Germans

Low-context/explicit communication cultures

Source: Adapted from Martin Rosch, "Communications: Focal Point of Culture," *Management International Review* 27, no. 4 (1987), p. 60. Used with permission.

In low-context cultures, people often meet only to accomplish objectives. Since they do not know each other very well, they tend to be direct and focused in their communications.

One way of comparing these two kinds of culture—high context and low context—is by finding out what types of questions are typically asked when someone is contacted and told to attend a meeting. In a high-context culture it is common for the person to ask, "Who will be at this meeting?" so he or she knows how to prepare for appropriate personal interactions. In contrast, in a low-context culture the individual is likely to ask, "What is the meeting going to be about?" so he or she knows how to properly organize for the engagement. In the high-context society, the person focuses on the environment

Table 7–1
Major Characteristics of Verbal Styles

Verbal Style	Major Variation	Interaction Focus and Content	Cultures in Which Characteristic Is Found
Indirect vs. direct	Indirect	Implicit messages	Collective, high context
	Direct	Explicit messages	Individualistic, low context
Succinct vs. elaborate	Elaborate	High quantity of talk	Moderate uncertainty avoidance, high context
	Exacting	Moderate amount of talk	Low uncertainty avoidance, low context
	Succinct	Low amount of talk	High uncertainty avoidance, high context
Contextual vs. personal	Contextual	Focus on the speaker and role relationships	High power distance, collective, high context
	Personal	Focus on the speaker and personal relationships	Low power distance, individualistic, low context
Affective vs. instrumental	Affective	Process-oriented and receiver-focused language	Collective, high context
	Instrumental	Goal-oriented and sender-focused language	Individualistic, low context

in which the meeting will take place. In the low-context society, the individual is most interested in the objectives that are to be accomplished at the meeting.

Elaborate to Succinct Styles   There are three degrees of communication quantity—elaborate, exacting, and succinct. In high-context societies, the elaborate style is often very common. There is a great deal of talking, description includes much detail, and people often repeat themselves. This elaborate style is widely used in Arabic countries.

The exacting style is more common in nations such as England, Germany, and Sweden. This style focuses on precision and the use of the right amount of words to convey the message. If a person uses too many words, this is considered exaggeration; if the individual relies on too few, the result is an ambiguous message.

The succinct style is most common in Asia, where people tend to say few words and allow understatements, pauses, and silence to convey meaning. In particular, in unfamiliar situations, communicators are succinct in order to avoid risking a loss of face.

Researchers have found that the elaborating style is more popular in high-context cultures that have a moderate degree of uncertainty avoidance. The exacting style is more common in low-context, low-uncertainty-avoidance cultures. The succinct style is more common in high-context cultures with considerable uncertainty avoidance.

Contextual and Personal Styles   A contextual style is one that focuses on the speaker and relationship of the parties. For example, in Asian cultures people use words that reflect the role and hierarchical relationship of those in the conversation. As a result, in an organizational setting, speakers will choose words that indicate their status relative to the status of the others. Commenting on this idea, Yoshimura and Anderson have noted that white-collar, middle-management employees in Japan, commonly known as salarymen, quickly learn how to communicate with others in the organization by understanding the context and reference group of the other party:

> A salaryman can hardly say a word to another person without implicitly defining the reference groups to which he thinks both of them belong. . . . [This is because] failing to use proper language is socially embarrassing, and the correct form of Japanese to use with someone else depends not only on the relationship between the two people, but also on the relationship between their reference groups. Juniors defer to seniors in Japan, but even this relationship is complicated when the junior person works for a much more prestigious organization (for example, a government bureau) than the senior. [As a result, it is] likely that both will use the polite form to avoid social embarrassment.[17]

A personal style focuses on the speaker and the reduction of barriers between the parties. In the United States, for example, it is common to use first names and to address others informally and directly on an equal basis.

Researchers have found that the contextual style is often associated with high-power-distance, collective, high-context cultures. Examples include Japan, India, and Ghana. In contrast, the personal style is more popular in low-power-distance, individualistic, low-context cultures. Examples include the United States, Australia, and Canada.

Affective and Instrumental Styles   The affective style is characterized by language that requires the listener to carefully note what is being said and to observe how the sender is presenting the message. Quite often the meaning that is being conveyed is nonverbal and requires the receiver to use his or her intuitive skills in deciphering what is being said. The part of the message that is being left out may be just as important as the part that is being included. In contrast, the instrumental style is goal-oriented and focuses on the sender. The individual clearly lets the other party know what he or she wants the other party to know.

The affective style is common in collective, high-context cultures such as the Middle East, Latin America, and Asia. The instrumental style is more commonly found in individualistic, low-context cultures such as Switzerland, Denmark, and the United States.

Table 7–2
Verbal Styles Used in 10 Select Countries

Country	Indirect vs. Direct	Elaborate vs. Succinct	Contextual vs. Personal	Affective vs. Instrumental
Australia	Direct	Exacting	Personal	Instrumental
Canada	Direct	Exacting	Personal	Instrumental
Denmark	Direct	Exacting	Personal	Instrumental
Egypt	Indirect	Elaborate	Contextual	Affective
England	Direct	Exacting	Personal	Instrumental
Japan	Indirect	Succinct	Contextual	Affective
Korea	Indirect	Succinct	Contextual	Affective
Saudi Arabia	Indirect	Elaborate	Contextual	Affective
Sweden	Direct	Exacting	Personal	Instrumental
United States	Direct	Exacting	Personal	Instrumental

Source: Anne Marie Francesco and Barry Allen Gold, *International Organizational Behavior: Text, Readings, Cases, and Skills,* 1st Edition © 1998. Reproduced by permission of Barry Allen Gold.

Table 7–2 provides a brief description of the four verbal styles that are used in select countries. A close look at the table helps explain why managers in Japan can have great difficulty communicating with their counterparts in the United States and vice versa: The verbal styles do not match in any context.

Interpretation of Communications

The effectiveness of communication in the international context often is determined by how closely the sender and receiver have the same meaning for the same message.[18] If this meaning is different, effective communication will not occur. A good example is the U.S. firm that wanted to increase worker output among its Japanese personnel. This firm put an individual incentive plan into effect, whereby workers would be given extra pay based on their work output. The plan, which had worked well in the United States, was a total flop. The Japanese were accustomed to working in groups and to being rewarded as a group. In another case, a U.S. firm offered a bonus to anyone who would provide suggestions that resulted in increased productivity. The Japanese workers rejected this idea, because they felt that no one working alone is responsible for increased productivity. It is always a group effort. When the company changed the system and began rewarding group productivity, it was successful in gaining support for the program.

A related case occurs when both parties agree on the content of the message but one party believes it is necessary to persuade the other to accept the message. Here is an example:

> Motorola University recently prepared carefully for a presentation in China. After considerable thought, the presenters entitled it "Relationships do not retire." The gist of the presentation was that Motorola had come to China in order to stay and help the economy to create wealth. Relationships with Chinese suppliers, subcontractors and employees would constitute a permanent commitment to building Chinese economic infrastructure and earning hard currency through exports. The Chinese audience listened politely to this presentation but was quiet when invited to ask questions. Finally one manager put up his hand and said: "Can you tell us about pay for performance?"[19]

Quite obviously, the Motorola presenter believed that it was necessary to convince the audience that the company was in China for the long run. Those in attendance, however, had already accepted this idea and wanted to move on to other issues.

Still another example has been provided by Adler, who has pointed out that people doing business in a foreign culture often misinterpret the meaning of messages. As a result, they arrive at erroneous conclusions, as in the following story of a Canadian doing business in the Middle East. The Canadian was surprised when his meeting with a high-ranking official was not held in a closed office and was constantly interrupted:

> Using the Canadian-based cultural assumptions that (a) important people have large private offices with secretaries to monitor the flow of people into the office, and (b) important business takes precedence over less important business and is therefore not interrupted, the Canadian interprets the . . . open office and constant interruptions to mean that the official is neither as high ranking nor as interested in conducting the business at hand as he had previously thought.[20]

■ Communication Flows

Communication flows in international organizations move both down and up. However, as Figure 7–2 humorously, but in many ways accurately, portrays, there are some unique differences in organizations around the world.

Downward Communication

Downward communication is the transmission of information from manager to subordinate. The primary purpose of the manager-initiated communication flow is to convey orders and information. Managers use this channel to let their people know what is to be done and how well they are doing. The channel facilitates the flow of information to those who need it for operational purposes.

Communicating with subordinates can be both challenging and difficult, especially if the manager delivering the news does not believe in the decision. Some suggest that managers should consider pushing back with superiors to gauge whether there is some flexibility. If you haven't fully bought into it, "your employees will be able to tell in the tone of your voice or your body language that you do not believe in what you are doing," says Ray Skiba, director of human resources at Streck, a manufacturer of clinical laboratory products in Omaha, Nebraska. Whether or not this is successful, sending a mixed signal is never helpful.

> "Once you've done your internal work, prepare yourself to deliver the message. If there was team involvement in the decision, ask one of the team members to listen to how you plan to address your employees. The more prepared you are, the better the outcome," says Mr. Skiba. Next, consider your communication strategy. "Explain why the decision is important to the business, how the decision was made, and why it is important that the plan be executed," says Kimberly Bishop, founder of a career management and leadership services consulting firm in New York. Give your employees ample time to digest the message. Since it took you some time to accept the information, realize that your employees will need time as well. "When the message has been delivered, be available to answer questions, be visible and approachable to help individuals get to the point of acceptance," says Mr. Skiba.[21]

In the international context, downward communication poses special challenges. For example, in Asian countries, as noted earlier, downward communication is less direct than in the United States. Orders tend to be implicit in nature. Conversely, in some European countries, downward communication is not only direct but extends beyond business matters. For example, one early study surveyed 299 U.S. and French managers regarding the nature of downward communication and the managerial authority they perceived themselves as having. This study found that U.S. managers basically used downward communication for work-related matters. A follow-up study investigated matters that U.S. and French managers felt were within the purview of their authority.[22] The major differences involved work-related and nonwork-related activities: U.S. managers felt that it was within their authority to communicate or attempt to influence their people's

downward communication
The transmission of information from manager to subordinate.

There are a number of different "organization charts" that have been constructed to depict international organizations. An epigram is a poem or line of verse that is witty or satirical in nature. The following organization designs are epigrams that show how communication occurs in different countries. In examining them, remember that each contains considerable exaggeration and humor, but also some degree of truth.

In America, everyone thinks he or she has a communication pipeline directly to the top.

America

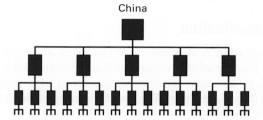

There are so many people in China that organizations are monolithic structures characterized by copious levels of bureaucracy. All information flows through channels.

China

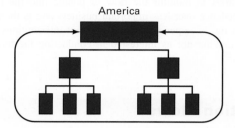

At the United Nations everyone is arranged in a circle so that no one is more powerful than anyone else. Those directly in front or behind are philosophically aligned, and those nearby form part of an international bloc.

United Nations

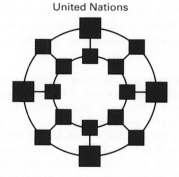

In France some people in the hierarchy are not linked to anyone, indicating how haphazard the structure can be.

France

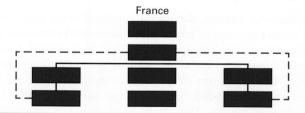

Source: Adapted from Simcha Ronen, *Comparative and Multinational Management* (New York: Wiley, 1986), pp. 318–319. The epigrams in turn were derived from a variety of sources, including Robert M. Worchester of the U.K.-based Market and Opinion Research International (MORI), Ole Jacob Raad of Norway's PM Systems, and anonymous managers.

social behavior only if it occurred on the job or it directly affected their work. For example, U.S. managers felt that it was proper to look into matters such as how much an individual drinks at lunch, whether the person uses profanity in the workplace, and how active the individual is in recruiting others to join the company. The French managers were not as supportive of these activities. The researcher concluded that "the Americans find it as difficult [as] or more difficult than the French to accept the legitimacy of managerial authority in areas unrelated to work."[23]

Harris and Moran have noted that, when communicating downward with nonnative speakers, it is extremely important to use language that is easy to understand and allows the other person to ask questions. Here are 10 suggestions that apply not only for downward but for all types of communication with nonnative speakers:

1. Use the most common words with their most common meanings.

2. Select words that have few alternative meanings.

3. Strictly follow the basic rules of grammar—more so than would be the case with native speakers.

4. Speak with clear breaks between the words so that it is easier for the person to follow.

5. Avoid using words that are esoteric or culturally biased such as "he struck out" or "the whole idea is Mickey Mouse" because these clichés often have no meaning for the listener.

6. Avoid the use of slang.

7. Do not use words or expressions that require the other person to create a mental image such as "we were knee deep in the Big Muddy."

8. Mimic the cultural flavor of the nonnative speaker's language, for example, by using more flowery communication with Spanish-speaking listeners than with Germans.

9. Continually paraphrase and repeat the basic ideas.

10. At the end, test how well the other person understands by asking the individual to paraphrase what has been said.[24]

Upward Communication

Upward communication is the transfer of information from subordinate to superior. The primary purpose of this subordinate-initiated upward communication is to provide feedback, ask questions, or obtain assistance from higher-level management. In recent years, there has been a call for and a concerted effort to promote more upward communication in the United States. In other countries, such as in Japan, Hong Kong, and Singapore, upward communication has long been a fact of life. Managers in these countries have extensively used suggestion systems and quality circles to get employee input and always are available to listen to their people's concerns.

upward communication
The transfer of meaning from subordinate to superior.

Here are some observations from the approach the Japanese firm Matsushita uses in dealing with employee suggestions:

> Matsushita views employee recommendations as instrumental to making improvements on the shop floor and in the marketplace. [It believes] that a great many little people, paying attention each day to how to improve their jobs, can accomplish more than a whole headquarters full of production engineers and planners. Praise and positive reinforcement are an important part of the Matsushita philosophy. . . . Approximately 90 percent of . . . suggestions receive rewards; most only a few dollars per month, but the message is reinforced constantly: "Think about your job; develop yourself and help us improve the company." The best suggestions receive company-wide recognition and can earn substantial monetary rewards. Each year, many special awards are also given, including presidential prizes and various divisional honors.[25]

Matsushita has used the same approach wherever it has established plants worldwide, and the strategy has proved very successful. The company has all its employees

---

Table 7–3
Matsushita's Philosophy

Basic Business Principles

To recognize our responsibilities as industrialists, to foster progress, to promote the general welfare of society, and to devote ourselves to the further development of world culture.

Employees Creed

Progress and development can be realized only through the combined efforts and cooperation of each member of the company. Each of us, therefore, shall keep this idea constantly in mind as we devote ourselves to the continuous improvement of our company.

The Seven Spiritual Values

1. National service through industry
2. Fairness
3. Harmony and cooperation
4. Struggle for betterment
5. Courtesy and humility
6. Adjustment and assimilation
7. Gratitude

---

begin the day by reciting its basic principles, beliefs, and values, which are summarized in Table 7–3, to reinforce in all employees the reason for the company's existence and to provide a form of spiritual fabric to energize and sustain them. All employees see themselves as important members of a successful team, and they are willing to do whatever is necessary to ensure the success of the group.

Outside these Asian countries, upward communication is not as popular. For example, in South America, many managers believe that employees should follow orders and not ask a lot of questions. German managers also make much less use of this form of communication. In most cases, however, evidence shows that employees prefer to have downward communication at least supplemented by upward channels. Unfortunately, such upward communication does not always occur because of a number of communication barriers.

■ Communication Barriers

A number of common communication barriers are relevant to international management. The more important barriers involve language, perception, culture, and nonverbal communication.

Language Barriers

Knowledge of the home country's language (the language used at the headquarters of the MNC) is important for personnel placed in a foreign assignment. If managers do not understand the language that is used at headquarters, they likely will make a wide assortment of errors. Additionally, many MNCs now prescribe English as the common language for internal communication, so that managers can more easily convey information to their counterparts in other geographically dispersed locales.[26] Despite such progress, however, language training continues to lag in many areas, although in an increasing number of European countries, more and more young people are becoming multilingual.[27] Table 7–4 shows the percentage of European students who are studying English, French, or German.

Language education is a good beginning, but it is also important to realize that the ability to speak the language used at MNC headquarters is often not enough to ensure that the personnel are capable of doing the work. Stout recently noted that many MNCs worldwide place a great deal of attention on the applicant's ability to speak English without considering if the person has other necessary skills, such as the ability to interact well with others and the technical knowledge demanded by the job.[28] Additionally, in interviewing people for jobs, he has noted that many interviewers fail to take into

Table 7–4
Multilingualism in the EU Classroom

	Percentage of Pupils in General Secondary Education Learning English, French, or German as a Foreign Language, 2009/2010		
	English	**French**	**German**
European Union	92.7	23.2	23.9
Finland	99.1	17.4	25.7
Germany	91.1	27.3	–
Denmark	91.7	10.6	34.7
Spain	94.7	22.3	1.0
France	99.5	–	21.6
Greece	91.4	6.9	2.9
Italy	97.7	19.5	6.9
Romania	98.7	86.3	11.8
Britain	–	27.4	10.3
Ireland	–	58.2	16.4
Poland	92.4	8.6	52.4

Source: Eurostat (2011).
http://eacea.ec.europa.eu/education/eurydice/documents/key_data_series/143EN.pdf

account the applicant's culture. As a result, interviewers misinterpret behaviors such as quietness or shyness and use them to conclude that the applicant is not sufficiently confident or self-assured. Still another problem is that nonnative speakers may know the language but not be fully fluent, so they end up asking questions or making statements that convey the wrong message. After studying Japanese for only one year, Stout began interviewing candidates in their local language and made a number of mistakes. In one case, he reports, "a young woman admitted to having an adulterous affair—even though this was not even close to the topic I was inquiring about—because of my unskilled use of the language."[29]

Written communication has been getting increased attention, because poor writing is proving to be a greater barrier than poor talking. For example, Hildebrandt has found that among U.S. subsidiaries studied in Germany, language was a major problem when subsidiaries were sending written communications to the home office. The process often involved elaborate procedures associated with translating and reworking the report. Typical steps included (1) holding a staff conference to determine what was to be included in the written message; (2) writing the initial draft in German; (3) rewriting the draft in German; (4) translating the material into English; (5) consulting with bilingual staff members regarding the translation; and (6) rewriting the English draft a series of additional times until the paper was judged to be acceptable for transmission. The German managers admitted that they felt uncomfortable with writing, because their command of written English was poor. As Hildebrandt noted:

> All German managers commanding oral English stated that their grammatical competence was not sufficiently honed to produce a written English report of top quality. Even when professional translators from outside the company rewrote the German into English, German middle managers were unable to verify whether the report captured the substantive intent or included editorial alterations.[30]

Problems associated with the translation of information from one language to another have been made even clearer by Schermerhorn, who conducted research among 153 Hong Kong Chinese bilinguals who were enrolled in an undergraduate management course at a major Hong Kong university. The students were given two scenarios, written in either

English or Chinese. One scenario involved a manager who was providing some form of personal support or praise for a subordinate. The research used the following procedures:

> [A] careful translation and back-translation method was followed to create the Chinese language versions of the research instruments. Two bilingual Hong Kong Chinese, both highly fluent in English and having expertise in the field of management, shared roles in the process. Each first translated one scenario and the evaluation questions into Chinese. Next they translated each other's Chinese versions back into English, and discussed and resolved translation differences in group consultation with the author. Finally, a Hong Kong professor read and interpreted the translations correctly as a final check of equivalency.[31]

The participants were asked to answer eight evaluation questions about these scenarios. A significant difference between the two sets of responses was found. Those who were queried in Chinese gave different answers from those who were queried in English. This led Schermerhorn to conclude that language plays a key role in conveying information between cultures and that in cross-cultural management research, bilingual individuals should not be queried in their second language.

Cultural Barriers in Language   Geographic distance poses challenges for international managers, but so do cultural and institutional distance. Previous research has conceptualized and measured cross-national differences primarily in terms of dyadic cultural distance; that is, comparing the "distance" of one culture to another. Some, however, have suggested that distance is a multidimensional construct which includes economic, financial, political, administrative, cultural, demographic, knowledge, and global connectedness as well as geographic distance and cannot be summarized in one "score."[32] Nowhere does such cultural distance show up more vividly than in challenges to accurate communications.

As one dimension of such distance, cultural barriers have significant ramifications for international communications. For example, research by Sims and Guice compared 214 letters of inquiry written by native and nonnative speakers of English to test the assumption that cultural factors affect business communication. Among other things, the researchers found that nonnative speakers used exaggerated politeness, provided unnecessary professional and personal information, and made inappropriate requests of the other party. Commenting on the results and implications of their study, the researchers noted that their investigation indicated that the deviations from standard U.S. business communication practices were not specific to one or more nationalities. The deviations did not occur among specific nationalities but were spread throughout the sample of nonnative letters used for the study. Therefore, we can speculate that U.S. native speakers of English might have similar difficulties in international settings. In other words, a significant number of native speakers in the U.S. might deviate from the standard business communication practices of other cultures. Therefore, these native speakers need specific training in the business communication practices of the major cultures of the world so they can communicate successfully and acceptably with readers in those cultures.[33]

Research by Scott and Green has extended these findings, showing that even in English-speaking countries, there are different approaches to writing letters. In the United States, for example, it is common practice when constructing a bad-news letter to start out "with a pleasant, relevant, neutral, and transitional buffer statement; give the reasons for the unfavorable news before presenting the bad news; present the refusal in a positive manner; imply the bad news whenever possible; explain how the refusal is in the reader's best interest; and suggest positive alternatives that build goodwill."[34] In Great Britain, however, it is common to start out by referring to the situation, discussing the reasons for the bad news, conveying the bad news (often quite bluntly), and concluding with an apology or statement of regret (something that is frowned on by business-letter experts in the United States) designed to keep the reader's goodwill. Here is an example:

> Lord Hanson has asked me to reply to your letter and questionnaire of February 12 which we received today.

As you may imagine, we receive numerous requests to complete questionnaires or to participate in a survey, and this poses problems for us. You will appreciate that the time it would take to complete these requests would represent a full-time job, so we decided some while ago to decline such requests unless there was some obvious benefit to Hanson PLC and our stockholders. As I am sure you will understand, our prime responsibility is to look after our stockholders' interests.

I apologize that this will not have been the response that you were hoping for, but I wish you success with your research study.[35]

U.S. MNC managers would seldom, if ever, send that type of letter; it would be viewed as blunt and tactless. However, the indirect approach that Americans use would be viewed by their British counterparts as overly indirect and obviously insincere.

On the other hand, when compared to Asians, many American writers are far more blunt and direct. For example, Park, Dillon, and Mitchell reported that there are pronounced differences between the ways in which Americans and Asians write business letters of complaint. They compared the approach used by American managers for whom English is a first language, who wrote international business letters of complaint, with the approach of Korean managers for whom English is a second language, who wrote the same types of letters. They found that American writers used a direct organizational pattern and tended to state the main idea or problem first before sharing explanatory details that clearly related to the stated problem. In contrast, the standard Korean pattern was indirect and tended to delay the reader's discovery of the main point. This led the researchers to conclude that the U.S.-generated letter might be regarded as rude by Asian readers, while American readers might regard the letter from the Korean writer as vague, emotional, and accusatory.[36]

Perceptual Barriers

Perception is a person's view of reality. How people see reality can vary and will influence their judgment and decision making.[37] Examples abound, of course, of how perceptions play an important role in international management. Japanese stockbrokers who perceived that the chances of improving their career would be better with U.S. firms have changed jobs. Hong Kong hoteliers bought U.S. properties because they had the perception that if they could offer the same top-quality hotel service as back home, they could dominate the U.S. markets. Unfortunately, misperceptions can become a barrier to effective communication and thus decision making. For example, when the Clinton administration decided to allow Taiwan President Lee Tenghui to visit the United States, the Chinese (PRC) government perceived this as a threatening gesture and took actions of its own. Besides conducting dangerous war games very near Taiwan's border as a warning to Taiwan not to become too bold in its quest for recognition as a sovereign nation, the PRC also snubbed U.S. car manufacturers and gave a much-coveted $1 billion contract to Mercedes-Benz of Germany.[38] In international incidents such as this, perception is critical, and misperceptions may get out of hand. The following sections provide examples of perceptual barriers and their results in the international business arena.

perception
A person's view of reality.

Advertising Messages   One way that perception can prove to be a problem in international management communication is the very basic misunderstandings caused when one side uses words or symbols that simply are misinterpreted by others. Many firms have found to their dismay that a failure to understand home-country perceptions can result in disastrous advertising programs, for instance. Here are two examples:

Ford . . . introduced a low cost truck, the "Fiera," into some Spanish-speaking countries. Unfortunately, the name meant "ugly old woman" in Spanish. Needless to say, this name did not encourage sales. Ford also experienced slow sales when it introduced a top-of-the-line automobile, the "Comet," in Mexico under the name "Caliente." The puzzling low sales were finally understood when Ford discovered that "caliente" is slang for a street walker.[39]

One laundry detergent company certainly wishes now that it had contacted a few locals before it initiated its promotional campaign in the Middle East. All of the company's advertisements pictured soiled clothes on the left, its box of soap in the middle, and clean clothes on the right. But, because in that area of the world people tend to read from the right to the left, many potential customers interpreted the message to indicate the soap actually soiled the clothes.[40]

There have been countless other such advertising blunders. Some speak to the political context, such as when Mercedes-Benz introduced its Grand Sports Tourer, or Mercedes GST, in Canada. Canadians were not very impressed, since they used the letters GST to refer to Canadian socialism. Other times, the advertising is simply offensive. Bacardi, for example, advertised the fruity drink "Pavian" in Germany, believing that it was tres chic. "Pavian" to the German population, however, meant "baboon." Needless to say, sales did not exceed expectations. The food and beverage industry may have experienced the worst string of bloopers. The Coors slogan "Turn It Loose" dismayed the Spanish who thought it would cause intestinal problems. In Taiwan, Pepsi's "Come alive with Pepsi" frightened consumers, since it literally meant "Pepsi will bring your ancestors back from the grave." Finally, even though Kentucky Fried Chicken is performing better in the Chinese market than in America, its catchphrase "Finger-licking good" was originally translated as "Eat your fingers off."[41]

Managers must be very careful when they translate messages. As mentioned, some common phrases in one country will not mean the same thing in others. Evidently from the many examples, errors in translation occur frequently, but MNCs can still come out on top with care and persistence, always remembering that perception may create new reality.

View of Others   Perception influences how individuals "see" others. A good example is provided by the perception of foreigners who reside in the United States by Americans and the perception of Americans by the rest of the world. Most Americans see themselves as extremely friendly, outgoing, and kind, and they believe that others also see them in this way. At the same time, many are not aware of the negative impressions they give to others. This has become especially salient in light of Americans' reaction to September 11, 2001, and their conduct of the Iraq War, which have at times shaken the world view of the United States. It becomes a trying exercise to sort through truth and error in such circumstances.

An example in the business world where perception is all important and misperception may abound is the way in which people act, or should act, when initially meeting others. The International Management in Action feature, "Doing It Right the First Time," provides some insight regarding how to conduct oneself when doing business in Japan.

Perceptions of others obviously may play a major role in the context of international management in the effects of the ways that international managers perceive their subordinates and their peers. For example, a study examined the perceptions that German and U.S. managers had of the qualifications of their peers (those on the same level and status), managers, and subordinates in Europe and Latin America.[42] The findings showed that both the German and the U.S. respondents perceived their subordinates to be less qualified than their peers. However, although the Germans perceived their managers to have more managerial ability than their peers, the Americans felt that their South American peers in many instances had qualifications equal to or better than the qualifications of their own managers. Quite obviously, these perceptions will affect how German and U.S. expatriates communicate with their South American and other peers and subordinates, as well as how the expatriates communicate with their bosses.

Another study found that Western managers have more favorable attitudes toward women as managers than do Asian or Saudi managers.[43] Japanese managers, according to one survey, also still regard women as superfluous to the effective running of their organizations and generally continue to not treat women as equals.[44] Such perceptions obviously affect the way these managers interact and communicate with their female counterparts.

Doing It Right the First Time

Like other countries of the world, Japan has its own business customs and culture. And when someone fails to adhere to tradition, the individual runs the risk of being perceived as ineffective or uncaring. The following addresses three areas that are important in being correctly perceived by one's Japanese counterparts.

Business Cards

The exchange of business cards is an integral part of Japanese business etiquette, and Japanese business-people exchange these cards when meeting someone for the first time. Additionally, those who are most likely to interface with non-Japanese are supplied with business cards printed in Japanese on one side and a foreign language, usually English, on the reverse side. This is aimed at enhancing recognition and pronunciation of Japanese names, which are often unfamiliar to foreign businesspeople. Conversely, it is advisable for foreign businesspeople to carry and exchange with their Japanese counterparts a similar type of card printed in Japanese and in their native language. These cards can often be obtained through business centers in major hotels.

When receiving a card, it is considered common courtesy to offer one in return. In fact, not returning a card might convey the impression that the manager is not committed to a meaningful business relationship in the future.

Business cards should be presented and received with both hands. When presenting one's card, the presenter's name should be facing the person who is receiving the card so the receiver can easily read it. When receiving a business card, it should be handled with care, and if the receiver is sitting at a conference or other type of table, the card should be placed in front of the individual for the duration of the meeting.

It is considered rude to put a prospective business partner's card in one's pocket before sitting down to discuss business matters.

Bowing

Although the handshake is increasingly common in Japan, bowing remains the most prevalent formal method of greeting, saying goodbye, expressing gratitude, or apologizing to another person. When meeting foreign businesspeople, however, Japanese will often use the handshake or a combination of both a handshake and a bow, even though there are different forms and styles of bowing, depending on the relationship of the parties involved. Foreign businesspeople are not expected to be familiar with these intricacies, and therefore a deep nod of the head or a slight bow will suffice in most cases. Many foreign businesspeople are unsure whether to use a handshake or to bow. In these situations, it is best to wait and see if one's Japanese counterpart offers a hand or prefers to bow and then to follow suit.

Attire

Most Japanese businessmen dress in conservative dark or navy blue suits, although slight variations in style and color have come to be accepted in recent years. As a general rule, what is acceptable business attire in virtually any industrialized country is usually regarded as good business attire in Japan as well. Although there is no need to conform precisely to the style of dress of the Japanese, good judgment should be exercised when selecting attire for a business meeting. If unsure about what constitutes appropriate attire for a particular situation, it is best to err on the conservative side.

The Impact of Culture

Besides language and perception, another major barrier to communication is culture, a topic that was given detailed attention in Chapter 4. Culture can affect communication in a number of ways, and one way is through the impact of cultural values.

Cultural Values   One expert on Middle Eastern countries notes that people there do not relate to and communicate with each other in a loose, general way as do those in the United States. Relationships are more intense and binding in the Middle East, and a wide variety of work-related values influence what people in the Middle East will and will not do.

In North American society, the generally professed prevalent pattern is one of nonclass-consciousness, as far as work is concerned. Students, for example, make extra pocket money by taking all sorts of part-time jobs—manual and otherwise—regardless of the socioeconomic stratum to which the individual belongs. The attitude is uninhibited. In the Middle East, the overruling obsession is how the money is made and via what kind of job.[45]

Table 7–5
U.S. Proverbs Representing Cultural Values

Proverb	Cultural Value
A penny saved is a penny earned.	Thriftiness
Time is money.	Time thriftiness
Don't cry over spilt milk.	Practicality
Waste not, want not.	Frugality
Early to bed, early to rise, makes one healthy, wealthy, and wise.	Diligence; work ethic
A stitch in time saves nine.	Timeliness of action
If at first you don't succeed, try, try again.	Persistence; work ethic
Take care of today, and tomorrow will take care of itself.	Preparation for future

Source: Adapted from Nancy J. Adler (with Allison Gunderson), *International Dimensions of Organizational Behavior,* 5th ed. (Mason, OH: South-Western, 2008), p. 84.

These types of values indirectly, and in many cases directly, affect communication between people from different cultures. For example, one would communicate differently with a "rich college student" from the United States than with one from Saudi Arabia. Similarly, when negotiating with managers from other cultures, knowing the way to handle the deal requires an understanding of cultural values.[46]

Another cultural value is the way that people use time. In the United States, people believe that time is an asset and is not to be wasted. This is an idea that has limited meaning in some other cultures. Various values are reinforced and reflected in proverbs that Americans are taught from an early age. These proverbs help to guide people's behavior. Table 7–5 lists some examples.

Misinterpretation   Cultural differences can cause misinterpretations both in how others see expatriate managers and in how the latter see themselves. For example, U.S. managers doing business in Austria often misinterpret the fact that local businesspeople always address them in formal terms. They may view this as meaning that they are not friends or are not liked, but in fact, this formal behavior is the way that Austrians always conduct business. The informal, first-name approach used in the United States is not the style of the Austrians.

Culture even affects day-to-day activities of corporate communications.[47] For example, when sending messages to international clients, American managers have to keep in mind that there are many things that are uniquely American and overseas managers may not be aware of them. As an example, daylight savings time is known to all Americans, but many Asian managers have no idea what the term means. Similarly, it is common for American managers to address memos to their "international office" without realizing that the managers who work in this office regard the American location as the "international" one! Other suggestions that can be of value to American managers who are engaged in international communications include:

- Be careful not to use generalized statements about benefits, compensation, pay cycles, holidays, or policies in your worldwide communications. Work hours, vacation accrual, general business practices, and human resource issues vary widely from country to country.

- Since most of the world uses the metric system, be sure to include converted weights and measures in all internal and external communications.

- Keep in mind that even in English-speaking countries, words may have different meanings. Not everyone knows what is meant by "counterclockwise," or "quite good."

- Remember that letterhead and paper sizes differ worldwide. The 8½ × 11 inch page is a U.S. standard, but most countries use an A4 (8¼ × 11½ inch) size for their letterhead, with envelopes to match.

- Dollars are not unique to the United States. There are Australian, Bermudian, Canadian, Hong Kong, Taiwanese, and New Zealand dollars, among others. So when referring to American dollars, it is important to use "US$."

Many Americans also have difficulty interpreting the effect of national values on work behavior. For example, why do French and German workers drink alcoholic beverages at lunchtime? Why are many European workers unwilling to work the night shift? Why do overseas affiliates contribute to the support of the employees' work council or donate money to the support of kindergarten teachers in local schools? These types of actions are viewed by some people as wasteful, but those who know the culture of these countries realize that such actions promote the long-run good of the company. It is the outsider who is misinterpreting why these culturally specific actions are happening, and such misperceptions can become a barrier to effective communication.

Nonverbal Communication

Another major source of communication and perception problems is **nonverbal communication**, which is the transfer of meaning through means such as body language and use of physical space. Table 7–6 summarizes a number of dimensions of nonverbal communication. The general categories that are especially important to communication in international management are kinesics, proxemics, chronemics, and chromatics.

Kinesics   **Kinesics** is the study of communication through body movement and facial expression. Primary areas of concern include eye contact, posture, and gestures. For example, when one communicates verbally with someone in the United States, it is good manners to look the other person in the eye. This area of communicating through the use of eye contact and gaze is known as **oculesics**. In some areas of the world oculesics is an important

nonverbal communication
The transfer of meaning through means such as body language and the use of physical space.

kinesics
The study of communication through body movement and facial expression.

oculesics
The area of communication that deals with conveying messages through the use of eye contact and gaze.

Table 7–6
Common Forms of Nonverbal Communication

1. Hand gestures, both intended and self-directed (autistic), such as the nervous rubbing of hands.
2. Facial expressions, such as smiles, frowns, and yawns.
3. Posture and stance.
4. Clothing and hair styles (hair being more like clothes than like skin, both subject to the fashion of the day).
5. Interpersonal distance (proxemics).
6. Eye contact and direction of gaze, particularly in "listening behavior."
7. "Artifacts" and nonverbal symbols, such as lapel pins, walking sticks, and jewelry.
8. Paralanguage (though often in language, just as often treated as part of nonverbal behavior—speech rate, pitch, inflections, volume).
9. Taste, including symbolism of food and the communication function of chatting over coffee or tea, and oral gratification such as smoking or gum chewing.
10. Cosmetics: temporary—powder; permanent—tattoos.
11. Time symbolism: when is too late or too early to telephone or visit a friend, or what is too long or too short to make a speech or stay for dinner.
12. Timing and pauses within verbal behavior.

Source: From John C. Condon and Fathi S. Yousef, *An Introduction to Intercultural Communication,* 1st Edition. Published by Allyn and Bacon, Boston, MA. Copyright © 1975 by Pearson Education. Reprinted by permission of the publisher.

consideration because of what people should not do, such as stare at others or maintain continuous eye contact, because it is considered impolite to do these things.

Another area of kinesics is posture, which can also cause problems. For example, when Americans are engaged in prolonged negotiations or meetings, it is not uncommon for them to relax and put their feet up on a chair or desk, but this is insulting behavior in the Middle East. Here is an example from a classroom situation:

> In the midst of a discussion of a poem in the sophomore class of the English Department, the professor, who was British, took up the argument, started to explain the subtleties of the poem, and was carried away by the situation. He leaned back in his chair, put his feet up on the desk, and went on with the explanation. The class was furious. Before the end of the day, a demonstration by the University's full student body had taken place. Petitions were submitted to the deans of the various facilities. The next day, the situation even made the newspaper headlines. The consequences of the act, that was innocently done, might seem ridiculous, funny, baffling, incomprehensible, or even incredible to a stranger. Yet, to the native, the students' behavior was logical and in context. The students and their supporters were outraged because of the implications of the breach of the native behavioral pattern. In the Middle East, it is extremely insulting to have to sit facing two soles of the shoes of somebody.[48]

Gestures are also widely used and take many different forms. For example, Canadians shake hands, Japanese bow, and Middle Easterners of the same sex kiss on the cheek. Communicating through the use of bodily contact is known as **haptics**, and it is a widely used form of nonverbal communication.

Sometimes gestures present problems for expatriate managers because these behaviors have different meanings depending on the country. For example, in the United States, putting the thumb and index finger together to form an "O" is the sign for "okay." In Japan, this is the sign for money; in southern France, the gesture means "zero" or "worthless"; and in Brazil, it is regarded as a vulgar or obscene sign. In France and Belgium, snapping the fingers of both hands is considered vulgar; in Brazil, this gesture is used to indicate that something has been done for a long time. In Britain, the "V for victory" sign is given with the palm facing out; if the palm is facing in, this roughly means "shove it"; in non-British countries, the gesture means two of something and often is used when placing an order at a restaurant.[49] Gibson, Hodgetts, and Blackwell found that many foreign students attending school in the United States have trouble communicating because they are unable to interpret some of the most common nonverbal gestures.[50] A survey group of 44 Jamaican, Venezuelan, Colombian, Peruvian, Thai, Indian, and Japanese students at two major universities were given pictures of 20 universal cultural gestures, and each was asked to describe the nonverbal gestures illustrated. In 56 percent of the choices the respondents either gave an interpretation that was markedly different from that of Americans or reported that the nonverbal gesture had no meaning in their culture. These findings help to reinforce the need to teach expatriates about local nonverbal communication.

Proxemics   **Proxemics** is the study of the way that people use physical space to convey messages. For example, in the United States, there are four "distances" people use in communicating on a face-to-face basis (see Figure 7–3). **Intimate distance** is used for very confidential communications. **Personal distance** is used for talking with family and close friends. **Social distance** is used to handle most business transactions. **Public distance** is used when calling across the room or giving a talk to a group.

One major problem for Americans communicating with people from the Middle East or South America is that the intimate or personal distance zones are violated. Americans often tend to be moving away in interpersonal communication with their Middle Eastern or Latin counterparts, while the latter are trying to physically close the gap. The American cannot understand why the other is standing so close; the latter cannot understand why the American is being so reserved and standing so far away. The result is a breakdown in communication.

Office layout is another good example of proxemics. In the United States, the more important the manager, the larger the office, and often a secretary screens visitors and

---

haptics
Communicating through the use of bodily contact.

proxemics
The study of the way people use physical space to convey messages.

intimate distance
Distance between people that is used for very confidential communications.

personal distance
In communicating, the physical distance used for talking with family and close friends.

social distance
In communicating, the distance used to handle most business transactions.

public distance
In communicating, the distance used when calling across the room or giving a talk to a group.

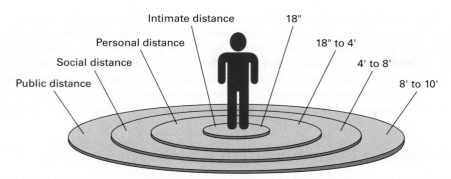

Source: Adapted from Richard M. Hodgetts and Donald F. Kuratko, *Management,* 2nd ed. (San Diego, CA: Harcourt Brace Jovanovich, 1991), p. 384.

keeps away those whom the manager does not wish to see. In Japan, most managers do not have large offices, and even if they do, they spend a great deal of time out of the office and with the employees. Thus, the Japanese have no trouble communicating directly with their superiors. A Japanese manager staying in his office would be viewed as a sign of distrust or anger toward the group.

Another way that office proxemics can affect communication is that in many European companies, no wall separates the space allocated to the senior-level manager from that of the subordinates. Everyone works in the same large room. These working conditions often are disconcerting to Americans, who tend to prefer more privacy.

Chronemics   **Chronemics** refers to the way in which time is used in a culture. When examined in terms of extremes, there are two types of time schedules: *monochronic* and *polychronic*. A **monochronic time schedule** is one in which things are done in a linear fashion. A manager will address Issue A first and then move on to Issue B. In individualistic cultures such as the United States, Great Britain, Canada, and Australia, as well as many of the cultures in Northern Europe, managers adhere to monochronic time schedules. In these societies, time schedules are very important, and time is viewed as something that can be controlled and should be used wisely.

This is in sharp contrast to **polychronic time schedules**, which are characterized by people tending to do several things at the same time and placing higher value on personal involvement than on getting things done on time. In these cultures, schedules are subordinated to personal relationships. Regions of the world where polychronic time schedules are common include Latin America and the Middle East.

When doing business in countries that adhere to monochronic time schedules, it is important to be on time for meetings. Additionally, these meetings typically end at the appointed time so that participants can be on time for their next meeting. When doing business in countries that adhere to polychronic time schedules, it is common to find business meetings starting late and finishing late.

Chromatics   **Chromatics** is the use of color to communicate messages. Every society uses chromatics, but in different ways. Colors that mean one thing in the United States may mean something entirely different in Asia. For example, in the United States it is common to wear black when one is in mourning, while in some locations in India people wear white when they are in mourning. In Hong Kong red is used to signify happiness or luck and traditional bridal dresses are red; in the United States it is common for the bride to wear white. In many Asian countries shampoos are dark in color because users want the soap to be the same color as their hair and believe that if it were a light color, it would remove color from their hair. In the United States shampoos tend to be light in color because people see this as a sign of cleanliness and hygiene. In Chile a gift of yellow roses conveys the message "I don't like you," but in the United States it says quite the opposite.

---

chronemics
The way in which time is used in a culture.

monochronic time schedule
A time schedule in which things are done in a linear fashion.

polychronic time schedule
A time schedule in which people tend to do several things at the same time and place higher value on personal involvement than on getting things done on time.

chromatics
The use of color to communicate messages.

Knowing the importance and the specifics of chromatics in a culture can be very helpful because, among other things, such knowledge can help you avoid embarrassing situations. A good example is the American manager in Peru who, upon finishing a one-week visit to the Lima subsidiary, decided to thank the assistant who was assigned to him. He sent her a dozen red roses. The lady understood the faux pas, but the American manager was somewhat embarrassed when his Peruvian counterpart smilingly told him, "It was really nice of you to buy her a present. However, red roses indicate a romantic interest!"

■ Achieving Communication Effectiveness

A number of steps can be taken to improve communication effectiveness in the international arena. These include improving feedback systems, providing language and cultural training, and increasing flexibility and cooperation.

Improve Feedback Systems

One of the most important ways of improving communication effectiveness in the international context is to open up feedback systems. Feedback is particularly important between parent companies and their affiliates. There are two basic types of feedback systems: personal (e.g., face-to-face meetings, telephone conversations, and personalized e-mail) and impersonal (e.g., reports, budgets, and plans). Both systems help affiliates keep their home office aware of progress and, in turn, help the home office monitor and control affiliate performance as well as set goals and standards.

At present, there seem to be varying degrees of feedback between the home offices of MNCs and their affiliates. For example, one study evaluated the communication feedback between subsidiaries and home offices of 63 MNCs headquartered in Europe, Japan, and North America.[51] A marked difference was found between the way that U.S. companies communicated with their subsidiaries and the way that European and Japanese firms did. Over one-half of the U.S. subsidiaries responded that they received monthly feedback from their parent companies, in contrast to less than 10 percent for the subsidiaries of European and Japanese firms. In addition, the Americans were much more inclined to hold regular management meetings on a regional or worldwide basis. Seventy-five percent of the U.S. companies had annual meetings for their affiliate top managers, compared with less than 50 percent for the Europeans and Japanese. These findings may help explain why many international subsidiaries and affiliates are not operating as efficiently as they should. The units may not have sufficient contact with the home office. They do not seem to be getting continuous assistance and feedback that are critical to effective communication.

Provide Language Training

Besides improving feedback systems, another way to make communication more effective in the international arena is through language training. Many host-country managers cannot communicate well with their counterparts at headquarters. Because English has become the international language of business, those who are not native speakers of English should learn the language well enough so that face-to-face and telephone conversations and e-mail are possible. If the language of the home office is not English, this other language also should be learned. As a U.S. manager working for a Japanese MNC recently told one of the authors, "The official international language of this company is English. However, whenever the home-office people show up, they tend to cluster together with their countrymen and speak Japanese. That's why I'm trying to learn Japanese. Let's face it. They say all you need to know is English, but if you want to really know what's going on, you have to talk their language."

Written communication also is extremely important in achieving effectiveness. As noted earlier, when reports, letters, and e-mail messages are translated from one language to another, preventing a loss of meaning is virtually impossible. Moreover, if the communications are not written properly, they may not be given the attention they deserve. The reader will allow poor grammar and syntax to influence his or her interpretation and subsequent actions. Moreover, if readers cannot communicate in the language of those who will be receiving their comments or questions about the report, their messages also must be translated and likely will further lose meaning. Therefore, the process can continue on and on, each party failing to achieve full communication with the other. Hildebrandt has described the problems in this two-way process when an employee in a foreign subsidiary writes a report and then sends it to his or her boss for forwarding to the home office:

> The general manager or vice president cannot be asked to be an editor. Yet they often send statements along, knowingly, which are poorly written, grammatically imperfect, or generally unclear. The time pressures do not permit otherwise. Predictably, questions are issued from the States to the subsidiary and the complicated bilingual process now goes in reverse, ultimately reaching the original . . . staff member, who receives the English questions retranslated.[52]

Language training would help to alleviate such complicated communication problems.

Provide Cultural Training

It is very difficult to communicate effectively with someone from another culture unless at least one party has some understanding of the other's culture.[53] Otherwise, communication likely will break down. This is particularly important for multinational companies that have operations throughout the world.[54] Although there always are important differences between countries, and even between subcultures of the same country, firms that operate in South America find that the cultures of these countries have certain commonalities. These common factors also apply to Spain and Portugal. Therefore, a basic understanding of Latin cultures can prove to be useful throughout a large region of the world. The same is true of Anglo cultures, where norms and values tend to be somewhat similar from one country to another. When a multinational has operations in South America, Europe, and Asia, however, multicultural training becomes necessary. The International Management in Action on the following page, "Communicating in Europe," provides some specific examples of cultural differences.

As Chapter 4 pointed out, it is erroneous to generalize about an "international" culture, because the various nations and regions of the globe are so different. Training must be conducted on a regional or country-specific basis. Failure to do so can result in continuous communication breakdown.[55] Many corporations are investing in programs to help train their executives in international communication. Such training has become more common since it began in the 1970s as many Americans returned from the Peace Corps with increased awareness of cultural differences. And this training is not limited to those who travel themselves but is increasingly important for employees who frequently interact with individuals from other cultures in their workplace or in their communication.

"Whether a multinational or a start-up business out of a garage, everybody is global these days," said Dean Foster, president of Dean Foster Associates, an intercultural consultancy in New York. "In today's economy, there is no room for failure. Companies have to understand the culture they are working in from Day 1." Mr. Foster recounted how an American businessman recently gave four antique clocks wrapped in white paper to a prospective client in China. What the man did not realize, he said, was that the words in Mandarin for clock and the number four are similar to the word for death, and white is a funeral color in many Asian countries. "The symbolism was so powerful," Mr. Foster said that the man lost the deal.[56] Chapter 14 will give considerable attention to cultural training as part of selection for overseas assignments and human resource development.

Increase Flexibility and Cooperation

Effective international communications require increased flexibility and cooperation by all parties.[57] To improve understanding and cooperation, each party must be prepared to give a little.[58] Take the case of International Computers Ltd., a mainframe computer firm

Communicating in Europe

In Europe, many countries are within easy commuting distance of their neighbors, so an expatriate who does business in France on Monday may be in Germany on Tuesday, Great Britain on Wednesday, Italy on Thursday, and Spain on Friday. Each country has its own etiquette regarding how to greet others and conduct oneself during social and business meetings. The following sections examine some of the things that expatriate managers need to know to communicate effectively.

France

When one is meeting with businesspeople in France, promptness is expected, although tardiness of 5 to 10 minutes is not considered a major gaffe. The French prefer to shake hands when introduced, and it is correct to address them by title plus last name. When the meeting is over, a handshake again is proper manners.

French executives try to keep their personal and professional lives separate. As a result, most business entertaining is done at restaurants or clubs. When gifts are given to business associates, they should appeal to intellectual or aesthetic pursuits as opposed to being something that one's company produces for sale on the world market. In conversational discussions, topics such as politics and money should be avoided. Also, humor should be used carefully during business meetings.

Germany

German executives like to be greeted by their title, and one should never refer to someone on a first-name basis unless invited to do so. When introducing yourself, do not use a title, just state your last name. Business appointments should be made well in advance, and punctuality is important. Like the French, the Germans usually do not entertain clients at home, so an invitation to a German manager's home is a special privilege and always should be followed with a thank-you note. Additionally, as is the case in France, one should avoid using humor during business meetings. They are very serious when it comes to business, so be as prepared as possible and keep light-hearted banter to the German hosts' discretion.

Great Britain

In Britain, it is common to shake hands on the first meeting, and to be polite one should use last names and appropriate titles when addressing the host, until invited to use their first name. Punctuality again is important to the British, so be prepared to be on time and get down to business fairly quickly. The British are quite warm, though, and an invitation to a British home is more likely than in most areas of Europe. You should always bring a gift if invited to the host's house; flowers, chocolates, or books are acceptable.

During business meetings, suits and ties are common dress; however, striped ties should be avoided if they appear to be a copy of those worn by alumni of British universities and schools or by members of military or social clubs. Additionally, during social gatherings it is a good idea not to discuss politics, religion, or gossip about the monarchy unless the British person brings the topic up first.

Italy

In traditional companies, executives are referred to by title plus last name. It is common to shake hands when being introduced, and if the individual is a university graduate, the professional title *dottore* should be used.

Business appointments should be made well in advance, and if you expect to be late, call the host and explain the situation. In most cases, business is done at the office, and when someone is invited to a restaurant, this invitation is usually done to socialize and not to continue business discussions. If an expatriate is invited to an Italian home, it is common to bring a gift for the host, such as a bottle of wine or a box of chocolates. Flowers are also acceptable, but be sure to send an uneven number and avoid chrysanthemums, a symbol of death, and red roses, a sign of deep passion. Be sure to offer high-quality gifts with the wrapping done well, as the Italians are very generous when it comes to gifts. It is not a common practice to exchange them during business, but it is recommended that you are prepared. During the dinner conversation, there is a wide variety of acceptable topics, including business, family matters, and soccer.

Spain

It is common to use first names when introducing or talking to people in Spain, and close friends typically greet each other with an embrace. Appointments should be made in advance, but punctuality is not essential.

If one is invited to the home of a Spanish executive, flowers or chocolates for the host are acceptable gifts. If the invitation includes dinner, any business discussions should be delayed until after coffee is served. During the social gathering, some topics that should be avoided include religion, family, and work. Additionally, humor rarely is used during formal occasions.

that does a great deal of business in Japan. This firm urges its people to strive for successful collaboration in their international partnerships and ventures. At the heart of this process is effective communication. As Kenichi Ohmae put it:

> We must recognize and accept the inescapable subtleties and difficulties of intercompany relationships. This is the essential starting point. Then we must focus not on contractual or equity-related issues but on the quality of the people at the interface between organizations. Finally, we must understand that success requires frequent, rapport-building meetings by at least three organizational levels: top management, staff, and line management at the working level.[59]

■ Managing Cross-Cultural Negotiations

Closely related to communications but deserving special attention is managing negotiations.[60] **Negotiation** is the process of bargaining with one or more parties to arrive at a solution that is acceptable to all. It has been estimated that managers can spend 50 percent or more of their time on negotiation processes.[61] Therefore, it is a learnable skill that is imperative not only for the international manager but for the domestic manager as well, since more and more domestic businesses are operating in multicultural environments (see Chapter 6). Negotiation often follows assessing political environments and is a natural approach to conflict management. Often, the MNC must negotiate with the host country to secure the best possible arrangements. The MNC and the host country will discuss the investment the MNC is prepared to make in return for certain guarantees or concessions. The initial range of topics typically includes critical areas such as hiring practices, direct financial investment, taxes, and ownership control. Negotiation also is used in creating joint ventures with local firms and in getting the operation off the ground. After the firm is operating, additional areas of negotiation include expansion of facilities, use of more local managers, additional imports or exports of materials and finished goods, and recapture of profits.

On a more macro level of international trade are the negotiations conducted between countries. The current balance-of-trade problem between the United States and China is one example. The massive debt problems of less developed countries and the opening of trade with Eastern European and newly emerging economies are other current examples.

negotiation
Bargaining with one or more parties for the purpose of arriving at a solution acceptable to all.

Types of Negotiation

People enter into negotiations for a multitude of reasons, but the nature of the goal determines what kind of negotiation will take place. There are two types of negotiations that we will discuss here: distributive and integrative negotiation. **Distributive negotiations** occur when two parties with opposing goals compete over a set value.[62] Consider a person who passes a street vendor and sees an item he likes but considers the price, or set value, a bit steep. The goal of the buyer is to procure the item at the lowest price, getting more value for his money, while the goal of the seller is to collect as much as possible to maximize profits. Both are trying to get the best deal, but what translates into a gain by one side is usually experienced as a loss by the other, otherwise known as a win-lose situation. The relationship is focused on the individual and based on a short-term interaction. More often than not, the people involved are not friends, or at least their personal relationship is put aside in the matter. Information also plays an important role, since you do not want to expose too much and be vulnerable to counterattack.

distributive negotiations
Bargaining that occurs when two parties with opposing goals compete over a set value.

Research has shown that first offers in a negotiation can be good predictors of outcomes, which is why it is important to have a strong initial offer.[63] This does not imply that overly greedy or aggressive behavior is acceptable; this could be off-putting to the other negotiator, causing her or him to walk away. In addition to limiting the amount of information you disclose, it can be advantageous to know a little about the other side.

Table 7–7
Negotiation Types and Characteristics

Characteristic	Distributive Negotiations	Integrative Negotiations
Objective	Claim maximum value	Create and claim value
Motivation	Individual-selfish benefit	Group-cooperative benefit
Interests	Divergent	Overlapping
Relationship	Short term	Long term
Outcome	Win-lose	Win-win

Source: Adapted from *Harvard Business Essentials: Negotiation* (Boston: Harvard Business School Press, 2003), pp. 2–6.

integrative negotiation
Bargaining that involves cooperation between two groups to integrate interests, create value, and invest in the agreement.

Integrative negotiation involves cooperation between the two groups to integrate interests, create value, and invest in the agreement. Both groups work toward maximizing benefits for both sides and distributing those benefits. This method is sometimes called the win-win scenario, which does not mean that everyone receives exactly what they wish for, but instead that the compromise allows both sides to keep what is most important and still gain on the deal. The relationship in this instance tends to be more long term, since both sides take time to really get to know the other side and what motivates them. The focus is on the group, reaching for a best-case outcome where everyone benefits. This is the most useful tactic when dealing with business negotiation, so from this point on, we assume the integrative approach. Table 7–7 provides a summary of the two types of negotiation.

The Negotiation Process

Several basic steps can be used to manage the negotiation process. Regardless of the issues or personalities of the parties involved, this process typically begins with planning.

Planning   Planning starts with the negotiators identifying the objectives they would like to attain. Then they explore the possible options for reaching these objectives. Research shows that the greater the number of options, the greater the chances for successful negotiations. While this appears to be an obvious statement, research also reveals that many negotiators do not alter their strategy when negotiating across cultures.[64] Next, consideration is given to areas of common ground between the parties. Other major areas include (1) the setting of limits on single-point objectives, such as deciding to pay no more than $10 million for the factory and $3 million for the land; (2) dividing issues into short- and long-term considerations and deciding how to handle each; and (3) determining the sequence in which to discuss the various issues.

Interpersonal Relationship Building   The second phase of the negotiation process involves getting to know the people on the other side. This "feeling out" period is characterized by the desire to identify those who are reasonable and those who are not. In contrast to negotiators in many other countries, those in the United States often give little attention to this phase; they want to get down to business immediately, which often is an ineffective approach. Adler notes:

> Effective negotiators view luncheon, dinner, reception, ceremony, and tour invitations as times for interpersonal relationship building and therefore as key to the negotiating process. When American negotiators, often frustrated by the seemingly endless formalities, ceremonies, and "small talk," ask how long they must wait before beginning to "do business," the answer is simple: wait until your counterparts bring up business (and they will). Realize that the work of conducting a successful negotiation has already begun, even if business has yet to be mentioned.[65]

Exchanging Task-Related Information In this part of the negotiation process, each group sets forth its position on the critical issues. These positions often will change later in the negotiations. At this point, the participants are trying to find out what the other party wants to attain and what it is willing to give up.

Persuasion This step of negotiations is considered by many to be the most important. No side wants to give away more than it has to, but each knows that without giving some concessions, it is unlikely to reach a final agreement. The success of the persuasion step often depends on (1) how well the parties understand each other's position; (2) the ability of each to identify areas of similarity and difference; (3) the ability to create new options; and (4) the willingness to work toward a solution that allows all parties to walk away feeling they have achieved their objectives.

Agreement The final phase of negotiations is the granting of concessions and hammering out a final agreement. Sometimes, this phase is carried out piecemeal, and concessions and agreements are made on issues one at a time. This is the way negotiators from the United States like to operate. As each issue is resolved, it is removed from the bargaining table, and interest is focused on the next. Asians and Russians, on the other hand, tend to negotiate a final agreement on everything, and few concessions are given until the end.

Once again, as in all areas of communication, to negotiate effectively in the international arena, it is necessary to understand how cultural differences between the parties affect the process.

Cultural Differences Affecting Negotiations

In international negotiations, participants tend to orient their approach and interests around their home culture and their group's needs and aspirations. This is natural. Yet, to negotiate effectively, it is important to have a sound understanding of the other side's culture and position to better empathize and understand what they are about.[66] The cultural aspects managers should consider include communication patterns, time orientation, and social behaviors.[67] A number of useful steps can help in this process of understanding. One negotiation expert recommends the following:

1. Do not identify the counterpart's home culture too quickly. Common cues (e.g., name, physical appearance, language, accent, location) may be unreliable. The counterpart probably belongs to more than one culture.

2. Beware of the Western bias toward "doing." In Arab, Asian, and Latin groups, ways of being (e.g., comportment, smell), feeling, thinking, and talking can shape relationships more powerfully than doing.

3. Try to counteract the tendency to formulate simple, consistent, stable images.

4. Do not assume that all aspects of the culture are equally significant. In Japan, consulting all relevant parties to a decision is more important than presenting a gift.

5. Recognize that norms for interactions involving outsiders may differ from those for interactions between compatriots.

6. Do not overestimate your familiarity with your counterpart's culture. An American studying Japanese wrote New Year's wishes to Japanese contacts in basic Japanese characters but omitted one character. As a result, the message became "Dead man, congratulations."[68]

Other useful examples have been offered by Trompenaars and Hampden-Turner, who note that a society's culture often plays a major role in determining the effectiveness of a negotiating approach. This is particularly true when the negotiating groups come from decidedly different cultures such as an ascription society and an achievement society.

As noted in Chapter 4, in an ascription society status is attributed based on birth, kinship, gender, age, and personal connections. In an achievement society, status is determined by accomplishments. As a result, each side's cultural perceptions can affect the outcome of the negotiation. Here is an example:

> Sending whiz-kids to deal with people 10–20 years their senior often insults the ascriptive culture. The reaction may be: "Do these people think that they have reached our own level of experience in half the time? That a 30-year-old American is good enough to negotiate with a 50-year-old Greek or Italian?" Achievement cultures must understand that some ascriptive cultures, the Japanese especially, spend much on training and in-house education to ensure that older people actually are wiser for the years they have spent in the corporation and for the sheer number of subordinates briefing them. It insults an ascriptive culture to do anything which prevents the self-fulfilling nature of its beliefs. Older people are held to be important so that they will be nourished and sustained by others' respect. A stranger is expected to facilitate this scheme, not challenge it.[69]

U.S. negotiators have a style that often differs from that of negotiators in many other countries. Americans believe it is important to be factual and objective. In addition, they often make early concessions to show the other party that they are flexible and reasonable. Moreover, U.S. negotiators typically have authority to bind their party to an agreement, so if the right deal is struck, the matter can be resolved quickly. This is why deadlines are so important to Americans. They have come to do business, and they want to get things resolved immediately.

A comparative example would be the Arabs, who in contrast to Americans, with their logical approach, tend to use an emotional appeal in their negotiation style. They analyze things subjectively and treat deadlines as only general guidelines for wrapping up negotiations. They tend to open negotiations with an extreme initial position. However, the Arabs believe strongly in making concessions, do so throughout the bargaining process, and almost always reciprocate an opponent's concessions. They also seek to build a long-term relationship with their bargaining partners. For these reasons, Americans typically find it easier to negotiate with Arabs than with representatives from many other regions of the world.

Another interesting comparative example is provided by the Chinese. In initial negotiation meetings, it is common for Chinese negotiators to seek agreement on the general focus of the meetings. The hammering out of specific details is postponed for later get-togethers. By achieving agreement on the general framework within which the negotiations will be conducted, the Chinese seek to limit and focus the discussions. Many Westerners misunderstand what is happening during these initial meetings and believe the dialogue consists mostly of rhetoric and general conversation. They are wrong and quite often are surprised later on when the Chinese negotiators use the agreement on the framework and principles as a basis for getting agreement on goals—and then insist that all discussions on concrete arrangements be in accord with these agreed-upon goals. Simply put, what is viewed as general conversation by many Western negotiators is regarded by the Chinese as a formulation of the rules of the game that must be adhered to throughout the negotiations. So in negotiating with the Chinese, it is important to come prepared to ensure that one's own agenda, framework, and principles are accepted by both parties.

Before beginning any negotiations, negotiators should review the negotiating style of the other parties. (Table 7–8 provides some insights regarding negotiation styles of the Americans, Japanese, Arabs, and Mexicans.) This review should help to answer certain questions: What can we expect the other side to say and do? How are they likely to respond to certain offers? When should the most important matters be introduced? How quickly should concessions be made, and what type of reciprocity should be expected? These types of questions help effectively prepare the negotiators. In addition, the team will work on formulating negotiation tactics. The International Management in Action on page 228, "Negotiating with the Japanese," demonstrates such tactics, and the following discussion gets into some of the specifics.

Table 7–8
Negotiation Styles from a Cross-Cultural Perspective

Element	United States	Japanese	Arabians	Mexicans
Group composition	Marketing oriented	Function oriented	Committee of specialists	Friendship oriented
Number involved	2–3	4–7	4–6	2–3
Space orientation	Confrontational; competitive	Display harmonious relationship	Status	Close, friendly
Establishing rapport	Short period; direct to task	Longer period; until harmony	Long period; until trusted	Longer period; discuss family
Exchange of information	Documented; step by step; multimedia	Extensive; concentrate on receiving side	Less emphasis on technology, more on relationship	Less emphasis on technology, more on relationship
Persuasion tools	Time pressure; loss of saving/making money	Maintain relation-ship references; intergroup connections	Go-between; hospitality	Emphasis on family and on social concerns; goodwill measured in generations
Use of language	Open, direct, sense of urgency	Indirect, appreciative, cooperative	Flattery, emotional, religious	Respectful, gracious
First offer	Fair ±5 to 10%	±10 to 20%	±20 to 50%	Fair
Second offer	Add to package; sweeten the deal	−5%	−10%	Add an incentive
Final offer package	Total package	Makes no further concessions	−25%	Total
Decision-making process	Top management team	Collective	Team makes recommendation	Senior manager and secretary
Decision maker	Top management team	Middle line with team consensus	Senior manager	Senior manager
Risk taking	Calculated personal responsibility	Low group responsibility	Religion based	Personally responsible

Source: Lillian H. Chaney and Jeanette S. Martin, *International Business Communication*, 3rd Edition © 2004. Electronically reproduced by permission of Pearson Education, Inc., Upper Saddle River, New Jersey.

Sometimes, simply being familiar with the culture is still falling short of being aptly informed. We discussed in Chapter 2 how the political and legal environment of a country can have an influence over an MNC's decision to open operations, and those external factors are good to bear in mind when coming to an agreement. Both parties may believe that the goals have been made clear, and on the surface a settlement may deliver positive results. However, the subsequent actions taken by either company could prove to exhibit even more barriers. Take Pirelli, an Italian tire maker that acquired Continental Gummiwerke, its German competitor. Pirelli purchased the majority holdings of Continental's stock, a transaction which would translate into Pirelli having control of the company if it occurred in the United States. When Pirelli attempted to make key managerial decisions for its Continental unit, it discovered that in Germany, the corporate governance in place allows German companies to block such actions, regardless of the shareholder position. Furthermore, the labor force has quite a bit of leverage with its ability to elect members of the supervisory board, which in turn chooses the management board.[70] Pirelli essentially lost on an investment; that is, unless Continental can be profitable under its current management. If Pirelli had known that this was going to happen, it probably would have reconsidered. One solution could be for Pirelli's management to begin some positive rapport with the labor force to try to sway viewpoints internally. The better option, though, would be for international managers to be as informed as possible and avoid trouble before it occurs.

Some people believe that the most effective way of getting the Japanese to open up their markets to the United States is to use a form of strong-arm tactics, such as putting the country on a list of those to be targeted for retaliatory action. Others believe that this approach will not be effective, because the interests of the United States and Japan are intertwined and we would be hurting ourselves as much as them. Regardless of which group is right, one thing is certain: U.S. MNCs must learn how to negotiate more effectively with the Japanese. What can they do? Researchers have found that besides patience and a little table pounding, a number of important steps warrant consideration.

First, business firms need to prepare for their negotiations by learning more about Japanese culture and the "right" ways to conduct discussions. Those companies with experience in these matters report that the two best ways of doing this are to read books on Japanese business practices and social customs and to hire experts to train the negotiators. Other steps that are helpful include putting the team through simulated negotiations and hiring Japanese to assist in the negotiations.

Second, U.S. MNCs must learn patience and sincerity. Negotiations are a two-way street that require the mutual cooperation and efforts of both parties. The U.S. negotiators must understand that many times, Japanese negotiators do not have full authority to make on-the-spot decisions. Authority must be given by someone at the home office, and this failure to act quickly should not be interpreted as a lack of sincerity on the part of the Japanese negotiators.

Third, the MNC must have a unique good or service. So many things are offered for sale in Japan that unless the company has something that is truly different, persuading the other party to buy it is difficult.

Fourth, technical expertise often is viewed as a very important contribution, and this often helps to win concessions with the Japanese. The Japanese know that the Americans, for example, still dominate the world when it comes to certain types of technology and that Japan is unable to compete effectively in these areas. When such technical expertise is evident, it is very influential in persuading the Japanese to do business with the company.

These four criteria are critical to effective negotiations with the Japanese. MNCs that use them report more successful experiences than those that do not.

Negotiation Tactics

A number of specific tactics are used in international negotiation. The following discussion examines some of the most common.

Location   Where should negotiations take place? If the matter is very important, most businesses will choose a neutral site. For example, U.S. firms negotiating with companies from the Far East will meet in Hawaii, and South American companies negotiating with European firms will meet halfway, in New York City. A number of benefits derive from using a neutral site. One is that each party has limited access to its home office for receiving a great deal of negotiating information and advice and thus gaining an advantage on the other. A second is that the cost of staying at the site often is quite high, so both sides have an incentive to conclude their negotiations as quickly as possible. (Of course, if one side enjoys the facilities and would like to stay as long as possible, the negotiations could drag on.) A third is that most negotiators do not like to return home with nothing to show for their efforts, so they are motivated to reach some type of agreement.

Time Limits   Time limits are an important negotiation tactic when one party is under a time constraint. This is particularly true when this party has agreed to meet at the home site of the other party. For example, U.S. negotiators who go to London to discuss a joint venture with a British firm often will have a scheduled return flight. Once their hosts find out how long these individuals intend to stay, the British can plan their strategy accordingly. The "real" negotiations are unlikely to begin until close to the time that the Americans must leave. The British know that their guests will be anxious to strike some type of deal before returning home, so the Americans are at a disadvantage.

Time limits can be used tactically even if the negotiators meet at a neutral site. For example, most Americans like to be home with their families for Thanksgiving, Christmas, and the New Year holiday. Negotiations held right before these dates put

Americans at a disadvantage, because the other party knows when the Americans would like to leave.

Buyer-Seller Relations   How should buyers and sellers act? As noted earlier, Americans believe in being objective and trading favors. When the negotiations are over, Americans walk away with what they have received from the other party, and they expect the other party to do the same. This is not the way negotiators in many other countries think, however.

The Japanese, for example, believe that the buyers should get most of what they want. On the other hand, they also believe that the seller should be taken care of through reciprocal favors. The buyer must ensure that the seller has not been "picked clean." For example, when many Japanese firms first started doing business with large U.S. firms, they were unaware of U.S. negotiating tactics. As a result, the Japanese thought the Americans were taking advantage of them, whereas the Americans believed they were driving a good, hard bargain.

The Brazilians are quite different from both the Americans and Japanese. Researchers have found that Brazilians do better when they are more deceptive and self-interested and their opponents more open and honest than they are.[71] Brazilians also tend to make fewer promises and commitments than their opponents, and they are much more prone to say no. However, Brazilians are more likely to make initial concessions. Overall, Brazilians are more like Americans than Japanese in that they try to maximize their advantage, but they are unlike Americans in that they do not feel obligated to be open and forthright in their approach. Whether they are buyer or seller, they want to come out on top.

Negotiating for Mutual Benefit

When managers enter a negotiation with the intent to win and are not open to flexible compromises, it can result in a stalemate. Ongoing discussion with little progress can increase tensions between the two groups and create an impasse where groups become more frustrated and aggressive, and no agreement can be reached.[72] Ultimately, too much focus on the plan with little concern for the viewpoint of the other group can lead to missed opportunities. It is important to keep objectives in mind and at the forefront, but it should not be a substitute for constructive discussions. Fisher and Ury, authors of the book *Getting to Yes*, present five general principles to help avoid such disasters: (1) separate the people from the problem, (2) focus on interests rather than positions, (3) generate a variety of options before settling on an agreement (as mentioned earlier in this section), (4) insist that the agreement be based on objective criteria, and (5) stand your ground.[73]

Separating the People from the Problem   Often, when managers spend so much time getting to know the issue, many become personally involved. Therefore, responses to a particular position can be interpreted as a personal affront. In order to preserve the personal relationship and gain a clear perspective on the issue, it is important to distinguish the problem from the individual.

When dealing with people, one barrier to complete understanding is the negotiating parties' perspectives. Negotiators should try to put themselves in the other's shoes. Avoid blame, and keep the atmosphere positive by attempting to alter proposals to better translate the objectives. The more inclusive the process, the more willing everyone will be to find a solution that is mutually beneficial.

Emotional factors arise as well. Negotiators often experience some level of an emotional reaction during the process, but it is not seen by the other side. Recognize your own emotions, and be open to hearing and accepting emotional concerns of the other party. Do not respond in a defensive manner or give in to intense impulses. Ignoring the intangible tension is not recommended; try to alleviate the situation through sympathetic gestures such as apologies.

As mentioned earlier, good communication is imperative to reaching an agreement. Talk to each other, instead of just rehashing grandiose aspects of the proposal. Listen to responses, and avoid passively sitting there while formulating a response. When appropriate, summarize the key points by vocalizing your interpretation to the other side to ensure correct evaluation of intentions.

Overall, don't wait for issues to arise and react to them. Instead, go into discussion with these guidelines already in play.

Focusing on Interests over Positions   The position one side takes can be expressed through a simple outline, but still does not provide the most useful information. Focusing on interests gives one insight into the motivation behind why a particular position was chosen. Digging deeper into the situation by both recognizing your own interests and becoming more familiar with others' interests will put all active partners in a better position to defend their proposal. Simply stating, "This model works, and it is the best option," may not have much leverage. Discussing your motivation, such as, "I believe our collaboration will enhance customer satisfaction, which is why I took on this project," will help others see the why, not just the what.

Hearing the incentive behind the project will make both sides more sympathetic, and may keep things consistent. Be sure to consider the other side, but maintain focus on your own concerns.

Generating Options   Managers may feel pressured to come to an agreement quickly for many reasons, especially if they hail from a country that puts a value on time. If negotiations are with a group that does not consider time constraints, there may be temptation to have only a few choices to narrow the focus and expedite decisions. It turns out, though, that it is better for everyone to have a large number of options in case some proposals prove to be unsatisfactory.

How do groups go about forming these proposals? First, they can meet to brainstorm and formulate creative solutions through a sort of invention process. This includes shifting thought focus among stating the problem, analyzing the issue, pondering general approaches, and strategizing the actions. After creating the proposals, the groups can begin evaluating the options and discuss improvements where necessary. Try to avoid the win-lose approach by accentuating the points of parity. When groups do not see eye to eye, find options that can work with both viewpoints by "look[ing] for items that are of low cost to you and high benefit to them, and vice versa."[74] By offering proposals that the other side will agree to, you can pinpoint the decision makers and tailor future suggestions toward them. Be sure to support the validity of your proposal, but not to the point of being overbearing.

Using Objective Criteria   In cases where there are no common interests, avoid tension by looking for objective options. Legitimate, practical criteria could be formed by using reliable third-party data, such as legal precedent. If both parties would accept being bound to certain terms, then chances are the suggestions were derived from objective criteria. The key is to emphasize the communal nature of the process. Inquire about why the other group chose its particular ideas. It will help you both see the other side and give you a springboard from which you can argue your views, which can be very persuasive. Overall, effective negotiations will result from international managers being flexible but not folding to external pressures.

These are just general guidelines to abide by to try and reach a mutual agreement. The approaches will be more effective if the group adhering to the outline was the one with more power. Fisher and Ury also looked at what managers should do if the other party has the power.

Standing Ground   Every discussion will have some imbalance of power, but there is something negotiators can do to defend themselves. It may be tempting to create a "bottom line," or lowest possible set of options that one will accept, but it does not necessarily accomplish the objective. When negotiators make a definitive decision before engaging in discussion, they may soon find out that the terms never even surface. That is not to say that their bottom line is below even the lowest offer, but instead that without working with the other negotiators, they cannot accurately predict the proposals that will be devised. So what should the "weaker" opponent do?

The reason two parties are involved in a negotiation is because they both want a situation that will leave them better off than before. Therefore, no matter how long negotiations drag on, neither side should agree to terms that will leave it worse off than its best alternative to a negotiated agreement, or BATNA. Clearly defining and understanding the BATNA will make it easier to know when it is time to leave a negotiation and empower that side. An even better scenario would be if the negotiator learns of the other side's BATNA. As Fisher and Ury say: "Developing your BATNA thus not only enables you to determine what is a minimally acceptable agreement, it will probably raise that minimum."[75]

Even the most prepared manager can walk into a battle zone. At times, negotiators will encounter rigid, irritable, caustic, and selfish opponents. A positional approach to bargaining can cause tension, but the other side can opt for a principled angle. This entails a calm demeanor and a focus on the issues. Instead of counterattacking, redirect the conversation to the problem, and do not take any outbursts as personal attacks. Inquire about their reasoning and try to take any negative statements as constructive. If no common ground is reached, a neutral third party can come in to assess the desires of each side and compose an initial proposal. Each group has the right to suggest alternative approaches, but the third-party person has the last word in what the true "final draft" is. If the parties decide it is still unacceptable, then it is time to walk away from negotiations.

Fisher and Ury compiled a comprehensive guide as to how to approach negotiations. While no guideline has a 100 percent effective rate, their method helps gain a position where both sides win.

Bargaining Behaviors

Closely related to the discussion of negotiation tactics are the different types of bargaining behaviors, including both verbal and nonverbal behaviors. Verbal behaviors are an important part of the negotiating process, because they can improve the final outcome. Research shows that the profits of the negotiators increase when they make high initial offers, ask a lot of questions, and do not make many verbal commitments until the end of the negotiating process. In short, verbal behaviors are critical to the success of negotiations.

Use of Extreme Behaviors Some negotiators begin by making extreme offers or requests. The Chinese and Arabs are examples. Some negotiators, however, begin with an initial position that is close to the one they are seeking. The Americans and Swedes are examples here.

Is one approach any more effective than the other? Research shows that extreme positions tend to produce better results. Some of the reasons relate to the fact that an extreme bargaining position (1) shows the other party that the bargainer will not be exploited; (2) extends the negotiation and gives the bargainer a better opportunity to gain information on the opponent; (3) allows more room for concessions; (4) modifies the opponent's beliefs about the bargainer's preferences; (5) shows the opponent that the bargainer is willing to play the game according to the usual norms; and (6) lets the bargainer gain more than would probably be possible if a less extreme initial position had been taken.

Although the use of extreme position bargaining is considered to be "un-American," many U.S. firms have used it successfully against foreign competitors. When Peter Ueberroth managed the Olympic Games in the United States in 1984, he turned a profit of well over $100 million—and that was without the participation of Soviet-bloc countries, which would have further increased the market potential of the games. In past Olympiads, sponsoring countries had lost hundreds of millions of dollars. How did Ueberroth do it? One way was by using extreme position bargaining. For example, the Olympic Committee felt that the Japanese should pay $10 million for the right to televise the games in the country, so when the Japanese offered $6 million for the rights, the Olympic Committee countered with $90 million. Eventually, the two sides agreed on $18.5 million. Through the effective use of extreme position bargaining, Ueberroth got the Japanese to pay over three times their original offer, an amount well in excess of the committee's budget.

Promises, Threats, and Other Behaviors   Another approach to bargaining is the use of promises, threats, rewards, self-disclosures, and other behaviors that are designed to influence the other party. These behaviors often are greatly influenced by the culture. Graham conducted research using Japanese, U.S., and Brazilian businesspeople and found that they employed a variety of different behaviors during a buyer-seller negotiation simulation.[76] Table 7–9 presents the results.

Table 7–9
Cross-Cultural Differences in Verbal Behavior of Japanese, U.S., and Brazilian Negotiators

Behavior and Definition	Number of Times Tactic Was Used in a Half-Hour Bargaining Session		
	Japanese	United States	Brazilian
Promise. A statement in which the source indicated an intention to provide the target with a reinforcing consequence which source anticipates target will evaluate as pleasant, positive, or rewarding.	7	8	3
Threat. Same as promise, except that the reinforcing consequences are thought to be noxious, unpleasant, or punishing.	4	4	2
Recommendation. A statement in which the source predicts that a pleasant environmental consequence will occur to the target. Its occurrence is not under the source's control.	7	4	5
Warning. Same as recommendation except that the consequences are thought to be unpleasant.	2	1	1
Reward. A statement by the source that is thought to create pleasant consequences for the target.	1	2	2
Punishment. Same as reward, except that the consequences are thought to be unpleasant.	1	3	3
Positive normative appeal. A statement in which the source indicates that the target's past, present, or future behavior was or will be in conformity with social norms.	1	1	0
Negative normative appeal. Same as positive normative appeal, except that the target's behavior is in violation of social norms.	3	1	1
Commitment. A statement by the source to the effect that its future bids will not go below or above a certain level.	15	13	8
Self-disclosure. A statement in which the source reveals information about itself.	34	36	39
Question. A statement in which the source asks the target to reveal information about itself.	20	20	22
Command. A statement in which the source suggests that the target perform a certain behavior.	8	6	14
First offer. The profit level associated with each participant's first offer.	61.5	57.3	75.2
Initial concession. The differences in profit between the first and second offer.	6.5	7.1	9.4
Number of no's. Number of times the word "no" was used by bargainers per half-hour.	5.7	9.0	83.4

Source: Adapted from John L. Graham, "The Influence of Culture on the Process of Business Negotiations in an Exploratory Study," *Journal of International Business Studies,* Spring 1983, p. 88. Reprinted by permission from Macmillan Publishers Ltd., *Journal of International Business Studies,* March 1, 1985. Published by Palgrave Macmillan. Palgrave Macmillan.

The table shows that Americans and Japanese make greater use of promises than do Brazilians. The Japanese also rely heavily on recommendations and commitment. The Brazilians use a discussion of rewards, commands, and self-disclosure more than Americans and Japanese. The Brazilians also say no a great deal more and make first offers that have higher-level profits than those of the others. Americans tend to operate between these two groups, although they do make less use of commands than either of their opponents and make first offers that have lower profit levels than their opponents'.

Nonverbal Behaviors   Nonverbal behaviors also are very common during negotiations. These behaviors refer to what people do rather than what they say. Nonverbal behaviors sometimes are called the "silent language." Typical examples include silent periods, facial gazing, touching, and conversational overlaps. As seen in Table 7–10, the Japanese tend to use silent periods much more often than either Americans or Brazilians during negotiations. In fact, in this study, the Brazilians did not use them at all. The Brazilians did, however, make frequent use of other nonverbal behaviors. They employed facial gazing almost four times more often than the Japanese and almost twice as often as the Americans. In addition, although the Americans and Japanese did not touch their opponents, the Brazilians made wide use of this nonverbal tactic. They also relied heavily on conversational overlaps, employing them more than twice as often as the Japanese and almost three times as often as Americans. Quite obviously, the Brazilians rely very heavily on nonverbal behaviors in their negotiating.

The important thing to remember is that in international negotiations, people use a wide variety of tactics, and the other side must be prepared to counter or find a way of dealing with them. The response will depend on the situation. Managers from different cultures will employ different tactics. Table 7–11 suggests some characteristics needed in effective negotiators, as exemplified by various cultures. To the extent that international managers have these characteristics, their success as negotiators should increase.

Table 7–10
Cross-Cultural Differences in Nonverbal Behavior of Japanese, U.S., and Brazilian Negotiators

Behavior and Definition	Number of Times Tactic Was Used in a Half-Hour Bargaining Session		
	Japanese	United States	Brazilian
Silent period. The number of conversational gaps of 10 seconds or more per 30 minutes.	5.5	3.5	0
Facial gazing. The number of minutes negotiators spend looking at their opponent's face per randomly selected 10-minute period.	1.3 minutes	3.3 minutes	5.2 minutes
Touching. Incidents of bargainers' touching one another per half-hour (not including handshakes).	0	0	4.7
Conversational overlaps. The number of times (per 10 minutes) that both parties to the negotiation would talk at the same time.	12.6	10.3	28.6

Source: Adapted from John L. Graham, "The Influence of Culture on the Process of Business Negotiations in an Exploratory Study," *Journal of International Business Studies,* Spring 1983, p. 88. Reprinted by permission from Macmillan Publishers Ltd., *Journal of International Business Studies,* March 1, 1985. Published by Palgrave Macmillan. Palgrave Macmillan.

Table 7–11
Culture-Specific Characteristics Needed by International Managers for Effective Negotiations

U.S. managers	Preparation and planning skill
	Ability to think under pressure
	Judgment and intelligence
	Verbal expressiveness
	Product knowledge
	Ability to perceive and exploit power
	Integrity
Japanese managers	Dedication to job
	Ability to perceive and exploit power
	Ability to win respect and confidence
	Integrity
	Listening skill
	Broad perspective
	Verbal expressiveness
Chinese managers (Taiwan)	Persistence and determination
	Ability to win respect and confidence
	Preparation and planning skill
	Product knowledge
	Interesting
	Judgment and intelligence
Brazilian managers	Preparation and planning skill
	Ability to think under pressure
	Judgment and intelligence
	Verbal expressiveness
	Product knowledge
	Ability to perceive and exploit power
	Competitiveness

Source: Adapted from Nancy J. Adler, *International Dimensions of Organizational Behavior,* 2nd ed. (Boston: PWS-Kent Publishing, 1991), p. 187; and from material provided by Professor John Graham, School of Business Administration, University of Southern California, 1983.

■ The World of International Management—Revisited

The chapter's opening World of International Management surveyed some of the international communication and negotiation challenges that have emerged as a result of the increasing prevalence of offshoring. Offshoring has increased telephone and e-mail communication, which may exacerbate already substantial cultural differences in communication. In the opening World of International Management, recall how an e-mailed reply from an Indian colleague stating "I will do the needful" resulted in confusion on the part of an American manager. Even cultures that are speaking the same language (English, in this instance) may experience such difficulties. Understanding the communication styles of different cultures is a critical variable in managing relationships among employees and customers, managers and subordinates, and in all business relationships.

A key to success in today's global economy is being able to communicate effectively within and across national boundaries and to engage in effective negotiations across cultures. Considering the communication challenges faced by offshoring firms, along with what you have read in this chapter, answer the following questions: (1) How is communication in India similar to that of Europe and North America? How is it different? (2) What kind of managerial relationships could you assume exist between the American financial services firm (mentioned in The World of International Management) and its employees in India? (3) What kind of negotiations could help engage Indian employees and overcome some of the cultural problems encountered? How might culture play a role in the approach the Indian employees take in their negotiation with the financial firm?

SUMMARY OF KEY POINTS

1. Communication is the transfer of meaning from sender to receiver. The key to the effectiveness of communication is how accurately the receiver interprets the intended meaning.

2. Communicating in the international business context involves both downward and upward flows. Downward flows convey information from superior to subordinate; these flows vary considerably from country to country. For example, the downward system of organizational communication is much more prevalent in France than in Japan. Upward communication conveys information from subordinate to superior. In the United States and Japan, the upward system is more common than in South America or some European countries.

3. The international arena is characterized by a number of communication barriers. Some of the most important are intrinsic to language, perception, culture, and nonverbal communication. Language, particularly in written communications, often loses considerable meaning during interpretation. Perception and culture can result in people's seeing and interpreting things differently, and as a result, communication can break down. Nonverbal communication such as body language, facial expressions, and use of physical space, time, and even color often varies from country to country and, if improper, often results in communication problems.

4. A number of steps can be taken to improve communication effectiveness. Some of the most important include improving feedback, providing language and cultural training, and encouraging flexibility and cooperation. These steps can be particularly helpful in overcoming communication barriers in the international context and can lead to more effective international management.

5. Negotiation is the process of bargaining with one or more parties to arrive at a solution that is acceptable to all. There are two basic types of negotiation: distributive negotiation involves bargaining over opposing goals while integrative negotiation involves cooperation aimed at integrating interests. The negotiation process involves five basic steps: planning, interpersonal relationship building, exchanging task-related information, persuasion, and agreement. The way in which the process is carried out often will vary because of cultural differences, and it is important to understand them.

6. There are a wide variety of tactics used in international negotiating. These include location, time limits, buyer-seller relations, verbal behaviors, and nonverbal behaviors.

7. Negotiating for mutual benefit is enhanced by separating the people from the problem, focusing on interests rather than positions, generating a variety of options, insisting that the agreement be based on objective criteria, and standing one's ground.

KEY TERMS

REVIEW AND DISCUSSION QUESTIONS

1. How does explicit communication differ from implicit communication? Which is one culture that makes wide use of explicit communication? Implicit communication? Describe how one would go about conveying the following message in each of the two cultures you identified: "You are trying very hard, but you are still making too many mistakes."

2. One of the major reasons that foreign expatriates have difficulty doing business in the United States is that they do not understand American slang. A business executive recently gave the authors the following three examples of statements that had no direct meaning for her because she was unfamiliar with slang: "He was laughing like hell." "Don't worry; it's a piece of cake." "Let's throw these ideas up against the wall and see if any of them stick." Why did the foreign expat have trouble understanding these statements, and what could be said instead?

3. Yamamoto Iron & Steel is considering setting up a minimill outside Atlanta, Georgia. At present, the company is planning to send a group of executives to the area to talk with local and state officials regarding this plant. In what way might misperception be a barrier to effective communication between the representatives for both sides? Identify and discuss two examples.

4. Diaz Brothers is a winery in Barcelona. The company would like to expand operations to the United States and begin distributing its products in the Chicago area. If things work out well, the company then will expand to both coasts. In its business dealings in the Midwest, how might culture prove to be a communication barrier for the company's representatives from Barcelona? Identify and discuss two examples.

5. Why is nonverbal communication a barrier to effective communication? Would this barrier be greater for Yamamoto Iron & Steel (question 3) or Diaz Brothers (question 4)? Defend your answer.

6. For U.S. companies going abroad for the first time, which form of nonverbal communication barrier would be the greatest, kinesics or proxemics? Why? Defend your answer.

7. If a company new to the international arena was negotiating an agreement with a potential partner in an overseas country, what basic steps should it be prepared to implement? Identify and describe them.

8. Which elements of the negotiation process should be done with only your group? Which events should take place with all sides present? Why?

9. An American manager is trying to close a deal with a Brazilian manager, but has not heard back from him for quite some time. The American is getting very nervous that if he waits too long, he is going to miss out on any backup options lost while waiting for the Brazilian. What should the American do? How can the American tell it is time to drop the deal? Give some signs that suggest negotiations will go no further.

10. Wilsten Inc. has been approached by a Japanese firm that wants exclusive production and selling rights for one of Wilsten's new high-tech products. What does Wilsten need to know about Japanese bargaining behaviors to strike the best possible deal with this company? Identify and describe five.

INTERNET EXERCISE: WORKING EFFECTIVELY AT TOYOTA

For 11 straight years, the Toyota Camry has been the best-selling car in the United States, and the firm's share of the American automobile market was solid. However, the company is not resting on its laurels. Toyota has expanded worldwide and is now doing business in scores of countries. Visit the firm's website and find out what it has been up to lately. The address is www.toyota.com. Then take a tour of the company's products and services including cars, air services, and sports vehicles. Next, go to the jobs section site, and see what types of career opportunities there are at Toyota. Finally, find out what Toyota is doing in your particular locale. Then, drawing upon this information and the material you read in the chapter, answer these three questions: (1) What type of communication and negotiation challenges do you think you would face if you worked for Toyota and were in constant communication with home-office personnel in Japan? (2) What type of communication training do you think the firm would need to provide to you to ensure that you were effective in dealing with senior-level Japanese managers in the hierarchy? (3) Using Table 7–1 as your guide, what conclusions can you draw regarding communicating with the Japanese managers, and what guidelines would you offer to a non-Japanese employee who just entered the firm and is looking for advice and guidance regarding how to communicate and negotiate more effectively?

China

China, with more than 1.3 billion people, is the world's most populous country and has a rapidly growing economy. Economic development has proceeded unevenly. Urban coastal areas, particularly in the southeast, are experiencing more rapid economic development than other areas of the country. By 2011, just 10.1 percent of the GDP consisted of agriculture, while industry constituted 46.8 percent. China has a mixed economy, with a combination of state-owned and private firms. A number of state-owned enterprises (SOEs) have undergone partial or full privatization in recent years. The Chinese government has encouraged foreign investment—in some sectors of the economy and subject to constraints—since the 1980s, defining several "special economic zones" in which foreign investors receive preferable tax, tariff, and investment treatment. Since 2003 Hu Jintao has been the country's president and he also has the chairmanship of the Central Military Commission.

With China's entry into the World Trade Organization in November 2001, the Chinese government made a number of specific commitments to trade and investment liberalization that have substantially opened the Chinese economy to foreign firms. In telecommunications, this means the lifting or sharp reduction of tariffs and foreign ownership limitations, although China retains the right to limit foreign majority ownership of telecom firms. There has been increasing concern on the part of foreign MNCs that China has not moved fast enough in opening up previously protected sectors and generally favors Chinese firms for large government tenders such as those issued as part of the government's US$586 billion stimulus package, designed to counteract the effects of the global economic crisis. China's successful hosting of the 2008 Summer Olympics in Beijing reinforced the country's pride and position as a global leader in economics, culture, foreign relations, and sports.

China's real GDP grew by 9.2 percent in 2011, an impressive performance given the global economic crisis.

This growth brought China's GDP to US$7.3 trillion and boosted per capita GDP to US$8,500.

Despite this impressive growth, employees are increasingly demanding higher wages and better working conditions. Widespread strikes at firms such as Foxconn (a large contract manufacturer that assembles Apple's iPhone, along with many other products), Honda, and Toyota underscore the desire by workers to receive a greater share of company profits and to have a stronger voice in decisions that affect them. In June 2010 a plant of Toyoda Gosei, a car parts manufacturer affiliated with Toyota, was forced to halt production in Tianjin due to a strike. The cause of the strike was the workers' demand for higher wages.

Some analysts believe that the era of China's reliance on low-cost labor to fuel its economic growth may be coming to an end. Increasingly, the Chinese government and Chinese industry are investing in higher value-added products such as clean energy technology, aviation and avionics, and health care equipment. China's growth has been unparalleled and China will no doubt play an increasingly important role in global economic affairs in the future.

www.cnbc.com/id/37768476,
www.1stheadlines.com/china.htm,
www.infoplease.com

Questions

1. Do you think China will continue to achieve record growth? What factors could hurt its prospects?

2. Because of an abundance of cheap labor, China has been called "the workshop of the world." Do you think this will still be the case a decade from now? Why or why not?

3. What communication and negotiation approaches are likely to work best when foreign MNCs experience demands from Chinese workers for higher wages?

Coca-Cola in India

Coca-Cola is a brand name known throughout the entire world. It covers 60 percent of the $1.6 billion soft drink market. In 2006–2007, Coca-Cola faced some difficult challenges in the region of Kerala, India. The company was accused of using water that contained pesticides in its bottling plants in Kerala. An environmental group, the Center for Science and Environment (CSE), found 57 bottles of Coke and Pepsi products from 12 Indian states that contained unsafe levels of pesticides.[1]

The Kerala minister of health, Karnataka R. Ashok, imposed a ban on the manufacture and sale of Coca-Cola products in the region. Coca-Cola then arranged to have its drinks tested in a British lab, and the report found that the amount of pesticides found in Pepsi and Coca-Cola drinks was harmless to the body.[2] Coca-Cola then ran numerous ads to regain consumers' confidence in its products and brand. However, these efforts did not satisfy the environmental groups or the minister of health.

India's Changing Marketplace

During the 1960s and 1970s, India's economy faced many challenges, growing only an average of 3–3.5 percent per year. Numerous obstacles hindered foreign companies from investing in India, and many restrictions on economic activity caused huge difficulties for Indian firms and a lack of interest among foreign investors. For many years the government had problems implementing reform and overcoming bureaucratic and political divisions. Business activity has traditionally been undervalued in India; leisure is typically given more value than work. Stemming from India's colonial legacy, Indians are highly suspicious of foreign investors. Indeed, there have been a few well-publicized disputes between the Indian government and foreign investors.[3]

More recently, however, many Western companies are finding an easier time doing business in India.[4] In 1991, political conditions had changed, many restrictions were eased, and economic reforms came into force. With more than 1 billion consumers, India has become an increasingly attractive market.[5] From 2003–2006, foreign investment doubled to $6 billion. Imported goods have become a status symbol for the burgeoning middle class.[6]

Coca-Cola has been targeting India for potential growth, as Indians consume an average of 12 eight-ounce beverages per year. In comparison, Brazil consumers drink roughly 240 beverages per year on average. Despite the relatively low amount of beverages consumed by India on average, India has been one of Coke's best emerging market plays.

During the January to March period of 2012, sales in India increased 20 percent. This compares very favorably with Coca-Cola's other emerging market operations in China (9 percent growth over the same period) and Brazil (4 percent growth over the same period). As part of the investment plan, Coca-Cola plans to expand capacity at all 13 of its bottling plants, which should help expand the company's distribution throughout the country. Coca-Cola is aiming to double both revenue and volume in India by the year 2020.[7]

In 2008–2009 FDI in India stood at $27.31 billion.[8] In 2009, India was the third highest recipient of FDI and was likely to continue to remain among the top five attractive destinations for international investors during the following two years, according to a United Nations Conference on Trade and Development (UNCTAD) report.[9] The 2009 survey of the Japan Bank for International Cooperation conducted among Japanese investors continued to rank India as the second most promising country for overseas business operations, after China. According to the Minister of Commerce and Industry, Mr. Anand Sharma, FDI equity inflows as a percentage of GDP have grown from 0.75 percent in 2005–2006 to nearly 2.49 percent in 2008–2009.[10]

India's GDP has grown at the impressive average annual rate of 8.5 percent during the six years spanning 2003/04–2008/09. Even the global financial crisis, which began in September 2008, has cut the rate of growth by only 2–3 percentage points, and the economy continued to grow at the annual rate of 6 percent during the three quarters following the crisis.[11] But the country needs more investment in manufacturing if it hopes to improve the lives of the 350 million people living in poverty.[12]

Coca-Cola and Other Soft Drink Investment in India

Coca-Cola had experienced previous confrontations with the Indian government. In 1977, Coke had pulled out of India when the government demanded its secret formula.[13]

Circumstances have dramatically improved over the years for soft drink providers of India. Coke and Pepsi have invested nearly $2 billion in India over the years. They employ about 12,500 people directly and support 200,000 indirectly through their purchases of sugar, packaging material, and shipping services. Coke is India's number-one consumer of mango pulp for its local soft drink offerings.[14] Coca-Cola in India is also the largest domestic buyer of sugar and green coffee beans.[15] From 1994 to 2003, Coca-Cola sales in India more than doubled.

In 2008–2009 Coca-Cola announced its plans to invest more than $250 million in India over the next three years. The money would be used for everything from expanding bottling capacity to buying delivery trucks and refrigerators for small retailers. The new money will mean around a 20 percent increase in the total Coca-Cola has invested in India.[16] Coca-Cola's sales in India climbed 31 percent in the three months ended March 31, 2009, compared to a year earlier. That's the highest volume growth of any of Coke's markets.[17]

Furthermore, Coca-Cola announced plans in 2012 to invest upwards of US$5 billion in India by 2020. This investment marks a 150 percent increase over the announced plans from 2011 to invest up to US$2 billion in India over the next five years. Putting this investment in perspective, Coca-Cola has invested a total of just over US$2 billion in its India operations over the past 20 years. Despite the large investment in India, Coca-Cola will see serious competition from Pepsi in this market. Together Coke and Pepsi make up 97 percent of the market for carbonated soft drinks in India, where soda sales overall are estimated to be US$1.05 billion. Coke accounted for 60 percent of all sales in 2011 while Pepsi received 37 percent of the market share.[18]

Royal Crown Cola (RC Cola) is the world's third largest brand of soft drinks. The brand was purchased in 2000 by Cadbury Schweppes and entered the Indian market in 2003. For production in India, the company hired three licensing and franchising bottlers. In order to ensure that it was not associated with the pesticide accusations against Pepsi and Coke, RC Cola immediately had its groundwater tested by the testing institute SGS India Pvt Ltd.[19]

The Charges against Coke

The pesticide issue began in 2002, in Plachimada, India. Villagers thought that water levels had sunk and the drinking water was contaminated by Coke's plant. They launched a vigil at the plant, and two years later, Coke's license was canceled. Coca-Cola's most recent pesticide issue began at a bottling plant in Mehdiganj. The plant was accused of exploiting the groundwater and polluting it with toxic metals.[20] Karnataka R. Ashok, the health minister of Kerala, India, banned the sale of all Coca-Cola and PepsiCo products, claiming that the drinks contained unsafe levels of pesticides.

The alleged contamination of the water launched a debate on everything from pesticide-polluted water to the Indian middle-class's addiction to unhealthy, processed foods. "It's wonderful," said Sunita Narin, director of CSE. "Pepsi and Coke are doing our work for us. Now the whole nation knows that there is a pesticide problem."[21]

Coca-Cola fought back against the accusations. "No Indian soft drink makers have been tested for similar violations even though pesticides could be in their products such as milk and bottled teas. If pesticides are in the groundwater, why isn't anyone else being tested? We are continuously being challenged because of who we are," said Atul Singh, CEO of Coca-Cola India.[22]

Some believe that Coca-Cola was targeted to bring the subject of pesticides in consumer products to light. "If you target multinational corporations, you get more publicity," adds Arvind Kumar, a researcher at the watchdog group Toxic Links. "Pesticides are in everything in India."[23]

India's Response to the Allegations

After CSE's discovery of the unsafe levels of pesticides,[24] some suggested the high levels of pesticides came from sugar, which is 10 percent of the soft drink content. However laboratories found the sugar samples to be pesticide free.[25]

Kerala is run by a communist government and a chief minister who still claims to have a revolutionary objection to the evils of capitalism.[26] Defenders of Coca-Cola claim that this is a large reason for the pesticide findings in Coca-Cola products. After the ban was placed on all Coca-Cola and PepsiCo products in the region of Kerala, Coca-Cola took its case to the state court to defend its products and name. The court said that the state government had no jurisdiction to impose a ban on the manufacture and sale of products.[27] Kerala then lifted the statewide ban on Coke products.[28]

In March 2010, after several years of tense battles, the Indian unit of Coca-Cola Company was asked to pay $47 million in compensation for causing environmental damage at its bottling plant in the southern Indian state of Kerala. A state government panel said Coca-Cola's subsidiary, Hindustan Coca-Cola Beverages Pvt Ltd (HCBPL), was responsible for depleting groundwater and dumping toxic waste around its Palakkad plant between 1999 and 2004. Protests by farmers, complaining about the alleged pollution, forced Coca-Cola to close down the plant in 2005. Coca-Cola responded that HCBPL was not responsible for pollution in Palakkad, but the final decision on the compensation will be taken by the state government.[29]

Pepsi's Experience in India

PepsiCo has had an equally noticeable presence in India; and it is not surprising that the company has weathered the same storms as its rival Coca-Cola. In addition to claims of excessive water use, a CSE pesticide study, performed in August 2006, accused Pepsi of having 30 times the "unofficial" pesticide limit in its beverages (Coke was claimed to be 27 times the limit in this study).[30] These findings, coupled with the original 2003 CSE study that first tarnished the cola companies' image, have prompted numerous consumers to stop their cola consumption. Some have even taken to the streets, burning pictures of Pepsi bottles in protest.

Indra Nooyi, CEO of PepsiCo Inc. and a native of India, is all too familiar with the issues of water contamination and water shortages. Yet, in light of the recent claims made against Pepsi, she has expressed frustration with the exaggerated CSE findings (local tea and coffee have thousands of times the alleged pesticide level found in Pepsi products) and the disproportionate reaction to Pepsi's water-use practices (pointing out that soft drinks and bottled water account for less than 0.04 percent of industrial water usage in India).[31]

In order to reaffirm the safety and popularity of its products, Pepsi has taken on a celebrity-studded ad campaign across India, as well as continued its legacy of corporate social responsibility (CSR). Some of Pepsi's CSR efforts have involved digging village wells, "harvesting" rainwater, and teaching better techniques for growing rice and tomatoes.[32] Pepsi has also initiated efforts to reduce water waste at its Indian facilities.

Although Pepsi sales are back on the rise, Nooyi realizes that she should have acted sooner to counteract CSE's claims about Pepsi products. From here on out, the company must be more attentive to its water-use practices; but Nooyi also notes, "We have to invest, too, in educating communities in how to farm better, collect water, and then work with industry to retrofit plants and recycle."[33]

Coke's Social Responsibility Commitments

Coca-Cola has recently employed The Energy and Resources Institute (TERI) to assess its operations in India. The investigations have been conducted because of claims that Coca-Cola has engaged in unethical production practices in India. These alleged practices include causing severe water shortages, locating water-extracting plants in "drought prone" areas, further limiting water access by contaminating the surrounding land and groundwater, and irresponsibly disposing of toxic waste. Colleges and universities throughout the United States, U.K., and Canada have joined in holding the company accountable for its overseas business practices by banning Coca-Cola products on their campuses until more positive results are reported. However, critics have argued that TERI's assessment would undoubtedly be biased since the organization has been largely funded by the Coca-Cola Company.[34]

Coca-Cola stands behind the safety of its products. "Multinational corporations provide an easy target," says Amulya Ganguli, a political analyst in New Delhi. "These corporations are believed to be greedy, devoted solely to profit, and uncaring about the health of the consumers." There is also a deeply rooted distrust of big business, and particularly foreign big business, in India.[35] This is a reminder that there will continue to be obstacles, as there were in the past, to foreign investments in India.

In order to reaffirm their presence in India, Coke and Pepsi have run separate ads insisting that their drinks are safe. Coke's ad said, "Is there anything safer for you to drink?" and invited Indians to visit its plants to see how the beverage is made.[36] Nevertheless, in July 2006, Coke reported a 12 percent decline in sales.[37]

Coca-Cola has undertaken various initiatives to improve the drinking water conditions around the world. It has formally pledged support for the United Nations Global Compact and co-founded the Global Water Challenge, which improves water access and sanitation in countries in critical need. It is improving energy efficiency through the use of hydrofluorocarbon-free insulation for 98 percent of new refrigerater sales and marketing equipment. Specifically, in India, Coke has stated, "More than one-third of the total water that is used in operations is renewed and returned to groundwater systems."[38] Among its first water renewal projects was installation of 270 rainwater catching devices.[39]

Table 1   A Timeline of Coca-Cola in Kerala, India

1977:	Coca-Cola pulls out of India when the government demands its secret formula.
1991:	Restrictions are eased in India for easier international business development.
1999:	A report is published by the All-Indian Coordinated Research Program stating that 20% of all Indian food commodities exceed the maximum pesticide residue level and 43% of milk exceeds the maximum residue levels of DDT.
2002:	Villagers in Plachimada, India, make the accusation that Coke's bottling plant is contaminating their drinking water.
2003:	The Center for Science and Environment produces a study that finds unsafe levels of pesticides in Coca-Cola products in India.
January 2004:	Parliament in India forms a Joint Parliamentary Committee to investigate the charges by the CSE.
March 2004:	A Coca-Cola bottling facility is shut down in Plachimada, India.
2004:	Indian government announces new regulations for carbonated soft drinks based on European Union standards.
2005:	Coca-Cola co-founds the Global Water Challenge, develops the Global Community-Watershed Partnership, and establishes the Ethics and Compliance Committee.
August 2006:	The CSE produces another report finding 57 Coke and Pepsi products from 12 Indian states that contain unsafe pesticide levels.
September 2006:	India's high court overturns the ban on the sale of Coke products in Kerala.
March 2010:	Indian unit of Coca-Cola Co asked by state government to pay $47 million compensation for causing environmental damage at its bottling plant in Kerala.

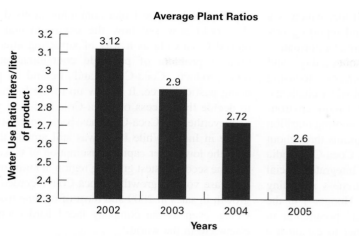

Source: The Coca-Cola Company, *2005 Environmental Report,* www.thecocacolacompany.com/citizenship/environmental_report2005.pdf.

Later, Coca-Cola expanded the number of rainwater harvesting projects by partnering with the Central Ground Water Authority (CGWA), State Ground Water Boards, schools, colleges, NGOs, and local communities to combat water scarcity. According to Coca-Cola India's 2007–2008 Environment Report, the company was actively engaged in 400 rainwater harvesting projects running across 17 states. These efforts were contributing to the company's eventual target of being a "net zero" user of groundwater by the end of 2009.[40]

Having inspected its own water-use habits, Coca-Cola has vowed to reduce the amount of water it uses in its bottling operations. As of June 2007, Coca-Cola had reduced the amount of water needed to make one liter of Coke to 2.54 liters (compared with 3.14 liters five years earlier).[41]

At the June 2007 annual meeting of the World Wildlife Fund (WWF) in Beijing, Coca-Cola announced its multiyear partnership with the organization "to conserve and protect freshwater resources." E. Neville Isdell, chairman and CEO of the Coca-Cola Company, said, "Our goal is to replace every drop of water we use in our beverages and their production. For us that means reducing the amount of water used to produce our beverages, recycling water used for manufacturing processes so it can be returned safely to the environment, and replenishing water in communities and nature through locally relevant projects." Coca-Cola hopes to spread these practices to other members of its supply chain, particularly the sugar cane industry. The Coca-Cola–WWF partnership is also focused on climate protection and protection of seven of the world's "most critical freshwater basins," including the Yangtze in China. Although Coca-Cola's corporate social responsibility efforts have included other projects with the WWF in the past, it hopes that this official partnership will help achieve larger-scale results.[42] Figures 1 and 2 show Coca-Cola's declining water use on a per-plant and systemwide basis.

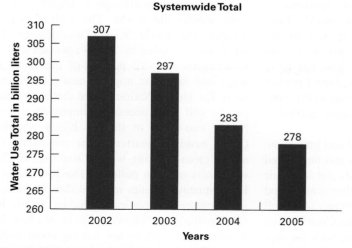

Source: The Coca-Cola Company, *2005 Environmental Report,* www.thecocacolacompany.com/citizenship/environmental_report2005.pdf.

Coca-Cola has also established EthicsLine, which is a global Web and telephone information and reporting service that allows anyone to report confidential information to a third party. Service is toll free—24 hours a day—and translators are available. Coca-Cola is currently focusing on improving standards through the global water challenge and enhancing global packaging to make it more environmentally friendly. It is also working on promoting nutrition and physical education by launching programs throughout the world. For example, in January 2009, Coca-Cola India announced a partnership with the Bharat Integrated Social Welfare Agency (BISWA) to build awareness regarding micro-nutrient malnutrition (or "Hidden Hunger") in the "bottom of the socio-economic pyramid" population in India. The two partners will work together to establish a successful income-generation model for communities through Self-Help Groups in Sambalpur in Orissa and also provide them with affordable alternatives to alleviate "Hidden Hunger." The first product developed by Coca-Cola India to address the issue of "hidden hunger" is Vitingo, a tasty, affordable and refreshing orange-flavored beverage fortified with micro-nutrients.

During the past decade, the Coca-Cola Company has invested more than US$1 billion in India, making it one of India's top international investors. Almost all the goods and services required to produce and market Coca-Cola are made in India. The Coca-Cola Company directly employs approximately 5,500 local people in India; and indirectly, its business in India creates employment for more than 150,000 people.[43] Hindustan Coca-Cola Beverages Pvt Ltd operates 22 bottling plants, some of which are located in economically underdeveloped areas of the country. The Coca-Cola system also includes 23 franchise operated plants, and has one facility that manufactures concentrates or beverage bases.[44]

Lessons Learned

Yet Coca-Cola was caught off guard by its experience in India. Coke did not fully appreciate how quickly local politicians would attack Coke in light of the test results, nor did it respond quickly enough to the anxieties of its consumers. The company failed to realize how fast news travels in modern India. India represents only about 1 percent of Coca-Cola's global volume, but it is central to the company's long-term growth strategy. The company needed to take action fast.[45]

In what Coke thought to be a respectful and immediate time frame, it formed committees in India and the United States. The committees worked on rebuttals and had their own labs commission the tests, and then they commented in detail. Coke also directed reporters to Internet blogs full of entries that were pro-Coke. Critics say that Coke focused too much on the charges instead of winning back the support of its customers. "Here people interpret silence as guilt," said Mr. Seth, Coke's Indian public relations expert.

Ms. Bjorhus, the Coke communications director, said she could now see how the environmental group had picked Coca-Cola as a way of attracting attention to the broader problem of pesticide contamination in Indian food products. Coca-Cola stands behind its products as being pesticide free. It is now up to the Indian consumer to decide the success of Coca-Cola in future years.

Nevertheless, Coca-Cola has been optimistic about its future in India. While India was still among the countries with the lowest per capita consumption of Coke, in 2009 it was the second fastest growing region in terms of Coca-Cola unit case volume growth.[46] Coca-Cola recorded a 3 percent growth in sales in 2009 and most of it came from India and China, even as the company faced hard economic times elsewhere in the world.[47]

The Global Water Challenge

In 2007, one out of every five people globally lacked access to clean drinking water.[48] In August 2006, an international conference was held in Stockholm, Sweden, to discuss global water issues. A UN study reported that many large water corporations have decreased their investments in developing countries because of high political and financial risks. Even nations that have had abundant water supplies are experiencing significant reductions. These reductions are believed to be caused by two factors: the decline in rainfall and increased evaporation of water due to global warming and the loss of wetlands. Water is something that affects every person each and every day. The executive director of the Stockholm Water Institute, Anders Berntell, noted that water affects the areas of agriculture, energy, transportation, forestry, trade, financing, and social and political security. The Food and Agriculture Organization points out, "Agriculture is the world's largest water consumer. Any water crisis will therefore also create a food crisis."

There have been attempts to improve the water conditions around the world. The United Nations recently released the World Water Development Report. This report was compiled by 24 UN agencies and claimed that, in actuality, only 12 percent of the funds targeted for water and sanitation improvement reached those most in need. The United Nations stated that more than 1.1 billion people still lack access to improved water resources. Nearly two-thirds of the 1.1 billion live in Asia.[49] In China, nearly a quarter of the population is unable to access clean drinking water. Over half of China's major waterways are also polluted. The Institute of Public and Environmental Affairs reported that 34 foreign-owned or joint-venture companies, including Pepsi, have caused water pollution problems in China. Ma Jun, the institute's founder, said, "We're not talking about very high standards. These companies are known for their commitment to the environment."[50]

According to the 2009 UN World Water Development Report, the world's population is growing by about 80 million people a year, implying increased freshwater demand of about 64 billion cubic meters a year. An estimated 90 percent of the 3 billion people who are expected to be added to the population by 2050 will be in developing countries, many in regions where the current population does not have sustainable access to safe drinking water or adequate sanitation. The world will have substantially more people in vulnerable urban and coastal areas in the next 20 years.[51]

With businesses expanding globally every day, water is a crucial resource, and water issues will increasingly affect all industries. With water conditions improving at a slower rate than business development, businesses will have to take on the responsibility of not only finding an adequate supply of the diminishing resource but also making sure the water is safe for all to consume. This responsibility is going to be an additional cost to companies, but a necessary one that will prevent loss of sales in the future. Coca-Cola's specific situation in India is a reminder for all global corporations.

Questions for Review

1. What aspects of U.S. culture and of Indian culture may have been causes of Coke's difficulties in India?

2. How might Coca-Cola have responded differently when this situation first occurred, especially in terms of responding to negative perceptions among Indians of Coke and other MNCs?

3. If Coca-Cola wants to obtain more of India's soft drink market, what changes does it need to make?

4. How might companies like Coca-Cola and PepsiCo demonstrate their commitment to working with different countries and respecting the cultural and natural environments of those societies?

Source: This case was prepared by Jaclyn Johns of Villanova University under the supervision of Professor Jonathan Doh as the basis for class discussion. It is not intended to illustrate either effective or ineffective managerial capability or administrative responsibility. Research assistance was provided by Courtney Asher, Tetyana Azarova, and Benjamin Littell.

Brief Integrative Case 2.2

Danone's Wrangle with Wahaha

In 1996, Danone Group and Wahaha Group combined forces in a joint venture (JV) to form the largest beverage company in China. A longstanding trademark dispute between the JV members, embedded within a broader clash of national and organizational cultures, came to a head. Valuable lessons can be learned from this dispute for investors considering joint ventures in China.[1]

The Wahaha Joint Venture was established in 1996 by Hangzhou Wahaha Food Group Co. Ltd., Danone Group, and Bai Fu Qin Ltd. In 1997, Danone bought the interests of Bai Fu Qin and gained legal control of the JV with 51 percent of shares. While members of the JV are entitled to use the JV's Wahaha trademark, in 2000, the Wahaha Group developed companies outside of the JV that sold products similar to those of the JV and used the JV's trademark. The Danone Group objected and sought to purchase those non-JV companies.[2]

In April 2007, Danone offered RMB4 billion to acquire 51 percent of the shares of Wahaha's five non-JV companies. Wahaha Group rejected the offer. Subsequently, Danone filed more than 30 lawsuits against Wahaha for violating the contract and illegally using the JV's Wahaha trademark in countries such as France, Italy, the U.S., and China.[3]

Danone's Background

Danone traces its routes to Europe in the early 20th century. In 1919, Isaac Carasso opened a small yogurt stand in Spain. He named it "Danone," meaning "Little Daniel," after his son. Carasso was aware of new methods of milk fermentation conducted at the Pasteur Institute in Paris. He decided to merge these new techniques with traditional practices for making yogurt. The first industrial manufacturer of yogurt was started.[4]

Following his success in Europe, Carasso immigrated to the U.S. to expand his market. He changed the Danone name to Dannon Milk products, Inc., and founded the first American yogurt company in 1942 in New York. Distribution began on a small scale. When Dannon introduced the "fruit on the bottom" line in 1947, sales soared. The following year, he sold his company's interest and returned to Spain to manage his family's original business.[5]

By 1950, Dannon had expanded to other U.S. states in the Northeast. It also broadened the line by introducing low-fat yogurt that targeted the health-conscious consumer. Sales continued to rise. Dannon expanded across the country throughout the 1960s and 1970s. In 1979,

Dannon became the first company to sell perishable dairy products coast to coast in the U.S.[6]

In 1967, Danone merged with leading French fresh cheese producer Gervais to become Gervais Danone. In 1973, Gervais Danone merged with Boussois-Souchon-Neuvesel (BSN), a company which had also acquired the Alsacian brewer Kronenbourg and Evian mineral water.[7] In 1987, Gervais Danone acquired European biscuit manufacturer Général Biscuit, owners of the LU brand, and in 1989, it bought out the European biscuit operations of Nabisco.

In 1994, BSN changed its name to Groupe Danone, adopting the name of the Group's best known international brand. Under its current CEO, Franck Riboud, the company has pursued its focus on the three product groups: dairy, beverages, and cereals.[8]

Today, Danone is a Fortune 500 company with a mission to produce healthy, nutritious, and affordable food and beverage products for as many people as possible.

Danone's Global Growth

Danone, with 160 plants and around 80,000 employees, has a presence in all five continents and over 120 countries. In 2008, Danone recorded €15.2 billion in sales. Danone enjoys leading positions in healthy food:[9]

- No. 1 worldwide in fresh dairy products
- No. 2 worldwide in bottled water
- No. 2 worldwide in baby nutrition
- No. 1 in Europe in medical nutrition

Its portfolio of brands and products includes Activia, a probiotic dairy product line; Danette, a brand of cream desserts; Nutricia, an infant product line; Danonino, a brand of yogurts; and Evian, a brand of bottled water.[10]

Listed on Euronext Paris, Danone is also ranked among the main indexes of social responsibility: Dow Jones Sustainability Index Stoxx and World, ASPI Eurozone (Advanced Sustainable Performance Indices), and Ethibel Sustainability index.[11] Danone has ranked number 60 in top 100 international brands according to Interbrand 2009 Best Global Brand valuation, with the brand value of $5.96 billion.[12]

In 2008, Danone recorded an organic growth rate of 8.4 percent. With its operating margin increasing for the 14th year running, the group further strengthened its global standing. The group's performance is the result of a balanced strategy that builds on international expansion, a growing commitment to innovation, and strengthening health-oriented brands. Danone invests heavily in research and development—€208 million in 2008. One hundred percent of projects currently in the pipeline focus on health and nutrition.[13]

With a total of roughly 18 billion liters of bottled water marketed in 2008, Danone is the world's second largest producer (its global market share is approximately 11 percent). Danone owns the world's top-selling brand of packaged water, Aqua, which recorded sales of 6 billion liters. With Evian and Volvic, Danone also owns two of the five worldwide brands of bottled water.[14] Its revenue from water products amounted to €2.9 billion in 2008: Europe accounted for 47 percent of this total, Asia 31 percent, and the rest of the world 22 percent. At constant structure and exchange rates, the proportion of sales in emerging countries rose in 2008 to 52 percent.[15]

In the mid-1990s, Danone did 80 percent of its business in Western Europe. Until 1996, the company was present in about a dozen markets including pasta, confectionery, biscuits, ready-to-serve meals, and beer. The company realized that it is difficult to achieve simultaneous growth in all these markets. Therefore, they decided to concentrate on the few markets that showed the most growth potential and were consistent with Danone's focus on health. Starting in 1997, the Group decided to focus on three business lines worldwide (Fresh Dairy Products, Beverages, as well as Biscuits and Cereal Products), and the rest of the business lines were divested. This freed the company's financial and human resources and allowed for quick expansion into new markets in Asia, Africa, Eastern Europe, and Latin America. In less than 10 years, the contribution of emerging markets to sales rose from zero to 40 percent while that of Western Europe went below 50 percent.[16]

The 2007 year marked the end of a 10-year refocusing strategy period during which the Group's activities were refocused in the area of health. That year, the Group sold nearly all of its Biscuits and Cereal Products business to the Kraft Foods group, while adding Baby Nutrition and Medical Nutrition to its portfolio by acquiring Numico.

Danone is now centered on 4 business lines:

1. Fresh Dairy Products, representing approximately 57 percent of consolidated sales for 2008

2. Waters, representing approximately 19 percent of consolidated sales for 2008

3. Baby Nutrition, representing approximately 18 percent of consolidated sales for 2008

4. Medical Nutrition, representing approximately 6 percent of consolidated sales for 2008

Danone Strategy in China

Danone entered the Chinese market in the late 1980s. Since then, it has invested heavily in China, building factories and expanding production. Today, Danone has 70 factories in China, including Danone Biscuits, Robust, Wahaha, and Health. Danone sells primarily yogurt, biscuits, and beverages in China.[17]

Danone's Asia-Pacific division employs 23,000 people in the Asia-Pacific area, which is almost 30 percent of Danone's total employees. Of Danone's Asian sales, 57 percent were in China. Danone's Wahaha was China's largest beverage company. Two billion liters of Wahaha were sold in 2004, making it the market leader in China with a 30 percent market share.[18] In Asia, in 2007, Danone Group was the market leader with a 20 percent share of a 34-billion liter market. In comparison, rivals Coca-Cola and Nestlé had a 7 percent and 2 percent share, respectively. Evian, its global brand, was sold alongside of local brands such as China's Wahaha.

In the past 20 years, Danone has purchased shares of many of the top beverage companies in China: 51 percent of shares of the companies owned by Wahaha Group, 98 percent of Robust Group, 50 percent of Shanghai Maling Aquarius Co., Ltd., 54.2 percent of Shenzhen Yili Mineral Water Company, 22.18 percent of China Huiyuan Group, 50 percent of Mengniu, and 20.01 percent of Bright dairy. These companies, leaders in their industry, all own trademarks that are well-known in China.[19]

However, while expanding into the Chinese market, Danone faced challenges due to lack of market knowledge. In 2000, Danone purchased Robust, the then-second-largest company in the Chinese beverage industry. Sales of Robust had reached RMB2 billion in 1999. After the purchase, Danone dismissed the original management and managed Robust directly. Because its new management was not familiar with the Chinese beverage market, Robust struggled. Its tea and milk products almost disappeared from the market. During 2005–2006, the company lost RMB 150 million.[20]

Wahaha Company

The Wahaha company was established in 1987 by a retired teacher, Mr. Zong Qinghou. In 1989, the enterprise opened its first plant, Wahaha Nutritional Food Factory, to produce "Wahaha Oral Liquid for Children," a nutritional drink for kids. The name Wahaha was meant to evoke a laughing child, combining the character for baby (wa) with the sound of laughter.[21] After its launch, Wahaha won a rapid public acceptance. By 1991, the company's sales revenue grew beyond 100 million renminbi (¥).[22]

In 1991, with the support of the Hangzhou local district government, Wahaha Nutritional Food Factory merged with Hangzhou Canning Food Factory, a state-owned enterprise, to form the Hangzhou Wahaha Group Corporation. After mergers with three more companies, Wahaha became the biggest corporation of its district.[23]

Since 1997, Wahaha has set up new many subsidiaries. It was aided by state and local government since its continuous expansion helped create new jobs and its increased profits led to more tax revenues.

In 1996, the Hangzhou Wahaha Group Corporation began a joint venture with Danone Group and formed five new subsidiaries, which attracted a $45 million foreign investment and then added another $26.2 million investment. With the investment funds, Wahaha brought world-class advanced production lines from Germany, America, Italy, Japan, and Canada into its sites. The terms of the Danone–Wahaha joint venture allowed Wahaha to retain all managerial and operating rights as well as the brand name Wahaha. In the next eight years, the company established 40 subsidiaries in China, and in 1998 launched its own brand, "Future Cola," to compete against Coke and Pepsi.[24]

In 2000, the company produced 2.24 million tons of beverages with sales revenue of $5.4 billion. The production accounted for 15 percent of the Chinese output of beverages. The group became the biggest company in the beverage industry of China with total assets of $4.4 billion.[25]

In 2007, it produced 6.89 million tons of beverage with a sales revenue of $25.8 billion. Today, Hangzhou Wahaha Group Co., Ltd., is still the leading beverage producer in China and has more than 100 subsidiary companies with total assets of $17.8 billion. The company product category contains more than 100 varieties, such as milk drinks, drinking water, carbonated drinks, tea drinks, canned food, and health care products.[26]

According to a report on the "Top 10 Beverage Companies" released by the China Beverage Industry Association, Wahaha contributed 55.57 percent to the Association Top 10's overall production, 65.84 percent to its revenue, and 73.16 percent to its profit tax. According to Zong Qinghou, the president of Wahaha: "As China becomes the world's largest food and beverage market, we'll be a major player in the global market." Wahaha implements a strategy of "local production and local distribution" and has built an excellent production-distribution network. Its Wahaha R&D center and Analysis Center provide guarantees for high product quality.[27]

Danone–Wahaha Joint Venture Conflict

The Wahaha joint venture (JV) was formed in 1996 with three participants: Hangzhou Wahaha Food Group (Wahaha Group); Danone Group, a French corporation (Danone); and Bai Fu Qin, a Hong Kong corporation (Baifu). Danone and Baifu did not invest directly in the JV. Instead, Danone and Baifu formed Jin Jia Investment, a Singapore corporation (Jinjia). Upon the formation of the JV, Wahaha Group owned 49 percent of the shares of the JV and Jinjia owned 51 percent of the shares of the JV. This structure led to immediate misunderstandings between the participants. From Wahaha Group's point of view—with the division of ownership at 49 percent Wahaha Group, 25.5 percent Danone, and 25.5 percent Baifu—it was the majority shareholder in the JV. Since Wahaha Group felt it controlled the JV, it was relatively unconcerned when it transferred its trademark to the JV.[29]

In 1998, Danone bought out the interest of Baifu in Jinjia, becoming 100 percent owner of Jinjia and effectively the 51 percent owner of the JV. This gave it legal control over the JV because of its right to elect the board of directors. For the first time, the Wahaha Group and Zong realized two things: (1) They had given complete control over their trademark to the JV; (2) A foreign company was now in control of the JV. From a legal standpoint, this result was implied by the structure of the JV from the very beginning. However, it is clear from public statements that the Wahaha Group did not understand the implications when they entered into the venture. The Danone "takeover" in 1998 therefore produced significant resentment on the part of Wahaha Group. Rightly or not, Wahaha felt that Danone misled them from the very beginning.[30]

Figure 1
Structure of Initial Wahaha Joint Venture[28]

Hierarchy of the Initial Wahaha Joint Venture

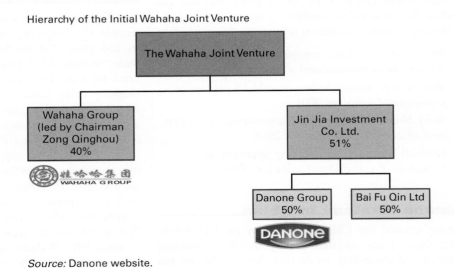

Source: Danone website.

When the JV was formed, Wahaha Group was a state-owned enterprise owned by the Hangzhou city government. After formation of the JV, it was converted into a private corporation, effectively controlled by Zong. This set the stage for Wahaha Group's decision to take back control of the trademark it felt had been unfairly transferred to Danone. Zong and his employees now viewed the transferred trademark as their personal property.[31]

When the JV was formed, Wahaha Group obtained an appraisal of its trademark valuing it at RMB100 million (US$13.2 million). The trademark was its sole contribution to the JV, while Jinjia contributed RMB500 million (US$66.1 million) in cash. Wahaha Group also agreed not to use the trademark for any independent business activity or allow it to be used by any other entity. However, the trademark transfer was rejected by China's Trademark Office. It took the position that, as the well-known mark of a state-owned enterprise, the trademark belonged to the state and Wahaha Group did not have the right to transfer it to a private company.[32]

Rather than terminate the JV, the shareholders (now Danone and Wahaha Group) decided to work around the approval issue by entering into an exclusive license agreement for the trademark in 1999. Since the license agreement was intended to be the functional equivalent of a sale of the trademark, they were concerned the Trademark Office would refuse to register the license. Therefore, they only registered an abbreviated license. This was accepted by the Trademark Office, which never saw the full license. As a result, Wahaha Group never transferred ownership of the Wahaha trademark to the JV, just the exclusive license. Thus, Wahaha Group never complied with its basic obligation for capitalization of the JV. It does not appear that any of the JV documents were revised to deal with this changed situation.[33]

Although Danone was the majority shareholder and maintained a majority interest on the board of directors, day-to-day management of the JV was delegated entirely to Zong. He filled management positions with his family members and employees of the Wahaha Group. Under Zong's management, the JV became the largest Chinese bottled water and beverage company.[34]

Beginning in 2000, the Wahaha Group created a series of companies that sold the same products as the JV and used the Wahaha trademark. The non-JV companies appear to have been owned in part by Wahaha Group and in part by an offshore British Virgin Islands company controlled by Zong's daughter and wife. Neither Danone nor Wahaha group receives any benefits from the profits of these non-JV companies. According to press reports in China, products from the non-JV companies and the JV were sold by the same sales staff working for the same sales company, all ultimately managed by Zong.[35]

In 2005, Danone realized the situation and insisted it be given a 51 percent ownership interest in the non-JV companies. Wahaha Group and Zong, who by this time was one of the richest men in China, refused.[36]

Details of the Dispute

In April 2006, Wahaha was informed by its 10-year JV partner Danone that it had breached the contract by establishing nonjoint ventures, which had infringed upon the interests of Danone. Danone proposed to purchase 51 percent of shares of Wahaha's nonjoint ventures.[37] The move was opposed by Wahaha. In May 2007, Danone formally initiated a proceeding, claiming that Wahaha's establishment of nonjoint ventures as well as the illegal use of "Wahaha" trademark had seriously violated the noncompete clause. The two parties carried on 10 lawsuits in and out of China, and all the ruled cases between Wahaha and Danone have ended in Wahaha's favor.[38]

On February 3, 2009, a California court in the United States dismissed Danone's accusation against the wife and daughter of Zong Qinghou and ruled that the dispute between Danone and Wahaha should be settled in China. In addition, Danone's lawsuits against Wahaha were rejected by courts in Italy and France; and a series of lawsuits brought by Danone in China against Zong Qinghou and Wahaha's nonjoint ventures all ended in failure.[39]

The rationality of the existence of the nonjoint ventures, the ownership of the "Wahaha" trademark, and the noncompete clause issue were the key points of the Danone-Wahaha dispute.[40] In 1996, Wahaha offered a list of 10 subsidiaries to Danone, which after evaluation selected four. Jinja Investments Pte Ltd. (a Singapore-based joint venture between Danone Asia Pte Ltd. and Hong Kong Peregrine Investment, of which Danone is the controlling shareholder), Hangzhou Wahaha Group Co., Ltd., and Zhejiang Wahaha Industrial Holdings Ltd. jointly invested to form five joint venture enterprises, with shareholdings of 51 percent, 39 percent, and 10 percent, respectively. In 1998, Hong Kong Peregrine sold its stake in Jinja Investments to Danone, which makes Danone the sole shareholder of Jinja Investments, giving it the control of over 51 percent of the joint ventures. Wahaha and Danone cooperated on the basis of joint venture enterprises, rather than the complete acquisition of Wahaha by Danone. As a result, Wahaha was always independent, and its nonjoint ventures have existed and developed since 1996. Relevant transactions of Wahaha's nonjoint ventures and joint ventures were disclosed fully and frankly by the auditing reports of PricewaterhouseCoopers, an accounting firm appointed by Danone. Meanwhile, during the 11-year cooperation, Danone assigned a Finance Director to locate in the headquarters of Wahaha Group to audit the latter's financial information.[41]

Danone and Wahaha had signed in succession three relevant agreements concerning the ownership of the "Wahaha" brand name. In 1997, the two parties signed a trademark transfer agreement, with an intention to transfer the "Wahaha" trademark to the joint ventures. The move, however, was not approved by the State Trademark Office.[42] For this reason, the two parties signed in 1999 the trademark licensing contract. According to law, the same subject cannot be synchronously transferred and licensed the use to others by the same host. Therefore, the signing and fulfillment of the trademark licensing contract showed that the two parties had agreed to the invalidation of the transfer agreement. The "Wahaha" brand should belong to the Wahaha Group, while the joint ventures only have right of use.[43]

In October 2005, the two parties signed the No. 1 amendment agreement to the trademark licensing contract, in which it confirmed Party A (Hangzhou Wahaha Group Co., Ltd.) as owner of the trademark. In addition, the second provision of the amendment agreement clearly stated that the several Wahaha subsidiaries listed in the fifth annex of the licensing contract as well as other Wahaha subsidiaries (referred to as "licensed Wahaha enterprises") established by Party A or its affiliates following the signing of the licensing contract also have right granted by one party to use the trademark. The "licensed Wahaha enterprises" involved in the amendment agreement refer to the nonjoint ventures.[44] According to related files, Wahaha owns the ownership of the "Wahaha" trademark, while its nonjoint ventures have the right to use the trademark.[45] The Wahaha brand is among the most famous in China. It ranked No. 16 among domestic brands and is worth $2.2 billion, according to a recent report by Shanghai research firm Hurun Report. Wahaha doesn't publicly disclose financial figures.[46]

Ventures and Acquisitions

Several years ago, as Wahaha sought to expand its market, Wahaha suggested adding online new production lines by increasing investment, while Danone requested Wahaha outsource to product processing suppliers for its joint ventures. Wahaha saw the shortcomings in using product processing suppliers, so it set up nonjoint ventures to meet production needs. Wahaha believed that the existence and operation of the nonjoint ventures did not adversely affect the interest of Danone.[47]

During the 11 years that followed 1996, Danone invested less than RMB1.4 billion in Wahaha's joint ventures, but received a profit of RMB3.554 billion as of 2007. On the other hand, Danone acquired several strong competitors of Wahaha including Robust, Huiyuan, and Shanghai Maling Aquariust. Wahaha saw Robust as its biggest rival. Wahaha was disappointed that Danone failed to hold up its end of the bargain of "jointly exploring markets in and out of China" listed in the JV contract.[48]

Through influence of the Chinese and French governments, Danone and Wahaha reached a peaceful settlement in late 2007. However, Danone's proposal to sell its shares in the joint ventures to Wahaha for RMB50 billion (finally reduced to approximately RMB20 billion) was rejected by Wahaha.[49]

After the negotiations were suspended, the two parties again turned to legal action. As of April 2009, all the ruled cases both in China and abroad have ruled against Danone.[50]

Conflict Resolution

In late September 2009, France's Groupe Danone SA agreed to accept a cash settlement to relinquish claims to the name Wahaha. In a joint statement issued September 30, 2009, Danone announced a settlement with China's Hangzhou Wahaha Group Co. by saying its 51 percent share in joint ventures that make soft drinks and related products will be sold to the businesses' Chinese partners. "The completion of this settlement will put an end to all legal proceedings related to the disputes between the two parties," the statement said.[51]

The feud over control of the Wahaha empire offered a glimpse into the breakup of a major Asian-foreign joint venture. Danone's strategy to publicly confront its partner and Wahaha's strategy to respond with its own accusations marked a break with prevailing business practice in China, where problems have usually been settled with face-saving, private negotiations.[52]

Analysts said the case served to reinforce how difficult it is to operate a partnership in China. "That's a key lesson: To build a [brand] business in China you need to build from the ground up," said Jonathan Chajet, China managing director for consultancy Interbrand.[53] Foreign firms such as Procter & Gamble, Starbucks, and General Motors have operated wholly or in part through joint ventures in China. But executives involved say the expectations of foreign and local parties can conflict in a JV, for instance, when an international company is striving for efficiencies and profits that match its global goals while the local partner—sometimes an arm of the Chinese government—strives to maximize employment or improve technology. At other times, partners have stolen corporate secrets or cheated and otherwise sabotaged a venture, while legal avenues have had little effect on disputes over operations.[54]

Danone, which reported the Wahaha business generated about 10 percent of its global revenue in 2006 but has since adjusted how it accounted for Wahaha, said it expects no impact on its income statement from the settlement. In China, it will be left with a much smaller footprint and is essentially starting over.[55] Danone's CEO Franck Riboud stated: "Danone has a long-standing commitment to China, where it has been present since 1987, and we are keen to accelerate the success of our Chinese activities." China is Danone's fourth-largest market after France, Spain, and the U.S., contributing about €1bn, or 8 percent, of Danone's revenues.[56]

Lessons Learned[57]

What can potential foreign investors learn from this dispute? Although JVs in China can be quite difficult, with proper planning and management, they can be successful. In the case of the Wahaha-Danone JV, many basic rules of JV operations in China were violated, virtually guaranteeing the JV's destruction. According to Steve Dickinson, lawyer at Harris Moure PLC, the primary rules violated are as follows:[58]

1. Don't use technical legal techniques to assert or gain control in a JV.
2. Do not expect that a 51 percent ownership interest in a JV will necessarily provide effective control.
3. Do not proceed with a JV formed on a weak or uncertain legal basis.
4. The foreign party must actively supervise or participate in the day-to-day management of the JV.

Questions for Review

1. When and how did Danone expand into the Chinese market? What problems did Danone Group encounter while operating in China?

2. How was the Danone and Wahaha JV formed? What was its structure? Why did Danone decide to form a joint venture rather than establish a 100 percent–owned subsidiary?

3. What was the problem of Danone Wahaha joint venture that triggered the conflict between the companies? What were the differences in Danone's and Wahaha's understanding of their own respective roles and responsibilities in this venture? What aspects of national and organizational culture affected this perspective?

4. Was Danone successful in proving its claims in court? How was the conflict between the two companies resolved? What were the key lessons for Danone about doing business in China?

5. Did Danone follow the advice regarding JVs in China mentioned in the list just above? Which aspects did it follow and which did it not?

Source: This case was prepared by Tetyana Azarova of Villanova University under the supervision of Professor Jonathan Doh as the basis for class discussion. Research assistance was provided by Kelley Bergsma and Benjamin Littell. It is not intended to illustrate either effective or ineffective managerial capability or administrative responsibility.

In-Depth Integrative Case 2.1a

Euro Disneyland

On January 18, 1993, Euro Disneyland chairperson Robert Fitzpatrick announced he would leave that post on April 12 to begin his own consulting company. Quitting his position exactly one year after the grand opening of Euro Disneyland, Fitzpatrick with his resignation removed U.S. management from the helm of the French theme park and resort.

Fitzpatrick's position was taken by a Frenchman, Philippe Bourguignon, who had been Euro Disneyland's senior vice president for real estate. Bourguignon, 45 years old, faced a net loss of FFr 188 million for Euro Disneyland's fiscal year, which ended September 1992. Also, between April and September 1992, only 29 percent of the park's total visitors were French. Expectations were that closer to half of all visitors would be French.

It was hoped that the promotion of Philippe Bourguignon would have a public relations benefit for Euro Disneyland—a project that had been a publicist's nightmare from the beginning. One of the low points was at a news conference prior to the park's opening when protesters pelted Michael Eisner, CEO of the Walt Disney Company, with rotten eggs. Within the first year of operation, Disney had to compromise its "squeaky clean" image and lift the alcohol ban at the park. Wine is now served at all major restaurants.

Euro Disneyland, 49 percent owned by Walt Disney Company, Burbank, California, originally forecasted 11 million visitors in the first year of operation. In January 1993 it appeared attendance would be closer to 10 million. In response, management temporarily slashed prices at the park for local residents to FFr 150 ($27.27) from FFr 225 ($40.91) for adults and to FFr 100 from FFr 150 for children in order to lure more French during the slow, wet winter months. The company also reduced prices at its restaurants and hotels, which registered occupancy rates of just 37 percent.

Bourguignon also faced other problems, such as the second phase of development at Euro Disneyland, which was expected to start in September 1993. It was unclear how the company planned to finance its FFr 8–10 billion cost. The company had steadily drained its cash reserves (FFr 1.9 billion in May 1993) while piling up debt (FFr 21 billion in May 1993). Euro Disneyland admitted that it and the Walt Disney Company were "exploring potential sources of financing for Euro Disneyland." The company was also talking to banks about restructuring its debts.

Despite the frustrations, Eisner was tirelessly upbeat about the project. "Instant hits are things that go away quickly, and things that grow slowly and are part of the culture are what we look for," he said. "What we created in France is the biggest private investment in a foreign country by an American company ever. And it's gonna pay off."

In the Beginning

Disney's story is the classic American rags-to-riches story, which started in a small Kansas City advertising office where Mickey was a real mouse prowling the unknown Walt Disney floor. Originally, Mickey was named Mortimer, until a dissenting Mrs. Disney stepped in. How close Mickey was to Walt Disney is evidenced by the fact that when filming, Disney himself dubbed the mouse's voice. Only in later films did Mickey get a different voice. Disney made many sacrifices to promote his hero-mascot, including selling his first car, a beloved Moon Cabriolet, and humiliating himself in front of Louis B. Mayer. "Get that mouse off the screen!" was the movie mogul's reported response to the cartoon character. Then, in 1955, Disney had the brainstorm of sending his movie characters out into the "real" world to mix with their fans, and he battled skeptics to build the very first Disneyland in Anaheim, California.

When Disney died in 1966, the company went into virtual suspended animation. Its last big hit of that era was 1969's *The Love Bug,* about a Volkswagen named Herbie. Today, Disney executives trace the problem to a tyrannical CEO named E. Cardon Walker, who ruled the company from 1976 to 1983, and to his successor, Ronald W. Miller. Walker was quick to ridicule underlings in public and impervious to any point of view but his own. He made decisions according to what he thought Walt would have done. Executives clinched arguments by quoting Walt like the Scriptures or Marx, and the company eventually supplied a little book of the founder's sayings. Making the wholesome family movies Walt would have wanted formed a key article of Walker's creed. For example, a poster advertising the unremarkable Condorman featured actress Barbara Carrera in a slit skirt. Walker had the slit painted over. With this as the context, studio producers ground out a thin stream of tired, formulaic movies that fewer and fewer customers would pay to see. In mid-1983, a similar low-horsepower approach to television production led to CBS's cancellation of the hour-long program *The Wonderful World of Disney,* leaving the company without a regular network show for the first time in 29 years. Like a reclusive hermit, the company lost touch with the contemporary world.

Ron Miller's brief reign was by contrast a model of decentralization and delegation. Many attributed Miller's ascent to his marrying the boss's daughter rather than to any special gift. To shore Miller up, the board installed Raymond L. Watson, former head of the Irvine Co., as part-time chairperson. He quickly became full time.

Miller sensed the studio needed rejuvenation, and he managed to produce the hit film *Splash,* featuring an apparently (but not actually) bare-breasted mermaid, under the newly devised Touchstone label. However, the reluctance of freelance Hollywood talent to accommodate Disney's narrow range and stingy compensation often kept his sound instincts from bearing fruit. "Card [Cardon Walker] would listen but not hear," said a former executive. "Ron [Ron Miller] would listen but not act."

Too many box office bombs contributed to a steady erosion of profit. Profits of $135 million on revenues of $915 million in 1980 dwindled to $93 million on revenues of $1.3 billion in 1983. More alarmingly, revenues from the company's theme parks, about three-quarters of the company's total revenues, were showing signs of leveling off. Disney's stock slid from $84.375 a share to $48.75 between April 1983 and February 1984.

Through these years, Roy Disney Jr. simmered while he watched the downfall of the national institution that his uncle, Walt, and his father, Roy Disney Sr., had built. He had long argued that the company's constituent parts all worked together to enhance each other. If movie and television production weren't revitalized, not only would that source of revenue disappear but the company and its activities would also grow dim in the public eye. At the same time the stream of new ideas and characters that kept people pouring into the parks and buying toys, books, and records would dry up. Now his dire predictions were coming true. His own personal shareholding had already dropped from $96 million to $54 million. Walker's treatment of Ron Miller as the shining heir apparent and Roy Disney as the idiot nephew helped drive Roy to quit as Disney vice president in 1977 and to set up Shamrock Holdings, a broadcasting and investment company.

In 1984, Roy teamed up with Stanley Gold, a tough-talking lawyer and a brilliant strategist. Gold saw that the falling stock price was bound to flush out a raider and afford Roy Disney a chance to restore the company's fortunes. They asked Frank Wells, vice chairperson of Warner Bros., if he would take a top job in the company in the event they offered it. Wells, a lawyer and a Rhodes scholar, said yes. With that, Roy knew that what he would hear in Disney's boardroom would limit his freedom to trade in its stock, so he quit the board on March 9, 1984. "I knew that would hang a 'For Sale' sign over the company," said Gold.

By resigning, Roy pushed over the first of a train of dominoes that ultimately led to the result he most desired. The company was raided, almost dismantled, greenmailed, raided again, and sued left and right. But it miraculously emerged with a skilled new top management with big plans for a bright future. Roy Disney proposed Michael Eisner as the CEO, but the board came close to rejecting Eisner in favor of an older, more buttoned-down candidate. Gold stepped in and made an impassioned speech to the directors. "You see guys like Eisner as a little crazy . . . but every studio in this country has been run by crazies. What do you think Walt Disney was? The guy was off the goddamned wall. This is a creative institution. It needs to be run by crazies again."[1]

Meanwhile Eisner and Wells staged an all-out lobbying campaign, calling on every board member except two, who were abroad, to explain their views about the company's future. "What was most important," said Eisner, "was that they saw I did not come in a tutu, and that I was a serious person, and I understood a P&L, and I knew the investment analysts, and I read Fortune."

In September 1984, Michael Eisner was appointed CEO and Frank Wells became president. Jeffrey Katzenberg, the 33-year-old, maniacal production chief, followed Fisher from Paramount Pictures. He took over Disney's movie and television studios. "The key," said Eisner, "is to start off with a great idea."

Disneyland in Anaheim, California

For a long time, Walt Disney had been concerned about the lack of family-type entertainment available for his two daughters. The amusement parks he saw around him were mostly filthy traveling carnivals. They were often unsafe and allowed unruly conduct on the premises. Disney envisioned a place where people from all over the world would be able to go for clean and safe fun. His dream came true on July 17, 1955, when the gates first opened at Disneyland in Anaheim, California.

Disneyland strives to generate the perfect fantasy. But magic does not simply happen. The place is a marvel of modern technology. Literally dozens of computers, huge banks of tape machines, film projectors, and electronic controls lie behind the walls, beneath the floors, and above the ceilings of dozens of rides and attractions. The philosophy is that "Disneyland is the world's biggest stage, and the audience is right here on the stage," said Dick Hollinger, chief industrial engineer at Disneyland. "It takes a tremendous amount of work to keep the stage clean and working properly."

Cleanliness is a primary concern. Before the park opens at 8 a.m., the cleaning crew will have mopped, hosed, and dried every sidewalk, street, floor, and counter. More than 350 of the park's 7,400 employees come on duty at 1 a.m., to begin the daily cleanup routine. The thousands of feet that walk through the park each day and chewing gum do not mix; gum has always presented major cleanup problems. The park's janitors found long ago that fire hoses with 90 pounds of water pressure would not do the job. Now they use steam machines, razor scrapers, and mops towed by Cushman scooters to literally scour the streets and sidewalks daily.

It takes one person working a full eight-hour shift to polish the brass on the Fantasyland merry-go-round. The scrupulously manicured plantings throughout the park are treated with growth-retarding hormones to keep the trees and bushes from spreading beyond their assigned spaces and destroying the carefully maintained five-eighths scale modeling that is utilized in the park. The maintenance supervisor of the Matterhorn bobsled ride personally walks every foot of track and inspects every link of tow chain every night, thus trusting his or her own eyes more than the $2 million in safety equipment that is built into the ride.

Eisner himself pays obsessive attention to detail. Walking through Disneyland one Sunday afternoon, he peered at the plastic leaves on the Swiss Family Robinson tree house noting that they periodically wear out and need to be replaced leaf by leaf at a cost of $500,000. As his family strolled through the park, he and his eldest son Breck stooped to pick up the rare piece of litter that the cleanup crew had somehow missed. This old-fashioned dedication has paid off. Since opening day in 1955, Disneyland has been a consistent moneymaker.

Disney World in Orlando, Florida

By the time Eisner arrived, Disney World in Orlando was already on its way to becoming what it is today—the most popular vacation destination in the United States. But the company had neglected a rich niche in its business: hotels. Disney's three existing hotels, probably the most profitable in the United States, registered unheard-of occupancy rates of 92 percent to 96 percent versus 66 percent for the industry. Eisner promptly embarked on an ambitious $1 billion hotel expansion plan. Two major hotels, Disney's Grand Floridian Beach Resort and Disney's Caribbean Beach Resort, were opened during 1987–89. Disney's Yacht Club and Beach Resort along with the Dolphin and Swan Hotels, owned and operated by Tishman Realty & Construction, Metropolitan Life Insurance, and Aoki Corporation opened during 1989–90. Adding 3,400 hotel rooms and 250,000 square feet of convention space made it the largest convention center east of the Mississippi.

In October 1982, Disney made a new addition to the theme park—the Experimental Prototype Community of Tomorrow, or EPCOT Center. E. Cardon Walker, then president of the company, announced that EPCOT would be a "permanent showcase, industrial park, and experimental housing center." This new park consists of two large complexes: Future World, a series of pavilions designed to show the technological advances of the next 25 years, and World Showcase, a collection of foreign "villages."

Tokyo Disneyland

It was Tokyo's nastiest winter day in four years. Arctic winds and 8 inches of snow lashed the city. Roads were clogged and trains slowed down. But the bad weather didn't keep 13,200 hardy souls from Tokyo Disneyland. Mikki Mausu, better known outside Japan as Mickey Mouse, had taken the country by storm.

Located on a fringe of reclaimed shoreline in Urayasu City on the outskirts of Tokyo, the park opened to the public on April 15, 1983. In less than one year, over 10 million people had passed through its gates, an attendance figure that has been bettered every single year. On August 13, 1983, 93,000 people helped set a one-day attendance record that easily eclipsed the old records established at the two parent U.S. parks. Four years later, records again toppled as the turnstiles clicked. The total this time: 111,500. By 1988, approximately 50 million people, or nearly half of Japan's population, had visited Tokyo Disneyland since its opening. The steady cash flow pushed revenues for fiscal year 1989 to $768 million, up 17 percent from 1988.

The 204-acre Tokyo Disneyland is owned and operated by Oriental Land under license from the Walt Disney Co. The 45-year contract gives Disney 10 percent of admissions and 5 percent of food and merchandise sales, plus licensing fees. Disney opted to take no equity in the project and put no money down for construction. "I never had the slightest doubt about the success of Disneyland in Japan," said Masatomo Takahashi, president of Oriental Land Company. Oriental Land was so confident of the success of Disney in Japan that it financed the park entirely with debt, borrowing ¥180 billion ($1.5 billion at February 1988 exchange rates). Takahashi added, "The debt means nothing to me," and with good reason. According to Fusahao Awata, who co-authored a book on Tokyo Disneyland: "The Japanese yearn for [American culture]."

Soon after Tokyo Disneyland opened in April 1983, five Shinto priests held a solemn dedication ceremony near Cinderella's castle. It is the only overtly Japanese ritual seen so far in this sprawling theme park. What visitors see is pure Americana. All signs are in English, with only small katakana (a phonetic Japanese alphabet)

Exhibit 1   How the Theme Parks Grew

1955	Disneyland
1966	Walt Disney's death
1971	Walt Disney World in Orlando
1982	Epcot Center
1983	Tokyo Disneyland
1992	Euro Disneyland

Stephen Koepp, "Do You Believe in Magic?" *Time*, April 25, 1988, pp. 66–73.

translations. Most of the food is American style, and the attractions are cloned from Disney's U.S. parks. Disney also held firm on two fundamentals that strike the Japanese as strange—no alcohol is allowed and no food may be brought in from outside the park.

However, in Disney's enthusiasm to make Tokyo a brick-by-brick copy of Anaheim's Magic Kingdom, there were a few glitches. On opening day, the Tokyo park discovered that almost 100 public telephones were placed too high for Japanese guests to reach them comfortably. And many hungry customers found countertops above their reach at the park's snack stands.

"Everything we imported that worked in the United States works here," said Ronald D. Pogue, managing director of Walt Disney Attractions Japan Ltd. "American things like McDonald's hamburgers and Kentucky Fried Chicken are popular here with young people. We also wanted visitors from Japan and Southeast Asia to feel they were getting the real thing," said Toshiharu Akiba, a staff member of the Oriental Land publicity department.

Still, local sensibilities dictated a few changes. A Japanese restaurant was added to please older patrons. The Nautilus submarine is missing. More areas are covered to protect against rain and snow. Lines for attractions had to be redesigned so that people walking through the park did not cross in front of patrons waiting to ride an attraction. "It's very discourteous in Japan to have people cross in front of somebody else," explained James B. Cora, managing director of operations for the Tokyo project. The biggest differences between Japan and America have come in slogans and ad copy. Although English is often used, it's "Japanized" English—the sort that would have native speakers shaking their heads while the Japanese nod happily in recognition. "Let's Spring" was the motto for one of their highly successful ad campaigns.

Pogue, visiting frequently from his base in California, supervised seven resident American Disney managers who work side by side with Japanese counterparts from Oriental Land Co. to keep the park in tune with the Disney doctrine. American it may be, but Tokyo Disneyland appeals to such deep-seated Japanese passions as cleanliness, order, outstanding service, and technological wizardry. Japanese executives are impressed by Disney's detailed training manuals, which teach employees how to make visitors feel like VIPs. Most worth emulating, say the Japanese, is Disney's ability to make even the lowliest job seem glamorous. "They have changed the image of dirty work," said Hakuhodo Institute's Sekizawa.

Disney Company did encounter a few unique cultural problems when developing Tokyo Disneyland:

> The problem: how to dispose of some 250 tons of trash that would be generated weekly by Tokyo Disneyland visitors?
> The standard Disney solution: trash compactors.
> The Japanese proposal: pigs to eat the trash and be slaughtered and sold at a profit.

Exhibit 2 Investor's Snapshot: The Walt Disney Company (December 1989)

Sales (latest four quarters)	$4.6 billion
Change from year earlier	Up 33.6%
Net profit	$703.3 million
Change	Up 34.7%
Return on common stockholders' equity	23.4%
Five year average	20.3%
Stock price average (last 12 months)	$60.50–$136.25
Recent share price	$122.75
Price/Earnings Multiple	27
Total return to investor (12 months to 11/3/89)	90.6%

Source: Fortune, December 4, 1989.

James B. Cora and his team of some 150 operations experts did a little calculating and pointed out that it would take 100,000 pigs to do the job. And then there would be the smell . . .

The Japanese relented.

The Japanese were also uneasy about a rustic-looking Westernland, Tokyo's version of Frontierland. "The Japanese like everything fresh and new when they put it in," said Cora. "They kept painting the wood and we kept saying, 'No, it's got to look old.'" Finally the Disney crew took the Japanese to Anaheim to give them a firsthand look at the Old West.

Tokyo Disneyland opened just as the yen escalated in value against the dollar, and the income level of the Japanese registered a phenomenal improvement. During this era of affluence, Tokyo Disneyland triggered an interest in leisure. Its great success spurred the construction of "leisurelands" throughout the country. This created an increase in the Japanese people's orientation toward leisure. But demographics are the real key to Tokyo Disneyland's success. Thirty million Japanese live within 30 miles of the park. There are three times more than the number of people in the same proximity to Anaheim's Disneyland. With the park proven such an unqualified hit, and nearing capacity, Oriental Land and Disney mapped out plans for a version of the Disney-MGM studio tour next door. This time, Disney talked about taking a 50 percent stake in the project.

Building Euro Disneyland

On March 24, 1987, Michael Eisner and Jacques Chirac, the French prime minister, signed a contract for the building of a Disney theme park at Marne-la-Vallee. Talks between Disney and the French government had dragged on for more than a year. At the signing, Robert Fitzpatrick, fluent in French, married to the former Sylvie Blondet, and the recipient of two awards from the French government, was introduced as the president of Euro Disneyland. He was expected to be a key player in wooing support from the French establishment for the theme park. As one analyst put it, Disney selected him to set up the park because he is "more French than the French."

Disney had been courted extensively by Spain and France. The prime ministers of both countries ordered their governments to lend Disney a hand in its quest for a site. France set up a five-person team headed by Special Advisor to Foreign Trade and Tourism Minister Edith Cresson, and Spain's negotiators included Ignacio Vasallo, Director-General for the Promotion of Tourism. Disney pummeled both governments with requests for detailed information. "The only thing they haven't asked us for is the color of the tourists' eyes," moaned Vasallo.

The governments tried other enticements too. Spain offered tax and labor incentives and possibly as much as 20,000 acres of land. The French package, although less generous, included spending of $53 million to improve highway access to the proposed site and perhaps speeding up a $75 million subway project. For a long time, all that smiling Disney officials would say was that Spain had better weather while France had a better population base.

Officials explained that they picked France over Spain because Marne-la-Vallee is advantageously close to one of the world's tourism capitals, while also being situated within a day's drive or train ride of some 30 million people in France, Belgium, England, and Germany. Another advantage mentioned was the availability of good transportation. A train line that serves as part of the Paris Metro subway system ran to Torcy, in the center of Marne-la-Vallee, and the French government promised to extend the line to the actual site of the park. The park would also be served by A-4, a modern highway that runs from Paris to the German border, as well as a freeway that runs to Charles de Gaulle airport.

Once a letter of intent had been signed, sensing that the French government was keen to not let the plan fail, Disney held out for one concession after another. For example, Disney negotiated for VAT (value-added tax) on ticket sales to be cut from a normal 18.6 percent to 7 percent. A quarter of the investment in building the park would come from subsidized loans. Additionally, any disputes arising from the contract would be settled not in French courts but by a special international panel of arbitrators. But Disney did have to agree to a clause in the contract which would require it to respect and utilize French culture in its themes.

The park was built on 4,460 acres of farmland in Marne-la-Vallee, a rural corner of France 20 miles east of Paris known mostly for sugar beets and Brie cheese. Opening was planned for early 1992, and planners hoped to attract some 10 million visitors a year. Approximately $2.5 billion was needed to build the park, making it the largest single foreign investment ever in France. A French "pivot" company was formed to build the park with starting capital of FFr 3 billion, split 60 percent French and 40 percent foreign, with Disney taking 16.67 percent. Euro Disneyland was expected to bring $600 million in foreign investment into France each year.

As soon as the contract had been signed, individuals and businesses began scurrying to somehow plug into the Mickey Mouse money machine—all were hoping to benefit from the American dream without leaving France. In fact, one Paris daily, *Liberation,* actually sprouted mouse ears over its front-page flag.

The $1.5 to $2 billion first phase investment would involve an amusement complex including hotels and restaurants, golf courses, and an aquatic park in addition to a European version of the Magic Kingdom. The second phase, scheduled to start after the gates opened in 1992, called for the construction of a community around the park, including a sports complex, technology park, conference center, theater, shopping mall, university campus, villas, and condominiums. No price tag had been put on the second phase, although it was expected to rival, if not surpass, the first phase investment. In November 1989, Fitzpatrick announced that the Disney–MGM Studios, Europe, would also open at Euro Disneyland in 1996, resembling the enormously successful Disney–MGM Studios theme park at Disney World in Orlando. The new studios would greatly enhance the Walt Disney Company's strategy of increasing its production of live action and animated filmed entertainment in Europe for both the European and world markets.

"The phone's been ringing here ever since the announcement," said Marc Berthod of EpaMarne, the government body that oversees the Marne-la-Vallee region. "We've gotten calls from big companies as well as small—everything from hotel chains to language interpreters all asking for details on Euro Disneyland. And the individual mayors of the villages around here have been swamped with calls from people looking for jobs," he added.

Euro Disneyland was expected to generate up to 28,000 jobs, providing a measure of relief for an area that had suffered a 10 percent–plus unemployment rate for the previous year. It was also expected to light a fire under France's construction industry, which had been particularly hard hit by France's economic problems over the previous year. Moreover, Euro Disneyland was expected to attract many other investors to the depressed outskirts of Paris. International Business Machines (IBM) and Banque National de Paris were among those already building in the area. In addition one of the new buildings going up was a factory that would employ 400 outside workers to wash the 50 tons of laundry expected to be generated per day by Euro Disneyland's 14,000 employees.

The impact of Euro Disneyland was also felt in the real estate market. "Everyone who owns land around here is holding on to it for the time being, at least until they know what's going to happen," said Danny Theveno, a spokesman for the town of Villiers on the western edge of Marne-la-Vallee. Disney expected 11 million visitors in the first year. The break-even point was estimated to be between 7 and 8 million. One worry was that Euro Disneyland would cannibalize the flow of European visitors to Walt Disney World in Florida, but European travel agents said that their customers were still eagerly signing up for Florida, lured by the cheap dollar and the promise of sunshine.

Protests of Cultural Imperialism

Disney faced French communists and intellectuals who protested the building of Euro Disneyland. Ariane Mnouchkine, a theater director, described it as a "cultural Chernobyl." "I wish with all my heart that the rebels would set fire to Disneyland," thundered a French intellectual in the newspaper *La Figaro*. "Mickey Mouse," sniffed another, "is stifling individualism and transforming children into consumers." The theme park was damned as an example of American "neoprovincialism."

Farmers in the Marne-la-Vallee region posted protest signs along the roadside featuring a mean looking Mickey Mouse and touting sentiments such as "Disney go home," "Stop the massacre," and "Don't gnaw away our national wealth." Farmers were upset partly because under the terms of the contract, the French government would expropriate the necessary land and sell it without profit to the Euro Disneyland development company.

While local officials were sympathetic to the farmers' position, they were unwilling to let their predicament interfere with what some called "the deal of the century." "For many years these farmers have had the fortune to cultivate what is considered some of the richest land in France," said Berthod. "Now they'll have to find another occupation."

Also less than enchanted about the prospect of a magic kingdom rising among its midst was the communist-dominated labor federation, the Confédération Générale du Travail (CGT). Despite the job-creating potential of Euro Disney, the CGT doubted its members would benefit. The union had been fighting hard to stop the passage of a bill which would give managers the right to establish flexible hours for their workers. Flexible hours were believed to be a prerequisite to the profitable operation of Euro Disneyland, especially considering seasonal variations.

However, Disney proved to be relatively immune to the anti-U.S. virus. In early 1985, one of the three state-owned television networks signed a contract to broadcast two hours of dubbed Disney programming every Saturday evening. Soon after, *Disney Channel* became one of the top-rated programs in France.

In 1987, the company launched an aggressive community relations program to calm the fears of politicians, farmers, villagers, and even bankers that the project would bring traffic congestion, noise, pollution, and other problems to their countryside. Such a public relations program was a rarity in France, where businesses make little effort to establish good relations with local residents. Disney invited 400 local children to a birthday party for Mickey Mouse, sent Mickey to area hospitals, and hosted free trips to Disney World in Florida for dozens of local officials and children.

"They're experts at seduction, and they don't hide the fact that they're trying to seduce you," said Vincent Guardiola, an official with Banque Indosuez, one of the 17 banks wined and dined at Orlando and subsequently one of the venture's financial participants. "The French aren't used to this kind of public relations—it was unbelievable." Observers said that the goodwill efforts helped dissipate initial objections to the project.

Financial Structuring at Euro Disneyland

Eisner was so keen on Euro Disneyland that Disney kept a 49 percent stake in the project, while the remaining 51 percent of stock was distributed through the London, Paris, and Brussels stock exchanges. Half the stock under the offer was going to the French, 25 percent to the English, and the remainder distributed in the rest of the European community. The initial offer price of FFr 72 was considerably higher than the pathfinder prospectus estimate because the capacity of the park had been slightly extended. Scarcity of stock was likely to push up the price, which was expected to reach FFr 166 by opening day in 1992. This would give a compound return of 21 percent.

Exhibit 3 Chronology of the Euro Disneyland Deal

1984–85	Disney negotiates with Spain and France to create a European theme park. Chooses France as the site.
1987	Disney signs letter of intent with the French government.
1988	Selects lead commercial bank lenders for the senior portion of the project. Forms the Société en Nom Collectif (SNC). Begins planning for the equity offering of 51% of Euro Disneyland as required in the letter of intent.
1989	European press and stock analysts visit Walt Disney World in Orlando. Begin extensive news and television campaign. Stock starts trading at 20–25 percent premium from the issue price.

Source: Geraldine E. Willigan, "The Value-Adding CFO: An Interview with Disney's Gary Wilson," *Harvard Business Review*, January–February 1990, pp. 85–93.

Walt Disney Company maintained management control of the company. The U.S. company put up $160 million of its own capital to fund the project, an investment which soared in value to $2.4 billion after the popular stock offering in Europe. French national and local authorities, by comparison, were providing about $800 million in low-interest loans and poured at least that much again into infrastructure.

Other sources of funding were the park's 12 corporate sponsors, and Disney would pay them back in kind. The "autopolis" ride, where kids ride cars, features coupes emblazoned with the "Hot Wheels" logo. Mattel Inc., sponsor of the ride, was grateful for the boost to one of its biggest toy lines.

The real payoff would begin once the park opened. The Walt Disney Company would receive 10 percent of admission fees and 5 percent of food and merchandise revenue, the same arrangement as in Japan. But in France, it would also receive management fees, incentive fees, and 49 percent of the profits.

A Saloman Brothers analyst estimated that the park would pull in 3 to 4 million more visitors than the 11 million the company expected in the first year. Other Wall Street analysts cautioned that stock prices of both Walt Disney Company and Euro Disney already contained all the Euro optimism they could absorb. "Europeans visit Disney World in Florida as part of an 'American experience,'" said Patrick P. Roper, marketing director of Alton Towers, a successful British theme park near Manchester. He doubted they would seek the suburbs of Paris as eagerly as America and predicted attendance would trail Disney projections.

The Layout of Euro Disneyland

Euro Disneyland is determinedly American in its theme. There was an alcohol ban in the park despite the attitude among the French that wine with a meal is a God-given right. Designers presented a plan for a Main Street USA based on scenes of America in the 1920s, because research indicated that Europeans loved the Prohibition era. Eisner decreed that images of gangsters and speakeasies were too negative. Though made more ornate and Victorian than Walt Disney's idealized Midwestern small town, Main Street remained Main Street. Steamships leave from Main Street through the Grand Canyon Diorama en route to Frontierland.

The familiar Disney Tomorrowland, with its dated images of the space age, was jettisoned entirely. It was replaced by a gleaming brass and wood complex called Discoverland, which was based on themes of Jules Verne and Leonardo da Vinci. Eisner ordered $8 or $10 million in extras to the "Visionarium" exhibit, a 360-degree movie about French culture which was required by the French in their original contract. French and English are the official languages at the park, and multilingual guides are available to help Dutch, German, Spanish, and Italian visitors.

With the American Wild West being so frequently captured on film, Europeans have their own idea of what life was like back then. Frontierland reinforces those images. A runaway mine train takes guests through the canyons and mines of Gold Rush country. There is a paddle wheel steamboat reminiscent of Mark Twain, Indian explorer canoes, and a phantom manor from the Gold Rush days.

In Fantasyland, designers strived to avoid competing with the nearby European reality of actual medieval towns, cathedrals, and chateaux. While Disneyland's castle is based on Germany's Neuschwanstein and Disney World's is based on a Loire Valley chateau, Euro Disney's *Le Château de la Belle au Bois Dormant,* as the French insisted Sleeping Beauty be called, is more cartoonlike with stained glass windows built by English craftspeople and depicting Disney characters. Fanciful trees grow inside as well as a beanstalk.

The park is criss-crossed with covered walkways. Eisner personally ordered the installation of 35 fireplaces in hotels and restaurants. "People walk around Disney World in Florida with humidity and temperatures in the 90s and they walk into an air-conditioned ride and say, 'This is the greatest,'" said Eisner. "When it's raining and miserable, I hope they will walk into one of these lobbies with the fireplace going and say the same thing."

Children all over Europe were primed to consume. Even one of the intellectuals who contributed to *Le Figaro's* Disney-bashing broadsheet was forced to admit with resignation that his 10-year-old son "swears by Michael Jackson." At Euro Disneyland, under the name "Captain EO," Disney just so happened to have a Michael Jackson attraction awaiting him.

Food Service and Accommodations at Euro Disneyland

Disney expected to serve 15,000 to 17,000 meals per hour, excluding snacks. Menus and service systems were developed so that they varied both in style and price. There is a 400-seat buffeteria, 6 table service restaurants, 12 counter service units, 10 snack bars, 1 Discovery food court seating 850, 9 popcorn wagons, 15 ice-cream carts, 14 specialty food carts, and 2 employee cafeterias. Restaurants were, in fact, to be a showcase for American foods. The only exception to this is Fantasyland which re-creates European fables. Here, food service will reflect the fable's country of origin: Pinocchio's facility having German food; Cinderella's, French; Bella Notte's, Italian; and so on.

Of course recipes were adapted for European tastes. Since many Europeans don't care much for very spicy food, Tex-Mex recipes were toned down. A special coffee blend had to be developed which would have universal appeal. Hot dog carts would reflect the regionalism of

Exhibit 4   The Euro Disneyland Resort

5,000 acres in size
30 attractions
12,000 employees
6 hotels (with 5,184 rooms)
10 theme restaurants
414 cabins
181 camping sites

Source: Roger Cohen, "Threat of Strikes in Euro Disney Debut," *New York Times,* April 10, 1992, p. 20.

American tastes. There would be a ball park hot dog (mild, steamed, a mixture of beef and pork), a New York hot dog (all beef, and spicy), and a Chicago hot dog (Vienna-style, similar to bratwurst).

Euro Disneyland has six theme hotels which would offer nearly 5,200 rooms on opening day, a campground (444 rental trailers and 181 camping sites), and single family homes on the periphery of the 27-hole golf course.

Disney's Strict Appearance Code

Antoine Guervil stood at his post in front of the 1,000-room Cheyenne Hotel at Euro Disneyland, practicing his "Howdy!" When Guervil, a political refugee from Haiti, said the word, it sounded more like "Audi." Native French speakers have trouble with the aspirated "h" sound in words like "hay" and "Hank" and "howdy." Guervil had been given the job of wearing a cowboy costume and booming a happy, welcoming howdy to guests as they entered the Cheyenne, styled after a Western movie set.

"Audi," said Guervil, the strain of linguistic effort showing on his face. This was clearly a struggle. Unless things got better, it was not hard to imagine objections from Renault, the French car company that was one of the corporate sponsors of the park. Picture the rage of a French auto executive arriving with his or her family at the Renault-sponsored Euro Disneyland, only to hear the doorman of a Disney hotel advertising a German car.

Such were the problems Disney faced while hiring some 12,000 people to maintain and populate its Euro Disneyland theme park. A handbook of detailed rules on acceptable clothing, hairstyles, and jewelry, among other things, embroiled the company in a legal and cultural dispute. Critics asked how the brash Americans could be so insensitive to French culture, individualism, and privacy. Disney officials insisted that a ruling that barred them from imposing a squeaky-clean employment standard could threaten the image and long-term success of the park.

"For us, the appearance code has a real effect from a product identification standpoint," said Thor Degelmann, vice president for human resources for Euro Disneyland. "Without it we wouldn't be presenting the Disney product that people would be expecting."

The rules, spelled out in a video presentation and detailed in a guide handbook, went beyond height and weight standards. They required men's hair to be cut above the collar and ears with no beards or mustaches. Any tattoos must be covered. Women must keep their hair in one "natural color" with no frosting or streaking, and they may make only limited use of makeup like mascara. False eyelashes, eyeliners, and eye pencil were completely off limits. Fingernails can't pass the end of the fingers. As for jewelry, women can wear only one earring in each ear, with the earring's diameter no more than three-quarters of an inch. Neither men nor women can wear more than one ring on each hand. Further, women were required to wear appropriate undergarments and only transparent panty hose, not black or anything with fancy designs. Though a daily bath was not specified in the rules, the applicant's video depicted a shower scene and informed applicants that they were expected to show up for work "fresh and clean each day." Similar rules are in force at Disney's three other theme parks in the United States and Japan.

In the United States, some labor unions representing Disney employees have occasionally protested the company's strict appearance code, but with little success. French labor unions began protesting when Disneyland opened its "casting center" and invited applicants to "play the role of [their lives]" and to take a "unique opportunity to marry work and magic." The CGT handed out leaflets in front of the center to warn applicants of the appearance code, which they believed represented "an attack on individual liberty." A more mainstream union, the Confédération Française Démocratique du Travail (CFDT), appealed to the Labor Ministry to halt Disney's violation of "human dignity." French law prohibits employers from restricting individual and collective liberties unless the restrictions can be justified by the nature of the task to be accomplished and are proportional to that end.

Degelmann, however, said that the company was "well aware of the cultural differences" between the United States and France and as a result had "toned down" the wording in the original American version of the guidebook. He pointed out that many companies, particularly airlines, maintained appearance codes just as strict. "We happened to put ours in writing," he added. In any case, he said that he knew of no one who had refused to take the job because of the rules and that no more than 5 percent of the people showing up for interviews had decided not to proceed after watching the video, which also detailed transportation and salary.

Fitzpatrick also defended the dress code, although he conceded that Disney might have been a little naive in presenting things so directly. He added, "Only in France is there still a communist party. There is not even one in Russia any more. The ironic thing is that I could fill the park with CGT requests for tickets."

Another big challenge lay in getting the mostly French "cast members," as Disney calls its employees, to break their ancient cultural aversions to smiling and being consistently polite to park guests. The individualistic French had to be molded into the squeaky-clean Disney image. Rival theme parks in the area, loosely modeled on the Disney system, had already encountered trouble keeping smiles on the faces of the staff, who sometimes took on the demeanor of subway ticket clerks.

The delicate matter of hiring French citizens as opposed to other nationals was examined in the more than two-year-long preagreement negotiations between the French government and Disney. The final agreement called for Disney to make a maximum effort to tap into the local labor market. At the same time, it was understood that for Euro Disneyland to work, its staff must mirror the multicountry makeup of its guests. "Casting centers" were set up in Paris, London, Amsterdam, and Frankfurt. "We are concentrating on the local labor market, but we are also looking for workers who are German, English, Italian, Spanish, or other nationalities and who have good communication skills, are outgoing, speak two European languages—French plus one other—and like being around people," said Degelmann.

Stephane Baudet, a 28-year-old trumpet player from Paris, refused to audition for a job in a Disney brass band when he learned he would have to cut his ponytail. "Some people will turn themselves into a pumpkin to work at Euro Disneyland," he said. "But not me."

Opening Day at Euro Disneyland

A few days before the grand opening of Euro Disneyland, hundreds of French visitors were invited to a preopening party. They gazed perplexed at what was placed before them. It was a heaping plate of spare ribs. The visitors were at the Buffalo Bill Wild West Show, a cavernous theater featuring a panoply of "Le Far West," including 20 imported buffaloes. And Disney deliberately didn't provide silverware. "There was a moment of consternation," recalls Fitzpatrick. "Then they just kind of said, 'The hell with it,' and dug in." There was one problem. The guests couldn't master the art of gnawing ribs and applauding at the same time. So Disney planned to provide more napkins and teach visitors to stamp with their feet.

On April 12, 1992, the opening day of Euro Disneyland, France-Soir enthusiastically predicted Disney dementia. "Mickey! It's Madness" read its front-page headline, warning of chaos on the roads and suggesting that people might have to be turned away. A French government survey indicated that half a million might turn up with 90,000 cars trying to get in. French radio warned traffic to avoid the area.

By lunchtime on opening day, the Euro Disneyland car park was less than half full, suggesting an attendance of below 25,000, less than half the park's capacity and way below expectations. Many people may have heeded the advice to stay home or, more likely, were deterred by a one-day strike that cut the direct rail link to Euro Disneyland from the center of Paris. Queues for the main rides, such as Pirates of the Caribbean and Big Thunder Mountain railroad, were averaging around 15 minutes less than on an ordinary day at Disney World, Florida.

Disney executives put on a brave face, claiming that attendance was better than at first days for other Disney theme parks in Florida, California, and Japan. However, there was no disguising the fact that after spending thousands of dollars on the preopening celebrations, Euro Disney would have appreciated some impressively long traffic jams on the auto route.

Other Operating Problems

When the French government changed hands in 1986, work ground to a halt, as the negotiator appointed by the Conservative government threw out much of the groundwork prepared by his Socialist predecessor. The legalistic approach taken by the Americans also bogged down talks, as it meant planning ahead for every conceivable contingency. At the same time, right-wing groups who saw the park as an invasion of "chewing-gum jobs" and U.S. pop culture also fought hard for a greater "local cultural context."

On opening day, English visitors found the French reluctant to play the game of queuing. "The French seem to think that if God had meant them to queue, He wouldn't have given them elbows," they commented. Different cultures have different definitions of personal space, and Disney guests faced problems of people getting too close or pressing around those who left too much space between themselves and the person in front.

Exhibit 5 **What Price Mickey?**

	Euro Disneyland	Disney World, Orlando
Peak Season Hotel Rates		
4-person room	$97–$345	$104–$455
Campground Space		
	$48	$30–$49
One-Day Pass		
Children	$26	$26
Adults	$40	$33

Source: BusinessWeek, March 30, 1992.

A Further Look at Euro Disneyland in Recent Years:

As discussed in In-Depth Integrative Case 2.1a, Euro Disneyland faced major hurdles in its early years. In May 1992, roughly 25 percent of Euro Disney's workforce (approximately 3,000 people) resigned from their jobs citing unacceptable working conditions. As a result, the Euro Disney Company stock price declined and Euro Disney announced an expected net loss in its first year of operation of approximately 300 million French francs in July of 1992.[1] Since then, Euro Disneyland has enacted some major changes—many with great success.

In an effort to improve attendance, Disney began serving alcoholic beverages with meals inside the Euro Disneyland Park in June of 1993.[2] In March of 1994, Disney offered the banks a deal: Disney would provide additional capital to ensure that it continues to operate if the banks agreed to restructure the US$1 billion of debt. If the banks did not agree, Disney was prepared to close the park and default on the loans. Disney put additional pressure on the banks by publically announcing the possible closure of the park unless the debt was restructured. The banks agreed to Disney's demands and wrote off the next two years of interest payments along with a three year period where loan repayments would be postponed. In return, The Walt Disney Company agreed to restructure its own loan arrangements at the new park valued at US$210 million.[3]

A turnaround began to blossom shortly after restructuring. In 1995, Disney reported that attendance had increased 21 percent from 8.8 million to 10.7 million year over year with hotel occupancy also increasing from 60 percent to 68.5 percent.[4] The Euro Disney Resort was renamed to Disneyland Paris in 1994 and, in July of 1995, the company reported its first quarterly profit of US$35.3 million. Disneyland Paris ended 1995 with a profit of US$22.8 million. Disney opened a second theme park in France, Walt Disney Studios Park in March of 2002.[5] The two combined parks had a total attendance in 2012 of over 15 million, making it Europe's most visited themed attraction.[6]

In September 2012, the Walt Disney Co. assumed Euro Disney S.C.A.'s debt under a new refinancing deal. The new 1.23 billion euro loan aims to free Euro Disney of debt covenants that have restricted capital expenditures and future investments.[7]

Disney placed its first ads for work bids in English, leaving small- and medium-sized French firms feeling like foreigners in their own land. Eventually, Disney set up a data bank with information on over 20,000 French and European firms looking for work, and the local Chamber of Commerce developed a video text information bank with Disney that small- and medium-sized companies through France and Europe would be able to tap into. "The work will come, but many local companies have got to learn that they don't simply have the right to a chunk of work without competing," said a chamber official.

Efforts were made to ensure that sooner, rather than later, European nationals take over the day-to-day running of the park. Although there were only 23 U.S. expatriates among the employees, they controlled the show and held most of the top jobs. Each senior manager had the task of choosing his or her European successor.

Disney was also forced to bail out 40 subcontractors who were working for the Gabot-Eremco construction contracting group, which had been unable to honor all of its commitments. Some of the subcontractors said they faced bankruptcy if they were not paid for their work on Euro Disneyland. A Disney spokesperson said that the payments would be less than $20.3 million and the company had already paid Gabot-Eremco for work on the park. Gabot-Eremco and 15 other main contractors demanded $157 million in additional fees from Disney for work that they said was added to the project after the initial contracts were signed. Disney rejected the claim and sought government intervention. Disney said that under no circumstances would it pay Gabot-Eremco and accused its officers of incompetence. As Bourguignon thought about these and other problems, the previous year's losses and the prospect of losses again in the current year, with their negative impact on the company's stock price, weighed heavily on his mind.

Questions for Review

1. Using Hofstede's four cultural dimensions as a point of reference, what are some of the main cultural differences between the United States and France?

2. In what way has Trompenaars's research helped explain cultural differences between the United States and France?

3. In managing its Euro Disneyland operations, what are three mistakes that the company made? Explain.

4. Based on its experience, what are three lessons the company should have learned about how to deal with diversity? Describe each.

Source: This case was prepared by Research Assistant Sonali Krishna under the direction of Professors J. Stewart Black and Hal B. Gregersen as the basis for class discussion. It is not intended to illustrate either effective or ineffective managerial capability or administrative responsibility. Reprinted by permission of the authors.

Beyond Tokyo: Disney's Expansion in Asia

After its success with Tokyo Disneyland in the 1980s, Disney began to realize the vast potential of the Asian market. The theme park industry throughout Asia has been very successful in recent years, with a range of regional and international companies all trying to enter the market. Disney has been one of the major participants, opening Hong Kong Disneyland in 2005 and discussing future operations in at least three other Asian cities.

Disney in China

After Disney's success in Tokyo, China, in particular, became a serious option for its next theme park venture in light of the country's impressive population and economic growth throughout the 1990s. Successful sales associated with the Disney movie *The Lion King*, in 1996, also convinced Disney officials that China was a promising location. However, consumer enthusiasm for theme parks in China was at a low in the late 1990s. "Between 1993 and 1998, more than 2,000 theme parks had been opened in China," and "many projects were swamped by excessive competition, poor market projections, high costs, and relentless interference from local officials," forcing several hundred to be closed.[8] Nevertheless, Disney continued to pursue plans in both Shanghai and Hong Kong.

Shanghai, known as the "Paris of the Orient," was an attractive site for Disney officials because of its growing commercialization and industrialization and its already extant transportation access. The projected $1 billion project was scheduled to be built across the Huangpu River from Shanghai's world-famous waterfront promenade, the Bund, on a 200-square-mile expanse called The Pudong New Area. The first phase of construction included a Magic Kingdom park, while an EPCOT-style theme park was to be added after at least five years of operations.[9]

A Disney theme park in Shanghai would be mutually beneficial for the company and the nation of China. From Disney's perspective, it would gain access to one of the world's largest potential markets (and also compete with Universal Studios' new theme park). From the perspective of Chinese government officials, Disney's park would be a long-awaited mark of international success for a communist nation.[10]

Initially planners hoped to have a Disneyland operating in Shanghai prior to the World Expo in 2010. However the project stalled, and as of late 2006, "the chances of Beijing approving the project have shrunk since Shanghai's Communist Party boss was implicated in a big corruption investigation in September [2005]." This led Disney to consider other options for the construction of a new park.[11]

Hong Kong Disneyland

Plans in Hong Kong, which culminated in the opening of Hong Kong Disneyland in September 2005, began after the 1997–1998 Asian financial crisis. Despite the poor economic condition of Hong Kong in the late 1990s, Disney was still optimistic about prospects for a theme park in the "city of life." Hong Kong, already an international tourist destination, would draw Disneyland patrons primarily from China, Taiwan, and Southeast Asia.

The official park plans were announced in November 1999 as a joint venture between the Walt Disney Company and the Hong Kong SAR Government. Unlike its experience in Tokyo, where Disney handed the reins over completely to a foreign company (the Oriental Land Company), Disney decided to take more direct control over this new park. The park was built on Lantau Island at Penny's Bay, within the 6-mile stretch separating the international airport and downtown. Hong Kong Disneyland was estimated to create 18,000 jobs upon opening and ultimately 36,000 jobs. The first phase of the park was to include a 10 million annual visitor Disneyland-based theme park, 2,100 hotel rooms, and a 300,000-square-foot retail, dining and entertainment complex.[12]

In order to make the park "culturally sensitive," Jay Rasulo, president of Walt Disney Parks & Resorts, announced that Hong Kong Disneyland would be trilingual with English, Cantonese, and Mandarin. The park would also include a fantasy garden for taking pictures with the Disney characters (popular among Asian tourists), as well as more covered and rainproof spaces to accommodate the "drizzly" climate.[13]

Unfortunately, Disney soon realized that its attempts at cultural sensitivity had not gone far enough. For instance, the decision to serve shark fin soup, a local favorite, greatly angered environmentalists. The park ultimately had to remove the dish from its menus. Park executives also failed to plan for the large influx of visitors around the Chinese New Year in early 2006, forcing them to turn away numerous patrons who had valid tickets. Unsurprisingly, this led to customer outrage and negative media coverage of the relatively new theme park.

Other criticisms of the park have included its small scale and slow pace of expansion. Hong Kong Disneyland has only 16 attractions and "one classic Disney thrill ride, Space Mountain, compared to 52 at Disneyland Resort Paris [formerly Euro Disneyland]."[14] However the government has made plans to increase the size of the park by acquiring land adjacent to the existing facilities. Likely due to its small size and fewer attractions, Hong Kong Disneyland pulled in only 5.2 million guests during its first 12 months, less than the estimated 5.6 million.[15] Failure to meet its projected levels of attendance and guest spending could cause the park to look toward other sources of funding for these expansions.

Battle over Hong Kong Park Expansion

Disney had plans to expand the size of the theme park in Hong Kong by about a third and it had been trying to obtain the local government's financial support for these plans since 2007. However, Disney's Park in Hong Kong had been performing well below the projected sales number in 2007–2008, and the government, which is 57 percent stockholder in this business, has expressed serious doubts in the need to fund the further expansion. As noted by *Financial Times* analysts, in one of the March 2009 reports, Hong Kong Disneyland has attracted about 15m visitors since its opening in September 2005, or about 4.3m a year. That figure fell short of the original projection of more than 5m a year.[16] Although Disney did not release financial figures to the public, Euromonitor estimated the park had an operating loss of $46 million in the year ended June 2006, and lost $162 million the following year.[17]

Disney's officials have been trying to stress the importance of park expansion for the overall viability of the project. So far, the park occupied 126 hectares and had only four "lands"—Fantasyland, Tomorrowland, Adventureland, and Main Street USA—and two hotels. Hong Kong Disneyland Managing Director Andrew Kam said expansion is vital to the park's success. In one of the September 2008 releases, Kam said the park had plenty of room to grow, since it was only using half of the land available. "Expansion is part of the strategy to make this park work for Hong Kong," he said.[18] An expansion could cost as much as 3 billion Hong Kong dollars, or $387 million, local media have reported. In December 2008, the Sing Tao Daily newspaper in Hong Kong reported that Disney, in what was deemed an unusual concession, might give the government a greater share in the project in repayment of a cash loan of nearly $800 million that the city had extended previously to the theme park.[19]

Unable to come to agreement with the Hong Kong government, Disney has indicated that it is putting on hold long-awaited plans to expand the park. In a statement from Disney's Burbank (Calif.) office released in March 2009, the company said it was laying off employees in Hong Kong after failing to reach an agreement with the Hong Kong government to fund a much-needed expansion. According to Disney, "The uncertainty of the outcome requires us to immediately suspend all creative and design work on the project." Thirty Hong Kong–based Disney "Imagineers," who helped to plan and design new parks, will be losing their jobs.[20] Business news sources had noted that one reason Disney might be willing to end negotiations with the Hong Kong government is the company's progress in negotiations with Shanghai officials to open a theme park there that would be much larger and arguably a more exciting China project. This park is expected to be easier for many Chinese families to visit. However, the possible shift of mainland Chinese away from Hong Kong to Shanghai could mean a drop of as much as 60 percent in visitor numbers to the Hong Kong park, according to Euromonitor's estimates.[21]

In June of 2009 Disney and Hong Kong's government finally reached a deal to expand the territories of the Disneyland theme park at a cost of about $465 million. Under terms of the deal, the entertainment giant will contribute all the necessary new capital for construction as well as sustaining the park's operation during the building phases. It will also convert into equity about $350 million in loans to the venture to help with funding and will keep open a credit facility of about $40 million. Hong Kong, which shouldered much of the $3.5 billion original construction cost, will not add any new capital. "Disney is making a substantial investment in this important project," Leslie Goodman, a Disney vice president, said in a statement.[22]

Disney Gets Green Light for Shanghai Park

In spite of the global economic downturn, Walt Disney Co. has revisited its plans to build a park in Shanghai, China. In January 2009 Disney presented to the Chinese central government a $3.59 billion proposal that outlined the plans for a jointly owned park, hotel, and shopping development. Shanghai Disneyland, if the project succeeds, would be one of the largest-ever foreign investments in China.[23] Though Disney had been unsuccessful in its negotiations with the Chinese government a few years earlier, and almost abandoned its plans of expansion to Shanghai, the global economic crisis played a role making the prospective creation of 50,000 new jobs amid a cooling Chinese economy especially attractive, and gave Disney the grounds to revisit its plans.[24]

The preliminary agreement signed in January represented a framework to be considered by China's State Council, the central government's highest administrative body. According to the proposal Disney would take a 43 percent equity stake in Shanghai Disneyland with 57 percent owned by the Shanghai government forming a joint-venture company.[25] The park's first phase would include building a theme park, a hotel, and shopping outlets on about 1.5 square kilometers (371 acres) site near

Shanghai's Pudong International Airport.[26] The preliminary agreement outlined a six-year construction period for the first phase with the projected opening of the park in 2014. Disney will likely pay $300 million to $600 million in capital expenses for the park in exchange for 5 percent of the ticket sales and 10 percent of the concessions.[27] Shanghai Disneyland will incorporate Chinese cultural features as well as attractions built around traditional Disney characters and themes. The ownership structure will contain some aspects of Disney's Hong Kong joint venture agreement. But the details of the Shanghai project will need to be further negotiated and the actual contract will have to be approved by the central government. According to *The Wall Street Journal,* a newly formed Shanghai company named Shendi will hold the local government's interest in the park. Shendi is owned by two business entities under district governments in Shanghai, as well as a third company owned by the municipal government's propaganda bureau.[28]

After almost a year of negotiation, in November 2009, Disney finally received an approval from the Chinese government to proceed with its Shanghai park plan.[29] The new park planned for the Pudong new district of China's financial capital will take years to contribute to a company that takes in more than $30 billion in annual revenue. But analysts see the move as an important step forward for Disney and other Western media firms to make inroads into the vast and untapped Chinese media and entertainment market.

"They've been laying the groundwork for a park for many years by exposing the population to Disney properties, film, TV and merchandising," said Christopher Marangi, senior analyst with Gabelli and Co in New York.[30]

There are certain public concerns that the new Shanghai park, which would be Disney's sixth, will inevitably affect the Hong Kong park. The main concern is that Hong Kong park's revenue may be cannibalized which will make the financial perspectives of this underperforming park even sadder looking. However, Disney thinks that both parks will complement each other rather than be competitors. Disney's main points are that Shanghai is close to a number of other major cities within easy driving distance, including Nanjing, Suzhou, and Hangzhou, and that Shanghai's own population of around 19 million, combined with tens of millions more within a three-hour driving radius, would provide a more-than-ample base of local users for the park. There are analysts, like Paul Tang, chief economist at Bank of East Asia, who share this optimism, projecting that "visitors from Guangdong and southern China will still find Hong Kong more convenient, while Shanghai will attract visitors from northern and eastern China."[31] Indeed, when Disney reported its 2012 results, it noted that the Hong Kong park turned a modest profit, its first since opening, with overall attendance up 13 percent to 6.7 million, and revenue up 18 percent.[32]

The critics of the Shanghai park on the other hand are convinced that this project is a bigger threat to the Hong Kong park than anybody can imagine. According to Parita Chitakasem, research manager at Euromonitor International in Singapore, who specializes in theme parks, "Disneyland Shanghai will have two big features which will make it more attractive than its Hong Kong counterpart: Although it is still early days, Disneyland in Shanghai will probably offer a much better experience for your money than Disneyland in Hong Kong—initial plans show that Shanghai's Disneyland will be six times bigger compared to the current size of Hong Kong Disneyland, which is very small (only 16 attractions). Also, for visitors from mainland China, it will be much easier to travel to Disneyland in Shanghai, as there are no visa/cross border concerns to take care of."[33]

While the public is debating the project, Disney is not wasting time and moves on with getting all other necessary approvals and documents that are needed for the park construction, which still may take long to obtain. In April 2010 the company received approval for the land. Authorities have also confirmed that 97 percent of residents have been already relocated, and the land would be transferred over to Disney in July. Over 2,000 households and 297 companies have to be relocated to make way for the first phase of construction. The head of Pudong New District where Shanghai Disney will be sited informed the public that the first phase of the project, including a theme park and supporting facilities, will span four square km with the theme park covering one square km. The project would take five to six years to finish.[34]

Other Asian Ventures

The Walt Disney Company has also looked into building other theme parks and resorts in Asia. Based on its successful operation of two theme parks in the United States (at Anaheim and Orlando), Disney believes that it can have more than one park per region. Another strategically located park in Asia, officials agreed, would not compete with Tokyo Disneyland or Hong Kong Disneyland, but rather bring in a new set of customers.

One such strategic location is the state of Johor in Malaysia. Malaysian officials wanted to develop Johor in order to rival its neighbor, Singapore, as a tourist attraction. (Two large casinos were built in Singapore in 2006.) However, Disney claimed to have no existing plans or discussions for building a park in Malaysia. Alannah Goss, a spokeswoman for Disney's Asian operations based in Hong Kong, said, "We are constantly evaluating strategic markets in the world to grow our park and resort business and the Disney brand. We continue to evaluate markets but at this time, we have no plans to announce regarding a park in Malaysia."[35]

Singapore, in its effort to expand its tourism industry, had also expressed interest in being host to the next Disneyland theme park. Although rumors of a Singapore Disneyland were quickly dismissed, some reports suggested there were exploratory discussions of locations at either Marina East or Seletar. Residents of Singapore expressed concern that the park would not be competitive, even against the smaller-scale Hong Kong Disneyland. Their primary fears included limited attractions (based on size and local regulations), hot weather, and high ticket prices.

Disney's Future in Asia

Although Disney is wise to enter the Asian market with its new theme parks, it still faces many obstacles. One is finding the right location. Lee Hoon, professor of tourism management at Yanyang University in Seoul, noted, "Often, more important than content is whether a venue is located in a metropolis, whether it's easily accessible by public transportation." Often tied to issues of location is the additional threat of competition, both from local attractions and those of other international corporations. It seems that Asian travelers are loyal to their local attractions, evidenced by the success of South Korea's Everland theme park and Hong Kong's own Ocean Park (which brought in more visitors than Hong Kong Disneyland in 2006).[36] The stiff competition of the theme park industry in Asia will center on not only which park can create a surge of interest in its first year but also which can build a loyal base of repeat customers.

Despite its already large size, the Asian theme park industry is still developing. Disney officials will need to be innovative and strategic in order to maintain sales. After Universal Studios in Japan witnessed a 20 percent drop in attendance between 2001 and 2006 and Hong Kong Disneyland failed to meet its estimated attendance level in 2006, Disney officials might want to think twice about building additional parks in Asia.[37]

In spite of underperformance of some theme parks, and a recent world economic crisis, Asia is still viewed by many as the most attractive region for the entertainment industry. Attendance may be stagnating in some parts of the world, but a growing middle class with disposable incomes to match is making the Asia-Pacific region a prime target for investors and theme park owners. "China will lead the way," said Kelven Tan, Southeast Asia's representative for the International Association of Amusement Parks and Attractions, an industry group. "The critical mass really came about with the resurgence of China. You need a good source of people; you also need labor and you need cheap land."[38]

That's what the people behind the just-completed Universal Studios in Singapore are betting. Developers aim to tap the wallets of Singapore's 4.6 million residents and 9.7 million tourists a year and its proximity to populous areas of Indonesia and southern Malaysia. After opening in spring of 2010, it will be the island nation's first bona fide amusement park. Outside this and other foreign brands like Legoland, which plan to open a park in Johor, Malaysia, for 2013, home-grown companies like Genting in Malaysia and OTC Enterprise Corp. in China are aggressively looking to take advantage of the burgeoning market in their backyards.[39]

Overall spending on entertainment and media in Asia Pacific is set to increase 4.5 percent each year, jumping to $413 billion in 2013 from $331 billion in 2008, according to PricewaterhouseCoopers, with places like South Korea, Australia, and China posting the biggest increases. "It's an up-and-coming market, and growing quite fast," said Christian Aaen, Hong Kong–based regional director for AECOM Economics, a consulting firm that specializes in the entertainment and leisure industries. MGM Studios and Paramount, too, are scouting around Asia for future projects. PricewaterhouseCoopers predicted the region's market will be worth nearly $8.5 billion by 2012, up from $6.4 billion in 2007.[40]

In light of these optimistic projections, it is reasonable to assume that Disney may consider expansion to other Asian countries such as Malaysia, South Korea, or Singapore, where Disney appeared to have seriously considered a park. Given that the Hong Kong park expansion and Shanghai park construction are on track, Disney now has the experience and motivation to further penetrate the Asian region. In this regard, Disney announced in mid-2010 a comprehensive plan to develop and operate English language schools throughout China.[41] Such a move could constitute a broader push by Disney to establish a strong Asian presence across its businesses and brands, a move that would undoubtedly involve the theme park operations as a central component.

Questions for Review

1. What cultural challenges are posed by Disney's expansion into Asia? How are these different from those in Europe?

2. How do cultural variables influence the location choice of theme parks around the world?

3. Why was Disney's Shanghai theme park so controversial? What are the risks and benefits of this project?

4. What location would you recommend for Disney's next theme park in Asia? Why?

Source: This case was prepared by Courtney Asher under the supervision of Professor Jonathan Doh of Villanova University as the basis for class discussion. Additional research assistance was provided by Benjamin Littell.

In-Depth Integrative Case 2.2

Walmart's Global Strategies

Introduction

In 1991, Walmart became an international company when it opened a Sam's Club near Mexico City. Just two years later, Walmart International was created. Since venturing into Mexico in 1991, Walmart International has grown somewhat erratically. During the 1990s the retailer exported its big-box, low-price model, an approach the company expected to be as successful in foreign markets as it was in the United States. Although Walmart has had success in several overseas markets, this success has been far from universal. For example, in Mexico, China, and the U.K., the company's efforts to offer the lowest price to customers backfired because of resistance from established retailers. And in Germany, Walmart could not seem to fit its model to local tastes and preferences. In Japan, its joint venture had a series of setbacks, many related to buying habits for which the Walmart model did not respond well. In Mexico, three of the largest domestic retailers constructed a joint buying and operational alliance solely to compete with Walmart.[1] Its presence in Hong Kong ended after only two years during the 1990s, and it shuttered operations in Indonesia in the mid-1990s after rioting incidents in Jakarta. Walmart also owned approximately 16 stores in South Korea and 85 in Germany; however, it sold off these operations in 2006 after merchandise failed to match consumer tastes, distribution and re-bagging problems arose, and strong loyalties to other brands made attracting customers difficult and expensive.[2]

In addition, labor advocates and environmentalists have created headaches for the U.S. behemoth, making continued expansion both cumbersome and expensive. For instance, in 2006, Walmart faced a strong public relations campaign from the All-China Federation of Trade Unions (ACFTU) over Walmart's refusal to let its workers in China unionize. Walmart was eventually forced to concede, perhaps because the Chinese government also lent its weight to the ACFTU's campaign in its effort to establish unions in all foreign-funded enterprises throughout the country. As of October 2006, almost 6,000 of Walmart China's 30,000 employees were union members.[3] Despite its public battle with the ACFTU, Fortune China and Watson Wyatt still voted Walmart China as one of the "Top 10 Best Companies to Work for" in 2005.[4] As Walmart continues to expand its global operations, analysts are curious to see how the company is received and whether consumers' opinions in fragmented market settings are a match with Walmart's low price model.

Notwithstanding these challenges, today, Walmart International is a fast-growing part of Walmart's overall

Exhibit 1 Walmart International Operations, April 2010[8]

Market	Retail Units (04/2010)	Date of Entry
Mexico	1,479	November 1991
Canada	317	November 1994
Brazil	438	May 1995
Argentina	44	August 1995
China	284	August 1996
United Kingdom	374	July 1999
Japan	371	March 2002
Costa Rica	170	September 2005
El Salvador	77	September 2005
Guatemala	164	September 2005
Honduras	53	September 2005
Nicaragua	55	September 2005
Chile	254	January 2009
India	1	May 2009

operations, with 6,155 stores and more than 800,000 associates in 26 countries outside the continental U.S.[5] (See Exhibit 1.) According to international chief C. Douglas McMillon, Walmart is "progressing from being a domestic company with an international division to being a global company." In two decades Walmart International had become a $100 billion business. Had it been a stand-alone company, it would have ranked among the top five global retailers.[6] (See Exhibit 2.) Walmart International's business represents a solid chunk of Walmart's overall $405 billion revenues for the fiscal year 2010.[7]

With a market capitalization of more than $200 billion in 2010, Walmart is worth as much as the gross domestic product of Nigeria. Four of America's 10 richest individuals are from Walmart's low-profile Walton family, which still owns a 40 percent controlling stake. The company's portfolio ranges from superstores in the U.S. to neighborhood markets in Brazil, bodegas in Mexico, the ASDA supermarket chain in Britain, and Japan's nationwide network of Seiyu shops. Walmart sources many of its products from low-cost Chinese suppliers. The pressure group China Labour Watch estimates that if it were a country, Walmart would rank as China's seventh largest trading partner, just ahead of the U.K., spending more than $18bn annually on Chinese goods.[9]

Walmart Early Internationalization

In venturing beyond its large domestic market, Walmart had a number of regional options, including entering

Exhibit 2 **The Largest Global Companies and Retailers, 2008**

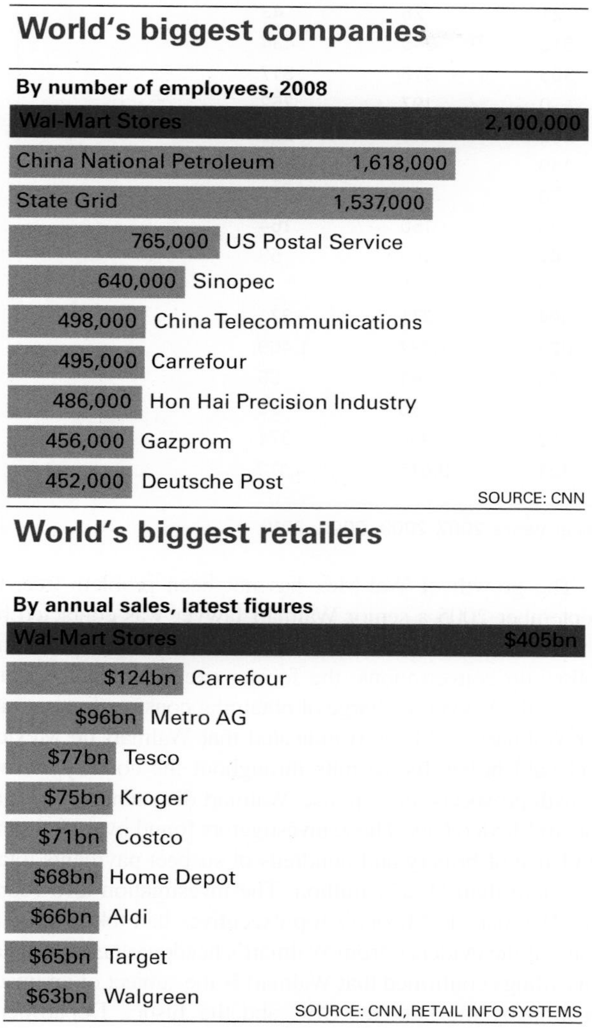

World's biggest companies

By number of employees, 2008

Company	Employees
Wal-Mart Stores	2,100,000
China National Petroleum	1,618,000
State Grid	1,537,000
US Postal Service	765,000
Sinopec	640,000
China Telecommunications	498,000
Carrefour	495,000
Hon Hai Precision Industry	486,000
Gazprom	456,000
Deutsche Post	452,000

SOURCE: CNN

World's biggest retailers

By annual sales, latest figures

Retailer	Sales
Wal-Mart Stores	$405bn
Carrefour	$124bn
Metro AG	$96bn
Tesco	$77bn
Kroger	$75bn
Costco	$71bn
Home Depot	$68bn
Aldi	$66bn
Target	$65bn
Walgreen	$63bn

SOURCE: CNN, RETAIL INFO SYSTEMS

Source: Guardian (http://www.guardian.co.uk/business/2010/jan/12/walmart-companies-to-shape-the-decade).

Europe, Asia, or other countries in the Western hemisphere. (See Exhibits 3 and 4.) At the time, however, Walmart lacked the requisite financial, organizational, and managerial resources to pursue multiple countries simultaneously. Instead, it opted for a logically sequenced approach to market entry that would allow it to apply the learning gained from its initial entries to subsequent ones. In the end, during the first five years of its globalization (1991 to 1995), Walmart decided to concentrate heavily on establishing a presence in the Americas: Mexico, Brazil, Argentina, and Canada. Obviously, Canada had the business environment closest to the U.S. and appeared the easiest entry destination. The other countries that Walmart chose as its first global points of entry—Mexico (1991), Brazil (1994), and Argentina (1995)—were those with the three largest populations in Latin America.[10]

The European market had certain characteristics that made it less attractive to Walmart as a first point of entry. The European retail industry was mature, implying that a new entrant would have to take market share away from an existing player—a very difficult task. Additionally, there were well-entrenched competitors on the scene (e.g., Carrefour in France and Metro A.G. in Germany) that would likely retaliate vigorously against any new player. Further, as with most newcomers, Walmart's relatively small size and lack of strong local customer relationships would be severe handicaps in the European arena. In addition, the higher growth rates of Latin American and Asian markets would have made a delayed entry into those markets extremely costly in terms of lost opportunities. In contrast, the opportunity costs of delaying acquisition-based entries into European markets appeared to be relatively small.[11]

While the Asian markets had huge potential when Walmart launched its globalization effort in 1991, they were the most distant geographically and different culturally and logistically from the United States market. It would have taken considerable financial and managerial resources to establish a presence in Asia.[12] However, by 1996, Walmart

Exhibit 3 **Walmart International Retail Unit Count (2001–2006)**

Country	2001	2002	2003	2004	2005	2006
Argentina	11	11	11	11	11	11
Brazil	20	22	22	25	149	295
Canada	174	196	213	235	262	278
China	11	19	26	34	43	56
Germany	94	95	94	92	91	88
Japan	0	0	0	0	0	398
Mexico	499	551	597	623	679	774
Puerto Rico	15	17	52	53	54	54
UK	241	250	258	267	282	315
South Korea	6	9	15	15	16	16
Total	1,071	1,170	1,288	1,355	1,587	2,285

Source: Walmart Annual Reports for fiscal years 2001, 2002, 2003, 2004, 2005, 2006.

Exhibit 4 **Walmart International Retail Unit Count (2006–2010)**

Country	2007	2008	2009	2010
Argentina	13	21	28	43
Brazil	299	313	345	434
Canada	289	305	318	317
Chile	0	0	197	252
China	73	202	243	279
Costa Rica	137	149	164	170
El Salvador	63	70	77	77
Guatemala	132	145	160	164
Honduras	41	47	50	53
India	0	0	0	1
Japan	392	394	371	371
Mexico	889	1,023	1,197	1,469
Nicaragua	40	46	51	55
Puerto Rico	54	54	56	56
UK	335	352	358	371
Total	2,757	3,121	3,615	4,112

Source: Walmart Annual Reports for fiscal years 2007, 2008, 2009, 2010.

felt ready to take on the Asian challenge and it targeted China. This choice made sense in that the lower purchasing power of the Chinese consumer offered huge potential to a low-price retailer like Walmart. Still, China's cultural, linguistic, and geographical distance from the United States presented relatively high entry barriers, so Walmart decided to use two beachheads as learning vehicles for establishing an Asian presence.[13]

During 1992–93, Walmart agreed to sell low-priced products to two Japanese retailers, Ito-Yokado and Yaohan, that would market these products in Japan, Singapore, Hong Kong, Malaysia, Thailand, Indonesia, and the Philippines. Then, in 1994, Walmart entered Hong Kong through a joint venture with the C.P. Pokphand Company, a Thailand-based conglomerate, to open three Value Club membership discount stores in Hong Kong.[14]

Success in Mexico and China

Overall, Walmart has had a very successful experience in Mexico. In 1991 Walmart entered into a joint venture with retail conglomerate Cifra and opened a Sam's Club in Mexico City. In 1997 it gained a majority position in the company and in 2001 changed the store name to Walmart de Mexico, or more commonly, "Wal-Mex." In addition to its 195 Walmart Supercenters and Sam's Club warehouses, Wal-Mex also operates Bodega food and general merchandise discount stores, Superama supermarkets, Suburbia apparel stores, and Vips and El Portón restaurants. The majority of its stores are located in and around Mexico City; however, it does business in over 145 cities throughout Mexico. Wal-Mex has shown no signs of slowing down. In 2005 Walmart opened 93 new stores and saw a 13.7 percent increase in net sales overall. As of February 2007, it operated 889 stores in Mexico and had plans to open another 125 that year.[15]

The growth of Wal-Mex has not been problem-free. In September 2005 a senior Walmart lawyer was contacted by a former executive at Walmart de Mexico. In the e-mail and follow-up conversations, the former executive (later identified as the lawyer in charge of obtaining construction permits for Walmart de Mexico) indicated that Walmart de Mexico had paid bribes for permits throughout the country to fuel growth prospects. In response, Walmart dispatched investigators to Mexico City. Those investigators found overwhelming evidence of bribery and hundreds of suspect payments totaling more than US$24 million. The investigation also found that Walmart de Mexico's top executives had taken steps to conceal the evidence from Walmart's headquarters.[16] Regulatory filings confirmed that Walmart is the subject of an investigation by the both the SEC and the Justice Department. Walmart warned shareholders that its reputation could be affected by the bribery scandal. In a statement Walmart said that inquiries from media and law enforcement could affect the "perception among certain audiences of its role as a corporate citizen."[17] In response to the investigation and bribery charges, Walmart has created a new executive position to ensure that all Walmart employees are complying with the U.S. Foreign Corrupt Practices Act.[18]

In late 2006 the company was also approved by Mexico's Finance Ministry to open its own bank. In a country where 75 percent of citizens have never had a bank account due to high fees, "Banco Walmart de Mexico Adelante" added much-needed competition to the financial services industry and it was hoped would begin to offer consumers lower fees than traditional banks.[19] In November 2007, Wal-Mex opened its first consumer bank, Banco Walmart, in Toluca; by August 2010, the company had opened nearly 250 branches. Banco Walmart is especially targeting the low-income market in a country where just 24 percent of households have savings accounts, compared with 55 percent in Chile. Wal-Mex plans to boost sales via debit cards, later ease users into more profitable services like insurance, and make money on interest-rate spreads. Wal-Mex's mission is to lure newcomers with easy instructions and entry points, like minimum balances of less than $5 and no commissions, compared with $100 minimums at competing banks. Wal-Mex is also eyeing the $23 billion remittances market—the amount sent home every year by Mexican immigrants in the U.S.[20]

Wal-Mex's plans for future growth involve more heavily targeting the 16–24-year-old age group, which constitutes 55 percent of Mexico's population. In April 2010, Mexico ranked as Walmart's number one international destination with 1,479 retail outlets, far ahead of its second major international destination Brazil, which had only 438 stores.[21] In 2011, Walmart de Mexico was a top performer globally with an operating margin of 7.9 percent, compared to 4.9 percent in total for all global operations during this same time.[22]

Though not as easy as its experience in Mexico, Walmart has also found decent success in China. Walmart entered the Chinese market in 1996 when it opened a Supercenter and Sam's Club in Shenzen. As of late 2006 the company had expanded to 73 stores in 36 cities. In order to cater to its Chinese shoppers, Walmart has introduced "retail-tainment" and attempted to create a more hands-on shopping experience.[23] China's Tourism Bureau even named one underground Walmart store a tourist destination.[24]

In addition to its own stores, Walmart has had a stake in the Taiwanese Bounteous Company Ltd., which owned the popular chain of Trust-Mart stores.[25] In late 2006, *The Wall Street Journal* publicized a $1 billion deal between Walmart and Bounteous, in which Walmart would acquire Trust-Mart's 100 stores over the course of three years. In light of Walmart's slowing U.S. sales and the termination of its operations in Germany and South Korea, the company's expansion in China is quite timely. Like its operations in Mexico, Walmart has also entered the Chinese financial service industry, by introducing a credit card with Bank of Communications Ltd. in late 2006.[26]

Walmart's expansion has not gone unnoticed. Domestic Chinese rivals have also built up their businesses in order to compete. In 2005 Shanghai Bailan Group purchased four rival supermarkets and department stores and now operates over 5,000 stores. China Resources Enterprise has hired away managers from foreign chains and cut staff in order to increase its profitability.[27] While these efforts signal greater competition for Walmart in particular, they are necessary for domestic companies to survive in China's $841 billion retail market,[28] which has been increasingly competitive ever since the country joined the WTO and dropped restrictions on foreign retailers.

Mixed Results in Europe and Japan

In 1998 Walmart entered the European market through Germany by acquiring 21 Wertkauf hypermarkets, one-stop shopping centers that offered a broad assortment of high quality general merchandise and food. Germany was seen as the largest single base for retailing in Europe. Wertkauf's annual sales were about $1.4 billion, and its stores operated similar to the popular Walmart Supercenter format in the U.S. Walmart's executives considered Wertkauf as an "excellent fit" for Walmart and hoped that it would provide the company with an ideal entry into a new market.[29]

However, Walmart's operations in Germany quickly turned into a costly struggle. There were a number of critical factors that the company underestimated when it entered the new market. First of all, the stores of the acquired German retail chain were geographically dispersed and often in poor locations. Also, Walmart had faced some serious cultural differences, which it tried to resolve by making one error after another. For example, the company initially installed American managers, who made some well-intentioned cultural gaffes, like offering to bag groceries for customers (Germans prefer to bag their own groceries) or instructing clerks to smile at customers (Germans, used to brusque service, were put off).[30]

Other problems, however, were largely outside Walmart's control. Two German discounters, Aldi and Lidl, dominated the grocery business, with smaller shops that featured cut-rate, though still good-quality, food. Aldi also heavily promoted one-week sales, featuring deeply discounted merchandise, ranging from wine to garden hoses, which draw customers back. While Walmart's vast size gave it enormous leverage in purchasing clothing and other goods, it had to buy much of the food for its German stores locally. And there, it lacked the muscle of Aldi, which had 4,100 shops and a presence in nearly every town in the country.[31]

"Germany is the home of the discounter," said Mark Josefson, a retail analyst at Kepler Securities in Frankfurt. "Walmart is not competing on price, and that is one of its main attributes in its home market." Beyond these competitive pressures there was another serious factor to consider, namely that the German consumer was one of the most parsimonious and price-conscious in Europe. Profit margins in German retailing were the lowest in Europe.[32]

Walmart had struggled in Germany for almost 8 years. Analysts said that Walmart Germany was losing about €200 million (£137 million) a year on a turnover of about €2 billion, despite several attempts to turn around the business. In 2006 it finally made the decision to withdraw from the German market, by selling its 85 German stores to the rival supermarket chain Metro and taking a pre-tax loss of about $1 billion (£536 million) on the failed venture.[33] The decision to sell out to the Metro Group came two months after Walmart sold its 16 stores in South Korea and it appeared a rare retreat by the world's largest retailer from its breakneck global expansion.[34]

In contrast, Walmart's second retail destination in Europe, the United Kingdom, has brought the company much needed success. Walmart entered the U.K. market in June 1999 by acquiring ASDA Group PLC, Britain's third-largest food retailer. Walmart offered £6.7 billion ($10.8 billion). The cash deal, which topped a rival bid from the British retail group Kingfisher PLC, was predicted to double Walmart's international business at a stroke and put it in a position to expand its retailing expertise throughout Europe.[35]

Walmart executives said they hoped to draw upon ASDA's management talent and experience. ASDA's 229 stores are a little less than half the size of Walmart's supercenters of more than 200,000 square feet (18,000 square meters) in the United States, but the lack of space in much of Europe for new out-of-town shopping developments could make ASDA's formula more relevant as a platform for expansion.[36]

However, while the chain has been only a moderate success, delivering consistent results, Walmart has been frustrated in its efforts to expand, though competing in Britain's feverishly competitive supermarket industry has taught Walmart a good deal. Nevertheless, ASDA is now something of a center for excellence for its global grocery sales. The head of global marketing for Walmart is based at ASDA's head office in Leeds. And, in an example of Walmart's global distribution muscle, *The Wall Street Journal* recently reported that the best-selling wine in the whole of Japan is an own-label ASDA Bordeaux.[37]

The third major strategic step in Walmart's early 2000s global expansion was entering the Japanese market. In 2002 Walmart set foot in Japan with the purchase of a 6 percent stake in the 371-store Seiyu chain. Despite continued losses, Walmart gradually raised its stake, making Seiyu a wholly owned subsidiary in June 2008. Walmart has had to confront numerous issues in Japan, from longtime Seiyu managers resisting its initiatives to a tendency among Japanese shoppers to equate low prices with inferior products. Also, bulk deals did not play well in a country where many lived in small urban apartments, and the country's grocery distribution system was populated with wholesalers who brokered deals between suppliers and retailers, skimming profits. Even rival Carrefour abandoned this market.[38]

Edward J. Kolodzieski was the man in charge of turning Seiyu around. As CEO of Walmart Japan, Kolodzieski has slashed expenses, closed 20 stores, and cut 29 percent of corporate staff. In-store butchers were removed, with most meat now processed in a central facility. With the freed-up floor space, Seiyu bulked up meals-to-go offerings. To bypass the middlemen, Seiyu has also boosted the number of products it imports directly from manufacturers by 25 percent in 2009, and was also focusing on increasing sales of its own private-label brands.[39]

The biggest change, however, was a shift away from weekly specials to "everyday low prices" in areas like baby care and pet products, and, eventually, throughout the store. Taking a page from Britain's ASDA, Seiyu instead used its marketing dollars to compare prices against competitors. With the pressure of prolonged recession Japanese consumers have finally accepted that they can buy quality merchandise for a lower price.[40] After spending 100 billion yen (roughly $1.2 billion), by 2010, Walmart's situation in Japan had stabilized, with two years of profits and reports that it was looking for further expansion through acquisition.[41]

After 2005: Refocusing on Latin America

2005 became another turning point in Walmart's strategy. Somewhat frustrated by strategic failure in Germany, and very slow expansion in the developed countries like Canada and the U.K., the company has turned its focus toward Latin America. Walmart has decided to leverage its positive experience in Mexico toward other South American countries. In 2005 Walmart successfully entered this market with the purchase of a 33-ss 1/3 percent interest in Central American Retail Holding Company (CARHCO) from the Dutch retailer Royal Ahold NV. CARHCO is Central America's largest retailer, with 363 supermarkets and other stores in the following five countries: Guatemala (120), El Salvador (57), Honduras (32), Nicaragua (30), and Costa Rica (124). CARHCO has approximately 23,000 associates. Its sales during 2004 were approximately $2.0 billion.[42]

Prior to that, in March 2004, Walmart bought a 118-store supermarket chain, Bompreco, in northeastern Brazil for $300 million, also from Royal Ahold of the Netherlands. This acquisition has significantly increased Walmart's competitive position in the country. In 2006 the company made another successful deal with Portugal-based Sonae by purchasing its 140 Brazilian stores for $757 million. The Sonae purchase was expected to boost Walmart's presence in Brazil's wealthier southern states. With the Sonae acquisition, Walmart store count increased to 295 units in 17 of Brazil's 26 states. However, this move made Walmart only the third-largest retailer in Brazil, following Carrefour of France and Companhia Brasileira de Distribuio Po de Acar.[43]

The last step in the sequence of its strategic moves in Latin America was Walmart's expansion into Chile. In 2009 Walmart acquired a majority stake of D&S (short for Distribución y Servicio) 224-store chain for $1.6 billion. In acquiring D&S, the nation's leading grocer and third-largest retailer, Walmart hopes to cement its dominance in Latin America, where it is by far the biggest retailer with $38 billion in sales, estimates research firm Planet Retail, double that of its closest rival, Carrefour. In Chile, Walmart enters a market that has long been inhospitable to foreign retailers. Home Depot, Carrefour, and JC Penney are among the companies that have tried, and failed, to make it in Chile, a nation of 17 million with the sixth-largest retail market in Latin America.[44]

Walmart has increased D&S's expansion budget from $150 million to $250 million, which would go toward opening nearly 70 stores in fiscal year 2010, many of them small stores that cater to lower-income shoppers, according to Vicente Trius, Walmart Latin America's president and CEO.

The appeal of D&S goes well beyond its stores. About 1.7 million Chileans carry a Presto card issued by its financial services unit, up from 1.2 million in 2004. "There is a saying here that large retailers generate sales with [stores] and earnings with their credit cards," says Rodrigo Rivera, a partner with the Boston Consulting Group in Santiago.[45]

Indeed, analysts estimate some South American retail chains generate upwards of 70 percent of their profits from financial services. (At D&S that figure is just 17 percent.) Walmart already offers financial services in Mexico and Brazil, though its attempts to launch a bank in the U.S. have failed. The retailer is keen to grow the Presto business by adding more low-risk services such as selling life insurance for outside vendors.[46]

Walmart's Plans for 2010–2011

In October 2009 Walmart Stores, Inc., presented its global plans for store and club growth in the next year at its annual conference for the investment community and updated its projections for capital expenditures through the fiscal year ending on January 31, 2011. According to this plan, total capital spending for the fiscal year ending January 31, 2010, is projected to be in a range of $12.5 to $13.1 billion, up from approximately $11.5 billion in fiscal year 2009. Total capital spending for the fiscal year ending January 31, 2011, is projected to be in a range of $13.0 to $15.0 billion.[47]

"Our plan for growth is clearly intended to increase shareholder value," said Tom Schoewe, executive vice president and chief financial officer. "In the U.S., we're building new stores and accelerating the pace of our remodels because they have been so successful at winning and retaining customers. We're stepping up growth in our International operations to take advantage of growing economies and opportunities in emerging markets, such as China and Brazil."[48] Capital expenditures for all purposes are projected as shown in Exhibit 5 and exclude the impact of any future acquisitions.

If fiscal year 2009 were placed on a constant currency basis with fiscal year 2010, international capital expenditures in fiscal year 2009 would have been approximately $3.8 billion. In the fiscal year ending January 31, 2010, the company expected to add approximately 38 million square feet globally, compared to approximately 44 million

Exhibit 5 **Walmart Actual and Projected Capital Expenditure 2009–2011 (US$ billions)**

Segment	Actual	Projected	
	FY09	FY10	FY11
Walmart U.S.	$5.8	$6.6–6.8	$7.0–8.0
Sam's Club U.S.	$0.8	$0.8–0.9	$0.7–1.0
Walmart International	$4.1	$4.2–4.4	$4.5–5.0
Corporate	$0.8	$0.9–1.0	$0.8–1.0
Total	$11.5	$12.5–13.1	$13.0–15.0

Source: walmartstores.com.

Exhibit 6 **Walmart Actual and Projected Square Footage Growth by Segment (in millions)**

Additional Square Footage for:	Actual	Projected	
	FY09	FY10	FY11
Walmart U.S.	23	14	11
Sam's Club U.S.	2	1	1
Walmart International	19	23	25
Total Company	44	38	37

Source: walmartstores.com.

square feet added in the prior year (excluding square footage added by acquisition). Walmart expects to increase global square footage by approximately 37 million square feet in fiscal year 2011.[49] Square footage growth (excluding any acquisitions) is projected as shown in Exhibit 6.

Walmart International plans aggressive investment, particularly in growth markets such as China and Brazil. The International portfolio includes a variety of formats, from supercenters to small grocery stores. New stores are expected to add approximately 23 million square feet in fiscal year 2010, and approximately 25 million more square feet in fiscal year 2011. These projections are based on the existing store base and do not include possible acquisitions.[50]

"We will continue our organic growth strategy, with strong capital discipline and optimization of our portfolio of formats and brands worldwide," said Doug McMillon, president and CEO of Walmart International in a company press release in October 2009. "We will allocate capital, by country and by format, to improve returns from these investments."[51]

Walmart, whose international business is its fastest growing segment and already makes up roughly one-quarter of its total business, is positioning itself for 20 years of worldwide growth according to the CEO.[52] Walmart is projected to spend up to US$750 million to build, renovate, or relocate roughly 73 stores in Canada in 2012.[53] If Walmart International (with over 9,000 stores under 60 different names in 15 foreign countries) was viewed as a stand-alone company, it would be the third largest retailer in the world as of 2010 with sales of US$109 billion and a growth rate of 12.1 percent. Seventy-five percent of Walmart's stores outside of the U.S. operate under a different name as Walmart has shifted towards smaller formats and smaller acquisitive growth for global strategy. In comparison, Walmart's domestic unit did not experience any significant growth and virtually remained flat for 2010.[54]

China

In March 2010, the official website of China's Ministry of Commerce reported that Walmart had set up a new wholly owned subsidiary in Hebei. This move is reportedly designed to help Walmart's smooth expansion and localization of Walmart in China. An insider from Walmart revealed to the local media that the company will continue to speed up its expansion in China in 2010 and in the future the Chinese market is expected to have the most Walmart stores worldwide, exceeding even its domestic American market.[55]

Since 2009, Walmart has set up more than 10 wholly owned subsidiaries in Chinese cities and provinces, including Hunan, Chongqing, Hubei, and Dongguan. Before setting up these regional subsidiaries, Walmart cooperated with Chinese companies, including Shenzhen International Trust & Investment, for expansion in China. However, the complicated operating processes slowed down the retailer's expansion. With the help of these new subsidiaries, Walmart opened nearly 40 new outlets in 2009 and the total number of Walmart stores in China exceeded that of its competitor Carrefour for the first time.[56]

Brazil

In this most open of the large emerging economies, the world's two biggest supermarket chains and a homegrown competitor are battling for dominance. Leading the field is Companhia Brasileira de Distribuicão Grupo Pão de Açúcar, with revenues of $13 billion in 2009. Close behind is France's Carrefour, with sales last year of $12.6 billion. In third place, but making a big push, is the world's No. 1 retailer, Walmart Stores, which operates under several names in Brazil. It racked up $9.5 billion in sales in Brazil in 2009.[57]

All three plan to invest big in Brazil in coming years. As its middle class expands, annual spending on food is expected to rise 50 percent over the next five years, to $406 billion, says Carlos Hernandez, a Madrid-based analyst at consultant Planet Retail. Among the emerging nations known as the BRICs, Brazil offers fewer barriers to business than Russia, India, and China. India bans foreign stores that sell multiple brands, and Russia limits expansion by retailers. China is attractive because of its rapid economic growth, expected to be 8 percent in 2010, versus 5.8 percent in Brazil. However, "Brazil is more developed in terms of infrastructure and wealth creation," says Justin Scarborough, a retail analyst at Royal Bank of Scotland in London. "Consumers are used to shopping in hypermarkets, whereas retail in China is more traditional."[58]

Already No. 1 in Mexico, Walmart aims to overtake Carrefour to become No. 2 or No. 1 in Latin America's largest market. The Bentonville (Arkansas) retailer plans to spend $1.2 billion this year to open 110 new stores in Brazil, on top of the 436 it now operates. It may also scout out an acquisition, says Héctor Núñez, president of Walmart Brazil. "We have a very, very clear plan to win here in Brazil," he says. "We are investing heavily to start having a much more solid and persuasive presence."[59]

Walmart is opening the cash spigot at a time when Carrefour is contending with the recession in Europe, which accounts for 80 percent of its revenues. Annual sales growth for the Paris-based chain at home has averaged less than 1 percent over the last 10 years. To defend its No. 2 position in Brazil, Carrefour is planning to spend $1.4 billion over the next two years. The goal: to add 70 stores and double

Brazil's share of Carrefour's overall sales to 20 percent by 2015. Pão de Açúcar, which is 34 percent owned by French supermarket chain Casino, says it will invest $2.8 billion to add 300 stores to its 1,080-store chain by 2012.[60]

India and Russia

The other two attractive growing markets from the BRIC group that also draw Walmart's attention are India and Russia. India and Russia are widely regarded as two of the world's fastest-growing retail markets—and two of the most frustrating for foreign retailers. Walmart boasts one wholesale outlet so far in India, and it has only a 30-person development administrative office in Moscow to show after more than five years of scouting in Russia. But through a combination of joint ventures, acquisitions, and expansion, the retailer is hoping to become a major player in both countries.[61]

India's $350 billion retail sector is composed of small family-run ventures, with organized chains accounting for less than 5 percent of sales. To get around government restrictions on foreign retailers selling to consumers, Walmart recently teamed up with Bharti Enterprises to open a cash-and-carry operation in the northern city of Amritsar. Best Price Modern Wholesale, as it's called, technically caters to merchants and small businesses. But with few restrictions, more than 30,000 members have signed up for the first store.[62]

As in the U.S., the emphasis is on a wide selection of goods in one location at a low cost—everything from Castrol motor oil and sneakers to milk in large canisters that can be tied to the side of bicycles. Best Price employs 25 people to go around the region each week and check prices at mom-and-pop shops, to ensure that they're consistently offering the best value. Raj Jain, a former Whirlpool executive who now heads Walmart's Indian operations, also opened a training institute in Amritsar last December in partnership with Bharti and the Punjab government.[63]

Walmart plans to open 10 to 15 outlets through the partnership over the next three years, eventually employing about 5,000 people. But McMillon wants to see Walmart running its own retail stores there, too. He pressed his case with commerce and agriculture ministers in New Delhi in July. "What I tried to convey is that we would invest more, and faster, if we had the opportunity to do so," he says. A representative from the Indian government declined to comment.[64] As of 2013, Walmart only had 20 wholesale stores in India.[65]

In April of 2010 Scott Price, president and CEO of Walmart Asia, reinforced the major points of Walmart's Asian strategy: "We will capture 10 to 15 markets in Asia in ten years. At present, expansion plans for India alone is the full time job for us." He also noted that India has a lot of potential as it has availability of a highly educated workforce. "The retail giant would also like to increase sourcing from India for their stores all over the world," he said.[66]

In Russia, the impediments to retail development are less visible but no less worrisome. Corruption is rampant with various administrative authorities capable of gumming up operations if payments are not made. Anticorruption group Transparency International ranked Russia 147th out of 180 countries on its most recent corruption perception index. While Walmart is looking at opening its own stores in Russia, it's far more likely it will start by acquiring a local retailer. Analysts say the prime candidate is Lenta, a fast-growing, privately held chain of 34 hypermarkets and the nation's fifth-largest retailer. Lenta founder Oleg Zherebtsov is saddled with debts and sold his 35 percent stake to the investment group of private equity firm TPG and the private equity arm of Russian state bank VTB in early September 2010.[67]

According to another source Walmart made a preliminary offer to the Kopeika store chain in June 2009.[68] Walmart is not the first retailer Kopeika has dealt with. X5 Retail Group tried to negotiate a deal at the end of 2008 and it was in discussions with Magnit in January 2009. Kopeika operates a network of around 500 supermarkets in Moscow and the Moscow region, where it competes with around 400 X5 Retail Group Pyaterochka stores and Dixy Group's outlets. Walmart is actively seeking a partner in Russia. It was in negotiations with St. Petersburg–based hypermarket operator Lenta in 2008, but no deal was reached.[69] With rivals such as Metro expanding their presence through new stores, and Carrefour opening its second outlet in September, "they cannot wait," says Planet Retail analyst Milos Ryba.[70]

Canada

Established in 1994 and headquartered in Mississauga, Ontario, Walmart Canada currently operates 317 stores and serves more than 1 million customers each day across Canada. Walmart is Canada's third-largest employer with more than 85,000 associates, and was recently named one of Canada's top 10 corporate cultures by Waterstone Human Capital.[71]

In February 2010 Walmart Canada announced that the company will open 35 to 40 supercentres in 2010. According to Walmart, the projects will include new stores, relocations of existing stores, store expansions, and store remodels, representing a combined investment of almost half a billion dollars in Canadian communities. The supercentres are expected to generate approximately 6,500 store and construction jobs, with specific store locations to be announced over the coming weeks and months. "The combination of one-stop shopping and low prices that our supercentres provide has been embraced by our customers," said David Cheesewright, president and CEO of Walmart Canada. "We look forward to bringing this popular format to a new range of shoppers."[72]

In addition to store expansions, Walmart Canada is investing in its first sustainable refrigerated distribution center, which is anticipated to open in Balzac, Alberta, in the fall of this year. The company is investing $115 million in its construction. The center will create 1,400 jobs, including trade and construction jobs.[73]

Expected to be one of the most energy-efficient distribution facilities of its kind in North America, the cutting-edge distribution center will be an estimated 60 percent more energy-efficient than Walmart's traditional refrigerated distribution centers. The center will include a pilot of fuel cell technology and many other sustainable features. Walmart Canada is committed to reducing costs while implementing energy-saving strategies across its operations. The company's new stores are now 30 percent more energy-efficient than previous prototypes.[74]

Despite its growth in Canada, Walmart is not without competition. Target opened 150 locations in Canada in 2011 alone.[75]

South Africa

In October of 2010, it was announced that Walmart was conducting due diligence on Massmart, a leading retailer in South Africa which operates 288 large stores located in 14 African countries, most of them in South Africa where it has a strong presence catering to a range of customers. Initially, reports suggested that Walmart would offer 32 billion rand ($4.63 billion) to own Massmart outright.[76] Subsequently, it was reported that Walmart would bid only for a majority controlling share (more than 50 percent but less than 100 percent) in order to preserve Massmart's listing on the Johannesburg stock exchange.[77] If either deal goes through, it would place Walmart ahead of its European competitors Tesco PLC and Carrefour SA, which don't have any stores in Africa.

Walmart's Global.com Challenge to Amazon.com

In January 2010 Vice Chairman Eduardo Castro-Wright announced that Walmart is creating a new unit that will be responsible for driving online growth around the world, both in developed markets where the company has stores and an online presence and in markets it doesn't. This new organization will be called Global.com.[78]

Wan Ling Martello, formerly the Ccief financial officer of Walmart International, will be the executive vice president and chief operating officer of Global.com. In her new role, Wan Ling's primary responsibilities will include (1) development and execution of a global strategy for e-commerce; (2) establishing cross-functional and cross-border Walmart relationships designed to accelerate and broaden growth in the global online channel; and (3) the creation of technology platforms and applications that can be used effectively in every Walmart market.[79]

In early 2008, the retailer said it would invest "millions of dollars" in its global e-commerce initiative, which it labeled "a multi-billion dollar opportunity over the next three to five years." Walmart, with stores in 15 countries, currently operates separate e-commerce sites in the U.S., U.K., Mexico, and Brazil. It has been working on developing a single global e-commerce platform that would be replicable in all of its markets, similar to the model developed by its rival Amazon.[80]

In the U.S., where the retailer competes directly with Amazon, Walmart has named Steve Nave, currently chief operating officer, as general manager of its website, taking over from Raul Vazquez, who has taken a new position as head of the retailer's new Walmart West division.

But Mr. Nave will now report directly to John Fleming, the chief merchandising officer who himself previously served as CEO of Walmart.com. Mr. Castro-Wright said Walmart hopes to "integrate merchandising and operations capabilities of the dot-com organization with those of our traditional retail business." Walmart's online marketing will now be overseen directly by Stephen Quinn, its chief marketing officer.

The changes reflect Walmart's strategy of tying its website closely to its stores, which some argue could give it a long-term strategic advantage over Amazon. Currently around 40 percent of its U.S. business is delivered to stores for pickup under its "site to store" service, which it sees as also augmenting the development of smaller format stores in the future.[81]

Continued Challenges with Corporate Responsibility

Like other retailers, Walmart continues to face challenges from its exposure to the realities of production and sales in emerging and developing regions. On the sales side, as noted above, Walmart has been embroiled in corruption scandals in Mexico and India. On the production side, a fire at a Bangalore textile factory in late 2012, and two horrific accidents at garment factories in Bangladesh in 2013, have placed renewed pressure on U.S. and European clothing brands to take greater responsibility for the working conditions of the factories from which they source products. What happened in Bangladesh has underscored the difficulties and vulnerabilities of outsourcing production to sometimes unreliable and unethical suppliers.

In early 2013, more than 1,000 workers were killed when an eight-story garment factory in Dhaka caught firewhile thousands worked inside. Not two weeks later, a fire killed eight workers in another site in Bangladesh. After initially denying it had production at these locations, Walmart eventurlly confirmed that it had ordered garments from a supplier who utilized the plant.[82] Then on June 11 another fire erupted at a Dickies garment factory on the outskirts of Dhaka, causing employees to run from the building, raising further questions about safety in Bangladeshi factories.[83]

As a result Walmart and the Gap Inc. subsequently announced their signing of the Bangladesh Worker Safety Initiative to ensure factory safety in Bangladesh. This agreement, backed by a $50 million commitment, will be overseen by the Bipartisan Policy Center, a nonprofit group based in Washington. As part of this effort, various U.S. retail trade groups who had been concerned about the legal liability associated with the competing, European-dominated agreement will join with Walmart and the Gap.[84] On June 25, the Obama Administration announced it was suspending trade privileges with Bangladesh, removing the country from the list of countries with most favored trade status. The move came after pressure from unions and continuing concerns about the Bangladeshi government's ability to maintain safe working conditions in its factories.[85] Walmart and other retailers continue to struggle with how to manage extended global supply chains with multiple layers of suppliers.

Questions for Review

1. What was Walmart's early global expansion strategy? Why did it choose to first enter Mexico and Canada rather than expand into Europe and Asia?

2. What cultural problems did Walmart face in some of the international markets it entered? Which early strategies succeeded and which failed? Why? What lessons did Walmart learn from its experience in Germany and in Japan?

3. How would you characterize Walmart's Latin America strategy? What countries were targeted as part of this strategy? What potential does this region brings to Walmart's future global expansion? What cultural challenges and opportunities have Walmart faced in Latin America?

4. What group of countries will be targeted for Walmart's future growth? What are the attractiveness and risk profiles of these countries? What regions of the world do you think will be vital for Walmart's future global expansion?

5. How would you characterize Walmart's response to pressure for greater ethics and social responsibilities in its expansion strategy and supply chain? Are its responses appropriate and adequate?

Exercise

You are part of Walmart's global strategic planning group and have been asked to explore the benefits and challenges of expansion into the following regions. Divide your group into six teams, each representing a country or region of the world other than North America.

Team	Country/Region
1	Latin America
2	Western Europe
3	Central/Eastern Europe
4	Japan
5	China
6	Russia

Describe the opportunities and challenges of expansion in your assigned country or region. Be sure to summarize the cultural environment, how it differs from the U.S., and what challenges that might pose for the company.

Source: This case was prepared by Tetyana Azarova of Villanova University under the supervision of Professor Jonathan Doh as the basis for class discussion. Additional research assistance was provided by Benjamin Littell.

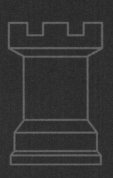

PART THREE

INTERNATIONAL
STRATEGIC
MANAGEMENT

STRATEGY FORMULATION AND IMPLEMENTATION

The World of *International Management*

Big Pharma Goes Global

The pharmaceutical industry is getting a facelift. Its fastest growing market is no longer in the developed world—it's in emerging markets. Its main revenue stream is no longer "blockbuster" drugs—patents are expiring (see the accompanying chart). Even the physical makeup of the pharmaceutical industry has changed as major pharmaceutical companies have acquired other firms from related industries, including generics and biotech companies. These changes mean that pharmaceutical executives must craft a new global strategy to adapt to industry trends.

Pharmerging Markets

The Policy and Medicine website IMS Health "reported that the size of the global market for pharmaceuticals is expected to grow nearly $300 billion over the next five years, reaching $1.1 trillion in 2014."[1] A majority of this growth, however, will come from emerging markets—what IMS calls "pharmerging markets."[2] Murray Aitken, IMS's senior vice president, Healthcare Insight, states: "Patient demand for pharmaceuticals will remain robust. . . . In developed markets with publicly funded health care plans, pressure by payers to curb drug spending growth will only intensify, but that will be more than offset by the ongoing, rapid expansion of demand in the pharmerging markets."[3] IMS estimates that pharmerging markets will grow at 14–17 percent through 2014, whereas developed markets will grow at 3–6 percent.[4]

The profit margins in the pharmerging market, however, may be limited. Individuals with lower incomes may not be able to afford expensive medicines and many people do not have access to health insurance. Still, as the standard of living rises in emerging economies, pharmaceutical companies see potential in these markets, particularly in India.

Destination India

During 2008–2010, there was significant alliance, merger, and acquisition activity in the global pharma industry. This included partnerships and alliances among traditional pharmaceutical companies, generic firms, and biotechnology firms.

In India alone, according to the *New York Times,* "GlaxoSmithKline formed a partnership with Dr. Reddy's Laboratories; Pfizer tied up with Claris Lifesciences; Sanofi-Aventis took control of Shantha Biotechnics, and Bristol-Myers Squibb opened a research center in India with Biocon."[5] All of these were overshadowed by Abbott Laboratories' $3.7 billion deal to acquire Piramal's Healthcare Solutions business, one of India's top branded generics companies.[6]

The Burrill Report quoted Miles D. White, chairman and CEO of Abbott, who said: "Emerging markets represent one of the greatest opportunities in health care not only in pharmaceuticals but across all of our business segments. Today, emerging markets represent more than 20 percent of Abbott's total business."[7] As one of the fastest growing pharmaceutical markets in the world, India "will generate nearly $8 billion in pharmaceutical annual sales this year, a number that is expected to more than double by 2015."[8]

Not only is there an Indian market for pharmaceutical products, but India herself is now manufacturing drugs on a large scale and even doing research and development. G.V. Prasad, chief executive of Dr. Reddy's Laboratories, told the *New York Times* that Indian drug makers have the "ability to handle product development on a massive scale at a low cost."[9] Dr. Reddy's diabetes drug has completed Phase 3 clinical trials, the last step before seeking FDA approval.[10]

Yet, the pharmaceutical industry in India is not without its problems. Pfizer and Sanofi-Aventis both had to recall drugs made by their respective acquired firms in India. Also, the protection of intellectual property rights is an issue. According to the *New York Times:* "Trying to change its outlaw image as a maker of illegal knock-offs, India toughened its patent laws in 2005. But dozens of intellectual property suits are still being fought between Indian and foreign firms in courts around the world. And big pharmaceutical companies still find securing protection of their intellectual property in India difficult."[11]

"Cost is one issue, and yes it is important, but there are two other critical factors: intellectual property and quality and safety issues," said Panos Kalaritis, the chief operating officer of Irix Pharmaceuticals, a Florence, S.C.,

contract research and manufacturing company, which competes with Indian laboratories and factories.[12]

A former executive at GlaxoSmithKline noted that there are large short-term cost-saving gains by outsourcing to India. He asserted, however, that these gains may fall over time. Indian workers' wages may rise substantially and shipping materials to India may become more expensive as the price of oil increases.[13] A good manager assesses all risks from a long-term perspective; therefore, pharmaceutical executives need to take all these factors into consideration.

Patent Expiration

In addition to market growth shifting to emerging economies, the global pharmaceutical industry is facing another huge paradigm shift: patents are expiring. IMS reported that "Patent expires in the U.S. will peak in 2011 and 2012 when six of today's ten largest products are expected to face generic competition."[14]

When companies lose their patent protection, they lose the ability to charge premiums for their products. These premiums are used to fund investments in research and development. At the same time, governments are putting pressure on pharmaceutical companies to cut prices. As a result of these price pressures, many pharmaceutical companies have chosen to reduce research and development and let go thousands of scientists, especially in the U.S. and the U.K.

Most pharmaceutical companies' strategies have focused on developing and marketing blockbuster drugs targeted at major diseases. During the 1990s, firms profited from their blockbuster drugs, but now they are struggling. As their patents expire, generic competition will decrease their revenues by an estimated $140 billion over the next five years, according to *Bloomberg Business-Week.* Also, their drug pipelines are not promising. *Bloomberg BusinessWeek* reported that only eight new or first-in-class drugs reached the market in 2008, half as many as in 2001.[15]

New Strategies for New Times

Nevertheless, pharmaceutical companies have adopted different strategies which the companies hope will enable them to thrive in spite of the current challenges.

Some companies, such as Pfizer, are looking to enter what is viewed as the cutting edge of biologically derived compounds (versus those that are derived from generally "small" chemical compounds). These companies are moving into the territory in search of heftier margins and better protection from generics. Pfizer, which bought Wyeth in part to acquire biotech experience, is seeking to use biologics to improve aspects of drugs such as Rituxan, a treatment for blood cancers and rheumatoid arthritis, and Enbrel, an arthritis medicine.[16] Roche Holding's purchase of the entirety of biopharmaceutical company Genentech (it has held a majority stake since 1990) may have been driven by a desire to further integrate management and product development and achieve substantial cost savings. And Genzyme, one of the largest biopharma firms, has most recently entertained overtures from French drug maker Sanofi-Aventis, while GlaxoSmithKline, Johnson & Johnson, and Pfizer have also expressed interest.[17,18,19]

Others are reemphasizing their vaccines businesses, which had been viewed as relatively low margin products with little scope for dramatic innovation that could command premium prices. At the same time, these firms are under pressure to provide greater access and cheaper prices for those vaccines, challenging their ability to depend upon these revenues.[20] (See the In-Depth Integrative Case 1.2 at the end of Part One.)

Some traditional "branded" companies are linking up with generics in order to lower costs and reach broader markets. In addition to the deals in India mentioned above, the most recent wave of integration between traditional pharma companies and generics includes Novartis's acquisitions of German generics firm Hexal and U.S.-based Eon Labs in 2005, and its more recent purchase of the injectable generic drugs business of Austria's Ebewe Pharma. Pfizer has expanded its licensing agreement with Indian generics maker Aurobindo and has licensed 15 injectable products from Indian generics

firm Claris Lifesciences. Sanofi-Aventis has purchased a number of South American generics companies and GSK bought a 16 percent share of its South African generics partner, Aspen Pharmacare.[21] And Daiichi Sankyo Co, a Japanese pharma firm, bought a controlling stake in Ranbaxy, India's largest drug maker by revenue, in 2008.[22] This mixing of premium and low cost products was unheard of just a decade ago.

Others are diversifying into a wider range of health care products to generate more predictable income and avoid the gyrations associated with "winner take all" blockbuster drugs. For example, Merck's mergers with Schering-Plough may have been motivated, in part, by a desire to balance the volatility of Merck's drug portfolio with Schering-Plough's extensive human and animal health care product line.[23]

One company is taking a more focused approach. In 2002, Novartis CEO Daniel L. Vasella declared that "Novartis would investigate only diseases for which new drugs were desperately needed and where the genetics of the target illnesses were well understood," according to *Bloomberg BusinessWeek*.[24] Vasella reasoned that by concentrating on smaller, well-defined groups of patients, Novartis can develop effective drugs with fewer side effects that regulators will be more likely to approve.[25]

Vasella's strategy has paid off. *Bloomberg BusinessWeek* indicated that "Today, Novartis has 93 drug candidates in the pipeline, 40 percent more than three years ago, and 80 percent of Novartis' drugs [in 2008] made it from early testing to late-stage development."[26] William W. George, professor of management practice at Harvard Business School and the former CEO of Medtronic, told *Bloomberg BusinessWeek* that Vasella "has the mind of a long-term strategist."[27]

The pharmaceutical industry certainly needs managers who are long-term strategists in order to navigate through the waves of change that it is facing today.

Top 10 Drug Patents That Expired In 2013

Company	Drug Patents Expiring	Revenue in 2012 from Drug (in billions)
Eli Lilly	Cymbalta	$4.9
Biogen Idec	Avonex	$2.9
Eli Lilly	Humalog	$2.5
Purdue Pharma	OxyContin	$2.4
Merck KGaA	Rebif	$2.3
Eisai, J&J	Aciphex	$1.9
Roche	Xeloda	$1.6
J&J	Procrit	$1.4
Novartis	Zometa	$1.3
Amgen, Kirin, Roche	Neupogen	$1.3

Source: "Top 15 drug patent losses for 2013," *FiercePharma,* November 1, 2012, http://www.fiercepharma.com/special-reports/top-15-patent-expirations-2013.

Strategic management—the formulation and implementation of a strategy—is a critical function in today's global business environment. The large pharmaceutical companies are increasingly drawn to the international markets because of their growth prospects and potential. At the same time, changes in health care markets in the U.S. and Europe, including the expiration of patents and calls for greater cost containment, are exerting pressures on traditional companies to seek alternative income streams but also to reshape their basic business models. The traditional approach to R&D and drug development, which emphasized massive investments in a few potential "blockbusters," may be giving way to alternative strategies, including greater emphasis on what used to be considered "low margin" vaccines, which companies increasingly find provide a dependable income stream, and to Novartis's approach which focuses on diseases for which new drugs are desperately needed and where the genetics are well understood.[28]

This chapter will examine how multinational corporations use strategic management in their global operations. When formulated and implemented wisely, strategic management sets the course for a company's future. It should answer two simple questions, "Where are we going?" and "How are we going to get there?" Some strategies are consistent across markets, while others must be adapted to regional situations, but in either case, a firm's global strategy should support decision making in all major operations. In the case of large pharma companies, those questions are still being asked as the industry undergoes a dramatic transformation, much of it associated with globalization and its implications for strategy.

As you read this chapter, think of yourself as a manager in a large pharmaceutical company firm. How might you go about developing a strategic plan to capture greater market share and expand the types of products you are selling? There are some basic steps involved in creating a strategy, but first, let us take a look at what strategic management is and why it is so important.

■ Strategic Management

Strategic management is the process of determining an organization's basic mission and long-term objectives and then implementing a plan of action for pursuing this mission and attaining these objectives. For most companies, regardless of how decentralized, the top management team is responsible for setting the strategy. Middle management has sometimes been viewed as primarily responsible for the strategic implementation process, but now companies are realizing how imperative all levels of management are to the entire process. For example, Volvo discovered that while managers do inform team members of new strategic plans, the most informed, enthusiastic, and effective managers were those who were involved in the entire process.[29]

strategic management
The process of determining an organization's basic mission and long-term objectives, then implementing a plan of action for attaining these goals.

As companies go international, strategic processes take on added dimensions. A good example is provided by Citibank (a unit of Citicorp), which opened offices in China in 1902 and continued to do business there until 1949, when communists took power. However, in 1984 Citibank quietly returned, and over the last two decades the firm has been slowly increasing its presence in China.[30] Some ways Citibank has done this include opening new branches, expanding the employee base, and increasing stakes in local companies such as Shanghai Pudon Development Bank Co.[31] The Chinese banking environment is closely regulated by the government, and Citibank's activities are currently restricted to making local currency loans to foreign multinationals and their joint-venture partners. As a result, the bank does only about 20 percent as much business here as it does in South Korea. However, China's admission into the World Trade Organization (WTO) is changing all of this. Under WTO provisions, local corporations, such as the personal computer maker Legend, electronic goods manufacturer Konda, consumer appliance maker Haier, and telecom service provider China Telecom, will all be able to turn to foreign banks for local currency loans. This will give Citibank a major opportunity to expand operations. Additionally, under WTO rules the bank is allowed to offer consumer financial services such as credit cards and home mortgages. Though the Chinese government originally resisted, Citibank was officially given the authorization to offer its own independent credit cards in 2012.[32] Citibank believes that there is a large pent-up demand for credit cards, especially among businesspeople and yuppies who now carry thick wads of currency to pay their bills and make purchases. Another opportunity Citibank sees is in the area of business-to-business (B2B) commerce. As more Chinese firms conduct commerce over the Internet, there will be an increase in Net-related financial services. Citibank has now hooked up with U.S.-based B2B site Commerce One to run its Net-based payment systems, and the bank believes that it can provide this same service for Chinese exporters. Notwithstanding the dramatic losses at Citibank as part of the global financial crisis, and the move to downsize the firm and spin off some units, Citibank remains committed to expansion in Asia. Over 700 branches are currently operating in 14 different Asian markets.[33] In fact, Citibank plans to double its number of retail branches in China by 2015.[34] "We're investing more in Asia now than at any time in our history," said Stephen Bird, co-chief executive officer of Citi Asia Pacific.[35]

While this chapter focuses on the larger picture of strategic planning, it is important to remember that all stages of organizational change incorporate levels of strategy from planning to implementation. This includes innovative ways to improve a product to expanding to international operations.

The Growing Need for Strategic Management

One of the primary reasons that MNCs such as Citibank need strategic management is to keep track of their increasingly diversified operations in a continuously changing international environment. This need is particularly obvious when one considers the amount of foreign direct investment (FDI) that has occurred in recent years. Statistics reveal that FDI has grown three times faster than trade and four times faster than world gross domestic product (GDP).[36] These developments are resulting in a need to coordinate and integrate diverse operations with a unified and agreed-on focus. There are many examples of firms that are doing just this.

One is Ford Motor, which has reentered the market in Thailand and has built a strong sales force to garner market share. The firm's strategic plan here is based on offering the right combination of price and financing to a carefully identified market segment. In particular, Ford is working to keep down the monthly payments so that customers can afford a new vehicle. Despite political unrest in 2009 and 2010, Ford restated its commitment to build a $450 million automotive assembly plant, its first wholly owned one in Thailand.[37] The plant officially opened in May, 2012.[38] Ford and its Japanese partner Mazda Motor Corp. invested about $1.5 billion in pickup truck and passenger-car factories in Thailand. Toyota, Honda Motor Co., and General Motors Co. have also built plants in Thailand, Southeast Asia's second-biggest economy, lured by tax incentives and demand amid a domestic population of 70 million. Automakers produced over 2.4 million vehicles in Thailand in 2012, surpassing Canada to become the ninth-largest automobile manufacturer globally.[39]

General Electric provides another example that reflects the challenge managers face in shedding unprofitable businesses in order to generate capital for expansion into higher growth product and/or geographic markets. Several years ago General Electric Co. shed its plastics business, selling it to a Saudi Arabian company for $11.6 billion, and it has also signaled it wanted to exit its iconic "white goods" (home appliances) business.[40] In its place, GE is aggressively expanding its infrastructure, health care, and environmental technologies businesses, which it sees as providing better growth opportunities in emerging markets. More recently, Genzyme, the large biotech company, indicated in 2010 that it was pursuing "strategic alternatives" for its genetic-testing, diagnostics, and pharmaceutical intermediates businesses, with potential options including a sale, spin-out, or management buyout because these businesses did not fit with its longer-term strategy.[41] Many thought this strategy could, in part, be in preparation for an eventual sale to a larger pharmaceutical company, as a number of global firms have expressed interest in acquiring the firm.[42] Sure enough, in 2011, Genzyme was acquired by Sanofi, a French MNC, for US$20.1 billion.[43]

Benefits of Strategic Planning

Now that the needs for strategic planning have been explored in our discussion, what are some of the benefits? Many MNCs are convinced that strategic planning is critical to their success, and these efforts are being conducted both at the home office and in the subsidiaries. For example, one study found that 70 percent of the 56 U.S. MNC subsidiaries in Asia and Latin America had comprehensive 5- to 10-year plans.[44] Others found that U.S., European, and Japanese subsidiaries in Brazil were heavily planning-driven[45] and that Australian manufacturing companies use planning systems that are very similar to those of U.S. manufacturing firms.[46]

Do these strategic planning efforts really pay off? To date, the evidence is mixed. Certainly, strategic planning helps an MNC to coordinate and monitor its far-flung operations and deal with political risk (see Chapter 10), competition, and currency instability.

Despite some obvious benefits, there is no definitive evidence that strategic planning in the international arena always results in higher profitability, especially when MNCs try to use home strategies across different cultures (see Chapter 6). Most studies that report favorable results were conducted at least a decade ago. Moreover, many of these findings are tempered with contingency-based recommendations. For example, one study found that when decisions were made mainly at the home office and close coordination between the subsidiary and home office was required, return on investment was negatively affected.[47] Simply put, the home office ends up interfering with the subsidiary, and profitability suffers.

Another study found that planning intensity (the degree to which a firm carries out strategic planning) is an important variable in determining performance.[48] Drawing on results from 22 German MNCs representing 71 percent of Germany's multinational enterprises, the study found that companies with only a few foreign affiliates performed best with medium planning intensity. Those firms with high planning intensity tended to exaggerate the emphasis, and profitability suffered. Companies that earned a high percentage of their total sales in overseas markets, however, did best with a high-intensity planning process and poorly with a low-intensity process. Therefore, although strategic planning usually seems to pay off, as with most other aspects of international management, the specifics of the situation will dictate the success of the process.

Approaches to Formulating and Implementing Strategy

Four common approaches to formulating and implementing strategy are (1) focusing on the economic imperative; (2) addressing the political imperative; (3) emphasizing the quality imperative; and (4) implementing an administrative coordination strategy.

Economic Imperative MNCs that focus on the **economic imperative** employ a worldwide strategy based on cost leadership, differentiation, and segmentation. Middle managers are the key to stimulating profit growth within a company, so expanding those efforts on an international level is a necessary tool to learn for today's new managers.[49] Many of these companies typically sell products for which a large portion of value is added in the upstream activities of the industry's value chain. By the time the product is ready to be sold, much of its value has already been created through research and development, manufacturing, and distribution. Some of the industries in this group include automobiles, chemicals, heavy electrical systems, motorcycles, and steel. Because the product is basically homogeneous and requires no alteration to fit the needs of the specific country, management uses a worldwide strategy that is consistent on a country-to-country basis.

The strategy is also used when the product is regarded as a generic good and therefore does not have to be sold based on name brand or support service. A good example is the European PC market. Initially, this market was dominated by such well-known companies as IBM, Apple, and Compaq. However, more recently, clone manufacturers have begun to gain market share. This is because the most influential reasons for buying a PC have changed. A few years ago, the main reasons were brand name, service, and support. Today, price has emerged as a major input into the purchasing decision. Customers now

economic imperative
A worldwide strategy based on cost leadership, differentiation, and segmentation.

are much more computer literate, and they realize that many PCs offer identical quality performance. Therefore, it does not pay to purchase a high-priced name brand when a lower-priced clone will do the same things. As a result, the economic imperative dominates the strategic plans of computer manufacturers. This process has repeated in many industries as those products become commoditized.

Another economic imperative concept that has gained prominence in recent years is global sourcing, which is proving very useful in formulating and implementing strategy.[50] A good example is provided by the way in which manufacturers are reaching into the supply chain and shortening the buying circle. Li & Fung, Hong Kong's largest export trading company, is one of the world's leading innovators in the development of supply chain management, and the company has managed to use its expertise to whittle costs to the bone. Instead of buying fabric and yarn from one company and letting that firm work on keeping its costs as low as possible, Li & Fung gets actively involved in managing the entire process. How does it keep costs down for orders it receives from The Limited? The chairman of the company explained the firm's economic imperative strategy this way:

> We come in and look at the whole supply chain. We know The Limited is going to order 100,000 garments, but we don't know the style or the colors yet. The buyer will tell us that five weeks before delivery. The trust between us and our supply network means that we can reserve undyed yarn from the yarn supplier. I can lock up capacity at the mills for the weaving and dying with the promise that they'll get an order of a specified size; five weeks before delivery, we will let them know what colors we want. Then I say the same thing to the factories, "I don't know the product specs yet, but I have organized the colors and the fabric and the trim for you, and they'll be delivered to you on this date and you'll have three weeks to produce so many garments."
>
> I've certainly made life harder for myself now. It would be easier to let the factories worry about securing their own fabric and trim. But then the order would take three months, not five weeks. So to shrink the delivery cycle, I go upstream to organize production. And the shorter production time lets the retailer hold off before having to commit to a fashion trend. It's all about flexibility, response time, small production runs, small minimum-order quantities, and the ability to shift direction as the trends move.[51]

political imperative
Strategic formulation and implementation utilizing strategies that are country-responsive and designed to protect local market niches.

Political Imperative MNCs using the **political imperative** approach to strategic planning are country-responsive; their approach is designed to protect local market niches. The nearby International Management in Action, "Point/Counterpoint," demonstrates this political imperative. The products sold by MNCs often have a large portion of their value added in the downstream activities of the value chain. Industries such as insurance and consumer packaged goods are examples—the success of the product or service generally depends heavily on marketing, sales, and service. Typically, these industries use a country-centered or multi-domestic strategy.

A good example of a country-centered strategy is provided by Thums Up, a local drink that Coca-Cola bought from an Indian bottler in 1993. This drink was created back in the 1970s, shortly after Coca-Cola pulled up stakes and left India. In the ensuing two decades the drink, which is similar in taste to Coke, made major inroads in the Indian market. But when Coca-Cola returned and bought the company, it decided to put Thums Up on the back burner and began pushing its own soft drink. However, local buyers were not interested. They continued to buy Thums Up, and Coca-Cola finally relented. Today Thums Up is the firm's biggest seller in India, holding an overall 15 percent market share in the carbonated beverage market.[52] The company spends more money on this soft drink than it does on any of its other product offerings, including Coke.[53] As one observer noted, "In India the 'Real Thing' for Coca-Cola is its Thums Up brand." Recently, Coke has encountered challenges in India, as described in the Brief Integrative Case at the end of Part Two, but the acknowledgment that Thums Up was the best vehicle for expansion appears to have been validated: By 2009, the company's sales volume grew more than 30 percent and it turned a profit for the first time since it returned to the country in 1993 after a 16-year hiatus, partly via a strategy of seeking to penetrate rural consumers, something Thums Up is uniquely qualified to advance.[54] Additionally, traditional Coke sales have improved, and it is now the fastest growing soft drink in the country.[55]

Point/Counterpoint: Boeing vs. Airbus

A good example of the political imperative in action is the Boeing-Airbus dispute. The two largest aircraft manufacturers in the world have been engaged in a longstanding dispute over the degree to which government subsidies distort trade and contribute to unfair trade between the U.S. and EU. Specifically, Boeing has alleged that as a result of longstanding government support, Airbus, and its parent, European Aeronautic Defense and Space Company, or EADS, have gained unfair advantage for civilian and military contracts in the U.S. and around the world. The World Trade Organization ruled in June of 2010 that Airbus had received billions of dollars in European government subsidies for its aircraft and the practice must end. The case dates back to 2004, when the U.S. Trade Representative filed a complaint with the WTO alleging Airbus had received $200 billion worth of launch aid from the governments of France, Germany, the United Kingdom, and Spain. The U.S. alleged the aid allowed Airbus to win more than half the commercial airplane market from Boeing which for years had been the leading manufacturer of passenger jets in the world.

Airbus maintains that the aid it has received from various European governments is much less than Boeing and the U.S. government allege and has all been consistent with international trade rules. It also argues that Boeing has been a large recipient of U.S. federal and state government subsidization: $16 billion in R&D subsidies, almost $6 billion in local and state government subsidies, more than $2 billion in export-related tax subsidies, and even $2 billion in foreign subsidies in exchange for moving operations and jobs overseas. And the EU has brought its own case before the W.T.O., claiming that Boeing has benefited from more than $20 billion in subsidies since the 1980s from its military business and tax breaks.

This dispute has played out in the context of a number of large commercial and defense contracts. In June 2010, Boeing and EADS submitted proposals to supply the Air Force's next-generation aerial-refueling tanker. The service plans to buy 179 modified commercial transports in the first phase of a multi-decade program that eventually will replace all 509 tankers in the aerial-refueling fleet. Nine out of ten tankers in the current fleet are KC-135 jets similar to the old Boeing 707 airliner that were built during the Eisenhower and Kennedy administrations. The tanker program has been tangled in controversy since 2002, when the Pentagon planned to lease a fleet of new tankers from Boeing, a plan that was later revoked. In 2008, the Defense Department awarded a contract to Northrop Grumman and EADS to build the fleet using the Airbus A330 jetliner. Boeing successfully protested that award and the Pentagon restarted the process again in 2009. Boeing officials have said they fear the subsidies could allow EADS to undercut their price in the tanker competition even though the A300-200 is larger than Boeing's plane. Some of Boeing's backers in Congress have called on the Pentagon to add the estimated value of the subsidies to the EADS bid price. Other members of Congress in whose districts EADS now employs thousands of workers objected, saying no such premium is warranted.

Will the U.S. government prevail in its efforts to help Boeing? Will Airbus be able to make further gains in the U.S. market? What role will political intervention play? These questions are yet to be answered. In the meantime, the two firms continue to compete.

Quality Imperative A **quality imperative** takes two interdependent paths: (1) a change in attitudes and a raising of expectation for service quality and (2) the implementation of management practices that are designed to make quality improvement an ongoing process.[56] Commonly called total quality management, or simply TQM, the approach takes a wide number of forms, including cross-training personnel to do the jobs of all members in their work group, process re-engineering designed to help identify and eliminate redundant tasks and wasteful effort, and reward systems designed to reinforce quality performance.

TQM covers the full gamut, from strategy formulation to implementation. TQM can be summarized as follows:

> **quality imperative**
> Strategic formulation and implementation utilizing strategies of total quality management to meet or exceed customers' expectations and continuously improve products or services.

1. Quality is operationalized by meeting or exceeding customer expectations. Customers include not only the buyer or external user of the product or service but also the support personnel both inside and outside the organization who are associated with the good or service.

2. The quality strategy is formulated at the top management level and is diffused throughout the organization. From top executives to hourly employees, everyone operates under a TQM strategy of delivering quality products or services to internal and external customers. Middle managers will better understand and implement these strategies if they are a part of the process.

3. TQM techniques range from traditional inspection and statistical quality control to cutting-edge human resource management techniques, such as self-managing teams and empowerment.[57]

Many MNCs make quality a major part of their overall strategy, because they have learned that this is the way to increase market share and profitability. Take the game console industry, for example. Nintendo lived in the shadow of Sony's PlayStation success as it fought for market share with the GameCube. Years later, Nintendo proved to have superior game console quality when it introduced the Wii. Now, the tables have turned, and it is Sony which is scrambling after its less than successful launch of the PlayStation 3. In fact, Nintendo is now challenging Sony's market leadership, with Microsoft also entering the market with a competitive product.

The auto industry is also a good point of reference. While the U.S. automakers have dramatically increased their overall quality in recent years to close the gap with Japanese auto quality, Japanese firms continue to have fewer safety recalls. Up until 2010, Toyota and Honda continued to be ranked very high by American consumers, and Nissan and Subaru's recent performance were also strong. In light of the Toyota recalls in 2010 and continued improvements by U.S.-based producers, for the first time in years, North American-based manufacturers topped many Japanese brands in J.D. Power and Associates' 2010 Automotive Performance, Execution and Layout Study. Ford had more standout vehicles than any other manufacturer, with five of the 20 models leading their segments. GM also came out well with its four core brands, Chevrolet, Buick, GMC, and Cadillac, all exceeding the industry average. Overall, the domestic brands scored higher than the import brands for the first time since 1997.[58]

Apple Inc. has experienced rave quality reviews from customers and electronics analysts for its line of Mac products, iPod, iPhone, and iPad. These devices have demonstrated global appeal as Apple's stock soared. Apple introduced the iPhone 5 concurrently in the U.S., U.K., France, Germany, Canada, Hong Kong, Singapore, and Japan and made it available in over 100 countries within four months of its launch, a more aggressive worldwide launch timetable than in the past.[59] In response to several quality-related issues that arose with the iPhone 4 and 4s, Apple improved the size, weight, and battery life on its iPhone5 model.[60]

A growing number of MNCs are finding that they must continually revise their strategies and make renewed commitment to the quality imperative because they are being bested by emerging market forces. Motorola, for example, found that its failure to anticipate the industry's switch to digital cell technology was a costly one.[61] In 1998 the company dominated the U.S. handset market, and its StarTAC was popular worldwide. Five years later the firm's share of the then $160 billion global market for handsets had shrunk from 22 percent to 10 percent and was continuing to fall, while Nokia, Ericsson, and Samsung in particular, with smaller, lighter, and more versatile offerings, were now the dominant players.[62] Motorola's wireless network business also suffered, and in 2011, Motorola partitioned its wireless company from its primary operations. Later that year, Google acquired the new Motorola Mobility wireless division for US$12.5 billion.[63] The quality imperative is never-ending, and MNCs such as Motorola must meet this strategic challenge or pay the price.

administrative coordination
Strategic formulation and implementation in which the MNC makes strategic decisions based on the merits of the individual situation rather than using a predetermined economically or politically driven strategy.

Administrative Coordination   An **administrative coordination** approach to formulation and implementation is one in which the MNC makes strategic decisions based on the merits of the individual situation rather than using a predetermined economic or political strategy. A good example is provided by Walmart, which has expanded rapidly into Latin America in recent years. While many of the ideas that worked well in the North American market served as the basis for operations in the Southern Hemisphere, the company soon realized that it was doing business in a market where local tastes were different and competition was strong.

Walmart is counting on its international operations to grow 25–30 percent annually, and Latin American operations are critical to this objective. Despite this objective, the company has faced losses in several of its Latin American businesses as it strives to adapt to the local markets. The firm is learning, for example, that the timely delivery of merchandise in places such as São Paulo, where there are continual traffic snarls and the company uses contract truckers for delivery, is often far from ideal. Another challenge is finding suppliers who can produce products to Walmart's specification for easy-to-handle packaging and quality control. A third challenge is learning to adapt to the culture. For example, in Brazil, Walmart brought in stock-handling equipment that did not work with standardized local pallets. It also installed a computerized bookkeeping system that failed to take into account Brazil's wildly complicated tax system. The In-Depth Integrative Case at the end of Part Two provides more detail on Walmart's successes and challenges in the international marketplace, including those related to administrative coordination.

Many large MNCs work to combine the economic, political, quality, and administrative approaches to strategic planning. For example, IBM relies on the economic imperative when it has strong market power (especially in less developed countries), the political and quality imperatives when the market requires a calculated response (European countries), and an administrative coordination strategy when rapid, flexible decision making is needed to close the sale. Of the four, however, the first three approaches are much more common because of the firm's desire to coordinate its strategy both regionally and globally.

Global and Regional Strategies

A fundamental tension in international strategic management is the question of when to pursue global or regional (or local) strategies. This is commonly referred to as the globalization vs. national responsiveness conflict. As used here, **global integration** is the production and distribution of products and services of a homogeneous type and quality on a worldwide basis.[64] To a growing extent, the customers of MNCs have homogenized tastes, and this has helped to spread international consumerism. For example, throughout North America, the EU, and Japan, there has been a growing acceptance of standardized, yet increasingly personally, customized goods such as automobiles and computers. This goal of efficient economic performance through a globalization and mass customization strategy, however, has left MNCs open to the charge that they are overlooking the need to address national responsiveness through Internet and intranet technology.

National responsiveness is the need to understand the different consumer tastes in segmented regional markets and respond to different national standards and regulations imposed by autonomous governments and agencies.[65] For example, in designing and building cars, international manufacturers now carefully tailor their offerings in the American market. Toyota's "full-size" T100 pickup proved much too small to attract U.S. buyers. So the firm went back to the drawing board and created a full-size Tundra pickup that is powered by a V-8 engine and has a cabin designed to "accommodate a passenger wearing a 10-gallon cowboy hat." Honda has developed its new Model X SUV with more Americanized features, including enough interior room so that travelers can eat and sleep in the vehicle. Mitsubishi has abandoned its idea of making a global vehicle and has brought out its new Montero Sport SUV in the U.S. market with the features it learned that Americans want: more horsepower, more interior room, more comfort. Meanwhile, Nissan is doing what many foreign carmakers would have thought to be unthinkable just a few years ago. Today, U.S. engineers and product designers are now completely responsible for the development of most Nissan vehicles sold in North America. Among other things, they are asking children between the ages of 8 and 15, in focus-group sessions, for ideas on storage, cup holders, and other refinements that would make a full-size minivan more attractive to them.[66]

National responsiveness also relates to the need to adapt tools and techniques for managing the local workforce. Sometimes what works well in one country does not work in another, as seen in the following example:

> An American computer company introduced pay-for-performance in both the USA and the Middle East. It worked well in the USA and increased sales briefly in the Middle East before a serious slump occurred. Inquiries showed that indeed the winners among salesmen in the Middle East had done better, but the vast majority had done worse. The wish for their

global integration
The production and distribution of products and services of a homogeneous type and quality on a worldwide basis.

national responsiveness
The need to understand the different consumer tastes in segmented regional markets and respond to different national standards and regulations imposed by autonomous governments and agencies.

fellows to succeed had been seriously eroded by the contest. Overall morale and sales were down. Ill-will was contagious. When the bosses discovered that certain salespeople were earning more than they did, high individual performances also ceased. But the principal reason for eventually abandoning the system was the discovery that customers were being loaded up with products they could not sell. As A tried to beat B to the bonus, the care of customers began to slip, with serious, if delayed, results.[67]

Global Integration vs. National Responsiveness Matrix   The issue of global integration versus national responsiveness can be further analyzed conceptually via a two-dimensional matrix. Figure 8–1 provides an example.

The vertical axis in the figure measures the need for global integration. Movement up the axis results in a greater degree of economic integration. Global integration generates economies of scale (takes advantage of large size) and also capitalizes on further lowering unit costs (through experience curve benefits) as a firm moves into worldwide markets selling its products or services. These economies are captured through centralizing specific activities in the value-added chain. They also occur by reaping the benefits of increased coordination and control of geographically dispersed activities.

The horizontal axis measures the need for multinationals to respond to national responsiveness or differentiation. This suggests that MNCs must address local tastes and government regulations. The result may be a geographic dispersion of activities or a decentralization of coordination and control for individual MNCs.

Figure 8–1 depicts four basic situations in relation to the degrees of global integration versus national responsiveness. Quadrants 1 and 4 are the simplest cases. In quadrant 1, the need for integration is high and awareness of differentiation is low. In terms of economies of scale, this situation leads to **global strategies** based on price competition. A good example of this is Matsushita, which has standardized many aspects of its operations and marketing over the years, including its name. To gain global recognition, Matsushita changed the name of all its products to then have the Panasonic brand. Even before that, Matsushita, along with the Toshiba Corporation, the Victor Company of Japan, and others worked to standardize the digital videocassette recording (VCR) industry. Matsushita's

global strategy
Integrated strategy based primarily on price competition.

Figure 8–1

Global Integration vs. National Responsiveness

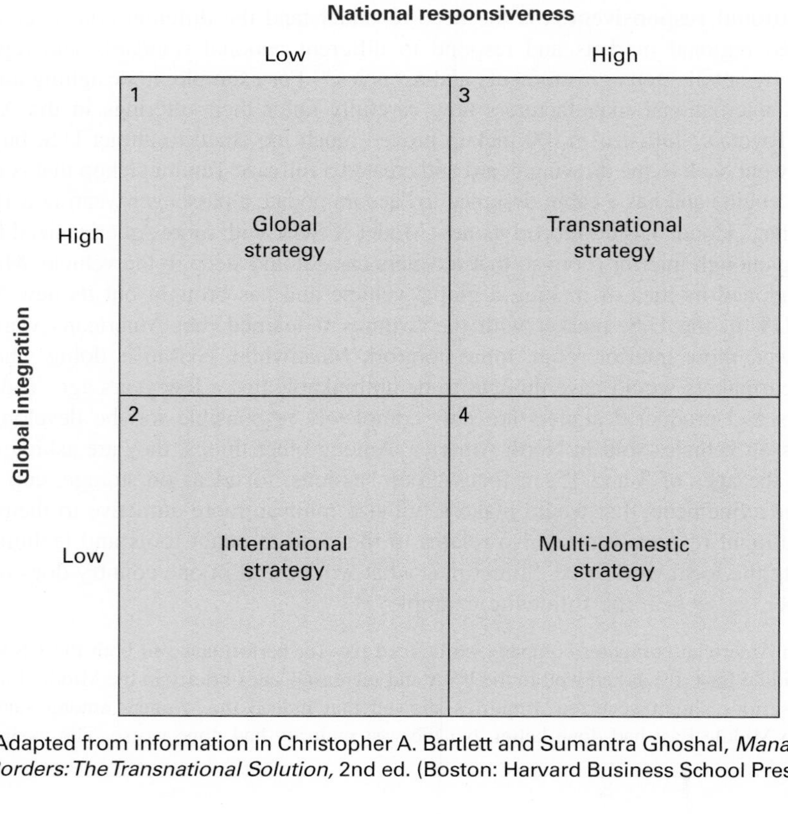

Source: Adapted from information in Christopher A. Bartlett and Sumantra Ghoshal, *Managing Across Borders: The Transnational Solution,* 2nd ed. (Boston: Harvard Business School Press, 1998).

strong global distribution network, companywide mission statements, financial control, and ability to get to the market quickly allowed the company to offer the VCR at an economy of scale and, in turn, gained a sizable portion of the market.[68] In this quadrant-1 type of environment, mergers and acquisitions often occur.

The opposite situation is represented by quadrant 4, where the need for differentiation is high but the concern for integration low. This quadrant is referred to as **multi-domestic strategy**. In this case, niche companies adapt products to satisfy the high demands of differentiation and ignore economies of scale because integration is not very important. An example of this is Philips, which provides medical equipment to doctors worldwide. As diagnoses become more complex, Philips has to find new innovative ways to simplify the machines used by doctors so that they can spend more time with patients. Yet the medical systems of each country are so different that products must be adapted and adjusted to the particular medical environment. Philips recently sought out opinions from board members, and even asked for participation of fashion designers, to better understand different strategic methods. By using this multidimensional information pool, Philips is moving toward offering even more differentiated products.[69]

multi-domestic strategy
Differentiated strategy emphasizing local adaptation.

Quadrants 2 and 3 reflect more complex environmental situations. Quadrant 2 incorporates those cases in which both the need for integration and awareness of differentiation are low. Both the potential to obtain economies of scale and the benefits of being sensitive to differentiation are of little value. Typical strategies in quadrant 2 are characterized by increased international standardization of products and services. This mixed approach is often referred to as **international strategy**.

international strategy
Mixed strategy combining low demand for integration and responsiveness.

This situation can lead to lower needs for centralized quality control and centralized strategic decision making while eliminating requirements to adapt activities to individual countries. This strategy is decreasingly employed as most industries and products face one or both pressures for global integration and local responsiveness. Nonetheless, companies may experience a very temporary phase in this quadrant, but the standards lie in the other three.

In quadrant 3, the needs for integration and differentiation are high. There is a strong need for integration in production along with higher requirements for regional differentiation in marketing. MNCs trying to simultaneously achieve these objectives often refer to them as **transnational strategy**. Quadrant 3 is the most challenging quadrant and the one where successful MNCs seek to operate. The problem for many MNCs, however, is the cultural challenges associated with "localizing" a global focus. One good example of a transnational company is Monsanto. Monsanto offers a very diverse line of hybrid seeds to the agricultural industry. Hybrid seeds are genetically modified seeds which are sterile and must be purchased at the beginning of each season for the specified crop. Monsanto's operations, discussed in Chapter 2, include finding new ways to differentiate its product to best fit the surrounding market. The company offers products which can withstand the various environments and climates of its global customers, from herbicide and insect resistant strains to drought tolerance.[70]

transnational strategy
Integrated strategy emphasizing both global integration and local responsiveness.

Summary and Implications of the Four Basic Strategies MNCs can be characterized as using one of four basic international strategies: an international strategy, a multi-domestic strategy, a global strategy, and a transnational strategy. The appropriateness of each strategy depends on pressures for cost reduction and local responsiveness in each country served. Firms that pursue an international strategy have valuable core competencies that host-country competitors do not possess and face minimal pressures for local responsiveness and cost reductions. International firms such as McDonald's, Walmart, and Microsoft have been successful using an international strategy. Organizations pursuing a multi-domestic strategy should do so when there is high pressure for local responsiveness and low pressures for cost reductions. Changing offerings on a localized level increases a firm's overall cost structure but increases the likelihood that its products and services will be responsive to local needs and therefore be successful.[71]

A global strategy is a low-cost strategy. Firms that experience high cost pressures should use a global strategy in an attempt to benefit from scale economies in production, distribution, and marketing. By offering a standardized product worldwide, firms can leverage their experience and use aggressive pricing schemes. This strategy makes most sense where there are high cost pressures and low demand for localized product offerings. A transnational strategy should be pursued when there are high cost pressures and high demands for local responsiveness. However, a transnational strategy is very difficult to pursue effectively. Pressures for cost reduction and local responsiveness put contradictory demands on a company because localized product offerings increase cost. Organizations that can find appropriate synergies in global corporate functions are the ones that can leverage a transnational strategy effectively.[72]

Recent analyses of the strategies of MNCs confirm these basic approaches. The globalization–national responsiveness model, which was initially developed from nine in-depth case studies, has been corroborated in large-scale empirical settings. Moreover, it appears as if there are positive performance effects from tailoring the strategy to particular industry and country characteristics.[73]

■ The Basic Steps in Formulating Strategy

The needs, benefits, approaches, and predispositions of strategic planning serve as a point of departure for the basic steps in formulating strategy. In international management, strategic planning can be broken into the following steps: (1) scanning the external environment for opportunities and threats; (2) conducting an internal resource analysis of company strengths and weaknesses; and (3) formulating goals in light of the external scanning and internal analysis. These steps are graphically summarized in Figure 8–2. The following sections discuss each step in detail.

Environmental Scanning

environmental scanning
The process of providing management with accurate forecasts of trends related to external changes in geographic areas where the firm currently is doing business or is considering setting up operations.

Environmental scanning attempts to provide management with accurate forecasts of trends that relate to external changes in geographic areas where the firm is currently doing business or considering setting up operations. These changes relate to environmental factors that can affect the company and include the industry or market, technology, regulatory, economic, social, and political aspects. Figure 8–3 shows how this dynamic is set up.

MNCs observe and evaluate an exorbitant amount of information, and while data are usually collected for all forms of environmental factors, the order in which they approach each factor and the extent to which they are studied depend on the industry and the goals of the MNC.[74] One of the most important foci is the industry or the market. This includes the role of all potential competitors and the relationships surrounding those competitors, such as affiliation with one another or the connection between the company and its customers and suppliers. Monitoring changes in technology will also help keep the company modern and innovative. Some technologic options managers may wish to follow are those that influence business efficiencies or changes in production. From a competitor standpoint, it is good to familiarize oneself with the rise of new products or services and the existing infrastructure.

The regulatory environment can also change at any time, shifting laws or regulatory guidelines. Managers should be aware of ownership or property rights within an area and also what kind of employment practices are exhibited in a region. Minimum wage laws and tax rates should also be considered, since they can affect the hiring process and company finances.

Figure 8–2

Basic Elements of Strategic Planning for International Management

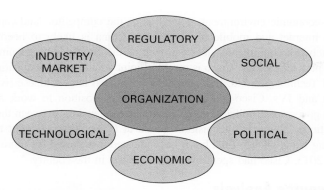

Source: Kendra S. Albright, "Environmental Scanning: Radar for Success," *Information Management Journal* 38, no. 3 (May/June 2004), p. 42. Reprinted with permission.

Figure 8–3

Environmental Factors Affecting Organizations

This is different from the economic environment, which mainly highlights rates, namely, rates of employment, exchange rates, inflation rates, and the level of GNP for a country.

Appropriate observation of the social environment can help the company. Awareness of demographic shifts including age, education, and income, coupled with in-depth knowledge of consumer attitudes, is imperative for a company to assess whether its services would be welcomed or not within a region. Finally, the political environment can impact how a company runs operations. We discussed in Chapter 2 the different political systems that exist across the world, and an understanding of those systems, along with the current state of affairs, can alert MNCs to any warnings that may impede expansion.

After obtaining the information, MNCs then go through an analyzing process which gives rise to the relevant features of the external environment. By performing analyses, the company can discover the risks and opportunities involved in expanding to that region. Typically, managers would communicate the results and then try to formulate the best strategy to take advantage of a ripening market. However, the external environment is not the only aspect to consider, and more information must be reviewed before those steps can be applied.

Environmental scanning is central to discovering if an MNC can survive in a particular region; however, it is only effective if it is done consistently. The environment changes very rapidly, and in order for firms to continually adapt, they must assess the external dynamics that could bolster or hinder future productivity. Each country will have a different perspective as to which factors create the most roadblocks and therefore must be evaluated on a more consistent basis. For example, a recent study showed that while both Malaysian and U.S. managers see competitors and the market as highly important, the U.S. managers considered regulatory issues more relevant than the Malaysians did. In this case, Malaysian MNCs have not been exposed to the sometimes strict directives that U.S. MNCs can face.[75]

OpenTV Inc. provides an example of how this environmental scanning process works. The firm analyzed the environment in China and concluded that the market in Shanghai was ideal for its software. As a result, it signed a deal with Shanghai Cable Network to provide this company with "middleware." When this software is installed in a subscriber's set-top box, it allows the user to interact with the television and do a number of different things—from shopping online to ordering a movie for viewing. Shanghai Cable has over 3 million customers, and one-third of them have broadband cable that lets them access the Internet and interact with television programs in what industry analysts say is one of the world's most advanced cable systems. By 2010, OpenTV had also launched its middleware solution for Southern Yinshi Network Media Ltd., a subsidiary of Southern Media Corporation, one of China's leading broadcasting groups. Southern Yinshi is responsible for the digital conversion of 18 municipal and city cable networks of Southern Media Corporation. If OpenTV's scan of the environment is correct, these arrangements will help provide revenue and profits to help support the firm's global expansion to India and elsewhere.[76] Another example is Cisco Systems, the world's largest maker of networking equipment, which continues to grow rapidly through acquisitions. From 2000 to 2009, it acquired more start-up companies than any other firm in the world. Cisco's China strategy has resulted from careful scanning of the broad macro political-economic environment as well as of the competitor landscape. Already the world's largest Internet and mobile phone market, China is likely to become even more crucial to the network equipment maker's growth as the country's burgeoning middle class gains access to new technology. Cisco is pursuing joint ventures and acquisitions to compete against Huawei Technologies Co. Ltd. and ZTE Corp., two large Chinese rivals. By relying on acquisitions and JVs, Cisco would be in a stronger position to work around difficult regulations and government policies, even if overall trade tensions between the United States and China continue. In its first acquisition aimed at China, Cisco bought the set-top box business of Hong Kong's DVN Ltd., but it has indicated it is poised for more acquisitions in China.[77] As of 2013, Cisco had spent over US$1 billion in the country.[78]

Internal Resource Analysis

When formulating strategy, some firms wait until they have completed their environmental scanning before conducting an internal resource analysis, which is a microeconomic aspect of activity. Others perform these two steps simultaneously. Internal resource analysis helps the firm to evaluate its current managerial, technical, material, and financial resources and capabilities to better assess its strengths and weaknesses. This assessment then is used by the MNC to determine its ability to take advantage of international market opportunities. The primary thrust of this analysis is to match external opportunities (gained through the environmental scan) with internal capabilities (gained through the internal resource analysis). In other words, these evaluations should not be viewed as how the environment creates a barrier to entry, but rather how companies can utilize their resources and capabilities to best take advantage of environmental opportunities.

key success factor (KSF)
A factor necessary for a firm to effectively compete in a market niche.

An internal analysis identifies the key factors for success that will dictate how well the firm is likely to do. A **key success factor (KSF)** is a factor that is necessary for a firm to compete effectively in a market niche. For example, a KSF for an international airline is price. An airline that discounts its prices will gain market share vis-à-vis competitors that do not. A second KSF for the airline is safety, and a third is quality of service in terms of on-time departures and arrivals, convenient schedules, and friendly, helpful personnel. In the automobile industry, quality of products has emerged as the number-one KSF in world markets. Japanese firms have been able to invade the U.S. auto market successfully because they have been able to prove that the quality of their cars is better than that of the average domestically built U.S. car. Toyota and Honda have had a quality edge over the competition in recent years in the eyes of U.S. car buyers. A second KSF is styling. The redesigned Mini-Cooper has been successful, in part, because customers like its unique look.

The key question for the management of an MNC is, Do we have the people and resources that can help us to develop and sustain the necessary KSFs, or can we acquire them? If the answer is yes, the recommendation would be to proceed. If the answer is no, management would begin looking at other markets where it has, or can develop, the necessary KSFs.

The balance between environmental scanning and internal resource analysis can be quite delicate. Managers do not want to spend too much time looking inward; otherwise, they could miss changes in the environment that would alter the company's strengths and weaknesses based on that market. Conversely, managers do not want to appraise the outward view for too long as they could take time away from improving internal systems and taking advantage of opportunities.

Goal Setting for Strategy Formulation

In practice, goal formulation often precedes the first two steps of environmental scanning and internal resource analysis. As used here, however, the more specific goals for the strategic plan come out of external scanning and internal analysis. MNCs pursue a variety of such goals; Table 8–1 provides a list of the most common ones. These goals typically serve as an umbrella beneath which the subsidiaries and other international groups operate.

Profitability and marketing goals almost always dominate the strategic plans of today's MNCs. Profitability, as shown in Table 8–1, is so important because MNCs generally need higher profitability from their overseas operations than they do from their

Table 8–1
Areas for Formulation of MNC Goals

Profitability

Level of profits
Return on assets, investment, equity, sales
Yearly profit growth
Yearly earnings per share growth

Marketing

Total sales volume
Market share—worldwide, region, country
Growth in sales volume
Growth in market share
Integration of country markets for marketing efficiency and effectiveness

Operations

Ratio of foreign to domestic production volume
Economies of scale via international production integration
Quality and cost control
Introduction of cost-efficient production methods

Finance

Financing of foreign affiliates—retained earnings or local borrowing
Taxation—minimizing tax burden globally
Optimum capital structure
Foreign exchange management—minimizing losses from foreign fluctuations

Human Resources

Recruitment and selection
Development of managers with global orientation
Management development of host-country nationals
Compensation and benefits

domestic operations. The reason is quite simple: Setting up overseas operations involves greater risk and effort. In addition, a firm that has done well domestically with a product or service usually has done so because the competition is minimal or ineffective. Firms with this advantage often find additional lucrative opportunities outside their borders. Moreover, the more successful a firm is domestically, the more difficult it is to increase market share without strong competitive response. International markets, however, offer an ideal alternative to the desire for increased growth and profitability.

Another reason that profitability and marketing top the list is that these tend to be more externally environmentally responsive, whereas production, finance, and personnel functions tend to be more internally controlled. Thus, for strategic planning, profitability and marketing goals are given higher importance and warrant closer attention. Ford's European operations offer an example. In recent years the automaker has been losing market share in the EU. GM, Ford, and Chrysler have all been focusing on regaining profitability in light of the global economic crisis and the lower shares in most global markets. In 2010, Ford continued to restructure and streamline its operations in Europe, even as market share declined to 7.8 percent in the European marketplace. After unloading the Land Rover and Jaguar to Tata of India, and its share of Volvo to China's Geely, Ford posted pretax profits of $8.8 billion in 2011 and $8.0 billion in 2012, despite slumping European sales. In seeking to improve performance in Europe, Ford is shipping more cars from its factory in Thailand and, in so doing, saving on costs and increasing margins.[79,80]

Once the strategic goals are set, the MNC will develop specific operational goals and controls, usually through a two-way process at the subsidiary or affiliate level. Home-office management will set certain parameters, and the overseas group will operate within these guidelines. For example, the MNC headquarters may require periodic financial reports, restrict on-site decisions to matters involving less than $100,000, and require that all client contracts be cleared through the home office. These guidelines are designed to ensure that the overseas group's activities support the goals in the strategic plan and that all units operate in a coordinated effort.

■ Strategy Implementation

strategy implementation
The process of providing goods and services in accord with a plan of action.

Once formulated, the strategic plan next must be implemented. **Strategy implementation** provides goods and services in accord with a plan of action. Quite often, this plan will have an overall philosophy or series of guidelines that direct the process. In the case of Japanese electronic-manufacturing firms entering the U.S. market, Chang has found a common approach:

> To reduce the risk of failure, these firms are entering their core businesses and those in which they have stronger competitive advantages over local firms first. The learning from early entry enables firms to launch further entry into areas in which they have the next strongest competitive advantages. As learning accumulates, firms may overcome the disadvantages intrinsic to foreignness. Although primary learning takes place within firms through learning by doing, they may also learn from other firms through the transfer or diffusion of experience. This process is not automatic, however, and it may be enhanced by membership in a corporate network: in firms associated with either horizontal or vertical business, groups were more likely to initiate entries than independent firms. By learning from their own sequential entry experience as well as from other firms in corporate networks, firms build capabilities in foreign entry.[81]

International management must consider three general areas in strategy implementation. First, the MNC must decide where to locate operations. Second, the MNC must carry out entry and ownership strategies (discussed in Chapter 9). Finally, management must implement functional strategies in areas such as marketing, production, and finance.

Location Considerations for Implementation

In choosing a location, today's MNC has two primary considerations: the country and the specific locale within the chosen country. Quite often, the first choice is easier than the second, because there are many more alternatives from which to choose a specific locale.

The Country   Traditionally, MNCs have invested in highly industrialized countries, and research reveals that annual investments have been increasing substantially.

In the case of Japan, multinational banks and investors from around the world have been looking for properties that are being jettisoned by Japanese banks that are trying to unload some of their distressed loans. The Japanese commercial property market collapsed starting in the mid-1990s, creating many opportunities for investors. MNCs are also actively engaged in mergers and acquisitions in Japan. Intuit Inc. of Menlo Park, California, purchased a financial software specialist in Japan for $52 million in stock and spent $30 million for the Nihon Mikon Company, which sells small business accounting software. These purchases point to a new trend in Japan—the acquisition of small firms. However, many larger purchases have also been made.

Foreign investors are also pouring into Mexico, although this investment activity has generated some political controversy in the United States.[82] One reason is that it is a gateway to the American and Canadian markets. A second reason is that Mexico is a very cost-effective place in which to manufacture goods. A third is that the declining value of the peso after Mexico's economic crisis in 1994 and 1995 hit many Mexican businesses hard and left them vulnerable to mergers and acquisitions—an opportunity not lost on many large multinationals. In the period 1996–1997, Britain's B.A.T. Industries PLC took control of Cigarrera La Moderna, Mexico's tobacco giant, in a $1.5 billion deal. A few days earlier, Philip Morris Cos. increased its stake in the second-largest tobacco company, Cigarros La Tabacalera Mexicana SA, to 50 percent from about 29 percent for $400 million. Walmart Stores Inc. announced plans to acquire control of Mexico's largest retailer, Cifra SA, in a deal valued at more than $1 billion. eventually becoming part of Wal-Mex, Walmart's Mexican subsidiary (see In-Depth Integrative Case 2.2). A month later, Procter & Gamble Co. acquired a consumer-products concern, Loreto y Pena Pobre, for $170 million. Bell Atlantic Co. has acquired full control of its cellular-phone partner, Grupo Iusacell SA, with total investments of more than $1 billion.[83] More recently, acquisitions of Mexican companies have continued, although for more strategic reasons. For example, in June, 2013, Anheuser-Busch InBev and Grupo Modelo, Mexico's largest brewer, announced completion of their integration in a deal valued at $20.1 billion. In its press release, AB Inbev said. "The combination is a natural next step given the successful long-term partnership between AB InBev and Grupo Modelo, which started more than 20 years ago. The combined company will benefit from the significant growth potential that Modelo brands such as Corona have globally outside of the U.S., as well as locally in Mexico, where there will also be opportunities to introduce AB InBev brands through Modelo's distribution network."[84]

MNCs often invest in advanced industrialized countries because they offer the largest markets for goods and services. In addition, the established country or geographic locale may have legal restrictions related to imports, encouraging a local presence. Japanese firms, for example, in complying with their voluntary export quotas of cars to the United States as well as responding to dissatisfaction in Washington regarding the continuing trade imbalance with the United States, have established U.S.-based assembly plants. In Europe, because of EU regulations for outsiders, most U.S. and Japanese MNCs have operations in at least one European country, thus ensuring access to the European community at large. In fact, the huge U.S. MNC ITT now operates in each of the original 12 EU countries.

Another consideration in choosing a country is the amount of government control and restrictions on foreign investment. Traditionally, MNCs from around the world resisted anything but very limited business in Eastern European countries with central planning economies. The recent relaxing of the trade rules and move toward free-market economies in the republics of the former Soviet Union and the other Eastern European nations, however, have encouraged MNCs to rethink their positions; more and more are making moves into this largely untapped part of the global market. The same is true in India, although the political climate can be volatile and MNCs must carefully weigh the risks of investing here. Restrictions on foreign investment also play a factor. Countries such as China and India have required that control of the operation be in the hands of local partners. MNCs that are reluctant to accept such conditions will not establish operations there.

In addition to these considerations, MNCs examine the specific benefits offered by host countries, including low tax rates, rent-free land and buildings, low-interest or no-interest loans, subsidized energy and transportation rates, and a well-developed infrastructure that provides many of the services found back home (good roads, communication systems, schools, health care, entertainment, and housing). These benefits will be weighed against any disincentives or performance requirements that must be met by the MNC, such as job-creation quotas, export minimums for generating foreign currency, limits on local market growth, labor regulations, wage and price controls, restrictions on profit repatriation, and controls on the transfer of technology.

Local Issues   Once the MNC has selected the country in which to locate, the firm must choose the specific locale. A number of factors influence this choice. Common considerations include access to markets, proximity to competitors, availability of transportation and electric power, and desirability of the location for employees coming in from the outside.

One study found that in selecting U.S. sites, both German and Japanese firms place more importance on accessibility and desirability and less importance on financial considerations.[85] However, financial matters remain important: Many countries attempt to lure MNCs to specific locales by offering special financial packages.

Another common consideration is the nature of the workforce. MNCs prefer to locate near sources of available labor that can be readily trained to do the work. A complementary consideration that often is unspoken is the presence and strength of organized labor. Japanese firms in particular tend to avoid heavily unionized areas.

Still another consideration is the cost of doing business. Manufacturers often set up operations in rural areas, commonly called "greenfield locations," which are much less expensive and do not have the problems of urban areas. Conversely, banks often choose metropolitan areas, because they feel they must have a presence in the business district.

Some MNCs opt for locales where the cost of running a small enterprise is significantly lower than that of running a large one. In this way, they spread their risk, setting up many small locations throughout the world rather than one or two large ones. Manufacturing firms are a good example. Some production firms feel that the economies of scale associated with a large-scale plant are more than offset by potential problems that can result should economic or political difficulties develop in the country. These firms' strategy is to spread the risk by opting for a series of small plants throughout a wide geographic region.[86] This location strategy can also be beneficial for stockholders. Research has found that MNCs with a presence in developing countries have significantly higher market values than MNCs that operate only in countries that have advanced economies.[87]

Frontier Markets   Sometimes referred to as pre-emerging, frontier markets are a unique subset of emerging economies. Whereas most traditional emerging markets are financially linked to the economies of their more developed counterparts, frontier markets are less correlated to the ups and downs of the global economy. From an investment point of view, these markets offer potentially high rewards, but with high risk. The most commonly cited frontier markets are located in Africa and Asia.

Business initiatives in frontier markets require careful strategic considerations. One potential approach is to joint-venture with a local company that specializes in the cultural knowledge of the marketplace. The Mara Group, for example, is an African conglomerate that conducts business in a variety of unrelated ventures across the continent. Rather than focus on the financial and technical aspects of the business, the Mara Group provides the marketing, logistical, and bureaucratic assistance to its international partners. The Mara Group also provides a trusted, recognizable brand name to foreign products. IBM is an example of a MNC that has conducted business in frontier markets using a partnership with the Mara Group.[88]

Combining Country and Firm-Specific Factors in International Strategy

International management scholars have developed a simple framework that builds upon the integration-responsiveness framework to help managers understand the interaction between the relative attractiveness of different country locations for a given activity and the firm-level attributes or strengths that can be leveraged in that location.[89] The first set of factors are referred to as CSAs, or country-specific advantages, while the second are referred to as FSAs, or firm-specific advantages. CSAs can be based on natural resource endowments (minerals, energy, forests), the labor force, or on less tangible factors that include education and skills, institutional protections of intellectual property, entrepreneurial dynamism, or other factors unique to a given market. FSAs are unique capabilities proprietary to the organization that may be based on product or process technology, marketing or distributional skills, or managerial know-how.

Managers of MNCs use strategies that build upon the interactions of CSAs and FSAs. Figure 8–4 provides a graphical depiction of this framework. It should be emphasized that the "strength" or "weakness" of FSAs and CSAs is a relative notion that depends on the relevant market and the CSAs and FSAs of potential competitors.

MNCs in quadrants 1, 2, and 3 would be expected to pursue different strategies. Quadrant 1 firms would tend to emphasize cost leadership; they are likely to be resource-based and/or mature, internationally oriented firms producing a commodity-type product. Given these factors, FSAs tend to be less important compared to the CSAs of location and energy costs, which are the main sources of the firm's competitive advantage.

Quadrant 2 firms represent less efficient firms with few intrinsic CSAs or FSAs. Quadrant 2 could also represent domestically based small and medium-sized firms with

Firm-specific advantages (FSAs)

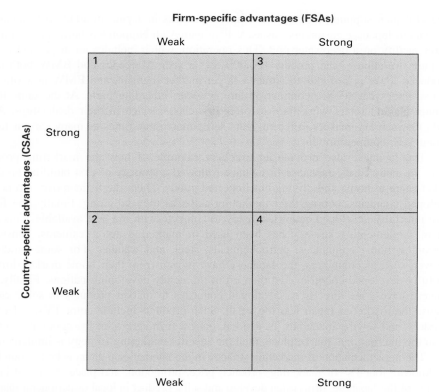

Figure 8–4

The CSA-FSA Matrix

little global exposure. Firms in quadrant 4 are generally differentiated firms with strong FSAs
in marketing and customization. These firms usually have strong brands. In quadrant 4 the
FSAs dominate, so in world markets the home-country CSAs are not essential in the long
run. Quadrant 3 firms generally can choose either the cost or differentiation strategies, or
perhaps combine them because of the strength of both their CSAs and FSAs.

In terms of business strategy, firms in quadrants 2 and 3 can benefit from strategies
of both low cost and differentiation. Such a firm is constantly evaluating its production
mix. Quadrants 4 and 1 require specific strategies for different types of firms. For
instance, a quadrant 4 firm that has strong FSAs in marketing (customization) can operate internationally without reliance on its home-market CSA, or the CSAs of the host
nation. For such a firm, in quadrant 4, the CSA is not relevant. In contrast, quadrant 1
has mature multinationals or product divisions determined more by CSAs than by FSAs.
By improving potential FSAs in marketing or product innovation and increasing value
added through vertical integration, the quadrant 1 firm can move to quadrant 3.

The Role of the Functional Areas in Implementation

To implement strategies, MNCs must tap the primary functional areas of marketing,
production, and finance. The following sections examine the roles of these functions in
international strategy implementation.

Marketing   The implementation of strategy from a marketing perspective must be determined on a country-by-country basis. What works from the standpoint of marketing in
one locale may not necessarily succeed in another. In addition, the specific steps of a
marketing approach often are dictated by the overall strategic plan, which in turn is based
heavily on market analysis.

German auto firms in Japan are a good example of using marketing analysis to
meet customer needs. Over the past 15 years, the Germans have spent millions of dollars

to build dealer, supplier, and service-support networks in Japan, in addition to adapting their cars to Japanese customers' tastes. Volkswagen Audi Nippon has built a $320 million import facility on a deepwater port. This operation, which includes an inspection center and parts warehouse, can process 100,000 cars a year. Mercedes and BMW both have introduced lower-priced cars to attract a larger market segment, and BMW now offers a flat-fee, three-year service contract on any new car, including parts. At the same time, German manufacturers work hard to offer first-class service in their dealerships. As a result, German automakers in recent years sell almost three times as many cars in Japan as their U.S. competitors do.

The Japanese also provide an excellent example of how the marketing process works. In many cases, Japanese firms have followed a strategy of first building up their market share at home and driving out imported goods. Then, the firms move into newly developed countries, honing their marketing skills as they go along. Finally, the firms move into fully developed countries, ready to compete with the best available. This pattern of implementing strategy has been used in marketing autos, cameras, consumer electronics, home appliances, petrochemicals, steel, and watches. For some products, however, such as computers, the Japanese have moved from their home market directly into fully developed countries and then on to the newly developing nations. Finally, the Japanese have gone directly to developed countries to market products in some cases, because the market in Japan was too small. Such products include color TVs, videotape recorders, and sewing machines. In general, once a firm agrees on the goods it wants to sell in the international marketplace, then the specific marketing strategy is implemented.

The implementation of marketing strategy in the international arena is built around the well-known "four Ps" of marketing: product, price, promotion, and place. As noted in the example of the Japanese, firms often develop and sell a product in local or peripheral markets before expanding to major overseas targets. If the product is designed specifically to meet an overseas demand, however, the process is more direct. Price largely is a function of market demand.[90] For example, the Japanese have found that the U.S. microcomputer market is price-sensitive; by introducing lower-priced clones, the Japanese have been able to make headway, especially in the portable laptop market. The last two Ps, promotion and place, are dictated by local conditions and often left in the hands of those running the subsidiary or affiliate. Local management may implement customer sales incentives, for example, or make arrangements with dealers and salespeople who are helping to move the product locally.

Production Although marketing usually dominates strategy implementation, the production function also plays a role. If a company is going to export goods to a foreign market, the production process traditionally has been handled through domestic operations. In recent years, however, MNCs have found that whether they are exporting or producing the goods locally in the host country, consideration of worldwide production is important. For example, goods may be produced in foreign countries for export to other nations. Sometimes, a plant will specialize in a particular product and export it to all the MNC's markets; other times, a plant will produce goods only for a specific locale, such as Western Europe or South America. Still other facilities will produce one or more components that are shipped to a larger network of assembly plants. That last option has been widely adopted by pharmaceutical firms and automakers such as Volkswagen and Honda.

As mentioned in the first part of the chapter, if the firm operates production plants in different countries but makes no attempt to integrate its overall operations, the company is known as a multi-domestic. A recent trend has been away from this scattered approach and toward global coordination of operations.

Finally, if the product is labor-intensive, as in the case of microcomputers, then the trend is to farm the product out to low-cost sites such as Mexico or Brazil, where the cost of labor is relatively low and the infrastructure (electric power, communications systems, transportation systems) is sufficient to support production. Sometimes, multiple sources of individual components are used; in other cases, one or two sources are sufficient. In any event, careful coordination of the production function is needed when implementing the strategy, and the result is a product that is truly global in nature.

Finance   Use of the finance function to implement strategy normally is developed at the home office and carried out by the overseas affiliate or branch. When a firm went international in the past, the overseas operation commonly relied on the local area for funds, but the rise of global financing has ended this practice. MNCs have learned that transferring funds from one place in the world to another, or borrowing funds in the international money markets, often is less expensive than relying on local sources. Unfortunately, there are problems in these transfers.

Such a problem is representative of those faced by MNCs using the finance function to implement their strategies. One of an MNC's biggest recent headaches when implementing strategies in the financial dimension has been the revaluation of currencies. For example, in the late 1990s the U.S. dollar increased in value against the Japanese yen. American overseas subsidiaries that held yen found their profits (in terms of dollars) declining. The same was true for those subsidiaries that held Mexican pesos when that government devalued the currency several years ago. When this happens, a subsidiary's profit will decline. After its initial introduction in 1999, the euro declined against the U.S. dollar, but when the dollar subsequently came under pressure, the euro regained strength. One of the more recent examples of financial issues is the expansive U.S. trade deficit with China, where the potentially undervalued yuan has played a role.

When dealing with the inherent risk of volatile monetary exchange rates, some MNCs have bought currency options that (for a price) guarantee convertibility at a specified rate. Others have developed countertrade strategies, whereby they receive products in exchange for currency. For example, PepsiCo received payment in vodka for its products sold in Russia. Countertrade continues to be a popular form of international business, especially in less developed countries and those with nonconvertible currencies.

■ Specialized Strategies

In addition to the basic steps in strategy formulation, the analysis of which strategies may be appropriate based on the globalization vs. national responsiveness framework, and the specific processes in strategy implementation, there are some circumstances that may require specialized strategies. Two that have received considerable attention in recent years are strategies for developing and emerging markets and strategies for international entrepreneurship and new ventures.

Strategies for Emerging Markets

Emerging economies have assumed an increasingly important role in the global economy and are predicted to compose more than half of global economic output by midcentury. Partly in response to this growth, MNCs are directing increasing attention to those markets. Foreign direct investment (FDI) flows into developing countries—one measure of increased integration and business activity between developed and emerging economies—grew from $23.7 billion in 1990 to $680 billion in 2012. For the first time ever, FDI inflows into developing countries surpassed that of developed countries, which drew only $550 billion.[91] In particular, the "BRIC" economies have been among the largest recipients of FDI. In 2008, Brazil, Russia, India, and China attracted, respectively, $65.3 billion, $44.1 billion, $27.3 billion, and $119.7 billion in FDI.[92]

At the same time, emerging economies pose exceptional risks due to their political and economic volatility and their relatively underdeveloped institutional systems. These risks show up in corruption, failure to enforce contracts, red tape and bureaucratic costs, and general uncertainty in the legal and political environment.[93] MNCs must adjust their strategy to respond to these risks. For example, in these risky markets, it may be wise to engage in arm's-length or limited equity investments or to maintain greater control of operations by avoiding joint ventures or other shared ownership structures. In other circumstances, it may be wiser to collaborate with a local partner who can help buffer risks through its political connections. Some of the factors relating to these conditions will be discussed in Chapters 9 and 10. However, two unique types of strategies for emerging markets deserve particular attention here.

First-Mover Strategies   Recent research has suggested that entry order into developing countries may be particularly important given the transitional nature of these markets. In general, in particular industries and economic environments, significant economies are associated with first-mover or early-entry positioning—being the first or one of the first to enter a market. These include capturing learning effects important for increasing market share, achieving scale economies that accrue from opportunities for capturing that greater share, and development of alliances with the most attractive (or in some cases the only) local partner. In emerging economies that are undergoing rapid changes such as privatization and market liberalization, there may be a narrow window of time within which these opportunities can be best exploited. In these conditions, first-mover strategies allow entrants to preempt competition, establish beachhead positions, and influence the evolving competitive environment in a manner conducive to their long-term interests and market position.

One study analyzed these benefits in the case of China, concluding that early entrants have reaped substantial rewards for their efforts, especially when collaborations with governments provided credible commitments that the deals struck in those early years of liberalization would not later be undone. First-mover advantages in some other transitional markets, such as Russia and Eastern Europe, are not so clear. Moreover, there may be substantial risks to premature entry—that is, entry before the basic legal, institutional, and political frameworks for doing business have been established.[94]

Privatization presents a particularly powerful case supporting the competitive effects of first-mover positioning. First movers who succeed in taking over newly privatized state-owned enterprises, such as telecom and energy firms, possess a significant advantage over later entrants, especially when market liberalization is delayed and the host government provides protection to the newly privatized incumbent firms. This was the case in 1998 when the Mexican government accepted a $1.757 billion bid for a minority (20.4 percent) but controlling interest in Telefonos de Mexico (Telmex) from an international consortium composed of Grupo Carso, Southwestern Bell, and France Cable et Radio, an affiliate of France Telecom. Although the Mexican market subsequently opened to competition, Telmex and its foreign partners (the first movers) maintained monopoly control over local networks and were able to bundle local and long-distance service, cross-market, and cross-subsidize, giving Telmex a strong advantage. Moreover, the Mexican government was responsive to providing the Telmex consortium protection and financial support for infrastructure investment, and it did so partly by charging new carriers to help Telmex pay for improvements needed for the long-distance network. In addition, Telmex was able to charge relatively high fees to connect to its network, and the long delay between the initial privatization and market opening allowed these advantages to persist.[95]

base of the pyramid strategy
Strategy targeting low-income customers in developing countries.

Strategies for the "Base of the Pyramid"   Another area of increasing focus for MNCs is the 5 billion or more potential customers around the world who have heretofore been mostly ignored by international business, even within emerging economies, where most MNCs target only the wealthiest consumers. Although FDI in emerging economies has grown rapidly, most has been directed at the big emerging markets previously mentioned—China, India, and Brazil—and even there, most MNC emerging-market strategies have focused exclusively on the elite and emerging middle-class markets, ignoring the vast majority of people considered too poor to be viable customers.[96] Because of this focus, MNC strategies aimed at tailoring existing practices and products to better fit the needs of emerging-market customers have not succeeded in making products and services available to the mass markets in the developing world—the 4–5 billion people at the bottom of the economic pyramid who represent fully two-thirds of the world's population. Figure 8–5 shows the distribution of population and income around the world.

A group of researchers and companies have begun exploring the potentially untapped markets at the base of the pyramid (BOP). They have found that incremental adaptation of existing technologies and products is not effective at the BOP and that the BOP forces MNCs to fundamentally rethink their strategies.[97] Companies must consider smaller-scale strategies and build relationships with local governments, small entrepreneurs, and nonprofits

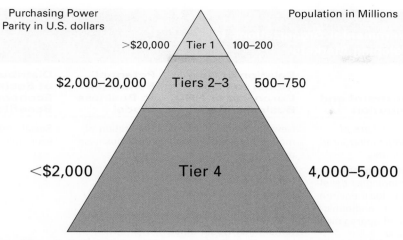

Purchasing Power Parity in U.S. dollars

Population in Millions

>$20,000 / Tier 1 \ 100–200

$2,000–20,000 / Tiers 2–3 \ 500–750

<$2,000   Tier 4   4,000–5,000

Figure 8–5

The World Population and Income Pyramid

Source: Adapted from C. K. Prahalad and Stuart L. Hart, "The Fortune at the Bottom of the Pyramid," *Strategy + Business* 26 (2002), pp. 54–67.

rather than depend on established partners such as central governments and large local companies. Building relationships directly and at the local level contributes to the reputation and fosters the trust necessary to overcome the lack of formal institutions such as intellectual property rights and the rule of law. The BOP may also be an ideal environment for incubating new, leapfrog technologies, including "disruptive" technologies that reduce environmental impacts and increase social benefit such as renewable energy and wireless telecom. Finally, business models forged successfully at the base of the pyramid have the potential to travel profitably to higher-income markets because adding cost and features to a low-cost model may be easier than removing cost and features from high-cost models.[98] This last finding has significant implications for the globalization–national responsiveness framework introduced at the beginning of the chapter and for the potential for MNCs to achieve a truly transnational strategy.[99]

Some researchers have proposed that collaboration and alliances with nonprofit nongovernmental organizations (NGOs) can be a means to jump-start market entry in BOP markets. Dahan, Doh, Oetzel, and Yaziji documented how collaborating with NGOs can contribute complementary capabilities—both intangible assets such as knowledge, reputation, and brand and tangible resources, such as human capital, production capabilities, and market access—along each stage of the value chain, affecting many aspects of the business model. These initiatives enable participating firms to create and deliver value in novel ways, while minimizing costs and risks. They highlight, in particular, the competencies and resources that NGOs can bring to such partnerships, including market expertise (needs identification, knowledge of certain market segments); the value of NGO brands to customers, customer relationships, legitimacy with civil society players and governments; and ownership of—or access to—local distribution systems and local sourcing ability.[100] Among the cross-sectoral initiatives they profile is Nestlé's cocoa initiatives in Africa. Together with a dozen other major chocolate manufacturers, Nestlé has partnered with NGOs and local governments in setting up programs to improve labor conditions and promote sustainable farming practices in West Africa. Nestlé is at the forefront of the latter objective, with its sponsorship of "farmers field schools" on the Ivory Coast,[101] which support both the production of higher quality cocoa (thus ensuring Nestlé has access to that labor and production) and the social benefits of that production. Table 8–2 summarizes the findings of this research by presenting how NGOs and MNCs can build a business model that creates both economic and social value.

Danone is another company that has targeted poor consumers through innovative strategy and marketing. It is marketing a single serving yogurt drink in many developing country markets around the world, some living on dollar-a-day food budgets, selling the drinkable yogurts for as little as 10 cents. In 2009, 42 percent of Danone's sales were from emerging markets—up from just 6 percent 10 years ago. Danone seeks to reach 1 billion

Table 8–2
Contributions by Nongovernmental Organizations to Business Models in Developing Markets

Business Activity and Example	Market Constraint and NGO Contribution	Relation of New Model to Prior Corporate or NGO Business Model	Potential Benefit(s) to Business Model	Distribution of Social and Economic Benefits
Market research: Ashoka/FEC project to provide irrigation to small farmers in Latin America	*Market constraint:* Lack of knowledge; overcoming information asymmetries *NGO contribution:* Identifying innovative technologies developed for unique local environment and market conditions; identification and aggregation of customer base	New co-created business model that enabled the provision of irrigation service to farmers resulting in a doubling or tripling of their incomes; enabled private sector firm to reach new customers that would otherwise be inaccessible	Generation of novel business model	Social and economic
R&D: Cemex's Patrimonio Hoy program	*Market constraint:* Lack of appropriately priced and designed construction materials for self-construction of housing and financing *NGO contribution:* Market testing of products, incorporation of customer feedback; use of internal microcredit system to facilitate purchase of newly developed materials	New co-created business model that enabled Cemex to expand its market through reconfiguration of its business model and made it possible for Patrimonio Hoy to expand housing opportunities for low income families	Generation of novel business model; Value creation; cost minimization	Social and economic
Procurement and Production: Nestlé's cocoa farming initiatives	*Market constraint:* Underdeveloped human capital; need access to local networks and supply chains *NGO contribution:* Established relations with local communities and host-country governments	Extends Nestlé's existing business model (supply chain) and enables local NGOs to increase employment and other social benefits for residents	Value creation; value delivery; cost minimization	Primarily economic
Marketing: P&G/PSI and the Safe Drinking Water Alliance	*Market constraint:* Lack of knowledge surrounding distribution and use of water in developing countries *NGO contribution:* Input in product development, co-branding, customer education	Extends P&G's and PSI's existing business models by expanding the market for and the affordable availability of water-purification products (P&G product development; PSI's distribution networks)	Value creation	Social and economic
Distribution: HSBC Amah and Islamic Relief	*Market constraint:* Access to local networks and supply chains *NGO contribution:* May take on the provision of some services itself	Extends HSBC Amah's existing business model	Value creation; value delivery; cost minimization	Primarily economic
Comprehensive: AtoZ Mosquito Net Venture	*Market constraint:* No single organization was able to develop and distribute affordable mosquito nets *NGO contribution:* Holistic and fundamental rethinking of product/process and construction of new model tailored to specific context	Creation of new product based on shared technology and expertise. WHO participation makes product accessible to many people in Africa. Substantial financial and social value created		Social and economic

Source: Nicolas Dahan, Jonathan P. Doh, Jennifer Oetzel, and Michael Yaziji, "Corporate-NGO Collaboration: Creating New Business Models for Developing Markets," *Long Range Planning* 43, no. 2, pp. 337–338.

Can Internet and Mobile Access Transform Poor Economies at the Base of the Pyramid?

Developed countries have experienced dramatic advances in Information and Communications Technology (ITC), notably, sharp increases in penetration of both Internet and wireless phone networks. Developing countries, especially the poorest countries of South Asia and Africa, have not benefited from these trends. Some entrepreneurs, however, see great potential in reaching these "bottom of the pyramid markets," although these efforts have, to date, been challenging. Low literacy rates, poor infrastructure, corruption and other political interference, and incomplete business models have all contributed to still-born efforts. Yet, these entrepreneurs have persevered.

In terms of wireless service and Internet services, many view Africa as the next great frontier, despite the fact that more than half the population lives on less than $2 a day. From 2000 to 2009, Internet penetration in Africa grew 1,809.8 percent, from just over 4 million in 2000 to 86 million in 2009 (see Table 2–2 in Chapter 2). The total number of mobile subscribers in Africa stood at 296 million in 2008 and increased by more than 74 million subscribers, reaching 370 million subscribers as of the fourth quarter of 2008. In the top nine African telecom countries, users are expected to reach 444 million by 2013, with Nigeria alone expected to add more than 58 million mobile subscribers from 2009 to 2013.

The increase in the number of mobile cellular subscriptions over the last five years has defied all predictions and Africa remains the region with the highest mobile growth rate, according to an ITU document, "Information Society Statistical Profiles 2009: Africa." It says the high ratio of mobile cellular subscriptions to fixed telephone lines and the high mobile cellular growth rate suggest that Africa has taken the lead in the shift from fixed to mobile telephony, a trend that can be observed worldwide. The number of Internet users has also grown faster than in other regions. However, the report notes that despite rapid growth, "Africa's ICT penetration levels in 2009 are still far behind the rest of the world and very few African countries reach ICT levels comparable to global averages." Fewer than 5 percent of Africans use the Internet, and fixed and mobile broadband penetration levels are negligible. "Indeed, the digital divide between the African region and the rest of the world is much more pronounced than the divide within the region, with very few countries reaching ICT levels comparable to global averages," says the ITU document. The research shows that African countries are facing a number of challenges in increasing ICT levels. These include the lack of full liberalization of markets and the limited availability of infrastructure, such as shortage of international Internet bandwidth. "In addition, prices for ICT services remain very high compared to income levels." On the question of infrastructure, the report says there are practically no cable networks and many countries face a shortage of international Internet bandwidth.

According to the ITU the figures highlight the acceleration of growth in African mobile and Internet markets outside of South Africa in less than a decade. Growth in Nigeria has been very strong. Kenya, Ghana, Tanzania, and Cote d'Ivoire have also accounted for the change in the distribution of mobile connections.

European companies were among the first to aggressively pursue African cellular markets. Ericsson, Alcatel, and Motorola have pushed into the region, and England's Vodafone Group PLC and France Télécom's Orange unit have set up operations around the region. But other entrepreneurs have identified mobile service and Internet services as a way to make money and empower individuals.

Terracom, an Internet venture started by Greg Wyler, an American tech entrepreneur, entered Rwanda and was granted a contract to connect 300 schools to the Internet. Later, the company bought 99 percent of the shares in Rwandatel, the country's national telecommunications company, for $20 million. Africa's only connection to the network of computers and fiber optic cables that are the Internet's backbone is a $600 million undersea cable running from Portugal down the west coast of Africa. Built in 2002, the cable was supposed to provide cheaper and faster Web access, but didn't deliver. Adding to the problem is that most of the satellites serving Africa were launched nearly 20 years ago and are aging or going out of commission. A satellite set to go into service last year blew up on the launching pad. Power is also an issue, as intermittent power failures in Rwanda hamper efforts to provide a steady electricity source. Meanwhile, Terracom's venture has been plagued by repeated setbacks with both sides accusing the other of failing to deliver on its promise. "The bottom line is that he promised many things and didn't deliver," said Albert Butare, the country's telecommunications minister.

Africa Online, another venture, was the first Internet service provider in Kenya (1995) and Cote d'Ivoire (1996). It grew to span eight countries across Africa. The company was founded in 1994 by three Kenyans who met each other while students at MIT and Harvard. The idea began as an online news service for Kenyans, which developed from an online community hosted at MIT called KenyaNet, one of several online communities that were among the most fervent virtual communities in the early pre-Web 1990s. With the commercialization of the Internet, Africa Online moved its focus away from providing news to connecting Africans on the continent to the Internet. In 1995, the company was bought by International Wireless of Boston, which ultimately became Prodigy. During this period, Africa Online expanded rapidly from its original operation in Kenya to Ghana, Cote d'Ivoire, Tanzania, Uganda, Zambia, Zimbabwe, and Swaziland, with the three Kenyans continuing to manage the operation. Africa Online was the first commercial Internet provider in Kenya and Cote d'Ivoire. In 2007, Africa Online was purchased by South Africa's Telkom.

What makes Africa's mobile and Internet revolution significant is its potential economic impact. The World Bank has been a strong supporter of deploying wireless and Internet communication to improve food production and other development. To some, mobile has become a means to economic empowerment. For example, farmers in Senegal now use their one mobile phone to find eggplant buyers in Dakar willing to pay three times the rate offered by local middlemen. These and other examples suggest the information and communication technology revolution may reap benefits for multinational and local companies, as well as others who may improve their economic situation by exploiting these new communication opportunities.

customers a month by 2013, up from 700 million today. Other companies are pursuing similar strategies, including Adidas, which is experimenting with a one-euro sneaker for barefoot Bangladeshis. L'Oréal is selling sample-sized containers of shampoo and face cream in India for a few pennies each and Unilever developed Cubitos, small cubes of flavoring that cost as little as two cents apiece, for poor markets. Danone says that the yogurt is a good match in Senegal because it is meant as an on-the-go snack—well adapted for Senegalese consumers who have three or four snacks during a day and only one main meal. The first yogurt debuted in Indonesia at the end of 2004 and was an instant hit, selling 10 million bottles in its first three months on the market. It is still one of Danone's most popular products in Indonesia, where the average per-capita income is about $11 a day. Danone partnered with Muhammad Yunus, the Bangladeshi who later won the Nobel Peace Prize for pioneering work in microfinance, to set up a joint venture called Grameen Danone Foods Ltd. to sell a seven-cent yogurt product called Shokti Doi—which means "strong yogurt." Rich with vitamins and minerals, it was to be sold through local women who would peddle it door to door on commission.[102]

The BOP strategy is challenging to implement. Companies have to offer affordable goods that are highly available in a community that is willing to accept the product. Most importantly, however, is that the company must bring awareness of the product to the general populace. Balancing these is not a simple task, since advertising and efficient distribution networks, for example, cost a significant amount, yet the companies cannot add a high price tag. Furthermore, illiteracy issues, poor infrastructure, corruption, and nonexistent distribution channels often associated with poverty-stricken societies deter companies from wanting to invest. Despite the many barriers, companies can be successful. Smart Communications Inc. saw that there was a great opportunity to expand in the Philippines, where about half the population lived in poverty. In 2002, the market forecasted that approximately 30 percent of the population would be using mobile phones by 2008. Smart offered pay-as-you-go phones that could be recharged using a microchip that was already in the cellular phones, making it possible to recharge "over the air." The company then began to offer pricing plans that consisted of extremely small increments, so even the low-income consumer could take advantage of the opportunity. It worked in Smart's favor, as more and more people began using the service daily, and the cellular industry reached a 30 percent margin in 2004, changing forecasts to a shocking 70 percent mobile phone usage rate by 2008. Smart's parent company experienced a more than tenfold increase in profits in 2004 as compared to 2003, due in large part to focusing on the very lucrative market at the base of the pyramid.[103] To learn more about how mobile technology is reaching impoverished countries, see the nearby International Management in Action box.

The Danone venture with Grameen also faced setbacks: milk prices soared, factory openings were delayed, and the saleswomen couldn't earn a living selling yogurt alone. The Danone venture shifted strategies and now sells the bulk of Shokti Doi in urban stores, not rural villages. But the knowledge gained through these experiences can be essential for MNCs: Danone maintained the project in Bangladesh, which it says provided useful insights for other parts of its business, and subsequently built a factory in Thailand modeled on the Bangladesh facility.

Entrepreneurial Strategy and New Ventures

In addition to strategies that must be tailored for the particular needs and circumstances in emerging economies, specialized strategies are also required for the international management activities of entrepreneurial and new-venture firms. Most international management activities take place within the context of medium-large MNCs, but, increasingly, small and medium companies, often in the form of new ventures, are getting involved in international management. This has been made possible by advances in telecommunication and Internet technologies and by greater efficiencies and lower costs in shipping, allowing firms that were previously limited to local or national markets to access international customers. These new access channels, however, suggest particular strategies that must be customized and tailored to the unique situations and resource limitations of small, entrepreneurial firms.[104]

International Entrepreneurship **International entrepreneurship** has been defined as "a combination of innovative, proactive, and risk-seeking behavior that crosses national borders and is intended to create value in organizations."[105] The internationalization of the marketplace and the increasing number of entrepreneurial firms in the global economy have created new opportunities for small and new-venture firms to accelerate internationalization. This international entrepreneurial activity is being observed in even the smallest and newest organizations. Indeed, one study among 57 privately held Finnish electronics firms during the mid-1990s showed that firms that internationalize after they are established domestically must overcome a number of barriers to that international expansion, such as their domestic orientation, internal domestic political ties, and domestic decision-making inertia. In contrast, firms that internationalize earlier face fewer barriers to learning about the international environment.[106] Thus, the earlier in its existence that an innovative firm internationalizes, the faster it is likely to grow both overall and in foreign markets.

> **international entrepreneurship**
> A combination of innovative, proactive, and risk-seeking behavior that crosses national boundaries and is intended to create value in organizations.

However, despite this new access, there remain limitations to international entrepreneurial activities. In another study, researchers show that deploying a technological learning advantage internationally is no simple process. They studied more than 300 private independent and corporate new ventures based in the United States. Building on past research about the advantages of large, established multinational enterprises, their results from 12 high-technology industries show that greater diversity of national environments is associated with increased technological learning opportunities even for new ventures, whose internationalization is usually thought to be limited.[107] In addition, the breadth, depth, and speed of technological learning from varied international environments is significantly enhanced by formal organizational efforts to integrate knowledge throughout a firm such as cross-functional teams and formal analysis of both successful and failed projects. Further, the research shows that venture performance (growth and return on equity) is improved by technological learning gained from international environments.

International New Ventures and "Born-Global" Firms Another dimension of the growth of international entrepreneurial activities is the increasing incidence of international new ventures, or **born-global firms**—firms that engage in significant international activity a short time after being established. Building on an empirical study of small firms in Norway and France, researchers found that more than half of the exporting firms established there since 1990 could be classified as "born globals."[108] Examining the differences between newly established firms with high or low export involvement levels revealed that a decision maker's global orientation and market conditions are important factors.

> **born-global firms**
> Firms that engage in significant international activities a short time after being established.

Another study highlighted the critical role of innovative culture, as well as knowledge and capabilities, in this unique breed of international, entrepreneurial firms. An analysis of case studies and surveys revealed key strategies that engender international success among these innovative firms.[109] Successful born-global firms leverage a distinctive mix of orientations and strategies that allow them to succeed in diverse international markets. Their possession of the foundational capabilities of international entrepreneurial orientation and international marketing orientation engender the development of a specific collection of organizational strategies. The most important business strategies employed by born-global firms are global technological competence, unique-products development, quality focus, and leveraging of foreign distributor competences.[110]

There is a difference between born-global firms and born-international firms, as one study showed. Born-international firms tend to export products close to markets, and revenues from these outside markets contribute 25 percent or less of total revenues. Truly born-global firms, however, tend to distribute goods to distant markets in multiple regions, and revenues from international activities tend to surpass 25 percent. It has been found that truly born-global firms tend to survive longer than other seemingly global companies.[111] However, being born global can simply be seen as accelerated internationalization. Another study compared born-global firms to those which sought out joint ventures or acquisitions (see Chapter 9) as a method to expand internationally. Results showed that while the market responds more positively to joint ventures or "partnerships," the extent to which a born-global is successful greatly depends on how developed the area is that the company is moving into. In other words, while the market appreciates already established firms because they are familiar, if a start-up does not have the capital to partner with well-known organizations and the international markets are open, then born-global companies may show slightly lower returns in the beginning, but this is not an indicator of survival or ultimate success.[112]

One clear example of a born-global firm is California-based Amazon.com. Like most U.S. Internet firms, Amazon.com has been able to distribute its products and services on an international scale from the outset. Although differing levels of cultural similarities and technological sophistication impact Amazon's potential for success internationally, the Internet as a medium has removed certain entry barriers that have historically restricted quick market entry.[113] Another example is New York–based online trading and investing services E*Trade. The company was able to bring in revenues from 33 countries in only three years, clearly making it a global brand. Allowing customers to actively participate in their investments while offering multilingual technical and professional customer support allowed E*Trade to integrate its services in many countries. The simplified website does not bombard consumers with extraneous information, and allows each person to trade as much or as little as desired, making it inherently customized. It has not been a success story for its entire existence, however. The company was in danger of being left behind when it could not get out of the red, but in 2005, the company was able to become profitable due to the low cost of Internet business and its extremely diverse customer base. Although it had its ups and downs in the following years, it survived the financial crisis with fewer problems than many "bricks and mortar" brokerages.

The Internet clearly provides one of the easiest and most efficient methods of becoming global quickly, but it is important that awareness is brought to the business, or it too can be lost in the digital maze of the World Wide Web.[114] Now more than ever, born-global as a corporate strategy is becoming more attractive and less risky. The opening World of International Management feature of Chapter 11 provides a discussion of the globalization and strategy of two online retailers.

■ The World of International Management—Revisited

Recall the World of International Management's discussion of the pharma industry that opened this chapter. It is easy to see why pharmaceutical companies are expanding globally and reshaping their business strategies accordingly. Large, traditional pharmaceutical companies are facing pressures from a range of quarters, including new competition from emerging markets. These firms are attempting to lower costs by collaborating with or merging with generic companies, diversifying their product portfolio to provide more consistent revenue streams, investing in newer higher value-added compounds that require biologic expertise, and leveraging their research and development across products and geographies. This is truly an industry in transition, with globalization itself as a major driver of the transformation.

Drawing on your understanding of the need for and the benefits of strategic management, answer these questions: (1) Which imperative is likely to be relatively most important to MNCs in the coming decade: economic, political, or quality? (2) When MNCs scan the environment, what are two key areas for consideration that they must address? (3) Choose one of the pharma companies mentioned in the chapter's opening World of International Management. How would you characterize its strategy within the globalization–national responsiveness framework? (4) Which FSAs and CSAs does it primarily rely upon? To what extent does the company use a "base-of-pyramid approach"? How would it affect the company if low-income markets turned out to be a bust?

SUMMARY OF KEY POINTS

1. There is a growing need for strategic management among MNCs. Some of the primary reasons include: foreign direct investment is increasing; planning is needed to coordinate and integrate increasingly diverse operations via an overall focus; and emerging international challenges require strategic planning.

2. A strategic plan can take on an economic focus, a political focus, a quality focus, an administrative coordination focus, or some variation of the four. The global integration–national responsiveness framework defines the four basic strategies employed by MNCs: international, global, multi-domestic, and transnational. Although transnational is often the preferred strategy, it is also the most difficult to implement.

3. Strategy formulation consists of several steps. First, the MNC carries out external environmental scanning to identify opportunities and threats. Next, the firm conducts an internal resource analysis of company strengths and weaknesses. Strategic goals then are formulated in light of the results of these external and internal analyses.

4. Strategy implementation is the process of providing goods and services in accord with the predetermined plan of action. This implementation typically involves such considerations as deciding where to locate operations, carrying out an entry and ownership strategy, and using functional strategies to implement the plan. Functional strategies focus on marketing, production, and finance.

5. Strategies for emerging markets and international entrepreneurship/new ventures may require specialized approaches targeted to these unique circumstances.

KEY TERMS

administrative coordination, *282*

base of the pyramid strategy, *296*

born-global firms, *301*

economic imperative, *279*

environmental scanning, *286*

global integration, *283*

global strategy, *284*

international entrepreneurship, *301*

international strategy, *285*

key success factor (KSF), *288*

multi-domestic strategy, *285*

national responsiveness, *283*

political imperative, *280*

quality imperative, *281*

strategic management, *277*

strategy implementation, *290*

transnational strategy, *285*

REVIEW AND DISCUSSION QUESTIONS

1. Of the four imperatives discussed in this chapter—economic, political, quality, and administration—which would be most important to IBM in its efforts to make inroads in the Pacific Rim market? Would this emphasis be the same as that in the United States, or would IBM be giving primary attention to one of the other imperatives? Explain.

2. Define global integration as used in the context of strategic international management. In what way might globalization be a problem for a successful national organization that is intent on going international? In your answer, provide an example of the problem.

3. Some international management experts contend that globalization and national responsiveness are diametrically opposed forces, and that to accommodate one, a multinational must relax its efforts in the other. In what way is this an accurate statement? In what way is it incomplete or inaccurate?

4. Consider that both a retail chain and a manufacturing company want to expand overseas. What environmental factors would have the most impact on these companies? What ratio of environmental scanning to internal analysis should each employ? What key factors of success differentiate the two?

5. Anheuser-Busch is attempting to expand in India, where beer is not widely consumed and liquor dominates the market. What areas should be targeted for strategic goals? What could be some marketing implications in the Indian market?

6. What particular conditions that MNCs face in emerging markets may require specialized strategies?

What strategies might be most appropriate in response? How might a company identify opportunities at the "base of the pyramid" (i.e., low-income markets)?

7. What conditions have allowed some firms to be born global? What are some examples of born-global companies?

8. Mercedes changed its U.S. strategy by announcing that it is developing cars for the $30,000 to $45,000 price range (as well as its typical upper-end cars). What might have accounted for this change in strategy? In your answer, include a discussion of the implications from the standpoints of marketing, production, and finance.

INTERNET EXERCISE: INFOSYS'S GLOBAL STRATEGY

Infosys is one of the world's largest IT service providers. It started in India but has rapidly expanded around the world. It offers consulting services, outsourcing, data storage, and other informational management services to all industries. Go to Infosys's website and review the various services it offers. Then answer these questions: How do you think international strategic management is reflected in what you see on the website? What major strategic planning steps would Infosys need to carry out in order to remain a world leader with such diverse offerings? What potential threat, if it occurred, would prove most disastrous for Infosys, and what could the company do to deal with the possibility of this negative development?

Poland

Poland is the sixth-largest country in Europe. It is bordered by Germany, the Czech Republic, and Slovakia in the west and south and by the former Soviet Union republics of Ukraine in the south, Belarus in the east, and Lithuania in the northeast. The northwest section of the country is located on the Baltic Sea. Named after the Polane, a Slavic tribe that lived more than a thousand years ago, Poland has beautiful countryside and rapidly growing cities. Rolling hills and rugged mountains rise in southern Poland.

In 2012, there were approximately 38 million Poles, and GDP was around $514 billion. A shift to industry and services has made Poland attractive to MNCs. There are many facets that make Poland attractive, one of which is that the central location to other European countries provides MNCs with easy access to competitive markets nearby. A policy of economic liberalization, which Poland has been pursuing since 1990, has converted the country that had not been known for ranking high in business into a success story among transition economies.

Despite continuing problems, the Poles have made some progress in establishing a viable economy. Poland has proven to be very attractive for U.S. investors; in the last 20 years, U.S. companies have poured over US$20 billion in the country. There are approximately 350 U.S. firms that have offices, factories, joint ventures, or subsidiaries on Polish ground. A basis for foreign cooperation is the broad consensus across political lines, which welcomes foreign direct investment. Many incentives to attract new firms that can bring capital, technology, and jobs to Poland are offered by the government. Poland's economy has performed considerably better than its Eastern and Central European neighbors, especially during difficult economic times such as the 2009–2010 global recession and subsequent slowdown in Europe.

To take advantage of this economic situation, a medium-sized Canadian manufacturing firm has begun thinking about renovating a plant near Warsaw and building small power tools for the expanding Central and Eastern European market. The company's logic is fairly straightforward. There appears to be no competition in this niche, because there has been little demand for power tools in this area. As the postcommunist countries continue to struggle in their transition to a market economy, they will have to increase their productivity if they hope to compete with Western European nations. Small power tools are one of the products they will need to accomplish this goal.

Other than the relatively open market, why would Poland seem so attractive to U.S. and Canadian companies? The people of Poland have a great deal to offer. The highly educated populace includes a great many individuals who are multilingual and are extremely hard working, second only to Korea in hours worked per year. Furthermore, low labor costs in a country where almost 13 percent of the people are still unemployed are a huge incentive. Poland also has a vast modern transportation system including seaports, major airports, railroad systems, and roadways. The government attempts to bring in new companies by offering grants or tax exemptions. While the Canadian firm considers moving the manufacturing of small power tools to Poland, it might be favorably impressed by the vast and successful R&D projects that are in progress in the country, including institutions such as Siemens, Avio, IBM, Intel, Motorola, GlaxoSmithKline, and more.

There likely will be little competition for the Canadian firm for the next couple of years, because small power tools do not carry a very large markup and no other manufacturer is attempting to tap what the Canadian firm views as "an emerging market for the 21st century." However, a final decision on this matter is going to have to wait until the company has made a thorough evaluation of the market and the competitive nature of the industry.

www.poland.pl, www.buyusa.gov, www.infoplease.com/ipa

Questions

1. What are some current issues facing Poland? What is the climate for doing business in Poland today?
2. Is the Canadian manufacturing firm using an economic, political, or quality imperative approach to strategy?
3. How should the firm carry out the environmental scanning process? Would the process be of any practical value?
4. What are two key factors that will be important if this project is to succeed?

Chapter 9

ENTRY STRATEGIES AND ORGANIZATIONAL STRUCTURES

The World of *International Management*

Volkswagen's Comeback: Aligning Strategy and Structure

In the fiercely competitive global automotive industry, Volkswagen has pursued an ongoing global strategy that emphasizes both centralization and regional adaptation and leverages the range of capabilities from its various brands and their production. The Volkswagen Group makes 245 models of passenger cars, trucks, and buses under 10 brands. In 2012, it sold 9.3 million vehicles in 153 countries on five continents, adding more than 1 million passenger cars over 2011 and catapulting it ahead of both General Motors and Toyota to become the largest automaker in the world.[1] Despite the tough global environment for automotive sales, especially in Europe, VW's home base, the Volkswagen Group outperformed the market in 2012, growing in almost all key regions. Deliveries of all vehicles climbed 12.2 percent, increasing the Group's global share of the passenger car market to 12.8 percent from 12.3 percent in the prior year. Volkswagen's revenue increased by 20.9 percent in fiscal year 2012 to €192.7 billion from the previous year's €159.3 billion. Like many leading automotive companies, including Ford, GM, and Toyota, VW operates a joint venture in China that generated a €3.7 billion (€2.6 billion) share of the 2012 operating profit.[2] In 2013, VW extended its lead over its rivals in market share for passenger vehicles and trucks through its many brands, including the Volkswagen Passenger Cars brand; the Audi brand; ŠKODA, a car and truck manufacturer; SEAT, an entry level vehicle brand; Bentley, the luxury car maker; sports car manufacturer Porsche; the Commercial Vehicles group; Scania, a truck maker; and a financial services group.[3]

Despite these successes, as recently as 2007, VW was facing severe challenges with slow sales, meager margins, and no clear global strategy. What factors led to the impressive comeback?

First VW, which had always had solid technology, sought to better integrate technological development with production. Beginning in the early 1990s, VW has increasingly perfected the "world car" strategy of producing platforms that can be used in multiple brands, while retaining the uniqueness and cache of those individual brands.[4] This approach can be challenging, with the potential of undermining the luster of the higher end counterpart. VW, however, has struck this balance better than any other assembler, allowing tremendous scale economies while

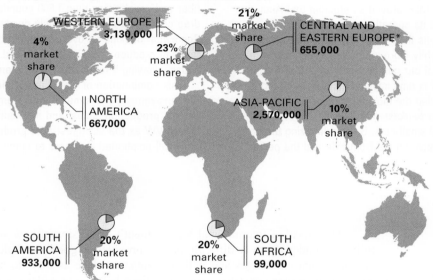

Volkswagen Sales Around the World
Passenger-car and light-commercial-vehicle deliveries in 2011

WESTERN EUROPE
3,130,000

4% market share

23% market share

21% market share

CENTRAL AND EASTERN EUROPE*
655,000

NORTH AMERICA
667,000

ASIA-PACIFIC
2,570,000

10% market share

SOUTH AMERICA
933,000

20% market share

20% market share

SOUTH AFRICA
99,000

*Includes Turkey units number: unshown remaining markets: 106,000 units.
Source: Volkswagen group

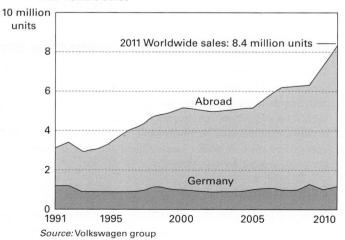

_VW_ Vehicle Sales

10 million units

2011 Worldwide sales: 8.4 million units

Abroad

Germany

1991   1995   2000   2005   2010

Source: Volkswagen group

maintaining brand identity. Since then, this approach—which combines global integration with local responsiveness—has allowed it to realize tremendous economies among cars of a similar vehicle class—subcompact, compact, and so on—by putting different bodies, or "hats," on identical chassis platforms. For example, the A3, produced in Gyor, Hungary, uses the same chassis as the Golf. More than any other strategy, this has allowed VW to realize cost savings while pushing distinctive models to the regions and markets that most demand them.[5]

In 2007 the company launched what it calls its modular longitudinal matrix (MLB) for large cars. It enabled the automaker to use the same key components (VW calls them assembly kits) in 16 new vehicles. For example, Audi could now build its entire product line with the same parts. It was separated from lesser brands by the creation of a unique upper structure, with "plug and play" inner pressings that made variations in body style possible with a minimum of additional parts. The MLB proved so efficient that Audi was able to nearly double its operating profit in 2011 and achieve higher margins than either BMW or Mercedes. "We may have a slightly more intensive relationship with our cars than some of our competitors," says Volkswagen CEO Winterkorn. VW is now implementing an even more ambitious system called the modular transverse matrix, or MQB (*modularer Querbaukasten* in German) that will be used in more than 40 small cars. By standardizing the parts in the critical area between the front axle and the pedals

that represent 60 percent of a car's cost, VW can use the same transmission, front axle, steering, heating, air conditioning, and ventilation system. MQB is flexible enough to accommodate a wide range of wheelbases, track widths, and wheel sizes that previously were immovable, giving designers more flexibility. When the integration of MQB is complete, it will underpin more than 7 million units across VW's brands, providing unequaled scale and cost advantages. VW figures that standardization will cut product development costs by 20 percent, parts costs by another 20 percent, and production time by 30 percent. Add it all up and the analysts at Société Générale believe the annual savings could reach $3 billion, or about $500 per car.[6]

Although VW emphasizes efficiency, it also stresses distinctiveness. Part of this distinctiveness is a concurrent emphasis on efficiency and sustainability as part of the same imperative. It is working on a "radical" new vehicle known by the code name XL1. The vehicle is built of carbon fiber and weighs less than 1,800 pounds and has a lower drag coefficient than any vehicle currently on the market.[7] Somewhat bucking an overall trend in the industry, VW tends to produce much of its parts and components in-house, allowing it to maintain control and materials flow.[8]

This combination of global integration and local responsiveness, and simultaneous commitment to global design, production, sales, and marketing integration, leaves VW as the strongest auto producer in the world and well-positioned for years to come.[9]

The World of International Management's discussion of how Volkswagen successfully rebounded from a difficult period provides a good example of the entry and organizational challenges and options companies face as they do business around the world. Volkswagen centralizes some functions but also provides considerable autonomy to individual bands as they focus on particular geographies. It also demonstrates the necessity of using joint ventures to enter some markets such as China, where overt and implicit expectations make JVs a must. In this chapter we review the basic entry strategies and organizational structures available to firms as they expand their global reach.

■ Entry Strategies and Ownership Structures

There are a number of common entry strategies and ownership structures in international operations. The most common entry approaches are wholly owned subsidiaries, mergers and acquisitions, alliances and joint ventures, licensing agreements, franchising, and basic export and import operations. Depending on the situation, any one of these can be a very effective way to implement an MNC's strategy. We first look at exporting and importing, since it is not only one of the oldest approaches, but one that requires the least investment by the MNC.

Export/Import

As noted in the discussion in Chapter 8 on international entrepreneurship and new ventures, exporting and importing often are the only available choices for small and new firms wanting to go international.[10] These choices also provide an avenue for larger firms that want to begin their international expansion with minimum investment and risk. The paperwork associated with documentation and foreign-currency exchange can be turned over to an export management company to handle, or the firm can handle things itself by creating its own export department. Additionally, the firm can turn to major banks or other specialists that, for a fee, will provide a variety of services, including letters of credit, currency conversion, and related financial assistance.

A number of potential problems face firms that plan to export. For example, if a foreign distributor does not work out well, some countries have strict rules about dropping that distributor. So an MNC with a contractual agreement with a distributor could be stuck with that distributor. On the other hand, if the firm decides to get more actively involved, it may make direct investments in marketing facilities, such as warehouses, sales offices, and transportation equipment, without making a direct investment in manufacturing facilities overseas.

When importing goods, many MNCs source products from a wide range of suppliers from all over the world. It is common to find U.S. firms purchasing supplies and components from Korea, Taiwan, and Hong Kong. In Europe, there is so much trade between EU countries that the entire process seldom is regarded as "international" in focus by the MNCs that are involved.

Exporting and importing can provide easy access to overseas markets; however, the strategy usually is transitional in nature. If the firm wishes to continue doing business internationally, it will need to get more actively involved in terms of investment and take on new risks.

Wholly Owned Subsidiary

Increasing in risk and involvement, a **wholly owned subsidiary** is an overseas operation that is totally owned and controlled by an MNC. This option is often pursued by smaller companies, especially if international or transaction costs, such as the cost of negotiating and transferring information, are high.[11] When MNCs make an initial investment in the form of a wholly owned subsidiary in a foreign country, it is sometimes referred to as "greenfield" or de novo (new) investment.

> **wholly owned subsidiary**
> An overseas operation that is totally owned and controlled by an MNC.

The primary reason for the use of wholly owned subsidiaries is a desire by the MNC for total control and the belief that managerial efficiency will be better without outside partners. Due to the sole ownership, it has been found that profits can be higher with this venture and that there are clearer communications and shared visions. However, there are some drawbacks. Typically, wholly owned subsidiaries face a high risk with such a large investment in one area and are not very efficient with entering multiple countries or markets. This can also lead to low international integration or multinational involvement.[12] Furthermore, host countries often feel that the MNC is trying to gain economic control by setting up local operations but refusing to include local partners. Some countries are concerned that the MNC will drive out local enterprises as opposed to helping develop them. In dealing with these concerns, many newly developing countries prohibit wholly owned subsidiaries. Another drawback is that home-country unions sometimes oppose the creation of foreign subsidiaries, which they see as an attempt to "export jobs," particularly when the MNC exports goods to another country and then decides to set up manufacturing operations there. As a result, today many multinationals opt for a merger, alliance, or joint venture rather than a wholly owned subsidiary.[13]

Mergers/Acquisitions

In recent years, a growing number of multinationals have acquired (fully or in part) their subsidiaries through **mergers/acquisitions**. MNCs may choose this route in order to quickly expand resources or construct high-profit products in a new market.[14] Purchasing a majority interest in another company is an expedient way to expand. A recent example of a sizeable cross-border acquisition was GDF Suez's purchase of International Power plc (see Table 9–1, which shows the top M&A deals in 2011). International Power plc, a British power company, has invested significant resources in emerging markets across Asia and South America. Many of these investments will begin reaping profits by 2017. With

> **merger/acquisition**
> The cross-border purchase or exchange of equity involving two or more companies.

Table 9–1
Completed Cross-Border M&A Deals Worth over $3 Billion in 2011

Rank	Value ($ billion)	Acquired Company	Host Economy	Industry of the Acquired Company	Acquiring Company	Home Economy	Industry of the Acquiring Company	Shares Acquired (percent)
1	25.1	International Power PLC	United Kingdom	Electric services	GDF Suez SA	France	Natural gas transmission	100
2	22.4	Weather Investments Srl	Italy	Telephone communications, except radiotelephone	VimpelCom Ltd	Netherlands	Radiotelephone communications	100
3	21.2	Genzyme Corp	United States	Biological products, except diagnostic substances	Sanofi-Aventis SA	France	Pharmaceutical preparations	100
4	13.7	Nycomed International Management GmbH	Switzerland	Pharmaceutical preparations	Takeda Pharmaceutical Co Ltd	Japan	Pharmaceutical preparations	100
5	11.8	Petrohawk Energy Corp	United States	Crude petroleum and natural gas	BHP Billiton PLC	United Kingdom	Steel works, blast furnaces, and rolling mills	100
6	10.8	Foster's Group Ltd	Australia	Malt beverages	SABMiller Beverage Investments Pty Ltd	Australia	Investors, nec	100
7	9.4	Centro Properties Group-US Property Portfolio	United States	Land subdividers and developers, except cemeteries	BRE Retail Holdings Inc	United States	Real estate investment trusts	100
8	9.0	Reliance Industries Ltd-21 Oil & Gas Blocks	India	Crude petroleum and natural gas	BP PLC	United Kingdom	Oil and gas field exploration services	30
9	8.5	Skype Global Sarl	Luxembourg	Prepackaged software	Microsoft Corp	United States	Prepackaged software	100
10	7.8	Morgan Stanley	United States	Offices of bank holding companies	Mitsubishi UFJ Financial Group Inc	Japan	Banks	22
11	7.4	Equinox Minerals Ltd	Australia	Copper ores	Barrick Canada Inc	Canada	Gold ores	98
12	7.3	Pride International Inc	United States	Drilling oil and gas wells	Ensco PLC	United Kingdom	Drilling oil and gas wells	100
13	7.2	Danisco A/S	Denmark	Food preparations, nec	DuPont Denmark Holding ApS	Denmark	Offices of holding companies, nec	100
14	7.1	AXA Asia Pacific Holdings Ltd	Australia	Life insurance	AMP Ltd	Australia	Investment advice	54
15	6.6	Polkomtel SA	Poland	Radiotelephone communications	Spartan Capital Holdings Sp zoo	Poland	Investment offices, nec	100
16	6.5	Central Networks PLC	United Kingdom	Electric services	PPL Corp	United States	Electric services	100

Rank	Value ($ billion)	Acquired Company	Host Economy	Industry of the Acquired Company	Acquiring Company	Home Economy	Industry of the Acquiring Company	Shares Acquired (percent)
17	6.3	Cephalon Inc	United States	Pharmaceutical preparations	Teva Pharmaceutical Industries Ltd	Israel	Pharmaceutical preparations	100
18	6.3	Chrysler Financial Corp	United States	Personal credit institutions	TD Bank NA	United States	National commercial banks	100
19	6.3	OAO "Polyus Zoloto"	Russian Federation	Gold ores	KazakhGold Group Ltd	Kazakhstan	Gold ores	73
20	6.0	AXA Asia Pacific Holdings Ltd	Australia	Life insurance	AMP Ltd	Australia	Investment advice	46
21	5.6	Bank Zachodni WBK SA	Poland	Banks	Banco Santander SA	Spain	Banks	96
22	5.5	Vivo Participacoes SA	Brazil	Radiotelephone communications	Telecommunicacoes de Sao Paulo SA	Brazil	Telephone communications, except radiotelephone	100
23	5.5	OAO "Polimetall"	Russian Federation	Gold ores	PMTL Holding Ltd	Jersey	Offices of holding companies, nec	83
24	5.4	Anglo American Sur SA	Chile	Copper ores	Mitsubishi Corp	Japan	Chemicals and chemical preparations, nec	25
25	5.1	Kinetic Concepts Inc	United States	Surgical and medical instruments and apparatus	Chiron Holdings Inc	United States	Investment offices, nec	100
26	5.0	Cia Espanola de Petroleos SA {CEPSA}	Spain	Crude petroleum and natural gas	International Petroleum Investment Co{IPIC}	United Arab Emirates	Investors, nec	49
27	4.9	Macarthur Coal Ltd	Australia	Coal mining services	PEAMCoal Pty Ltd	Australia	Investment offices, nec	100
28	4.9	Vale SA-Aluminum Operations	Brazil	Iron ores	Norsk Hydro ASA	Norway	Crude petroleum and natural gas	100
29	4.9	Shell International Petroleum Co Ltd-Brazilian Assets	Brazil	Industrial organic chemicals, nec	Cosan SA Industria e Comercio- Brazilian Assets	Brazil	Petroleum and petroleum products wholesalers, nec	100
30	4.8	AIG Star Life Insurance Co Ltd	Japan	Life insurance	Prudential Financial Inc	United States	Life insurance	100
31	4.8	Chesapeake Energy Corp- Fayetteville Shale Assets	United States	Crude petroleum and natural gas	BHP Billiton Ltd	Australia	Copper ores	100
32	4.7	Tognum AG	Germany	Internal combustion engines, nec	Engine Holding GmbH	Germany	Investors, nec	98
33	4.7	Nuon NV	Netherlands	Electric services	Vattenfall AB	Sweden	Electric services	15

(continued)

Table 9–1
Completed Cross-Border M&A Deals Worth over $3 Billion in 2011 *(continued)*

Rank	Value ($ billion)	Acquired Company	Host Economy	Industry of the Acquired Company	Acquiring Company	Home Economy	Industry of the Acquiring Company	Shares Acquired (percent)
34	4.6	Rhodia SA	France	Manmade organic fibers, except cellulosic	Solvay SA	Belgium	Plastics materials and synthetic resins	100
35	4.5	Porsche Holding GmbH	Austria	Automobiles and other motor vehicles	Volkswagen AG	Germany	Motor vehicles and passenger car bodies	100
36	4.5	Cairn India Ltd	India	Crude petroleum and natural gas	Vedanta Resources PLC	United Kingdom	Copper ores	30
37	4.5	Musketeer GmbH	Germany	Cable and other pay television services	UPC Germany HoldCo 2 GmbH	Germany	Offices of holding companies, nec	100
38	4.4	Consolidated Thompson Iron Mines Ltd	Canada	Iron ores	Cliffs Natural Resources Inc	United States	Iron ores	100
39	4.2	OAO "Pervaya Gruzovaya Kompaniya"	Russian Federation	Railroads, line-haul operating	OOO "Nezavisimaya Transportnaya Kompaniya"	Russian Federation	Courier services, except by air	75
40	4.1	Marshall & Ilsley Corp, Milwaukee,Wisconsin	United States	National commercial banks	Bank of Montreal, Ontario, Canada	Canada	Banks	100
41	4.0	OAO "Novatek"	Russian Federation	Crude petroleum and natural gas	Total SA	France	Crude petroleum and natural gas	12
42	3.9	Riversdale Mining Ltd	Australia	Bituminous coal and lignite surface mining	Rio Tinto PLC	United Kingdom	Gold ores	100
43	3.9	Baldor Electric Co	United States	Motors and generators	ABB Ltd	Switzerland	Switchgear, switchboard equip	90
44	3.8	Alberto-Culver Co	United States	Perfumes, cosmetics, and other toilet preparations	Unilever PLC	United Kingdom	Food preparations, nec	100
45	3.8	Northumbrian Water Group PLC	United Kingdom	Water supply	UK Water(2011)Ltd	United Kingdom	Investment offices, nec	100
46	3.8	Turkiye Garanti Bankasi AS	Turkey	Banks	Banco Bilbao Vizcaya Argentaria SA{BBVA}	Spain	Banks	19
47	3.8	OAO "Vimm-Bill'-Dann Produkty Pitaniya"	Russian Federation	Fluid milk	Pepsi-Cola (Bermuda) Ltd	Bermuda	Bottled & canned soft drinks & carbonated waters	66
48	3.8	Universal Studios Holding III Corp	United States	Television broadcasting stations	General Electric Co {GE}	United States	Power, distribution, and specialty transformers	62

Rank	Value ($ billion)	Acquired Company	Host Economy	Industry of the Acquired Company	Acquiring Company	Home Economy	Industry of the Acquiring Company	Shares Acquired (percent)
49	3.6	ING Groep NV-Insurance & Pension Operations,Latin America	Mexico	Insurance agents, brokers, and service	Investor Group	Colombia	Investors, nec	100
50	3.6	Parmalat SpA	Italy	Fluid milk	Investor Group	France	Investors, nec	52
51	3.6	Talecris Biotherapeutics Holdings Corp	United States	Pharmaceutical preparations	Grifols SA	Spain	Pharmaceutical preparations	100
52	3.5	EMI Group PLC	United Kingdom	Services allied to motion picture production	Citigroup Inc	United States	National commercial banks	100
53	3.5	Phadia AB	Sweden	Surgical and medical instruments and apparatus	Thermo Fisher Scientific Inc	United States	Measuring & controlling devices	100
54	3.5	Frac Tech Holdings LLC	United States	Oil and gas field services, nec	Investor Group	Singapore	Investors, nec	70
55	3.4	Securitas Direct AB	Sweden	Security systems services	Investor Group	United States	Investors, nec	100
56	3.3	Hutchison Essar Ltd	India	Telephone communications, except radiotelephone	Vodafone Group PLC	United Kingdom	Radiotelephone communications	22
57	3.3	GDF Suez SA-Exploration and Production Business Operations	France	Electric services	China Investment Corp {CIC}	China	Management investment offices, open-end	30
58	3.2	Converteam Group SAS	France	Motors and generators	GE Energy	United States	Turbines and turbine generator sets	90
59	3.1	Distribuidora Internacional de Alimentacion SA{Dia}	Spain	Grocery stores	Shareholders	France	Investors, nec	100
60	3.1	Peregrino Project,Campos Basin	Brazil	Crude petroleum and natural gas	Sinochem Group	China	Crude petroleum and natural gas	40
61	3.0	SPIE SA	France	Electrical work	Investor Group	United States	Investors, nec	100
62	3.0	Global Crossing Ltd	Bermuda	Telephone communications, except radiotelephone	Level 3 Communications Inc	United States	Telephone communications, except radiotelephone	100

Source: Global Finance Magazine, *Cross-border M&A deals over US$3 billion - 2011. Data gathered from UNCTAD, World Investment Report 2012,* (http://www.gfmag.com/tools/global-database/economic-data/).

the aim of expanding its reach within these growing economies, GDF Suez originally acquired 70 percent of International Power in 2011. Increased success from this initial purchase led GDF Suez to purchase the remaining 30 percent in 2012. GDF Suez expects profits to grow by as much as 9 percent annually due to the acquisition.[15] At the same time, the record of success for cross-border mergers is decidedly mixed.

Cultural differences (see Chapter 6) and time constraints are the two most pervasive barriers.[16] Even before agreements are reached, time is of great concern. While managers do not want to force negotiations or rush a potential subsidiary's decision, waiting too long could result in missed opportunities due to bids from competitors or a rapid change in the market. Once a merger or acquisition occurs, managers may find it difficult to clearly communicate new operational goals to the foreign subsidiary, which not only highlights cultural differences but also adds time and risk to a company's activities.

Transition costs also pose a problem in the postmerger environment. In 2006, French telecommunication company Alcatel merged with U.S. telecommunication company Lucent in an $11.6 billion deal. Alcatel-Lucent, which provides hardware, software, and services in the telecommunication industry, did not turn a profit until 2011, five years after the merger. Since the merger, the stock price of the company has dropped 87 percent, and Alcatel-Lucent has spent billions in free cash on restructuring efforts. This counteracted the original purpose of the merger, namely to deflect worldwide competition, since other companies such as Ericsson had been experiencing a gain in profits and were then better equipped to weaken the already stumbling newborn. Alcatel-Lucent attributes the loss to postmerger complications due to heavy investments which were necessary to migrate customer networks. The future of this company is bleak for the moment, as the company lost US$1.85 billion in the fourth quarter of 2012. Managers need to be wary of such common complications and attempt to move forward by enhancing communication and operational efficiency.[17, 18]

Alliances and Joint Ventures

alliance
Any type of cooperative relationship among different firms.

joint venture (JV)
An agreement under which two or more partners own or control a business.

An **alliance** is any type of cooperative relationship among two or more different firms. An international alliance is composed of two or more firms from different countries. Some alliances are temporary; others are more permanent. A **joint venture (JV)** can be considered a specific type of alliance agreement under which two or more partners own or control a business. An international joint venture (IJV) is a JV composed of two or more firms from different countries. Alliances and joint ventures can take a number of different forms, including cross-marketing arrangements, technology-sharing agreements, production-contracting deals, and equity agreements. In some instances, two parties may create a third, independent entity expressly for the purpose of developing a collaborative relationship outside their core operations. Just like mergers and acquisitions, alliances and joint ventures can pose substantial managerial challenges. We discuss some of these at the end of the chapter and again in Chapter 10.

There are two types of alliances and joint ventures. The first type is the nonequity venture, which is characterized by one group's merely providing a service for another. The group providing the service typically is more active than the other. Examples include a consulting firm that is hired to provide analysis and evaluation and then make its recommendations, an engineering or construction firm that contracts to design or build a dam or series of apartment complexes in an undeveloped area of a partner's country, or a mining firm that has an agreement to extract a natural resource in the other party's country.

The second type is the equity joint venture, which involves a financial investment by the MNC parties involved. Many variations of this arrangement adjust the degree of control that each of the parties will have and the amount of money, technological expertise, and managerial expertise each will contribute to the JV.[19]

Most MNCs are more interested in the amount of control they will have over the venture rather than their share of the profits. Similarly, local partners feel the same way, which can result in problems. Nevertheless, alliances and joint ventures have become very popular in recent years because of the significant operational benefits they offer to both parties. Some of the most commonly cited advantages include:

1. *Improvement of efficiency.* The creation of an alliance or JV can help the partners achieve economies of scale and scope that would be difficult for one firm operating alone to accomplish. Additionally, the partners can spread the risks among themselves and profit from the synergies that arise from the complementary resources.[20]

2. *Access to knowledge.* In alliances and JVs each partner has access to the knowledge and skills of the others. So one partner may bring financial and technological resources to the venture while another brings knowledge of the customer and market channels.

3. *Mitigating political factors.* A local partner can be very helpful in dealing with political risk factors such as a hostile government or restrictive legislation.

4. *Overcoming collusion or restriction in competition.* Alliances and JVs can help partners overcome the effects of local collusion or limits being put on foreign competition by becoming part of an "insider" group.[21]

As noted above, alliance and JV partners often complement each other and can thus reduce the risks associated with their operations and entering a foreign market. A good example is European truck manufacturing and auto component industries. Firms in both groups have found that the high cost of developing and building their products can be offset through joint ventures.

One industry that has been very active in cross-border alliances is airlines. These alliances have been prompted by slow growth in some markets, increased global competition, and the competitive dynamics among domestic and global carriers. In 2013, British Airways of the UK, Iberia of Spain, and American Airlines of the United States expanded their existing alliance with the addition of Finnair, headquartered in Finland.[22] The original alliance, formed in 2010, was prompted, in part, by the merger of Air France and KLM. Each carrier maintains its brand identity, with Iberia and British Airways owned under new British-Spanish holding company, International Airlines Group.[23] The structure mirrors those used by Air France and Lufthansa in their European acquisitions.[24] In general, airlines are discouraged from formal alliances because of concerns about collusion and price-fixing, but many airlines have been granted waivers because of a recognition by regulatory authorities that their very survival may depend on consolidation. More broadly, the structure of the global airline industry has evolved into three large alliances in which member firms agree to code-sharing and reciprocity in their frequent flyer programs. Table 9–2 shows the major alliances, their current members, and their geographic scope and coverage.

Alliances and JVs are proving to be particularly popular as a means for doing business in emerging-market countries. For example, in the early 1990s, foreigners signed more than 3,000 joint-venture agreements in Eastern Europe and the former republics of the Soviet Union, and such interest remains high today. However, careful analysis must be undertaken to ensure that the market for the desired goods and services is sufficiently large, that all parties understand their responsibilities, and that all are in agreement regarding the overall operation of the venture. If these issues can be resolved, the venture stands a good chance of success. The International Management in Action on page 318, "Joint Venturing in Russia," illustrates some of the problems that need to be overcome in order for a JV to be successful. Some of the other suggestions that have been offered by researchers regarding participation in strategic alliances include:

1. Know your partners well before an alliance is formed.

2. Expect differences in alliance objectives among potential partners headquartered in different countries.

3. Realize that having the desired resource profiles does not guarantee that they are complementary to your firm's resources.

Table 9–2
Membership and Market Data for the Largest Airline Alliances (as of December 2012)

	Star Alliance (27 members, Founded 1997)	Sky Team (19 members, Founded 2000)	One World (13 members, Founded 1999)	Rest of Industry (selected major nonaligned carriers)
Passengers per year	649 million	506 million	303 million	
Destinations	1,293	1,000	766	
Revenue (billion US$)	160.9	97.9	89.9	
Market share	29.3%	24.6%	23.2%	22.9%
Major airlines	Air Canada (founder) Air China (2007) Air New Zealand (1999) ANA (1999) Avianca (2012) Copa Airlines (2012) Lufthansa (founder) SAS (founder) Singapore Airlines (2000) TAM Airlines (2010) United Airlines (founder) US Airways (2004)	Aeroflot (2006) Aeroméxico (founder) Air France (founder) Alitalia (2001) China Southern (2007) Delta (founder) KLM (2004) Saudia (2012)	American Airlines (founder) British Airways (founder) Cathay Pacific (founder) Iberia (1999) Japan Airlines (2007) Korean Air (founder) Qatar (2013)	JetBlue Southwest Aer Lingus Icelandair Virgin Atlantic Emirates Air India Gulf Air Qantas (founder) China Airlines Jet Airways
Network capacity				
Within North America	23%	28%	15%	34%
Within South America	1	2	14	83
Within Europe	20	16	11	53
Within Middle East	2	0	3	95
Within Africa	23	10	4	63
Within Asia	35	11	9	45
Within Oceania	11	0	32	57
Between N. America and Europe	27	34	21	18
Between N. America and S. America	9	29	40	22
Between Europe and S. America	20	28	22	30
Between N. America and Asia	41	29	10	20
Between Europe and Asia	36	22	19	23

Source: Adapted from Wikipedia, based on airline websites. www.wikipedia.com

4. Be sensitive to your alliance partner's needs.
5. After identifying the best partner, work on developing a relationship that is built on trust, an especially important variable in some cultures.[25]

Alliances, Joint Ventures, and M&A: The Case of the Automotive Industry

One industry that has been actively engaging in both alliances/JVs and mergers and acquisitions is the global automotive industry. Indeed, often alliances and joint ventures are the first step toward a merger or acquisition. In the 1970s, as domestic producers in the United States and Europe began to face competition from abroad, alliances and joint ventures were fueled in part by auto companies' desire to adapt and adjust to the changing global dynamics, especially the interest in smaller, high quality cars built by Japanese manufacturers. With periods of contraction during the recessions of the early 1990s, late 1990s, and late 2000s, producers were pressured to consolidate as a way to streamline production and cut costs. More recently, alliances, JVs, M&A have been stimulated by a range of factors, including continued overcapacity, emerging markets expansion, and demand for new types of vehicles, including hybrid and electric.[26]

As discussed in Chapter 1, Renault and Nissan maintain a broad-based alliance that includes an equity joint venture arrangement. As a result of Chrysler's bankruptcy, Fiat took a 20 percent stake in Chrysler, with plans to increase it to a majority ownership share.[27]

As discussed in this chapter's opening article, Volkswagen—like many other U.S. and European companies—entered China via a joint venture. GM has long maintained a joint venture with China's Shanghai Automotive Industries Corporation (SAIC). Fiat signed a joint venture in with GAC (Guangzhou AutomobileGroup) in 2010, forming GAC Fiat Automobiles Co., Ltd., which is an automobile manufacturing company headquartered in Changsha, China. More recently, the rising power of China and India in the global automotive industry has been made clear by the growth of brands such as Cherry and Tata, and by two recent acquisitions. On March 28, 2010, the Chinese auto company Geely bought Ford's Volvo car unit for $1.8 billion. Reuters declared the deal to be China's "biggest overseas auto purchase" which "underscores China's arrival as a major force in the global auto industry." Two years earlier, another historic deal took place. On March 26, 2008, the Indian auto company Tata bought Ford's Land Rover and Jaguar brands. Volvo, Land Rover, and Jaguar are all European brands that Ford had previously purchased.[28]

Finally, development of hybrid and electric vehicles has often taken the form of joint ventures because (a) the technologies often do not exist in traditional automotive companies, and (b) the market prospect and regulatory uncertainties are high, prompting companies to want to share risks with partners.

All of these collaborations—whether alliances, joint ventures, mergers or acquisitions—are fueled by opportunities created by integrating some combination of market knowledge and access, technological and managerial capability, scale economies and efficiency, and political and legal imperatives.

Licensing

Another way to gain market entry, which may also be considered a form of alliance, is to acquire the right to a particular product by getting an exclusive license to make or sell the good in a particular geographic locale. A **license** is an agreement that allows one party to use an industrial property right in exchange for payment to the owning party. In a typical arrangement, the party giving the license (the licensor) will allow the other (the licensee) to use a patent, a trademark, or proprietary information in exchange for a fee. The fee usually is based on sales, such as 1 percent of all revenues earned from an industrial motor sold in Asia. The licensor typically restricts licensee sales to a particular geographic locale and limits the time period covered by the arrangement. The firm in this example may have an exclusive right to sell this patented motor in Asia for the next five years. This allows the licensor to seek licensees for other major geographic locales, such as Europe, South America, and Australia.

Licensing is used under a number of common conditions. For example, the product typically is in the mature stage of the product life cycle, competition is strong, and profit margins are declining. Under these conditions, the licensor is unlikely to want to spend money to enter foreign markets. However, if the company can find an MNC that is already there and willing to add the product to its own current offerings, both sides can benefit from the arrangement. A second common instance of licensing is evident when foreign governments require newly entering firms to make a substantial direct investment in the country. By licensing to a firm already there, the licensee avoids these high entry costs. A third common condition is that the licensor usually is a small firm that lacks

license
An agreement that allows one party to use an industrial property right in exchange for payment to the owning party.

Joint venturing is becoming an increasingly popular strategy for setting up international operations. Russia is particularly interested in these arrangements because of the benefits they offer for attracting foreign capital and helping the country tap its natural resource wealth. However, investors are finding that joint venturing in Russia and the other republics of the former Soviet Union can be fraught with problems. For example, Royal Dutch Shell was recently pressured to give up its majority stake in Sakhalin Island to Gazprom. BP has been forced to renegotiate its contracts with its Russian joint-venture partner, TNK. New laws will require foreign investors interested in Russian energy projects to pair with Kremlin-approved organizations, further empowering the Russian company and government. Kremlin power is not the only problem facing joint-venture investors in Russia. Others include the following:

1. Many Russian partners view a joint venture as an opportunity to travel abroad and gain access to foreign currency; the business itself often is given secondary consideration.

2. Finding a suitable partner, negotiating the deal, and registering the joint venture often take up to a year, mainly because the Russians are unaccustomed to some of the basic steps in putting together business deals.

3. Russian partners typically try to expand joint ventures into unrelated activities.

4. Russians do not like to declare profits, because a two-year tax holiday on profits starts from the moment the first profits are declared.

5. The government sometimes allows profits to be repatriated in the form of countertrade. However, much of what can be taken out of the country has limited value, because the government keeps control of those resources that are most saleable in the world market.

These representative problems indicate why there is reluctance on the part of some MNCs to enter into joint ventures in Russia. As one of them recently put it, "The country may well turn into an economic sink hole." As a result, many MNCs are wary of potential contracts and are proceeding with caution.

financial and managerial resources. Finally, companies that spend a relatively large share of their revenues on research and development (R&D) are likely to be licensors, and those that spend very little on R&D are more likely to be licensees. In fact, some small R&D firms make a handsome profit every year by developing and licensing new products to large firms with diversified product lines.

Some licensors use their industrial property rights to develop and sell goods in certain areas of the world and license others to handle other geographic locales. This provides the licensor with a source of additional revenues, but the license usually is not good for much more than a decade. This is a major disadvantage of licensing. In particular, if the product is very good, the competition will develop improvement patents that allow it to sell similar goods or even new patents that make the current product obsolete. Nevertheless, for the period during which the agreement is in effect, a license can be a very low-cost way of gaining and exploiting foreign markets. Table 9–3 provides some comparisons between licensing and joint ventures and summarizes the major advantages and disadvantages of each.

Licenses are also common among large firms seeking to acquire technology to bolster an existing product. For example, Microsoft announced it had agreed to a licensing arrangement with ARM Holdings PLC that allows the software giant to design chips based on ARM's technology, a common component in smartphones and tablets. According to *The Wall Street Journal*, most of ARM's licensees "take complete designs for application processors—which run software in cellphones—often combining them with other circuitry, like baseband processors for managing cellphone radios. But Microsoft signed up for what ARM calls an 'architectural license,' a more comprehensive agreement that allows a company to take the underlying instructions used in ARM chips and create wholly original designs."[29]

Table 9–3
Partial Comparison of Global Strategic Alliances

Strategy	Organization Design	Advantages	Disadvantages	Critical Success Factors	Strategic Human Resources Management
Licensing—manufacturing industries	Technologies	Early standardization of design Ability to capitalize on innovations Access to new technologies Ability to control pace of industry evolution	New competitors created Possible eventual exit from industry Possible dependence on licensee	Selection of licensee unlikely to become a competitor Enforcement of patents and licensing agreements	Technical knowledge Training of local managers on-site
Licensing—servicing and franchises	Geography	Fast market entry Low capital cost	Quality control Trademark protection	Partners compatible in philosophies/values Tight performance standards	Socialization of franchisees and licensees with core values
Joint ventures—specialization across partners	Function	Learning a partner's skills Economies of scale Quasivertical integration Faster learning	Excessive dependence on partner for skills Deterrent to internal investment	Tight and specific performance criteria Entering a venture as "student" rather than "teacher" to learn skills from partner Recognizing that collaboration is another form of competition to learn new skills	Management development and training Negotiation skills Managerial rotation
Joint venture—shared value-adding	Product or line of business	Strengths of both partners pooled Faster learning along value chain Fast upgrading of technologic skills	High switching costs Inability to limit partner's access to information	Decentralization and autonomy from corporate parents Long "courtship" period Harmonization of management styles	Team-building Acculturation Flexible skills for implicit communication

Source: Reprinted from *Organizational Dynamics*, Winter 1991, David Lei and John W. Slocum, Jr., "Global Strategic Alliances: Payoffs and Pitfalls," p. 48. Copyright © 1991, with permission from Elsevier.

Franchising

Closely related to licensing is franchising. A **franchise** is a business arrangement under which one party (the franchisor) allows another (the franchisee) to operate an enterprise using its trademark, logo, product line, and methods of operation in return for a fee. Franchising is widely used in the fast-food and hotel-motel industries. The concept is very adaptable to the international arena, and with some minor adjustments for the local market, it can result in a highly profitable business. In fast foods, McDonald's, Burger King, and Kentucky Fried Chicken have used franchise arrangements to expand into new markets. In the hotel business, Holiday Inn, among others, has been very successful in gaining worldwide presence through the effective use of franchisees.

Franchise agreements typically require payment of a fee up front and then a percentage of the revenues. In return, the franchisor provides assistance and, in some instances, may require the purchase of goods or supplies to ensure the same quality of goods or services worldwide. Franchising can be beneficial to both groups: It provides the franchisor with a new stream of income and the franchisee with a time-proven concept and products or services that can be quickly brought to market.

■ The Organization Challenge

A natural outgrowth of general international strategy formulation and implementation and specific decisions about how best to enter international markets is the question of how best to structure the organization for international operations. A number of MNCs have recently been rethinking their organizational approaches to international operations.

An excellent illustration of worldwide reorganizing is provided by Coca-Cola, which now delegates a great deal of authority for operations to the local level. This move is designed to increase the ability of the worldwide divisions to respond to their local markets. As a result, decisions related to advertising, products, and packaging are handled by international division managers for their own geographic regions. As an example, in Turkey the regional division has introduced a new pear-flavored drink, while Coke's German operation launched a berry-flavored Fanta. This "local" approach was designed to help Coke improve its international reputation, although Coke's new management is rethinking some aspects of this approach in the face of increasing cost pressures.[30] Even so, Coke continues to diversify its offerings, despite an initial increase in cost. In Brazil, for example, Coke was losing market share as local soda companies were offering low-priced carbonated beverages. Coke offered only three bottle sizes, and simply cutting the price of those did not seem to gain anything for the company. Now, Coke offers 18 different sizes in Brazil, which include many reusable glass bottles that can be returned for credit. While this has not increased market share, it has boosted profits.[31] In India, Coca-Cola has notoriously experienced difficulty gaining market share for its classic Coke brand. Rather than continue to push its signature product in India, Coke purchased the local brand, Thums Up, in 1993. As of 2012, Thums Up maintained a 42 percent market share while Pepsi only holds a 36 percent share.[32]

A second example of how firms are meeting international challenges through reorganization is provided by Li & Fung, Hong Kong's largest export trading company and an innovator in the development of supply chain management. The company has global suppliers worldwide that are responsible for providing the firm with a wide range of consumer goods ranging from toys to fashion accessories to luggage. In recent years Li & Fung reorganized and now manages its day-to-day operations through a group of product managers who are responsible for their individual areas. This new organizational arrangement emerged in a series of steps. In the late 1970s, the company was a regional sourcing agent. Big international buyers would come to Li & Fung for assistance in getting materials and products because the MNC was familiar with the producers throughout Asia and it knew the complex government regulations and how to successfully work through them. The MNC then moved into a more sophisticated stage in which it began developing the entire process for the buyer from concept to prototype to delivery of the goods. By the late 1980s, however, Hong Kong had become a very expensive place to manufacture products, and Li & Fung changed its approach and began organizing around a new concept called "dispersed manufacturing," which draws heavily on dissection of the value chain and coordinating the operations of many suppliers in different geographic locations. For example, when the MNC receives an order from a European retailer to produce a large number of dresses, it has to decide where to buy the yarn in the world market, which companies should get the orders to weave and dye the cloth, where supplemental purchases such as buttons and zippers should be made, and how final shipment must be made to the customer. Commenting on this overall process, the company president noted:

> This is a new type of value added, a truly global product that has never been seen before. The label may say "Made in Thailand," but it's not a Thai product. We dissect the manufacturing process and look for the best solution at each step. We're not asking which country can do the best job overall. Instead, we're pulling apart the value chain and optimizing each step—and we're doing it globally. Not only do the benefits outweigh the costs of logistics and transportation, but the higher value added also lets us charge more for our services. We deliver a sophisticated product and we deliver it fast. If you talk to the big global consumer products companies, they are all moving in this direction—toward being best on a global scale.[33]

■ Basic Organizational Structures

The preceding examples of Coca-Cola and Li & Fung suggest how MNCs are dramatically reorganizing their operations to compete more effectively in the international arena. For all MNCs following this strategic route, a number of basic organization structures need to be considered. In many cases, the designs are similar to those used domestically; however, significant differences may arise depending on the nature and scope of the overseas businesses and the home office's approach to controlling the foreign operation. Ideally, an overseas affiliate or subsidiary will be designed to respond to specific concerns, such as production technology or the need for specialized personnel. The overall goal, however, is to meet the needs of both the local market and the home-office strategy of globalization.

Figure 9–1 illustrates how the pressures for global integration and local responsiveness play out in a host of industries. As an MNC tries to balance these factors, an if-then contingency approach can be used. If the strategy needed to respond quickly to the local market changes, then there will be accompanying change in the organizational structure. Despite the need for such a flexible, fast-changing, contingency-based approach, most MNCs still slowly evolve through certain basic structural arrangements in international operations. The following sections examine these structures, beginning with initial, pre-international patterns.[34]

Initial Division Structure

Many firms make their initial entry into international markets by setting up a subsidiary or by exporting locally produced goods or services. A subsidiary is a common organizational arrangement for handling finance-related businesses or other operations that require an on-site presence from the start. In recent years, many service organizations have begun exporting their expertise. Examples include architectural services, legal services, advertising, public relations, accounting, and management consulting. Research and development firms also fall into this category, exporting products that have been successfully developed and marketed locally.

Figure 9–1

Organizational Expectations of Internationalization

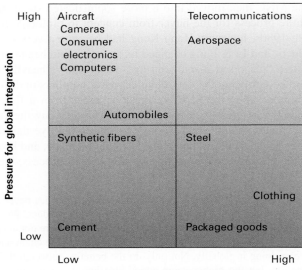

Source: Adapted from Paul W. Beamish, J. Peter Killing, Donald J. LeCraw, and Harold Crookell, *International Management: Text and Cases* (Homewood, IL: Irwin, 1991), p. 99.

An export arrangement is a common first choice among manufacturing firms, especially those with technologically advanced products. Because there is little, if any, competition, the firm can charge a premium price and handle sales through an export manager. If the company has a narrow product line, the export manager usually reports directly to the head of marketing, and international operations are coordinated by this department. If the firm has a broad product line and intends to export a number of different products into the international market, the export manager will head a separate department and often report directly to the president. These two arrangements work well as long as the company has little competition and is using international sales only to supplement domestic efforts. Furthermore, an export arrangement allows the firm to reduce the risk and size of investment in establishing significant international operations while at the same time testing the size of international markets.

If overseas sales continue to increase, local governments often exert pressure in these growing markets for setting up on-site manufacturing operations. A good example is the General Motors-Shanghai Automotive Industry Group (SAIC) joint venture in China mentioned earlier, in which a large percentage of all parts are made locally.[35] Additionally, many firms find themselves facing increased competition in the foreign market. Establishing foreign manufacturing subsidiaries can help the MNC deal with both of these pressures. The overseas plants show the government that the firm wants to be a good local citizen. At the same time, these plants help the MNC greatly reduce transportation costs, thus making the product more competitive. This new structural arrangement often takes a form similar to that shown in Figure 9–2. Each foreign subsidiary is responsible for operations within its own geographic area, and the head of the subsidiary reports either to a senior executive who is coordinating international operations or directly to the home-office CEO.

International Division Structure

international division structure
A structural arrangement that handles all international operations out of a division created for this purpose.

If international operations continue to grow and require more control, subsidiaries commonly are grouped into an **international division structure**, which handles all international operations out of a division that is created for this purpose. In other words, a unit is added on simply to deal with international issues, while the original organizational

structure is left intact. This structural arrangement is useful as it takes a great deal of the burden off the CEO for monitoring the operations of a series of overseas subsidiaries as well as domestic operations. Instead, the new head of the international division coordinates and monitors overseas activities and reports directly to the CEO on these matters. Figure 9–3 provides an example. PepsiCo reorganized its international soft drink division into six such geographic business units covering the nearly 200 countries in which Pepsi does business. Each geographic unit has self-sufficient operations and broad local authority.

Companies still in the developmental stages of international business involvement are most likely to adopt the international division structure. Others that use this structural arrangement include those with small international sales, limited geographic diversity, or few executives with international expertise.

A number of advantages are associated with use of an international division structure. The grouping of international activities under one senior executive ensures that the international focus receives top management's attention. This structural arrangement also allows the company to develop an overall, unified approach to international operations, as well as a cadre of internationally experienced managers.

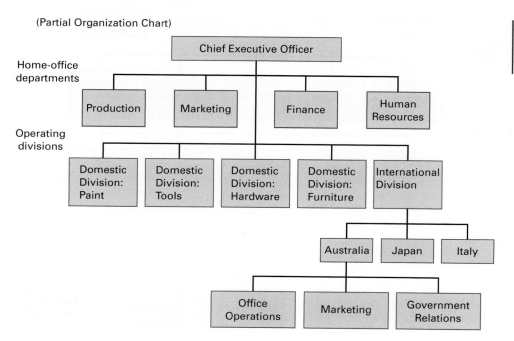

Figure 9–3

An International Division Structure

At the same time, the use of this structure does have a number of drawbacks. The structure separates the domestic and international managers, which can result in two different camps with divergent objectives. Also, as the international operation grows larger, the home office may find it difficult to think and act strategically and to allocate resources on a global basis; thus, the international division may be penalized. Finally, most R&D efforts are domestically oriented, so ideas for new products or processes in the international market often are given low priority.

Global Structural Arrangements

MNCs typically turn to global structural arrangements when they begin acquiring and allocating their resources based on international opportunities and threats. The global structural arrangement differs from the international division structure because, while both have an international scope, the former focuses on greater expansion and integration among international operations. This international perspective signifies a major change in management strategy, and it is supported by the requisite changes in organization structure. It is important to remember that a structural framework is chosen only after the basic strategy is formulated, not vice versa. Global structures come in three common types: product, area, and functional.

global product division
A structural arrangement in which domestic divisions are given worldwide responsibility for product groups.

Global Product Division   A **global product division** is a structural arrangement in which domestic divisions are given worldwide responsibility for product groups. Figure 9–4 provides an illustration. As shown, the manager who is in charge of product division C has authority for this product line on a global basis. This manager also has internal functional support related to the product line. For example, all marketing, production, and finance activities associated with product division C are under the control of this manager.

Figure 9–4

A Global Product Division Structure

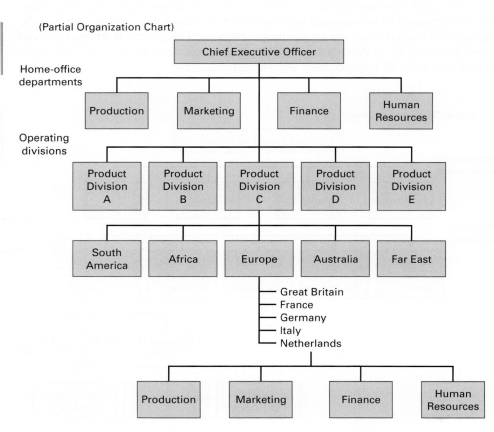

(Partial Organization Chart)

Home-office departments

Operating divisions

The global product divisions operate as profit centers. The products are generally in the growth stage of the product life cycle, so they need to be promoted and marketed carefully. In doing so, global product division managers generally run the operation with considerable autonomy; they have the authority to make many important decisions regarding the product. However, corporate headquarters usually will maintain control in terms of budgetary constraints, home-office approval for certain decisions, and mainly "bottom-line" (i.e., profit) results.

A global product structure provides the most benefits when the need for product specification or differentiation in different markets is high. This often occurs when companies offer a variety of products, the customer base is extremely diverse, or goods must be modified to match local tastes (e.g., food or toys). Creating divisions which specialize in each product set results in efficient alterations, especially since marketing, production, and finance can be coordinated on a product-by-product basis. Furthermore, if a product is in a different life cycle (mature versus growth stage) across regions, global product divisions can ensure that each location responds appropriately. Other advantages of a global product division structure can be summarized as follows:

> It preserves product emphasis and promotes product planning on a global basis; it provides a direct line of communication from the customer to those in the organization who have product knowledge and expertise, thus enabling research and development to work on development of products that serve the needs of the world customer; and it permits line and staff managers within the division to gain an expertise in the technical and marketing aspects of products assigned to them.[36]

Unfortunately, the approach also has some drawbacks. One is the necessity of duplicating facilities and staff personnel within each division. A second is that division managers may pursue currently attractive geographic prospects for their products and neglect other areas with better long-term potential. A third is that many division managers spend too much time trying to tap the local rather than the international market because it is more convenient and they are more experienced in domestic operations.

Global Area Division Instead of a global product division, some MNCs prefer to use a **global area division**. In this structure, illustrated in Figure 9–5, global operations are organized based on a geographic rather than a product orientation. This approach often signals a major change in company strategy, because now international operations are put on the same level as domestic operations. In other words, European or Asian operations are just as important to the company as North American operations. For example, when British Petroleum purchased Standard Oil of Ohio, the firm revised its overall structure and adopted a global area division structure. Under this arrangement, global division managers are responsible for all business operations in their designated geographic area. The CEO and other members of top management are charged with formulating the overall strategy that ensures that the global divisions all work in harmony.

A global area division structure most often is used by companies that are in mature businesses and have narrow product lines which are differentiated by geographic area. For example, the product has a strong demand in Europe but not in South America, or the type of product that is offered in France differs from that sold in England. This is different from the global product division structure because each division focuses on regional tastes and offers specialized products for and within that area, as opposed to focusing on a product set and discovering where it can survive and subsequently distributing it to that region. In addition, the MNC usually seeks high economies of scale for production, marketing, and resource-purchase integration in a particular area. Thus, by manufacturing in this region rather than bringing the product in from somewhere else, the firm is able to reduce cost per unit and offer a very competitive price. The geographic structure also allows the division manager to cater to the tastes of the local market and

global area division
A structure under which global operations are organized on a geographic rather than a product basis.

Figure 9–5

A Global Area Division Structure

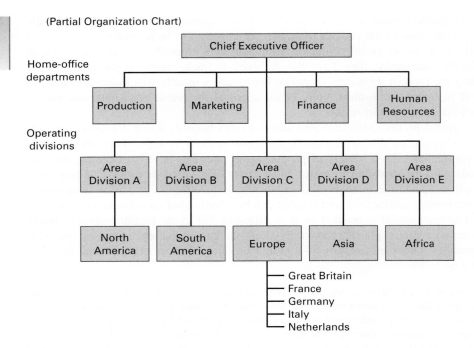

(Partial Organization Chart)

A Global Area Division Structure

make rapid decisions to accommodate environmental changes. A good example is food products. In the United States, soft drinks have less sugar than in South America, so the manufacturing process must be slightly different in these two locales. Similarly, in England, people prefer bland soups, but in France, the preference is for mildly spicy. A global area structure allows the geographic unit in a foods company to accommodate such local preferences.

The primary disadvantage of the global area division structure is the difficulty encountered in reconciling a product emphasis with a geographic orientation. For example, if a product is sold worldwide, a number of different divisions are responsible for sales. This lack of centralized management and control can result in increased costs and duplication of effort on a region-by-region basis. A second drawback is that new R&D efforts often are ignored by division groups because they are selling goods that have reached the maturity stage. Their focus is not on the latest technologically superior goods that will win in the market in the long run but on those that are proven winners and now are being marketed conveniently worldwide.

Global Functional Division A **global functional division** organizes worldwide operations based primarily on function and secondarily on product. This approach is not widely used other than by extractive companies, such as oil and mining firms. Figure 9–6 provides an example.

A number of important advantages are associated with the global functional division structure. These include (1) an emphasis on functional expertise, (2) tight centralized control, and (3) a relatively lean managerial staff. There also are some important disadvantages: (1) Coordination of manufacturing and marketing often is difficult; (2) managing multiple product lines can be very challenging because of the separation of production and marketing into different departments; and (3) only the chief executive officer can be held accountable for the profits. As a result, the global functional process structure typically is favored only by firms that need tight, centralized coordination and control of integrated production processes and firms that are

global functional division
A structure that organizes worldwide operations primarily based on function and secondarily on product.

(Partial Organization Chart)

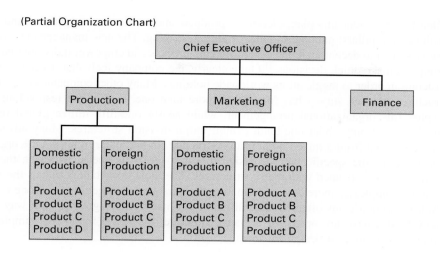

Figure 9–6

A Global Functional Structure

involved in transporting products and raw materials from one geographic area to another.

Mixed Organization Structures   Some companies find that neither a global product, an area, or a functional arrangement is satisfactory. Instead they opt for a **mixed organization structure**, which combines all three into an MNC that supplements its primary structure with a secondary one and, perhaps, a tertiary one. For example, if a company uses a global area approach, committees of functional managers may provide assistance and support to the various geographic divisions. Conversely, if the firm uses a global functional approach, product committees may be responsible for coordinating transactions that cut across functional lines. In other cases, the organization will opt for a matrix structure that results in managers' having two or more bosses. Figure 9–7 illustrates this structure. In this arrangement, the MNC coordinates geographic and product lines through use of a matrix design.

In recent years, mixed organization structures have become increasingly popular. In 2012, Sony's electronic businesses, including personal computers, mobile phones, and cable-television set-top boxes, were unified under a new management structure called

mixed organization structure
A structure that is a combination of a global product, area, or functional arrangement.

(Partial Organization Chart)

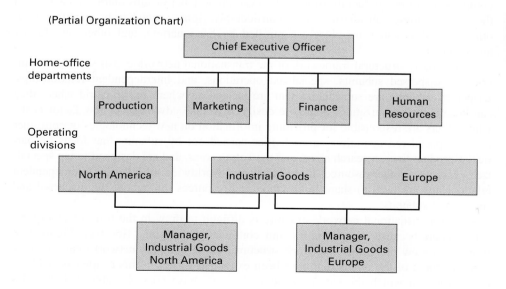

Figure 9–7

A Multinational Matrix Structure

"One Sony." Under this plan, electronic products and services are organized under one of three core pillars: gaming, mobile, or digital imaging. The new management structure was designed to decentralize the design-making process and empower individual business groups to make quick decisions.[37] Quite clearly, the company feels that it needs a mixed structure in order to juggle all its worldwide holdings. Many other companies use a mixed structure, and one survey has found that more than one-third of the responding firms employ this organizational arrangement, while nearly one-fifth utilize global product divisions, and only about one-tenth exhibit initial division structures. Many advantages can be gleaned from a mixed organization structure. In particular, it allows the organization to create the specific type of design that best meets its needs. However, there are shortcomings associated with matrix structures. The most important is that as the matrix design's complexity increases, coordinating the personnel and getting everyone to work toward common goals often become difficult; too many groups go their own way. Thus, many MNCs have not opted for a matrix structure; they have found that simple, lean structures are the best design for them.

Transnational Network Structures

transnational network structure
A multinational structural arrangement that combines elements of function, product, and geographic designs, while relying on a network arrangement to link worldwide subsidiaries.

Besides matrix structures, another alternative international organizational design to recently emerge is the **transnational network structure**. This is designed to help MNCs take advantage of global economies of scale while also being responsive to local customer demands. The design combines elements of classic functional, product, and geographic structures while relying on a network arrangement to link the various worldwide subsidiaries. This configuration may appear very similar to the matrix, but it is much more complex. While the matrix may use more than one strategy to supplement inefficient operations, it is still fairly centralized in the sense that decisions are balanced between the main headquarters and international subsidiaries. Transnational networks, however, are convoluted integrations of business functions and communications where decisions are made at the local level, but each grouping informs headquarters and sometimes each other. At the center of the transnational network structure are nodes, which are units charged with coordinating product, functional, and geographic information. Different product line units and geographical area units have different structures depending on what is best for their particular operations. A good example of how the transnational network structure works is provided by Koninklijke Philips Electronics N.V. (commonly known as Philips), which has operations in more than 60 countries and produces a diverse product line ranging from light bulbs to defense systems. In all, the company has three product divisions with a varying number of subsidiaries in each—and the focus of these subsidiaries varies considerably. Some specialize in manufacturing, others in sales; some are closely controlled by headquarters, and others are highly autonomous.

The basic structural framework of the transnational network consists of three components: dispersed subunits, specialized operations, and interdependent relationships. Dispersed subunits are subsidiaries that are located anywhere in the world where they can benefit the organization. Some are designed to take advantage of low factor costs, while others are responsible for providing information on new technologies or consumer trends. Specialized operations are activities carried out by subunits that focus on particular product lines, research areas, and marketing areas, and are designed to tap specialized expertise or other resources in the company's worldwide subsidiaries. Interdependent relationships are used to share information and resources throughout the dispersed and specialized subunits.

The transnational network structure is difficult to draw in the form of an organization chart because it is complex and continually changing. However, Figure 9–8 provides a view of Philips's network structure. These complex networks can be compared to some of the others that have been examined earlier in this chapter by looking at the ways in which the enterprise attempts to exercise control. Table 9–4 provides such a comparison.

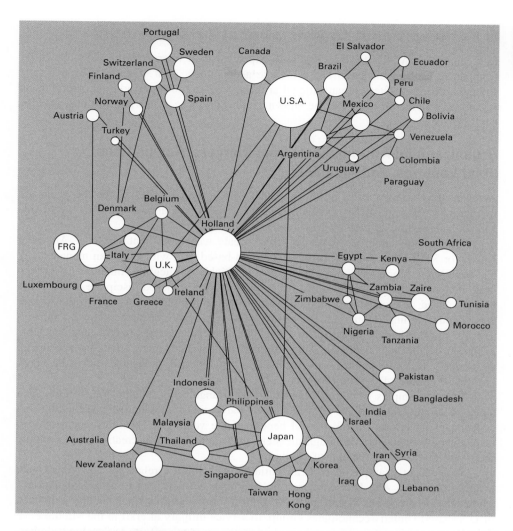

Figure 9–8

The Network Structure of N.V. Philips

Table 9–4
Control Mechanisms Used in Select Multinational Organization Structures

Type of Multinational Structure	Output Control	Bureaucratic Control	Decision-Making Control	Cultural Control
International division structure	Profit control.	Have to follow company policies.	Typically there is some centralization.	Treated like all other divisions.
Global area division	Use of profit centers.	Some policies and procedures are necessary.	Local units are given autonomy.	Local subsidiary culture is often the most important.
Global product division	Unit output for supply; sales volume for sales.	Tight process controls are used to maintain product quality and consistency.	Centralized at the product-division headquarters level.	Possible for some companies, but not always necessary.
Matrix structure	Profit responsibility is shared with product and geographic units.	Not very important.	Balanced between the global area and product units.	Culture must support the shared decision making.
Transnational network structure	Used for supplier units and for some independent profit centers.	Not very important.	Few decisions are centralized at headquarters; most are centralized in the key network nodes.	Organization culture transcends national cultures, supports sharing and learning, and is the most important control mechanism.

■ Nontraditional Organizational Arrangements

In recent years, MNCs have increasingly expanded their operations in ways that differ from those used in the past. These include acquisitions, joint ventures, keiretsus, and strategic alliances. These organizational arrangements do not use traditional hierarchical structures and therefore cannot be shown graphically. The following sections describe how they work.

Organizational Arrangements from Mergers, Acquisitions, Joint Ventures, and Alliances

A recent development affecting the way that MNCs are organized is the increased use of mergers and acquisitions (M&As). In recent years, the annual value of worldwide M&As has reached as high as $6 trillion!

Among the larger cross-border M&A deals was Inbev's purchase of Anheuser Busch for $52 billion in 2009. Inbev, a Belgium-based firm with Brazilian management, had been known for a ruthless style and moved quickly to integrate Anheuser Busch into its global structure. It cut costs, laid off employees, and imposed discipline on a culture that it viewed as bloated and inefficient. From November 2008, just before the merger was announced, until January 2010, ABInbev (the new name for the combined company) saw its stock price increase nearly triple in value, suggesting analysts and investors approved of the new approach.[38] By contrast the Roche-Genentech tie-up appears to deliberately seek to maintain some postmerger separation in order to preserve the more innovative culture of the biotech firm.[39]

Other examples of recent organizational arrangements include joint-venture and strategic alliance agreements in which each party contributes to the undertaking and coordinates its efforts for the overall benefit of the venture.[40] These arrangements can take a variety of forms,[41] although the steps that are followed in creating and operating them often have a fair amount of similarity.

One recent example of such an initiative was when a relatively new Abu Dhabi aviation company, Abu Dhabi Aircraft Technologies, owned by the oil-rich sheikdom's Mubadala Development, began an $800 million joint venture with Sikorsky, a division of U.S.-based United Technologies Group, to service military aircraft in the Middle East. This JV was designed, in part, to help support the emirate's efforts to develop a domestic aircraft and avionics industry. The JV will provide maintenance, repair, and overhaul services to the Emirati armed forces and other military forces in the region. "Putting these two companies together will be the right move to capture the lucrative market in the region," Homaid al-Shemmari, chairman of Abu Dhabi Aircraft, told the Associated Press. "With our local knowledge and reach . . . and the capabilities Sikorsky can bring from the U.S., it's a perfect match."

The JV will initially be housed at a facility in Al Ain, an Emirati city about 100 miles east of the capital Abu Dhabi, on the border with Oman. Interestingly, it will also operate on Emirati military bases, with an initial focus on servicing some of the country's more than 400-strong fleet, which includes Mirage fighters from France and American-made F-16 planes and Apache attack helicopters.[42]

Another example is the longstanding joint venture between General Motors and Shanghai Automotive Industry Corporation (S.A.I.C.), which produces the Wuling line of trucks and vans targeted to rural areas of China. Recently, these JV partners announced they would introduce a new passenger-car brand called Baojun, which means "treasured horse." This basic car line will be targeted at buyers outside China's major metropolitan areas. This joint venture became the first automaker to sell more than 1 million vehicles in China.[43]

These joint ventures require carefully formulated structures that allow each partner to contribute what it does best and to coordinate their efforts efficiently. This calls for clearly spelling out the responsibilities of all parties and identifying the authority that each will have for meeting specific targets.

One of the main objectives in developing the structure for joint ventures is to help the partners address and effectively meld their different values, management styles, action orientation, and organization preferences. Figure 9–9 illustrates how Western and Asian firms differ in these four areas; the figure also is useful for illustrating the types of considerations that need to be addressed by MNCs from the same area of the world. Consider, for example, Matsushita Electric Industrial and Hitachi Ltd. The two agreed to join forces to develop new technology in three areas: smart cards, home network systems, and recyclable and energy-efficient consumer electronics.[44] The two firms will need to structure their organizational interface carefully to ensure effective interaction, coordination, and cooperation.

In each of these examples, the purchasing MNCs fashioned a structural arrangement that attempts to promote synergy while encouraging local initiative by the acquired firm. The result is an organization design that draws on the more traditional structures that have been examined here but still has a unique structure specifically addressing the needs of the two firms.

In fact, strategic partners are so important to the success of many MNCs that it is common to find them giving their partners direct access to their own computer systems. In this way, for example, an outsourcer can quickly determine the MNC's supply needs

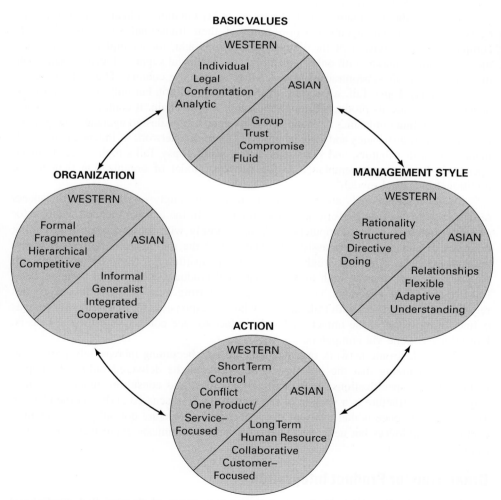

Figure 9–9

A Comparison of Asian and Western Management Features

Source: Frederic Swierczek and Georges Hirsch, "Joint Ventures in Asia and Multicultural Management," *European Management Journal,* June 1994, p. 203. Copyright European Management Journal.

and adjust its own production schedule to meet these demands. This same type of close working B2B arrangement is used when providing services. For example, IBM works closely with the giant French MNC Thomson Multimedia SA, managing the firm's data centers, desktops, help desk, disaster recovery, and support services.[45]

Many companies are finding that M&As do not work out or they involve a considerable financial risk because of the high sales price. Joint ventures and strategic alliances are a good alternative. They provide MNCs with the opportunity to access a wide variety of competencies, thus reducing their own costs while ensuring that they have a reliable provider. In addition, joint ventures and strategic alliances help promote cooperation between the participating organizations.[46]

■ The Emergence of the Network Organizational Forms

Over the last few years there has been a major increase in the number of "electronic freelancers"—individuals who work on a project for a company, usually via the Internet, and move on to other employment when the assignment is done. In a way, these individuals represent a new type of electronic network organization—"temporary companies"—that serve a particular, short-term purpose and then go on to other assignments. There are numerous examples.

Consider the way many manufacturers are today pursuing radical outsourcing strategies, letting external agents perform more of their traditional activities. The U.S. computer-display division of the Finnish company Nokia, for example, chose to enter the U.S. display market with only five employees. Technical support, logistics, sales, and marketing were all subcontracted to specialists around the country. The fashion accessories company Topsy Tail, which has revenues of $80 million but only three employees, never even touches its products through the entire supply chain. It contracts with various injection-molding companies to manufacture its goods; uses design agencies to create its packaging; and distributes and sells its products through a network of independent fulfillment houses, distributors, and sales reps. Nokia's and Topsy Tail's highly decentralized operations bear more resemblance to the network model of organization than to the traditional industrial model.[47]

Many multinationals are beginning to rely increasingly on electronic freelancers (e-lancers, for short) to perform key tasks for them. In the case of General Motors, for example, outsourcers via computers work very closely with the company in providing both design and engineering assistance. The rise of the multinational university is yet another example. Growing numbers of academic institutions from Europe to North America are now offering both undergraduate and graduate courses, and in some cases full-fledged degree programs, via the Internet. In staffing these courses, the universities rely heavily on e-lancers with PhD degrees who are responsible for delivering the courses online. In most cases, the university has little face-to-face contact with these e-lancers. Everything is done via computers.

These electronic network organizations are now becoming increasingly prominent. MNCs are realizing that the outsourcing function can be delivered online. Examples include design specifications, analytical computations, and consulting reports. So, in a way, this new structure is a version of the matrix design discussed earlier in the chapter. The major difference is that many of the people in the structure not only are temporary, contingent employees but never see each other and communicate exclusively in an electronic environment.

Organizing for Product Integration

Another recent organizing development is the emergence of designs that are tailored toward helping multinationals integrate product development into their worldwide operations. In the recent past, the use of cross-functional coordination was helpful in achieving this goal. However, MNCs have found that this arrangement results in people spending less time within their functions and thus becoming less knowledgeable regarding developments that are occurring in their specialized areas. A second shortcoming of the cross-functional approach is that it often leads to product teams becoming autonomous and thus failing to integrate their overall efforts with the organization at large.

Toyota created a structure that combines a highly formalized system with new structural innovations that ensure that projects are flexibly managed and, at the same time, able to benefit from the learning and experiences of other projects. In accomplishing this, Toyota employs six organizational mechanisms.

One of these is called mutual adjustment. In most companies this is achieved by assigning people to a specific project and having them meet face to face and work out a plan of action for designing the new product. At Toyota, however, design engineers are not assigned to specific projects; rather they remain in their functional area and typically communicate through written messages. This approach ensures that all members remain dedicated to their primary functional area and that they communicate succinctly and directly with each other—thus saving time.

A second mechanism employed by Toyota is the use of direct, technically skilled supervisors. In a typical arrangement, design engineers are led by individuals who are no longer doing engineering work; they are primarily responsible for seeing that others do this work. However, at Toyota supervisors remain highly skilled in the technical side of the work and are responsible for mentoring, training, and developing their engineers. So if anyone has a design-related problem, the supervisor is technically skilled and can provide this assistance.

A third mechanism is the use of integrative leadership. In typical product design structures, the manager in charge has full authority and relies on the engineering personnel to get the work done within time, cost, and quality parameters. At Toyota, however, these managers are responsible for coordinating the work of the functional specialists and serving less as a manager than as a lead designer on the entire project. In this way, they serve as the glue that binds together the whole process.

In typical design operations, engineers are hired from universities or from other companies where they have gained experience, and they remain in their engineering position indefinitely. At Toyota most of the technical training is provided in-house, and people are rotated within only one function, such as body engineers who work on autobody subsystems for most, if not all, of their careers. As a result, they are able to get more work done faster because they do not have to communicate and coordinate continually with their counterparts regarding what needs to be done. They are so familiar with their jobs that they know what needs to be done.

Another organizational difference is that in typical design work each new product calls for a new development process, and there are complex forms and bureaucratic procedures for ensuring that everything is done correctly. At Toyota, standard milestones are created by the project leader, and simple forms and procedures are employed so that the work can be done simply and efficiently.

A final difference is that in many organizations design standards are obsolete and rigid. At Toyota, these standards are maintained by the people who are doing the work and are continually changed to meet new design demands.

The organizational approach used at Toyota is being carefully studied by other world-class auto manufacturers, who are coming to realize that the old way of organizing for product design is not sufficiently effective for dealing with the competitive challenges of the new millennium. In particular, a new organizational emphasis has to be placed on better blending the personnel and the work. Commenting on all of this, a group of experts who studied Toyota's approach wrote:

> The success of Toyota's system rides squarely on the shoulders of its people. Successful product development requires highly competent, highly skilled people with a lot of hands-on experience, deep technical knowledge, and an eye for the overall system. When we look at all the things that Toyota does well, we find two foundations for its product-development

system: chief engineers using their expertise to gain leadership, and functional engineers using their expertise to reduce the amount of communication, supervision, trial and error, and confusion in the process. All the other coordinating mechanisms and practices serve to help highly skilled engineers do their job effectively. By contrast, many other companies seem to aspire to develop systems "designed by geniuses to be run by idiots." Toyota prefers to develop and rely on the skill of its personnel, and it shapes its product-development process around this central idea: people, not systems, design cars.[48]

■ Organizational Characteristics of MNCs

Although MNCs have similar organizational structures, they do not all operate in the same way. A variety of factors that help explain the differences have been identified.[49] These include overall strategy, employee attitudes, and local conditions. Of particular significance to this discussion are the organizational characteristics of formalization, specialization, and centralization.

Formalization

formalization
The use of defined structures and systems in decision making, communicating, and controlling.

Formalization is the use of defined structures and systems in decision making, communicating, and controlling. Some countries make greater use of formalization than others; in turn, this affects the day-to-day organizational functioning. One large research study of Korean firms found that, unlike employees in the United States, Korean workers perceive more positive work environments when expectations for their jobs are set forth more strictly and formally. In short, Koreans respond very favorably to formalization.[50] Korean firms tend to be quite formal, but this may not hold throughout Asia. For example, a study that investigated whether Japanese organizations are more formalized than U.S. organizations found that although Japanese firms tend to use more labor-intensive approaches to areas such as bookkeeping and office-related work than their U.S. counterparts, no statistical data support the contention that Japanese firms are more formalized.[51]

Another study of U.S. and Japanese firms in Taiwan divided formalization into two categories: objective and subjective.[52] Objective formalization was measured by things such as the number of different documents given to employees, organizational charts, information booklets, operating instructions, written job descriptions, procedure manuals, written policies, and work-flow schedules and programs. Subjective formalization was measured by the extent to which goals were left vague and unspecified, informal controls were used, and culturally induced values facilitated getting things done.

Commenting on differences in the use of formalization, the researchers concluded that American and Japanese firms appear to have almost the same level of written goals or objectives for subordinates, written standards of performance appraisals, written schedules, programs, and work specifications, written duties, authority, and accountability. However, managers in Japanese firms perceive less formalization than do managers in American firms. Less reliance on formal rules and structure in Japanese firms is also revealed by the emphasis on a face-to-face or behavioral mode of control indicated by the ratio of foreign expatriates to total employees in subsidiaries.[53]

The study also found that U.S. MNCs tend to rely heavily on budgets, financial data, and other formalized tools in controlling their subsidiary operations. This contrasts with Japanese MNCs, in which wider use is made of face-to-face, informal controls. These findings reveal that although the outward structural design of overseas subsidiaries may appear to be similar, the internal functioning in characteristics such as formalization may be quite different.

In recent years, this formal-informal characteristic of organizations has become the focal point of increased scrutiny.[54] One reason is that MNCs now realize there are two dimensions of formality-informality that must be considered: internal and external. Moreover, to a large degree, these formal-informal relationships require different types of networking. As Yoshino and Rangan noted, there are two approaches that firms that must

Table 9–5 **Internal versus External Networks**		
Managerial Dimensions	**Internal Network**	**External Network**
Shared vision	Yes	No
Animating mindset	Cooperation	Cooperation and competition
Organizational mandates	Clear	Ambiguous
Organizational objective	Global optimization	Develop win-win approaches
Emphasis on systems	More	Less
Emphasis on people	Less	More
Lines of authority	Clear	Ambiguous at best

Source: Information drawn from Michael Yoshino and N. S. Rangan, *Strategic Alliances* (Boston: Harvard Business School Press, 1995), p. 203.

compete globally—and that includes most major firms—employ to achieve the layering of competitive advantages: (1) development of extensive internal networks of international subsidiaries in major national or regional markets and (2) forging external networks of strategic alliances with firms around the world. These approaches are not mutually exclusive, and increasingly firms are striving to build both types of networks.[55]

What is particularly interesting about these networking relationships is that each places a different set of demands on the MNC. In particular, external networking with joint-venture partners often involves ambiguous organizational mandates, less emphasis on systems and more on people, and ambiguous lines of authority. This is a marked difference from internal networking characteristics, where formality is much stronger than informality and the enterprise can rely on a shared vision, clear organizational mandates, and well-developed systems and lines of authority. Table 9–5 summarizes the characteristics of these internal and external networks.

Specialization

As an organizational characteristic, **specialization** is the assigning of individuals to specific, well-defined tasks. Specialization in an international context can be classified into horizontal and vertical specialization.

Horizontal specialization assigns jobs so that individuals are given a particular function to perform, and people tend to stay within the confines of this area. Examples include jobs in areas such as customer service, sales, recruiting, training, purchasing, and marketing research. When there is a great deal of horizontal specialization, personnel will develop functional expertise in one particular area.

Vertical specialization assigns work to groups or departments where individuals are collectively responsible for performance. Vertical specialization also is characterized by distinct differences between levels in the hierarchy such that those higher up are accorded much more status than those farther down, and the overall structure usually is quite tall.

In the earlier comparative study of 55 U.S. and 51 Japanese manufacturing plants, Japanese organizations had lower functional specialization of employees. Specifically, three-quarters of the functions listed were assigned to specialists in the U.S. plants, but less than one-third were assigned in the Japanese plants.[56] Later studies with regard to formalization have echoed this finding on specialization.

By contrast, studies find that the Japanese rely more heavily on vertical specialization. They have taller organization structures in contrast to the flatter designs of their U.S. counterparts. Japanese departments and units also are more differentiated than departments and units in U.S. organizations. Vertical specialization can be measured by

specialization
An organizational characteristic that assigns individuals to specific, well-defined tasks.

horizontal specialization
The assignment of jobs so that individuals are given a particular function to perform and tend to stay within the confines of this area.

vertical specialization
The assignment of work to groups or departments where individuals are collectively responsible for performance.

the amount of group activity as well, such as in quality circles. Japanese firms make much greater use of quality circles than do U.S. firms. Vertical specialization also can result in greater job routinization. Because one is collectively responsible for the work, strong emphasis is placed on everyone's doing the job in a predetermined way, refraining from improvising, and structuring the work so that everyone can do the job after a short training period. Again, Japanese organizations make much wider use of job routinization than do U.S. organizations.

Centralization

centralization
A management system in which important decisions are made at the top.

decentralization
Pushing decision making down the line and getting the lower-level personnel involved.

Centralization is a management system in which important decisions are made at the top. In an international context, the value of centralization will vary according to the local environment and the goals of the organization. Many U.S. firms tend toward **decentralization**, pushing decision making down the line and getting the lower-level personnel involved. German MNCs centralize strategic headquarter-specific decisions independent of the host country and decentralize operative decisions in accordance with the local situation in the host country. The International Management in Action, "Organizing in Germany," describes how relatively small German MNCs have been very successful with such a decentralization strategy. In some cases, large firms have also been very successful using a decentralized approach. Nokia, for example, has been described as "one of the least hierarchical big companies on earth, a place where it is often profoundly unclear who's in charge."[57] This hands-off approach promotes creativity, entrepreneurial effort, and personal responsibility. At the same time, however, in order to prevent operations from spinning out of control, the company exercises very tight financial discipline.

In contrast, researchers have found that Japanese organizations delegate less formal authority than their U.S. counterparts but permit greater involvement in decisions by employees lower in the hierarchy. At the same time, the Japanese manage to maintain strong control over their lower-level personnel by limiting the amount of authority given to the latter and carefully controlling and orchestrating worker involvement and participation in quality circles.[58] Other studies show similar findings.[59] When evaluating the presence of centralization by examining the amount of autonomy that Japanese give to their subordinates, one study concluded:

> In terms of job autonomy, employees in American firms have greater freedom to make their decisions and their own rules than in Japanese firms. . . . Results show that managers in American firms perceive a higher degree of delegation than do managers in Japanese firms. Also, managers in American firms feel a much higher level of participation in the coordinating with other units, . . . in influencing the company's policy related to their work, and in influencing the company's policy in areas not related to their work.[60]

The finding related to influence is explained in more detail in Table 9–6. U.S. managers in Taiwanese subsidiaries felt that they had greater influence than did their Japanese counterparts. Moreover, when statistically analyzed, these data proved to be significant.

Putting Organizational Characteristics in Perspective

MNCs tend to organize their international operations in a manner similar to that used at home. If the MNC tends to have high formalization, specialization, and centralization at its home-based headquarters, these organizational characteristics probably will occur in the firm's international subsidiaries.[61] Japanese and U.S. firms are good examples. As the researchers of the comparative study in Taiwan concluded: "Almost 80 percent of Japanese firms and more than 80 percent of American firms in the sample have been operating in Taiwan for about ten years, but they maintain the traits of their distinct

Like every other place in the world, Europe in general and Germany in particular have gone through economic ups and downs. German labor unions, the most powerful in Europe, were having to give ground, and major corporations were scaling back operations and reporting losses. At the same time, a number of medium-sized and small German companies continued to be some of the most successful in the world. Part of this success resulted from their carefully designed decentralized organization structures, a result of company efforts to remain close to the customer. The goal of these German MNCs is to establish operations in overseas locales where they can provide on-site assistance to buyers. Moreover, in most cases these subsidiaries are wholly owned by the company and have centralized controls on profits.

A common practice among German MNCs is to overserve the market by providing more than is needed. For example, when the auto firm BMW entered Japan, its initial investment was several times higher than that required to run a small operation; however, its high visibility and commitment to the market helped to create customer awareness and build local prestige.

Another strategy is to leave expatriate managers in their positions for extended periods of time. In this way, they become familiar with the local culture and thus the market, and they are better able to respond to customer needs as well as problems. As a result, customers get to know the firm's personnel and are more willing to do repeat business with them.

Still another strategy the German MNCs use is to closely mesh the talents of the people with the needs of the customers. For example, there is considerable evidence that most customers value product quality, closeness to the customer, service, economy, helpful employees, technologic leadership, and innovativeness. The German firms will overperform in the area that is most important and thus further bond themselves to the customer.

A final strategy is to develop strong self-reliance so that when problems arise, they can be handled with in-house personnel. This practice is a result of German companies' believing strongly in specialization and concentration of effort. They tend to do their own research and to master production and service problems so that if there is a problem, they can resolve it without having to rely on outsiders.

How well do these German organizing efforts pay off? Many of these relatively small companies hold world market shares in the 70 to 90 percent range. These are companies that no one has ever heard of, such as Booder (fish-processing machines), Gehring (honing machines), Korber/Hauni (cigarette machines), Marklin & Cle (model railways), Stihl (chain saws), and Webasto (sunroofs for cars). Even so, every one of these companies is the market leader not only in Europe but also throughout the world, and in some cases its relative market strength is up to 10 times greater than that of the nearest competitor.

Table 9–6
Managers' Influence in U.S. and Japanese Firms in Taiwan

Managers' Work-Related Activity	U.S. Firm Average	Japanese Firm Average
Assigning work to subordinates	4.72	3.96
Disciplining subordinates	4.07	3.82
Controlling subordinates' work (quality and pace)	3.99	3.82
Controlling salary and promotion of subordinates	3.81	3.18
Hiring and placing subordinates	3.94	3.24
Setting the budget for own unit	3.45	3.16
Coordinating with other units	3.68	3.52
Influencing policy related to own work	3.22	2.85
Influencing policy not related to own work	2.29	1.94
Influencing superiors	3.02	3.00

Note: The highest score of means is 5 (very great influence); the lowest score is 1 (very little influence). The *T*-value for all scores is significant at the .01 level.

Source: Adapted from Rhy-song Yeh and Tagi Sagafi-nejad, "Organizational Characteristics of American and Japanese Firms in Taiwan," *National Academy of Management Proceedings* (New Orleans, 1987), p. 114.

cultural origins even though they have been operating in the same (Taiwanese) environment for such a long time."[62]

These findings also reveal that many enterprises view their international operations as extensions of their domestic operations, thus disproving the widely held belief that convergence occurs between overseas operations and local customs. In other words, there is far less of an "international management melting pot" than many people realize. European countries are finding that as they attempt to unify and do business with each other, differing cultures (languages, religions, and values) are very difficult to overcome. A major challenge for the years ahead will be bringing subsidiary organizational characteristics more into line with local customs and cultures.

■ The World of International Management—Revisited

In this chapter, a number of different entry strategies and organizational arrangements were discussed. Some of these are fairly standard approaches used by MNCs; others represent hybrid or flexible arrangements. Increasingly, entry modes and organizational structures involve collaborative relationships in which control and oversight are shared. Review the chapter opening World of International Management discussion of Volkswagen's integrated approach to global strategy, emphasizing both global and regional aspects. Then think about the major themes of the chapter, forms of entry and organization structure, and answer the following questions: (1) Which organizational structure described in the chapter does Volkswagen's "customer oriented" structure most closely resemble? (2) How might such a structure help or hinder entry into new markets? (3) Does a matrix or customer-oriented structure lend itself better to forming joint ventures and alliances?

SUMMARY OF KEY POINTS

1. MNCs pursue a range of entry strategies in their international operations. These include wholly owned subsidiaries, mergers and acquisitions, alliances and joint ventures, licensing and franchising, and exporting. In general, the more cooperative forms of entry (alliances, joint ventures, mergers, licensing) are on the rise.

2. A number of different organizational structures are used in international operations. Many MNCs begin by using an export manager or subsidiary to handle overseas business. As the operation grows or the company expands into more markets, the firm often will opt for an international division structure. Further growth may result in adoption of a global structural arrangement, such as a global production division, global area division structure, global functional division, or a mixture of these structures.

3. Although MNCs still use the various structural designs that can be drawn in a hierarchical manner, they recently have begun merging or acquiring other firms or parts of other firms, and the resulting organizational arrangements are quite different from

those of the past. The same is true of the many joint ventures now taking place across the world. One change stems from the Japanese concept of keiretsu, which involves the vertical integration and cooperation of a group of companies. Other examples of new MNC organizational arrangements include the emergence of electronic networks, new approaches to organizing for production development, and the more effective use of IT.

4. A variety of factors help to explain differences in the way that international firms operate. Three organizational characteristics that are of particular importance are formalization, specialization, and centralization. These characteristics often vary from country to country, so that Japanese firms will conduct operations differently from U.S. firms, for example. When MNCs set up international subsidiaries, they often use the same organizational techniques they do at home without necessarily adjusting their approach to better match the local conditions.

KEY TERMS

alliance, *314*

centralization, *336*

decentralization, *336*

formalization, *334*

franchise, *320*

global area division, *325*

global functional division, *326*

global product division, *324*

horizontal specialization, *325*

international division structure, *322*

joint venture (JV), *314*

license, *317*

merger/acquisition, *309*

mixed organization structure, *327*

specialization, *335*

transnational network structure, *328*

vertical specialization, *325*

wholly owned subsidiary, *309*

REVIEW AND DISCUSSION QUESTIONS

1. One of the most common entry strategies for MNCs is the joint venture. Why are so many companies opting for this strategy? Would a fully owned subsidiary be a better choice?

2. A small manufacturing firm believes there is a market for handheld tools that are carefully crafted for local markets. After spending two months in Europe, the president of this firm believes that his company can create a popular line of these tools. What type of organization structure would be of most value to this firm in its initial efforts to go international?

3. If the company in question 2 finds a major market for its products in Europe and decides to expand into Asia, would you recommend any change in its organization structure? If yes, what would you suggest? If no, why not?

4. If this same company finds after three years of international effort that it is selling 50 percent of its output overseas, what type of organizational structure would you suggest for the future?

5. In what way do the concepts of formalization, specialization, and centralization have an impact on MNC organization structures? In your answer, use a well-known firm such as IBM or Ford to illustrate the practical expressions of these three characteristics.

INTERNET EXERCISE: ORGANIZING FOR EFFECTIVENESS

Every MNC tries to drive down costs by getting its goods and services to the market in the most efficient way. Good examples include auto firms such as Ford Motor and Volkswagen, which have worldwide operations. In recent years Ford has been expanding into Europe and VW has begun setting up operations in Latin America. By building cars closer to the market, these companies hope to reduce their costs and be more responsive to local needs. At the same time this strategy requires a great deal of organization and coordination.

Visit the websites of both firms and examine the scope of their operations. The Web address for Ford Motor is www.ford.com, and for Volkswagen it is www.vw.com. Then, based on your findings, answer these questions: What type of organizational arrangement(s) do you see the two firms using in coordinating their worldwide operations? Which of the two companies has the more modern arrangement? Do you think this increases that firm's efficiency, or does it hamper the company's efforts to contain costs and be more competitive? Why?

Australia

Australia is the smallest continent but the sixth-largest country in the world. It lies between the Indian and Pacific oceans in the Southern Hemisphere and has a landmass of almost 3 million square miles (around 85 percent the size of the United States). Referred to as being "down under" because it lies entirely within the Southern Hemisphere, it is a dry, thinly populated land. The outback is famous for its bright sunshine, enormous numbers of sheep and cattle, and unusual wildlife, such as kangaroos, koalas, platypuses, and wombats. Over 22 million people live in this former British colony. Although many British customs are retained, Australians have developed their own unique way of life. One of the world's most developed countries, Australia operates under a democratic form of government somewhat similar to that of Great Britain. Gross domestic product was US$907.7 billion in 2011. Services constitute about two-thirds of GDP. Unemployment in 2011 hovered around 5 percent.

A large financial services MNC in the United States examined the demographic and economic data of Australia. This MNC concluded that there would be increased demand for financial services in Australia. As a result, the company set up an operation in the capital, Canberra, which is slightly inland from Sydney and Melbourne, the two largest cities.

This financial services firm began in Chicago and now has offices in seven countries. Many of these foreign operations are closely controlled by the Chicago office. The overseas personnel are charged with carefully following instructions from headquarters and implementing centralized decisions. However, the Australian operation will be run differently. Because the country is so large and the population spread along the coast and to Perth in the west, and because of the "free spirit" cultural values of the Aussies, the home office feels compelled to give the manager of Australian operations full control over decision making. This manager will have a small number of senior-level managers brought from the United States, but the rest of the personnel will be hired locally. The office will be given sales and profit goals, but specific implementation of strategy will be left to the manager and his or her key subordinates onsite.

The home office believes that in addition to providing direct banking and credit card services, the Australian operation should seek to gain a strong foothold in insurance and investment services. As the country continues to grow economically, this sector of the industry should increase relatively fast. Moreover, few multinational firms are trying to tap this market in Australia, and those that are doing so are from British Commonwealth countries, with some exceptions. The CEO believes that the experience of the people being sent to Australia (the U.S. expatriates) will be particularly helpful in developing this market. He recently noted, "We know that the needs of the Australian market are not as sophisticated or complex as those in the United States, but we also know that they are moving in the same direction as we are. So we intend to tap our experience and knowledge and use it to garner a commanding share of this expanding market."

www.csu.edu.au/australia, www.cia.gov

Questions

1. What are some current issues facing Australia? What is the climate for doing business in Australia today?
2. What type of organizational structure arrangement is the MNC going to use in setting up its Australian operation?
3. Can this MNC benefit from any of the new organizational arrangements, such as a joint venture, the Japanese concept of keiretsu, or electronic networks?
4. Will this operation be basically centralized or decentralized?

Chapter 10

MANAGING POLITICAL RISK, GOVERNMENT RELATIONS, AND ALLIANCES

Firms go international to become more competitive and profitable. Unfortunately, many risks accompany internationalization. One of the biggest risks emerges from the political situation of the countries in which the MNC does business. Terrorism is also a worldwide concern which can create a large barrier to MNC entry or survival in a country. MNCs must be able to assess political risk and conduct skillful negotiations. An overview of the political environment in selected areas of the world was provided in Chapter 2. This chapter specifically examines the impact of political risk on MNCs and their subsequent decisions in managing it. One major way is through effective evaluation and risk reduction. This process extends from risk identification and quantification to the formulation of appropriate responses, such as integration and protective and defensive techniques.

This chapter also describes the process for developing productive relationships with governments and for managing alliances with foreign partners, many of which are influenced by home- and host-government relations. The specific objectives of this chapter are:

1. **EXAMINE** how MNCs evaluate political risk.

2. **PRESENT** some common methods used for managing and reducing political risk.

3. **DISCUSS** strategies to mitigate political risk and develop productive relations with governments.

4. **DESCRIBE** challenges to and strategies for effectively managing alliances.

The World of *International Management*

Shell's Russian Roulette

█ n early 2006, investors in Royal Dutch Shell had reason to be excited. With a 55 percent stake in the Sakhalin-II energy project, Shell owned the majority share of the world's largest oil and gas project. The $22 billion project, centered off the coast of mainland Russia, promised production of billions of barrels of oil and gas.[1] Within a few months, however, shareholder optimism transformed into confusion and anger.

First, Shell agreed to give up half of its interest in the project for a meager $7.5 billion, allowing for majority control by the Russian-based energy company Gazprom. In so doing, Shell was foregoing billions in future earnings.[2] To outsiders, this apparently one-sided deal appeared to provide little benefit to Shell. What prompted Shell to cede such a large amount of potential profit to a Russian-based company?

1990s: Production Sharing Agreements

Shell's involvement in Russia traces back to the early 1990s. Following the collapse of the Soviet Union, the Russian economy was stuck at a standstill. The country's untapped fossil fuel reserves, which potentially contained billions of barrels of oil and gas, appeared to be a possible solution to some of the country's financial problems. However, the Russian government lacked the necessary infrastructure to bring the fossil fuels to market. The proposed solution: encourage foreign energy companies to do the drilling through production-sharing agreements. These agreements, signed in the mid-1990s when oil was selling for just $22 a barrel, provided Shell with significant financial incentive to explore and drill in the Russian reserves, while guaranteeing the Russian government some much-needed future financial returns. To outsiders, the agreements seemed very favorable to the foreign companies. The terms of the 1996 agreement with Shell, for example, included a 100-percent recoup on all of

Shell's initial costs and a 17.5-percent return on its initial investments before Russia would collect any royalties. In 1997, Shell projected that initial investments would total $10 billion, leaving plenty of room for the Russian government to make a future profit.[3,4]

1997 to 2005: Russian Government Frustration

As work progressed on necessary infrastructure over the next decade, Shell's cost estimates began to swell. By 2005, projected costs reached $20 billion—more than double the original estimates. Because the 1996 production-sharing agreement allowed Shell to recoup all of its costs before paying the Russian government any royalty, cost overruns meant delayed and lost funds for the Russian government. Furthermore, as the Russian economy had improved significantly, the government began to realize how unfavorable the production-sharing agreements would be to emerging Russia. Russia was no longer as desperate for capital, and the country, now with its own oil and gas company Gazprom, could remove the fossil fuels itself. By early 2006, the Russian government openly expressed frustration with frequent cost overruns on the project, leading many outsiders to predict that Shell's future in the Sakhalin-II project was in jeopardy.[5]

2006: Shell Is Backed into a Corner

Later that year, after Shell announced that the project's projected annual cost for the following year was going to double, the Russian Ministry of Natural Resources announced it would revoke the environmental permits for Sakhalin-II. Work on the two 400-mile long pipelines—critical to the completion of the project—was halted. The entire Sakhalin-II project, and Shell's enormous investment, was suddenly in jeopardy. Although the government claimed that whale migration patterns were threatened by the project, hence requiring the revocation of the permits, many analysts saw this action as an effort by the frustrated Russian government to force Shell to renegotiate its 1996 agreement, giving Russia a larger slice of the profit pool. Environmental issues were never a previous problem on the project—in fact, Shell was seen as more environmentally-conscious than the Russian company Gazprom.[6] With $13 billion of shareholder money invested in Sakhalin-II, and

profitability still a few years away, Shell was forced into a corner with only two options: withdraw from Russia completely and take a massive loss, or accept the consequences of doing business in Russia, concede to the Russian government's demands, and renegotiate its previous contract.

Shell decided that the only way restart the project, and ultimately make a return for the shareholders, would be to accept the new conditions established by the Russian government. The renegotiated December 2006 deal included selling half of Shell's shares to Gazprom at discounted prices. Foreign partners Mitsubishi and Mitsui also were forced to sell shares to Gazprom. As a result, Shell was left with only a 27.5 percent share, while Gazprom gained 50-percent plus one share, giving it majority control. Shell also agreed to absorb over $3 billion in cost overruns, meaning an additional $3 billion in future profits for the Russian government. To stockholders, this new deal appeared to provide no upside. Immediately following the 2006 deal, environmental restrictions were lifted on the project and work was permitted to continue.[7]

The Risks of Doing Business in Russia: Shell Is Not Alone

Shell's experience with Sakhalin-II is not an isolated incident in Russia's energy sector. BP's joint venture with Russian investors AAR, TNK-BP, was plagued by similar frustrations. Formed in 2003, the joint venture's goal was to bring almost 12 billion barrels of Russian oil to the marketplace—constituting a quarter of BP's reserves. From the beginning of the alliance, however, BP faced obstacles at almost every turn. In 2008, when disagreements over future strategy emerged between BP and AAR, BP executives suddenly experienced visa problems, and BP CEO Robert Dudley became the subject of a Russian criminal investigation. With talks at a standstill and Dudley forced from the country, BP was strong-armed into giving up most of its influence in the joint alliance to AAR.[8] CEO Dudley was forced to remove himself from the project, and AAR installed a new CEO.[9] A few years later in 2011, BP was blocked from creating a second Russian joint venture, this time with Rosneft, following complaints from AAR.[10] Frustrated, BP finally sold its 50 percent stake in TNK-BP in 2013, netting $12.5 billion in cash and an 18.5 percent stake in Rosneft.[11]

International managers interested in expanding into Russia, or any emerging economy, must make a thorough assessment of its political risk and the costs and benefits of joint ventures with local partners. The World Bank is an excellent resource for assessing political risk. In the latest IFC/World Bank report "Doing Business 2013: Russian Federation," Russia is ranked 178 out of 185 in the category of "Dealing with Construction Permits." The report states that it takes 42 different procedures and at least 344 days (almost a full year) to gather all of these permits.[12]

Russia is one of the most challenging countries in which to do business. Corruption, red tape, security concerns, and overall lack of faith in governmental policies result in an especially difficult political environment. Foreign energy companies faced all of these issues and more in their effort to expand and operate in Russia. At first, these risks appeared manageable and worth the lucrative returns, but over time, the environment was just too much of a deterrent to their growth plans.

MNCs must be able to evaluate and manage political risks on a global scale and contemplate the potential of alliances and other long-term cooperative relationships to help mitigate risks. In this chapter, we explore strategies for evaluating political risks, managing government relations, and developing and managing alliances with private and public partners.

■ The Nature and Analysis of Political Risk

Both domestic and international political developments have a major impact on MNCs' strategic plans. MNCs face hazards that originate directly from variation and unpredictability in political and governance systems around the world. The state and its various institutions and agencies continue to pose a direct threat to MNCs through policy shifts in taxation or regulation, through outright or de facto expropriation, or by allowing the exploitation of assets by local firms. As government policies change, MNCs must be willing and able to adjust their strategies and practices to accommodate the new perspectives and actual requirements. Moreover, in a growing number of geographic regions and countries, governments appear to be less stable; therefore, these areas carry more risk than they did in the past. Applied to international management, **political risk** is the unanticipated likelihood that an MNC's foreign investment will be constrained by a host government's policies. Since the terrorist attacks of 9/11, political risk assessment has become especially vital to MNCs. Today, almost all countries are interested in sustaining investment from MNCs.[13] Yet political risks persist, especially in the emerging economies of the world, which continue to struggle with political and institutional instability. Examples of risk factors include freezing the movement of assets out of the host country, placing limits on the remittance of profits or capital, devaluing the currency, appropriating assets, and refusing to abide by the contractual terms of agreements previously signed with the MNC. As rapid globalization continues, MNCs must be aware of the political risk factors present in doing business abroad and develop strategies to respond to them. Policy and control mechanisms, along with awareness of the historical treatment of MNCs within certain nations, allow firms to evaluate the inherent risk of doing business there.

The government of China, for example, was for years very anxious to see the country admitted to the World Trade Organization (WTO). Yet even after its entry into the WTO, China made decisions that were in its own best short-run interests but that created new political risks for MNCs doing business there. One analyst noted:

> A series of recent moves by Chinese authorities—price controls, currency restrictions, limits on sale of state-owned companies—seem to reflect a slowdown in the nation's effort to shift from a planned to a market economy. Whether such steps are justifiably cautious or simply timid, economists and business executives agree that they are likely to further deter trade and investment in the near future. Today, China's central bank announced new restrictions on foreign exchange transactions, an attempt to control the flow of convertible currency out of the country. Officially described as a crackdown on illegal transactions, the moves will effectively make it more difficult for both domestic and international companies to move money in and out of China.[14]

political risk
The unanticipated likelihood that a business's foreign investment will be constrained by a host government's policy.

Some of the policies have since been relaxed; however, political risk still continues to be a major consideration for multinationals doing business there. As was brought out in Chapter 3, industrial piracy continues to be a big problem, and the Chinese government has yet to take effective action against it. Counterfeit goods produced in China cost American businesses an estimated US$48 billion every year.[15] One reason for the reluctance of the Chinese government to take action may well be that state-owned factories are some of the biggest counterfeiters. Yamaha estimates that five of every six motorcycles and scooters bearing its name in China are fake; some state-owned factories turn out copies four months after Yamaha introduces a new model. Yamaha did win a trademark case in 2007, but the penalty was relatively modest and it was not clear if a broader crackdown would have the desired effect.[16] Sometimes, counterfeiters are so efficient that the fake goods reach the market even before the actual product. Nike, for example, experienced this with its Air Max 360 when someone at the China office stole blueprints and began manufacturing. This is not the first instance of fake Nikes being sold in China and abroad. The company often receives shipments of shoes or returns from customers which bear the very recognizable swoosh logo but which are in fact cheap knockoffs of the original.

Another common complaint is the way rules and regulations are interpreted in China. Google's attempted entry into China is an example. The cyber attacks on Google, apparently linked to government concerns about Google's content and a desire to limit that content, and ongoing negotiations with the government as to what services and links would be available in China, have resulted in a difficult and ambiguous situation for the company. Noting that the Chinese government can "arbitrarily decide" the level of service Google Inc. can provide in China, the company's chief executive, Eric Schmidt, said, "'We don't know' if what seems to have been a relatively minor disruption of Google's search availability in China Thursday was evidence of that government power."[17]

These types of actions by the Chinese government increase the political risk of doing business in China. On the other side of the coin, Chinese MNCs must also assess the political risk inherent in doing business in the United States. The U.S. government has begun to review its trade policy with China. In particular, American trade officials claim that China has taken for granted its relationship with the United States and warn that if markets there are not opened for American goods, there will be reciprocal action against Chinese firms that are selling in the United States.[18] Given the enormous trade deficit that the United States has with China, this situation could end up creating major political risks for Chinese MNCs doing business in the politically stable but very risky United States. In fact, tensions continue to rise as U.S. politicians have become frustrated by China's unwillingness to revalue the yuan, and concerns have grown over the safety of goods imported from China. Tainted pet food, unsafe toys, suspect drywall imported from China, and recalls by many U.S. companies that import products from China, such as the massive toy recall by Mattel, have caused many in the United States to question the safety and reliability of Chinese products.[19]

Macro and Micro Analysis of Political Risk

Firms evaluate political risk in a number of ways. One is through **macro political risk analysis**, which reviews major political decisions that are likely to affect all business conducted in the country. For example, China's decision regarding restrictions on foreign-exchange transactions represents a macro political risk because it affects all MNCs. Another approach is **micro political risk analysis**, which is directed toward government policies and actions that influence selected sectors of the economy or specific foreign businesses. China's government policies regarding investment in the telecommunications industry fall into the micro political risk category. The following two sections examine both of these areas requiring analysis—macro political risk and micro political risk—in more depth.

macro political risk analysis
Analysis that reviews major political decisions likely to affect all enterprises in the country.

micro political risk analysis
Analysis directed toward government policies and actions that influence selected sectors of the economy or specific foreign businesses in the country.

Macro Risk Issues and Examples   In recent years, macro risk analysis has become of increasing concern to MNCs because of the growing number of countries that are finding their economies in trouble, as in Southeast Asia, or, even worse, that are unable to make the transition to a market-driven economy. A good example of the latter is Russia, as we saw in The World of International Management. Russia has been tightening controls on the flow of foreign currencies. This decision represents a change in direction from the free-market principles that Russia had been following in order to ensure that it continued to receive assistance from the International Monetary Fund.

India provides plenty of examples of macro political risks for MNCs. India's legal system is stymied by a labyrinth of laws and bureaucratic red tape. In recent years, the Indian courts have had a backlog of over 32 million cases.[20] Moreover, approximately one-quarter of these cases have been winding their way through the legal system for more than five years. So while the government touts the fact that Indian law offers strong protection to foreign firms against counterfeiters, an MNC finding that it must rely on the Indian judicial system to enforce its proprietary rights is likely to be sadly disappointed. As a result, many MNCs accept this risk as a cost of doing business in India and formulate strategies for managing the problem. A good example is provided by the Timken Company of Canton, Ohio, which makes bearings and alloy steel. When Timken found that the Indian market was rampant with fake Timken products, the MNC's initial reaction was to sue the counterfeiters. However, after realizing how long this would take, the MNC opted for a different strategy. Management switched the packaging of its products from cardboard boxes to heat-sealed plastic with eight-color printing and a hologram that could not be forged. Result: Within months the counterfeit market began drying up. Timken is not alone; there are many counterfeit operations in India because the slow-moving judicial system encourages noncompliance. In fact, some counterfeiters have found that by filing countersuits, they can tie up a case in court for years.

Many other newly emerging economies, besides the big countries China, Russia, and India, also present macro political risks for MNCs. In Vietnam, the communist government earned a bad name among foreign investors because of all the pitfalls they have to face. Until recently the Vietnamese government required all foreign investors to establish joint ventures with local partners. But even with this arrangement, getting things done proved to be extremely slow and difficult because of the numerous levels of bureaucracy to be dealt with. One international manager described his MNC's experience this way: "The negotiations would follow a serpentine path, with breakthroughs in one session often being erased in the next."[21] To date, macro political risks in Vietnam remain high, although there is little risk of political instability. Investors continue to proceed with caution, which may be a wise approach in an economy that could prove to be challenging for an increasingly integrated global marketplace.[22]

An example of a macro consideration of political risk would be an analysis of what would happen to a company's investment if opposition government leaders were to take control. In the 1970s U.S. companies in Iran failed to forecast the fall of the shah and rise of Khomeini and, as a result, they lost their investment. Because of this Iranian experience, the situation in Iraq under militant dictator Saddam Hussein and the subsequent instability after his removal, the 9/11 terrorist attacks on New York by ethnic Middle Easterners, and the recent Arab Spring uprisings, many MNCs now are reluctant to invest very heavily in most Middle Eastern countries. Recently, the government of Iran appeared to be interested in attracting foreign investment, but there is still a great deal of concern that this region is too politically explosive.

Central, if not Eastern, Europe appears to be a better bet, as seen by the millions of dollars that MNCs have poured into transition postcommunist countries such as Hungary and Poland. This geographic region is also regarded as politically risky, however, given the ongoing conflict in the Balkans, the breakup of Czechoslovakia into the independent Czech Republic and Slovak Republic, the continuing problems in the former Soviet republics, and the political instability in the entire region. As a result, many MNCs have been tempering their expansion plans in these still emerging economies. Recently, populist governments, somewhat hostile to capitalism and foreign investment, have emerged in a number of Latin American countries, including Bolivia, Ecuador, and Venezuela. In some cases, these governments have effectively forced divestment by MNCs, as was the case in Venezuela in the petrochemical sector.

Still another area of consideration for MNCs regarding macro political risks is government corruption, such as prevalence of bribery and government rules and regulations that require the inclusion of certain locals in lucrative business deals. One of the most commonly cited reasons for the severe economic problems in Indonesia in recent years is the corrupt practices of the government. Because the family of former president Suharto was involved in virtually every big business deal that took place under his regime, many loans and major projects were approved by banks and government agencies simply because these family members were part of the process. When these loans and projects ran into trouble, more money was poured in to shore up things—and no one dared to challenge these unsound decisions.

Which are the most and the least corrupt nations in the world? Table 10–1 provides the results for 2012 of the Corruption Perceptions Index, which measures the perceived level of public-sector corruption, in which 180 countries/territories were ranked. The United States ended up in 19th position, illustrating that even the U.S. has work to do in improving its business environment.

Micro Risk Issues and Examples   Micro risk issues often take such forms as industry regulation, taxes on specific types of business activity, and restrictive local laws. The essence of these micro risk issues is that some MNCs are treated differently from others, thus increasing the cost of doing business for some.

Table 10–1
Select Countries in the 2012 Transparency International Corruption Perceptions Index (Note: Some countries are "tied")

Rank	Country/Territory	Rank	Country/Territory
1	New Zealand	80	China
1	Denmark	88	Thailand
1	Finland	89	Swaziland
4	Sweden	94	India
5	Singapore	105	Mexico
6	Switzerland	118	Egypt
9	Canada	118	Indonesia
12	Luxembourg	123	Vietnam
13	Germany	133	Russia
17	Japan	133	Iran
17	United Kingdom	139	Pakistan
19	United States	139	Kenya
20	Chile	144	Ukraine
30	Spain	154	Kyrgyzstan
37	Taiwan	157	Cambodia
39	Israel	157	Angola
41	Poland	165	Venezuela
45	Korea (South)	165	Haiti
66	Saudi Arabia	169	Iraq
69	Brazil	170	Uzbekistan
69	South Africa	174	Afghanistan
72	Italy	174	Somalia

Source: © Transparency International. All rights reserved. For more information visit http://cpi.transparency.org

In 1992 American steel makers filed more than 80 complaints against 20 nations on a single day. They charged that foreign steel makers were dumping their products in the U.S. market at artificially low prices. In the first six months of 1998, the industry again demanded action against foreign producers in Brazil, Japan, and Russia who were dumping steel in the United States at unfairly low prices. What was even more troubling was that the American producers were in the process of negotiating with big auto and appliance makers for the steel that is sold under long-term contracts. Since steel prices had dropped sharply because of the alleged "dumping," the American firms were concerned that they would end up getting locked into contracts that offered very little, if any, profit. The American steel makers were insisting that their government force foreign producers to raise their prices.[23] The George W. Bush administration did ultimately impose tariffs on steel (these were, in part, subsequently rescinded). Such events underscore the uncertainty and volatility associated with micro political risks, even in the United States.

World Trade Organization (WTO) and European Union (EU) regulations on American MNCs have created new sorts of micro political risk. For example, the WTO ruled that the United States' 1916 Anti-Dumping Act violates global trade regulations and cannot be used by American firms to fend off imports.[24] Meanwhile on the European continent, the European Commission is investigating complaints by PepsiCo and other competitors that Coca-Cola has improperly attempted to shut down sales of its rivals.[25] The EU examines all major mergers and acquisitions and has the authority to block them. For example, the EU refused to allow the General Electric (GE) and Honeywell merger, a prime example of the forces of globalization (the EU was able to stop the actions of perhaps the most powerful U.S. firm) as well as of the need for political risk analysis (GE needed to better assess and manage the risk posed by the politicians and government bureaucrats in Brussels).

Other examples have included the EU's denying Volvo and Scania approval to merge and preventing Alcan Aluminum of Canada, Pechiney of France, and the Alusuisse Lonza Group of Switzerland, the world's three largest aluminum companies, from combining forces.[26] Microsoft has also faced challenges in the EU, including over a billion dollars in fines between 2004 and 2013. In 2004, the European Commission issued its decision regarding allegations of anticompetitive practices by Microsoft, finding that Microsoft had engaged in such practices and issuing a sweeping set of penalties, including the biggest fine it has ever levied, $613 million. The EC also says it will require that the company offer computer makers in Europe two versions of its monopoly Windows operating system, one with Windows Media Player, which lets users watch videos and hear music, and one without. Microsoft must share technical information with rivals that will help their server software work better with Windows: "We are simply ensuring that anyone who develops new software has a fair opportunity to compete in the marketplace," said Mario Monti, competition commissioner for the EU. Although Microsoft had emerged generally unscathed from the extended litigation in the U.S. related to a variety of allegedly anticompetitive practices, this EU decision constituted a major setback for the firm, and reflected the uniquely European perspective on these practices. In 2007, Microsoft lost its appeal and the ruling stood.[27] In 2013, Microsoft was again fined, this time for US$731 million, for ignoring previous promises and failing to give customers a choice of web browser.[28] These regulatory actions are good examples of the types of micro risk issues that MNCs face from industry regulation.

In some instances, it is not clear whether macro or micro political risk is at work. Research in Motion Ltd., the maker of the Blackberry line of smartphones, was threatened with expulsion from a number of markets, including Saudi Arabia, United Arab Emirates, and India, because of its proprietary encryption technology which makes it hard for countries to access calls and messages, which some claim is necessary to protect national security. The concerns center around corporate e-mail routed through the handsets and instant-messaging, which use high levels of encryption and proprietary technology. Consumer e-mails sent over the devices are lightly encrypted and can be decoded by local wireless phone companies. The governments have focused on RIM because it operates its own network of servers, and is therefore outside their legal jurisdiction and monitoring reach. RIM also features corporate e-mail services that are heavily encrypted and which only each corporate customer can access. This security has made RIM popular among companies and governments, but the target for governments. In this example, a company has been targeted because of its unique product features and their implications for government security.[29]

Terrorism and Its Overseas Expansion

Terrorism has existed for centuries, but terrorism has become more of a concern everywhere over the last few years, and especially so in the United States in light of the September 11, 2001, attacks. **Terrorism** is the use of force or violence against others to promote political or social views. The ultimate goal of the violence is for government and citizens to change policies and ultimately yield to the beliefs of the terrorist group.[30] Three types of terrorism exist: classic, amateur, and religiously motivated.[31] *Classic terrorism* entails a specific, well-defined objective pursued by well-trained, professional, underground members. *Amateur terrorism* tends to occur once and often has poorly defined objectives, and therefore members are not as committed. *Religiously motivated terrorism* is carried out by individuals holding very strong core beliefs, regardless of how well defined their objectives are. The latter tends to be more chaotic and scattered, since the individuals involved are extremely passionate about the cause, despite the lack of unified goals.

MNCs need to be wary of the combative political environment that may exist when they seek to engage in overseas expansion in certain geographic areas. For example, the Al Qaeda group has attacked in Yemen, Pakistan, Kuwait, Tunisia, and Kenya, to name a few. Palestinian suicide bombers have blown up buses in Israel. Australian tourists were killed in a massive attack in Bali, and a restaurant in the Philippines was the target of similar assaults. The United States' invasions of Afghanistan and Iraq have harmed political relations with countries that did not agree with those actions.[32] Violent conflicts in Africa are ongoing and endemic. There have been bombings in the U.K. In 2004, a terrorist group took over a school in Russia, resulting in the deaths of about 325 people when the Russian military recaptured the school.[33] As you well know, the list is long and likely to get longer.

It is clear that terrorism within a country can have a significant impact on the MNC in the macro sense. If a country has a high incidence of terrorist attacks against commercial businesses specifically, companies will need to be even more wary about setting up operations. Typically, terrorists target business areas or businesses that have high status or those that have great influence on initiating change. While terrorists now use an extensive array of attack methods, they tend to avoid institutions with high security; most attacks on private businesses are either driven by the amateur terrorist or those that are religiously motivated.[34] There is no way to guarantee that companies can fully avoid harm, but political risk analysis and preparation may forestall it. MNCs must thoroughly evaluate the political environment, install modern security systems, compile a crisis handbook, and prepare employees for situations that may arise.

Analyzing the Expropriation Risk

Expropriation is the seizure of businesses with little, if any, compensation to the owners. Such seizures of foreign enterprises by developing countries were quite common in the old days. In addition, some takeovers were caused by **indigenization laws**, which required that nationals hold a majority interest in the operation. Generally, expropriation is more likely to occur in non-Western countries that are poor, relatively unstable, and suspicious of foreign multinationals.

Some firms are more vulnerable to expropriation than others. Often, those at greatest risk are in extractive, agricultural, or infrastructure industries such as utilities and transportation, because of their importance to the country. In addition, large firms often are more likely targets than small firms, because more is to be gained by expropriating large firms.

terrorism
The use of force or violence against others to promote political or social views.

expropriation
The seizure of businesses by a host country with little, if any, compensation to the owners.

indigenization laws
Laws that require nationals to hold a majority interest in an operation.

MNCs can take a wide variety of strategies to minimize their chances of expropriation. They can bring in local partners. They can limit the use of high technology so that if the firm is expropriated, the country cannot duplicate the technology. They also can acquire an affiliate that depends on the parent company for key areas of the operation, such as financing, research, and technology transfer, so that no practical value exists in seizing the affiliate.

■ Managing Political Risk and Government Relations

For well over two decades, businesses have been looking for ways to manage their political risk. Quite often, the process begins with a detailed analysis of the various risks with which the MNC will be confronted, including development of a comprehensive framework that identifies the various risks and then assigns a quantitative risk or rating factor to them.

Developing a Comprehensive Framework or Quantitative Analysis

A comprehensive framework for managing political risk should consider all political risks and identify those that are most important. Schmidt has offered a three-dimensional framework that combines political risks, general investments, and special investments.[35] Figure 10–1 illustrates this framework, and the following sections examine each dimension in detail.

Political Risks Political risks can be broken down into three basic categories: transfer risks, operational risks, and ownership-control risks. **Transfer risks** stem from government policies that limit the transfer of capital, payments, production, people, and technology in or out of the country. Examples include tariffs on exports and imports as well as restrictions on exports, dividend remittance, and capital repatriation. **Operational risks** result from government policies and procedures that directly constrain the management and performance of local operations. Examples include price controls, financing restrictions, export commitments, taxes, and local sourcing requirements. **Ownership-control risks** are embodied in government policies or actions that inhibit ownership or control of local operations. Examples include foreign-ownership limitations, pressure for local participation, confiscation, expropriation, and abrogation of proprietary rights. For example, the Russian government canceled an agreement with the Exxon Corporation that would have allowed the firm to tap huge oil deposits in the country's far north. The Russian minister for natural resources cited "legal irregularities" as the reason for the decision. As a result, the $1.5 billion project came to a grinding halt.

transfer risks
Government policies that limit the transfer of capital, payments, production, people, and technology in and out of the country.

operational risks
Government policies and procedures that directly constrain management and performance of local operations.

ownership-control risks
Government policies or actions that inhibit ownership or control of local operations.

Figure 10–1

A Three-Dimensional Framework for Assessing Political Risk

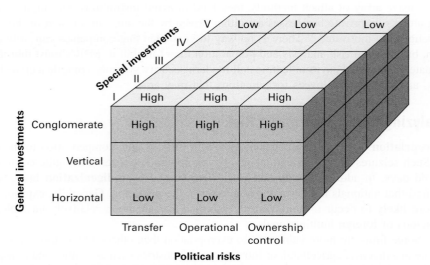

Source: David A. Schmidt, "Analyzing Political Risk," *Business Horizons,* August 1986, p. 50. Copyright 1986 Elsevier. Reprinted with premission.

One of the biggest problems in doing business internationally is that yesterday's agreement with a government may be canceled or delayed by today's politicians who disagree with that earlier decision. Enron, the now bankrupt Houston-based U.S. energy consortium, discovered this when its power project in Dabhol, India, became the focal point of political interest. India's economic nationalists began accelerating a campaign to scrap a high-profile, U.S.-backed power project despite warnings of potential damage to the confidence of foreign investors in the country. These politicians wanted to abandon the $2.8 billion deal as well as all other power projects in the country that had been approved under the government's "fast track" provisions. The contract for the two-stage, 2,000 megawatt plant was signed before the current politicians came to power in Maharashtra, the state where Dabhol is located.

What effect would this political move have on foreign investment in India? A number of foreign investors indicated that if the Enron project were canceled, they would review their investment plans for the country. A survey of international energy companies by the East-West Center in Hawaii found that of 13 Asian economies, India's investment climate ranked fifth from the bottom for power-sector investment. This seemed to have little effect on the politicians, who proceeded to cancel the project. Members of the political opposition, who supported the project, called it a mere political ploy designed to appeal to voters in the upcoming elections, and they urged foreign investors to sit tight and ride out the political storm. Many of these investors appeared to be apprehensive about taking such advice, and Enron announced plans for taking the case to international arbitration to reclaim the $300 million it had invested in the project—as well as $300 million in damages.

Eventually things were straightened out, but only for a while. Later the Maharashtra State Electric Board defaulted on $64 million in unpaid power bills. The board said that the company was charging too much for power, and Enron served notice that it would terminate the power supply contract and pull out. As of fall 2002, following Enron's own collapse, the power purchase agreement was to be reworked, and the foreign investors—Enron's creditors, GE, and Bechtel—were looking to divest their stakes in the venture, scrambling to recover whatever they could from the project.

The political climate in India is not unique. Russia also offers its share of jitters to investors. In particular, many joint ventures that were created during the Gorbachev era now are having problems. A good example is Moscow's Radisson-Slavjanskaya Hotel venture, in which American Business Centers of Irvine, California, owns a 40 percent stake. American Business Centers manages several floors of offices in the hotel, and now that the venture is making money, it appears that the Irvine firm's Russian partners and the Radisson hotel people are trying to oust them. The president of American Business Centers claims that his partners feel they do not need him any longer.

The dilemma faced by American Business Centers is becoming increasingly common in Russia. For example, the Seattle-based firm Radio Page entered into a joint venture with Moscow Public Telephone Network and another Russian company to offer paging services. Together, they built a system of telephone pagers in the Moscow region. Radio Page held a 51 percent stake. When annual revenues hit $5 million and the venture was on the verge of making $1 million, the agreement began to unravel. The Russian partners demanded control of the operation and even threatened to pull the critical radio frequencies if they did not get their way.

There is little that foreign joint-venture firms doing business in high-risk countries can do except try to negotiate with their partners. For instance, the political situation in Russia is so unstable that support from one government ministry may be offset by opposition from another, or, worse yet, the individuals supporting the foreign firm may be ousted from their jobs tomorrow. Economic considerations tend to be the main reason why firms seek international partners, but sometimes it seems that everything boils down to politics and the risks associated with dealing in this political environment.

Commenting on the government's action, one Western investment banker in Russia said that "it raises the question of whether a deal is a deal in Russia, because Exxon is meticulous to a fault in following the letter of the law."[36] Abrogation of the agreement is an example of ownership-control risks.

For some other examples of political risks that must be managed, see the International Management in Action box, "Sometimes It's All Politics," on the following page.

General Nature of Investment The general nature of investment examines whether the company is making a conglomerate, vertical, or horizontal investment (see Figure 10–1). In a **conglomerate investment**, the goods or services produced are not similar to those produced at home. These types of investments usually are rated as high risk, because foreign governments see them as providing fewer benefits to the country and

conglomerate investment
A type of high-risk investment in which goods or services produced are not similar to those produced at home.

vertical investment
The production of raw materials or intermediate goods that are to be processed into final products.

horizontal investment
An MNC investment in foreign operations to produce the same goods or services as those produced at home.

greater benefits to the MNC than other investments. **Vertical investments** include the production of raw materials or intermediate goods that are to be processed into final products. These investments run the risk of being taken over by the government because they are export-oriented, and governments like a business that helps them generate foreign capital. **Horizontal investments** involve the production of goods or services that are the same as those produced at home. These investments typically are made with an eye toward satisfying the host country's market demands. As a result, they are not very likely to be takeover targets.

Special Nature of Investment   The special nature of foreign direct investment (FDI) relates to the sector of economic activity, technological sophistication, and pattern of ownership. There are three sectors of economic activity: (1) the primary sector, which consists of agriculture, forestry, and mineral exploration and extraction; (2) the industrial sector, consisting of manufacturing operations; and (3) the service sector, which includes transportation, finance, insurance, and related industries. Levels of technological sophistication characterize science-based industry and non-science-based industry. The difference between them is that science-based industry requires the continuous introduction of new products or processes. Patterns of ownership relate to whether businesses are wholly or partially owned.

The special nature of FDI can be categorized as one of five types (see Figure 10–1). Type I is the highest-risk venture; type V is the lowest-risk venture. This risk factor is assigned based on sector, technology, and ownership. Primary sector industries usually have the highest risk factor, service sector industries have the next highest, and industrial sector industries have the lowest. Firms with technology that is not available to the government should the firm be taken over have lower risk than those with technology that is easily acquired. Wholly owned subsidiaries have higher risk than partially owned subsidiaries.

Using a framework similar to that provided in Figure 10–1 helps MNCs to understand and manage their political risks. A way to complement this framework approach is to give specific risk ratings to various criteria and make a final compilation.

Quantifying the Variables in Managing Political Risk   Some MNCs attempt to manage political risk through a quantification process in which a range of variables are simultaneously analyzed to derive an overall rating of the degree of political risk in a given jurisdiction. This would allow an MNC, for example, to compare how risky a particular venture would be in Russia and in Argentina.

Factors that are typically quantified reflect the political and economic environment, domestic economic conditions, and external economic conditions. Each factor is given a minimum or maximum score, and the scores are tallied to provide an overall evaluation of the risk. Table 10–2 provides an example of a quantitative list of political risk criteria.

Techniques for Responding to Political Risk

Once political risk has been analyzed by a framework, quantitative analysis, or both, the MNC then will attempt to manage the risk further through a carefully developed response. The MNC can also proactively improve its relationship with governments by means of pre-emptive political strategies to mitigate risk before it appears. Three related strategies should be considered: (1) relative bargaining power analysis; (2) integrative, protective, and defensive techniques; and (3) proactive political strategies.

Relative Bargaining Power Analysis

The theory behind relative bargaining power is quite simple. The MNC works to maintain a bargaining power position stronger than that of the host country. A good example

Table 10–2
Criteria for Quantifying Political Risk

Major Area	Criteria	Scores	
		Minimum	Maximum
Political and economic environment	1. Stability of the political system	3	14
	2. Imminent internal conflicts	0	14
	3. Threats to stability emanating from the outside world	0	12
	4. Degree of control of the economic system	5	9
	5. Reliability of the country as a trading partner	4	12
	6. Constitutional guarantees	2	12
	7. Effectiveness of public administration	3	12
	8. Labor relations and social peace	3	15
Domestic economic conditions	9. Size of population	4	8
	10. Per capita income	2	10
	11. Economic growth during previous 5 years	2	7
	12. Prospective growth during next 3 years	3	10
	13. Inflation during previous 2 years	2	10
	14. Accessibility of domestic capital market to foreigners	3	7
	15. Availability of high-quality local labor	2	8
	16. Possibility of giving employment to foreign nationals	2	8
	17. Availability of energy resources	2	14
	18. Legal requirements concerning environmental protection	4	8
	19. Traffic system and communication	2	14
External economic relations	20. Restrictions imposed on imports	2	10
	21. Restrictions imposed on exports	2	10
	22. Restrictions imposed on foreign investments in the country	3	9
	23. Freedom to set up or engage in partnerships	3	9
	24. Legal protection for brands and products	3	9
	25. Restrictions imposed on monetary transfers	2	8
	26. Reevaluations against the home market currency during previous 5 years	2	7
	27. Development of the balance of payments	2	9
	28. Drain on foreign funds through oil and other energy imports	3	14
	29. International financial standing	3	8
	30. Restrictions imposed on the exchange of local money into foreign currencies	2	8

Source: From E. Diehtl and H. G. Koglmayr, "Country Risk Ratings," *Management International Review,* Vol. 26, No. 4, 1986, p. 6. Reprinted with permission.

arises when the MNC has proprietary technology that will be unavailable to the host country if the operation is expropriated or the firm is forced to abide by government decisions that are unacceptable to it. Over time, of course, this technology may become common, and the firm will lose its bargaining power. To prevent this from happening, the firm will work to develop new technology that again establishes the balance of power in its favor. As long as the host country stands to lose more than it will gain by taking action against the company, the firm has successfully minimized its political risk by establishing an effective bargaining position. Figure 10–2 provides an example. As long as the MNC's bargaining power remains at or above the diagonal line, the government will not intervene. At point E in the figure, this power declines, and the host country will begin to intervene.[37]

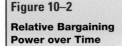

Figure 10–2

Relative Bargaining Power over Time

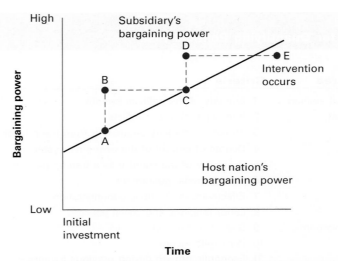

Source: Adapted from Thomas A. Pointer, "Political Risk: Managing Government Intervention," in *International Management: Text and Cases,* ed. Paul W. Beamish, J. Peter Killing, Donald J. LeCraw, and Harold Crookell (Homewood, IL: Irwin, 1991), p. 125.

Gaining bargaining power depends on many factors, such as the host country's perception of the MNC's size, experience, and legitimacy. Furthermore, the ability to bargain and achieve security does not necessarily mean that the MNC must be aggressive or engage in a "power play." Enticing the host country with products or services which could benefit it in the short run could result in retaliatory actions if the MNC is not able to innovate or the host country grows weary of a lack of power.

Integrative, Protective, and Defensive Techniques Another way that MNCs attempt to protect themselves from expropriation or minimize government interference in their operations is to use integration and the implementation of protective and defensive techniques. **Integrative techniques** are designed to help the overseas operation become part of the host country's infrastructure. The objective is to be perceived as "less foreign" and thus unlikely to be the target of government action. Some of the most integrative techniques include (1) developing good relations with the host government and other local political groups; (2) producing as much of the product locally as possible with the use of in-country suppliers and subcontractors, thus making it a "domestic" product; (3) creating joint ventures and hiring local people to manage and run the operation; (4) doing as much local research and development as possible; and (5) developing effective labor-management relations.

At the same time, MNCs should be cognizant of how integrated they become in foreign markets. It is recommended that managers seek to maintain close ties between the subsidiary and the parent company, and not fully integrate into the host country. There is no guarantee that host countries will completely treat the MNC as a domestic company, making true competition difficult. Therefore, other, more distant techniques may be beneficial.

Protective and defensive techniques are designed to discourage the host government from interfering in operations, mainly by avoiding complex ties to the host country's economy. In contrast to the integrative techniques, these actually encourage nonintegration of the enterprise in the local environment. Examples include (1) doing as little local manufacturing as possible and conducting all research and development outside the country; (2) limiting the responsibility of local personnel and hiring only those who are vital to the operation; (3) raising capital from local banks and the host government as well as outside sources; and (4) diversifying production of the product among a number of countries.

integrative techniques
Techniques that help the overseas operation become a part of the host country's infrastructure.

protective and defensive techniques
Techniques that discourage the host government from interfering in operations.

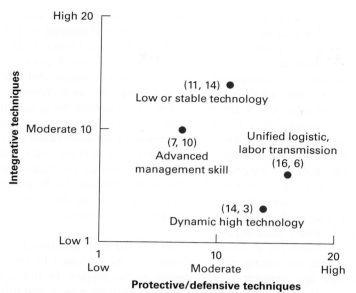

Source: Adapted from Ann Gregory, "Firm Characteristic and Political Risk Reduction in Overseas Ventures," *National Academy of Management Proceedings* (New York, 1982), p. 77.

Companies are more likely to use a protective-defensive strategy or a balance over completely integrating into another country, as illustrated in Figure 10–3. Organizations with an emphasis on innovative technology, such as Microsoft, prefer a protective technique as a way to safeguard against actions such as counterfeiting. MNCs that have products which are labor-intensive and have a high value to weight ratio also prefer protective methods, though there exists some integration. Here, strong global marketing systems are needed to sell the product, which is why integration occurs on some level despite the more cost-efficient method of either manufacturing in the home country or simply outsourcing construction to lower-wage regions.

Developing countries do not hold advanced management skills in as high regard as developed countries. For this reason, when selling products such as food, which requires advanced marketing and management skills, it is best to employ a mixed strategy (see Figure 10–3). That is, integration is necessary in order to effectively manufacture the product to local tastes and advertise, and there is little need for the company to distance operations from the host country in a manner tailored to local preferences. Finally, industries that utilize little technology, such as steel manufacturing, exhibit the strongest integrative technique while still employing a defensive strategy. These companies require integration to ensure long-term production for projects, but may not desire to become completely enveloped in the host country's economy due to possibilities such as the host government suddenly requiring a greater share of profits generated by the MNC.

Proactive Political Strategies As mentioned at the beginning of the chapter, despite the general trend of developing countries seeking MNC investment, many developing-country governments continue to engage in practices that effectively overturn or renege on past deals.[38] In the last half of the 1990s, leaders of a number of countries in which autocratic or dictatorial governments controlled negotiations with foreign investors were toppled. The ousting of leaders in Peru, Indonesia, Malaysia, the Philippines, and Venezuela led to a backlash against incumbent foreign investors and forced many project leaders to withdraw or renegotiate the terms of their investments.[39]

In Indonesia, President Suharto's 30 years of dictatorial and nepotistic government were totally discredited, and investors whose reputations were closely associated with his legacy face a challenging environment for preserving the economic viability of their presence. For example, the government of Indonesia reneged on its commitment to buy power from two projects sponsored by MidAmerica Energy Holdings, arguing that the projects, both of which were awarded on a sole-source contract basis under the Suharto regime, were overpriced and the government simply could not afford to pay.[40] Indonesia's former minister of mines and energy, Purnamo Yusgiantora, said his government would fight in U.S. courts to release $130 million being held in a Bank of America escrow account after Karaha Bodas, a power developer, won an arbitration award in its dispute with the Indonesian government over cancelation of a geothermal plant that Karaha had agreed to build in collaboration with Indonesia's state electricity company.[41] The Bolivian government rescinded a 40-year contract with Aguas del Tunari—a consortium that included London-based International Water Ltd., Bechtel Enterprise Holdings, Italy's Montedison Energy Services, Spain's Abengoa Servicios Urbanos, and four of Bolivia's largest construction companies—to supply water to Cochabamba, Bolivia's third-largest city.

Often the challenges and complexity associated with government's tendency to seek to renegotiate investment rules and contracts are worsened by the participation of both national and subcentral governments in the project. In India, Brazil, and, increasingly, China, states and provinces wield significant power, and this has been a particular problem in the development and financing of power, water, and transport projects. The Linha Amarela project in Rio de Janeiro, an urban expressway that begins in the residential area of Rio and provides a direct link to the downtown area, was initially bid with an official traffic estimate of around 55,000 cars per day in 1993–1994. However, when construction was complete and the road opened for business in 1998, traffic exceeded that amount, reaching 80,000 vehicles per day in early 2001. When the new mayor of Rio, Cesar Maia, took office on January 1, 2001, he issued a number of decrees overturning policies of his predecessor. One of these decrees unilaterally dropped the toll by 20 percent, squeezing the foreign owner of the concession.

In addition to the approaches mentioned above, how else can MNCs respond to such unpredictable government decisions? Because government policies can have a significant impact on business activities and many governments face competing pressures from a range of stakeholders, corporations must adopt various **proactive political strategies** both to affect government policy and to respond to competitors' efforts to influence that policy. Comprehensive strategies are especially important in unstable and transitional policy environments.[42] These strategies are designed, in part, to develop and maintain ongoing favorable relationships with government policy makers as a tool to mitigate risk before it becomes unmanageable. Broadly, strategies may include leveraging bilateral, regional, and international trade and investment agreements, drawing on bilateral and multilateral financial support, and using project finance structures to separate project exposure from overall firm risk. They also can include entering markets early in the privatization-liberalization cycle (the first-mover strategy discussed in Chapter 8), establishing a local presence and partnering with local firms, and pursuing pre-emptive stakeholder management strategies to secure relationships with all relevant actors.[43]

More specific proactive political strategies include formal lobbying, campaign financing, seeking advocacy through the embassy and consulates of the home country, and more formal public relations and public affairs activities such as grassroots campaigning and advertising.[44] Strategies must vary based on the particular political system (parliamentary vs. non-parliamentary), distribution of power (highly centralized vs. decentralized), and other variations in political systems.[45] However, MNCs have the option of purchasing political risk insurance, which could be used across cultures and systems and protect the company from inherent uncertainty. This option has been available for decades, but many have not utilized it because risk assessment

proactive political strategies
Lobbying, campaign financing, advocacy, and other political interventions designed to shape and influence the political decisions prior to their impact on the firm.

is so subjective and unpredictable, that most companies choose to forgo coverage.[46] MNCs that are concerned with currency convertibility issues, political unrest, or exporting matters may want to take a closer look. Insurance terms range anywhere from 3 to 15 years or more and can cover up to $80 million per risk.[47] As an MNC increases exporting or overseas operations, the benefits of coverage may outweigh the cost of the insurance.

Developing and maintaining ongoing relationships with political actors, including officials in power and in opposition parties, and with the range of stakeholders, including nongovernmental organizations (NGOs) and others, can help buffer host-government actions that may constrain or undermine MNC strategies and plans.[48] In the previous examples, had investors made low-level contacts with opposition groups, they might have aggravated existing strains in relationships with governments but secured some protections for the future. Knowing when—and how—to exercise such relationships is a difficult but necessary strategy.

How does an MNC know which strategy to pursue? There is no straightforward answer to this question, since strategic responses depend on a multitude of factors. The nature of the industry, the firm's technological capabilities, local conditions in a host country, management skills and philosophies, logistics, and labor transmission are just a few ways decisions are impacted. No one strategy is guaranteed to work, but building a relationship with all parties involved could assist in the betterment of any method an MNC employs.

■ Managing Alliances

Another dimension of management strategy related to political risk and government relations is managing relationships with alliance partners. Some partners may be current or former state-owned enterprises; others may be controlled or influenced by government agencies. For example, in China, most foreign investors have some sort of alliance or joint-venture relationships with Chinese state-owned enterprises. AB Volvo, which had not been able to previously penetrate the Chinese truck market, entered into a strategic alliance with state-owned automobile producer Dongfeng Motors in 2013. The deal not only expands Volvo's heavy-duty truck presence in China but will also result in Volvo becoming the largest truck manufacturer in the world.[49] In 2004, Siemens AG chief executive Heinrich von Pierer announced a sweeping expansion of the company's business in China using its more than 45 joint ventures as the primary vehicle for expansion.[50] Some recent examples of Siemens' strategy in action include a 2012 deal with the Wasion Group to expand the market for its meter data management solutions and a 2011 deal with Shanghai Electric to penetrate the Chinese wind power market, which is the largest in the world.[51,52] As mentioned in Chapter 9, alliances and joint ventures can significantly improve the success of MNC entry and operation in many international markets, especially emerging economies. Managing the relationships inherent in alliances, especially when governments are involved, can be especially challenging.

The Alliance Challenge

A rich and increasingly diverse recent literature has examined the motivations for collective action through international strategic alliances (ISAs). Researchers have begun to focus on specific explanations of ISA formation, the conditions that appear to lead to better or worse ISA performance and endurance, and the primary factors motivating firms to enter into such relationships.[53] Motivating factors include faster entry and payback, economies of scale and rationalization, complementary technologies and patents, and co-opting or blocking competition.[54]

In the strategic alliance literature, several researchers have argued that learning can be a powerful force in the initial motivations for, and ultimate success of, ISAs.[55] Some kinds of local knowledge cannot be internalized simply as a result of an MNC entering and operating in a foreign market; acquisition of some kinds of local knowledge requires local firm participation. Collaboration facilitates rapid market entry by allowing firms to share costs and risks, combine product and market complementarities, and reduce the time-to-market.[56]

How an alliance relationship is developed is largely a function of interfirm negotiation. Alliances are an arena where both value-claiming activities (competitive, distributive negotiation) and value-creating activities (collaborative, integrative negotiation) take place. In order to lay claim to a larger share of the alliance pie, firms tend to seek an advantage over their partners. Firms do this by possessing superior resources or alternatives beyond the scope of the alliance. However, in order to create a "larger pie" through the combination of partner-firm resources and activities, firms must balance authority, allowing each firm to dictate certain activities within the alliance, and to commit to sharing and reciprocity where each partner firm plays some decision-making role. In these instances, alliance partners can create value through specialization gains or when the rationalization of redundant activities results in enhanced performance for the partners.[57]

A fundamental challenge of alliances is managing operations with partners from different national cultures (as previously discussed in Chapter 5). Cultural differences may create uncertainties and misunderstandings in the relationship, which may lead to conflict and even dissolution of the venture. Indeed, an alliance may be viewed as a temporal structure designed to address a particular problem during a period in time; all alliances eventually outlast their purpose.

Differences in the cultural backgrounds of partners can potentially cause problems in alliances. One study tried to determine whether some differences are more disruptive than others. The researchers found that differences in uncertainty avoidance and in long-term orientation, in particular, cause problems (see Chapter 4 for cultural dimensions). These differences have a negative impact on survival and decrease the likelihood that firms will enter a foreign country through an alliance rather than a wholly owned subsidiary.[58] Apparently, these differences, which translate into differences in how partners perceive and adapt to opportunities and threats in their environment, are more difficult to resolve than differences in other cultural dimensions. Perhaps cultural differences in power distance, individualism, and masculinity are more easily resolved because they are mainly reflected in different attitudes toward the management of personnel—something firms can make explicit.

Successful management of alliances depends on situational conditions, management instruments, and performance criteria. Success factors may include partner selection, cooperation agreement, management structure, acculturation process, and knowledge management.[59] In particular, partner selection and task selection criteria have been identified as critical variables that influence alliance success or failure. Conducting due diligence, choosing the right partners, and defining the scope and limit of the alliance appear to be the most important elements in determining if an alliance will succeed or fail.

One difficult but important aspect of successful alliance management is preparation for the likely eventual termination of the alliance.[60] Many firms are caught off guard when their partners are better prepared to deal with issues related to termination of the alliance than they are. After studying two dozen successful alliance "divorces," a group of researchers identified a number of legal and business issues that were critical to successful divorces. Legal issues include the conditions of termination, the disposition of assets and liabilities, dispute resolution, distributorship arrangements, protection of proprietary information and property, and rights over sales territories and obligations to customers. Business issues include the basic decision to exit, people-related issues, and relations with the host government. Alliances, like individual businesses, experience a life

| **Figure 10–4** | **Alliance Life Cycle** |

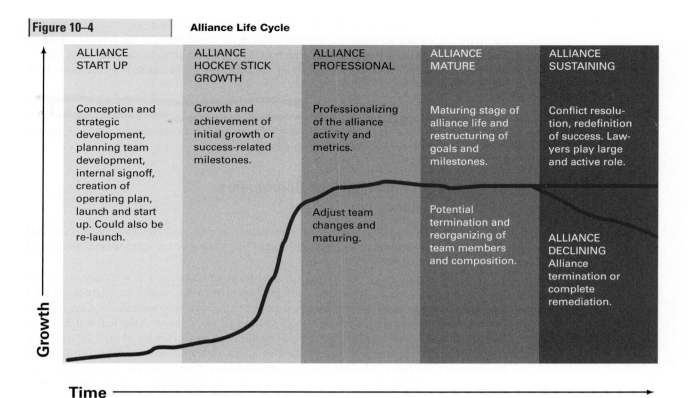

Source: From Larraine Segil, "Metrics to Successfully Manage Alliances," *Strategy & Leadership,* Vol. 22, No. 5 (2005), p. 47. Reprinted with permission of the author.

cycle, as illustrated in Figure 10–4. Recognizing the point at which your alliance exists in the life cycle can help determine a proactive strategy to sustain the relationship and work toward a common goal.

The Role of Host Governments in Alliances

As previously mentioned, host governments are active in mandating that investors take on partners, and these mandates can pose managerial and operational challenges for MNCs. Many host governments require investors to share ownership of their subsidiaries with local partners—in some cases, state-owned or state-controlled partners. These mandates can include specific requirements that investors select local state-owned firms (China) or that investors form joint ventures to meet local regulatory requirements where restrictions or local-content rules apply (Central and Eastern Europe).[61]

Even when host governments do not require alliances or JV as a condition for entry, many MNCs find that having alliance or JV partners is advantageous to their entry and expansion. This is especially so in highly regulated industries such as banking, telecommunications, and health care. In a study conducted of alliances among global telecommunications firms, firms were found to establish alliances with local partners primarily to gain market access and to contend with local regulations.[62] In another study, also of telecommunications projects in emerging markets, firms were found to take on local partners as a way to cope with emerging-market environments characterized by arbitrary and unpredictable corruption.[63]

Even when alliances are dissolved, host governments can have a role. In particular, the host government of a partner may be unwilling to permit the alliance to terminate. It could object to the termination in an overt way, such as not permitting a foreign partner to sell its interest in the alliance.[64] There are also subtle ways to discourage a partner from leaving an alliance, such as blocking the repatriation of the foreign partner's investments in the alliance. It is also important to consider carefully the long-term effects of terminating an alliance on the ability of the company to do business in the same host country in the future.

In sum, host governments have a substantial role in the terms under which alliances are initially formed, the way in which they are managed, and even the terms of their dissolution. MNCs must be aware of these influences and use carefully crafted strategies to manage host-government involvement in their alliances.

Examples of Challenges and Opportunities in Alliance Management

Alliances and JVs are increasingly common modes of entry and operation in international business. A number of recent examples illustrate the challenges and opportunities associated with managing alliances.

A good example is provided by Ford Motor and Mazda. For a number of years the two had a strategic alliance. With guidance from its American partner, Mazda was able to trim costs and introduce a host of popular new models in Asia. At the same time, the company began to gain ground in both North America and Europe. Part of this success was accounted for by Ford executives who reined in Mazda's freewheeling engineers and forced them to share auto platforms and to source more components overseas. Mazda also began following Ford's advice to use customer clinics, thus helping the company to develop low-priced, compact sport vehicles that have proved to be very popular in the Japanese market. Although Ford divested the majority of its Mazda shares and severed production ties in 2010, the two automakers continue to share technology and work together on mutually beneficial joint ventures.[65]

Starbucks Coffee International of Seattle, Washington, developed a joint venture with the Beijing Mei Da Coffee Company to open coffee houses in China. Getting local consumers to switch from tea to coffee is likely to be a major challenge. However, for the moment, the joint venture is focusing on the training of local managers who will run the coffee shops. Recruits are sent to Tacoma, Washington, to learn how to make the various types of Starbucks coffee and to get a firsthand look at the company's culture. As one of the general managers for the Mei Da Company put it, "People don't go to Starbucks for the coffee but for the experience. Focusing on the development of employees so that they can deliver that experience is our priority for now."[66] Part of Starbucks' strategy is also to show the new recruits that there are career and personal development opportunities in this new venture. This is an important area of emphasis for the firm because there is a major shortage of management personnel in China. As a result, many companies raid the management ranks of others, offering lucrative financial arrangements to those who are willing to change companies. One way that Starbucks is trying to deal with this is by encouraging the trainees to take responsibility, question the system, take risks, and make changes that will keep the customers coming back. Although the relationship began as a joint venture, Starbucks ultimately bought out its joint venture partner, a common progression as foreign and local partners begin to collaborate more closely and complete integration is desirable. The latest acquisition, which gives Starbucks a 90 percent controlling stake in Beijing Mei Da, will help the coffee company "achieve greater operational efficiencies and accelerate our expansion in China," said Wang Jinlong, president of Starbucks Greater China.[67] More recently, Starbucks has entered India via a JV with Tata, the conglomerate involved in automotive production, informational systems, and beverages such as tea.

As these examples show, MNCs are and will be making a host of decisions related to IJVs. In Russia, the current trend is to renegotiate many of the old agreements and seek smaller deals that entail less bureaucratic red tape and are easier to bring to fruition. At the same time, the U.S. administration is trying to create a plan for providing assistance to the former Soviet republics, and this likely will generate increased interest in the use of IJVs.

Besides the former Soviet Union, other areas of the world previously closed to foreign investment are beginning to open up. One of these is Vietnam, which had a very auspicious beginning in the early 1990s when investors began flocking there. During this time period, Japan's Idemitsu Oil Development Company signed a deal with the Vietnamese government that gave the company the right to explore an off-shore oil and gas field in the Gulf of Tonkin. A number of U.S. companies also targeted Vietnam for investment, and Citibank and Bank of America both were approved for branch status by the government. The bulk of their business was to be in wholesale banking and, in the case of Bank of America, advising the government on financing the rebuilding of the nation's weak power sector. Other firms that began giving serious consideration to Vietnam included AT&T, Coca-Cola, General Electric, ExxonMobil, and Ralston Purina, to name but five. As a result, by 1996 the country was attracting over $8 billion annually in foreign direct investment (FDI). In the late 1990s and early 2000s, however, FDI dropped sharply. In recent years, it has risen sharply again.

The sometimes bureaucratic communist government often sends mixed signals to foreign investors. Ford Motor, for example, had spent over $100 million to build a factory near Hanoi, but because of pressure from its local rival, the Vietnam Motor Corporation, it took 16 months for Ford to get approval to sell its Laser sedan. By the end of 2000, the company had sold fewer than 1,000 vehicles, a far cry from the 14,000 that had been initially projected.[68] Many other firms reported similar experiences. Consequently, the Vietnamese government tried to turn things around by undertaking domestic economic reform, pursuing international trade agreements, and encouraging foreign investment, especially joint ventures.[69] Among other things, the country's coffee production was skyrocketing, and Vietnam exported over 20 percent of its coffee to the United States; so it is in the best interests of the country to open its markets. At the same time, a growing number of multinationals were re-examining Vietnam's potential and looking to create strategic alliances that will help them establish a foothold in one of the more promising emerging economies in Asia.[70] After several years, this approach seemed to be paying off. Vietnam had passed a domestic enterprise law and investment law easing and clarifying foreign investment and business rules, including those pertaining to joint ventures, signed a trade agreement with the United States, and, in 2005, joined the WTO. As a result, foreign investment was once again on the rise, reaching US$9.6 billion in 2008. In 2009, Ford had its best ever sales year in Vietnam, selling 8,286 units. To help support the growth of its business and increasing demand for Ford vehicles, Ford Vietnam continued with its expansion plans in 2009 by completing a new, state-of-the-art assembly line at its Hai Duong facility and increasing production capacity by 25 percent.[71] Now over a decade later, Ford is approaching the 10,000 vehicle per year mark.[72]

■ The World of International Management—Revisited

A wide range of risks emanate from the political environment in which MNCs operate, and firms can employ an equally diverse set of strategies to mitigate those risks and improve their relations with governments. Shell faced a series of challenges in Russia which it sought to overcome using a range of strategies. Initially, Shell chose to continue with its ongoing operations but to defer further investment, but ultimately Shell was forced to exit and under unfavorable conditions. After reading this chapter and considering the challenges associated with doing business in Russia, answer the following questions: (1) What are two main concerns that MNCs should evaluate when doing business in Russia? (2) How can MNCs protect themselves from government action? (3) What proactive political strategies might help protect MNCs from future changes in the political environment? (4) How might alliances and joint ventures reduce risk and help relationships with government actors and other stakeholders?

SUMMARY OF KEY POINTS

1. Political risk is the likelihood that the foreign investment of a business will be constrained by a host government's policies. In dealing with this risk, companies conduct both macro and micro political risk analyses. Specific consideration is given to changing host-government policies, expropriation, and operational profitability risk.

2. MNCs attempt to manage their political risk in two basic ways. One is by developing a comprehensive framework for identifying and describing these risks. This includes consideration of political, operational,

and ownership-control risks. A second is by quantifying the variables that constitute the risk.

3. Common risk management strategies are the use of relative bargaining power, integrative, protective, and defensive techniques, and proactive political strategies.

4. Effective alliance management includes careful selection of partners, defining the tasks and scope of the alliance, addressing cross-cultural differences, and responding to host-government requirements.

KEY TERMS

conglomerate investment, *351*

expropriation, *350*

horizontal investment, *351*

indigenization laws, *350*

integrative techniques, *354*

macro political risk analysis, *345*

micro political risk analysis, *345*

operational risks, *350*

ownership-control risks, *351*

political risk, *344*

proactive political strategies, *356*

protective and defensive techniques, *355*

terrorism, *349*

transfer risks, *350*

vertical investment, *351*

REVIEW AND DISCUSSION QUESTIONS

1. What types of political risk would a company entering Russia face? Identify and describe three. What types of political risk would a company entering France face? Identify and describe three. How are these risks similar? How are they different?

2. Most firms attempt to quantify their political risk, although they do not assign specific weights to the respective criteria. Why is this approach so popular? Would the companies be better off assigning weights to each of the risks being assumed? Defend your answer.

3. How has terrorism impacted foreign interest in Iran and Saudi Arabia, considering the vast oil

reserves that are there? How have terrorist attacks affected political relationships between countries such as the United States and Russia?

4. If a high-tech firm wanted to set up operations in Iran, what steps might it take to ensure that the subsidiary would not be expropriated? Identify and describe three strategies that would be particularly helpful. How might proactive political strategies help protect firms from future changes in the political environment?

5. What are some of the challenges associated with managing alliances? How do host governments affect these?

INTERNET EXERCISE: NOKIA IN CHINA

Asia still offers great opportunities for multinational firms. However, given the slowdown that has occurred in this region in recent years, there are also great risks associated with doing business there. The large Finnish-based MNC, Nokia, has determined that the opportunities are worth the risk and has staked a large claim in China and is determined to be a major player in the emerging Asian market. Visit its website at www.nokia.com and focus your attention on what this well-known MNC is now doing in Asia. Drawing from specific information obtained from the website, this chapter, and your reading of the current news, answer these questions: What political risks does Nokia face in Asia, particularly China? How can Nokia manage these risks? How can effective international negotiating skills be of value to the firm in reducing its political risk and increasing its competitive advantage in this area of the world?

Brazil

After three centuries under the rule of Portugal, Brazil became an independent nation in 1822. By far the largest and most populous country in South America, with a population of over 205 million, Brazil has overcome more than a half century of military intervention in the governance of the country to pursue industrial and agricultural growth and the development of the interior.

After crafting a fiscal adjustment program and pledging progress on structural reform, Brazil received a $41.5 billion IMF-led international support program in November 1998. In January 1999, the Brazilian Central Bank announced that the real would no longer be pegged to the U.S. dollar. The consequent devaluation helped moderate the downturn in economic growth in 1999, and the country posted moderate GDP growth in 2000. Economic growth slowed considerably in 2001–2003—to less than 2 percent—because of a slowdown in major markets and the hiking of interest rates by the Central Bank to combat inflationary pressures. President Luiz Inácio Lula da Silva, who took office on January 1, 2003, gave high priority to reforming the complex tax code, trimming the overblown civil service pension system, and continuing the fight against inflation. By exploiting vast natural resources and a large labor pool, Brazil is today South America's leading economic power and a regional bellwether as it continues toward a free-market society.

After winning a landslide victory in 2002 on a campaign to revamp the economy and battle for the poor, President Lula da Silva reassured worried investors when he continued his predecessor's plan of strict financial austerity. Instead of catching the jitters as predicted, the country's bond and stock markets enjoyed stellar returns in 2003 and are still going strong. But within a year, pressure was mounting on Lula da Silva to keep true to his populist roots. After riding a wave of popular support through his first year, Lula da Silva faced some criticism from within his own Workers' Party and governing coalition as well as from ordinary voters. Lula has also gained a reputation for being thin-skinned when it comes to criticism; he expelled a foreign journalist critical of his policies. Although Lula's popularity dipped through this period, da Silva was reelected in 2006, and received more votes than any other Brazilian elected president. During his second term, Brazil continued its progress in modernization and da Silva's support gained steam again. In 2010, da Silva entered the final year of his second four-year term as one of the most popular Brazilian politicians

of all time. But in Latin America, any change in leadership is always met with nervousness from financial markets because it creates uncertainty and reminds business of previous transitions that have been disruptive.

Brazil's economy rebounded sharply from the global economic recession in 2009, with GDP growth of 2.7 percent and unemployment of 6 percent in 2011. With a GDP of US$2.5 trillion, Brazil ranks ninth globally in GDP in terms of purchasing power parity. According to The Economist, Brazil is likely to become the world's fifth largest economy, overtaking Britain and France before 2025. Brazil's progress in fighting poverty has been one of the most impressive of any developing country. Brazil boasts a number of world class companies, including Embraer, the global leader in short- and mid-range jet aircraft. In addition, Brazil will be host to the World Cup soccer match in 2014 and Rio will host the summer Olympic games in 2016. Substantial infrastructure investment is expected in advance of these two events. Brazil announced in early 2007 the discovery of the Tupi and Carioca oil fields off the coast of Rio de Janeiro. The oil reserves in these fields are conservatively estimated at between 30 billion and 80 billion barrels, which would put Brazil in the top ten countries in the world by reserves. In May of 2010, Brazil announced another large discovery in the Santos Basin. By 2012, oil exports exceeded 800,000 bbl/day, making Brazil the 24th largest oil exporter globally. Output from the existing Campos Basin and the discovery of the new fields could make Brazil an even more significant oil exporter by 2015. Brazil's national oil company, Petrobras, is one of the largest in the world. The government has created a new state-owned company called Petrosal to manage licensing in the new fields. This new company will award some exploration and production rights straight to Petrobras without options for foreign firms. Also, by mandate, it will award over half of the shallow-water contracts to locally owned Oil Service Companies (LOSCs). In deeper and more challenging waters beyond the capacity of local companies, foreign companies will be invited to bid. Those pledging to incorporate Brazilian "content" would be more likely to succeed. Higher taxes and fees are expected as well. Nonetheless, this sector is likely to create substantial new opportunities for foreign firms in Brazil.

Most recently, the government of President Delma Rousseff, who succeeded da Silva, has faced street protests over corruption, taxation, and poor public services. While Brazil has made great strides, challenges remain.

Questions

1. In your opinion, is there still political uncertainty in Brazil?

2. What strategy would be the most useful to companies interested in Brazilian investment?

3. Considering the economic and political environment, what types of companies would benefit the most by expanding operations to Brazil?

4. How should BellSouth, AES, and other companies address concerns about government policies in Brazil?

Chapter 11

MANAGEMENT DECISION AND CONTROL

Although they are not directly related to internationalization, decision making and control are two management functions that play critical roles in international operations. In *decision making,* a manager chooses a course of action among alternatives. In *controlling,* the manager evaluates results in relation to plans or objectives and decides what action, if any, to take. How these functions are carried out is influenced by the international context. An organization can employ a centralized or decentralized management system depending on such factors as company philosophy or competition. The company also has an array of measures and tools it can use to evaluate firm performance and restructuring options. As with most international operations, culture plays a significant role in what is important in both decision-making processes and control features, and can affect MNC decisions when forming relationships with subsidiaries.

This chapter examines the different decision-making and controlling management functions used by MNCs, notes some of the major factors that account for differences between these functions, and identifies the major challenges of the years ahead. The specific objectives of this chapter are:

1. **PROVIDE** comparative examples of decision making in different countries.

2. **PRESENT** some of the major factors affecting the degree of decision-making authority given to overseas units.

3. **COMPARE and CONTRAST** direct controls with indirect controls.

4. **DESCRIBE** some of the major differences in the ways that MNCs control operations.

5. **DISCUSS** some of the specific performance measures that are used to control international operations.

The World of *International Management*

Global Online Retail: Amazon v. Alibaba

Over the last two decades, the Internet has revolutionized the way customers around the world shop. According to Forrester Research, U.S. online retail sales alone will reach $370 billion by 2017.[1] Within the U.S., no online merchant has had more success than Amazon. Started in 1995 as a small bookseller, the ecommerce website now sells a variety of products to individuals across North America. While the U.S. has traditionally been the leader in ecommerce, online retail in countries around the world has been growing at a rapid pace.

Perhaps most surprising is the sudden surge of the Alibaba Group, an online Chinese retail conglomerate. Consisting of multiple ecommerce-related websites, the Alibaba Group's combined US$170 billion in transactions in 2012 totaled more than EBay and Amazon combined.[2] And Alibaba's Tmall, the direct competitor to Amazon, is expected to become the largest individual ecommerce site in the world by 2015, surpassing Amazon in total revenue.[3] Despite similar successes in the ecommerce marketplace, managers at Amazon and Alibaba have taken different approaches to the marketplace. What competitive strategies do these two companies use, and which company stands a better shot at long-term success?

Conglomerate versus Specializer

The Alibaba Group is a conglomerate of over a half-dozen individual ecommerce websites, combining business-to-business, business-to-consumer, and consumer-to-consumer transactions under a single ownership umbrella. Through its diverse set of websites, the company can cater to virtually any type of transaction, whether it is a small personal purchase or a multi-million dollar business transaction. In addition to providing traditional ecommerce services, the Alibaba Group has branched into web-based business solutions. Utilizing its existing infrastructure, Alibaba provides cloud computing and data services to

US online retail sales will reach $248.7 billion by 2014

US Online Retail Sales*
($ billions)

	2009	2010	2011	2012	2013	2014
US Online Retail Sales	$155.2	$172.9	$191.7	$210.0	$229.8	$248.7
% of Total U.S. Retail Sales	6%	7%	7%	7%	8%	8%

companies of all sizes, and has even created its own mobile operating system. Alibaba also operates Alipay, a secure payment transfer service, giving the company control over the entire purchase process. Together, the Alibaba Group conglomerate now accounts for 60 percent of all packages shipped within China.[4]

Amazon, unlike Alibaba, specializes primarily in just business-to-consumer sales. As a result, Amazon's target market is significantly smaller, but more loyal, than Alibaba's. With a primarily focus on personal purchases, Amazon has grown into the world's largest online retailer. Recently, however, Amazon has made an effort to expand its offerings. Utilizing the information infrastructure that it established for its traditional business operations, Amazon now offers video streaming, cloud storage, and other web services. And in an attempt to enter the growing tablet market, Amazon released its Kindle Fire in 2011. The core of Amazon's revenue, however, is still generated from its specialization in business-to-consumer transactions.[5]

Merchant versus Facilitator

Amazon not only hosts third-party sellers, but the company also acts as a direct merchant itself. Amazon buys and sells merchandise, ships products, and warehouses inventory. The company currently has over 50 distribution centers strategically spread across the United States, with roughly one million square feet of storage space per center. This direct-seller approach allows Amazon to quickly adapt to changes in demand. The company can directly control the timeliness and quality of most products sold over its interface, giving it the ability to provide unmatched service features, like single-day delivery. Furthermore, by hosting third-party merchants, Amazon is able to generate additional revenue on products sold by its users. However, Amazon's merchant strategy, requiring a large investment in fixed assets, has resulted in minimal profits for the company. Though it does not have quite the level of expenses that traditional physical stores have, Amazon's margin is tightened by the other necessary investments, like labor and warehouses.[6]

Alibaba, on the other hand, acts solely as a facilitator for sales between third parties. The company does not carry an inventory, directly sell products, or control distribution. Rather, it simply provides a digital space for those activities to happen. As a result, fixed assets are kept to a minimum. Going forward, the Alibaba Group sees this "efficiency" as a key business strength. While Amazon's scale of operations is capital intensive, Alibaba's approach allows for extra financial flexibility, as it does not need to build, staff, and maintain regional warehouses. One major downside, however, is that Alibaba gives up control over the shipping and distribution operations of its merchants, meaning that mistakes by third-party businesses could reflect negatively on the company as a whole. Furthermore, the company misses out on possible financial gains from direct-to-consumer selling.[7]

Growth Potential

Although both companies are online, and therefore "global," the geographic positioning of Amazon and Alibaba affects their potential future growth. Amazon, founded nearly 20 years ago, grew into the largest online retailer in the world due to its geographic advantages. The North American ecommerce market accounts for over 30 percent of all global online sales, and this region is overwhelmingly dominated by Amazon. In fact, Alibaba has not even attempted to enter the North American marketplace due to Amazon's strength. Although Amazon will likely continue to lead business-to-consumer sales in North America, the future growth potential of Amazon is somewhat limited. North America has nearly 80 percent Internet penetration, and the population growth of the region has rapidly slowed. Unless Amazon actively expands into other regions across the globe, its revenues will likely stagnate.[8]

Alibaba's foothold in Asia holds far more growth potential. Internet penetration in China currently stands at just 50 percent, leaving plenty of room for growth with unreached customers. Furthermore, nearly 40 percent of the world's population resides in Asia, and the population growth rates within Southeast Asia far exceed those of North America. As wealth continues to accumulate in the region, Internet access and ecommerce will likely expand. If the Alibaba Group can maintain its strong standing in Asia, revenue will grow significantly over the next decade.[9]

Whether Amazon's strategy as a specialized direct seller or Alibaba's strategy as a third-party facilitator will lead to greater long-term success is yet to be seen. As Internet usage increases and ecommerce expands beyond North America, managers of companies like Amazon and Alibaba will need to implement new strategies to adapt to the changing marketplace. The advent of online retail has certainly challenged some aspects of managerial decision making for all ecommerce companies.

■ Decision-Making Process and Challenges

decision making
The process of choosing a course of action among alternatives.

The managerial **decision-making** process, choosing a course of action among alternatives, is a common business practice becoming more and more relevant for the international manager as globalization becomes more pervasive. The decision-making process is often linear, though looping back is common, and consists of the general phases outlined in Figure 11–1. The degree to which managers are involved in this procedure depends on the structure of the subsidiaries and the locus of decision making. If decision making is centralized, most important decisions are made at the top; if decision making is decentralized, decisions are delegated to operating personnel. Decision making is used to solve a myriad of issues, including helping the subsidiary respond to economic and political demands of the host country. Decisions which are heavily economic in orientation concentrate on such aspects as return on investment (ROI) for overseas operations. In other instances, cultural differences can both inspire and motivate the process and outcome of decision making.

For example, Ford Motor Company designed and built an inexpensive vehicle, the Ikon, for the Indian market. Engineers took apart the Ford Fiesta and totally rebuilt the car to address buyer needs. Some of the changes that were made included raising the amount of rear headroom to accommodate men in turbans, adjusting doors so that they opened wider in order to avoid catching the flowing saris of women, fitting intake valves to avoid auto flooding during the monsoon season, toughening shock absorbers to handle the pockmarked city streets, and adjusting the air-conditioning system to deal with the intense summer heat.[10] As a result of these decisions, the car sold very well in India. Ford is now replicating that same strategy with the Ikon's successor, the Fiesta Mark VI. Santander, the second largest bank in Europe by market capitalization, is vesting more autonomy in its subsidiaries by listing subsidiaries in its principal foreign markets and thereby strengthening their independence and autonomy from the Spanish headquarters. A number of European banks, including Santander and HSBC Holdings PLC (see case at end of Part Four) establish foreign subsidiaries as opposed to direct branches. Santander Chief Executive Officer Alfredo Saenz said, "We also believe it's good for the local

Stage	Process

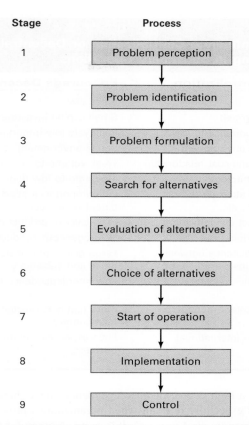

Figure 11–1

Decision-Making Process

Source: From Jette Schramm-Nielsen, "Cultural Dimensions of Decision Making: Denmark and France Compared," *Journal of Managerial Psychology* 16, no. 6 (2001), p. 408. Reprinted with permission of Emerald Insight.

management teams, because having local minority shareholders breathing down their neck keeps them on their toes, and it's a good way of identifying the franchise as local, instead of foreign." In addition, the IPO boosted the visibility of the bank in Brazil, resulted in greater access to local capital, and put a higher value on the franchise than what analysts were giving it before the float. When Santander sold 15 percent of its Brazilian unit, the unit alone was valued at €34 billion, more than European rivals Deutsche Bank or Société Générale.[11]

The way in which decision making is carried out will be influenced by a number of factors. We will first look at some of the factors, then provide some comparative examples in order to illustrate some of the differences.

Factors Affecting Decision-Making Authority

A number of factors influence international managers' conclusions about retaining authority or delegating decision making to a subsidiary. Table 11–1 lists some of the most important situational factors, and the following discussion evaluates the influential aspects.

One of the major concerns for organizations is how efficient the processes are which are put in place. The size of a company can have great importance in this realm. Larger organizations may choose to centralize authority for critical decisions in order to ensure efficiency through greater coordination and integration of operations. An example of this occurred after PetroChina's initial public offering (IPO) in 2001. The company consisted of 53 subsidiaries which then had sub-subsidiaries. Overall, there were more than 100 bank accounts which ultimately belonged to PetroChina, and the company was losing money by thinly spread resources. Through consolidation, the company realized over $241 million in savings and achieved greater efficiency.[12] The same holds true for

Table 11–1

Factors That Influence Centralization or Decentralization of Decision Making in Subsidiary Operations

Encourage Centralization	Encourage Decentralization
Large size	Small size
Large capital investment	Small capital investment
Relatively high importance to MNC	Relatively low importance to MNC
Highly competitive environment	Stable environment
Strong volume-to-unit-cost relationship	Weak volume-to-unit-cost relationship
High degree of technology	Moderate to low degree of technology
Strong importance attached to brand name, patent rights, etc.	Little importance attached to brand name, patent rights, etc.
Low level of product diversification	High level of product diversification
Homogeneous product lines	Heterogeneous product lines
Small geographic distance between home office and subsidiary	Large geographic distance between home office and subsidiary
High interdependence between the units	Low interdependence between the units
Fewer highly competent managers in host country	More highly competent managers in host country
Much experience in international business	Little experience in international business

companies that have a high degree of interdependence, since there is a greater need for coordination. This is especially relevant when organizations provide a large investment since they prefer to keep track of progress. It is quite common for the investing company to send home-office personnel to the subsidiary and report on the situation, and for subsidiary managers to submit periodic reports. Both of the above scenarios imply that the subsidiary is of great importance to the MNC, and it is customary in these situations for subsidiary managers to clear any decisions with the home office before implementation. In fact, MNCs often will hire someone who they know will respond to their directives and will regard this individual as an extension of the central management staff.

Another efficiency checkpoint arises when competition is high. In domestic situations, when competition increases, management will decentralize authority and give the local manager greater decision-making authority. This reduces the time that is needed for responding to competitive threats. In the international arena, however, sometimes the opposite approach is used. As competition increases and profit margins are driven down, home-office management often seeks to standardize product and marketing decisions to reduce cost and maintain profitability. Many upper-level operating decisions are made by central management and merely implemented by the subsidiary, although in some instances, companies still opt to decentralize operations if product diversification is necessary. An example of a newly centralized company was Cadbury, as it sought to improve efficiency and competitiveness in part to ward off a take-over. Cadbury recently decided to shed 15 percent of its workforce by closing 12 of its 81 factories, dropping the beverage sector of its subsidiaries and centralizing the management of its larger brands such as Trident, Dentyne, and Halls in order to better compete against candy rivals Hershey and Wrigley's.[13] Cadbury products also have a strong volume-to-unit cost relationship, as the low-cost edibles are purchased often.[14] In the end, Cadbury succumbed to a buyout by Kraft, but these moves helped strengthen the acquired company and make the combined firm leaner and better positioned globally. Firms that are able to produce large quantities will have lower cost per unit than those that produce at smaller amounts, and home-office management will often take the initiative to oversee sourcing, marketing, and overall strategy to keep subsidiary costs down.

Efficient processes become increasingly important as diversification or differences between the parent and subsidiary increase. This refers not only to specific products and services that may need to be tailored to geographic areas, but also to the socioeconomic, political, legal, and cultural environments in which the subsidiary exists. In this case, the subsidiary would have superior staff and resources which would only become increasingly skilled in manufacturing and marketing products at the local level over time. Decentralization is emphasized here, and there exists a direct relationship between the physical distance and different environments between the parent and subsidiary and the level of decentralization. In other words, the farther apart the two units are in either geographical area or cultural beliefs, the higher the level of decentralization.

Experience proves to be a simple indicator of efficiency. For example, if the subsidiary has highly competent local managers, the chances for decentralization are increased, because the home-office has more confidence in delegating to the local level and less to gain by making all the important decisions. Conversely, if the local managers are inexperienced or not highly effective, the MNC likely will centralize decision making and make many of the major decisions at headquarters. Furthermore, if the firm itself has a great deal of international experience, its operations will likely be more centralized as it has already exhibited a high efficiency level and increasing management decision making at the local level may slow processes.

Protection of goods and services is also important to an MNC. It would not be a very lucrative experience to spend valuable time and money on R&D processes only to have competitors successfully mimic products and essentially take away market share. For this reason and many others, it is common for MNCs to centralize operations when dealing with sophisticated levels of technology. This is particularly true for high-tech, research-intensive firms such as computer and pharmaceutical companies, which do not want their technology controlled at the local level. Furthermore, a company is likely to centralize decision-making processes when there are important brand names or patent rights involved as it wants to create as much protection as possible. For example, Ranbaxy Laboratories Ltd., one of the largest generic drug makers in the world, transferred its new drug discovery research capabilities to Japanese parent Daiichi Sankyo Co., while focusing its own efforts on generic discovery. The higher value-added and high-risk, high-return new drug research operations will be transferred to parent Daiichi Sankyo, while Ranbaxy will retain the research and development functions related to making generic drugs (Daiichi Sankyo bought a controlling stake in Ranbaxy, India's largest drug maker by revenue, in 2008).[15]

In some areas of operation, MNCs tend to retain decision making at the top (centralization); other areas fall within the domain of subsidiary management (decentralization). It is most common to find finance, R&D, and strategic planning decisions being made at MNC headquarters with the subsidiaries working within the parameters established by the home office. In addition, when the subsidiary is selling new products in growing markets, centralized decision making is more likely. As the product line matures and the subsidiary managers gain experience, however, the company will start to rely more on decentralized decision making. These decisions involve planning and budgeting systems, performance evaluations, assignment of managers to the subsidiary, and use of coordinating committees to mesh the operations of the subsidiary with the worldwide operations of the MNC. The right degree of centralized or decentralized decision making can be critical to the success of the MNC.

Deloitte, the accounting and management consulting firm, describes some of the challenges associated with postmerger integration in the area of centralization and decentralization:

> The union of two European engineering companies is a prime example of a merger that brought together companies with very different structures—a business unit of a much larger corporation and a stand-alone company. The business unit had a more decentralized management approach with responsibilities delegated within functional areas such as

procurement and IT. In contrast, the stand-alone company had a more centralized approach with a strong corporate headquarters retaining control over IT, finance, procurement and HR. Bringing these two disparate structures together without reconciling these differences almost destroyed the new company. Sales plummeted and key people left, unable to adjust to the new corporate structure. Within three years the company collapsed, to be swiftly scooped up by a competitor.[16]

Cultural Differences and Comparative Examples of Decision Making

Culture, whether outside or within the organization (see Chapters 4 and 6, respectively), has an effect on how individuals and businesses perceive situations and subsequently react. This knowledge raises the question: Do decision-making philosophies and practices differ from country to country? Research shows that to some extent they do, although there also is evidence that many international operations, regardless of foreign or domestic ownership, use similar decision-making norms.

One study showed that French and Danish managers do not approach the decision-making process in the same manner.[17] The French managers tend to spend ample time on searching for and evaluating alternatives (see Figure 11–1), exhibiting rationality and intelligence in each option. While the French approach each opportunity with a sense of creativity and logic, they tend to become quite emotionally charged rather quickly if challenged. Middle managers report to higher-level managers who ultimately make the final decision. Therefore, the individualistic nature of the French creates an environment in which middle managers vie for the recognition and praise of the upper management. Furthermore, middle-management implementation of ideas tends to be lacking since that stage is often seen as boring, practical work which lacks the prestige managers strive to achieve. Control, discussed later in the chapter, is quite high in the French firms at every level, so where implementation fails, control will compensate.

Danish managers tend to emphasize different stages in the decision-making process (see Figure 11–1). They do not spend as much time searching or analyzing alternatives to optimize production but instead choose the option that can be started and implemented quickly and still bring about the relative desired results. They are less emotionally responsive and tend to take a straightforward approach. Danes do not emphasize control in operations, since it tends to be a sign that management lacks confidence in the areas that "require" high control. The cooperative as opposed to individualistic emphasis in Danish corporations, coupled with a results-oriented environment, breeds a situation in which decisions are made quickly and middle managers are given autonomy.

Overall, the pragmatic nature of the Danes and the French need for intellectual prowess mark why each is more adept at different stages of the decision-making process. The French tend to be better at stages 4, 5, and 9, while the Danes are more adept at stages 6, 7, and 8 (see Figure 11–1). As one Danish manager in France says:

> They [Danes and Frenchmen] do not analyze and synthesize the same way. The French tend to think that the Danes are not thorough enough, and the Danes tend to think that the French are too complicated. At his desk, the Frenchman tends to keep on working on the case. He seems to agree neither with his surroundings nor with himself. This means that when he has analyzed a case and has come to a conclusion, then he would like to go over it once more. I think that Frenchmen think in a more synthetic way . . . and he has a tendency to say: "well, yes, but what if it can still be done in another maybe smarter way." This means that in fact he is wasting time instead of making improvements.[18]

In Germany, managers focus more on productivity and quality of goods and services than on managing subordinates, which often translates into companies pursuing long-term approaches. In addition, management education is highly technical, and a legal system called **codetermination** requires workers and their managers to discuss major decisions. As a result, German MNCs tend to be fairly centralized, autocratic, and hierarchical. Scandinavian countries also have codetermination, but the Swedes focus much more on quality of work life and the importance of the individual in the organization. As a result, decision making in Sweden is decentralized and participative.

The Japanese are somewhat different from the Europeans, though they still employ a long-term focus. They make heavy use of a decision-making process called **ringisei**, or decision making by consensus. Under this system any changes in procedures and routines, tactics, and even strategies of a firm are organized by those directly concerned with those changes. The final decision is made at the top level after an elaborate examination of the proposal through successively higher levels in the management hierarchy, and results in acceptance or rejection of a decision only through consensus at every echelon of the management structure.[19]

Sometimes Japanese consensus decision making can be very time-consuming. However, in practice most Japanese managers know how to respond to "suggestions" from the top and to act accordingly—thus saving a great deal of time. Many outsiders misunderstand how Japanese managers make such decisions. In Japan, what should be done is called **tatemae**, whereas what one really feels, which may be quite different, is **honne**. Because it is vital to do what others expect in a given context, situations arise that often strike Westerners as a game of charades. Nevertheless, it is very important in Japan to play out the situation according to what each person believes others expect to happen.

Another cultural difference is how managers view time in the decision-making process. As we saw from the French-Danish example earlier, the French do not value time as much as their counterparts. The French want to ensure that the best alternative was put into action, whereas the Danes want to act first and take advantage of opportunities. This is key in many international decision-making processes, as globalization has opened the door to extreme competition, and all players need to be able to both identify and make the most of profitable prospects.

In another study of decision making in teams composed of Swedes, Germans, and combinations of the two, researchers found Swedish teams featured higher team orientation, flatter organizational hierarchies, and more open-minded and informal work attitudes. In this study, German team members were perceived to be faster in decision making, to have clearer responsibilities for the individual, and to be more willing to accept a changed or unpopular decision. In Swedish teams, decision making appeared more transparent and less formal. On German teams, the process is largely dominated by the decision authority of an expert in the field. This is in contrast to the group decision-making style used in Swedish teams.[20]

Total Quality Management Decisions

To achieve world-class competitiveness, MNCs are finding that a commitment to total quality management is critical. **Total quality management (TQM)** is an organizational strategy and accompanying techniques that result in delivery of high-quality products or services to customers.[21] The concept and techniques of TQM, which were introduced in Chapter 8 in relation to strategic planning, also are relevant to decision making and controlling.

One of the primary areas where TQM is having a big impact is in manufacturing. A number of TQM techniques have been successfully applied to improve the quality of manufactured goods. One is the use of concurrent engineering/interfunctional teams in which designers, engineers, production specialists, and customers work together to develop new products. This approach involves all the necessary parties and overcomes what used to be an all-too-common procedure: The design people would tell the manufacturing group what to produce, and the latter would send the finished product to retail stores for sale to

codetermination
A legal system that requires workers and their managers to discuss major decisions.

ringisei
A Japanese term that means "decision making by consensus."

tatemae
A Japanese term that means "doing the right thing" according to the norm.

honne
A Japanese term that means "what one really wants to do."

total quality management (TQM)
An organizational strategy and the accompanying techniques that result in the delivery of high-quality products or services to customers.

the customer. Today, MNCs taking a TQM approach are customer-driven. They use TQM techniques to tailor their output to customer needs, and they require the same approach from their own suppliers.[22] IBM followed a similar approach in developing its AS/400 computer systems. Customer advisory councils were created to provide input, test the product, and suggest refinements. The result was one of the most successful product launches in the company's history.

A particularly critical issue is how much decision making to delegate to subordinates. TQM uses employee **empowerment**. Individuals and teams are encouraged to generate and implement ideas for improving quality, and are given the decision-making authority and necessary resources and information to implement them. Many MNCs have had outstanding success with empowerment. For example, General Electric credits employee empowerment for cutting in half the time needed to change product-mix production of its dishwashers in response to market demand.

Another TQM technique that is successfully employed by MNCs is rewards and recognition. These range from increases in pay and benefits to the use of merit pay, discretionary bonuses, pay-for-skills and knowledge plans, plaques, and public recognition. The important thing to realize is that the rewards and recognition approaches that work well in one country may be ineffective in another. For example, individual recognition in the U.S. may be appropriate and valued by workers, but in Japan, group rewards are more appropriate as Japanese do not like to be singled out for personal praise. Similarly, although putting a picture or plaque on the wall to honor an individual is common practice in the United States, these rewards are frowned on in Finland, for they remind the workers that their neighbors, the Russians, used this system to encourage people to increase output (but not necessarily quality), and while the Russian economy is beginning to make headway, it was once in shambles in part due to poor decision making.

Still another technique associated with TQM is the use of ongoing training to achieve continual improvement. This training takes a wide variety of forms, ranging from statistical quality control techniques to team meetings designed to generate ideas for streamlining operations and eliminating waste. In all cases, the objective is to apply what the Japanese call **kaizen**, or continuous improvement. By adopting a TQM perspective and applying the techniques discussed earlier, MNCs find that they can both develop and maintain a worldwide competitive edge. A good example is Zytec, the world-class, Minnesota-based manufacturer of power supplies. The customer base for Zytec ranges from the United States to Japan to Europe. One way in which the firm ensures that it maintains a total quality perspective is to continually identify client demands and then work to exceed these expectations. Another is to totally revise the company's philosophy and beliefs regarding what quality is all about and how it needs to be implemented. Table 11–2 provides some examples of the new thinking that is now emerging regarding quality.

Toyota's recent challenges with safety recalls have prompted the firm to integrate the term "kaizen" in its North American marketing initiatives designed to reassure the public about Toyota's commitment to safety. In one commercial, a worker says, "Kaizen is a real core principle at Toyota, and it means continuous improvement." The concept is so integral to Toyota's culture and ethos, the firm felt it necessary to share it with the general public as a means to restore trust and confidence in the company.[23]

Indirectly related to TQM is ISO 9000, International Standards Organization (ISO) certification, to ensure quality products and services. Areas that are examined by the ISO certification team include design (product or service specifications), process control (instruction for manufacturing or service functions), purchasing, service (e.g., instructions for conducting after-sales service), inspection and testing, and training. ISO 9000 certification is becoming a necessary prerequisite to doing business in the EU, but it also is increasingly used as a screening criterion for bidding on contracts or getting business in the United States and other parts of the world.

empowerment
The process of giving individuals and teams the resources, information, and authority they need to develop ideas and effectively implement them.

kaizen
A Japanese term that means "continuous improvement."

Table 11–2
The Emergence of New Beliefs Regarding Quality

Old Myth	New Truth
Quality is the responsibility of the people in the Quality Control Department.	Quality is everyone's job.
Training is costly.	Training does not cost; it saves.
New quality programs have high initial costs.	The best quality programs do not have up-front costs.
Better quality will cost the company a lot of money.	As quality goes up, costs come down.
The measurement of data should be kept to a minimum.	An organization cannot have too much relevant data on hand.
It is human to make mistakes.	Perfection—total customer satisfaction—is a standard that should be vigorously pursued.
Some defects are major and should be addressed, but many are minor and can be ignored.	No defects are acceptable, regardless of whether they are major or minor.
Quality improvements are made in small, continuous steps.	In improving quality, both small and large improvements are necessary.
Quality improvement takes time.	Quality does not take time; it saves time.
Haste makes waste.	Thoughtful speed improves quality.
Quality programs are best oriented toward areas such as products and manufacturing.	Quality is important in all areas, including administration and service.
After a number of quality improvements, customers are no longer able to see additional improvements.	Customers are able to see all improvements, including those in price, delivery, and performance.
Good ideas can be found throughout the organization.	Good ideas can be found everywhere, including in the operations of competitors and organizations providing similar goods and services.
Suppliers need to be price competitive.	Suppliers need to be quality competitive.

Source: Reported in Richard M. Hodgetts, *Measures of Quality and High Performance* (New York: American Management Association, 1998), p. 14.

Decisions for Attacking the Competition

Another series of key decisions relates to MNC actions that are designed to attack the competition and gain a foothold in world markets. An example is General Motors' decision to establish production operations on a worldwide basis and to be a major player throughout Asia, Australia, Europe, and South America, as well as in select areas of Africa. As a result of this decision, the company is now closing U.S. factories and building new assembly plants abroad. Between 1995 and 1999 GM opened a host of new international facilities, including a plant in Brazil that has an annual capacity of 120,000 units, as well as factories in Poland, India, Mexico, Thailand, and Shanghai, each of which has annual capacity of 100,000 units. By locating closer to the final customer and offering a well-designed and efficiently built car, the company has been able to increase its worldwide market share, thus more than offsetting the downturn it has encountered in the U.S. market, where overall share has dropped below 30 percent.

Another example of decision making for attacking the competition is provided by BMW. While GM is trying to tap the upper market, BMW has made the decision to move down the line and gain small-car market share. The company is building small cars with a sales price in the range of $20,000. By sharing engines, gearboxes, and electrical systems from its other offerings, the firm intends to reduce its development and production costs and offer a reliable and competitively priced auto.[24] Other firms, including Mercedes and Audi, have done this and have not been particularly profitable, but BMW believes that it can succeed where they have not. BMW's introduction of the MINI Cooper is an interesting example of the integration of efficiency, sportiness, and nostalgia.

NEC offers a further example of how decision making is being used for attacking the competition. In 2001 the company held 8 percent of the world market for mobile transmitting infrastructure and was vying with major competitors such as Ericsson, Lucent, Nokia, and Nortel. Most of NEC's revenues come from its contracts with NTT, Japan's phone monopoly. However, the company is moving aggressively into the worldwide arena. Its prowess in fiber optics resulted in its winning a big AT&T network installation contract, and as the demand for fiber optics increases, NEC intends to exploit this strength.[25] The firm recently announced that it had developed a fiber-optic cable that is four times more powerful than that currently on the market. The company is also a world leader in manufacturing mobile handsets and the semiconductors used in mobiles and other devices. Its folding phones, for example, account for 40 percent of the Internet-capable handset market in Japan, and NEC is looking to expand its international sales of these products.

Intel has made a number of interesting decisions designed to stymie the competition. One is to bring out a new version of its Pentium chip at a much lower-than-expected price and cut the prices of its other chips, thus creating a strong demand for its products and forcing competitors to cut their prices. In a market where overall demand has been slowing, this strategy wreaks havoc on the competition. At the same time, lower prices mean that Intel must sell more products in order to increase revenues. One of the ways in which the firm is trying to do this is with an extension of its Xeon microprocessor family, which is aimed at more powerful desktop workstations and server systems than the firm has targeted in the past. Intel's server offerings generally were used in relatively lightweight machines such as those that serve up Web pages. This new push is designed to provide chips that are used in midsize servers, such as those that run databases, as well as in some larger systems used in mission-critical tasks. These machines typically cost millions of dollars and run on dozens of microprocessors operating in parallel.[26] The company also teamed up with Hewlett-Packard to develop the Itanium chip, which offers greater speed because it can process 64 bits of data at a time rather than 32 bits. Working with HP, Intel is building servers for telecommunications and making three-in-one chips that have the ability to radically reduce the size of cell phones and handheld computers.

■ Decision and Control Linkages

controlling
The process of evaluating results in relation to plans or objectives and deciding what action, if any, to take.

Decision making and **controlling** are two vital and often interlinked functions of international management. As an example of a company struggling with control issues, Siemens has long been praised for its engineering abilities, but its slow market response has left the company struggling to reach internal earnings targets, which it has fallen short of for years. Klaus Kleinfeld took over as CEO in 2005 in a move to change management and improve profits. Almost immediately, Kleinfeld was able to encourage faster decision-making processes and stressed a customer spotlight as passionate as Siemens's technology focus. This proved successful, as 2006 sales increased by 16 percent and profits by 35 percent. There have been ongoing discussions about expansion, including building cement plants in Yemen and improving plants in Russia. Most would believe that the German company would have been pleased by the turn of events, but the U.S. management style that Kleinfeld employed did not sit well with the parent company, especially as questions arose over specific growth strategies. The culture clash led to Kleinfeld stepping down, but not before a foundation of change was implemented. Whether the company returns to slow responses and lack of control is something only time can tell, but Siemens's taste of success may be enough to sustain its new aggressive posture.[27]

Another example of how the control function plays out is Universal Studios Japan. To attract visitors to the Osaka location, this new theme park was specially built based on feedback from Japanese tourists at Universal parks in Orlando and Los Angeles. The company wanted to learn what these visitors liked and disliked and then use this information in its Osaka park. One theme clearly emerged: The Japanese wanted an authentic American experience but also expected the park to cater to their own cultural preferences. In the process of controlling the creation of the new park, thousands of decisions were made regarding what to include and what to leave out. For example, seafood pizza and gumbo-style soup were put on the menu, but a fried-shrimp concoction with colored rice crackers was rejected. It was decided that in a musical number based on the movie Beetlejuice, the main character should talk in Japanese and his sidekicks would speak and sing in English. The decision to put in a restaurant called Shakin's, based on the 1906 San Francisco earthquake, turned out to be not a good idea because Osaka has had terrible earthquakes that killed thousands of people.

Other decisions were made to give the "American" park a uniquely Japanese flavor. The nation's penchant for buying edible souvenirs inspired a 6,000-square-foot confection shop packed with Japanese sweets such as dinosaur-shaped bean cakes. Restrooms include Japanese-style squat toilets. Even the park layout caters to the tendency of Japanese crowds to flow clockwise in an orderly manner, contrary to more chaotic U.S. crowds that steer right. And millions of dollars were spent on the Jurassic Park water slide to widen the landing pond, redesign boat hulls, and install underwater wave-damping panels to reduce spray. Why? Many fastidious Japanese don't like to get wet, even on what's billed as one of the world's biggest water slides.[28]

Over the next few years, as Universal Studios Japan evaluates park revenues and feedback from visitors, it will be able to judge how well it is doing in giving customers an American experience in an environment that also addresses local cultural considerations. After a period of reduced attendance, the company has discovered that creating an emotional connection between the consumer and the park, instead of focusing on the power of Hollywood, encourages people to frequent the park. The quick and adept response to profit losses shows that management has a concrete idea of how to deal with other cultures. In fact, plans are already in place to open Universal Studios in Dubai, Singapore, and South Korea.[29] (See related discussion in the case at end of Part Two on Disney in Asia.)

■ The Controlling Process

As we've stated, controlling involves evaluating results in relation to plans or objectives and deciding what action to take next. An excellent illustration of this process was Mitsubishi's purchase of 80 percent of Rockefeller Center in the late 1980s. The Japanese firm paid $1.4 billion for this choice piece of Manhattan real estate, and it looked like a very wise decision. Over the next six years, however, depressed rental prices and rising maintenance costs resulted in Mitsubishi sinking an additional $500 million into the project. Finally, in late 1995, the company decided it had had enough and announced that it was walking away from the investment. Mitsubishi passed ownership to Rockefeller Center Properties Inc., the publicly traded real-estate investment trust that held the mortgage on the center. The cost of keeping the properties was too great for the Japanese firm, which decided to cut its losses and focus efforts on more lucrative opportunities elsewhere.

The control process is of course crucial for MNCs in the fast-moving personal computer (PC) business. Until the mid-1990s, PCs were built using the traditional model shown in Figure 11–2. Today the direct-sales model and the hybrid model are the most common. PC firms are finding that they must keep on the cutting edge more than any other industry because of the relentless pace of technological change. This is where the control function becomes especially critical for success. For example, stringent controls keep the inventory in the system as small as possible. PCs are manufactured using a just-in-time approach (a customer orders the unit and has it made to specifications) or an almost just-in-time approach (a retailer orders 30 units and sells them all within a few weeks). Because technology in the PC industry changes so quickly, any units that are not sold in retail outlets within 60 days may be outdated and must be severely discounted and sold for whatever the market will bear. In turn, these costs are often assumed by the manufacturer. As a result, PC manufacturers are very much inclined to build to order or to ship in quantities that can be sold quickly. In this way the firm's control system helps ensure that inventory moves through the system profitably.[30]

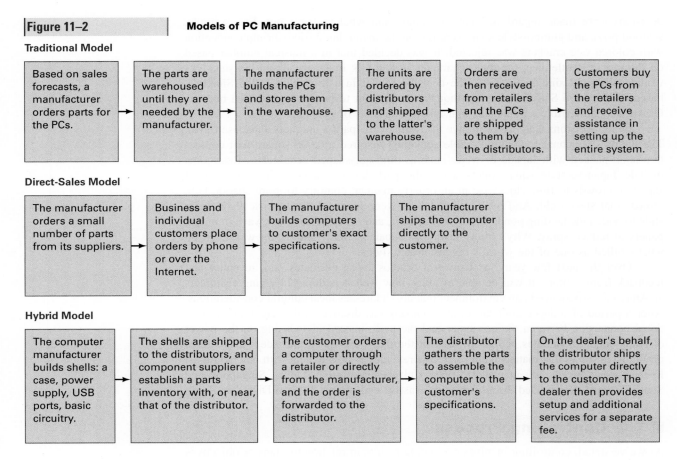

| Figure 11–2 | Models of PC Manufacturing |

Traditional Model

| Based on sales forecasts, a manufacturer orders parts for the PCs. | → | The parts are warehoused until they are needed by the manufacturer. | → | The manufacturer builds the PCs and stores them in the warehouse. | → | The units are ordered by distributors and shipped to the latter's warehouse. | → | Orders are then received from retailers and the PCs are shipped to them by the distributors. | → | Customers buy the PCs from the retailers and receive assistance in setting up the entire system. |

Direct-Sales Model

| The manufacturer orders a small number of parts from its suppliers. | → | Business and individual customers place orders by phone or over the Internet. | → | The manufacturer builds computers to customer's exact specifications. | → | The manufacturer ships the computer directly to the customer. |

Hybrid Model

| The computer manufacturer builds shells: a case, power supply, USB ports, basic circuitry. | → | The shells are shipped to the distributors, and component suppliers establish a parts inventory with, or near, that of the distributor. | → | The customer orders a computer through a retailer or directly from the manufacturer, and the order is forwarded to the distributor. | → | The distributor gathers the parts to assemble the computer to the customer's specifications. | → | On the dealer's behalf, the distributor ships the computer directly to the customer. The dealer then provides setup and additional services for a separate fee. |

Of particular interest is how companies attempt to control their overseas operations to become integrated, coordinated units. A number of control problems may arise: (1) The objectives of the overseas operation and the corporation conflict. (2) The objectives of joint-venture partners and corporate management are not in accord. (3) Degrees of experience and competence in planning vary widely among managers running the various overseas units. (4) Finally, there may be basic philosophic disagreements about the objectives and policies of international operations, largely because of cultural differences between home- and host-country managers. The following discussion examines the various types of control that are used in international operations and the approaches that are often employed in dealing with typical problems.

Types of Control

There are two common, complementary ways of looking at how MNCs control operations. One way is by determining whether the enterprise chooses to use internal or external control in devising its overall strategy. The other is by looking at the ways in which the organization uses direct and indirect controls.

Internal and External Control From an internal control standpoint, an MNC will focus on the things that it does best. At the same time, of course, management wants to ensure that there is a market for the goods and services that it is offering. So the company first needs to find out what the customers want and be prepared to respond appropriately. This requires an external control focus. Naturally, every MNC will give consideration to both internal and external perspectives on control. However, one is often given more attention than the other. In explaining this idea, Trompenaars and Hampden-Turner set forth four management views regarding how a control strategy should be devised and implemented:

1. No one dealing with customers is without a strategy of sorts. Our task is to find out which of these strategies work, which don't, and why. Devising our own strategy in the abstract and imposing it downwards only spreads confusion.

2. No one dealing with customers is without a strategy of sorts. Our task is to find out which of these strategies work and then create a master strategy from proven successful initiatives by encouraging and combining the best.

3. To be a leader is to be the chief deviser of strategy. Using all the experience, information, and intelligence we can mobilize, we need to devise an innovative strategy and then cascade it down the hierarchy.

4. To be a leader is to be the chief deviser of strategy. Using all the experience, information, and intelligence we can mobilize, we must create a broad thrust, while leaving it to subordinates to fit these to customer needs.

Trompenaars and Hampden-Turner ask managers to rank each of these four statements by placing a "1" next to the one they feel would most likely be used in their company, a "2" next to the second most likely, on down to a "4" next to the one that would be the last choice. This ranking helps managers better see whether they use an external or an internal control approach. Answer 1 focuses most strongly on an external-directed approach and rejects the internal control option. Answer 3 represents the opposite. Answer 2 affirms a connection between an external-directed strategy and an inner-directed one, whereas answer 4 does the opposite.[31]

Cultures differ in the control approach they use. For example, among U.S. MNCs it is common to find managers using an internal control approach. Among Asian firms an external control approach is more typical. Table 11–3 provides some contrasts between the two.

Direct Controls   **Direct controls** involve the use of face-to-face or personal meetings to monitor operations. A good example is how International Telephone and Telegraph (ITT) holds monthly management meetings at its New York headquarters. These meetings are run by the CEO of the company, and reports are submitted by each ITT unit manager

direct controls
The use of face-to-face or personal meetings for the purpose of monitoring operations.

Table 11–3
The Impact of Internal- and External-Oriented Cultures on the Control Process

Key Differences Between . . .

Internal Control	External Control
Often dominating attitude bordering on aggressiveness toward the environment.	Often flexible attitude, willing to compromise and keep the peace.
Conflict and resistance mean that a person has convictions.	Harmony, responsiveness, and sensibility are encouraged.
The focus is on self, function, one's own group, and one's own organization.	The focus is on others such as customers, partners, and colleagues.
There is discomfort when the environment seems "out of control" or changeable.	There is comfort with waves, shifts, and cycles, which are regarded as "natural."

Tips for Doing Business with . . .

Internally Controlled (for externals)	Externally Controlled (for internals)
Playing "hardball" is legitimate to test the resilience of an opponent.	Softness, persistence, politeness, and long patience will get rewards.
It is most important to "win your objective."	It is most important to maintain one's relationships with others.
Win some, lose some.	Win together, lose apart.

Source: Adapted from Fons Trompenaars and Charles Hampden-Turner, *Riding the Waves of Culture: Understanding Diversity in Global Business,* 2nd ed. (New York: McGraw-Hill, 1998), pp. 160–161.

throughout the world. Problems are discussed, goals set, evaluations made, and actions taken that will help the unit improve its effectiveness.

Another common form of direct control is visits by top executives to overseas affiliates or subsidiaries. During these visits, top managers can learn firsthand the problems and challenges facing the unit and offer assistance.

A third form is the staffing practices of MNCs. By determining whom to send overseas to run the unit, the corporation can directly control how the operation will be run. The company will want the manager to make operating decisions and handle day-to-day matters, but the individual also will know which decisions should be cleared with the home office. In fact, this approach to direct control sometimes results in a manager who is more responsive to central management than to the needs of the local unit.

And finally, a fourth form is the organizational structure itself. By designing a structure that makes the unit highly responsive to home-office requests and communications, the MNC ensures that all overseas operations are run in accord with central management's desires. This structure can be established through formal reporting relationships and chain of command (who reports to whom).

indirect controls
The use of reports and other written forms of communication to control operations.

Indirect Controls   **Indirect controls** involve the use of reports and other written forms of communication to control operations. One of the most common examples is the use of monthly operating reports that are sent to the home office. Other examples, which typically are used to supplement the operating report, include financial statements, such as balance sheets, income statements, cash budgets, and financial ratios that provide insights into the unit's financial health. The home office will use these operating and financial data to evaluate how well things are going and make decisions regarding necessary changes. Three sets of financial statements usually are required from subsidiaries: (1) statements prepared to meet the national accounting standards and procedures prescribed by law and other professional organizations in the host country; (2) statements prepared to comply with the accounting principles and standards required by the home country; and (3) statements prepared to meet the financial consolidation requirements of the home country.

Indirect controls are particularly important in international management because of the great expense associated with direct methods of control. Typically, MNCs will use indirect controls to monitor performance on a monthly basis, whereas direct controls are used semi-annually or annually. This dual approach often provides the company with effective control of its operations at a price that also is cost-effective.

Approaches to Control

International managers can employ many different approaches to control. These approaches typically are dictated by the MNC's philosophy of control, the economic environment in which the overseas unit is operating, and the needs and desires of the managerial personnel who staff the unit. Working within control parameters, MNCs will structure their processes so that they are as efficient and effective as possible. Typically, the tools used will give the unit manager the autonomy needed to adapt to changes in the market as well as to attract competent local personnel. These tools will also provide for coordination of operations with the home office, so that the overseas unit operates in harmony with the MNC's overall strategic plan.

Some control tools are universal. For example, all MNCs use financial tools in monitoring overseas units. This was true as long as three decades ago, when the following was reported:

> The cross-cultural homogeneity in financial control is in marked contrast to the heterogeneity exercised over the areas of international operations. American subsidiaries of Italian and Scandinavian firms are virtually independent operationally from their parents in functions pertaining to marketing, production, and research and development; whereas, the subsidiaries of German and British firms have limited freedom in these areas. Almost no autonomy on financial matters is given by any nationality to the subsidiaries.[32]

Some Major Differences   MNCs control operations in many different ways, and these often vary considerably from country to country. For example, how British firms monitor their overseas operations often is different from how German or French firms do. Similarly, U.S. MNCs tend to have their own approach to controlling, and it differs from both European and Japanese approaches. When Horovitz examined the key characteristics of top management control in Great Britain, Germany, and France, he found that British controls had four common characteristics: (1) Financial records were sophisticated and heavily emphasized. (2) Top management tended to focus its attention on major problem areas and did not get involved in specific, detailed matters of control. (3) Control was used more for general guidance than for surveillance. (4) Operating units had a large amount of marketing autonomy.[33]

This model was in marked contrast to that of German managers, who employed very detailed control and focused attention on all variances large and small. These managers also placed heavy control on the production area and stressed operational efficiency. In achieving this centralized control, managers used a large central staff for measuring performance, analyzing variances, and compiling quantitative reports for senior executives. Overall, the control process in the German firms was used as a policing and surveillance instrument. French managers employed a control system that was closer to that of the Germans than to the British. Control was used more for surveillance than for guiding operations, and the process was centrally administered. Even so, the French system was less systematic and sophisticated.[34]

How do U.S. MNCs differ from their European counterparts? One comparative study found that a major difference is that U.S. firms tend to rely much more heavily on reports and other performance-related data. Americans make greater use of output control, and Europeans rely more heavily on behavioral control. Commenting on the differences between these two groups, the researcher noted: "This pattern appears to be quite robust and continues to exist even when a number of common factors that seem to influence control are taken into account."[35] Some specific findings from this study include:

1. Control in U.S. MNCs focuses more on the quantifiable, objective aspects of a foreign subsidiary, whereas control in European MNCs tends to be used to measure more qualitative aspects. The U.S. approach allows comparative analyses between other foreign operations as well as domestic units; the European measures are more flexible and allow control to be exercised on a unit-by-unit basis.

2. Control in U.S. MNCs requires more precise plans and budgets in generating suitable standards for comparison. Control in European MNCs requires a high level of companywide understanding and agreement regarding what constitutes appropriate behavior and how such behavior supports the goals of both the subsidiary and the parent firm.

3. Control in U.S. MNCs requires large central staffs and centralized information-processing capability. Control in European MNCs requires a larger cadre of capable expatriate managers who are willing to spend long periods of time abroad. This control characteristic is reflected in the career approaches used in the various MNCs. Although U.S. multinationals do not encourage lengthy stays in foreign management positions, European MNCs often regard these positions as stepping-stones to higher offices.

4. Control in European MNCs requires more decentralization of operating decision making than does control in U.S. MNCs.

5. Control in European MNCs favors short vertical spans or reporting channels from the foreign subsidiary to responsible positions in the parent.[36]

As noted in the discussion of decision making, these differences help explain why many researchers have found European subsidiaries to be more decentralized than U.S. subsidiaries. Europeans rely on the managerial personnel they assign from headquarters to run the unit properly. Americans tend to hire a greater percentage of local management people and control operations through reports and other objective, performance-related data. The difference results in Europeans' relying more on socio-emotional control systems and Americans' opting for task-oriented, objective control systems.

Evaluating Approaches to Control   Is one control approach any better than the other? The answer is that each seems to work best for its respective group. Some studies predict that as MNCs increase in size, they likely will move toward the objective orientation of the U.S. MNCs. Commenting on the data gathered from large German and U.S. MNCs, two researchers concluded:

> Control mechanisms have to be harmonized with the main characteristics of management corporate structure to become an integrated part of the global organization concept and to meet situational needs. Trying to explain the differences in concepts of control, we have to consider that the companies of the U.S. sample were much larger and more diversified. Accordingly, they use different corporate structures, combining operational units into larger units and integrating these through primarily centralized, indirect, and task-oriented control. The German companies have not (yet) reached this size and complexity, so a behavioral model of control seems to be fitting.[37]

So in deciding which form of control to use, MNCs must determine whether they want a more bureaucratic or a more cultural control approach; and from the cultural perspective, it must be remembered that this control will vary across subsidiaries.

■ Performance Evaluation as a Mechanism of Control

A number of performance measures are used for control purposes. Three of the most common evaluate financial performance, quality performance, and personnel performance.

Financial Performance

Financial performance evaluation of a foreign subsidiary or affiliate is usually based on profit and loss, and return on investment. **Profit** and loss (P&L) is the amount remaining after all expenses are deducted from total revenues. **Return on investment (ROI)** is measured by dividing profit by assets; some firms use profit divided by owners' equity (return on owners' investment, or ROOI) in referring to the return-on-investment performance measure. In any case, the most important part of the ROI calculation is profits, which often can be manipulated by management. Thus, the amount of profit directly relates to how well or how poorly a unit is judged to perform. For example, if an MNC has an operation in both country A and country B and taxes are lower in country A, the MNC may be able to benefit if the two units have occasion to do business with each other. This benefit can be accomplished by having the unit in country A charge higher prices than usual to the unit in country B, thus providing greater net profits to the MNC. Simply put, sometimes differences in tax rates can be used to maximize overall MNC profits. This same basic form of manipulation can be used in transferring money from one country to another, which can be explained as follows:

> Transfer prices are manipulated upward or downward depending on whether the parent company wishes to inject or remove cash into or from a subsidiary. Prices on imports by a subsidiary from a related subsidiary are raised if the multinational company wishes to move funds from the receiver to the seller, but they are lowered if the objective is to keep the funds in the importing subsidiary. . . . Multinational companies have been known to use transfer pricing for moving excess cash from subsidiaries located in countries with weak currencies to countries with strong currencies in order to protect the value of their current assets.[38]

The so-called bottom-line (i.e., profit or loss) performance of subsidiaries also can be affected by a devaluation or revaluation of local currency. For example, if a country devalues its currency, then subsidiary export sales will increase, because the

profit
The amount remaining after all expenses are deducted from total revenues.

return on investment (ROI)
Return measured by dividing profit by assets.

price of these goods will be lower for foreign buyers, whose currencies now have greater purchasing power. If the country revalues its currency, then export sales will decline because the price of goods for foreign buyers will rise, since their currencies now have less purchasing power in the subsidiary's country. Likewise, a devaluation of the currency will increase the cost of imported materials and supplies for the sub- sidiary, and a revaluation will decrease these costs because of the relative changes in the purchasing power of local currency. Because devaluation and revaluation of local currency are outside the control of the overseas unit, bottom-line performance some- times will be a result of external conditions that do not accurately reflect how well the operation actually is being run, which should be considered when evaluating a subsidiary's performance.

Of course, not all bottom-line financial performance is a result of manipulation or external economic conditions. Frequently, other forces account for the problem. For example, one of Volkswagen's goals for a recent year was to earn a pre-tax 6.5 percent on revenues. The firm fell far short of this goal, earning only 3.5 percent before taxes. One reason for this poor performance was that labor costs in Lower Saxony, where approximately half its workforce is located, are very high. Workers here produce only 40 vehicles per employee annually in contrast to the VW plant in Navarra, Spain, which turns out 79 vehicles per employee per year. Why doesn't VW move work to lower-cost production sites? The major reason is that the state of Lower Saxony owns 19 percent of the company's voting stock, so the workers' jobs are protected.[39] Simply put, relying solely on financial results to evaluate performance can result in misleading conclusions.

Quality Performance

Just as quality has become a major focus in decision making, it also is a major dimen- sion of the modern control process of MNCs. The term quality control (QC) has been around for a long time, and it is a major function of production and operations manage- ment. Besides the TQM techniques of concurrent engineering/interfunctional teams, employee empowerment, reward/recognition systems, and training, discussed earlier in this chapter in the context of decision making, another technique more directly associated with the control function is the use of quality circles, which have been popularized by the Japanese. A **quality control circle (QCC)** is a group of workers who meet on a regular basis to discuss ways of improving the quality of work. This approach has helped many MNCs improve the quality of their goods and services dramatically.

Why are Japanese-made goods of higher quality than the goods of many other countries? The answer cannot rest solely on technology, because many MNCs have the same or superior technology, or the financial ability to purchase it. There must be other causal factors. On the following page, the International Management in Action, "How the Japanese Do Things Differently," gives some details about these factors. One study attempted to answer the question by examining the differences between Japanese and U.S. manufacturers of air conditioners.[40] In this analysis, many of the commonly cited reasons for superior Japanese quality were discovered to be inaccurate. So what were the reasons for the quality differences?

One reason was the focus on keeping the workplace clean and ensuring that all machinery and equipment were properly maintained. The Japanese firms were more careful in handling incoming parts and materials, work-in-process, and finished products than their U.S. counterparts. Japanese companies also employed equipment fixtures to a greater extent than did U.S. manufacturers in ensuring proper alignment of parts during final assembly.

The Japanese minimized worker error by assigning new employees to existing work teams or pairing them with supervisors. In this way, the new workers gained important experience under the watchful eye of someone who could correct their mistakes.

Another interesting finding was that the Japanese made effective use of QCCs. Quality targets were set, and responsibility for their attainment then fell on the circle while management provided support assistance. This was stated by the researcher as follows:

quality control circle (QCC)
A group of workers who meet on a regular basis to discuss ways of improving the quality of work.

How the Japanese Do Things Differently

Japanese firms do a number of things extremely well. One is to train their people carefully, a strategy that many successful U.S. firms also employ. Another is to try to remain on the technological cutting edge. A third, increasingly important because of its uniqueness to the Japanese, is to keep a keen focus on developing and bringing to market goods that are competitively priced.

In contrast to Western firms, many Japanese companies use a "target cost" approach. Like other multinational firms, Japanese companies begin the new product development process by conducting marketing research and examining the characteristics of the product to be produced. At this point, however, the Japanese take a different approach. The traditional approach used by MNCs around the world is next to go into designing, engineering, and supplier pricing and then to determine if the cost is sufficiently competitive to move ahead with manufacturing. Japanese manufacturers, in contrast, first determine the price that the consumer most likely will accept, and then they work with design, engineering, and supply people to ensure that the product can be produced at this price. The other major difference is that after most firms manufacture a product, they will engage in periodic cost reductions. The Japanese, however, use a kaizen approach, which fosters continuous cost-reduction efforts.

The critical difference between the two systems is that the Japanese get costs out of the product during the planning and design stage. Additionally, they look at profit in terms of product lines rather than just individual goods, so a consumer product that would be rejected for production by a U.S. or European firm because its projected profitability is too low may be accepted by a Japanese firm because the product will attract additional customers to other offerings in the line. A good example is Sony, which decided to build a smaller version of its compact personal stereo system and market it to older consumers. Sony knew that the profitability of the unit would not be as high as usual, but it went ahead because the product would provide another market niche for the firm and strengthen its reputation. Also, a side benefit is that once a product is out there, it may appeal to an unanticipated market. This was the case with Sony's compact personal stereo system. The unit caught on with young people, and Sony's sales were 50 percent greater than anticipated. Had Sony based its manufacturing decision solely on "stand-alone" profitability, the unit never would have been produced.

These approaches are not unique to Japanese firms. Foreign companies operating in Japan are catching on and using them as well. Coca-Cola Japan is the leading company in the Japanese soft drink market, which sees the introduction of more than 1,000 new products each year. Most offerings do not last very long, and a cost accountant might well argue that it is not worth the effort to produce them. However, Coca-Cola introduces one new product a month. Most of these sodas, soft drinks, and cold coffees survive less than 90 days, but Coke does not let the short-term bottom line dictate the decision. The firm goes beyond quick profitability and looks at the overall picture. Result: Coca-Cola continues to be the leading soft drink firm in Japan despite competition that often is more vigorous than that in the United States.

In supporting the activities of their QCCs, the Japanese firms in this industry routinely collected extensive quality data. Information on defects was compiled daily, and analyzed for trends. Perhaps most important, the data were made easily accessible to line workers, often in the form of publicly posted charts. More detailed data were available to QCCs on request.[41]

This finding pointed out an important difference between Americans and Japanese. The Japanese pushed data on quality down to the operating employees in the quality circles, whereas Americans tended to aggregate the quality data into summary reports aimed at middle and upper management.

Another important difference is that the Japanese tend to build in early warning systems so that they know when something is going wrong. Incoming field data, for example, are reviewed immediately by the quality department, and problems are assigned to one of two categories: routine or emergency. Special efforts then are made to resolve the emergency problems as quickly as possible. High failure rates attributable to a single persistent problem are identified and handled much faster than they would be in U.S. firms. Still another reason is that the Japanese work closely with their suppliers so that the latter's quality increases. In fact, research shows that among suppliers that have contracts with both American and Japanese auto plants in the United States, the Japanese plants get higher performance from their suppliers than do the Americans.[42] The Japanese are able to accomplish this because they work closely with their suppliers and help them develop lean manufacturing capabilities. Some of the steps that Japanese manufacturers take in doing this include (1) leveling their own production schedules in order to avoid big spikes in demand, thus allowing their suppliers to hold less inventory; (2) encouraging their suppliers to ship only what is needed by the assembly plant at a particular time, even if this means sending partially filled trucks; and (3) creating a disciplined system of delivery time windows during which all parts have to be received at the delivery plant. A close look at Table 11–4 shows that the 91 suppliers who were working for both Japanese and American auto firms performed more efficiently for their Japanese customers than for their American customers.

Management attitudes toward quality also were quite different. The Japanese philosophy is: "Anything worth doing in the area of quality is worth overdoing." Workers are trained for all jobs on the line, even though they eventually are assigned to a single workstation. This method of "training overkill" ensures that everyone can perform every job perfectly and results in two important outcomes: (1) If someone is moved to another job, he or she can handle the work without any additional assistance. (2) The workers realize that management puts an extremely high value on the need for quality. When questioned regarding whether their approach to quality resulted in spending more money than was necessary, the Japanese managers disagreed. They believed that quality improvement was technically possible and economically feasible. They did not accept the common U.S. strategy of building a product with quality that was "good enough."

These managers were speaking only for their own firms, however. Some evidence shows that, at least in the short run, an overfocus on quality may become economically unwise. Even so, firms must remember that quality goods and services lead in the long run to repeat business, which translates into profits and growth. From a control standpoint, the major issue is how to identify quality problems and resolve them as efficiently as possible. One approach that has gained acceptance in the United States is outlined by Genichi Taguchi, one of the foremost authorities on quality control. Taguchi's method is to dispense with highly sophisticated statistical methods unless more fundamental ways

Table 11–4
Performance of Suppliers When Serving U.S.- and Japanese-Owned Auto Plants

Performance Indicators	Chrysler Suppliers (n = 26)	Ford Suppliers (n = 42)	GM Suppliers (n = 23)	Honda Suppliers (n = 22)	Nissan Suppliers (n = 16)	Toyota Suppliers (n = 37)
Inventory turnover	28.3	24.4	25.5	38.4	49.2	52.4
Work-in-process	3.0	3.9	7.2	4.0	3.8	3.0
Finished-goods storage time	4.8	5.4	6.6	5.3	4.9	3.2
Inventory on the truck	2.1	4.5	2.6	2.8	2.08	1.61
Inventory maintained at the customer's site	3.5	4.8	3.1	4.0	2.8	2.3
Percentage change in manufacturing costs compared to the previous year	0.69%	0.58%	0.74%	−0.9%	−0.7%	−1.3%
Percentage of late deliveries	4.4%	7.70%	3.04%	2.11%	1.08%	0.44%
Emergency shipping cost (per million sales dollars) in previous year	$1,235	$446	$616	$423	$379	$204

Source: Adapted from Jeffrey K. Liker and Yen-Chun Wu, "Japanese Automakers, U.S. Suppliers and Supply-Chain Superiority," *Sloan Management Review,* Fall 2000, p. 84.

| **Figure 11-3** | **Solving a Quality Problem: Taguchi Method vs. Traditional Method** |

Traditional Method Possible causes are studied one by one while holding the other factors constant.

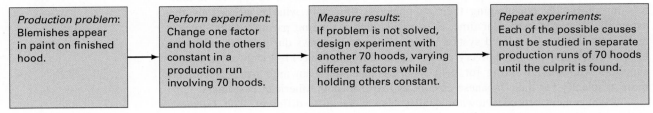

Production problem: Blemishes appear in paint on finished hood. → *Perform experiment:* Change one factor and hold the others constant in a production run involving 70 hoods. → *Measure results:* If problem is not solved, design experiment with another 70 hoods, varying different factors while holding others constant. → *Repeat experiments:* Each of the possible causes must be studied in separate production runs of 70 hoods until the culprit is found.

Taguchi Method Brainstorming and a few bold experiments seek to quickly find the problem.

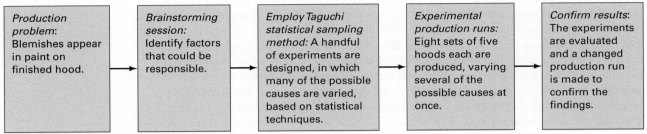

Production problem: Blemishes appear in paint on finished hood. → *Brainstorming session:* Identify factors that could be responsible. → *Employ Taguchi statistical sampling method:* A handful of experiments are designed, in which many of the possible causes are varied, based on statistical techniques. → *Experimental production runs:* Eight sets of five hoods each are produced, varying several of the possible causes at once. → *Confirm results:* The experiments are evaluated and a changed production run is made to confirm the findings.

Source: From information reported in John Holusha, "Improving Quality, the Japanese Way," *New York Times,* July 20, 1988, p. 35.

do not work. Figure 11–3 compares the use of the Taguchi method and the traditional method to identify the cause of defects in the paint on a minivan hood. The Taguchi approach to solving quality control problems is proving to be so effective that many MNCs are adopting it. They also are realizing that the belief that Japanese firms will correct quality control problems regardless of the cost is not true. As Taguchi puts it, "the more efficient approach is to identify the things that can be controlled at a reasonable cost in an organized manner, and simply ignore those too expensive to control."[43] To the extent that U.S. MNCs can do this, they will be able to compete on the basis of quality.

Personnel Performance

Besides financial techniques and the emphasis on quality, another key area of control is personnel performance evaluation. This type of evaluation can take a number of different forms, although there is a great deal of agreement from firm to firm about the general criteria to be measured. Table 11–5 provides a list of the most reputable companies as calculated by the Reputation Institute in conjunction with Forbes magazine. The "reputation pulse" measure incorporates a range of criteria, including the trust, admiration, and esteem that stakeholders have for a company.

In describing what makes another group of companies successful—the "World's Most Admired" firms—consultants at the Hay Group made an analysis of the best global firms, focusing especially on their personnel and talent management systems, identifying seven common themes:

1. Top managers at the most-admired companies take their mission statements seriously and expect everyone else to do the same.
2. Success attracts the best people—and the best people sustain success.
3. The top companies know precisely what they are looking for.
4. These firms see career development as an investment, not a chore.
5. Whenever possible, these companies promote from within.
6. Performance is rewarded.
7. The firms are genuinely interested in what their employees think, and they measure work satisfaction often and thoroughly.[44]

Table 11–5
World's Most Reputable Companies, 2012

RepTrak™ 100: The Most Reputable Companies in the World:
Pulse Score and Rank

Company	Home Country	Rank	RepTrak™ Pulse Score
BMW	Germany	1	80.08
Sony	Japan	2	79.31
The Walt Disney Company	U.S.	3	78.92
Daimler (Mercedes-Benz)	Germany	4	78.54
Apple	U.S.	5	78.49
Google	U.S.	6	78.05
Microsoft	U.S.	7	77.98
Volkswagen	Germany	8	77.04
Canon	Japan	9	76.98
LEGO Group	Denmark	10	76.35
Adidas Group	Germany	11	76.00
Nestle	Switzerland	12	75.88
Colgate-Palmolive	U.S.	13	75.75
Panasonic	Japan	14	75.71
Nike	U.S.	15	75.43
Intel	U.S.	16	75.42
Michelin	France	17	75.32
Johnson & Johnson	U.S.	18	75.17
IBM	U.S.	19	75.08
Ferrero	Italy	20	74.90
Samsung Electronics	South Korea	21	74.81
Honda Motor	Japan	22	74.80
L'Oreal	France	23	74.35
Nokia	Finland	24	73.33
Philips Electronics	Netherlands	25	74.33
Kellogg	U.S.	26	74.32
Goodyear	U.S.	27	74.28
Amazon.com	U.S.	28	74.07

Source: Reputation Institute: Global RepTrak™ 100. http://www.rankingthebrands.com/
PDF/2012%20RepTrak%20100 Global_Report,%20Reputation%20Institute.pdf.

One of the most common approaches to personnel performance evaluation is the periodic appraisal of work performance. Although the objective is similar from country to country, how performance appraisals are done differs. For example, effective employee performance in one country is not always judged to be effective in another. Awareness of international differences is particularly important when expatriate managers evaluate local managers on the basis of home-country standards. A good example comes out of a survey that found Japanese managers in U.S.-based manufacturing firms gave higher evaluations to Japanese personnel than to Americans. The results led the researcher to conclude: "It seems that cultural differences and diversified approaches to management in MNCs of different nationalities will always create a situation where some bias in performance appraisal may exist."[45] Dealing with these biases is a big challenge facing MNCs.

Another important difference is how personnel performance control actually is conducted. A study that compared personnel control approaches used by Japanese managers in Japan with those employed by U.S. managers in the United States found marked differences.[46] For example, when Japanese work groups were successful because of the actions of a particular individual, the Japanese manager tended to give credit to the whole group. When the group was unsuccessful because of the actions of a particular individual, however, the Japanese manager tended to perceive this one employee as responsible. In addition, the more unexpected the poor performance, the greater was the likelihood that the individual would be responsible. In contrast, individuals in the United States typically were given the credit when things went well and the blame when performance was poor.

Other differences relate to how rewards and monitoring of personnel performance are handled. Both U.S. and Japanese managers offered greater rewards and more freedom from close monitoring to individuals when they were associated with successful performance, no matter what the influence of the group on the performance. The Americans carried this tendency further than the Japanese in the case of rewards, including giving high rewards to a person who was a "lone wolf."[47]

A comparison of these two approaches to personnel evaluation shows that the Japanese tend to use a more social or group orientation, while the Americans are more individualistic (for more, see Chapter 4). The researchers found that overall, however, the approaches were quite similar and that the control of personnel performance by Japanese and U.S. managers is far more similar than different.

assessment center
An evaluation tool used to identify individuals with the potential to be selected for or promoted to higher-level positions.

Such similarity also can be found in assessment centers used to evaluate employees. An **assessment center** is an evaluation tool that is used to identify individuals with the potential to be selected for or promoted to higher-level positions. Used by large U.S. MNCs for many years, these centers also are employed around the world. A typical assessment center would involve simulation exercises such as these: (1) in-basket exercises that require managerial attention; (2) a committee exercise in which the candidates must work as a team in making decisions; (3) business decision exercises in which participants compete in the same market; (4) preparation of a business plan; and (5) a letter-writing exercise. These forms of evaluation are beginning to gain support, because they are more comprehensive than simple checklists or the use of a test or an interview and thus better able to identify those managers who are most likely to succeed when hired or promoted.

■ The World of International Management—Revisited

This chapter focuses on two areas that are essential to any company joining the race to compete in online retail or to develop productive contracting relationships for outsourcing in this area: management decision and control systems. The rapid growth in online retail poses substantial challenges in the areas of management decision and control. For example, many companies rely on extensive and sophisticated Web infrastructure to market and fulfill orders; any breakdown in these systems can have substantial ramifications for smooth operations and overall reputation. The implications for these firms' control process are obvious. Further, many companies, even large ones, outsource these functions to one of the large online retailers such as Amazon.com, further exacerbating the possible misconnection between management and customers.

Review the opening World of International Management discussion of online retailers and think about the principal considerations in international management decision making and control processes you have read about in this chapter. Then, answer the following questions: (1) How might differences in national and corporate culture impede timely decisions and control processes among existing and potential competitors in online retail? (2) To what extent should total quality management and quality control be considered when establishing an online retail presence or contracting with another firm to provide it? (3) What specific decision and control systems or tools would be helpful in overseeing an online presence (either internal or outsourced)?

SUMMARY OF KEY POINTS

1. Decision-making involves choosing from among alternatives. Some countries tend to use more centralized decision making than do others, so that more decisions are made at the top of the MNC than are delegated to the subsidiaries and operating levels.

2. A number of factors help influence whether decision making will be centralized or decentralized, including company size, amount of capital investment, relative importance of the overseas unit to the MNC, volume-to-unit-cost relationship, level of product diversification, distance between the home office and the subsidiary, and the competence of managers in the host country.

3. There are a number of decision-making challenges with which MNCs currently are confronted. These include total quality management (TQM) decisions and strategies for attacking the competition, among others.

4. Controlling involves evaluating results in relation to plans or objectives and then taking action to correct deviations. MNCs control their overseas operations in a number of ways. Most combine direct and indirect controls. Some prefer heavily quantifiable methods, and others opt for more qualitative approaches. Some prefer decentralized approaches; others opt for greater centralization.

5. Three of the most common performance measures used to control subsidiaries are in the financial, quality, and personnel areas. Financial performance typically is measured by profit and return on investment. Quality performance often is controlled through quality circles. Personnel performance typically is judged through performance evaluation techniques.

KEY TERMS

assessment center, *388*

codetermination, *373*

controlling, *376*

decision making, *368*

direct controls, *379*

empowerment, *374*

honne, *373*

indirect controls, *380*

kaizen, *374*

profit, *382*

quality control circle (QCC), *383*

return on investment (ROI), *382*

ringisei, *373*

tatemae, *373*

total quality management (TQM), *373*

REVIEW AND DISCUSSION QUESTIONS

1. A British computer firm is acquiring a smaller competitor located in Frankfurt. What are two likely differences in the way these two firms carry out the decision-making process? How could these differences create a problem for the acquiring firm? Give an example in each case.

2. Which cultures would be more likely to focus on external controls? Which cultures would consider direct controls to be more important than indirect controls?

3. How would you explain a company's decision to employ centralized decision-making processes and decentralized control processes, considering the two are so interconnected? Provide an industry example of where this may occur.

4. How are U.S. multinationals trying to introduce total quality management into their operations? Give two examples. Would a U.S. MNC doing business in Germany find it easier to introduce TQM concepts into German operations, or would there be more receptivity to them back in the United States? Why? What if the U.S. multinational were introducing these ideas into a Japanese subsidiary?

5. In what ways could an accelerated decision-making process harm a company? Using Figure 11–1, which stage(s) do you think would be most in danger of being overlooked?

6. A company practices personnel performance evaluation through reviewing financial decisions management has made, specifically focusing on ROI. How is this approach beneficial to the company? Which aspects could the company be neglecting? Which cultures are most likely to employ this method? Which cultures would avoid this tactic?

INTERNET EXERCISE: LOOKING AT THE BEST

In Table 11–5, the most reputable global companies are listed. Each company uses decision making and controlling to help ensure its success in the world market. Visit these two companies' corporate sites: Procter & Gamble and Panasonic. Carefully examine what these firms are doing. For example, what markets are they targeting? What products and services are they offering? What new markets are they entering? Then, after you are as familiar with their operations as possible, answer these two questions: (1) What types of factors may influence future management decision making in these two companies? (2) What types of control criteria would you expect these companies to use in evaluating their operations and determining how well they are doing?

Turkey

Located at the strategic intersection of Asia, Europe, and the Middle East, the Republic of Turkey is about the size of Texas and contains a population of roughly 80 million people. Turkey sits in a region that has a rich history of economic prosperity. For nearly 600 years, the Ottoman Empire, governed from modern-day Istanbul, controlled lucrative trade routes between the East and West that crossed its territory. Today, Turkey is a multi-party parliamentary republic, governed by a Prime Minister, a legislative 550-member Grand National Assembly, and a largely ceremonial President. Despite 99 percent of its citizens identifying as Islamic, the government of Turkey remains secularly governed—unique to a region that is dominated by theocratic nations.

For the first 60 years following the collapse of the Ottoman Empire, Turkey's industries were primarily government-owned and controlled. During this period, many industries suffered from inefficiencies and large financial losses. Government restrictions placed on foreign direct investment (FDI) and foreign trade limited economic growth, leading to government debt and a large trade deficit. Moderate economic gains were frequently offset by sharp recessions. Following a period of high inflation and severe economic crisis in the late 1970s, government reforms were enacted in 1983 to begin the process of privatizing the economy and increasing exports.

Turkey's newly open economy has rapidly diversified over the past 30 years. Fueled by FDI and private enterprise, Turkish exports now include automotive, construction, and electronic goods. Services account for 63 percent of gross domestic product (GDP), while agriculture only accounts for 8 percent. Raw materials and fossil fuels have entered Turkey's export mix. Oil exports, delivered from the Caspian Sea through a 1000-mile-long pipeline, first began operation in 2006. With a skilled workforce and increased demand for its exports, unemployment has dropped to 9 percent. Increases in trade between Turkey and its European neighbors have helped expand GDP to US$1.125 trillion, ranking it 17th in the world. Since 1983, GDP has averaged a 4 percent per year growth. Turkey applied for full European Union membership in 1987 and negotiations for admission began in 2004.

The transition toward a private-sector economy has not been without setbacks, however. With a per-capita income of roughly US$15,000, Turkey remains behind most of its European neighbors. Rapid growth has led to high inflation, which now stands at 9 percent. External conflicts, such as the Persian Gulf War in 1991 and the resulting trade embargo against Iraq, have sharply cut into Turkey's exports. And alleged human rights violations against Kurdish citizens have damaged relations with Western Europe. If Turkey is admitted to the European Union, it will likely not occur for several more years.

In June of 2013, a group of demonstrators who were protesting the construction of a major commercial and retail project on one of Istanbul's last remaining green spaces were brutally suppressed by police, setting off a series of broader protests in Istanbul and around the country over the government's sometimes authoritarian policies. These protests—and the government's response to them—underscored the uneven process of democracy and the influence of political issues on economic progress.

www.mongabay.com, www.cia.gov

Questions

1. Why did Turkey decide to privatize its economy in 1983?

2. What effect has privatization had on Turkey?

3. What challenges does Turkey face as it continues to develop and expand?

Google in China: Protecting Property and Rights

Google in China

In early 2008 Guo Quan announced plans to sue Google in the United States for blocking his entire name from search results in China. But why was his name blocked from search results? Guo Quan had published an open letter in early January to his government leaders Hu Jintao and Wu Bangguo, calling "for government reform [with] multi-party democratic elections" that served the interests of the common people.[1] In response to his letter, the government labeled Guo as a dissident and a political danger. He was ultimately arrested on charges of "subversion of state power."[2]

Guo Quan's name might have forever been lost in the shadow of the then-upcoming 2008 Beijing Summer Olympics, but formal and informal networks of information helped publicize his case, his harsh sentence which will have him imprisoned until at least 2019, and the fact that he named Google in his suit, have made him infamous. The story of Guo Quan reflects the many challenges faced by Google over the course of the past decade as it has attempted to expand globally. During this period, Google's relationship with China has undergone a series of advances and setbacks, each reflecting in some way China's response to the challenges of the Internet and social networking as well as Google's difficulties of translating a uniquely North American business model to countries and environments with different regulatory regimes, legal environments, and fundamental values.

Rough Beginnings

At the break of the new millennium, Google began to offer its search services in a Chinese-language format with the hope of furthering its mission "to organize the world's information and make it universally accessible and useful."[3] Disappointingly, the website was consistently unavailable "about 10 percent of the time . . . [and] slow and unreliable" due to "extensive filtering performed by China's licensed Internet service providers."[4] This sense of distrust persisted for another two years until the autumn of 2002, when Google first became completely unavailable in China, because Google claimed to have "stood by its principles and not subject itself to Chinese laws and regulations."[4] The dysfunctional use of Google search services for mainlanders continued and in December 2003, Google.com was again blocked in China.

Three years later, in 2006, Google.com was again blocked while Google.cn, Google's Chinese subsidiary, remained in operation. The following year, in 2007, CEO Eric Schmidt gave an upbeat assessment of Google's outlook in China amidst challenges of censorship issues and competition from Baidu.com.

More Than a BackRub: Google's Rise to Power

But how did Google come to such international prominence? In 1996, Stanford graduate students Larry Page and Sergey Brin began collaborating on a search engine called BackRub. This search engine got its name because Page and Brin used backlinks to measure the importance of a site.[5] By using the innovation called PageRank, a new system of ranking a website's relevance using "an objective measure of its citation importance . . . according to an idealized model of user behavior,"[6] Page and Brin dramatically increased search relevance compared to other search engines like Yahoo.

A little more than a year later, BackRub's massive bandwidth usage, which had downloaded over 30 million indexable HTML pages, made it inoperable on the Stanford server.[7] From then on, Larry and Sergey realized the potential of BackRub, changed its name to Google, and moved their office to a colleague's garage.[8]

Google's first investor became interested in 1996 when Sun Microsystem founder Andy Bechtolsheim provided a $100,000 check, allowing Google to incorporate and become officially Google Inc. In 1999, more investors grew attracted to Page and Brin's idea and, with an increased budget of around $1 million, Google Inc. was able to relocate to a real office in Palo Alto, where a staff of only eight answered about 500,000 queries per day.[9]

In mid-1999 Google received an additional $25 million in equity funding for their search engine from two venture capital firms: Sequoia Capital and Kleiner Perkins Caufield & Buyers. The confidence to invest such a large amount of capital came from the previous experience these VC's had in funding high-tech companies, such as Amazon.com and Cisco Systems. Google's engineering genius and a monthly growth rate of 50 percent fueled only by word of mouth easily proved its value to these seasoned investors.[10]

By the year 2000, Google became the world's largest search engine, supporting 15 languages.[11] Google's service was nothing new considering the existing search engines at the time, like Yahoo and AOL, but it was indisputable that Google offered the best search services.

The innovative PageRank algorithm was combined with a minimalist homepage that focused on its search tool and reminded the user of its chief focus while helping to reinforce confidence in its best feature. Having secured a solid foothold in America, Google continued to seek more ways to expand. Visionaries from the very beginning, Page and Brin created Google to have "simplicity in our user interface and the scalability in our back-end systems [that] enables us to expand very quickly."[12]

By anticipating the need to be flexible in order to expand, Google was set to go global. And as Larry Page remarked: "Google's search engine has always had strong global appeal. We attribute this success to the site's simplicity of design, ease of use, and highly relevant results. By localizing our search services to new international communities, Google will open up a host of new revenue, sales, and partnership channels."[13]

Unfortunately, Asian countries in general had always been more difficult to penetrate because of competition from well-established local search engines. For example, in 2010, Korea's search engine Naver had a market share of 47.32 percent, while Google had 45.29 percent.[14] Furthermore, China posed the greatest roadblock with censorship and competition from Baidu. However, with a population of one billion people and Internet usage on a steady climb, Google was determined to establish a stronger foothold in China.

China's Internet Users and Population

	Users (millions)	Population (millions)	Percent
2002	59	1,284.5	**4.6**
2003	69	1,292.3	**5.3**
2004	94	1,299.9	**7.2**
2005	103	1,307.6	**7.9**
2006	137	1,314.5	**10.4**
2007	162	1,284.5	**12.6**
2008	253	1,321.3	**19.1**
2009	384	1,328.0	**28.9**
2010	420	1,334.7	**31.5**
2011	508	1,341.4	**37.9**
2012	538	1,354.0	**39.7**

2012 figures for Internet users are estimates.
Source: ITU, China Population Buruea.[15] Author's calculations.

Google vs. Baidu

China's policies have directly influenced the competitive landscape for search firms in China. In the space of Internet search, Baidu is usually referred to as China's Google. But in reality, Baidu holds a strong market share lead over Google.[16] Prior to the launch of Google.cn in 2006 in China, Google held 33.3 percent of the search engine market share between Shanghai, Beijing, and Guangzhou while Baidu held 47.9 percent.[17] Google was optimistic about the close margin in market share and considered the possibility of perhaps buying out Baidu in competition. But instead, in mid-2006, Google made a fatal mistake, selling its 2.6 percent stake of more than $60 million in Baidu shares and introducing Google.cn to China.[18]

Nevertheless, Google.cn was launched with the promise that it would agree to block certain websites in return for the opportunity to run local Chinese services.[19] Google promised to notify Chinese users when their search results would be censored and also promised not to maintain any services that involved personal or confidential data, like Gmail or Blogger, on the mainland. Google.cn was a response to improve the poor service Google believed it was providing in China. As senior policy counsel Andrew McLaughlin put it, "Google users in China today struggle with a service that, to be blunt, isn't very good . . . the website is slow, and sometimes produces results that when clicked on, stall out the user's browser. Our Google News service is never available; Google Images is accessible only half the time . . . the level of service we've been able to provide in China is not something we're proud of."[20]

Fundamentally, Google's strategic move to create a local presence with Google.cn was driven by its desire to follow its mission of creating the most organized and efficient search engine. However, while Google thought it had the flexibility to set up a better search engine in China, Baidu CEO Robin Li was already ahead of the curve. While PageRank was being developed by Page and Brin, Robin Li was simultaneously working on a similar strategy for site-ranking called RankDex. As a result, this similar search concept was brought to Baidu. In the end, Google had erroneously presumed that it could overtake Baidu by maximizing its core competencies within China.[21]

Not only did Baidu have a strong competing search engine against Google but it also provided several innovative search features customized for more local tastes. It introduced community-oriented services, including information exchanging bulletin boards and instant messaging. These extra services appealed strongly to Chinese Internet users and put Baidu ahead of a foreign Google that did not seem to understand the Chinese market as well.

In addition, Baidu also took an extra step that Google missed by setting up "a national network of advertising resellers in 200 Chinese cities to educate businesses about the power of online advertising."[22] By specifically targeting the business market segment, Baidu aimed to secure the Shanghai business sector. To secure the more general student population in Beijing, Baidu also offered a search engine that provided easy access to pirated film and music downloads.[23]

While Baidu strategically offered services that targeted specific market segments, Google was at a loss because of its slow comprehension of the Chinese market. Among one of the failures Google made was its attempt to rebrand Google.cn to Guge, which was Chinese for Harvest Song. Six months after the launch of Guge, "72.6 percent (62.8 percent of the users whose first choice was Google) of the interviewed users still weren't able to [recall] the Chinese name of Google."[24] The lack in brand loyalty was reflected in the insignificant number of Google users who were willing to convert from using the Chinese version of Google.com to Guge. Most users still preferred to use the original Google.com that was only censored by the People's Republic of China.[25]

Google seemed to be fighting a losing battle while Baidu continued to receive positive press coverage during its 2005 IPO on NASDAQ. Consequently, in just one year, Baidu gained 14 percent of the search engine market share while Google lost 8 percent. [26]

In the following year, 2007, Google fought hard to hold onto its piece of the China market, increasing its total market share from 19.2 percent to 22.8 percent while Baidu fell from 63.7 percent to 58.1 percent. Google increased its efforts by "hiring Chinese employees and . . . partnering with Chinese technology firms . . . [and establishing] two research centers, one in Beijing and one in Shanghai."[27]

The small victory was short-lived as Google was soon met with conflict from both China's and the U.S.'s government.

The Challenge of Censorship: Google under Fire

Shortly after Google.cn received its license from the Chinese government in 2007, Google proceeded to sign a set of guidelines, designed to reduce the risk that their actions would lead to human rights abuses in China and other countries.[28] By promising to comply with censorship when the government filed a formal request, this effectively removed Google's presence from the majority of human rights activities.

From this point forward, Google was fiercely criticized for running advertisements from nonlicensed medical websites in 2008, launching free music services, scanning books without proper copyright laws, and making pornographic content easily available multiple times in 2009.[29] What has unfolded in the most recent years has been the climax of this drama between country and company.

On January 13, 2010, in response to an attack on the Gmail accounts of human rights activists by the Chinese government, Google released an initial statement saying that it was ready to end censorship of its search service.[30] The announcement caused a stir, with speculations that Google would pull out of China completely.

Soon afterwards, however, CEO Eric Schmidt released a counterstatement stating that Google was planning to stay in China, even if it was forced to close down its local search services and just carry through with its other range of services.[31] In the same month, Hilary Clinton, the U.S. Secretary of State, called upon Beijing to carry out a thorough and transparent investigation regarding the cyber hacks of human rights activists' e-mail accounts. Ultimately, she threw her weight behind Google's threat to pull out of China unless Beijing permitted an "unfiltered search engine."[32]

Following the conflict in January, Google formally announced in March that all Google.cn users would be directed to the uncensored Google.com.hk website instead. According to Google, the decision reflected a legal move that still allowed mainland users access to their search engine.[33] The move to stop offering a local search engine and battling with China over censorship reflected a shift in Google's attitude, giving up competing with Baidu for Internet usage. In April, Google's share of Chinese Internet searches dropped from 35.6 percent to 30.9 percent and Baidu rose from 58.4 percent to 64 percent.[34] Despite no longer providing Google.cn to China, Google still cannot escape the censorship battles and attacks on its server. Even as recently as 2012, Google services were still being temporarily blocked in China.[35]

But criticisms of Google have not always been from China. On March 22, 2011, New York Judge Denny Chin rejected a settlement between Google and both the Authors Guild and the Association of American Publishers (AAP). The original settlement had included an annual payment of $125 million in royalties to the copyright owners in order for Google to continue its project of scanning and selling online access to 150 million books.[36] But copyright concerns persisted since no one could establish ownership of the digitized and scanned pages. It was concluded that Google's current pact would simply give the company an unfair advantage over its competitors while rewarding it for engaging in wholesale copying of copyrighted works without permission.

Since October 2012, the AAP has announced a new settlement deal with Google. For each book already scanned by Google, publishers could choose to contact Google for removal. Moving forward, every digitized book catalog would first require an express opt-in from publishers. None of the financial terms of the deal were released. The Authors Guild, on the other hand, still remains in litigation, leading a class-action lawsuit criticizing Google for its opt-out approach.[37]

Google's Future

The challenges of censorship in China have forced Google to look beyond the appeal of China's gargantuan search market. Instead, Google has shifted its focus to the operating systems of smartphones. At the end of the second quarter of 2012, Google's Android operating system enjoyed an 83 percent lead in market share. Android is closely held by Google; so closely, in fact, that Google had been unwilling to share the most recent versions of code with Chinese smartphone developers. The most recent example of this is when Google forced the delayed release of a smartphone manufactured by Acer Inc., which ran an operating system called Aliyun. This operating system was allegedly created by taking Android's software and making unapproved changes which were headed by the Chinese e-commerce organization Alibaba.[38]

Relationships are extremely hostile between Google and China, and the options for China are quickly disappearing. The only course of action left for China is to build its own Chinese mobile-OS for Chinese mobile devices.[39] Mobile continues to dominate a large portion of Google's strategy. When Google purchased Motorola Mobility in May 2012, it had hoped that the accompanying treasure trove of over 17,000 patents would yield innumerable benefits. But this has not been the case. After the $12.4 billion purchase, Google still has yet to win a decisive legal case with a big payoff.[40]

Regardless of the challenges, Google still has accumulated a powerful tool. In acquiring Motorola Mobility and its store of patents, Google now possesses among the best IPR for designing devices, and Google has the software to supplement those devices and integrate them vertically into its online systems.[41] Ultimately, this purchase was consistent with Google's hope to reposition itself as a bigger player in the space of mobile technology.

The rate at which technology is becoming even more integrated into our lives is astounding, and Google is on the forefront of that mission. With its newest app for Android users, called "Google Keep," it hopes to target early software-adopters looking for another way to manage all of their sticky notes, photos, and lists. But yet again, a central component to this new advancement is trust. While some users are easily giving up more private ground in the routine of their daily lives, others are questioning whether or not the free services are worth it, especially since similar projects like Google Reader or iGoogle have been terminated.[42]

For Google, these privacy issues have taken off internationally. In April 2013, Germany prosecuted Google for "scooping up sensitive personal information in the Street View mapping project." The total fine added up to $189,225, which is a drop in the bucket compared to Google's profits of $10.7 billion in 2012. Such fees are usually already factored into the business expenses of large data-mining corporations like Google. But these fines are not uncommon. Rather, it is the opposite, and often considered regular behavior. Google has accumulated several violations over the years. In 2012, Google paid $7 million to settle with 38 states that had filed against the company. In a separate case related to the Safari browser, the Federal Trade Commission penalized Google for $22.5 million, "the largest civil penalty ever levied." In 2011, France also fined Google 100,000 euros.[43]

Google's extensive reach in data is only growing in size. At around the same time that Germany was bringing its charges against Google, Google cemented its Global Human Trafficking Hotline Network, committing $3 million to bring together three NGOs: Polaris Project, Liberty Asia, and La Strada International. But one question still remains, even in the face of Google's good intentions: Can this company be trusted, with sensitive information now regarding potentially trafficked victims? Have we gone too far by giving Google so much credit and by painting Google with a philanthropic stroke? In response to these questions, head of philanthropy at Palantir Technologies Jason Payne points out, "Just because someone's human rights have been eviscerated, doesn't mean that their civil liberties and electronic rights can be eviscerated."[44]

Regardless of Google's legal efforts and privacy challenges, it is still pressing on with several innovative projects. The most imaginative of these projects is a wearable beta technology device called Google Glass. The thrust of this new device is in the power of voice-command for queries such as the weather, a built-in GPS, and being able to take point-of-view photos and videos from an intimate perspective. All of this self-generated media is then directly uploaded to a user's Google+ account in private mode by default.[45]

Google is also considering several other projects including Android@Home, Google's attempt at Home Automation, connecting lightbulbs, coffee pots, and alarm clocks.[46] Another project is Google Fiber, which focuses on delivering Internet speeds "100 times faster than the average Internet connection in the United States."[47] Driverless cars is also another ambitious goal for the company, which would go nicely with its current database of road maps. Google's strategy is clear: With billions of dollars spent on research and development, Google knows that it has a responsibility to push out products that no other company would dare to dream about, all the while pursuing high-tech inventions that integrate with our daily lives.

Technology is inevitable and the Internet has reached nearly every corner of the world. For the countries that do not adopt the Internet as a part of their economic activity, it will be an uphill struggle to receive new information and new ideas, especially if those new ideas mean the difference for whether or not change happens in societies.

In March 2013, CEO Eric Schmidt and Jared Cohen, director of Google Ideas, made a trip to Burma. Cohen commented: "This whole concept of cyberspace has come to serve in some respects as a global version of the American dream. They think it's going to make them economically better off; they think it's going to make them more free."[48]

Schmidt shared similar hopes about the power of the Internet during their stop in North Korea. "In many countries, the Internet is the only way to get an alternative point of view in, and the Internet's arrival could destabilize some of these autocratic regimes, who we believe will fight it."[49]

As Google expands, and its presence permeates developing markets, its opportunities are abundant. This is especially true since most of the newly connected Internet users are living in areas of conflict and could potentially experience drastic changes to their social structures as a result of interacting with Google. A company such as Google could extend its influence beyond that of a nation-state by empowering desperate citizens with the ideas or information they need to incite a revolution.

Ultimately, Google's international strategy will continue to align itself with its information strategy, continually leveraging the opportunities of both computational science and human ingenuity. At the same time, Google will continue to face political threats of censorship and information restriction and challenges to its privacy policies and practices. But the reverberations from its new technology will continue to generate commotion in the markets and challenges to governments and their information policies.

Questions for Review

1. How would you characterize China's market for online search and related services?

2. Why was Google initially attracted to China? What changed its perspective?

3. Should companies like Google conform to the Chinese government's expectation regarding privacy, censorship, and distribution of information?

4. What advantages does Baidu have over Google in the Chinese marketplace? How might Google overcome those advantages?

5. What recommendations would you make for Google in China going forward?

Source: This case was prepared by Karl Li and Pin-Pin Liao of Villanova University under the supervision of Professor Jonathan Doh as the basis for class discussion.

Brief Integrative Case 3.2

Can Sony Regain Its Innovative Edge?
The OLED Project

Sony Corporation, once an undeniable innovation leader, has struggled recently to bring new innovative technologies to the market. Sony's next-generation television, an ultrathin model hailed by executives as a symbol of the company's technological comeback, is now a symbol of another kind: the dilemma facing its TV business. The essence of the dilemma involves Sony's ability to hold its position as an innovation leader and stay profitable at the same time.[1]

Sony developed a new flat-panel technology, called organic light-emitting diode (OLED), to produce a brilliant picture on a screen only 3 millimeters thick. The technology is so new that Sony is barely breaking even on the pricey sets.[2] In November 2007, Sony introduced the world's first OLED TV, the 11" XEL-1. Initially priced at US$2,500, the XEL-1 was more of a prototype than a commercial set. In January of 2009, Sony introduced the new 'X' series OLED Walkman with a 432×240 touch OLED.[3] Despite these two releases, Sony announced it would postpone mass production of the new TV for several years, and halted production of the XEL-1 three years after it was brought to market citing the global downturn.[4] Working in conjunction with Panasonic to jointly develop technologies for OLED TV panel mass production, Sony does not anticipate low-cost mass production by 2013.[5]

The decision to postpone mass production sent a clear message to Sony's engineers and R&D staff that returning its TV business to profitability is a priority. The business is on track to lose money for the sixth straight year. In the past, Sony's engineers could push the company to roll out products that were technological marvels but struggled to turn a profit. Sony's TV division lost 127 billion yen ($1.34 billion) in 2008, representing more than half of the company's operating losses for the fiscal year which ended March 31, 2009. Televisions accounted for 16.5 percent of Sony's 7.73 trillion yen in revenue.[6]

Sony has a lot to lose. The Japanese electronics giant has invested more than $78 million in OLED, which it thinks may eventually replace plasma and liquid crystal display (LCD) as the dominant TV technology. According to tech analyst Paul Semenza at researcher iSuppli, 2.8 million OLED TVs will be sold in 2013. That's a promising opportunity for Sony, which has lost market share in music players, video game systems, and other types of TVs in recent years. "Sony desperately needs a new (television)

technology," says Semenza. "They haven't had a blockbuster since the Trinitron" cathode-ray-tube (CRT) televisions of the 1970s, 1980s and 1990s.[7]

According to analysts, Sony was slow to embrace the shift from cathode-ray-tube televisions to LCDs. Once the world's top TV maker, Sony now trails both Samsung and LG in terms of revenue, according to DisplaySearch.[8] And commercialization of this new technology brings about operational and supply chain challenges to the electronic giant: Manufacturing costs for new technology are very high, and the needed components are hard to procure. Research firm DisplaySearch estimates Sony's production yield for its 11-inch OLED panel is below 60 percent, meaning at least 4 of every 10 panels its factories produce aren't up to par and can't be sold. Production of larger panels would likely introduce more difficulties.[9]

Sony's New OLED TV Features

Limited quantities of Sony's first OLED TV model ("XEL-1") came to the U.S. market in January 2008 at strikingly high prices—$2,500 for a tiny 11-inch TV set.[10] Sony executives tried to persuade the market that the new technology brought so many benefits that it was worth every penny. According to Sony, the main features of the "XEL-1" TV include:[11]

1. Thinness: Introduces new TV form factor measuring approximately 3mm thinness (at its thinnest point).

2. High contrast: Reproduces realistic images using exquisite shades of black and flexible control of color tone and gradation.

3. High peak brightness: Faithfully reproduces picture glow.

4. Excellent color reproduction: Delivers pure and vivid colors in both dark and bright images.

5. Rapid response time: Smoothly reproduces fast-moving images such as sports scenes.

6. Low power consumption.

"The launch of an OLED TV is one of the most important industry landmarks," said Randy Waynick, senior vice president of Sony Electronics' Home Products Division. "Not only does the technology change the form factor of television, it delivers flawless picture quality that will soon become the standard against which all TVs are measured."[12]

Under development for more than 10 years, OLED displays not only offer a striking form factor, they deliver "unmatched performance" in key picture quality categories, according to Waynick. With their light-emitting structure, OLED displays can prevent light emission when reproducing shades of black, resulting in very deep blacks and a contrast ratio of over 1,000,000:1. The lack of a backlight allows the device to control all phases of light emission from zero to peak brightness. The innovative technology delivers exceptional color expression and detail without wasting power, so it is an exceptional energy-saver.[13]

The other advantage of new technology cited by Sony officials is that the OLED display panel uses extremely low power levels since the light-emitting structure of the panel eliminates the need for a separate light source. As a result, OLED panels can be up to 40 percent more efficient per panel inch compared with a conventional 20-inch LCD panel. Additionally, since OLED displays create their own light, any mercury associated with traditional backlighting is eliminated.[14]

"Super Top Emission," a technology unique to Sony and incorporated in its "Organic Panel," has a high aperture ratio which allows for efficient light emission from the organic materials, realizing high peak brightness. This enables "XEL-1" to faithfully reproduce light flow such as reflections of sunlight or camera flashlights through the image reproduced on the display. This "Super Top Emission" and the color extracting technology within its embedded color filter enable "XEL-1" to reproduce natural colors beautifully. As a result, the fresh colors of ripe fruit and shades of deep cobalt blue can be stunningly reproduced. In order to use OLED to generate the full spectrum of Sony's TV color requirements, Sony developed its own proprietary organic materials, with bright coloration. The "Organic Panel" can also sustain its color reproduction capability in scenes of diminished brightness, enabling "XEL-1" to faithfully re-create even dark movie scenes using the colors that were originally intended.[15]

A final advantage of the OLED technology is its rapid response time, enabling it to smoothly reproduce fast moving images such as sports scenes. This response time is attributed to newly developed OLED drive circuits which spontaneously turn the light emitted from the organic material layer on and off.

Weaknesses of the OLED Technology

In spite of all the features that new OLED technology delivers, it has a number of shortcomings, some of which may take years for the manufacturers to overcome in order to make the technology commercially attractive. According to analysts, among the weaknesses of this new technology were the following:[16]

1. *Lifespan*
   The biggest technical problem for OLEDs is the limited lifetime of the organic materials. In particular, blue OLEDs historically have had a lifetime of around 14,000 hours to half original brightness (five years at 8 hours a day) when used for flat-panel displays, which is lower than the typical lifetime of LCD, LED, or PDP (plasma display) technology—each currently rated for about 60,000 hours to half brightness, depending on manufacturer and model. However, some manufacturers of OLED displays aim to increase the lifespan of OLED displays, pushing their expected life past that of LCD displays by improving light outcoupling, thus achieving the same brightness at a lower drive current.

2. *Color balance issues*
   Additionally, as the OLED material used to produce blue light degrades significantly more rapidly than the materials that produce other colors, blue light output will decrease relative to the other colors of light. This differential color output change will change the color balance of the display and is much more noticeable than a decrease in overall luminance. This can be partially avoided by adjusting color balance, but this may require advanced control circuits and interaction with the user, which is unacceptable for some uses. In order to delay the problem, manufacturers bias the color balance toward blue so that the display initially has an artificially blue tint, leading to complaints of artificial-looking, over-saturated colors.

3. *Water damage*
   The intrusion of water into displays can damage or destroy the organic materials. Therefore, improved sealing processes are important for practical manufacturing and may limit the longevity of more flexible displays.

4. *Outdoor performance*
   As an emissive display technology, OLEDs are 100 percent reliant converting electricity to light whereas most LCD displays contain at least some portion of reflective technology, and e-ink leads the way in efficiency with ~33 percent reflectivity of sunlight, enabling the display to be used without any artificial light source. OLEDs typically have poor readability in bright ambient light, such as outdoors, whereas displays that use reflective light are able to increase their brightness in the presence of ambient light to help overcome unwanted surface reflections without using any additional power.

5. *Power consumption*
   While an OLED will consume around 40 percent of the power of an LCD displaying an image which is primarily black, for the majority of images it will

consume 60–80 percent of the power of an LCD; however, it can use over three times as much power to display an image with a white background such as a document or a website. This can lead to disappointing real-world battery life in mobile devices.

6. *Screen burn-in*
   Unlike displays with a common light source, the brightness of each OLED pixel fades depending on the content displayed. Combined with the short lifetime of the organic dyes, this leads to screen burn-in, worse than was common in the days of CRT-based displays.

Competition

The postponement also opens the door to competitors such as LG Electronics Inc. and Samsung Electronics Co. to assume leadership in a promising technology, touted as a potential replacement to liquid-crystal displays. LG plans to one-up Sony with a 15-inch OLED TV for the Korean and overseas markets. Pricing hasn't yet been determined.[17]

Samsung showcased a 31-inch OLED model in January 2009, but said it is a few years away from release.[18] "OLED is probably the best technology we see out there in terms of picture quality," said S. I. Lee, a Samsung senior vice president. But Samsung isn't ready to bring the sets to market. If the 31-inch were commercially available, it would cost $15,000 to $20,000, Lee said. "There isn't enough high-definition programming to make such a pricey set worth it," he said. "We want to continue to work on this, to bring the price down to a level that makes sense," he said.[19] Samsung Electronics and LG Electronics, Sony's primary market competitor in this field, introduced a 98-inch OLED television prototype in 2013.[20]

The biggest threat to OLED's future could be LCDs. Prices of LCDs are falling rapidly even as their quality improves. Newer LCD models are thinner, use less energy, and can offer brighter colors. Also, as is often the case with new display technology, producing an OLED television is expensive and the product can cause sticker shock. As we mentioned, Sony's first model, the 11-inch XEL-1, sells for $2,500—a price reserved for the latest LCD TVs with screens of 50 inches and above.[21]

All new products take time and money to develop, but television technology is particularly difficult. It's complicated and tough to manufacture in large quantities. LCD screens were first tested in the 1970s, but were not commonly used in TVs until 30 years later.[22]

OLED, which goes back to the 1970s, is used in a few tiny products today. One of the most common applications is the small, secondary screen on the outside of some flip-style cell phones. (These relatively low-quality OLED screens usually display the time and date when the phone is closed.) But the technology can't yet produce a TV screen size "at a price that will be accepted by the consumer," says Bob Scaglione, senior vice president at TV maker Sharp.[23] Analysts forecast that even if OLED does do well, it will be years before it will really take on plasma and LCD. Sizes won't be comparable until 2012 at the earliest.[24] That's why Sharp is betting on LCD. In 2008 the company showed off an experimental, 52-inch LCD that's less than 1 inch thick. Samsung, too, demonstrated thinner, bigger LCDs, including one monster that's 82 inches.[25]

According to Sharp's representatives, LCD has more room to improve. The sets will get at least 40 percent better than they are today as the technology is refined. Such improvements are a moving target that OLED manufacturers must constantly chase. And quickly producing larger OLED TVs is crucial, because everyone is looking for the biggest TV they can afford. The analysts are skeptical that OLED can get there fast enough.[26]

Sony's Overall Performance

A brief look at Sony's 2009 Annual Report for fiscal year 2008 (year-end of March 31, 2009) shows a grim picture of overall company performance. Sony has been lagging in its core businesses. Electronics and games divisions that together comprise 78 percent of Sony's sales both had posted losses.[27] The 2009 Annual Report outlined a wide array of changes to be implemented over the next couple of years. However, the most recent 2010 Annual Report for fiscal year 2009 (year-end of March 31, 2010) showed only slight improvement.

An analysis of Sony's market performance illustrates many current operational problems, including:

1. *Basic profitability problems*
   Sony's net loss reported in the 2009 Annual Report for fiscal year (FY) 2008 amounted to ¥98.9 billion (approximately $1 billion). This was Sony's first annual loss in 14 years. For FY 2009, the net loss had been reduced to ¥40.8 (about $453 million) compared to the prior year.[28,29] The company's FY 2008 year operating loss amounted to ¥227.8 billion. Among the largest contributors to the loss were (1) the Electronics division with ¥168 billion operating loss (declining earnings from Sony Ericsson, VAIO PCs, Handycam video cameras, BRAVIA LCD TVs), (2) the Games division with ¥58.5 billion operation loss (this division had losses for three years in a row), and (3) the Financial Services division with ¥31 billion operating loss. Only Sony's noncore businesses (Sony Pictures and Sony Music, shown in the graphs as the "All Other" division) had operated profitably in 2008–2009.[30] In FY 2009, the company was able to generate a ¥31.8 billion operating income; its revenue-generating forces were again only noncore divisions: Sony Music, Sony Pictures, and Financial Services.[31] Another disturbing sign for the company was a steady decrease in overall sales. Total sales reported for FY 2008 were ¥7.7 trillion (approximately $86 billion),

down 13 percent from the prior year.[32] For FY 2009, sales dropped further to ¥7.2 trillion.[33]

2. *Operations and supply-chain problems*
Analysts viewed the company's supply chain as too large, complex, and poorly managed. In 2004–2005 Sony tried to optimize its supply chain by reducing the number of suppliers from 4,700 to 2,500.[34] Major restructuring initiatives were announced by new CEO Howard Stringer, the first non-Japanese CEO, after taking the position in 2005.[35] In spite of the restructuring, operations were not synchronized between divisions and departments, and it became apparent that Sony's operations and supply chain needed further improvement.[36] In FY 2008, additional restructuring ambitions were detailed: (1) Cut suppliers from 2,500 to 1,200 by March 2011; (2) place higher volume orders with fewer suppliers to gain more purchasing power and extract better prices; (3) reduce the number of plants from 57 to 49 and outsource a portion of production to low-cost OEM/ODM partners; (4) reduce the workforce by 16,000 (8,000 in the Electronics division); and (5) reorganize/merge several divisions (particularly Electronics and Games divisions) to enhance competitiveness, improve profitability, and accelerate innovation and growth.[37]

3. *Diversification problems*
Many believed the company had become overdiversified, which posed a threat to core business dilution. Many believed the company comprised too many divisions (electronics, games, pictures, music, financial services, etc.) and subdivisions.[38] One example of this problem was mounting losses at Sony's mobile phone venture with the Swedish company Ericsson. Sony recorded equity in net loss of Sony Ericsson of ¥34.5 billion for the fiscal year 2009, compared to a loss of ¥30.3 billion in the prior fiscal year.[39,40,41]

4. *Misdirected consumer focus*
Sony has been frequently criticized for being too focused on the Japanese market and on the consumer segment that is willing to pay a higher price for the product.[42] However, according to the 2009 and 2010 annual reports Sony's sales outside of Japan were 76 percent and 71 percent, respectively.[43,44] While Sony's penetration of global markets is impressive, it is notable that the percentage of sales outside of Japan fell over these two reporting periods. In addition, Sony has been criticized for not meeting consumer expectations and losing market share in different industries. For example, it gave up the lead in personal music players to Apple's popular iPod.[45] Also, it has been struggling to develop a telephone device that can compete with the iPhone.[46] A particularly bitter loss for Sony was when Nintendo outsold Sony's powerful PlayStation 3 video game console with the Wii, a simpler console for novice players.[47] For example, in November of 2006 Sony experienced production constraints with projected components shortages and quality problems. Sony could make only 400,000 units of PS3 in North America compared to Nintendo's 1.2 million due to lack of components for the Blu-Ray drive. In addition, Nintendo was lower priced ($250 compared to PS3 $500), which boosted consumer demand during the holiday season.[48]

Where Did Sony Go Wrong?

Sony's upsetting financial performance in recent years had posed questions about the company's deviation from its image of innovation and excellence. An interesting analysis of the various factors that were pivotal to Sony's leadership success and failure was presented by business and brand strategist Martin Roll.[49] Three major factors contributed to Sony's ascent to global supremacy in the consumer electronics sector:[50]

1. *Innovation.* Innovation, to a great extent, defined the brand character of Sony. Sony grew to global prominence due to its ability to constantly create products even before other companies could conceptualize them. Further, Sony had the ability to sense the hidden consumer demand and create entire product categories through its innovative products. When the Walkman was introduced into the market, there was no existing market for portable music. But Sony's innovative product brought about an entire generation of products and created a new category altogether. Such an innovative culture differentiated Sony from the other consumer electronics brands for a very long time.

2. *Visionary leadership.* Sony is a classic case proving the strategic importance of a visionary leader in carrying a brand to dizzying heights. Sony's management team, along with the CEO, was responsible for creating an environment that nurtured experimentation and innovation. Further, Sony was one of the early Asian brands to recognize the importance of branding, which was again supported and led by the management team.

3. *Pioneer advantage.* Given its innovative edge, Sony emerged as the pioneer in almost every sector that it was operating in. Being the first mover, or in many cases, the inventor of the category, Sony had great leeway in defining the rules of the game, as it were. It set the expectations for the other companies that entered the category. Also, the brand image was enhanced every time a competitor imitated Sony as it became an indirect way to accept Sony's leadership position. Being the pioneer also offered Sony an opportunity to make more mistakes, test new ideas, and experiment with innovative concepts.

Together these three factors were mutually supportive and, in effect, created a virtuous circle. The combination of factors pushed Sony into the exclusive club of iconic brands. But over the last decade, Sony seemed to have lost the magic formula. A number of critical missteps contributed to Sony's decline:[51]

1. *Unrelated diversification.* An important and unique factor that has distinguished several Asian businesses from other Western business is the extent of diversification. Controlled and managed largely by business families, companies blow up into conglomerates that do business in very diverse and unrelated industries. Many Asian companies such as Samsung and LG that have become global forces to reckon with also started as bloated conglomerates. But these companies still focused on core competencies. For example, Samsung trimmed down its organization, withdrew from unrelated industries and channeled its resources around one or two dominant businesses. But Sony stuck to maintaining a presence—even expanding its multiple businesses. In some cases, this kind of unrelated or at best quasi-related diversification can drain the brand's resources and divert focus from the core of the brand.

2. *Innovation shortfall.* The Walkman made Sony the undisputed leader in the portable music player category. As is often the case, success can breed complacency. Sony did not follow up with any outstanding and innovative product lines to sustain the initial success. Apple came out with the iPod, which appealed to the younger generation worldwide, and also established iTunes as the standard from which consumers could download songs for a low price. This not only established Apple as the undisputed leader in the mobile music market but also helped to establish the industry standard. Sony has suffered similar challenges from many brands such as Samsung, Nokia, LG, and others in different product categories. Sony's lack of consumer-oriented innovation has contributed greatly to its decline in recent years.

3. *Lack of brand evolution.* Sony's brand identity surely is informed by an enormous amount of heritage, history, and achievements. But for a brand to be successful in the current ultra-competitive market, it has to make itself very relevant to the current customer segments. Resting on past laurels and expecting customers to support the brand due to its past achievements is not realistic. Sony has not been very successful in evolving as the brand for the masses of the 21st century. Apple, Samsung, and others have appropriated Sony's past position. The Sony brand has not been up with the times, and that has contributed to its slide from the top.

Despite a small profit in 2010, fueled by rising consumer interest in 3-D televisions and price cuts in the PlayStation game series,[52] Sony reported a loss of 520 billion yen for 2011. On April 9, 2012, Sony's chief financial officer Masaru Kato stated that "The situation is critical and we will carry out drastic reform. Nothing is sacred, turning around our TV business is a top priority." It was also reported that Sony may eliminate as many as 10,000 positions, but Kato did not elaborate on the exact number of job cuts. Sony, which had a market capitalization of more than $125 billion in 2000, is now valued at less than $19 billion.[53]

Growth for the OLED industry will no doubt be subdued as long as LCD TVs of similar size are selling at a fifth of the cost of OLED sets. Sales projections of OLED TVs are estimated to reach 2.1 million by 2015, as compared to only 34,000 projected for 2012.[54] Growth has also been hampered by excessive inventory, as global TV shipments fell in 2011 for the first time in six years.[55] Whether the OLED project can help bolster this performance and restore the once dominant home and personal electronics company is unclear. Sony has a lot to gain or lose, depending on the outcome.

Questions for Review

1. Why did Sony push back introduction of the OLED television? What was the advantage in waiting? What were the drawbacks? Was there a threat of moving to market with new technology too fast? How might the delayed introduction affect Sony's reputation among consumers, enthusiasts, and Sony's own R&D personnel?

2. What competitive threats does Sony face? From which companies and geographic regions? How does Sony stack up against these competitors?

3. Is it possible for a diversified company like Sony to be an innovation leader and stay profitable? What does its recent company performance suggest?

4. Should Sony's R&D efforts be focused on a limited number of "core" products or should it aim to be an innovation leader in each single business subsegment that it has? Do you think Sony should subsidize the unsuccessful R&D efforts that produce products which do not turn profits?

5. Do you think excessive diversification is Sony's problem? Do you think the problem is that Sony's products are targeting the upscale high-income consumer group, when most consumers are looking for cheap affordable goods? Why or why not?

Source: This case was prepared by Tetyana Azarova of Villanova University under the supervision of Professor Jonathan Doh as the basis for class discussion. It is not intended to illustrate either effective or ineffective managerial capability or administrative responsibility.

In-Depth Integrative Case 3.1

Tata "Nano": The People's Car

Nano, India's first "People's Car," may soon earn a place in history alongside Ford's Model T, Volkswagen's Beetle, and the British Motor Corp.'s Mini, all of which made automotive travel within reach of millions of customers who had previously been locked out of the car market. In January 2008 during India's main auto show in New Delhi, Tata Motors introduced to the Indian public its ultra-cheap car "Nano" that was expected to retail for as little as the equivalent of $2,500, or about the price of the optional DVD player on the Lexus LX 470 sport utility vehicle.[1] This event had driven unprecedented public attention, since Tata's new vehicle was projected to revolutionize the auto industry.[2]

The emergence of Tata Motors on the global auto scene marks the advent of India as a global center for small-car production and represents a victory for those who advocate making cheap goods for potential customers at the "bottom of the pyramid" in emerging markets. Most of all, the car could give millions of people now relegated to lesser means of transportation the chance to drive cars.[3] In India, there were an estimated 18 cars for every thousand people in 2009, compared with 47 per thousand in China, and 802 in the U.S. Far more middle-class Indians bought and transported their entire families on scooters.[4]

According to some analysts, Tata Motor's Chairman Ratan Tata hopes to use the Nano to become the Henry Ford of emerging India, in part, by offering a car at a fraction of the price of rival products. The company is gambling that its tiny price tag will make it appealing to Indians who now drive motorcycles and scooters.

While India's population is more than 1 billion people, only around 1 million passenger cars were sold in the country in 2007, one-tenth as many as in China. By contrast, more than 7 million motorcycles and scooters were sold. Mr. Tata said the tiny car is aimed at keeping the families of India's growing middle class from having to travel with as many as four people on a scooter.[5]

Speaking at the unveiling ceremony at the 9th Auto Expo in New Delhi, Ratan Tata said, "I observed families riding on two-wheelers—the father driving the scooter, his young kid standing in front of him, his wife seated behind him holding a little baby. It led me to wonder whether one could conceive of a safe, affordable, all-weather form of transport for such a family. Tata Motors' engineers and designers gave their all for about four years to realize this goal. Today, we indeed have a People's Car, which is affordable and yet built to meet safety requirements and emission norms, to be fuel efficient and low on emissions. We are happy to present the People's Car to India and we hope it brings the joy, pride and utility of owning a car to many families who need personal mobility."[6]

Middle-class household incomes in India start at roughly $6,000 a year, so a $3,000 car is the kind of innovation that could create millions of new drivers. Eight million Indians currently own cars, according to the Mumbai-based credit-rating agency Crisil. Another 18 million have the means to buy one. However, the Nano could increase that pool of potential auto owners by as much as 65 percent, to 30 million. "This goes beyond economics and class," says Ravi Kant, managing director of Tata Motors. "This crosses the urban-rural divide. Now a car is within the reach of people who never imagined they would own a car. It's a triumph for our company. And for India."[7]

Designed with a Family in Mind

Though Nano's design triggered different comments from the public—some people called it handsome;[8] others called it egg shaped[9]—overall Tata Motors was very proud of the design, which was developed with a family in mind.[10] From Tata's perspective the new Nano addresses several key characteristics that Indian families would prize in a car: low price, adequate comfort, fuel-efficiency, and safety.

According to Tata, Nano has a roomy passenger compartment with generous leg space and head room, and it can comfortably seat four persons. Four doors with high seating position make ingress and egress easy. With a snub nose and a sloping roof, the world's cheapest car can hold five people—if they squeeze.[11] Nano's dimensions are as follows: length of 3.1 meters, width of 1.5 meters, and height of 1.6 meters. Tata suggests these compact dimensions should allow the car to effortlessly maneuver on busy roads in cities as well as in rural areas. Its mono-volume design, with wheels at the corners and the power train at the rear, enables it to combine both space and maneuverability.[12] At 10 feet long, the Nano is about 2 feet shorter than a Mini Cooper.[13]

The car is available in both standard and deluxe versions. According to the company, both versions offer a wide range of body colors and other accessories so that the car can be customized to an individual's preferences.[14] But reviewers called the basic version spare: There's no radio, no air bags, no passenger-side mirror, and only one windshield wiper. If you want air conditioning to cope with India's brutal summers, you need to get the deluxe version.

According to the company, Nano has a fuel-efficient engine powered by the lean design strategy that has helped minimize weight, maximize performance per unit of energy consumed, and deliver higher fuel efficiency.[15] The final design stands at 1,322 pounds, 528 pounds lighter than the flyweight Honda Insight. To power it, the engineers settled on a 33-horsepower, 623-cc, two-cylinder engine housed in the rear; to service it, the mechanic must remove a set of bolts in the 5.4-cubic-foot trunk. The payoff: an uncommonly efficient 47 miles per gallon running at top speed (65 mph). But that doesn't mean Nano owners won't spend a lot of time pumping gas—the minuscule tank holds just 3.9 gallons.[16]

According to the company, the People's Car's safety performance exceeds current Indian regulatory requirements. With an all-sheet-metal body, it has a strong passenger compartment, with safety features such as crumple zones, intrusion-resistant doors, seat belts, strong seats and anchorages, and the rear tailgate glass bonded to the body. Tubeless tires further enhance safety. Tata also placed emphasis on environmental friendliness. According to a corporate press release the People's Car's tailpipe emission performance exceeds regulatory requirements. In terms of overall pollutants, it has a lower pollution level than two-wheelers being manufactured in India today.[17]

About Tata Motors

Tata Motors is a part of the Tata Group. The Tata Group is considered the General Electric of India, a sprawling conglomerate with a commanding presence in media, telecom, outsourcing, retailing, and real estate. Started in 1868 as a textile wholesaler, the company branched out into luxury hotels after, as legend has it, founder Jamsetji Tata was turned away from a posh establishment because of his skin color. In 1945, a few years before the British left India, Tata created Tata Motors and started producing locomotives and, eventually, autos. In 1998, Tata Motors introduced the country's first indigenously designed car. The homegrown Indica, which now sells for around $6,000, became ubiquitous as a taxi.[18]

Meanwhile, the Tata Group has been expanding globally. It bought the tea company Tetley in 2000 and acquired Anglo-Dutch steel giant Corus in 2007. It maintains Tata Consultancy Services offices in 54 countries and owns hotels in Boston, New York, and San Francisco. In March 2008, Tata Motors bought Jaguar and Land Rover from the financially strangled Ford Motors.[19]

Tata Motors listed on the New York Stock Exchange in 2004. After thousands of changes, in the quarter ending December 2006 Tata earned $116 million on revenue of $1.55 billion. Annual revenue grew to $5.2 billion for the fiscal year ending in March 2006.[20] Now Tata Motors Limited is India's largest automobile company, with consolidated revenues of Rs.70,938.85 crores (US$14 billion) in 2008–2009. It is the leader in commercial vehicles in each segment, and among the top three in passenger vehicles with winning products in the compact, midsize car, and utility vehicle segments. The company is the world's fourth largest truck manufacturer, and the world's second largest bus manufacturer. The company's 24,000 employees are guided by the vision to be "best in the manner in which we operate, best in the products we deliver, and best in our value system and ethics."[21]

Established in 1945, Tata Motors' presence cuts across the length and breadth of India. Over 4 million Tata vehicles ply on Indian roads, since they first rolled out in 1954. The company's manufacturing base in India is spread across Jamshedpur (Jharkhand), Pune (Maharashtra), Lucknow (Uttar Pradesh), Pantnagar (Uttarakhand), and Dharwad (Karnataka). Following a strategic alliance with Fiat in 2005, it has set up an industrial joint venture with Fiat Group Automobiles at Ranjangaon (Maharashtra) to produce both Fiat and Tata cars and Fiat powertrains. The company is establishing a new plant at Sanand (Gujarat). The company's dealership, sales, services, and spare parts network comprises over 3,500 touch points; Tata Motors also distributes and markets Fiat branded cars in India.[22]

Tata Motors has also emerged as an international automobile company. Through subsidiaries and associate companies, Tata Motors has operations in the U.K., South Korea, Thailand, and Spain. Among them is Jaguar Land Rover, a business comprising the two iconic British brands that was acquired in 2008. In 2004, it acquired the Daewoo Commercial Vehicles Company, South Korea's second largest truck maker. The rechristened Tata Daewoo Commercial Vehicles Company has launched several new products in the Korean market, while also exporting these products to several international markets. Today two-thirds of heavy commercial vehicle exports out of South Korea are from Tata Daewoo.[23]

In 2005, Tata Motors acquired a 21 percent stake in Hispano Carrocera, a well regarded Spanish bus and coach manufacturer, and subsequently the remaining stake in 2009. Hispano's presence is being expanded in other markets. In 2006, Tata Motors formed a joint venture with the Brazil-based Marcopolo, a global leader in body building for buses and coaches, to manufacture fully built buses and coaches for India and select international markets. In 2006, Tata Motors entered into joint venture with Thonburi Automotive Assembly Plant Company of Thailand to manufacture and market the company's pickup vehicles in Thailand. The new plant of Tata Motors (Thailand) has begun production of the Xenon pickup truck, with the Xenon having been launched in Thailand in 2008.[24]

Tata Motors is also expanding its international footprint, established through exports since 1961. The company's commercial and passenger vehicles are already being marketed in several countries in Europe, Africa, the

Middle East, South East Asia, South Asia, and South America. It has franchisee/joint venture assembly operations in Kenya, Bangladesh, Ukraine, Russia, Senegal, and South Africa. Through its subsidiaries, the company is engaged in engineering and automotive solutions, construction equipment manufacturing, automotive vehicle components manufacturing and supply chain activities, machine tools and factory automation solutions, high-precision tooling and plastic and electronic components for automotive and computer applications, and automotive retailing and service operations.[25]

The foundation of the company's growth over the last 50 years is a deep understanding of economic stimuli and customer needs, and the ability to translate them into customer-desired offerings through leading-edge R&D. With over 3,000 engineers and scientists, the company's Engineering Research Centre, established in 1966, has enabled pioneering technologies and products. The company today has R&D centers in Pune, Jamshedpur, Lucknow, Dharwad in India, and in South Korea, Spain, and the U.K. It was Tata Motors which developed the first indigenously developed Light Commercial Vehicle, India's first Sports Utility Vehicle, and, in 1998, the Tata Indica, India's first fully indigenous passenger car. Within two years of launch, Tata Indica became India's largest selling car in its segment. In 2005, Tata Motors created a new segment by launching the Tata Ace, India's first indigenously developed mini-truck. In January 2008, Tata Motors unveiled its People's Car, the Tata Nano, which was launched in India in March 2009.[26]

Tata Motors is equally focused on environment-friendly technologies in emissions and alternative fuels. It has developed electric and hybrid vehicles both for personal and public transportation. It has also been implementing several environment-friendly technologies in manufacturing processes, significantly enhancing resource conservation.[27]

Tata Motors is committed to improving the quality of life of communities by working on four thrust areas: employability, education, health, and environment. The firm's activities touch the lives of more than a million citizens. Its support for education and employability is focused on youth and women, ranging from schools to technical education institutes, to actual facilitation of income generation. In health, Tata's intervention is in both preventive and curative health care. The goal of environment protection is achieved through tree plantations, conserving water and creating new water bodies, and, last but not least, introducing appropriate technologies in Tata vehicles and operations for constantly enhancing environment care.[28]

Tata Motors Milestones

It has been a long and accelerating journey for Tata Motors until it became India's leading automobile manufacturer. Here are some significant milestones in the company's journey toward excellence and leadership:[29]

1945	• Tata Engineering and Locomotive Co. Ltd. was established to manufacture locomotives and other engineering products.
1948	• Steam road roller introduced in collaboration with Marshall Sons (U.K.).
1954	• Collaboration with Daimler Benz AG, West Germany, for manufacture of medium commercial vehicles. The first vehicle rolled out within 6 months of the contract.
1959	• Research and Development Centre set up at Jamshedpur.
1961	• Exports begin with the first truck being shipped to Ceylon, now Sri Lanka.
1966	• Setting up of the Engineering Research Centre at Pune to provide impetus to automobile Research and Development.
1971	• Introduction of DI engines.
1977	• First commercial vehicle manufactured in Pune.
1983	• Manufacture of Heavy Commercial Vehicle commences.
1985	• First hydraulic excavator produced with Hitachi collaboration.
1986	• Production of first light commercial vehicle, Tata 407, indigenously designed, followed by Tata 608.
1989	• Introduction of the Tatamobile 206—3rd LCV model.
1991	• Launch of the 1st indigenous passenger car Tata Sierra. • TAC 20 crane produced. • One millionth vehicle rolled out.
1992	• Launch of the Tata Estate.
1993	• Joint venture agreement signed with Cummins Engine Co. Inc. for the manufacture of high horse-power and emission friendly diesel engines.
1994	• Launch of Tata Sumo—the multi utility vehicle. • Launch of LPT 709—a full forward control, light commercial vehicle. • Joint venture agreement signed with M/s Daimler-Benz/Mercedes-Benz for manufacture of Mercedes Benz passenger cars in India. • Joint venture agreement signed with Tata Holset Ltd., U.K., for manufacturing turbochargers to be used on Cummins engines.
1995	• Mercedes Benz car E220 launched.
1996	• Tata Sumo deluxe launched.
1997	• Tata Sierra Turbo launched. • 100,000th Tata Sumo rolled out.
1998	• Tata Safari—India's first sports utility vehicle launched. • 2 millionth vehicle rolled out. • Indica, India's first fully indigenous passenger car, launched.
1999	• 115,000 bookings for Indica registered against full payment within a week. • Commercial production of Indica commences in full swing.
2000	• First consignment of 160 Indicas shipped to Malta. • Indica with Bharat Stage 2 (Euro II) compliant diesel engine launched. • Utility vehicles with Bharat 2 (Euro II) compliant engine launched.

- Indica 2000 (Euro II) with multi point fuel injection petrol engine launched.
- Launch of CNG buses.
- Launch of 1109 vehicle—an Intermediate commercial vehicle.

2001
- Indica V2 launched—2nd generation Indica.
- 100,000th Indica wheeled out.
- Launch of CNG Indica.
- Launch of the Tata Safari EX.
- Indica V2 becomes India's number one car in its segment.
- Exits joint venture with Daimler Chrysler.

2002
- Unveiling of the Tata Sedan at Auto Expo 2002.
- Petrol version of Indica V2 launched.
- Launch of the EX series in commercial vehicles.
- Launch of the Tata 207 DI.
- 200,000th Indica rolled out.
- 500,000th passenger vehicle rolled out.
- Launch of the Tata Sumo'1' Series.
- Launch of the Tata Indigo.
- Tata Engineering signed a product agreement with MG Rover of the U.K.

2003
- Launch of the Tata Safari Limited Edition.
- The Tata Indigo Station Wagon unveiled at the Geneva Motor Show.
- On 29th July, J. R. D. Tata's birth anniversary, Tata Engineering becomes Tata Motors Limited.
- 3 millionth vehicle produced.
- First CityRover rolled out.
- 135 PS Tata Safari EXi Petrol launched.
- Tata SFC 407 EX Turbo launched.

2004
- Tata Motors unveils new product range at Auto Expo '04.
- New Tata Indica V2 launched.
- Tata Motors and Daewoo Commercial Vehicle Co. Ltd. sign investment agreement.
- Indigo Advent unveiled at Geneva Motor Show.
- Tata Motors completes acquisition of Daewoo Commercial Vehicle Company.
- Tata LPT 909 EX launched.
- Tata Daewoo Commercial Vehicle Co. Ltd. (TDCV) launches the heavy duty truck NOVUS, in Korea.
- Sumo Victa launched.
- Indigo Marina launched.
- Tata Motors lists on the NYSE.

2005
- Tata Motors rolls out the 500,000th passenger car from its Car Plant Facility in Pune.
- The Tata Xover unveiled at the 75th Geneva Motor Show.
- Branded buses and coaches—Starbus and Globus—launched.
- Tata Motors acquires 21% stake in Hispano Carrocera SA, Spanish bus manufacturing company.
- Tata Ace, India's first mini truck launched.
- Tata Motors wins JRD QV award for business excellence.
- The power packed Safari Dicor is launched.
- Introduction of Indigo SX series, luxury variant of Tata Indigo.
- Tata Motors launches Indica V2 Turbo Diesel.

- One millionth passenger car produced and sold.
- Inauguration of new factory at Jamshedpur for Novus.
- Tata TL 4×4, India's first Sports Utility Truck (SUT), is launched.
- Launch of Tata Novus.
- Launch of Novus range of medium trucks in Korea, by Tata Daewoo Commercial Vehicle Co. (TDCV).

2006
- Tata Motors vehicle sales in India cross four million mark.
- Tata Motors unveils new long wheel base premium Indigo & X-over concept at Auto Expo 2006.
- Indica V2 Xeta launched.
- Passenger vehicle sales in India cross one-million mark.
- Tata Motors and Marcopolo, Brazil, announce joint venture to manufacture fully built buses and coaches for India and markets abroad.
- Tata Motors first plant for small car to come up in West Bengal.
- Tata Motors extends CNG options on its hatchback and estate range.
- TDCV develops South Korea's first LNG-Powered Tractor-Trailer.
- Tata Motors and Fiat Group announce three additional cooperation agreements.
- Tata Motors introduces a new Indigo range.

2007
- Construction of Small Car plant at Singur, West Bengal, begins on January 21.
- New 2007 Indica V2 range is launched.
- Tata Motors launches the longwheel base Indigo XL, India's first stretch limousine.
- Common rail diesel (DICOR) engine extended to Indigo sedan and estate range.
- Tata Motors and Thonburi Automotive Assembly Plant Co. (Thonburi) announce formation of a joint venture company in Thailand to manufacture, assemble, and market pickup trucks.
- Rollout of 100,000th Ace.
- Tata-Fiat plant at Ranjangaon inaugurated.
- Launch of a new upgraded range of its entry level utility vehicle offering, the Tata Spacio.
- CRM-DMS initiative crosses the 1,000th location milestone.
- Launch of Magic, a comfortable, safe, four-wheeler public transportation mode, developed on the Ace platform.
- Launch of Winger, India's only maxi-van.
- Fiat Group and Tata Motors announce establishment of Joint Venture in India.
- Launch of the Sumo Victa Turbo DI, the new upgraded range of its entry-level utility vehicle, the Sumo Spacio.
- Tata Motors launches Indica V2 Turbo with dual airbags and ABS.
- Launch of new Safari DICOR 2.2 VTT range, powered by a new 2.2 L Direct Injection Common Rail (DICOR) engine.
- Rollout of the one millionth passenger car off the Indica platform.

2008
- Ace plant at Pantnagar (Uttarakhand) begins production.
- Indica Vista, the new generation Indica, is launched.
- Tata Motors' new plant for Nano to come up in Gujarat.
- Latest common rail diesel offering, the Indica V2 DICOR, launched.
- Indigo CS (Compact Sedan), world's first sub four-metre sedan, launched.
- Launch of the new Sumo—Sumo Grande, which combines the looks of an SUV with the comforts of a family car.
- Tata Motors unveils its People's Car, Nano, at the ninth Auto Expo.
- Xenon, 1-ton pickup truck, launched in Thailand.
- Tata Motors signs definitive agreement with Ford Motor Company to purchase Jaguar and Land Rover.
- Tata Motors completes acquisition of Jaguar Land Rover.
- Tata Motors introduces new Super Milo range of buses.
- Tata Motors is Official Vehicle Provider to Youth Baton Relay for The III Commonwealth Youth Games, Pune 2008.
- Indica Vista, the second generation Indica, is launched.
- Tata Motors launches passenger cars and the new pickup in D.R. Congo.

2009
- Tata Motors begins distribution of Prima World truck.
- Tata Motors launches the next generation all-new Indigo MANZA.
- FREELANDER 2 launched in India.
- Tata Marcopolo Motors' Dharwad plant begins production.
- Tata Motors launches Nano—The People's Car.
- Introduction of new world standard truck range.
- Launch of premium luxury vehicles Jaguar XF, XFR, and XKR and Land Rover Discovery 3, Range Rover Sport, and Range Rover from Jaguar and Land Rover in India.

Secrets behind the Low Price

How could Tata Motors make a car so inexpensively? It started by looking at everything from scratch, applying what some analysts have described as "Gandhian engineering" principles—deep frugality with a willingness to challenge conventional wisdom. A lot of features that Western consumers take for granted—air conditioning, power brakes, radios, etc.—are missing from the entry-level model.[30]

In order to succeed with building a low-cost affordable car, Tata Motors began by studying and trying to understand the customer. What do the customers need? What do they really want? What can they afford? The customer was ever-present in the development of the Nano. Tata didn't set the price of the Nano by calculating the cost of production and then adding a margin. Rather it set $2,500 as the price that it thought customers could pay and then worked backward, with the help of partners willing to take on a challenge, to build a $2,500 car that would reward all involved with a small profit.[31]

More fundamentally, the engineers worked to do more with less. Tata has been able to slash the price by asking his engineers and suppliers to redesign the many components to cut costs. The speedometer, for example, is in the center of the dashboard over the air vents, not behind the steering wheel, so the dashboard can be built with fewer parts.[32] To save $10, Tata engineers redesigned the suspension to eliminate actuators in the headlights, the levelers that adjust the angle of the beam depending on how the car is loaded, according to Mr. Chaturvedi of Lumax. In lieu of the solid steel beam that typically connects steering wheels to axles, one supplier, Sona Koyo Steering Systems, used a hollow tube, said Kiran Deshmukh, the chief operating officer of the company, which is based in Delhi.[33]

Also, Nano is smaller in overall dimensions than the Suzuki Maruti, a similar but higher priced low-cost competitor assembled in India, but it offers about 20 percent more seating capacity as a result of design choices such as putting the wheels at the extreme edges of the car. The Nano is also much lighter than comparable models as a result of a reduction in the amount of steel in the car (including the use of an aluminum engine) and the use of lightweight steel where possible.[34]

However, Nano engineers and partners didn't simply strip features out of an existing car to create a new low-cost model, which most other manufacturers have done when making affordable cars. Instead, they looked at their target customers' lives for cost-cutting ideas. So, for instance, the Nano has a smaller engine than other cars because more horsepower would be wasted in India's jam-packed cities, where the average speed is 10 to 20 miles per hour.[35] The car currently meets all Indian emission, pollution, and safety standards, although it only attains a maximum speed of about 65 mph. The fuel efficiency is also attractive to economy-driven consumers—nearly 50 miles to the gallon.[36]

Nano ultimately became a triumph of creativity and innovation. For example, Tata Motors has filed for 34 patents associated with the design of the Nano, although some suggest that measuring progress solely by patent creation misses a key dimension of innovation. Some of the most valuable innovations take existing, patented components and remix them in ways that more effectively serve the needs of large numbers of customers. The most innovative aspect of the Nano is its modular design. The Nano is constructed of components that can be built and shipped separately to be assembled in a variety of locations. In effect, the Nano is being sold in kits that are distributed, assembled, and serviced by local entrepreneurs.[37]

As Ratan Tata, chairman of the Tata group of companies, observed in an interview with The Times of London: "A bunch of entrepreneurs could establish an assembly operation and Tata Motors would train their people, would oversee their quality assurance and they would become satellite assembly operations for us. So we would create entrepreneurs across the country that would produce the car. We would produce the mass items and ship it to them as kits. That is my idea of dispersing wealth. The service person would be like an insurance agent who would be trained, have a cell phone and scooter and would be assigned to a set of customers."[38]

This is part of a broader pattern of innovation emerging in India in a variety of markets, ranging from diesel engines and agricultural products to financial services. In fact, Tata envisions going even further, providing the tools for local mechanics to assemble the car in existing auto shops or even in new garages created to cater to remote rural customers.[39]

Struggling with a Production Site

In spite of Tata's great commitment to meet the transportation needs of the poor Indian population and its pledge that the price of the car would not exceed $2,500 equivalent, the company experienced a major challenge due to unexpected problems at Tata's proposed manufacturing plant in Singur, in the eastern state of West Bengal, India, that could have stopped the whole Nano project right at the start.

In May 2006 Tata Motors announced that it would be manufacturing Nano in Singur, West Bengal, India.[40] Tata made plans to acquire the land and build the plant for the sole purpose of producing the Nano. The entire project, including the purchase of more than 600 acres of land, reportedly cost Tata Motors upwards of $350 million.[41]

The problems began immediately following Tata's purchase of the property from the West Bengal government.[42] Prior to the purchase, the government didn't actually own the land, but acquired it from local farmers by imposing the force of eminent domain.[43] The Communist government of West Bengal was interested in bringing Tata Motors to its state since it saw the Nano project as key to rejuvenating industries in West Bengal, a poor region that was traditionally focused on farming. Trouble began after the government took over 1,000 acres (400 hectares) of farmland for the factory. The government offered compensation, but some farmers with smaller land holdings refused that compensation, demanding that land be given back to them. The disputed land measured about 400 acres.[44]

The protests hinged upon allegations that Tata forced farmers from their land and handed out payments that were a fraction of the land's value. Mamata Banerjee, the fiery chief of the Trinamool Congress, the West Bengali political party staging the protest, demanded that Tata Motors return 400 acres of land surrounding the Nano

factory to these farmers. Tata Motors stated that this land was necessary for 60 parts suppliers to the Nano. The company argued that keeping parts suppliers close to the plant was vital to maintaining the Nano's extremely low cost.[45]

At the peak of the protests in September 2008, over 30,000 activists and farmers besieged Singur, in West Bengal state, to rally against the plant, reiterating their claim that the land was forcibly taken from farmers and that compensation was inadequate. The highway leading to Singur was blockaded and Tata Motors was forced to evacuate employees from the plant site. In response, the company threatened to walk out of West Bengal if the agitation was not quickly quelled.[46]

According a statement released by Tata Motors in September 2008, work on the factory was close to completion. Up to 4,000 workers, including "several hundred young residents from around the [Singur] region" were said to have been employed by the factory during its construction. But continuing the work with the ongoing protests proved too risky. Employees failed to show up for work after threats from protestors. The protests also snarled traffic in the region. Trucks loaded with food were left on highways, their contents rotting in the sun.[47]

Ratan Tata, chairman of the Tata Group and Tata Motors, expressed concern that the factory in Singur was at serious risk. Commenting on the situation, a Tata Motors spokesperson said, "The situation around the Nano plant continues to be hostile and intimidating. There is no way this plant could operate efficiently unless the environment became congenial and supportive of the project. We came to West Bengal hoping we could add value, prosperity and create job opportunities in the communities in the state."[48]

The dispute reflected a larger standoff between industry in India and farmers unwilling to part with land in a country where two-thirds of the billion-plus population depends on agriculture. Unable to get satisfactory resolution of the dispute, on September 2, 2008, Tata Motors announced that violent protests had forced it to suspend all work at the plant. Tata Motors also said it was putting together a detailed plan for the relocation of the plant and machinery, and was evaluating options for manufacturing the Nano at other company facilities.[49]

By October, the Singur protests had grown in size and intensity. Highways surrounding the factory were at a standstill, and workers were being threatened. Tata finally abandoned the Singur factory, in which it had invested $350 million.[50] However, by that time the company had received an invitation from another state to relocate its Nano project. On October 7, 2008, the Gujarat government and Tata Motors signed a MoU (memorandum of understanding)[51] in Ahmedabad, bringing the ambitious Nano project to that state. Gujarat Chief Minister Narendra Modi announced allocation of 11,000 acres of land at Sanand near Ahmedabad to Tata Motors. The state government promised Tata various tax rebates and ready land along with connectivity to the national highway. In addition, the company was assured that no bandh (*bandh*, originally a Hindi word meaning "closed," is a form of protest used by political activists in some countries in South Asia like India and Nepal)[52] or labor unrest would delay the project.[53]

Despite the Gujarat government's assurances regarding the safe and friendly business environment in its state, the relocation of the plant to a new state was not painless. In December 2008, several farmers filed a case against the local Indian government and Tata Motors, demanding better compensation for land sold to support the Gujarat factory, India.[54] Tata was pressured to find a quick solution. Ultimately, it decided that Nano production would begin at Tata's existing factory in Pantnagar in the northern state of Uttarakhand after receiving an additional allotment of land from the Uttarakhand government to expand the Pantnagar factory for Nano production. It became apparent that sales of the Nano in India, originally scheduled for October of 2008, would not begin until spring of 2009.[55]

Nano's 2009 Launch

Even though Tata was expected to solve the transportation problem for thousands of Indians, and Nano's launch was a highly awaited public event, sales of the Nano were delayed by at least six months after the land disputes.[56] However, when Tata eventually announced Nano's 2009 production plans, it quickly started generating the orders at volumes that far exceeded expectations. As of May 2009, according to Bloomberg analysts, Tata Motors had received 203,000 orders for its Nano, more than double the initial sales plan. The company accepted the bookings between April 9 and April 25, amounting to almost 25 billion rupees ($501 million), according to a Tata Motors release. Deliveries were planned to start in July of 2009 and were expected to be completed in the last quarter of 2010, according to the company.[57]

Surging demand from first-time buyers and motorcyclists in India contrasted with plunging automobile sales in the U.S. and Europe where job losses and economic recession were keeping consumers away from showrooms. "The Nano has the potential to become a game-changer for Tata in the long run," said Gaurav Lohia, an analyst at K.R. Choksey Shares & Securities Pvt. in Mumbai. "Once you generate the volumes, you are the king."[58]

According to the Society of Indian Automobile Manufacturers, the [Nano] bookings represented about 17 percent of the 1.22 million passenger cars sold in India, Asia's fourth-largest automobile market, in the fiscal year ended March. Maruti Suzuki India Ltd., maker of half the cars sold in the country, sold 636,707 units while Hyundai Motor Co. sold 244,030 and Tata Motors sold 160,446.[59]

Due to its manufacturing capacity constraints, Tata Motors would not be able to fill all the orders as quickly as expected. The first Nanos were to roll out of the Pantnagar plant which could produce only 60,000 units a year. Annual output was projected to increase by a further 350,000 units when the facility at Sanand in western India was completed at the end of 2009. Therefore, Tata Motors announced that it would choose the first 100,000 customers for the $2,500 Nano by a lottery, leaving the company with at least a year of production as backlog.[60]

Production for the Nano switched to Sanand in the summer of 2010, but the factory was still unable to produce enough Nanos to meet the initial demand.[61]

Global Race for Low-Cost Cars

The Nano is part of a global race to lower the prices of entry-level cars for millions of new developing world consumers. As growth slows in developed markets in the West, auto makers are looking to tap the rapid growth in countries like India, China, and Brazil, where the lowest priced cars are often the best sellers. Maruti Suzuki India Ltd., which is controlled by Japan's Suzuki Motor Corp., has dominated the Indian market for decades; its least expensive model today sells for around $5,000.[62]

Now that Tata Motors has shown the way, competitors are scrambling to offer their own budget vehicles. For example, Ford Motor Co. announced plans to build a new small car in India that will have a sticker price as low as $7,500. Nissan Motor Co. has plans for a $7,000 and then a $5,000 car in the next few years. German auto maker Volkswagen AG said it would also start to make small cars at a new plant in 2010.[63] Hyundai has announced a $3,700 car. Renault-Nissan has teamed with Indian motorcycle maker Bajaj to put 400,000 of its own ultra-low-cost cars on the road by 2011. General Motors is rumored to be working on a Nano-killer with China's Wuling Automotive. By 2020, millions of ultra-low-cost vehicles will crowd narrow alleyways throughout the world. Thus, what happened in Bangalore would presage changes to come in Lagos, Rio de Janeiro, and Budapest.[64]

The global market for the Nano and similarly low-priced cars could be immense—the World Bank counts more than 800 million people who earn between $3,600 and $11,000 annually. In India, the new vehicle could change the taxi business overnight and energize a cadre of small-time entrepreneurs by providing new levels of mobility, carrying capacity, and social status.[65]

In spite of glamorous projections of high demand for low-cost cars, some analysts pose serious concerns of the overall profitability of budget car manufacturing. With the rising competition in the low-cost vehicle market, increasing cost pressure and small profit margins, will the new budget car models be able to recoup the R&D investment and generate any profits? For example, on the eve of the Nano launch, Mr. Tata said in an interview that developing the new model cost between $380 million and $435 million. He said without a better idea of future input costs and demand, he could not predict how soon the project would turn a profit or what the profit margin on the cars would be. Should steel prices continue to rise, prices may have to be adjusted.[66]

As long as the Nano runs as well as it looks and avoids major quality issues, Tata Motors should have no trouble selling it to hundreds of thousands of Indian families a year, analysts say. Still, at such a low price it could take a long time for Tata to recoup its investment in developing the world's cheapest car. With profit margins as low as 5 percent, it could take more than five years for the project to be in the black, estimated Vaishali Jajoo, senior research analyst at Angel Broking in Mumbai. "It depends on how the margins will be," and at this price they are going to be very low, she said.[67]

However, although the competition in the low-cost vehicle market will remain fierce, Tata Motors now has a significant benefit relative to its competitors, which is called in business language "the first mover advantage." Anil K. Gupta and Haiyan Wang, two experts on India and China, said in a BusinessWeek article that Tata's Nano should be viewed as not just a product for an identified market need today but also as a platform for tomorrow. The key to leveraging any product or service as a platform for future growth is to treat it as a bundle of capabilities instead of becoming overly constrained by its current features, branding, distribution channels, or targeted customers. Underlying capabilities—either singly or in combination—can be leveraged across different markets far more easily than is the case with end products or services (look at corporate intranet searches powered by Google). They can also be upgraded and/or combined with new capabilities to create entirely new products and services (this is how the iPod led to the iPhone/iPod Touch).[68]

According to Gupta and Wang, many companies overlook this aspect of global production and marketing. Tata Motors, on the other hand, shows a grasp of this concept in establishing the Nano as a platform for further growth. While competitors are struggling to develop low-cost models for the Indian market, Tata has now broadened its plans and will bring its low budget car to other markets, including Europe and North America. As a start, it will begin selling its car in Nigeria in 2010. Tata is talking about launching upgraded models of the car at about $8,000 in Europe by 2011 and in North America by 2012. (The Nano has already passed European crash-test safety standards.) The company is reportedly also working on hybrid and all-electric versions of the Nano.[69]

The entrance of Tata's Nano into European and U.S. markets may be potentially devastating to financially strangled automakers such as Ford and GM. As Gupta and Wang have pointed out, viewed from the lens of underlying capabilities, the Nano is not just a particular type of car designed for the peculiarities of the Indian market. It is also a bundle of proprietary technologies, supplier relationships, and a mindset that prizes frugal engineering. These capabilities, when applied to the needs of the rich European and North American markets, could easily result in an upgraded car that may sell for, say, $8,000 and give a competitor whose product sells for $12,000 a run for its money. As global auto companies look at the Nano, the question they should ask is not whether customers in the rich economies would care for such an inexpensive-but-simple car, but whether Tata Motors could show up in their backyards with a competitive or better product that sells for 30–35 percent lower prices than their own in these markets.[70]

Tata Touching U.S. Ground

Tata showcased its Nano in United States in January 2010 at the Detroit auto show and generated its first feedback from potential American customers. The comments ranged from highly skeptical to very optimistic. Some people said that Nano would have to go through many upgrades in order to win the American consumer and in order to meet the safety requirements. For example, in most American cars, safety features alone cost more than $2,500, according to Adrian Lund, president of the Insurance Institute for Highway Safety in Arlington, VA.[71]

As far as American consumer preferences are concerned, a "U.S. Nano would also need to be nicer inside to be attractive to buyers," Tata representatives told Autoblog Green. Reps from the blog drove the car around Judson College in Alabama and concluded that Tata will need to significantly improve the comfort level in the car. Students all asked where the iPod connector was and why there weren't any cupholders. Those sorts of features would be a part of the program if the car actually gets the official green light. Thankfully, Tata Motors designers have time to iron out these details, because any potential U.S. launch is likely to be years away.[72]

Optimists suggest that there is a big segment of American consumers for whom Nano will be a "just good enough" car since they do not need any fancy features. For example, Volkswagen built millions of Beetles for people who wanted a car for a simple reason—to avoid walking—and this car became very successful on the market since it resonated with the needs of a large consumer segment that was looking for this type of car. As inexpensive as Nano would be when entering the U.S. market, it might challenge not only new car models, but also the used car markets, since the American consumer would have the ability to buy a new Nano model for the price of a used car. This purchase alternative may be another benefit attracting the economy-driven consumers in the U.S., especially in times of prolonged economic crisis and rising gasoline prices.[73]

Source: Anugraph Adams.

After making a strong debut, in late 2010 Tata announced somewhat disappointing sales figures for the Nano. In November 2010, just 509 Nanos were sold, despite brisk sales for more expensive cars. Mercedes sells more than 500 cars a month in India. After selling nearly 10,000 cars a month through the summer and early fall of 2010, sales dropped off when stories circulated that some Nanos had caught fire and other tales were related of poor service and performance.[74] Sales temporary recovered to 10,000 a month in the spring of 2011, but were still well below the predicted demand of 20,000 per month. Tata received only 3,260 orders in July of 2011. Rising interest rates and fuel prices also had a negative effect on demand. Carl-Peter Forster (Head of Tata Motors) discussed some of the areas for improvement surrounding the Nano; namely, the distribution scheme, marketing, advertising and an effective consumer finance system.[75] In an effort to counteract the disappointing sales, Tata announced it was launching distribution in six new provinces where the Nano had not yet been available. Tata also unveiled a new finance scheme with 26 local banks with interest rates from between 8 percent and 20 percent.[76] Through mid-2012, roughly 200,000 Nanos had been sold. This number is significantly less than the 250,000 cars the Nano was initially expected to sell annually.[77] Despite the performance of the Nano, Tata Motors reported growth in consolidated revenues of 44.3 percent in the first quarter of 2012, when compared to the first quarter of 2011. Standalone revenues for FY 2011-2012 grew by 15.3 percent over the previous year and vehicle sales for the quarter increased 16.2 percent over the sales figures from the first quarter of 2011.[78] It is yet too early to tell if these setbacks will halt the Nano's penetration in India and around the world, or whether they are simply the natural growing pains of a new approach to passenger vehicles that will continue to permeate global markets for decades to come.

Questions for Review

1. What inspired Tata Motors to build the Nano? Why was there a need for an inexpensive car in India?

2. What innovative steps did Tata undertake to design the Nano in a way that would meet the $2,500 price tag? Do you think that the low price automatically means poor quality? How did Tata Motors address the quality issue while developing its budget car?

3. What caused delay in Nano's launch? What important features of the Indian economic environment were the key factors that caused the problem? What does this story teach about risks of doing business in India?

4. Would you agree that introduction of the Nano to the world auto market will be setting new trends in the auto industry, and possibly reshaping the industry? What did Tata Motors teach other automakers in terms of leadership and innovation?

5. Do you agree that there is a future for low budget cars like Nano in other markets besides India? Do you think Tata Motors is going in the right direction by trying to develop its low cost Nano models adapted to European and U.S. markets? How would you evaluate a likelihood of success of the Nano on the U.S. market? What should Tata Motors do to win American consumers?

Source: This case was prepared by Tetyana Azarova of Villanova University under the supervision of Professor Jonathan Doh as the basis for class discussion. It is not intended to illustrate either effective or ineffective managerial capability or administrative responsibility. Ben Littell provided research assistance.

In-Depth Integrative Case 3.2

The Ascendance of AirAsia: Building a Successful Budget Airline in Asia

IVEY | Publishing

Source: Professors Thomas Lawton and Jonathan Doh wrote this case solely to provide material for class discussion. The authors do not intend to illustrate either effective or ineffective handling of a managerial situation. The authors may have disguised certain names and other identifying information to protect confidentiality.

One time permission to reproduce granted by Richard Ivey School of Business Foundation on (Effective Date)

Introduction

In September 2001, Tony Fernandes left his job as vice president and head of Warner Music's Southeast Asian operations, one of the most visible and prominent positions in Asia's music industry. He reportedly cashed in his stock options, took out a mortgage on his house, and lined up investors to take control of a struggling Malaysian airline with two jets and US$37 million in debt. Three days later, terrorists destroyed the World Trade Center.[1]

Within two years, AirAsia had demonstrated that the low-fare model epitomized by Southwest and JetBlue in the United States, and by Ryanair and easyJet in Europe, had great potential in the Asian marketplace. AirAsia's success rapidly spawned numerous imitators and competitors. Despite its success to date and continued growth, could AirAsia maintain momentum and continue to expand across Asia and globally? Would the influx of new entrants result in a shakeout such as had occurred in North America and Europe, compromising AirAsia's future in this increasingly competitive market?[2]

Market Liberalization and the Rise of Low-Fare Airlines in the Asia-Pacific Region

Following late on the global trend, low-fare, budget airlines (LFAs) were rapidly established across Asia. Air Do began operating in Japan in 1998, followed by Skymark in 2000. Carriers modeled on leading American and European budget airlines also emerged in Thailand (PBAir and Air Andaman) and in Cambodia (Siem Reap Air). In late 2001, AirAsia was relaunched in Malaysia as a no-frills operation. In the Philippines, Cebu Pacific Airways, also expressly modeled on Southwest, focused on cost containment by selling online and operating out of secondary airports. India's first budget airline, Air Deccan (now Kingfisher Red), was launched in late August 2003. China entered the game in 2005 with the creation of Spring Airlines, based in Shanghai.

Budget airlines were making inroads into most Asian markets, but the long-term survival of these carriers depended on their ability to compete with Asia's traditional, full-service airlines. The prevailing sentiment among some of the Asian majors, expressed by the Asia Pacific Airlines Association in early 2003, was that "no-frill fliers are not a threat to Asian airlines." This view was based in part on the perception that many established Asian airlines were highly cost competitive relative to their global peers. It also illustrates a perception that Asian air passengers valued high service more than low price.

As early as the late 1990s, most observers questioned whether Asia would ever emerge as a viable market for no-frills budget carriers similar to the United States' Southwest and Europe's Ryanair and easyJet. But the environment had since changed dramatically. According to Peter Harbison of the Centre for Asia Pacific Aviation, a consultancy in Sydney, Australia, "the key ingredient is liberalization."[3]

Air transport liberalization in the Asia-Pacific region began in the 1990s when Australia deregulated its domestic market. Virgin Blue was one of the few carriers that survived this initial battle with incumbents, and it succeeded in establishing its position in the market. New Zealand was one of the first countries to privatize its national flag carrier and embrace airline liberalization. Japan and India subsequently pursued air transport deregulation in order to stimulate competition. Elsewhere in Asia, several countries publicly embraced liberalization in the form of reciprocal access agreements: Singapore, Malaysia, Taiwan, South Korea, Brunei, and Pakistan all negotiated open-skies air service agreements with the United States. In Taiwan and South Korea, liberalization measures in the late 1980s and early 1990s spawned the birth of carriers that, by the turn of the century, had all become major players in their countries' air service sectors, both domestic and international. In Thailand, the domestic market underwent deregulation, and new private players were looking to expand. Indonesia witnessed the emergence of a large number of new entrants, following government moves to allow more competition.

In India, Pakistan, Bangladesh, Nepal, the Philippines, and Malaysia, domestic markets underwent varying forms of deregulation in the early-to-mid-1990s, and within a decade, despite some glitches, passengers generally experienced much greater choice in domestic travel. The People's Republic of China also began opening up its air transport market and system. Foreign investors were permitted to enter joint ventures with, or buy stock of, domestic Chinese airlines. The first outside investment in China was George Soros's US$25 million acquisition of a 25 percent stake in Hainan Airlines in 1995. China Eastern and China Southern Airlines had also issued shares on international capital markets.[4] In Hong Kong, restrictions barring more than one locally based airline from operating on a particular route had been eased. These moves were long overdue in a region that had been resistant to change in the airline sector.

Association of Southeast Asian Nation (ASEAN) leaders announced plans to fully liberalize air travel by the end of 2008. However, there were doubts as to whether that deadline would mean much in practice, since countries were allowed to opt out and delay liberalization until 2015. Still, according to the Centre for Asia Pacific Aviation, many ASEAN states were prepared to open the skies between their capital cities in 2008[5]; and by 2010, significant liberalization had taken place, although with some countries lagging in their progress.

Low-Fare Airlines in Japan

Japan was the first Asian country to experience a real boom in both domestic and international travel in the 1960s. Subsequently, Japan retained the status of the largest air travel market among all Asia-Pacific countries as a result of the combination of its population size and a steadily growing disposable income level. Japanese air travel growth rates increased rapidly until the late 1980s, when the market became more mature and reached a plateau. The total Japanese travel market (both international and domestic) grew by only 6 percent from 1990 to 2000, which, even allowing for domestic economic slowdown, indicates that it was saturated with the product offered by the traditional, full-service carriers.[6] Japan undertook comprehensive deregulation and liberalization in a range of sectors throughout the 1990s, partly as a strategy to jump-start its stagnant economy. One sector that was partly liberalized was air transport. Future growth in air transport could come from the introduction of the new business model represented by low-cost, low-fare carriers. Although the total supply of seats provided by the budget airlines in the Japanese domestic market was still very small when compared to Japan Airlines (JAL)[7] and All Nippon Airways (ANA), the two large traditional carriers, the potential for growth was significant as long as new entrants could successfully compete both with the full-service majors and with intermodal competition from high-speed rail.

Skymark Airlines, one of Japan's first budget carriers, pursued a business model similar to JetBlue and easyJet's differentiated low-fare airline approach rather than the traditional Southwest or Ryanair no-frills, price leadership model. Skymark was established in 1996 and commenced operations in 1998. By 2007, it was flying between five domestic points in Japan—Haneda (Tokyo), Sapporo, Kobe, Fukuoka, and Naha on Okinawa—and operating an international charter service to Seoul. It had a fleet of nine aircraft, six Boeing 767s, and three Boeing 737s. The service was basic although all aircraft were equipped with a satellite TV entertainment system. Skymark's onboard product was further differentiated through offering a small number of first-class seats on some routes, e.g., 12 seats out of 309 on its Fukuoka route. Such additional features put Skymark closer to a hybrid budget airline model. An advanced entertainment package drew parallels with the JetBlue onboard TV model, while the availability of business-class seats placed Skymark in the same category as AirTran and Spirit in the United States.[8] Despite challenges, by 2010 Skymark had become Japan's third largest carrier in terms of passenger numbers and consistently outperformed its larger, full-service rivals in terms of cost, load factor, and price. Skymark's share value quadrupled in the 2009–2010 period and it was predicted to turn a profit in 2010, despite the adverse economic conditions. JAL's bankruptcy and consequent restructuring (including cutting many domestic routes) provided further growth opportunities for Skymark over the coming years.

Low-Fare Airlines in Malaysia

The emergence of the budget model in Malaysia resulted from market deregulation and the Malaysian government's desire to release Malaysia Airlines (MAS) from its obligation to serve perpetually money-losing domestic routes. Malaysia's geographic position and land structure provided natural conditions that encouraged air travel, but only 6 percent of the adult population traveled by air in 2001.[9] This low figure indicated an underdeveloped aviation market that could be grown significantly through the introduction of low fares on domestic routes. The policy of highly regulated domestic fares had been long maintained by the Malaysian government.[10] Such a policy created many headaches for the management of MAS, which had "reportedly been losing up to US$79 million annually" on its domestic routes.[11] The initial success of AirAsia may well have validated the Malaysian government's role in encouraging a budget airline to enter the domestic market. However, the government-controlled MAS did show initial concern about that same success. In fall 2002, MAS introduced discounted fares on limited seats on domestic routes. Meanwhile, after its initial failure, a revamped AirAsia was transformed from a money-losing full-service airline into a low-cost, low-fare airline when a new group of investors, Tune Air Sdn Bhd, bought the shares and half the share of liabilities in the original airline in September 2001.[12]

How did Malaysians react to the introduction of this new business model? The anecdotal evidence points out that they were as eager to embrace it as residents of the United States, United Kingdom, Australia, Canada, Ireland, and elsewhere were when they were first given an opportunity to travel for a fraction of historical fares.[13] Conor McCarthy, AirAsia's co-founder and a former director of operations for Ryanair, had specifically noted that the management of AirAsia was encouraged by the similarities between the consumer market in Malaysia and in Ireland, the United Kingdom, and Germany when Ryanair first entered those markets.[14] One traveler offered the following comment on an online discussion site after traveling on AirAsia in March 2003 from Kuala Lumpur to Penang:

> It is good to see the no-frills model finally making headway in the Asia-Pacific region. No food, total scrum for the plane at the boarding announcement, crammed seats . . . but for the equivalent of around US$15, you can't complain. . . . Let's hope that the governments around the region put consumer interests ahead of protecting state-owned airlines.[15]

But 2006 data[16] comparing the types of aircraft in use in major world regions showed that on average, Asian airlines had fleets comprising 71 percent wide-body aircraft (such as the Boeing 747 or the Airbus 340) and only 29 percent narrow-body (such as the Boeing 737 or the Airbus 320). This compared with North America and Europe, where the average airline fleet was 23 percent wide-body and 77 percent narrow-body. This underscored the relative underdevelopment of the Asian market, where narrow-body fleets, typically used for shorter haul intraregional service, were not widely used. Most of the air passenger market remained long haul, often intercontinental and usually full service in nature.

The Rise of AirAsia

The emergence of Malaysian-based AirAsia resembled the story of Ryanair, the Irish low-cost carrier that has dramatically altered the passenger air transport landscape in Europe since the mid-1990s. Both carriers underwent a remarkable transformation from money-losing regional operators into profitable low-cost, low-fare airlines. AirAsia was initially launched in 1996 as a full-service regional airline offering slightly cheaper fares than its main competitor, Malaysia Airlines.[17] This business model failed because AirAsia could neither sufficiently stimulate the market nor attract enough passengers away from Malaysia Airlines to establish its own market niche.

Fernandes's Entrepreneurial Venture

Tony Fernandes had a history of going his own way. Shipped off to boarding school in Britain to become a doctor like his father, Fernandes rebelled, earning an accounting degree

and landing a job with the Virgin Group instead. Eventually he left Virgin for Warner Music, which sent him back to Malaysia in 1992. In 1997, he became vice president for the company's Southeast Asian operations. By 2001, however, he had tired of the politics at what had become AOL Time Warner and decided to start his own airline. This came as no surprise to those who knew him. Unlike many kids, who aspired to become airline pilots, from an early age Fernandes had wanted to own his own airline.[18]

On a trip to Europe, he met Conor McCarthy, Ryanair's former director of group operations.[19] Fernandes had envisioned a low-cost airline competing on long-haul routes. McCarthy encouraged him to focus closer to home. In late 2001, AirAsia was up for sale. Founded in 1996 as Malaysia's second airline, AirAsia had been beset by problems from the beginning and failed to turn a profit. Fernandes enlisted leading low-cost airline experts to restructure AirAsia's business model, and he persuaded McCarthy to join the executive team and become one of the investors.[20]

The investors announced an agreement on September 8, 2001, to buy AirAsia for a symbolic one ringgit (26 cents) and to assume 50 percent of net liabilities, or around 40 million ringgit.[21] Paradoxically, the September 11 attacks resulted in lower costs for purchasing and leasing used airplanes. The new AirAsia was relaunched in January 2002 with three Boeing 737 aircraft as a low-fare, low-cost domestic airline. Its value proposition was described as being based on "a Ryanair operational strategy, a Southwest people strategy, and an easyJet branding strategy."[22] Fulfilling his boyhood dream, Fernandes was running an airline company in which he had a personal stake of around 35 percent.

AirAsia co-founder Conor McCarthy noted that one thing which strikes him when telling the story of the AirAsia journey, is how much timing and luck had huge parts to play. AirAsia got its first batch of aircraft when the market was down, then locked in some purchases and long-term leases when the market was still very weak in 2003. In 2004 and 2005, the market was picking up and management concluded only short-term contracts for the necessary aircraft. Management pursued a similar strategy with regard to maintenance contracts and fuel hedging. The one thing the company managed to keep consistent was its no-frills model and always offering value in low fares. In distribution, it kept the largest majority of bookings via the Web but in coming to terms with local markets where payment type in particular was an issue, AirAsia did open up some billing and settlement plan (BSP) and computer reservation system (CRS) channels[23]—under its own control—as to stick rigidly to the direct sales-only channel would have been value-destroying. Also, as McCarthy noted, "Competition was complacent when we took over AirAsia in late 2001 and this enabled us to get a toehold, followed by a foothold, followed by a large niche followed by market leadership in our key Malaysian domestic market."[24]

The Malaysian government recognized early on that AirAsia could help the economy overall and specifically assisted in infrastructure development (providing huge freedom of movement advantages with none of the associated subsidies/tax expenditure that is required of road and rail) and tourism growth (amplifying the number of visitors per aircraft through the high seat density, short flights, and superior utilization). It also could play a role in distributing wealth from the main cities to the outlying areas and in connecting a previously fragmented East (Borneo)-West (Peninsular) Malaysia through a phenomenal increase in flights, seats, and destinations at much lower fares. Government support for a more competitive domestic market paid off handsomely and also reduced the need to subsidize Malaysian Airlines (MAS) domestic services. This was a major change and, as McCarthy argued, one for which the policy and decision makers in the Malaysian government deserved genuine credit.

AirAsia's Strategy and Operations

AirAsia focused on ensuring a very low cost structure as a cornerstone of its business strategy. It was able to achieve a cost per available-seat-kilometer (ASK) early in its development of 2.5 cents, half that of Malaysia Airlines and Ryanair and a third that of easyJet.[25] UBS research indicated that AirAsia was the lowest cost airline in the world by 2007 (see Exhibit 1). The company continued to retain that position, as it consistently pushed down cost year on year (Exhibit 2). Similar to budget airlines elsewhere in the world, AirAsia's revenue model was driven by the visiting friends and relatives (VFR) market and small business travelers.

Fernandes acknowledged that the timing of the AirAsia start-up in the aftermath of the tragic events of September 11, 2001, helped ensure the lowest possible cost structure, with both leasing and operating aircraft costs sharply declining year over year. By 2007, AirAsia was handling 51,000 passengers a day with a fleet of 54 planes, offering fares as low as 50 Malaysia ringgit (less than US$15).[26] The revenue formula of AirAsia mostly followed the traditional low-fare approach; only three different fare types were offered.[27] AirAsia's focus on Internet bookings and ticketless travel allowed it to emphasize simplicity for the customer while securing low distribution costs. With the average fare 40 to 60 percent lower than the fares of its full-service competitors, AirAsia was able to achieve strong market stimulation in the domestic Malaysian air market.[28] For example, when AirAsia started out, the lowest fare it offered for the trip from Kuala Lumpur to Penang started at 39 ringgit. The same trip by bus cost 40 ringgit and increased to about 80 ringgit if

Exhibit 1   The Operating Costs of Global Low-Cost Carriers

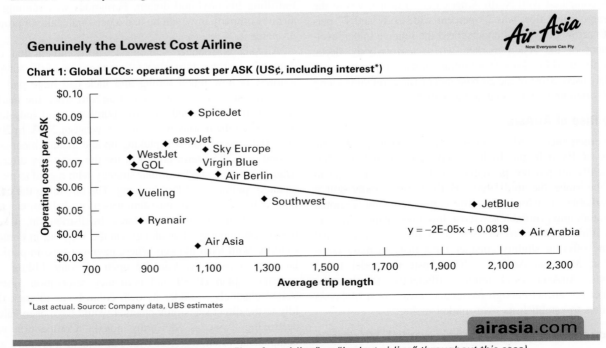

LCC = Low-Cost Carrier (we use the terms "low-fare airline" or "budget airline" throughout this case)
ASK = Average-seat-kilometer

Source: Company files.

Exhibit 2   Cost/ASK—AirAsia's Year on Year Comparison

Cost Breakdown (US cents/ASK)	Jan-Mar 2009	Jan-Mar 2008	Δ (%)	Reason
Staff	0.34	0.36	−6%	Productivity gains
Fuel and Oil	1.04	1.93	−46%	Lower jet fuel price
User & Station Charges	0.26	0.20	29%	More international routes bias
Maintenance and Overhaul	0.17	0.16	3%	Redelivery of Boeing 737-300 cost
Cost of Aircraft	(0.25)	(0.08)	212%	Sub-lease income from associates
Depreciation & Amortisation	0.52	0.48	9%	More number of owned aircraft
Sales and Marketing	0.11	0.14	−19%	Economies of scale
Others	0.20	0.11	84%	Higher overheads
Cost/ASK	2.38	3.30	−28%	
Cost/ASK-excluding fuel	1.35	1.37	−2%	
Finance Cost	0.51	0.34	49%	More aircraft being financed
Cost/ASK inc. finance cost	2.90	3.64	−20%	

Source: Company files.

traveling by car. The introduction of such super-competitive fares began to produce the same market growth effect that was achieved by the entry of Ryanair (in its low-fare form) into the U.K.-Ireland air travel market—travelers' switching from sea, train, and bus to air transportation. In the case of Malaysia, consumers increasingly switched from bus to air travel. Starting with two planes bought from a Malaysian conglomerate in late 2001, the airline had expanded to 54 aircraft by 2007 and more than 70 by 2010, with plans to grow to more than 180 aircraft by 2014. This was impressive growth, but it also raised concerns because other budget airlines had faced their most serious challenges when they attempted to expand too fast.[29]

AirAsia expanded quickly. The airline handled 1.5 million passengers in 2003 and this number almost doubled the following year and rose to 6.3 million in 2005. By June 2007, this number had climbed to almost 14 million passengers. In early 2010, despite a fall in global passenger demand, AirAsia had grown its passenger numbers by a further 24 percent, taking the group total (combining the Malaysian, Thai, and Indonesian operations) to 22.7 million. The company quickly repaid its inherited debt and was profitable from the outset. Its profit margins (before interest, depreciation, amortization, and aircraft leasing costs) have been as high as 35 percent, among the highest in the world, according to Michael McGhee, Credit Suisse First Boston's airline analyst. AirAsia announced net profits of RM549 million (US$162 million) for the full year 2009, despite what was described by many as the worst year in aviation history.

Reaction to AirAsia's Success

The Malaysian government was supportive of AirAsia so long as it was assuming previously money-losing domestic routes and serving as a benchmark for the restructuring of Malaysia Airlines. In August 2006, AirAsia took over 96 of Malaysia Airlines' 118 domestic routes, only four of which had previously been profitable. AirAsia's plans to enter the traditionally profitable intraregional markets of Thailand and other neighboring countries met with less enthusiasm from the Malaysian government. The Malaysian regulatory authorities faced the knotty problem of accommodating the growth plans of a new budget airline at the cost of reducing the market value of government-owned Malaysia Airlines.

Given the initial uncertainty about its ability to fly outside of Malaysia, AirAsia sought creative ways to expand its market coverage by targeting cross-border markets. AirAsia entered into a number of joint ventures, including Thai AirAsia, Indonesia AirAsia, and AirAsia X.[30] In its cross-border joint ventures with Indonesia and Thailand, AirAsia urged harmonization of national regulations in the areas of pilot hours and maintenance oversight. AirAsia also won greater favor with the Malaysian government, which endorsed AirAsia X (the group's low-cost, long-haul airline) and built the region's first low-cost terminal at Kuala Lumpur International Airport in March 2006.[31] As with the Thai and Indonesian operations, AirAsia X was a legally separate company in which AirAsia held just a 16 percent stake. However, a consortium that included Tony Fernandes owned 48 percent. Virgin Group also had a 16 percent stake in the long-haul budget carrier.

The Malaysian towns serviced by AirAsia attracted residents of neighboring countries to try AirAsia when they traveled to Kuala Lumpur, as it often meant saving half the airfare by taking a simple car trip across the border. This elicited a response from some of AirAsia's competitors, most notably Singapore Airlines, Asia's largest carrier by market capitalization. Singapore Airlines announced a low-fare subsidiary, and a former Singapore Airlines deputy chairman, Lim Chin Beng, registered "Valuair" in June 2003, intending it to operate as Singapore's third airline. Thai Airways International also launched its own low-fare spin-off, Nok Air, in 2004, which it co-owned as part of a consortium.[32] The Sri Lankan government launched a fully state-owned budget carrier, Mihin Lanka, in 2007. In sum, AirAsia was causing competitive ripples that were likely to grow in scale and scope.

Going International: The Response of Incumbent Carriers

In January 2004, AirAsia started its first international service, from Kuala Lumpur to the Thai holiday island of Phuket. In February, it began flying from Johor Bahru, across the border from Singapore. In 2005, it began flying to Indonesia, a country with 235 million potential passengers. Expansion to India and China was also in the cards, two markets with a combined population of 2.5 billion. By early 2008, AirAsia X was flying to Hangzhou (Shanghai) and by late 2008 AirAsia was connecting Malaysia to Kolkata, Trichy, Kochi, and Trivandrum in India. This proved only the tip of the iceberg for both markets, as AirAsia and AirAsia X continued a relentless growth strategy vis-à-vis China and India.

At the same time, incumbents were striking back. Of the 50 or so budget airlines serving East, South, and Southeast Asia, many came from spin-offs of traditional airlines. For example, Thai Airways announced an international carrier, Nok Air, and Singapore Airlines established its own budget airline, Tiger Airways, together with the founders of Ryanair. In 2004, Australia's Qantas announced that it was starting a new Singapore-based low-fare airline, subsequently called Jetstar. Qantas invested about 50 million Singapore dollars (US$30 million) for a 49 percent stake in the new airline; Temasek Holdings, the powerful investment arm of the Singapore government, owned 19 percent, and two local businessmen held the remainder. Although Temasek owned 57 percent of Singapore Airlines, Temasek officials denied that its ownership in the two carriers represented a conflict of interest. "We think this new player will increase the pie," said Rachel Lin, a spokeswoman for Temasek. "Our interest is strictly for financial returns; we see both of them as potentially attractive investments." Moreover, as the government moved to defend its role as a hub for air travel by building an airport terminal designed to accommodate budget airlines,

Singapore's founding prime minister and elder statesman, Lee Kuan Yew, warned Singapore Airlines that the government intended to protect Changi Airport's competitiveness, even at the flag carrier's expense.[33]

Some believed many of the incumbents in Asia—like those in the United States—faced inherent disadvantages in their ability to compete on cost and price because they did not have the cost discipline or the entrepreneurial culture of budget start-ups. Thai Airways hired an advertising executive to run Nok, apparently with the intention of mimicking Fernandes, but its choice appeared to lack Fernandes's marketing and operational ability. Eric Kohn, who was number two at Deutsche BA, initially organized as a German-based low-price offshoot of British Airways, argued that established carriers are not set up to succeed in the low-cost space: "People at big airlines don't have accountability or a focus on costs. It is a lot easier to start an airline from scratch than to take a legacy airline and make a profit."

"We feel pretty vindicated," Fernandes said in a telephone interview from his office at Kuala Lumpur International Airport. "A lot of people laughed at us at first."[34] Fernandes disputed analysts' warnings that AirAsia was likely to run into more difficulties as it went more international. "I don't see why it makes any difference," he said. As for Asia's relative lack of bilateral agreements to allow new carriers to ferry passengers from country to country, Fernandes argued that competition for tourist revenue is pushing more countries to open up.

Moving Forward at AirAsia: Regional and Global Expansion

As more and more countries opened their skies, AirAsia was quick to start cross-border joint ventures, most notably in Thailand and Indonesia. AirAsia prompted increased passenger travel with its 2007–2008 "To Malaysia with Love" campaign. The campaign celebrated 50 years of nationhood for Malaysia, and offered travelers affordable fares "starting from MYR0.50 (about 15 cents), available for all destinations to/from its Malaysian hubs."[35] Cheaper airfares were also made possible by the low-cost carrier terminal at Kuala Lumpur Airport, with a throughput of about 10 million passengers annually.

International route expansion continued unabated. This combined shorter routes (typically up to four hours' flying time) undertaken by AirAsia (Malaysia), Thai AirAsia, or Indonesia AirAsia, with longer routes operated by AirAsia X. By early 2010, AirAsia X was flying long haul from Malaysia to three cities in China and AirAsia was flying shorter routes to a further six cities (including Hong Kong and Macau) from both Malaysia and Thailand. CEO Fernandes declared 2010 his "India year," with plans to gradually link New Delhi, Chennai, Bangalore, Hyderabad, and Mumbai to Kuala Lumpur and Penang, and from there to more than 130 routes.[36] In addition, AirAsia X offered daily services to three destinations in Australia, as well as to

Exhibit 3   **AirAsia and AirAsia X Route Network (2009)**

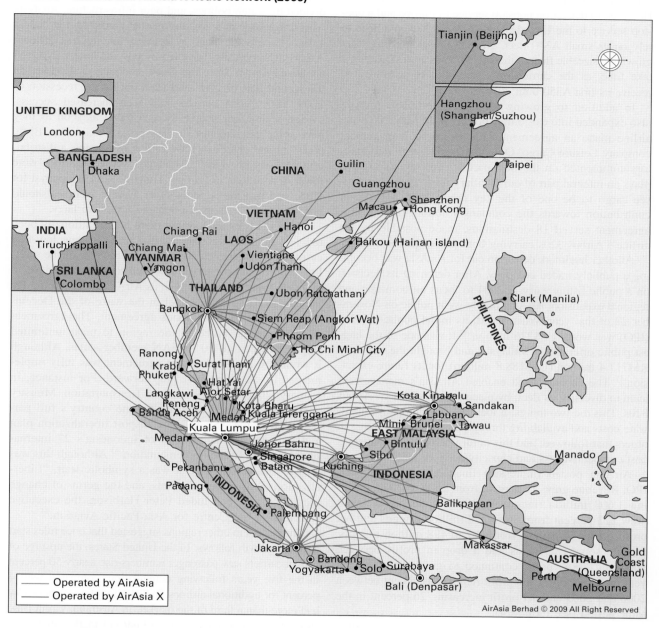

Source: Company files.

Taiwan and London. Plans for further long-haul expansion included more Australian routes, Paris, and the United States. AirAsia's sponsorship of sports teams such as Manchester United helped build up brand recognition in many markets. In the United States, the airline signed a sponsorship deal with the Oakland Raiders football team in early 2009, raising the group's profile in northern California; AirAsia was reportedly exploring Oakland as an alternative airport to San Francisco and investigating additional airports in the Los Angeles and New York City areas. A prerequisite to any of these forays was that the airports must support the needs of

budget airlines, including quick turnaround and taxi times.[37] An airport such as Oakland was also attractive because of its large base for Southwest Airlines, allowing passengers to connect onwards to hundreds of domestic U.S. routes at a low price. AirAsia X would serve future U.S. west coast routes from Kuala Lumpur via Taipei, Seoul, or Honolulu and any east coast routes would route via London Stansted. Another 16 Airbus aircraft were expected during 2010, mostly A320s to serve short-haul routes but including several A330s to support projected growth for long-haul operator AirAsia X.[38] The A330 was ideal for long-haul flights between Southeast Asia and Australia or the Middle East. However, to deliver on nonstop service to Europe and a one-stop service to the United States, AirAsia X would need to rely on its small A340 fleet, gradually replacing these and growing a sizeable fleet of the new A350 aircraft. This might take time, as the carrier was currently not scheduled to receive its first A350 until 2016.

In addition to growing its passenger travel, AirAsia also expanded into cargo transportation. In May 2007, the airline made an agreement with the cargo management company Leisure Cargo. One of AirAsia's regional directors commented on the new partnership, saying, "Cargo plays an integral part of our ancillary income and we foresee cargo to be one of the key drivers with significant contribution towards the company's bottom line."[39] This agreement served 18 destinations, made possible by the airline's Airbus 320s carrying both passengers and cargo.

Another landmark development for AirAsia was becoming a publicly traded company. After deferring its decision on a public listing early in 2004 to focus on domestic and regional expansion, AirAsia finally went public on November 22 of that year. When it did, its initial public offering (IPO) was worth US$226 million.[40] It was one of the largest public offerings in Malaysia, and brought the company RM717.4 million (US$188.8 million) for its future expansion.[41] The capital raised enabled AirAsia's management team to diversify its fleet, by placing orders for new Airbus 320s. This did two things: it locked in the company's hardware costs and availability through the very strong surge in orders that followed; and this in turn helped the company's cost competitiveness and capacity/network build out.

AirAsia posted impressive financial results in post-IPO: Revenue grew 52 percent from 2006 to 2007, reaching 1,603 million ringgits in 2007, while pretax profit grew 223 percent from 86 to 278 million ringgits and net profit grew 147 percent from 202 to 498 million ringgits. Despite some challenges and a drop in profits between 2007 and 2008, profit continued to grow the following year with core operating profit rising 591 percent between 2008 and 2009 and net profit increasing 26 percent in the same period (see Exhibit 4).

The Budget Airline Future in Asia

In 2010, views on whether low-fare airlines would continue to flourish in Asia varied. Three factors—regulation, population, and demographics—drove this calculus. Although the target consumer base for AirAsia was enormous—more than 500 million people lived within three hours of AirAsia's hubs in Kuala Lumpur and Bangkok, more than Western Europe's entire population—the failure of Asia's regulatory environment to keep pace and the uncertain demand for low-fare services created uncertainty.

Those who sold airplanes, airports, or advice tended to be of the opinion that low-fare carriers would redraw Asia's socioeconomic map, offering affordable international travel to millions and thereby fostering the integration of a region divided by water, politics, and poor infrastructure. Analysts who saw a large and growing market predicted that budget airlines would tap pent-up demand among less affluent Asians, who typically travelled by bus and hardly expected attentive service. Since the global economy had peaked in the second half of 2006 and even during the recession of 2008–2009, Asian carriers had seen increased success. "We're seeing that people in Asia travel as soon as they have some extra money in their pocket," said Don Birth, president and chief executive officer of Abacus, a distribution services provider.[42] Although average incomes were lower in Asia than in Europe, Timothy Ross, an analyst for UBS, said that the region's lower average incomes should boost rather than constrain demand for cheap fares.

Other analysts argued that there had traditionally been too few bilateral agreements that allowed new low-fare carriers to fly between countries and too few of the satellite airports that the airlines needed to keep costs low. In that vein, budget airlines such as AirAsia were hoping for increased cross-border travel in the wake of the December 2008 ASEAN open skies agreement. The agreement allowed carriers based in the region to make unlimited flights between all 10 ASEAN member states. Although it would be 2015 before the agreement was fully implemented, it was a positive step forward. For instance, in January 2010, the Indonesian Transportation Ministry announced it was gearing up for the country's full participation in the ASEAN air transport liberalization plan and intended to include five of Indonesia's 27 international airports in the implementation.[43] Although this was only a small proportion, it was a symbolic start. "Liberalization tends to be infectious, and the germs of change are in the air," concluded Peter Harbison, the executive chairman of the Centre for Asia Pacific Aviation.[44]

The pattern in other regions suggested that once rules start to relax, growth follows. In the United States, the upsurge of budget carriers saw passenger numbers rise nearly 50 percent in the five years following deregulation, compared with 4 percent for traditional airlines. In 2010, low-fare carriers now had more than a third of the market. In Australia, Virgin Blue took only three years to win a 30 percent market share.[45]

The growth of low-fare carriers had great potential to spill over into the broader tourist and business travel economy: Having more air passengers generates higher demand for hotel rooms. This connection had been seen in Australia, where Virgin Blue took nearly one-third of the domestic market from Qantas Airways (which responded in part by setting up Jetstar). This resulted in a sharp upturn in demand for economy hotels, such as Accor. "In many cases, it's entirely new business that wouldn't have happened if it weren't for cheap air tickets," commented Peter Hook, general manager for communications at Accor Asia Pacific.[46] In addition, low-fare carriers might offer options for Asian travelers to mix business with pleasure, as many North

Exhibit 4   **AirAsia's Profit and Expanding Margins**

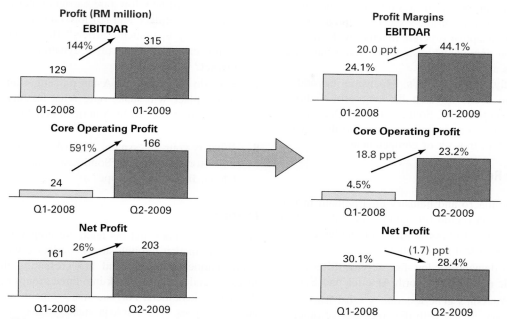

RM = Ringgit (Malaysia's unit of currency; on June 1, 2008, RM1 was equal to US$.30)
EBITDAR = Earnings Before Interest, Taxes, Depreciation, Amortization, and Restructuring or Rent Costs
EBIT = Earnings Before Interest, Taxes
Source: Company files.

American and European business travelers did, by extending trips or bringing family members to accompany them. Ultimately, Fernandes pointed out, budget airlines in Asia had an advantage in that Asia had almost no interregional highways and no high-speed international rail. "There's a lot of sea in between," he said. "Air travel is the only way to develop interconnectivity in Asia."

But competition was growing. In addition to the many upstart carriers and joint ventures with majors, some significant players from outside the region were also making rumbles. After his success with Virgin Blue, Richard Branson expressed interest in investing in a low-fare operation specifically in Asia. His stake in AirAsia X ensured he was an ally rather than an adversary of Tony Fernandes. David Bonderman, an airline financier who helped found Ireland's Ryanair, took a stake in Tiger Airways, Singapore Airlines' budget venture. So far, Hong Kong–based Cathay Pacific Airways was one of the few regional heavyweights to say it was not likely to enter the fray.[47]

With all of the new competitors for low-fare air travel in the region, AirAsia needed to stay ahead. In order to do so, it was important to focus on profits, not just cost-cutting, in order to win investors, thereby increasing capital. According to the Centre for Asia Pacific Aviation, "With financial experts predicting that funding aircraft acquisitions with equity and affordable debt will be much more difficult in the near future, only those airlines that have

exhibited an ability to wisely increase capacity will be able to grow their operations."[48]

External, industry-wide challenges—particularly the escalating cost of fuel—also posed a threat to AirAsia. As the lowest cost carrier in the world, the company suffered more from high fuel prices, as they were a higher percentage of total costs, than any other airline (assuming similar equipment and seat density). Surcharges and baggage fees covered some of this but the airline was conscious that if it loaded on the full charge, it might find no demand on some flights due to a high base price (e.g., minimum or zero fare plus taxes, fees, and surcharges). To offset this eventuality, AirAsia did a lot to improve operations and efficiency and also saw the benefits of the fuel efficient Airbus 320 help to maintain its low-fares brand position. But what were the business implications for AirAsia if oil prices remained above $100 a barrel for the foreseeable future?

To retain its cost advantage in the wake of the global recession, AirAsia entered into an alliance in January 2010 with Jetstar, the low-fare subsidiary of Australia's flag carrier, Qantas. This was the first time two leading budget airlines had collaborated in this fashion. The alliance allowed the companies to explore joint aircraft purchasing, passenger and ground handling services cooperation, and the transportation of each other's passengers in the event of a disruption.[49] Assuming the focus of the alliance was on cost sharing for services and aircraft procurement, it might prove effective. However, any alliance—but particularly with another airline—is always difficult to manage for budget airlines. A budget airline's success is predicated on a lean and highly adaptive structure together with an autonomous and often unpredictable strategy. Would the Jetstar alliance put this at risk?

More broadly, did AirAsia's expansion beyond its Southeast Asian focus threaten its long-term viability? Even if expansion to China, South Asia, and Oceania was consistent with its core capabilities, how did the AirAsia X initiative fit with this set of competencies?

Questions for Review

1. What is the macro and industry environment in the Southeast Asian region for the entrance of new budget airlines? What opportunities and challenges are associated with that environment?

2. How might demand for low-fare service differ in the Asia-Pacific region from North America and Europe?

3. Compare AirAsia's generic strategy (cost leadership, differentiation, focus) with the strategies of other incumbent carriers and with Southwest and Ryanair. How is it similar to and different from the strategies of those carriers?

4. Did Fernandes weigh the range of political, economic, and operational uncertainties and risks when he took over AirAsia? What risks might he have overlooked?

5. How would you describe Fernandes's entrepreneurial strategy?

6. How should AirAsia respond to the challenges posed by (a) new low-fare carriers entering the Asian marketplace and (b) low-fare strategies pursued by incumbent carriers? How would you characterize the competitive dynamics in this market?

7. How do you think the Asian passenger air transport marketplace will shake out? What lessons can be drawn from the North American and European experience?

8. What is your assessment of AirAsia moving beyond its historic strength in Southeast Asia to Australia, China, India, and Europe?

Exercise

Anthony Fernandes and his team are preparing to enter a new Asian market through strategic alliance with an indigenous partner company and are presenting the case to investors and workers. Break into three groups representing the key stakeholders: AirAsia management, shareholders, and employees. The AirAsia management group should make the case for the alliance to support expansion, describe the impact of this expansion on future earnings growth, and support this pitch with specific information about opportunities in the new Asian market. The groups representing workers and investors should ask questions and seek clarification about the validity of the expansion plans, the financial and operational implications, and the likely overall market and customer receptivity to the alliance.

(Daily flights are available to all destinations.)

PART FOUR

ORGANIZATIONAL
BEHAVIOR AND
HUMAN RESOURCE
MANAGEMENT

Chapter 12

MOTIVATION ACROSS CULTURES

Motivation is closely related to the performance of human resources in modern organizations. Although the motivation process may be similar across cultures, there are clear differences in motivation that are culturally based. What motivates employees in the United States may be only moderately effective in Japan, France, or Nigeria. Therefore, although motivation in the workplace is related to stimulating and encouraging employee performance in many situations and environments, an international context requires country-by-country, or at least regional, examination of differences in motivation and its sources.

This chapter examines motivation as a psychological process and explores how motivation can be used to understand and improve employee performance. It also identifies and describes internationally researched work-motivation theories and discusses their relevance for international human resource management. The specific objectives of this chapter are:

1. **DEFINE** *motivation,* and explain it as a psychological process.

2. **EXAMINE** the hierarchy-of-needs, two-factor, and achievement motivation theories, and assess their value to international human resource management.

3. **DISCUSS** how an understanding of employee satisfaction can be useful in human resource management throughout the world.

4. **EXAMINE** the value of process theories in motivating employees worldwide.

5. **UNDERSTAND** the importance of job design, work centrality, and rewards in motivating employees in an international context.

The World of *International Management*

Motivating Employees in a Multicultural Context: Insights from Emerging Markets

According to Patricia Odell of PROMO magazine, "As U.S. companies continue to expand globally, currently employing more than 60 million overseas workers, motivating and rewarding these diverse workforces is a significant challenge to organizations." Bob Nelson, Ph.D., author of *1001 Ways to Reward Employees,* told PROMO magazine, "One size doesn't fit all when it comes to employee motivation—rewards that motivate best are those that are most valued by the person you are trying to thank."[1]

According to *BusinessWeek,* numerous well-known firms have enlisted the help of Globoforce, an Irish company, to design their corporate recognition programs. Globoforce's program lets employees choose a reward they want, such as tickets to a concert or a $50 gift card to their favorite store. In this way, Globoforce tailors rewards to specific employee preferences.[2]

These employee preferences are often correlated with culture. To illustrate this, Bob Nelson provides an example of a certain Indonesian company. If this company has a good year, employees receive extra pay at year end. The amount of pay an employee receives is "not a function of individual performance, but rather of one's loyalty to the organization as measured by the number of years one had worked with the company, plus the size of one's family." The company demonstrates an Indonesian cultural value: the employee is loyal to the employer and the employer takes care of the employee's family.[3]

Furthermore, managers must be aware that a reward in one culture may be viewed differently in another culture. Bob Nelson shares a story of how a pharmaceutical company decided to give customized watches bearing the company logo to all 44,000 employees around the world. When Nelson told this story to Taiwanese employees of a different company, they remarked that such a gift would never work in their culture. Timepieces are associated with death in Taiwan and China.[4]

So, as a manager, how does one motivate employees? There are general management principles that can be applied to most cultural settings. But also, there are specific considerations for each individual culture. Next, we mention some general concepts that have proved useful and then discuss motivating Chinese employees in particular.

Motivating Employees: General Principles

In its guide on how to motivate employees, *The Wall Street Journal* outlines several findings on the subject:

- The goal of management . . . [is] not simply to direct and control employees seeking to shun work, but rather to create conditions that make people want to offer maximum effort.
- Having employees harness self-direction and self-control in pursuit of common objectives . . . was far preferable to imposing a system of controls designed to force people to meet objectives they didn't understand or share.
- Rewarding people for achievement was a far more effective way to reinforce shared commitment than punishing them for failure.
- Giving people responsibility caused them to rise to the challenge.
- Unleashing their imagination, ingenuity, and creativity resulted in their contributions to the organization being multiplied many times over.[5]

In addition, Bob Nelson notes that today employees "expect work to be an integrated part of their lives—not their entire lives." Thus, managers can likely increase employee motivation by offering more flexible working hours. With technology, it has become much easier for employees to work from home. Nelson also emphasizes that discussing career options in the organization and providing learning and development opportunities often motivates employees.[6]

Frequently, managers focus on extrinsic rewards, such as pay, to motivate employees, while ignoring intrinsic rewards. Kenneth Thomas told *BusinessWeek*, "Research shows that managers underestimate the importance of intrinsic rewards." *BusinessWeek* describes intrinsic

rewards as "the psychological lift that employees get from doing work that matters to them."[7]

In a collectivistic culture, such as China, an intrinsic reward may be the satisfaction of helping the group complete a project.

Motivating Employees in China

Watson Wyatt conducted a WorkChina™ employee opinion survey of 10,000 employees from 67 companies in China. The WorkChina™ survey found that compensation had a limited role in motivating Chinese employees. Jim Leininger of Watson Wyatt Beijing wrote:

> Increasing employee satisfaction by raising salaries may result in short-term retention, but employees who stay in your organization because of high salaries may also leave for higher salaries. Thus, compensation is sometimes called a "hygiene issue." It is something that is not noticed until it is missing. A non-competitive compensation system is easily "noticed" by employees and can lead to turnover. However, having high salary levels does not necessarily lead to highly committed employees or lower turnover. Other things become the distinguishing factors once average compensation levels are satisfied.[8]

The following factors were found to be strong drivers of employee commitment:

- *Management effectiveness.* Employees are motivated when their managers have sound decision-making ability, successfully engage their employees, and value their employees.
- *Positive work environment.* To be productive, employees need a healthy, safe workplace with access to information needed to do their jobs.
- *Objective performance management system.* Watson Wyatt's 2003 compensation survey demonstrated that, for the typical employee, at least one month's salary will be tied to a performance measure—either for the employee personally or for the company itself. Managers must ensure that the performance management system is objective, fair, and clearly communicated to employees.
- *Clear communication.* Managers can increase commitment by making sure employees understand their company's goals, their own job, and the link between their job and the customer.[9]

In contrast, Fisher and Yuan's case study of Chinese employees of a major hotel in Shanghai found that good wages and good working conditions were the most important motivating factors. They discovered that employees' intrinsic needs for interesting work, personal growth, and involvement tended to be lower, especially among older Chinese workers, as compared with employees in Western cultures. According to Fisher and Yuan, managers of MNCs with ventures in China should take note that Chinese employees appreciate wage raises, increased housing subsidies, and employee share ownership. Chinese employees are also grateful when a manager is loyal to them. This loyalty can be demonstrated through renewing employment contracts and showing concern for employees' families.[10]

Motivating Employees in the Global Workplace

In her article "Motivating Employees from Other Cultures," Sondra Thiederman offers tips to adapt one's management style to fit a multicultural context. First,

she underscores the importance of interpreting situations accurately. For instance, many managers "misinterpret the speaking of a foreign language in the workplace as a sign of laziness, rudeness, and disrespect." In reality, "using another language is an effort to communicate a job-related message accurately, a sign of extreme stress or fatigue, or an effort to speed up the communication process."[11]

Second, Thiederman notes that managers need to explain their expectations to employees in such a way that they can be understood by someone not raised in American culture. For example, many cultures view complaining to superiors as a sign of disloyalty. For an American manager, however, complaints provide an opportunity to identify problems. Managers need to explain to their workforce that good employees can bring up problems to managers. Third, managers can motivate employees by offering positive reinforcement. Kind words can go a long way in affirming the value of people of any culture.[12]

Clearly, motivation is a matter of critical importance to international managers in organizations around the world that is much discussed and debated, as are the similarities and differences among cultures as touching on what are perceived to be effective incentives and rewards. While there are some common elements in effective motivation across cultures, the role of pay (versus other forms of incentives) varies somewhat. Moreover, the form and structure of financial rewards are distinct in different cultures. For instance, the Indonesian example in the World of International Management above demonstrates how a U.S. approach to end-of-year bonuses, which would typically be based on individual merit and accomplishments, might be poorly received in Indonesia, where the collectivist culture would encourage a bonus based on tenure and family size.

The role of intrinsic rewards—the psychological rewards that employees get from doing work that matters to them—is important around the world; however, what is meaningful and rewarding may vary from culture to culture. As MNCs shift from simply finding inexpensive employment bases to discovering new ways to enhance employee satisfaction, important questions begin to surface. Why does a relationship with an employee's family make a difference? What truly motivates workers in different cultures? What do they consider important with regard to their perception of satisfaction? Employees typically seek more than just fair compensation. They want to believe that they are making a difference in some way. Effectively motivating across cultures can create competitive advantages that are difficult for competitors to match. In this chapter we provide some of the background discussion about motivation, explore research in the area of motivation, and discuss the implications of our knowledge about motivating employees across cultures.

motivation
A psychological process through which unsatisfied wants or needs lead to drives that are aimed at goals or incentives.

intrinsic
A determinant of motivation by which an individual experiences fulfillment through carrying out an activity itself and helping others.

extrinsic
A determinant of motivation by which the external environment and result of the activity in the form of competition and compensation or incentive plans are of great importance.

■ The Nature of Motivation

Motivation is a psychological process through which unsatisfied wants or needs lead to drives that are aimed at goals or incentives. A person with an unsatisfied need will undertake goal-directed behavior to satisfy the need. Figure 12–1 shows the motivation process. The three basic elements in this process are needs, drives, and goal attainment. The determinants of motivation could be **intrinsic**, by which an individual experiences fulfillment through carrying out an activity itself and helping others, or **extrinsic**, in the

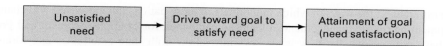

| Unsatisfied need | → | Drive toward goal to satisfy need | → | Attainment of goal (need satisfaction) |

Figure 12–1

The Basic Motivation Process

sense that the external environment and result of the activity in the form of competition and compensation or incentive plans are of greater importance.[13] Motivation is an important topic in international human resource management, especially so because many MNC managers tend to assume they can motivate their overseas personnel with the same approaches that are used in the home country. Whether this is true, or to what extent major differences in culture require tailor-made, country-by-country motivation programs, is the source of debate. As described in earlier chapters (especially Chapter 4), there obviously are some motivational differences caused by culture. The major question is: Are these differences highly significant, or can an overall theory of work motivation apply throughout the world? Considerable research on motivating human resources has been conducted in a large number of countries. Before reviewing these findings, let's take a look at two generally agreed-on starting assumptions about work motivation in the international arena.

The Universalist Assumption

The first assumption is that the motivation process is universal, that all people are motivated to pursue goals they value—what the work-motivation theorists call goals with "high valence" or "preference." The process is universal; however, culture influences the specific content and goals that are pursued. For example, one analysis suggests that the key incentive for many U.S. workers is money; for Japanese employees, it is respect and power; and for Latin American workers, it is an array of factors including family considerations, respect, job status, and a good personal life. Similarly, the primary interest of the U.S. worker is him- or herself; for the Japanese, it is group interest; and for the Latin American employee, it is the interest of the employer.[14] Simply put, motivation is universal but its specific nature differs across cultures, so no one motivation theory can be universally applied across cultures.

In the United States, personal success and professional achievement are important motivators, and promotions and increased earnings are important goals. In China, group affiliation is an important need, and social harmony is an important goal. Obviously, Americans may value teamwork too, and Chinese workers wish to be well paid. However, clearly, some of the ways to motivate U.S. employees and Chinese workers will differ. The motivational process may be the same, but the specific needs and goals can be different between the two cultures. This conclusion was supported in a study by Welsh, Luthans, and Sommer that examined the value of extrinsic rewards, behavioral management, and participative techniques among Russian factory workers. The first two of these motivational approaches worked well to increase worker performance, but the third did not. The researchers noted that this study provides at least beginning evidence that U.S.-based behavioral theories and techniques may be helpful in meeting the performance challenges facing human resources management in rapidly changing and different cultural environments. They found that two behavioral techniques—administering desirable extrinsic rewards to employees contingent upon improved performance, and providing social reinforcement and feedback for functional behaviors and corrective feedback for dysfunctional behaviors—significantly improved Russian factory workers' performance. By the same token, the study also points out the danger of making universalist assumptions about U.S.-based theories and techniques. In particular, the failure of the participative intervention does not indicate so much that this approach just won't work across cultures, as that historical and cultural values and norms need to be recognized and overcome for such a relatively sophisticated theory and technique to work effectively.[15]

At the same time, it is important to remember that as a growing number of countries begin moving toward free-market economies and as new opportunities for economic rewards emerge, the ways in which individuals in these nations are motivated will change. Commenting on the management of Chinese personnel, for example, Sergeant and Frenkel have pointed out that new labor laws now allow both state enterprises and foreign-invested Chinese enterprises to set their own wage and salary levels. However, companies have to be careful about believing that they can simply go into the marketplace, pay high wages, and recruit highly motivated personnel. In particular, the researchers note that:

> Devising reward packages for Chinese employees has been difficult because of the range and complexity of nonwage benefits expected by workers as a legacy of the "iron rice bowl" tradition. However, health and accident insurance, pensions, unemployment and other benefits are increasingly being taken over by the state. There are two cultural impediments to introducing greater differentials in pay among workers of similar status: importance accorded to interpersonal harmony which would be disrupted by variations in earnings; and distrust of performance appraisals because in state enterprises evaluations are based on ideological principles and guanxi [connections].[16]

So some of what foreign MNCs would suspect about how to motivate Chinese employees is accurate, but not all. The same is true, for example, about Japanese employees. Many people believe that all Japanese firms guarantee lifetime employment and that this practice is motivational and results in a strong bond between employer and employee. In truth, much of this is a myth. Actually, less than 28 percent (and decreasing) of the workforce has any such guarantee, and in recent years a growing number of Japanese employees have been finding that their firms may do the best they can to ensure jobs for them but will not guarantee jobs if the company begins to face critical times. As in the West, when a Japanese firm has a crisis, people are often let go. This was clearly seen in recent years when the Japanese economy was stalled and the country's jobless rate hit new highs.[17]

In a test of the universalist assumption in developing countries, researchers measured the frequency that managers were involved with certain skill activities, such as negotiation, job planning, motivation, and decision making. Drawing from a sample that included managers from Hungary and Senegal, they found that the relative frequency with which managers from one stratum of one nation are involved in various skill activities reflects the relative frequency with which managers from other strata within the same nation and from nations of different cultural-industrialized standing are also involved in the same activities, providing in this case at least some general support for the universalist hypothesis.[18]

The Assumption of Content and Process

content theories of motivation
Theories that explain work motivation in terms of what arouses, energizes, or initiates employee behavior.

process theories of motivation
Theories that explain work motivation by how employee behavior is initiated, redirected, and halted.

The second starting assumption is that work-motivation theories can be broken down into two general categories: content and process. **Content theories** explain work motivation in terms of what arouses, energizes, or initiates employee behavior. **Process theories** of work motivation explain how employee behavior is initiated, redirected, and halted.[19] Most research in international human resource management has been content-oriented, because these theories examine motivation in more general terms and are more useful in creating a composite picture of employee motivation in a particular country or region. Process theories are more sophisticated and tend to focus on individual behavior in specific settings. Thus, they have less value to the study of employee motivation in international settings, although there has been some research in this area as well. By far the majority of research studies in the international arena have been content-driven, but this chapter examines research findings exploring both the content and the process theories.

The next sections examine work motivation in an international setting by focusing on the three content theories that have received the greatest amount of attention: the hierarchy-of-needs theory, the two-factor motivation theory, and the achievement motivation theory. Then we focus on three process theories: equity theory, goal-setting theory, and expectancy theory. Each theory offers important insights regarding the motivation process for personnel in international settings.

■ The Hierarchy-of-Needs Theory

The hierarchy-of-needs theory is based primarily on work by Abraham Maslow, a well-known humanistic psychologist.[20] Maslow's hierarchy of needs has received a great deal of attention in the U.S. management and organizational behavior field and from international management researchers, who have attempted to show its value in understanding employee motivation throughout the world.[21]

The Maslow Theory

Maslow postulated that everyone has five basic needs which constitute a need hierarchy. In ascending order, beginning with the most basic need and going up to the highest, they are physiological, safety, social, esteem, and self-actualization needs. Figure 12–2 illustrates this hierarchy.

Physiological needs are basic physical needs for water, food, clothing, and shelter. Maslow contended that an individual's drive to satisfy these physiological needs is greater than the drive to satisfy any other type of need. In the context of work motivation, these physiological needs often are satisfied through the wages and salaries paid by the organization.

Safety needs are desires for security, stability, and absence of pain. Organizations typically help personnel to satisfy these needs through safety programs and equipment, and by providing security through medical insurance, unemployment and retirement plans, and similar benefits.

Social needs are needs to interact and affiliate with others and the need to feel wanted by others. This desire for "belongingness" often is satisfied on the job through social interaction within work groups in which people give and receive friendship. Social needs can be satisfied not only in formally assigned work groups but also in informal groups.

Esteem needs are needs for power and status. Individuals need to feel important and receive recognition from others. Promotions, awards, and feedback from the boss lead to feelings of self-confidence, prestige, and self-importance.

Self-actualization needs reflect a desire to reach one's full potential, to become everything that one is capable of becoming as a human being. In an organization, an individual may achieve self-actualization not so much through promotion but instead by mastering his or her environment and setting and achieving personal goals.[22]

Maslow's theory rests on a number of basic assumptions. One is that lower-level needs must be satisfied before higher-level needs can be achieved. A second is that a need that is satisfied no longer serves as a motivator. A third is that there are more ways to satisfy higher-level needs than there are ways to satisfy lower-level needs. Some of these assumptions came from Maslow's original work, some came from others' work, and some were later modifications by Maslow himself. These assumptions have driven much of the international research on the theory.

International Findings on Maslow's Theory

Do people throughout the world have needs that are similar to those described in Maslow's need hierarchy? Research generally shows that they do. For example, in a classic study

physiological needs
Basic physical needs for water, food, clothing, and shelter.

safety needs
Desires for security, stability, and the absence of pain.

social needs
Desires to interact and affiliate with others and to feel wanted by others.

esteem needs
Needs for power and status.

self-actualization needs
Desires to reach one's full potential, to become everything one is capable of becoming as a human being.

Figure 12–2

Maslow's Need Hierarchy

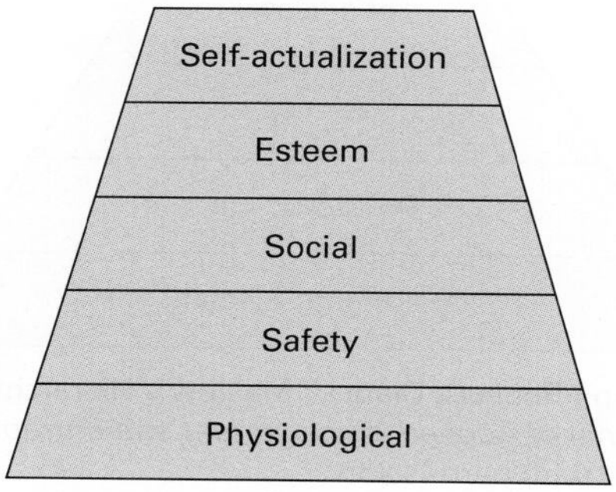

undertaken by Haire, Ghiselli, and Porter, a sample of 3,641 managers from 14 countries was surveyed. Although this study is quite dated it remains the most comprehensive and relevant one for showing different cultural impacts on employee motivation. Countries in this survey included the United States, Argentina, Belgium, Chile, Denmark, England, France, Germany, India, Italy, Japan, Norway, Spain, and Sweden.[23] With some minor modification, the researchers examined the need of satisfaction and need of importance of the four highest-level needs in the Maslow hierarchy. Esteem needs were divided into two groups: esteem and autonomy. The former included needs for self-esteem and prestige; the latter, desires for authority and for opportunities for independent thought and action.

The results of the Haire group's study showed that all these needs were important to the respondents across cultures. It should be remembered, however, that the subjects in this huge international study were managers, not rank-and-file employees. Upper-level needs were of particular importance to these managers. The findings for select country clusters (Latin Europe, United States/United Kingdom, and Nordic Europe) show that autonomy and self-actualization were the most important needs for the respondents. Interestingly, these same managers reported that those were the needs with which they were least satisfied, which led Haire and his associates to conclude:

> It appears obvious, from an organizational point of view, that business firms, no matter what country, will have to be concerned with the satisfaction of these needs for their managers and executives. Both types of needs were regarded as relatively quite important by managers, but, at the present time at least, the degree to which they were fulfilled did not live up to their expectations.[24]

Each country or geographic region appears to have its own need-satisfaction profile. When using this information to motivate managers, MNCs would be wise to consider the individual country's or region's profile and adjust their approach accordingly.

Some researchers have suggested that Maslow's hierarchy is too Western, and a more collectivist, Eastern perspective is necessary. Nevis believes that the Maslow hierarchy reflects a culture that is Western-oriented and focused on the inner needs of individuals.[25] Obviously, not all cultures function in this way: Asian cultures emphasize the needs of society. Nevis suggested that a Chinese hierarchy of needs would have four levels, which from lowest to highest would be (1) belonging (social), (2) physiological, (3) safety, and (4) self-actualization in the service of society, as seen in Figure 12–3. If this is true, MNCs attempting to do business in China must consider this revised hierarchy and determine how they can modify their compensation and job-design programs to accommodate the requisite motivational needs. In any event, Nevis's idea is worth considering, because it forces the multinational firm to address work motivation based on those cultural factors that are unique to its surroundings as opposed to a universal approach.

Figure 12–3

Collectivist Need Hierarchy

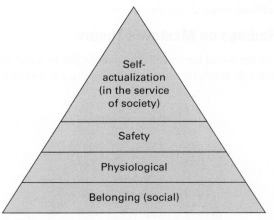

Source: Patrick A. Gambrel and Rebecca Cianci, "Maslow's Hierarchy of Needs: Does It Apply in a Collectivist Culture?" *Journal of Applied Management and Entrepreneurship* 8, no. 2 (April 2003), p. 157. Reprinted with permission.

Table 12–1
Top-Ranking Goals for Professional Technical Personnel from a Large Variety of Countries

Rank	Goal	Questionnaire Wording
1	Training	Have training opportunities (to improve your present skills or learn new skills)
2	Challenge	Have challenging work to do—work from which you can get a personal sense of accomplishment
3	Autonomy	Have considerable freedom to adopt your own approach to the job
4	Up-to-dateness	Keep up-to-date with the technical developments relating to your job
5	Use of skills	Fully use your skills and abilities on the job
6	Advancement	Have an opportunity for advancement to higher-level job
7	Recognition	Get the recognition you deserve when you do a good job
8	Earnings	Have an opportunity for high earnings
9	Cooperation	Work with people who cooperate well with one another
10	Manager	Have a good working relationship with your manager
11	Personal time	Have a job which leaves you sufficient time for your personal or family life
12	Friendly department	Work in a congenial and friendly atmosphere
13	Company contribution	Have a job which allows you to make a real contribution to the success of your company
14	Efficient department	Work in a department which is run efficiently
15	Security	Have the security that you will be able to work for your company as long as you want to
16	Desirable area	Live in an area desirable to you and your family
17	Benefits	Have good fringe benefits
18	Physical conditions	Have good physical working conditions (good ventilation and lighting, adequate work space, etc.)
19	Successful company	Work in a company which is regarded in your country as successful

Source: From Geert H. Hofstede, "The Colors of Collars," *Columbia Journal of World Business,* September 1972, p. 74. Copyright © 1972 Elsevier. Reprinted with permission.

The discussion so far indicates that even though the need-hierarchy concept is culturally specific, it offers a useful way to study and apply work motivation internationally. However, the well-known Dutch researcher Geert Hofstede and others have suggested that need-satisfaction profiles are not a very useful way of addressing motivation, because there often are so many different subcultures within any given country that it may be difficult or impossible to determine which culture variables are at work in any particular work setting. The Haire and follow-up studies dealt only with managers. Hofstede found that job categories are a more effective way of examining motivation. He reported a linkage between job types and levels and the need hierarchy. Based on survey results from over 60,000 people in more than 50 countries who were asked to rank a series of 19 work goals (see Tables 12–1 and 12–2), he found that:

- The top four goals ranked by professionals corresponded to "high" Maslow needs.
- The top four goals ranked by clerks corresponded to "middle" Maslow needs.
- The top four goals ranked by unskilled workers corresponded to "low" Maslow needs.
- Managers and technicians showed a mixed picture—having at least one goal in the "high" Maslow category.[26]

Table 12-2
The Four Most Important Goals Ranked by Occupational Group and Related to the Need Hierarchy

Goals Ranked in "Need Hierarchy"	Professionals (Research Laboratories)	Professionals (Branch Offices)	Managers	Technicians (Branch Offices)	Technicians (Manufacturing Plants)	Clerical Workers (Branch Offices)	Unskilled Workers (Manufacturing Plants)
High—Self-Actualization and Esteem Needs							
Challenge	1	2	1	3	3		
Training		1		1			
Autonomy	3	3	2				
Up-to-dateness	2	4		4			
Use of skills	4						
Middle—Social Needs							
Cooperation			3/4			1	
Manager			3/4		4	2	
Friendly department						3	
Efficient department						4	
Low—Security and Physiological Needs							
Security				2	1		2
Earnings					2		3
Benefits							4
Physical conditions							1

Source: From Geert H. Hofstede, "The Colors of Collars," *Columbia Journal of World Business*, September 1972, p. 78. Copyright © 1972 Elsevier. Reprinted with permission.

The tables from Hofstede's research show that self-actualization and esteem needs rank highest for professionals and managers, and that security, earnings, benefits, and physical working conditions are most important to low-level, unskilled workers. These findings illustrate that job categories and levels may have a dramatic effect on motivation and may well offset cultural considerations. As Hofstede noted, "There are greater differences between job categories than there are between countries when it comes to employee motivation."[27]

In deciding how to motivate human resources in different countries or help them to attain need satisfaction, researchers such as Hofstede recommend that MNCs focus most heavily on giving physical rewards to lower-level personnel and on creating for middle- and upper-level personnel a climate in which there is challenge, autonomy, the ability to use one's skills, and cooperation. Some companies are finding innovative ways to create motivation throughout the organization, from lower-level employees to middle management, by altering HR strategies. The International Management in Action on page 432, "McDonald's New Latin Flavor," provides an example of how focusing on employees' needs can both increase sales for the company and keep personnel on board.

Overall, there seems to be little doubt that need-hierarchy theory is useful in helping to identify motivational factors for international human resource management. This theory alone is not sufficient, however. Other content theories, such as the two-factor theory, add further understanding and effective practical application for motivating personnel.

■ The Two-Factor Theory of Motivation

The two-factor theory was formulated by well-known work-motivation theorist Frederick Herzberg and his colleagues. Like Maslow's theory, Herzberg's has been a focus of attention in international human resource management research over the years. This two-factor theory is closely linked to the need hierarchy.

The Herzberg Theory

The **two-factor theory of motivation** holds that two sets of factors influence job satisfaction: hygiene factors and motivators. The data from which the theory was developed were collected through a critical incident methodology that asked the respondents to answer two basic types of questions: (1) When did you feel particularly good about your job? (2) When did you feel exceptionally bad about your job? Responses to the first question generally related to job content and included factors such as achievement, recognition, responsibility, advancement, and the work itself. Herzberg called these job-content factors **motivators**. Responses to the second question related to job context and included factors such as salary, interpersonal relations, technical supervision, working conditions, and company policies and administration. Herzberg called these job-context variables **hygiene factors**. Table 12–3 lists both groups of factors. A close look at the two lists shows that the motivators are heavily psychological and relate to Maslow's upper-level needs and the hygiene factors are environmental in nature and relate more to Maslow's lower-level needs. Table 12–4 illustrates this linkage.

two-factor theory of motivation
A theory that identifies two sets of factors that influence job satisfaction: hygiene factors and motivators.

motivators
In the two-factor motivation theory, job-content factors such as achievement, recognition, responsibility, advancement, and the work itself.

hygiene factors
In the two-factor motivation theory, job-context variables such as salary, interpersonal relations, technical supervision, working conditions, and company policies and administration.

Table 12–3
Herzberg's Two-Factor Theory

Hygiene Factors	Motivators
Salary	Achievement
Technical supervision	Recognition
Company policies and administration	Responsibility
Interpersonal relations	Advancement
Working conditions	The work itself

International Management in Action

McDonald's Latin Flavor

www.hewittassociates.com/intl/na/en-us/
KnowledgeCenter/Magazine/vol9_iss1/
departments-upclose.html

McDonald's was once the leader of "fast and friendly" service, according to customer opinions of Latin American restaurants. Over time, the company saw its margins quickly shrinking, and in some areas of Latin America, competitors were edging ahead. With managerial turnover at 40 percent, and an astounding 90 to 100 percent turnover rate among employees between 16 and 18 years old, it was clear that motivation and morale were too low for a sustainable work environment. Clearly, something had to change.

In the past, organizational operations were carried out on a country-by-country basis, where initiatives were created to mirror the specific region in a way McDonald's calls "freedom within a framework." The stagnant sales and dissatisfied employees indicated that while the company could survive, altering initiatives could lead to further success. The human resources department recognized its crucial role in changing the atmosphere, and soon plans emerged. First, it modified the HR board to include one member from each country. This provided efficient communication, collaboration, and coordination among the Latin American countries. A three-year plan was then set in place, accentuating a continuous-improvement mentality which would keep processes and employee satisfaction in check. However, no plan is effective unless it is put into action.

McDonald's began a point reward system in which each store was allotted a base number of points, depending on sales for that store. A competitive structure was then furthered by allowing lower-level employees to increase points by filling out operational surveys, a tactic used to promote product knowledge and enhance employee skills. These points could then be cashed in for prizes such as backpacks and even an iPod. Furthermore, global recognition programs were instilled that rewarded top-performing employees. For example, McDonald's sent the top 300 performers from around the world to the Turin Winter Olympics, where crew members attended various McDonald's sponsored events and, of course, the Olympic games. Managers were also given the opportunity to profit from their actions, and the company stressed creativity throughout the process. Periodic meetings among regional managers allowed each to share "best practices" that have helped each store, and company strategies were often brought to the table to better inform those in charge. A Latin American Ray Kroc Award program was created to bring the top 1 percent of managers in the region to McDonald's headquarters, where participants had a chance to meet with top executives and engage in forums. The company further encouraged success through offering managers the opportunity to take business classes at surrounding universities and work toward a degree. Furthermore, managers engaged in training courses which shifted focus from administrative work to customers and employees under the assumption that given a more hands-on approach, personnel can better understand and achieve organizational and personal satisfaction goals.

McDonald's seems to have made all the right moves. Employees at every level are more motivated, and it shows in the numbers. After implementing the new HR strategy, sales in Latin America initially increased by 13 percent and continued to grow by 11.6 percent the next year. More crew members and managers remained at the stores as well, with turnover reducing to 70 percent and 25 percent, respectively. Furthermore, employee surveys indicated that there was an increase of overall commitment to the company by 9 percent, far surpassing the goal of 3–4 percent projected by the company.

Latin America sent a strong message to McDonald's without having to say a word. Personnel originally did not feel challenged and therefore sought other lucrative endeavors. McDonald's global strategy clearly was not universal, and in order to successfully integrate, local responses were imperative (see Chapter 8). The company's ability to balance its global HR standardization with regional cultures proved to be beneficial to all. Motivating personnel to achieve goals through rewards programs keeps morale high, and could save McDonald's a great deal of money as retention rates rise and the need for new worker training declines. Employees have had a taste of the revised HR programs, and it shows they like the new Latin flavor.

The two-factor theory holds that motivators and hygiene factors relate to employee satisfaction. This relationship is more complex than the traditional view that employees are either satisfied or dissatisfied. According to the two-factor theory, if hygiene factors are not taken care of or are deficient, there will be dissatisfaction (see Figure 12–4). Importantly, however, if hygiene factors are taken care of, there may be no dissatisfaction, but there also may be no satisfaction. Only when motivators are present will there be satisfaction. In short, hygiene factors help prevent dissatisfaction (thus the term hygiene, as it is used in the health field), but only motivators lead to satisfaction. Therefore, according to this theory, efforts to motivate human resources must provide recognition, a chance to achieve and grow, advancement, and interesting work.

Table 12–4 The Relationship between Maslow's Need Hierarchy and Herzberg's Two-Factor Theory	
Maslow's Need Hierarchy	**Herzberg's Two-Factor Theory**
Self-actualization	Motivators
	Achievement
	Recognition
	Responsibility
Esteem	Advancement
	The work itself
Social	Hygiene factors
	Salary
	Technical supervision
Safety	Company policies and administration
	Interpersonal relations
Physiological	Working conditions

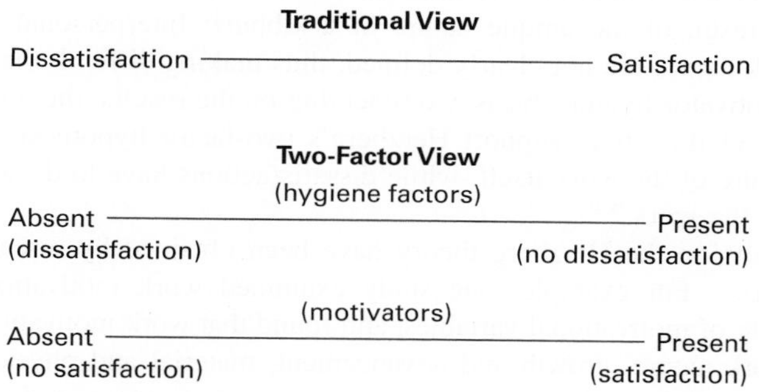

Traditional View

Dissatisfaction —————————————— Satisfaction

Two-Factor View

(hygiene factors)

Absent ——————————————— Present
(dissatisfaction)   (no dissatisfaction)

(motivators)

Absent ——————————————— Present
(no satisfaction)   (satisfaction)

Figure 12–4

Views of Satisfaction/ Dissatisfaction

Before examining the two-factor theory in the international arena, it is important to note that Herzberg's theory has been criticized by some organizational-behavior academics. One criticism involves the classification of money as a hygiene factor and not as a motivator. There is no universal agreement on this point. Some researchers report that salary is a motivator for some groups, such as blue-collar workers, or those for whom money is important for psychological reasons, such as a score-keeping method for their power and achievement needs.

A second line of criticism is whether Herzberg developed a total theory of motivation. Some argue that his findings actually support a theory of job satisfaction. In other words, if a company gives its people motivators, they will be satisfied; if it denies them motivators, they will not be satisfied; and if the hygiene factors are deficient, they may well be dissatisfied. Much of the international research on the two-factor theory discussed next is directed toward the satisfaction-dissatisfaction concerns rather than complex motivational needs, drives, and goals.

International Findings on Herzberg's Theory

International findings related to the two-factor theory fall into two categories. One consists of replications of Herzberg's research in a particular country. This research asks whether managers in country X give answers similar to those in Herzberg's original studies. In the other category are cross-cultural studies that focus on job satisfaction. This research asks what factors cause job satisfaction and how these responses differ from country to country. The latter studies are not a direct extension of the two-factor theory, but they do offer insights regarding the importance of job satisfaction in international human resource management.

Two-Factor Replications A number of research efforts have been undertaken to replicate the two-factor theory, and in the main, they support Herzberg's findings. George Hines, for example, surveyed 218 middle managers and 196 salaried employees in New Zealand using ratings of 12 job factors and overall job satisfaction. Based on these findings, he concluded that "the Herzberg model appears to have validity across occupational levels."[28]

Another similar study was conducted among 178 managers in Greece who were Greek nationals. Overall, this study found that Herzberg's two-factor theory of job satisfaction generally held true for these managers. The researchers summarized their findings as follows:

> As far as job dissatisfaction was concerned, no motivator was found to be a source of dissatisfaction. Only categories traditionally designated as hygiene factors were reported to be sources of dissatisfaction for participating Greek managers. . . . Moreover . . . motivators . . . were more important contributors to job satisfaction than to dissatisfaction . . . (66.8% of the traditional motivator items . . . were related to satisfaction and 31.1% were related to dissatisfaction). Traditional hygiene factors, as a group, were more important contributors to job dissatisfaction than to job satisfaction (64% of the responses were related to dissatisfaction and 36% were related to satisfaction).[29]

Another study tested the Herzberg theory in an Israeli kibbutz (communal work group). Motivators there tended to be sources of satisfaction and hygiene factors sources of dissatisfaction, although interpersonal relations (a hygiene factor) were regarded more as a source of satisfaction than of dissatisfaction. The researcher was careful to explain this finding as a result of the unique nature of a kibbutz: Interpersonal relations of a work and nonwork nature are not clearly defined, thus making difficult the separation of this factor on a motivator-hygiene basis. Commenting on the results, the researcher noted that "the findings of this study support Herzberg's two-factor hypothesis: Satisfactions arise from the nature of the work itself, while dissatisfactions have to do with the conditions surrounding the work."[30]

Similar results on the Herzberg theory have been obtained by research studies in developing countries. For example, one study examined work motivation in Zambia, employing a variety of motivational variables, and found that work motivation was a result of six factors: work nature, growth and advancement, material and physical provisions, relations with others, fairness/unfairness in organizational practices, and personal problems. These variables are presented in Figure 12–5. They illustrate that, in general, the two-factor theory of motivation was supported in this African country.[31] Furthermore, a

Figure 12–5

Motivation Factors in Zambia

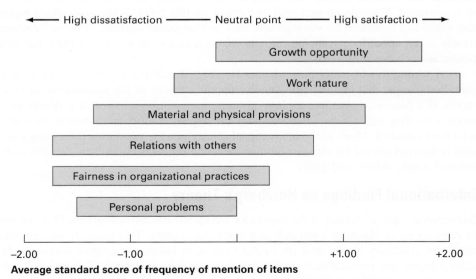

Average standard score of frequency of mention of items

Source: Adapted from Peter D. Machungwa and Neal Schmitt, "Work Motivation in a Developing Country," *Journal of Applied Psychology,* February 1983, p. 41. Reprinted with permission of the American Psychological Association and the author.

study performed in Romania indicated that hygiene factors (salary, working conditions, and supervision), though important, were not the driving forces in deciding to accept a senior manager position. The most important aspects of a job to Romanians were how much recognition and appreciation they would receive. This was followed by a desire for salary incentives, though the need for increased knowledge and skills, along with being involved in teams and improving competence and self development, was also significant.[32]

Cross-Cultural Job-Satisfaction Studies   A number of cross-cultural studies related to job satisfaction also have been conducted in recent years. These comparisons show that Herzberg-type motivators tend to be of more importance to job satisfaction than are hygiene factors. A comparison from selected Herzberg studies is provided in Figure 12–6.

Figure 12–6	Selected Countries Hygiene and Motivation

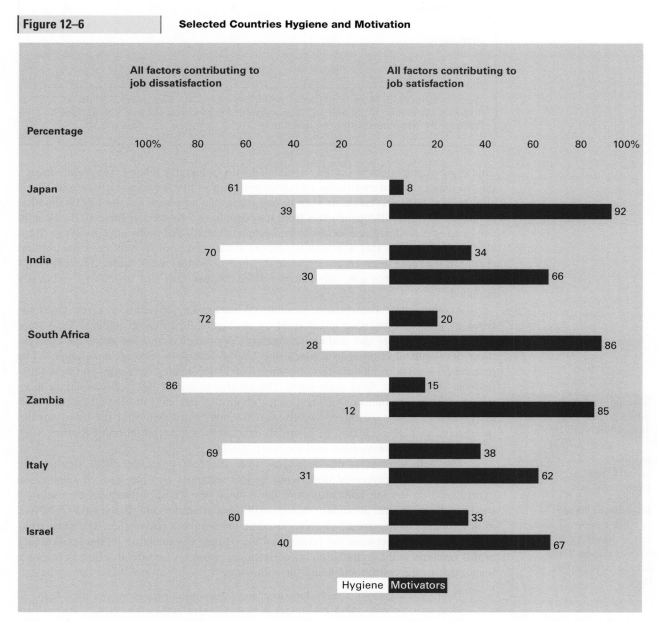

Source: Reprinted by permission of *Harvard Business Review* from "One More Time: How Do You Motivate Employees?" by Frederick Herzberg, September–October 1987, p. 118. Copyright © 1987 by the Harvard Business School Publishing Corporation; all rights reserved.

Table 12–5
The Results of Administering the JOI to Four Cross-Cultural Groups

	Relative Rankings			
	United States (*n* = 49)	Australia (*n* = 58)	Canada (*n* = 25)	Singapore (*n* = 33)
Achievement	2	2	2	2
Responsibility	3	3	3	3
Growth	1	1	1	1
Recognition	10	10	8	9
Job status	7	7	7	7
Relationships	5	5	10	6
Pay	8	8	6	8
Security	9	9	9	10
Family	6	6	5	5
Hobby	4	4	4	4

Source: From G. E. Popp, H. J. Davis, and T. T. Herbert, "An International Study of Intrinsic Motivation Composition," *Management International Review,* Vol. 26, No. 3 1986, p. 31. Reprinted with permission.

This shows that hygiene is strongly associated with factors that relate to job dissatisfaction (or avoidance of), and motivation correlates with factors that drive job satisfaction. This is also evident in the research, as seen in one study that administered the Job Orientation Inventory (JOI) to MBA candidates from four countries.[33] As seen in Table 12–5, the relative ranking placed hygiene factors at the bottom of the list and motivators at the top. What also is significant is that although Singapore students do not fit into the same cultural cluster as the other three groups in the study, their responses were similar. These findings provide evidence that job-satisfaction-related factors may not always be culturally bounded.[34]

Another, more comprehensive study of managerial job attitudes investigated the types of job outcomes that are desired by managers in different cultures. Data were gathered from lower- and middle-management personnel who were attending management development courses in Canada, the United Kingdom, France, and Japan.[35] The researchers sought to identify the importance of 15 job-related outcomes and how satisfied the respondents were with each. The results indicated that job content is more important than job context. Organizationally controlled factors (**job-context factors**, such as conditions, hours, earnings, security, benefits, and promotions) for the most part did not receive as high a ranking as internally mediated factors (**job-content factors**, such as responsibility, achievement, and the work itself).

The data also show that managers from the four countries differ significantly regarding both the perceived importance of job outcomes and the level of satisfaction experienced on the job with respect to these outcomes. These differences are useful in shedding light on what motivates managers in these countries and, in the case of MNCs, in developing country-specific human resource management approaches. The most striking contrasts were between the French and the British. Commenting on the applicability of this research to the formulation of motivational strategies for effective human resource management, the researchers noted the following:

> The results suggest . . . that efforts to improve managerial performance in the UK should focus on job content rather than on job context. Changes in the nature of the work itself are likely to be more valued than changes in organizational or interpersonal factors. Job enrichment programs which help individuals design their own goals and tasks, and which downplay formal rules and structure, are more likely to improve performance in an intrinsically

job-context factors
In work motivation, those factors controlled by the organization, such as conditions, hours, earnings, security, benefits, and promotions.

job-content factors
In work motivation, those factors internally controlled, such as responsibility, achievement, and the work itself.

oriented society such as Britain, where satisfaction tends to be derived from the job itself, than in France, where job context factors such as security and fringe benefits are more highly valued. The results suggest that French managers may be more effectively motivated by changing job situation factors, as long as such changes are explicitly linked to performance.[36]

In summary, Herzberg's two-factor theory appears to reinforce Maslow's need hierarchy through its research support in the international arena. As with the application of Maslow's theory, however, MNCs would be wise to apply motivation-hygiene theory on a country-by-country or a regional basis. Although there are exceptions, such as France, there seems to be little doubt that job-content factors are more important than job-context factors in motivating not only managers but also lower-level employees around the world, as Hofstede pointed out.

■ Achievement Motivation Theory

In addition to the need-hierarchy and two-factor theories of work motivation, achievement motivation theory has been given a relatively great amount of attention in the international arena. Achievement motivation theory has been more applied to the actual practice of management than the others, and it has been the focus of some interesting international research.

The Background of Achievement Motivation Theory

Achievement motivation theory holds that individuals can have a need to get ahead, to attain success, and to reach objectives. Note that like the upper-level needs in Maslow's hierarchy or like Herzberg's motivators, the need for achievement is learned. Therefore, in the United States, where entrepreneurial effort is encouraged and individual success promoted, the probability is higher that there would be a greater percentage of people with high needs for achievement than, for example, in China, Russia, or Eastern European countries,[37] where cultural values have not traditionally supported individual, entrepreneurial efforts.

Researchers such as the late Harvard psychologist David McClelland have identified a characteristic profile of high achievers.[38] First, these people like situations in which they take personal responsibility for finding solutions to problems. They want to win because of their own efforts, not because of luck or chance. Second, they tend to be moderate risk takers rather than high or low risk takers. If a decision-making situation appears to be too risky, they will learn as much as they can about the environment and try to reduce the probability of failure. In this way, they turn a high-risk situation into a moderate-risk situation. If the situation is too low risk, however, there usually is an accompanying low reward, and they tend to avoid situations with insufficient incentive.

Third, high achievers want concrete feedback on their performance. They like to know how well they are doing, and they use this information to modify their actions. High achievers tend to gravitate into vocations such as sales, which provide them with immediate, objective feedback about how they are doing. Finally, and this has considerable implications for human resource management, high achievers often tend to be loners, and not team players. They do not form warm, close relationships, and they have little empathy for others' problems. This last characteristic may distract from their effectiveness as managers of people.

Researchers have discovered a number of ways to develop high-achievement needs in people. These involve teaching the individual to do the following: (1) obtain feedback on performance and use this information to channel efforts into areas where success likely will be attained; (2) emulate people who have been successful achievers; (3) develop an internal desire for success and challenges; and (4) daydream in positive terms by picturing oneself as successful in the pursuit of important objectives.[39] Simply put, the need for achievement can be taught and learned.

Before examining international research on achievement motivation theory, it is important to realize that the theory has been cited as having a number of shortcomings. One is that it relies almost solely on the projective personality Thematic Apperception Test (TAT) to measure individual achievement, and a number of recent studies have questioned the validity and reliability of this approach.[40] Another concern is that

achievement motivation theory
A theory which holds that individuals can have a need to get ahead, to attain success, and to reach objectives.

achievement motivation is grounded in individual effort, but in many countries group harmony and cooperation are critically important to success. Simply put, the original theory does not satisfactorily explain the need for achievement in cultures in which individual accomplishment is neither valued nor rewarded.[41]

International Findings on Achievement Motivation Theory

A number of international researchers have investigated the role and importance of high-achievement needs in human resource management.[42]

Early research among Polish industrialists found that many of them were high achievers.[43] The average high-achievement score was 6.58, quite close to U.S. managers' average score of 6.74. This led some to conclude there is evidence that managers in countries as diverse as the United States and those of the former Soviet bloc in Central Europe have high needs for achievement.[44] In later studies, however, researchers did not find a high need for achievement in Central European countries. One study, for example, surveyed Czech industrial managers and found that the average high-achievement score was 3.32, considerably lower than that of U.S. managers.[45] Because the need for achievement is learned, differences in these samples can be attributed to cultural differences. By the same token, given the dramatic, revolutionary changes that occurred in Central and Eastern Europe with the end of communism and of centrally planned economies, one could argue that the achievement needs of postcommunist Europeans, now able to be freely expressed, may well be high today. The important point is that because achievement is a learned need and thus largely determined by the prevailing culture, it is not universal and may change over time.

The ideal profile for high-achieving societies can be described in terms of the cultural dimensions examined in Chapter 4. In particular, two cultural dimensions identified by Hofstede in Chapter 4—uncertainty avoidance and masculinity—best describe high-achieving societies (see Figure 12–7). These societies tend to have weak uncertainty avoidance. People in high-achieving societies are not afraid to take at least moderate risks or to live with ambiguity. These societies also tend to have moderate-to-high masculinity, as measured by the high importance they assign to the acquisition of money and other

Figure 12–7

Selected Countries on the Uncertainty-Avoidance and Masculinity Scales

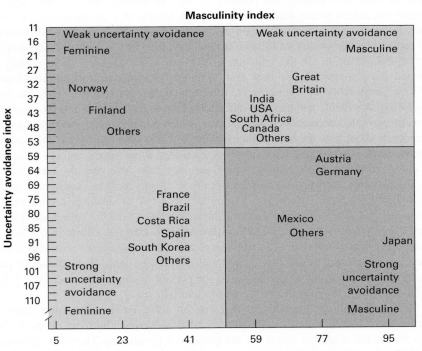

Source: Adapted from Geert Hofstede, "The Cultural Relativity of Organizational Practices and Theories," *Journal of International Business Studies*, Fall 1983, p. 86.

physical assets and the low value they give to caring for others and for the quality of work life. This combination (see the upper right quadrant of Figure 12–7) is found almost exclusively in Anglo countries or in nations that have been closely associated with them through colonization or treaty, such as India, Singapore, and Hong Kong (countries associated with Great Britain) and the Philippines (associated with the United States).

Countries that fall into one of the other three quadrants of Figure 12–7 will not be very supportive of the high need for achievement. MNCs in these geographic regions, therefore, would be wise to formulate a human resource management strategy for either changing the situation or adjusting to it. If they decide to change the situation, they must design jobs to fit the needs of their people or put people through an achievement motivation training program to create high-achieving managers and entrepreneurs.

A number of years ago, McClelland was able to demonstrate the success of such achievement motivation training programs with underdeveloped countries. For example, in India, he conducted such a program with considerable success. In following up these Indian trainees over the subsequent 6 to 10 months, he found that two-thirds were unusually active in achievement-oriented activities. They had started new businesses, investigated new product lines, increased profits, or expanded their present organizations. For example, the owner of a small radio store opened a paint and varnish factory after completing the program. McClelland concluded that this training appeared to have doubled the natural rate of unusual achievement-oriented activity in the group studied.[46]

If international human resource managers cannot change the situation or train the participants, then they must adjust to the specific conditions of the country and formulate a motivation strategy that is based on those conditions. In many cases, this requires consideration of a need-hierarchy approach blended with an achievement approach. Hofstede offers such advice in dealing with the countries in the various quadrants of Figure 12–7:

> The countries on the feminine side . . . distinguish themselves by focusing on quality of life rather than on performance and on relationships between people rather than on money and things. This means social motivation: quality of life plus security and quality of life plus risk.[47]

In the case of countries that are attempting to introduce changes that incorporate values from one of the other quadrants in Figure 12–7, the challenge can be even greater.

In summary, achievement motivation theory provides additional insights into the motivation of personnel around the world. Like the need-hierarchy and two-factor theories, however, achievement motivation theory must be modified to meet the specific needs of the local culture. The culture of many countries does not support high achievement. However, the cultures of Anglo countries and those that reward entrepreneurial effort do support achievement motivation, and their human resources should probably be managed accordingly.

■ Select Process Theories

While content theories are useful in explaining motivation for managing international personnel, process theories can also lead to better understanding. As noted earlier, the process theories explain how employee behavior is initiated, redirected, and halted; and some of these theories have been used to examine motivation in the international arena. Among the most widely recognized are equity theory, goal-setting theory, and expectancy theory. The following briefly examines each of these three and their relevance to international human resource management.

Equity Theory

Equity theory focuses on how motivation is affected by people's perception of how fairly they are being treated. The theory holds that if people perceive that they are being treated equitably, this perception will have a positive effect on their job performance and satisfaction, and there is no need to strive for equity. Conversely, if they believe they are not being treated fairly, especially in relation to relevant others, they will be dissatisfied,

equity theory
A process theory that focuses on how motivation is affected by people's perception of how fairly they are being treated.

and this belief will have a negative effect on their job performance and they will strive to restore equity.

There is considerable research to support the fundamental equity principle in Western work groups.[48] However, when the theory is examined on an international basis, the results are mixed. Yuchtman, for example, studied equity perceptions among managers and nonmanagers in an Israeli kibbutz production unit.[49] In this setting everyone was treated the same, but the managers reported lower satisfaction levels than the workers. The managers perceived their contributions to be greater than those of any other group in the kibbutz. As a result of this perception, they felt that they were undercompensated for their value and effort. These findings support the basic concepts of equity theory.

One study, which assumed that Western thought was synonymous with individualism and Eastern thought with collectivism, indicated that there are both similarities and differences between how cultures view the equity model. The model consists of employee inputs, subsequent outcomes, areas employees choose to compare the self to, and the motivation to change any perceived inequity that may exist between the self and the point of comparison (such as co-workers or employees in similar industries and positions).[50] A summary comparison is provided in Table 12–6.

Table 12–6
Individualistic and Collectivist Approaches to Equity Model

	Western (Individualistic) Cultures	Eastern (Collectivist) Cultures
Inputs	Effort Intelligence Education Experience Skill Social status	Loyalty Support Respect Organizational tenure Organizational status Group member
Outcomes	Pay Autonomy Seniority status Fringe benefits Job status Status symbol	Harmony Social status Acceptance Solidarity Cohesion
Comparisons	*Situation* Physical proximity Job facet *Personal* Gender Age Position Professionalism	*Organizational Group* Similar industry Similar product/service *In-Group* Status Job Tenure Age Position
Motivation to Reduce Inequity	Change personal inputs Provoke alternate outcomes Psychologically distort inputs and outcomes Leave the field Change points of comparison	*Organizational Group* Change points of comparison Psychologically distort inputs and outcomes *In-Group* Alter inputs of self Psychologically distort inputs and outcomes

Source: Adapted from Paul A. Fadil et al., "Equity or Equality? . . ." *Cross-Cultural Management* 12, no. 4 (2005), p. 23.

On the other hand, a number of studies cast doubt on the relevance of equity theory in explaining motivation in an international setting. Perhaps the biggest shortcoming is that the theory appears to be culture-bound. For example, equity theory postulates that when people are not treated fairly, they will take steps to reduce the inequity by, for example, doing less work, filing a grievance, or getting a transfer to another department. In Asia and the Middle East, however, employees often readily accept inequitable treatment in order to preserve group harmony. Additionally, in countries such as Japan and Korea, men and women typically receive different pay for doing the same work, yet because of years of cultural conditioning, women may not feel they are being treated inequitably.[51] Some researchers have explained this finding by suggesting that these women compare themselves only to other women and in this comparison feel they are being treated equitably. While this may be true, the results still point to the fact that equity theory is not universally applicable in explaining motivation and job satisfaction. In short, although the theory may help explain why "equal pay for equal work" is a guiding motivation principle in countries such as the United States and Canada, it may have limited value in other areas of the world, including Asia and Latin America, where compensation differences based on gender, at least traditionally, have been culturally acceptable.

Goal-Setting Theory

Goal-setting theory focuses on how individuals go about setting goals and responding to them and the overall impact of this process on motivation. Specific areas that are given attention in goal-setting theory include the level of participation in setting goals, goal difficulty, goal specificity, and the importance of objective, timely feedback to progress toward goals. Unlike many theories of motivation, goal setting has been continually refined and developed.[52] There is considerable research evidence showing that employees perform extremely well when they are assigned specific and challenging goals that they have had a hand in setting.[53] But most of these studies have been conducted in the United States, while few of them have been carried out in other cultures.[54] One study that did examine goal setting in an international setting looked at Norwegian employee participation in goal setting.[55] The researchers found that the Norwegian employees shunned participation and preferred to have their union representatives work with management in determining work goals. This led the researchers to conclude that individual participation in goal setting was seen as inconsistent with the prevailing philosophy of participation through union representatives. Unlike the United States, where employee participation in setting goals is motivational, it had no value for the Norwegian employees in this study.

Similar results to the Norwegian study have been reported by Earley, who found that workers in the U.K. responded more favorably to a goal-setting program sponsored by the union stewards than to one sponsored by management. This led Earley to conclude that the transferability across cultural settings of management concepts such as participation in goal setting may well be affected by the prevailing work norms.[56] In order to further test this proposition, Erez and Earley studied American and Israeli subjects and found that participative strategies led to higher levels of goal acceptance and performance in both cultures than did strategies in which objectives were assigned by higher-level management.[57] In other words, the value of goal-setting theory may well be determined by culture. In the case, for example, of Asian and Latin work groups, where collectivism is very high, the theory may have limited value for MNC managers in selected countries.

Expectancy Theory

Expectancy theory postulates that motivation is largely influenced by a multiplicative combination of a person's belief that (a) effort will lead to performance, (b) performance will lead to specific outcomes, and (c) the outcomes will be of value to the individual.[58] In addition, the theory predicts that high performance followed by high rewards will lead

goal-setting theory
A process theory that focuses on how individuals go about setting goals and responding to them and the overall impact of this process on motivation.

expectancy theory
A process theory that postulates that motivation is influenced by a person's belief that (a) effort will lead to performance, (b) performance will lead to specific outcomes, and (c) the outcomes will be of value to the individual.

to high satisfaction.[59] Does this theory have universal application? Eden used it in studying workers in an Israeli kibbutz and found some support;[60] and Matsui and colleagues reported that the theory could be applied successfully in Japan.[61] On the other hand, it is important to remember that expectancy theory is based on employees having considerable control over their environment, a condition that does not exist in many cultures (e.g., Asia). In particular, in societies where people believe that much of what happens is beyond their control, this theory may have less value. It would seem that expectancy theory is best able to explain worker motivation in cultures where there is a strong internal locus of control (e.g., in the United States). In short, the theory seems culture-bound, and international managers must be aware of this limitation in their efforts to apply this theory to motivate human resources.

■ Motivation Applied: Job Design, Work Centrality, and Rewards

Content and process theories provide important insights into and understanding of ways to motivate human resources in international management. So, too, do applied concepts such as job design, work centrality, and rewards.

Job Design

job design
A job's content, the methods that are used on the job, and the way the job relates to other jobs in the organization.

Job design consists of a job's content, the methods that are used on the job, and the way in which the job relates to other jobs in the organization. Job design typically is a function of the work to be done and the way in which management wants it to be carried out. These factors help explain why the same type of work may have a different impact on the motivation of human resources in various parts of the world and result in differing qualities of work life.

Quality of Work Life: The Impact of Culture Quality of work life (QWL) is not the same throughout the world. For example, assembly-line employees in Japan work at a rapid pace for hours and have very little control over their work activities. In Sweden, assembly-line employees work at a more relaxed pace and have a great deal of control over their work activities. U.S. assembly-line employees are somewhere in between; they typically work at a pace that is less demanding than that in Japan but more structured than that in Sweden.

What accounts for these differences? One answer is found in the culture of the country. QWL is directly related to culture. Table 12–7 compares the United States, Japan, and Sweden along the four cultural dimensions described in Chapter 4. A brief look shows that each country has a different cultural profile, helping explain why

---

Table 12–7
Cultural Dimensions in Japan, Sweden, and the United States

Cultural Dimension	Degree of Dimension					
	High/Strong X ←		**Moderate** — X —		**Low/Weak** → X	
Uncertainty avoidance		J			USA	S
Individualism	USA		S		J	
Power distance			J	USA	S	
Masculinity	J			USA		S

Source: From Geert Hofstede, "The Cultural Relativity of the Quality of Life Concept," *Academy of Management Review,* July 1984, pp. 391, 393. Reproduced with permission of Academy of Management via Copyright Clearance Center.

similar jobs may be designed quite differently from country to country. Assembly-line work provides a good basis for comparison.

In Japan, there is strong uncertainty avoidance. The Japanese like to structure tasks so there is no doubt regarding what is to be done and how it is to be done. Individualism is low, so there is strong emphasis on security, and individual risk taking is discouraged. The power-distance index is high, so Japanese workers are accustomed to taking orders from those above them. The masculinity index for the Japanese is high, which shows that they put a great deal of importance on money and other material symbols of success. In designing jobs, the Japanese structure tasks so that the work is performed within these cultural constraints. Japanese managers work their employees extremely hard. Although Japanese workers contribute many ideas through the extensive use of quality circles, Japanese managers give them very little say in what actually goes on in the organization (in contrast to the erroneous picture often portrayed by the media, which presents Japanese firms as highly democratic and managed from the bottom up)[62] and depend heavily on monetary rewards, as reflected by the fact that the Japanese rate money as an important motivator more than the workers in any other industrialized country do.

In Sweden, uncertainty avoidance is low, so job descriptions, policy manuals, and similar work-related materials are more open-ended or general in contrast with the detailed procedural materials developed by the Japanese. In addition, Swedish workers are encouraged to make decisions and to take risks. Swedes exhibit a moderate-to-high degree of individualism, which is reflected in their emphasis on individual decision making (in contrast to the collective or group decision making of the Japanese). They have a weak power-distance index, which means that Swedish managers use participative approaches in leading their people. Swedes score low on masculinity, which means that interpersonal relations and the ability to interact with other workers and discuss job-related matters are important. These cultural dimensions result in job designs that are markedly different from those in Japan.

Cultural dimensions in the United States are closer to those of Sweden than to those of Japan. In addition, except for individualism, the U.S. profile is between that of Sweden and Japan (again see Table 12–7). This means that job design in U.S. assembly plants tends to be more flexible or unstructured than that of the Japanese but more rigid than that of the Swedes.

This same pattern holds for many other jobs in these three countries. All job designs tend to reflect the cultural values of the country. The challenge for MNCs is to adjust job design to meet the needs of the host country's culture. For example, when Japanese firms enter the United States, they often are surprised to learn that people resent close control. In fact, there is evidence that the most profitable Japanese-owned companies in the United States are those that delegate a high degree of authority to their U.S. managers.[63] Similarly, Japanese firms operating in Sweden find that quality of work life is a central concern for the personnel and that a less structured, highly participative management style is needed for success. Some of the best examples of efforts to integrate job designs with culture and personality are provided by sociotechnical job designs.

Sociotechnical Job Designs

Sociotechnical designs are job designs that blend personnel and technology. The objective of these designs is to integrate new technology into the workplace so that workers accept and use it to increase overall productivity. Because new technology often requires people to learn new methods and, in some cases, work faster, employee resistance is common. Effective sociotechnical design can overcome these problems. There are a number of good examples, and perhaps the most famous is that of Volvo, the Swedish automaker.

Sociotechnical changes reflective of the cultural values of the workers were introduced at Volvo's Kalmar plant. Autonomous work groups were formed and given the authority to elect their own supervisors as well as to schedule, assign, and inspect their

sociotechnical designs
Job designs that blend personnel and technology.

own work. Each group was allowed to work at its own pace, although there was an overall output objective for the week, and each group was expected to attain this goal.[64] The outcome was very positive and resulted in Volvo building another plant that employed even more sophisticated sociotechnical job-design concepts. Volvo's plant layout, however, did not prevent the firm from having some problems. Both Japanese and North American automakers were able to produce cars in far less time, putting Volvo at a cost disadvantage. As a result, stagnant economies in Asia, coupled with weakening demand for Volvo's product lines in both Europe and the United States, resulted in the firm laying off workers and taking steps to increase its efficiency. More recently, Volvo's performance has rebounded, bolstered in part by its truck sales and reputation for safety in its passenger car division.[65]

Without sacrificing efficiency, other firms have introduced sociotechnical designs for better blending of their personnel and technology. A well-known U.S. example is General Foods, which set up autonomous groups at its Topeka, Kansas, plant to produce Gaines pet food. Patterned after the Volvo example, the General Foods project allowed workers to share responsibility and work in a highly democratic environment. Other U.S. firms also have opted for a self-managed team approach. In fact, research reports that the concept of multifunctional teams with autonomy for generating successful product innovation is more widely used by successful U.S., Japanese, and European firms than any other teamwork concept.[66] Its use must be tempered by the cultural situation, however. And even the widely publicized General Foods project at Topeka had some problems. Some former employees indicate that the approach steadily eroded and that some managers were openly hostile because it undermined their power, authority, and decision-making flexibility. The most effective job design will be a result of both the job to be done and the cultural values that support a particular approach.[67] For MNCs, the challenge will be to make the fit between the design and the culture.

At the same time, it is important to realize that functional job descriptions now are being phased out in many MNCs and replaced by more of a process approach. The result is a more horizontal network that relies on communication and teamwork. This approach also is useful in helping create and sustain partnerships with other firms.

Work Centrality

work centrality
The importance of work in an individual's life relative to other areas of interest.

Work centrality, which can be defined as the importance of work in an individual's life relative to his or her other areas of interest (family, church, leisure), provides important insights into how to motivate human resources in different cultures.[68] After conducting a review of the literature, Bhagat and associates found that Japan has the highest level of work centrality, followed by moderately high levels for Israel, average levels for the United States and Belgium, moderately low levels for the Netherlands and Germany, and low levels for Britain.[69] These findings indicate that successful multinationals in Japan must realize that although work is an integral part of the Japanese lifestyle, work in the United States must be more balanced with a concern for other interests. Unfortunately, this is likely to become increasingly more difficult for Japanese firms in Japan because stagnant population growth is creating a shortage of personnel. As a result, growing numbers of Japanese firms are now trying to push the mandatory retirement age to 65 from 60 and, except for workers in the United States, Japanese workers put in the most hours.[70]

Value of Work   Although work is an important part of the lifestyles of most people, this emphasis can be attributed to a variety of conditions. For example, one reason that Americans and Japanese work such long hours is that the cost of living is high, and hourly employees cannot afford to pass up the opportunity for extra money. Among salaried employees who are not paid extra, most Japanese managers expect their subordinates to stay late at work, and overtime has become a requirement of the job. Moreover, there is recent evidence that Japanese workers may do far less work in a business day than outsiders would suspect.

Many people are unaware of these facts and have misperceptions of why the Japanese and Americans work so hard and the importance of work to them. The same is true of Germans and Americans. In recent years, the number of hours worked annually by German workers has been declining, while the number for Americans has been on the rise. What accounts for this trend? Some observers have explained it in cultural terms, noting that Germans place high value on lifestyle and often prefer leisure to work, while their American counterparts are just the opposite. In fact, research reveals that culture may have little to do with it. A study by the National Bureau of Economic Research (NBER) found a far wider range of wages within American companies than in German firms, and this large pay disparity has created incentives for American employees to work harder. For instance, Table 12–8 compares U.S. and German salaries based on a "Step 1" or entry-level pay scale. In particular, many U.S. workers believe that if they work harder, their chances of getting pay hikes and promotions will increase, and there are historical data to support this belief. An analysis of worker histories in the United States and Germany led NBER researchers to estimate that American workers who increase their working time by 10 percent, for example, from 2,000 to 2,200 hours annually, will raise their future earnings by about 1 percent for each year in which they put in extra hours.

Obviously, factors other than culture—such as gender, industry, and organizational characteristics—influence the degree and type of work centrality within a country. These factors, in turn, interact with national cultural characteristics. One study of work centrality examined the effect of parenthood on men and on women regarding the centrality of and investment in work and family in the bicultural context of the Israeli high-tech industry (i.e., the family-centered Israeli society on the one hand, and the masculine work-centered high-tech industry on the other hand). This study found a contrasting parenthood effect on men and women. Fathers showed higher relative work centrality than childless men, whereas mothers showed lower relative work centrality than women without children. Fathers invested more weekly hours in paid work than childless men, whereas mothers invested fewer weekly hours in paid work than women without children.

Table 12–8
2013 Annual Salaries: U.S. and Germany

Grade	U.S. Salary (Annual, in US$)	German Salary (Annual, in US$)
1	17,803	23,722
2	20,017	29,478
3	21,840	31,970
4	24,518	32,486
5	27,431	34,117
6	30,577	35,662
7	33,979	36,349
8	37,631	38,842
9	41,563	41,505
10	45,771	47,001
11	50,287	48,718
12	60,274	50,518
13	71,674	56,360
14	84,697	61,084
15	99,628	67,439

Source: http://www.opm.gov/policy-data-oversight/pay-leave/salaries-wages#url=2013 and calculated from http://oeffentlicher-dienst.info/beamte/land/.

Doing business in Japan can be a real killer. Overwork, or *karoshi,* as it is called in Japan, claims 10,000 lives annually in this hard-driving, competitive economic society according to Hiroshi Kawahito, a lawyer who founded the National Defense Council for Victims of Karoshi.

One of the cases is Jun Ishii of Mitsui & Company. Ishii was one of the firm's only speakers of Russian. In the year before his death, Ishii made 10 trips to Russia, totaling 115 days. No sooner would he arrive home from one trip than the company would send him out again. The grueling pace took its toll. While on a trip, Ishii collapsed and died of a heart attack. His widow filed a lawsuit against Mitsui & Company, charging that her husband had been worked to death. Tokyo labor regulators ruled that Ishii had indeed died of karoshi, and the government now is paying annual worker's compensation to the widow. The company also cooperated and agreed to make a one-time payment of $240,000.

The reason that the case received so much publicity is that this is one of the few instances in which the government ruled that a person died from overwork. Now regulators are expanding karoshi compensation to salaried as well as hourly workers. This development is receiving the attention of the top management of many Japanese multinationals, and some Japanese MNCs are beginning to take steps to prevent the likelihood of overwork. For example, Mitsui & Company now assesses its managers based on how well they set overtime hours, keep subordinates healthy, and encourage workers to take vacations. Matsushita Electric has extended vacations from 16 days annually to 23 days and now requires all workers to take this time off. One branch of Nippon Telegraph & Telephone found that stress made some workers irritable and ill, so the company initiated periods of silent meditation. Other companies are following suit, although there still are many Japanese who work well over 2,500 hours a year and feel both frustrated and burned out by job demands.

On the positive side, the Ishii case likely will bring about some improvements in working conditions for many Japanese employees. Experts admit, however, that it is difficult to determine if karoshi is caused by work demands or by private, late-night socializing that may be work-related. Other possible causes include high stress, lack of exercise, and fatty diets, but whatever the cause, one thing is clear: More and more Japanese families no longer are willing to accept the belief that karoshi is a risk that all employees must accept. Work may be a killer, but this outcome can be prevented through more carefully implemented job designs and work processes.

At the same time, recent reports show that there is still a long way to go. In Saku, Japan, for example, the city's main hospital has found that 32 percent of the patients hospitalized in the internal medicine and psychiatric wards are being treated for chronic fatigue syndrome, a diagnosis that is made only after six months of severe, continuous fatigue in the absence of any organic illness. Japanese doctors attribute this explosion of chronic fatigue syndrome to stress. Moreover, during the prolonged economic downturn, a growing number of businesspeople found themselves suffering from these symptoms. And to make matters worse, there is growing concern about alcoholism among workers. Over the past four decades, per capita alcohol consumption in most countries has declined, but in Japan it has risen fourfold. The per capita consumption of alcohol in Japan is equal to that in the United States. Even this comparison is misleading because researchers have found that most Japanese women do not drink at all, but Japanese men in their 50s drink more than twice as much as their American counterparts. Additionally, young Japanese employees find that drinking is considered necessary, and some of them have raised complaints about *alru-hara,* or alcohol harassment (forced/pressured alcohol consumption).

Dealing with overwork will continue to be a challenge both for Japanese firms and for the government. The same is true of the growing problems associated with alcohol that are being brought on by stress and business cultures that have long supported alcohol consumption as a way of doing business and fitting into the social structure.

In the parents' sub-sample, mothers evinced higher relative family centrality than fathers. Mothers also invested more weekly hours in child care and core housework tasks than fathers. A key finding was that the contrasting parenthood effect prevails even in the demanding high-tech sector, in which women are expected to work long hours and play down their care-giving activities.[71]

Another important area of consideration is the importance of work as a part of overall lifestyle. In the case of Japanese workers, in particular, there has been a growing interest in the impact of overwork on the physical condition of employees. A report by the Japanese government noted that one-third of the working-age population suffers from chronic fatigue, and a recent survey by the Japanese prime minister's office found that a majority of those who were surveyed complained of being chronically tired and feeling emotionally stressed and some complained about abusive conditions in the workplace.[72] Fortunately, as seen in the International Management in Action box, "Karoshi: Stressed Out in Japan," the effects of overwork or job burnout—**karoshi** in Japanese—are beginning to be recognized as a real social problem. Other Asian countries which are subject to accelerated development are also experiencing job stress. Chinese workers, for example, are exhibiting classic Western signs of stress and overwork. Burnout, substance abuse, eating disorders, and depression abound, not to mention time away from the family. The culture is such that employees will not seek counseling, as it is a sign of weakness and embarrassment. However, like the Japanese, the Chinese are seeing the issue and attempting to approach a solution that will alleviate stress and save face.[73]

karoshi
A Japanese term that means "overwork" or "job burnout."

Job Satisfaction In addition to the implications that value of work has for motivating human resources across cultures, another interesting contrast is job satisfaction. For example, one study found that Japanese office workers may be much less satisfied with their jobs than their U.S., Canadian, and EU counterparts are. The Americans, who reported the highest level of satisfaction in this study, were pleased with job challenges, opportunities for teamwork, and ability to make a significant contribution at work. Japanese workers were least pleased with these three factors.[74] Similar findings were uncovered by Luthans and his associates, who reported that U.S. employees had higher organizational commitment than Japanese or Korean workers in their cross-cultural study. What makes these findings particularly interesting is that a large percentage of the Japanese and Korean workers were supervisory employees, who could be expected to be more committed to their organization than nonsupervisory employees, and a significant percentage of these employees also had lifetime guarantees.[75] This study also showed that findings related to job satisfaction in the international arena often are different from expected.[76]

Conventional wisdom not always being substantiated has been reinforced by cross-cultural studies that found Japanese workers who already were highly paid, and then received even higher wages, experienced decreased job satisfaction, morale, commitment, and intention to remain with the firm. This contrasts sharply with U.S. workers, who did not experience these negative feelings.[77] These findings show that the motivation approaches used in one culture may have limited value in another.[78]

Research by Kakabadse and Myers also has brought to light findings that are contradictory to commonly accepted beliefs. These researchers examined job satisfaction among managers from the United Kingdom, France, Belgium, Sweden, and Finland. It has long been assumed that satisfaction is highest at the upper levels of organizations; however, this study found varying degrees of satisfaction among managers, depending on the country. The researchers reported that senior managers from France and Finland display greater job dissatisfaction than the managers from the remaining countries. In terms of satisfaction with and commitment to the organization, British, German, and Swedish managers display the highest levels of commitment. Equally, British and German managers highlight that they feel stretched in their job, but senior managers from French organizations suggest that their jobs lack sufficient challenge and stimulus. In keeping with the job-related views displayed by French managers, they equally indicate their desire to leave their job because of their unsatisfactory work-related circumstances.[79]

On the other hand, research also reveals that some of the conditions that help create organizational commitment among U.S. workers also have value in other cultures. For example, a large study of Korean employees ($n = 1,192$ in 27 companies in 8 major industries) found that consistent with U.S. studies, Korean employees' position in the hierarchy, tenure in their current position, and age all related significantly to organizational commitment. Also, as in previous studies in the United States, as the size of the Korean organizations increased, commitment decreased, and the more positive the climate perceptions, the greater was the commitment.[80] In other words, there is at least beginning evidence that the theoretic constructs predicting organizational commitment may hold across cultures.

Also related to motivation are job attitudes toward quality of work life. Recent research reports that EU workers see a strong relationship between how well they do their jobs and the ability to get what they want out of life. U.S. workers were not as supportive of this relationship, and Japanese workers were least likely to see any connection.

This finding raises an interesting motivation-related issue regarding how well, for example, American, European, and Japanese employees can work together effectively. Some researchers have recently raised the question of how Japanese firms will be able to have effective strategic alliances with American and European companies if the work values of the partners are so different. Tornvall, after conducting a detailed examination of the work practices of five companies—Fuji-Kiku, a spare-parts firm in Japan; Toyota Motor Ltd. of Japan; Volvo Automobile AB of Sweden; SAAB Automobile AB, Sweden; and the General Motors plant in Saginaw, Michigan—concluded that there were benefits from the approaches used by each. This led him to recommend what he calls a "balance in the synergy" between the partners.[81] Some of his suggestions included the following:

Moving away from	Moving toward
Logical and reason-centered, individualistic thinking	A more holistic, idealistic, and group thinking approach to problem solving
Viewing work as a necessary burden	Viewing work as a challenging and development activity
The avoidance of risk taking and the feeling of distrust of others	An emphasis on cooperation, trust, and personal concern for others
The habit of analyzing things in such great depth that it results in "paralysis through analysis"	Cooperation built on intuition and pragmatism
An emphasis on control	An emphasis on flexibility

In large degree, this balance will require all three groups—Americans, Europeans, and Asians—to make changes in the way they approach work.

In conclusion, it should be remembered that work is important in every society. The extent of importance varies, however, and much of what is "known" about work as a motivator often is culture-specific. Again, the lesson to be learned for international management is that although the process of motivation may be the same, the content may change from one culture to another.

Reward Systems   Besides the content and process theories, another important area of motivation is that of rewards. Managers everywhere use rewards to motivate their personnel. Sometimes these are financial in nature such as salary raises, bonuses, and stock options. At other times they are nonfinancial such as feedback and recognition.[82] The major challenge for international managers is that there are often significant differences between the reward systems that work best in one country and those that are most effective in another. Some of these differences are a result of the competitive environment[83] or of government legislation that dictates such things as minimum wages, pensions, and perquisites.[84] In other cases, the differences are accounted for very heavily by culture.[85] For example, while many American companies like to use merit-based reward systems, firms in Japan, Korea, and Taiwan, where individualism is not very high, often feel that this form of reward system is too disruptive of the corporate culture and traditional values.[86]

■ Incentives and Culture

Use of financial incentives to motivate employees is very common, especially in countries with high individualism. In the United States, a number of chief executive officers earn over $100 million a year thanks to bonuses, stock options, and long-term incentive payments.[87] These pay systems are common when companies attempt to link compensation to performance. Typically, these systems range from individual incentive-based pay systems in which workers are paid directly for their output, to systems in which employees earn individual bonuses based on how well the organization at large achieves certain goals such as sales growth, total revenue, or total profit. These reward systems are designed to stress equity. However, they are not universally accepted.

In many cultures compensation is based on group membership or group effort. In these cases the systems are designed to stress equality, and employees will oppose the use of individual incentive plans. One example of this is the American multinational corporation that decided to institute an individually based bonus system for the sales representatives in its Danish subsidiary. The sales force rejected the proposal because it favored one group over another and employees felt that everyone should receive the same size bonus.[88] Another example, reported by Vance and associates, was Indonesian oil workers who rejected a pay-for-performance system that would have resulted in some work teams making more money than others.[89]

While financial rewards such as pay, bonuses, and stock options are important motivators, in many countries workers are highly motivated by other things as well. For example, Sirota and Greenwood studied employees of a large multinational electrical equipment manufacturer with operations in 40 countries. They found that in all of these locales the most important rewards involved recognition and achievement. Second in importance were improvements in the work environment and employment conditions including pay and work hours.[90] Beyond this, a number of differences emerged in preferred types of rewards. For example, employees in France and Italy highly valued job security, while for American and British workers it held little importance. Scandinavian workers placed high value on concern for others on the job and for personal freedom and autonomy, but they did not rate "getting ahead" as very important. German workers ranked security, fringe benefits, and "getting ahead" as very important, while Japanese employees put good working conditions and a congenial work environment high on their list but ranked personal advancement quite low.

Very simply, the types of incentives that are deemed important appear to be culturally influenced. Moreover, culture can even affect the overall cost of an incentive system. In Japan, efforts to introduce Western-style merit pay systems typically lead to an increase in the overall labor costs because the companies find that they cannot reduce the pay of less productive workers for fear of causing them to lose face and thus disturb group harmony.[91] As a result, everyone's salary increases. Culture also impacts profit in that people tend to perform better under management systems that are supportive of their own values. Nam, for example, studied two Korean banks that operated under different management systems.[92] One was owned and operated as a joint venture with an American bank, and the other was owned and operated as a joint venture with a Japanese bank. The American bank put into place management practices and personnel policies that were common in its own organization. The Japanese bank put together a blend of Japanese and Korean human resource management policies. Nam found that employees in the joint venture with the Japanese bank were significantly more committed to the organization than were their counterparts in the American joint venture and the Japanese-affiliated bank had significantly higher financial performance.

Sometimes, however, reward systems can be transferred and used successfully. For example, Welsh, Luthans, and Sommer examined the effectiveness of common Western incentive systems in a Russian textile factory.[93] They found that both contingently administered extrinsic rewards and positive recognition and attention from the supervisor led to significantly enhanced job performance, while participative techniques had little impact on job behavior and performance. Similarly, many people believe that large annual financial packages and lucrative golden parachutes are used only in American firms, but this is untrue. Senior-level managers in many MNCs now earn large salaries, and large financial packages for executives who are terminated or whose company is acquired by another firm are gaining in popularity, especially in Europe.[94] In other words, the type of rewards that are used is not culture-bound.

Overall, however, cultures do greatly influence the effectiveness of various rewards. What works in one country may not work in another. For example, research shows that Swedish workers with superior performance often prefer a reward of time off rather than additional money, while high-performing Japanese workers tend to opt for financial incentives—as long as they are group-based and not given on an individual basis.[95] It is also important to realize that the reasons why workers choose one form of motivation over another—for example, days off rather than more money—may not be immediately obvious or intuitively discernible. For example, research has found that Japanese workers tend to take only about half of their annual holiday entitlements, while French and German workers take all of the days to which they are entitled. Many people believe the Japanese want to earn more money, but the primary reason why they do not take all their holiday entitlements is that they believe taking all of those days shows a lack of commitment to their work group. The same is true for overtime: Individuals who refuse to work overtime are viewed as selfish. One of the results of these Japanese cultural values is karoshi, which we discussed a bit earlier in the chapter.

The World of *International Management*—Revisited

The World of International Management at the start of the chapter introduced you to how important it is for MNCs and international managers to understand the underlying motivators of workers' performance. It also discussed various sources of employee satisfaction or dissatisfaction and how these factors may differ among countries and cultures or how they may be the same. By ignoring such crucial issues, companies risk losing a vast talent pool and incurring costs through new hires, training, or settling for less experienced personnel.

While workers in some countries may be lured into attractive jobs provided by MNCs through relatively good salary compensation and the promise of upward mobility, many have become impatient from the lack of institutional follow-through in various dimensions. Companies moving to other countries may initially save money from low introductory wages, but they need to consider the costs involved in retaining (or losing) valuable talent. Until recently, awareness of the needs of employees in the international context was reflected simply in wage incentives, but more and more organizations are realizing that the less tangible values of work environment, recognition of intertwined work/family relationships, and the opportunity to continue education are highly regarded in many cultures. Identifying specific cultural viewpoints early can help MNCs in any country to grow and may be the key to continued survival.

The challenge for international managers is to put together a motivational package that addresses the specific needs of the employee or group in each region where an MNC serves. Applying the ideas presented in this chapter, answer the following questions: (1) What are some of the things that successful MNCs do to effectively motivate European employees? Chinese employees? Southeast-Asian (Indonesian) employees? (2) What kinds of incentives do scientific and technical employees respond to that might not be as meaningful to other categories of employees? (3) What advantages might employees see in working for a truly global company (as opposed to a North American MNC)?

SUMMARY OF KEY POINTS

1. Two basic types of theories explain motivation: content and process. Content theories of motivation have received much more attention in international management research because they provide the opportunity to create a composite picture of the motivation of human resources in a particular country or region. In addition, content theories more directly provide ways for managers to improve the performance of their human resources.

2. Maslow's hierarchy-of-needs theory has been studied in a number of different countries. Researchers have found that regardless of the country, managers have to be concerned with the satisfaction of these needs for their human resources.

3. Some researchers have suggested that satisfaction profiles are not very useful for studying motivation in an international setting because there are so many different subcultures within any country or even at different levels of a given organization. These researchers have suggested that job categories are more effective for examining motivation, because job level (managers versus operating employees) and the need hierarchy have established correspondences.

4. Like Maslow's theory, Herzberg's two-factor theory has received considerable attention in the international arena, and Herzberg's original findings from the United States have been replicated in other countries. Cross-cultural studies related to job satisfaction also have been conducted. The data show that job content is more important than job context to job satisfaction.

5. The third content theory of motivation that has received a great amount of attention in the international arena is the need for achievement. Some current findings show that this need is not as widely held across cultures as was previously believed. In some parts of the world, however, such as Anglo countries, cultural values encourage people to be high achievers. In particular, Dutch researcher Geert Hofstede suggested that an analysis of two cultural dimensions, uncertainty avoidance and masculinity, helps to identify high-achieving societies. Once again, it can be concluded that different cultures will support different motivational needs, and that international managers developing strategies to motivate their human resources for improved performance must recognize cultural differences.

6. Process theories have also contributed to the understanding of motivation in the international arena. Equity theory focuses on how motivation is affected by people's perception of how fairly they are being treated, and there is considerable research to support the fundamental equity principle in Western work groups. However, when the theory is examined on an international basis, the results are mixed. Perhaps the biggest shortcoming of the theory is that it appears to be culture-bound. For example, in Japan and Korea, men and women typically receive different pay for doing precisely the same work, and this is at least traditionally not perceived as inequitable to women.

7. Goal-setting theory focuses on how individuals go about setting goals and responding to them and the overall impact of this process on motivation. There is evidence showing that employees perform extremely well when they are assigned specific and challenging goals that they had a hand in setting.

However, most of these goal-setting studies have been conducted in the United States; few of them have been carried out in other cultures. Additionally, research results on the effects of goal setting at the individual level are very limited, and culture may well account for these outcomes.

8. Expectancy theory postulates that motivation is largely influenced by a multiplicative combination of a person's belief that effort will lead to performance, that performance will lead to specific outcomes, and that these outcomes are valued by the individual. There is mixed support for this theory. Many researchers believe that the theory best explains motivation in countries characterized by an internal locus of control.

9. Although content and process theories provide important insights into the motivation of human resources, three additional areas that have received a great deal of recent attention in the application of motivation theory are job design, work centrality, and reward systems. Job design is influenced by culture as well as the specific methods that are used to bring together the people and the work. Work centrality helps to explain the importance of work in an individual's life relative to other areas of interest. In recent years work has become a relatively greater part of the average U.S. employee's life and perhaps less a part of the average Japanese worker's life. Research also indicates that Japanese office workers are less satisfied with their jobs than are U.S., Canadian, and EU workers, suggesting once again that MNCs need to design motivation packages that address the specific needs of different cultures. This is also true for rewards. Research shows that the relative motivational value of monetary and nonmonetary rewards is influenced by culture. Countries with high individualism, such as the United States and the U.K., tend to make wide use of individual incentives, while collectivistic countries such as those in Asia prefer group-oriented incentives.

10. A central point of the chapter is that some motivational practices may have universal appeal, but more often they need tailoring to fit to the culture in which an MNC may be working. Research shows that some motivational approaches in the United States have been successfully transferred to Russia. More often creative modification to familiar approaches is necessary. The importance for international managers of focusing on employee motivation is unquestioned. The challenge lies in finding the appropriate applications of motivational theory to the specific culture at hand.

KEY TERMS

achievement motivation theory, *437*

content theories of motivation, *426*

equity theory, *439*

esteem needs, *427*

expectancy theory, *441*

extrinsic, *424*

goal-setting theory, *441*

hygiene factors, *431*

intrinsic, *424*

job-content factors, *436*

job-context factors, *436*

job design, *442*

karoshi, *447*

motivation, *424*

motivators, *431*

physiological needs, *427*

process theories of motivation, *426*

safety needs, *427*

self-actualization needs, *427*

social needs, *427*

sociotechnical designs, *443*

two-factor theory of motivation, *431*

work centrality, *444*

REVIEW AND DISCUSSION QUESTIONS

1. Do people throughout the world have needs similar to those described in Maslow's need hierarchy? What does your answer reveal about using universal assumptions regarding motivation?

2. Is Herzberg's two-factor theory universally applicable to human resource management, or is its value limited to Anglo countries?

3. What are the dominant characteristics of high achievers? Using Figure 12–7 as your point of reference, determine which countries likely will have the greatest percentage of high achievers. Why is this so? Of what value is your answer to the study of international management?

4. A U.S. manufacturer is planning to open a plant in Sweden. What should this firm know about the quality of work life in Sweden that would have a

direct effect on job design in the plant? Give an example.

5. What does a U.S. firm setting up operations in Japan need to know about work centrality in that country? How would this information be of value to the multinational? Conversely, what would a Japanese firm need to know about work centrality in the United States? Explain.

6. In managing operations in Europe, which process theory—equity theory, goal-setting theory, or expectancy theory—would be of most value to an American manager? Why?

7. What do international managers need to know about the use of reward incentives to motivate personnel? What role does culture play in this process?

INTERNET EXERCISE: MOTIVATING POTENTIAL EMPLOYEES

In order for multinationals to continue expanding their operations, they must be able to attract and retain highly qualified personnel in many countries. Much of their success in doing this will be tied to the motivational package that they offer, including financial opportunities, benefits and perquisites, meaningful work, and an environment that promotes productivity and worker creativity. Automotive firms, in particular, are a good example of MNCs that are trying very hard to increase their worldwide market share. So for them, employee motivation is an area that is getting a lot of attention.

Go to the Web and look at the career opportunities that are currently being offered by Nestlé, Unilever, and Procter & Gamble (websites: nestle.com, unilever.com, png.com). All three of these companies provide information about the career opportunities they offer. Based on this information, answer these questions: (1) What are some of the things that all three firms offer to motivate new employees? (2) Which of the three has the best motivational package? Why? (3) Are there any major differences between P&G and European-based rivals? What conclusion can you draw from this?

Indonesia

Located along the Equator between the Indian and Pacific Oceans, Indonesia is a tropical, volcanic archipelago of over 6,000 inhabited islands. The island nation is home to hundreds of native ethnic groups, multiple languages, and the world's largest Muslim population. With a combined land area equivalent to roughly the size of Alaska, 60 percent of Indonesia is covered by tropical forest. Indonesia is second only to Brazil in biodiversity, and its land holds access to countless natural resources. Currently, Indonesia is the world's fourth most-populous nation, with over 250 million citizens. The economy has been rapidly emerging over the past 15 years. GDP, in terms of purchasing power parity, measured $1.212 trillion in 2012, ranking it 16th in the world. This equates to $5000 per capita. Colonized by the Dutch in the 1600s and briefly occupied by the Japanese during World War II, Indonesia is a parliamentary democracy.

For the first 50 years after gaining independence from the Dutch in 1949, Indonesia's economy was government-controlled by corruptly elected leaders. In 1999, following constitutional reforms, truly free elections for both houses of parliament occurred for the first time since 1955. Over 40 political parties participated in the process. These free elections marked the end of the government-controlled economy and the start of more open economic policies and prosperity. Despite a slight setback in 2005, the economy has continued to expand, and diversify, at a rapid pace since 1999. Exports of fossil fuels, textiles, and electronic equipment have grown significantly, increasing individual wealth. Indonesia posted positive growth during the global recession of 2009 and is currently the third fastest–growing G20 country, eclipsed by only China and India.

With this new prosperity, however, has come rapid environmental destruction. Industries such as mining, timbering, and agriculture have cleared Indonesia's rainforests at record paces. Many in the environmental community have called for increased environmental protections over Indonesia's unique habitats. The elected government representatives, now held responsible by the ballot box, have been hesitant to impose regulations which may stunt business growth and wealth accumulation. In December 2012, 200,000 acres of carbon-rich land were set aside by the government for permanent conservation to prevent the release of greenhouse gases—the first conservation of its kind for Indonesia. Private industry is slowly making environmental changes as well, though resistance is strong. As a result of international pressure, the world's third largest paper manufacturer, Asia Pulp and Paper Company, vowed to end its practice of logging in natural rainforests in Indonesia in February 2013. Other companies have yet to make the same commitment. In June 2013, massive forest fires broke out on the island of Sumatra, an annual event that results from clearing forests. The fires resulted in widespread air pollution that drifted to Malaysia and Singapore with air quality reaching very dangerous levels. Although the Indonesian president apologized to the neighboring countries, this event underscored the ongoing challenges of managing a rapidly growing emerging market while preserving the natural environment.

www.nytimes.com, www.cia.gov

Questions

1. What unique problems does Indonesia face as its economy continues to expand?
2. What problems does the freely-elected government face in protecting Indonesia's environmental habitats?

Chapter 13

LEADERSHIP ACROSS CULTURES

Leadership is often credited (or blamed) for the success (or failure) of international operations. As with other aspects of management, leadership styles and practices that work well in one culture are not necessarily effective in another. The leadership approach commonly used by U.S. managers would not necessarily be the same as that employed in other parts of the world. Even within the same country, effective leadership tends to be very situation-specific. However, as with the other areas of international management you have studied in this text, certain leadership styles and practices may be more or less universally applicable and transcend international boundaries. This chapter examines some differences and similarities in leadership styles across cultures.

First, we review the basic foundation for the study of leadership. Next, we examine leadership in various parts of the world, Europe, East Asia, and the Middle East, including some developing countries. Finally, we'll analyze specific types of leadership, drawing from recent research on leadership across cultures. The specific objectives of this chapter are:

1. **DESCRIBE** the basic philosophic foundation and styles of managerial leadership.

2. **EXAMINE** the attitudes of European managers toward leadership practices.

3. **COMPARE** and **CONTRAST** leadership styles in Japan with those in the United States.

4. **REVIEW** leadership approaches in China, the Middle East, and developing countries.

5. **EXAMINE** recent research and findings regarding leadership across cultures.

6. **DISCUSS** the relationship of culture clusters and leader behavior on effective leadership practices, including increasing calls for more responsible global leadership.

The World of *International Management*

Global Leadership Development: An Emerging Need

Firms are currently bolstering their leadership development programs to prevent a future shortage of managers. As reported in *The Wall Street Journal* in August 2010, the number of potential managers has decreased as a result of layoffs and cuts in training during the economic downturn. Larry Looker, Amway Corp.'s manager of global leadership development, told *The Wall Street Journal,* "We're finding times when we want to open a new market but don't have anyone with the capabilities to do it. It's a real weakness."[1] When Amway needed country managers for an expansion in Latin America, it could not find qualified candidates in its local operations. During the recession, Amway put on hold two leadership development programs. In 2011, it restarted these programs with the hope of training future managers. It's a positive sign that companies are growing their global leadership development programs.[2] What does a global leadership development program look like? What qualities are companies looking for in candidates for these programs? What are the benefits to the individual in participating in such a program? To answer these questions, one MNC will be examined in detail.

Spotlight on Roche

The worldwide health care company, Roche, has extensive global leadership development programs. Roche has 81,507 employees and is active in 150 countries. Roche's training for employees includes language courses, interpersonal skills training, and individual coaching and programs on leadership and change management.[3]

According to Roche's website, "Every Roche site has its own training and development programs geared to local needs and resources, and in line with local legal and regulatory requirements."[4] One such program is

Shanghai Roche Pharma's "People & Leadership Development Program." Shanghai Roche has a specific training program for managers to reinforce leadership skills, such as strategic leadership. Furthermore, each employee has an individualized development plan. Based on the Roche 3E (Experience, Education, and Exposure) development model, each employee works with his or her manager to work out a customized development plan together.[5]

To prepare its future leaders, Roche offers two distinct leadership programs, especially designed for managers:

1. *Leadership Impact.* Through this program, managers can build their
   - People management skills (developing, coaching, etc.).
   - Functional management skills (process knowledge and compliance).
   - Leadership skills (creating a vision, guiding a team, etc.).

2. *Leadership Excellence.* Through this program, senior level managers can
   - Remain honest and transparent regarding the realities of their roles.
   - Provide each other with support through peer networking.
   - Increase their collective competencies while sharing common challenges.[6]

Moreover, Roche has a special global leadership development program in its home country, Switzerland. One of Roche's programs has been highlighted on LinkedIn. The following is adapted from a description of the Perspectives Global Accelerated Talent Development Program at Roche:

> Our success is built on innovation, curiosity, and diversity, and on seeing each other's differences as an advantage. The headquarters in Basel is one of Roche's largest sites; over 8,000 people from approximately 80 countries work at Roche Basel.
>
> The Perspectives Global Accelerated Talent Development Program is a Roche Corporate program designed to provide a "rapid fire" induction experience to one of the two divisions of Roche

(Pharmaceuticals/Diagnostics). It is targeted at talented individuals who are at a very early stage of their career and are seeking to make significant contributions to the industry. Roche is looking for highly energetic and globally mobile future business leaders from around the globe.[7]

Recognizing the central importance of experiential learning and development, Perspectives provides a unique opportunity to build a broad global network, experience different areas of the business, and gain skills that will be necessary for a career in general management in an accelerated timeframe.

Features of the Perspectives program include:
- Two years (temporary contract), four assignments of six months (three or four are typically international assignments).
- Completely tailored to your development needs and areas of interest in line with Roche needs.
- Diverse experience: different areas of the business, functions, countries, sites, markets, leadership styles, business and ethnic cultures.
- Training targeted at accelerating your leadership capabilities.
- Personal Development Coach: dedicated senior management support throughout the program and beyond.[8]

For this program, Roche is looking for candidates with master's degrees, fluency in two languages, global mindset and mobility, strong leadership potential and business acumen, and excellent communication skills.[9]

Employee Development Yields Results

Two Roche employees' experiences demonstrate the results of Roche's training programs.

At age 24, Luciana, an employee at the Roche Diagnostics affiliate in São Paolo, Brazil, participated in one of Roche's programs. As part of the program, she had the opportunity to work at Roche Diagnostics in Rotkreuz, Switzerland, and the Roche Diagnostics affiliate in Burgess Hill, U.K. Those at Roche believe, "Experiencing new ways of working and thinking inspires creativity in employees, advancing their careers and the company."[10]

This appears to have been the case for Luciana. As a result of her experience, Luciana said, "I have no words to describe how it changes your point of view of life. In two and a half years at Roche, I feel I've gained five years' growth. I have opportunities to grow every day, with challenging projects, good professionals around me, and space to express myself and to learn how to express myself better."[11]

Tuygan Goeker has been at Roche for 30 years. His career "has scarcely stood still, punctuated by a change in responsibilities or a country move every three to four years." He has worked in Roche Istanbul, Roche Indonesia, and at the Roche headquarters in Switzerland. Today, he is Head of the Central and Eastern Europe, Middle East, Africa, and Indian subcontinent region. He is currently working on developing strategies for maximizing market potential in Brazil, Russia, India, China, South Korea, Mexico, and his native Turkey. As an international manager, Tuygan has learned adaptability. Tuygan said, "Along the way I've had to expand the way I define success. Sometimes the scope or budget of a new role has been tiny in comparison to a previous position. On the other hand, the number of employees and indirect responsibilities turn out to be infinitely greater."[12]

Roche considers its key to success to be: "Placing the best people with the most advanced skills and attributes in the right place, at the right time, focused on the right priorities." This focus on what's right requires good leadership. Thus, good leadership is essential to corporate success. When companies invest in global leadership development programs, they are investing in their firms' future.[13]

Effective global leadership is an essential competency of leading MNCs, and therefore companies are investing in programs to ensure effective global leadership development. Having leaders who can help companies enter and operate in new markets is especially important. At Amway, Roche, and other companies, a shortage of such employees could constrain global growth. Roche like many MNCs has developed a series of formal, structured programs that are available to employees around the world. These programs are designed to develop skills and capabilities that will help the firms become more culturally sensitive, adaptable, and able to effectively manage in challenging global environments. In this chapter we address different leadership styles as a platform for building effective leadership across cultures.

■ Foundation for Leadership

More academic research over the years has focused on leadership than on nearly any other social science topic. Much of historical studies, political science, and the behavioral sciences is either directly or indirectly concerned with leadership. Despite all this attention there still is no generally agreed-on definition of leadership, let alone sound answers to the question of which leadership approach is more effective than others in the international arena. For our present purposes, **leadership** can be defined simply as the process of influencing people to direct their efforts toward achievement of some particular goal or goals.[14] Leadership is widely recognized as being very important in the study of international management, which raises the question, What is the difference between being a manager and being a leader? While there is no concise answer to this either, some interesting and helpful perspectives have emerged.

leadership
The process of influencing people to direct their efforts toward the achievement of some particular goal or goals.

The Manager-Leader Paradigm

While the terms *manager* and *leader* have often been used interchangeably in the business environment, many believe that there exist clear distinctions in characteristics and behaviors between the two. Some believe that leaders are born, but managers can be shaped. MNCs that have simply sought out employees with appropriate skill sets now face a new challenge: clarifying the seemingly dichotomous roles of managers and leaders to ensure a cohesive vision going forward.

It has been postulated that managers may provide leadership and leaders perform management functions. But managers don't perform the unique functions of leaders.[15] Managerial positions often consist of sheer responsibility. The attributes necessary to make a successful manager can be learned through academic study or observation and training.[16] Behaviors of managers vary greatly, but fundamentally they tend to follow company objectives and rules while attempting to maintain stability as they react to inevitable change. Essentially, management is something that one does, and the journey consists of striving to always do things right (as opposed to doing the right thing). Unfortunately this often results in focusing on failures as a basis for identifying what needs improvement and ignoring success or denying praise.[17]

Leadership is more difficult to articulate as views of what makes a leader are inconsistent across studies. Leader status is not something that can be learned, but something that must be earned through respect.[18] In other words, people are not hired as leaders, but appointed as such via employee perspective on the individual. Leaders guide and motivate team members and are extremely visible. While managers often merely focus on reaching objectives by mastering financial information, leaders work to get the right people in the right positions and motivate them; money matters become a secondary objective. Proactive behavior is often crucial as these individuals create change on the basis of a vision of the future. To sum it up in a word, leadership is about the drive to ultimately do the right thing.[19] The focus of the leader is on the success of team members and building their morale and motivation, as the firm seeks to implement and execute the right strategy.

Many firms are beginning to search for an all-encompassing package of skill sets, and while it is imperative for the survival of a business to have both managers and leaders, it is extremely difficult, if not impossible, to find someone who fits the inclusive criteria of both roles.[20] Still, hope abounds that it is a reasonable venture to search for individuals with the latent attributes of the leader-manager, who may benefit from training methods that can magnify the most relevant qualities. Skills in effective communication, planning, organizing, and problem solving are what both leaders and managers should develop in order to live up to their roles. The manager-leader must exhibit the ability to focus on the future while maintaining current organizational trends. After that a certain undefined charisma must come into play, evoking the support and respect of subordinates, since the leadership role is ultimately determined by team member perspectives.[21]

Table 13–1 provides a comparison of perceived differences between leadership and management. Again, whether or not these contrasting qualities and abilities are mutually exclusive or if one list is a subset of the other is highly debatable. But it seems clear that pitfalls loom when individuals who do not really exhibit the capacities of both a leader and a manager attempt to fill both sets of shoes. Uncertain and shifting roles and practices can lead to inconsistencies in execution, leading to a belief among subordinates that those in positions of authority may not have the qualifications to serve in either capacity.[22] In the context of our discussion of international management, it is important to note that cultural perspectives are often responsible for how the roles of managers and

Table 13–1
Perceived Differences: Managers vs. Leaders

Managers	Leaders
Can learn skills necessary	Harbor innate characteristics
Take care of where you are	Bring you to new horizons
Oversee	Motivate
Point out flaws to improve on	Give recognition for good work
Deal with complexity	Deal with ambiguity
Are fact finders	Are decision makers
Focus on efficiency	Focus on effectiveness
Are given immediate authority	Earn respect through actions
Follow company objectives	Set new standards
Have present vision	Have future vision
Do things right	Do the right things

leaders are seen to overlap, and in some cases, viewed as synonymous. In some cultures, especially those characterized by high power distance, the aura of leader is projected onto the manager whether or not he or she is ready for it. At the same time, globalization and international operations are evolving such that the manager may be cast into the role of leader out of necessity because there is no one else or no other choice available. Today, managers that seek to do more than balance the budget may be shaped through appropriate training into the leaders of tomorrow.

For the purpose of this book and the multiple challenges associated with managing in an international context we may assume a high level of overlap in characteristics such that international managers will often be called upon to assume the role of manager-leader, or leader-manager. Indeed, in our discussion in the international context we use the terms "supervisor," "leader," and "manager" somewhat interchangeably.

Leadership definitions may not be universal, yet it is true that relatively little effort has been made to systematically study and compare leadership approaches throughout the world. Most international research efforts on leadership have been directed toward a specific country or geographic area. Two comparative areas provide a foundation for understanding leadership in the international arena: (1) the philosophical grounding of how leaders view their subordinates and (2) leadership approaches as reflected by autocratic-participative behaviors of leaders. The philosophies/approaches common in the United States often are quite different from those employed by leaders in overseas organizations. At the same time, the differences often are not as pronounced as is commonly believed. First, we will review historical viewpoints on leadership and then move on to exploring new findings.

Philosophical Background: Theories X, Y, and Z

One primary reason that leaders behave as they do is rooted in their philosophy or beliefs regarding how to direct their subordinates most effectively. Managers who believe their people are naturally lazy and work only for money will use a leadership style that is different from the style of managers who believe their people are self-starters and enjoy challenge and increased responsibility. Douglas McGregor, the pioneering leadership theorist, labeled these two sets of assumptions "Theory X" and "Theory Y."

Theory X manager
A manager who believes that people are basically lazy and that coercion and threats of punishment often are necessary to get them to work.

A **Theory X manager** believes that people are basically lazy and that coercion and threats of punishment must be used to get them to work. The specific philosophical assumptions of Theory X managers or leaders are:

1. By their very nature, people do not like to work and will avoid it whenever possible.
2. Workers have little ambition, try to avoid responsibility, and like to be directed.
3. The primary need of employees is job security.
4. To get people to attain organizational objectives, it is necessary to use coercion, control, and threats of punishment.[23]

Theory Y manager
A manager who believes that under the right conditions people not only will work hard but will seek increased responsibility and challenge.

A **Theory Y manager** believes that under the right conditions people will not only work hard but will seek increased responsibility and challenge. In addition, a great deal of creative potential basically goes untapped, believes Theory Y, and if these abilities can be tapped, workers will provide much higher quantity and quality of output. The specific philosophical assumptions of Theory Y leaders are:

1. The expenditure of physical and mental effort at work is as natural to people as resting or playing.
2. External control and threats of punishment are not the only ways of getting people to work toward organizational objectives. If people are committed to the goals, they will exercise self-direction and self-control.

3. Commitment to objectives is determined by the rewards that are associated with their achievement.

4. Under proper conditions, the average human being learns not only to accept but to seek responsibility.

5. The capacity to exercise a relatively high degree of imagination, ingenuity, and creativity in the solution of organizational problems is widely distributed throughout the population.

6. Under conditions of modern industrial life, the intellectual potential of the average human being is only partially tapped.[24]

The reasoning behind these beliefs will vary by culture. U.S. managers believe that to motivate workers, it is necessary to satisfy their higher-order needs. This is done best through a Theory Y leadership approach. In China, Theory Y managers act similarly—but for different reasons. After the 1949 revolution, two types of managers emerged in China: Experts and Reds. The Experts focused on technical skills and primarily were Theory X advocates. The Reds, skilled in the management of people and possessing political and ideological expertise, were Theory Y advocates. The Reds also believed that the philosophy of Chairman Mao supported their thinking (i.e., all employees had to rise together both economically and culturally). Both Chinese and U.S. managers support Theory Y, but for very different reasons.[25]

The same is true in the case of Russian managers. In a survey conducted by Puffer, McCarthy, and Naumov, 292 Russian managers were asked about their beliefs regarding work.[26] Table 13–2 shows the six different groupings of the responses. Drawing together the findings of the study, the researchers pointed out the importance of Westerners getting beyond the stereotypes of Russian managers and learning more about the latter's beliefs in order to be more effective in working with them as employees and as joint-venture partners. Obviously, the assumption that Russian managers are strict adherents of Theory X may be common, but it may also be erroneous.[27]

The assumptions of Theory X or Y are most easily seen in the managers' behaviors, such as giving orders, getting and giving feedback, and creating an overall climate within which the work will be done.

William Ouchi proposed an additional perspective, which he called "Theory Z," that brings together Theory Y and modern Japanese management techniques. A **Theory Z manager** believes that workers seek opportunities to participate in management and are motivated by teamwork and responsibility sharing.[28] The specific philosophical assumptions of a Theory Z leader are:

Theory Z manager
A manager who believes that workers seek opportunities to participate in management and are motivated by teamwork and responsibility sharing.

1. People are motivated by a strong sense of commitment to be part of a greater whole—the organization in which they work.

2. Employees seek out responsibility and look for opportunities to advance in an organization. Through teamwork and commitment to common goals, employees derive self-satisfaction and contribute to organizational success.

3. Employees who learn different aspects of the business will be in a better position to contribute to the broader goals of the organization.

4. By making commitments to employees' security through lifetime or long-term employment, the organization will engender in employees strong bonds of loyalty, making the organization more productive and successful.

In sum, each of these three theories, Theory X, Y, and Z, provide useful insights that reveal how different leadership approaches and styles appeal to different constituencies and to certain aspects of human behavior. Theory X has generally fallen out of fashion and managers and leaders are increasingly aware of nonpecuniary (nonfinancial) incentives and rewards. Theories Y and Z are somewhat complementary in that each assumes some degree of intrinsic motivation on the part of employees.

Table 13–2
Russian Managerial Beliefs about Work

A. Humanistic Beliefs

Work can be made meaningful.

One's job should give one a chance to try out new ideas.

The workplace can be humanized.

Work can be made satisfying.

Work should allow for the use of human capabilities.

Work can be a means of self-expression.

Work should enable one to learn new things.

Work can be organized to allow for human fulfillment.

Work can be made interesting rather than boring.

The job should be a source of new experiences.

B. Organizational Beliefs

Survival of the group is very important in an organization.

Working with a group is better than working alone.

It is best to have a job as part of an organization where all work together even if you don't get individual credit.

One should take an active part in all group affairs.

The group is the most important entity in any organization.

One's contribution to the group is the most important thing about one's work.

Work is a means to foster group interests.

C. Work Ethic

Only those who depend on themselves get ahead in life.

To be superior a person must stand alone.

A person can learn better on the job by striking out boldly on his own than by following the advice of others.

One must avoid dependence on other persons whenever possible.

One should live one's life independent of others as much as possible.

D. Beliefs about Participation in Managerial Decisions

The working classes should have more say in running society.

Factories would be better run if workers had more of a say in management.

Workers should be more active in making decisions about products, financing, and capital investment.

Workers should be represented on the boards of directors of companies.

E. Leisure Ethic

The trend toward more leisure is not a good thing. (R)

More leisure time is good for people.

Increased leisure time is bad for society. (R)

Leisure-time activities are more interesting than work.

The present trend toward a shorter workweek is to be encouraged.

F. Marxist-Related Beliefs

The free-enterprise system mainly benefits the rich and powerful.

The rich do not make much of a contribution to society.

Workers get their fair share of the economic rewards of society. (R)

The work of the laboring classes is exploited by the rich for their own benefit.

Wealthy people carry their fair share of the burdens of life in this country. (R)

The most important work is done by the laboring classes.

Notes: 1. Response scales ranged from 1 (strongly disagree) to 5 (strongly agree).

2. R denotes reverse-scoring items.

3. The 45 individual items contained in the 6 belief clusters were presented to respondents in a mixed fashion, rather than categorized by cluster as shown above.

4. Participation was a subset of Marxist-related values in Buchholz's original study, but was made a separate cluster in his later work.

Source: Adapted from Sheila M. Puffer, Daniel J. McCarthy, and Alexander I. Naumov, "Russian Managers' Beliefs about Work: Beyond the Stereotypes," *Journal of World Business* 32, no. 3 (1997), p. 262;

Leadership Behaviors and Styles

Leader behaviors can be translated into three commonly recognized styles: (1) authoritarian, (2) paternalistic, and (3) participative. **Authoritarian leadership** is the use of work-centered behavior that is designed to ensure task accomplishment. As shown in Figure 13–1, this leader behavior typically involves the use of one-way communication from manager to subordinate. The focus of attention usually is on work progress, work procedures, and roadblocks that are preventing goal attainment. There is a managerial tendency toward a lack of involvement with subordinates, where final decisions are in the hands of the higher-level employees. The distance translates into a lack of a relationship where managers focus on assignments over the needs of the employees. At times, the organizational leadership behavior is reflective of the political surroundings, as indicated in one study which focused on Romania.[29] Leaders in this region were slightly more authoritarian (55 percent), which could have been influenced by the Romanian communistic roots that stressed the importance of completing planned productions. Although this leadership style often is effective in handling crises, some leaders employ it as their primary style regardless of the situation. It also is widely used by Theory X managers, who believe that a continued focus on the task is compatible with the kind of people they are dealing with.

authoritarian leadership
The use of work-centered behavior designed to ensure task accomplishment.

Figure 13–1

Leader-Subordinate Interactions

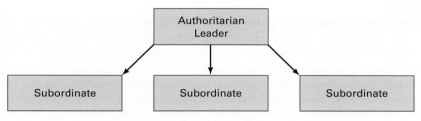

One-way downward flow of information and influence from authoritarian leader to subordinates.

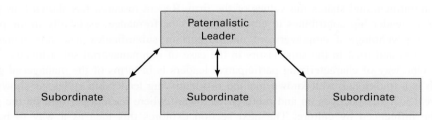

Continual interaction and exchange of information and influence between leader and subordinates.

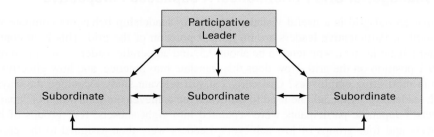

Continual interaction and exchange of information and influence between leader and subordinates and between subordinates.

Source: Adapted from Richard M. Hodgetts, *Modern Human Relations at Work,* 8th ed. (Ft. Worth, TX: Harcourt, 2002), p. 264.

paternalistic leadership
The use of work-centered behavior coupled with a protective employee-centered concern.

Paternalistic leadership uses work-centered behavior coupled with a protective employee-centered concern. This leadership style can be best summarized by the statement, "Work hard and the company will take care of you." Paternalistic leaders expect everyone to work hard; in return, the employees are guaranteed employment and given security benefits such as medical and retirement programs. Usually, this leadership behavior satisfies some employee needs, and in turn subordinates tend to exhibit loyalty and compliance.[30]

Studies have shown that this behavior is seen throughout Latin America, including Argentina, Bolivia, Chile, and Mexico,[31] but also in China, Pakistan, India, Turkey, and the United States.[32] Mexico appears to be a country that has high paternalistic values, owing in part to Mexican cultural values of respect for hierarchical relations and strong family and personal relationships[33] and the fact of the absence of welfare or employment benefits.[34] There is also some evidence that paternalistic leadership is still a common leadership approach in greater China, stemming from Confucian ideology, which is founded on social relations, such as "benevolent leader with loyal minister" and "kind father with filial son." In Malaysia, paternalistic leadership acts as a positive reinforcer because paternalistic treatment is contingent on subordinates' task accomplishment. More broadly, paternalistic leadership has been shown to have a positive impact on employees' attitudes in collectivistic cultures because the care, support, and protection provided by paternalistic leaders may address employees' need for frequent contact and close personal relationships.[35]

participative leadership
The use of both work- or task-centered and people-centered approaches to leading subordinates.

Participative leadership is the use of both work-centered and people-centered approaches. Participative leaders typically encourage their people to play an active role in assuming control of their work, and authority usually is highly decentralized. The way in which leaders motivate employees could be through consulting with employees, encouraging joint decisions, or delegating responsibilities. Regardless of the method, employees tend to be more creative and innovative when driven by leaders exhibiting this behavior.[36] Participative leadership is very popular in many technologically advanced countries. Such leadership has been widely espoused in the United States, England, and other Anglo countries, and it is currently very popular in Scandinavian countries as well. At General Electric, managers are encouraged to use a participative style that delivers on commitment and shares the values of the firm. Recent research has shown how participative leadership contributes to employees' task performance, especially in the presence of psychological empowerment on the part of subordinates who are managers themselves and trust in the supervisors in the case of nonmanagerial subordinates.[37]

One way of characterizing participative leaders is in terms of the managerial grid, which is a traditional, well-known method of identifying leadership styles, as shown in Figure 13–2. Perspectives on and preferences toward where leaders perform on the grid can be influenced by culture. The next section explores this idea as a way to better illustrate the managerial grid.

The Managerial Grid Performance: A Japanese Perspective

The managerial grid is a useful visual to chart how leadership behaviors compare with one another. Participative leaders are on the 9,9 position of the grid. This is in contrast to paternalistic leaders, who tend to be about 9,5, and autocratic leaders, who are in more of a 9,1 position on the grid. How does this translate into practice, and how effective are these in motivating employees? One early but still relevant study examined the ways in which leadership style could be used to influence the achievement motivation of Japanese subjects.[38] Japanese participants were separated into eight subsets: four groups of high achievers and four groups of low achievers. Leaders were then assigned to the groups. The first leader focused on performance (called "P supervision" in the study) and mirrored the autocratic style. There was a work-centered focus where subordinates were compared to other groups, and if they were behind, they were pressed to catch up. This correlates to point 9,1 on the grid (high on task, low on people). The second leadership

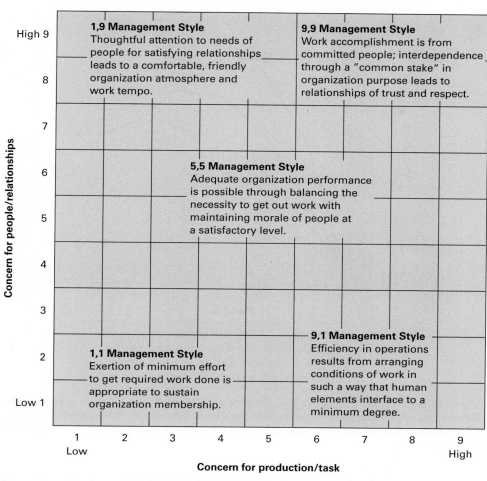

Figure 13-2

The Managerial Grid

1,9 Management Style Thoughtful attention to needs of people for satisfying relationships leads to a comfortable, friendly organization atmosphere and work tempo.

9,9 Management Style Work accomplishment is from committed people; interdependence through a "common stake" in organization purpose leads to relationships of trust and respect.

5,5 Management Style Adequate organization performance is possible through balancing the necessity to get out work with maintaining morale of people at a satisfactory level.

1,1 Management Style Exertion of minimum effort to get required work done is appropriate to sustain organization membership.

9,1 Management Style Efficiency in operations results from arranging conditions of work in such a way that human elements interface to a minimum degree.

Concern for people/relationships

High 9 · 8 · 7 · 6 · 5 · 4 · 3 · 2 · Low 1

1 Low · 2 · 3 · 4 · 5 · 6 · 7 · 8 · 9 High

Concern for production/task

Source: Adapted from Robert S. Blake and Jane S. Mouton, "Managerial Facades," *Advanced Management Journal,* July 1966, p. 31.

style focused on maintaining and strengthening the group (called "M supervision" in the study). The individual used a 1,9 (low on task, high on people) leadership style on the managerial grid, and created a warm, friendly, sympathetic environment where tensions were reduced, interpersonal relationships strengthened, and suggestions welcomed.

The third leader combined the first two methods into a performance-maintenance style (called "PM supervision" in the study). While pressure to complete tasks was prevalent, supervisors still offered encouragement and support. This style correlates with participative leadership, and is at point 9,9 on the managerial grid. Finally, the fourth leader exhibited more absenteeism, as the focus was neither on performance nor maintenance (called "pm supervision" in the study). This supervisor simply did not get very involved in either the task or the people side of the group being led. In other words, the supervisor used a 1,1 leadership style on the grid.

The results of these four leadership styles among the high-achieving and low-achieving groups are reported in Figures 13–3 and 13–4. In the high-achieving groups, the PM, or participative (9,9) style, was most effective across all phases. The P, or authoritarian (9,1—high on task, low on people), leadership style was second most effective during early and middle phases of the study, but later phases proved M supervision (1,9—low on task, high on people) to be more relevant, possibly suggesting that the more familiar the supervisor and subordinate become with one another, the more significant a personal relationship is over a task-focused objective. Finally, the pm (1,1) leadership style was consistently ineffective.

Figure 13–3

Productivity of Japanese Groups with High-Achievement Motivation under Different Leadership Styles

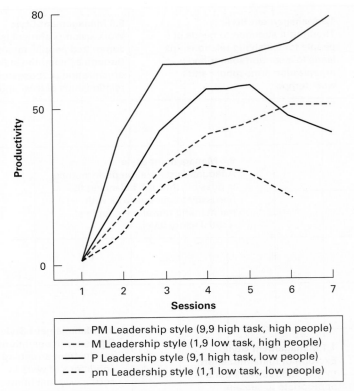

PM Leadership style (9,9 high task, high people)
M Leadership style (1,9 low task, high people)
P Leadership style (9,1 high task, low people)
pm Leadership style (1,1 low task, low people)

Source: Reprinted from "Effects of Achievement Motivation on the Effectiveness of Leadership Patterns," by Jyuji Misumi and Fumiyasu Seki, published in Volume 16, No. 1, March 1971, of *Administrative Science Quarterly.* Copyright © 1971 Johnson Graduate School of Management, Cornell University.

Figure 13–4

Productivity of Japanese Groups with Low-Achievement Motivation under Different Leadership Styles

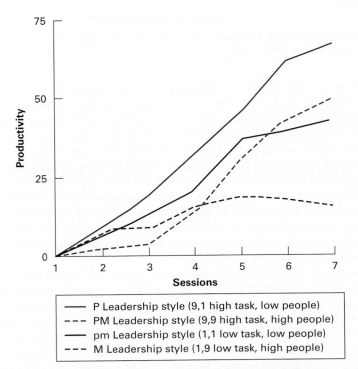

P Leadership style (9,1 high task, low people)
PM Leadership style (9,9 high task, high people)
pm Leadership style (1,1 low task, low people)
M Leadership style (1,9 low task, high people)

Source: Reprinted from "Effects of Achievement Motivation on the Effectiveness of Leadership Patterns," by Jyuji Misumi and Fumiyasu Seki, published in Volume 16, No. 1, March 1971, of *Administrative Science Quarterly.* Copyright © 1971 Johnson Graduate School of Management, Cornell University.

Among low-achieving groups, the P, or authoritarian (9,1), supervision was most effective. The M (1,9) leadership style was the second most effective during early sessions, but eventually led to negative results. The PM, or participative (9,9), style was moderately ineffective during the first three stages but improved rapidly and was the second most effective by the end of the seventh session. The pm (1,1) leadership style was consistently effective until the fifth session; then productivity began to level off.

So what does this all mean? One can infer from the results that if an individual is high-achieving, then he or she may be driven by intrinsic factors. This translates into being the most motivated when a creative and supportive environment is provided, as indicated by the success of the participative leadership style. This group preferred to be actively challenged, and became unproductive when faced with absentee leadership. On the other hand, low-achieving groups seemed to be driven by extrinsic factors, such as supervisor behavior toward subordinates. The success of the authoritarian style indicates that this group prefers to be told what to do, and a creative environment that encouraged participation was not a successful motivator until after the supervisors and subordinates were familiar with one another. This group tended to be more self-motivated, as absentee leadership initially resulted in satisfactory production, but this did not last throughout the study. This could be an indication that subordinates were active because of the uncertainty involved, but relaxed efforts when it was clear that supervisors would not intervene.

While results of this study were not specific as to what actually occurs in Japan, other studies from high-achieving societies have supported the findings. Korean firms, for example, are relying more heavily on 9,9, or participatory, leadership. Sang Lee and associates have reported that among Korea's largest firms, a series of personality criteria are used in screening employees, and many of these directly relate to 9,9 leadership: harmonious relationships with others, creativeness, motivation to achieve, future orientation, and a sense of duty.[39] These findings have important implications as to what it means to be a leader in different cultures. The next section looks at leadership in the international context in more detail.

■ Leadership in the International Context

How do leaders in other countries attempt to direct or influence their subordinates? Are their approaches similar to those used in the United States? Research shows that there are both similarities and differences. Most international research on leadership has focused on Europe, East Asia, the Middle East, and developing countries such as India, Peru, Chile, and Argentina.

Attitudes of European Managers toward Leadership Practices

In recent years, much research has been directed at leadership approaches in Europe. Most effort has concentrated on related areas, such as decision making, risk taking, strategic planning, and organization design, which have been covered in previous chapters. Some of this previous discussion is relevant to an understanding of leadership practices in Europe. For example, British managers tend to use a highly participative leadership approach. This is true for two reasons: (1) the political background of the country favors such an approach and (2) because most top British managers are not highly involved in the day-to-day affairs of the business, they prefer to delegate authority and let much of the decision making be handled by middle- and lower-level managers. This preference contrasts sharply with that of the French and the Germans,[40] who prefer a more work-centered, authoritarian approach. In fact, if labor unions had no legally mandated seats on the boards of directors, participative management in Germany likely would be even less pervasive than it is, a problem that currently confronts firms like Volkswagen that are trying to reduce sharply their overhead to meet increasing competition in Europe.[41] Scandinavian countries, however, make wide use of participative leadership approaches, with worker representation on the boards of directors and high management-worker interaction regarding workplace design and changes.

As a general statement, most evidence indicates that European managers tend to use a participative approach. They do not entirely subscribe to Theory Y philosophical assumptions, however, because an element of Theory X thinking persists. This was made clear by the Haire, Ghiselli, and Porter study of 3,641 managers from 14 countries.[42] (The motivation-related findings of this study were reported in Chapter 12.) The leadership-related portion of this study sought to determine whether these managers were basically traditional (Theory X, or system 1/2) or democratic-participative (Theory Y, or system 3/4) in their approach. Specifically, the researchers investigated four areas relevant to leadership:

1. *Capacity for leadership and initiative.* Does the leader believe that employees prefer to be directed and have little ambition (Theory X), or does the leader believe that characteristics such as initiative can be acquired by most people regardless of their inborn traits and abilities (Theory Y)?

2. *Sharing information and objectives.* Does the leader believe that detailed, complete instructions should be given to subordinates and that subordinates need only this information to do their jobs, or does the leader believe that general directions are sufficient and that subordinates can use their initiative in working out the details?

3. *Participation.* Does the leader support participative leadership practices?

4. *Internal control.* Does the leader believe that the most effective way to control employees is through rewards and punishment or that employees respond best to internally generated control?

Overall Results of Research on Attitudes of European Managers   Responses by managers to the four areas covered in the Haire, Ghiselli, and Porter study, as noted in Chapter 12, are quite dated but remain the most comprehensive available and are relevant to the current discussion of leadership similarities and differences. The specifics by country may have changed somewhat over the years, but the leadership processes revealed should not be out of date. The clusters of countries studied by these researchers are shown in Table 13–3. Results indicate that none of the leaders from various parts of the world, on average, were very supportive of the belief that individuals have a capacity for leadership and initiative. The researchers put it this way: "In each country, in each group of countries, in all of the countries taken together, there is a relatively low opinion of the capabilities of the average person, coupled with a relatively positive belief in the necessity for democratic-type supervisory practices."[43]

An analysis of standard scores compared each cluster of countries against the others, and it revealed that Anglo leaders tend to have more faith in the capacity of their people for leadership and initiative than do the other clusters. They also believe that

Table 13–3 Clusters of Countries in the Haire, Ghiselli, and Porter Study	
NORDIC-EUROPEAN COUNTRIES Denmark Germany Norway Sweden	**ANGLO-AMERICAN COUNTRIES** England United States
	DEVELOPING COUNTRIES Argentina Chile India
LATIN-EUROPEAN COUNTRIES Belgium France Italy Spain	**JAPAN**

sharing information and objectives is important; however, when it comes to participation and internal control, the Anglo group tends to give relatively more autocratic responses than all the other clusters except developing countries. Interestingly, Anglo leaders reported a much stronger belief in the value of external rewards (pay, promotion, etc.) than did any of the clusters except that of the developing countries. These findings clearly illustrate that attitudes toward leadership practices tend to be quite different in various parts of the world.

The Role of Level, Size, and Age on European Managers' Attitudes toward Leadership The research of Haire and associates provided important additional details within each cluster of European countries. These findings indicated that in some countries, higher-level managers tended to express more democratic values than lower-level managers; however, in other countries, the opposite was true. For example, in England, higher-level managers responded with more democratic attitudes on all four leadership dimensions, whereas in the United States, lower-level managers gave more democratically oriented responses on all four. In the Scandinavian countries, higher-level managers tended to respond more democratically; in Germany, lower-level managers tended to have more democratic attitudes.

Company size also tended to influence the degree of participative-autocratic attitudes. There was more support among managers in small firms than in large ones regarding the belief that individuals have a capacity for leadership and initiative; however, respondents from large firms were more supportive of sharing information and objectives, participation, and use of internal control.

There were findings that age also had some influence on participative attitudes. Younger managers were more likely to have democratic values when it came to capacity for leadership and initiative and to sharing information and objectives, although on the other two areas of leadership practices older and younger managers differed little. In specific countries, some important differences were found. For example, younger managers in both the United States and Sweden espoused more democratic values than did their older counterparts; in Belgium, the opposite was true.

Japanese Leadership Approaches

Japan is well known for its paternalistic approach to leadership. As noted in Figure 12–7, Japanese culture promotes a high safety or security need, which is present among home country–based employees as well as MNC expatriates. For example, one study examined the cultural orientations of 522 employees of 28 Japanese-owned firms in the United States and found that the native Japanese employees were more likely than their U.S. counterparts to value paternalistic company behavior.[44] Another study found that Koreans also value such paternalism.[45] However, major differences appear in leadership approaches used by the Japanese and those in other locales.

For example, the comprehensive Haire, Ghiselli, and Porter study found that Japanese managers have much greater belief in the capacity of subordinates for leadership and initiative than do managers in most other countries.[46] In fact, in the study, only managers in Anglo-American countries had stronger feelings in this area. The Japanese also expressed attitudes toward the use of participation to a greater degree than others. In the other two leadership areas, sharing information and objectives and using internal control, the Japanese respondents were above average but not distinctive. Overall, however, this study found that the Japanese respondents scored highest on the four areas of leadership combined. In other words, these findings provide evidence that Japanese leaders have considerable confidence in the overall ability of their subordinates and use a style that allows their people to actively participate in decisions.

In addition, the leadership process used by Japanese managers places a strong emphasis on ambiguous goals. Subordinates are typically unsure of what their manager wants them to do. As a result, they spend a great deal of time overpreparing their assignments. Some observers believe that this leadership approach is time-consuming and wasteful. However, it has a number of important benefits. One is that the leader is able to maintain stronger control of the followers because the latter do not know with certainty what is expected of them. So they prepare themselves for every eventuality. Second, by placing the subordinates in a position where they must examine a great deal of information, the manager ensures that the personnel are well prepared to deal with the situation and all its ramifications. Third, the approach helps the leader maintain order and provide guidance, even when the leader is not as knowledgeable as the followers.

Two experts on the behavior of Japanese management have noted that salarymen (middle managers) survive in the organization by anticipating contingencies and being prepared to deal with them. So when the manager asks a question and the salaryman shows that he has done the research needed to answer the question, the middle manager also shows himself to be a reliable person. The leader does not have to tell the salaryman to be prepared; the individual knows what is expected of him.

Japanese managers operate this way because they usually have less expertise in a division's day-to-day business than their subordinates do. It is the manager's job to maintain harmony, not to be a technical expert. Consequently, a senior manager doesn't necessarily realize that E, F, G, and H are important to know. He gives ambiguous directions to his subordinates so they can use their superior expertise to go beyond A, B, C, and D. One salaryman explained it this way: "When my boss asks me to write a report, I infer what he wants to know and what he needs to know without being told what he wants." Another interviewee added that subordinates who receive high performance evaluations are those who know what the boss wants without needing to be told. What frustrates Japanese managers about non-Japanese employees is the feeling that, if they tell such a person they want A through D, they will never extract E through H; instead, they'll get exactly what they asked for. Inferring what the boss would have wanted had he only known to ask is a tough game, but it is the one salarymen must play.[47]

As we saw in 2010 with the massive safety recall of certain Toyota vehicles (see Chapter 4), some researchers believe that this paternalistic approach may have impeded and constrained Toyota's ability to respond quickly to vehicle quality safety problems. The Financial Times reported that, in response, Toyota is shifting more responsibility to non-Japanese managers by promoting North Americans and Europeans to run factories outside Japan. Toyota officials concluded that poor communication between local managers and their bosses in Japan contributed to the crisis. In the U.S., especially, warnings from local managers about the outcry were either passed on too slowly or not at all.[48]

Differences between Japanese and U.S. Leadership Styles

In a number of ways, Japanese leadership styles differ from those in the United States. For example, the Haire and associates study found that except for internal control, large U.S. firms tend to be more democratic than small ones, whereas in Japan, the profile is quite different.[49] A second difference is that younger U.S. managers appear to express more democratic attitudes than their older counterparts on all four leadership dimensions, but younger Japanese fall into this category only for sharing information and objectives and in the use of internal control.[50] Simply put, evidence points to some similarities between U.S. and Japanese leadership styles, but major differences also exist.

A number of reasons have been cited for these differences. One of the most common is that Japanese and U.S. managers have a basically different philosophy of managing people. Table 13–4 provides a comparison of seven key characteristics that come from Ouchi's *Theory Z,* which combines Japanese and U.S. assumptions and approaches. Note in the table that the Japanese leadership approach is heavily group-oriented, paternalistic, and concerned with the employee's work and personal life. The U.S. leadership approach is almost the opposite.[51]

Another difference between Japanese and U.S. leadership styles is how senior-level managers process information and learn. Japanese executives are taught and tend to use

Table 13-4
Japanese vs. U.S. Leadership Styles

Philosophical Dimension	Japanese Approach	U.S. Approach
Employment	Often for life; layoffs are rare	Usually short-term; layoffs are common
Evaluation and promotion	Very slow; big promotions may not come for the first 10 years	Very fast; those not quickly promoted often seek employment elsewhere
Career paths	Very general; people rotate from one area to another and become familiar with all areas of operations	Very specialized; people tend to stay in one area (accounting, sales, etc.) for their entire careers
Decision making	Carried out via group decision making	Carried out by the individual manager
Control mechanism	Very implicit and informal; people rely heavily on trust and goodwill	Very explicit; people know exactly what to control and how to do it
Responsibility	Shared collectively	Assigned to individuals
Concern for employees	Management's concern extends to the whole life, business and social, of the worker	Management concerned basically with the individual's work life only

Source: Adapted from William Ouchi, *Theory Z: How American Business Can Meet the Japanese Challenge* (Reading, MA: Addison-Wesley, 1981).

variety amplification, which is the creation of uncertainty and the analysis of many alternatives regarding future action. By contrast, U.S. executives are taught and tend to use **variety reduction**, which is the limiting of uncertainty and the focusing of action on a limited number of alternatives.[52] Through acculturation, patterning, and mentoring, as well as formal training, U.S. managers tend to limit the scope of questions and issues before them, emphasize one or two central aspects of that topic, identify specific employees to respond to it, and focus on a goal or objective that is attainable. Japanese managers, in contrast, tend to be inclusive in their consideration of issues or problems, seek a large quantity of information to inform the problem, encourage all employees to engage in solutions, and aim for goals that are distant in the future.

> **variety amplification**
> The creation of uncertainty and the analysis of many alternatives regarding future action.
>
> **variety reduction**
> The limiting of uncertainty and the focusing of action on a limited number of alternatives.

Further, this research found that Japanese focused very heavily on problems, while the U.S. managers focused on opportunities.[53] The Japanese were more willing to allow poor performance to continue for a time so that those who were involved would learn from their mistakes, but the Americans worked to stop poor performance as quickly as possible. Finally, the Japanese sought creative approaches to managing projects and tried to avoid relying on experience, but the Americans sought to build on their experiences.

Still another major reason accounting for differences in leadership styles is that the Japanese tend to be more ethnocentric than their U.S. counterparts. The Japanese think of themselves as Japanese managers who are operating overseas; most do not view themselves as international managers. As a result, even if they do adapt their leadership approach on the surface to that of the country in which they are operating, they still believe in the Japanese way of doing things and are reluctant to abandon it.

Despite these differences, managerial practices indicate that there may be more similarities than once believed. For example, in the United States, the approach used in managing workers at the Saturn plant was quite different from that employed in other GM plants. (Saturn was once one of General Motors' most successful auto offerings; as a result of GM's restructuring it has since been folded back into GM proper.) Strong attention was given to allowing workers a voice in all management decisions, and pay was linked to quality, productivity, and profitability. Japanese firms such as Sony use a similar approach, encouraging personnel to assume authority, use initiative, and work as a team. Major emphasis also is given to developing communication links between management and the employees and to encouraging people to do their best.

Another common trend is the movement toward team orientation and away from individualism. International Management in Action, "Global Teams," illustrates this point.

Institutional productivity used to involve a cavalcade of employees manning factory floors, where meetings with international subsidiaries had to be carefully planned. As technology continues to evolve and the window for decision making periods quickly closes, the need to instantly connect and coordinate with regional and transnational offices becomes imperative to stay competitive. But how is this implemented? International leaders now put increasing focus on developing global teams that are capable of overcoming cultural barriers and working together in an efficient, harmonious manner. At Dallas-based Maxus Energy (a wholly owned subsidiary of YPF, the largest Argentinean corporation in the world), teams consist of Americans, Dutch, British, and Indonesians who have been brought together to pursue a common goal: maximize oil and gas production. Capitalizing on the technical expertise of the members and their willingness to work together, the team has helped the company to achieve its objective and add oil reserves to its stockpiles—an almost unprecedented achievement. This story is only one of many that help illustrate the way in which global teams are being created and used to achieve difficult international objectives.

In developing effective global teams, companies are finding there are four phases in the process. In phase one, the team members come together with their own expectations, culture, and values. In phase two, members go through a self-awareness period, during which they learn to respect the cultures of the other team members. Phase three is characterized by a developing trust among members, and in phase four, team members begin working in a collaborative way.

How are MNCs able to create the environment that is needed for this metamorphosis? Several specific steps are implemented by management, including:

1. The objectives of the group are carefully identified and communicated to the members.

2. Team members are carefully chosen so that the group has the necessary skills and personnel to reinforce and complement each other.

3. Each person learns what he or she is to contribute to the group, thus promoting a feeling of self-importance and interdependency.

4. Cultural differences between the members are discussed so that members can achieve a better understanding of how they may work together effectively.

5. Measurable outcomes are identified so that the team can chart its progress and determine how well it is doing. Management also continually stresses the team's purpose and its measurable outcomes so that the group does not lose sight of its goals.

6. Specially designed training programs are used to help the team members develop interpersonal, intercultural skills.

7. Lines of communication are spelled out so that everyone understands how to communicate with other members of the group.

8. Members are continually praised and rewarded for innovative ideas and actions.

MNCs now find that global teams are critical to their ability to compete successfully in the world market. As a result, leaders who are able to create and lead interdisciplinary, culturally diverse groups are finding themselves in increasing demand by MNCs.

Leadership in China

In the past few years a growing amount of attention has been focused on leadership in China. In particular, international researchers are interested in learning if the country's economic progress is creating a new cadre of leaders whose styles are different from the styles of leaders of the past. In one of the most comprehensive studies to date, Ralston and his colleagues found that, indeed, a new generation of Chinese leaders is emerging and they are somewhat different from past leaders in work values.[54]

The researchers gathered data from a large number of managers and professionals ($n = 869$) who were about to take part in management development programs. These individuals were part of what the researchers called the "New Generation" of Chinese organizational leaders. The researchers wanted to determine if this new generation of managers had the same work values as those of the "Current Generation" and "Older Generation" groups. In their investigation, the researchers focused their attention on the importance that the respondents assigned to three areas: individualism, collectivism, and Confucianism. Individualism was measured by the importance assigned to self-sufficiency and personal accomplishments. Collectivism was measured by the person's willingness to subordinate personal goals to those of the work group with an emphasis on sharing and group harmony. Confucianism was measured by the importance the respondent assigned to societal harmony, virtuous interpersonal behavior, and personal and interpersonal harmony.

The researchers found that the new generation group scored significantly higher on individualism than did the current and older generation groups. In addition, the new generation leaders scored significantly lower than the other two groups on collectivism and Confucianism. These values appear to reflect the period of relative openness and freedom, often called the "Social Reform Era," during which these new managers grew up. They have had greater exposure to Western societal influences, and this may well be resulting in leadership styles similar to those of Western managers.

These research findings show that leadership is culturally influenced, but as the economy of China continues to change and the country moves more and more toward capitalism, the work values of managers may also change. As a result, the new generation of leaders may well use leadership styles similar to those in the West, something that has also occurred in Japan, as seen in Figures 13–3 and 13–4.

Leadership in the Middle East

Research also has been conducted on Middle East countries to determine the similarities and differences in managerial attitudes toward leadership practices. For example, in a follow-up study to that of Haire and associates, midlevel managers from Arab countries were surveyed and found to have higher attitude scores for capacity for leadership and initiative than those from any of the other countries or clusters reported in Table 13–3.[55] The Arab managers' scores for sharing information and objectives, participation, and internal control, however, all were significantly lower than the scores of managers in the other countries and clusters reported in Table 13–3. The researcher concluded that the results were accounted for by the culture of the Middle East region. Table 13–5 summarizes not only the leadership differences between Middle Eastern and Western managers but also other areas of organization and management.

More recent research provides some evidence that there may be much greater similarity between Middle Eastern leadership styles and those of Western countries.[56] In particular, the observation was made that Western management practices are very evident in the Arabian Gulf region because of the close business ties between the West and this oil-rich area and the increasing educational attainment, often in Western universities, of Middle Eastern managers. A study on decision-making styles in the United Arab Emirates showed that organizational culture, level of technology, level of education, and management responsibility were good predictors of decision-making styles in such an environment.[57] These findings were consistent with similar studies in Western environments. Also, results indicated a tendency toward participative leadership styles among young Arab middle management, as well as among highly educated managers of all ages.[58]

Leadership Approaches in India

India is developing at a rapid rate as MNCs increase investment. India's workforce is quite knowledgeable in the high-tech industry, and society as a whole is moving toward higher education. However, India is still bound by old traditions. This raises the question, What kind of leadership style does India need to satisfy its traditional roots while heading into a high-tech future? One study showed that Indian workers were more productive when managers took a high people and high task approach (participative). Meanwhile, the less productive workers were managed by individuals who showed high people orientation, but low focus on task-related objectives.[59] These findings may indicate that it is important in India to focus on the individual, but in order to be efficient and produce results, managers need to maintain awareness of the tasks that need to be completed.

Table 13–5
Differences between Middle Eastern and Western Management

Management Dimensions	Middle Eastern Management	Western Management
Leadership	Highly authoritarian tone, rigid instructions. Too many management directives.	Less emphasis on leader's personality, considerable weight on leader's style and performance.
Organizational structures	Highly bureaucratic, overcentralized, with power and authority at the top. Vague relationships. Ambiguous and unpredictable organization environments.	Less bureaucratic, more delegation of authority. Relatively decentralized structure.
Decision making	Ad hoc planning, decisions made at the highest level of management. Unwillingness to take high risk inherent in decision making.	Sophisticated planning techniques, modern tools of decision making, elaborate management information systems.
Performance evaluation and control	Informal control mechanisms, routine checks on performance. Lack of vigorous performance evaluation systems.	Fairly advanced control systems focusing on cost reduction and organizational effectiveness.
Personnel policies	Heavy reliance on personal contacts and getting individuals from the "right social origin" to fill major positions.	Sound personnel management policies. Candidates' qualifications are usually the basis for selection decisions.
Communication	The tone depends on the communicants. Social position, power, and family influence are ever-present factors. Chain of command must be followed rigidly. People relate to each other tightly and specifically. Friendships are intense and binding.	Stress usually on equality and a minimization of difference. People relate to each other loosely and generally. Friendships not intense and binding.

Source: From M. K. Badawy, "Styles of Mid-Eastern Managers," *California Management Review*, Spring 1980. Copyright © 1980, by The Regents of the University of California. Reprinted from the California Management review, Vol. 22, No. 3. By permission of The Regents. All rights reserved. This article is for personal viewing by individuals accessing this site. It is not to be copied, reproduced, or otherwise disseminated without written permission from the California Management Review. By viewing this document, you hereby agree to these terms. For permission or reprints, contact: cmr@haas.berkeley.edu.

Because of India's long affiliation with Great Britain, leadership styles in India would seem more likely to be participative than those in the Middle East or in other developing countries. Haire and associates found some degree of similarity between leadership styles in India and Anglo-American countries, but it was not significant. The study found Indians to be similar to the Anglo-Americans in managerial attitudes toward capacity for leadership and initiative, participation, and internal control. The difference is in sharing information and objectives. The Indian managers' responses tended to be quite similar to those of managers in other developing countries.[60] These findings from India show that a participative leadership style may be more common and more effective in developing countries than has been reported previously. Over time, developing countries (as also shown in the case of the Persian Gulf nations) may be moving toward a more participative leadership style. Recently, researchers have suggested there may be some unique management and leadership styles that emerge from the polyglot nature of India's population and some of the unique challenges of doing business there. For example, some suggest that Indian leaders can improvise quickly to overcome hurdles, a concept sometimes referred to here as *jugaad*.[61]

Leadership Approaches in Latin America

Research pertaining to leadership styles in Latin America has indicated that as globalization increases, so does the transitional nature of managers within these regions. One study that compared Latin American leadership styles reviewed past research indicating an initial universality among the countries.[62] In Mexico, leaders tended to have a combination of authoritarian and participative behaviors, while Chile, Argentina, and Bolivia also showed signs of authoritarian behaviors. Typically, Mexican managers who welcomed input from subordinates were viewed as incompetent and weak. This may be the reason that in Mexico, as well as in Chile, managers tend to be socially distant from those working below them. Romero found that Mexican managers who worked close to the U.S. border, however, exhibited even more participative behavior, and that trend enhanced as globalization increased.[63] Overall, the study found that Mexico is moving toward a modern leadership style, while other Latin American countries continue to lead based on tradition. However, this is not the only viewpoint.

Haire and associates originally found quite different results for Chile and Argentina, and one can only assume that Peru would be similar to the aforementioned countries due to their geographic and cultural similarities. The results from the study for those two developing countries were similar to those for India.[64] Additional research, however, has found that leadership styles in Peru may be much closer to those in the United States than was previously assumed.

As in the case of Middle Eastern managers, these findings in South America indicate there indeed may be more similarities in international leadership styles than previously assumed. As countries become more economically advanced, participative styles may well gain in importance. Of course, this does not mean that MNCs can use the same leadership styles in their various locations around the world. There still must be careful contingency application of leadership styles (different styles for different situations); however, many of the more enlightened participative leadership styles used in the United States and other economically advanced countries, such as Japan, also may have value in managing international operations even in developing countries as well as in the emerging Eastern European countries.

■ Recent Findings and Insights about Leadership

In recent years researchers have begun raising the question of universality of leadership behavior. Do effective leaders, regardless of their country culture or job, act similarly? A second, and somewhat linked, research inquiry has focused on the question, Are there a host of specific behaviors, attitudes, and values that leaders in the 21st century will need in order to be successful? Thus far the findings have been mixed. Some investigators have found that there is a trend toward universalism for leadership; others have concluded that culture continues to be a determining factor and that an effective leader, for example, in Sweden will not be as effective in Italy if he or she employs the same approach, most likely due to motivational factors being different (see Chapter 12). One of the most interesting recent efforts has been conducted by Bass and his associates, and has focused on the universality and effectiveness of both transformational and transactional leadership.

Transformational, Transactional, and Charismatic Leadership

Transformational leaders are visionary agents with a sense of mission who are capable of motivating their followers to accept new goals and new ways of doing things. One recent variant on transformational leadership focuses on the individual's charismatic traits and abilities. This research stream, known as the study of **charismatic leaders**, has explored how the individual abilities of an executive work to inspire and motivate her or his subordinates.[65] **Transactional leaders** are individuals who exchange rewards for effort and performance and work on a "something for something" basis.[66] Do these types of leaders exist worldwide, and is their effectiveness consistent in terms of performance? Drawing on an analysis of studies conducted in Canada, India, Italy, Japan, New Zealand, Singapore, and Sweden, as well as in the United States, Bass discovered that very little of the variance in leadership behavior could be attributed to culture. In fact, in many cases he found that national differences accounted for less than 10 percent of the results.

transformational leaders
Leaders who are visionary agents with a sense of mission and who are capable of motivating their followers to accept new goals and new ways of doing things.

charismatic leaders
Leaders who inspire and motivate employees through their charismatic traits and abilities.

transactional leaders
Individuals who exchange rewards for effort and performance and work on a "something for something" basis.

This led him to create a model of leadership and conclude that "although this model . . . may require adjustments and fine-tuning as we move across cultures, particularly into non-Western cultures, overall, it holds up as having considerable universal potential."[67]

Simply stated, Bass discovered that there was far more universalism in leadership than had been believed previously. Additionally, after studying thousands of international cases, he found that the most effective managers were transformational leaders and they were characterized by four interrelated factors. For convenience, the factors are referred to as the "4 I's," and they can be described this way:

1. *Idealized influence.* Transformational leaders are a source of charisma and enjoy the admiration of their followers. They enhance pride, loyalty, and confidence in their people, and they align these followers by providing a common purpose or vision that the latter willingly accept.

2. *Inspirational motivation.* These leaders are extremely effective in articulating their vision, mission, and beliefs in clear-cut ways, thus providing an easy-to-understand sense of purpose regarding what needs to be done.

3. *Intellectual stimulation.* Transformational leaders are able to get their followers to question old paradigms and to accept new views of the world regarding how things now need to be done.

4. *Individualized consideration.* These leaders are able to diagnose and elevate the needs of each of their followers through individualized consideration, thus furthering the development of these people.[68]

Bass also discovered that there were four other types of leaders. All of these are less effective than the transformational leader, although the degree of their effectiveness (or ineffectiveness) will vary. The most effective of the remaining four types was labeled the *contingent reward (CR) leader* by Bass. This leader clarifies what needs to be done and provides both psychic and material rewards to those who comply with his or her directives. The next most effective manager is the *active management-by-exception (MBE-A) leader.* This individual monitors follower performance and takes corrective action when deviations from standards occur. The next manager in terms of effectiveness is the *passive management-by-exception (MBE-P) leader.* This leader takes action or intervenes in situations only when standards are not met. Finally, there is the *laissez-faire (LF) leader.* This person avoids intervening or accepting responsibility for follower actions.

Bass found that through the use of higher-order factor analysis it is possible to develop a leadership model that illustrates the effectiveness of all five types of leaders: I's (transformational), CR, MBE-A, MBE-P, and LF. Figure 13–5 presents this model. The higher the box in the figure and the farther to the right on the shaded base area, the more effective and active is the leader. Notice that the 4 I's box is taller than any of the others in the figure and is located more to the right than any of the others. The CR box is second tallest and second closest to the right, on down to the LF box, which is the shortest and farthest from the right margin.

Bass also found that the 4 I's were positively correlated with each other, but less so with contingent reward. Moreover, there was a near zero correlation between the 4 I's and management-by-exception styles, and there was an inverse correlation between these four factors and the laissez-faire leadership style.

Does this mean that effective leader behaviors are the same regardless of country? Bass concluded that this statement is not quite true—but there is far more universalism than people believed previously. In putting his findings in perspective, he concluded that there certainly would be differences in leadership behavior from country to country.[69] For example, he noted that transformational leaders in Honduras would have to be more directive than their counterparts in Norway. Moreover, culture can create some problems in using universal leadership concepts in countries such as Japan, where the use of contingent reward systems is not as widespread as in the West. These reward systems can also become meaningless in Arab and Turkish cultures where there is a strong belief that

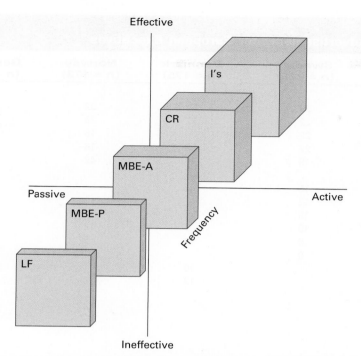

Figure 13–5

An Optimal Profile of Universal Leadership Behaviors

Source: Adapted from Bernard M. Bass, "Is There Universality in the Full Range Model of Leadership?" *International Journal of Public Administration* 16, no. 6 (1996), p. 738.

things will happen "if God wills" and not because a leader has decided to carry them out. Yet even after taking these differences into consideration, Bass contends that universal leadership behavior is far more common than many people realize.[70]

Qualities for Successful Leaders

Another recent research approach that has been used to address the issue of international leadership is that of examining the characteristics that companies are looking for in their new executive hires. Are all firms seeking the same types of behaviors or qualities or, for example, are companies in Sweden looking for executives with qualities that are quite different from those being sought by Italian firms? The answer to this type of question can help shed light on international leadership because it helps focus attention on the behaviors that organizations believe are important in their managerial workforce. It also helps examine the impact, if any, of culture on leadership style.

Tollgerdt-Andersson examined thousands of advertisements for executives in the European Union (EU). She began by studying ads in Swedish newspapers and journals, noting the qualities, characteristics, and behaviors that were being sought. She then expanded her focus to publications in other European countries including Denmark, Norway, Germany, Great Britain, France, Italy, and Spain. The results are reported in Table 13–6. Based on this analysis, she concluded:

> Generally, there seem to be great differences between the European countries regarding their leadership requirements. Different characteristics are stressed in the various countries. There are also differences concerning how frequently various characteristics are demanded in each country. Some kind of personal or social quality is mentioned much more often in the Scandinavian countries than in the other European countries. In the Scandinavian advertisements, you often see many qualities mentioned in a single advertisement. This can be seen in other European countries too, but it is much more rare. Generally, the characteristics mentioned in a single advertisement do not exceed three and fairly often, especially in Mediterranean countries (in 46–48% of the advertisements) no personal or social characteristics are mentioned at all.[71]

Table 13–6
Qualities Most Demanded in Advertisements for European Executives

Quality	Sweden (*n* = 225)	Denmark (*n* = 175)	Norway (*n* = 173)	Germany (*n* = 190)
Ability to cooperate (interpersonal ability)	25	42	32	16
Independence	22	22	25	9
Leadership ability	22		16	17
Ability to take initiatives	22	12	16	
Aim and result orientation	19	10	42	
Ability to motivate and inspire others	16	11		
Business orientation	12			
Age	10	25		13
Extrovert personality/contact ability	10	8	12	11
Creativity	9	10	9	9
Customer ability	9			
Analytic ability		10		
Ability to communicate		12	15	
High level of energy/drive			12	
Enthusiasm and involvement			14	14
Organization skills				7
Team builder				
Self-motivated				
Flexibility				
Precision				
Dynamic personality				
Responsibility				

Quality	Great Britain (*n* = 163)	France (*n* = 164)	Italy (*n* = 132)	Spain (*n* = 182)
Ability to cooperate (interpersonal ability)	7	9	32	18
Independence			16	4
Leadership ability	10		22	16
Ability to take initiatives			10	8
Aim and result orientation	5			2
Ability to motivate and inspire others		9	26	20
Business orientation				8
Age		12	46	34
Extrovert personality/contact ability				
Creativity	5			4
Customer ability				2
Analytic ability			10	
Ability to communicate	23			8
High level of energy/drive	8			20
Enthusiasm and involvement				
Organization skills		6	12	12
Team builder	10	5		
Self-motivated	10			
Flexibility				2
Precision		7		
Dynamic personality		6		6
Responsibility				10

Note: The qualities most demanded in Swedish, Danish, Norwegian, German, British, French, Italian, and Spanish advertisements for executives are expressed in percentage terms. *n* = total number of advertisements analyzed in each country. Each entry represents the percentage of the total advertisements requesting each quality.

Source: Adapted from Ingrid Tollgerdt-Andersson, "Attitudes, Values and Demands on Leadership—A Cultural Comparison among Some European Countries," in *Managing Across Cultures,* ed. Pat Joynt and Malcolm Warner (London: International Thomson Business Press, 1996), p. 173.

At the same time, Tollgerdt-Andersson did find that there were similarities between nations. For example, Italy and Spain had common patterns regarding desirable leadership characteristics. Between 52 and 54 percent of the ads she reviewed in these two countries stated specific personal and social abilities that were needed by the job applicant. The same pattern was true for Germany and Great Britain, where between 64 and 68 percent of the advertisements set forth the personal and social abilities required for the job. In the Scandinavian countries these percentages ranged between 80 and 85.

Admittedly, it may be difficult to determine the degree of similarity between ads in different countries (or cultural clusters) because there may be implied meanings in the messages or it may be the custom in a country not to mention certain abilities but simply to assume that applicants know that these will be assessed in making the final hiring decision. Additionally, Tollgerdt-Andersson did find that all countries expected executive applicants to have good social and personal qualities. So some degree of universalism in leadership behaviors was uncovered. On the other hand, the requirements differed from country to country, showing that effective leaders in northern Europe may not be able to transfer their skills to the southern part of the continent with equal results. This led Tollgerdt-Andersson to conclude that multicultural understanding will continue to be a requirement for effective leadership in the 21st century. She put it this way: "If tomorrow's leaders possess international competence and understanding of other cultures it will, hopefully, result in the increased competitive cooperation which is essential if European commerce and industry is to compete with, for example, the USA and Asia."[72]

Culture Clusters and Leader Effectiveness

Although the foregoing discussion indicates there is research to support universalism in leadership behavior, recent findings also show that effective leader behaviors tend to vary by cultural cluster. Brodbeck and his associates conducted a large survey of middle

Table 13–7
Rankings of the Most Important Leadership Attributes by Region and Country Cluster

North/West European Region

Anglo Culture (Great Britain, Ireland)	Nordic Culture (Sweden, Netherlands, Finland, Denmark)	Germanic Culture (Switzerland, Germany, Austria)	Czech Republic	France
Performance-oriented	Integrity	Integrity	Integrity	Participative
Inspirational	Inspirational	Inspirational	Performance-oriented	Nonautocratic
Visionary	Visionary	Performance-oriented	Administratively skilled	
Team integrator	Team integrator	Nonautocratic	Inspirational	
Decisive	Performance-oriented	Visionary	Nonautocratic	

South/East European Region

Latin Culture (Italy, Spain, Portugal, Hungary)	Central Culture (Poland, Slovenia)	Near East Culture (Turkey, Greece)	Russia	Georgia
Team integrator	Team integrator	Team integrator	Visionary	Administratively skilled
Performance-oriented	Visionary	Decisive	Administratively skilled	Decisive
Inspirational	Administratively skilled	Visionary	Inspirational	Performance-oriented
Integrity	Diplomatic	Integrity	Decisive	Visionary
Visionary	Decisive	Inspirational	Integrity	Integrity

Source: Adapted from Felix C. Brodbeck et al., "Cultural Variation of Leadership Prototypes Across 22 European Countries," *Journal of Occupational and Organizational Psychology* 73 (2000), p. 15.

managers ($n = 6,052$) from 22 European countries.[73] Some of the results, grouped by cluster, are presented in Table 13–7. A close look at the data shows that while there are similarities between some of the cultures, none of the lists of leadership attributes are identical. For example, managers in the Anglo cluster reported that the five most important attributes of an effective manager were a performance orientation, an inspirational style, having a vision, being a team integrator, and being decisive. Managers in the Nordic culture ranked these same five attributes as the most important but not in this order. Moreover, although the rankings of clusters in the North/West European region were fairly similar, they were quite different from those in the South/East European region, which included the Latin cluster, countries from Eastern Europe that were grouped by the researchers into a Central cluster and a Near East cluster, and Russia and Georgia, which were listed separately.

Leader Behavior, Leader Effectiveness, and Leading Teams

Culture is also important in helping explain how leaders ought to act in order to be effective. A good example is provided by the difference in effective behaviors in Trompenaars's categories (covered in Chapter 4) of affective (or emotional) cultures and neutral cultures. In affective cultures, such as the United States, leaders tend to exhibit their emotions. In neutral cultures, such as Japan and China, leaders do not tend to show their emotions. Moreover, in some cultures people are taught to exhibit their emotions but not let emotion affect their making rational decisions, while in other cultures the two are intertwined.

Researchers have also found that the way in which managers speak to their people can influence the outcome. For example, in Anglo cultures it is common for managers to raise their voices in order to emphasize a point. In Asian cultures managers generally speak at the same level throughout their communication, using a form of self-control that shows respect for the other person. Latin American managers, meanwhile, vary their tone of voice continually, and this form of exaggeration is viewed by them as showing that they are very interested in what they are saying and committed to their point of view. Knowing how to communicate can greatly influence leadership across cultures. Here is an example:

> A British manager posted to Nigeria found that it was very effective to raise his voice for important issues. His Nigerian subordinates viewed that unexpected explosion by a normally self-controlled manager as a sign of extra concern. After success in Nigeria he was posted to Malaysia. Shouting there was a sign of loss of face; his colleagues did not take him seriously and he was transferred.[74]

One of the keys to successful global leadership is knowing which style and which behavior work best in a given culture and adapting appropriately. In the case of affective and neutral cultures, for example, Trompenaars and Hampden-Turner have offered the specific tips provided in Table 13–8.

Cross-Cultural Leadership: Insights from the GLOBE Study

As discussed in Chapter 4, the GLOBE (Global Leadership and Organizational Behavior Effectiveness) research program, a 20-year, multimethod, three-phased study, is examining the relationships among societal and organizational culture, societal and organizational effectiveness, and leadership. In addition to the identification of nine major dimensions of culture described in Chapter 4, the GLOBE program also includes the classification of six global leadership behaviors. Through a qualitative and quantitative analysis of leadership, GLOBE researchers determined that leadership behaviors can be summarized into six broad categories:

- **Charismatic/Value-Based** leadership captures the ability of leaders to inspire, motivate, and encourage high performance outcomes from others based on a foundation of core values.
- **Team-Oriented** leadership places emphasis on effective team building and implementation of a common goal among team members.

Table 13–8
Leadership Tips for Doing Business in Affective and Neutral Cultures

When Managing or Being Managed in . . .

Affective Cultures	Neutral Cultures
Avoid a detached, ambiguous, and cool demeanor because this will be interpreted as negative behavior.	Avoid warm, excessive, or enthusiastic behaviors because these will be interpreted as a lack of personal control over one's feelings and be viewed as inconsistent with one's high status.
Find out whose work and enthusiasm are being directed into which projects, so you are able to appreciate the vigor and commitment they have for these efforts.	Extensively prepare the things you have to do and then stick tenaciously to the issues.
Let people be emotional without personally becoming intimidated or coerced by their behavior.	Look for cues regarding whether people are pleased or angry and then amplify their importance.

When Doing Business with Individuals in . . .

Affective Cultures (for Those from Neutral Cultures)	Neutral Cultures (for Those from Affective Cultures)
Do not be put off stride when others create scenes and get histrionic; take time-outs for sober reflection and hard assessments.	Ask for time-outs from meetings and negotiations where you can patch each other up and rest between games of poker with the "impassive ones."
When others are expressing goodwill, respond warmly.	Put down as much as you can on paper before beginning the negotiation.
Remember that the other person's enthusiasm and readiness to agree or disagree do not mean that the individual has made up his or her mind.	Remember that the other person's lack of emotional tone does not mean that the individual is uninterested or bored, only that the person does not like to show his or her hand.
Keep in mind that the entire negotiation is typically focused on you as a person and not so much on the object or proposition that is being discussed.	Keep in mind that the entire negotiation is typically focused on the object or proposition that is being discussed and not on you as a person.

Recognize the Way in Which People Behave in . . .

Affective Cultures	Neutral Cultures
They reveal their thoughts and feelings both verbally and nonverbally.	They often do not reveal what they are thinking or feeling.
Emotions flow easily, vehemently, and without inhibition.	Emotions are often dammed up, although they may occasionally explode.
Heated, vital, and animated expressions are admired.	Cool and self-possessed conduct is admired.
Touching, gesturing, and strong facial expressions are common.	Physical contact, gesturing, or strong facial expressions are not used.
Statements are made fluently and dramatically.	Statements are often read out in a monotone voice.

Source: Adapted from Fons Trompenaars and Charles Hampden-Turner, *Riding the Waves of Culture: Understanding Diversity in Global Business,* 2nd ed. (New York: McGraw-Hill, 1998), pp. 80–82.

- **Participative** leadership reflects the extent to which leaders involve others in decisions and their implementation.
- **Humane-Oriented** leadership comprises supportive and considerate leadership.
- **Autonomous** leadership refers to independent and individualistic leadership behaviors.
- **Self-Protective** leadership "focuses on ensuring the safety and security of the individual and group through status-enhancement and face-saving."[75]

As is the case in the classification of culture dimensions, these categories build on and extend classifications of leadership styles described earlier in this chapter.

Phases 1 and 2 of the GLOBE study, like earlier research, found that certain attributes of leadership were universally endorsed, while others were viewed as effective only in certain cultures. Among the leadership attributes found to be effective across cultures are being trustworthy, just, and honest (having integrity); having foresight and planning ahead; being positive, dynamic, encouraging, and motivating and building confidence; and being communicative and informed and being a coordinator and a team integrator.[76] Several attributes were also found to be universally undesirable in leadership. Traits such as irritable, malevolent, and ruthless were rated as inhibitors of strong leadership across all cultures.[77]

In linking the cultural dimensions of the GLOBE study with the leadership styles described above, the GLOBE researchers investigated the association between cultural values and leadership attributes, and cultural practices and leadership attributes. With regard to the relationship between cultural values and leadership attributes, the GLOBE researchers concluded the following:

- Collectivism I values, as found in Sweden and other Nordic and Scandinavian countries, were likely to view Participative and Self-Protective leadership behaviors favorably while viewing Autonomous leadership behaviors negatively.[78]

- In-Group Collectivism II values, as found in societies such as the Philippines and other East Asian countries, were positively related to Charismatic/Value-Based leadership and Team-Oriented leadership.[79]

- Gender Egalitarian values, as found in countries such as Hungary, Russia, and Poland, were positively associated with Participative and Charismatic/Value-Based leader attributes.[80]

- Performance Orientation values, as found in countries such as Switzerland, Singapore, and Hong Kong, were positively associated with Participative and Charismatic/Value-Based leader attributes.[81]

- Future Orientation values, as found in societies such as Singapore, were positively associated with Self-Protective and Humane-Oriented leader attributes.[82]

- Societal Uncertainty Avoidance values, as found in Germany, Denmark, and China, were positively associated with Team-Oriented, Humane-Oriented, and Self-Protective leader attributes.[83]

- Societal Humane Orientation values, as found in countries such as Zambia, the Philippines, and Ireland, were positively associated with Participative leader attributes.[84]

- Societal Assertiveness values, as found in countries such as the United States, Germany, and Austria, were positively associated with Humane-Oriented leader attributes.[85]

- Societal Power Distance values, as found in countries such as Morocco, Nigeria, and Argentina, were positively correlated with Self-Protective and Humane-Oriented leader attributes.[86]

One of the most influential and possibly universal leadership attributes is future orientation. An extension of the GLOBE project compared the future orientation of select countries, and surprisingly found that "the greater a society's future orientation, the higher its average GDP per capita and its levels of innovativeness, happiness, confidence, and . . . competitiveness."[87] Figure 13–6 illustrates the findings. As shown, Singapore is the most future-oriented country, while Slovenia is the most competitive. Other extremely competitive cultures include Switzerland, the Netherlands, and Malaysia. Conversely, Russia, Argentina, Poland, and Hungary were the least future-oriented, with Germany, Taiwan, Korea, and Ireland posed somewhere in between.

Phase 3 of the GLOBE project, which was completed in 2012, expanded on the middle-management studies of phases 1 and 2 by exploring the relationship between the

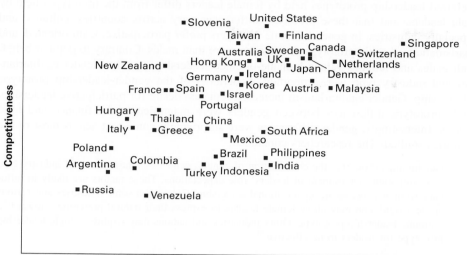

Future Orientation
(cultural support for delayed gratification, planning, and investment)

Source: Reprinted by permission of *Harvard Business Review* from "Forward Thinking Cultures" by Mansour Javidan, July–August 2007, p. 20. Copyright © 2007 by the Harvard Business School Publishing Corporation; all rights reserved.

Figure 13–6

Cross-Country Comparison: Future Orientation and Competitiveness

leadership behavior of CEOs and the effectiveness of their companies. It had been long assumed, yet unproven, that successful executives behave and lead in a manner that is consistent with the preferred leadership style of that particular culture; phase 3 was intended to fill in this gap in the research.[88]

Using a survey of over 1000 CEOs and 5000 direct reports, phase 3 determined that CEOs tend to lead in a way that is consistent with the culturally-desired leadership dimensions of that society. For example, in societies that prefer participatory leadership (such as Germany), CEOs tend to lead in a participatory manner. In southern Asia, where the society prefers more humane leadership, CEOs act in a humane way. If the ideal type of leadership of a society is known, the actions and behaviors of the CEOs in that society can likely be predicted. Furthermore, the study found that CEOs tend to lead in the culturally-desired style of their society not just because they were raised in that particular culture, but because leading in the desired manner of the society leads to success. In the most successful companies, leaders exceeded the cultural expectations of their society. In the least productive and inefficient companies, CEOs fell short of the idealized leadership style. Across all cultures, CEOs who exhibited charismatic, value-based, and team-oriented leadership traits were more likely to also exhibit the desired leadership characteristics of their society.[89]

In summarizing the GLOBE findings, researchers suggest that cultural values influence leadership preferences. Specifically, societies that share particular values prefer leadership attributes or styles that are congruent with or supportive of those values, with some exceptions. The studies also resulted in some unexpected findings. For example, societies that valued assertiveness were positively correlated with valuing Humane-Oriented leadership. According to one interpretation, some of these contradictions may reflect desires by societies to make up for or mitigate some aspects of cultural values with seemingly opposing leadership attributes. In the case of societies that value assertiveness, a preference for Humane-Oriented leader attributes may reflect a desire to provide a social support structure in an environment characterized by high competition.[90]

A recent study that used GLOBE data explored preferred leadership styles and approaches and their effectiveness across gender. As reported in Chapter 4 and elsewhere in Part Two, gender roles differ greatly in various cultures around the world, although there is some evidence of convergence among many of these cultures. One study showed preferred leadership prototypes held by female leaders differ from the prototypes held by male leaders, and that these prototype differences vary across countries, cultures, and especially industries. In general, female managers prefer participative, team oriented, and charismatic leadership prototype dimensions more than males. Contrary to popular belief, both males and females valued humane-oriented leadership equally. Gender egalitarianism and industry type were important moderators of the gender-leadership prototype relationship. Gender egalitarianism increased females' desire for participative leadership, while prototype differences between genders were magnified in the finance and food sectors. Interestingly, gender differences were surprisingly consistent across most of the countries studied. The researchers concluded:

> Our findings show that the combination of gender, gender egalitarianism and industry type is an important determinant of leaders' role expectations. These factors are likely to influence women's success in organizational leadership. Cultures in some industries and nations are less rigid, and may allow female leaders to express their natural preferences towards a feminine leadership prototype. Other industries and nations may require a single leadership prototype for leaders to be effective.[91]

Positive Organizational Scholarship and Leadership

positive organizational scholarship (POS)
A method that focuses on positive outcomes, processes, and attributes of organizations and their members.

Positive organizational scholarship (POS) focuses on positive outcomes, processes, and attributes of organizations and their members.[92] This is a dynamic view that factors in fundamental concerns, but ultimately emphasizes positive human potential, something of obvious relevance as MNCs are increasingly called upon to make contributions to society beyond the bottom line. It consists of three subunits: enablers, motivations, and outcomes or effects. Enablers could be capabilities, processes or methods, and structure of the environment, which are all external factors. Motivations focus inward, and are categorized as unselfish, altruistic, or as having the ability to contribute without self-regard. Finally, the outcomes or effects in this model accentuate vitality, meaningfulness, exhilaration, and high-quality relationships.[93]

The way POS relates to leadership is encompassed in the name. POS recognizes the positive potential that people have within. Constructive behavior will yield desired outcomes, in the sense that those who are able to create meaning in actions and are relatively flexible will be more successful in receiving praise and creating lasting relationships. These are characteristics that could be attributed to leaders, as future vision and relating to employees are positive driving forces that encourage leadership progress. Next, this method outlines positive organizational actions. For instance, if a firm is doing financially well due to actions such as downsizing, POS would accentuate the revenue and its potentials, instead of harping on the negative side effects. As indicated earlier in the chapter, leaders tend to reward for good things, and deemphasize the general tendency to motivate through pointing out issues. Effective leaders seem to live by the POS model, as they are constantly innovating, creating relationships, striving to bring the organization to new heights, and ultimately working for the greater global good through self-improvement. While positive internal and external factors provide a general framework for what makes a leader, how does one know that the person in power is a true leader?

Authentic Leadership

What makes a leader "authentic"? Researchers have sought to explain what makes a leader authentic and why leaders are important to today's organizations.

As indicated throughout the chapter, leaders tend to be dynamic, forward-thinking, and pioneers in setting new standards. Therefore, individuals who are stagnant or meet the status quo without reaching for higher realms could be considered ineffectual, or inauthentic, leaders. Just as with positive organizational scholarship, authentic leadership accentuates the positive. Authentic leaders are defined by an all-encompassing package of personality traits, styles, behaviors, and credits.[94] Many interpretations exist as to what makes a leader authentic. For example, authentic leaders could be defined as "those who are deeply aware of how they think and behave and are perceived by others as being aware of their own and others' values/moral perspectives, knowledge, and strengths; aware of the context in which they operate; and who are confident, hopeful, optimistic, resilient, and of high moral character."[95] An interpretation by Shamir and Eilam suggested that authentic leaders have four distinct characteristics: (1) authentic leaders do not fake their actions; they are true to themselves and do not adhere to external expectations; (2) authentic leaders are driven from internal forces, not external rewards; (3) authentic leaders are unique and guide based on personal beliefs, not others' orders; and (4) authentic leaders act based on individual passion and values.[96] However, the authors did not accentuate personal moral drive, which is elsewhere considered to be of great importance to the authentic leader.

Authentic leaders must possess several interrelated qualities. First, they must have positive psychological aspects, such as confidence and optimism. Next, leaders should have positive morals to guide them through processes. However, these aspects are not effective unless the leader is self-aware, as it is essential for leaders to be cognizant of their duties and be true to themselves. This also means that leaders should periodically check their actions and make sure they are congruous with ultimate goals, and that they do not stray from internal standards or expected outcomes. Authentic leaders are expected to lead by example, and therefore their processes and behaviors should be virtuous and reflect the positive moral values inherent in the leader. However, a leader cannot exist without followers, and if the methods are effective, then the open communication and functionality will motivate followers to exhibit the same characteristics. In other words, followers will become self-aware, and a new clarity will be created in relation to values, morals, and drivers.[97] This could eventually result in followers being indirectly molded into leaders, as inspiration is quite effective. Furthermore, followers will tend toward a sense of trust in their leader, actively engage in processes, and experience a sense of overall workplace well-being.[98] Environment also plays a role in leadership development, and in order for an authentic leader to succeed, the organization should be evaluated. An optimal situation would be one in which the organization values open communication and sharing, where leaders can both promote the company values and still have room to improve through learning and continued self-development. Finally, an authentic leader consistently performs above expected standards. In other words, in a competitive environment, it is imperative for the leader to sustain innovation, and avoid the tendency to remain stagnant. Future orientation and personal drives will motivate the leader to perform above expectations, as long as he or she remains true to him- or herself and is not simply acting out a part for superiors.[99]

How are authentic leaders different from traditional leaders? We discussed transformational leadership earlier in the chapter. Authentic leadership and transformational leadership are similar but with one important difference. Authentic leadership focuses mainly on the internal aspects of the leader, such as morals, values, motivators, and so forth. While transformational leaders may have all the characteristics of an authentic leader, the key to transformational leadership is how the leader motivates others, which is a secondary concern with authentic leadership. In other words, transformational leaders may very well be authentic, but not all authentic leaders are inherently transformational. Charismatic leadership, on the other hand, does not seem to encompass a sense of self-awareness, with either the leader or the follower. Since this is an important component of authentic leadership, it is also a key point of differentiating between the charismatic and authentic leader. Again, charismatic leaders may have similar attributes to the authentic cohorts, but the individual is just not aware of it.[100] Table 13–9 outlines some other areas where these may differ and where they overlap.

Authentic leadership, while similar to traditional leadership, is becoming more important in today's globally marketed world. Through a sense of higher awareness, authentic leadership can create a better understanding within the organization. As cohesive relationships form, understanding is created, and the authentic leaders' drive to reach new standards will motivate everyone to attain their future-oriented goals.

Table 13–9
Comparative Leadership Styles

Components of Authentic Leadership Development Theory	TL	CL(B)	CL(SC)
Positive psychological capital	×	×	×
Positive moral perspective	×	×	×
Leader self-awareness			
Values	×	×	×
Cognitions	×	×	×
Emotions	×	×	×
Leader self-regulation			
Internalized	×		×
Balanced processing	×		
Relational transparency	×		
Authentic behavior	×	×	×
Leadership processes/behaviors			
Positive modeling	×	×	×
Personal and social identification	×	×	×
Emotional contagion			
Supporting self-determination	×	×	×
Positive social exchanges	×	×	×
Follower self-awareness			
Values	×		×
Cognitions	×		×
Emotions	×		×
Follower self-regulation			
Internalized	×	×	×
Balanced processing	×		
Relational transparency	×		×
Authentic behavior	×		×
Follower development			
Organizational context			
Uncertainty	×	×	×
Inclusion	×		
Ethical	×		
Positive, strengths-based			
Performance			
Veritable			
Sustained	×	×	
Beyond expectations	×	×	

Note: ×—Focal Component.

×—Discussed.

Key: TL—Transformational Leadership Theory.

CL(B)—Behavioral Theory of Charismatic Leadership.

CL(SC)—Self-Concept Based Theory of Charismatic Leadership.

Source: Reprinted from *The Leadership Quarterly,* Vol. 15, Bruce J. Avolio and William L. Gardner, "Authentic Leadership Development: Getting to the Root of Positive Forms of Leadership," p. 323. Copyright © 2005 with permission from Elsevier.

Ethical, Responsible, and Servant Leadership

Related to the concept of authentic leadership is ethically responsible leadership. As discussed in Part One of the text, globalization and MNCs have come under fire from a number of areas. Criticisms have been especially sharp in relation to the activities of companies—such as Nike, Levi's, and United Fruit—whose sourcing practices in developing countries have been alleged to exploit low-wage workers, take advantage of lax environmental and workplace standards, and otherwise contribute to social and economic degradation. Ethical principles provide the philosophical basis for responsible business practices, and leadership defines the mechanism through which these principles become actionable.

As a result of scandals at Royal Ahold, Andersen, BP, Enron, Tyco, WorldCom, and others, there is decreasing trust of global leaders. A recent public opinion survey conducted for the World Economic Forum by Gallup and Environics found that leaders have suffered declining public trust in recent years and enjoy less trust than the institutions they lead. The survey asked respondents questions about how much they trust various leaders "to manage the challenges of the coming year in the best interests of you and your family." Leaders of nongovernmental organizations (NGOs) were the only ones receiving the trust of a clear majority of citizens across the countries surveyed.[101] Leaders at the United Nations and spiritual and religious leaders were the next-most-trusted leaders; over 4 in 10 citizens said they had a lot or some trust in them. Next most trusted were leaders of Western Europe, "individuals responsible for managing the global economy," those "responsible for managing our national economy," and executives of multinational companies. Those four groups were trusted by only one-third of citizens.[102] Over 4 in 10 citizens reported decreased trust in executives of domestic companies. Figure 3–2 in Chapter 3 summarizes these findings.

The decline in trust in leaders is prompting some companies to go on the offensive and to develop more ethically oriented and responsible leadership practices in their global operations. Some researchers link transformational leadership and corporate social responsibility, arguing that transformational leaders exhibit high levels of moral development, including a sense of obligation to the larger community.[103] According to this view, authentic charismatic leadership is rooted in strong ethical values, and effective global leaders are guided by principles of altruism, justice, and humanistic notions of the greater good.

On a more instrumental basis, another research effort linking leadership and corporate responsibility defines "responsible global leadership" as encompassing (1) values-based leadership, (2) ethical decision making, and (3) quality stakeholder relationships.[104] According to this view, global leadership must be based on core values and credos that reflect principled business and leadership practices, high levels of ethical and moral behavior, and a set of shared ideals that advance organizational and societal well-being. The importance of ethical decision making in corporations, governments, not-for-profit organizations, and professional services firms is omnipresent. In addition, the quality of relationships with internal and external stakeholders is increasingly critical to organizational success, especially to governance processes. Relationships involving mutual trust and respect are important within organizations, between organizations and the various constituencies that they affect, and among the extended networks of individuals and their organizational affiliates.

Leaders at many companies have dedicated themselves to responsible global leadership with apparent benefits for their companies' reputations and bottom lines. Even British Petroleum (BP), whose drilling practices in the Gulf of Mexico resulted in the worst oil spill in history in 2010, has attempted to accentuate responsible global leadership. BP will have to work harder now than ever, but keeping a socially responsible and clear objective will certainly aid in its continued global success. Executives at ICI India, a manufacturer and marketer of paints and various specialty chemicals, believe that adhering to global standards, even though doing so increases costs, can boost competitiveness. Aditya Narayan, president of ICI India, explains: "At ICI, standards involving ethics, safety, health, and environment policies are established by headquarters but are adapted to meet national laws. I can benefit by drawing on these corporate policies and in some cases we do far more than required by Indian laws."[105]

A concept related to ethical and responsible leadership is *servant leadership.* Servant-leaders achieve results for their organizations by giving priority attention to the needs of their colleagues and those they serve. Servant-leaders are often seen as humble stewards of their organization's resources (human, financial, and physical). In order to be a servant leader, one needs the following qualities: listening, empathy, healing, awareness, persuasion, conceptualization, foresight, stewardship, growth, and building community. Acquiring these qualities tends to give a person authority versus power. Some trace the concept of servant leadership to ancient Indian and Chinese thought. In the 4th century BC, Chanakya wrote in his book *Arthashastra:* "the king [leader] shall consider as good, not what pleases himself but what pleases his subjects [followers]"; "the king [leader] is a paid servant and enjoys the resources of the state together with the people." The following statement appears in the *Tao Te Ching,* attributed to Lao-Tzu, who is believed to have lived in China sometime between 570 and 490 BC: "The highest type of ruler is one of whose existence the people are barely aware. Next comes one whom they love and praise. Next comes one whom they fear. Next comes one whom they despise and defy. When you are lacking in faith, others will be unfaithful to you. The Sage is self-effacing and scanty of words. When his task is accomplished and things have been completed, all the people say, 'We ourselves have achieved it!'"[106]

More recently, an intellectual movement, led by Robert Greenleaf, but with many followers, has proposed servant leadership as an underlying philosophy of leadership, demonstrated through specific characteristics and practices. Larry Spears, one of Greenleaf's disciplines, identifies 10 characteristics of servant leaders in the writings of Greenleaf. The 10 characteristics are listening, empathy, healing, awareness, persuasion, conceptualization, foresight, stewardship, commitment to the growth of others, and building community. Kent Keith, author of *The Case for Servant Leadership* and the current CEO of the Greenleaf Center, states that servant leadership is ethical, practical, and meaningful. He identifies seven key practices of servant leaders: self-awareness, listening, changing the pyramid, developing your colleagues, coaching not controlling, unleashing the energy and intelligence of others, and foresight. Unlike leadership approaches with a top-down hierarchical style, servant leadership instead emphasizes collaboration, trust, empathy, and the ethical use of power. At heart, the individual is a servant first, making the conscious decision to lead in order to better serve others, not to increase her or his own power. The objective is to enhance the growth of individuals in the organization and increase teamwork and personal involvement. Large MNCs, such as Starbucks, have adopted aspects of servant leadership in their global operations.[107]

Entrepreneurial Leadership and Mindset

As discussed in Chapter 8, an increasing share of international management activities is occurring in entrepreneurial new ventures. But given the high failure rate for international new ventures, what leadership characteristics are important for such ventures to succeed?

Promising start-ups fail for many reasons, including lack of capital, absence of clear goals and objectives, and failure to accurately assess market demand and competition. For international new ventures, these factors are significantly complicated by differences in cultures, national political and economic systems, geographic distance, and shipping, tax, and regulatory costs. A critical factor in the long-term success of a new venture—whether domestic or international—is the personal leadership ability of the entrepreneurial CEO.

Entrepreneurship research has examined some of the key personal characteristics of entrepreneurs, some of which coincide with those of strong leaders. In comparison to nonentrepreneurs, entrepreneurs appear to be more creative and innovative. They tend to break the rules and do not need structure, support, or an organization to guide their thinking. They are able to see things differently and add to a product, system, or idea value that amounts to more than an adaptation or linear change. They are more willing to take personal and business risks and to do so in visible and salient ways. They are opportunity seekers—solving only those problems that limit their success in reaching the vision—and are comfortable with failure, rebounding quickly to pursue another opportunity.[108] Others characterize them as adventurous, ambitious, energetic, domineering, and self-confident.

In addition to these traits, entrepreneurial leaders operating internationally must also possess the cultural sensitivity, international vision, and global mindset to effectively lead their venture as it confronts the challenges of doing business in other countries. Well-known entrepreneurs such as Richard Branson (Virgin Group), Arthur Blank (Home Depot), and Russell Simmons (Def Jam Recordings) have all been successful leading their companies on a global scale while preserving the integrity and values of the host country.[109] As Yang Yuanqing (Lenovo) has shown, this is a trend that is growing, and soon we may see more entrepreneurs emerge from countries where such ventures are not common practice.

The World of *International Management*—Revisited

The World of International Management that opens this chapter underscores the importance and value of understanding differences in leadership styles and approaches across cultures. It also emphasizes the related need to prepare prospective international managers so that they can be successful in these varying environments. A number of global companies—including Roche, Amway, and others—have developed comprehensive and challenging programs to help provide their employees with experiences to understand when consistent, "universalist" approaches may be appropriate, and when adaptation to local practices, norms, and expectations is called for.

In this chapter, it was noted that effective leadership is often heavily influenced by culture. The approach that is effective in Europe is different from approaches used in the United States or Latin America. For example, according to one Roche employee, defining success may mean different things in different contexts. Even so, there are threads of universalism evident, for example, in the case of Japanese and U.S. leadership styles in managing both high- and low-achieving workers. The research by Bass also lends support to universalism. But can Roche rely on the leadership style that has served it well in Europe to oversee operations in other countries as it looks to expand? In most cases, leadership styles need to be adjusted to fit the cultural subtleties of disparate markets.

After reviewing the chapter and considering the experience of Roche, Amway, and other companies mentioned in the chapter, respond to the following questions: (1) Do the leadership programs developed by Roche emphasize development of managerial characteristics, leadership characteristics, or a combination of the two? (2) How do Roche's programs prepare prospective leaders to manage in differing cultural contexts? (3) How might deeper understanding of the GLOBE dimensions and the different leadership behaviors across countries help Roche in developing future leaders?

SUMMARY OF KEY POINTS

1. Leadership is a complex and controversial process that can be defined simply as influencing people to direct their efforts toward the achievement of some particular goal or goals. While some claim that managers and leaders conduct two separate job functions, the lack of a universal definition of leadership allows both terms to be used interchangeably, especially as the world moves toward a manager-leader model. Two areas warrant attention as a foundation for the study of leadership in an international setting: philosophical assumptions about people in general and leadership styles. The philosophical foundation is heavily grounded in Douglas McGregor's Theories X and Y and William Ouchi's Theory Z. Leadership styles relate to how managers treat their subordinates and

incorporate authoritarian, paternalistic, and participative approaches. These styles can be summarized in terms of the managerial grid shown in Figure 13–2 (1,1 through 9,9).

2. The attitudes of European managers toward dimensions of leadership practice, such as the capacity for leadership and initiative, sharing information and objectives, participation, and internal control, were examined in a classic study by Haire, Ghiselli, and Porter. They found that Europeans, as a composite, had a relatively low opinion of the capabilities of the average person coupled with a relatively positive belief in the necessity for participative leadership styles. The study also found that these European managers' attitudes were affected by hierarchical level, company size, and age. Overall, however, European managers espouse a participative leadership style.

3. The Japanese managers in the Haire and associates study had a much greater belief in the capacity of subordinates for leadership and initiative than managers in most other countries. The Japanese managers also expressed a more favorable attitude toward a participative leadership style. In terms of sharing information and objectives and using internal control, the Japanese responded above average but were not distinctive. In a number of ways, Japanese leadership styles differed from those of U.S. managers. Company size and age of the managers are two factors that seem to affect these differences. Other reasons include the basic philosophy of managing people, how information is processed, and the high degree of ethnocentrism among the Japanese. However, some often overlooked similarities are important, such as how effective Japanese leaders manage high-achieving and low-achieving subordinates.

4. Leadership research in China shows that the new generation of managers tends to have a leadership style that is different from the styles of both the current generation and the older generation. In particular, new generation managers assign greater importance to individualism as measured by such things as self-sufficiency and personal accomplishments. They also assign less importance to collectivism as measured by subordination of personal goals to those of the group and to Confucianism as measured by such things as societal harmony and virtuous interpersonal behavior.

5. Leadership research in the Middle East traditionally has stressed the basic differences between Middle Eastern and Western management styles. Other research, however, shows that many managers in multinational organizations in the Persian Gulf region operate in a Western-oriented participative style. Such findings indicate that there may be more similarities in leadership styles between Western and Middle Eastern parts of the world than has previously been assumed.

6. Leadership research also has been conducted among managers in India and Latin American countries. These studies show that Indian managers have a tendency toward participative leadership styles while Latin America wavers between participative and authoritarian styles. Although there always will be important differences in styles of leadership between various parts of the world, participative leadership styles may become more prevalent as countries develop and become more economically advanced.

7. In recent years, there have been research efforts to explore new areas in international leadership. In particular, Bass has found that there is a great deal of similarity from culture to culture and that transformational leaders, regardless of culture, tend to be the most effective. In addition, the GLOBE study has confirmed earlier research that specific cultural values and practices are associated with particular leadership attributes. Moreover, there is increasing pressure for MNCs to engage in globally responsible leadership that incorporates (a) values-based leadership; (b) ethical decision making, and (c) quality stakeholder relationships. Leaders of international new ventures face particularly challenging obstacles; however, the integration of a global orientation and entrepreneurial flair can contribute to successful "born global" leaders and firms.

KEY TERMS

authoritarian leadership, *461*

charismatic leaders, *473*

leadership, *456*

participative leadership, *462*

paternalistic leadership, *462*

positive organizational scholarship (POS), *482*

Theory X manager, *458*

Theory Y manager, *458*

Theory Z manager, *459*

transactional leaders, *473*

transformational leaders, *473*

variety amplification, *469*

variety reduction, *469*

REVIEW AND DISCUSSION QUESTIONS

1. What cultures would be the most likely to perceive differences between managerial and leadership duties? What cultures would view them as the same? Use evidence to support your answer.

2. Using the results of the classic Haire and associates study as a basis for your answer, compare and contrast managers' attitudes toward leadership practices in Nordic-European and Latin-European countries. (The countries in these clusters are identified in Table 13–3.)

3. Is there any relationship between company size and European managers' attitude toward participative leadership styles?

4. Using the GLOBE study results and other supporting data, determine what Japanese managers believe about their subordinates. How are these beliefs similar to those of U.S. and European managers? How are these beliefs different?

5. A U.S. firm is going to be opening a subsidiary in Japan within the next six months. What type of leadership style does research show to be most effective for leading high-achieving Japanese? Low-achieving Japanese? How are these results likely to affect the way that U.S. expatriates should lead their Japanese employees?

6. What do U.S. managers need to know about leading in the international arena? Identify and describe three important guidelines that can be of practical value.

7. Is effective leadership behavior universal, or does it vary from culture to culture? Explain.

8. What is authentic leadership? What is ethically responsible leadership?

INTERNET EXERCISE: TAKING A CLOSER LOOK

Over the last three decades, one of the most successful global firms has been General Electric. Although GE has faced challenges, and has shed some of its businesses, such as the sale of GE Plastics to Saudia Arabian SABIC in 2007, and sold its stake in broadcaster NBC Universal to Comcast in 2013. It remains a global powerhouse in energy and power systems, health care, finance, and appliances. Go to the company's website at www.ge.com, and review its latest annual report. Pay close attention to the MNC's international operations and to its product lines. Also read about the new members on the board of directors, and look through the information on the company's Six Sigma program. Then, aware of what GE is doing worldwide as well as in regard to its quality efforts, answer these questions:

On how many continents does the company currently do business? Based on this answer, is there one leadership style that will work best for the company, or is it going to have to choose managers on a country-by-country basis? Additionally, if there is no one universal style that is best, how can current CEO Jeffrey Immelt effectively lead so diverse a group of worldwide managers? In what way would an understanding of the managerial grid be useful in explaining leadership behaviors at GE? Finally, if GE were advertising for new managers in England, Italy, and Japan, what qualities would you expect the firm to be seeking in these managers? Would there be a universal list, or would lists differ on a country-by-country basis?

Germany

The reunification of Germany was a major event of modern times. Despite problems, Germany remains a major economic power. The unified Germany is big, though only about the size of the state of Nevada in the United States. With a population of about 81.3 million, Germany has about three times the population of California. Despite being the largest economy in Europe, Germany still is far behind the economic size of Japan and 20 percent that of the United States. Because Germany was rebuilt almost from the ground up after World War II, however, many feel that Germany, along with Japan, is an economic miracle of modern times. Unified Germany's GDP of $3.6 trillion is behind that of both the United States and Japan, but Germany exports more than Japan, its gross investment as a percentage of GDP, at 17 percent, is higher than that of the United States, and its average compensation with benefits to workers is higher than that of the United States or Japan. It is estimated that Germany has direct control of about one-fourth of Western Europe's economy, which gives it considerable power in Europe. The German people are known for being thrifty, hardworking, and obedient to authority. They love music, dancing, good food and beer, and fellowship. The government is a parliamentary democracy headed by a chancellor. Although Germany has experienced a difficult economic environment in recent years, governments have pushed through labor reforms designed to improve productivity and stem unemployment. Unemployment currently stands at about 6 percent.

For the last 13 years, the Wiscomb Company has held a majority interest in a large retail store in Bonn. The store has been very successful and also has proved to be an excellent training ground for managers whom the company wanted to prepare for other overseas assignments. First, the managers would be posted to the Bonn store.

Then after three or four months of international seasoning, they would be sent on to other stores in Europe. Wiscomb has holdings in the Netherlands, Luxembourg, and Austria. The Bonn store has been the primary training ground because it was the first store the company had in Europe, and the training program was created with this store in mind.

Some time ago, the Wiscomb management and its German partners decided to try a new approach to selling. The plan called for some young U.S. managers to be posted to the Bonn store for a three-year tour, while some young German managers were sent stateside. Both companies hoped that this program would provide important training and experience for their people; however, things have not worked out as hoped. The U.S. managers have reported great difficulty in supervising their German subordinates. Three of their main concerns are as follows: (1) Their subordinates do not seem to like to participate in decision making, preferring to be told what to do. (2) The German nationals in the store rely much more heavily on a Theory X approach to supervising than the Americans are accustomed to using, and they are encouraging their U.S. counterparts to follow their example. (3) Some of the German managers have suggested to the young Americans that they not share as much information with their own subordinates. Overall, the Americans believe that the German style of management is not as effective as their own, but they feel equally ill at ease raising this issue with their hosts. They have asked if someone from headquarters could come over from the United States and help resolve their problem. A human resources executive is scheduled to arrive next week and meet with the U.S. contingent.

www.tradingeconomics.com, www.cia.gov

Questions

1. What are some current issues facing Germany? What is the climate for doing business in Germany today?
2. Are the leadership styles used by the German managers really much different from those used by the Americans?
3. Do you think the German managers are really more Theory X–oriented than their U.S. counterparts? Why, or why not?
4. Are the German managers who have come to the United States likely to be having the same types of problems?
5. Using the GLOBE study as a guide, what are some leadership attributes you would expect from the Germans? How does this affect the way German subordinates view U.S. leaders?

Chapter 14

HUMAN RESOURCE SELECTION AND DEVELOPMENT ACROSS CULTURES

OBJECTIVES OF THE CHAPTER

Firms conducting international business need to be particularly concerned with human resource management issues—including selection, training, and development—to better prepare their personnel for overseas assignments. This chapter focuses on potential sources of human resources that can be employed for overseas assignments, procedures that are used in their selection process, and compensation issues. In this chapter we discuss training and development and the various types of training that are commonly offered. The specific objectives of this chapter are:

1. IDENTIFY the three basic sources that MNCs can tap when filling management vacancies in overseas operations in addition to options of subcontracting and outsourcing.

2. DESCRIBE the selection criteria and procedures used by organizations and individual managers when making final decisions.

3. DISCUSS the reasons why people return from overseas assignments, and present some of the strategies used to ensure a smooth transition back into the home-market operation.

4. DESCRIBE the training process, the most common reasons for training, and the types of training that often are provided.

5. EXPLAIN how cultural assimilators work and why they are so highly regarded.

The World of *International Management*

The Challenge of Talent Retention in India

Retaining talented employees is a challenge for managers around the world. Somewhat to the surprise of MNCs, this challenge has become particularly acute in India. More than 80 percent of CEOs in India say they have serious concerns about the lack of availability of people with key skills and the threat this poses to business growth, according to PricewaterhouseCoopers' 16th annual CEO survey.[1]

A study conducted by the Chambers of Commerce of India found that employee turnover averaged 25–30 percent in the IT sector and averaged 30–35 percent in the business process outsourcing (BPO) sector.[2] Such high employee turnover has a cost. Shyamal Majumdar of India's Business Standard explained that frontline employees in a top company cost 40 percent of their salaries to replace and top managers cost 150–200 percent of their salaries to replace.[3]

Right Management's Executive Overview described the business implications of high Indian employee turnover:

> In IT, for example, it is important for clients to develop close relationships with employees working on projects. Frequent turnover means continually building new relationships with replacements, thereby slowing down projects and harming both efficiency and client trust. In manufacturing, high attrition results in the expensive and time-consuming exercise of training recent hires about new technologies.[4]

Because of the cost of hiring and retraining employees, MNCs in India may not be able to secure the cost savings that led them to India in the first place.

More than Money

Discussing retaining talent in India, Elena Groznaya points out that MNCs sometimes mistakenly use the same methods to try to retain employees in India as in the home country. These methods are often compensation driven. In India's relationship-oriented culture, however, employees are primarily motivated not by compensation, but by a sense of "family" in their companies. Groznaya states: "Traditional Indian companies often play the role of a family extension for their staff" and give employees a feeling of belonging.[5]

A comprehensive talent management and HR practices study in India supported the conclusion that compensation is not the main factor in retaining Indian employees. At the end of 2007, Villanova School of Business and Right Management conducted a survey of 4,811 individuals from 28 Indian companies in five industries. According to Right Management's Executive Overview, the researchers found:

> While the common perception is that pay is the key element in attracting and retaining talent in India, as well as other emerging countries, our results showed a more complex array of factors played a significant role. Most notably, they included the value of intrinsic rewards—the employees' sense of progress, competence, influence/choice, and opportunity to do meaningful work. Compensation was not the most significant factor in either retention or engagement, a phenomenon that held true across all industries. Among respondents who indicated an intent to stay, only 30 percent were "very satisfied" with their compensation.[6]

The key to high retention is keeping employees engaged. The researchers discovered that "lack of engagement was by far the strongest single factor leading to intent to leave an organization. The lesson is clear: The more engaged an employee, the likelier he or she will stay."[7]

Four Factors Correlated to Employee Engagement

What steps can managers take to keep employees engaged? The researchers identified four HR practices that are correlated with employee engagement, as measured by employees' feelings of pride and satisfaction in the organization. These factors were performance management, professional development, manager support, and an organizational commitment to a larger social purpose.[8]

Performance Management The researchers found a significant relationship between retention and a favorable assessment of a firm's performance management system. Of employees who were in the top third of those who rated their company's performance management practices highly, "56.1 percent had strong pride in the organization, 65.9 percent had strong satisfaction with the organization, and only 23.5 percent indicated a strong intention to leave." In contrast, of the bottom third, "only 17.3 percent had strong pride in the organization, 11.1 percent had strong satisfaction, and 48.8 percent expressed a strong intention to leave."[9]

When setting up performance management systems at Indian firms, managers need to be coached on how to provide constructive feedback. Indian managers are often hesitant to criticize their employees, but with coaching, they can learn how to use criticism to help employees improve their performance.[10]

Professional Development Employees who are satisfied with their firm's professional development opportunities are more likely to remain at the firm. For instance, the researchers found that of those respondents who did not like the professional development practices at their companies, "52.3 percent indicated intent to leave within 12 months vs. 18.7 percent in organizations that strongly supported those practices." Employees are more engaged when they have clear opportunities for growth in their career. A typical career path may involve the opportunity to work on different projects, participate in overseas assignments, and eventually take on a managerial role.[11]

Employee assessments should be an important part of the development process. These assessments "can ensure that companies hire the right people for the right jobs and . . . will also help to pinpoint those people with the potential to move into management roles."[12]

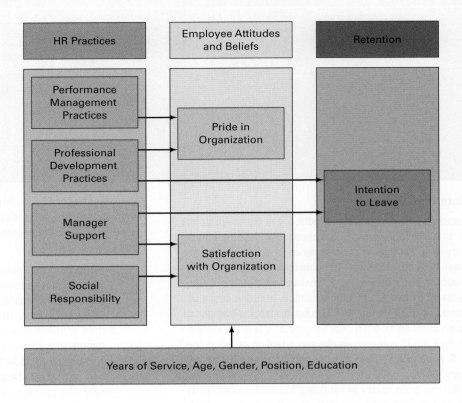

Management Support From the study, the researchers found that "Due to the urgent need for managerial level personnel, employees in India are often promoted to supervisory roles before they're ready to assume such responsibilities." Furthermore, many respondents in the study were dissatisfied with their manager's ability to engage with their team: "Only 47 percent of respondents agreed that their immediate supervisor was able to provide support and develop his or her team effectively." This gap in management skills has a negative impact on employee retention. If employees are working for a supervisor who lacks management skills, they are more likely to leave the company.[13]

Thus, Indian firms need to train new managers in the basics of management, such as how to reach team objectives and how to mentor employees. Mentoring is an essential management skill in India, where leaders often act as personal advisers. Having effective managers to support their employees is critical to increasing employee retention.[14]

Social Responsibility Many Indian employees highly value commitment to the community. Firms can engage employees by providing them with opportunities to participate in initiatives to help social causes, such as alleviating poverty. These initiatives should be highlighted in annual reports.[15]

Start on the First Day

The highlights of the research study mentioned were published in an article in *MIT Sloan Management Review*. According to the article, "The best companies drive employee satisfaction and pride by providing management support, training, and professional opportunities early on. . . . Employers should start an employee's professional development plan on his or her *first day*."[16]

One of the researchers in the study, Dr. Jonathan Doh, told the *MIT Sloan Management Review*, "Our findings suggest that even six months from the start date is probably too late. [At that point] the employee is already making decisions about whether to stay around or not." MNCs can make the decision to stay an easy one by offering employees effective professional development, performance management systems, and manager support.[17]

Once, India was seen as a source of never-ending talent. Today, India poses some of the same challenges in attracting, hiring, and retaining talent as do many developed countries, with some issues that are particular to the Indian context. Originally, MNCs searched overseas for inexpensive labor, but as countries become more developed and education levels increase, and as employers in home countries worry about a diminishing labor force, the search has shifted. As more highly skilled workers become available in other countries, MNCs have a growing number of sources for their human resources; however, as more MNCs and local firms vie for this talent, a "talent war" may ensue. MNCs may also be able to access foreign human resources by hiring them on a temporary or permanent basis in the home country. Often, they will subcontract or outsource work to foreign employees in home and host countries. This complex web of relationships creates significant managerial challenges and opportunities and suggests that there will always be a need for highly skilled, culturally sensitive, and geographically mobile managerial talent.

In this chapter we explore the procedure of international human resource (HR) selection and training and examine the difficulties of developing a global human resource management process in the presence of dissimilar cultural norms. At the same time, we survey emerging trends in international human resource management, including the increasing use of temporary and contingent staffing to fill the growing global HR needs of MNCs. We also review training and development programs designed to help employees prepare for and succeed in their foreign assignments and adjust to conditions once they return home.

■ The Importance of International Human Resources

Human resources is an essential part of any organization since it provides the human capital that keeps operations running. Human resource management is also key to an efficient, productive workplace. We discussed in Chapter 12 how financial compensation can motivate employees, but creative human resource management can play an even more important role. By focusing on the employees, or the human resources themselves, organizations have found that positive organizational structure leads to company success in the market.[18] Sometimes this is recognized through compensation, such as competitive salaries, good benefits, promotions, training, education opportunities, and so forth, which has been known to motivate employees and reduce turnover, since there are further incentives to strive for. Other times, companies will provide employees with daily comforts such as meals where an employee's family is welcome to attend, fitness centers, laundry rooms, or even services such as oil changes while at work. Showing the employees that they are not simply cogs in a machine, but that their time is valued and they are thanked for it, often builds morale and can increase company sales through a shared drive to succeed. Furthermore, recognizing the potential in employees and encouraging teamwork can lead to greater risk taking and innovations.[19]

Getting the Employee Perspective

Whether managers are trying to increase productivity or decrease turnover rates, it is good to get a sense of how the employees feel they are being treated. Times continue to change, and while employees in the past could be considered one unit, today people are realizing their individual talents and their need to be recognized. For instance, global companies are experiencing a labor shortage as skilled workers are in high demand.[20] In essence, skilled workers can almost walk in and request the kind of compensation they desire, and companies may be willing to accept the terms. Even outside this context of labor shortages, firms are restructuring how they look at employees for many good reasons. By segmenting the workforce into categories (but avoiding differentiation based on age or gender since that may imply a form of discrimination) and by offering choices, flexibility, and a personal touch to each employee package, employers are able to provide an underlying sense of commitment since the employee is getting what he or she wants. In other words, by focusing on employees and tailoring human resource management to the individual, people are naturally influenced to stay longer and be more committed to the organization they have joined.[21] However, before a company can keep the employee, it must first hire.

Employees as Critical Resources

Attracting the most qualified employees and matching them to the jobs for which they are best suited are important for the success of any organization. For international organizations, the selection and development of human resources are especially challenging and vitally important. As prevalent and useful as e-mail and Web- and teleconferencing have become, and despite the increasing incidence of subcontracting and outsourcing, face-to-face human contact will remain an important means of communication and transferring "tacit" knowledge—knowledge that cannot be formalized in manuals or written guidelines. Hence, most companies continue to deploy human resources around the world as they are needed, although the range of options for filling human resources needs is expanding.

Investing in International Assignments

MNCs must send expatriate ("expat") managers overseas, no matter how good "virtual" communications become. There are quite a few costs involved, including pre-assignment training, and potential costs due to failure. According to one estimate, the cost of one assignment failure is between $100,000 and $300,000 per employee.[22] Given these high costs, many MNCs are turning to locally engaged employees or third-country nationals.[23] In addition, the improved education of many populations around the world gives MNCs more options when considering international human resource needs. The emergence of highly trained technical and scientific employees in emerging markets and the increased prevalence of MBA-type training in many developed and developing countries have dramatically expanded the pool of talent from which MNCs can draw. Yet some companies are still having difficulty in winning the "war for talent." A recent report from China noted that despite much greater levels of advanced education, there is still a shortage of skilled management. "We need a lot more people than we have now, and we need a higher caliber of people," said Guo Ming, Coca-Cola's human resource director for Greater China.[24]

Adjustment problems of expats undertaking international assignments can be reduced through careful selection and training. Language training and cross-culture training are especially important, but they are often neglected by MNCs in a hurry to deploy resources to meet critical needs.[25] The demand for globally adept managers will likely grow, and MNCs will need to continue to invest in recruiting and training the best future leaders.

MNCs are also under increasing pressure to keep jobs at home, and their international HR practices have come under close scrutiny. In particular, the "importing" of programmers from India at a fraction of domestic wages, combined with the offshore outsourcing of work to high-tech employees in lower cost countries, has created political and social challenges for MNCs seeking to manage their international human resources efficiently and effectively. All of this suggests an ongoing need for attention to and investment in this challenging area.

Economic Pressures

It is important to note that the human resources function within MNCs is itself changing as a result of ongoing pressures for reduced costs and increased efficiencies. There was a time when human resources departments handled every staffing need at a company, from hiring and firing to administering benefits and determining salaries. According to a study by the Society for Human Resource Management, the profession's largest association, the head count at the average HR department fell from 13 in 2007 to 9 in 2008. According to one senior HR manager, "HR departments are under pressure like never before." Further, some of what in-house HR departments oversaw is now being outsourced, because the costs associated with these "staff" (versus revenue-generating "line") functions are under increasing scrutiny. For those that remain in-house, HR departments are now focusing on boosting productivity by helping employees better understand what's expected of them and by showing managers how to be more effective.[26]

Table 14–1 shows how companies have indicated they are responding to the economic recession in terms of employee compensation and benefits. Despite these cutbacks, companies remain concerned about retaining their most talented employees, according

Table 14–1
How Companies Are Responding to the Economic Crisis

	Completed	Planned	Considering	Not Considering	Too Soon to Tell
Freeze or reduce hiring	42%	18%	14%	22%	4%
Cut travel and entertainment spending	40	20	22	12	6
Reduce pay/merit increase budget	36	24	21	14	5
Scale back employee events	36	15	24	17	8
Reduce training budgets	20	12	26	32	10
Targeted reduction in head count (focus on less critical roles or lower performers)	19	21	18	30	12
Freeze salaries	18	7	16	50	9
Delay planned merit increases	12	6	14	62	6
Significant reduction in head count (10 percent or more)	11	8	11	55	15
Cut back on perquisites	10	3	20	58	9
Cut back on benefits	7	3	14	68	8
Provide lump-sum increase in lieu of merit increases	2	1	7	84	6
Reduce salaries across the board	1	1	7	85	6

Source: Towers Perrin.

to a study from Towers Perrin, The Towers Perrin Pulse Survey. The Towers Perrin survey, conducted in January 2009, found that 42 percent of organizations were planning hiring freezes and reductions as well as pay cuts. Another survey, an update to ECA International's Salary Trends Survey, conducted annually for more than 50 countries, found that 40 percent of companies planned to freeze pay. On average, salary increases were half as high as anticipated before the economic crisis set in. In Canada, increases dropped from 4 percent to 1 percent. In South America, wage increases are only slightly lower than last year's forecasts, with some countries, such as Brazil, Chile, and Venezuela, expecting higher salaries. Salary increases in Western Europe averaged around 2 percent, according to the survey, while those in Eastern Europe were just under 5 percent. Russia, Romania, and Latvia saw the greatest increases, while workers in Lithuania, the Irish Republic, and Switzerland were expected to receive the smallest pay raises in the region. Despite plans for slow pay growth, 62 percent of companies in the Towers Perrin survey say they are concerned about the potential impact on their ability to retain high-performing talent or those in pivotal roles. In response, organizations reserved their salary increases and cash rewards for their most talented and top-performing employees, even while pay is cut for the rest of the workforce. The 2009 HR Executive's Agenda, a study from Aberdeen Group, found that the five most critical workforce challenges the respondents faced in 2009 were:

- Retaining top talent (rated 4.03 on a one-to-five scale)
- Developing leadership skills of existing managers (3.94)
- Recruiting top talent (3.9)
- Workforce productivity (3.87)
- Developing future leaders (3.82)[27]

■ Sources of Human Resources

MNCs can tap four basic sources for positions: (1) home-country nationals; (2) host-country nationals; (3) third-country nationals; and (4) inpatriates. In addition, many MNCs are outsourcing aspects of their global operations and in so doing are engaging temporary or contingent employees. The following sections analyze each of these major sources.

Home-Country Nationals

home-country nationals
Expatriate managers who are citizens of the country where the multinational corporation is headquartered.

expatriates
Managers who live and work outside their home country. They are citizens of the country where the multinational corporation is headquartered.

Home-country nationals are managers who are citizens of the country where the MNC is headquartered. In fact, sometimes the term *headquarters nationals* is used. These managers commonly are called **expatriates**, or simply "expats," which refers to those who live and work outside their home country. Historically, MNCs have staffed key positions in their foreign affiliates with home-country nationals or expatriates. For many companies and for the most senior positions, that trend persists. Major U.S. and European companies such as Cisco Systems have been sending expats to India, and according to a recent estimate, about 1,000 expat senior managers are there now, almost seven times that of two years ago. However, some research has shown that in many instances, host-country nationals may be better suited for the job. Richards, for example, investigated staffing practices for the purpose of determining when companies are more likely to use an expatriate rather than a local manager. She conducted interviews with senior-level headquarters managers at 24 U.S. multinational manufacturing firms and with managers at their U.K. and Thai subsidiaries. This study found that local managers were most effective in subsidiaries located in developing countries or those that relied on a local customer base. In contrast, expatriates were most effective when they were in charge of larger subsidiaries or those with a marketing theme similar to that at headquarters.[28]

There are a variety of reasons for using home-country nationals. One of the most common is to start up operations. Another is to provide technical expertise. A third is to help the MNC maintain financial control over the operation.[29] Other commonly cited reasons include the desire to provide the company's more promising managers with international experience to equip them better for more responsible positions; the need to maintain and facilitate organizational coordination and control; the unavailability of managerial talent in the host country; the company's view of the foreign operation as short lived; the host country's multiracial population, which might mean that selecting a manager of either race would result in political or social problems; the company's conviction that it must maintain a foreign image in the host country; and the belief of some companies that a home country manager is the best person for the job.[30]

In recent years, there has been a trend away from using home-country nationals, given the costs, somewhat uncertain returns, and increasing availability of host-country and third-country nationals and inpatriates.

Host-Country Nationals

host-country nationals
Local managers who are hired by the MNC.

Host-country nationals are local managers who are hired by the MNC. For a number of reasons, many MNCs use host-country managers at the middle- and lower-level ranks. One reason in particular is that many countries expect the MNC to hire local talent, and the use of host-country nationals is a good way to meet this expectation. Also, even if an MNC wanted to staff all management positions with home-country personnel, it would be unlikely to have this many available managers, and the cost of transferring and maintaining them in the host country would be prohibitive.

In some cases government regulations dictate selection practices and mandate at least some degree of "nativization." In Brazil, for example, two-thirds of the employees

International Management in Action
Important Tips on Working for Foreigners
www.overseasjobs.com

As the Japanese, South Koreans, and Europeans continue to expand their economic horizons, increased employment opportunities will be available worldwide. Is it a good idea to work for foreigners? Those who have done so have learned that there are both rewards and penalties associated with this career choice. Following are some useful tips that have been drawn from the experiences of those who have worked for foreign MNCs.

First, most U.S. managers are taught to make fast decisions, but most foreign managers take more time and view rapid decision making as unnecessary and sometimes bad. In the United States, we hear the cliché, "The effective manager is right 51 percent of the time." In Europe, this percentage is perceived as much too low, which helps explain why European managers analyze situations in much more depth than most U.S. managers do. Americans working for foreign-owned firms have to focus on making slower and more accurate decisions.

Second, most Americans are taught to operate without much direction. In Latin countries, managers are accustomed to giving a great deal of direction, and in East Asian firms, there is little structure and direction. Americans have to learn to adjust to the decision making process of the particular company.

Third, most Americans go home around 5 p.m. If there is more paperwork to do, they take it with them. Japanese managers, in contrast, stay late at the office

and often view those who leave early as being lazy. Americans either have to adapt or have to convince the manager that they are working as hard as their peers but in a different physical location.

Fourth, many international firms say that their official language is English. However, important conversations always are carried out in the home-country's language, so it is important to learn that language.

Fifth, many foreign MNCs make use of fear to motivate their people. This is particularly true in manufacturing work, where personnel are under continuous pressure to maintain high output and quality. For instance, those who do not like to work under intense conditions would have a very difficult time succeeding in Japanese auto assembly plants. Americans have to understand that humanistic climates of work may be the exception rather than the rule.

Finally, despite the fact that discrimination in employment is outlawed in the United States, it is practiced by many MNCs, including those operating in the United States. Women seldom are given the same opportunities as men, and top-level jobs almost always are reserved for home-office personnel. In many cases, Americans have accepted or accommodated to this ethnocentric (nationalistic) approach.

Nevertheless, as Chapter 3 discussed, ethics and social responsibility are becoming a major issue in the international arena, and these moral challenges must be met now and in the future.

in any foreign subsidiary traditionally had to be Brazilian nationals. In addition, many countries exert real and subtle pressures to staff the upper-management ranks with nationals. In the past, these pressures by host countries have led companies such as Standard Oil to change their approach to selecting managers. These regulations have substantial costs in that shielding local employees from international competition may create a sense of entitlement and result in low productivity.

Sony is trying the host-country approach in the United States. Employees are encouraged to accept or decline styles that emerge from Japanese headquarters, depending on American tastes. Furthermore, innovative creations are birthed at the U.S. site, all with an American flavor. Sony believes that local citizens are the best qualified for the job, as opposed to Japanese managers, because they already have a working knowledge of the language and culture, and it may be difficult for Sony to understand preferred styles otherwise.[31] The International Management in Action box, "Important Tips on Working for Foreigners," gives examples of how Americans can better adapt to foreign bosses.

Third-Country Nationals

Third-country nationals (TCNs) are managers who are citizens of countries other than the country in which the MNC is headquartered or the one in which they are assigned to work by the MNC. Available data on third-country nationals are not as extensive as those on home- or host-country nationals.

third-country nationals (TCNs)
Managers who are citizens of countries other than the country in which the MNC is headquartered or the one in which they are assigned to work by the MNC.

A number of advantages have been cited for using TCNs. One is that the salary and benefit package usually is less than that of a home-country national, although in recent years, the salary gap between the two has begun to diminish. A second reason is that the TCN may have a very good working knowledge of the region or speak the same language as the local people. This helps explain why many U.S. MNCs hire English or Scottish managers for top positions at subsidiaries in former British colonies such as Jamaica, India, the West Indies, and Kenya. It also explains why successful MNCs such as Gillette, Coca-Cola, and IBM recruit local managers and train them to run overseas subsidiaries. Other cited benefits of using TCNs include:

1. TCN managers, particularly those who have had assignments in the headquarters country, can often achieve corporate objectives more effectively than expatriates or local nationals. In particular, they frequently have a deep understanding of the corporation's policies from the perspective of a foreigner and can communicate and implement those policies more effectively to others than can expats.

2. During periods of rapid expansion, TCNs can not only substitute for expatriates in new and growing operations but also offer different perspectives that can complement and expand on the sometimes narrowly focused viewpoints of both local nationals and headquarters personnel.

3. In joint ventures, TCNs can demonstrate a global or transnational image and bring unique cross-cultural skills to the relationship.[32]

inpatriates
Individuals from a host country or third-country nationals who are assigned to work in the home country.

In recent years a new term has emerged in international management—inpatriates. An **inpatriate**, or inpat, is an individual from a host country or a third-country national who is assigned to work in the home country. Even Japanese MNCs are now beginning to rely on inpatriates to help them meet their international challenges. Harvey and Buckley report:

> The Japanese are reducing their unicultural orientation in their global businesses. Yoichi Morishita, president of Matsushita, has ordered that top management must reflect the cultural diversity of the countries where Matsushita does business. Sony sells 80 percent of its products overseas and recently recognized the need to become multicultural. It has appointed two foreigners to its board of directors and has plans to hire host-country nationals who are to be integrated into the top management of the parent organization. At the same time, the Chairman of Sony has stated that in five years the board of directors of Sony will reflect the diversity of countries that are important to the future of the company. Similarly, Toshiba plans to have a more representative top management and board of directors to facilitate long-run global strategies.[33]

This growing use of inpats is helping MNCs better develop their global core competencies. As a result, today a new breed of multilingual, multiexperienced, so-called global managers or transnational managers is truly emerging.[34] These new managers are part of a growing group of international executives who can manage across borders and do not fit the traditional third-country nationals mold. With a unified Europe and other such developments in North America and Asia, these global managers are in great demand. Additionally, with labor shortages developing in certain regions, there is a wave of migration from regions with an abundance of personnel to those where the demand is strongest.

Subcontracting and Outsourcing

Other potential sources of international management talent are subcontracting and offshore outsourcing (introduced in Chapter 1). Offshore outsourcing is made possible by the increasing organizational and technological capacity of companies to separate, coordinate, and integrate geographically dispersed human resources—whether employed directly by the firm or contracted out—across distant geographic borders. The development of this capacity can be traced to the earlier growth of international sub-contracting as well as to the international diffusion of lean production systems (which originated with Japanese auto manufacturers) to other manufacturing and service sectors. In particular, service industries are exploiting inexpensive telecommunications to transmit engineering, medical, legal, and accounting services to be performed in locations previously viewed as remote. Rising levels of educational attainment in developing countries such as China, India, and the Philippines, especially in the scientific and technical fields, make offshoring increasingly attractive for a range of international human resource needs.

These developments are not without controversy, however. On the one hand, offshore outsourcing, as well as the hiring of temporary workers from abroad on special visas, similar to inpatriates, presents significant opportunities for cost savings and lower overhead. On the other hand, the recent wave of media attention has focused on widespread concern that in an age of cheap telecommunications, almost any job—professional or blue collar—can be performed in India for a fraction of U.S. wages. In particular, as discussed in Chapter 1, union groups, politicians, and NGOs have challenged MNCs' right to engage in labor "arbitrage."

Offshoring is reaching a new era, and while the top reason that MNCs look to other countries for labor is still to save money, there has been a decline all around in qualified personnel, which has brought about an emerging focus on other factors, notably access to qualified personnel. Figure 14–1 illustrates this.

Moreover, although the cost for a computer programmer or a middle manager in India remains a small fraction of the cost for a similar employee in the United States

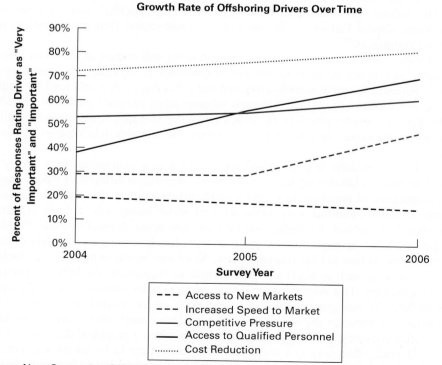

Growth Rate of Offshoring Drivers Over Time

Figure 14–1

Reasons MNCs Look Abroad for Workforce

Source: *Next Generation Offshoring: The Globalization of Innovation* by Arie Y. Lewin and Vinay Couto; *2006 Survey Report*, Booz Allen Hamilton/Duke University Offshoring Research Network 2006 Survey. Reprinted with permission.

(a programmer with three to five years' experience makes about $25,000 in India but about $65,000 in the United States), the wage savings do not necessarily translate directly into overall savings because the typical outsourcing contract between an American company and an Indian vendor saves less than half as much as the wage differences would imply.[35] Microsoft recently revealed that it has been paying two Indian outsourcing companies, Infosys and Satyam, to provide skilled software architects for Microsoft projects. In this case, the work of software architects and developers was being done by employees of the Indian companies working at Microsoft facilities in the United States. Although the actual employees were paid much less than U.S. counterparts ($30,000 to $40,000), Microsoft was billed $90 an hour for software architects, or at a yearly rate of more than $180,000. The on-site work was done by Indian software engineers who came to the United States on H-1B visas, which allow foreign workers to be employed in the United States for up to six years. Microsoft also contracted work in India through the firms, with billing rates of $23 to $36 an hour.[36]

Though politically controversial, outsourcing can save companies significant costs and is very profitable for firms that specialize in providing these services on a contract basis. U.S.-based firms such as EDS, IBM, and Deloitte have developed specific competencies in global production and HR coordination, including managing the HR functions that must support it. These firms combine low labor costs, specialized technical capabilities, and coordination expertise.

Outsourcing can also create quality control problems for some companies, as demonstrated in Dell's decision to repatriate some of its call-center staff from India to Texas because of quality control problems. Because Dell is a company that has little on-site service, the call-center capability is core to Dell's competitive position. "We felt a little noise and angst from our customers, and we decided to make some changes," said Gary Cotshott, vice president of Dell's services division. "Sometimes, we move a little too far, too fast."[37] In addition, Indian companies are beginning to develop their own approaches to outsourcing, including investing in U.S. call centers and business-processing outsourcers. The Indians "are looking to build a global model quickly," said a partner with WestBridge Capital Partners, a Silicon Valley venture-capital firm that invests in outsourcing companies.[38]

Despite these limitations, offshore subcontracting will remain an important tool for managing and deploying international human resources. If anything, the trend is accelerating. Forrester Research recently estimated that U.S. companies would send 3.4 million service jobs offshore by 2015.[39] Although subcontracting provides important flexibility in the human resource practices of MNCs operating globally, it also requires skilled international managers to coordinate and oversee the complex relationships that arise from it.

This is especially true as offshoring begins a new generation. In a survey by Duke University's Offshoring Research Network, significant differences were found in the perspectives of home (source) and host (destination) countries. Specifically, individuals in home countries were often worried about losing jobs to host countries, exacerbated by the fact that higher-end jobs are now being shipped overseas.[40] This is not the case from the organizations' point of view. It is becoming increasingly difficult for managers to find the appropriate talent. More and more, companies are looking overseas in areas such as R&D and procurement to supplement the lack of experts in the home country. This does not take jobs away from home countries; it simply opens jobs globally as managers attempt to fit the skills of the worker to the job itself.[41] Furthermore, companies are very specific about which country they search when looking to fill particular job functions. Figure 14–2 provides a graphical depiction of this reality. Overall, offshoring is a trend that does not appear to be on its way out, but instead is evolving through alternative motivators and continuing to innovatively help the company grow.

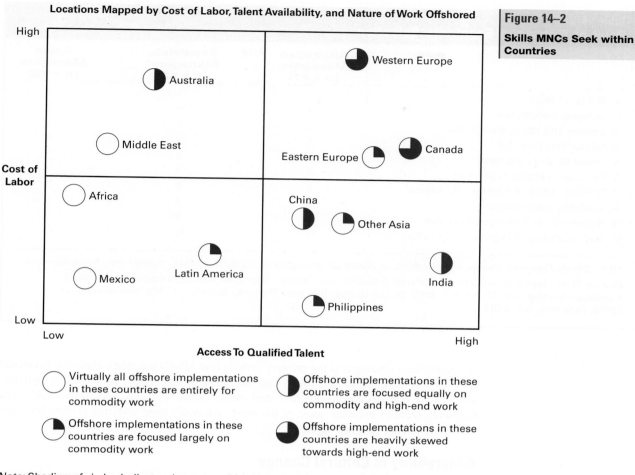

Locations Mapped by Cost of Labor, Talent Availability, and Nature of Work Offshored

Figure 14–2

Skills MNCs Seek within Countries

○ Virtually all offshore implementations in these countries are entirely for commodity work

◐ Offshore implementations in these countries are focused equally on commodity and high-end work

◖ Offshore implementations in these countries are focused largely on commodity work

● Offshore implementations in these countries are heavily skewed towards high-end work

Note: Shading of circles indicates degree to which high skilled work is currently offshored to the specific country.

Source: Next Generation Offshoring: The Globalization of Innovation by Arie Y. Lewin and Vinay Couto; *2006 Survey Report,* Booz Allen Hamilton/Duke University Offshoring Research Network 2006 Survey. Reprinted with permission.

■ Selection Criteria for International Assignments

Making an effective selection decision for an overseas assignment can prove to be a major problem. Typically, this decision is based on **international selection criteria,** which are factors used to choose international managers. These selections are influenced by the MNC's experience and often are culturally based. Sometimes as many as a dozen criteria are used, although most MNCs give serious consideration to only five or six.[42] Table 14–2 reports the importance of some of these criteria as ranked by Australian, expatriate, and Asian managers from 60 leading Australian, New Zealand, British, and U.S. MNCs with operations in South Asia.[43]

international selection criteria
Factors used to choose personnel for international assignments.

General Criteria

Some selection criteria are given a great deal of weight; others receive, at best, only lip service. A company sending people overseas for the first time often will have a much longer list of criteria than will an experienced MNC that has developed a "short list."

Typically, both technical and human criteria are considered. Firms that fail to consider both often find that their rate of failure is quite high. For example, Peterson, Napier,

Table 14–2
Rank of Criteria in Expatriate Selection

	Australian Managers (*n* = 47)	Expatriate Managers* (*n* = 52)	Asian Managers (*n* = 15)
1. Ability to adapt	1	1	2
2. Technical competence	2	3	1
3. Spouse and family adaptability	3	2	4
4. Human relations skill	4	4	3
5. Desire to serve overseas	5	5	5
6. Previous overseas experience	6	7	7
7. Understanding of host-country culture	7	6	6
8. Academic qualifications	8	8	8
9. Knowledge of language of country	9	9	9
10. Understanding of home-country culture	10	10	10

*U.S., British, Canadian, French, New Zealand, or Australian managers working for an MNC outside their home countries.

Source: From Raymond J. Stone, "Expatriate Selection and Failure." Reprinted with permission from *Human Resource Planning,* Vol. 14, Issue 1, 1991, by The Human Resource Planning Society, 317 Madison Avenue, Suite 12509, New York, NY 10017.

and Shul-Shim investigated the primary criteria that MNCs use when choosing personnel for overseas assignments and found that the Japanese and American MNCs in their survey ranked both technical expertise and interpersonal skills as very important.[44] The following sections examine some of the most commonly used selection criteria for overseas assignments in more depth.

Adaptability to Cultural Change

Overseas managers must be able to adapt to change. They also need a degree of cultural toughness. Research shows that many managers are exhilarated at the beginning of their overseas assignment. After a few months, however, a form of culture shock creeps in, and they begin to encounter frustration and feel confused in their new environment. This may be a good sign because it shows that the expatriate manager is becoming involved in the new culture and not just isolating himself or herself from the environment.

As this initial and trying period comes to an end, expatriates tend to identify more with the host-country culture, which only increases as managers become more adept at the position. As seen in Figure 14–3, upon first arrival, the expatriates identify almost wholly with the home country. Over time, they become more familiar with their surroundings and become more of an integral part of the environment. This integration can lead to a higher sense of satisfaction with the job and a lessening of stress and alienation.[45]

Organizations examine a number of characteristics to determine whether an individual is sufficiently adaptable. Examples include work experiences with cultures other than one's own, previous overseas travel, knowledge of foreign languages (fluency generally is not necessary), and recent immigration background or heritage. Others include (1) the ability to integrate with different people, cultures, and types of business organizations; (2) the ability to sense developments in the host country and accurately evaluate them; (3) the ability to solve problems within different frameworks and from different perspectives; (4) sensitivity to the fine print of differences of culture, politics, religion, and ethics, in addition to individual differences; and (5) flexibility in managing operations on a continuous basis despite lack of assistance and gaps in information.

In research conducted among expatriates in China, Selmar found that those who were best able to deal with their new situation had developed coping strategies characterized by

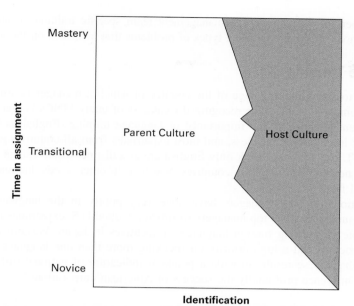

Figure 14–3

Evolution of Parent and Host Culture Identification

Source: Juan Sanchez, Paul Spector, and Cary Cooper, "Adapting to a Boundaryless World: A Developmental Expatriate Model," *Academy of Management Executive* 14, no. 2 (2000), p. 100.

socio-cultural and psychological adjustments including (1) feeling comfortable that their work challenges can be met; (2) being able to adjust to their new living conditions; (3) learning how to interact well with host-country nationals outside of work; and (4) feeling reasonably happy and being able to enjoy day-to-day activities.[46] And Caligiuri, after examining how host nationals help expatriates adjust, reported that certain types of personality characteristics are important in this process. In particular, her findings suggest that greater contact with host nationals helps with cross-cultural adjustment when the person also possesses the personality trait of openness. She also found that sociability was directly related to effective adjustment.[47]

Physical and Emotional Health

Most organizations require that their overseas managers have good physical and emotional health. Some examples are fairly obvious. An employee with a heart condition or a nervous disorder would not be considered. The psychological ability of individuals to withstand culture shock, if this could be discerned, would be an issue, as would the current marital status as it affected an individual's ability to cope in a foreign environment. For example, one U.S. oil company operating in the Middle East considers middle-aged men with grown children to be the best able to cope with culture shock, and for some locations in the desert, considers people from Texas or southern California to be a better fit than those from New England.

Age, Experience, and Education

Most MNCs strive for a balance between age and experience. There is evidence that younger managers are more eager for international assignments. These managers tend to be more "worldly" and have a greater appreciation of other cultures than older managers do. By the same token, young people often are the least developed in management experience and technical skills; they lack real-world experience. To gain the desired balance, many firms send both young and seasoned personnel to the same overseas post. Many companies consider an academic degree, preferably a graduate degree, to be of critical importance to an international executive; however, universal agreement regarding the ideal type of degree is nonexistent. MNCs, of course, use formal education only as a point of departure for their own training and development efforts. For example, Siemens of Germany gives members of its international management team specific training designed to help them deal more effectively with the types of problems they will face on the job.

Language Training

The ability to speak the language of the country in which a manager is doing business can be extremely valuable. One recognized weakness of many MNCs is that they do not give sufficient attention to the importance of language training. English is the primary language of international business, and most expatriates from all countries can converse in English. Those who can speak only English are at a distinct disadvantage when doing business in non-English-speaking countries, however. In other words, language can be a very critical factor.

Traditionally, U.S. managers have done very poorly in the language area. For example, a survey of 1,500 top managers worldwide faulted U.S. expatriates for minimizing the value of learning foreign languages. Executives in Japan, Western Europe, and South America placed a high priority on speaking more than one language. The report concludes that "these results provide a poignant indication of national differences that promise to influence profoundly the success of American corporations."[48]

Motivation for a Foreign Assignment

Although individuals being sent overseas should have a desire to work abroad, this usually is not sufficient motivation. International management experts contend that the candidate also must believe in the importance of the job and even have something of an element of idealism or a sense of mission. Applicants who are unhappy with their current situation at home and are looking to get away seldom make effective overseas managers.

Some experts believe that a desire for adventure or a pioneering spirit is an acceptable reason for wanting to go overseas. Other motivators that often are cited include the desire to increase one's chances for promotion and the opportunity to improve one's economic status. For example, many U.S. MNCs regard international experience as being critical for promotion to the upper ranks. In addition, thanks to the supplemental wage and benefit package, U.S. managers sometimes find that they can make, and especially save, more money than if they remained stateside.

And while many may romanticize the expatriate life, it is clear that the travel mystique continues to motivate professionals to desire and seek an assignment abroad. A recent survey found that at least 40 percent of Britons say that they would like to work or retire abroad. And according to a report in the British Daily Telegraph:

> And it's not just about the sunshine. Becoming an expatriate is an adventure, a new beginning, a fresh start, and it is in human nature to want to explore. Global mobility is as old as human-kind itself. The ancient migration routes of our earliest ancestors are well documented and the distances travelled by primitive man still continue to amaze. There were even expatriates in the Bible—consider the exodus from Egypt for example. Indeed, the forced expatriation of Adam and Eve from the garden of Eden is the starting point for the entire Biblical narrative. Was Eve the very first "trailing spouse"? In more recent times entire civilizations have been influenced by explorers such as Marco Polo, Christopher Columbus, Captain Cook and the Pilgrim Fathers. So moving across continents is nothing new but its continued rise has been underpinned by the drive towards globalisation aided by the revolution in communication throughout the 20th century. Technologies have allowed companies to globalise in ways which were simply unimaginable in earlier times. Indeed such is the commitment to globalisation, that many major companies now structure their reporting lines along global delivery lines rather than local geographic control.[49]

Spouses and Dependents or Work-Family Issues

Spouses and dependents are another important consideration when a person is to be chosen for an overseas assignment. If the family is not happy, the manager often performs poorly and may either be terminated or simply decide to leave the organization. Shaffer and her associates recently collected multisource data from 324 expatriates in 46 countries and found that the amount of organizational support that an expatriate feels he or she is receiving and the interplay between the person's work and family domains have a direct and unique influence on the individual's intentions regarding staying with or leaving the enterprise.[50] For this reason, some firms interview both the spouse and the manager before deciding whether to approve the assignment. This can be a very important decision for the firm because it focuses on the importance of family as a critical issue to a successful assignment. One popular approach in appraising the family's suitability for an overseas assignment is called **adaptability screening**. This process evaluates how well the family is likely to stand up to the rigors and stress of overseas life. The company will look for a number of things in this screening, including how closely knit the family is, how well it can withstand stress, and how well it can adjust to a new culture and climate. The reason this family criterion receives so much attention is that MNCs have learned that an unhappy executive will be unproductive on the job and the individual will want to transfer home long before the tour of duty is complete. These findings were affirmed and extended by Borstorff and her associates, who examined the factors associated with employee willingness to work overseas and concluded that:

adaptability screening
The process of evaluating how well a family is likely to stand up to the stress of overseas life.

1. Unmarried employees are more willing than any other group to accept expat assignments.

2. Married couples without children at home or those with non-teenage children are probably the most willing to move.

3. Prior international experience appears associated with willingness to work as an expatriate.

4. Individuals most committed to their professional careers and to their employing organizations are prone to be more willing to work as expatriates.

5. Careers and attitudes of spouses will likely have a significant impact on employee willingness to move overseas.

6. Employee and spouse perceptions of organizational support for expatriates are critical to employee willingness to work overseas.[51]

These findings indicate that organizations cannot afford to overlook the role of the spouse in the expat selection decision process. What, in particular, can be done to address their concerns?[52] Table 14–3 provides some insights into this answer. Additionally, the table adds a factor often overlooked in this process—situations in which the wife is being assigned overseas and the husband is the "other" spouse. Although many of the concerns of the male spouse are similar to those of spouses in general, a close look at Table 14–3 shows that some of the concerns of the males are different in their rank ordering.

Leadership Ability

The ability to influence people to act in a particular way—leadership—is another important criterion in selecting managers for an international assignment. Determining whether a person who is an effective leader in the home country will be equally effective in an overseas environment can be difficult, however. When determining whether an applicant has the desired leadership ability, many firms look for specific characteristics, such as maturity, emotional stability, the ability to communicate well, independence, initiative, creativity, and good health. If these characteristics are present and the person has been an effective leader in the home country, MNCs assume that the individual also will do well overseas.

Other Considerations

Applicants also can take certain steps to prepare themselves better for international assignments. Tu and Sullivan suggest the applicant can carry out a number of different phases of preparation.[53] In phase one, they suggest focusing on self-evaluation and general awareness.

Table 14–3
Activities That Are Important for Expatriate Spouses
(scale: 1–5, 5 = Very important)

Mean Score	Activity
Average from All Respondents	
4.33	Company help in obtaining necessary paperwork (permits, etc.) for spouse
4.28	Adequate notice of relocation
4.24	Predeparture training for spouse and children
4.23	Counseling for spouse regarding work/activity opportunities in foreign location
4.05	Employment networks coordinated with other international networks
3.97	Help with spouse's reentry into home country
3.93	Financial support for education
3.76	Compensation for spouse's lost wages and/or benefits
3.71	Creation of a job for spouse
3.58	Development of support groups for spouses
3.24	Administrative support (office space, secretarial services, etc.) for spouse
3.11	Financial support for research
3.01	Financial support for volunteer activities
2.90	Financial support for creative activities
Average from Male Spouses	
4.86	Employment networks coordinated with other international organizations
4.71	Help with spouse's reentry into home country
4.71	Administrative support (office space, secretarial services, etc.) for spouse
4.57	Compensation for spouse's lost wages and/or benefits
4.29	Adequate notice of relocation
4.29	Counseling for spouse regarding work/activity opportunities in foreign location
3.86	Predeparture training for spouse and children
3.71	Creation of a job for spouse
3.71	Financial support for volunteer activities
3.43	Financial support for education
3.14	Financial support for research
3.14	Financial support for creative activities
3.00	Development of support groups for spouses

Source: Adapted from Betty Jane Punnett, "Towards Effective Management of Expatriate Spouses," *Journal of World Business* 33, no. 3 (1997), p. 249.

This includes answering the question, Is an international assignment really for me? Other questions in the first phase include finding out if one's spouse and family support the decision to go international and collecting general information on the available job opportunities.

Phase two is characterized by a concentration on activities that should be completed before a person is selected. Some of these include (1) conducting a technical skills match to ensure that one's skills are in line with those that are required for the job; (2) starting to learn the language, customs, and etiquette of the region where one will be posted; (3) developing an awareness of the culture and value systems of this geographic area; and (4) making one's superior aware of this interest in an international assignment.

The third phase consists of activities to be completed after being selected for an overseas assignment. Some of these include (1) attending training sessions provided by the company; (2) conferring with colleagues who have had experience in the assigned region; (3) speaking with expatriates and foreign nationals about the assigned country; and (4) if possible, visiting the host country with one's spouse before the formally scheduled departure.

■ Economic Pressures and Trends in Expat Assignments

Despite the economic recession of 2008–2010, most MNCs continue to make overseas assignments. A survey in 2009 found that 95 percent of MNCs responding to GMAC Global Relocation Services' 13th annual Global Relocation Trends Survey said they are optimistic about their global business outlook and plan to send more employees on overseas assignments in the future. The survey of 154 multinational companies, with a total worldwide employee population of 4.3 million, found that 68 percent of the corporations are ramping up their employee assignment efforts. Apparently, this optimism was driven in part by assessments of the growth of emerging markets, especially China as well as the continued integration of the European Union, allowing continued consolidation and integration of European operations. "The survey identified three significant challenges facing corporations: finding suitable candidates for assignments, helping employees—and their families—complete their assignments, and retaining these employees once their assignments end," said Rick Schwartz, president and chief executive officer of GMAC Global Relocation Services in Woodridge, Illinois.

Not surprisingly, family concerns were cited as the most common reason for assignment refusal, with 89 percent of those surveyed identifying families as the primarily reason employees turn down an assignment. This was followed by spousal career concerns, indicated by 62 percent. Family-related concerns also were important in the duration of international assignments and were the main driver of early returns from assignments. "Not surprisingly, children's education, family adjustment, partner resistance and difficult locations were identified as the top four critical family challenges in this year's survey," Schwartz said. "That's underscored by the fact that 61 percent of respondents noted that the impact of family issues on early returns from assignment was very critical or of high importance."

The lack of relevance of assignments to one's career progress was also identified as a major issue. In addition, the general inconveniences caused by assignments were also identified as not fully appreciated by their companies. Moreover, some employees lack opportunities to leverage their international experiences into better positions within their companies. Finally, the annual turnover rate for expatriates on assignment is 25 percent. In addition, it's 27 percent for expatriates within one year of completing assignments, compared to 13 percent average annual turnover for all employees. Other findings from the survey included:

- 19 percent of expatriates were women; the historical average was 15 percent.
- 50 percent of expatriates were 20 to 39 years old.
- 60 percent of expatriates were married, less than the 66 percent historical average. The percentage of married men, 51 percent, was the lowest in the report's history.
- 51 percent of expatriates had children accompanying them, matching the previous all-time low in the 2003–2004 report; the historical average was 57 percent.
- Spouses and partners accompanied 83 percent of expatriates, compared to the historical average of 85 percent.
- 54 percent of spouses were employed before an assignment but not during it; 12 percent were employed during an assignment but not before; 20 percent were employed both before and during the assignment.
- 56 percent of expatriates were relocated to or from the headquarters country, below the historical average of 65 percent.
- The United States, China, and United Kingdom were the most frequently cited locations for expatriate assignments.
- China, India, and Russia were the primary emerging destinations.
- China, India, and Russia also were cited as the most challenging locations for administrators overseeing employee relocations.[54]

■ International Human Resource Selection Procedures

MNCs use a number of selection procedures. The two most common are tests and interviews. Some international firms use one; a smaller percentage employ both. Theoretical models containing the variables that are important for adjusting to an overseas assignment have been developed. These adjustment models can help contribute to more effective selection of expatriates. The following sections examine traditional testing and interviewing procedures and then present an adjustment model.

Testing and Interviewing Procedures

Some evidence suggests that although some firms use testing, it is not extremely popular. For example, an early study found that almost 80 percent of the 127 foreign operations managers who were surveyed reported that their companies used no tests in the selection process.[55] This contrasts with the more widespread testing that these firms use when selecting domestic managers. Many MNCs report that the costs, questionable accuracy, and poor predictive record make testing of limited value.

Many firms do use interviews to screen people for overseas assignments. One expert notes: "It is generally agreed that extensive interviews of candidates (and their spouses) by senior executives still ultimately provide the best method of selection."[56] Tung's research supports these comments. For example, 52 percent of the U.S. MNCs she surveyed reported that in the case of managerial candidates, MNCs conducted interviews with both the manager and his or her spouse, and 47 percent conducted interviews with the candidate alone. Concerning these findings, Tung concluded:

> These figures suggest that in management-type positions which involve more extensive contact with the local community, as compared to technically oriented positions, the adaptability of the spouse to living in a foreign environment was perceived as important for successful performance abroad. However, even for technically oriented positions, a sizable proportion of the firms did conduct interviews with both candidate and spouse. This lends support to the contention of other researchers that MNCs are becoming increasingly cognizant of the importance of this factor to effective performance abroad.[57]

The Adjustment Process

In recent years, international human resource management specialists have developed models that help to explain the factors involved in effectively adjusting to overseas assignments.[58] These adjustment models help to identify the underpinnings of the effective selection of expatriates.

There are two major types of adjustments that an expatriate must make when going on an overseas assignment: anticipatory and in-country adjustment. Anticipatory adjustment is carried out before the expat leaves for the assignment and is influenced by a number of important factors. One factor is the pre-departure training that is provided. This often takes the form of cross-cultural seminars or workshops, and it is designed to acquaint expats with the culture and work life of the country to which they will be posted. Another factor affecting anticipatory adjustment is the previous experience the expat may have had with the assigned country or with countries with similar cultures. The organizational input into anticipatory adjustment is most directly related and concerned with the selection process. Traditionally, MNCs relied on only one important selection criterion for overseas assignments: technical competence. Obviously, technical competence is important, but it is only one of a number of skills that will be needed. If the MNC concentrates only on technical competence as a selection criterion, then it is not properly preparing the expatriate managers for successful adjustment in overseas assignments. As a result, expats are going to go abroad believing that they are prepared to deal with the challenges awaiting them, and they will be wrong.

In-country adjustment takes place once the expatriate is on site, and a number of factors will influence his or her ability to adjust effectively. One factor is the expat's ability to maintain a positive outlook in the face of a high-pressure situation, to interact well with host nationals, and to perceive and evaluate the host country's cultural values and norms correctly. A second factor is the job itself, as reflected by the clarity of the role the expat plays in the host management team, the authority the expat has to make decisions, the newness of the work-related challenges, and the amount of role conflict that exists. A third factor is the organizational culture and how easily the expat can adjust to it. A fourth is nonwork matters, such as the toughness with which the expatriate faces a whole new cultural experience and how well his or her family can adjust to the rigors of the new assignment. A fifth and final factor identified in the adjustment model is the expat's ability to develop effective socialization tactics and to understand "what's what" and "who's who" in the host organization.

Another model of expatriate adjustment emphasized the formation of network ties in the host country to obtain critical informational and emotional support resources, proposing a five-stage process model that delineates how expatriates form adjustment-facilitating support ties in a culturally unfamiliar context. These include

- Stage 1: Factors influencing expatriates' motivation to seek support from actors in the host country.
- Stage 2: Factors influencing expatriates' selection of and support seeking toward actors.
- Stage 3: Factors influencing contacted actors' ability and willingness to provide support.
- Stage 4: Factors influencing expatriates' utilization of received support.
- Stage 5: Factors influencing expatriates' addition of actors to network.[59]

These anticipatory and in-country factors will influence the expatriate's mode and degree of adjustment to an overseas assignment. They can help to explain why effective selection of expatriates is multifaceted and can be very difficult and challenging. But if all works out well, the individual can become a very important part of the organization's overseas operations. McCormick and Chapman illustrated this by showing the changes that an expat goes through as he or she seeks to adjust to the new assignment.[60] As seen in Figure 14–4, early enthusiasm often gives way to cold reality, and the expat typically

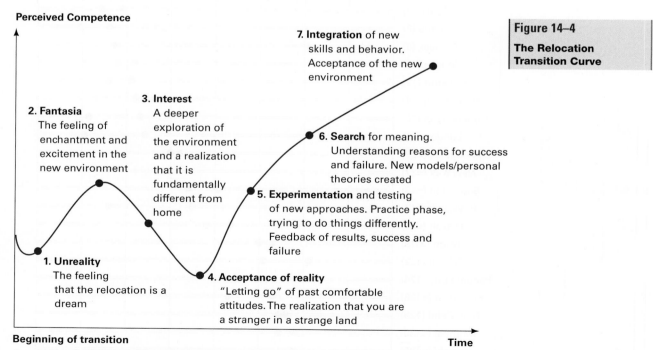

Figure 14–4

The Relocation Transition Curve

Source: Adapted from Iain McCormick and Tony Chapman, "Executive Relocation: Personal and Organizational Tactics," in *Managing Across Cultures: Issues and Perspectives,* ed. Pat Joynt and Malcolm Warner (London: International Thomson Business Press, 1996), p. 368.

ends up in a search to balance personal and work demands with the new environment. In many cases, fortunately, everything works out well. Additionally, one of the ways in which MNCs often try to put potential expats at ease about their new assignment is by presenting an attractive compensation package.

■ Compensation

One of the reasons there has been a decline in the number of expats in recent years is that MNCs have found that the expense can be prohibitive. Reynolds estimated that, on average, "expats cost employers two to five times as much as home-country counterparts and frequently ten or more times as much as local nationals in the country to which they are assigned."[61] As seen in Figure 14–5, the cost of living in some of the major cities is extremely high, and these expenses must be included somewhere in the compensation package.

The recession of the late 2000s placed additional pressure on firms to control costs associated with expatriate assignments. Mercer reported in 2009 that nearly 40 percent of MNCs were planning on revising their current international assignment policy in the face of declining corporate growth and profitability, as well as an uncertain economic environment. The increasing trend toward localization reflects companies' efforts to either tap into the local

Figure 14–5

Cost-of-Living Index

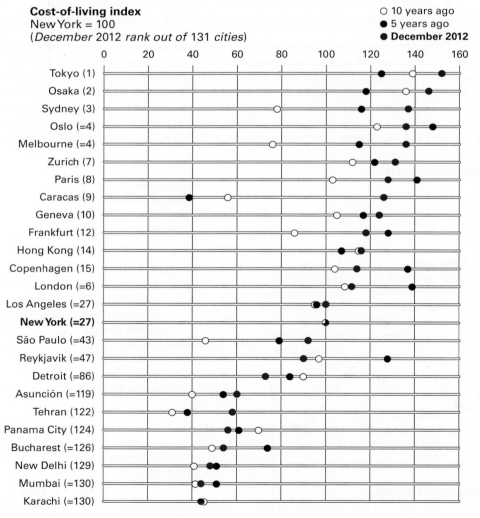

Cost-of-living index
New York = 100
(*December* 2012 *rank out of* 131 *cities*)

○ 10 years ago
● 5 years ago
● December 2012

Source: Economist Intelligence Unit

talents or to offer less generous packages to locally hired foreign workers. This localization approach was quite consistent among regions and countries around the world, including for companies operating in emerging markets (such as China, India, and Vietnam), where the local compensation and benefits packages are less generous than home-country plans. In terms of expatriate benefits and allowances, the elements that are least likely to be eliminated for localized employees are housing allowances and education benefits. Mercer did find that localization is practiced in Europe and in North America more than in Latin America and Asia Pacific. In recent years, however, localization has picked up in the Asia Pacific region, particularly as companies want to tap into the regional talent pool and contain costs.[62]

Common Elements of Compensation Packages

The overall compensation package often varies from country to country. As Bailey noted:

> Compensation programs implemented in a global organization will not mirror an organization's domestic plan because of differences in legally mandated benefits, tax laws, cultures, and employee expectation based on local practices. The additional challenge in compensation design is the requirement that excessive costs be avoided and at the same time employee morale be maintained at high levels.[63]

There are five common elements in the typical expatriate compensation package: base salary, benefits, allowances, incentives, and taxes.

Base Salary Base salary is the amount of money that an expatriate normally receives in the home country. In the United States this has often been in the range of $200,000–$300,000 for upper-middle managers in recent years, and this rate is similar to that paid to managers in both Japan and Germany. The exchange rates, of course, also affect the real wages.

Expatriate salaries typically are set according to the base pay of the home countries. Therefore, a German manager working for a U.S. MNC and assigned to Spain would have a base salary that reflects the salary structure in Germany. U.S. expatriates have salaries tied to U.S. levels. The salaries usually are paid in home currency, local currency, or a combination of the two. The base pay also serves as the benchmark against which bonuses and benefits are calculated.

Benefits Approximately one-third of compensation for regular employees is benefits. These benefits compose a similar, or even larger, portion of expat compensation. A number of thorny issues surround compensation for expatriates, however. These include:

1. Whether MNCs should maintain expatriates in home-country benefit programs, particularly if these programs are not tax-deductible.
2. Whether MNCs have the option of enrolling expatriates in host-country benefit programs or making up any difference in coverage.
3. Whether host-country legislation regarding termination of employment affects employee benefits entitlements.
4. Whether the home or host country is responsible for the expatriates' social security benefits.
5. Whether benefits should be subject to the requirements of the home or host country.
6. Which country should pay for the benefits.
7. Whether other benefits should be used to offset any shortfall in coverage.
8. Whether home-country benefits programs should be available to local nationals.

Most U.S.-based MNCs include expatriate managers in their home-office benefits program at no additional cost to the expats. If the host country requires expats to contribute to their social security program, the MNC typically picks up the tab. Fortunately, several international agreements between countries recently have eliminated such dual coverage and expenses.

Additionally, MNCs often provide expatriates with extra vacation and with special leaves. The MNC typically will pay the airfare for expats and their families to make an annual visit home, for emergency leave, and for expenses when a relative in the home country is ill or dies.

Allowances   Allowances are an expensive feature of expatriate compensation packages. One of the most common parts is a cost-of-living allowance—a payment for differences between the home country and the overseas assignment. This allowance is designed to provide the expat with the same standard of living that he or she enjoyed in the home country, and it may cover a variety of expenses, including relocation, housing, education, and hardship.

Relocation expenses typically involve moving, shipping, and storage charges that are associated with personal furniture, clothing, and other items that the expatriate and his or her family are (or are not) taking to the new assignment. Related expenses also may include cars and club memberships in the host country, although these perks commonly are provided only to senior-level expats.

Housing allowances cover a wide range. Some firms provide the expat with a residence during the assignment and pay all associated expenses. Others give a predetermined housing allotment each month and let expats choose their own residence. Additionally, some MNCs help those going on assignment with the sale or lease of the house they are leaving behind; if the house is sold, the company usually pays closing costs and other associated expenses.

Education allowances for the expat's children are another integral part of the compensation package. These expenses cover costs such as tuition, enrollment fees, books, supplies, transportation, room, board, and school uniforms. In some cases, expenses to attend postsecondary schools also are covered.

Hardship allowances are designed to induce expats to work in hazardous areas or in an area with a poor quality of life. Those who are assigned to Eastern Europe, China, and some Middle Eastern countries sometimes are granted a hardship premium. These payments may be in the form of a lump sum ($10,000 to $50,000) or a percentage (15 to 50 percent) of the expat's base compensation.

Incentives   In recent years some MNCs have also been designing special incentive programs for keeping expats motivated. In the process, a growing number of firms have dropped the ongoing premium for overseas assignments and replaced it with a one-time, lump-sum premium. For example, in the early 1990s over 60 percent of MNCs gave ongoing premiums to their expats. Today that percentage is under 50 percent and continuing to decline. Peterson and his colleagues, for example, examined the human resource policies of 24 U.S., British, German, and Japanese subsidiaries and found that in only 10 of the cases did the multinational have a policy of paying expatriates higher compensation than they would have received if they had stayed in their home country.[64]

The lump-sum payment has a number of benefits. One is that expats realize that they will be given this payment just once—when they move to the international locale. So the payment tends to retain its value as an incentive. A second is that the costs to the company are less because there is only one payment and no future financial commitment. A third is that because it is a separate payment, distinguishable from regular pay, it is more readily available for saving or spending.

The specific incentive program that is used will vary, and expats like this. Researchers, for example, have found that some of the factors that influence the type and amount of incentive include whether the person is moving within or between continents and where the person is being stationed. Table 14–4 provides some of the latest survey information related to worldwide employer incentive practices.

Finally, it is important to recognize that growing numbers of MNCs are beginning to phase out incentive premiums. Instead, they are focusing on creating a cadre of expats who are motivated by nonfinancial incentives.

Table 14–4
Employer Incentive Practices Around the World

Percent of MNCs Paying for Moves Within Continents				
Type of Premium	Asia	Europe	North America	Total
Ongoing	62%	46%	29%	42%
Lump sum	21	20	25	23
None	16	27	42	32

Percent of MNCs Paying for Moves Between Continents				
Type of Premium	Asia	Europe	North America	Total
Ongoing	63%	54%	39%	49%
Lump sum	24	18	30	26
None	13	21	27	22

Source: Derived from Geoffrey W. Latta, "Expatriate Incentives: Beyond Tradition," *HR Focus,* March 1998, p. S4.

Taxes Another major component of expatriate compensation is tax equalization. For example, an expat may have two tax bills, one from the host country and one from the U.S. Internal Revenue Service, for the same pay. IRS Code Section 911 permits a deduction of up to $80,000 on foreign-earned income. Top-level expats often earn far more than this, however; thus, they may pay two tax bills for the amount by which their pay exceeds $80,000.

Usually, MNCs pay the extra tax burden. The most common way is by determining the base salary and other extras (e.g., bonuses) that the expat would make if based in the home country. Taxes on this income then are computed and compared with the taxes due on the expat's income. Any taxes that exceed what would have been imposed in the home country are paid by the MNC, and any windfall is kept by the expat as a reward for taking the assignment.

Tailoring the Package

Working within the five common elements just described, MNCs will tailor compensation packages to fit the specific situation. For example, senior-level managers in Japan are paid only around four times as much as junior staff members. This is in sharp contrast to the United States, where the multiple is much higher. A similar situation exists in Europe, where many senior-level managers make far less than their U.S. counterparts and stockholders, politicians, and the general public oppose U.S.-style affluence. Can a senior-level U.S. expat be paid a salary that is significantly higher than local senior-level managers in the overseas subsidiary, or would the disparity create morale problems? This is a difficult question to answer and must be given careful consideration. One solution is to link pay and performance to attract and retain outstanding personnel.

In formulating the compensation package, a number of approaches can be used. The most common is the **balance-sheet approach**, which involves ensuring that the expat is "made whole" and does not lose money by taking the assignment. A second and often complementary approach is negotiation, which involves working out a special, ad hoc arrangement that is acceptable to both the company and the expat. A third approach, **localization**, involves paying the expat a salary that is comparable to the salaries of local nationals. This approach most commonly is used with individuals early in their careers who are being given a long-term overseas assignment. A fourth approach is the **lump-sum method**, which involves giving the expat a predetermined amount of money and letting the individual make his or her own decisions regarding how to spend it. A fifth is the

balance-sheet approach
An approach to developing an expatriate compensation package that ensures the expat is "made whole" and does not lose money by taking the assignment.

localization
An approach to developing an expatriate compensation package that involves paying the expat a salary comparable to that of local nationals.

lump-sum method
An approach to developing an expatriate compensation package that involves giving the expat a predetermined amount of money and letting the individual make his or her own decisions regarding how to spend it.

cafeteria approach
An approach to developing an expatriate compensation package that entails giving the individual a series of options and letting the person decide how to spend the available funds.

regional system
An approach to developing an expatriate compensation package that involves setting a compensation system for all expats who are assigned to a particular region and paying everyone in accord with that system.

cafeteria approach, which entails giving expats a series of options and letting them decide how to spend the available funds. For example, expats who have children may opt for private schooling; expats who have no children may choose a chauffeur-driven car or an upscale apartment. A sixth method is the **regional system**, under which the MNC sets a compensation system for all expats who are assigned to a particular region, so that (for example) everyone going to Europe falls under one particular system and everyone being assigned to South America is covered by a different system.[65] The most important thing to remember about global compensation is that the package must be cost-effective and fair. If it meets these two criteria, it likely will be acceptable to all parties.

As a result of the 2008–2010 recession, many companies are making changes to their expatriate staffing and compensation practices. While many companies have developed short-term assignment and business-travel policies to more efficiently fill their staffing needs, more comprehensive measures, such as shifting home country employees working in foreign locations from expatriate to "local plus" packages, are becoming more common.[66] Participants in two surveys by HR consultancy ORC Worldwide—Survey on Local-Plus Packages in Hong Kong and Singapore and Survey on Local-Plus Packages for Expatriates in China—report a growing trend toward expatriate "light" or "local-plus" packages. "These alternative packages often base the assignee's salary on host country pay structures," says Phil Stanley, managing director of ORC Worldwide's Asia-Pacific region, "but then tack on a few expatriate type benefits, such as some form of housing assistance and possibly an allowance to partially cover children's education."[67]

■ Individual and Host-Country Viewpoints

Until now, we have examined the selection process mostly from the standpoint of the MNC: What will be best for the company? However, two additional perspectives for selection warrant consideration: (1) that of the individual who is being selected and (2) that of the country to which the candidate will be sent. Research shows that each has specific desires and motivations regarding the expatriate selection process.

Candidate Motivations

Why do individuals accept foreign assignments? One answer is a greater demand for their talents abroad than at home. For example, a growing number of senior U.S. managers have moved to Mexico because of Mexico's growing need for experienced executives. The findings of one early study grouped the participating countries into clusters: Anglo (Australia, Austria, Canada, India, New Zealand, South Africa, Switzerland, United Kingdom, and United States); Northern European (Denmark, Finland, Norway); French (Belgium and France); Northern South American (Colombia, Mexico, and Peru); Southern South American (Argentina and Chile); and Independent (Brazil, Germany, Israel, Japan, Sweden, and Venezuela).[68] Within these groupings, researchers were able to identify major motivational differences. Some of their findings included:

1. The Anglo cluster was more interested in individual achievement and less interested in the desire for security than any other cluster.
2. The French cluster was similar to the Anglo cluster, except that less importance was given to individual achievement and more to security.
3. Countries in the Northern European cluster were more oriented to job accomplishment and less to getting ahead; considerable importance was assigned to jobs not interfering with personal lives.
4. In South American clusters, individual achievement goals were less important than in most other clusters. Fringe benefits were particularly important to South American groups.
5. Germans were similar to those in the South American clusters, except that they placed a greater emphasis on advancement and earnings.

6. The Japanese were unique in their mix of desires. They placed high value on earnings opportunities but low value on advancement. They were high on challenge but low on autonomy. At the same time, they placed strong emphasis on working in a friendly, efficient department and having good physical working conditions.

Another interesting focus of attention has been on those countries that expatriates like best. A study conducted by Ingemar Torbiorn found that the 1,100 Swedish expatriates surveyed were at least fairly well satisfied with their host country and in some cases were very satisfied. Five of the countries that they liked very much were Switzerland, Belgium, England, the United States, and Portugal.[69] These countries are still popular today, which makes sense since they are included in the top tier of countries with the highest quality of life. The criteria include such things as family life, economic life, unemployment rates, political stability, and so forth to determine how safe or attractive the country is.

Host-Country Desires

Although many MNCs try to choose people who fit in well, little attention has been paid to the host country's point of view. Whom would it like to see put in managerial positions? One study that compared U.S., Indonesian, and Mexican managers found that behaviors can distinguish them from one another and that host countries would prefer a managerial style similar to that of their country.[70] For example, positive managerial behaviors, such as honesty and follow-through with employees, distinguish Indonesian and U.S. managers from Mexican managers. As seen in Chapter 4, this could partially be due to the power distance suggested by Hofstede. Furthermore, negative managerial behaviors, such as public criticism and discipline toward employees, also distinguish Indonesian and U.S. managers from Mexican managers. It has been suggested that the dynamic in the workplace has to do with the familial structure, namely that Mexican workers place a higher value on family over work than do the U.S. or Indonesian counterparts. This can be a factor in how the positive and negative behaviors are expressed in each country, as outlined in Table 14–5. Overall, it is important for managers to take the host-country perspectives into consideration, or it could result in an ineffectual endeavor.

Table 14–5
Comparative Positive and Negative Managerial Behavior by Country

Positive Behaviors	Negative Behaviors
Indonesia	
Is honest with employees	Engages in unfair discrimination
Provides clear work expectations	Disciplines and criticizes in public
Shows confidence in employee	Flaunts power
Provides regular feedback	
Mexico	
Shows respect for employees	Practices favoritism
Shows confidence in employees	Does not understand employee values
Is flexible to individual employee needs	and traditions
Provides clear work expectations	
United States	
Is honest with employees	Disciplines and criticizes in public
Shows loyalty to employees	Flaunts power
Shows respect for employees	
Shows confidence in employees	

Source: From Charles M. Vance and Yongsun Paik, "One Size Fits All in Expatriate Pre-departure Training?" *Journal of Management Development* 21, No. 7/8, 2002, p. 566. Reprinted with permission of Emerald Insight.

■ Repatriation of Expatriates

For most overseas managers, **repatriation**, the return to one's home country, occurs within five years of the time they leave. Few expatriates remain overseas for the duration of their stay with the firm.[71] When they return, these expatriates often find themselves facing readjustment problems, and some MNCs are trying to deal with these problems through use of transition strategies.

Reasons for Returning

The most common reason that expatriates return home from overseas assignments is that their formally agreed-on tour of duty is over. Before they left, they were told that they would be posted overseas for a predetermined period, often two to three years, and they are returning as planned. A second common reason is that expatriates want their children educated in a home-country school, and the longer they are away, the less likely it is that this will happen.[72]

A third reason expatriates return is that they are not happy in their overseas assignment. Sometimes unhappiness is a result of poor organizational support by the home office, which leaves the manager feeling that the assignment is not a good one and it would be best to return as soon as possible. Kraimer, Wayne, and Jaworski found that lack of this kind of support has a negative effect on the expat's ability to adjust to the assignment.[73] At other times an expat will want to return home early because the spouse or children do not want to stay. Because the company feels that the loss in managerial productivity is too great to be offset by short-term personal unhappiness, the individual is allowed to come back even though typically the cost is quite high.[74] A fourth reason that people return is failure to do a good job. Such failure often spells trouble for the manager and may even result in demotion or termination.

Readjustment Problems

Many companies that say that they want their people to have international experience often seem unsure of what to do with these managers when they return. One recent survey of midsize and large firms found that 80 percent of these companies send people abroad and more than half of them intend to increase the number they have on assignment overseas. However, responses from returning expats point to problems. Three-quarters of the respondents said that they felt their permanent position upon returning home was a demotion. Over 60 percent said that they lacked the opportunities to put their foreign experience to work, and 60 percent said that their company had not communicated clearly about what would happen to them when they returned. Perhaps worst of all, within a year of returning, 25 percent of the managers had left the company.[75] These statistics are not surprising to those who have been studying repatriation problems. In fact, one researcher reported the following expatriate comments about their experiences:

> My colleagues react indifferently to my international assignment. . . . They view me as doing a job I did in the past; they don't see me as having gained anything while overseas.

> I had no specific reentry job to return to. I wanted to leave international and return to domestic. Working abroad magnifies problems while isolating effects. You deal with more problems, but the home office doesn't know the details of the good or bad effects. Managerially, I'm out of touch.

> I'm bored at work. . . . I run upstairs to see what [another returning colleague] is doing. He says, "Nothing." Me, too.[76]

Other readjustment problems are more personal in nature. Many expatriates find that the salary and fringe benefits to which they have become accustomed in the foreign assignment now are lost, and adjusting to this lower standard of living is difficult. In addition, those who sold their houses and now must buy new ones find that the monthly cost often is much higher than when they left. The children often are placed in public schools, where classes are much larger than in the overseas private schools. Many also miss the cultural lifestyles, as in the case of an executive who is transferred from Paris, France, to a medium-sized city in the United States, or from any developed country to an underdeveloped country. Additionally, many returning expatriates have learned that their international experiences are not viewed as important. Many Japanese expatriates, for example, report that when they return, their experiences should be downplayed if they want to "fit in" with the organization. In fact, reports one recent New York Times article, a substantial number of Japanese expatriates "are happier overseas than they are back home."[77]

Other research supports the findings noted here and offers operative recommendations for action. Based on questionnaires completed by 174 respondents who had been repatriated from four large U.S. MNCs, Black found the following:

1. With few exceptions, individuals whose expectations were met had the most positive levels of repatriation adjustment and job performance.

2. In the case of high-level managers in particular, expatriates whose job demands were greater, rather than less, than expected reported high levels of repatriation adjustment and job performance. Those having greater job demands may have put in more effort and had better adjustment and performance.

3. Job performance and repatriation adjustment were greater for individuals whose job constraint expectations were undermet than for those individuals whose expectations were overmet. In other words, job constraints were viewed as an undesirable aspect of the job, and having them turn out to be less than expected was a pleasant surprise that helped adjustment and performance.

4. When living and housing conditions turned out to be better than expected, general repatriation adjustment and job performance were better.

5. Individuals whose general expectations were met or overmet had job evaluations that placed them 10 percent higher than those whose general expectations were unmet.[78]

Transition Strategies

To help smooth the adjustment from an overseas to a stateside assignment, some MNCs have developed **transition strategies**, which can take a number of different forms. One is the use of **repatriation agreements**, whereby the firm tells an individual how long she or he will be posted overseas and promises to give the individual, on return, a job that is mutually acceptable. This agreement typically does not promise a specific position or salary, but the agreement may state that the person will be given a job that is equal to, if not better than, the one held before leaving.[79]

Some firms also rent or otherwise maintain expatriates' homes until they return. The Aluminum Company of America and Union Carbide both have such plans for managers going overseas. This plan helps reduce the financial shock that often accompanies home shopping by returning expatriates. A third strategy is to use senior executives as sponsors of managers abroad.

Still another approach is to keep expatriate managers apprised of what is going on at corporate headquarters and to plug these managers into projects at the home office whenever they are on leave in the home country. This helps maintain the person's visibility and ensures the individual is looked on as a regular member of the management staff.

One study surveyed 99 employees and managers with international experience in 21 corporations.[80] The findings reveal that cultural reentry, financial implications, and the nature of job assignments are three major areas of expatriate concern. In particular, some of the main problems of repatriation identified in this study include (1) adjusting to life back home; (2) facing a financial package that is not as good as that overseas; (3) having less autonomy in the stateside job than in the overseas position; and (4) not receiving any career counseling from the company. To the extent that the MNC can

transition strategies
Strategies used to help smooth the adjustment from an overseas to a stateside assignment.

repatriation agreements
Agreements whereby the firm tells an individual how long she or he will be posted overseas and promises to give the individual, on return, a job that is mutually acceptable.

address these types of problems, the transition will be smooth, and the expatriate's performance effectiveness once home will increase quickly. Some additional steps suggested by experts in this area include:

1. Arrange an event to welcome and recognize the employee and family, either formally or informally.
2. Establish support to facilitate family reintegration.
3. Offer repatriation counseling or workshops to ease the adjustment.
4. Assist the spouse with job counseling, résumé writing, and interviewing techniques.
5. Provide educational counseling for the children.
6. Provide the employee with a thorough debriefing by a facilitator to identify new knowledge, insights, and skills and to provide a forum to showcase new competencies.
7. Offer international outplacement to the employee and reentry counseling to the entire family if no positions are possible.
8. Arrange a postassignment interview with the expatriate and spouse to review their view of the assignment and address any repatriation issues.[81]

Hammer and his associates echo these types of recommendations. Based on research that they conducted in two multinational corporations among expats and their spouses, they concluded:

> The findings from the present study suggest that one of the key transitional activities for returning expatriates and their spouses from a corporate context should involve targeted communication from the home environment concerning the expectations of the home office toward the return of the repatriate executive and his/her family (role relationships). Further, reentry training should focus primarily on helping the repatriate manager and spouse align their expectations with the actual situation that will be encountered upon arrival in the home culture both within the organizational context as well as more broadly within the social milieu. To the degree that corporate communication and reentry training activities help the returning executive and spouse in expectation alignment, the executive's level of reentry satisfaction should be higher and the degree of reentry difficulties less.[82]

Additionally, in recent years many MNCs have begun using inpatriates to supplement their home-office staff and some of the same issues discussed here with repatriation come into play.

■ Training in International Management

training
The process of altering employee behavior and attitudes in a way that increases the probability of goal attainment.

Training is the process of altering employee behavior and attitudes in a way that increases the probability of goal attainment. Training is particularly important in preparing employees for overseas assignments because it helps ensure that their full potential will be tapped.[83] One of the things that training can do is to help expat managers better understand the customs, cultures, and work habits of the local culture. The simplest training, in terms of preparation time, is to place a cultural integrator in each foreign operation. This individual is responsible for ensuring that the operation's business systems are in accord with those of the local culture. The integrator advises, guides, and recommends actions needed to ensure this synchronization.[84]

Unfortunately, although using an integrator can help, it is seldom sufficient. Recent experience clearly reveals that in creating an effective global team, the MNC must assemble individuals who collectively understand the local language, have grown up in diverse cultures or neighborhoods, have open, flexible minds, and will be able to deal with high degrees of stress.[85] In those cases where potential candidates do not yet possess all these requisite skills or abilities, MNCs need a well-designed training program that is administered before the individuals leave for their overseas assignment (and, in some cases, also on-site) and then evaluated later to determine its overall effectiveness. One review of 228 MNCs found that cross-cultural training, which can take many forms, is becoming increasingly popular. Some of these findings included the following:

1. Of organizations with cultural programs, 58 percent offer training only to some expatriates, and 42 percent offer it to all of them.

2. Ninety-one percent offer cultural orientation programs to spouses, and 75 percent offer them to dependent children.

3. The average duration of the cultural training programs is three days.

4. Cultural training is continued after arrival in the assignment location 32 percent of the time.

5. Thirty percent offer formal cultural training programs.

6. Of those without formal cultural programs, 37 percent plan to add such training.[86]

The most common topics covered in cultural training are social etiquette, customs, economics, history, politics, and business etiquette. However, the MNC's overall philosophy of international management and the demands of the specific cultural situation are the starting point. This is because countries tend to have distinctive human resource management (HRM) practices that differentiate them from other countries. For example, the HRM practices that are prevalent in the United States are quite different from those in France and Argentina. This was clearly illustrated by Sparrow and Budhwar, who compared data from 13 different countries on the basis of HRM factors. Five of these factors were the following:

1. Structural empowerment that is characterized by flat organization designs, wide spans of control, the use of flexible cross-functional teams, and the rewarding of individuals for productivity gains.

2. Accelerated resource development that is characterized by the early identification of high-potential employees, the establishment of both multiple and parallel career paths, the rewarding of personnel for enhancing their skills and knowledge, and the offering of continuous training and development education.

3. Employee welfare emphasis that is characterized by firms offering personal family assistance, encouraging and rewarding external volunteer activities, and promoting organizational cultures that emphasize equality in the workplace.

4. An efficiency emphasis in which employees are encouraged to monitor their own work and to continually improve their performance.

5. Long-termism, which stresses long-term results such as innovation and creativity rather than weekly and monthly short-term productivity.[87]

When Sparrow and Budhwar used these HRM approaches on a comparative country-by-country basis, they found that there were worldwide differences in human resource management practices. Table 14–6 shows the comparative results after each of the 13 countries was categorized as being either high or low on the respective factors. These findings reveal that countries are unique in their approach to human resource management. What works well in the United States may have limited value in France. In fact, a close analysis of Table 14–6 shows that none of the 13 countries had the same profile; each was different. This was true even in the case of Anglo nations such as the United States, Canada, Australia, and the United Kingdom, where differences in employee welfare emphasis, accelerated resource development, efficiency emphasis orientation, and long-termism resulted in unique HRM profiles for each. Similarly, Japan and Korea differed on two of the factors, as did Germany and France; and India, which many people might feel would be more similar to an Anglo culture, because of the British influence, than to an Asian one, differed on two factors with Canada, on three factors with both the United States and the United Kingdom, and on four factors with Australia.

Table 14–6
Human Resource Management Practices in Select Countries

	Structural Empowerment		Accelerated Resource Development		Employee Welfare Emphasis		Efficiency Emphasis		Long-Termism	
	High	Low	High	Low	High	Low	High	Low	High	Low
United States	X			X	X		X			X
Canada	X			X	X			X		X
United Kingdom	X			X		X		X		X
Italy		X		X		X		X		X
Japan		X		X	X		X		X	
India		X		X	X			X	X	
Australia	X		X			X	X		X	
Brazil	X			X	X			X	X	
Mexico	X			X	X			X		X
Argentina		X		X	X			X		X
Germany		X		X		X		X	X	
Korea		X		X		X	X		X	
France		X		X		X	X			X

Source: Adapted from Paul R. Sparrow and Pawan S. Budhwar, "Competition and Change: Mapping the Indian HRM Recipe Against Worldwide Patterns," *Journal of World Business* 32, no. 3 (1997), p. 233.

These findings point to the fact that MNCs will have to focus increasingly on HRM programs designed to meet the needs of local personnel. A good example is provided in the former communist countries of Europe, where international managers are discovering that in order to effectively recruit college graduates, their firms must provide training programs that give these new employees opportunities to work with a variety of tasks and to help them specialize in their particular fields of interest. At the same time the MNCs are discovering that these recruits are looking for companies that offer a good social working environment. A recent survey of over 1,000 business and engineering students from Poland, the Czech Republic, and Hungary found that almost two-thirds of the respondents said that they wanted their boss to be receptive to their ideas; 37 percent wanted to work for managers who had strong industry experience; and 34 percent wanted a boss who was a good rational decision maker. These findings indicate that multinational human resource management is now becoming much more of a two-way street: Both employees and managers need to continually adjust to emerging demands.[88]

The Impact of Overall Management Philosophy on Training

The type of training that is required of expatriates is influenced by the firm's overall philosophy of international management. For example, some companies prefer to send their own people to staff an overseas operation; others prefer to use locals whenever possible.[89] Briefly, four basic philosophical positions of multinational corporations can influence the training program:

ethnocentric MNC
An MNC that stresses nationalism and often puts home-office people in charge of key international management positions.

polycentric MNC
An MNC that places local nationals in key positions and allows these managers to appoint and develop their own people.

1. An **ethnocentric MNC** puts home-office people in charge of key international management positions. The MNC headquarters group and the affiliated world company managers all have the same basic experiences, attitudes, and beliefs about how to manage operations. Many Japanese firms follow this practice.

2. A **polycentric MNC** places local nationals in key positions and allows these managers to appoint and develop their own people. MNC headquarters gives

the subsidiary managers authority to manage their operations just as long as these operations are sufficiently profitable. Some MNCs use this approach in East Asia, Australia, and other markets that are deemed too expensive to staff with expatriates.

3. A **regiocentric MNC** relies on local managers from a particular geographic region to handle operations in and around that area. For example, production facilities in France would be used to produce goods for all EU countries. Similarly, advertising managers from subsidiaries in Italy, Germany, France, and Spain would come together and formulate a "European" advertising campaign for the company's products. A regiocentric approach often relies on regional group cooperation of local managers. The Gillette MNC uses a regiocentric approach.

4. A **geocentric MNC** seeks to integrate diverse regions of the world through a global approach to decision making. Assignments are based on qualifications, and all subsidiary managers throughout the structure are regarded as equal to those at headquarters. IBM is an excellent example of an MNC that attempts to use a geocentric approach.

All four of these philosophical positions can be found in the multinational arena, and each puts a different type of training demand on the MNC.[90] For example, ethnocentric MNCs will do all training at headquarters, but polycentric MNCs will rely on local managers to assume responsibility for seeing that the training function is carried out.

The Impact of Different Learning Styles on Training and Development

Another important area of consideration for development is learning styles. **Learning** is the acquisition of skills, knowledge, and abilities that result in a relatively permanent change in behavior.[91] Over the last decade, growing numbers of multinationals have tried to become "learning organizations," continually focused on activities such as training and development. In the new millennium, this learning focus applied to human resource development may go beyond learning organizations to "teaching organizations." For example, Tichy and Cohen, after conducting an analysis of world-class companies such as General Electric, PepsiCo, AlliedSignal, and Coca-Cola, found that teaching organizations are even more relevant than learning organizations because they go beyond the belief that everyone must continually acquire new knowledge and skills and focus on ensuring that everyone in the organization, especially the top management personnel, passes the learning on to others. Here are their conclusions:

> In teaching organizations, leaders see it as their responsibility to teach. They do that because they understand that it's the best, if not only, way to develop throughout a company people who can come up with and carry out smart ideas about the business. Because people in teaching organizations see teaching as critical to the success of their business, they find ways to do it every day. Teaching every day about critical business issues avoids the fuzzy focus that has plagued some learning organization efforts, which have sometimes become a throwback to the 1960s and 1970s style of self-exportation and human relations training.[92]

Of course, the way in which training takes place can be extremely important. A great deal of research has been conducted on the various types and theories of learning. However, the application of these ideas in an international context often can be quite challenging because cultural differences can affect the learning and teaching. Prud'homme van Reine and Trompenaars, commenting on the development of expats, noted that national cultural differences typically affect the way MNCs train and develop their people. For example, Americans like an experiential learning style, while Germans prefer a theoretical-analytical learning approach.[93] Moreover, there can be sharp learning preferences between groups that are quite similar in terms of culture. Hayes and Allinson, after

regiocentric MNC
An MNC that relies on local managers from a particular geographic region to handle operations in and around that area.

geocentric MNC
An MNC that seeks to integrate diverse regions of the world through a global approach to decision making.

learning
The acquisition of skills, knowledge, and abilities that result in a relatively permanent change in behavior.

studying cultural differences in the learning styles of managers, reported, "Two groups can be very similar in ecology and climate and, for example, through a common legacy of colonialism, have a similar language and legal, educational and governmental infra-structure, but may be markedly different in terms of beliefs, attitudes, and values."[94] Moreover, research shows that people with different learning styles prefer different learning environments, and if there is a mismatch between the preferred learning style and the work environment, dissatisfaction and poor performance can result.

In addition to these conclusions, those responsible for training programs must remember that even if learning does occur, the new behaviors will not be used if they are not reinforced. For example, if the head of a foreign subsidiary is highly ethnocentric and believes that things should be done the way they are in the home country, new managers with intercultural training likely will find little reward or reinforcement for using their ideas. This cultural complexity also extends to the way in which the training is conducted.

Reasons for Training

Training programs are useful in preparing people for overseas assignments for many reasons. These reasons can be put into two general categories: organizational and personal.

ethnocentrism
The belief that one's own way of doing things is superior to that of others.

Organizational Reasons Organizational reasons for training relate to the enterprise at large and its efforts to manage overseas operations more effectively.[95] One primary reason is to help overcome **ethnocentrism**, the belief that one's way of doing things is superior to that of others. Ethnocentrism is common in many large MNCs where managers believe that the home office's approach to doing business can be exported intact to all other countries because this approach is superior to anything at the local level. Training can help home-office managers understand the values and customs of other countries so that when they are transferred overseas, they have a better understanding of how to interact with local personnel. This training also can help managers overcome the common belief among many personnel that expatriates are not as effective as host-country managers. This is particularly important given that an increasing number of managerial positions now are held by foreign managers in U.S. MNCs.[96]

Another organizational reason for training is to improve the flow of communication between the home office and the international subsidiaries and branches. Quite often, overseas managers find that they are not adequately informed regarding what is expected of them although the home office places close controls on their operating authority. This is particularly true when the overseas manager is from the host country. Effective communication can help minimize these problems.

Finally, another organizational reason for training is to increase overall efficiency and profitability. Research shows that organizations that closely tie their training and human resource management strategy to their business strategy tend to outperform those that do not.[97] Stroh and Caligiuri conducted research on 60 of the world's major multi-nationals and found that effective HRM programs pay dividends in the form of higher profits. Additionally, their data showed that the most successful MNCs recognized the importance of having top managers with a global orientation. One of the ways in which almost all these organizations did this was by giving their managers global assignments that not only filled technical and managerial needs but also provided developmental experiences for the personnel—and this assignment strategy included managers from every geographic region where the firms were doing business. Drawing together the lessons to be learned from this approach, Stroh and Caligiuri noted:

> The development of global leadership skills should not stop with home-country nationals. Global HR should also be involved in developing a global orientation among host-country nationals as well. This means, for example, sending not only home-country managers on global assignments but host national talent to the corporate office and to other divisions around the world. Many of the managers at the successful MNCs talked about how their

companies develop talent in this way. In addition, they described a "desired state" for human resources, including the ability to source talent within the company from around the world. Victor Guerra, an executive at Prudential, commented: *We need to continually recognize that there are bright, articulate people who do not live in the home country. U.S. multinationals are especially guilty of this shortsightedness.* Acknowledging that talent exists and using the talent appropriately are two different issues—one idealist, the other strategic.[98]

Personal Reasons   The primary reason for training overseas managers is to improve their ability to interact effectively with local people in general and with their personnel in particular. Increasing numbers of training programs now address social topics such as how to take a client to dinner, effectively apologize to a customer, appropriately address one's overseas colleagues, communicate formally and politely with others, and learn how to help others "save face."[99] These programs also focus on dispelling myths and stereotypes by replacing them with facts about the culture. For example, in helping expatriates better understand Arab executives, the following guidelines are offered:

1. There is a close relationship between the Arab executive and his environment. The Arab executive is looked on as a community and family leader, and there are numerous social pressures on him because of this role. He is consulted on all types of problems, even those far removed from his position.

2. With regard to decision making, the Arab executive likely will consult with his subordinates, but he will take responsibility for his decision himself rather than arriving at it through consensus.

3. The Arab executive likely will try to avoid conflict. If there is an issue that he favors but that is opposed by his subordinates, he tends to impose his authority. If it is an issue favored by the subordinates but opposed by the executive, he will likely let the matter drop without taking action.

4. The Arab executive's style is very personal. He values loyalty over efficiency. Although some executives find that the open-door tradition consumes a great deal of time, they do not feel that the situation can be changed. Many executives tend to look on their employees as family and will allow them to bypass the hierarchy to meet them.

5. The Arab executive, contrary to popular beliefs, puts considerable value on the use of time. One thing he admires most about Western or expatriate executives is their use of time, and he would like to encourage his own employees to make more productive use of their time.[100]

Another growing problem is the belief that foreign language skills are not really essential to doing business overseas. Effective training programs can help to minimize these personal problems.

A particularly big personal problem that managers have in an overseas assignment is arrogance. This is the so-called Ugly American problem that U.S. expatriates have been known to have. Many expatriate managers find that their power and prestige are much greater than they were in their job in the home country. This often results in improper behavior, especially among managers at the upper and lower positions of overseas subsidiaries. This arrogance takes a number of different forms, including rudeness to personnel and inaccessibility to clients.

Another common problem is expatriate managers' overruling of decisions, often seen at lower levels of the hierarchy. When a decision is made by a superior who is from the host country and the expatriate does not agree with it, the expatriate may appeal to higher authority in the subsidiary. Host-country managers obviously resent this behavior, because it implies that they are incompetent and can be second-guessed by expatriate subordinates.

Still another common problem is the open criticizing by expatriate managers of their own country or the host country. Many expatriates believe that this form of criticism is regarded as constructive and shows them to have an open mind. Experience has found, however, that most host-country personnel view such behavior negatively and feel that the manager should refrain from such unconstructive criticism. It creates bad feelings and lack of loyalty.

In addition to helping deal with these types of personal problems, training can be useful in improving overall management style. Research shows that many host-country nationals would like to see changes in some of the styles of expatriate managers, including their leadership, decision making, communication, and group work. In terms of leadership, the locals would like to see their expatriate managers be more friendly, accessible, receptive to subordinate suggestions, and encouraging to subordinates to make their best efforts. In decision making, they would like to see clearer definition of goals, more involvement in the process by those employees who will be affected by the decision, and greater use of group meetings to help make decisions. In communication, they would like to see more exchange of opinions and ideas between subordinates and managers. In group work, they would like to see more group problem solving and teamwork.

The specific training approach used must reflect both the industrial and the cultural environment. For example, there is some evidence that Japanese students who come to the United States to earn an MBA degree often find this education of no real value back home. One graduate noted that when he tactfully suggested putting to use a skill he had learned during his U.S. MBA program, he got nowhere. An analysis of Japanese getting an outside education concluded:

> Part of the problem is the reason that most Japanese workers are sent to business schools. Whatever ticket the MBA degree promises—or appears to promise—Americans, the diploma has little meaning within most Japanese companies. Rather, companies send students abroad under the life-time employment system to ensure that there will be more English speakers who are familiar with Western business practices. Some managers regard business schools as a kind of high-level English language school, returning students say, or consider the two years as more or less a paid vacation.[101]

However, as the Japanese economy continues to have problems, American-style business education is beginning to receive attention and respect. In the 1980s American managers went to Japan to learn; now Japanese managers are coming to the United States in increasing numbers to see what they can pick up to help them better compete.

■ Types of Training Programs

There are many different types of multinational management training programs. Some last only a few hours; others last for months. Some are fairly superficial; others are extensive in coverage. Organizations can decide what training program works best by determining the effectiveness of the program, and altering it accordingly. Typically, a combination of standardized and tailor-made training and development approaches are used.

Standardized vs. Tailor-Made

Some management training is standard, or generic. For example, participants often are taught how to use specific decision-making tools, such as quantitative analysis, and regardless of where the managers are sent in the world, the application is the same. These tools do not have to be culturally specific. Research shows that small firms usually rely on standard training programs. Larger MNCs, in contrast, tend to design their own. Some of the larger MNCs are increasingly turning to specially designed video and PowerPoint programs for their training and development needs.

Tailor-made training programs are created for the specific needs of the participants. Input for these offerings usually is obtained from managers who currently are working (or have worked) in the country to which the participants will be sent as well as from local managers and personnel who are citizens of that country. These programs often are designed to provide a new set of skills for a new culture. For example, MNCs are now learning that in managing in China, there is a need to provide directive leadership training because many local managers rely heavily on rules, procedures, and orders from their superiors to guide their behaviors.[102] So training programs must explain how to effectively use this approach. Quite often, the offerings are provided before the individuals leave for their overseas assignment; however, there also are postdeparture training programs that are conducted on-site. These often take the form of systematically familiarizing the individual with the country through steps such as meeting with government officials and other key personnel in the community; becoming acquainted with managers and employees in the organization; learning the host-country nationals' work methods, problems, and expectations; and taking on-site language training.

Training approaches that are successful in one geographic region of the world may need to be heavily modified if they are to be as effective elsewhere. Sergeant and Frenkel conducted interviews with expatriate managers with extensive experience in China in order to identify HRM issues and the ways in which they need to be addressed by MNCs going into China.[103] As seen in Table 14–7, many of the human resource management approaches that are employed are different from those used in the United States or other developed countries because of the nature of Chinese culture and China's economy.

Table 14–7
Human Resources Management Challenges Facing MNCs in China

Human Resource Management Function	Comments/Recommendations
Employee recruitment	The market for skilled manual and white-collar employees is very tight and characterized by rapidly rising wages and high turnover rates. Nepotism and overhiring remain a major problem where Chinese partners strongly influence HR policies; and transferring employees from state enterprises to joint ventures can be difficult because it requires approval from the employee's old work unit.
Reward system	New labor laws allow most companies to set their own wage and salary levels. As a result, there is a wide wage disparity between semiskilled and skilled workers. However, these disparities must be balanced with the negative effect they can have on workers' interpersonal relations.
Employee retention	It can be difficult to retain good employees because of poaching by competitive organizations. In response, many American joint-venture managers are learning to take greater control of compensation programs in order to retain high-performing Chinese managers and skilled workers.
Work performance and employee management	Local managers are not used to taking the initiative and are rarely provided with performance feedback in their Chinese enterprises. As a result, they tend to be risk-averse and are often unwilling to innovate. In turn, the workers are not driven to get things done quickly and they often give little emphasis to the quality of output. At the same time, it is difficult to dismiss people.
Labor relations	Joint-venture regulations give workers the right to establish a trade union to protect employee rights and to organize. These unions are less adversarial than in the West and tend to facilitate operational efficiency. However, there is concern that with the changes taking place in labor laws and the possibility of collective bargaining, unions may become more adversarial in the future.
Expatriate relations	Many firms have provided little cross-training to their people and family, education, and health issues limit the attractiveness of a China assignment. Some of the major repatriation problems include limited continuity in international assignments and difficulties of adjusting to more specialized and less autonomous positions at home, lack of career prospects, and undervaluation of international experience. Management succession and the balancing of local and international staff at Chinese firms are also problematic.

Source: Adapted from Andrew Sergeant and Stephen Frenkel, "Managing People in China: Perceptions of Expatriate Managers," *Journal of World Business* 33, no. 1 (1998), p. 21.

One of the major reasons expatriates have trouble with overseas assignments is that their teenage children are unable to adapt to the new culture, and this has an impact on the expat's performance. To deal with this acculturation problem, many U.S. MNCs now are developing special programs for helping teenagers assimilate into new cultures and adjust to new school environments. A good example is provided by General Electric Medical Systems Group (GEMS), a Milwaukee-based firm that has expatriates in France, Japan, and Singapore. As soon as GEMS designates an individual for an overseas assignment, this expat and his or her family are matched up with those who have recently returned from this country. If the family going overseas has teenage children, the company will team them up with a family that had teenagers during its stay abroad. Both groups then discuss the challenges and problems that must be faced. In the case of teenagers, they are able to talk about their concerns with others who already have encountered these issues, and the latter can provide important information regarding how to make friends, learn the language, get around town, and turn the time abroad into a pleasant experience. Coca-Cola uses a similar approach. As soon as someone is designated for an overseas assignment, the company helps initiate cross-cultural discussions with experienced personnel. Coke also provides formal training through use of external cross-cultural consulting firms that are experienced in working with all family members.

A typical concern of teenagers going abroad is that they will have to go away to boarding school. In Saudi Arabia, for example, national law forbids expatriate children's attending school past the ninth grade, so most expatriate families will look for European institutions for these children. GEMS addresses these types of problems with a specially developed education program. Tutors, schools, curricula, home-country requirements, and host-country requirements are examined, and a plan and specific program of study are developed for each school-age child before he or she leaves.

Before the departure of the family, some MNCs will subscribe to local magazines about teen fashions, music, and other sports or social activities in the host country, so that the children know what to expect when they get there. Before the return of the family to the United States, these MNCs provide similar information about what is going on in the United States, so that when the children return for a visit or come back to stay, they are able to quickly fit into their home-country environment once again.

An increasing number of MNCs now give teenagers much of the same cultural training they give their own managers; however, there is one area in which formal assistance often is not as critical for teens as for adults: language training. While most expatriates find it difficult and spend a good deal of time trying to master the local language, many teens find that they can pick it up quite easily. They speak it at school, in their social groups, and out on the street. As a result, they learn not only the formal language but also clichés and slang that help them communicate more easily. In fact, sometimes their accent is so good that they are mistaken for local kids. Simply put: The facility of teens to learn a language often is greatly underrated. A Coca-Cola manager recently drove home this point when he declared: "One girl we sent insisted that, although she would move, she wasn't going to learn the language. Within two months she was practically fluent."

A major educational benefit of this emphasis on teenagers is that it leads to an experienced, bicultural person. So when the young person completes college and begins looking for work, the parent's MNC often is interested in this young adult as a future manager. The person has a working knowledge of the MNC, speaks a second language, and has had overseas experience in a country where the multinational does business. This type of logic is leading some U.S. MNCs to realize that effective cross-cultural training can be of benefit for their workforces of tomorrow as well as today.

Some organizations have extended cross-cultural training to include training for family members, especially children who will be accompanying the parents. International Management in Action, "U.S.-Style Training for Expats and Their Teenagers," explains how this approach to cultural assimilation is carried out.

In addition to training expats and their families, effective MNCs also are developing carefully crafted programs for training personnel from other cultures who are coming into their culture. These programs, among other things, have materials that are specially designed for the target audience. Some of the specific steps that well-designed cultural training programs follow include:

1. Local instructors and a translator, typically someone who is bicultural, observe the pilot training program or examine written training materials.

2. The educational designer then debriefs the observation with the translator, curriculum writer, and local instructors.

3. Together, the group examines the structure and sequence, ice breaker, and other materials that will be used in the training.

4. The group then collectively identifies stories, metaphors, experiences, and examples in the culture that will fit into the new training program.

5. The educational designer and curriculum writer make the necessary changes in the training materials.

6. The local instructors are trained to use the newly developed materials.

7. After the designer, translator, and native-language trainers are satisfied, the materials are printed.

8. The language and content of the training materials are tested with a pilot group.[104]

In developing the instructional materials, culturally specific guidelines are carefully followed so that the training does not lose any of its effectiveness.[105] For example, inappropriate pictures or scenarios that might prove to be offensive to the audience must be screened out. Handouts and other instructional materials that are designed to enhance the learning process are provided for all participants. If the trainees are learning a second language, generous use of visuals and live demonstrations will be employed. Despite all these efforts, however, errors sometimes occur.

■ Cultural Assimilators

The cultural assimilator has become one of the most effective approaches to cross-cultural training. A **cultural assimilator** is a programmed learning technique that is designed to expose members of one culture to some of the basic concepts, attitudes, role perceptions, customs, and values of another culture. These assimilators are developed for each pair of cultures. For example, if an MNC is going to send three U.S. managers from Chicago to Caracas, a cultural assimilator would be developed to familiarize the three Americans with Venezuelan customs and cultures. If three Venezuelan managers from Caracas were to be transferred to Singapore, another assimilator would be developed to familiarize the managers with Singapore customs and cultures.

In most cases, these assimilators require the trainee to read a short episode of a cultural encounter and choose an interpretation of what has happened and why. If the trainee's choice is correct, he or she goes on to the next episode. If the response is incorrect, the trainee is asked to reread the episode and choose another response.

cultural assimilator
A programmed learning technique designed to expose members of one culture to some of the basic concepts, attitudes, role perceptions, customs, and values of another culture.

Choice of Content of the Assimilators One of the major problems in constructing an effective cultural assimilator is deciding what is important enough to include. Some assimilators use critical incidents that are identified as being important. To be classified as a critical incident, a situation must meet at least one of the following conditions:

1. An expatriate and a host national interact in the situation.

2. The situation is puzzling or likely to be misinterpreted by the expatriate.

3. The situation can be interpreted accurately if sufficient knowledge about the culture is available.

4. The situation is relevant to the expatriate's task or mission requirements.[106]

These incidents typically are obtained by asking expatriates and host nationals with whom they come in contact to describe specific intercultural occurrences or events that made a major difference in their attitudes or behavior toward members of the other culture. These incidents can be pleasant, unpleasant, or simply nonunderstandable occurrences.

validity
The quality of being effective, of producing the desired results. A valid test or selection technique measures what it is intended to measure.

Validation of the Assimilator The term **validity** refers to the quality of being effective, of producing the desired results. It means that an instrument—in this case, the cultural assimilator—measures what it is intended to measure. After the cultural assimilator's critical incidents are constructed and the alternative responses are written, the process is validated. Making sure that the assimilator is valid is the crux of its effectiveness. One way to test an assimilator is to draw a sample from the target culture and ask these people to read the scenarios that have been written, choosing the alternative they feel is most appropriate. If a large percentage of the group agrees that one of the alternatives is preferable, this scenario is used in the assimilator. If more than one of the four alternatives receives strong support, however, either the scenario or the alternatives are revised until there is general agreement or the scenario is dropped.

After the final incidents are chosen, they are sequenced in the assimilator booklet and can be put online to be taken electronically. Similar cultural concepts are placed together and presented, beginning with simple situations and progressing to more complex ones. Most cultural assimilator programs start out with 150 to 200 incidents, of which 75 to 100 eventually are included in the final product.

The Cost-Benefit Analysis of Assimilators The assimilator approach to training can be quite expensive. A typical 75- to 100-incident program often requires approximately 800 hours to develop. Assuming that a training specialist is costing the company $50 an hour including benefits, the cost is around $40,000 per assimilator. This cost can be spread over many trainees, and the program may not need to be changed every year. An MNC that sends 40 people a year to a foreign country for which an assimilator has been constructed is paying only $200 per person for this programmed training. In the long run, the costs often are more than justified. In addition, the concept can be applied to nearly all cultures. Many different assimilators have been constructed, including Arab, Thai, Honduran, and Greek, to name but four. Most importantly, research shows that these assimilators improve the effectiveness and satisfaction of individuals being trained as compared with other training methods.

Positive Organizational Behavior

We discussed in Chapter 13 how leaders can increase motivation and morale if they focus on the positives, or strengths, of individuals. The positive internal traits of the leader, along with the other factors, tend to lead to consistent positive behaviors. Luthans has done extensive research on **positive organizational behavior (POB)**. He defines it as:

positive organizational behavior (POB)
The study and application of positively oriented human resource strengths and psychological capacities that can be measured, developed, and effectively managed for performance improvement in today's workplace.

> The study and application of positively oriented human resource strengths and psychological capacities that can be measured, developed, and effectively managed for performance improvement in today's workplace.[107]

Positivity in the workplace has been connected to employee satisfaction. The positive environment, however, consists of many layers. Luthans and Youssef postulated that in order for an organization to be the most efficient and innovative, it must have positive traits, states, and systems in order to promote positive behavior. The positive traits were covered in Chapter 13 and consist of conscientiousness, emotional stability, extroversion, agreeableness, openness to experience, core self-evaluations, and positive psychological traits. A positive state is domain-specific, and reactions and behaviors may change depending on the environment. Research has shown that other "states" are self-efficacy, hope, optimism, resiliency, and psychological capital.[108]

Finally, positive organizations focus on the selection, development, and management of human resources. This positive approach attempts to match employee skills and talents with organizational goals and expectations. When employees are treated well, they will be motivated to give back to the institution. Therefore, when these individual traits, internal and external states, and organizations all focus on the positive, the resulting organizational citizenship behavior (OCB) will also be positive. Furthermore, altruism, conscientiousness, and courtesy will be inadvertently emphasized.[109]

As with most examples, the description above is culturally specific. That is, what seems to be positive internal or external factors in one country may not be the same in another. However, human resources are essential to an organization no matter its location, and MNCs should do all they can to focus on the power of human capital to drive organizational success.

■ Future Trends

The coming decades will be important and transformational ones for international human resources. A recent report from Brookfield Global Relocation Services concludes that several issues will emerge as critical for managing a global workforce. At the top of the list, according to Brookfield, will be linking talent management and employee mobility. As the nature of temporary assignments evolves, companies and employees will be more closely scrutinizing the costs and benefits of the assignments.

Some companies are questioning the basic decision of supporting expensive international assignments. Employees are also questioning the personal and professional value of an overseas assignment, especially if such assignments have little influence in helping them to advance in their careers. The Brookfield survey found that 38 percent of employees leave their company within just one year of repatriation, in line with industry estimates that range between 25 percent and 45 percent. "This is a key issue for global organizations, since this is a population of employees that they have invested so heavily in," Sullivan said. "Losing these employees represents a significant loss of experience and talent. Many of the companies we surveyed are beginning to see the integration of talent management and international assignment mobility as a strategy to turn this loss into a competitive gain."

Another trend is the emergence of "cross-border" commuters, employees who regularly move back and forth between countries. Commuter assignments, as an alternative to short-term (and even long-term) assignments, have begun to take a larger role, especially in Europe, given the deepening integration of the European Union and the resultant cross-border employee mobility. The report suggests this trend is likely to continue and accelerate.[110]

One of the most profound trends, first explored in Chapter 1 of this book, is the dramatic rise and growth of emerging markets. Brookfield's survey notes that emerging locations run the spectrum of countries from those that are long-time assignment destinations to those that are just this year appearing as locations for expatriate assignments. To some degree, this trend may offset the effects of the other trends, suggesting that although the particular structure and duration may evolve, expatriate assignments are likely to continue as part of the arsenal of MNCs seeking to leverage talent for global success.

The World of International Management—Revisited

The World of International Management that opened this chapter illustrated how the desire to source and retain talent has become a global phenomenon, affecting most major markets, including India. In a time of increased globalization, firms must be able to source talent from a range of locations. Given the increasing presence of foreign MNCs in India—and the dramatic growth of India's domestic offshore outsourcing sector—employee retention has become a critical issue. One interesting observation is that employees are motivated by intrinsic rewards that go beyond financial compensation. Attracting and retaining talent turns out be a complex process in which both financial and nonfinancial issues come into play.

As outlined in this chapter, MNCs are realizing the intense challenges associated with the selection, development, and training of international human resources. MNCs have a range of options when selecting employees for overseas assignments, and increasing numbers of tools and resources are available to help develop, train, and deploy those individuals. Human resource selection and development across cultures cannot be taken lightly. Firms that do not invest in their human resource processes will face additional costs related to poor labor relations, quality control, and other issues. Now that you have read the chapter

Lessons in Global Leadership Development: The PWC Ulysses Program

PricewaterhouseCoopers (PwC), one of the "Final 4" global accounting firms, has for several years sent top midcareer talent to the developing world for eight-week service projects under its "Ulysses" Program. After the merger of Price Waterhouse and Coopers Lybrand in 1998, the combined firm decided it needed a new model for a global professional services organization. Executives recognized that global problems were not increasing or decreasing, but changing and reshaping, the way business is done. In response, the firm created "Project Ulysses" in 2001, which sends a number of emerging leaders each year to a developing nation for two and a half months to work on service projects and programs. The purpose is not only to aid those in need, but to develop leadership skills on an individual level by taking executives out of their comfort zone, on a team level by pairing two to three partners together from different nations, and on the organizational level by creating stakeholder networks on a much broader level. For a relatively modest investment—about $15,000 per person, plus salaries—Ulysses both tests the talent and expands the world view of the accounting firm's future leaders. Since the company started the program in 2000, it has attracted the attention of Johnson & Johnson, Cisco Systems, and other big companies considering their own programs.

The projects, which range from helping an ecotourism collective in Belize to AIDS work in Namibia and organic farming in Zambia, take the participants out of their comfort zone and force them to build upon their leadership skills in a new and challenging environment. The benefit of pairing partners from three different places is that they draw on their own cultures to make decisions. As one participant noted, "You realize that perhaps the way you see things isn't necessarily the best way." In 2003, PwC partner Tahir Ayub was assigned a consulting gig unlike anything he had done before. His job was helping village leaders in the Namibian outback grapple with their community's growing AIDS crisis. Faced with language barriers, cultural differences, and scant access to electricity, Ayub, 39, and two colleagues had to scrap their PowerPoint presentations in favor of a more low-tech approach: face-to-face discussion. The village chiefs learned that they needed to garner community support for programs to combat the disease, and Ayub learned an important lesson as well: Technology isn't always the answer. "You better put your beliefs and biases to one side and figure out new ways to look at things," he said.

Although traditional business education and training has historically focused on helping firms improve financial performance, increasingly, B-schools and training programs are adding social responsibility to their curriculum. Further, graduates are increasingly signaling they want to work for firms with a positive reputation for social responsibility and service. According to a *Wall Street Journal* article, top corporate executives are now pairing with MBA programs across the country to help students gain a better understanding of responsible global leadership. In fact, a recent study showed that 75 percent of Americans consider a company's commitment to social issues when deciding where to work, and that 6 out of 10 employees wish their companies did more to help globally. According to Liz Maw, executive director of Net Impact, a corporate nonprofit dedicated to social responsibility, "The companies most involved in corporate social responsibility are the ones that have already seen their bottom line and brand awareness increase."

While results are hard to quantify, PwC is convinced that the program works. All two dozen of the initial graduates are still working at the company. Half of them have been promoted, and most have new responsibilities. Just as important, all 24 people say they have a stronger commitment to PwC—in part because of the commitment the firm made to them and in part because of their new vision of the firm's values. Says global managing partner Willem Bröcker: "We get better partners from this exercise." The Ulysses Program is PwC's answer to one of the biggest challenges confronting professional services companies: identifying and training up-and-coming leaders who can find unconventional answers to intractable problems. By tradition and necessity, new PwC leaders are nurtured from within. With 8,000 partners, identifying those with the necessary business savvy and relationship-building skills isn't easy. But just as the program gives partners a new view of PwC, it also gives PwC a new view of them, particularly their ability to hold up under pressure.

PwC says the program, now in its third cycle, gives participants a broad, international perspective that's crucial for a company that does business around the world. Traditional executive education programs turn out men and women who have specific job skills but little familiarity with issues outside their narrow specialty, according to Douglas Ready, director of the International Consortium for Executive Development Research. PwC says Ulysses helps prepare participants for challenges that go beyond the strict confines of accounting or consulting and instills values such as community involvement that are essential to success in any field.

Ulysses has also given PwC a very positive name in the accounting and broader professional services community. The project has taught the partners to understand risks more holistically, to consider all stakeholders that are involved, and to realize that doing business is not about one goal, but many.

and reflected back on the chapter's opening World of International Management about employee retention in India, answer the following questions: (1) What are the costs and benefits of hiring home-, host-, and third-country nationals for overseas assignments? (2) What skill sets are important for international assignments, and how can employees be prepared for such assignments? (3) What are the implications of offshore outsourcing for the management of human resources globally and in India in particular?

SUMMARY OF KEY POINTS

1. MNCs can use four basic sources for filling overseas positions: home-country nationals (expatriates), host-country nationals, third-country nationals, and inpatriates. The most common reason for using home-country nationals, or expatriates, is to get the overseas operation under way. Once this is done, many MNCs turn the top management job over to a host-country national who is familiar with the culture and language and who often commands a lower salary than the home-country national. The primary reason for using third-country nationals is that these people have the necessary expertise for the job. The use of inpatriates (a host-country or third-country national assigned to the home office) recognizes the need for diversity at the home office. This movement builds a transnational core competency for MNCs. In addition, MNCs can subcontract or outsource to take advantage of lower human resource costs and increase flexibility.

2. Many criteria are used in selecting managers for overseas assignments. Some of these include adaptability, independence, self-reliance, physical and emotional health, age, experience, education, knowledge of the local language, motivation, the support of spouse and children, and leadership.

3. Individuals who meet selection criteria are given some form of screening. Some firms use psychological testing, but this approach has lost popularity in recent years. More commonly, candidates are given interviews. Theoretical models that identify important anticipatory and in-country dimensions of adjustment offer help in effective selection.

4. Compensating expatriates can be a difficult problem, because there are many variables to consider. However, most compensation packages are designed around five common elements: base salary, benefits, allowances, incentives, and taxes. Working within these elements, the MNC will tailor the package to fit the specific situation. In doing so, there are five different approaches that can be used: balance-sheet approach, localization, lump-sum method, cafeteria approach, and regional method. Whichever one

(or combination) is used, the package must be both cost-effective and fair.

5. A manager might be willing to take an international assignment for a number of reasons: increased pay, promotion potential, the opportunity for greater responsibility, the chance to travel, and the ability to use his or her talents and skills. Research shows that most home countries prefer that the individual who is selected to head the affiliate or subsidiary be a local manager, even though this often does not occur.

6. At some time, most expatriates return home, usually when their predetermined tour is over. Sometimes, managers return because they want to leave early; at other times, they return because of poor performance on their part. In any event, readjustment problems can arise back home, and the longer a manager has been gone, the bigger the problems usually are. Some firms are developing transition strategies to help expatriates adjust to their new environments.

7. Training is the process of altering employee behavior and attitudes to increase the probability of goal attainment. Many expatriates need training before (as well as during) their overseas stay. A number of factors will influence a company's approach to training. One is the basic type of MNC: ethnocentric, polycentric, regiocentric, or geocentric. Another factor is the learning style of the trainees.

8. There are two primary reasons for training: organizational and personal. Organizational reasons include overcoming ethnocentrism, improving communication, and validating the effectiveness of training programs. Personal reasons include improving the ability of expatriates to interact locally and increasing the effectiveness of leadership styles. There are two types of training programs: standard and tailor-made. Research shows that small firms usually rely on standard programs and larger MNCs tailor their training. Common approaches to training include elements such as cultural orientation, cultural assimilators, language training, sensitivity training, and field experience.

9. A cultural assimilator is a programmed learning approach that is designed to expose members of one culture to some of the basic concepts, attitudes, role perceptions, customs, and values of another.

Assimilators have been developed for many different cultures. Their validity has resulted in the improved effectiveness and satisfaction of those being trained as compared with other training methods.

KEY TERMS

adaptability screening, *507*

balance-sheet approach, *515*

cafeteria approach, *516*

cultural assimilator, *529*

ethnocentric MNC, *522*

ethnocentrism, *524*

expatriates, *498*

geocentric MNC, *523*

home-country nationals, *498*

host-country nationals, *498*

inpatriates, *500*

international selection criteria, *503*

learning, *523*

localization, *515*

lump-sum method, *515*

polycentric MNC, *522*

positive organizational behavior (POB), *530*

regiocentric MNC, *523*

regional system, *516*

repatriation, *518*

repatriation agreements, *519*

third-country nationals (TCNs), *499*

training, *520*

transition strategies, *519*

validity, *529*

REVIEW AND DISCUSSION QUESTIONS

1. A New York–based MNC is in the process of staffing a subsidiary in New Delhi, India. Why would it consider using expatriate managers in the unit? Local managers? Third-country managers?

2. What selection criteria are most important in choosing people for an overseas assignment? Identify and describe the four that you judge to be of most universal importance, and defend your choice.

3. What are the major common elements in an expat's compensation package? Besides base pay, which would be most important to you? Why?

4. Why are individuals motivated to accept international assignments? Which of these motivations would you rank as positive reasons? Which would you regard as negative reasons?

5. Why do expatriates return early? What can MNCs do to prevent this from happening? Identify and discuss three steps they can take.

6. What kinds of problems do expatriates face when returning home? Identify and describe four of the most important. What can MNCs do to deal with these repatriation problems effectively?

7. How do the following types of MNCs differ: ethnocentric, polycentric, regiocentric, and geocentric? Which type is most likely to provide international management training to its people? Which is

least likely to provide international management training to its people?

8. IBM is planning on sending three managers to its Zurich office, two to Madrid, and two to Tokyo. None of these individuals has any international experience. Would you expect the company to use a standard training program or a tailor-made program for each group?

9. Zygen Inc., a medium-sized manufacturing firm, is planning to enter into a joint venture in China. Would training be of any value to those managers who will be part of this venture? If so, what types of training would you recommend?

10. Hofstadt & Hoerr, a German-based insurance firm, is planning on expanding out of the EU and opening offices in Chicago and Buenos Aires. How would a cultural assimilator be of value in training the MNC's expatriates? Is the assimilator a valid training tool?

11. Ford is in the process of training managers for overseas assignments. Would a global leadership program be a useful approach? Why or why not?

12. Microsoft is weighing setting up an R&D facility in India to develop new software applications. Should it staff the new facility with Microsoft employees? Indian employees? Or should it subcontract with an Indian firm? Explain your answer and some of the potential challenges in implementing it.

INTERNET EXERCISE: GOING INTERNATIONAL WITH COKE

As seen in this chapter, the recruiting and selecting of managers is critical to effective international management. This is particularly true in the case of firms that are expanding their international operations or currently do business in a large number of countries. These MNCs are continually having to replace managers who are retiring or moving to other companies. Coca-Cola is an excellent example. Go to the company's website at www.coke.com and look at the career opportunities that it offers overseas. In particular, pay close attention to current opportunities in Europe, Africa, and Asia. Read what the company has to say, and then contact one of the individuals whose e-mail address is provided.

Ask this company representative about the opportunities and challenges of working in that country or geographic area. Then using this information, coupled with the chapter material, answer these questions: (1) From what you have learned from the Coca-Cola inquiry, what types of education or experience would you need to be hired by the company? (2) What kinds of international career opportunities does Coke offer? (3) If you were hired by Coke, what type of financial package could you expect? (4) In what areas of the world is Coke focusing more of its attention? (5) What kinds of management and leadership training programs does Coke offer?

Russia

Russia is by far the largest of the former Soviet republics. Russia stretches from Eastern Europe across northern Asia to the Pacific Ocean. The 138 million people in Russia consist of 79.8 percent Russians, 4.8 percent Tartars, and a scattering of various others. The largest city and capital is Moscow, with about 12 million people. At present, there is continuing social and economic turmoil in Russia. Although prices are no longer controlled and privatization is well under way, the value of the ruble has been deteriorating. At the same time, there are many pockets of prosperity in the country, and under former President Vladimir Putin positive efforts were made to bolster the economy with some tangible results.

By 2012, Russia's GDP had reached $2.1 trillion, which is a lot more than the $1.75 trillion of 2006. Russia's privatization and liberalization program has attracted substantial foreign investment. One MNC that has been extremely interested in the country is Earth, Inc. (EI), a farm-implement company headquartered in Birmingham, Alabama. EI entered into an agreement with the government of Russia to set up operations near Moscow in a factory that was operating at about one-half of capacity. The factory will produce farm implements for the newly emerging Eastern European market. EI will supply the technical know-how and product design as well as assume responsibility for marketing the products. The Russian plant will build the equipment and package it for shipping.

The management of the plant operation will be handled on a joint basis. EI will send a team of five management and technical personnel from the United States to the Russian factory site for a period of 12 to 18 months. After this time, EI hopes to send three of them home, and the two who remain will continue to provide ongoing assistance. At the same time, EI intends to hire four middle-level managers and eight first-level supervisors from Italy and Germany, because the operation will need Europeans who are more familiar with doing manufacturing in this part of the world. Very few locals have inspired EI with confidence that they can get the job done. However, over a two-year period, EI intends to replace the third-country nationals with trained local managers. "We need to staff the management ranks with knowledgeable, experienced people," the CEO explained, "at least until we get the operation up and running successfully with our own people. Then we can turn more and more of the operation over to local management, and run the plant with just a handful of headquarters people on-site."

This arrangement has been agreed to by the Russian government, and EI currently is identifying and recruiting managers both in the United States and in Europe. Initially, the firm thought that this would be a fairly simple process, but screening and selecting are taking much longer than anticipated. Nevertheless, EI hopes to have the plant operating within 12 months.

Questions

1. What are some current issues facing Russia? What is the climate for doing business in Russia today?

2. What are some of the benefits of using home-country nationals in overseas operations? What are some of the benefits of using host-country nationals?

3. Why would a multinational such as EI be interested in bringing in third-country nationals?

4. What criteria should EI use in selecting personnel for the overseas assignment in Russia?

IKEA's Global Renovations

In late January 2013, Swedish furniture retailer IKEA announced record revenue of $36 billion for 2012 and an 8 percent increase in profit over 2011. Sales of $4.1 billion came from the U.S. market, a dramatic figure given that IKEA opened its first store in the United States in 1985 and was now the largest U.S. furniture retailer after Ashley Furniture. Not three weeks later, however, IKEA was embroiled in another scandal—this one over the apparent use of horsemeat in some of its iconic meatballs. This setback was one of many over the past two decades, as IKEA has attempted to balance its unique approach to both the retail shopping experience and its own expansion as it has sought to achieve a reputation for social responsibility and sustainability.

IKEA's Humble Beginnings

The idea of IKEA began in 1935 in the small province of southern Sweden, Smaland, where the people are known for their hard work and for making the most from very little means.[1] Ingvar Kamprad, a 9-year-old boy with a strong entrepreneurial spirit, began by selling fish and Christmas decorations to those in the local community. By age 17, using a gift of money from his father, Kamprad established the company IKEA. Kamprad created the name IKEA by combining his initials, the initials of his hometown farm, and the initials of a nearby village. During that period he sold everything from pens to gadgets to stockings, and within a short time he was able to put together a mail order catalog. By 1947 Kamprad decided to introduce home furnishings to the product mix and by 1951 eliminated all other products lines, focusing solely on the home furniture market.[2]

Kamprad built his empire on the foundation of offering a "wide range of home furnishings of good design and functionality at a price low enough to be affordable to most people."[3] With this idea in hand, he set out to build a business that met the needs of the Swedish people, showing no differentiation between rich and poor.

Around this time he was seeing a great deal of pressure from other furniture providers in his direct market. In 1956, with his suppliers facing pressure to boycott due to increased competition, Kamprad decided to design his own furniture and have a manufacturer produce it.[4] This seemingly small decision led IKEA to offer low prices and efficient packaging, which are still the capstones of the business today.

It is universally believed that IKEA's growth and success is a direct result of Kamprad's vision, values, and culture, which he cultivated in all aspects of IKEA's business model. His openness to change, his drive for innovation, and his focus on his stakeholders have made IKEA what it is today: the largest and most successful furniture retailer in the world.[5]

Growth and Expansion

The first IKEA store opened in Almhult, Sweden, in 1958. In 1963 IKEA opened its first international store in Oslo, Norway, and two years after that opened a flagship store near Stockholm. In 1973 IKEA spread to mainland Europe, opening stores in Switzerland and Germany. Germany, to this day, remains IKEA's largest market.[6] Following these markets a store was opened in Australia in 1977 and in the Netherlands in 1979. The first store in the United States did not arrive until 1985, which is surprising given IKEA's record-breaking $36 billion in revenue in the U.S. in 2012. The U.S. opening was quickly followed by the first one in the United Kingdom.[7] See Table 1 for a more detailed timeline of IKEA's expansion.

IKEA now operates over 338 stores in 41 countries, with more than 150,000 employees as of 2013.[8] The fast growth was primarily organic, with IKEA maintaining full control over the company, as it still does today.[9] Several "business format franchises" currently exist, where local entrepreneurs took on the capital investment and the management, and left the merchandising and marketing to IKEA.[10] Since 1982, IKEA has been owned by a foundation, and remaining private is a keystone of success to ensure that the culture and values remain intact.

Specifically, the Netherlands-based company, Inter IKEA Systems BV, owns the franchise, and Inka holding company, of which Kamprad is the senior advisor, operates over 300 stores worldwide.[11] In addition, a separate company, Ikano, manages the Kamprad fortune and owns several other IKEA stores in its own right.[12]

IKEA's success cannot be ignored in today's turbulent market, with IKEA being commended for entering and remaining in traditionally difficult markets. What keeps the IKEA group going strong is its corporate initiatives embedded in Swedish heritage. These corporate initiatives are visually apparent throughout the stores and have been considered a "significant force of competitive advantage."[13]

The Swedish lifestyle incorporates a "fresh, healthy way of life" with bright colors and textiles even though Sweden does not see a great amount of sunlight.[14] The high quality, stress-free furniture and the caring employees represent a Swedish tradition where "rich and poor

Table 1

1926:	Founder Ingvar Kamprad is born in Smaland, Sweden.
1931:	Kamprad begins selling matches to nearby neighbors.
1933–1935:	Kamprad uses his bicycle to expand territory, and begins selling flower seeds, greeting cards, Christmas tree decorations.
1943:	Using money from his father, Kamprad founds IKEA, selling pens, wallets, picture frames, table runners, watches, jewelry, and nylon stockings.
1945:	First IKEA advertisement is in a local newspaper.
1948:	IKEA begins selling furniture.
1951:	The first IKEA catalog is published and Kamprad decides to focus solely on selling furniture.
1953:	First showroom opens in Almhult, Sweden.
1956:	IKEA decides to design its own furniture and flat pack it for self-assembly.
1958:	First IKEA opens in Sweden.
1960:	First IKEA restaurant opens at the Almhult location.
1963:	IKEA enters Oslo, Norway.
1969:	IKEA enters Copenhagen, Denmark.
1973:	IKEA enters Zurich, Switzerland.
1975:	IKEA enters Sydney, Australia.
1976:	IKEA enters Vancouver, Canada.
1977:	IKEA enters Vienna, Austria.
1979:	IKEA enters Rotterdam, Netherlands.
1981:	IKEA enters Paris, France.
1982:	The IKEA Group is formed.
1984:	IKEA enters Brussels, Belgium.
1985:	IKEA enters Philadelphia, USA.
1986:	A new president and CEO, Anders Moberg, takes over.
1987:	IKEA enters Manchester, UK.
1989:	IKEA enters Milan, Italy.
1990:	The IKEA Group develops its first environmental policy.
1990:	IKEA enters Budapest, Hungary.
1991:	IKEA enters Prague, Czech Republic, and Poznan, Poland.
1993:	IKEA Group becomes a member of the global forest certification organization Forest Stewardship Council (FSC).
1996:	IKEA enters Madrid, Spain.
1997:	Global website is launched.
1997:	IKEA's sustainable approach to shipping, titled "IKEA, Transport and the Environment" is created.
1998:	IKEA enters Shanghai, China.
1999:	New president and CEO, Anders Dahlvig, is named.
2000:	IKEA enters Moscow, Russia, Kamprad's "last big hobby."
2000:	IKEA code of conduct, IWAY, is launched.
2000:	Online shopping begins.
June 2004:	IKEA enters Lisbon, Portugal.
July 2004:	The 200th store opens.
December 2004:	Opening ceremonies in Moscow are cancelled due to protracted disputes with government over corruption.
May 2006:	IKEA enters Tokyo, Japan.
January 2006:	IKEA Food is launched.
June 2009:	IKEA halts further investment in Russia.
October 2, 2012:	IKEA is criticized for removing women from Saudi Arabia ads.
November 16, 2012:	IKEA publicly apologizes for forced labor practices in East Germany 25-30 years prior.
February 25, 2013:	IKEA is under attack for horsemeat found in European meatballs.
March 5, 2013:	IKEA now admits to contamination of chocolate cake in China.
March 5, 2013:	IKEA announces future partnership with Marriott for budget hotel chains in Europe.

alike were well looked after."[15] Food stands with Swedish snacks are prominent in every store. Also the do-it-yourself requirement of customers to perform some of the work by putting together and/or transporting the furniture facilitates low prices.

Every IKEA store is built fundamentally similar, but each has a distinct local flare. Within any IKEA there are "free pushchairs, supervised childcare and sometimes children's playgrounds as well as wheelchairs for the disabled."[16] In addition, a receptionist's desk holds catalogs, tape measures, pens and pencils, and a wide range of staff members are always throughout the store to aid any customer in need of help.[17]

One of the biggest reasons for IKEA's success on a global level has been its ability to enter new international markets yet keep its core values and brand image consistent. This is something that other companies have not been able to tackle as successfully, and a brief look into IKEA's international strategy will provide a strong understanding of why the company has been so successful with global expansion while at the same time maintaining a positive corporate image.

Global Expansion

IKEA is a unique case, not only because its founder wrote a vision and a set of core values over 60 years ago that are still in use today, but also because the founder is still a part of everyday management. Ingvar Kamprad, now Sweden's richest man at 86 years old, created these core values that have driven business growth, shaped culture, and ultimately built a brand image that has propelled IKEA to huge success. In fact, some believe that the culture, embedded deep in every store, transcends the actual products.[18]

Vision, Core Values, Brand

Kamprad began with his vision to offer "a wide range of well-designed, functional home furnishing products at prices so low that as many people as possible will be able to afford them."[19] From this vision came a set of corporate values that are still followed today. The three defining values that drive operations to this day are "common sense and simplicity," "dare to be different," and "working together."[20]

Common sense and simplicity, created as a value in 1943, follows the belief that "complicated rules paralyze!"[21] The principle that simplicity prevails both internally and externally has been a major driving force in operations since IKEA's inception. Simplicity can be seen in large warehouse stores, in interactions between management, suppliers, and customers, and in cost cutting.[22]

Cost cutting is seen throughout the business, especially at the management level. One will not find management flying first class or staying in luxury hotels. Cost-saving techniques are seen at every level, allowing IKEA to not just verbalize their commitment to low prices, but to physically have significantly lower prices than the competition.

Dare to be different, also created in 1943, is about always finding a new path by asking the question, "why."[23] By constantly questioning the status quo, IKEA has found success in innovation and in its ability to continually change and evolve. For instance, Ingvar Kamprad, when conceiving IKEA, asked himself, "Why must well-designed furniture always be so expensive? Why do the most famous designers always fail to reach the majority of people with their ideas?"[24]

That simple question has led IKEA to create what it is known for today, and will continue to guide the company moving forward. Kamprad believes that it is more difficult now than ever before to find new ways to solve problems and, in the face of strong competition, will allow IKEA to differentiate even further from the competition.[25]

Working together was added to IKEA's values in 1956 when the furniture was recreated for self-assembly by customers.[26] IKEA even released this statement in 1999: "You (the customer) do your part. We (IKEA) do our part. Together we save money."[27] It is very representative of their belief to work together in every aspect of the business and help each other along the way.

According to Tarnovskaya et al. (2008), the vision, values, and culture, taken together with systems and networks, form the "value proposition for customers."[28] In other words, how these values permeate into the business will be apparent to customers, allowing them to form their own opinion on the brand. The customers and stakeholders of IKEA, therefore, ultimately define the brand essence.

Corporate brand is a construct of "intangible nature," built through relationships, perceptions, and behaviors.[29] It involves all stakeholders, including "customers, competitors, employees, and other business actors"[30] By taking the values created by Ingvar Kamprad years ago, and embedding them in all company stakeholders, IKEA has developed strong corporate brand values that have led them to success both domestically and internationally.

Internationalization Strategies

As the number of stakeholders increases, especially across country borders, the more difficult it is to maintain a uniform brand image and goals.[31] IKEA has found success when expanding internationally by staying consistent with the global values described while still allowing some room for a unique local flare.[32]

"Employees become the ambassadors of the brand values," as they are the salesmen of the firm.[33] If employees do not believe in the values and live them, the customers surely won't either. IKEA succeeds by bringing in a staff of experienced IKEA employees, traditionally Swedish, to train and reshape the culture in each new market.[34] For instance, IKEA trains all new staff members on the core competencies seen as most important to support brand vision and values, and the success of this lies not only in training, but also in recruitment.

An IKEA HR corporate manager was quoted as saying "Our goal is to employ co-workers who understand and embrace our core values and will reflect and reinforce those."[35] By focusing heavily on the recruitment process, IKEA is able to ensure they hire the right type of employee who can potentially change his own personal traditional values, and become a believer and salesman of the IKEA brand. Edvardsson et al., (2006), even argued that values are coproduced with customers, and given that employees are communicating the brand to the customer, communication becomes a value in itself.[36]

Another important stakeholder that plays a strong role in internationalization is the supplier. The global supplier plays a large role because it needs to act as a firm base for the company when entering new markets, to continually support IKEA in order to avoid the necessity of constantly forming new relationships. Just as important, though, is the need for local suppliers, who are very beneficial and most often necessary within each market, but who typically hold views contradictory to Swedish values.

In 2000, IKEA created a code called "The IKEA Way," or "IWAY," that puts forth standards of acceptable working conditions for suppliers.[37] The code touches on many aspects such as child labor, forestry, and corruption, with the main goal to make "sustainable development the core business value."[38]

With 1,500 suppliers in 55 countries, IKEA focuses on long-term relationships with suppliers who not only produce low cost, high quality goods, but who positively impact working conditions, the commodities, and the environment as well.[39] "On a global scale, IKEA has more than 1,000 employees involved in purchasing. Purchasing is divided into 16 regional 'trading areas,' encompassing 43 trading service offices in 33 countries."[40]

Every supplier is chosen based on his or her ability to meet predetermined standards set forth in the IWAY, focusing specifically around management style, financial situation, sourcing of materials, equipment, impact on the environment, and location.[41,42] The IWAY is made up of 19 areas containing over 90 issues that must be met. It is revised every two years and IKEA has a staff of internal auditors selected to research the suppliers' ability to meet the IWAY requirements.[43] Once a supplier makes it to the final stage of approval, goals and plans are set in place to further improve working conditions.[44]

When entering a new market, IKEA chooses and trains local suppliers similarly to its processes for recruiting and hiring employees. For instance, when entering Russia, IKEA's strategy was to build a local supplier base through "active cooperation in the Russian wood industry."[45] IKEA's proactive strategy was difficult, given that IKEA bases its strategy for long-term commitments on feelings of trust, which was very uncommon for Russians who "operate under great uncertainty and are reluctant to enter into long-term commitments."[46] However, IKEA took the time to understand the Russian positions and invested heavily to change their opinions and behaviors.[47]

Global expansion has proven historically difficult, yet IKEA has found a way to not only balance the entire customer experience, but also achieve a reputation for social responsibility and sustainability in the process. One of their greatest impacts thus far has been on the environment. In 1997, before the IWAY was even finalized, IKEA sought to increase the efficiency of transportation by writing "IKEA, transport and the environment."[48] Its purpose was to limit pollution from travel and strategically place all stakeholders geographically.[49] Based on responses gathered by a University of Bari study, 60 percent of stakeholders lived less than 20 km from the store.[50] According to one author, "IKEA's intuition was not so

much to involve some vendors in this program, but more to formalize this synergy through the sharing of an ethical code. A code whose purpose is not only practical in terms of production, but also symbolic of the ability of the Swedish corporation to use its brand as a means to ensure the work of all those with whom it collaborates."[51]

The goal is to limit manpower and trips by using flat-packs, and ultimately limit CO_2 emissions through decreased travel.[52] In 2001, with 170 carriers, IKEA asked its suppliers to meet certain requirements—". . . IKEA recommended they update transport vehicles to more modern models. The company also required a switch to less polluting fuels as well as the establishment of environmental protection policies and action plans to control pollution."[53] By 2010, results in Italy, for example, showed a decrease from 75 percent to 65 percent of road transport as well as CO_2 emissions reductions.[54]

According to the chief sustainability officer Steve Howard, IKEA has also installed 50,000 solar panels across its stores in 2012, and plans to invest $2 billion in renewable energy by 2015. IKEA also now owns wind farms in six countries and has committed to use 100 percent renewable energy sources by 2020.[55]

IKEA's dedication to the environment and strong network of stakeholders has been yet another point of success when entering international markets. A look into a few internationalization examples will provide further information on IKEA's global practices.

IKEA's Internationalization Journey

China Entry and Expansion

IKEA entered China in 1998 and moved slower than they had in other locations. By 2006, they opened three stores, and there were a total of nine stores by 2011.[56] The plan is to have 17 stores in China by 2017.[57] The Beijing location, which opened in 2011, has been tagged as IKEA's largest-volume store globally with over 6 million visitors in 2011.[58]

IKEA originally entered China as a joint venture with the Chinese government. In 2004, China entered the World Trade Organization and, as a result, the third location in Quangzhou was able to be wholly owned by IKEA, as well as all subsequent openings.

Asia has been a difficult market for IKEA, notably because of the extreme cultural differences between Asia and Sweden. It has not been an easy road for IKEA, yet even in difficult times, Asia cannot be ignored given its sheer size.

Asia makes up 30 percent of IKEA's sourcing, and the large population results in daily visitors, for instance, on a Saturday in Beijing equaling the number of weekly visitors to a store in the West.[59,60] The size and population, though, also come at a price for the company that created a successful business based on principles of standardization with local adaptation.

China is vastly different from all western markets in size, culture. and tastes, and has forced IKEA to alter their marketing strategies to meet demand. The core strategy of the company is to offer low cost, high quality furniture, meaning the cost must be low in comparison to other furniture providers in the country,[61] Other businesses in China, though, are traditionally providing the lowest cost options. Therefore, IKEA, faced with extreme competition and copycats, had to alter its emphasis to the higher income population who see their furniture as more of a luxury purchase.[62,63]

IKEA has also seen challenges in the open showroom-selling environment, which is designed to allow customers to envision the design of a room and touch the furniture. The Chinese are not accustomed to this, and view it as a hangout. Customers can often be found reading, lounging, and napping on the furniture, or gathering around looking for freebies.[64] In fact, several China locations have now become hotspots for senior citizen romance.[65]

The seniors show up in groups, sit for hours in the cafeteria and bring their own food and tea.[66] To deal with these groups taking up all the space without actually making a purchase, IKEA has added guards and created special seating areas for those patrons who only want to sit, and not shop.[67] Because of these situations, IKEA had to adapt each store to its unique surroundings and cultural differences in order to successfully meet the needs of the Chinese economy.

Although it has been a difficult undertaking, China has become a $2.7 trillion dollar market, with growth up 16 percent from 2010 to 2011, as compared to 8 percent growth in the U.S., making China one of the fastest growing markets in the world.[68]

Russia Entry and Setbacks

IKEA entered Russia in 2000 as a "last big hobby" for founder Ingvar Kamprad, then age 81.[69] Amid large changes in culture and a great deal of training, IKEA was a huge success with its "mega-mall" business model.[70] The first store in Russia drew 40,000 shoppers on the first day, and as of 2010 IKEA has opened twelve more stores with approximately 200 million visitors each year.[71,72]

Although IKEA has seen success in Russia, the road to get there was not always easy. Like China, Russia's culture is extremely different from Sweden, and changing a culture without changing the IKEA brand values proved to be extremely difficult. For instance, when hiring, IKEA wants its employees to have a personality that lends to the IKEA business model rather than a comprehensive resume, whereas Russians place a great deal of emphasis on education and experience.[73]

Training was also an issue for the Russian employees, who value academic training and had a negative perception of the "shop floor training" provided by IKEA trainers.[74] However, the IKEA trainers stuck to the IKEA model and began reaching their new Russian counterparts by altering the Russians' previously held views.

In 1998, after the currency devaluation and economic collapse seen throughout Russia, IKEA stood by their side, refusing to abandon the country IKEA worked so hard to enter.[75] This dedication created a strong outlook among the Russian population. However, IKEA's challenges in Russia did not diminish following this symbol of perseverance.

After entering Russia in 2000, IKEA invested $4 billion in 10 years. This amount would seem to be a plan that would pay in dividends, when looking at the original statistics, but, according to Kamprad, IKEA "had been 'cheated' out of $190 million" due to the rampant corruption running through Russia.[76] According to the 2009 Corruption Perception Index, Russia ranked 146th out of 180 countries as the most corrupt, whereas Sweden ranked 3rd.[77,78] In addition, Transparency International's Bribe Payer Index, 2009, ranked Russia in the top five countries where bribes are "likely to be paid."[79]

What is a company dedicated to fair business practices supposed to do in an opportunistic market flooded with corruption? IKEA played fair, and dealt with blow after blow from the Russian government. In 2004, the opening ceremonies of a new store in Moscow were cancelled last minute due to the location being too near a gas pipeline.[80] Following that, in 2007, the company planned on opening a Samara, Russia, location, which a year and a half later still remained closed.

In June 2009, IKEA announced it would suspend all further investment in the country due to the troubles it previously faced with the government.[81] And in 2010, the company announced that two expatriate executives were fired for taking part in bribes involving the Russian utility company, Lenenergo, in the prior year.[82]

IKEA took a great deal of heat for taking bribes during an anticorruption campaign put forth by the company during the Russian turbulence. Although it is never acceptable to participate in corruption in any way, even turning a blind eye to it, anticorruption experts were quoted as saying: "How to reconcile tough antibribery corporate policies back home with the corrupt rules of the game in Russia is a nigh-impossible task."[83]

It has been pointed out that, given IKEA's role as one of Russia's largest foreign investors, the fact that the company has always previously performed business ethically as proven by Sweden's place on the Corruption Perception Index shows just how difficult it is to perform business, and perform it well, in Russia.[84]

Although IKEA is driven by a positive social mission and proactively seeks out stakeholders who support its core values, it does not always work out ideally. IKEA has recently been in the negative media spotlight as a result of a few cases that go against its code of conduct. It is important to mention, though, that IKEA was not acting in haste, but rather these examples should highlight why the company must stay on its toes in the midst of ubiquitous

Exhibit 1

Year	City/Country
1958	Almhult, Sweden
1963	Oslo, Norway
1969	Copenhagen, Denmark
1973	Zurich, Switzerland
1975	Sydney, Australia
1976	Vancouver, Canada
1977	Vienna, Austria
1979	Rotterdam, Netherlands
1981	Paris, France
1984	Brussels, Belgium
1985	Philadelphia, USA
1987	Manchester, UK
1989	Milan, Italy
1990	Budapest, Hungary
1991	Proague, Czech Republic
1991	Poznan, Poland
1996	Madrid, Spain
1998	Shanghai, China
2000	Moscow, Russia
2004	Lisbon, Portugal
2006	Tokyo, Japan

information, social networks, and media and governments eager to take advantage of companies in general.

Recent Challenges and Opportunities

Images in Saudi Arabia

IKEA came under attack in October 2012 for removing pictures of women from catalogs destined for Saudi Arabia. That year alone, IKEA planned to produce over 200 million copies of its catalog in 62 different versions.[85] However, it admitted to tailoring the images "to suit fashion-related tastes of local markets."[86]

IKEA publicly apologized for altering the Saudi images in a statement, noting that such self-censorship was inconsistent with its values.[87] "We're deeply sorry for what has happened," Ulrika Englesson Sandman said. "It's not the local franchisee that has removed the photos. The error has occurred in the process of producing the proposal to Saudi Arabia, and that is ultimately our responsibility."[88]

Catalogs still remain the primary source of marketing for IKEA, and it comes at a time that Saudi Arabia is in a political firestorm over their treatment of women.[89] The same photographs had been published in 27 languages for 37 countries with the women present, leaving many to wonder about IKEA's stance on gender equality.[90]

Forced Labor Practices

IKEA publicly apologized in November 2012 for having profited by the use of prisoners in East Germany 25 to 30 years prior. The issue was publicized when, earlier in the year, the media began reporting on the connection. In response to the accusation, IKEA hired Ernst & Young, who researched 20,000 pages of internal records and 80,000 pages of state and federal documents in addition to interviews of 90 former employees and witnesses.[91]

It was realized that political prisoners were in fact used in the production of IKEA merchandise during that time, even though IKEA initially questioned the use of prisoners by suppliers. Jeanette Skjelmose, sustainability manager, showed her remorse in a public statement: "We deeply regret that this could happen... The use of political prisoners in production has never been acceptable to the IKEA Group. At the time, we didn't have today's well-developed control systems and obviously didn't do enough to prevent such production conditions among our former G.D.P. suppliers."[92]

When speaking of their current control systems, Skjelmose was probably referring to the previously mentioned IWAY code of conduct standards. In addition to placing provisions on working conditions, touched on in the code, IKEA also conducts audits on suppliers over 1,000 times every year just to ensure a situation like this will not arise again.[93]

This news comes as a large surprise to those who follow IKEA and their traditionally positive social impact. IKEA has even been commended many times over the years for their strong stance on social issues, such as child labor. Susan Bissell of UNICEF (the United Nations Children's Fund) in South Asia was quoted as saying, "The risk of falling into disrepute and becoming the victim of consumer boycotts has driven many companies to move production from South Asia to areas which are easier to control. Those companies which stay on do everything they can to conceal their presence. I wish more companies had the courage to follow IKEA's example: stay on and actively work on the problems and take genuine social responsibility. IKEA is a sponsor of UNICEF [...] but we regard IKEA as a cooperation partner rather than a contributor [...]."[94]

Many even commended IKEA for how they handled this situation. IKEA took on the responsibility of hiring Ernst & Young to investigate the situation at the first mention of forced labor. They are not the only company to have profited from such actions, but one of the few who took action against their prior role. In fact, Christian Sachse, a Berlin historian, spoke of how common this act was, and said it would "take years of research to properly understand the field."[95]

For now, IKEA has accepted its wrongdoing and is moving forward while trying to make things right. The company has vowed its commitment to donate funds and provide an effort to research the issue of forced labor in East Germany, and stand as one of the only companies who is coming forward and taking action to turn the negative into a positive.

Horsemeat Scandal

In rise of the horsemeat scandal raging across Europe, inspectors from the Czech Republic found traces of the meat in IKEA's European signature meatballs in February 2013.[96] Although the United States' supply remained unaffected, customer morale will surely be impacted. One customer was even quoted as saying, "I am more trusting of Swedish companies and it makes me wonder about corporate integrity in a way I never have questioned Swedes before."[97]

In a public statement, IKEA reassured communities and supporters across the world that they are committed to high quality, safe food and will not stand for any ingredients other than those listed in the recipe.[98] The company guaranteed the public that it is taking all concerns very seriously, and assured all that no product is actually harmful if eaten. The real issue is the discrepancy in labeling.[99]

Five percent of IKEA's total revenue comes from food, and currently meatballs in 13 countries have been removed. It is a situation affecting many of Europe's leading food companies, including Nestle SA and ABP Food Group's Silvercrest Food. As IKEA's private investigation continues, it will need to continue to ease the nerves of the disheartened public.

Cake Contamination

Just one month after the horsemeat scandal took place, IKEA again found itself in the news for chocolate cake that was discovered to contain traces of coliform bacteria, a contaminant found in the environment and in the feces of humans and warm-blooded animals, according to *The Wall Street Journal*.[100] Although the cakes posed no true health hazards, as the issue was caught before the cakes hit stores, it came at a bad time publicly.

The Shanghai quarantine bureau destroyed two tons of the cake, and IKEA performed a formal investigation and removed the cakes from restaurants in 23 countries.[101] The company has released a formal apology for all concerns raised regarding the issue.

Budget Hotel Chain

IKEA, in a more positive light, announced a new partnership with Marriott to open a budget-friendly hotel chain called "Moxy," targeted toward next-generation travelers in Europe.[102] The partnership aims to sneak into the economy sector of the European travel market, which represents half of the largest travel market worldwide.[103]

The hope is to secure locations of 50 hotels in the next five years, as well as 150 hotels in the next 10 years.[104] The first is scheduled to open in Milan, Italy, in 2014. All rooms will be designed to be the same size with the same décor, typically contemporary with large wall art, a flat-screen TV and USB ports.[105] The hotel stay will also include a continental breakfast, bars, and public spaces for the low price of 60 to 85 euros a night.[106,107]

This comes as a new initiative for the largest furniture retailer, as well as for Marriott who currently owns over 3,700 properties in 74 countries, but is now seeking a spot in the economy segment.[108] The brand will be operated by a franchise, and will stay in line with IKEA's low cost, high quality mentality.

Amidst IKEA's international success, president of the U.S. IKEA, Mike Ward, believes this is just the beginning. In addition to entering new markets as seen in its partnership with Marriott, IKEA is also placing a strong focus on making its current line of business even better.[109] The company is investing heavily in core products, particularly in the U.S. market, to battle the predisposition that the product line is primarily for those in their "starting-up phase."[110] IKEA has also begun offering delivery service in some markets and plans on putting other strategies into place throughout 2013 to further highlight itself as a quality brand that not only acts responsibly, but also listens to its customers.

There will also be a shift in leadership structure moving forward, as CEO Mikael Ohlsson plans to leave IKEA by early September 2013.[111] Although there has been much speculation as to succession plans for Ingvar Kamprad, he does plan on providing his three sons with larger ownership roles moving forward, while Kamprad himself will continue his role as senior advisor to the Ingka holding company.[112] He plans on staying with the company for years to come as its key decision maker.[113]

Questions for Review

1. How would you describe IKEA's overall approach to international expansion? What were some of the important successes and challenges it experienced along the way?
2. What macro- and micro-political risks did IKEA face when it first considered entry into Russia? What kinds of preemptive and/or proactive political strategies might it have pursued to mitigate these risks?
3. How should IKEA respond to some of the recent scandals concerning product contamination, sourcing, and working conditions?
4. What motivation, leadership and international HR approaches has IKEA pursued to achieve its international success? What additional steps might it consider given its expanding global reach and impending change in leadership?

Source: This case was prepared by Deborah Zachar of Villanova University under the supervision of Professor Jonathan Doh as the basis for class discussion.

HSBC in China

Introduction

After years of negotiations, China finally acceded to the World Trade Organization (WTO) in December 2001 (see Exhibit 1). This development was a significant milestone in China's integration with the global economy. One of the most important and far-reaching consequences was the transformation of China's financial sector. China's banking, insurance, and securities industries were long due for a major overhaul, and the WTO requirements guaranteed that the liberalization of China's economy would extend to the important financial sector. China's banking sector had become a casualty of the state. Banks and other financial institutions haphazardly extended loans to state-owned enterprises (SOEs) based not on sound credit analysis but favoritism and government-directed policy. As a consequence, crippling debt from bad and underperforming loans mounted, with no effective market disciplines to rein it in.

China recognized that opening up the banking sector could bolster its financial system. Foreign management would help overhaul the banking sector and put the focus on returns, instead of promoting a social agenda. This fiscal agenda would ultimately lead to a stronger and more stable economy. Yet after years of direction from the state, Chinese bank managers did not have the necessary skills to transform the banks on their own. Guo Shuqing, shortly after being promoted to chairman of China Construction Bank, admitted that, "more than 90 percent of the bank's risk managers are unqualified."[1]

Immediately upon accession to the WTO, China's banking sector began to open to foreign banks. Initially, foreign banks were allowed to conduct foreign currency business without any market access restrictions and conduct local currency business with foreign-invested enterprises and foreign individuals. In addition, the liberalization of foreign investment rules made Chinese banks attractive targets for foreign financial institutions. Sweeping domestic changes have followed. Strong emphasis has been placed on interest rate liberalization, clearer and more consistent regulation, and a frenzy of IPOs of state owned banks has followed. It was in this context that HSBC rapidly expanded its presence in China.

Exhibit 1 China's WTO Commitments

General Cross-Sector Commitments

➤ Reforms to lower trade barriers in every sector of the economy, opening its markets to foreign companies and their exports from the first day of accession.

➤ Provide national treatment and improved market access to goods and services from other WTO members.

➤ Special rules regarding subsidies and the operation of state-owned enterprises, in light of the state's large role in China's economy.

➤ Undertake important changes to its legal framework, designed to add transparency and predictability to business dealings and improve the process of foreign market entry.

➤ Agreement to assume the obligations of more than 20 *existing* multilateral WTO agreements, covering all areas of trade.

➤ Under the acquired rights commitment, agreed that the conditions of ownership, operation, and scope of activities for a foreign company under any existing agreement would not be made more restrictive than they were on the date of China's accession to the WTO.

➤ Licensing procedures that were streamlined, transparent, and more predictable.

Commitments Specific to the Financial Services Industry

➤ Allow foreign banks to conduct *foreign currency business* without any market access or national treatment limitations.

➤ Allow foreign banks to conduct *local currency business* with foreign-invested enterprises and foreign individuals (subject to geographic restrictions).

➤ Banking services (with a five-year transitional plan) by foreign banks:
  Within two years after accession, foreign banks would be able to conduct *domestic* currency business with Chinese enterprises (subject to geographic restrictions).
  Within five years after accession, foreign banks would be able to conduct domestic currency business with Chinese individuals, and all geographic restrictions will be lifted.
  Foreign banks also would be permitted to provide financial leasing services at the same time that Chinese banks are permitted to do so.

HSBC, known for its international scope and careful, judicious strategy, made a series of key investments between 2001 and 2005 that arguably gave it the most extensive position in China of any foreign financial group. These investments included two separate transactions that resulted in a 19.9 percent stake in Ping An insurance, and, in June 2004, a $1.8 billion successful tender for a 19.9 percent stake in Bank of Communications, the fifth largest bank in China. HSBC had a long history in Asia, and was uniquely positioned to take advantage of China's vast population and mushrooming middle class, high savings rates (in the range of 40 percent), and huge capital investments (US$50 billion FDI in 2005). HSBC recognized that the current banking system was not capitalizing on this vast opportunity, and sought to get in on the ground floor in this new environment. Perhaps, with further liberalization, however, China would allow future investors to establish even greater claims to Chinese banks. Citigroup's successful effort to gain a controlling stake in Guandgong Development Bank appeared to undermine earlier investors who had been limited by China's rule that allowed foreigners to own no more than 19.9 percent of domestic financial institutions. Did the huge potential rewards of being an early mover in China mitigate the promise of uncertainty and risks of doing business in an emerging market? After being burned in Argentina, could HSBC relax its conservative philosophy in its China strategy? If the economy took a turn for the worse, HSBC could face heavy losses. On the other hand, could HSBC afford not to be an early mover in a region where it had a longstanding presence?

Background on HSBC

History

Thomas Sutherland founded the Hongkong and Shanghai Banking Corporation (Hongkong Bank) in 1865 to finance the growing trade between Europe, India, and China.[2] Sutherland, a Scot, was working for the Peninsular and Oriental Steam Navigation Company when he recognized a considerable demand for local banking facilities in Hong Kong and on the China coast. Hongkong Bank opened in Hong Kong in March 1865 and in Shanghai a month later.

The bank rapidly expanded by opening agencies and branches across the globe, reaching as far as Europe and North America, but maintained a distinct focus on China and the Asia-Pacific region. Hongkong Bank helped pioneer modern banking during this time in a number of countries, such as Japan, where it opened a branch in 1866 and advised the government on banking and currency, and Thailand, where it opened the country's first bank in 1888 and printed the country's first banknotes. By the 1880s, the bank issued banknotes and held government funds in Hong Kong, and also helped manage British government accounts in China, Japan, Penang,

and Singapore. In 1876, the bank handled China's first public loan, and thereafter issued most of China's public loans. Hongkong Bank had become the foremost financial institution in Asia by the close of the 19th century.[3]

After the First World War, the Hongkong Bank anticipated an expansion in its Asian markets, and took a leading role in stabilizing the Chinese national currency. The tumultuous Second World War, for its part, saw most of the bank's European staff become prisoners of war to the advancing Japanese.

The Postwar Years

In the postwar years, Hongkong Bank turned to dramatic expansion through acquisitions and alliances in order to diversify. The acquisitions began with the British Bank of the Middle East (Persia and the Gulf states) and the Mercantile Bank (India and Malaya) in 1959, and were followed by acquiring a majority interest in Hong Kong's Hang Seng Bank in 1965. The 51 percent controlling interest in Hang Seng Bank was acquired during a local banking crisis for $12.4 million. As of 2002, HSBC's interest in the bank was 62 percent and was over $13 billion. Hang Seng, which retained its name and management, has been a consistently strong performer. The bank made further acquisitions in the United Kingdom and Europe (from 1973), North America (from 1980), and Latin America (from 1997), as well as other Asian markets.

Under Chairman Michael Sandberg, Hongkong Bank entered the North American market with a $314 million, 51 percent acquisition of Marine Midland, a regional bank in upstate New York. In 1987, the bank purchased the remaining 49 percent, doubling Hongkong Bank's investment and providing the bank a significant U.S. presence. As a condition of the acquisition, however, Marine Midland retained its senior management.

Move to London and Acquisitions

In 1991, Hongkong Bank reorganized as HSBC Holdings and moved its headquarters in 1993 to London from Hong Kong. Sandberg's successor, William Purves, led HSBC's purchase of the U.K.'s Midland Bank in 1992. This acquisition fortified HSBC's European presence and doubled its assets. The move also enhanced HSBC's global presence and advanced the bank's reputation as a global financial services company.

Other major acquisitions of the 1990s included Republic Bank and Safra Holdings in the United States, which doubled HSBC's private banking business investments moves in Brazil and Argentina in 1997, and acquisition of Mexico's Bital in 2002. In 2000, HSBC acquired CCF in France. By 2006, HSBC had assets exceeding $1,860 billion, customers numbering close to 100 million, and operations in six continents. In recent years, HSBC has made a major commitment to emerging markets, especially China and Mexico, but also Brazil, India, and smaller developing economies.

Expansion, Acquisition, and Succession

The World's Local Bank

HSBC holding company set up a group policy in 1991 that established 11 quasi-independent banks, each a separate subsidiary with its own balance sheet.[4] The head office provided essential functions, such as strategic planning, human resource management, and legal, administrative, and financial planning and control. This setup promoted prompter decision making at a local level and greater accountability.[5] HSBC portrays itself as "the world's local bank," recognizing the importance of globalization, flexibility, and local responsiveness.

As of 1998, HSBC established distinct customer groups or lines of business that would overlay existing geographic designations. This encouraged maximizing the benefits of its universal scope, such as sharing best practices of product development, management, and marketing. The geographic perspective was melded closely with a customer group perspective, demanding both global and local thinking.

Traditionally, HSBC's culture has embraced caution, thrift, discipline, and risk avoidance. The bank looked at long-term survival and considered markets in 50-year views. Thrift manifested through the company, and even the chairman flew economy class on flights less than three hours.[6] In 2005, incoming Chairman Stephen Green recognized the company's rule "to follow the letter and spirit of regulations" and signaled his intention to protect the bank's reputation as it extends into consumer finance.[7]

Bond's Rein and Move to "HSBC"

Sir John Bond became CEO of HSBC in 1993, and chairman in 1998, bringing with him a hands-on entrepreneurial style and exceptionally ambitious goals.[8] He pursued acquisitions beyond HSBC's traditional core, in pursuit of such attractive financial segments as wealth management, investment banking, online retail financing, and consumer finance. Bond considered shareholder value and economic profit in deciding when acquisition premiums were in order, which was in contrast to his predecessor's "three times book value" rule.[9] By 2001, Bond had authorized investments of over $21 billion on acquisitions and new ventures.[10]

In 1998, Bond adopted the HSBC brand, and preserved "The Hongkong & Shanghai Banking Corp." name only for its bank based in Hong Kong. HSBC branded its subsidiary banks across the world with the parent bank's acronym and greatly expanded marketing efforts in 2000. In March 2002, HSBC's marketing message became "the world's local bank," which would help the brand become one of the world's top 50 most recognizable brands by 2003.[11]

Household Acquisition

In 2003, a $15.5 billion acquisition of Household International,[12] the U.S. consumer lending business, became the basis of HSBC's Consumer Finance customer group. Household utilized a unique system to forecast the likelihood that customers would repay debt, which used a 13-year database of consumer behavior. Household was controversial and yet presented great opportunity. HSBC desired to leverage this new skill in developing countries, yet was unable to find all demographic and credit data that Household normally relies on in the United States. HSBC particularly looked to extend the Household model into China and Mexico. However, the subprime mortgage crisis hit the United States hard in 2007–2008 and had a major impact on Household operations.

Six years after acquiring Household International, HSBC effectively conceded that the deal was a mistake. In March 2009 HSBC made public that it would close all 800 remaining branches of HSBC Finance Corp., the former Household Financial, resulting in 6,100 job cuts nationwide. HSBC had already closed about 600 HFC and Beneficial branches over the past two years.[13] "High levels of delinquency, given rising levels of unemployment, mean that the business model for subprime home equity refinancing is not sustainable," said Niall Booker, HSBC Finance chief executive during one of the media conferences.[14] HSBC Finance said it would retain its credit card business, and HSBC Holdings would keep its New York–based HSBC Bank USA. HSBC officials also said that the bank would continue to help mortgage customers with loan repayments and foreclosure-prevention efforts.

The HSBC Finance (Household) executives pointed out that it was hard to predict in 2003 that global financial crisis and the recession would occur. When the crisis hit hard in 2008, the subprime mortgage market led to more than $1.15 trillion of credit losses and writedowns at financial institutions and government bailouts of companies ranging from Citigroup Inc. to Royal Bank of Scotland Group Plc of Edinburgh as noted by Bloomberg analysts. HSBC was one of the first banks to acknowledge the possibility of upcoming subprime mortgage problems, and set aside about $53 billion to cover bad loans during the past three years.[15]

Economic Crisis and Financial Performance

The consequences of global economic crisis were severe for the world's banking system, prompting thousands of banks to seek financial assistance from their local government. Many banks were burdened with highly overvalued "bad loans" and suffered huge losses. Unlike many global players, HSBC reported a profit for 2008 but it still took a hit: Its pretax profit of $9.3 billion was 62 percent below the $24.2 billion reported for 2007.

The bank also cut its dividend for the full year by 29 percent to 64 cents per share. The slide in profits was largely the result of a goodwill impairment charge of $10.6 billion in the United States.[16] In spite of the bitter loss in North America, HSBC performed much better in the other parts of the world. For example, in Europe, pretax profit rose to $10.9 billion from $8.6 billion. Profit from Hong Kong fell to $5.46 billion from $7.34 billion, while earnings from the rest of Asia rose to $6.47 billion from $6.01 billion.[17] HSBC is still considered one of the world's strongest banks by some measures. The bank's market value of $68.2 billion in early 2009 ranked it behind only Industrial & Commercial Bank of China Ltd., China Construction Bank Corp., Bank of China Ltd., and JPMorgan Chase & Co.[18]

To the credit of HSBC management, the bank avoided taking U.K. government "bailout" funding unlike other big banks. Instead, HSBC made plans to raise £12.5 billion ($17.9 billion) in capital to prepare for further deterioration of the global economy.[19] Also, responding to growing public anger over the scale of bonuses paid to many senior bankers, HSBC said no performance share awards would be made for 2008 and that no executive director would receive a cash bonus.[20]

Managing for Growth

HSBC's strategic plan, "Managing for Growth," was launched in the fall of 2003. This strategy builds on HSBC's global, international scope and seeks to grow by focusing on the key customer groups of personal financial services; consumer finance; commercial banking; corporate, investment banking, and markets; and private banking.[21] "Managing for Growth" is intended to be "evolutionary, not revolutionary," and aims to vault HSBC to the world's leading financial services company. HSBC seeks to grow earnings over the long term, using its peers as a benchmark. It also plans to invest in delivery platforms, technology, its people, and brand name to prop up the future value of HSBC's stock market rating and total shareholder return. HSBC retains its core values of communication, long-term focus, ethical relationships, teamwork, prudence, creativity, high standards, ambition, customer-focused marketing, and corporate social responsibility, all with an international outlook.[22]

Strategic Pillars

As part of the growth strategy, HSBC identified eight strategic pillars:

> *Brand:* continue to establish HSBC and its hexagon symbol as one of the top global brands for customer experience and corporate social responsibility.
> *Personal Financial Services:* drive growth in key markets and through appropriate channels; emerging markets are essential markets with a burgeoning demand.

> *Consumer Finance:* offer both a wider product range and penetrate new markets, such as the emerging country markets.
> *Commercial Banking:* leverage HSBC's international reach through effective relationship management and improved product offerings.
> *Corporate, Investment Banking, and Markets:* accelerate growth by enhancing capital markets and advisory capabilities.
> *Private Banking:* a focus on serving the highest value personal clients.
> *People:* draw in, develop and motivate HSBC's people.
> *TSR:* fulfill HSBC's TSR target by achieving strong competitive performances in earnings per share growth and efficiency.[23]

Focus on Emerging Markets

In 2000, HSBC had half of its assets in developing countries.[24] Most earnings, however, stemmed from mature markets, such as Hong Kong and Britain. All but 5 percent of group profits came from five economies, while India and Latin America each added only 1 percent to group profit.[25]

In 2005 incoming Chairman Stephen Green underlined HSBC's focus on the potential of emerging markets: "There is a general rule of thumb that says the emerging markets grow faster than mature markets as economies and the financial services sector grows faster than the real economy in emerging markets because you are starting from very low penetration of financial services in general."[26]

Specifically in consumer finance, Green recognized the importance of importing HSBC's model into markets starved for credit cards and loans, saying, "Any analysis of the demographics of emerging markets tells you that consumer finance is going to be an important part, and a rapidly growing part, of the financial-services spectrum for a long time to come."[27]

The Draw of Emerging Markets

Recognition of the impact of emerging markets is an essential thread running throughout the elements of the "Managing for Growth" strategy. Since 2000, many of HSBC's emerging markets' profits have increased dramatically (see Exhibit 2). Across the board, HSBC's pretax profits in emerging markets have increased from $905 million in 2000 to $3,439 million in 2005. In January 2010, HSBC Global Asset Management reported that despite high volatility throughout 2009, Asian and emerging market equities gained around 100 percent. The Brazilian equity market was the best performer with a return of over 140 percent in 2009. In contrast, major markets such as the U.S., Europe, and Japan were all up between 39 and 82 percent for the same period. Meanwhile, HSBC Global Asset Management expects the pace of economic growth in global emerging markets to be faster than that of developed markets over the medium to long term.[28]

Exhibit 2 HSBC Emerging Markets
Pretax Profits 2005 vs. 2004, 2000 **Pretax Profits 2005 vs. 2006**

Country	2000 (US$ mil)	2004 (US$ mil)	2005 (US$ mil)	% Change 2004–2005	Country	2006 (US$ mil)	% Change (2006 over 2005)
Argentina	112	154	244	58	Argentina	157	236
Brazil	208	281	406	44	Brazil	526	30
China	226	32	334	944	China	708	112
India	87	178	212	19	India	393	85
Indonesia	70	76	113	49	Indonesia	71	237
Malaysia	116	214	236	10	Malaysia	274	16
Mexico	9	774	923	19	Mexico	1,009	9
Saudi Arabia	30	122	236	93	Saudi Arabia	181	41
South Korea	65	89	94	6	South Korea	48	213
Taiwan	45	107	68	236	Taiwan	(23)	NA
Turkey	59	142	265	87	Turkey	217	218
UAE	130	192	308	60	Middle East	730	25
					Other	166	215
Total	**905**	**2,361**	**3,439**	**146**	**Total**	**4,533**	**19**
Total profit before tax (all countries)		18,943	20,966	110.7	Total profit before tax (all countries)	22,086	5

Liberalization of China's Banking Sector

China's Banking Sector Pre-WTO

Before the WTO accession negotiations, China's banking industry operated as a cog in China's centrally planned economy. The state commercial banks performed a social function, during China's post-Mao drive to industrialize, instead of operating for economic return. Consequently, the banks adhered to directed lending practices from the government and in turn created some of China's most successful enterprises, but also supported thousands of other inefficient and unprofitable state-owned enterprises. This practice left state commercial banks with massive amounts of debt that were largely unrecoverable and hordes of nonperforming loans.

In addition to widespread losses, instability ensued in the banking system overall. To make matters worse, corruption and mismanagement ran rampant throughout the sector, sapping away consumer and investor confidence.

WTO Accession

Following 15 years of negotiation and two decades of economic reform in China, December 11, 2001, marked China's accession to the World Trade Organization. The main objective of the WTO agreement was to open China's market up to foreign competition. The deadline for complete implementation was December 11, 2006.

China made a number of implementations immediately. To begin with, foreign banks were allowed to conduct foreign currency business without any market access restrictions. Also, foreign banks were allowed to conduct local currency business with foreign-invested enterprises and foreign individuals (with geographic restrictions). Within two years of accession, China agreed to allow foreign banks to conduct domestic currency business with Chinese enterprises (geographic restrictions). Within five years, foreign banks could conduct domestic currency business with Chinese individuals (no geographic restrictions); and foreign banks were able to provide financial leasing services at the same time as Chinese banks. Under the WTO investment provisions, China agreed to allow foreign ownership of Chinese banks (up to 25 percent), with no single foreign investor permitted to own more than 20 percent.

"Bank reform has become the most crucial task for the government in pushing forward economic reforms," said Yi Xianrong, an economist at the Chinese Academy of Social Sciences in Beijing.[29] Indeed, bank reform is critical to stabilizing and advancing the Chinese economy.

Domestic Reform

China has undertaken a number of domestic reforms in order to overhaul the banking industry. China has engaged in interest rate liberalization by removing certain interest rate and price controls. Instead of being pegged to the U.S. dollar, as it once was, China's currency exchange rate is now pegged to within 0.3 percent of a basket of currencies, dominated by a group including the U.S. dollar, euro, Japanese yen, South Korean won, British pound, Thai baht, and Russian ruble. The yuan was revalued by 2.1 percent against the dollar in July 2005, but analysts estimate that it remains 10–30 percent undervalued.

Regulation has long been a concern in the Chinese banking industry. China has made major progress by creating regulatory agencies. In 2003, China created a central regulator, the China Banking Regulatory Commission (CBRC), out of the central bank. The regulator's 20,000 staff members endeavor to shift the banks' focus from senseless loans and grow mind-sets to a goal of preserving capital and generating returns. Lenders not meeting a capital ratio of 8 percent of risk-weighted assets (as decreed by Basel I, a global standard) by 2007 may face sanctions, which could include the removal of senior management. Still, the CBRC faces an uphill battle. Han Mingzhi, as head of the CBRC's international department, admitted in 2004 that "we lack people who understand commercial banking and microeconomics. It is a headache for the CBRC."[30]

Concurrently, China is striving to make regulatory and reporting requirements more clear, because they have often proved confusing barriers to foreign investment. Since 1998, China has intensified accounting, prudential, and regulatory standards. Prior to 1998, the banks booked interest income for up to three years even if it was not being paid. Now, the banks can do so for only 90 days, which is the international norm. Still, it has been all too common for Chinese banks to ignore regulations and not monitor loans. As a result of poor accounting, the banks themselves are sometimes unsure of their bad loans. Lai Xiaomin, head of the CBRC's Beijing office, admits that "when our banks disclose information, they don't always do so in a totally honest manner."[31] Indeed, the lack of reliable accounting can hamper investment. As one Hong Kong investor put it, "When you take a state-owned enterprise that has had weak internal controls, it can be enormously labor-intensive to come up with financials we can work with."[32]

In 2006, regulators overhauled the system in which almost one-third of a company's shares were "nontradable." Fixing this problem has helped energize the market and welcome in individual investors.[33]

Recent Regulatory Moves

New regulations, it is hoped, will address China's history of dishonesty and embezzlement. With the tight connection of Chinese banks with local governments, corruption has choked the Chinese banking system. Some common practices have historically encouraged corruption, such as allowing the same person to make and approve a loan. Former bank Chairman Zhang Enzhao himself was arrested in June 2005 for allegedly taking bribes. At the China Construction Bank alone, there were more than 100 cases of theft and embezzlement between 2002 and 2004.[34] These old habits have to be rooted out.

China is working hard to transition its traditional banks into "universal" banks. Most of China's 128 commercial banks have introduced better governance, shareholding, and incentive structures, while also adding independent directors to their boards.[35] Foreign management and

Exhibit 3 Foreign Bank Investments in China

PRC Bank	Foreign Partner	% Stake	Price	Date
Bank of Shanghai	HSBC	8.00	$62.6 m	12/2001
	IFC	7.00	$25.0 m	
	Shanghai Commercial Bank (HK)	3.00	$15.7 m	
Shanghai Pudong Dev Bank	Citigroup	4.62	$72.0 m	12/2003
Fujian Asian Bank	HSBC	50	Less than $20 m[1]	12/2003
Bank of Communications	HSBC	19.90	$1.75 b	6/2004
Xian CCB	Scotia Bank	12.4	$3.2 m	10/2004
Jinan City CCB	Commonwealth Bank of Australia	11.0	$17 m[2]	11/2004
Shenzhen Dev. Bank	Newbridge Capital	17.9	$1.23 b	12/2004
Minsheng Bank	Temasek	4.9		1/2005
Hangzhou CCB	Commonwealth Bank of Australia	19.90	$78.0 m	4/2005
China Construction Bank	Bank of America	9.00	$3.0 b	6/2005
	Temasek	5.1	$1.5 m[3]	
Bank of China	Royal Bank of Scotland	5.00	$3.1 b	8/2005
	UBS	1.6	$500 m[4]	9/2005
	Temasek	10.00	$3.1 b[5]	9/2005
Industrial Commercial BOC	Goldman, Allianz, AmEx			8/2005
Nanjing CCB	BNP Paribas	19.20	$27.0 m	10/2005
Hua Xia Bank	Deutsche Bank	9.9	$329 m[6]	10/2005
	Sal. Oppenheim Jr.	4.1		10/2005
Bank of Beijing	ING	19.90	$214 m	3/2005

[1]HSBC Press Article, accessed October 3, 2006, www.hsbc.com.cn/cn/aboutus/press/content/03dec29a.htm.

[2]Guonan Ma, "Sharing China's Bank Restructuring," *China and World Economy* 14, no. 3 (2006), p. 8.

[3]David Lague and Donald Greenlees, "China's Troubled Banks Lure Investors," *International Herald Tribune*, www.iht.com/articles/2005/09/21/business/bank.php, accessed on October 4, 2006.

[4]"UBS to Invest $500 million in Bank of China," CBS News, www.cbsnews.com/stories/2005/09/27/ap/business/main D8CSHPLO0.shtml, assessed October 4, 2006.

[5]Luo Jun and Xiao Yu, "Temasek to Buy 10% of China Bank," *International Herald Tribune*, www.iht.com/articles/2005/09/01/bloomberg/sxboc.php, accessed on October 4, 2006.

[6]"Deutsche Bank Seals Chinese Deal," BBC News, news.bbc.co.uk/2/hi/business/4348560.stm, accessed October 4, 2006.

knowledge are intended to flush the Chinese banking system with managerial talent. To help encourage foreign banks, China is relaxing some foreign bank restrictions. The Chinese government has also taken steps to eliminate bad loans by bailing out banks.

IPO Explosion

China has aggressively pursued IPOs of state-owned banks, a policy which has been met with a strong response from investors eager to tap into the populous country and seize first-mover advantages (see Exhibit 3). HSBC's purchase of a 19.9 percent stake in Bank of Communications (BoCOM) in June 2004 was the pioneering, substantial foreign bank investment in China. HSBC had previously made large investments in Fujian Asian Bank (50 percent) and Bank of Shanghai (8 percent). In 2005, foreign banks invested $18 billion in several of China's largest banks. The October 2005 listing of China Construction Bank (CCB), China's largest at the time, raised $8 billion from foreign investors for 12 percent of its shares. CCB further obtained an additional $4 billion ahead of its float by selling stakes of 9 percent to Bank of America and 5.1 percent to Temasek, Singapore's investment agency. In the following months, the Royal Bank of Scotland put $3.1 billion into Bank of China, Temasek another $3.1 billion, and Switzerland's UBS $500 million.

In May 2006, Bank of China, the country's second-largest lender, raised $11.2 billion in a Hong Kong stock sale, which was the fifth-largest initial public offering in history. In July 2006, the Chinese government announced approval for an even larger IPO of the country's largest bank, Industrial & Commercial Bank of China, to raise $18 billion or more in one of the largest stock offerings ever.[36] The central bank expects foreigners to bring much needed improvements to the state banks' risk-management and internal control systems, including credit-risk assessment and more transparent reporting. With capital allocated more efficiently, a more stable financial system will follow, and the economy will become more open to foreign competition.

Two Steps Forward

Pulling back from some of its commitments, China indirectly delayed the implementation of its WTO commitments. On February 1, 2002, the People's Bank of China (PBOC) issued regulations and implementation rules governing foreign-funded banks. While these measures met the commitments of the WTO agreement, the PBOC was taking a very conservative approach in opening up the banking sector. For example, foreign-funded banks could open only one branch every 12 months.

In the wake of these early obstacles, there have been positive changes. Capital requirements were reduced, additional cities were opened up to foreign banking, and the "one branch every 12 months" restriction was lifted. Central bank officials have indicated willingness to eventually elevate the foreign ownership limit above the current 25 percent, but experts doubt it will ever go beyond 50 percent.[37]

A 2006 study by McKinsey found that underperforming loans with merely negligible returns are also very damaging to the Chinese economy. McKinsey estimates that reforming China's financial system could boost GDP by $321 billion annually.[38]

Exhibit 4   Financial Depth in Major Market

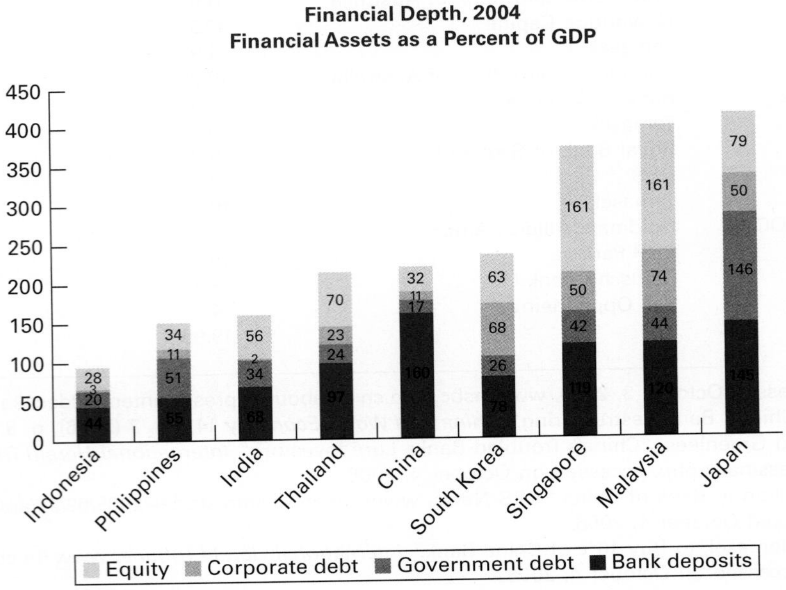

Financial Depth, 2004
Financial Assets as a Percent of GDP

Legend: Equity Corporate debt Government debt Bank deposits

Source: McKinsey.

China's banking sector plays an excessive role in the overall financial system. The share of bank deposits in the financial system ranges from less than 20 percent in developed economies to around half in emerging markets. China, however, has a share of bank deposits at a sky-high 75 percent of the capital in the economy, which practically doubles any other Asian nation (see Exhibit 4).[39]

Capital is still mostly allocated to state-owned enterprises even though private companies have been China's growth engine. Private companies produce 52 percent of GDP in China, but only account for 27 percent of outstanding loans.[40] By sinking money into state-owned enterprises, China's banks are dragging the economy. China's banks had difficulty lending to private companies in the past, because of challenges related to gathering and processing the necessary information on them. As a response, China launched its first national credit bureau in early 2006. China's banks have been satisfying a social role, but now must allocate capital efficiently in order to generate positive economic return.

Investments in Ping An and BoCOM

With its longstanding presence in China, HSBC was among the best positioned financial institutions to take advantage of China's market opening.

Ping An Investments

In October of 2002, HSBC announced that it had taken a 10 percent stake in Ping An Insurance, China's second largest insurer, for $600 million. U.S. investment banks Goldman Sachs and Morgan Stanley already had a combined 14 percent stake in Ping An. Chairman Sir John Bond indicated that HSBC was particularly attracted to the long-term prospects in the insurance and asset management sectors.

In May 2005, HSBC indicated it was investing an additional HK$8.1 billion ($1.04 billion) for an additional 9.91 percent stake in Ping An, doubling its holding in the number-two life insurer. HSBC paid HK$13.20 a share for the stakes held by investment banks Goldman Sachs and Morgan Stanley, lifting HSBC's holding to 19.9 percent, the maximum stake allowed by a single foreign investor.

"This is good news for Ping An," said Kenneth Lee, an analyst at Daiwa Institute of Research. "HSBC is buying at a premium and is replacing Goldman Sachs and Morgan Stanley, which are venture capital investors. HSBC is a long-term investor and will help Ping An to develop its insurance platform," he said.

The company's market share of more than 15 percent of the Chinese market puts it behind domestic competitor China Life Insurance Co., which underwrites about half of all Chinese life insurance premiums. In 2005, HSBC Chairman John Bond commented, "We are optimistic about the long-term prospects of the insurance industry in mainland China and believe Ping An is well-positioned to benefit from the sector's development."[41]

In 2011, China's insurance market reported an 18.5 percent increase in premium income as compared to 2010. Total premium income in China experienced a 5.3 percent increase during this same time period. In 2011, Ping An reported premiums increasing by 28 percent year-over-year, while China Life, China's largest insurer, reported premiums virtually unchanged from 2010.

In addition to holding a stake in Ping An Insurance, HSBC has applied for its own life insurance license in China. Foreign firms account for only 5 percent of the life insurance market in China, while three domestic firms (China Life Insurance, Ping An Insurance, and China Pacific Insurance) hold 76 percent of the market share. The bank hopes to start operations in 2008, and says it will maintain its relationship with Ping An.[42]

The BoCOM Deal

HSBC invested $1.8 billion for a 19.9 percent stake in BoCOM in June 2004. HSBC's chairman at the time, Sir John Bond, commented on the company's long-term perspective: "[I]t is inevitable that China will become a superpower. And indeed, desirable. And we are positioning our business for the decades ahead accordingly."[43] HSBC wanted a piece of the alluring Chinese market, which Goldman Sachs predicts will overtake the United States as the number-one economy in the world by 2040, and wanted to deepen its international scope in line with the "Managing for Growth" strategy.

Speaking one month after HSBC's big move, then-CEO and future Chairman Stephen Green expounded upon China: "[T]he potential in China's domestic market is the largest in history." China is the "world's manufacturer," and as the population continues to urbanize and industrialize, it increasingly has more disposable income, the workers become greater consumers, and the middle class expands.[44] China has one of the world's highest savings rates, at around 40 percent, and already has around one-third of the $1.2 trillion of central bank foreign exchange reserves sitting in Asia. Further, access to capital is not a problem, as FDI floods the country. The challenge facing China is to recycle and invest its pool of savings efficiently.

HSBC recognized the huge potential in the market for banking services, as well as credit cards. As part of its emerging market strategy, HSBC wanted to feed the demand for credit cards in these markets. Green commented: "[O]ur joint venture with Bank of Communications for credit cards is one which we think has a lot of exciting prospects. Bank of Communications has over 30 million debit cards in issue. Over time, a proportion of those is going to convert to credit cards. And we are issuing co-branded credit cards with the Bank of Communications."[45] HSBC saw an opportunity to shepherd millions of new people into the banking system.

HSBC's Green acquiesced that emerging markets do carry risk. This risk was starkly evident during the HSBC debacle in Argentina during the country's economic crisis. China's epic turnaround could conceivably flop, and heavily invested banks could pay dearly. The banking system in China was and is very fragile. Would China's banks be able to break away from state-directed lending and its lasting effects? The banks further rely on the continued acceleration of the economy, and many rely on volatile real estate loans.[46] HSBC recognized other challenges for China, including the need to strengthen regulations, build social security, stem corruption, and fortify the financial system.[47]

Margaret Leung, general manager and global co-head of commercial banking for the HSBC Group, commented, "[W]e believe we have a unique advantage [in China]. A lot of analysts . . . have been saying that if any foreign bank is going to succeed in China, that would be HSBC."[48] BoCOM's net profit soared from Rmb1.604bn (US$200m) in 2004 to Rmb9.249bn in 2005, and a BoCOM-HSBC credit card has successfully been issued to over 650,000 people.[49] However, with the passing of the WTO deadline, BoCOM now faces greater competition from foreign banks, which are now better able to compete under the new Regulation on Administration of Foreign-Funded Banks (adopted in late 2006). Under these new regulations, foreign banks are allowed to issue local currency loans and are no longer limited in the size and scope of their business.

Recent Developments and Future Competitive Conditions

Current Strategies in China

Foreign banks that operate in China have different strategies. Some of them have purchased smaller stakes of Chinese financial institutions, while some prefer to buy a bigger stake of a small bank. Nevertheless, they all want to be in China. The best strategy, in theory, has turned out to be with a local partner. Bob Edgar, senior managing director at Australia and New Zealand Banking Group Ltd., said that "it would be very difficult to go into a market like that and undertake the cost of establishing a branch network, getting a customer base of hundreds of thousands if not millions of customers. That already exists, so why would we want to set it up again?"[50]

Many foreign banks, however, experience difficulties when working with a local partner. The credit standards are not as strict as they should be, and there is still endemic corruption at different levels. In addition, the partners gain influence in the foreign bank. This is the reason why HSBC has decided to invest "outside the Big Four": so it would have bigger control in operations. Peter Wong, executive director of HSBC's Hong Kong and Mainland China operations, has commented: "[T]he state-owned banks would be too big." So only the future will tell what is the best strategy.[51]

Recent Developments

One significant development in the bank sector in China was the IPO of Industrial and Commercial Bank of China. As expected, it was the world's biggest IPO. ICBS raised $19.1 billion, exceeding investors' predictions, valuing the bank at more than $108 billion. The previous IPO record was $18.4 billion and was held by NTT DoCoMo Inc., a Japanese mobile company.[52] The bank has announced that the money will be used to fund its expansion.

The competition in China's banking industry is continuing to grow. Recently, Morgan Stanley announced its expansion into China, given the company's desire to tap into the growing Chinese market and become competitive there. The company chief executive commented, "[T]his platform will allow us to provide a wider array of new product capabilities that are currently offered only by commercial banks with a presence within China."[53]

Another important development was the deal in which a consortium led by Citigroup took control over the Guangdong Development Bank (GDB). The agreement was reached on November 16, 2006, after a year of negotiations. Citigroup and its investors' partners have agreed to pay about $3.1 billon for 85.6 percent of Guangdong Development Bank.[54] The deal is significant since this is the first time that a foreign investor has been able to gain control in a Chinese bank. It is expected that Citigroup alone would purchase only 20 percent of Guangdong Development Bank; however, its partners would split the remaining 65.6 percent. The China Life Insurance Co. and State Grid Corporation each own 20 percent, followed by Citic Trust & Investment Co. with 12.9 percent and Yangpu Puhua Investment and Development Co. with 8 percent. Interestingly, IBM also has a stake at GDB, owning 4.74 percent of Guangdong Development Bank.

Another issue that makes the deal special is the fact that in January 2007, China opened its financial sector to foreign investors, which was one of its last WTO membership commitments. Under the new rules, foreign banks in China finally have the opportunity to offer services in the local currency—yuan—which was previously prohibited.[55] In a statement issued after the deal was announced, William R. Rhodes, the chairman and chief executive of Citibank, said, "The continued emergence of China's economy represents a tremendous opportunity for Citigroup."[56]

Although Citigroup has gained more market opportunities since the deal was approved, analysts say that there are certain risks involved. It is publicly known that the Guangdong Development Bank has been struggling financially, and there is speculation about the amount of bad loans that have not been put on the books. Bad loans have been an issue for the Chinese banks. However, it seems that the experience in banking and asset management that Citigroup possesses, in addition to the IT support offered by IBM, would make this investment beneficial to Guangdong Development Bank and could turn the bank around.[57] In June 2007, the Guangdong

Development Bank issued an outline of its five-year plan. The bank aims to reach the average levels of its Chinese bank peers for all major operational indicators in the next two to three years and become a leader among midsized Chinese banks within three to five years.[58]

Other recent developments include the Ping An and China Life Insurance initial public offerings in China. Ping An raised 38.9 billion yuan ($5 billion) with its February 2007 IPO and plans to use those funds to finance operations. In January 2007, its main competitor, China Life Insurance Co., was also listed on the Shanghai Stock Exchange, making an IPO of $3.6 billion.

On September 11, 2006, HSBC opened a new sub-branch in Beijing. With the opening of its fourth branch in Beijing, HSBC became the foreign bank with the most branches in Beijing. Richard Yorke, chief executive officer China at the Hongkong and Shanghai Banking Corporation Limited, commented: "[We] are delighted to be able to further expand our service network in Beijing. It is part of our overall network expansion in China where HSBC has a long-term commitment. Beijing is a key retail market for HSBC in the Mainland and we shall provide diversified products to meet our customers' growing needs for world-class banking services."[59] As of 2012, HSBC's network in mainland China has roughly 120 outlets with a branch network across 35 different cities. It has the largest number of outlets of any foreign bank in mainland China.

In addition, HSBC continues to invest in fast-growing emerging markets, including Asia, Latin America, and the Middle East. Malaysia is one country where HSBC's expansion is quite noticeable. It operated 40 branches there as of June 2010.[60] HSBC also has plans to extend its insurance business to other countries.[61]

HSBC Plans to Expand in Vietnam, Laos, and Cambodia

In the beginning of 2009 HSBC Holdings PLC announced plans to increase its branches in Vietnam and to set up operations in Laos and Cambodia. HSBC's moves were part of its broader expansion in developing Asian markets. Solid financial results from this region have helped outweigh losses at the bank's U.S. business. "It's something that we keep an eye on. We visit there [Laos and Cambodia] regularly, and we're in close contact with the customers and the regulators. We see tremendous potential in both those countries. So for sure, within the next five years, we'll keep an eye on it," said HSBC Vietnam President and Chief Executive Thomas Tobin.[62]

In March 2008, HSBC won approval from the Vietnamese government to become the first foreign bank to set up a locally incorporated entity. New laws that have helped open Vietnam's banking sector to foreign companies were introduced as part of the communist country's inclusion in the World Trade Organization. The change in legal status in Vietnam has made it easier for HSBC's local operations to set up branches across the country. That year, HSBC hired more than 400 additional staff in Vietnam in anticipation of its expansion. This has brought the number of staff numbers there to more than 1,000. In Vietnam, HSBC also owns 10 percent of Bao Viet Holdings, an insurance company, and 20 percent of Vietnam Technological & Commercial Joint Stock Bank, or Techcombank.[63]

Future Competitive Conditions

Despite the economic crisis, there were several geographical regions that did not fall into economic recession in

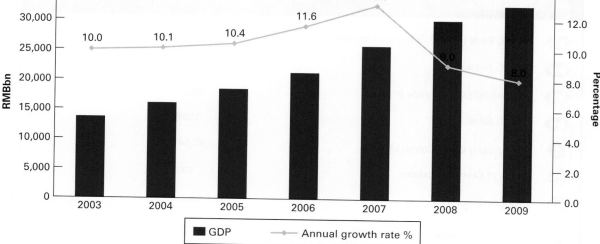

China: continued growth

Note: The Chinese government targets GDP growth for 2009 at about 8%

Source: HSBC, "China Strategy," May 26, 2009.

the 2008–2010 period. China, foremost, experienced strong economic growth throughout this period.

China's gross domestic product expanded 10.7 percent in the fourth quarter of 2009, bringing full-year growth to 8.7 percent. That came in above the government's targeted 8 percent growth and well above many economists' estimates. China officially surpassed Japan as the world's second-largest economy in mid 2010. The growth numbers demonstrate that Beijing's stimulus program—a response to the global economic slowdown that focused on massive bank lending and public investments in infrastructure—helped

avert an economic slowdown. But now that China is growing so rapidly, in part thanks to a real-estate boom fueled by government lending, some economists warned that it was time for Beijing to adjust its policies to better manage growth.[64]

China has the highest foreign direct investment (FDI) in Asia; however, as of 2010, FDI was beginning to slow. China had long been preferred as an attractive FDI destination due to its low labor costs and land rental fees. But such advantages are now diminishing and the nation is facing stiff competition from other Asian nations like Vietnam and India. In 2009, China's FDI decreased by 2.6 percent to

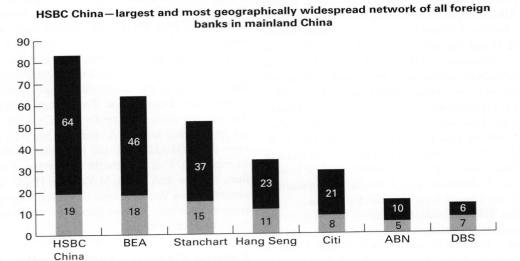

Locally incorporated foreign banks by network

HSBC China—largest and most geographically widespread network of all foreign banks in mainland China

■ Sub-branches   ▨ Branches

Note: As of end-April 2009 (excluding representative offices, administrative offices, etc.)

HSBC's investments in China

HSBC in China (US$m)	% Ownership	Outlets
HSBC Bank (China) Company Limited	100%	83
HSBC Jintrust	49.0%	1
Beijing HSBC Insurance Broker	24.9%	1
HSBC Rural Bank	100%	5
Hang Seng Bank (China) Limited	62.14%	34
Bank of Communications	19%	2,600+
Ping An Insurance	16.8%	356,000 agents
Bank of Shanghai	8.0%	200+
Industrial Bank	12.78% (via Hang Seng Bank)	400+

Source: HSBC, "China Strategy," May 26, 2009.

PwC Report 2008—Foreign banks in China

	First		Second	Third
Corporate lending	HSBC	→	Standard Chartered	Citibank
Retail banking	HSBC	→	Citibank	Standard Chartered
Private wealth management*	HSBC		UBS	Citibank
Foreign exchange and Treasury	HSBC	↗	Citibank	Standard Chartered
Trade finance	HSBC	→	Standard Chartered	Citibank
Credit cards	HSBC	↗	Citibank	Standard Chartered
Brand awareness*	HSBC		Citibank	Standard Chartered
	First		**Second**	**Third**
Derivatives	Citibank		HSBC →	Deutsche Bank
Corporate finance	Goldman Sachs		HSBC ↗	Standard Chartered
Cash management*	Citibank		HSBC	Standard Chartered
Debt capital markets*	Citibank		HSBC	Deutsche Bank
	First		**Second**	**Third**
Project financing	Citibank		Standard Chartered	HSBC ↘
Asset management	JPMorgan Chase		Fortis	HSBC ↘
	First		**Second**	**Third**
Mergers and acquisitions	Goldman Sachs		Morgan Stanley	UBS
Equity capital markets	Goldman Sachs		Morgan Stanley	UBS
Investment banking	Goldman Sachs		Morgan Stanley	UBS

*New category in 2008

Source: HSBC, "China Strategy," May 26, 2009.

$90.03 billion.[65] In response, the government relaxed rules to lure investors amid a sustained economic expansion. As a result, total FDI for the first four months of 2010 was $30.8 billion, up 11.3 percent from a year earlier.[66]

HSBC's future development will depend heavily on two things. First, the competition will play a major role in HSBC's strategy. HSBC competitors are aggressively seeking opportunities in China, and HSBC has to constantly work to maintain and expand its market position. Second, HSBC's success will depend on the opportunities that the company sees in the other emerging markets of the world.

HSBC Current China Strategy

HSBC's strategy in China is carried out by its 100 percent subsidiary HSBC Bank (China) Company Limited. As of April of 2009 HSBC Bank (China) was a network of 83 bank outlets (19 branches and 64 sub-branches) with 5,376 employees and registered capital of RMB 8 billion. At this time HSBC had the largest and most geographically widespread network of banks in mainland China compared to other foreign banks operating in China. Moody's has rated HSBC Bank (China) as A1 (long-term), which was the highest rating for a locally incorporated bank in China.[67]

Among the list of foreign banks in China, HSBC identifies itself as the largest and it provides a greater number of

bank services than other foreign banks (UBS, Citibank, Goldman Sachs Standard Chartered, JPMorgan Chase, etc.).

In its attempt to mitigate the negative impact of economic crisis and strengthen its competitive position, HSBC took several measures to redefine and clarify its strategies for the nearest future. In May 26, 2009, new China strategy was outlined by Richard Yorke, chief executive of HSBC Bank (China) Co. in London.[68] China was identified to be the center of the Group's emerging markets strategy.

Two elements of this strategy were:

1. *Organic growth*—organic business growth via own branch network.

2. *Strategic investments*—creating value and synergies from HSBC's investment in strategic partners.

The 2009 strategy focused on further expansion in Bohai Rim, Yangtze River, Pearl River Delta, and western regions.[69]

Later in July of 2009, HSBC opened a branch in Jinan, the capital of the eastern Shandong Province. It became the first foreign bank operating in that area. HSBC Bank (China) Co. confirmed its plans to further expand its presence in China's Bohai Rim region and said it is strengthening its network in inland cities. The Bohai Rim region, which includes Jinan, offers great potential and is one of its key areas for business development. HSBC has also obtained

Organic strategy—expand network

- 83 service outlets
- Regional focus: Bohai Rim, Yangtze River Delta, Pearl River Delta, and western region

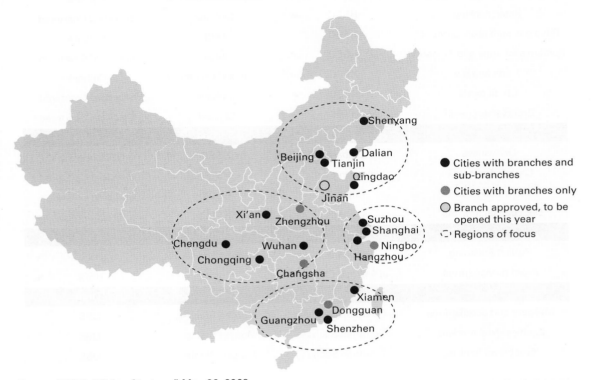

Source: HSBC, "China Strategy," May 26, 2009.

approval to establish a branch in Taiyuan, the capital of the northwest Shanxi Province.[70]

HSBC Group Strategy for 2010

HSBC continued to track its performance and global expansion in emerging markets compared to the developed markets. At the end of 2009, it conducted another assessment of its performance in various markets and noted that emerging markets, especially the Asian region, were taking the lead. Based on the first half of 2009, HSBC reported the following results:[71]

North America
- In the U.S. consumer finance run-off portfolio, loan impairment allowances declined in Q3 2009, first quarterly fall since start of 2006.
- Did not require any capital support from Group in Q3 2009.

Asia
- Continued to perform strongly.
- Lending growing as regional economies move out of recession.
- Loan impairment charges moderated in Q3 2009.

Latin America and Middle East
- Positive contribution; revenue held up well.
- In Latin America loan impairment charges declined in Q3 2009.

Europe
- In Middle East lending portfolios continued to reduce though loan impairment charges were higher than Q2 2009. Credit conditions remained difficult.
- UK mortgage lending continued to perform well, with our market share increasing to 9.9%.
- Overdraft utilization by our Commercial Banking customers remained stable at under 50%.

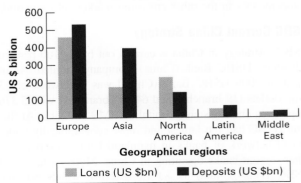

HSBC Loans vs. Deposits, by region (based on 1H09 results)

Source: HSBC, "Strategy Reconfirmed in a Period of Regulatory Change," December 2, 2009.

The key points of HSBC Group's current strategy are based on three world trends:

Group strategy
Aligned with key trends

> Developing markets are growing faster than mature economies

> World trade expanding at a greater rate than gross domestic product

> Life expectancy increasing around the world

> Combine emerging markets leadership with global network

> Build on international connectivity and scale

In a December 2, 2009 report, HSBC management identified the following three key opportunities in Asia region:[72]

1. Asia to contribute largest share of global GDP, surpassing EU and U.S. by 2016.

2. Asian consumers to become biggest incremental spenders, overtaking U.S. and European consumers by 2013.

3. Asian intra-regional trade growing significantly faster than world trade overall.

Presence
Largest foreign bank[1] in mainland China, Hong Kong, Indonesia, and Malaysia

▶ Footprint in Asia

- History in Asia spans nearly 150 years
- Presence in 22 countries and territories[2]
- Access to half of the world's population with combined GDP of US$21.3trn, the size of the combined GDP of the US, UK, Germany, and France[3]
- Nearly 1,000 branches and offices in the region
- Over 3 million internet banking customers in Asia, over half located in Hong Kong

Notes:
(1) In respect of branch network
(2) Includes a representative office in Nigeria
(3) CIA The World Factbook 2009: Population and GDP (purchasing power parity)

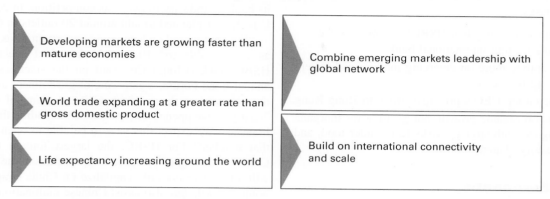

Japan, 1866
South Korea, 1897
Mainland China, 1865
Pakistan
Taiwan, 1884
Macau, 1972
Bangladesh, 1996
Hong Kong, 1865
Philippines, 1875
India, 1867
Thailand, 1870
Libya
Algeria   Egypt
Vietnam, 1870
Sri Lanka, 1892
Nigeria, 2009
Malaysia, 1884
Brunei, 1947
Maldives, 2002
Mauritius, 1894
Singapore, 1877
Indonesia, 1895
Australia, 1964
South Africa, 1995

● Middle East
● Asia

New Zealand, 1987

Source: HSBC, "Strategy Reconfirmed in a Period of Regulatory Change," December 2, 2009.

HSBC management has re-affirmed that the core of its strategy for 2010 will be to continue positioning the Group for long-term growth and attractive returns. Within this framework, HSBC management outlined the following four tasks:[73]

1. Continue to strengthen HSBC's position as the world's leading international bank.
2. Concentrate more on emerging markets and faster growing businesses.
3. Move Group CEO's principal office to Hong Kong.
4. Focus on organic growth, but position for inorganic if aligned with strategy, risks fully understood, and regulatory changes allow.

2010 Forecasts

HSBC's Global Asset Management division issued a statement in January 2010 saying that emerging markets will sustain high momentum to lead the global recovery in 2010, particularly countries with favorable demographics and solid fundamentals, like China and India. The bank's optimism toward emerging markets was in stark contrast with its conservative viewpoint toward developed economies.[74]

"We expect that global economic growth is likely to be moderate in 2010, hindered by unsolved structural problems, particularly in developed markets with personal wealth and balance sheets to be rebuilt," said Leon Goldfeld, chief investment officer of HSBC Global Asset Management (Hong Kong) in a press conference on its 2010 investment outlook on January 11, 2010. As governments were expected to begin winding down their stimulus programs by the second half of the year, Goldfeld said unless consumption and business investment picked up, the momentum of global growth will slow down in the latter part of this year.[75]

Goldfeld said the collapse over the past 18 months brought the level of economic activity to a very low base, which provides an easy comparison when the economy springs back. "Our concern is that due to the structural constraints of excessive household debt as well as the conservative stances by banks in terms of new lending, the private sector will struggle to deliver sufficient growth," said Goldfeld.[76] Goldfeld also predicted that official interest rates across the world would be tightened very gradually from the middle of the year, noting that bonds should provide a good opportunity against cash. Emerging markets, on the other hand, are in a better position, with more to sustain their growth story and outperform developed markets.[77]

2010 China Strategy in Motion

In April of 2010 HSBC Holdings PLC re-affirmed that it is capitalizing on China's fast-growing economy and a government-led campaign aimed at expanding rural

financial services to ramp up its business in the country. HSBC reported that it now has 99 outlets across 23 cities in mainland China, a sharp increase from fewer than 30 in mid-2006, a year before China fully opened its banking industry to overseas competition. In 2010, the U.K. lender planned to add around 20 outlets in China.[78]

"We are focused on leveraging opportunities as quickly as we are able to," Richard Yorke, chief executive of HSBC Bank (China) Co., said on the sidelines of the annual Boao Forum, a gathering of government and business leaders on the southern Chinese island of Hainan. "Last year we opened 19 new outlets, including three new branches. We expect this year to be able to open at least that number." For HSBC, the largest foreign bank in China, extending its presence to more cities in the country will allow it to not only capitalize on China's rapid economic growth, but also assist Chinese multinational companies looking to expand overseas, Mr. Yorke said.[79]

In addition, HSBC has been strengthening its presence in China's rural areas, targeting the two-thirds of the nation's 1.3 billion population, who lack easy access to funding sources. Providing financial services to people who don't live in China's large cities has become a concern for Beijing's leadership in recent years, as China's rural population continues to miss out on the strong economic growth and rising living standards in the country's urban areas.[80]

The bank announced it had set up seven standalone rural-banking branches in China since August 2007, and hoped to maintain the growth rate to expand HSBC's rural-banking business in the coming years. "The rural banking sector is under-banked, so we are seeing strong demand for the right product and for the right services. There is strong untapped demand in that market," said HSBC Bank (China) CEO Yorke. HSBC's oldest rural bank is just over two years old, he said, adding that the rural outlets will likely start breaking even at the three-year mark.[81]

The bank is also working toward being one of mainland China's first foreign-listed companies to tap into the country's liquidity and to raise its overall profile there. In addition, HSBC is seeking regulatory approval to set up a credit-card joint venture with Bank of Communications and is seeking licenses to access China's securities business. Foreign banks have been allowed to issue credit cards in China since 2004 in conjunction with their local partners. Since then HSBC and Bank of Communications have issued over 20 million co-branded credit cards in China.[82]

HSBC's China experience has been one of steady and consistent expansion and success. While there have been some setbacks, its overall approach, emphasizing close collaboration with the Chinese government and local partners, reliance on local staff and talent, and its overall shift in global strategy from developed to emerging markets, has served it well.

Questions for Review

1. How has HSBC adapted its global strategy to operate in China, both before and after China's WTO accession?

2. Discuss HSBC's strategy for entering and operating in other emerging markets. Where has it found success, and where has it faced setbacks? Why?

3. What are the pros and cons of HSBC's "Managing for Growth" strategy?

4. How did HSBC withstand the world economic crisis? Was HSBC's position weakened or strengthened as result of the crisis? What were the results of HSBC group strategy in 2009? What regions were identified as new global opportunities?

5. What is the core of HSBC's current "Organic Growth Strategy" in China? Why did HSBC decide to expand its financial services in China's rural areas? What are the pros and cons of the rural expansion?

Exercise

HSBC is considering asking the government of China (China Banking Regulatory Commission—CBRC) to allow it to increase its stake in BoCom above the limit currently in place (25% total foreign ownership; 20% for an individual foreign investor). Break into four groups:

1. HSBC
2. BoCom
3. Citibank
4. CBRC

Groups 1–3 should prepare a 5-minute presentation on whether the government of China should grant the request and, if so, what the ownership limit should be (30%? 50%?) and whether it should be extended to other foreign financial institutions (e.g., Citibank). Then, Group 4 should discuss the question and report its decision.

Source: This case was prepared by Jonathan Doh of Villanova University as the basis for class discussion. Research assistance was provided by Courtney Asher, Elizabeth Stewart, Tetyana Azarova, and Benjamin Littell.

Chiquita's Global Turnaround

On January 12, 2004, Chiquita named Fernando Aguirre as the company's new president and CEO, replacing Cyrus Freidhem, who had held the position since the company's emergence from bankruptcy in March 2002. In his 23 years with Cincinnati-based Procter & Gamble (P&G), Aguirre served in a variety of positions, including president of P&G Brazil and president of P&G Mexico. In his first remarks to Chiquita employees and investors, Aguirre reiterated the importance of corporate responsibility: "In terms of managing businesses and people, while I am profit-conscious, I make decisions first and foremost based on values and principles. In that respect, I'm proud to be joining a company with Core Values that guide day-to-day operations and one where corporate responsibility is an important part of our company culture."[1]

Over the past several years, social responsibility has become the watchword of this traditional company with midwestern roots but a checkered history. In 2004, Chiquita scarcely resembled the company that once held a reputation as cold, uncaring, and indifferent, frustrated with mediocre returns, a lack of innovation, and a demoralized workforce. Throughout the 20th century, hostile relationships with its labor unions and employees and a reputation for immorality solidified by the actions of its predecessor company, United Fruit, helped to slow Chiquita's growth. In addition, by the late 1990s, consumption of bananas had declined in major markets, and Chiquita's position in Europe had been compromised by the European Union's preferential import relationships with its members' former colonies in the Caribbean, Africa, and the Pacific. These factors helped push Chiquita to seek Chapter 11 bankruptcy protection in November 2001.

Through a serious and dedicated internal analysis, a thorough reevaluation of its core mission and business principles, and a concerted effort to reach out to some of its primary stakeholders—such as employees—who had become disenchanted and alienated, by early 2003, Chiquita had engineered the beginnings of a turnaround. One of the most impressive aspects of this recovery was Chiquita's success in redirecting and redefining its reputation through a more open and transparent approach to its global operations and to the various stakeholder groups with which it interacted. In addition, Chiquita had substantially reformed its labor practices and relations and initiated a set of projects in sustainable development and community action in its various locations around the world. Both labor unions and nongovernmental organizations (NGOs) lauded these steps.

Yet despite Chiquita's apparent turnaround, lingering problems remained in financial performance, organizational efficiency, and a strategy for the future. How could Chiquita sustain the positive momentum from its turnaround in reputation and employee relations to deliver improved and sustainable business performance in a global industry environment plagued by low margins and intense competition?

Chiquita's Background

Chiquita Brands International Inc. is a multinational producer, distributor, and marketer of bananas and other fresh produce. The company also distributes and markets fresh-cut fruit and other branded, value-added fruit products. Approximately 60 percent of its 2003 revenues of $2.6 billion came from bananas.[2] Since adding new products and acquiring Fresh Express, the U.S. market leader in fresh salads, in 2005, bananas totaled 43 percent of Chiquita's net sales.[3] In 2003, the banana division consisted of 19,000 employees, mainly working on more than 100 banana farms in countries throughout Latin America, including Guatemala, Honduras, Nicaragua, Ecuador, Costa Rica, Panama, and Colombia. Approximately 45 percent of all bananas sold by Chiquita are from Chiquita-owned farms; independent suppliers in Latin America produce the remainder. Chiquita is one of the global market leaders in banana supply and production (see Table 1). Since Chiquita's exports are often a substantial part of the foreign trade of the Latin American countries in which the company operates, relationships with suppliers, workers' unions, and communities are critical elements for success.

Chiquita sources bananas from many developing Latin American countries, countries that historically have struggled with poverty, literacy, access to affordable health care, and limited infrastructure. The image of the banana industry has long been tarnished by its historical support of the failed U.S. invasion of Cuba in 1961, child labor, unsafe

Table 1 Banana World Market Share Leaders, 1999, 2002, and 2005

	2005	2002	1999
Chiquita	25%	23%	25%
Dole	25	25	25
Del Monte	15	16	15
Fyfess	8	8	8
Noboa	11	11	11

Source: Banana Link.

working conditions, sexual discrimination, low wages, and accusations of serious brutality against unionizing workers.[4] Chiquita's reputation was damaged by past events, notably those associated with its predecessor company, United Fruit. These included allegations of the company's participation in labor rights suppression in Colombia in the 1920s, the use of company ships in the U.S. government–backed overthrow of the Guatemalan government in 1954, and involvement in a bribery scandal in Honduras in 1975.[5] In the 1980s and 1990s, Chiquita clearly projected a defensive and protective culture, conveying a closed-door impression of its policies and practices.

Because bananas are produced all year long, local communities are closely tied together by the performance of farms. Many employees live in houses owned by the company, most of which are located on the farms themselves. In many areas, Chiquita provides electricity, potable water, medical facilities, and other basic services.[6] However, labor relations remained strained throughout the 1980s and 1990s.

Chiquita's Downward Spiral

Although Chiquita improved its environmental procedures throughout the 1990s, many human rights groups, including Banana Link and US/Labor Education in the Americas, organized an outspoken campaign against all banana companies to improve social conditions on their plantations. One morning in early 1998, executives at Chiquita were devastated to see their company splashed all over the newspapers after an undercover investigation into "dangerous and illegal business practices" throughout Chiquita's Latin American operations. This was a watershed moment for the company.

The Cincinnati Enquirer, a paper based in the same town as Chiquita's corporate headquarters, printed an exposé contending that Chiquita was guilty of "labor, human rights, environmental and political violations in Central America."[7] Although the newspaper was later forced to retract the series after it was discovered that a reporter had illegally penetrated Chiquita's voicemail system, the damage was done. Corporate image was further damaged when the firm emphasized the violation of its privacy instead of addressing the possible validity of the claims made. According to Jeff Zalla, current corporate responsibility officer at Chiquita,

the strategy backfired. "It left some people with an unsavory impression of our company," he said.[8]

Damaging media coverage and a renewed desire to evaluate its own ethics performance and gain support for a common set of values and standards for environmental and social performance served as catalysts for the institution of corporate social responsibility policies at Chiquita. After recognizing the need for a complete corporate makeover, Chiquita's then CEO, Steve Warshaw, declared his commitment to leading in the area of corporate responsibility and pledged that the company would do much more than just repair previous damage. Four years later, despite changes in the executive management group, Chiquita's corporate social responsibility programs were a positive example of leading responsibility change in today's multinational business environment.

In January 2001, Chiquita announced that it could no longer pay the interest on its $862 million debt. The fiercely competitive banana industry, downward trends in prices due to excess supply, EU restrictive trade quotas, poor labor-union relations, and the market view of bananas as a low-margin commodity all contributed to Chiquita's bankruptcy filing. Chiquita attributed much of the responsibility to the European Union. In 1993, the EU imposed quotas that gave preferential treatment to banana imports from ACP (Africa, Caribbean, and Pacific) countries that were former European colonies, ostensibly to help these former European colonies boost their international trade and commerce. Before the 1993 act, 70 percent of the bananas sold in Europe came from Latin America, and Chiquita had a 22 percent share of the world's banana market.[9] After the quotas were imposed, Chiquita claimed that its European market share was cut in half, costing $200 million a year in lost earnings.

Although many of its difficulties were intensified by the EU policy, Chiquita's problems had begun to develop before the 1993 decision. Most important, miscalculations of increases in European demand in the 1990s resulted in an oversupply, leading to depressed banana prices worldwide. Although prices recovered somewhat (see Table 2), CEO Keith Linder blamed $284 million in losses in 2001 on a "decline in product quality resulting from an extraordinary outbreak of disease and unusual weather patterns."[10]

Table 2 Banana Prices: Regional Year-over-Year Percentage Change, 2003 vs. 2002

Region	Q1, 03	Q2, 03	Q3, 03	Q4, 03	Year
North America	3%	24%	1%	22%	21%
European core markets—US$	11	12	5	18	12
European core markets—local currency	29	210	29	0	27
Central & E. Europe/Mediterranean—US$	4	23	4	2	22
Central & E. Europe/Mediterranean—local currency	215	222	210	214	219
Asia—US$	27	0	3	12	0
Asia—local currency	218	27	3	6	25

Source: Company reports.

Table 3   Key Developments in Chiquita's History

1899:   United Fruit Company is created through a merger of fruit companies.
1903:   The company is listed on the New York Stock Exchange; it builds refrigerated ships.
1918:   Thirteen banana ships are lost after being commissioned by Allied forces in World War I.
1941:   Allied forces in World War II commission company ships, and the banana industry nearly shuts down.
1945:   Twenty-seven ships and 275 men on company ships are lost serving Allied forces.
1950:   The company starts massive postwar banana-planting projects.
1961:   Company ships provide support for failed U.S. invasion of Cuba.
1964:   The company begins a large-scale branding program for produce and starts using banana stickers bearing the Chiquita name.
1970:   United Fruit merges with AMK Corp. and becomes United Brands Company.
1975:   United Brands is involved in Honduran bribery scandal, which leads to enactment of U.S. Foreign Corrupt Practices Act. Company stocks plunge, and CEO Eli Black commits suicide.
1990:   United Brands changes name to Chiquita Brands International.
1993:   EU banana regulations cut Chiquita's market share by more than 50 percent. Chiquita begins working with Rainforest Alliance and Better Banana Project.
1994:   Start of the "banana wars" between the EU and WTO. Follows complaints by Chiquita that EU favors Caribbean banana suppliers over Latin American importers.
1998:   Chiquita becomes largest U.S. private-label fruit canner. Becomes first large company to meet with COLSIBA, an affiliation of Latin American banana unions.
1999:   Faces possible auction proposed by large shareholder American Financial Group.
2000:   Adopts expanded code of conduct. All 115 Chiquita-owned farms achieve Better Banana certification.
2001:   Restructures debt after stopping payments on $862 million loan, cites prejudiced trade pacts by EU.
2001:   Files for Chapter 11 bankruptcy protection.
2001:   Issues first (2000) corporate responsibility report.
2002:   Chiquita shareholders and bondholders support reorganization plan.
2002:   Issues 2001 corporate responsibility report.
2003:   Chiquita reports positive net income under reorganized company.
2003:   SustainableBusiness.com names Chiquita one of the top 20 sustainable stock picks for the second year in a row.
2004:   Maintained market leadership in the growing EU.
2005:   Chiquita acquires Fresh Express, U.S. market leader in fresh salads.
2006:   Awarded the Contribution to the Community Award by the American–Costa Rican Chamber of Commerce for its Nature & Community Project in Costa Rica.
2007:   Chiquita faces a $25 million fine from the U.S. Department of Justice for payments made to Colombian paramilitary groups for the protection of its employees.

At the end of 2006, Chiquita still faced financial difficulties as a result of a "perfect storm" of higher tariffs, increased competition in the EU banana market, U.S. consumer concerns about the safety of fresh spinach (another Chiquita product), and higher industry costs overall. While the company expressed dissatisfaction with 2006 results, it also stated that "we firmly believe our 2006 results are not indicative of the underlying strengths of Chiquita's business or our long-term potential."[11] Table 3 provides a comprehensive summary of key developments in Chiquita's history.

Dispute over Access to European Banana Markets

Chiquita has long claimed that its recent struggles are a direct result of the 1993 EU decision to put restrictive quotas on imports from Latin American suppliers. Immediately after the decision by the EU in 1993 to extend preferential quotas to its former Caribbean and African colonies, Chiquita took the issue to the U.S. trade representative, suggesting violations of free trade. In 1994, a General Agreement on Tariffs and Trade (GATT) panel ruled that the new regime violates GATT obligations, but the EU blocked adoption of the ruling by the full GATT.

In 1996, the United States, along with Ecuador, Guatemala, Honduras, and Mexico, challenged the new regime under the new World Trade Organization (WTO) dispute-settlement mechanism, which came into force after the Uruguay Round of GATT negotiations.

In May 1997, a WTO panel ruled that the EU's banana import regime violated WTO obligations under the General Agreement on Trade in Services and the Agreement on Import Licensing Procedures. In September 1997, the WTO Appellate Body upheld the panel ruling, granting the EU 15 months, until January 1, 1999, to comply with the ruling. In January 1999, the deadline for EU compliance expired, and the United States sought WTO authorization to impose retaliatory tariffs. In April 1999, the WTO Dispute Settlement Body authorized U.S. retaliatory tariffs amounting to $191.4 million a year—the level of damage to U.S. companies calculated by arbitrators—and the United States immediately began steps to withhold liquidation of European imports, the first step in the imposition of the tariffs.[12]

In April 2001, the United States and the European Commission announced that they had reached agreement resolving their dispute. The agreement took effect on July 1, 2001, at which time the United States suspended the retaliatory sanctions imposed on EU imports in 1999. Import volumes of bananas were returned to levels comparable to those prior to 1993, and the EU committed to moving to a tariff-only system in 2006 as part of its overall WTO obligations.

The dispute has taken its toll on the banana trade by creating uncertainty for smaller producers reliant on EU markets under the quota system and for large producers such as Chiquita that were forced to expend considerable financial and other resources in the course of the dispute. High tariffs in the EU continue to be a financial burden for Chiquita.

Corporate Responsibility

Chiquita had begun to initiate corporate responsibility projects in 1992 when it adopted Better Banana Project standards designed to improve environmental and worker conditions on its farms. Then after the 1998 exposé in the Cincinnati Enquirer, Chiquita management began to conduct a series of broader companywide reviews of its conduct, policies, and internal and external operations and relationships, all designed to integrate corporate responsibility throughout the company's operations.

In 1998, Chiquita initiated several projects aimed at implementing its corporate responsibility efforts worldwide. Two internal groups were formed: the Senior Management Group and the Corporate Responsibility Steering Committee. The former consists of eight top managers of Chiquita's global businesses, including the president/CEO and COO of banana operations. The Senior Management Group is ultimately responsible for providing strategic vision and leadership for corporate responsibility. The Steering Committee, also consisting of eight members, was constructed to help streamline corporate social responsibility policies throughout each operational area of the firm.

In August 1999, Chiquita adopted the four key values that now guide all strategic business decision making worldwide. After a year of discussions, interviews, and debates on the merits of an internal corporate social responsibility policy, Chiquita defined the following four core values:

> *Integrity:* We live by our Core Values. We communicate in an open, honest and straightforward manner. We conduct our business ethically and lawfully.
> *Respect:* We treat people fairly and respectfully. We recognize the importance of family in the lives of our employees. We value and benefit from individual and cultural differences. We foster individual expression, open dialogue and a sense of belonging.
> *Opportunity:* We believe the continuous growth and development of our employees is key to our success. We encourage teamwork. We recognize employees for their contributions to the company's success.
> *Responsibility:* We take pride in our work, in our products and in satisfying our customers. We act responsibly in the communities and environments in which we live and work.

> We are accountable for the careful use of all resources entrusted to us and for providing appropriate returns to our shareholders.[13]

In support of the four core values, Chiquita undertook reforms to link its corporate governance and corporate responsibility policies. These reforms included expanding the role of the board's Audit Committee to oversee the firm's corporate responsibility (CR) mission and to evaluate whether the firm had the right people, policies, and programs in place to properly advance the CR agenda.[14] In addition, in May 2000, Chiquita appointed a full-time vice president and CR officer responsible for all aspects of corporate social responsibility. According to Chiquita, the four core values, supported by the senior management group and CR committee, have helped drive responsible change throughout the entire organization. Each business decision must be evaluated through the lens of CR policies.

Chiquita also began to realize that a corporate social responsibility platform could mean a competitive advantage in the banana market. Dennis Christou, vice president of marketing–Europe, explained: "Bananas are, by definition, a commodity and U.K. consumers do not generally see fruit as branded. Chiquita is trying to change this. We have a brand because we own certain values and a relationship with consumers. And we communicate with them. They have expectations about Chiquita."[15] In particular, environmental and social performance is of keen interest to some leading European customers. In 2002, 56 percent of Chiquita's sales in northern European markets were to customers who had either inspected farms or formally asked questions about environmental and social performance. This was a 5 percent increase—about 13,000 forty-pound boxes per week—over the prior year.

Chiquita also strengthened its commitment to the Better Bananas Project. Under this program, external auditors audit all Chiquita farms annually. Chiquita has made an important partnership with Rainforest Alliance, which has been integral in assessing Chiquita's environmental practices, especially related to deforestation. The Rainforest Alliance, which claims that the world's rainforests are being deforested at a rate of 1 percent per year (or two U.S. football fields every second),[16] has annually accredited every Chiquita farm since 2000. Chiquita also encourages its independent producers, which supply Chiquita with about 50 percent of its bananas, to achieve Rainforest Alliance certification. In 2002, the volume of bananas purchased from certified farms rose from 33 to 46 percent, and farms certified through June 2003 brought the total to 65 percent. As of August 2006, all of the farms owned by the Chiquita Company are certified by the Rainforest Alliance. Along with all of Chiquita's farms, the Rainforest Alliance has also certified the majority of the independent farms connected to Chiquita. TreeHugger.com also contends that "Chiquita now recycles 100 percent of its plastic bags into paving stones and has reduced pesticide

Table 4 Better Banana Project Principles

1. **Ecosystem Conservation.** Protect existing ecosystems; recovery of damaged ecosystems in plantation area.

2. **Wildlife Conservation.** Protect biodiversity, especially endangered species.

3. **Fair Treatment and Good Conditions for Workers.** Comply with local and international labor laws/norms; maintain policy of nondiscrimination; support freedom of association.

4. **Community Relations.** Be a "good neighbor," contributing to the social and economic development of local communities.

5. **Integrated Pest Management.** Reduction in use of pesticides; training for workers in pesticide use/management/risks.

6. **Integrated Waste Management.** Reduction of the production of wastes that contaminate the environment and harm human health; institute recycling.

7. **Conservation of Water Resources.** Reduce and reuse the water used in production; establish buffer zones of vegetation around waterways; protect water from contamination.

8. **Soil Conservation.** Control erosion; promote soil conservation and replenishment.

9. **Planning and Monitoring.** Plan and monitor banana cultivation activities according to environmental, social, and economic measures.

Source: Adapted from Rainforest Alliance, *Normas Generales Para la Certificación del Cultivo de Banano,* May 2002, www.rainforest-alliance.org/programs/cap/socios/banana-s.pdf.

use by 26 percent".[17] Table 4 presents the nine principles of the Better Banana Project. According to insiders, the adoption of third-party standards has helped Chiquita drive a stronger internal commitment to achieving excellence[18]—and to cut costs. In 2003, the Rainforest Alliance estimated that Chiquita reduced production spending by $100 million as a result of a $20 million investment to reduce agrochemical use.[19] In a more recent effort to increase its corporate responsibility profile, Chiquita Bananas pledged to boycott oil from Canada's tar sands in November 2011.[20]

Chiquita is receiving increasing recognition for its efforts. In 2005, SustainableBusiness.com, publisher of The Progressive Investor newsletter, named Chiquita to its list of the world's top 20 sustainable stock picks, known as the SB20, for the fourth year in a row. SustainableBusiness.com identifies its picks by asking leading investment advisers to recommend companies that stand out as world leaders in both sustainability and financial strength. In April 2004, the Trust for the Americas, a division of the Organization of Americas, selected Chiquita Brands as the winner of the 2004 Corporate Citizen of the Americas Award for Chiquita's Nuevo San Juan Home-Ownership Project in Honduras.[21] Also in 2004, Chiquita earned the Ethic Award from the AGEPE Editorial Group and KPMG

in Italy for its initiatives in the field of ethics, environmental protection, and workplace improvements.[22]

One recent setback for Chiquita's corporate responsibility profile involved its banana-producing subsidiary in Colombia. After a 2003 probe into the company's finances, Chiquita self-reported to the U.S. Department of Justice (DOJ) that it had made payments to left- and right-wing paramilitary groups in Colombia such as the AUC, ELN, and FARC. These payments, beginning in 1997, were made in order to protect the lives of its employees. Colombia has one of the highest kidnapping rates in the world and a murder rate 11 times that of the United States.[23] "It's certainly a common understanding that in order to do business in Colombia, payments have to be made for at best security, or at worst extortion," explained Ron Oswald, general secretary of the International Union of Foodworkers, which represents Chiquita workers in Latin America (including many in Colombia).[24]

The U.S. 1996 Anti-Terrorism Act makes it illegal to support any organizations identified as a terrorist threat. As of September 2001, the list of terrorist threats included the Colombian paramilitary groups. In a company press release, Chiquita chairman and CEO, Fernando Aguirre, explained, "The payments . . . were always motivated by our good faith concern for the safety of our employees. Nevertheless, we recognized—and acted upon—our legal obligation to inform the DOJ of this admittedly difficult situation."[25] Officially announced in 2007, Chiquita faced a $25 million fine for the payments it made in Colombia. In anticipation of the decision, the company set aside funds in 2006 to pay the fine. Chiquita does not believe the fines will hurt its operations.[26] Perhaps as a result of the pending DOJ investigation and decision, Chiquita sold its Colombian subsidiary in 2004.

Global Codes of Conduct, Standards, and Labor Practices

In late 2001, Ron Oswald, general secretary of the International Union of Food Workers, was asked if he had seen improvements in Chiquita's internal and external corporate policies. He responded, "Yes. It is a company that is totally unrecognizable from five years ago."[27] Clearly Chiquita had come a long way.

Traditionally, relations between Chiquita and labor unions in Latin America were mired in conflict and mistrust. In 1998, after recognizing the need for change in the way it deals with its line, Chiquita began striving to adhere to SA8000, the widely accepted international labor rights standard. Management struggled with the decision of whether to adopt an outside standard or to develop an internal measurement gauge for corporate responsibility. After much deliberation, management concluded that adopting the SA8000 standard would yield the most credibility with external stakeholders, because SA8000 gives detailed requirements for adequacy of management systems for implementation. Having an external standard forces Chiquita to push CR change down through each organizational level so that the firm is able to meet third-party requirements.

In May 2000 Chiquita expanded its code of conduct to include SA8000. Standards now included areas such as food safety, labor standards, employee health and safety, environmental protection, and legal compliance.[28] Recognizing the importance of labor support and its resounding effect on corporate image, Chiquita began an open dialogue with the International Union of Food Workers and the Coalition of Latin American Banana Workers' Unions (COLSIBA). By June 2001, the firm had reached an agreement with both organizations, pledging to respect worker rights as elaborated in ILO conventions, address long-standing health and safety concerns for workers, and ensure that its independent suppliers did likewise. This made Chiquita the first multinational corporation in the agricultural sector to sign a worker rights agreement.[29] Management credits this agreement as having helped to build a positive image, improving relations with both internal and external stakeholders. In mid-2001, Chiquita published its first corporate responsibility report detailing the firm's future CR strategies and goals. Both stakeholders and media outlets have been impressed with the complete turnaround in the transparency of Chiquita's corporate agenda, which has led to a much more favorable impression of the company.

In order to adhere to the organization's own core values and to the SA8000 labor standard, Chiquita routinely performs internal audits in all of its Latin American operations. NGOs also conduct external audits. After the audits are completed, each local management team plans corrective actions using the firm's code of conduct and core values as decision-making guides. At year-end 2003, independent auditors certified Chiquita's operations in Costa Rica, Colombia, and Panama to the SA8000 standard. Chiquita's operations were the first ever to earn SA8000 certification in each of these countries. In its 2006 corporate responsibility report, Chiquita announced that it has maintained 100 percent certification of its banana farms in Latin America in accordance with the Rainforest Alliance, Social Accountability 8000, and EurepGAP standards (environmental, labor, and human rights and food safety standards, respectively).

Marketing the Message

Although it would seem advantageous for Chiquita to communicate and leverage the great strides it has made through its corporate responsibility effort, management seems reluctant to promote its achievements through the typical mass communication vehicles. Indeed, when Chiquita attempted to advertise its certification process with commercials in Denmark that equated its Central American banana farms with a "glorious rainforest," the ads were met with skepticism and thought to be unrealistic.[30]

Instead of mass advertising, the firm has opted for a longer-term marketing strategy based on educating leading opinion makers and critics alike. According to Dennis Christou, vice president of marketing–Europe, there is a natural suspicion among consumers about commercially driven messages. He believes that customers feel more trust in the message if it's delivered by an external body rather than by the company or by a paid advocate of the business.[31] That is a main reason why the firm is relying on viral marketing tactics and third-party testimonials as the means of spreading its message. Retailers are treated differently: They must be exposed to improvements at Chiquita because they determine which exclusive brand to carry on an annual basis. However, Christou believes that creating brand recognition with consumers is possible through nonobtrusive, reputable means.

Defining and conveying a brand's differences in a commodities marketplace is difficult. Nevertheless, Chiquita believes it can carve out its own niche by distinguishing itself as a leader in corporate responsibility. Instead of positioning itself solely on the basis of price, Chiquita is hoping that its distinctive competency in CR will help it stand out from the pack. The company got a boost in this regard in April 2003, when Chiquita, along with Ben and Jerry's, received the first Award for Outstanding Sustainability Reporting presented by the Coalition for Environmentally Responsible Economies (CERES) and the Association of Chartered Certified Accountants.[32] In 2006, Chiquita won Costa Rica's Contribution to the Community Award for its Nature and Community Project, which preserves biodiversity and promotes nature conservation awareness.[33]

Recent Performance and Future Path

Chiquita has drastically shifted its strategic decision-making models and broader corporate operating principles. During its reorganization, debt repayments and other reorganization costs resulted in significant losses. Chiquita made great strides in improving its financial performance by cutting costs and streamlining its local and global operations. In 2003, the year after it filed for bankruptcy, Chiquita's net sales were $2.6 billion, up from $1.6 billion the year before. In 2006, net sales reached a record $4.5 billion (due in part to the acquisition of Fresh Express). Since its emergence from bankruptcy in early 2002, Chiquita has been profitable (see Tables 5 and 6).

After a minor setback due to the global recession, in 2011 the Chiquita Company celebrated its fourth consecutive year of increasing profitability. Chairman and CEO Fernando Aguirre stated that Chiquita "had a much better year in bananas driven by higher pricing and volume in North America, and initial recovery in Europe. Our salads business did not perform as well as expected

Table 5 **Chiquita Brands Balance Sheet as of December 31, 2005, 2003, 2002, 2001, 2000 (in thousands)**

	2005	2003	2002	2001	2000
Assets					
Cash and equivalents	89,020	—	—	—	26,715
Other current assets	31,388	951	810	732	42,375
Total current assets	900,075	951	810	732	69,090
Investments in and accounts with subsidiaries	—	1,035,915	908,404	1,424,961	1,399,708
Other assets	165,558	5,607	5,429	15,328	29,872
Total assets	2,833,099	1,042,473	914,643	1,441,021	1,498,625
Liabilities and Shareholders' Equity					
Accounts payable and accrued liabilities	569,648	17,182	16,541	10,735	86,930
Total current liabilities	600,857	17,182	16,451	10,735	125,833
Long-term debt	475,000	250,000	250,000	—	772,380
Total liabilities	1,839,598	285,127	285,354	992,427	916,082
Shareholders' equity	993,501	757,346	629,289	448,594	582,543
Total liabilities and shareholders' equity	2,833,099	1,042,473	914,643	1,441,021	1,498,625

Source: Company reports.

Table 6 **Chiquita Brands International Income Statement, 2001–2005 (in thousands)**

	Predecessor Company			Reorganized Company	
	Year Ended 12/31/2005	Year Ended 12/31/2003	9 Months Ended 12/31/2002	Three Months Ended 3/31/2002	Year Ended 12/31/2001
Net sales	3,904,361	—	—	—	—
Cost of sales	3,268,128	—	—	—	—
SG&A	(384,184)	(38,500)	(30,443)	(6,545)	(31,188)
Equity in earnings of subsidiaries (loss)		170,398	68,822	(368,899)	32,674
Operating income (loss)	187,633	131,898	38,379	(375,444)	1,486
Interest income	10,255	—	—	—	783
Interest expense	(60,294)	(27,392)	(20,384)	(1,250)	(81,633)
Financial restructuring items	—	—	—	124,394	(33,604)
Income before income taxes and accounting change	134,540	104,506	17,995	(252,300)	(112,968)
Income taxes	(3,100)	(5,300)	(4,800)	(1,000)	(5,800)
Income (loss) before accounting change		99,206	13,195	(253,300)	(118,768)
Cumulative effect of accounting change		—	—	(144,523)	—
Net income (loss)	134,440	99,206	13,195	(397,823)	(118,768)

Source: Company reports.

and we've taken a number of corrective actions and adapted our structure and strategy to be more successful and profitable." Moving forward, Aguirre stated that Chiquita is focused on growing revenues in their core businesses of bananas and salads. In order to grow their revenues, Chiquita is looking to enter new markets and offer a more diverse product selection.[34]

According to the 2011 full year results, Chiquita net sales for their banana division increased to US$2 billion (a 4 percent increase over 2010). Operating income for the banana division also increased US$51 million in 2011 as compared to 2010. Unlike the banana division, Chiquita's salads and healthy snacks division reflected a decrease in net sales of roughly 7 percent as compared to

2010. Chiquita attributed this decline to a combination of customer conversions to private label and growth in the food service and healthy snacks arena. Operating income also declined drastically from US$63 million in 2010 to US$8 million for 2011. Per Chiquita, this drop in operating income was due primarily to lower salad sales, inflation, and manufacturing disruptions.[35]

Chiquita's future financial stability depends, in part, on external market factors such as steady or rising international banana prices and consumer demand. Internally, the company's performance will result from the effectiveness of financial controls on the cost side, and successful marketing, emphasizing differentiation and value-added production, on the revenue side. Although Chiquita has gone to impressive lengths to turn around its reputation and performance, it continues to face a challenging and competitive international business environment and must make continuous progress in its management and operations in order to achieve a healthy and sustainable financial future.

Questions for Review

1. How would you characterize Chiquita's historical approach to global management?

2. Describe Chiquita's approach to human resource management in its global supply chain. What particular human resource challenges does Chiquita face as the purchaser, producer, and supplier of a commodity?

3. Does Chiquita's global corporate responsibility (CR) program create a conflict between shareholders and other stakeholders? Who are Chiquita's main stakeholders in the United States and around the world, and how are they affected by Chiquita's CR program?

4. How would you characterize Chiquita's past and present leadership? How does leadership affect a company's overall reputation?

5. Do you believe Chiquita would have changed its policies without the presence of damaging stories in the media? If not, what does this say about Chiquita's old management style?

6. What challenges does Chiquita's new CEO face in continuing to turn the company around and balance the interests of competing stakeholders?

Exercise

At its annual stakeholder/shareholder meeting, management, represented by Chiquita's CEO, is considering input from various groups about its strategic direction and continued reorganization. Your group represents one of the following interests:

1. Shareholders of the previous company who lost most of the value of the shares after the company declared bankruptcy.

2. Shareholders in the newly reorganized company.

3. Employees and union representatives of North American operations.

4. Employees and union representatives of South American operations.

5. Representatives of the nongovernmental organization Rainforest Action Network.

Spend five minutes preparing two or three requests to the management team about your group's interests and priorities for the company. Then conduct an open forum in which you discuss these requests among the different groups.

Source: © McGraw-Hill Irwin. This case was prepared by Professor Jonathan Doh and Research Associate Erik Holt of Villanova University as the basis for class discussion. Research assistance was provided by Courtney Asher and Benjamin Littell. We appreciate assistance from Sherrie Terry and Michael Mitchell of Chiquita International. Any errors remain those of the authors.

SKILL-BUILDING AND EXPERIENTIAL EXERCISES

- Personal Skill-Building Exercises
- In-Class Simulations (Available on the book website at www.mhhe.com/luthans9e)

1. The Culture Quiz

Objectives

- To stimulate awareness of cultural differences
- To promote consideration of the impact of cultural differences in a global economy
- To stimulate dialogue between domestic and international students
- To explore issues raised by culturally diverse workforces

Background

Few, if any, traditions and values are universally held. Many business dealings have succeeded or failed because of a manager's awareness or lack of understanding of the traditions and values of his/her foreign counterparts. With the world business community so closely intertwined and interdependent, it is critical that managers today become increasingly aware of the differences that exist.

How culturally aware are you? Try the questions below.

Instructions

Working alone or with a small group, answer the questions (without peeking at the answers). When you do look at the answers, be sure to read the explanations. If you are taking the quiz with students from countries other than your own, explore what the answer might be in your country and theirs.

1. In Japan, loudly slurping your soup is considered to be
   a. rude and obnoxious.
   b. a sign that you like the soup.
   c. okay at home but not in public.
   d. something only foreigners do.

2. In Korea, business leaders tend to
   a. encourage strong commitment to teamwork and cooperation.
   b. encourage competition among subordinates.
   c. discourage subordinates from reporting directly, preferring information to come through well-defined channels.
   d. encourage close relationships with their subordinates.

3. In Japan, virtually every kind of drink is sold in public vending machines except for
   a. beer.
   b. diet drinks with saccharine.
   c. already sweetened coffee.
   d. soft drinks from U.S. companies.

4. In Latin America, managers
   a. are most likely to hire members of their own families.
   b. consider hiring members of their own families to be inappropriate.
   c. stress the importance of hiring members of minority groups.
   d. usually hire more people than are actually needed to do a job.

5. In Ethiopia, when a woman opens the front door of her home, it means
   a. she is ready to receive guests for a meal.
   b. only family members may enter.
   c. religious spirits may move freely in and out of the home.
   d. she has agreed to have sex with any man who enters.

6. In Latin America, businesspeople
   a. consider it impolite to make eye contact while talking to one another.
   b. always wait until the other person is finished speaking before starting to speak.
   c. touch each other more than North Americans do under similar circumstances.
   d. avoid touching one another as it is considered an invasion of privacy.

7. The principal religion in Malaysia is
   a. Buddhism.
   b. Judaism.
   c. Christianity.
   d. Islam.

8. In Thailand
   a. it is common to see men walking along holding hands.
   b. it is common to see a man and a woman holding hands in public.
   c. it is rude for men and women to walk together.
   d. men and women traditionally kiss each other on meeting in the street.

9. When eating in India, it is appropriate to
   a. take food with your right hand and eat with your left.
   b. take food with your left hand and eat with your right.
   c. take food and eat it with your left hand.
   d. take food and eat it with your right hand.

10. Pointing your toes at someone in Thailand is
   a. a symbol of respect, much like the Japanese bow.
   b. considered rude even if it is done by accident.
   c. an invitation to dance.
   d. the standard public greeting.

11. American managers tend to base the performance appraisals of their subordinates on performance, while in Iran, managers are more likely to base their performance appraisals on
   a. religion.
   b. seniority.
   c. friendship.
   d. ability.

12. In China, the status of every business negotiation is
   a. reported daily in the press.
   b. private, and details are not discussed publicly.
   c. subjected to scrutiny by a public tribunal on a regular basis.
   d. directed by the elders of every commune.

13. When rewarding a Hispanic worker for a job well done, it is best not to
   a. praise him or her publicly.
   b. say "thank you."
   c. offer a raise.
   d. offer a promotion.

14. In some South American countries, it is considered normal and acceptable to show up for a social appointment
   a. ten to fifteen minutes early.
   b. ten to fifteen minutes late.
   c. fifteen minutes to an hour late.
   d. one to two hours late.

15. In France, when friends talk to one another
   a. they generally stand about three feet apart.
   b. it is typical to shout.
   c. they stand closer to one another than Americans do.
   d. it is always with a third party present.

16. When giving flowers as gifts in Western Europe, be careful not to give
   a. tulips and jonquils.
   b. daisies and lilacs.
   c. chrysanthemums and calla lilies.
   d. lilacs and apple blossoms.

17. The appropriate gift-giving protocol for a male executive doing business in Saudi Arabia is to
   a. give a man a gift from you to his wife.
   b. present gifts to the wife or wives in person.

   c. give gifts only to the eldest wife.
   d. not give a gift to the wife at all.

18. If you want to give a necktie or a scarf to a Latin American, it is best to avoid the color
   a. red.
   b. purple.
   c. green.
   d. black.

19. The doors in German offices and homes are generally kept
   a. wide open to symbolize an acceptance and welcome of friends and strangers.
   b. slightly ajar to suggest that people should knock before entering.
   c. half-opened, suggesting that some people are welcome and others are not.
   d. tightly shut to preserve privacy and personal space.

20. In the area that was formerly West Germany, leaders who display charisma are
   a. not among the most desired.
   b. the ones most respected and sought after.
   c. invited frequently to serve on boards of cultural organizations.
   d. pushed to get involved in political activities.

21. American managers running businesses in Mexico have found that by increasing the salaries of Mexican workers, they
   a. increased the number of hours the workers were willing to work.
   b. enticed more workers to work night shifts.
   c. decreased the number of hours workers would agree to work.
   d. decreased production rates.

22. Chinese culture teaches people
   a. to seek psychiatric help for personal problems.
   b. to avoid conflict and internalize personal problems.
   c. to deal with conflict with immediate confrontation.
   d. to seek help from authorities whenever conflict arises.

23. One wedding gift that should not be given to a Chinese couple would be
   a. a jade bowl.
   b. a clock.
   c. a basket of oranges.
   d. shifts embroidered with dragon patterns.

24. In Venezuela, New Year's Eve is generally spent

    a. in quiet family gatherings.

    b. at wild neighborhood street parties.

    c. in restaurants with horns, hats, and live music and dancing.

    d. at pig roasts on the beach.

25. If you order "bubble and squeak" in a London pub, you will get

    a. two goldfish fried in olive oil.

    b. a very cold beer in a chilled glass, rather than the usual warm beer.

    c. Alka Seltzer and a glass of water.

    d. chopped cabbage and mashed potatoes fried together.

26. When a stranger in India wants to know what you do for a living and how much you earn, he will

    a. ask your guide.

    b. invite you to his home and, after getting to know you, will ask.

    c. come over and ask you directly, without introduction.

    d. respect your privacy above all.

27. When you feel you are being taken advantage of in a business exchange in Vietnam, it is important to

    a. let the anger show in your face but not in your words.

    b. say that you are angry, but keep your facial expression neutral.

    c. not show any anger in any way.

    d. end the business dealings immediately, and walk away.

28. When a taxi driver in India shakes his head from side to side, it probably means

    a. he thinks your price is too high.

    b. he isn't going in your direction.

    c. he will take you where you want to go.

    d. he doesn't understand what you're asking.

29. In England, holding your index and middle fingers up in a V with the back of your hand facing another person is seen as

    a. a gesture of peace.

    b. a gesture of victory.

    c. a signal that you want two of something.

    d. a vulgar gesture.

Answers to the Culture Quiz

1. *b.* Slurping your soup or noodles in Japan is good manners in both public and private. It indicates enjoyment and appreciation of the quality. (Source: Eiji Kanno and Constance O'Keefe, *New Japan Solo,* Japan National Tourist Organization: Tokyo, 1990, p. 20.)

2. *b.* Korean managers use a "divide-and-rule" method of leadership that encourages competition among subordinates. They do this to ensure that they can exercise maximum control. In addition, they stay informed by having individuals report directly to them. This way, they can know more than anyone else. (Source: Richard M. Castaldi and Tjipyanto Soerjanto, "Contrasts in East Asian Management Practices," *The Journal of Management in Practice* 2, no. 1, 1990, pp. 25–27.)

3. *b.* Saccharine-sweetened drinks may not be sold in Japan by law. On the other hand, beer, a wide variety of Japanese and international soft drinks, and so forth, are widely available from vending machines along the streets and in buildings. You're supposed to be at least 18 to buy the alcoholic ones, however. (Source: Eiji Kanno and Constance O'Keefe, *New Japan Solo,* Japan National Tourist Organization: Tokyo, 1990, p. 20.)

4. *a.* Family is considered to be very important in Latin America, so managers are likely to hire their relatives more quickly than hiring strangers. (Source: Nancy J. Adler, *International Dimensions of Organizational Behavior,* 2nd ed., PWS-Kent: Boston, 1991.)

5. *d.* The act, by a woman, of opening the front door, signifies that she has agreed to have sex with any man who enters. (Source: Adam Pertman, "Wandering No More," *Boston Globe Magazine,* June 30, 1991, pp. 10 ff.)

6. *c.* Touching one another during business negotiations is common practice. (Source: Nancy J. Adler, *International Dimensions of Organizational Behavior,* 2nd ed., PWS-Kent: Boston, 1991.)

7. *d.* Approximately 45 percent of the people in Malaysia follow Islam, the country's "official" religion. (Source: Hans Johannes Hoefer, ed., *Malaysia,* Prentice Hall: Englewood Cliffs, NJ, 1984.)

8. *a.* Men holding hands is considered a sign of friendship. Public displays of affection between men and women, however, are unacceptable. (Source: William Warren, Star Black, and M. R. Priya Rangsit, eds., *Thailand,* Prentice Hall: Englewood Cliffs, NJ, 1985.)

9. *d.* In India, as in many Asian countries, toilet paper is not used. Instead, water and the left hand are used, after which the left hand is thoroughly cleaned. Still, the left hand is considered to be polluted and therefore inappropriate for use during eating or touching another person. (Source: Gitanjali Kolanad, *Culture Shock! India,* Graphic Arts Center Publishing Company: Portland, OR, 1996, p. 117.)

10. *b.* This is especially an insult if it is done deliberately, since the feet are the lowest part of the body. (Source: William Warren, Star Black, and M. R. Priya Rangsit, eds., *Thailand,* Prentice Hall: Englewood Cliffs, NJ, 1985.)

11. *c.* Adler suggests that friendship is valued over task competence in Iran. (Source: Nancy J. Adler, *International Dimensions of Organizational Behavior,* 2nd ed., PWS-Kent: Boston, 1991.)

12. *b.* Public discussion of business dealings is considered inappropriate. Kaplan et al. report that "the Chinese may even have used a premature announcement to extract better terms from executives" who were too embarrassed to admit that there was never really a contract. (Source: Frederic Kaplan, Julian Sobin, and Arne de Keijzer, *The China Guidebook,* Houghton Mifflin: Boston, 1987.)

13. *a.* Public praise for Hispanics and Asians is generally embarrassing because modesty is an important cultural value. (Source: Jim Braham, "No, You Don't Manage Everyone the Same," *Industry Week,* February 6, 1989.) In Japan, being singled out for praise is also an embarrassment. A common saying in that country is, "The nail that sticks up gets hammered down."

14. *d.* Though being late is frowned upon in the United States, being late is not only accepted but expected in some South American countries. (Source: Lloyd S. Baird, James E. Post, and John F. Mahon, *Management: Functions and Responsibilities,* Harper & Row: New York, 1990.)

15. *c.* Personal space in most European countries is much smaller than in the United States. Americans generally like at least two feet of space around themselves, while it is not unusual for Europeans to be virtually touching. (Source: Lloyd S. Baird, James E. Post, and John F. Mahon, *Management: Functions and Responsibilities,* Harper & Row: New York, 1990.)

16. *c.* Chrysanthemums and calla lilies are both associated with funerals. (Source: Theodore Fischer, *Pinnacle: International Issue,* March–April 1991, p. 4.)

17. *d.* In Arab cultures, it is considered inappropriate for wives to accept gifts or even attention from other men. (Source: Theodore Fischer, *Pinnacle: International Issue,* March–April 1991, p. 4.)

18. *b.* In Argentina and other Latin American countries, purple is associated with the serious fasting period of Lent. (Source: Theodore Fischer, *Pinnacle: International Issue,* March–April 1991, p. 4.)

19. *d.* Private space is considered so important in Germany that partitions are erected to separate people from one another. Privacy screens and walled gardens are the norm. (Source: Julius Fast, *Subtext: Making Body Language Work,* Viking Penguin Books: New York, 1991, p. 207.)

20. *a.* Though political leaders in the United States are increasingly selected on their ability to inspire, charisma is a suspect trait in what was West Germany, where Hitler's charisma is still associated with evil intent and harmful outcomes. (Source: Nancy J. Adler, *International Dimensions of Organizational Behavior,* 2nd ed., PWS-Kent: Boston, 1991, p. 149.)

21. *c.* Paying Mexican workers more means, in the eyes of the workers, that they can make the same amount of money in fewer hours and thus have more time for enjoying life. (Source: Nancy J. Adler, *International Dimensions of Organizational Behavior,* 2nd ed., PWS-Kent: Boston, 1991, pp. 30 and 159.)

22. *b.* Psychological therapy is not an accepted concept in China. In addition, communism has kept most Chinese from expressing opinions openly. (Source: James McGregor, "Burma Road Heroin Breeds Addicts, AIDS Along China's Border," *The Wall Street Journal,* September 29, 1992, p. 1.)

23. *b.* The Chinese regard a clock as a bad omen because the word for clock, pronounced *zhong,* is phonetically similar to another Chinese word that means the end. Jade is highly valued as symbolizing superior virtues, and oranges and dragon patterns are also auspicious symbols. (Source: Dr. Evelyn Lip, "Culture and Customs," *Silver Kris,* February 1994, p. 84.)

24. *a.* Venezuelans do the reverse of what most people in other countries do on Christmas and New Year's. On Christmas, they socialize. While fireworks are shot off on both nights, most restaurants are closed, and the streets are quiet. (Source: Tony Perrottet, ed., *Venezuela,* Houghton Mifflin: Boston, 1994, p. 97.)

25. *d.* Other popular pub food includes Bangers and Mash (sausages and mashed potatoes), Ploughman's lunch (bread, cheese, and pickled onions), and Cottage pie (baked minced meat with onions and topped with mashed potatoes). (Source: Ravi Desai, ed., *Let's Go: The Budget Guide to Britain and Ireland,* Pan Books: London, 1990, p. 83.)

26. *c.* Indians are generally uninhibited about staring at strangers and asking them about personal details in their lives. Social distance and personal privacy are not common social conventions in India. (Source: Frank Kusy, *India,* The Globe Pequot Press: Chester, CT, 1989, p. 27.)

27. *c.* Vernon Weitzel of the Australian National University advises never to show anger when dealing with Vietnamese officials or businesspeople. Showing anger causes you to lose face and is considered rude. Weitzel also recommends always smiling, not complaining or criticizing anyone, and not

being inquisitive about personal matters. (Source: Daniel Robinson and Joe Cummings, *Vietnam, Laos & Cambodia,* Lonely Planet Publications: Australia, 1991, p. 96.)

28. *c.* What looks to Westerners like a refusal is really an Indian way of saying "yes." It can also express general agreement with what you're saying or suggest that an individual is interested in what you have to say. (Source: Gitanjali Kolanad, *Culture Shock! India,* Graphic Arts Center Publishing Company: Portland, OR, 1996, p. 114.)

29. *d.* In England, this simple hand gesture is considered vulgar and obscene. In a report to *The Boston Globe,* an American who had been working in London wrote, "I wish someone had told me before I emphatically explained to one of the draftsmen at work why I needed two complete sets of drawings." (Source: "Finger Gestures Can Spell Trouble," *The Berkshire Eagle,* January 26, 1997, p. E5.)

2. Using Gung Ho to Understand Cultural Differences

Background

There is no avoiding the increasing globalization of management. Few, if any, current students of business can expect to pursue a successful career without some encounter of an international nature. Gaining early and realistic exposure to the challenges of cross-cultural dynamics will greatly aid any student of business.

The Pacific Rim will continue to play a dominant role in North American transnational organization and global markets. The opening doors to China offer an unprecedented market opportunity. Korea, Singapore, and Taiwan continue to be unsung partners in mutually beneficial trading relationships. And, of course, Japan will always be a dominant player in the international arena.

An important aspect of cross-cultural awareness is understanding actual differences in interpersonal style and cultural expectations, and separating this from incorrect assumptions. Many embellished stereotypes have flourished as we extend our focus and attention abroad. Unfortunately, many of these myths have become quite pervasive, in spite of their lack of foundation. Thus, North American managers frequently and confidently err in their cross-cultural interactions. This may be particularly common in our interactions with the Japanese. For example, lifetime employment has long been touted as exemplifying the superior practices of Japanese management. In reality, only one-third of Japanese *male* employees enjoy this benefit, and in 1993, many Japanese firms actually laid off workers for the first time. Also, Japan is promoted as a collectivist culture founded on consensus, teamwork, and employee involvement. Yet Japan is at the same time one of the most competitive societies, especially when reviewing how students are selected for educational and occupational placement.

Films can provide an entertaining yet potent medium for studying such complex issues. Such experiential learning is most effective when realistic and identifiable with one's own likely experiences. Case studies can be too sterile. Role plays tend to be contrived and void of depth. Both lack a sense of background to help one "buy into" the situation. Films, on the other hand, can promote a rich and familiar presentation that promotes personal involvement. This exercise seeks to capitalize on this phenomenon to explore cross-cultural demands.

Procedure

Step I (110 minutes) Watch the film *Gung Ho.* (This film can be obtained at any video store.)

Step II (30 minutes) Use one of the following four formats to address the discussion topics.

Option A Address each issue in an open class forum. This option is particularly appropriate for moderate class sizes (40 students) or for sections that do not normally engage in group work.

Option B Divide the class into groups of four to seven to discuss the assigned topics. This is a better approach for larger classes (60 or more students). This approach might also be used to assign the exercise as an extracurricular activity if scheduled class time is too brief.

Option C Assign one group to adopt the American perspective and another group to take the Japanese perspective. Using a confrontation meeting approach, have each side describe its perceptions and expected difficulties in collaborating with the other. Then, have the two sides break into small mixed groups to discuss methods to bridge the gap (or avoid its extreme escalation as portrayed in the film). Ideas should extend beyond those cited in the movie. Present these separate discussions to the class as a whole.

Option D Assign students to groups of four to seven to watch the film and write a six-page analysis addressing one or more of the discussion topics.

Discussion Topics

1. In the opening scenes, Hunt observes Kaz being berated in a Japanese "management development center." According to at least one expert, this is a close representation of Japanese disciplinary practices. Would such an approach be possible in an American firm? How does this scene illustrate the different perspectives and approaches to motivation? To reinforcement? To feedback?

2. The concepts of multiculturalism and diversity are emerging issues in modern management environments. The importance of recognizing and responding to racial, ethnic, and other demographic factors has been widely debated in the popular press. What does *Gung Ho* offer to the discussion (both within and across the two groups)? How does each culture respond to different races, genders, and cultures?

3. Individualism and collectivism represent two endpoints on a continuum used to analyze different cultural orientations. Individualism refers to a sense of personal focus, autonomy, and compensation. Collectivism describes a group focus, self-subjugation, obligation, and sharing of rewards. How do you see American and Japanese workers differing on this dimension? You might compare the reactions of the Japanese manager whose wife was about to give

birth with those of the American worker who had planned to take his child to a doctor's appointment.

4. How does the softball game illuminate cultural differences (and even similarities)? You might consider this question in reference to topic 3; to approaches to work habits; to having "fun"; to behavioral norms of pride, honor, and sportsmanship.

5. On several occasions we see George Wendt's openly antagonistic responses to the exercise of authority by Japanese managers. Discuss the concept of authority as seen in both cultures. Discuss expectations of compliance. How might George's actions be interpreted differently by each culture? Indeed, would they be seen as different by an American manager as compared with a Japanese manager?

6. Throughout the film, one gains an impression of how Americans and the Japanese might differ in their approach to resolving conflict. Separately describe how each culture tends to approach conflict, and how the cultures might be different from each other.

7. Experienced conflict between work and family demands has also gained attention as an important managerial issue. How do both cultures approach the role of work in one's life? The role of family? How does each approach balance the competing demands between the two? Have these expectations changed over time (from twenty years ago, forty years ago, sixty years ago)? How might they change now in the twenty-first century?

8. In reality, Japanese managers would be "shamed" if one of their subordinates was seriously injured on the job (the scene where the American worker's hand is caught in the assembly-line belt). Taking this into account, what other issues in the film might be used to illustrate differences or similarities between American and Japanese management and work practices?

Source: Steven M. Sommer, Pepperdine University. Used with permission.

3. "When in Bogotá..."

As Jim Reynolds looked out the small window of the Boeing 757, he saw the glimmer of lights in the distance. After a five-hour flight, he arrived in Bogotá, Colombia, at 9:35 P.M. on a clear Friday evening. It had been nearly five years since Jim had seen his best friend, Rodrigo Cardozo. The two had met in college and kept in touch over the years. During their school years, Rodrigo would often accompany Jim when he went home to Chicago for the holidays.

Entering the main terminal, Jim found himself in what looked like a recently bombed building. Piles of debris were everywhere. Lights hung from the ceiling by exposed electrical wires, and the walls and floors were rough, unfinished concrete. "Certainly, aesthetics are not a major concern at the Bogotá International Airport," Jim thought.

As he came to the end of the long, dimly lit corridor, an expressionless customs official reached out his hand and gestured for Jim's travel documents.

"Passaporte, por favor. Bienvenidos a Bogotá, Señor Reynolds. Estás en vacacciones?"

"Sí," Jim replied.

After a few routine questions, Jim was allowed to pass through customs feeling relatively unscathed.

"Loquillo! Loquillo! Estamos aquí! Jim, Jim," a voice shouted.

Trying to find the origin of the voice among the dense crowd, Jim finally spotted Rodrigo. "Hey, man. How've you been? You look great!"

"Jim, it's so good to see you. How've you been? I would like you to meet my wife, Eva. Eva, this is my best friend, Jim. He's the one in all those pictures I've shown you."

Late Night Begins the Day

Close to an hour later, Jim, Rodrigo, and Eva arrived at Rodrigo's parents' house on the other side of Bogotá from the airport. As Jim was aware, it is customary for couples to live with their parents for a number of years after their marriage, and Rodrigo and Eva were following that custom.

Darío, Rodrigo's father, owned an import/export business in Bogotá. He was a knowledgeable and educated man and, from what Jim knew, a master of business negotiations. Over the years, Darío had conducted business with people in nearly every country in Central and South America, the United States, Europe, Hong Kong, and some parts of Africa. Jim had first met Darío with Rodrigo in Boston in 1989.

"Jim, welcome to my house," Darío boomed effusively as the group walked in. "I am so pleased that you're finally in Bogotá. Would you like something to drink—whiskey, bourbon, Aguardiente?"

"Aguardiente!" Rodrigo urged.

"Yes, Jim would like some Aguardiente. I understand you're going to Bahía tonight," Darío added.

"Where?" Jim asked, looking around. "I didn't know we were going anywhere tonight."

"Don't worry, Jim, todo bien, todo bien," Rodrigo assured him. "We're going dancing, so get dressed. Let's go."

The reality of being in Colombia hit Jim at about 11:15 that night when he and his friends entered Bahía, a Bogotá nightclub. The rhythms of salsa and merengue filled the club. Jim's mind flashed back to the Latin dance parties he and Rodrigo had had in Boston with their friends from Central and South America.

"Jim, this is my cousin, Diana. She'll be your partner tonight," Rodrigo said. "You'll get to practice your Spanish too; she doesn't speak a word of English. Have fun."

For the next six hours, they danced and drank. This is the Colombian way. At 5:30 the next morning, Rodrigo decided it was time to leave to get something to eat. On the drive home, they stopped at an outdoor grill in the mountains where many people had congregated for the same reason. Everyone was eating arepas con queso and mazorca, and drinking Aguardiente.

Next, they continued to an outdoor party just down the street. Here, they danced and drank until the sun crested over the mountains of Bogotá. It was about 7:00 A.M. when they decided to conclude the celebration—for now.

Saturday was spent recovering from the previous evening and also touring some local spots in the country. However, Saturday night was a repeat of Friday. After being in Colombia for three days, Jim had slept a total of about four hours. Fortunately, Monday was a national holiday.

Business Before Pleasure Before Business?

Although Jim was having a great time, he had also scheduled a series of business meetings with directors of business schools at various Bogotá universities for the week to come. Jim worked as an acquisitions editor for Academia Press, a major publisher of college-level business textbooks. The purpose of the meetings was to establish business contacts in the Colombian market. It was hoped that these initial contacts would lead to others in Latin America.

At Academia Press headquarters in New York, Jim and Caroline Evans, his boss, had discussed the opportunities in Latin America. Although Academia Press routinely published international editions of its texts, total international sales never represented more than 15 percent of their gross. Consequently, international markets had never been pursued aggressively. Caroline, however, saw the Latin American markets as having a lot of potential within the next three to five years. She envisioned this market alone, in time, representing 15 to 20 percent of gross sales. Moreover, she felt that within the next ten years, international sales could reach 40 percent if developed properly. With numbers like that, it was evident to Jim that this deal was important, not only to the company but to his career as well. If Jim was able to open these markets, he might receive a promotion and be able to continue to work in Central and South America.

Jim's first meeting was scheduled for 11:00 A.M. on Tuesday, the second on Wednesday at 11:00 A.M., and the third on Friday at 3:00 P.M. At precisely 11:00 A.M. on Tuesday, Jim arrived at Javeriana University, where he was to meet with Professors Emilio Muñoz, Diana Espitia, and Enrique Ronderos. When he arrived, Professor Muñoz was waiting for him in the conference room.

"Señor Reynolds, I am delighted to meet you. How was your flight?"

"Wonderful," Jim replied.

"And how do you like Bogotá so far? Have you been able to sightsee?"

"No, I haven't had the chance to get around the city yet. I hope to see some things later in the week."

"Well, before you leave, you must visit *El Museo de Oro*. It is the finest collection of gold artifacts from the various indigenous Indian tribes in Colombia. Although much of the gold was stolen by the Spanish, many pieces have survived." For the next thirty minutes, Professor Muñoz spoke of everything from the upcoming presidential elections to World Cup soccer.

Jim looked at his watch, concerned about the other professors who had not yet arrived and about the meeting for which he had prepared.

"Is there something wrong, Señor Reynolds?"

"No, no, I was just wondering about the others; it's 11:30."

"Don't worry. They'll be here shortly. Traffic in Bogotá at this hour is terrible. They're probably caught in a traffic jam."

Just then, Professors Espitia and Ronderos walked in.

"Muy buenas, Señor Reynolds," Professor Espitia said warmly. "Please forgive us for the delay. Traffic is simply awful at this time of day."

"Oh, that's not necessary. I understand. Traffic in New York can be absolutely horrendous as well," Jim replied. "Sometimes it takes two hours to get from one end of the city to the other."

"Have you had lunch yet, Señor Reynolds?" asked Professor Ronderos.

Jim shook his head.

"Why don't we go to lunch, and we can talk there?" Professor Ronderos suggested.

After discussing the restaurants in the area, the professors decided on El Club Ejecutivo. It was nearly 12:30 P.M. when they arrived.

"It's been an hour and a half, and we haven't discussed anything," Jim thought. He was concerned that the Colombians were not very interested in what he had to offer. Throughout lunch, Jim grew increasingly concerned that the professors were more interested in his trying typical Colombian dishes and visiting the sights in Bogotá than in Academia's textbooks. They were fascinated that Jim knew how to dance salsa and merengue and impressed that he spoke Spanish with a slight Colombian accent; Señorita Espitia said she found it amusing. That seemed much more important than his knowledge of business textbooks and publishing in general.

By the end of lunch, Jim was nearly beside himself. It was now after 2:30 P.M. and nothing had been accomplished.

"Why don't we all go to Monserate tomorrow? It's absolutely beautiful up there, Señor Reynolds," Professor Ronderos suggested, going on to describe the mountain that overlooks Bogotá and the myths and traditions that surround it.

"That's a wonderful idea," Professor Espitia added.

"Monserate it is then. Jim, it has been a pleasure. I look forward to our meeting tomorrow," Professor Ronderos said with a slight bow.

"Señor Reynolds, would you like a ride home?" Professor Muñoz asked.

"Yes, if it's not too much trouble."

On the way home, Jim was relatively quiet.

"Do you feel okay?"

"It must be jet lag catching up to me. I'm sure it's nothing," Jim responded. Concerned about the way the meeting had gone, Jim realized that he had never even had a chance to mention Academia Press's various titles and how these texts could be used to create a new curriculum or supplement an existing curriculum at the professors' business school.

When in Bogotá

On arriving at the house, Jim went upstairs and sat in the living room glumly sipping a cup of aguapanela. "I just don't get it," he thought. "The Colombians couldn't have been happier with the way the meeting turned out, but we didn't do anything. We didn't even talk about one book. I just don't understand what went wrong."

In a short time, Darío arrived. "Muy buenas, Jim. How did your meetings go today with the directors?" he asked.

"I don't know. I don't know what to think. We didn't do anything. We didn't talk about business at all. We talked more about the sights I should see and the places I should visit before I leave Colombia. I'm supposed to call my boss this afternoon and tell her how the initial meeting went. What am I going to tell her? 'Sorry, we just decided to plan my vacation in Colombia instead of discussing business.' I can't afford to have this deal fall through."

Darío laughed.

"Señor, I'm serious."

"Jim, I understand. Believe me. Tell me about your meeting today."

Jim recounted every detail of the meeting to Darío, who smiled and nodded his head as he listened.

"Jim, you have to understand one thing before you continue negotiating with the directors."

"What's that?"

"You're in Colombia now," Darío said simply.

Jim stared at him with a puzzled look. "And?"

"And what, Jim?"

"Is there something else I should know?"

"That's where you need to start. You let the directors set the tone of the meeting. It's obvious they felt very comfortable with you, or they wouldn't have invited you to Monserate. Here in Colombia, Jim, we do business differently. Right now, you're building friendship. You're building their trust in you. This is very important in doing business in all of Latin America."

After a moment's pause, "Jim," Darío continued, "would you rather do business with a friend or someone you hardly know?"

As Darío went on to analyze the meeting, Jim realized that his perception of the situation had been formed by his experiences in the United States. "When in Bogotá," he thought, "I guess I had better think like the Colombians."

"Jim, you've gained the respect and the trust of the directors. In my opinion, your first meeting was a complete success."

"What should I expect in the meetings to come?" Jim asked.

"Don't worry," he responded. "Just let the directors worry about that. You'll come to an agreement before the end of the week. I guarantee it."

Questions for Discussion

1. What differences does Jim notice between life in the United States and life in Colombia?

2. What differences does Jim notice between doing business in the United States and doing business in Colombia? How might these same factors differ in other countries?

3. What advice would you give Jim for closing his deals? Why?

Source: Written by Matthew C. Shull, twitter.com/Matthew_Shull

4. The International Cola Alliances

Objectives

- To introduce some of the complexities involved in doing business across international borders
- To examine what happens when countries seek to do business with one another without the benefit of a common language and customs

Background

Even with a common language, communication can break down, and interpretations of words and actions often can confound understanding and incur negative attributions of purpose. Add to this the differences of personal needs that exist from individual to individual, as well as national and cultural needs that exist from country to country. These limitless variables make cooperation across borders even more complex.

The Story

You are a delegation from a country that would like to enter into a large cooperative effort with a number of other countries for the production and distribution of a popular soft drink produced by the American company International Cola. In the past, countries in your region of the world have been resistant to allowing foreign soft drinks into their markets, despite consumer demands. However, recent thinking is that the advantages of allowing this competition outweigh the disadvantages.

International Cola has expressed an interest in setting up a bottling plant, a regional corporate headquarters, and four distribution depots. Their goal, of course, is to do this in the most economically efficient way possible to maximize profits. However, because the executives at International Cola believe this area to be a rich new market with outstanding potential and are therefore eager to get in, they have ceded to the demands of the various governments in the proposed alliance. These require International Cola to allow for local control of the facilities; to maintain only 49 percent interest in the facilities with local partners holding 51 percent ownership; and to allow the participating governments to work out among themselves the details of where the facilities will be located.

For the countries involved, having one or more of these facilities located within their borders will bring jobs, revenue, and a certain amount of prestige. (It is possible for a single country to have all six of the facilities: regional headquarters, bottling plant, distribution depots.)

Each of the countries involved shares at least two borders with the other countries. This has not always been the most peaceful area. Border skirmishes are frequent, most stemming from minor misunderstandings that became inflated by vast cultural and religious differences.

These distinct cultural differences between your country and your neighbors will likely become even more evident as you pursue the negotiation. It will be up to you to decide how to respond to them. While it is important for you to retain your own cultural integrity—for example, when you first meet a delegate from another country you will likely greet him or her in the cultural style of your country—you understand the importance of being sensitive to one another. If you understand, for example, that the cultural style of another country is to bow on meeting, whereas you shake hands, you may wish to bow instead.

Since you are negotiating the venture across borders, and each country has a different primary language, you have agreed to negotiate in English, but none of you are entirely fluent. Therefore, a few phrases will creep in from your own languages.

Wear your country's flag in a visible place at all times.

Instructions

Step 1 (30–40 minutes—may be done before class) Working in small groups (5–7), develop a profile of your country and its people based on profile sheets 1 and 2.

After you have completed profile sheets 1 and 2, briefly discuss them to be sure there is mutual understanding of what the group's behavior and negotiating stance are to be during the negotiation.

Step 2 (20 minutes—may be done before class) Based on the profile sheets, decide which International Cola facilities you believe you should have in your country and why you believe they should be in your country rather than one of the others that will be represented. For example, if you have a highly educated population, you may argue that you should be the home of the regional corporate headquarters; be aware, however, that another country might argue that you should not have bottling and distribution facilities because these do not require a highly educated or skilled labor force.

On the negotiation sheet, make a list of the facilities you believe your country should have and some notes as to what your arguments will be for having them. Also, make some notes on what you believe the other countries' counterarguments will be and how you expect to respond to them.

Step 3 (30–45 minutes—in class) Everyone in your group should pin a copy of your country's flag and motto on himself or herself in a visible place. One to three representatives from your group (delegation) should negotiate the arrangements for International Cola's facilities with the representatives from the other delegations. Be sure to use the cultural norms of your country during the negotiation, but *do not tell* the others what your social norms are.

Representatives should introduce themselves to one another on an individual basis. After personal introductions, representatives should form a circle in the center of the room with their delegations behind them, briefly describe their countries, state their positions, and begin negotiations. During negotiations, representatives should make an effort to use their new language at least three times. They should not use English for any of the six phrases listed.

Delegation representatives and the other members of their groups may communicate with one another at any point during the negotiation, but only in writing. Group members may also communicate among themselves, but only in writing during the negotiation.

Any group or representative may ask for a side meeting with one or more of the other groups during the negotiation. Side meetings may not last more than five minutes.

At any time in the negotiation, the delegation may change its representative. When such a change is made, the new representative and the other delegates must reintroduce themselves and greet one another.

Those members of each delegation who are not directly negotiating should be active observers. Use the observer sheet to record situations in which other groups insulted them, shamed them, or were otherwise offensive.

At the end of 45 minutes, the negotiation should be concluded whether or not an agreement has been reached.

Questions for Discussion

1. What role did cultural differences play in the various phases of the negotiation process? Be careful not to overlook the introductory phase. Was the negotiation frustrating? Satisfying? Other? Why?

2. At any time, did delegations recognize the cultural differences between themselves and the others? If so, was any attempt made to try to adapt to another country's norms? Why? Why not? Would there have been a benefit in doing so? Why?

3. What role did language differences play during the negotiation? What was the effect of lack of understanding or miscommunication on the process?

4. Did the delegations from various countries attempt to find mutual goals and interests despite their differences? In what ways were the best interests of the overall plan subjugated to the individual interests of each country? What rhetoric was used to justify the personal interests?

5. To what degree did groups construct their countries to best justify their position? In situations where this happened, did it work? Why? Why not?

Profile Sheet 1

1. Select a name for your country:

_____

Be sure that the name of your country appears on or around the flag (see below).

2. In the space below, design your country's flag or emblem. Make enough copies so that each member of your group has one to wear.

3. Write a slogan for your country that best embodies your country's ideals and goals. Include the slogan on or around the flag.

_____

_____

_____

4. Make up a partial language with a vocabulary of up to twenty-five (25) words into which you should translate the following phrases for use during negotiations:

Phrase   *Translation*

I agree. _____

I disagree. _____

This is unacceptable. _____

I don't understand your point._____

_____

You have insulted me. _____

Please repeat that. _____

5. Briefly describe how people in your country react when they have been insulted.

_____

_____

_____

_____

_____

_____

Profile Sheet 2

Describe your country by selecting one element from each of the following lists. After you have made your selections, list the elements that make up your country's description on a separate piece of paper and add any additional elements you wish.

Population Density

_____ high density with overpopulation a problem

_____ moderate density—high end

_____ moderate density—average

_____ moderate density—low end

_____ low density

Average Educational Level

_____ less than 3 years—large percent totally illiterate

_____ 3–6 years—widespread functional illiteracy

_____ 6–9 years—functional illiteracy a problem in scattered areas

_____ 9–12 years—most read and write at functional levels

_____ 12+ years—a highly educated and functioning population

Per Capita Income

_____ under $1,000 per year

_____ $1,000–5,000 per year

_____ $5,000–10,000 per year

_____ $10,000–20,000 per year

_____ $20,000–30,000 per year

_____ $30,000–40,000 per year

_____ $40,000+ per year

Climate

_____ tropical

_____ arctic

_____ mixed in different areas

_____ runs range from season to season

Form of Government

_____ socialist

_____ democratic

_____ communist

_____ monarchy

_____ dictatorship

_____ other (specify)

Dominant Racial-Ethnic Group

_____ Asian

_____ black

_____ white

_____ other (specify)

Dominant Religion

_____ animist

_____ atheist/agnostic

_____ Buddhist

_____ Catholic

_____ Hindu

_____ Jewish

_____ Mormon

_____ Protestant (specify)

_____ other (specify)

Negotiation Sheet

1. What facilities do you believe your country should have?

_____

_____

_____

_____

2. What facilities of those listed above are you willing to relinquish to reach agreement?

_____

_____

3. On what bases will you justify your need or desire for having the facilities you have listed?

_____

_____

_____

_____

_____

_____

_____

_____

Observer Sheet

1. List actions taken by members of other delegations that were insulting, created shame for you and your delegation, or were otherwise offensive based on your country's norms. Include notes on the context in which the actions were taken.

_____

_____

_____

_____

2. Based on the above list, what happened to your interest in forming an alliance and your belief that a mutual agreement could be reached?

5. Whom to Hire?

Objectives

- To explore participants' cultural biases and expectations
- To examine cultural differences
- To consider the impact culture has on hiring decisions

Instructions

Step 1 (10–15 minutes)   Read the background information and descriptions of each of the applicants. Consider the job and the cultures within which the individual to be hired will be operating. Rank the candidates from 1 to 5, with 1 being your first choice, and enter your rankings on the ranking sheet in the column marked "My Ranking." Briefly, list the reasons for each of your rankings.

Do not discuss your rankings with your classmates until told to do so.

Step 2 (30–40 minutes)   Working with three to four of your classmates, discuss the applicants, and rank them in the order of group preference. Do not vote.

Rank the candidates from 1 to 5, with 1 being the group's first choice, and enter your group rankings on the ranking sheet in the column marked "Group Ranking." Briefly list the reasons for each of the group's rankings.

If your group represents more than one culture, explore the ways in which each person's cultural background may have influenced his or her individual decisions.

Step 3 (open-ended)   Report your rankings to the class, and discuss the areas of difference that emerged within your group while you were trying to reach consensus.

Questions for Discussion

1. Was your group able to explore openly any culturally based biases that came up—for example, feelings about homosexuality, religion, personality traits, politics?
2. Did you make any comments or observations that you feel would have been fully acceptable in your own culture but were not accepted by the group? Explain.
3. If the answer to question 2 was yes, how did the reaction of the group make you feel about your membership in it? How did you handle the situation?
4. What implications do you believe these cultural differences would have in business dealings?

Background

You are a member of the management committee of a multinational company that does business in 23 countries. While your company's headquarters are in Holland, your offices are scattered fairly evenly throughout the four hemispheres. Primary markets have been in Europe and North America; the strongest emerging market is the Pacific Rim. Company executives would like to develop what they see as a powerful potential market in the Middle East. Sales in all areas except the Pacific Rim have shown slow growth over the past two years.

At present, your company is seeking to restructure and revitalize its worldwide marketing efforts. To accomplish this, you have determined that you need to hire a key marketing person to introduce fresh ideas and a new perspective. There is no one currently in your company who is qualified to do this, and so you have decided to look outside. The job title is "vice-president for international marketing"; it carries with it a salary well into six figures (US$), plus elaborate benefits, an unlimited expense account, a car, and the use of the corporate jet. The person you hire will be based at the company's headquarters and will travel frequently.

A lengthy search has turned up five people with good potential. It is now up to you to decide whom to hire. Although all the applicants have expressed a sincere interest in the position, it is possible that they may change their minds once the job is offered. Therefore, you must rank them in order of preference so that if your first choice declines the position, you can go on to the second, and so on.

Applicants:
Park L., age 41, Married with Three Children

Park L. is currently senior vice president for marketing at a major Korean high-technology firm. You have been told by the head of your Seoul office that his reputation as an expert in international marketing is outstanding. The market share of his company's products has consistently increased since he joined the company just over fifteen years ago. His company's market share is now well ahead of that of competing producers in the Pacific Rim.

Park started with his present company immediately after his graduation from the University of Seoul and has worked his way up through the ranks. He does not have a graduate degree. You sense that Park has a keen understanding of organizational politics and knows how to play them. He recognizes that because the company he works for now is family controlled, it is unlikely that he will ever move much higher than his present situation. Park has told you that he is interested in the growth potential offered at your company.

In addition to his native tongue, Park is able to carry on a reasonably fluent conversation in English and has a minimal working knowledge of German and French. His wife, who appears quiet and quite traditional, and his children speak only Korean.

Kiran K., age 50, Widow with One Adult Child

Kiran K. is a Sikh woman living in Malaysia. She began her teaching career while finishing her DBA (doctorate in business administration) at the Harvard Business School and published her first book on international marketing 10 months after graduation. Her doctoral dissertation was based on the international marketing of pharmaceuticals, but she has also done research and published on other areas of international marketing.

Two months after the publication of her book, Kiran went to work in the international marketing department of a Fortune 500 company, where she stayed for the next 10 years. She returned to teaching when Maura University offered her a full professorship with tenure, and she has been there since that time. Her academic position has allowed her to pursue a number of research interests and to write authoritative books and papers in her field. At present, she is well published and internationally recognized as an expert on international marketing. In addition, she has an active consulting practice throughout Southeast Asia.

You have learned through your office in Kuala Lumpur that Kiran's only child, a 23-year-old son, is severely mentally and physically disabled. You sense that part of her interest in the job with your company is to have the income to guarantee his care should anything happen to her. Her son would go with her to Holland, should she be given the job, where he will need to be enrolled in special support programs.

In addition to fluency in Malay, English, and Hindi, Kiran speaks and writes German and Spanish and is able to converse in Japanese and Mandarin.

Peter V., age 44, Single

Peter is a white South African. He had worked in a key position in the international marketing division of an American Fortune 100 company until the company pulled out of his country eight months ago. While the company wanted to keep him on, offering to move him from Johannesburg to its New York headquarters, Peter decided that it was time to look elsewhere. He had begun to feel somewhat dead-ended in his position and apparently sees the position at your company as an opportunity to try out new territory. Like your other candidates for the position, Peter has a long list of accomplishments and is widely recognized as outstanding in his field. People in your company who have had contacts with him say that Peter is creative, hardworking, and loyal. In addition, you have been told that Peter is a top-flight manager of people who is able to push his

employees to the highest levels of performance. And, you are told, he is very organized.

Peter has a PhD in computer science from a leading South African university and an MBA from Purdue's Krannert School of Business.

Peter had been a vehement opponent of apartheid and is still very much a social activist. His high political visibility within South Africa had made his life there difficult, and even now, with the end of apartheid, he would like to get out. His constant male companion, P. K. Kahn, would be coming with him to Holland, and Peter would like your personnel office to help P. K. find an appropriate position.

Peter speaks and reads English, Dutch, Afrikaans, and Swahili and can converse in German.

Tex P., age 36, Divorced with One Child

Tex is currently job hunting. His former job as head of marketing for a single-product, high-technology firm—highly specialized workstations for sophisticated artificial intelligence applications—ended when the company was bought out by Texas Instruments. Tex had been with his previous company virtually from the time the company was started six years earlier. Having to leave his job was an irony to Tex as it was largely due to the success of his efforts that the company was bought out. You sense that he is a little bitter, and he tells you that jobs offered to him by TI were beneath him and not worthy of consideration.

Tex has both his undergraduate and MBA degrees from Stanford University. In addition, he was a Rhodes Scholar and won a Fulbright scholarship, which he used to support himself while he undertook a two-year research project on the marketing of high-technology equipment to Third World countries.

You have learned through your New York office that Tex has a reputation for being aggressive and hard driving. Apparently he is a workaholic who has been known to work eighteen to twenty hours a day, seven days a week. He seems to have little time for his personal life.

In addition to his native English, Tex has a minimal command of French—which he admits he hasn't used since his college days.

Zvi C., age 40, Married with Five Children

Zvi began his career after receiving his MBA from the Sloan School of Management at the Massachusetts Institute of Technology (MIT). His first job was as marketing manager for a German company doing business in Israel.

Zvi's phenomenal success with this company led to his being hired away by an international office equipment company in England. Again, he proved to be outstanding, boosting the company's market share beyond all expectations within two years. After five years, Zvi was offered a chance to go back to Israel, this time to oversee and coordinate all the international marketing programs for an industrial park of 14 companies run as an adjunct to Israel's leading scientific research institution. It has been his responsibility to interface the research component with product development and sales as well as to manage the vast marketing department. Again, he has shown himself to be a master.

You have learned through your Haifa office that Zvi is highly respected and has extensive contacts in the scientific and high-tech worlds. He is exceptionally creative in his approach to marketing, often trying bold strategies that most of his peers would dismiss as too risky. Zvi, however, has made them work and work well.

Zvi is a religious man who must leave work by noon on Friday. He will not work Saturdays nor any of his religion's major and minor holidays—about eighteen a year. He will, however, work on Sundays.

In addition to his native language, Dutch (Zvi and his family moved to Israel from Holland when Zvi was six), he speaks and writes fluent Hebrew, English, German, and Arabic.

Ranking Sheet

Rank candidates from one to five with one as your first choice.

| Applicant | My Ranking | | Group Ranking | |
	Rank	Reasons	Rank	Reasons
Park L.				
Kiran K.				
Peter V.				
Tex P.				
Zvi C.				

References

■ Chapter 1

International Management in Action: Tracing the Roots of Modern Globalization   Thomas Cahill, *Sailing the Wine Dark Sea: Why Greeks Matter* (New York: Doubleday, 2003), pp. 10, 56–57; Charles W. L. Hill, *International Business,* 4th ed. (New York: McGraw-Hill Irwin, 2003), p. 100; Nefertiti website, http://nefertiti. iweland.com/trade/internal_trade.htm, 2003 (ancient Egypt: domestic trade); Gavin Menzies, *1421: The Year China Discovered America* (New York: William Morrow/HarperCollins, 2003), pp. 26–27; Milton Viorst, *The Great Documents of Western Civilization* (New York: Barnes & Noble Books, 1994), p. 115 (Magna Carta) and p. 168 (Declaration of Independence).

International Management in Action: Brazilian Economic Reform   Simon Romero, "Brazil Still Embraces Globalization," *New York Times,* December 2, 1999, p. C1; "Beyond Europe: Brazil and China," *European Advertising & Media Forecast,* August 26, 2010, 21(2), pp. 26–27; "Brazil," *Financial Services Forecast World,* December 2005, pp. 77–85; "The Blessings of Stability," *Economist,* April 14, 2007, pp. 7–8.

International Management in Action: Recognizing Cultural Differences   Garry Kasparov, "Putin's Gangster State," *The Wall Street Journal,* March 30, 2007, p. A15; The Economist Intelligence Unit, *Country Report: Russia* (Kent, U.K.: EIU, 2007), p. 7; "Trust the Locals," *The Economist* 382, January 25, 2007, pp. 55–56.

In the International Spotlight: India   John F. Burns, "India Now Winning U.S. Investment," *New York Times,* February 6, 1995, pp. C1, C5; Rahual Jacob, "India Gets Moving," *Fortune,* September 5, 1994, pp. 101–102; Jon E. Hilsenrath, "Honda Venture Takes the Bumps in India," *The Wall Street Journal,* August 2, 2000, p. A18; Manjeet Kripalani and Pete Engardio, "India: A Shocking Election Upset Means India Must Spend Heavily on Social Needs," *Business-Week,* May 31, 2004; Steve Hamm, "The Trouble with India," BusinessWeek, March 19, 2007, pp. 48–58; "The World's Headache," *Economist,* December 6, 2008, p. 58; Gaurav Choudhury, "How Slow GDP Growth Affects You," *Hindustan Times,* December 4, 2012, http://www.hindustantimes.com/.

■ Chapter 2

International Management in Action: The U.S. Goes to the Mat   Brian Brenner, "Why Taming the China Dragon Is Tricky," *BusinessWeek Online,* April 23, 2007; "China Tries to Tap the Brakes on Economic Growth," *The Wall Street Journal,* December 26, 2003, p. A9; "US-China Trade Friction Getting Hotter," *China Economic Review,* as appearing in *BusinessWeek Online,* May 7, 2007; Michael M. Phillips, "Congress Fumes as China Talks Show Few Gains," *The Wall Street Journal,* May 24, 2007, p. A1; "Bending, not Bowing," *Economist,* April 10, 2010, p. 75.

In the International Spotlight: Vietnam   Frederik Balfour, "Back on the Radar Screen," *BusinessWeek,* November 20, 2000, pp. 56–57; Jon E. Hilsenrath, "U.S. Investors See Hope in Vietnam Trip," *The Wall Street Journal,* November 17, 2000, p. A17; Roy Rowan,

"25 Years After the Fall," Fortune, May 1, 2000, pp. 208–222; Wayne Arnold, "Trade Accord with Vietnam: Exports in Place of Enmity," *New York Times,* July 28, 2000, p. C4; Ha Thank Nguyen and Klaus E. Meyer, "Managing Partnerships with State-Owned Joint Venture Companies: Experiences From Vietnam," *Business Strategy Review* 15 (Spring 2004), p. 39; James Hookway, "WTO Entry No Cure-All for Vietnam," *The Wall Street Journal,* November 8, 2006, www.wsj.com; "AES Corporation; AES Signs Long Term Purchase Commitments in Vietnam, Achieving Key Development Milestone for 1,200 MW Mong Duong II Coal Plant," *China Weekly News,* May 4, 2010, p. 37; "Nokia on Schedule Despite Struggles," *TalkVietnam Business,* December 24, 2012, talkvietnam.com.

■ Chapter 3

International Management in Action: The Ethics of an Offshoring Decision   Jonathan Doh and Bret Wilmot, "The Ethics of Offshoring," Working Paper, Villanova University, 2010; David Smith, "Offshoring: Political Myths and Economic Reality," *World Economy,* March 2006, pp. 249–256.

In the International Spotlight: Saudi Arabia   Neil Macfarquhar, "After the Saudi Rampage, Questions and Few Answers," *New York Times,* June 1, 2004, p. A6; "Rising Stars," *Airfinance Journal,* September 2002, p. 50; Neil MacFarquhar, "Saudi Monarch Grants Women Right to Vote," *The New York Times Online,* September 25, 2012, www.nytimes.com.

■ Chapter 4

International Management in Action: Business Customs in South Africa   www.kwintessential.co.uk/resources/globaletiquette/ south-africa-country-profile.html; Going Global Inc., "Cultural Advice," *South Africa Career Guide,* 2006, content.epnet.com.ps2. villanova.edu/pdf18_21/pdf/2006/ONI/01Jan06/22291722.pdf.

International Management in Action: Common Personal Values   George W. England, "Managers and Their Value Systems: A Five-Country Comparative Study," *Columbia Journal of World Business,* Summer 1978, pp. 35–44; Geert Hofstede, *Culture's Conse-quences: International Differences in Work-Related Values* (Beverly Hills, CA: Sage, 1980); Geert Hofstede, *Cultures and Organizations: Software of the Mind* (London: McGraw-Hill U.K., 1991); Martin J. Gannon, *Understanding Global Cultures,* 2nd ed. (Thousand Oaks, CA: Sage, 2001), pp. 35–56.

In the International Spotlight: South Africa   The Economist Intelligence Unit, *Country Report: South Africa* (Kent, U.K.: EIU, 2009), pp. 7–10; "Still Everything to Play For," *Economist,* June 5, 2010, pp. 15–16; "The Darkening of White South Africa," *Economist,* May 20, 1995, pp. 18–20; Tom Nevin, "The World Cup Retail Windfall—Myth or Reality?" *African Business,* March 2010, pp. 58–59; "When the Whistle Blows," *Economist,* June 5, 2010, p. 15; "Buthelezi Slams Affirmative Action," Mail & Guardian, February 1, 2007; "Tutu Warns of Poverty 'Powder Keg'," BBC, November 23, 2004, news.bbc.co.uk.

■ Chapter 5

International Management in Action: Ten Key Factors for MNC Success   James F. Bolt, "Global Competitors: Some Criteria for Success," *Business Horizons*, January–February 1988, pp. 34–41; Alan S. Rugman and Richard M. Hodgetts, *International Business*, 2nd ed. (London: Pearson, 2000), chapter 1; Sheida Hodge, *Global Smarts: The Art of Communicating and Deal Making Anywhere in the World* (New York: Wiley, 2000).

International Management in Action: Managing in Hong Kong   J. Stewart Black and Lyman W. Porter, "Managerial Behaviors and Job Performance: A Successful Manager in Los Angeles May Not Succeed in Hong Kong," *Journal of International Business Studies* 22, no. 1 (First Quarter 1991), pp. 99–112; Geert Hofstede, *Cultures and Organizations: Software of the Mind* (London: McGraw-Hill U.K., 1991), chapters 4–6; Alan S. Rugman and Richard M. Hodgetts, *International Business*, 2nd ed. (London: Pearson, 2000), chapter 20; Benjamin Fulford, "Microwave Missionaries," *Forbes,* November 13, 2000, pp. 136–146.

In the International Spotlight: Mexico   David Wessel, Paul B. Carroll, and Thomas T. Vogel Jr., "How Mexico's Crisis Ambushed Top Minds in Officialdom, Finance," *The Wall Street Journal*, July 6, 1995, pp. A1, A4; Craig Torres and Paul B. Carroll, "Mexico's Mantra for Salvation: Export, Export, Export," *The Wall Street Journal,* March 17, 1995, p. A6; "Mexico," *Europa* (London: Europa Publications, 1995), pp. 429–444; Carlta Vitzthum and Nicole Harris, "Telefonica Makes Its Move into Mexico," *The Wall Street Journal*, October 5, 2000, p. A19; Joel Millman, "Mexico Factories See Growth Unchecked," *The Wall Street Journal,* November 6, 2000, p. A29; David Luhnow, "Mexico's Economy Hints at Rebound, Aided Once Again by U.S. Ties," *The Wall Street Journal,* January 13, 2004, p. A2; Ken Bensinger, "Trade Bandwagon Sweeps Up Mexico, but Critics Say Pacts Create Mixed Results," *Houston Chronicle*, April 2, 2004, p. 1; The Economist Intelligence Unit, *Country Report: Mexico* (Kent, U.K.: EIU, 2009), pp. 6–9; John Sargent and Linda Matthews, "Exploitation or Choice? Exploring the Relative Attractiveness of Employment in the Maquiladoras," *Journal of Business Ethics*, January 15, 1999, pp. 213–227; Joel Millman, "Maquiladoras Resumed Hiring Growth in 2004," *The Wall Street Journal*–Eastern Edition, March 22, 2005, p. A13; Rick Nelson, "Recovery and Jobs," *Test & Measurement World*, June 2010, pp. 9; "Mexico," The World Bank, 2013, http://data.worldbank.org/country/mexico/.

■ Chapter 6

International Management in Action: Doing Things the Walmart Way, Germans Say, "Nein, vielen Dank"   Mark Landler and Michael Barbaro, "Wal-Mart Finds That Its Formula Doesn't Fit Every Culture," *New York Times,* August 2, 2006, http://www.nytimes.com/2006/08/02/business/worldbusiness/02walmart.html.

International Management in Action: Matsushita Goes Global   P. Christopher Earley and Harbir Singh, "International and Intercultural Management Research: What's Next," *Academy of Management Journal*, June 1995, pp. 327–340; Karen Lowry Miller, "Siemens Shapes Up," *BusinessWeek,* May 1, 1995, pp. 52–53; Christine M. Riordan and Robert J. Vandenberg, "A Central Question in Cross-Cultural Research: Do Employees of Different Cultures Interpret Work-Related Measures in an Equivalent Manner?" *Journal of Management* 20, no. 3 (1994), pp. 643–671; Brenton R. Schlender, "Matsushita Shows How to Go Global," *Fortune*, July 11, 1994, pp. 159–166.

In the International Spotlight: Japan   Iain McDonald, "Japan's Industrial Production Rises 3.3% Amid Payroll Gains," *The Wall Street Journal,* June 1, 2004, p. A14; Ian Rowley, "Japan Isn't Buying the Wal-Mart Idea," *BusinessWeek,* February 28, 2005, www.businessweek. com/magazine/content/05_09/b3922073.htm; Yuka Hayashi, "Japan's GDP Shrinks as Consumer Spending Feels the Pinch," *The Wall Street Journal*–Eastern Edition, May 20, 2009, p. A11; "Economic and Financial Indicators," *Economist*, March 18, 2006, pp. 96–97; "Japan," The World Bank, 2013, http://data.worldbank.org/country/japan/.

■ Chapter 7

International Management in Action: Doing It Right the First Time   www.jetro.gp.ip/JETROINFO/DOING/4.html; Alan Rugman and Richard M. Hodgetts, *International Business*, 2nd ed. (London: Pearson, 2000), chapter 17; Philip R. Harris and Robert T. Moran, *Managing Cultural Differences,* 3rd ed. (Houston: Gulf Publishing, 1991), pp. 393–406; Sheida Hodge, *Global Smarts* (New York: Wiley, 2000), p. 76; Richard D. Lewis, *When Cultures Collide* (London: Nicholas Brealey, 1999), pp. 414–415.

International Management in Action: Communicating in Europe   Karen Matthes, "Mind Your Manners When Doing Business in Europe," *Personnel*, January 1992, p. 19; Philip R. Harris and Robert T. Moran, *Managing Cultural Differences: High-Performance Strategies for a New World of Bus*iness, 4th ed. (Houston: Gulf Publishing, 1994), chapter 13; Alan Rugman and Richard M. Hodgetts, *International Business*, 2nd ed. (London: Pearson, 2000), chapter 16; Richard Lewis, *When Cultures Collide* (London: Nicholas Brealey, 1999).

International Management in Action: Negotiating with the Japanese   Rosalie J. Tung, "How to Negotiate with the Japanese," *California Management Review*, Summer 1984, pp. 62–77; Carla Rapoport, "You Can Make Money in Japan," *Fortune*, February 12, 1990, pp. 85–92; Margaret A. Neale and Max H. Bazerman, "Negotiating Rationally," *Academy of Management Executive*, August 1992, pp. 42–51; Martin J. Gannon, *Understanding Global Cultures*, 2nd ed. (Thousand Oaks, CA: Sage, 2001), pp. 35–56; Sheida Hodge, *Global Smarts* (New York: Wiley, 2000), chapter 14; Richard D. Lewis, *When Cultures Collide* (London: Nicholas Brealey, 1999), pp. 400–415.

In the International Spotlight: China   "China's Economy: After the Stimulus," *China Business Review,* July 2010, pp. 30–33; Tran Van Hoa, "Impact of the WTO Membership, Regional Economic Integration, and Structural Change on China's Trade and Growth," *Review of Development Economics*, August 2010, pp. 577–591; James Miles, "After the Olympics," *Economist,* December 21, 2008, p. 58; "The Next China," *Economist,* July 31, 2010, pp. 48–50; "China Revises Up 2010 GDP Expansion," *People's Daily Online*, September 8, 2011, english.peopledaily.com.cn/.

■ Chapter 8

International Management in Action: Point/Counterpoint: Boeing vs. Airbus   "Start Your Engines," *Economist,* March 20, 2010, pp. 69–70; "Business," *Economist,* July 3, 2010, p. 8; "The Best Plane Loses," *Economist,* March 13, 2010, p. 66.

International Management in Action: Can Internet and Mobile Access Transform Poor Economies at the Base of the Pyramid?   Mike Powell, "Culture and the Internet in Africa, a Challenge for Political Economists," *Review of African Political Economy*, June 2001, p. 241; "The Digital Gap," *Economist,* October 20, 2007, p. 64; "The Mobile Revolution in Africa," *Global Finance,* December 2009, p. 49; "Reasons to Cut Off Mr. Mugabe," *Economist*, April 13, 1996, p. 339.

In the International Spotlight: Poland   David Fairlamb and Bogdan Turek, "Poland and the EU: Will the Dynamic Poles Energize Europe or Sink into a Bureaucratic, Slow-Growth Trap?" *BusinessWeek*, May 10, 2004, p. 54; Ben Arisin Prague, "Central European Entrants to EU

Have Most to Gain but Are Least Prepared," *Knight Ridder Tribune Business News*, March 14, 2004, p. 1; The Economist Intelligence Unit, *Country Report: Poland* (Kent, U.K.: EIU, 2009), p. 23; "Poland," The World Bank, 2013, http://data.worldbank.org/country/poland/.

■ Chapter 9

International Management in Action: Joint Venturing in Russia
Keith A. Rosten, "Soviet–U.S. Joint Ventures: Pioneers on a New Frontier," *California Management Review*, Winter 1991, pp. 88–108; Steven Greenhouse, "Chevron to Spend $10 Billion to Seek Oil in Kazakhstan," *New York Times,* May 19, 1992, pp. A1, C9; Louis Uchitelle, "Givebacks by Chevron in Oil Deal," *New York Times*, May 23, 1992, pp. 17, 29; Craig Mellow, "Russia: Making Cash from Chaos," *Fortune*, April 17, 1995, pp. 145–151; Daniel J. McCarthy and Sheila M. Puffer, "Strategic Investment Flexibility for MNE Success in Russia," *Journal of World Business* 32, no. 4 (1997), pp. 293–318; R. Bruce Money and Debra Colton, "The Response of the 'New Consumer' to Promotion in the Transition Economies of the Former Soviet Bloc," *Journal of World Business* 35, no. 2 (2000), pp. 189–206.

International Management in Action: Organizing in Germany
Hermann Simon, "Lessons from Germany's Midsize Giants," *Harvard Business Review*, March–April 1992, pp. 115–123; Carla Rapoport, "Europe's Slump Won't End Soon," *Fortune*, May 3, 1993, pp. 82–87; Robert Neff and Douglas Harbrecht, "Germany's Mighty Unions Are Being Forced to Bend," *BusinessWeek,* March 1, 1993, pp. 52–56.

In the International Spotlight: Australia Wayne Arnold, "World Business Briefing: Australia's Jobless Rate Falls," *New York Times*, April 9, 2004, p. W1; "Finance and Economics: A Wonder Down Under—The Australian Economy," *Economist*, March 20, 2004, p. 105; "Raising our Forecast," *Business Asia*, February 22, 2010, pp. 6–7; "Labour Force," Australian Bureau of Statistics, July, 2013, www.abs.gov.au/ausstats/.

■ Chapter 10

International Management in Action: Sometimes It's All Politics
John Stackhouse, "India Sours on Foreign Investment," *Globe and Mail*, August 10, 1995, sec. 2, pp. 1–2; Peter Galuszka and Susan Chandler, "A Plague of Disjointed Ventures," *BusinessWeek,* May 1, 1995, p. 55; Marcus W. Brauchli, "Politics Threaten Power Project in India," *The Wall Street Journal*, July 3, 1995, p. A14; "Enron, and On and On," *Economist*, April 21, 2001, pp. 56–57; Saritha Rai, "Enron Unit Moves to End India Contract for Power," *New York Times*, May 22, 2001, pp. W1, W7; "Enron Properties Outside the U.S. Hit Auction Block," *The Wall Street Journal*, January, 22, 2002, p. A6.

In the International Spotlight: Brazil *CIA Factbook* (2001); Jonathan Wheatley, "Is Lula's Honeymoon Winding Down?" *BusinessWeek,* April 26, 2004, p. 59; "BellSouth's Latin Ambitions," *BusinessWeek Online*, October 20, 2003; Larry Rohter, "Brazil's President Re-elected in Land-slide," *New York Times*, October 29, 2006, p. A1; "In Lula's Footsteps," *Economist*, July 3, 2010, pp. 35–38; "Brazil: A New Era," *Euromoney*, December 2009, pp. 8–9; "Condemned to Prosperity," *Economist*, November 14, 2009, pp. 11–14; "Free Kicks and Kickbacks," *Economist*, November 3, 2007, p. 43; *CIA Factbook* (2012).

■ Chapter 11

International Management in Action: How the Japanese Do Things Differently Ford S. Worthy, "Japan's Smart Secret Weapon," *Fortune,* August 12, 1991, pp. 72–75; Brenton R. Schlender, "Hard Times for High Tech," *Fortune*, March 22, 1993, p. 98; Ronald Henkoff, "Companies

That Train Best," *Fortune*, March 22, 1993; Jim Carlton, "Sega Leaps Ahead by Shipping New Player Early," *The Wall Street Journal,* May 11, 1995, pp. B1, B3; Jeffrey K. Liker and Yen-Chun Wu, "Japanese Auto-makers, U.S. Suppliers and Supply-Chain Superiority," *Sloan Management Review*, Fall 2000, pp. 81–93.

In the International Spotlight: Turkey "GDP, US$, Current Prices, Current PPPs, Millions," OECD, retrieved April 1, 2013; "World Development Indicators Database: Turkey," The World Bank, 2012; "Economic Outlook 2002–2011 & 2011–2017," *Turkish Statistical Institute*, 2012; "GDP Composition by Sector," *CIA World Factbook*, 2012, www.cia.gov; "Turkey: Istanbul Clashes Rage as Violence Spreads to Ankara," *The Guardian*, May 31, 2013, www.guardian.co.uk/.

■ Chapter 12

International Management in Action: McDonald's New Latin Flavor "Putting the Front Line First: McDonald's Commitment to Employees Bolsters the Bottom Line," *Hewitt*, vol. 9, issue 1, http://www.hewittassociates.com/intl/na/en-us/KnowledgeCenter/Magazine/vol9_iss1/departments-upclose.html.

International Management in Action: Karoshi: Stressed Out in Japan Michael Zielenziger, "Alcohol Consumption a Rising Problem in Japan," *Miami Herald*, December 28, 2000, p. 10A; Howard K. French, "A Postmodern Plague Ravages Japan's Workers," *New York Times*, February 21, 2000, p. A4; William S. Brown, Rebecca E. Lubove, and James Kwalwasser, "Karoshi: Alternative Perspectives of Japanese Management Styles," *Business Horizons*, March–April 1994, pp. 58–60; Karen Lowry Miller, "Now, Japan Is Admitting It: Work Kills Executives," *BusinessWeek,* August 3, 1992, p. 35.

In the International Spotlight: Indonesia "World Economic Outlook Database," *International Monetary Fund*, October 2012, www.imf.org; "Doing Business in Indonesia," *The World Bank*, 2012, www.doingbusiness.org; "Policy Watch: UN Climate Talks Wrap Up, Indonesia Approves Landmark Forest Protection Deal, and Africa's Largest Solar Plant Close to Breaking Ground," *Climate Policy Initiative*, December 2012, climatepolicyinitiative.org; "Indonesia Tries to Preserve Forests Using Carbon Credits," *Sustainable Business*, December 13, 2012, www.sustainablebusiness.com/.

■ Chapter 13

International Management in Action: Global Teams Jitao Li, Katherine R. Xin, Anne Tsui, and Donald C. Hambrick, "Building Effective International Joint Venture Leadership Teams in China," *Journal of World Business* 34, no. 1 (1999), pp. 52–68; Charlene Marmer Solomon, "Global Teams: The Ultimate Collaboration," *Personnel Journal*, September 1995, pp. 49–58; Andrew Kakabdse and Andrew Myers, "Qualities of Top Management: Comparison of European Manufacturers," *Journal of Management Development* 14, no. 1 (1995), pp. 5–15; Noel M. Tichy, Michael I. Brimm, Ram Chran, and Hiroraka Takeuchi, "Leadership Development as a Lever for Global Transformation," in *Globalizing Management: Creating and Leading the Competitive Organization*, ed. Vladimir Pucik, Noel M. Tichy, and Carole K. Barnett (New York: Wiley, 1993), pp. 47–60; Gloria Barczak and Edward F. McDonough III, "Leading Global Prod-uct Development Teams," *Research Technology Management* 46, no. 6 (November/December 2003), pp. 14–18; Michael J. Marquard and Lisa Horvath, *Global Teams* (Palo Alto, CA: Davies-Black, 2001).

In the International Spotlight: Germany "Leaders: Odd European Out; Germany's Economy," *Economist,* February 21, 2004, p. 13; Robert Metz, Rebecca Riley, and Martin Weale, "Economic

Performance in France, Germany and the United Kingdom, 1997–2002," *National Institute Economic Review*, April 2004, pp. 83–99; "The Lives of Others," *Economist,* August 8, 2009, pp. 65–66; "GDP 2008-2012," *The World Bank*, 2013, http://data.worldbank.org/indicator/.

■ Chapter 14

International Management in Action: Important Tips on Working for Foreigners   Martin J. Gannon, *Understanding Global Cultures*, 2nd ed. (Thousand Oaks, CA: Sage, 2001); Richard D. Lewis, *When Cultures Collide* (London: Nicholas Brealey, 1999); Roger E. Axtell, ed., *Do's and Taboos Around the World* (New York: Wiley, 1990); John Holusha, "No Utopia But to Workers It's a Job," *New York Times,* January 29, 1989, sec. 3, pp. 1, 10; Faye Rice, "Should You Work for a Foreigner?" *Fortune*, August 1, 1988, pp. 123–124; Jeanne Whalen, "American Finds Himself Atop Russian Oil Giant in Turmoil," *The Wall Street Journal,* October 30, 2003, p. B1.

International Management in Action: U.S.-Style Training for Expats and Their Teenagers   Dawn Anfuso, "HR Unites the World of Coca-Cola," *Personnel Journal*, November 1994, pp. 112–121; Karen Dawn Stuart, "Teens Play a Role in Moves Overseas," *Personnel Journal*, March 1992, pp. 72–78; Richard M. Hodgetts and Fred Luthans, "U.S. Multinationals' Expatriate Compensation Strategies," *Compensation and Benefits Review*, January–February 1993, p. 61; Philip R. Harris and Robert T. Moran, *Managing Cultural Differences: High-Performance Strategies for a New World of Business,* 3rd ed. (Houston: Gulf Publishing, 1991), Chapter 9.

International Management in Action: Lessons in Global Leadership Development: The PWC Ulysses Program   Alina Dizik, "Sustainability Is a Growing Theme," *The Wall Street Journal,* March 4, 2010, http://online.wsj.com/article/SB100014240527487045413045750 9514203847820.html?KEYWORDS=social+responsibility (accessed October 21, 2010); Global Giving Matters, "PricewaterhouseCoopers' Project Ulysses—Linking Global Leadership Training to a Community Development," September/October 2004, http://www.synergos.org/globalgivingmatters/features/0409ulysses.htm (accessed October 21, 2010); Jessi Hempel and Seth Porges, "It Takes a Village—And a Consultant; PricewaterhouseCoopers Tests Partners by Sending Them to Work in Poor Nations," *Bloomberg BusinessWeek,* September 6, 2004, http://www.businessweek.com/magazine/content/04_36/b3898097_mz056.htm (accessed October 21, 2010); Jessica Marquez, "Companies Send Employees on Volunteer Projects Abroad to Cultivate Leadership Skills," *All Business*, November 21, 2005, http://www.allbusiness.com/management/3495038-1.html (accessed October 21, 2010); Nicola Pless and Ralph Schneider, "Towards Developing Global Responsible Leaders: The PwC Ulysses Experience," *Scientific Commons*, 2006, http://www.scientificcommons.org/71 (accessed October 21, 2010).

In the International Spotlight: Russia   "Mixed Signals; Russian Reform," *Economist*, May 29, 2004, p. 39; "Command and Control; Russian Economy," *Economist*, April 10, 2004, p. 70; Jason Bush, "Russia's New Deal," *BusinessWeek Online*, March 29, 2007, www.businessweek.com/globalbiz/content/mar2007/gb20070329_226664.htm; The Economist Intelligence Unit, *Country Report: Russia* (Kent, U.K.: EIU, 2010), pp. 7–9; Lidia Kelly, "Russian Official Says Recession Has Already Started in Country," *The Wall Street Journal*, Eastern Edition, December 13, 2008, p. A10; "GDP 2008–2012," The World Bank, 2013, http://data.worldbank.org/indicator/.

Endnotes

■ Chapter 1

1. Lars Backstrom, "Anatomy of Facebook," *Facebook.com*, November 21, 2011, http://www.facebook.com/notes/facebook-data-team/anatomy-of-facebook/10150388519243859.

2. "Key Facebook Facts," *Facebook.com*, 2013, http://newsroom.fb.com/Key-Facts.

3. Backstrom, "Anatomy of Facebook."

4. ComScore, "The State of Social Media," 2012.

5. "Facebook Statistics," *Social Bakers*, 2013, http://www.socialbakers.com/facebook-statistics/.

6. *P&G*, http://www.facebook.com/futurefriendly/.

7. Lauren Coleman-Lochner, "Social Media Takes Center Stage at P&G," *Bloomberg BusinessWeek*, March 29, 2012, http://www.businessweek.com/articles/2012-03-29/social-networking-takes-center-stage-at-p-and-g.

8. Ibid.

9. Erik Qualman, *Socialnomics: How Social Media Transforms the Way We Live and Do Business*. Hoboken, NJ: Wiley, 2009, front flap, pp. 95, 110.

10. Ibid.

11. Rose Yu and Yajun Zhang, "China Car Sales Set to Surge in 2013," *The Wall Street Journal online*, January 11, 2013, http://online.wsj.com/article/SB10001424127887324081704578235150976448808.html?mod=googlenews_wsj.

12. Rajesh Mahapatra, "Cisco to Set Up Center in India," *Associated Press* online, December 6, 2006.

13. Joan Lublin, "India Could Provide Unique Opportunities for Expat Managers," *The Wall Street Journal*, May 8, 2007, p. B1.

14. Emily Glazer, "P&G Unit Bids Goodbye to Cincinnati, Hello to Asia," *The Wall Street Journal Online*, May 10, 2012, http://online.wsj.com/article/SB10001424052702304070304577396053688081544.html.

15. Laurie Burkitt, "GE Bases X-ray Unit in China," *The Wall Street Journal Online*, July 26, 2012, http://online.wsj.com/article/SB10001424053111904772304576467873321597208.html.

16. "American Powerhouse Builds Global Profile," *The Wall Street Journal Online*, November 4, 2012, http://online.wsj.com/article/SB10001424052970204712904578092182301796600.html.

17. Rick Newman, "Why U.S. Companies Aren't so American Anymore," *US News and World Report: Money*, June 30, 2011, http://money.usnews.com/money/blogs/flowchart/2011/06/30/why-us-companies-arent-so-american-anymore.

18. Quentin Hardy, "IBM's Continent Building In Africa," *Forbes*, September 2, 2011, http://www.forbes.com/sites/quentinhardy/2011/09/02/ibms-continent-building-in-africa/.

19. Roberta Prescott, "Emerging Markets to Represent 30% of IBM's Global Revenues by 2015," *RCRWireless.com*, November 28, 2011, http://www.rcrwireless.com/americas/20111128/finance/emerging-markets-to-represent-30-of-ibm%E2%80%99s-global-revenues-by-2015/.

20. "New IBM Research Lab to Open in Kenya," *IBM.com*, August 13, 2012, http://www-03.ibm.com/press/us/en/pressrelease/38568.wss.

21. Thomas Friedman, *The World Is Flat: A Brief History of the Twenty-first Century* (New York: Farrar, Straus and Giroux, 2005).

22. "Anti-forum Protests Turn Violent," Associated Press, February 2, 2009.

23. Michael Yaziji and Jonathan P. Doh, *NGOs and Corporations: Conflict and Collaboration* (Cambridge: Cambridge University Press, 2009).

24. For discussions of the benefits of globalization, see Jagdish Bhagwati, *In Defense of Globalization* (New York: Oxford University Press, 2004), and Edward Graham, *Fighting the Wrong Enemy: Antiglobal Activists and Multinational Enterprises* (Washington, DC: Institute for International Economics, 2000).

25. For discussion of some of the emerging concerns surrounding globalization, see Peter Singer, *One World: The Ethics of Globalization* (New Haven: Yale University Press, 2002); *George Soros*, George Soros on Globalization (New York: Public Affairs Books, 2002); Joseph Stiglitz, *Globalization and Its Discontents* (New York: Norton, 2002).

26. Steve Hamm, "The Trouble with India," *BusinessWeek*, March 19, 2007, pp. 48–58.

27. Paul Blustein, "EU Offers to End Farm Subsidies," *Washington Post*, May 11, 2004, p. E1.

28. "Developing Nations Call for WTO Deal to Help Poor," *Reuters.com*, November 29, 2009.

29. CIA, *The World Factbook* (2009), www.cia.gov/library/publications/the-world-factbook/geos/cs.html.

30. Office of the United States Trade Representative, "Trade Agreements," www.ustr.gov/Trade_Agreements/Section_Index.html.

31. Haydn Shaughnessy, "China Could Overtake U.S. by 2027," *Forbes*, November 21, 2011, http://www.forbes.com/sites/haydnshaughnessy/2011/11/21/china-could-overtake-us-by-2027/.

32. Office of the United States Trade Representative, "The United States in the Trans-Pacific Partnership." http://www.ustr.gov/about-us/press-office/fact-sheets/2011/november/united-states-trans-pacific-partnership.

33. Goldman Sachs, "Global Economics Paper No: 99: Dreaming with the BRICs: The Path to 2050," October 1, 2003.

34. Goldman Sachs, "Global Economics Paper No: 208: The BRICs 10 Years On: Halfway Through the Great Transformation," December 7, 2011.

35. Eric Martin, "Move Over BRICs. Here Comes the MISTs." *BusinessWeek*, August 9, 2012. Businessweek.com.

36. Alex Frangos, "Emerging World Loses Growth Lead," *The Wall Street Journal Online*, August 11, 2013, online.wsj.com.

37. Ibid.

38. Kenneth Rapoza, "This Year's World Growth Slowest Since 2008 Crisis, Forecasts 'The Economist'," *Forbes Online*, August 22, 2013, forbes.com.

39. WTO, International Trade Statistics (Switzerland, WTO, 2012).

40. UNCTAD, World Investment Report 2012 (Switzerland, United Nations, 2012).

41. R. Glenn Hubbard and Anthony Patrick O'Brien, *Essentials of Economics* (Upper Saddle River, NJ: Pearson Prentice Hall, 2007).

42. Ibid.

43. Ibid.

44. CIA, *The World Factbook* (2012), https://www.cia.gov/library/publications/the-world-factbook/geos/mx.html.

45. The Economist. "Mexico's President Working Through a Reform Agenda," April 16, 2013. *Economist.com.*

46. CIA, *The World Factbook* (2012), https://www.cia.gov/library/publications/the-world-factbook/geos/ee.html.

47. James Kanter and Judy Dempsey, "Europeans Move to Head Off Spread of Debt Crisis," *New York Times,* May 8, 2010, p. B1.

48. Jack Perkowski, "Managing the Dragon's 2013 China Predictions," *Forbes,* January 7, 2013, http://www.forbes.com/sites/jackperkowski/2013/01/07/managing-the-dragons-2013-china-predictions/.

49. John Boudreau and Brandon Bailey, "Doing Business in China Getting Tougher for U.S. Companies," *Mercury News,* March 27, 2010; Edward Wong and Mark Landler, "China Rejects U.S. Complaints on Its Currency," *New York Times online,* February 4, 2010.

50. Aaron Back and Andrew Browne, "Wen Defends Chinese Trade, Currency Policies," *The Wall Street Journal Online,* March 14, 2012, http://online.wsj.com/article/SB10001424052702304450004577280331907336736.html.

51. William R Cline and John Williamson, Policy Brief 11–18: The Current Currency Situation (Washington DC, Peterson Institute for International Economics, 2011).

52. Bloomberg News. "Yum's 29% Sales Collapse in China Goes Beyond Avian Flu." May 12, 2013. *Bloomberg.com.*

53. Keith Bradsher, "Chinese City Shuts Down 13 Wal-Marts." *New York Times,* October 10, 2011, p. B9.

54. Thomas Fuller, " Yingluck Shinawatra Is Elected Thai Prime Minister by Parliament," *New York Times,* August 5, 2011, p. A5.

55. Acha Leke, Susan Lund, Charles Roxburgh, and Arend van Wamelen, "What's Driving Africa's Growth," *McKinsey Quarterly,* June 2010, https://www.mckinseyquarterly.com/ Economic_Studies/Productivity_Performance/Whats_driving_Africas_growth_2601.

■ Chapter 2

1. John D. Sutter, "The Faces of Egypt's 'Revolution 2.0'," *CNN.com,* February 21, 2011, http://www.cnn.com/2011/TECH/innovation/02/21/egypt.internet.revolution/index.html.

2. E.B. Boyd, "How Social Media Accelerated the Uprising in Egypt," *Fast Company,* January 31, 2011, http://www.fastcompany.com/1722492/how-social-media-accelerated-uprising-egypt.

3. John D. Sutter, "The Faces of Egypt's 'Revolution 2.0'," *CNN.com,* February 21, 2011, http://www.cnn.com/2011/TECH/innovation/02/21/egypt.internet.revolution/index.html.

4. Carol Huang. "Facebook and Twitter key to Arab Spring uprisings: Report," *The National,* June 6, 2011, http://www.thenational.ae/news/uae-news/facebook-and-twitter-key-to-arab-spring-uprisings-report.

5. James Cowie, "Egypt leaves the Internet," *Renesys,* February 4, 2011, http://web.archive.org/web/20110205011946/http://www.renesys.com/blog/2011/01/egypt-leaves-the-internet.shtml.

6. Huang. "Facebook and Twitter key to Arab Spring uprisings: Report."

7. Vadim Lavrusik, "How Journalists Are Using Social Media to Report on the Egyptian Uprisings," *Mashable,* January 31, 2011, http://mashable.com/2011/01/31/journalists-social-media-egypt/.

8. Tanja Aitamurto, "How Social Media Is Keeping the Egyptian Revolution Alive," *PBS,* September 13, 2011, http://www.pbs.org/mediashift/2011/09/how-social-media-is-keeping-the-egyptian-revolution-alive256.html.

9. Huang. "Facebook and Twitter key to Arab Spring uprisings: Report."

10. E.B. Boyd, "How Social Media Accelerated the Uprising in Egypt," *Fast Company,* January 31, 2011, http://www.fastcompany.com/1722492/how-social-media-accelerated-uprising-egypt.

11. Ibid.

12. "Business Counts the Cost of the Arab Spring," *Grant Thornton,* June 21, 2011, http://www.gti.org/IBR2011/Arab-Spring.asp.

13. "The Economic Winners and Losers of the Arab Spring*,"* *EconMatters,* October 19, 2011, http://articles.businessinsider.com/2011-10-19/markets/30295935_1_exporters-arab-spring-libya.

14. Deena Kamel Yousef, "The Arab Spring Report: Uprisings Came at a Hefty Price," *GulfNews.com,* October 24, 2011, http://gulfnews.com/business/economy/the-arab-spring-report-uprisings-came-at-a-hefty-price-1.916915.

15. "Business Counts the Cost of the Arab Spring," *Grant Thornton,* June 21, 2011, http://www.gti.org/IBR2011/Arab-Spring.asp.

16. Ibid.

17. Michael Gundlach, "Understanding the Relationship Between Individualism-Collectivism and Team Performance Through an Integration of Social Identity Theory and the Social Relations Model," *Human Relations* 59, no. 12 (2006), pp. 1603–1632.

18. Donald Ball, Michael Geringer, Michael Minor, and Jeanne McNett, *International Business: The Challenge of Global Competition* (New York: McGraw-Hill, 2009).

19. Alessandra Galloni, Charles Forelle, and Stephen Fidler, "France, Germany Weigh Rescue Plan for Greece," *The Wall Street Journal online,* February 11, 2010.

20. Henry W. Spiegel and Ann Hubbard, *The Growth of Economic Thought* (Durham, NC: Duke University Press, 1991).

21. Ball et al., *International Business: The Challenge of Global Competition.*

22. Daniel J. McCarthy, Sheila M. Puffer, and Alexander I. Naumov, "Russia's Retreat to Statization and the Implications for Business," *Journal of World Business* 35, no. 3 (2000), p. 258.

23. Jason Bush, "Russia's New Deal," *BusinessWeek online,* March 29, 2007, www.businessweek.com/globalbiz/content/mar2007/gb20070329_226664.htm.

24. Transparency International, *Corruption Perceptions Index* 2012.

25. Heritage Foundation, Index of Economic Freedom 2013.

26. Steven Morris and Hannah Waldram, "David Cameron Warns Wales to Expect Budget Cuts," *GuardianUK.com,* May 17, 2010.

27. Keith Bradsher, "As China Stirs Economy, Some See Protectionism," *New York Times,* June 24, 2009, p. B1.

28. "When Opium Can Be Benign," *The Economist,* February 1, 2007, pp. 25–27.

29. John Child and David K. Tse, "China's Transition and Its Implications for International Business," *Journal of International Business Studies,* First Quarter 2001, pp. 5–21.

30. "Arab Spring Reignites Renewable Energy Debate," *Grant Thornton,* September 9, 2011.

31. "Business Counts the Cost of the Arab Spring." *Grant Thornton,* June 21, 2011.

32. Paul Nadler, "Making a Mystery out of How to Comply with Patriot Act," *American Banker,* May 19, 2004, p. 5.

33. "International: Financial Crisis Goes Global," *New York Times,* September 19, 2008.

34. David M. Herszenhorn, "Financial Overhaul Wins Final Approval in House," *New York Times,* June 30, 2010, p. A1.

35. John Graham, "Foreign Corrupt Practices Act: A Manager's Guide," *California Management Review,* Summer 1987, p. 9.

36. R. Christopher Cook and Stephanie Connor, "The Foreign Corruption Practices Act: 2010 and Beyond," *Jonesday.com,* January 2010.

37. Katsunori Nagayasu, "How Japan Restored Its Financial System," *The Wall Street Journal online,* August 6, 2009.

38. Robert Slate, "Chinese Role Models and Classic Military Philosophy in Dealing with Soldier Corruption and Moral Degeneration," *Journal of Third World Studies* 20, no. 1 (Spring 2003), p. 193.

39. Privatization Alert, Fdi.net, May 2010.

40. Thomas Friedman, *The World Is Flat (Updated and Expanded): A Brief History of the Twenty-first Century* (New York: Farrar, Straus and Giroux, 2006).

41. Charles W.L. Hill, *International Business* (New York: McGraw Hill/Irwin, 2011).

42. Rebecca Buckman, "China Keeps Telecom Firms Waiting on 3G," *The Wall Street Journal,* May 13, 2004, p. B4.

43. "China Telecom Sets Goal of 80mln Handsets in 2013," *Morning Whistle.* January 22, 2013. http://www.morningwhistle.com/html/2013/Company_Industry_0122/216797.html.

44. "China Set to Lead Smartphone Market in 2013," *China Daily.* January 18, 2013. http://www.chinadaily.com.cn/china/2013-01/18/content_16135904.htm.

45. "Microsoft Launches DreamSpark: Indian Students Get Access to Technical Software at No Charge," MS India Press Release, November 5, 2008, http://www.microsoft.com/india/msindia/Details.aspx?Id=108.

46. Andy Greenberg, "One Laptop Per Child Revamps Tablet Plans," *Forbes,* May 27, 2010, www.forbes.com.

47. Steve Hamm and Spencer E. Ante, "Underwater Peril," *BusinessWeek,* January 15, 2007, pp. 46–47.

48. "Supercomputers: The Race Is On," *BusinessWeek,* June 7, 2004, p. 76.

49. Nicholas Zamiska and Eric Bellman, "Ranbaxy Unveils Its Ambition to Be a Generics Powerhouse," *The Wall Street Journal,* January 10, 2007, p. A11.

50. John Carey, Adrienne Carter, and Assif Shameen, "Food vs. Fuel," *BusinessWeek,* February 5, 2007, pp. 80–83.

51. Christopher Leonard, "Monsanto, BASF Join Forces," *BusinessWeek Online,* March 21, 2007, www.businessweek.com.

52. Doris De Guzman, "Monsanto Sows More Seeds," *ICIS Chemical Business Americas* 270, no. 2 (2007), p. 26.

53. "World's First BSE-Immune Cow," *Asia Pacific Biotech News* 8, no. 12 (2004), p. 682.

54. www.fda.gov.

55. David Mildenberg, "SDN Sees Growth in High Speed Links," *The Business Journal,* May 14, 2004, p. 1.

56. Jean Halliday, "Car Renters Flock to Internet," *Advertising Age,* October 27, 2003, p. 44.

57. "Deutsche Bank Govvie Honcho: Business as Usual Now," *Bondweek,* June 22, 2003, p. 1.

58. "We the Savers" Blog, http://wethesavers.ingdirect.com/personal-finance-blog/.

59. Matt Richtel, "Wi-Fi Providers Rethink How to Make Money," *New York Times,* June 7, 2004, p. C1.

60. Allen Hammond, William J. Kramer, Julia Tran, Rob Katz, and Courtland Walker, "The Next 4 Billion: Market Size and Business Strategy at the Base of the Pyramid," *IFC & World Resource Institute,* March 2007, http://www.wri.org/publication/the-next-4–billion.

61. David Barboza, "In China, Knockoff Cellphones Are a Hit," *New York Times,* April 28, 2009, p. B1.

62. Jonathan P. Doh, Kraiwinee Bunyaratavej, and Eugene E. Hahn, "Separable but Not Equal: The Location Determinants of Discrete Offshoring Activities," *Journal of International Business Studies* 40, no. 6 (2009), pp. 926–943.

63. Bureau of Labor Statistics, *Economic News Release,* Table 3: "Private Sector Gross Job Gains and Losses by Industry, Seasonally Adjusted," May 20, 2010.

64. Jan Syfert, "Up There with the Best," *Productivity SA,* November–December 1998, p. 49.

65. Ashok Bhattacharjee, "India's Outsourcing Tigers Seek Cover, Markets, in Europe's East," *The Wall Street Journal,* December 18, 2003, p. A16.

■ Chapter 3

1. "Becoming a Responsible Company," *Environmental and Social Responsibility,* Patagonia.com, http://www.patagonia.com/us/environmentalism.

2. "Our Reason for Being," *Company Info,* Patagonia.com, http://www.patagonia.com/us/.

3. "Becoming a Responsible Company."

4. Ibid.

5. "Promoting Fair Labor Practices and Safe Working Conditions throughout Patagonia's Supply Chain," *Corporate Responsibility,* Patagonia.com, http://www.patagonia.com/us/.

6. Ibid.

7. "Becoming a Responsible Company."

8. "About us," *1% For The Planet,* http://www.onepercentfortheplanet.org/en/aboutus/.

9. "Our Switch to Organic Cotton," *Company Info,* Patagonia.com, http://www.patagonia.com/us/.

10. "Annual Report 2012," Philips, Retrieved March 20, 2013.

11. "EcoVision," *Sustainability,* Philips. http://www.philips.com/about/sustainability/ecovision/index.page.

12. "Meaningful Innovation: Improving People's Lives," Philips. http://www.philips.com/philips/shared/assets/global/sustainability/downloads/Philips-Sustainable-Innovation.pdf.

13. "Annual Report 2012."

14. "Meaningful Innovation: Improving People's Lives."

15. "Annual Report 2012."

16. Raz Godelnik, "Philips Makes the Business Case for Sustainability," TriplePundit, http://www.triplepundit.com/2012/03/philips-2011-report-great-example-business-case-sustainability/.

17. "Meaningful Innovation: Improving People's Lives."

18. Godelnik, "Philips Makes the Business Case for Sustainability."

19. "Awards and Recognition," Philips, http://www.philips.com/about/sustainability/awardsandrecognition.

20. "About Tesla," *Tesla Motors,* http://www.teslamotors.com/about.

21. "Features and Specs," *Tesla Motors,* http://www.teslamotors.com/roadster/specs.

22. "Features and Specs," *Tesla Motors,* http://www.teslamotors.com/models/features#/performance.

23. Chuck Squatriglia, "Tesla Motors Joins Daimler On a Smart EV | Autopia," *Wired.com,* January 13, 2009, http://www.wired.com/autopia/2009/01/tesla-motors-jo/.

24. Tori Tellem, "2012 Toyota RAV4-EV: Take Two," *The New York Times*. November 17, 2011.

25. "Mercedes Electric Car by Tesla Test Drive–Video Tesla Mercedes A Class," *The Daily Green,* September 3, 2010.

26. Press Release, "Tesla Initiates Voluntary Recall after Single Customer Incident," *Telsa Motors,* October 1, 2010, http://www.teslamotors.com/about/press/releases/tesla-initiates-voluntary-recall-after-single-customer-incident.

27. Suzanne Ashe, "Tesla Motors recalls electric Roadster," *CNET,* May 28, 2009, http://reviews.cnet.com/8301-13746_7-10251758-48.html.

28. John M. Broder, "Stalled on the E.V. Highway," *The New York Times,* February 8, 2013,

29. Paul Chesser, "Tesla CEO Elon Musk Fights Perceptions as Stock Drops," *NLPC.org,* February 26, 2013, http://nlpc.org/stories/2013/02/25/tesla-ceo-elon-musk-fights-perceptions-stock-drops.

30. Ibid.

31. Kristen Scholer and Lee Spears, "Tesla Posts Second-Biggest Rally for 2010 U.S. IPO," *Bloomberg Businessweek,* June 29, 2010.

32. Thomas Donaldson, *The Ethics of International Business* (New York: Oxford University Press, 1989).

33. I. Kant, *Fundamental Principles of the Metaphysics of Morals,* trans. Thomas K. Abbott (New York: Macmillan, 1949 [1785]), p. 18.

34. Aristotle, *Nicomachean Ethics,* trans. Martin Ostwald (New York: Macmillan, 1962), p. 153.

35. W. Frankena, *Ethics,* 2nd ed. (Engelwood Cliffs, NJ: Prentice Hall, 1973).

36. J. Bentham, *The Principles of Morals and Legislation* (Amherst, NY: Prometheus Books, 1988 [1789]); J. S. Mill, *Utilitarianism* (Indianapolis: Bobbs-Merrill, 1957 [1861]).

37. R. J. Vincent, *Human Rights and International Relations* (New York: Cambridge University Press, 1986).

38. Vladimir Kovalev, "EU Presses Russia on Human Trafficking," *BusinessWeek,* February 23, 2007, http://www.businessweek.com/globalbiz/content/feb2007/gb20070223_311905.htm?chan=globalbiz_europe_more+of+today's+top+stories; Amanda Walker, "Russia Accused over Trafficking Victims," Skynews, sky.com, May 27, 2010.

39. Andrew Pollack, "In Japan, It's See No Evil; Have No Harassment," *New York Times,* May 7, 1996, p. C5; Howard W. French, "Diploma at Hand, Japanese Women Find Glass Ceiling Reinforced with Iron," *New York Times,* January 1, 2001, p. A4.

40. Yuri Kageyama, "Beauty Care Executives Break Japanese Glass Ceiling," *Associated Press,* latimes.com, May 29, 2010.

41. Tackling child labour: From commitment to action (Geneva: International Labour Organization, 2012).

42. Ibid.

43. Mikey Campbell. "Foxconn promises to fix a multitude of violations found by FLA audit," *Apple Insider,* March 29, 2012. http://appleinsider.com/articles/12/03/29/foxconn_promises_to_fix_violations_found_by_fla_audit.html.

44. David Barboza, "After Spate of Suicides, Technology Firm in China Raises Workers' Salaries," *New York Times,* June 3, 2010, p. B3.

45. Mikey Campbell. "Foxconn Promises to Fix a Multitude of Violations found by FLA audit," *Apple Insider,* March 29, 2012. http://appleinsider.com/articles/12/03/29/foxconn_promises_to_fix_violations_found_by_fla_audit.html.

46. Shelly Banjo. "Wal-Mart toughens supplier policies," Wall Street Journal. January 21, 2013. http://online.wsj.com/article/SB10001424127887323301104578256183164905720.html.

47. Steven Greenhouse and Jim Yardley, " Global Retailers Join Safety Plan for Bangladesh." *New York Times,* May 14, 2013, p. A1.

48. David Stern, "The Rise and Fall of the Environmental Kuznets Curve," *World Development* 32, no. 8 (2004), pp. 1419–1439.

49. Ron Duska and Nicholas M. Rongione, *Ethics and Corporate Responsibility: Theory, Cases and Dilemmas* (New York: Thomas Custom Publishing, 2003).

50. Paul M. Minus, *The Ethics of Business in a Global Economy* (Boston: Kluwer Academic Publishers, 1993).

51. Steve Hamm, "How Accenture One-Upped Bangalore," *BusinessWeek,* April 23, 2007, pp. 98–99.

52. Thomas Donaldson and Thomas W. Dunfee, *Ties That Bind: A Social Contracts Approach to Business Ethics* (Cambridge, MA: Harvard Business Press, 1999).

53. Abigal McWilliams and Donald Siegel, "Corporate Social Responsibility: A Theory of the Firm Perspective," *Academy of Management Review* 26, no. 1 (2001), pp. 117–127.

54. "Non-governmental Organizations and Business: Living with the Enemy," *Economist,* August 9, 2002, pp. 49–50.

55. Edelman Trust Barometer 201209, http://www.edelman.com/trust/2012/.

56. "Environmentalists Get Citigroup Pledge," *New York Times,* January 22, 2004, p. C3.

57. "WTO to Allow Access to Cheap Drug Treatments," *Los Angeles Times,* August 31, 2003, p. A4.

58. USAS Press Release on Jerzees de Honduras victory, November 18, 2009, http://usas.org/2009/11/18/usas-press-release-on-jerzees-de-honduras-victory/.

59. Jonathan P. Doh and Terrence R. Guay, "Globalization and Corporate Social Responsibility: How Nongovernmental Organizations Influence Labor and Environmental Codes of Conduct," *Management International Review* 44, no. 3 (2004), pp. 7–30; Petra Christmann and Glen Taylor, "Globalization and the Environment: Strategies for International Voluntary Environmental Initiatives," *Academy of Management Executive* 16, no. 30 (2002), pp. 121–135.

60. More with less: Scaling Sustainable Consumption and Resource Efficiency (Geneva: World Economic Forum, 2012).

61. For more information visit www.epa.gov.

62. For more information regarding the role of the UNEP visit www.unep.org.

63. http://corporate.walmart.com/global-responsibility/environment-sustainability.

64. Marc Gunther, "The Green Machine," *Fortune,* August 7, 2006, pp. 42–57; Marc Gunther, "Wal-Mart: Still the Green Giant," May 19, 2010, www.marcgunther.com/2010/05/19/walmart-still-the-green-giant/.

65. http://www.walmartsustainabilityhub.com/

66. Gunther, "The Green Machine."

67. Ecomagination 2008 Annual Report, pp. 1–36, GE Ecomagination website; http://ge.ecomagination.com/_files/downloads/reports/ge_2008_ecomagination_report.pdf; Healthymagination 2009 Annual Report, pp. 1–40, GE Healthymagination website, http://files.gecompany.com/healthymagination/ar/healthymagination_annual_report.pdf; Stuart L. Hart and Mark B. Milstein, "In Search of Sustainable Enterprise: The Case of GE's Ecomagination Initiative," *Value News Network,* April 23, 2007, http://www.policyinnovations.org/ideas/innovations/data/ecomagination.

68. Organization for Economic Cooperation and Development, Corporate Governance: A Survey of OECD Countries (Paris: OECD, 2003).

69. Stijn Claessens and Joseph P. H. Fan, "Corporate Governance in Asia: A Survey," *International Review of Finance* 3, no. 2 (2002), pp. 71–103.

70. Bob Davis, "The Economy: U.S. Nears Pact on Corruption Treaty," *The Wall Street Journal,* August 13, 2003, p. A2. See also Jonathan P. Doh, Peter Rodriguez, Klaus Uhlenbruck, Jamie Collins, and Lorraine Eden, "Coping with Corruption in Foreign Markets," *Academy of Management Executive* 17, no. 3 (2003), pp. 114–127.

71. Ken Stier, "Too Big to Be Nailed," *Cnnmoney.com,* April 19, 2001.

72. Tipton F. McCubbins, "Somebody Kicked the Sleeping Dog—New Bite in the Foreign Corrupt Practices Act," *Business Horizons,* January–February 2001, p. 27.

73. Greg Steinmetz, "U.S. Firms Are among Least Likely to Pay Bribes Abroad, Survey Finds," *The Wall Street Journal,* August 25, 1997, p. 5.

74. Edmund L. Andrews, "29 Nations Agree to Outlaw Bribing Foreign Officials," *New York Times,* November 21, 1997, p. C2.

75. "Special Report: The Short Arm of the Law—Bribery and Business," *Economist,* March 2, 2002, p. 85.

76. "Putting the World to Rights," *Economist,* June 5, 2004, p. 63.

77. Gustavo Capdevilla, "Development: U.N. Report Calls for Urgent Action on Poverty," *Global Information Network,* July 9, 2003, p. 1.

78. http://www.un.org/millenniumgoals/beyond2015.shtml.

79. Strategic Investments for Impact: Global Fund results report 2012. (Geneva: The Global Fund, 2012).

■ Part 1 Integrative Cases

Brief Integrative Case 1.1

1. "Nike CEO Retracts University Donation over Human Rights," *SocialFunds.com,* May 3, 2000.

2. State of California, San Francisco Superior Court, Marc Kasky v. Nike Inc., 02 C.D.O.S. 3790, www.law.com/regionals/ca/opinions/may/s087859.shtml (accessed May 24, 2007).

3. Linda Greenhouse, "Free Speech for Companies on Justices' Agenda," *New York Times,* April 20, 2003, p. A17.

4. Linda Greenhouse, "Nike Free Speech Case Is Unexpectedly Returned to California," *New York Times,* June 27, 2003, p. A16.

5. "Corporate Social Responsibility—Companies in the News: Nike," www.mallenbaker.net/csr/CSRfiles/nike.html (accessed May 24, 2007).

6. Nike Inc. Press Release, "Nike Foundation Secures Footing in Helping to Reach Millennium Development Goals," www.nikebiz.com (accessed September 15, 2005).

7. Nike Inc. Press Release, "Nike Announces $200,000 Grant to Hillsboro Schools," www.nikebiz.com (accessed March 6, 2007).

Brief Integrative Case 1.2

1. "Dansko: Our Story." http://www.dansko.com/Our%20Story/ (accessed June 3, 2013).

2. "Dansko: Milestones." http://www.dansko.com/Press%20Room/Media%20Kit/History%20and%20Milestones/ (accessed June 3, 2013).

3. "Dansko: 20: Supplement to Footwear Daily. http://images.dansko.com/Dansko%20Twenty%20Celebrating%2020%20Years%20of%20Innovation%20and%20Inspiration.pdf (accessed June 3, 2013).

4. Maria Panaritis, "Dansko Stepping up its U.S. Footprint," *Philadelphia Inquirer,* March 11, 2012. http://articles.philly.com/2012-03-11/business/31145490.

5. "Dansko: 20: Supplement to Footwear Daily," p. 1.

6. Panaritis, "Dansko Stepping up its U.S. Footprint."

7. "Dansko: Milestones."

8. "Dansko: 20: Supplement to Footwear Daily," p. 1.

9. "Dansko: 20: Supplement to Footwear Daily," p. 4.

10. "Dansko: 20: Supplement to Footwear Daily," p. 5.

11. Panaritis, "Dansko Stepping up its U.S. Footprint."

12. Ibid.

13. Ibid.

14. Ibid.

In-Depth Integrative Case 1.1

1. USAS Press Release on Jerzees de Honduras victory, November 18, 2009, http://usas.org/2009/11/18/usas-press-release-on-jerzees-de-honduras-victory/.

2. David Barboza, "In Chinese Factories, Lost Fingers and Low Pay," *New York Times,* January 5, 2008, http://www.nytimes.com/2008/01/05/business/worldbusiness/05sweatshop.html.

3. Ibid.

4. "Tearing Down a Sweatshop," *Duke University News,* June 15, 2001, http://news.duke.edu/2001/06/peterle615.html.

5. Dexter Roberts and Aaron Bernstein, "Inside a Chinese Sweatshop: A Life of Fines and Beating," *BusinessWeek,* October 2, 2000, http://www.businessweek.com/2000/00_40/b3701119.htm.

6. Tim Connor, "Still Waiting for Nike to Do It," *Global Exchange,* May 2001, http://www.globalexchange.org/campaigns/sweatshops/nike/stillwaiting.html.

7. Ann Harrison and Jason Scorse, "Multinationals and Anti-Sweatshop Activism," *AEAweb,* May 2006, http://are.berkeley.edu/~harrison/Multinational&%20AntiSweat.pdf.

8. Ibid.

9. Ibid.

10. "Working in a Chinese Sweatshop for HP, Microsoft, Dell and IBM," *France 24,* December 2, 2009, http://observers.france24.com/en/content/20090212–working-hp-microsoft-china-serving-prison-sentence-sweatshop-dell-ibm-china.

11. Jonathan Adams and Kathleen E. McLaughlin, "Special Report: Silicon Sweatshops," *Globalpost,* November 17, 2009, http://www.globalpost.com/dispatch/china-taiwan/091103/silicon-sweatshops-globalpost-investigation.

12. Laura P. Hartman, *Encyclopedia of Business Ethics and Society,* vol. 4, ed. Robert W. Kolb (Thousand Oaks, CA: Sage Publications, 2008), pp. 2034–2041.

13. Richard A. Greenwald, *Dictionary of American History,* 3rd ed., vol. 8, ed. Stanley I. Kutler (New York: Charles Scribner's Sons, 2003), pp. 34–35.

14. Gary Chaison, *Encyclopedia of Clothing and Fashion,* vol. 3, ed. Valerie Steele (Detroit: Charles Scribner's Sons, 2005), pp. 247–250.

15. Ibid.

16. Ibid.

17. Ibid.

18. Greenwald, *Dictionary of American History,* pp. 34–35.

19. Chaison, *Encyclopedia of Clothing and Fashion,* pp. 247–250.

20. Ibid.

21. Hartman, *Encyclopedia of Business Ethics and Society,* pp. 2034–2041.

22. Chaison, *Encyclopedia of Clothing and Fashion,* pp. 247–250.

23. Ibid.

24. Hartman, *Encyclopedia of Business Ethics and Society,* pp. 2034–2041.

25. Ibid.

26. Ibid.

27. Ibid.

28. Laura Fitch, "Do Sweatshop Scandals Really Damage Brands?" *Brandchannel,* November 20, 2009, http://www.brandchannel.com/home/post/2009/11/20/Do-Sweatshop-Scandals-Really-Damage-Brands.aspx#continue.

29. Steven Greenhouse, "Labor Fight Ends in Win for Students," *New York Times,* November 17, 2009, http://www.nytimes.com/2009/11/18/business/18labor.html.

30. http://www.russell-brands.com/index.html.

31. USAS Press Release on Jerzees de Honduras victory.

32. "Russell Corporation's Rights Violations in Honduras," Worker Rights Consortium, News and Projects, http://workersrights.org/RussellRightsViolations.asp.

33. Ibid.

34. Greenhouse, "Labor Fight Ends in Win for Students."

35. "Mission," Worker Rights Consortium, http://workersrights.org/about/.

36. "Russell Corporation's Rights Violations in Honduras."

37. Greenhouse, "Labor Fight Ends in Win for Students."

38. USAS, "Mission and Vision," http://usas.org/about-us/.

39. Ibid.

40. Ibid.

41. http://hare.house.gov/uploads/Russell%20Letter.pdf.

42. FLA Board Resolution on Special Review for Russell Corporation, adopted June 25, 2009, http://www.fairlabor.org/images/NewsandPublications/NewsReleasesandStatements2009/board_resolution_russell_jun.25.09.pdf.

43. http://www.fairlabor.org/what_we_do.html.

44. http://www.fairlabor.org/about_us_board_directors_d1.html.

45. USAS Press Release on Jerzees de Honduras victory.

46. Ibid.

47. Greenhouse, "Labor Fight Ends in Win for Students."

48. Steven Greenhouse and Jim Yardley, " Global Retailers Join Safety Plan for Bangladesh." *New York Times,* May 14, 2013, p. A1.

In-Depth Integrative Case 1.2

1. "WTO to Allow Access to Cheap Drug Treatments," *Los Angeles Times,* August 31, 2003, p. A4.

2. Miriam Jordan, "Brazil to Stir Up AIDS-Drug Battle; Nation to Authorize Imports of Generics, Citing the Cost of Big Companies' Products," *The Wall Street Journal,* September 5, 2003, p. A3.

3. WHO, "Top 10 Causes of Death," Fact Sheet No. 310, November 2008.

4. Sushil Vachani, "South Africa and the AIDS Epidemic," *Vikalpa* 29, no. 1 (January–March 2004), pp. 101–109. HIV stands for human immunodeficiency virus; AIDS stands for acquired immunodeficiency syndrome.

5. Ibid.

6. UNAIDS, 2002 Report on Global AIDS, www.unaids.gov.

7. Donald G. McNeil, "Medicine Merchants: A Special Report: Drug Makers and 3rd World: Study in Neglect," *New York Times,* May 21, 2000, p. 1.

8. World Health Organization, World Health Report, 2003.

9. Bill Schiller, "Hope," *Toronto Star,* September 18, 1999.

10. Ibid.

11. Vachani, "South Africa and the AIDS Epidemic."

12. UNIAIDS, "Executive Director calls on African leaders to reduce the 'triple dependency' on external aid," June 6, 2012, http://www.unaids.org/en/resources/presscentre/featurestories/2012/june/2012060.

13. Pharmaceutical Research and Manufacturers of America, Pharmaceutical Industry Profile 2002 (Washington, DC, 2002).

14. McNeil, "Medicine Merchants."

15. Lawrence K. Altman, "In Effort to Save Lives, South Africa Creates an Anti-AIDS Campaign That Minces No Words," *New York Times,* July 9, 2000, p. 8.

16. Ibid.

17. This section draws from Sushil Vachani, "South Africa and the AIDS Epidemic," *Vikalpa* 29, no. 1 (January–March, 2004), pp. 101–109.

18. www.wto.org/english/tratop_e/trips_e/trips_e.htm (accessed July 26, 2002).

19. Vachani, "South Africa and the AIDS Epidemic."

20. UNAIDS, 2000 Report on the Global AIDS epidemic, www.unaids.gov.

21. Vachani, "South Africa and the AIDS Epidemic."

22. Pharmaceutical Research and Manufacturers of America, Pharmaceutical Industry Profile 2002, p. 36.

23. This section draws from Sushil Vachani, "South Africa and the AIDS Epidemic," *Vikalpa* 29, no. 1 (January–March, 2004), pp. 101–109.

24. Karl Vick, "African AIDS Victims Losers of a Drug War: U.S. Policy Keeps Price Prohibitive," *Washington Post,* December 4, 1999, p. A1.

25. Ibid.

26. Ibid.

27. Sarah Boseley, "Trade Terrorism," *The Guardian,* August 11, 1999.

28. Vick, "African AIDS Victims Losers of a Drug War."

29. Ibid.

30. Victor Mallet, "The Ravaged Continent: AIDS Is Now the Biggest Killer of Young Adults in Africa," *Financial Times,* December 3, 1999, p. 4.

31. Vachani, "South Africa and the AIDS Epidemic."

32. Justin Brown, "Spread of AIDS Raises Moral Issue for U.S.," *Christian Science Monitor,* July 12, 2000.

33. Ibid.

34. Nicol Degli Innocenti, "South Africa Hits Back at EU Criticism of AIDS Policy," *Financial Times,* April 5, 2001, p. 11.

35. Melody Petersen and Larry Rohter, "Maker Agrees to Cut Prices of 2 AIDS Drugs in Brazil," *New York Times,* March 31, 2001, p. 4.

36. Vachani, "South Africa and the AIDS Epidemic."

37. UNAIDS, 2002 Report on the Global AIDS Epidemic, www.unaids.gov.

38. Vachani, "South Africa and the AIDS Epidemic."

39. Rachel Zimmerman, "Jack Valenti Will Lobby for AIDS Fight," *The Wall Street Journal,* June 3, 2004, p. B1.

40. http://www.avert.org/aids-funding.htm.

41. http://www.theglobalfund.org/en/donors/?lang=en.

42. http://www.avert.org/aids-funding.htm.

43. Ibid.

44. Ibid.

45. www.wto.org/english/tratop_e/trips_e/pharmpatent_e.htm (accessed July 26, 2002).

46. Julia Flynn and Mark Schoofs, "Glaxo, Boeringer to Let Africa Make More Generics for AIDS," *The Wall Street Journal,* December 11, 2003, p. D4.

47. Hollister H. Hovey, "Religious Groups Push Drug Cost to Assess HIV," *Dow Jones Newswires,* March 24, 2004.

48. World Trade Organization, Press Release, "Members OK Amendment to Make Health Flexibility Permanent," December 6, 2005, www.wto.org/english/news_e/pres05_e/pr426_e.htm.

49. Ibid.

50. Doctors Without Borders, "HIV/AIDS," 2006, www.doctorswith outborders.org/news/hiv-aids/index.cfm.

51. Ibid.

52. Doctors Without Borders, "Access Denied to Crucial New AIDS Medications," March 15, 2006, www.doctorswithoutborders.org/pr/2006/03–15–2006.cfm.

53. Ibid.

54. World Health Organization, "WHO Discussion Paper: The Practice of Charging User Fees at the Point of Service Delivery for HIV/AIDS Treatment and Care," December 2005, www.who.int/hiv/pub/advocacy/promotingfreeaccess.pdf.

55. UNAIDS/WHO Press Release, "HIV Infection Rates Decreasing in Several Countries but Global Number of People Living with HIV Continues to Rise," November 21, 2005, www.who.int/hiv/epiupdate2005/en/index.html.

56. James Hookway and Nicholas Zamiska, "Thai Showdown Spotlights Threat to Drug Patents: Abbott Protests Move to Buy Copycat Pills, but It Yields on Price," *The Wall Street Journal,* April 24, 2007, p. A1.

57. Ibid.

58. Alastair Stewart, "Brazil Moves to Break Merck AIDS Drug Patent," *The Wall Street Journal,* May 5, 2007, p. B6.

59. Ibid.

60. "Clinton, Drug Companies Strike Deal to Lower AIDS Drug Prices," *Associated Press,* May 8, 2007, lists.essential.org/pipermail/ip-health/2007–May/011142.html.

61. Ibid.

62. Donald G. McNeil, "Plan to Bring Generic AIDS Drugs to Poor Nations," *New York Times,* April 6, 2004, p. F6.

63. "R&D Spending by U.S. Biopharmaceutical Companies Reaches Record Levels in 2008 Despite Economic Challenges," PhRMA Press Release, March 10, 2009, http://www.phrma.org/news_room/ press_releases/r%26d_spending_by_u.s._biopharmaceutical_companies_reaches_record_levels_in_2008_despite_economic_chal/.

64. "109 Medicines and Vaccines Now in Development for HIV/AIDS," PhRMA Press Release, December 1, 2008, http://innovation.org/index.cfm/FutureOfInnovation/NewMedicinesinDevelopment/HIV-AIDS.

65. "PhRMA 2008 Report: Medicines in Development for HIV/AIDS," http://www.phrma.org/files/New%20Meds%20for%20 HIV-AIDS%20report.pdf.

66. Ibid.

67. "109 Medicines and Vaccines Now in Development for HIV/AIDS," PhRMA Press Release, December 1, 2008, http://www.phrma.org/news_room/press_releases/109_medicines_and_vaccines_now_in_development_for_hiv%10aids/.

68. "Drug Firms Agree to Invest More in AIDS Research—UN," *Reuters,* October 9, 2008, http://www.reuters.com/article/asiaCrisis/idUSN09327729.

69. "New York, 9 October 2008—Secretary-General's Statement following Meeting with Pharmaceutical and Diagnostic Companies Working on HIV and AIDS," http://www.un.org/apps/sg/sgstats.asp?nid=3466.

70. Reuters, October 9, 2008.

71. Andrew Clarke, "GKS Joins Forces with Pfizer to Develop HIV/AIDS Drugs," *Guardian,* April 16, 2009, http://www.guardian.co.uk/business/2009/apr/16/gsk-pfizer-hiv-aids.

72. Ibid.

73. Graham Ruddick, "GlaxoSmithKline to Inject £60m into HIV and AIDS Drugs in Africa," *Telegraph,* July 14, 2009, http://www.telegraph.co.uk/finance/newsbysector/pharmaceuticalsandchemicals/5826930/GlaxoSmithKline-to-inject-60m-into-HIV-and-Aids-drugs-in-Africa.html.

74. Duff Wilson, "AIDS Activists Issue Grades to Drug Companies," *New York Times,* September 10, 2009, http://www.nytimes.com/2009/09/10/business/10aids.html.

75. ViiV Healthcare, "ViiV healthcare awards grants from the Positive Action for Children Fund of £3.6m," June 30, 2010, http://www.viivhealthcare.com/media-room/press-releases/2010-06-30.aspx.

76. ViiV Healthcare, "ViiV healthcare's Positive Action for Children Fund announces 16 new grantees for the year 2011/2012," October 13, 2011, http://www.viivhealthcare.com/media-room/press-releases/2011-10-.

77. UNAIDS, "UNITAID: Five years of health innovation brings new approach and new medicines to developing country markets," May 11, 2012, http://www.unaids.org/en/resources/presscentre/featurestories/2012/may/201205.

■ Chapter 4

1. Associated Press, "Dealers and Car Owners Await Answers as Toyota's Massive Recalls go Global," *New York Daily News Online,* January 28, 2010, http://www.nydailynews.com/news/money/dealers-car-owners-await-answers-toyota-massive-recalls-global-article-1.193302.

2. Jeff Kingston, "A Crisis Made in Japan," *The Wall Street Journal,* February 5, 2010, http://online.wsj.com/article/SB1000142405274 87045332045750473706332344414.html..

3. Joseph B. White, "U.S. Fines Toyota for Defect Report Delays," *The Wall Street Journal Online,* December 18, 2012, http://online.wsj.com/article/SB100014241278873244075045781869931 19562224.html?mg=id-wsj.

4. Jeff Kingston, "A Crisis Made in Japan," *The Wall Street Journal,* February 5, 2010, http://online.wsj.com/article/SB1000142405274 87045332045750473706332344414.html.

5. Ibid.

6. "Independent Commission Releases Report on Fukushima Meltdown: Blames Japanese Culture," *Time,* July 5, 2012, http://science.time.com/2012/07/05/independent-commission-releases-report-on-fukushima-meltdown-blames-japanese-culture/.

7. "Fukushima Disaster Due to Japan's Culture? Ruth Benedict Would Have Said So," *East Asia Gazette,* July 13, 2012, http://asia-gazette.com/news/japan/157.

8. Jeff Kingston, "A Crisis Made in Japan," *The Wall Street Journal,* February 5, 2010, http://online.wsj.com/article/SB1000142405274 87045332045750473706332344414.html.

9. Akio Toyoda, "Back to Basics for Toyota," *The Wall Street Journal,* February 23, 2010, http://online.wsj.com/article/SB10001424 0527487044543045750816440513217222.html.

10. Jeffrey Johnson, Seongbae Lim, and Prasad Padmanabhan, "Important Lessons Need to Be Learned from the Toyota Recall," *San Antonio Business Journal,* March 19, 2010, http://www.bizjournals.com/birmingham/othercities/sanantonio/stories/

2010/03/22/editorial1.html?b=1269230400%5E3064371&s=
industry&i=manufacturing.

11. Ibid.

12. Bill Fischer, "Lessons from the Toyota Recall," *Management Issues.com,* February 9, 2010, http://www.management-issues.com/2010/2/9/opinion/lessons-from-the-toyota-recall.asp.

13. Jeffrey Johnson, Seongbae Lim, and Prasad Padmanabhan, "Important Lessons Need to Be Learned from the Toyota Recall," *San Antonio Business Journal,* March 19, 2010, http://www.bizjournals.com/birmingham/othercities/sanantonio/stories/2010/03/22/editorial1.html?b=1269230400%5E3064371&s=industry&i=manufacturing.

14. Pat Joynt and Malcolm Warner, "Introduction: Cross-Cultural Perspectives," in *Managing Across Cultures: Issues and Perspectives,* ed. Pat Joynt and Malcolm Warner (London: International Thomson Business Press, 1996), p. 3.

15. For additional insights see Gerry Darlington, "Culture—A Theoretical Review," in Pat Joynt and Malcolm Warner, *Managing Across Cultures: Issues and Perspectives* (London: International Thomson Business Press, 1996), pp. 33–55.

16. Fred Luthans, *Organizational Behavior,* 7th ed. (New York: McGraw-Hill, 1995), pp. 534–535.

17. Gary Bonvillian and William A. Nowlin, "Cultural Awareness: An Essential Element of Doing Business Abroad," *Business Horizons,* November–December 1994, pp. 44–54.

18. Roger E. Axtell, ed., *Do's and Taboos Around the World,* 2nd ed. (New York: Wiley, 1990), p. 3.

19. Lillian H. Chaney and Jeanette S. Martin, *Intercultural Business Communication* (Englewood Cliffs, NJ: Prentice Hall, 1995), p. 115.

20. Fons Trompenaars and Charles Hampden-Turner, *Riding the Waves of Culture: Understanding Diversity in Global Business,* 2nd ed. (New York: McGraw-Hill, 1998), p. 23.

21. Christopher Orpen, "The Work Values of Western and Tribal Black Employees," *Journal of Cross-Cultural Psychology,* March 1978, pp. 99–111.

22. William Whitely and George W. England, "Variability in Common Dimensions of Managerial Values Due to Value Orientation and Country Differences," *Personnel Psychology,* Spring 1980, pp. 77–89.

23. Ibid., p. 87.

24. George W. England and Raymond Lee, "The Relationship Between Managerial Values and Managerial Success in the United States, Japan, India, and Australia," *Journal of Applied Psychology,* August 1974, pp. 418–419.

25. George W. England, "Managers and Their Value Systems: A Five-Country Comparative Study," *Columbia Journal of World Business,* Summer 1978, p. 39.

26. A. Reichel and D. M. Flynn, "Values in Transition: An Empirical Study of Japanese Managers in the U.S.," *Management International Review* 23, no. 4 (1984), pp. 69–70.

27. Yumiko Ono and Bill Spindle, "Japan's Long Decline Makes One Thing Rise: Individualism," *The Wall Street Journal,* December 29, 2000, pp. A1, A4.

28. Sang M. Lee and Suzanne J. Peterson, "Culture, Entrepreneurial Orientation, and Global Competitiveness," *Journal of World Business* 35, no. 4 (2000), pp. 411–412.

29. "Confucius Makes a Comeback," *The Economist,* May 17, 2007, www.economist.com/world/asia/displaystory.cfm?story_id=9202957.

30. Geert Hofstede, *Culture's Consequences: International Differences in Work-Related Values* (Beverly Hills, CA: Sage, 1980).

31. Geert Hofstede, *Cultures and Organizations: Software of the Mind* (London: McGraw-Hill U.K., 1991), pp. 251–252.

32. Ibid.

33. Geert Hofstede and Michael Bond, "The Need for Synergy Among Cross-Cultural Studies," *Journal of Cross-Cultural Psychology,* December 1984, p. 419.

34. A. R. Negandhi and S. B. Prasad, *Comparative Management* (New York: Appleton-Century-Crofts, 1971), p. 128.

35. For additional insights, see Mark F. Peterson et al., "Role Conflict, Ambiguity, and Overload: A 21–Nation Study," *Academy of Management Journal,* June 1995, pp. 429–452.

36. Hofstede, *Culture's Consequences.*

37. Ibid.

38. Ibid.

39. Also see Chao C. Chen, Xiao-Ping Chen, and James R. Meindl, "How Can Cooperation Be Fostered? The Cultural Effects of Individualism-Collectivism," *Academy of Management Review* 23, no. 2 (1998), pp. 285–304.

40. Hofstede, *Culture's Consequences,* pp. 419–420.

41. Ibid., p. 420.

42. Geert Hofstede, "National Culture: Dimensions," http://geert-hofstede.com/dimensions.html.

43. Ibid.

44. Geert Hofstede. "Dimensionalizing Cultures: The Hofstede Model in Context," *Online Readings in Psychology and Culture:* Unit 2, 2011, http://scholarworks.gvsu.edu/orpc/vol2/iss1/8.

45. Geert Hofstede, "National Culture: Dimensions," http://geert-hofstede.com/dimensions.html.

46. Geert Hofstede. "Dimensionalizing Cultures: The Hofstede Model in Context," *Online Readings in Psychology and Culture:* Unit 2, 2011, http://scholarworks.gvsu.edu/orpc/vol2/iss1/8.

47. Fons Trompenaars, *Riding the Waves of Culture: Understanding Diversity in Global Business* (New York: Irwin, 1994), p. 10.

48. Talcott Parsons, *The Social System* (New York: Free Press, 1951).

49. Also see Lisa Hoecklin, *Managing Cultural Differences* (Workingham, England: Addison-Wesley, 1995).

50. Charles M. Hampden-Turner and Fons Trompenaars, "A World Turned Upside Down: Doing Business in Asia," in *Managing Across Cultures,* ed. Joynt and Warner (London: International Thomson Business Press, 1996), p. 279.

51. Ibid., p. 288.

52. Trompenaars, *Riding the Waves of Culture,* p. 131.

53. Ibid., p. 140.

54. Peter Dorfman, Mansour Javidan, Paul Hanges, Ali Dastmalchian, and Robert House, "GLOBE: A Twenty Year Journey into the Intriguing World of Culture and Leadership," *Journal of World Business* 47, (2012), pp. 504–518.

55. Ibid.

56. Mansour Javidan and Robert House, "Leadership and Cultures around the World: Findings from GLOBE: An Introduction to the Special Issue," *Journal of World Business* 37, no. 1 (2002), pp. 1–2.

57. Robert House, Paul J. Hanges, Mansour Javidan, Peter W. Dorfman, and Vipin Gupta, *Culture, Leadership, and Organizations: The GLOBE Study of 62 Societies* (London: Sage, 2004).

58. Kwong Leung, "Editor's Introduction to the Exchange between Hofstede and GLOBE," *Journal of International Business Studies* 37 (2006), p. 881.

59. Peter Dorfman, Mansour Javidan, Paul Hanges, Ali Dastmalchian, and Robert House, "GLOBE: A Twenty Year Journey into the Intriguing World of Culture and Leadership," *Journal of World Business* 47, (2012), pp. 504–518.

60. House et al., *Culture, Leadership, and Organizations: The GLOBE Study.*

61. Mansour Javidan and Robert House, "Cultural Acumen for the Global Manager: Lessons from Project GLOBE," *Organizational Dynamics* 29, no. 4 (2001), pp. 289–305.

62. Robert House, Mansour Javidan, Paul Hanges, and Peter Dorfman, "Understanding Cultures and Implicit Leadership Theories Across the Globe: An Introduction to Project GLOBE," *Journal of World Business* 37, no. 1 (2002), pp. 3–10.

63. Ibid.

64. David A. Waldman, Mary Sully de Luque et al., "Cultural and Leadership Predictors of Corporate Social Responsibility Values of Top Management: A GLOBE Study of 15 Countries," *Journal of International Business Studies* 37 (2006), pp. 823–837.

65. Geert Hofstede, "What Did GLOBE Really Measure? Researchers' Minds versus Respondents' Minds," *Journal of International Business Studies* 37 (2006), pp. 882–896.

66. P. Christopher Earley, "Leading Cultural Research in the Future: A Matter of Paradigms and Taste," *Journal of International Business Studies* 37 (2006), pp. 922–931; Peter B. Smith, "When Elephants Fight, the Grass Gets Trampled: The GLOBE and Hofstede Projects," *Journal of International Business Studies* 37 (2006), pp. 915–921.

67. Mansour Javidan, Peter W. Dorfman, et al., "In the Eye of the Beholder: Cross Cultural Lessons in Leadership from Project GLOBE," *Academy of Management Perspectives* 20, no. 1 (2006), pp. 67–90.

68. Ibid.

■ Chapter 5

1. Nancy J. Adler, *International Dimensions of Organizational Behavior*, 5th ed. (Cincinnati, OH: Southwestern, 2007).

2. Dylan Love, "At Apple, They Really Are After You," *Business Insider*, January 9, 2013. http://www.businessinsider.com/apple-corporate-culture-2013-1.

3. Adam Lashinsky, "The Secrets Apple Keeps," *Fortune*, January 28, 2012. http://tech.fortune.cnn.com/2012/01/18/inside-apple-adam-lashinsky/.

4. Sam Grobart, "How Samsung became the World's No. 1 Smartphone Maker," *Bloomberg Businessweek*. March 28, 2013. http://www.businessweek.com/articles/2013-03-28/how-samsung-became-the-worlds-no-dot-1-smartphone-maker#p1.

5. Miyoung Kim, "Samsung's Crisis Culture: a Driver and a Drawback," *Reuters*, September 2, 2012. http://www.reuters.com/article/2012/09/02/us-samsung-culture-idUSBRE8810B320120902.

6. Sam Grobart, "How Samsung Became the World's No. 1 Smartphone Maker," *Bloomberg Businessweek*. March 28, 2013. http://www.businessweek.com/articles/2013-03-28/how-samsung-became-the-worlds-no-dot-1-smartphone-maker#p1.

7. David M. Barreda, "Who Supplies Apple?" *China File*, http://www.chinafile.com/who-supplies-apple-it-s-not-just-china-interactive-map.

8. Peter Cohan, "Apple Can't Innovate or Manage Supply Chain," *Forbes*, October 26, 2012. http://www.forbes.com/sites/petercohan/2012/10/26/apple-cant-innovate-or-manage-supply-chain/.

9. Miyoung Kim, "Samsung Says to Fix Outsourcing Issues, but Keep Most Production Inhouse," *Reuters*, November 11, 2012. http://www.reuters.com/article/2012/11/30/us-samsung-labour-idUSBRE8AT09220121130.

10. Sam Grobart, "How Samsung Became the World's No. 1 Smartphone Maker," *Bloomberg Businessweek,* March 28, 2013. http://www.businessweek.com/articles/2013-03-28/how-samsung-became-the-worlds-no-dot-1-smartphone-maker#p1.

11. Ibid.

12. Leo Kelion, "Apple v Samsung Patent Verdict Reconsidered in Court," *BBC,* December 6, 2012. http://www.bbc.co.uk/news/technology-20615376.

13. Jung-ah Lee and Evan Ramstad, "Samsung's Smartphone Sales Surpass Apple's," *Wall Street Journal,* October 28, 2011. http://online.wsj.com/article/SB10001424052970203687504577002571419254242.html.

14. Brian S. Hall, "Samsung vs. Apple: Samsung is Winning Every Way But One," *Readwrite Mobile.* March 5, 2013. http://readwrite.com/2013/03/05/samsung-vs-apple-samsung-is-winning-every-way-but-one-infographic.

15. Ibid.

16. Market Data, Income Statement, *The Wall Street Journal.*

17. World Motor Vehicle Production (OICA, November 2012).

18. Luca Ciferri, "How Renault's Low-cost Dacia has Become a 'Cash Cow'," *Automotive News Europe,* January 2, 2013, http://europe.autonews.com/apps/pbcs.dll/article?AID=/20130102/ANE/312259994/how-renaults-low-cost-dacia-has-become-a-cash-cow.

19. Laurence Frost and Gilles Guillaume, "Renault Taps Logan Creator for Low-Cost Car for India," *Livemint*, December 16, 2012, http://www.livemint.com/Industry/lHHQsNgTS3bJKWMa1jvicK/Renault-taps-Logan-creator-for-5500-India-car.html.

20. "Renault-Nissan Alliance Recognises Its 10–Year Anniversary," *The Auto Channel*, March 27, 2009, http://www.theautochannel.com/news/2009/03/26/454752.html.

21. Lisa Hoecklin, *Managing Cultural Differences: Strategies for Competitive Advantage* (Workingham, England: Addison-Wesley, 1995), pp. 98–99.

22. Marcy Beitle, Arjun Sethi, Jessica Milesko, and Alyson Potenza, "The Offshore Culture Clash," *AT Kearney Executive Agenda* XI, no. 2 (2008), pp. 32–39.

23. Matt Ackerman, "State St.: New Markets Key to Growth," *American Banker,* May 3, 2004, p. 1.

24. Linda M. Randall and Lori A. Coakley, "Building a Successful Partnership in Russia and Belarus: The Impact of Culture on Strategy," *Business Horizons,* March–April 1998, pp. 15–22.

25. Fons Trompenaars and Charles Hampden-Turner, *Riding the Waves of Culture: Understanding Diversity in Global Business*, 2nd ed. (New York: McGraw-Hill, 1998), p. 202.

26. See, for example, Anisya S. Thomas and Stephen L. Mueller, "A Case for Comparative Entrepreneurship: Assessing the Relevance of Culture," *Journal of International Business Studies*, Second Quarter 2000, pp. 287–301.

27. Adapted from Richard Mead, *International Management* (Cambridge, MA: Blackwell, 1994), pp. 57–59.

28. Derived from www.communicaid.com/Malaysia-business-culture.asp.

29. Fred Luthans, Dianne H. B. Welsh, and Stuart A. Rosenkrantz, "What Do Russian Managers Really Do? An Observational Study with Comparisons to U.S. Managers," *Journal of International Business Studies,* Fourth Quarter 1993, pp. 741–761.

30. Diane H. B. Welsh, Fred Luthans, and Steven M. Sommer, "Organizational Behavior Modification Goes to Russia: Replicating an Experimental Analysis Across Cultures and Tasks," *Journal of Organizational Behavior Management* 13, no. 2 (1993), pp. 15–35; Diane H. B. Welsh, Fred Luthans, and Steven M. Sommer, "Managing Russian Factory Workers: The Impact of

U.S.-Based Behavioral and Participative Techniques," *Academy of Management Journal*, February 1993, pp. 58–79.

31. Welsh, Luthans, and Sommer, "Organizational Behavior Modification," p. 31. The summary of positive (17 percent average) performance from O.B.Mod. for U.S. samples can be found in Fred Luthans and Alexander Stajkovic, "Reinforce for Performance," *Academy of Management Executive* 13, no. 2 (1999), pp. 49–57.

32. Steven M. Sommer, Seung-Hyun Bae, and Fred Luthans, "The Structure-Climate Relationship in Korean Organizations," *Asia Pacific Journal of Management* 12, no. 2 (1995), pp. 23–36. Also see Steven Sommer, Seung-Hyun Bae, and Fred Luthans, "Organizational Commitment Across Cultures: The Impact of Antecedents on Korean Employees," *Human Relations* 49, no. 7 (1996), pp. 977–993.

33. Sommer, Bae, and Luthans, "The Structure-Climate Relationship."

34. Trompenaars and Hampden-Turner, *Riding the Waves of Culture*, p. 196.

35. Shari Caudron, "Lessons for HR Overseas," *Personnel Journal*, February 1995, p. 92.

36. Richard M. Hodgetts and Fred Luthans, "U.S. Multinationals' Compensation Strategies for Local Management: Cross-Cultural Implications," *Compensation and Benefits Review*, March–April 1993, pp. 42–48.

37. Philip M. Rosenzweig and Nitin Nohria, "Influences on Human Resource Management Practices in Multinational Corporations," *Journal of International Business Studies*, Second Quarter 1994, pp. 229–251.

38. "Disillusioned Workers Cost Japanese Economy up to $180.18 Billion," *The Wall Street Journal*, September 5, 2001, p. B18.

39. Also see Richard W. Wright, "Trends in International Business Research: Twenty-Five Years Later," *Journal of International Business Studies*, Fourth Quarter 1994, pp. 687–701; Schon Beechler and John Zhuang Yang, "The Transfer of Japanese-Style Management to American Subsidiaries: Contingencies, Constraints, and Competencies," *Journal of International Business Studies*, Third Quarter 1994, pp. 467–491.

40. Jacob M. Schlesinger, "Another Foreign CEO Leaves Japan's Executive Ranks," *The Wall Street Journal online*, April 18, 2012.

41. Jean Lee, "Emerging Need: How Companies in Developing Markets Can Cultivate the Leaders They Lack," *The Wall Street Journal online*, May 24, 2010.

42. John Boudreau and Brandon Bailey, "Doing Business in China Getting Tougher for U.S. Companies," *Mercury News*, March 27, 2010; Emily Rauhala, "Q. and A.: Doing Business in China," *New York Times online*, June 16, 2010.

43. Eric W. K. Tsang, "Can Guanxi Be a Source of Sustained Competitive Advantage for Doing Business in China?" *Academy of Management Executive* 12, no. 2 (1998), p. 64.

44. Stephen S. Standifird and R. Scott Marshall, "The Transaction Cost Advantage of Guanxi-Based Business Practices," *Journal of World Business* 35, no. 1 (2000), pp. 21–42.

45. Lee Mei Yi and Paul Ellis, "Insider-Outsider Perspective of Guanxi," *Business Horizons*, January–February 2000, p. 28.

46. Rosalie L. Tung, "Managing in Asia: Cross-Cultural Dimensions," in *Managing Across Cultures: Issues and Perspectives,* ed. Pat Joynt and Malcolm Warner (London: International Thomson Business Press, 1996), p. 239.

47. Michelle Conlin, "Go-Go-Going to Pieces in China," *Business-Week*, April 23, 2007, p. 88.

48. For more on this topic, see Philip R. Harris and Robert T. Moran, *Managing Cultural Differences*, 3rd ed. (Houston: Gulf Publishing, 1991), pp. 410–411.

49. Ming-Jer Chen, *Inside Chinese Business* (Boston: Harvard Business School Press, 2001), p. 153.

50. Conlin, "Go-Go-Going to Pieces in China."

51. William B. Snavely, Serguel Miassaoedov, and Kevin McNeilly, "Cross-Cultural Peculiarities of the Russian Entrepreneur: Adapting to the New Russians," *Business Horizons*, March–April 1998, pp. 10–13.

52. For additional insights into how to interact and negotiate effectively with the Russians, see Richard D. Lewis, *When Cultures Collide* (London: Nicholas Brealey, 1999), pp. 314–318.

53. Snavely, Miassaoedov, and McNeilly, "Cross-Cultural Peculiarities," p. 13.

54. "The Challenges for India," *Chicago Tribune*, May 27, 2004, p. 28; Amy Waldman, "In India, Economic Growth and Democracy Do Mix," *New York Times*, May 26, 2004, p. A13.

55. Adapted from Harris and Moran, *Managing Cultural Differences*, p. 447.

56. Also see Lewis, *When Cultures Collide*, pp. 341–346.

57. Jean-Louis Barsoux and Peter Lawrence, "The Making of a French Manager," *Harvard Business Review*, July–August 1991, pp. 58–67.

58. Adapted from Harris and Moran, *Managing Cultural Differences*, p. 471.

59. Lewis, *When Cultures Collide*, pp. 231–232.

60. T. Lenartowicz and James Patrick Johnson, "A Cross-National Assessment of Values of Latin America Managers: Contrasting Hues or Shades of Gray?" *Journal of International Business Studies* 34, no. 3 (May 2003), p. 270.

61. Reed E. Nelson and Suresh Gopalan, "Do Organizational Cultures Replicate National Cultures? Isomorphism, Rejection and Reciprocal Opposition in the Corporate Values of Three Countries," *Organization Studies* 24, no. 7 (September 2003), pp. 1115–1154.

62. Derived from Raul Gouvea, "Brazil: A Strategic Approach," *Thunderbird International Business Review* 46, no. 2 (March–April 2004), pp. 183–184; David Hannon, "Brazil Offers the Best of Both Worlds," *Purchasing,* October 5, 2006, pp. 51–52, www.careerjournaleurope.com/myc/workabroad/countries/brazil.html.

63. Sean Van Zyl, "Global Political Risks: Post 9/11," *Canadian Underwriter* 71, no. 3 (March 2004), p. 16; Marvin Zonis, "Mideast Hopes: Endless Surprises," *Chicago Tribune*, January 18, 2004, p. 1.

64. Changiz Pezeshkpur, "Challenges to Management in the Arab World," *Business Horizons*, August 1978, p. 50.

65. Adapted from Harris and Moran, *Managing Cultural Differences*, p. 503.

■ Chapter 6

1. "Innovation through Diversity," *Applied Materials,* http://www.appliedmaterials.com/careers/diversity.html.

2. Bradley L. Kirkman, Benson Rosen, Cristina Gibson, and Paul E. Tesluk, "Five Challenges to Virtual Team Success: Lessons from Sabre, Inc.," *Academy of Management Executive* 16, no. 3 (August 2002), pp. 67–79, retrieved from EBSCOhost: http://turbo.kean.edu/~jmcgill/sabre.htm.

3. Ibid.

4. Surinder Kahai, "Culture Matters in Virtual Teams," *Leading Virtually: Leadership in the Digital Age*, December 31, 2007, http://www.leadingvirtually.com/?p=22.

5. Ibid.

6. Ibid.

7. Ibid.

8. Melanie Doulton, "Tips for Working in Global Teams," *Career Guidance, The Institute,* January 5, 2007, http://www.ieee.org/portal/site/tionline/menuitem.130a3558587d56e8fb2275875bac26c8/index.jsp?&pName=institute_level1_article&TheCat=1002&article=tionline/legacy/inst2007/jan07/career.xml.

9. Steven R. Rayner, "The Virtual Team Challenge," Rayner & Associates, Inc., 1997, http://raynerassoc.com/Resources/Virtual.pdf.

10. Bradley L. Kirkman, Benson Rosen, Cristina Gibson, and Paul E. Tesluk, "Five Challenges to Virtual Team Success: Lessons from Sabre, Inc.," *Academy of Management Executive* 16, no. 3 (August 2002), pp. 67–79, retrieved from EBSCOhost: http://turbo.kean.edu/~jmcgill/sabre.htm.

11. Steven R. Rayner, "The Virtual Team Challenge," Rayner & Associates, Inc., 1997, http://raynerassoc.com/Resources/Virtual.pdf.

12. Bradley L. Kirkman, Benson Rosen, Cristina Gibson, and Paul E. Tesluk, "Five Challenges to Virtual Team Success: Lessons from Sabre, Inc.," *Academy of Management Executive* 16, no. 3 (August 2002), pp. 67–79, retrieved from EBSCOhost: http://turbo.kean.edu/~jmcgill/sabre.htm.

13. Melanie Doulton, "Tips for Working in Global Teams," *Career Guidance, The Institute,* January 5, 2007, http://www.ieee.org/portal/site/tionline/menuitem.130a3558587d56e8fb2275875bac26c8/index.jsp?&pName=institute_level1_article&TheCat=1002&article=tionline/legacy/inst2007/jan07/career.xml.

14. Bradley L. Kirkman, Benson Rosen, Cristina Gibson, and Paul E. Tesluk, "Five Challenges to Virtual Team Success: Lessons from Sabre, Inc.," *Academy of Management Executive* 16, no. 3 (August 2002), pp. 67–79, retrieved from EBSCOhost: http://turbo.kean.edu/~jmcgill/sabre.htm.

15. Ibid.

16. Bradley L. Kirkman, Benson Rosen, Cristina Gibson, and Paul E. Tesluk, "Five Challenges to Virtual Team Success: Lessons from Sabre, Inc.," *Academy of Management Executive* 16, no. 3 (August 2002), pp. 67–79, retrieved from EBSCOhost: http://turbo.kean.edu/~jmcgill/sabre.htm.

17. Steven R. Rayner, "The Virtual Team Challenge," Rayner & Associates, Inc., 1997, http://raynerassoc.com/Resources/Virtual.pdf.

18. Ibid.

19. Lisa Hoecklin, *Managing Cultural Differences: Strategies for Competitive Advantage* (Workingham, England: Addison-Wesley, 1995), p. 146.

20. Edgar H. Schein, *Organizational Culture and Leadership,* 2nd ed. (San Francisco: Jossey-Bass, 1997), p. 12.

21. Fred Luthans, *Organizational Behavior,* 10th ed. (New York: McGraw-Hill/Irwin, 2005), pp. 110–111.

22. In addition see W. Mathew Jeuchter, Caroline Fisher, and Randall J. Alford, "Five Conditions for High-Performance Cultures," *Training and Development Journal,* May 1998, pp. 63–67.

23. AstraZeneca, *Diversity and Inclusion,* http://www.astrazeneca.com/Responsibility/Our-people/.

24. Ibid.

25. Ibid.

26. Hoecklin, *Managing Cultural Differences,* p. 145.

27. Andre Laurent, "The Cultural Diversity of Western Conceptions of Management," *International Studies of Management and Organization,* Spring–Summer 1983, pp. 75–96.

28. Nancy J. Adler, *International Dimensions of Organizational Behavior,* 2nd ed. (Boston: PWS-Kent Publishing, 1991), pp. 58–59.

29. Robert Frank and Thomas M. Burton, "Cross-Border Merger Results in Headaches for a Drug Company," *The Wall Street Journal,* February 4, 1997, p. A1.

30. Hoecklin, *Managing Cultural Differences,* p. 151.

31. Robert Hughes, "Weekend Journal: Futures and Options: Global Culture," *The Wall Street Journal,* October 10, 2003, p. W2.

32. Rita A. Numeroff and Michael N. Abrams, "Integrating Corporate Culture from International M&As," *HR Focus,* June 1998, p. 12.

33. See Maddy Janssens, Jeanne M. Brett, and Frank J. Smith, "Confirmatory Cross-Cultural Research: Testing the Viability of a Corporation-Wide Safety Policy," *Academy of Management Journal,* June 1995, pp. 364–382.

34. Fons Trompenaars, *Riding the Waves of Culture: Understanding Diversity in Global Business* (Burr Ridge, IL: Irwin, 1994), p. 154.

35. Ibid.

36. Ibid., p. 156.

37. Ibid., p. 164.

38. Ibid., p. 167.

39. Ibid., p. 172.

40. For more see Rose Mary Wentling and Nilda Palma-Rivas, "Current Status of Diversity Initiatives in Selected Multinational Corporations," *Human Resource Development Quarterly,* Spring 2000, pp. 35–60.

41. Adler, *International Dimensions of Organizational Behavior,* p. 121.

42. Jean Lee, "Culture and Management: A Study of Small Chinese Family Business in Singapore," *Journal of Small Business Management,* July 1996, p. 65.

43. Noboru Yoshimura and Philip Anderson, *Inside the Kaisha: Demystifying Japanese Business Behavior* (Boston: Harvard Business School Press, 1997).

44. Edmund L. Andrews, "Meet the Maverick of Japan, Inc." *New York Times,* October 12, 1995, pp. C1, C4.

45. Sheryl WuDunn, "Incubators of Creativity," *New York Times,* October 9, 1997, pp. C1, C21.

46. Adler, *International Dimensions of Organizational Behavior,* p. 132.

47. Adele Thomas and Mike Bendixen, "The Management Implications of Ethnicity in South Africa," *Journal of International Business Studies,* Third Quarter 2000, pp. 507–519.

48. John M. Ivencevich and Jacqueline A. Gilbert, "Diversity Management: Time for a New Approach," *Public Personnel Management,* Spring 2000, pp. 75–92.

49. "Over the Rainbow," *Economist online,* November 20, 1997, www.economist.com/business/displaystory.cfm?story_id=E1_TDGQRP.

50. See, for example, Betty Jane Punnett and Jason Clemens, "Cross-National Diversity: Implications for International Expansion Decisions," *Journal of World Business* 34, no. 2 (1999), pp. 128–138.

51. Adler, *International Dimensions of Organizational Behavior,* p. 137.

■ Chapter 7

1. Ed Hammond, "Offshoring: Still in Control although at Arm's Length," *Financial Times,* June 24, 2010, http://www.ft.com/cms/s/0/6769a858-7d8e-11df-a0f5-00144feabdc0.html.

2. Marcy Beitle, Arjun Sethi, Jessica Milesko, and Alyson Potenza, "The Offshore Culture Clash," A.T. Kearney Global Management Consultants, http://www.atkearney.com/index.php/Publications/the-offshore-culture-clash.html.

3. Ibid.

4. Ibid.

5. Ibid.

6. Ibid.

7. Ibid.

8. Ibid.

9. Kannan Srikanth and Phanish Puranam, "Business Insight (A Special Report): Global Business—Advice for Outsourcers: Think Bigger: Too Many Companies Mistakenly Limit Offshore Work to Routine Tasks," *The Wall Street Journal (Europe),* January 25, 2010, http://online.wsj.com/article/SB1000142405274 8704007804574574161967309526.html.

10. Ibid.

11. Ibid.

12. Ibid.

13. Marcy Beitle, Arjun Sethi, Jessica Milesko, and Alyson Potenza, "The Offshore Culture Clash," A.T. Kearney Global Management Consultants, http://www.atkearney.com/index.php/Publications/ the-offshore-culture-clash.html.

14. Ibid.

15. Nicholas Carr, *The Shallows* (New York: Norton, 2010).

16. E. T. Hall and E. Hall, "How Cultures Collide," in *Culture, Communication, and Conflict: Readings in Intercultural Relations,* ed. G. R. Weaver (Needham Heights, MA: Ginn Press, 1994).

17. Noboru Yoshimura and Philip Anderson, *Inside the Kaisha: Demystifying Japanese Business Behavior* (Boston: Harvard Business School Press, 1997), p. 59.

18. William C. Byham and George Dixon, "Through Japanese Eyes," *Training and Development Journal,* March 1993, pp. 33–36; Linda S. Dillon, "West Meets East," *Training and Development Journal,* March 1993, pp. 39–43.

19. Fons Trompenaars and Charles Hampden-Turner, *Riding the Waves of Culture: Understanding Diversity in Global Business,* 2nd ed. (New York: McGraw-Hill, 1998), p. 204.

20. Nancy J. Adler (with Allison Gunderson), *International Dimensions of Organizational Behavior,* 5th ed. (Mason, OH: South-Western, 2008), p. 80.

21. Toddi Gunter, "Delivering Unpopular News When You Haven't Bought In," *New York Times online,* June 14, 2010.

22. Giorgio Inzerilli, "The Legitimacy of Managerial Authority: A Comparative Study," *National Academy of Management Proceedings* (Detroit, 1980), pp. 58–62.

23. Ibid., p. 62.

24. Philip R. Harris and Robert T. Moran, *Managing Cultural Differences,* 3rd ed. (Houston: Gulf Publishing, 1996), pp. 36–37.

25. Richard Tanner Pascale and Anthony G. Athos, *The Art of Japanese Management* (New York: Warner Books, 1981), pp. 82–83.

26. Justin Fox, "The Triumph of English," *Fortune,* September 18, 2000, pp. 209–212.

27. See "Double or Quits," *Economist,* February 25, 1995, pp. 84–85.

28. Brock Stout, "Interviewing in Japan," *HR Magazine,* June 1998, p. 73.

29. Ibid., p. 75.

30. H. W. Hildebrandt, "Communication Barriers Between German Subsidiaries and Parent American Companies," *Michigan Business Review,* July 1973, p. 9.

31. John R. Schermerhorn Jr., "Language Effects in Cross-Cultural Management Research: An Empirical Study and a Word of Caution," *National Academy of Management Proceedings* (New Orleans, 1987), p. 103.

32. Heather Berry, Mauro F. Guillén, and Nan Zhou, "An Institutional Approach to Cross-national Distance," *Journal of International Business Studies* (advance online publication), July 1, 2010, doi: 10.1057/jibs.2010.28.

33. Brenda R. Sims and Stephen Guice, "Differences Between Business Letters from Native and Non-Native Speakers of English," *Journal of Business Communication,* Winter 1991, p. 37.

34. James Calvert Scott and Diana J. Green, "British Perspectives on Organizing Bad-News Letters: Organizational Patterns Used by Major U.K. Companies," *The Bulletin,* March 1992, p. 17.

35. Ibid., pp. 18–19.

36. Mi Young Park, W. Tracy Dillon, and Kenneth L. Mitchell, "Korean Business Letters: Strategies for Effective Complaints in Cross-Cultural Communication," *Journal of Business Communication,* July 1998, pp. 328–345.

37. As an example see Jeremiah Sullivan, "What Are the Functions of Corporate Home Pages?" *Journal of World Business* 34, no. 2 (1999), pp. 193–211.

38. Joseph Kahn, "Fraying U.S.-Sino Ties Threaten Business," *The Wall Street Journal,* July 7, 1995, p. A6; Nathaniel C. Nash, "China Gives Big Van Deal to Mercedes," *New York Times,* July 13, 1995, pp. C1, C5; Seth Faison, "China Times a Business Deal to Make a Point to America," *New York Times,* July 16, 1995, pp. 1, 6.

39. David A. Ricks, *Big Business Blunders: Mistakes in Multinational Marketing* (Homewood, IL: Dow Jones/Irwin, 1983), p. 39.

40. Ibid., p. 55.

41. John Kass, "Some Bright Ideas Get Lost in Translation," *Chicago Tribune online edition,* April 20, 2007, www.chicagotribune.com/ news/columnists/chi-0704190692apr20,1,6809930.column.

42. Edwin Miller, Bhal Bhatt, Raymond Hill, and Julian Cattaneo, "Leadership Attitudes of American and German Expatriate Managers in Europe and Latin America," *National Academy of Management Proceedings* (Detroit, 1980), pp. 53–57.

43. Abdul Rahim A. Al-Meer, "Attitudes Towards Women as Managers: A Comparison of Asians, Saudis and Westerners," *Arab Journal of the Social Sciences,* April 1988, pp. 139–149.

44. Sheryl WuDunn, "In Japan, Still Getting Tea and No Sympathy," *New York Times,* August 27, 1995, p. E3.

45. Fathi S. Yousef, "Cross-Cultural Communication: Aspects of the Contrastive Social Values Between North Americans and Middle Easterners," *Human Organization,* Winter 1974, p. 385.

46. Peter McKiernan and Chris Carter, "The Millennium Nexus: Strategic Management at the Crossroads," *European Management Review* 1, no. 1 (Spring 2004), p. 3.

47. R. Bruce Money, "Word-of-Mouth Referral Sources for Buyers of International Corporate Financial Services," *Journal of World Business* 35, no. 3 (2000), pp. 314–329.

48. Yousef, "Cross-Cultural Communication," p. 383.

49. See Roger E. Axtell, ed., *Do's and Taboos Around the World* (New York: Wiley, 1990), chapter 2.

50. Jane Whitney Gibson, Richard M. Hodgetts, and Charles W. Blackwell, "Cultural Variations in Nonverbal Communication," *55th Annual Business Communication Proceedings,* San Antonio, November 8–10, 1990, pp. 211–229.

51. William K. Brandt and James M. Hulbert, "Patterns of Communications in the Multinational Corporation: An Empirical Study," *Journal of International Business Studies,* Spring 1976, pp. 57–64.

52. Hildebrandt, "Communication Barriers," p. 9.

53. See for example George Ming-Hong Lai, "Knowing Who You Are Doing Business with in Japan: A Managerial View of Keiretsu

and Keiretsu Business Groups," *Journal of World Business* 34, no. 4 (1999), pp. 423–449.

54. Nicholas Athanassiou and Douglas Nigh, "Internationalization, Tacit Knowledge and the Top Management Teams of MNCs," *Journal of International Business Studies*, Third Quarter 2000, pp. 471–487.

55. Also see Linda Beamer, "Bridging Business Cultures," *China Business Review*, May–June 1998, pp. 54–58.

56. Tanya Mohn, "Going Global, Stateside," *New York Times*, March 9, 2010, p. B9.

57. Michael D. Lord and Annette L. Ranft, "Organizational Learning about New International Markets: Exploring the Internal Transfer of Local Market Knowledge," *Journal of International Business Studies*, Fourth Quarter 2000, pp. 573–589.

58. Jennifer W. Spencer, "Knowledge Flows in the Global Innovation System: Do U.S. Firms Share More Scientific Knowledge than Their Japanese Rivals?" *Journal of International Business Studies*, Third Quarter 2000, pp. 521–530.

59. Kenichi Ohmae, "The Global Logic of Strategic Alliances," *Harvard Business Review*, March–April 1989, p. 154.

60. See Hildy Teegen and Jonathan P. Doh, "U.S./Mexican Alliance Negotiations: Cultural Impacts on Trust, Authority and Performance," *Thunderbird International Business Review* 44, no. 6 (2002), pp. 749–775; Elise Campbell and Jeffrey J. Reuer, "International Alliance Negotiations: Legal Issues for General Managers," *Business Horizons*, January–February 2001, pp. 19–26.

61. Nina Reynolds, Antonis Simintiras, and Efi Vlachou, "International Business Negotiations: Present Knowledge and Direction for Future Research," *International Marketing Review* 20, no. 3 (2003), p. 236.

62. *Harvard Business Essentials: Negotiation* (Boston: Harvard Business School Press, 2003), p. 2.

63. Ibid., p. 4.

64. David K. Tse, June Francis, and Ian Walls, "Cultural Differences in Conducting Intra- and Inter-Cultural Negotiations: A Sino-Canadian Comparison," *Journal of International Business Studies,* Third Quarter 1994, pp. 537–555; Teegen and Doh, "U.S./Mexican Alliance Negotiations," pp. 749–775.

65. Adler and Gundersen, *International Dimensions of Organizational Behavior*, p. 241.

66. Daniel Druckman, "Group Attachments in Negotiation and Collective Action," *International Negotiation* 11 (2006), pp. 229–252.

67. Jeanne M. Brett, Debra L. Shapiro, and Anne L. Lytle, "Breaking the Bonds of Reciprocity in Negotiations," *Academy of Management Journal*, August 1998, pp. 410–424.

68. Stephen E. Weiss, "Negotiating with 'Romans'—Part 2," *Sloan Management Review,* Spring 1994, p. 89.

69. Trompenaars and Hampden-Turner, *Riding the Waves of Culture*, p. 112.

70. James K. Sebenius, "The Hidden Challenge of Cross-Border Negotiations," *Harvard Business Review*, March 2002, pp. 4–12.

71. John L. Graham, "Brazilian, Japanese, and American Business Negotiations," *Journal of International Business Studies*, Spring–Summer 1983, pp. 47–61; John L. Graham, "The Influence of Culture on the Process of Business Negotiations in an Exploratory Study," *Journal of International Business Studies,* Spring 1983, pp. 81–96.

72. William Zartman, "Negotiating Internal, Ethnic and Identity Conflicts in a Globalized World," *International Negotiation* 11 (2006), pp. 253–272.

73. Roger Fisher and William Ury, *Getting to Yes: Negotiating Agreement Without Giving In* (New York: Penguin Books, 1983), p. 11.

74. Ibid., p. 79.

75. Ibid., p. 111.

76. Graham, "The Influence of Culture on the Process of Business Negotiations in an Exploratory Study," pp. 84, 88.

■ Part 2 Integrative Cases

Brief Integrative Case 2.1

1. Peter Wonacott and Chad Terhune, "Politics & Economics: Path to India's Market Dotted with Potholes; Savvy Cola Giants Stumble over Local Agendas; KFC Climbs Back from Abyss," *Wall Street Journal*, September 12, 2006, p. A6.

2. "CSE Report on Pesticide Residue Inconclusive," *Businessline*, August 27, 2006, p. 1.

3. Rajesh Kumar and Verner Worm, "Institutional Dynamics and the Negotiation Process: Comparing India and China," *International Journal of Conflict Management* 15, no. 3 (2004), p. 304.

4. Wonacott and Terhune, "Politics & Economics."

5. Archna Shukla, "Message Will Always Be More Important than Medium," *Business Today*, August 27, 2006, p. 102.

6. Mark Sappenfield, "India's Cola Revolt Taps into Old Distrust: Behind Contradictory Reports of Pesticides in Coke and Pepsi Is an Underlying Wariness of Foreign Companies," *The Christian Science Monitor*, September 1, 2006, p. 6.

7. Nikhil Gulati and Runman Ahmed, "India has 1.2 Billion People But Not Enough Drink Coke," *The Wall Street Journal Online*, July 13, 2012, http://online.wsj.com/article/SB1000142405270230 4870304577490092413939410.

8. "India 2009/10 FDI Flows Seen at $18 bn—Trade Min," *Reuters*, December 4, 2009, http://www.reuters.com/article/idUSDEL00240820091204.

9. UNCTAD, *World Investment Prospects Survey*, 2010.

10. "Foreign Direct Investment," *India Brand Equity Foundation*, February 2010, http://www.ibef.org/economy/fdi.aspx.

11. Arvind Panagariya, "Building a Modern India," *Business Standard India 2010*.

12. Brian Bremner, Nandini Lakshman, and Diane Brady, "India: Behind the Scare over Pesticides in Pepsi and Coke," *BusinessWeek*, September 4, 2006, p. 43.

13. Sappenfield, "India's Cola Revolt Taps into Old Distrust."

14. Bremner, Lakshman, and Brady, "India: Behind the Scare over Pesticides in Pepsi and Coke."

15. Coca-Cola India, "Environment Report 2007–2008."

16. Eric Bellman, "Coke Sees Strong Demand across India, Plans Investment," *The Wall Street Journal*, June 30, 2009, http://online.wsj.com/article/SB124055692273452331.html?mod=googlenews_wsj.

17. Ibid.

18. Nikhil Gulati and Runman Ahmed, "India Has 1.2 Billion People But Not Enough Drink Coke," *The Wall Street Journal Online*, July 13, 2012, http://online.wsj.com/article/SB1000142405270230 4870304577490092413939410.

19. Ratna Bhushan, "RC Cola Comes to India," *Businessline*, October 7, 2003, p. 1.

20. "India: Reports of Contaminated Soda Dry up Coke, Pepsi Sales," *Global Information Network*, September 7, 2006, p. 1.

21. Aryn Baker, "India's Storm in a Cola Cup," *Time International*, August 21, 2006, p. 8.

22. Bremner, Lakshman, and Brady, "India: Behind the Scare over Pesticides in Pepsi and Coke."

23. Sappenfield, "India's Cola Revolt Taps into Old Distrust."

24. Wonacott and Terhune, "Politics & Economics."

25. "India: Reports of Contaminated Soda Dry up Coke, Pepsi Sales."

26. Sappenfield, "India's Cola Revolt Taps into Old Distrust."

27. "Coca-Cola Co.: India's Kerala State Cancels Ban on Coke, Pepsi Drinks," *The Wall Street Journal,* September 25, 2006, p. A11.

28. Ibid.

29. "Coca-Cola India Unit Asked to Pay $47 Million Damages," *Reuters,* March 23, 2010, http://www.reuters.com/article/idUSSGE62M0AV20100323.

30. Diane Brady, "Pepsi: Repairing a Poisoned Reputation in India," *BusinessWeek,* June 11, 2007.

31. Ibid.

32. Ibid.

33. Ibid.

34. Amit Srivastava, "Coca-Cola Funded Group Investigates Coca-Cola in India," India Resource Center, April 16, 2007, www.indiaresource.org/campaigns/coke/2007/coketeri.html.

35. Sappenfield, "India's Cola Revolt Taps into Old Distrust."

36. Amelia Gentleman, "For 2 Giants of Soft Drinks, a Crisis in Crucial Market," *New York Times,* August 23, 2006, p. C3.

37. Wonacott and Terhune, "Politics & Economics."

38. "Coca-Cola-India: Key Facts," www.cokefacts.org.

39. Ibid.

40. Coca-Cola India, "Environment Report 2007–2008."

41. Ben Blanchard, "Coke Vows to Reduce Water Used in Drink Production," June 5, 2007, www.reuters.com.

42. "The Coca-Cola Company Pledges to Replace the Water It Uses in Its Beverages and Their Production," press release, June 5, 2007, www.thecoca-colacompany.com/presscenter/nr_20070605_tccc_and_wwf_partnership.html.

43. Coca-Cola India, "Environment Report 2007–2008."

44. Ibid.

45. Gentleman, "For 2 Giants of Soft Drinks, a Crisis in Crucial Market."

46. Coca-Cola, "2009 Annual Review."

47. Brad Dorfman and Martinne Geller, "Coca-Cola Sales Rise, Led by Emerging Markets," *Reuters,* February 9, 2010, http://www.reuters.com/article/idUSTRE61829W20100209.

48. Kenneth E. Behring, "Water Research; Researchers Are Raising Awareness of the Global Drinking Water Crisis," *Health & Medicine Week,* October 16, 2006, p. 1339.

49. Thalif Deen, "Development: Water, Water Everywhere Is Thing of the Past," *Global Information Network,* August 22, 2006, p. 1.

50. Loretta Chao and Shai Oster, "China Study Says Foreigners Violate Clean-Water Rules," *The Wall Street Journal,* October 30, 2006, p. B7.

51. *The 3rd United Nations World Water Development Report: Water in a Changing World* (WWDR-3), 2009.

Brief Integrative Case 2.2

1. Steve Dickinson, JP Morgan's Hand-On China Series: "Views You Can Use," July 2007, http://query.jpmorgan.com/inetSearch/index_redesign.jsp?q=wahaha&image=Go+%BB&pageType=_JPMC&sort=2&num=10&lr=&site=jpmorgan.

2. J. Zhou, "Trademark Disputes between Danone and Wahaha Group," *China Business Law,* August 2009, http://www.china-business-law.com/trademark-disputes-between-danone-and-wahaha-group/.

3. "Danone Encounters Continuous Frustration in China and a Murky Future Due to Unsuccessful Litigations," Wahaha Group, October 9, 2008, *PR Newswire,* http://www.highbeam.com/doc/1G1–184638322.html.

4. http://www.brandchannel.com/features_profile.asp?pr_id=120.

5. Ibid.

6. Ibid.

7. B. Bruce, "Danone Celebrates Its 90th Birthday," March 14, 2009, http://www.foodbev.com/article/danone-celebrates-its-90th-birthday.

8. Ibid.

9. Danone, corporate press release, September 30, 2009, http://phx.corporate-ir.net/phoenix.zhtml?c=95168&p=irol-newsArticle&ID=1336626.

10. Danone S.A. Profile, *Reuters,* http://www.reuters.com/finance/stocks/companyProfile?symbol=DANO.PA.

11. http://www.finance.danone.com/phoenix.zhtml?c=95168&p=irol-newsArticle&ID=1336626&highlight=.

12. http://www.interbrand.com/best_global_brands.aspx?year=2009&langid=1000.

13. http://www.danone.com/en/company/introduction.html.

14. http://www.danone.com/en/brands/business/beverages.html.

15. Ibid.

16. Danone 2008 Annual Report: *Economic and Social Report.*

17. Shangguan Zhoudong, "Danone's Quick Expansion in China," *China Daily,* June 15, 2007, http://www.chinadaily.com.cn/bizchina/2007–06/15/content_895462.htm.

18. T. C. Melewar, E. Badal, and J. Small, "Danone Branding Strategy in China," *Brand Management* 13, no. 6 (July 2006), pp. 407–417.

19. "Danone Encounters Continuous Frustration in China and a Murky Future Due to Unsuccessful Litigations," *Thomson Reuters,* September 9, 2008, http://www.reuters.com/article/pressRelease/idUS113471+09–Sep-2008+PRN20080909.

20. Ibid.

21. Vivian Wai-yin Kwok, "A Pyrrhic Victory for Danone in China," *Forbes,* August 6, 2007, http://www.forbes.com/2007/06/08/wahaha-danone-zong-markets-equity-cx_vk_0608markets2.html.

22. http://en.wahaha.com.cn/aboutus/history/.

23. Ibid.

24. Ibid.

25. Ibid.

26. Ibid.

27. Ibid.

28. S. M. Dickinson, "Danone v. Wahaha," *China Economic Review,* September 2007, http://www.chinaeconomicreview.com/cer/2007_09/Danone_v_Wahaha.html.

29. Ibid.

30. Steve Dickinson, JP Morgan's Hand-On China Series: "Views You Can Use," July 2007, http://query.jpmorgan.com/inetSearch/index_redesign.jsp.

31. Dickinson, "Danone v. Wahaha."

32. Ibid.

33. Ibid.

34. Ibid.

35. Ibid.

36. Ibid.

37. Baoxiu Ye, "Wahaha Reviews 21:0 Whitewash Against Danone," *Thomson Reuters,* April 13, 2009, http://www.reuters.com/article/pressRelease/idUS69637+13–Apr-2009+PRN20090413.

38. Ibid.
39. Ibid.
40. Ibid.
41. Ibid.
42. Ibid.
43. Ibid.
44. Ibid.
45. Ibid.
46. Ibid.
47. Ibid.
48. Ibid.
49. Ibid.
50. Ibid.
51. J. T. Areddy, "Danone Pulls Out of Disputed China Venture," *The Wall Street Journal,* October 1, 2009, http://online.wsj.com/article/SB125428911997751859.html.
52. Ibid.
53. Ibid.
54. Ibid.
55. Ibid.
56. P. Waldmeir and S. Tucker, "Danone to Quit Joint Venture with Wahaha," *Financial Times,* September 30, 2009, http://www.ft.com/cms/s/0/849e7eda-ad87-11de-bb8a-00144feabdc0,dwp_uuid=eced8d08-6d64-11da-a4df-0000779e2340.html.
57. Dickinson, "Danone v. Wahaha."
58. Ibid.

In-Depth Integrative Cases 2.1a and 2.1b

1. Anna Willard, James Mackenzie, James Grubel, Wayne Cole, Tova Cohen, Alan Raybould and Jonathan Thatcher. "FACTBOX:Who's next? Countries at risk of recession." March 3, 2009. http://www.reuters.com.
2. "Euro Disney Adding Alcohol," *The New York Times,* June 12, 1993. http://www.nytimes.com/1993/06/12/business/euro-disney-adding-alcohol.html.
3. "The History of DisneyLand Paris," Solarius, July 4, 2006. http://www.solarius.com/dvp/dlp/dlp-history.htm.
4. Christian Sylt, "Magic Results: Euro Disney Plans New Hotels." August 17, 2008. http://www.independent.co.uk/news/business/news/magic-results-euro-disney-plans-new-hotels-899529.html.
5. Euro Disney S.C.A. "EURO DISNEY S.C.A. Reports Fiscal Year 2011 Results." November 9, 2011. http://corporate.disneylandparis.com/CORP/EN/Neutral/Images/uk-2011-11-09-euro-disney-sca-reports-annual-results-for-fiscal-year-2011.pdf.
6. Peter Gumbel, "Disney's $1.7 Billion French Birthday Gift." *Time,* September 19, 2012. http://business.time.com/2012/09/19/disneys-1-7-billion-french-birthday-gift/.
7. Ibid.
8. Raymond H. Lopez, "Disney in China Again?" March 2002, appserv.pace.edu/emplibrary/FINAL.Asiacasestudy.doc.
9. Ibid.
10. Ibid.
11. "Disney's Shanghai Park Plan in Doubt: Company Mulls Move to Another Location in China," *Msnbc.com,* December 11, 2006.
12. Lopez, "Disney in China Again?"
13. Thomas Crampton, "Disney's New Hong Kong Park to be 'Culturally Sensitive': Mickey Mouse Learns Chinese," *International Herald Tribune,* January 13, 2003, www.iht.com/articles/2003/01/13/disney_ed3__0.php.
14. Michael Schuman, "Disney's Hong Kong Headache," *Time Magazine,* May 8, 2006, www.time.com/time/magazine/article/0,9171,501060515-1191881,00.html.
15. Kim Soyoung and George Chen, "Hollywood Chases Asia Theme Park Rainbow," *Turkish Daily News*, May 29, 2007, www.turkishdailynews.com.tr/article.php?enewsid=74352.
16. "Cuts Cloud Hong Kong Disneyland Expansion," *Financial Times,* March 17, 2009, http://www.ft.com/cms/s/0/c59c5a72-12bb-11de-9848-0000779fd2ac.html.
17. "Hong Kong Disneyland's Future Is in Danger," *BusinessWeek,* March 17, 2009, http://www.businessweek.com/globalbiz/content/mar2009/gb20090317_923737.htm.
18. Ibid.
19. "Disney Puts Hong Kong Expansion on Hold," *Reuters,* March 16, 2009, http://www.reuters.com/article/industryNews/idUSTRE52G0I120090317.
20. "Hong Kong Disneyland's Future Is in Danger."
21. Ibid.
22. "Disney, Hong Kong Reach $465m Expansion Deal," *China Daily,* June 30, 2009, http://www.chinadaily.com.cn/china/2009-06/30/content_8338445.htm.
23. J. T. Areddy and P. Sanders, "Disney's Shanghai Park Plan Advances," *The Wall Street Journal,* January 12, 2009, p. A1.
24. Ibid.
25. "Disney Announces Shanghai Theme Park," Disney news release, January 11, 2009, http://www.magicalmountain.net/WDWNewsDetail.asp?page=4&NewsID=2103&type=1&tag=.
26. "Walt Disney, Shanghai Propose New Theme Park in China (Update 1)," *Bloomberg,* January 9, 2009, http://www.bloomberg.com/apps/news?pid=20601080&sid=atGa2ymXAMM8&refer=asia.
27. Ibid.
28. Areddy and Sanders, "Disney's Shanghai Park Plan Advances."
29. Samuel Shen and Sue Zeidler, "Disney Takes China Stride as Shanghai Park Gets Nod," *Reuters,* November 4, 2009, http://www.reuters.com/article/idUSTRE5A31TC20091104.
30. Ibid.
31. Ibid.
32. Brooks Barnes, "Hong Kong Disneyland turns a Profit." *New York Times*, February 18, 2013. NTY.com.
33. Frederik Balfour, "Disney Shanghai: Good for China, Bad for Hong Kong," *BusinessWeek,* November 5, 2009.
34. "Shanghai Disney to Get Approved Land in July," *China Daily,* April 4, 2010, http://www.chinadaily.com.cn/china/2010-04/14/content_9730662.htm.
35. "Malaysia Discussing Building Disney Park: Would Be First Such Attraction in Southeast Asia," *Associated Press,* May 30, 2006, www.msnbc.msn.com/id/13045465/.
36. Soyoung and Chen, "Hollywood Chases Asia Theme Park Rainbow."
37. Ibid.
38. Hana R. Alberts, "Tokyo Disneyland? Asia's Top 12 Amusement Parks," February 13, 2010, http://www.ctv.ca/servlet/ArticleNews/story/CTVNews/20100212/forbes_amusement_100213/20100213?hub=World.
39. Ibid.

40. Ibid.

41. James T. Areddy and Peter Sanders, "Chinese Learn English the Disney Way," *The Wall Street Journal,* April 20, 2009, p. B1.

In-Depth Integrative Case 2.2

1. Jennifer McTaggart, "Walmart versus the World," *Progressive Grocer,* October 15, 2003, p. 20.

2. "'Walmart' in Japan Sees Losses," *Associated Press,* August 23, 2006, www.sptimes.com/2006/08/23/Business/_Wal_Mart__in_Japan_s.shtml.

3. David Lague, "Unions Triumphant at Walmart in China," *International Herald Tribune,* October 12, 2006, www.iht.com/-articles/2006/10/12/business/unions.php.

4. Walmart Inc., "China Fact Sheet," www.walmartstores.com.

5. Walmart corporate website, "Where in the World Is Walmart?" retrieved April 1, 2013, http://corporate.walmart.com/our-story/locations.

6. Matthew Boyle, "Walmart's Painful Lessons," *BusinessWeek,* October 13, 2009, http://www.businessweek.com/managing/content/oct2009/ca20091013_227022.htm.

7. walmartstores.com.

8. International Data Sheet, April 2010, http://walmartstores.com/pressroom/news/9865.aspx.

9. Andrew Clark, "Walmart, the U.S. Retailer Taking Over the World by Stealth," *Guardian,* January 12, 2010, http://www.guardian.co.uk/business/2010/jan/12/walmart-companies-to-shape-the-decade.

10. Vijay Govindarajan and Anil K. Gupta, "Taking Walmart Global: Lessons From Retailing's Giant," *Strategy + Business,* June 19, 2002, http://www.strategy-business.com/article/13866?pg=all.

11. Ibid.

12. Ibid.

13. Ibid.

14. Ibid.

15. "Walmart to Add 125 Stores in Mexico," *Arkansas Business Staff,* February 14, 2007, www.arkansasbusiness.com/article.aspx?aID=97026.13096.109168.

16. David Barstow, "Vast Mexico Bribery Case Hushed Up by Walmart After Top-Level Struggle," *New York Times.* April 21, 2012. http://www.nytimes.com/2012/04/22/business/at-wal-mart-in-mexico-a-bribe-inquiry-silenced.html?_r=1.

17. Stephanie Clifford, "Bribery Case at Wal-Mart May Widen," *New York Times.* May 17, 2012. http://www.nytimes.com/2012/05/18/business/wal-mart-concedes-bribery-case-may-widen.html?pagewanted=all.

18. David Welch, (4/25/12). http://www.businessweek.com. In Wal-Mart Mexico Probe Threatening Global Growth Success: Retail, retrieved 7/24/12, from http://www.businessweek.com/news/2012-04-25/wal-mart-mexico-probe-threatening-global-growth-success-retail#p2.

19. Geri Smith, "In Mexico, Banco Walmart," *BusinessWeek,* November 20, 2006.

20. Carolyn Whelan, "Walmart Gets Its Bank—In Mexico," *Fortune,* January 29, 2008, www.fortune.com.

21. Walmart corporate website, "April 2010 Data Sheet," walmartstores.com.

22. David Welch, "Wal-Mart Mexico Probe Threatening Global Growth Success: Retail," *BusinessWeek.* April 25, 2012. http://www.businessweek.com/news/2012-04-25/wal-mart-mexico-probe-threatening-global-growth-success-retail#p1

23. Clay Chandler, "The Great Walmart of China," *Fortune,* July 25, 2005, money.cnn.com/magazines/fortune/fortune_archive/2005/07/25/8266651/index.htm.

24. Pallavi Gogoi, "Walmart's China Card," *BusinessWeek,* July 26, 2005.

25. "Walmart's Cheap Doubling in China," *24/7 Wall Street,* February 27, 2007, www.247wallst.com/2007/02/walmarts_cheap_.html.

26. "Walmart Buys China Grocery Chain," *Wire Services,* October 17, 2006, www.sptimes.com/2006/10/17/Business/Wal_Mart_buys_China_g.shtml.

27. Gogoi, "Walmart's China Card."

28. "Walmart Buys China Grocery Chain."

29. "Walmart Reaches Agreement to Acquire German Hypermarket Chain," *Business Wire,* December 18, 1997, http://www.allbusiness.com/company-activities-management/company-structures-ownership/7024566–1.html.

30. Mark Lander, "Walmart Gives Up Germany—Business—International Herald Tribune," *New York Times,* July 28, 2006, http://www.nytimes.com/2006/07/28/business/worldbusiness/28iht-walmart.2325266.html.

31. Ibid.

32. Ibid.

33. Allan Hall, Tom Bawden, and Sarah Butler, "Walmart Pulls out of Germany at Cost of $1bn," *The Times,* July 29, 2006.

34. Lander, "Walmart Gives Up Germany."

35. Tom Buerkle, "$10 Billion Gamble in U.K. Doubles Its International Business: Walmart Takes Big Leap into Europe," *New York Times,* June 15, 1999, http://www.nytimes.com/1999/06/15/news/15iht-walmart.2.t.html.

36. Ibid.

37. Clark, "Walmart, the U.S. Retailer Taking Over the World by Stealth."

38. Boyle, "Walmart's Painful Lessons."

39. Ibid.

40. Ibid.

41. Mariko Sanchanta, "Wal-Mart Bargain Shops for Japanese Stores to Buy," *The Wall Street Journal,* November 15, 2010, p. B1.

42. "Walmart Announces Central American Investment," September 20, 2005, http://walmartstores.com/pressroom/news/5384.aspx.

43. Gordon Platt, "Walmart Bets Big on Brazil's Market," *Global Finance,* January 1, 2006, http://www.allbusiness.com/public-administration/national-security-international/1138985–1.html.

44. Boyle, "Walmart's Painful Lessons."

45. Ibid.

46. Ibid.

47. Walmart, "Investors: News and Articles," October 22, 2009, http://investors.walmartstores.com/phoenix.zhtml?c=112761&p=irol-newsArticle&ID=1345359&highlight.

48. Ibid.

49. Ibid.

50. Ibid.

51. Ibid.

52. Chuck Bartels. "Wal-Mart has eye on global expansion." MSNBC. June 4, 2010. http://www.msnbc.msn.com/id/37509252/ns/business-us_business/t/wal-mart-has-eye-global-expansion/#.UA9b8bTY-88.

53. Shubh Datta. "Wal-Mart Targets More International Expansion." *Fool.com.* February 9, 2012. http://www.fool.com/investing/general/2012/02/09/wal-mart-targets-more-international-expansion.aspx#.UA9cq7TY-88.

54. Natalie Berg. 2011. "Walmart International Revs Up Growth." Planet Retail. http://www.planetretail.net/Presentations/Walmart-PLMagazine.pdf.

55. "Walmart Sets Up New Subsidiary in China," *ChinaRetailNews.com,* March 24, 2010, http://www.chinaretailnews.com/2010/03/24/3471–Walmart-sets-up-new-subsidiary-in-china/.

56. Ibid.

57. Ladka Bauerova, Chris Burritt, and Joao Oliveira, "The Three-Way Fight for Brazilian Shoppers," *BusinessWeek,* March 25, 2010, http://newsletters.businessweek.com/c.asp?836292&b4a6a1b99cb8d1fb&4.

58. Ibid.

59. Ibid.

60. Ibid.

61. Boyle, "Walmart's Painful Lessons."

62. Ibid.

63. Ibid.

64. Ibid.

65. David Welch, "Wal-Mart Mexico Probe Threatening Global Growth Success: Retail," *BusinessWeek*, April 25, 2012. http://www.businessweek.com/news/2012-04-25/wal-mart-mexico-probe-threatening-global-growth-success-retail#p1

66. Shruti Setia Chhabra, "India Critical for Global Growth: Walmart," *The Times of India,* April 14, 2010, http://timesofindia.indiatimes.com/biz/india-business/India-critical-for-global-growth-Walmart/articleshow/5798939.cms.

67. Boyle, "Walmart's Painful Lessons."

68. "Walmart Actively Seeking Russian Expansion," *Retail.ru,* July 16, 2009, http://en.retail.ru/news/38768/.

69. Ibid.

70. Boyle, "Walmart's Painful Lessons."

71. "Walmart Canada to Open 35 to 40 Supercentres in 2010," *finchannel.com,* February 24, 2010, http://www.finchannel.com/Main_News/Business/59058_Walmart_Canada_to_Open_35_to_40_Supercentres_in_2010/.

72. Ibid.

73. Ibid.

74. Ibid.

75. David Welch, "Wal-Mart Mexico Probe Threatening Global Growth Success: Retail," *BusinessWeek*, April 25, 2012. http://www.businessweek.com/news/2012-04-25/wal-mart-mexico-probe-threatening-global-growth-success-retail#p1.

76. Robb M. Stewart, "Wal-Mart Checks Out a New Continent," *The Wall Street Journal,* October 27, p. B1.

77. Robb M. Stewart, "Wal-Mart Reassesses Massmart Bid," *The Wall Street Journal,* October 29, p. B1.

78. "WalMart Announces Major Reorganization, New Online Initiative," *FoodBiz Daily,* January 29, 2010, http://foodbizdaily.com/articles/96121–walmart-announces-major-reorganization-new-online-initiative.aspx.

79. Ibid.

80. Jonathan Birchall, "Walmart Gears Up for Global Online Push," *Financial Times,* January 29, 2010, http://www.ft.com/cms/s/0/9f944f78–0c67–11df-a941–00144feabdc0.html.

81. Ibid.

82. Mathew Mosk, "Walmart Fires Supplier after Bangladesh Revelation," *ABC News Blotter,* May 15, 2013. http://abcnews.go.com/Blotter/wal-mart-fires-supplier-bangladesh-revelation/story?id=19188673#.Ua3fGEC7Itg.

83. Ulfikar Ali Manik and Jim Yardley, "Another Garment Factory Scare in Bangladesh," *New York Times,* June 14, 2013, p. A11.

84. Steven Greenhouse, "U.S. Retailers Announce Safety Plan," *New York Times,* May 31, 2013, p. B6.

85. Steven Greenhouse, "Obama to Suspend Trade Privileges with Bangladesh," *New York Times,* June 28, 2013, p. B1.

■ Chapter 8

1. Thomas Sullivan, "IMS Reports Significant Global Pharmaceutical Sales Growth in Emerging Markets," Pharmaceutical and Device, Policy and Medicine, April 21, 2010, http://www.policymed.com/2010/04/ims-reports-significant-global-pharmaceutical-sales-growth-in-emerging-markets.html.

2. Ibid.

3. Ibid.

4. Ibid.

5. Heather Timmons, "India Expands Role as Drug Producer," *New York Times Online,* July 6, 2010, http://www.nytimes.com/2010/07/07/business/global/07indiadrug.html?_r=2&scp=1&sq=pharmaceutical%20india&st=cse.

6. Ibid.

7. Maria Daghlian, "Big Pharma's Emerging Market Fever: Abbott Aims for the Top of India's Industry," The Burrill Report, Seeking Alpha, May 23, 2010, http://seekingalpha.com/article/206465-big-pharma-s-emerging-market-fever-abbott-aims-for-the-top-of-india-s-industry.

8. Ibid.

9. Heather Timmons, "India Expands Role as Drug Producer," *New York Times Online,* July 6, 2010, http://www.nytimes.com/2010/07/07/business/global/07indiadrug.html?_r=2&scp=1&sq=pharmaceutical%20india&st=cse.

10. Ibid.

11. Ibid.

12. Ibid.

13. Dr. Derk Bergsma, former vice president of drug discovery group at Glaxosmithkline, personal interview, July 16, 2010.

14. Gary Gatyas and Clive Savage, "IMS Forecasts Global Pharmaceutical Market Growth of 5–8% Annually through 2014; Maintains Expectations of 4–6% Growth in 2010," IMS Biopharma Forecasts & Trends, April 20, 2010, http://www.imshealth.com/portal/site/ims/menuitem.d248e29c86589c9c30e81c033208c22a/?vgnextoid=4b8c410b6c718210VgnVCM100000ed152ca2RCRD.

15. Kerry Capell, "Novartis: Radically Remaking Its Drug Business," *Bloomberg BusinessWeek,* June 11, 2009, http://www.businessweek.com/magazine/content/09_25/b4136030131343.htm

16. Jonathan D. Rockoff and Peter Loftus, "Pfizer Pushes on New Biotech Drugs," *The Wall Street Journal,* April 28, 2010, www.wjs.com.

17. Andrew Pollack, "Roche Agrees to Acquire Genentech for $46.8 Billion," *New York Times,* March 13, 2009, p. B6.

18. "Pharma Consolidation Continues Its $40 Billion March," *InTech,* March 12, 2009, http://www.isa.org/InTechTemplate.cfm?Section=Automation_Update&template=/ContentManagement/ContentDisplay.cfm&ContentID=74917.

19. Gina Chon and Anupreeta Das, "Genzyme in Talks with Sanofi," *The Wall Street Journal*, August 3, 2010, p. B1

20. Andrew Pollack, "Deal Provides Vaccines to Poor Nations at Lower Cost," *New York Times,* March 24, 2010, p. B2.

21. Matt Wilkinson, "Big Pharma Set for Generics Boost," *Chemistry World,* May 21, 2009, http://www.rsc.org/chemistryworld/News/2009/May/21050903.asp.

22. Rumman Ahmed, "Ranbaxy Transfers New Drug Research Operations," *The Wall Street Journal,* July 2, 1010, www.wsj.com.

23. Matt Wilkinson, "Big Pharma Set for Generics Boost," *Chemistry World,* May 21, 2009, http://www.rsc.org/chemistryworld/News/2009/May/21050903.asp.

24. Kerry Capell, "Novartis: Radically Remaking Its Drug Business," *Bloomberg BusinessWeek,* June 11, 2009.

25. Ibid.

26. Ibid.

27. Ibid.

28. Ibid.

29. Charlie Nordblom, "Involving Middle Managers in Strategy at Volvo Group," *Strategic Communication Management* 10, no. 2 (February–March 2006), pp. 26–29.

30. Joel Baglole, "Citibank Takes Risk by Issuing Cards in China," *The Wall Street Journal,* March 10, 2004, p. C1.

31. Wang Ming, "Citigroup Sets China Growth," *The Wall Street Journal,* March 15, 2007, p. C7.

32. Jennifer M. Freedman, "China Nod for Citibank Credit Cards May Show Market Opening," *Bloomberg,* February 6, 2012, http://www.bloomberg.com/news/2012-02-06/nod-for-citibank-s-credit-cards-may-signal-chinese-banking-market-opening.html.

33. Enoch Yiu, "Citi Continues to Expand Branches to Tap Asia Clients," *South China Morning Post,* September 3, 2012, http://www.scmp.com/business/banking-finance/article/1028510/citi-continues-expand-branches-tap-asia-clients.

34. Paul J. Davies, "Citigroup plans to double China branches," *Financial Times,* March 11, 2012.

35. Alison Tuder, "Citigroup Eyes More Asian Expansion," *The Wall Street Journal,* July 16, 2010, www.wsj.com.

36. "Foreign Investment Restrictions in OECD Countries" (Paris: Organization for Economic Cooperation and Development, June 2003), p. 167.

37. Anuchit Nguyen, "Ford Plans $450 Million Thailand Plant After Riots," *Bloomberg Businessweek,* June 24, 2010, www.businessweek.com.

38. Joe Hinrichs, "Ford Celebrates Opening of New US$450 Million (THB14 billion) Manufacturing Facility in Thailand," Ford Motor Company, http://corporate.ford.com/.

39. "Thailand Passes Canada in Car Production," *CBC News Online,* March 6, 2013, http://www.cbc.ca/news/business/story/2013/03/06/business-scotia-auto-car.html/.

40. "G.E. Acknowledges Plan to Sell Appliance Unit," *Associated Press,* May 17, 2008.

41. Thomas Gryta, "Genzyme Plans Buyback, to Shed Business," *The Wall Street Journal,* May 6, 2010, www.wsj.com.

42. Gina Chon and Anupreeta Das, "Genzyme in Talks with Sanofi," *The Wall Street Journal,* August 3, 2010, p. B1.

43. Nina Sovich and Noelle Mennella, "Sanofi to Buy Genzyme for More than $20 Billion," *Reuters,* February 16, 2011, http://www.reuters.com/article/2011/02/16/us-genzyme-sanofi-idUSTRE71E4XI20110216.

44. Barry Hopewell, "Strategic Management: A Multi-perspective Approach," *Long Range Planning* 36, no. 4 (July 2003), p. 317.

45. Sharon Watson O'Neil, "Managing Foreign Subsidiaries: Agents of Headquarters, or an Independent Network?" *Strategic Management Journal* 21, no. 5 (May 2000), p. 525.

46. Noel Capon, Chris Christodoulou, John U. Farley, and James Hulbert, "A Comparison of Corporate Planning Practice in American and Australian Manufacturing Companies," *Journal of International Business Studies,* Fall 1984, pp. 41–45.

47. Martin K. Welge, "Planning in German Multinational Corporations," *International Studies of Management and Organization,* Spring 1982, pp. 6–37.

48. Martin K. Welge and Michael E. Kenter, "Impact of Planning on Control Effectiveness and Company Performance," *Management International Review* 20, no. 2 (1988), pp. 4–15.

49. Johanna Mair, "Exploring the Determinants of Unit Performance: The Role of Middle Managers in Stimulating Profit Growth," *Group & Organization Management* 30, no. 3 (June 2005), pp. 263–288.

50. See, for example, M. Kotabe and J. Y. Murray, "Global Sourcing Strategy and Sustainable Competitive Advantage," *Industrial Marketing Management* 33 (2004), pp. 7–14.

51. Joan Magretta, "Fast, Global, and Entrepreneurial: Supply Chain Management, Hong Kong Style," *Harvard Business Review,* September–October 1998, p. 108.

52. Preethi Chamikutty, "Will Coke's 200ml Pack Price Cut Cannibalise Thumbs Up?" *The Economic Times,* February 29, 2012, http://articles.economictimes.indiatimes.com/2012-02-29/news/31110875_1_thums-cola-category-coca-cola.

53. Nikhil Deogun, "For Coke in India, Thumbs Up Is the Real Thing," *The Wall Street Journal,* April 29, 1998, pp. B1, B6.

54. *Knowledge@Wharton,* "Coca-Cola India: Winning Hearts and Taste Buds in the Hinterland," *The Wall Street Journal,* May 14, 2010, www.wsj.com.

55. Ratna Bhushan, "Coca-Cola's Bouquet of Brands Leads Those of PepsiCo in Soft Drinks Market, but Coke Not at the Top," *The Economic Times,* November 2, 2012, http://articles.economictimes.indiatimes.com/2012-11-02/news/34876016_1_brand-coke-coca-cola-india-drinks-brands.

56. Richard M. Hodgetts, *Measures of Quality and High Performance* (New York: American Management Association, 1998).

57. Sang M. Lee, Fred Luthans, and Richard M. Hodgetts, "Total Quality Management: Implications for Central and Eastern Europe," *Organizational Dynamics,* Spring 1992, pp. 44–45.

58. Christine Tierney, "U.S. Carmakers Top Imports in J.D. Power Survey—Revamped Lineups Credited for Improved Customer Enjoyment," *The Detroit News,* July 16, 2010, www.dtnews.com.

59. Dara Kerr, "iPhone 5 sales in China surpass 2 million In first weekend," *Cnet,* December 16, 2012, http://news.cnet.com/8301-13579_3-57559484-37/iphone-5-sales-in-china-surpass-2-million-in-first-weekend/.

60. Tim Stevens, "iPhone 5 review," *Engadget,* September 18, 2012, http://www.engadget.com/2012/09/18/apple-iphone-5-review/.

61. Leslie Wayne, "Chief Decided to Step Down at Motorola," *New York Times,* September 20, 2003, p. C1.

62. "Hip Cell," *Chicago Tribune,* June 3, 2004, p. 32.

63. Hayley Tsukayama, "Google Agrees to Acquire Motorola Mobility," *The Washington Post,* August 15, 2011, http://www.washingtonpost.com/blogs/faster-forward/post/google-agrees-to-acquire-motorola-mobility/2011/08/15/gIQABmTkGJ_blog.html.

64. Christopher A. Bartlett and Sumantra Ghoshal, *Managing Across Borders: The Transnational Solution,* updated 2nd ed. (Cambridge, MA: Harvard Business School Press, 2002).

65. Ibid.

66. Royal Ford, "Driven by Demand, Vehicle Buyers Want Versatility and Amenities, Too," *Boston Globe,* February 3, 2004, p. G1.

67. Fons Trompenaars and Charles Hampden-Turner, *Riding the Waves of Culture: Understanding Diversity in Global Business,* 2nd ed. (New York: McGraw-Hill, 1998), p. 188.

68. Andrew Pollack, "Japan's Companies Seek a Digital VCR Standard," *New York Times,* February 16, 1993, online edition, www.nytimes.com; also www.panasonic.com.

69. Kerry Capell, "Thinking Simple at Philips," *BusinessWeek,* December 11, 2006, p. 50.

70. www.monsanto.com.

71. Charles Hill, *Global Business Today,* 3rd ed. (New York: McGraw-Hill, 2004), pp. 376–380.

72. Ibid.

73. See Anne-Wil Harzing, "An Empirical Analysis and Extension of the Bartlett and Ghoshal Typology of Multinational Companies," *Journal of International Business Studies,* First Quarter 2000, pp. 101–120.

74. Kendra S. Albright, "Environmental Scanning: Radar for Success," *Information Management Journal* 38, no. 3 (May–June 2004), pp. 38–44.

75. Manuel Yunggar, "Environment Scanning for Strategic Information: Content Analysis from Malaysia," *Journal of American Academy of Business* 6, no. 2 (March 2005), pp. 324–331.

76. Mike Robuck, "Opentv Gears Up Digital Cable Launch in China," *CED Magazine,* June 23, 2009, CedMagazine.com.

77. Ritsuko Ando, "Cisco Takes Aim at China Despite Trade Tensions," *Reuters,* April 15, 2010, www.reuters.com.

78. Suzanne Miller, "Cisco's M&A Machine Gears Up," *The Deal,* January, 11, 2013, http://www.thedeal.com/content/tmt/ciscos-ma-machine-gears-up.php.

79. Jamie Butters, "Ford Posts $2.1 Billion Profit, Boosts 2010 Outlook (Update2)," *Bloomberg Businessweek,* April 27, 2010, www.businessweek.com.

80. "Ford Earns $1.6 Billion Net in 4Q; Average Profit-Sharing of $8,300," *Detroit Free Press,* January 29, 2013, http://www.freep.com/article/20130129/BUSINESS01/130129005/Ford-earns-1-6-billion-net-in-4Q-average-profit-sharing-of-8-300.

81. Sea Jin Chang, "International Expansion Strategy of Japanese Firms: Capacity Building Through Sequential Entry," *Academy of Management Journal,* April 1995, p. 402.

82. Mary Anastasia O'Grady, "Americas: Teamsters Give NAFTA a Flat Tire," *The Wall Street Journal,* April 16, 2004, p. A15.

83. Joel Millman, "The Economy: Mexican Mergers, Acquisitions Triple from 2001," *Economist,* December 27, 2002, p. A2.

84. Press release, "Anheuser-Busch InBev Completes Combination with Grupo Modelo," *Wall Street Journal,* June 4, 2013, http://online.wsj.com/article/PR-CO-20130604-909365.html.

85. Harry I. Chernotsky, "Selecting U.S. Sites: A Case Study of German and Japanese Firms," *Management International Review* 23, no. 2 (1983), pp. 45–55.

86. Also see Roland Calori, Leif Melin, Tugrul Atamer, and Peter Gustavsson, "Innovative International Strategies," *Journal of World Business* 35, no. 4 (2000), pp. 333–354.

87. Christos Pantzalis, "Does Location Matter? An Empirical Analysis of Geographic Scope and MNC Market Valuation," *Journal of International Business Studies,* First Quarter 2001, pp. 133–155.

88. "A Guide In Africa: Why Investors in Frontier Markets Need Someone to Show Them Around," *The Economist,* February 23, 2013, http://www.economist.com/news/business/21572172-why-investors-frontier-markets-need-someone-show-them-around-guide-africa.

89. This section is adapted from Alan Rugman and Jonathan P. Doh, *Multinationals and Development* (New Haven: Yale University Press, 2008), pp. 12–14.

90. Das Narayandas, John Quelch, and Gordon Swartz, "Prepare Your Company for Global Pricing," *Sloan Management Review,* Fall 2000, pp. 61–70.

91. United Nations Conference on Trade and Development, *Global Investment Trends Monitor, No. 11,* (New York and Geneva: UNCTAD, January 2013).

92. Ibid., Annex Table 1.

93. Jonathan P. Doh and Ravi Ramamurti, "Reassessing Risk in Developing Country Infrastructure," *Long Range Planning* 36, no. 4 (2003), pp. 337–353; Jonathan P. Doh, Peter Rodriguez, Klaus Uhlenbruck, Jamie Collins, and Loraine Eden, "Coping with Corruption in Foreign Markets," *Academy of Management Executive* 17, no. 3 (2003), pp. 114–127.

94. See Yudong Luo and Mike W. Peng, "First Mover Advantages in Investing in Transitional Economies," *Thunderbird International Business Review* 40, no. 2 (March–April 1998), pp. 141–163.

95. For a detailed analysis of first-mover effects of this case, see Jonathan P. Doh, "Entrepreneurial Privatization Strategies: Order of Entry and Local Partner Collaboration as Sources of Competitive Advantage," *Academy of Management Review* 25, no. 3 (2000), pp. 551–571.

96. C. K. Prahalad, *The Fortune at the Bottom of the Pyramid: Eradicating Poverty Through Profits* (revised and updated 5th Anniversary Edition: *Eradicating Poverty Through Profits*) (Philadelphia: Wharton School Publishing, 2009); Stuart Hart and Clayton Christensen, "The Great Leap: Driving Innovation from the Base of the Pyramid," *Sloan Management Review* 44, no. 1 (2002), pp. 51–56; C. K. Prahalad and Stuart L. Hart, "The Fortune at the Bottom of the Pyramid," *Strategy + Business* 26 (2002), pp. 54–67.

97. Joan Enric Ricart, Michael J. Enright, Pankaj Ghemawat, Stuart L. Hart, and Tarun Khanna, "New Frontiers in International Strategy," *Journal of International Business Studies* 35, no. 3 (May 2004), pp. 175–200.

98. Ibid., pp. 194–195.

99. Erik Simanis, "At the Base of the Pyramid," *MIT Sloan Management Review,* MIT Sloan Management Review Executive Advisory, October 20, 2009, http://sloanreview.mit.edu.

100. Nicolas Dahan, Jonathan P. Doh, Jennifer Oetzel, and Michael Yaziji, "Corporate-NGO Collaboration: Creating New Business Models for Developing Markets," *Long Range Planning* 43, no. 2, pp. 326–342.

101. See http://www.nestle.com/SharedValueCSR/FarmersAndAgriculture/Cocoa/Introduction.htm.

102. Christina Passariello, "Danone Expands Its Pantry to Woo the World's Poor," *The Wall Street Journal,* June 25, 2010, www.wsj.com.

103. Jamie Anderson and Niels Billou, "Serving the World's Poor: Innovation at the Base of the Economic Pyramid," *Journal of Business Strategy* 28, no. 2 (2007), pp. 14–21.

104. Benjamin M. Oviatt and Patricia P. McDougall, "The Internationalization of Entrepreneurship," *Journal of International Business Studies* 36 (2005), pp. 2–8; Patricia P. McDougall and Benjamin M. Oviatt, "International Entrepreneurship: The Intersection of Two Research Paths," *Academy of Management Journal* 43 (2000), pp. 902–908.

105. McDougall and Oviatt, "International Entrepreneurship," p. 902.

106. Erkko Autio, Harry J. Sapienza, and James G. Almeida, "Effects of Age at Entry, Knowledge Intensity, and Irritability on International Growth," *Academy of Management Journal* 43 (2000), pp. 909–924.

107. Shaker A. Zahra, Duane R. Ireland, and Michael A. Hitt, "International Expansion by New Venture Firms: International

Diversity, Mode of Market Entry, Technological Learning, and Performance," *Academy of Management Journal* 43 (2000), pp. 925–950.

108. Moen Oystein, "The Born Globals: A New Generation of Small European Exporters," *International Marketing Review* 19, no. 2/3 (2002), pp. 156–175.

109. Gary A. Knight and S. Tamar Cavusgil, "Innovation, Organizational Capabilities, and the Born-Global Firm," *Journal of International Business Studies* 35, no. 2 (2004), pp. 124–141.

110. Ibid.

111. Olli Kuivalainen, Sanna Sundqvist, and Per Servais, "Firms' Degree of Born-Globalness, International Entrepreneurial Orientation and Export Performance," *Journal of World Business* 42 (2007), pp. 253–267.

112. Kimberly C. Gleason and Joan Wiggenhorn, "Born Globals: The Choice of Globalization Strategy, and the Market's Perception of Performance," *Journal of World Business* 42 (2007), pp. 322–335.

113. J. de La Torre and R. W. Moxon, "Electronic Commerce and Global Business: Introduction to the Symposium," *Journal of International Business* 32, no. 1 (2001), pp. 617–640.

114. Joseph Weber, "E*Trade Rises from the Ashes," *BusinessWeek*, January 17, 2005, online edition, www.businessweek.com; Whitney Kisling, "E*Trade Gains Most Since December on Return to Profit," *Bloomberg BusinessWeek*, July 23, 2010, www.businessweek.com.

■ Chapter 9

1. Alex Taylor III, "Volkswagen: Das Auto Giant, " *Fortune*, July 23, 2012. pp. 150–155.

2. Volkswagen, Press Release: Volkswagen Group Achieves Key Milestones in 2012, March 14, 2013. https://www.volkswagen-media-services.com/medias_publish/ms/content/en/pressemitteilungen/2013/03/14/volkswagen_group_achieves.standard.gid-oeffentlichkeit.html.

3. Ibid.

4. Volkswagen, Press Release: Volkswagen Strengthens Position in Global Markets in First Quarter, April 29, 2013. Volkswagen Group Achieves Key Milestones in 2012. http://www.marketwire.com/press-release/volkswagen-strengthens-position-in-global-markets-in-first-quarter-1783911.htm

5. Taylor, op. cit.

6. Taylor, op. cit.

7. Taylor, op. cit.

8. John McElroy, "Today's VW Looks like Sloan's GM," *Final Inspection,* February 27, 2013. http://wardsauto.com/blog/today-s-vw-looks-sloan-s-gm.

9. Stefan Schmid and Philipp Grosche, "Managing the International Value Chain in the Automotive Industry: Strategy, Structure, and Culture," Bertelsmann Stiftung and ESCP-EAP European School of Management. http://www.escp-eap.eu/uploads/media/Managing_the_International_Value_Chain_in_the_Automotive_Industr.pdf.

10. For more on this see Donald F. Kuratko and Richard M. Hodgetts, *Entrepreneurship: A Contemporary Approach,* 5th ed. (Ft. Worth, TX: Harcourt, 2001), pp. 529–535.

11. J. Contractor, "Contractual and Cooperative Forms of International Business: Towards Unified Theory of Model Choice," *Management International Review* 30, no. 1 (1990), pp. 31–54.

12. Peng S. Chan, "International Joint Ventures vs. Wholly Owned Subsidiaries," *Multinational Business Review* 3, no. 1 (Spring 1995), pp. 37–44.

13. Harrry Barkema and Freek Vermeulen, "International Expansion Through Start-up or Acquisition: A Learning Perspective," *Academy of Management Journal,* February 1998, pp. 7–26.

14. K. Carow, R. Heron, and T. Saxton, "Do Early Birds Get the Returns? An Empirical Investigation of Early-Mover Advantages in Acquisitions," *Strategic Management Journal* 25 (2004), pp. 563–585.

15. Caroline Jacobs and Adveith Nair, "GDF Suez Takes Full Control of International Power." *Reuters*, April 16, 2012, http://www.reuters.com/article/2012/04/16/us-internationalpower-gdf-idUS-BRE83F0AM20120416.

16. Christine T. W. Huang and Brian H. Kleiner, "New Developments Concerning Managing Mergers and Acquisitions," *Management Research News* 27, no. 4–5 (2004), pp. 54–62.

17. Max Colchester, "Alcatel-Lucent Continues to Struggle," *The Wall Street Journal,* August 1, 2007, p. B4.

18. Sam Schechner and Dana Cimilluca, "Alcatel Chief Is Out as the Turnaround Stalls," *The Wall Street Journal,* February 7, 2013, http://online.wsj.com/article/SB10001424127887324906004578287852518071498.html?mg=id-wsj.

19. For additional insights into alliances and joint ventures, see William Newburry and Yoram Zeira, "General Differences Between Equity International Joint Ventures (EIJVs), International Acquisitions (IAs) and International Greenfield Investments (IGIs): Implications for Parent Companies," *Journal of World Business* 32, no. 2 (1997), pp. 87–102.

20. Also see David Lei, Robert A. Pitts, and John W. Slocum Jr., "Building Cooperative Advantage: Managing Strategic Alliances to Promote Organizational Learning," *Journal of World Business* 32, no. 3 (1997), pp. 203–222.

21. For more on this see Ana Valdes Llaneza and Esteban Garcia-Canal, "Distinctive Features of Domestic and International Joint Ventures," *Management International Review* 38, no. 1 (1998), pp. 49–66.

22. Felicity Long, "Finnair to Join Transatlantic Joint Venture," *Travel Weekly.com,* March 12, 2013, http://www.travelweekly.com/Travel-News/Airline-News/Finnair-to-join-transatlantic-joint-venture/.

23. "International Airlines Group formed as BA signs merger with Iberia," *IBTimes.com,* April 8, 2010, http://www.ibtimes.co.uk/articles/20100408/international-airlines-group-formed-ba-signs-merger-iberia.htm.

24. Daniel Michaels, "Looming Alliance to Boost BA," *The Wall Street Journal,* July 13, 2010, www.wsj.com.

25. For more on this see Hildy J. Teegen and Jonathan P. Doh, "U.S./Mexican Alliance Negotiations: Cultural Impacts on Trust, Authority and Performance," *Thunderbird International Business Review* 44, no. 6 (2002), pp. 749–775; Michael A. Hitt, M. Tina Dacin, Edward Levitas, Jean-Luc Arregle, and Anca Borza, "Partner Selection in Emerging and Developed Market Contexts: Resource-Based and Organizational Learning Perspectives," *Academy of Management Journal* 43, no. 3 (2002), pp. 449–467.

26. Alan Ohnsman, "Hyundai Leads Asian Brands' U.S. Gains as Sales Slow," *Bloomberg BusinessWeek,* July 1, 2010, http://www.businessweek.com/news/2010-07-01/hyundai-leads-asian-brands-u-s-gains-as-sales-slow.html.

27. Tommaso Ebhardt Marchionne Holds Talks to Push Ahead Fiat-Chrysler Merger, *Bloomberg,* June 7, 2013. http://www.bloomberg.com/news/2013-06-07/fiat-in-talks-to-push-ahead-with-chrysler-merger.html.

28. Mark Milner, "Indian Firm Buys Jaguar and Land Rover," *The Guardian,* March 26, 2008, http://www.guardian.co.uk/business/2008/mar/26/automotive.mergersandacquisitions; Bruce Nussbaum, "Tata Buys Land Rover and Jaguar, Now It Has to

'Nano' Them," *BusinessWeek Online*, March 27, 2008, http://www.businessweek.com/innovate/NussbaumOnDesign/archives/2008/03/tata_buys_land.html.

29. Don Clark, "Microsoft to License ARM Chip Technology," *The Wall Street Journal*, July 26, 2010, www.wsj.com.

30. Jenny Watts, "Is This the End for Coke's 'Think Local' Ad Strategy?" *Campaign*, October 12, 2001, p. 17.

31. Jonathan Wheatley, "Coke Pops the Top off an Emerging Market," *BusinessWeek*, May 2, 2005, online edition, www.businessweek.com.

32. Preethi Chamikutty, "Will Coke's 200ml Pack Price Cut Cannibalise Thumbs Up?" *The Economic Times*, February 29, 2012, http://articles.economictimes.indiatimes.com/2012-02-29/news/31110875_1_thums-cola-category-coca-cola.

33. Joan Magretta, "Fast, Global, and Entrepreneurial: Supply Chain Management, Hong Kong Style," *Harvard Business Review*, September–October 1998, p. 106.

34. See George S. Yip, *Total Global Strategy II* (Englewood Cliffs, NJ: Prentice Hall, 2003), chapter 8.

35. *Total Global Strategy II* (Englewood Cliffs, NJ: Prentice Hall, 2003), chapter 8.

36. A. V. Phatak, *International Dimensions of Management*, 2nd ed. (Boston: PWS-Kent, 1989), pp. 92–93.

37. Mark Hachman, "'One Sony' Reorganization Focuses on Games, Mobile, Imaging," *PCMag.com*, March 27, 2012, http://www.pcmag.com/article2/0,2817,2402217,00.asp.

38. "American Management, By Brazilians," *Exame*, May 4, 2010, http://thebrazilianeconomy.com/american_management_by_brazilians.php.

39. Pollack, "Roche Agrees to Acquire Genentech."

40. Also see Andrew C. Inkpen and Adva Dinur, "Knowledge Management Processes and International Joint Ventures," *Organization Science*, July–August 1998, pp. 454–468.

41. See for example John Child, "A Configurational Analysis of International Joint Ventures," *Organization Studies* 23, no. 5 (2002), pp. 781–815.

42. "Abu Dhabi Aircraft and Sikorsky in Joint Venture," *New York Times*, July 19, 2010, www.nyt.com.

43. Paul Stenquist, "G.M. Joint Venture Introduces New Brand to China," *New York Times*, July 19, 2010.

44. Miki Tanikawa, "Electronics Giants Join Forces in Japan," *New York Times*, May 24, 2001, p. W1.

45. Craig Zarley, "IBM Outsourcing Rolls On," *CRN*, January 13, 2003, p. 24.

46. Matthew Schifrin, "Partner or Perish," *Forbes*, May 21, 2001, p. 27.

47. Thomas W. Malone and Robert J. Laubacher, "The Dawn of the E-Lance Economy," *Harvard Business Review*, September–October 1998, p. 148.

48. Durward K. Sobek II, Jeffrey K. Liker, and Allen C. Ward, "Another Look at How Toyota Integrates Product Development," *Harvard Business Review*, July–August 1998, p. 49.

49. Anne-Wil Harzing, "An Empirical Analysis and Extension of the Bartlett and Ghoshal Typology of Multinational Companies," *Journal of International Business Studies*, First Quarter 2000, pp. 101–120.

50. Steven M. Sommers, Seung-Hyun Bae, and Fred Luthans, "The Structure-Climate Relationship in Korean Organizations," *Asia Pacific Journal of Management* 12, no. 2 (1995), pp. 23–36.

51. James R. Lincoln, Mitsuyo Hanada, and Kerry McBride, "Organizational Structures in Japanese and U.S. Manufacturing," *Administrative Science Quarterly*, September 1986, p. 356.

52. Rhy-song Yeh and Tagi Sagafi-nejad, "Organizational Characteristics of American and Japanese Firms in Taiwan," *National Academy of Management Proceedings*, 1987, pp. 111–115.

53. Ibid., p. 113.

54. Abbass F. Alkhafaji, *Competitive Global Management: Principles and Strategies* (Delray Beach, FL: St. Lucie Press, 1995), pp. 390–391.

55. Michael Yoshino and N. S. Rangan, *Strategic Alliances* (Boston: Harvard Business School Press, 1995), p. 195.

56. Lincoln, Hanada, and McBride, "Organizational Structures," p. 349.

57. Vito Racancelli, "Why Hung-Up Nokia Might Still Be Decent Value Play," *Barron's*, May 24, 2004, p. MW6.

58. Mark Lehrer and Kazuhiro Asakawa, "Unbundling European Operations: Regional Management and Corporate Flexibility in American and Japanese MNCs," *Journal of World Business* 34, no. 3 (1999), pp. 267–286.

59. Masumi Tsuda, "The Future of the Organization and the Individual to Japanese Management," *International Studies of Management and Organization*, Fall-Winter 1985, pp. 89–125.

60. Yeh and Sagafi-nejad, "Organizational Characteristics," p. 113.

61. Stephen Christophe and Ray Pfeiffer Jr., "The Valuation of MNC International Operations during the 1990s," *Review of Quantitative Finance and Accounting* 18, no. 2 (March 2002), p. 119.

62. Tsuda, "The Future of the Organization," p. 114.

■ Chapter 10

1. Abrahm Lustgarten, "Shell Shakedown: Fortune's Abrahm Lustgarten reports how the world's second-largest oil company lost control of its $22 billion project on Russia's Sakhalin Island," *CNN Money*, February 1, 2007, http://money.cnn.com/magazines/fortune/fortune_archive/2007/02/05/8399125/index.htm.

2. Ibid.

3. Ibid.

4. "Russia Turns Screws on Foreign Oil Groups," *AAJ News*, September 26, 2006, http://www.aaj.tv/2006/09/russia-turns-screws-on-foreign-oil-groups/.

5. Abrahm Lustgarten, "Shell Shakedown: Fortune's Abrahm Lustgarten reports how the world's second-largest oil company lost control of its $22 billion project on Russia's Sakhalin Island," *CNN Money*, February 1, 2007, http://money.cnn.com/magazines/fortune/fortune_archive/2007/02/05/8399125/index.htm.

6. Ibid.

7. Ibid.

8. Terry Macalister, "Oligarchs to Sue TNK-BP after Failing to Agree on Control of Company," *The Guardian*, June 11, 2008, http://www.guardian.co.uk/business/2008/jun/12/bp.oil1.

9. "TNK-BP Dispute Settled," *Euronews*, April 9, 2008, http://www.euronews.com/2008/09/04/tnk-bp-dispute-settled/.

10. Shamil Yenikeyeff, "BP, Russian Billionaires, and the Kremlin: a Power Triangle that Never Was," The Oxford Institute for Energy Studies, November 2011, http://www.oxfordenergy.org/wpcms/wp-content/uploads/2011/11/BP-Russian-billionaires-and-the-Kremlin.pdf.

11. Vladimir Soldatkin and Andrew Callus, "Rosneft Pays Out in Historic TNK-BP Deal Completion," *Reuters*, March 21, 2013, http://www.reuters.com/article/2013/03/21/us-rosneft-tnkbp-deal-idUSBRE92K0IZ20130321.

12. "Doing Business 2013: Russian Federation," *International Finance Corporation and The World Bank*, 2013, http://www.doingbusiness.org/data/exploreeconomies/russia/.

13. "Finance and Economics: Footloose Firms; Economic Focus," *Economist,* March 27, 2004, p. 99.

14. Seth Faison, "China Applies Brakes on Move toward Market Economy," *New York Times,* September 30, 1998, p. C3. See also Kathy Chen, "China's Party Line Is Capital," *The Wall Street Journal,* February 12, 2004, p. C20.

15. Doug Palmer, "China Piracy Cost U.S. Firms $48 Billion in 2009: Report," *Reuters,* May 18, 2011, www.reuters.com.

16. Olivia Chung, "A Trademark Milestone in China," *Asia Times,* June 29, 2007, www.asiatimes.com.

17. Neil Lipschutz, "Google Says China Remains Murky," *The Wall Street Journal,* July 31, 2010, www.wsj.com.

18. Elisabeth Rosenthal, "U.S. Trade Official Says China Market Is Closed Tighter," *New York Times,* September 23, 1998, p. C2.

19. Melanie Trottman, "U.S. to Press China on Drywall," *The Wall Street Journal,* October 16, 2009, p. A3.

20. Sunrita Sen, "Backlog Stalls Justice in India," *IOL News,* January 21, 2013, http://www.iol.co.za/news/world/backlog-stalls-justice-in-india-1.1455345#.UWMYLlddCSo.

21. Mark Landler, "Back to Vietnam, This Time to Build," *New York Times,* September 13, 1998, sec. 3, pp. 1, 11.

22. "Change Will Come . . . But Not Yet," *Asia Monitor,* January 2007, online edition, www.asia-monitor.com.

23. Todd Zaun, "The Economy: U.S. Trade Chief Seeks to Reassure a Very Weary Japan on Steel Tariffs," *The Wall Street Journal,* April 12, 2002, p. A2.

24. John McKinnon and Neil King, "EU Set to Impose Trade Sanctions if U.S. Fails to Act," *The Wall Street Journal,* January 26, 2004, p. A4.

25. "Coca-Cola Co.: Settlement of Anti-Trust Case Is Discussed with EU Officials," *The Wall Street Journal,* April 19, 2004, p. 1.

26. Edmund L. Andrews, "Why U.S. Giants Are Crying Uncle," *New York Times,* October 11, 2000, p. W1.

27. Leo Cendrowicz, "Microsoft Loses E.U. Anti-Trust Case," *Time,* September 17, 2007, www.time.com.

28. Foo Yun Chee, "EU Fines Microsoft $731 Million for Broken Promise, Warns Others," *Reuters,* March 6, 2013, www.reuters.com.

29. Prasanta Sahu, Phred Dvorak, and R. Jai, "Krishna India Sets Blackberry Showdown," *The Wall Street Journal,* August 13, 2010, www.wsj.com.

30. Jack N. Kondrasuk, "The Effects of 9/11 and Terrorism on Human Resource Management: Recovery, Reconsideration, and Renewal," *Employee Responsibilities and Rights Journal* 16, no. 1 (May 2004), pp. 25–35.

31. J. Hocking, *Beyond Terrorism: The Development of the Australian Security State* (Sydney: Allen & Unwin Pty Ltd, 1993).

32. Kondrasuk, "The Effects of 9/11."

33. Jack N. Kondrasuk, Daniel Bailey, and Mathew Sheeks, "Leadership in the 21st Century: Understanding Global Terrorism," *Employee Responsibilities and Rights Journal* 17, no. 4 (December 2005), pp. 263–280.

34. Sia Khiun Then and Martin Loosemore, "Terrorism Prevention, Preparedness, and Response in Built Facilities," *Facilities* 24, no. 5–6 (2006), pp. 157–176.

35. David A. Schmidt, "Analyzing Political Risk," *Business Horizons,* July–August 1986, pp. 43–50.

36. Matthew Brzezinski, "Russia Kills Huge Oil Deal with Exxon," *The Wall Street Journal,* August 28, 1997, p. A2.

37. For more, see Thomas A. Pointer, "Political Risk: Managing Government Intervention," in *International Management: Text and Cases,* ed. Paul W. Beamish, J. Peter Killing, Donald J.

LeCraw, and Harold Crookell (Homewood, IL: Irwin, 1991), pp. 119–133.

38. See Jonathan P. Doh and Ravi Ramamurti, "Reassessing Risk in Developing Country Infrastructure," *Long Range Planning* 36, no. 4 (2003), pp. 337–353.

39. Ravi Ramamurti and Jonathan Doh, "Rethinking Foreign Infrastructure Investment in Developing Countries," *Journal of World Business* 39, no. 2 (2004), pp. 151–167.

40. Michael M. Schuman, "Indonesia to Pay Reduced Claim to U.S. in Long-Disputed Overseas Insurance Case," *The Wall Street Journal,* May 11, 2001, p. A12.

41. Timothy Mapes, "Power Firm's Bid to Collect Funds from Pertamina Raises Hackles," *The Wall Street Journal,* April 1, 2002, p. A6.

42. See Jonathan P. Doh and John A. Pearce II, "Corporate Entrepreneurship and Real Options in Transitional Policy Environments: Theory Development," *Journal of Management Studies* 41, no. 4 (2004), pp. 645–664.

43. Doh and Ramamurti, "Reassessing Risk," pp. 344–349.

44. Amy Hillman and Michael A. Hitt, "Corporate Political Strategy Formulation: A Model of Approach, Participation, and Strategy Decisions," *Academy of Management Review* 24, no. 24 (1999), pp. 825–842.

45. Amy Hillman and Gerald Keim, "International Variation in the Business-Government Interface: Institutional and Organizational Considerations," *Academy of Management Review* 20, no. 1 (1995), pp. 193–214.

46. Robert J. Bowman, "Are You Covered?" *World Trade* 8, no. 2 (March 1995), pp. 100–103.

47. Mark A. Hofmann, "Political Risk Market Eases as Supply Outpaces Demand," *Business Insurance* 40, no. 8 (February 20, 2006), pp. 9–10.

48. Jonathan P. Doh and Hildy Teegen, "Nongovernmental Organizations as Institutional Actors in International Business: Theory and Implications," *International Business Review* 11, no. 6 (2002), pp. 665–684.

49. Carlos Tejada, "Truck Maker Volvo Sets Alliance to Enter China," *The Wall Street Journal Online,* January 27, 2013, http://online.wsj.com/article/SB10001424127887324039504578264611071184722.html.

50. Matthew Karnitschnig, "Siemens to Expand Business in China and Boost Sales," *The Wall Street Journal,* May 18, 2004, p. A6.

51. Press Release, "Siemens and Waison Establish Joint Venture for Smart Metering Solutions," Siemens, September 13, 2012, www.siemens.com/press/en/pressrelease.

52. Press Release, "Siemens and Shanghai Electric Agree on Strategic Wind Power Alliance for China," Siemens, December 9, 2011, www.siemens.com/press/en/pressrelease.

53. Peter J. Buckley and Mark Casson, "An Economic Model of International Joint Venture Strategy," *Journal of International Business Studies* 27 (1996), pp. 849–876.

54. Farok J. Contractor and Peter Lorange, eds., *Cooperative Strategies in International Business* (Lexington, MA: Lexington Books, 1998).

55. Andrew C. Inkpen, *The Management of International Joint Ventures: An Organizational Learning Perspective* (London: Routledge, 1995).

56. Shige Makino and Andrew Delios, "Local Knowledge Transfer and Performance: Implications for Alliance Formation in Asia," *Journal of International Business Studies* 27 (1996), pp. 905–927.

57. Hildy Teegen and Jonathan P. Doh, "U.S./Mexican Alliance Negotiations: Cultural Impacts on Trust, Authority and Performance," *Thunderbird International Business Review* 44, no. 6 (2002), pp. 749–775.

58. Harry G. Barkema and Freek Vermeulen, "What Differences in the Cultural Backgrounds of Partners Are Detrimental for International Joint Ventures?" *Journal of International Business Studies* 28, no. 4 (1997), pp. 845–864.

59. Dirk Holtbrugge, "Management of International Strategic Business Cooperation: Situation Conditions, Performance Criteria, and Success Factors," *Thunderbird International Business Review* 46, no. 3 (May–June 2004), pp. 255–274.

60. Manuel G. Serapio Jr. and Wayner F. Cascio, "End Games in International Alliances," *Academy of Management Executive* 10, no. 1 (February 1996), pp. 62–73.

61. Julia G. Djarova, "Foreign Investment Strategies and the Attractiveness of Central and Eastern Europe," *International Studies in Management and Organization* 29, no. 1 (Spring 1999), pp. 14–23.

62. Jonathan P. Doh and Hildy Teegen, "Government Mandates and Local Partner Participation in Emerging Markets: Policy and Performance Implications for Government and Business Strategies," Paper presented at the annual meeting of the Academy of International Business, Phoenix, AZ, November 20, 2002.

63. Jonathan P. Doh, Peter Rodriguez, Klaus Uhlenbruck, Jamie Collins, and Lorraine Eden, "Coping with Corruption in Foreign Markets," *Academy of Management Executive* 17, no. 3 (2003), pp. 114–127.

64. Serapio and Cascio, "End Games in International Alliances," pp. 71–72.

65. Press Release, "Ford to Change Stake in Mazda," Ford Motor Company, November 18, 2010, corporate.ford.com/news-center/.

66. Edward Norton, "Starbucks in China," *Economist*, October 4, 2001, pp. 80–82.

67. "Starbucks Acquires Beijing Mei Da Coffee," *Asia Times*, October 27, 2006, www.asiatimes.com.

68. Frederick Balfour, "Back on the Radar Screen," *BusinessWeek*, November 2000, p. 27.

69. Henry Gallagher, "A Private Sector Surfaces in Vietnam," *The World & I* 18, no. 11 (November 2003), p. 56.

70. Trien Nguyen, "From Plan to Market: The Economic Transition in Vietnam," *Journal of Economic Literature* 38, no. 3 (September 2000), p. 683.

71. "Ford Vietnam Records Best-Ever Full Year Sales in 2009," Ford press release, www.mediaford.com.

72. "Ford Vietnam's 2011 sales hit record," *Saigon Money*, January 13, 2012, http://www.saigonmoney.com/2012/01/13/ford-vietnam%E2%80%99s-2011-sales-hit-record/.

■ Chapter 11

1. Forrester Research, Inc.

2. Jon Berkeley. "The Alibaba Phenomenon." *The Economist*. March 23, 2013. http://www.economist.com/news/leaders/21573981-chinas-e-commerce-giant-could-generate-enormous-wealthprovided-countrys-rulers-leave-it.

3. Eric Jackson. "New Study Says Alibaba's Tmall Will Overtake Amazon as the World's Biggest Ecommerce Site by 2015." *Forbes*. November 29, 2012. http://www.forbes.com/sites/ericjackson/2012/11/29/new-study-says-alibabas-tmall-will-overtake-amazon-as-the-worlds-biggest-ecommerce-site-by-2015/.

4. Jon Berkeley. "The Alibaba Phenomenon." *The Economist*. March 23, 2013. http://www.economist.com/news/leaders/21573981-chinas-e-commerce-giant-could-generate-enormous-wealthprovided-countrys-rulers-leave-it.

5. Danielle Kucera. "Amazon Rises After Sales, North American Margins Improve." *Bloomberg*. January 30, 2013. http://www.bloomberg.com/news/2013-01-29/amazon-revenue-rises-22-percent-amid-record-holiday-spending.html.

6. Don Davis. "Amazon Will Top 100 Warehouses by the Holidays, ChannelAdvisor Says." *InternetRetailer*. April 29, 2013. http://www.internetretailer.com/2013/04/29/amazon-tops-100-warehouses.

7. Steven Millward. "Alibaba's Jack Ma Talks E-Commerce, Ecosystems, Slams the Broken 'Amazon Model'." *Tech In Asia*. March 21, 2013. http://www.techinasia.com/alibaba-jack-ma-talks-b2c-ecommerce/.

8. Clark Fredricksen. "Ecommerce Sales Topped $1 Trillion for First Time in 2012." *eMarketer*. February 5, 2013. http://www.emarketer.com/Article/Ecommerce-Sales-Topped-1-Trillion-First-Time-2012/1009649.

9. Ibid.

10. Jon E. Hilsenrath, "Ford Designs Ikon to Suit Indian Tastes," *Globe and Mail*, August 8, 2000, p. B10.

11. Christopher Bjork, "Santander Pursues Local Listings," *The Wall Street Journal*, August 2, 2010, www.wsj.com.

12. "Q&A with PetroChina's Huang Yan," *BusinessWeek*, July 2, 2001, online edition, www.businessweek.com.

13. Deborah Ball, "Cadbury Retools to Ward Off a Takeover," *The Wall Street Journal*, June 20, 2007, p. A8.

14. Anjali Cordeiro, "Kraft Gets Books from Cadbury," *The Wall Street Journal*, August 5, 2010, www.wsj.com.

15. Rumman Ahmed, "Ranbaxy Transfers New Drug Research Operations," *The Wall Street Journal*, July 2, 2010, www.wsj.com.

16. Johannes Gerds and Freddy Strottmann, "Post Merger Integration: Hard Data, Hard Truths," *Deloitte Review*, issue 6, 2010, www.deloitte.com.

17. Jette Schramm-Nielsen, "Cultural Dimensions of Decision Making: Denmark and France Compared," *Journal of Managerial Psychology* 16, no. 6 (2001), pp. 404–423.

18. Ibid., pp. 410–411.

19. Raghu Nath, *Comparative Management: A Regional View* (Cambridge, MA: Ballinger, 1988), pp. 74–75.

20. Konrad Spang and Sinan Ozcan, "Cultural Differences in Decision Making in Project Teams," *International Journal of Managing Projects in Business* 2, no. 1 (2009), pp. 70–93.

21. Sang M. Lee, Fred Luthans, and Richard M. Hodgetts, "Total Quality Management: Implications for Central and Eastern Europe," *Organizational Dynamics*, Spring 1992, p. 45.

22. Daewoo Park and Herna A. Krishnan, "Understanding Supplier Selection Practices: Differences Between U.S. and Korean Executives," *Thunderbird International Business Review*, March–April 2001, pp. 243–255.

23. Peter Landers, "How the U.S. Re-Interprets 'Kaizen,'" *The Wall Street Journal*, June 16, 2010, www.wsj.com.

24. "BMW: Up Close and Personal," *Marketing Week*, July 27, 2002, p. 42.

25. Christopher Gasper, "NEC Seeks Right Fits for Expansion," *Boston Globe*, May 13, 2004, p. C3.

26. Edward Moltzen, "Intel Highlights New Roadmap with Dual-Core Processors," *CRN*, May 31, 2004, p. 35.

27. Jack Ewing, "Siemens' Culture Clash," *BusinessWeek*, January 29, 2007, pp. 42–46.

28. Bill Spindle, "Cowboys and Samurai: The Japanizing of Universal," *The Wall Street Journal*, March 22, 2001, p. B6.

29. Kelly Olsen, "Universal Studios Plans Theme Park in South Korea," *USAToday*, May 23, 2007, online edition, www.usatoday.com.

30. Jim Middlemiss, "IT Challenge: Settlement," *Wall Street Week,* April 2004, p. 46.

31. Fons Trompenaars and Charles Hampden-Turner, *Riding the Waves of Culture: Understanding Diversity in Global Business,* 2nd ed. (New York: McGraw-Hill, 1998), pp. 157–159.

32. John D. Daniels and Jeffrey Arpan, "Comparative Home Country Influences on Management Practices Abroad," *Academy of Management Journal,* September 1972, p. 310.

33. Jacques H. Horovitz, "Management Control in France, Great Britain and Germany," *Columbia Journal of World Business,* Summer 1978, pp. 17–18.

34. Ibid., p. 18.

35. William G. Egelhoff, "Patterns of Control in U.S., U.K., and European Multinational Corporations," *Journal of International Business Studies,* Fall 1984, p. 81.

36. Ibid., pp. 81–82.

37. M. Kreder and M. Zeller, "Control in German and U.S. Companies," *Management International Review* 28, no. 3 (1988), pp. 64–65.

38. A. V. Phatak, *International Dimensions of Management,* 2nd ed. (Boston: PWS-Kent, 1989), p. 154.

39. William Boston and Paul Hofheinz, "Once Again, EU to Take Back Seat to VW," *The Wall Street Journal,* February 27, 2002, p. A16.

40. David A. Garvin, "Japanese Quality Management," *Columbia Journal of World Business,* Fall 1984, pp. 3–12.

41. Ibid., p. 6.

42. Jeffrey K. Liker and Yen-Chun Wu, "Japanese Automakers, U.S. Suppliers and Supply-Chain Superiority," *Sloan Management Review,* Fall 2000, pp. 81–93.

43. Cited in John Holusha, "Improving Quality, the Japanese Way," *New York Times,* July 20, 1988, p. 25. See also Richard Dauch, "Recipe for Success," *Manufacturing Engineering* 131, no. 2 (August 2003), p. 69.

44. "Key to Success: People, People, People," *Fortune,* October 27, 1997, p. 232.

45. Golpira Eshgi, "Nationality Bias and Performance Evaluations in Multinational Corporations," *National Academy of Management Proceedings,* San Diego, CA, 1985, p. 95.

46. Jeremiah Sullivan, Terukiho Suzuki, and Yasumasa Kondo, "Managerial Theories and the Performance Control Process in Japanese and American Work Groups," *National Academy of Management Proceedings,* San Diego, CA, 1985, pp. 98–102.

47. Ibid.

■ Part 3 Integrative Cases

Brief Integrative Case 3.1

1. "Wife & Son of Well-Known Political Prisoner & Christian, Guo Quan Arrive in US," ChinaAid.org, January 24, 2012. http://www.chinaaid.org/2012/01/wife-son-of-well-known-political.html.

2. "Guo Quan," *The New School for Social Research,* May 4, 2010. http://www.newschool.edu/cps/subpage.aspx?id=52996.

3. "About Google," *Google.com,* May 7, 2013. http://www.google.com/about/.

4. "A History of Google in China," *Financial Times Online,* July 9, 2010. http://www.ft.com/cms/s/0/faf86fbc-0009-11df-8626-00144feabdc0.html#axzz2MmJQVW1J.

5. "The Birth of Google," *Wired.com,* August 2005. http://www.wired.com/wired/archive/13.08/battelle.html?tw=wn_tophead_4.

6. "PageRank: Bringing Order to the Web," *Stanford Digital Library Project,* September 16, 1997. http://web.archive.org/web/20020506051802/www-diglib.stanford.edu/cgi-bin/WP/get/SIDL-WP-1997-0072?1.

7. "BackRub," Google Web Archives, December 4, 1997. http://web.archive.org/web/19971210065425/backrub.stanford.edu/backrub.html.

8. "Google: Our History in Depth," *Google.com,* May 7, 2013. http://www.google.com/about/company/history.

9. "If the Check Says 'Google Inc.,' We're 'Google Inc.,'" *Wired.com,* September 7, 2007. http://www.wired.com/science/discoveries/news/2007/09/dayintech_0907.

10. "Google Receives $25 million in Equity Funding," Google Web Archives, June 7, 1997. http://web.archive.org/web/20000309205910/http://www.google.com/pressrel/pressrelease1.html.

11. "Google Goes Global with Addition of 10 Languages," *Google.com,* May 9, 2000. http://googlepress.blogspot.com/2000/05/google-goes-global-with-addition-of-10.html.

12. "Internet and Search Engine Usage by Country," *Internet World Stats.* http://ptgmedia.pearsoncmg.com/images/9780789747884/supplements/9780789747884_appC.pdf.

13. "Google: Our History in Depth," Google.com, May 7, 2013. http://www.google.com/about/company/history.

14. "Internet and Search Engine Usage by Country," *Internet World Stats.* http://ptgmedia.pearsoncmg.com/images/9780789747884/supplement/978078974884_appC.pdf. http://money.cnn.com/2012/02/13/technology/thebuzz/index.htm.

15. "China: Internet Usage Stats and Population Report," *Internet World Stats,* 2010. http://www.internetworldstats.com/asia/cn.htm.

16. "Is China's Google Better than Google?" *CNNMoney.com,* February 13, 2012. http://money.cnn.com/2012/02/13/technology/the buzz/index.htm.

17. "Google Losing Market Share in China," *Search Engine Journal,* September 21, 2006. http://www.searchenginejournal.com/google-losing-market-share-in-china/3816.

18. "Why Google is Quitting China," *Forbes.com,* January 15, 2010. http://www.forbes.com/2010/01/15/baidu-china-search-intelligent-technology-google.html.

19. "Google: Our History in Depth," *Google.com,* May 7, 2013. http://www.google.com/about/company/history.

20. "Google in China," *Google's Official Blog,* January 27, 2006. http://googleblog.blogspot.com/2006/01/google-in-china.html.

21. "Why Google Is Quitting China," *Forbes.com,* January 15, 2010. http://www.forbes.com/2010/01/15/baidu-china-search-intelligent-technology-google.html.

22. Ibid.

23. "Google Losing Market Share in China," *Search Engine Journal,* September 21, 2006. http://www.searchenginejournal.com/google-losing-market-share-in-china/3816/.

24. Ibid.

25. Ibid.

26. Ibid.

27. "Web History of China," *Timetoast.com,* 2010. http://www.timetoast.com/timelines/web-history-of-china.

28. "A History of Google in China," *Financial Times Online,* July 9, 2010. http://www.ft.com/cms/s/0/faf86fbc-0009-11df-8626-00144feabdc0.html#axzz2MmJQVW1J.

29. Ibid.

30. Ibid.

31. "Google Aims to Stay in China Despite Censorship Clash," *Financial Times,* January 22, 2010. http://www.ft.com/intl/ cms/s/2/f9ff5bcc-06ce-11df-b058-00144feabdc0. html#axzz2RynyO1Rd.

32. "Hillary Clinton Criticises Beijing over Internet Censorship," *The Guardian,* January 21, 2010. http://www.guardian.co.uk/ world/2010/jan/21/hillary-clinton-china-internet-censorship.

33. "A New Approach to China: an Update," *Google's Official Blog,* March 22, 2010. http://googleblog.blogspot.com/2010/03/new- approach-to-china-update.html.

34. "Google Loses Chinese Market Share," *Wall Street Journal,* April 27, 2010. http://online.wsj.com/article/SB10001424052748703465 20457520783328199 3688.html.

35. "Google Services Blocked in China," *The Guardian,* November 9, 2012. http://www.guardian.co.uk/technology/2012/nov/09/google- services-blocked-china-gmail.

36. "US Judge Writes Unhappy Ending for Google's Online Library Plans," *The Guardian,* March 22, 2011. http://www.guardian.co. uk/technology/2011/mar/23/google-online-library-plans-thwarted.

37. "Google Strikes Deal with Publishers over Universal Library," *CNNMoney.com,* October 4, 2012. http://money.cnn.com/2012/10/04/ technology/google-books-settlement/index.html.

38. "China Criticizes Android's Dominance," *Wall Street Journal,* March 13, 2013. http://online.wsj.com/article/SB10001424127887 32453940457834213 2324098420.html.

39. "China: Google's too controlling. We should create our own damn smartphone OS," *Venturebeat.com,* March 5, 2013. http://venturebeat.com/2013/03/05/china-google-android- drama/.

40. "Motorola Buyout Fails to Yield Patent Jackpot for Google," *Business Report,* April 30, 2013. http://www.iol.co.za/business/ international/motorola-buyout-fails-to-yield-patent-jackpot-for- google-1.1508190#.UYQPdrXqnoI.

41. "Facts about Google's Acquisition of Motorola," *Google Press,* 2013. http://www.google.com/press/motorola/.

42. "Google's Trust Problem," *The Washington Post,* March 21, 2013. http://www.washingtonpost.com/blogs/wonkblog/wp/2013/03/21/ googles-trust-problem/.

43. "Stern Words and Pea Size Punishment for Google," *The New York Times,* April 23, 2013. http://www.nytimes.com/2013/04/23/ business/global/stern-words-and-pea-size-punishment-for-google. html?pagewanted=all&_r=0.

44. "Google Launches Global Human Trafficking Helpline and Data Network," *Arstechnica,* April 10, 2013. http://arstechnica.com/ tech-policy/2013/04/google-launches-global-human-trafficking- helpline-and-data-network/.

45. "This Is Why Google Glass Is the Future," *Mashable,* April 30, 2013. http://mashable.com/2013/04/30/google-glass-future/.

46. "Google Future Tech: 10 Coolest Google R&D Projects," *CIO.com,* 2013. http://www.cio.com/article/694854/Google_Future_ Tech_10_Coolest_Google_R_D_Projects?page= 11#slideshow.

47. "Google's Future: Doing the Impossible," *BGR,* April, 19, 2013. http://bgr.com/2013/04/19/google-earnings-analysis-q1-2013-449971/.

48. "Google Execs say the power of information is underrated," npr.org, April 23, 2013. http://www.npr.org/blogs/alltechconsidered/ 2013/04/23/178620215/google-execs-say-the-power-of- information-is-underrated.

49. "Google's Eric Schmidt Makes a Rare Visit to Myanmar," CNNMoney, March 22, 2013. http://money.cnn.com/2013/03/22/ news/google-eric-schmidt-myanmar/index.html.

Brief Integrative Case 3.2

1. Daisuke Wakabayashi, "Sony, Stung by Losses, Delays Thin TV," *The Wall Street Journal,* August 18, 2009, http://online.wsj.com/ article/SB125053074821237541.html.

2. Ibid.

3. Ron Mertens. 2012. "Sony OLED Displays, OLED TVs." http:// www.oled-info.com/sony-oled.

4. Reiji Murai and Mari Saito. "Sony, Panasonic in Talks to Make OLED TVs: Sources." *Reuters,* May 15, 2012. http://www. reuters.com/article/2012/05/15/us-sony-panasonic-oled- idUSBRE84D1EV20120515.

5. Ron Mertens. 2012. "Sony OLED Displays, OLED TVs." http:// www.oled-info.com/sony-oled.

6. Daisuke Wakabayashi, "Sony, Stung by Losses, Delays Thin TV," *The Wall Street Journal,* August 18, 2009, http://online.wsj.com/ article/SB125053074821237541.html.

7. Michelle Kessler, "Will Thin Be In, or Will Sony Be Out?" *USA Today,* January 9, 2008, http://www.usatoday.com/tech/ products/2008-01-06-consumer-electronics-show_N.htm.

8. Wakabayashi, "Sony, Stung by Losses, Delays Thin TV."

9. Ibid.

10. Ibid.

11. "Sony Launches World's First OLED TV," press release, October 1, 2007, http://www.sony.net/SonyInfo/News/Press/200710/ 07-1001E/.

12. "Sony Debuts First OLED Television in the United States," corporate press release, Las Vegas, January 6, 2008, http:// news.sel.sony.com/en/press_room/consumer/television/release/ 32499.html.

13. Ibid.

14. Ibid.

15. "Sony Launches World's First OLED TV."

16. Wikipedia, "Organic LED," http://en.wikipedia.org/wiki/ Organic_LED.

17. Wakabayashi, "Sony, Stung by Losses, Delays Thin TV."

18. Ibid.

19. Kessler, "Will Thin Be In, or Will Sony Be Out?"

20. Reiji Murai and Mari Saito. "Sony, Panasonic in Talks to Make OLED TVs: Sources." *Reuters.* May 15, 2012. http://www. reuters.com/article/2012/05/15/us-sony-panasonic-oled- idUSBRE84D1EV20120515.

21. Ibid.

22. Kessler, "Will Thin Be In, or Will Sony Be Out?"

23. Ibid.

24. Ibid.

25. Ibid.

26. Ibid.

27. Sony 2009 Annual Report, http://www.sony.net/SonyInfo/IR/ financial/ar/2009/index.html.

28. Ibid.

29. Sony 2010 Annual Report, http://www.sony.net/SonyInfo/IR/ financial/ar/2010/index.html.

30. Sony 2009 Annual Report.

31. Sony 2010 Annual Report.

32. Sony 2009 Annual Report.

33. Sony 2010 Annual Report.

34. Saiji Ugajin, "Sony Tries, Once Again, to Cut Number of Suppliers," *Nikkei Business,* June 15, 2009, http://business.nikkeibp.co.jp/article/eng/20090615/197558/.

35. Sir Howard Stringer Profile, Senior Management, http://www.sony.com/SCA/bios/stringer_profile.shtml.

36. Bob Ferrari, "Sony's Supply Chain Challenges," May 22, 2009, http://www.theferrarigroup.com/blog1/2009/05/22/sonys-supply-chain-challenges/.

37. Sony 2009 Annual Report.

38. Martin Roll, "Brand Rejuvenation—A Case Study of Sony," *Venture Republic,* http://www.venturerepublic.com/resources/Brand_Rejuvenation_SONY_brand_brand_leadership.asp.

39. Richard Wray, "Sony Ericsson Issues Profit Warning as Mobile Phone Sales Slump," *Guardian,* March 20, 2009, http://www.guardian.co.uk/technology/2009/mar/20/sony-mobilephones.

40. Hiroko Tabuchi, "Recession and Strong Yen Drive Sony to Annual Loss," *New York Times,* May 14, 2009, http://www.nytimes.com/2009/05/15/business/global/15sony.html.

41. Sony 2010 Annual Report.

42. Tabuchi, "Recession and Strong Yen Drive Sony to Annual Loss."

43. Sony 2009 Annual Report.

44. Sony 2010 Annual Report.

45. Tabuchi, "Recession and Strong Yen Drive Sony to Annual Loss."

46. Ibid.

47. Ibid.

48. "Console Wars: May the Best Supply Chain Win," Tuck School of Business at Dartmouth–Glassmeyer/McNamee Center for Digital Strategies, 2006, http://mba.tuck.dartmouth.edu/digital/Research/AcademicPublications/GameConsoles.pdf.

49. Martin Roll, "The Troubles with the Sony Brand," November 1, 2006, http://www.asianbrandstrategy.com/2006/11/troubles-with-sony-brand.asp.

50. Roll, "Brand Rejuvenation."

51. Ibid.

52. Hiroko Tabuchi, "In Comeback for Japan, Sony Swings to a Profit," *New York Times,* July 30, 2010, p. B7.

53. Reuters, "Sony, Panasonic to cooperate on OLED televisions," June 25, 2012, http://www.reuters.com/article/2012/06/25/us-sony-panasonic-oled-idUSBRE85O05R20120625.

54. Ibid.

55. Mariko Yasu and Shunichi Ozasa, "Sony, Sharp Losing $11 Billion Leaves Investors Let Down," *Bloomberg,* April 10, 2012, http://www.bloomberg.com/news/2012-04-10/sony-widens-net-loss-estimate-to-520-billion-yen.html.

In-Depth Integrative Case 3.1

1. Anand Giridharadas, "Four Wheels for the Masses: The $2,500 Car," *New York Times,* January 8, 2008, http://www.nytimes.com/2008/01/08/business/worldbusiness/08indiacar.html?_r=1&ei=5065&en=35aebdd89f67e699&ex=1200459600&partner=MYWAY&pagewanted=print.

2. "Tata Unveils Nano, Its $2,500 Car," *MSN Money,* January 10, 2008, http://articles.moneycentral.msn.com/Investing/Extra/WorldsCheapestCarArrivesTomorrow.aspx.

3. Robyn Meredith, "The Next People Car," *Forbes,* April 17, 2009, http://finance.yahoo.com/family-home/article/102865/the-next-peoples-car.

4. World Bank, 2009. Motor vehicles (per 1,000 people). http://data.worldbank.org/indicator/IS.VEH.NVEH.P3.

5. Eric Bellman, "Tata's High-Stakes Bet on Low-Cost Car," *The Wall Street Journal,* January 10, 2008, http://online.wsj.com/article/SB119993102461279857.html?mg=com-wsj.

6. "Tata Motors Unveils the People's Car," Tata Motors corporate press release, January 10, 2008, http://www.tatamotors.com/our_world/press_releases.php?ID=340&action=Pull.

7. Scott Carney, "India's 50–MPG Tata Nano: Auto Solution or Pollution?" *Wired Magazine,* June 23, 2008, http://www.wired.com/cars/coolwheels/magazine/16-07/ff_tata.

8. Bellman, "Tata's High-Stakes Bet on Low-Cost Car."

9. Vipin V. Nair, "Tata Motors Gets 203,000 Orders for Nano, World's Cheapest Car," *Bloomberg,* May 4, 2009, http://www.bloomberg.com/apps/news?pid=20601091&sid=aVxvdjaxd0dw&refer=india.

10. "Tata Motors Unveils the People's Car."

11. "Tata Unveils Nano, Its $2,500 Car."

12. "Tata Motors Unveils the People's Car."

13. "Tata Unveils Nano, Its $2,500 Car."

14. "Tata Motors Unveils the People's Car."

15. Ibid.

16. Carney, "India's 50–MPG Tata Nano: Auto Solution or Pollution?"

17. Ibid.

18. Ibid.

19. Ibid.

20. Meredith, "The Next People Car."

21. Tata Motors: Profile, http://www.tatamotors.com/our_world/profile.php.

22. Ibid.

23. Ibid.

24. Ibid.

25. Ibid.

26. Ibid.

27. Ibid.

28. Ibid.

29. Tata Motors: Milestones, http://www.tatamotors.com/our_world/rearview.php?version=text.

30. John Hagel and John Seely Brown, "Learning from Tata's Nano," *BusinessWeek,* February 27, 2008, http://www.businessweek.com/innovate/content/feb2008/id20080227_377233.htm.

31. Jessie Scanlon, "What Can Tata's Nano Teach Detroit?" *BusinessWeek,* March 18, 2009, http://www.businessweek.com/innovate/content/mar2009/id20090318_012120.htm.

32. Bellman, "Tata's High-Stakes Bet on Low-Cost Car."

33. Anand Giridharadas, "Four Wheels for the Masses: The $2,500 Car," January 8, 2008, *New York Times,* http://www.nytimes.com/2008/01/08/business/worldbusiness/08indiacar.html?_r=1&ei=5065&en=35aebdd89f67e699&ex=1200459600&partner=MYWAY&pagewanted=print.

34. Hagel and Brown, "Learning from Tata's Nano."

35. Scanlon, "What Can Tata's Nano Teach Detroit?"

36. Hagel and Brown, "Learning from Tata's Nano."

37. Ibid.

38. Ibid.

39. Ibid.

40. "Villagers Raise Slogans against Car Company," *The Hindu,* May 26, 2006, http://www.hindu.com/2006/05/26/stories/2006052618090900.htm.

41. Nick Kurczewski, "Tata Motors Shuts Down Nano Factory," September 3, 2008, http://www.insideline.com/tata/nano/tata-motors-shuts-down-nano-factory.html.

42. Stephanie Grimmett, "Tata Motors Makes Its Move Out of Singur," September 5, 2008, http://seekingalpha.com/article/94106–tata-motors-makes-its-move-out-of-singur.

43. Ibid.

44. Rina Chandran and Sujoy Dhar, "Tata Motors Says Looking for Alternative Nano Site," *Reuters,* September 2, 2008, http://www.reuters.com/article/idUSDEL24564.

45. Kurczewski, "Tata Motors Shuts Down Nano Factory."

46. Malini Hariharan, "Singur Dispute Could Hurt India Projects," September 1, 2008, http://www.icis.com/Articles/2008/09/01/9153231/insight-singur-dispute-could-hurt-india-projects.html.

47. Ibid.

48. Ibid.

49. Chandran and Dhar, "Tata Motors Says Looking for Alternative Nano Site."

50. Nick Kurczewski, "Tough Times for the Tata Nano," *New York Times,* December 26, 2008, http://wheels.blogs.nytimes.com/2008/12/26/tough-times-for-the-tata-nano/.

51. A memorandum of understanding (MOU or MoU) is a document describing a bilateral or multilateral agreement between parties. It expresses a convergence of will between the parties, indicating an intended common line of action. It is often used in cases where parties either do not imply a legal commitment or in situations where the parties cannot create a legally enforceable agreement. (Source: http://en.wikipedia.org/wiki/Memorandum_of_understanding.)

52. *Bandh,* originally a Hindi word meaning "closed," is a form of protest used by political activists in some countries in South Asia like India and Nepal. During a Bandh, a major political party or a large chunk of a community declares a general strike, usually lasting one day. Often Bandh means that the community or political party declaring a Bandh expects the general public to stay in their homes and strike work. (Source: http://en.wikipedia.org/wiki/Bandh.)

53. "Buddha's Loss Is Modi's Gain as Nano Goes to Gujarat," *NDTV,* October 7, 2008, http://www.ndtv.com/convergence/ndtv/story.aspx?id=NEWEN20080067901.

54. "Nano Car Project: Third Petition Filed in Gujarat High Court," December 18, 2008, http://economictimes.indiatimes.com/News/News_By_Industry/Auto/Automobiles/Nano_Car_Project_Third_petition_filed_in_Gujarat_High_Court/articleshow/3857739.cms.

55. Kurczewski, "Tough Times for the Tata Nano."

56. Nair, "Tata Motors Gets 203,000 Orders for Nano, World's Cheapest Car."

57. Ibid.

58. Ibid.

59. Ibid.

60. Ibid.

61. "Tata's Nano: Stuck in low gear." *The Economist,* August 20, 2011. http://www.economist.com/node/21526374.

62. Bellman, "Tata's High-Stakes Bet on Low-Cost Car."

63. Ibid.

64. Carney, "India's 50–MPG Tata Nano: Auto Solution or Pollution?"

65. Ibid.

66. Bellman, "Tata's High-Stakes Bet on Low-Cost Car."

67. Ibid.

68. Anil K. Gupta and Haiyan Wang, "Tata Nano: Not Just a Car but Also a Platform," *BusinessWeek,* January 29, 2010, http://www.businessweek.com/globalbiz/content/jan2010/gb20100129_489420.htm.

69. Ibid.

70. Ibid.

71. Giridharadas, "Four Wheels for the Masses: The $2,500 Car."

72. Matthew DeBord, "Is the Tata Nano America's Good Enough Car?" *The Big Money,* January 21, 2010, http://www.thebigmoney.com/blogs/shifting-gears/2010/01/21/tata-nano-america-s-good-enough-car.

73. Ibid.

74. Adam Werbach, "Fizzling Sales in India for the Tata Nano," *The Atlantic,* December 3, 2010, www.theatlantic.com.

75. "Tata's Nano: Stuck in Low Gear." *The Economist,* August 20, 2011. http://www.economist.com/node/21526374.

76. Tim Pollard, "Tata Ramps Up Production of Nano to Boost Slow Sales," *Automotive and Motoring News,* www.carmagazine.co.uk.

77. Sumant Banerji, "Tata Nano Turns Three; Life Has Just Begun for the World's Cheapest Car." July 16, 2012. http://www.hindustantimes.com/News-Feed/Auto/Tata-Nano-turns-three-life-has-just-begun-for-the-world-s-cheapest-car/Article1-890119.aspx.

78. Tata Motors, Consolidated Financial Results for the Quarter and Year ended March 31, 2012, May 29, 2012, http://tatamotors.com/media/press-releases.php?id=758.

In-Depth Integrative Case 3.2

1. Wayne Arnold, "A Continent Divided by Water, Now United by Air," *New York Times,* January 1, 2004, p. W1.

2. Ibid.

3. Scott Neuman, "Low-Fare Airlines Take Off in Asia," *The Wall Street Journal,* February 25, 2004, p. B6G.

4. A. Goldstein and C. Findlay, "Liberalisation and Foreign Direct Investment in Asian Transport Systems: The Case of Aviation," Asian Development Bank and OECD Development Centre, no. 26–27, November 2003, p. 11.

5. Centre for Asia Pacific Aviation, "Outlook 2007: Full Frontal Attack on Flag Carriers Begins," March 6, 2007, www.centreforaviation.com, accessed July 9, 2007.

6. Japan Travel Bureau, "Travel Trends and Prospects for 2003," *JTB Newsletter,* January 5, 2003.

7. JAL has since become one of Japan's most visible corporate failures, filing for bankruptcy protection in January 2010 and embarking on a major restructuring initiative.

8. Centre for Asia Pacific Aviation, "Low Cost Airlines in the Asia Pacific Region: An Exceptional Intra-Regional Traffic Growth Opportunity," September 2002, www.centreforaviation.com.

9. Ibid.

10. Goldman Sachs, "Asia Airlines," *Asia Research,* October 17, 1997, p. 9.

11. "Malaysian Airline Tests Asia's Resistance to No-Frills Flights," *Associated Press,* December 2002.

12. Centre for Asia Pacific Aviation, "Low Cost Airlines in the Asia Pacific Region: An Exceptional Intra-Regional Traffic Growth Opportunity."

13. "Malaysian Airline Tests Asia's Resistance to No-Frills Flights."

14. Interview with Conor McCarthy, April 25, 2003.

15. Comment of William Ng provided on www.airlinequality.com after traveling on AirAsia in March 2003 from Kuala Lumpur to Penang.

16. Data sourced from the Association of Asia Pacific Airlines, the Air Transport Association, and the Association of European Airlines.

17. G. Thomas, "In Tune with Low Fares in Malaysia," *Air Transport World,* May 2003, pp. 45–46.

18. Nicholas Ionides, "Man of the Moment," *Airline Business,* April 2004, p. 29.

19. Arnold, "A Continent Divided by Water."

20. Thomas, "In Tune with Low Fares in Malaysia."

21. Ionides, "Man of the Moment."

22. Interview with Conor McCarthy, May 8, 2003.

23. CRS and BSP refer to electronic information and commercial interfaces, typically between airlines and travel agents. A CRS is a system that stores and retrieves air transport data for airlines and enables a transactional interface with travel agents and online consolidators. Similarly, according to the International Air Transport Association (IATA), a BSP is the central point through which data and funds flow between travel agents and airlines. Instead of every agent having an individual relationship with each airline, all of the information is consolidated through the BSP. Agents make one single payment to the BSP (remittance), covering sales on all BSP airlines. The BSP makes one consolidated payment to each airline, covering sales made by all agents in the country/region.

24. Noted in discussion with Conor McCarthy, May 12, 2008.

25. McCarthy interview.

26. Centre for Asia Pacific Aviation, "To Malaysia with Love; AirAsia Goes Patriotic," May 31, 2007, www.centreforaviation.com.

27. Centre for Asia Pacific Aviation, "Low Cost Airlines in the Asia Pacific Region."

28. Thomas, "In Tune with Low Fares in Malaysia."

29. Goldman Sachs, "Asia Airlines."

30. Centre for Asia Pacific Aviation, "Who's Who in Low Cost Aviation: Air Asia," 2007.

31. Ibid.

32. Nicholas Ionides, "Third Japanese New-Start Fair Inc. Launches Services," *Air Transport Intelligence,* August, 2000.

33. Wayne Arnold, "Qantas Airways Discloses Plan for Low-Cost Singapore Carrier," *New York Times,* April 7, 2004, p. W1.

34. Arnold, "A Continent Divided by Water."

35. AirAsia, 2012. "About AirAsia." http://www.airasia.com/my/en/corporate/iraboutairasia.page.

36. Bong D. Fabe. "AirAsia Tops Other LCCs in Performance." July 8, 2012. http://businessmirror.com.ph/home/top-news/29590-airasia-tops-other-lccs-in-performance.

37. Centre for Asia Pacific Aviation, "To Malaysia with Love."

38. Cuckoo Paul, "AirAsia Aims for a Full Flight in India," *Business.in.com,* February 8, 2010.

39. Brandan Sobie, "AirAsia X Lands in US for First Times," *Air Transport Intelligence,* September 18, 2009.

40. Ghim-Lay Yeo, "AirAsia Outlines Priorities for Future Expansion," *Air Transport Intelligence,* January 26, 2010.

41. Centre for Asia Pacific Aviation, "AirAsia & Leisure Cargo Partnership to Generate RM12 million in Revenue per Annum," June 7, 2007, www.centreforaviation.com.

42. "AirAsia IPO Takes Off," *The Standard,* November 23, 2004.

43. AirAsia, "Corporate Profile," www.airasia.com, accessed July 2, 2007.

44. Centre for Aviation, "Bullish AirAsia Reports 2011 Profit and Accelerates Expansion," February 23, 2012. http://centreforaviation.com/analysis/financials/bullish-airasia-reports-2011-profit-and-accelerates-expansion-68729.

45. Centre for Asia Pacific Aviation, "Outlook for 2007: Prepare for Shakeout," November 10, 2006.

46. "Government Readies Airports for ASEAN Open Sky," *The Jakarta Post,* January 16, 2010.

47. Centre for Asia Pacific Aviation, "Asian Governments to Open Skies in 2007," March 8, 2007.

48. "Having Fun and Flying High," *Economist.*

49. Neuman, "Low-Fare Airlines Take Off in Asia."

50. Ibid.

51. Centre for Asia Pacific Aviation, "Outlook for 2007: Prepare for Shakeout."

52. Siva Govindasamy, "AirAsia and Jetstar Ink Wide-Ranging Cooperation Agreement," *Air Transport Intelligence,* January 6, 2010.

53. Centre for Aviation, "Bullish AirAsia Reports 2011 Profit and Accelerates Expansion," February 23, 2012. http://centreforaviation.com/analysis/financials/bullish-airasia-reports-2011-profit-and-accelerates-expansion-68729.

■ Chapter 12

1. Patricia Odell, "Motivating Employees on a Global Scale: Author Bob Nelson," PROMO Magazine, November 9, 2005, http://promomagazine.com/incentives/motivating_empployees_110905.

2. Matthew Boyle, "Motivating without Money," *BusinessWeek,* April 24, 2009, http://www.businessweek.com/managing/content/apr2009/ca20090424_985238.htm.

3. Patricia Odell, "Motivating Employees on a Global Scale: Author Bob Nelson," *PROMO Magazine,* November 9, 2005, http://promomagazine.com/incentives/motivating_empployees_110905.

4. Ibid.

5. "Motivating Employees," How-To Guide: Managing Your People, *The Wall Street Journal Online,* http://guides.wsj.com/management/managing-your-people/how-to-motivate-employees/.

6. Patricia Odell, "Motivating Employees on a Global Scale: Author Bob Nelson," *PROMO Magazine,* November 9, 2005, http://promomagazine.com/incentives/motivating_empployees_110905.

7. Matthew Boyle, "Motivating without Money," *BusinessWeek,* April 24, 2009, http://www.businessweek.com/managing/content/apr2009/ca20090424_985238.htm.

8. Jim Leininger, "Finding the Key to Commitment in China," Watson Wyatt Beijing, *Towers Watson,* http://www.watsonwyatt.com/asia-pacific/localsites/hongkong/research/Aug04_a3.asp.

9. Ibid.

10. Cynthia D. Fisher and Anne Xue Ya Yuan, "What Motivates Employees? A Comparison of U.S. and Chinese Employees," *The International Journal of Human Resource Management* 9, no. 3 (June 1998), https://classshares.student.usp.ac.fj/TS302/Assignment%20resources/What%20motivates%20employees.pdf.

11. Sondra Thiederman, "Motivating Employees from Other Cultures," *Monster.com,* http://career-advice.monster.com/in-the-office/workplace-issues/Motivating-Employees-from-Other-Cultures/article.aspx.

12. Ibid.

13. David Beswick, "Management Implications of the Interaction between Intrinsic Motivation and Extrinsic Rewards," Seminar notes, February 16, 2007.

14. Abbass F. Alkhafaji, *Competitive Global Management* (Delray Beach, FL: St. Lucie Press, 1995), p. 118.

15. Dianne H. B. Welsh, Fred Luthans, and Steven Sommer, "Managing Russian Factory Workers: The Impact of U.S.-Based Behavioral and Participative Techniques," *Academy of Management Journal,* February 1993, p. 75.

16. Andrew Sergeant and Stephen Frenkel, "Managing People in China: Perceptions of Expatriate Managers," *Journal of World Business* 33, no. 1 (1998), p. 21.

17. "Economic Tonic: Japan's Economy," *Economist,* May 22, 2004, p. 87.

18. Michael H. Lubatkin, Momar Ndiaye, and Richard Vengroff, "The Nature of Managerial Work in Developing Countries: A Limited Test of the Universalist Hypothesis," *Journal of International Business Studies* 28 (1997), pp. 711–733.

19. For a more detailed discussion, see Fred Luthans, *Organizational Behavior,* 12th ed. (New York: Irwin/McGraw-Hill, 2010), chapter 6.

20. A. H. Maslow, "A Theory of Human Motivation," *Psychological Review,* July 1943, pp. 390–396.

21. For more information on this topic, see Richard Mead, *International Management: Cross-Cultural Dimensions* (Cambridge, MA: Blackwell, 1994), pp. 209–212.

22. See Richard M. Hodgetts, *Modern Human Relations at Work,* 8th ed. (Hinsdale, IL: Dryden Press, 2002), chapter 2.

23. Mason Haire, Edwin E. Ghiselli, and Lyman W. Porter, *Managerial Thinking: An International Study* (New York: Wiley, 1966).

24. Ibid., p. 75.

25. Edwin C. Nevis, "Cultural Assumption and Productivity: The United States and China," *Sloan Management Review,* Spring 1983, pp. 17–29.

26. Geert H. Hofstede, "The Colors of Collars," *Columbia Journal of World Business,* September 1972, pp. 72–78.

27. Ibid., p. 72.

28. George H. Hines, "Cross-Cultural Differences in Two-Factor Motivation Theory," *Journal of Applied Psychology,* December 1973, p. 376.

29. Donald D. White and Julio Leon, "The Two-Factor Theory: New Questions, New Answers," *National Academy of Management Proceedings,* 1976, p. 358.

30. D. Macarov, "Work Patterns and Satisfactions in an Israeli Kibbutz: A Test of the Herzberg Hypothesis," *Personnel Psychology,* Autumn 1972, p. 492.

31. Peter D. Machungwa and Neal Schmitt, "Work Motivation in a Developing Country," *Journal of Applied Psychology,* February 1983, pp. 31–42.

32. Farhad Analoui, "What Motivates Senior Managers? The Case of Romania," *Journal of Managerial Psychology* 15, no. 4 (2000).

33. G. E. Popp, H. J. Davis, and T. T. Herbert, "An International Study of Intrinsic Motivation Composition," *Management International Review* 26, no. 3 (1986), pp. 28–35.

34. Also see Rabi S. Bhagat et al., "Cross-Cultural Issues in Organizational Psychology: Emergent Trends and Directions for Research in the 1990s," in *International Review of Industrial and Organizational Psychology,* ed. C. L. Cooper and I. Robertson (New York: Wiley, 1990), p. 76.

35. Rabindra N. Kanungo and Richard W. Wright, "A Cross-Cultural Comparative Study of Managerial Job Attitudes," *Journal of International Business Studies,* Fall 1983, pp. 115–129.

36. Ibid., pp. 127–128.

37. Fred Luthans, "A Paradigm Shift in Eastern Europe: Some Helpful Management Development Techniques," *Journal of Management Development* 12, no. 8 (1993), pp. 53–60.

38. For more information on the characteristics of high achievers, see David C. McClelland, "Business Drive and National Achievement," *Harvard Business Review,* July–August 1962, pp. 99–112.

39. For more detail on the achievement motive, see Luthans, *Organizational Behavior,* pp. 253–256.

40. S. Iwawaki and R. Lynn, "Measuring Achievement Motivation in Japan and Great Britain," *Journal of Cross-Cultural Psychology* 3 (1999), pp. 219–220.

41. For more on this, see J. C. Abegglen and G. Stalk, *Kaisha: The Japanese Corporation* (New York: Basic Books, 1985); R. M. Steers, Y. K. Shin, and G. R. Ungson, *The Chaebol: Korea's New Industrial Might* (New York: McGraw-Hill, 1989).

42. Fred Luthans, Brooke R. Envick, and Mary F. Sully, "Characteristics of Successful Entrepreneurs: Do They Fit the Cultures of Developing Countries?" *Proceedings of the Pan Pacific Conference,* 1995, pp. 25–27.

43. These data were reported in David C. McClelland, *The Achieving Society* (Princeton, NJ: Van Nostrand, 1961), p. 294.

44. E. J. Murray, *Motivation and Emotion* (Englewood Cliffs, NJ: Prentice Hall, 1964), p. 101.

45. David J. Krus and Jane A. Rysberg, "Industrial Managers and nAch: Comparable and Compatible?" *Journal of Cross-Cultural Psychology,* December 1976, pp. 491–496.

46. David C. McClelland, "Achievement Motivation Can Be Developed," *Harvard Business Review,* November–December 1965, p. 20.

47. Geert Hofstede, "Motivation, Leadership, and Organization: Do American Theories Apply Abroad?" *Organizational Dynamics,* Summer 1980, pp. 55–56.

48. For more on this, see Richard M. Steers and Carlos J. Sanchez-Runde, "Culture, Motivation, and Work Behavior," in *Handbook of Cross-Cultural Management,* ed. Martin J. Gannon and Karen L. Newman (London: Basil Blackwell, 2002).

49. E. Yuchtman, "Reward Distribution and Work-Role Attractiveness in the Kibbutz: Reflections on Equity Theory," *American Sociological Review* 37 (1972), pp. 581–595.

50. Paul A. Fadil, Robert J. Williams, Wanthanee Limpaphayom, and Cindi Smatt, "Equity or Equality? A Conceptual Examination of the Influence of Individualism/Collectivism on the Cross-Cultural Application of the Equity Theory," *Cross Cultural Management* 12, no. 4 (2005), pp. 17–35.

51. R. M. Steers, S. J. Bischoff, and L. H. Higgins, "Cross-Cultural Management Research: The Fish and the Fisherman," *Journal of Management Inquiry* 1 (1992), pp. 321–330; Ken I. Kim, Hun-Joon Park, and Nori Suzuki, "Reward Allocations in the U.S., Japan, and Korea: A Comparison of Individualistic and Collectivistic Cultures," *Academy of Management Journal,* March 1990, pp. 188–198.

52. Luthans, *Organizational Behavior,* p. 520.

53. Edwin A. Locke and Gary P. Latham, *A Theory of Goal-Setting and Task Performance* (Englewood Cliffs, NJ: Prentice Hall, 1990).

54. M. Erez, "The Congruence of Goal-Setting Strategies with Socio-Cultural Values and Its Effect on Performance," *Journal of Management* 12 (1986), pp. 585–592.

55. J. P. French, J. Israel, and D. As, "An Experiment in a Norwegian Factory: Interpersonal Dimension in Decision-Making," *Human Relations* 13 (1960), pp. 3–19.

56. P. C. Earley, "Supervisors and Shop Stewards as Sources of Contextual Information in Goal-Setting," *Journal of Applied Psychology* 71 (1986), pp. 111–118.

57. M. Erez and P. C. Earley, "Comparative Analysis of Goal-Setting Strategies across Cultures," *Journal of Applied Psychology* 72, no. 4 (1987), pp. 658–665.

58. Victor Vroom, *Work and Motivation* (New York: Wiley, 1964).

59. Lyman W. Porter and Edward E. Lawler III, *Managerial Attitudes and Performance* (Homewood, IL: Irwin, 1968).

60. Dov Eden, "Intrinsic and Extrinsic Rewards and Motives: Replication and Extension with Kibbutz Workers," *Journal of Applied Social Psychology* 5 (1975), pp. 348–361.

61. T. Matsui, T. Kakuyama, and M. L. Onglatco, "Effects of Goals and Feedback on Performance in Groups," *Journal of Applied Psychology* 72 (1987), pp. 407–415.

62. For a systematic analysis of this and other myths of Japanese management, see Richard M. Hodgetts and Fred Luthans, "Japanese HR Management Practices," *Personnel,* April 1989, pp. 42–45.

63. David Nicklaus, "Labor's Pains," *St. Louis Post-Dispatch,* September 2, 2002, p. A1.

64. For more on this topic, see Noel M. Tichy and Thore Sandstrom, "Organizational Innovations in Sweden," *Columbia Journal of World Business,* Summer 1974, pp. 18–28.

65. "Automotive Brief—Volvo AB: Profit Rose 80% in 4th Period, Bolstered by Truck Division," *The Wall Street Journal,* February 4, 2004, p. A1; "Cars Brief: Volvo," *The Wall Street Journal,* March 16, 2004, p. A1.

66. Edward McDonough, "Market-Oriented Product Innovation," *R&D Management,* June 2004, p. 335.

67. Eric Sundstrom, Kenneth P. DeMeuse, and David Futrell, "Work Teams: Application and Effectiveness," *American Psychologist,* February 1990, pp. 120–133.

68. See Lillian H. Chaney and Jeanette S. Martin, *Intercultural Business Communication* (Englewood Cliffs, NJ: Prentice Hall, 1995), pp. 46–47.

69. Bhagat et al., "Cross-Cultural Issues," p. 72.

70. Jonathan Watts, "Japan's Old Shy Away from Retiring," *The Guardian,* August 5, 2002, p. 12; "U.S. Workers Most Productive; but Study Says Europeans Have More Output per Hour," *Houston Chronicle,* September 1, 2003, p. 27.

71. Raphael Snir, Itzhak Harpaz, and Dorit Ben-Baruch, "Centrality of and Investment in Work and Family among Israeli High-Tech Workers: A Bicultural Perspective," *Cross-Cultural Research* 43, no. 4 (2009), p. 366–385.

72. Howard W. French, "A Postmodern Plague Ravages Japan's Workers," *New York Times,* February 21, 2000, p. A4; "Japanese Workers See Abuses by Bosses," *Los Angeles Times,"* June 30, 2003, p. C5.

73. Michelle Conlin, "Go-Go-Going to Pieces in China," *BusinessWeek,* April 23, 2007, p. 88.

74. "Satisfaction in the USA, Unhappiness in Japanese Offices," *Personnel,* January 1992, p. 8.

75. Fred Luthans, Harriette S. McCaul, and Nancy G. Dodd, "Organizational Commitment: A Comparison of American, Japanese, and Korean Employees," *Academy of Management Journal,* March 1985, pp. 213–219.

76. For other research on this topic, see Shahid N. Bhuian, Eid S. Al-Shammari, and Omar A. Jefri, "Work-Related Attitudes and Job Characteristics of Expatriates in Saudi Arabia," *Thunderbird International Business Review,* January–February 2001, pp. 21–31.

77. David I. Levine, "What Do Wages Buy?" *Administrative Science Quarterly,* September 1993, pp. 462–483.

78. David Heming, "What Wages Buy in the U.S. and Japan," *Academy of Management Executive,* November 1994, pp. 88–89.

79. Andrew Kakabadse and Andrew Myers, "Qualities of Top Management: Comparisons of European Manufacturers," *Journal of Management Development* 14, no. 1 (1995), p. 6.

80. Steven M. Sommer, Seung-Hyun Bae, and Fred Luthans, "Organizational Commitment across Cultures: The Impact of Antecedents on Korean Employees," *Human Relations* 49, no. 7 (1996), pp. 977–993.

81. Anders Tornvall, "Work-Values in Japan: Work and Work Motivation in a Comparative Setting," in *Managing Across Cultures: Issues and Perspectives,* ed. Pat Joynt and Malcolm Warner (London: International Thomson Business Press, 1996), p. 256.

82. Stephen Kerr, "Practical, Cost-Neutral Alternatives That You May Know, but Don't Practice," *Organizational Dynamics,* Summer 1999, pp. 61–70.

83. "U.S. Workers Most Productive."

84. Matthew O. Hughes and Andrew Pirnie, "Retirement Reform Worldwide," *LIMRA's MarketFacts Quarterly* 22, no. 2 (Spring 2003), p. 12.

85. In the case of money, for example, see Swee Hoon Ang, "The Power of Money: A Cross-Cultural Analysis of Business-Related Beliefs," *Journal of World Business* 35, no. 1 (2000), pp. 43–60.

86. J. Milliman, S. Nason, M. A. von Glinow, P. Hou, K. B. Lowe, and N. Kim, "In Search of 'Best' Strategies Pay Practices: An Exploratory Study of Japan, Korea, Taiwan, and the United States," in *Advances in International Comparative Management,* ed. S. B. Prasad (Greenwich, CT: JAI Press, 1995), pp. 227–252.

87. Louis Lavelle, "Executive Pay," *BusinessWeek,* April 19, 2004, pp. 106–110.

88. S. C. Schneider, S. A. Wittenberg-Cox, and L. Hansen, *Honeywell Europe* (Insead, 1991).

89. C. M. Vance, S. R. McClaine, D. M. Boje, and H. D. Stage, "An Examination of the Transferability of Traditional Performance Appraisal Principles across Cultural Boundaries," *Management International Review* 32, no. 4 (1992), pp. 313–326.

90. David Sirota and J. Michael Greenwood, "Understand Your Overseas Workforce," *Harvard Business Review,* January–February 1971, pp. 53–60.

91. D. E. Sanger, "Performance Related Pay in Japan," *International Herald Tribune,* October 5, 1993, p. 20.

92. S. H. Nam, "Culture, Control, and Commitment in International Joint Ventures," *International Journal of Human Resource Management* 6 (1995), pp. 553–567.

93. Dianne H. B. Welsh, Fred Luthans, and Steven Sommer, "Managing Russian Factory Workers: The Impact of U.S.-Based Behavioral and Participative Techniques," *Academy of Management Journal,* February 1993, pp. 58–79.

94. Anita Raghavan and G. Thomas Sims, "'Golden Parachutes' Emerge in European Deals," *The Wall Street Journal,* February 14, 2000, pp. A17, A18.

95. Susan C. Schneider and Jean-Louis Barsoux, *Managing Across Cultures,* 2nd ed. (London: Prentice Hall, 2003).

■ Chapter 13

1. Joe Light, "Leadership Training Gains Urgency Amid Stronger Economy," *The Wall Street Journal,* August 2, 2010, http://online.wsj.com/article/SB1000142405274870331490457539926097
6490670.html?KEYWORDS=leadership.

2. Ibid.

3. "Employees," *Roche,* http://www.roche.com/corporate_responsibility/employees.htm.

4. "Local Leadership Development," *Roche,* http://careers.roche.com/us/en-us/Our-Locations/Indianapolis-(Indiana)/Local-programs/Local-Leadership-Development-Programs.html.

5. "People & Leadership Development Program—Shanghai Roche Pharma," *Roche,* http://careers.roche.com/cn/en/index.php?ci=3413&language=2.

6. "Development," *Roche,* http://www.roche.com/corporate_responsibility/employees/faq_employees-development.htm.

7. "Perspectives—Global Accelerated Talent Development Program at Roche," *LinkedIn,* http://www.linkedin.com/jobs?viewJob=&jobId=877188.

8. Ibid.

9. Ibid.

10. "Case Study," *Roche,* http://www.roche.com/responsibility/employees/case_studies.htm.

11. Ibid.

12. Ibid.

13. Ibid.

14. Richard M. Hodgetts, *Modern Human Relations at Work,* 8th ed. (Ft. Worth, TX: Harcourt, 2002), p. 255. Also see Daniel Goleman, "What Makes a Leader?" *Harvard Business Review,* November–December 1998, pp. 93–102.

15. Abraham Zaleznik, "Managers & Leaders: Are They Different?" *Harvard Business Review,* March–April 1992, pp. 126–135; James E. Colvard, "Managers vs. Leaders," *Government Executive* 35, no. 9 (July 2003), p. 82.

16. Caroline Hulme, "The Right Place and the Right Style," *The British Journal of Administrative Management* 55 (October–November 2006), pp. i–iii.

17. Zaleznik, "Managers & Leaders: Are They Different?"

18. Mike Diamond, "Are You a Manager or a Leader?" *Reeves Journal* 87, no. 2 (2007), p. 66.

19. Thomas W. Kent, "Leading and Managing: It Takes Two to Tango," *Management Decision* 43, no. 7–8 (2005), pp. 1010–1017.

20. L. Gary Boomer, "Leadership and Management: Your Firm Needs Both," *Accounting Today* 21, no. 2 (2007), pp. 22–23.

21. Zaleznik, "Managers & Leaders: Are They Different?"

22. Matthew Fairholm, "I Know It When I See It: How Local Government Managers See Leadership Differently," *Public Management* 88, no. 9, pp. 10–14.

23. Douglas McGregor, *The Human Side of Enterprise* (New York: McGraw-Hill, 1960), pp. 33–34.

24. Ibid., pp. 47–48.

25. See Nancy J. Adler, *International Dimensions of Organizational Behavior,* 2nd ed. (Boston: PWS-Kent, 1991), p. 150.

26. Sheila M. Puffer, Daniel J. McCarthy, and Alexander I. Naumov, "Russian Managers' Beliefs About Work: Beyond the Stereotypes," *Journal of World Business* 32, no. 3 (1997), pp. 258–276.

27. For other insights into this area, see Manfred F. R. Kets de Vries, "A Journey into the 'Wild West': Leadership Style and Organizational Practices in Russia," *Organizational Dynamics,* Spring 2000, pp. 67–80.

28. William Ouchi, *Theory Z: How American Management Can Meet the Japanese Challenge* (New York: Addison-Wesley, 1981).

29. Ingrid Aioanei, "Leadership in Romania," *Journal of Organizational Change Management* 19, no. 6 (2006), pp. 705–712.

30. Jun Yan and James G. Hunt, "A Cross Cultural Perspective on Perceived Leadership Effectiveness," *International Journal of Cross Cultural Management* 5, no. 1 (2005), pp. 49–67.

31. For more, see review in Sergio Matviuk, "A Study of Leadership Prototypes in Colombia," *The Business Review* 7, no. 1 (Summer 2007), pp. 14–19.

32. Z. Aycan, R. N. Kanungo, M. Mendonca, K. Yu, J. Deller, G. Stahl et al., "Impact of Culture on Human Resource Management Practices: A 10-Country Comparison," *Applied Psychology: An International Review* 49 (2000), pp. 192–221.

33. For a review, see Ekin K. Pellegrini and Terri A. Scandura, "Paternalistic Leadership: A Review and Agenda for Future Research," *Journal of Management* 34, no. 3, pp. 566–593.

34. S. Martinez and P. Dorfman, "The Mexican Entrepreneur," *International Studies of Management and Organization* 28, no. 2 (1998), pp. 97–123.

35. M. A. Ansari, Z. A. Ahmad, and R. Aafaqi, "Organizational Leadership in the Malaysian Context," in D. Tjosvold and K. Leung (eds.), *Leading in High Growth Asia: Managing Relationships for Teamwork and Change* (Singapore: World Scientific, 2004), pp. 109–138.

36. For more, see C. M. Axtell, D. J. Holman, K. L. Unsworth, T. D. Wall, P. E. Waterson, and E. Harrington, "Shopfloor Innovation: Facilitating the Suggestion and Implementation of Ideas," *Journal of Occupational and Organizational Psychology* 73, (2000), pp. 265–285; R. K. Yukl, *Leadership in Organizations* (Englewood Cliffs: Prentice-Hall, 2002).

37. Xu Huang, Joyce Iun, Aili Liu, and Yaping Gong, "Does Participative Leadership Enhance Work Performance by Inducing Empowerment or Trust? The Differential Effects on Managerial and Non-managerial Subordinates," *Journal of Organizational Behavior* 31, no. 1 (2010), pp. 122–143.

38. Iyuji Misumi and Fumiyasu Seki, "Effects of Achievement Motivation on the Effectiveness of Leadership Patterns," *Administrative Science Quarterly,* March 1971, pp. 51–59.

39. Sang M. Lee, Sangjin Yoo, and Tosca M. Lee, "Korean Chaebols: Corporate Values and Strategies," *Organizational Dynamics,* Spring 1991, p. 41.

40. Michael Woywode, "Global Management Concepts and Local Adaptations: Working Groups in the French and German Car Manufacturing Industry," *Organization Studies* 23, no. 4 (2002), p. 497.

41. Chris Reiter and Neal Boudette, "VW Delays Launch of Microbus to Reduce Its Production Cost," *The Wall Street Journal,* May 20, 2004, p. D3.

42. Mason Haire, Edwin E. Ghiselli, and Lyman W. Porter, *Managerial Thinking: An International Study* (New York: Wiley, 1966).

43. Ibid., p. 21.

44. James R. Lincoln, Mitsuyo Hanada, and Jon Olson, "Cultural Orientation and Individual Reactions to Organizations: A Study of Employees of Japanese-Owned Firms," *Administrative Science Quarterly,* March 1981, pp. 93–115. Also see Karen Lowry Miller, "Land of the Rising Jobless," *BusinessWeek,* January 11, 1993, p. 47.

45. Sangjin Yoo and Sang M. Lee, "Management Style and Practice of Korean Chaebols," *California Management Review,* Summer 1987, pp. 95–110.

46. Haire, Ghiselli, and Porter, *Managerial Thinking,* p. 29.

47. Noboru Yoshimura and Philip Anderson, *Inside the Kaisha: Demystifying Japanese Business Behavior* (Boston: Harvard Business School Press, 1997), p. 167.

48. Jonathan Soble, "Toyota Promotes Non-Japanese Managers in Wake of Problems," *Financial Times,* June 25, 2010, p. 13.

49. Haire, Ghiselli, and Porter, *Managerial Thinking,* p. 140.

50. Ibid., p. 157.

51. For more on this topic, see Edgar H. Schein, "SMR Forum: Does Japanese Management Style Have a Message for American Managers?" *Sloan Management Review,* Fall 1981, pp. 55–68.

52. Jeremiah J. Sullivan and Ikujiro Nonaka, "The Application of Organizational Learning Theory to Japanese and American Management," *Journal of International Business Studies,* Fall 1986, pp. 127–147.

53. Ibid., pp. 130–131.

54. David A. Ralston, Carolyn P. Egri, Sally Stewart, Robert H. Terpstra, and Yu Kaicheng, "Doing Business in the 21st Century with the New Generation of Chinese Managers: A Study of Generational Shifts in Work Values in China," *Journal of International Business Studies,* Second Quarter 1999, pp. 415–428.

55. John Politis, "The Role of Various Leadership Styles," *Leadership and Organization Development Journal* 24, no. 4 (2003), pp. 181–195.

56. Darwish A. Yousef, "Predictors of Decision-Making Styles in Non-Western Countries," *Leadership and Organizational Development Journal* 19, no. 7 (1998), pp. 366–373.

57. Ibid.

58. Ibid.

59. James Thomas Kunnanatt, "Leadership Orientation of Service Sector Managers in India: An Empirical Study," *Business and Society Review* 122, no. 1 (2007), pp. 99–119.

60. Haire, Ghiselli, and Porter, *Managerial Thinking,* p. 22.

61. Peter Cappelli, Harbir Singh, Jitendra Singh, and Michael Useem, *The India Way: How India's Top Business Leaders Are Revolutionizing Management* (Cambridge, MA: Harvard Business School Publishing, 2010).

62. Eric J. Romero, "Latin American Leadership: El Patron & El Lider Moderno," *Cross Cultural Management* 11, no. 3 (2004), pp. 25–37.

63. Ibid.

64. Haire, Ghiselli, and Porter, *Managerial Thinking,* p. 22.

65. See Jay A. Conger, *The Charismatic Leader* (San Francisco: Jossey-Bass, 1989).

66. Hodgetts, *Modern Human Relations at Work,* pp. 275–276.

67. Bernard M. Bass, "Is There Universality in the Full Range Model of Leadership?" *International Journal of Public Administration* 16, no. 6 (1996), p. 731.

68. Ibid., pp. 741–742.

69. Ibid., p. 731.

70. For additional insights on recent research by Bass and his associates, see Bruce J. Avolio and Bernard M. Bass, "You Can Drag a Horse to Water but You Can't Make It Drink Unless It Is Thirsty," *Journal of Leadership Studies,* Winter 1998, pp. 4–17.

71. Ingrid Tollgerdt-Andersson, "Attitudes, Values and Demands on Leadership—A Cultural Comparison among Some European Countries," in *Managing Across Cultures,* ed. Pat Joynt and Malcolm Warner (London: International Thomson Business Press, 1996), p. 172.

72. Ibid., p. 176.

73. Felix C. Brodbeck et al., "Cultural Variation of Leadership Prototypes across 22 European Countries," *Journal of Occupational and Organizational Psychology* 73 (2000), pp. 1–29.

74. Ibid., p. 77.

75. Robert J. House and Mansour Javidan, "Overview of GLOBE," in *Culture, Leadership, and Organizations: The GLOBE Study of 62 Societies,* ed. Robert J. House, Paul J. Hanges, Mansour Javidan et al. (Thousand Oaks, CA: Sage, 2004), p. 14.

76. Peter Dorfman, Paul Hanges, and Felix Brodbeck, "Leadership and Cultural Variation: The Identification of Culturally Endorsed Leadership Profiles," in House et al., *Culture, Leadership, and Organizations,* pp. 669–720.

77. Peter Dorfman, Mansour Javidan, Paul Hanges, Ali Dastmalchian, and Robert House, "GLOBE: A Twenty Year Journey into the Intriguing World of Culture and Leadership," *Journal of World Business* 47, (2012), pp. 504–518.

78. Michele J. Gelfand, D. P. S. Bhawuk, Lisa H. Nishii, and David J. Bechtold, "Individualism and Collectivism," in House et al., *Culture, Leadership, and Organizations,* pp. 437–512.

79. Ibid.

80. Cynthia G. Emrich, Florence L. Denmark, and Deanne Den Hartog, "Cross-Cultural Differences in Gender Egalitarianism," in House et al., *Culture, Leadership, and Organizations,* pp. 343–394.

81. Mansour Javidan, "Performance Orientation," in House et al., *Culture, Leadership, and Organizations,* pp. 239–281.

82. Neal Ashkanasy, Vipin Gupta, Melinda Mayfield, and Edwin Trevor-Roberts, "Future Orientation," in House et al., *Culture, Leadership, and Organizations,* pp. 282–342.

83. Mary Sully De Luque and Mansour Javidan, "Uncertainty Avoidance," in House et al., *Culture, Leadership, and Organizations,* pp. 602–654.

84. Hayat Kabasakal and Muzaffer Bodur, "Humane Orientation in Societies, Organizations, and Leader Attributes," in House et al., *Culture, Leadership, and Organizations,* pp. 564–601.

85. Dean Den Hartog, "Assertiveness," in House et al., *Culture, Leadership, and Organizations,* pp. 395–436.

86. Dale Carl, Vipin Gupta, and Mansour Javidan, "Power Distance," in House et al., *Culture, Leadership, and Organizations,* pp. 513–563.

87. Mansour Javidan, "Forward Thinking Cultures," *Harvard Business Review,* July–August 2007, p. 20.

88. Peter Dorfman, Mansour Javidan, Paul Hanges, Ali Dastmalchian, and Robert House, "GLOBE: A Twenty Year Journey into the Intriguing World of Culture and Leadership," *Journal of World Business* 47, (2012), pp. 504–518.

89. Ibid.

90. Narda Quigley, Mary Sully De Luque, and Robert J. House, "Responsible Leadership and Governance in a Global Context: Insights from the GLOBE Study," in *Handbook of Responsible Leadership and Governance in Global Business,* ed. Jonathan P. Doh and Stephen A. Stumpf (London: Edward Elgar Publishing, 2005), pp. 352–379.

91. Lori D. Paris, Jon P. Howell, Peter W. Dorfman, and Paul J. Hanges, "Preferred Leadership Prototypes of Male and Female Leaders in 27 Countries," *Journal of International Business Studies* 40, no. 8 (2009), pp. 1396–1405.

92. Kim S. Cameron, Jane E. Dutton, and Robert E. Quinn, *Positive Organizational Scholarship* (San Francisco: Berrett-Koehler, 2003), p. 3.

93. Ibid.

94. C. Cooper, T. A. Scandura, and C. A. Schriesheim, "Looking Forward but Learning from Our Past: Potential Challenges to Developing Authentic Leadership Theory and Authentic Leaders," *The Leadership Quarterly* 16, no. 3 (2005), pp. 475–493.

95. B. Avolio, F. Luthans, and F. O. Walumba, *Authentic Leadership: Theory Building for Veritable Sustained Performance* (Gallup Leadership Institute, University of Nebraska-Lincoln, 2004), p. 4.

96. B. Shamir and G. Eilam, "What's Your Story? A Life-Stories Approach to Authentic Leadership Development," *The Leadership Quarterly* 16, no. 3 (2005), pp. 395–417.

97. William L. Gardner, Bruce J. Avolio, Fred Luthans, Douglas R. May, and Fred Walumbwa, "Can You See the Real Me? A Self-Based Model of Authentic Leader and Follower Development," *The Leadership Quarterly* 16 (2005), pp. 343–372.

98. Ibid.

99. Bruce J. Avolio and William L. Gardner, "Authentic Leadership Development: Getting to the Root of Positive Forms of Leadership," *The Leadership Quarterly* 16 (2005), pp. 315–338.

100. Ibid.

101. World Economic Forum, "Declining Public Trust Foremost a Leadership Problem," press release, January 14, 2003.

102. Ibid.

103. David Waldman, Donald Siegel, and Mansour Javidan, "Transformational Leadership and Corporate Social Responsibility," in Doh and Stumpf, *Handbook of Responsible Leadership and Governance in Global Business.*

104. Jonathan P. Doh and Stephen A. Stumpf, "Toward a Framework of Responsible Leadership and Governance," in Doh and Stumpf, *Handbook of Responsible Leadership and Governance in Global Business.*

105. Allen Morrison, "Integrity and Global Leadership," *Journal of Business Ethics* 31, no. 1 (May 2001), p. 65.

106. Lao Tzu, *Tao Te Ching,* trans. John C. H. Wu (Boston, MA: Shambhala, 2006), p. 35.

107. Robert Greenleaf, *Servant Leadership: A Journey into the Nature of Legitimate Power and Greatness,* 25th Anniversary Edition (Mahwah, NJ: Paulist Press, 2002).

108. Stephen A. Stumpf, "Career Goal: Entrepreneur?" *International Journal of Career Management* 4, no. 2 (1992), pp. 26–32.

109. T. K. Maloy, "Entrepreneurs Need Moms," United Press International, March 11, 2004.

■ Chapter 14

1. "16th Annual PwC Global CEO Survey," PricewaterhouseCoopers Private Limited, March 2013, p. 6.

2. Elena Groznaya, "Attrition and Motivation: Retaining Staff in India," tcWorld, July 2009, http://www.tcworld.info/index.php?id=63.

3. Shyamal Majumdar, "Retaining Talent: Are Companies Doing Enough?" *Business Standard,* March 19, 2010, http://business.rediff.com/column/2010/mar/19/guest-retaining-talent-are-companies-doing-enough.htm.

4. "Stemming the Tide of Attrition in India: Keys to Increasing Retention," Executive Overview, Right Management, Executive Summary of a paper by Jonathan P. Doh, Steven A. Stumpf, Walter Tymon, and Michael Haid, 2008.

5. Elena Groznaya, "Attrition and Motivation: Retaining Staff in India," tcWorld, July 2009, http://www.tcworld.info/index.php?id=63.

6. "Stemming the Tide of Attrition in India: Keys to Increasing Retention," Executive Overview, Right Management, Executive Summary of a paper by Jonathan P. Doh, Steven A. Stumpf, Walter Tymon, and Michael Haid, 2008.

7. Ibid.

8. Ibid.

9. Ibid.

10. Ibid.

11. Ibid.

12. Ibid.

13. Ibid.

14. Ibid.

15. Ibid.

16. Elaine Appleton Grant, "How to Retain Talent in India," Synopsis of a paper by Jonathan P. Doh, Steven A. Stumpf, Walter

Tymon, and Michael Haid, MIT Sloan Management Review 50, no. 1 (Fall 2008).

17. Ibid.

18. "How HR Contributes at Best Small and Midsize Companies to Work For," *Human Resource Department Management Report,* August 2004, p. 2.

19. Ann Pomeroy, "Cooking Up Innovation," *HR Magazine,* November 2004, pp. 46–53.

20. Peter Coy and Jack Ewing, "Where Are All the Workers?" *BusinessWeek,* April 9, 2007, pp. 28–31.

21. Susan Cantrell, "The Work Force of One," *The Wall Street Journal,* June 16, 2007, p. R10.

22. Gary M. Wederspahn, "Costing Failures in Expatriate Human Resources Management," *Human Resource Planning* 15, no. 3 (1992), pp. 27–35.

23. Also see Kenneth Groh and Mark Allen, "Global Staffing: Are Expatriates the Only Answer?" *HR Focus,* March 1998, pp. S1–S2.

24. Leslie Chang, "China's Grads Find Jobs Scarce," *The Wall Street Journal,* June 22, 2004, p. A17.

25. Nick Forster, "Expatriates and the Impact of Cross-Cultural Training," *Human Resource Management Journal* 10, no. 3 (2000), pp. 63–78.

26. Jim Rendon, "Ten Things Human Resources Won't Tell You," *The Wall Street Journal,* April 19, 2010, www.wsj.com.

27. "Compensation: Employer Pay Adjustments: An Update," *Human Resources,* no. 7, July 2009.

28. Malika Richards, "U.S. Multinational Staffing Practices and Implications for Subsidiary Performance in the U.K. and Thailand," *Thunderbird International Business Review,* March–April 2001, pp. 225–242.

29. Richard B. Peterson, Nancy K. Napier, and Won Shul-Shim, "Expatriate Management: A Comparison of MNCs Across Four Parent Countries," *Thunderbird International Business Review,* March–April 2000, p. 150.

30. Arvind V. Phatak, *International Dimensions of Management,* 2nd ed. (Boston: PWS-Kent Publishing, 1989), p. 106.

31. Cliff Edwards and Kenji Hall, "Remade in the USA," *BusinessWeek,* May 7, 2007, pp. 44–45.

32. Calvin Reynolds, "Strategic Employment of Third Country Nationals," *HR Planning* 20, no. 1 (1997), p. 38.

33. Michael G. Harvey and M. Ronald Buckley, "Managing Inpatriates: Building a Global Core Competency," *Journal of World Business* 32, no. 1 (1997), p. 36.

34. For some additional insights about inpatriates and worldwide staffing, see Michael Harvey and Milorad M. Novicevic, "Staffing Global Marketing Positions: What We Don't Know Can Make a Difference," *Journal of World Business* 35, no. 1 (2000), pp. 80–94.

35. Noam Scheiber, "As a Center for Outsourcing, India Could Be Losing Its Edge," *New York Times,* May 9, 2004, p. 3.

36. Steve Lohr, "Evidence of High-Skill Work Going Abroad," *New York Times,* June 16, 2004, p. C2.

37. "Dell to Bring Some Jobs Back Home," *Houston Chronicle,* November 23, 2003, p. 2.

38. Manjeet Kripalani, "Now It's Bombay Calling the U.S.," *BusinessWeek,* June 21, 2004, p. 26.

39. Marilyn Geewax, "Outsourcing of Service Jobs Grows Faster than Estimated," *Houston Chronicle,* May 18, 2004, p. 4.

40. Arie Lewin and Vinay Couto, *2006 Survey Report: Next Generation Offshoring, The Globalization of Innovation* (Durham: Booz Allen Hamilton, 2007), pp. 7–10.

41. Ibid.

42. Winfred Arthur Jr. and Winston Bennett Jr., "The International Assignee: The Relative Importance of Factors Perceived to Contribute to Success," *Personnel Psychology,* Spring 1995, pp. 99–114.

43. Also see Michael G. Harvey, Milorad M. Novicevic, and Cheri Speier, "An Innovative Global Management Staffing System: A Competency-Based Perspective," *Human Resource Management,* Winter 2000, pp. 381–394.

44. Peterson, Napier, and Shul-Shim, "Expatriate Management," p. 151.

45. Juan Sanchez, Paul Spector, and Cary Cooper, "Adapting to a Boundaryless World: A Developmental Expatriate Model," *Academy of Management Executive* 14, no. 2 (2000), pp. 96–106.

46. Jan Selmar, "Effects of Coping Strategies on Sociocultural and Psychological Adjustment of Western Expatriate Managers in the PRC," *Journal of World Business* 34, no. 1 (1999), pp. 41–51.

47. Paula M. Caligiuri, "Selecting Expatriates for Personality Characteristics: A Moderating Effect of Personality on the Relationship Between Host National Contact and Cross-Cultural Adjustment," *Management International Review* 40, no. 1 (2000), pp. 61–80.

48. The survey was conducted by executive recruiters for Korn-Ferry International and the Columbia Business School. Excerpts were reported in "Report: Shortage of Executives Will Hurt U.S.," *Omaha World Herald,* June 25, 1989, p. 1G.

49. Brian Friedman, "How to Move and Manage the Best People around the World; An Assignment Overseas Is Often Now Seen as a Vital Career Move," *The Daily Telegraph,* May 15, 2010, p. 8.

50. Margaret A. Shaffer, David A. Harrison, K. Matthew Gilley, and Dora M. Luk, "Struggling for Balance amid Turbulence on International Assignments: Work-Family Conflict, Support, and Commitment," *Journal of Management* 27 (2001), pp. 99–121.

51. Patricia C. Borstorff, Stanley G. Harris, Hubert S. Field, and William F. Giles, "Who'll Go? A Review of Factors Associated with Employee Willingness to Work Overseas," *Human Resource Planning* 20, no. 3 (1997), p. 38.

52. See Betty Jane Punnett, "Towards Effective Management of Expatriate Spouses," *Journal of World Business* 33, no. 3 (1997), pp. 243–256.

53. Howard Tu and Sherry E. Sullivan, "Preparing Yourself for an International Assignment," *Business Horizons,* January–February 1994, p. 68.

54. Theresa Minton-Eversole, "Overseas Assignments Keep Pace, But Economic Conditions Hold the Rein," *HR Magazine* 53, (2009), pp. 72–73.

55. James C. Baker and John M. Ivancevich, "The Assignment of American Executives Abroad: Systematic, Haphazard or Chaotic?" *California Management Review,* Spring 1971, p. 41.

56. Jean E. Heller, "Criteria for Selecting an International Manager," *Personnel,* May–June 1980, p. 53.

57. Rosalie L. Tung, "U.S. Multinationals: A Study of Their Selection and Training Procedures for Overseas Assignments," *National Academy of Management Proceedings* (Atlanta, 1979), p. 65.

58. This section is based on J. Stewart Black, Mark Mendenhall, and Gary Oddou, "Toward a Comprehensive Model of International Adjustment: An Integration of Multiple Theoretical Perspectives," *Academy of Management Review,* April 1991, pp. 291–317. For more on this area, see Jaime Bonache, Chris Brewster, and Vesa Suutari, "Expatriation: A Developing Research Agenda," *Thunderbird International Business Review,* January–February 2001, pp. 3–20.

59. Crystal I. C. Farh, Kathryn M. Bartol, Debra L. Shapiro, and Jiseon Shin, "Networking Abroad: A Process Model of How Expatriates Form Support Ties to Facilitate Adjustment," *Academy of Management Review* 35, no. 3 (2010), pp. 434–454.

60. Iain McCormick and Tony Chapman, "Executive Relocation: Personal and Organizational Tactics," in *Managing Across Cultures: Issues and Perspectives,* ed. Pat Joynt and Malcolm Warner (London: International Thomson Business Press, 1996), pp. 326–337.

61. Calvin Reynolds, "Expatriate Compensation in Historical Perspective," *Journal of World Business* 32, no. 2 (1997), p. 127.

62. Cathy Loose, "Home and Away," *China Staff* 16, no. 3, pp. 24–26.

63. Elaine K. Bailey, "International Compensation," in *Global Perspectives of Human Resource Management,* ed. Oded Shenkar (Englewood Cliffs, NJ: Prentice Hall, 1995), p. 148.

64. Peterson, Napier, and Shul-Shim, "Expatriate Management," p. 155.

65. See Dennis R. Briscoe, Randall S. Schuler, and Lisbeth Claus, *International Human Resource Management* (Global HRM) (Routledge, 2008); Ute Krudewagen and Susan Eandi, "Designing Employee Policies for an International Workforce," *Workspan* 53, no. 6 (2010), p. 74.

66. Cheryl Spielman and Gerald A. Tammaro, "8 Action Items for Expatriate Planning in an Economic Downturn," *Workspan* 52, no. 10 (2009), p. 58.

67. "Pay Variations in Asia," *HR Magazine,* 2010, p. 6.

68. David Sirota and J. Michael Greenwood, "Understand Your Overseas Workforce," *Harvard Business Review,* January–February 1971, pp. 53–60.

69. Ingemar Torbiorn, *Living Abroad* (New York: Wiley, 1982), p. 127.

70. Charles Vance and Yongsun Paik, "One Size Fits All in Expatriate Pre-departure Training? Comparing the Host Country Voices of Mexican, Indonesian and U.S. Workers," *The Journal of Management Development* 21, no. 7–8 (2002), pp. 557–572.

71. Chi-Sum Wong and Kenneth S. Law, "Managing Localization of Human Resources in the PRC: A Practical Model," *Journal of World Business* 34, no. 1 (1999), pp. 28–29.

72. Torbiorn, *Living Abroad,* p. 41.

73. Maria L. Kraimer, Sandy J. Wayne, and Renata A. Jaworski, "Sources of Support and Expatriate Performance: The Mediating Role of Expatriate Adjustment," *Personnel Psychology* 54 (2001), pp. 71–99.

74. Yoram Zeira and Moshe Banai, "Selection of Expatriate Managers in MNCs: The Host-Environment Point of View," *International Studies of Management & Organization* 15, no. 1 (1985), pp. 33–41.

75. Jobert E. Abueva, "Return of the Native Executive," *New York Times,* May 17, 2000, p. C1.

76. Adler, *International Dimensions of Organizational Behavior,* 2nd ed. (Boston: PWS-Kent Publishing, 1991), p. 236.

77. Howard W. French, "Japan Unsettles Returnees, Who Yearn to Leave Again," *New York Times,* May 2, 2000, p. A12.

78. J. Stewart Black, "Coming Home: The Relationship of Expatriate Expectations with Repatriate Adjustment and Job Performance," *Human Relations* 45, no. 2 (1992), p. 188.

79. Wong and Law, "Managing Localization of Human Resources," p. 36.

80. Nancy K. Napier and Richard B. Peterson, "Expatriate Reentry: What Do Expatriates Have to Say?" *Human Resource Planning* 14, no. 1 (1991), pp. 19–28.

81. Charlene Marmer Solomon, "Repatriation: Up, Down or Out?" *Personnel Journal,* January 1995, p. 32.

82. Mitchell R. Hammer, William Hart, and Randall Rogan, "Can You Go Home Again? An Analysis of the Repatriation of

Corporate Managers and Spouses," *Management International Review* 38, no. 1 (1998), p. 81.

83. Karen Roberts, Ellen Ernst Kossek, and Cynthia Ozeki, "Managing the Global Workforce: Challenges and Strategies," *Academy of Management Executive,* November 1998, pp. 93–106. See also Mark C. Blino and Daniel C. Feldman, "Increasing the Skill Utilization of Expatriates," *Human Resource Management* 39, no. 4 (Winter 2000), pp. 367–379; Ben L. Kedia and Ananda Mukherji, "Global Managers: Developing a Mindset for Global Competitiveness," *Journal of World Business* 34, no. 3 (1999), pp. 230–251.

84. Robert C. Maddox and Douglas Short, "The Cultural Integrator," *Business Horizons,* November–December 1988, pp. 57–59.

85. Michael Hickins, "Creating a Global Team," *Management Review,* September 1998, p. 6.

86. Charlene Marmer Solomon, "Global Operations Demand that HR Rethink Diversity," *Personnel Journal,* July 1994, p. 50.

87. Paul R. Sparrow and Pawan S. Budhwar, "Competition and Change: Mapping the Indian HRM Recipe Against Worldwide Patterns," *Journal of World Business* 32, no. 3 (1997), p. 231. See also Chi-Sum Wong and Kenneth S. Law, "Managing Localization of Human Resources in the PRC: A Practical Model," *Journal of World Business* 34, no. 1 (1999), pp. 32–33.

88. Bodil Jones, "What Future European Recruits Want," *Management Review,* January 1998, p. 6.

89. Filiz Tabak, Janet Stern Solomon, and Christine Nielsen, "Managerial Success: A Profile of Future Managers in China," *SAM Advanced Management Journal,* Autumn 1998, pp. 18–26.

90. Also see Allan Bird, Sully Taylor, and Schon Beechler, "A Typology of International Human Resource Management in Japanese Multinational Corporations: Organizational Implications," *Human Resource Management,* Summer 1998, pp. 159–176.

91. Fred Luthans, *Organizational Behavior,* 10th ed. (New York: McGraw-Hill/Irwin, 2004), chapter 16.

92. Noel M. Tichy and Eli Cohen, "The Teaching Organization," *Training and Development Journal,* July 1998, p. 27.

93. Peter Prud'homme van Reine and Fons Trompenaars, "Invited Reaction: Developing Expatriates for the Asia-Pacific Region," *Human Resource Development Quarterly* 11, no. 3 (Fall 2000), p. 238.

94. J. Hayes and C. W. Allinson, "Cultural Differences in the Learning Styles of Managers," *Management International Review* 28, no. 3 (1988), p. 76.

95. See for example Jennifer Smith, "Southeast Asia's Search for Managers," *Management Review,* June 1998, p. 9.

96. Also see Schon Beechler and John Zhuang Yang, "The Transfer of Japanese-Style Management to American Subsidiaries: Contingencies, Constraints, and Competencies," *Journal of International Business Studies,* Third Quarter 1994, pp. 467–491.

97. Allan Bird and Schon Beechler, "Links Between Business Strategy and Human Resource Management Strategy in U.S.-Based Japanese Subsidiaries: An Empirical Investigation," *Journal of International Business Studies,* First Quarter 1995, p. 40.

98. Linda K. Stroh and Paula M. Caligiuri, "Increasing Global Competitiveness Through Effective People Management," *Journal of World Business* 33, no. 1 (1998), p. 10.

99. For more on this, see Tomoko Yoshida and Richard W. Breslin, "Intercultural Skills and Recommended Behaviors," in Shenkar, *Global Perspectives of Human Resource Management,* pp. 112–131.

100. Alan M. Barrett, "Training and Development of Expatriates and Home Country Nationals," in Shenkar, *Global Perspectives of Human Resource Management,* p. 135.

101. Yukimo Ono, "Japanese Firms Don't Let Masters Rule," *The Wall Street Journal,* May 4, 1992, p. B1.

102. See Chi-Sum Wong and Kenneth S. Law, "Managing Localization of Human Resources in the PRC: A Practical Model," *Journal of World Business* 34, no. 1 (1999), pp. 32–33.

103. See Andrew Sergeant and Stephen Frenkel, "Managing People in China: Perceptions of Expatriate Managers," *Journal of World Business* 33, no. 1 (1998), pp. 17–34.

104. Michael J. Marquardt and Dean W. Engel, *Global Human Resource Management* (Englewood Cliffs, NJ: Prentice Hall, 1995), p. 44.

105. Ingmar Bjorkman and Yuan Lu, "A Corporate Perspective on the Management of Human Resources in China," *Journal of World Business* 34, no. 1 (1999), pp. 20–21.

106. Fred E. Fiedler, Terence Mitchell, and Harry C. Triandis, "The Culture Assimilator: An Approach to Cross-Cultural Training," *Journal of Applied Psychology,* April 1971, p. 97.

107. Fred Luthans, "Positive Organizational Behavior: Developing and Managing Psychological Strengths," *Academy of Management Executive* 16, no. 1 (2002), p. 59.

108. Fred Luthans and Carolyn M. Youssef, "Emerging Positive Organizational Behavior," *Journal of Management* 33, no. 3 (June 2007), pp. 321–349.

109. Ibid.

110. "What Are Companies' Top Concerns for Relocating Employees over the Next Decade?" *Business Wire,* June 28, 2010.

■ Part 4 Integrative Cases

Brief Integrative Case 4.1

1. Veronika Tarnovskaya, Ulf Elg, and Steve Burt, "The Role of Corporate Branding in a Market Driving Strategy," *International Journal of Retail & Distribution Management* 36, no. 11 (2008), pp. 941–965.

2. IKEA (2013). "History—IKEA," http://www.ikea.com/ms/en_US/about_ikea/the_ikea_way/history/index.html. Accessed March 6, 2013.

3. Bo Edvardsson, Bo Enquist, and Michael Hay, "Values-Based Service Brands: narratives from IKEA," *Managing Service Quality* 16, no. 3 (2006), pp. 230–246.

4. IKEA (2013). "1940s–1950s–IKEA," http://www.ikea.com/ms/en_US/about_ikea/the_ikea_way/history/1940_1950.html. Accessed March 6, 2013.

5. Bo Edvardsson, Bo Enquist, and Michael Hay, "Values-Based Service Brands: Narratives from IKEA," Managing Service Quality 16, no. 3 (2006), pp. 230–246.

6. IKEA (2013). "1960s–1970s—IKEA," http://www.ikea.com/ms/en_US/about_ikea/the_ikea_way/history/1960_1970.html. Accessed March 6, 2013.

7. Ibid.

8. Aman Singh, "IKEA's Sustainability Strategy: Save the World, One Product At a Time," *Forbes,* February 7, 2013, http://www.forbes.com/sites/csr/2013/02/07/ikea-sustainability-and-profitability-two-ends-of-the-same-stick/. Accessed April 13, 2013.

9. Gary Warnaby, "Strategic Consequences of Retail Acquisition: IKEA and Habitat," *International Marketing Review* 16, no. 4/5 (1999), pp. 406–416.

10. Ibid.

11. Jens Hansegard and Sven Grundberg, "IKEA Chief Executive to Step Down." *WSJ.com.* September 17, 2012. http://online.wsj.com/article/SB10000872396390443816804578001922463079746.html/ Accessed July 8, 2013.

12. Jens Hansegard and Sven Grundberg, "IKEA Chief Executive to Step Down." *WSJ.com.* September 17, 2012. http://online.wsj.com/article/SB10000872396390443816804578001922463079746.html/ Accessed July 8, 2013.

13. Ibid.

14. IKEA (2013). "Swedish Heritage—IKEA." http://www.ikea.com/ms/en_US/about_ikea/the_ikea_way/swedish_heritage/index.html. Accessed March 6, 2013.

15. Ibid.

16. "The Story of IKEA," *Management Practice,* no. 8 (1997), pp. 33–34.

17. Ibid.

18. "Globalization's Winners and Losers; Lessons from retailers J.C. Penny, Home Depot, Carrefour, Ikea and others," *Strategic Management* 22, no. 9 (2006), pp. 27–29.

19. Veronika Tarnovskaya, Ulf Elg, and Steve Burt, "The Role of Corporate Branding in a Market Driving Strategy," *International Journal of Retail & Distribution Management* 36, no. 11 (2008), pp. 941–965.

20. Mats Urde, "Uncovering the Corporate Brand's Core Values," *Management Decision* 47, no. 4 (2009), pp. 616–638.

21. Ibid.

22. Ingvar Kamprad, "The Testament of a Furniture Dealer; A Little IKEA Dictionary," 2007.

23. Mats Urde, "Uncovering the Corporate Brand's Core Values," *Management Decision* 47, no. 4 (2009), pp. 616–638.

24. Bo Edvardsson, Bo Enquist, and Michael Hay, "Values-Based Service Brands: Narratives from IKEA," *Managing Service Quality* 16, no. 3 (2006), pp. 230–246.

25. Mats Urde, "Uncovering the Corporate Brand's Core Values," *Management Decision* 47, no. 4 (2009), pp. 616–638.

26. Ibid.

27. Ibid.

28. Veronika Tarnovskaya, Ulf Elg, and Steve Burt, "The Role of Corporate Branding in a Market Driving Strategy," *International Journal of Retail & Distribution Management* 36, no. 11 (2008), pp. 941–965.

29. Ibid.

30. Ibid.

31. Ibid.

32. Ibid.

33. Ibid.

34. Ibid.

35. Ibid.

36. Bo Edvardsson, Bo Enquist, and Michael Hay, "Values-Based Service Brands: Narratives from IKEA," *Managing Service Quality* 16, no. 3 (2006), pp. 230–246.

37. Ibid.

38. Dario A. Schirone and Germano Torkan, "New Transport Organization by IKEA. An Example of Social Responsibility in Corporate Strategy," *Advances in Management & Applied Economics* 2, no. 3 (2012), pp. 181–193.

39. Mette Andersen and Tage Skjoett-Larsen, "Corporate Social Responsibility in Global Supply Chains," *Supply Chain Management: An International Journal* 13, no. 2 (2009), pp. 75–86.

40. Ibid.

41. Ibid.

42. Dario A. Schirone and Germano Torkan, "New Transport Organization by IKEA. An Example of Social Responsibility in Corporate Strategy," *Advances in Management & Applied Economics* 2, no. 3 (2012), pp. 181–193.

43. Mette Andersen and Tage Skjoett-Larsen, "Corporate Social Responsibility in Global Supply Chains," *Supply Chain Management: An International Journal* 13, no. 2 (2009), pp. 75–86.

44. Ibid.

45. Veronika Tarnovskaya, Ulf Elg, and Steve Burt, "The Role of Corporate Branding in a Market Driving Strategy," *International Journal of Retail & Distribution Management* 36, no. 11 (2008), pp. 941–965.

46. Ibid.

47. Ibid.

48. Dario A. Schirone and Germano Torkan, "New Transport Organization by IKEA. An Example of Social Responsibility in Corporate Strategy," *Advances in Management & Applied Economics* 2, no. 3 (2012), pp. 181–193.

49. Ibid.

50. Ibid.

51. Ibid.

52. Ibid.

53. Ibid.

54. Ibid.

55. Aman Singh, "IKEA's Sustainability Strategy: Save the World, One Product At a Time," *Forbes,* February 7, 2013, http://www.forbes.com/sites/csr/2013/02/07/ikea-sustainability-and-profitability-two-ends-of-the-same-stick/. Accessed April 13, 2013.

56. Jens Hansegard, "Ikea Taking China By Storm," *Wall Street Journal,* March 26, 2012, http://online.wsj.com/article/SB10001424052702304636404577293083481821536.html. Accessed April 13, 2013.

57. Laurie Burkitt. "In China, IKEA Is a Swede Place for Senior Romance, Relaxation; Free Coffee, Empty Beds Set Intimate Tone; Retailer Struggles to Police the Unruly." *WSJ.com,* December 1, 2011. http://online.wsj.com/article/SB10001424052970203503204577037991554068290.html/ Accessed July 8, 2013.

58. Ibid.

59. Ulf Johansson and Asa Thelander, "A Standardized Approach to the World? IKEA in China," *International Journal of Quality and Service Sciences* 1, no. 2 (2009), pp. 199–219.

60. Jens Hansegard, "Ikea Taking China By Storm," *Wall Street Journal,* March 26, 2012, http://online.wsj.com/article/SB10001424052702304636404577293083481821536.html. Accessed April 13, 2013.

61. Ulf Johansson and Asa Thelander, "A Standardized Approach to the World? IKEA in China," *International Journal of Quality and Service Sciences* 1, no. 2 (2009), pp. 199–219.

62. Ibid.

63. Jens Hansegard, "Ikea Taking China By Storm," *Wall Street Journal,* March 26, 2012, http://online.wsj.com/article/SB10001424052702304636404577293083481821536.html. Accessed April 13, 2013.

64. Ulf Johansson and Asa Thelander, "A Standardized Approach to the World? IKEA in China," *International Journal of Quality and Service Sciences* 1, no. 2 (2009), pp. 199–219.

65. Laurie Burkitt. "In China, IKEA Is a Swede Place for Senior Romance, Relaxation; Free Coffee, Empty Beds Set Intimate Tone; Retailer Struggles to Police the Unruly." *WSJ.com,* December 1, 2011. http://online.wsj.com/article/SB10001424052970203503204577037991554068290.html/ Accessed July 8, 2013.

66. Laurie Burkitt. "In China, IKEA Is a Swede Place for Senior Romance, Relaxation; Free Coffee, Empty Beds Set Intimate Tone; Retailer Struggles to Police the Unruly." *WSJ.com,* December 1, 2011. http://online.wsj.com/article/SB100014240529 70203503204577037991554068290.html/ Accessed July 8, 2013.

67. Laurie Burkitt. "In China, IKEA Is a Swede Place for Senior Romance, Relaxation; Free Coffee, Empty Beds Set Intimate Tone; Retailer Struggles to Police the Unruly." *WSJ.com,* December 1, 2011. http://online.wsj.com/article/SB100014240529 70203503204577037991554068290.html/ Accessed July 8, 2013.

68. Anne VanderMey, "IKEA Takes on China," *CNN Money,* November 30, 2011. http://features.blogs.fortune.cnn.com/2011/11/30/ ikea-china-stores/. Accessed April 12, 2013.

69. Jason Bush, "An Unpredictable Business Climate: IKEA Turns Sour on Russia," *Spiegel Online International,* June 25, 2009, http://www.spiegel.de/international/business/a-632507.html. Access April 13, 2013.

70. Lucy Scott, "Ikea's Russian Strategy Snaps into Place," *PropertyWeek.com,* March, 2010, http://www.propertyweek.com/ lucy-scott/17782.contributor. Accessed April 13, 2013.

71. Alexander Osipovich, "Bed, Bath & Bribes," *Foreign Policy,* September/October 2010, http://www.foreignpolicy.com/articles/ 2010/08/16/bed_bath_and_bribes. Accessed April 13, 2013.

72. Lucy Scott, "Ikea's Russian Strategy Snaps into Place," *PropertyWeek.com,* March, 2010, http://www.propertyweek.com/ lucy-scott/17782.contributor. Accessed April 13, 2013.

73. Veronika Tarnovskaya, Ulf Elg, and Steve Burt, "The Role of Corporate Branding in a Market Driving Strategy," *International Journal of Retail & Distribution Management* 36, no. 11 (2008), pp. 941–965.

74. Ibid.

75. Ibid.

76. Jason Bush, "An Unpredictable Business Climate: IKEA Turns Sour on Russia," *Spiegel Online International,* June 25, 2009, http://www.spiegel.de/international/business/a-632507.html. Accessed April 13, 2013.

77. Alexander Osipovich, "Bed, Bath & Bribes," *Foreign Policy,* September/October 2010, http://www.foreignpolicy.com/articles/ 2010/08/16/bed_bath_and_bribes. Accessed April 13, 2013.

78. Jesse Heath, "Ikea in Russia: Now 'Everything is Possible' . . . for a price," *oD Russia; Post Soviet world,* February 22, 2010, http://www.opendemocracy.net/od-russia/jesse-heath/ikea-in-russia-now-everything-is-possiblefor-price. Accessed April 13, 2013.

79. Oleg Nikishenkov, "Ikea Case Exposes Bribe Culture in Russia," *The Moscow News,* February 23, 2010, http://themoscownews.com/ news/20100223/55414629.html. Accessed April 13, 2013.

80. Jason Bush, "An Unpredictable Business Climate: IKEA Turns Sour on Russia," *Spiegel Online International,* June 25, 2009, http://www.spiegel.de/international/business/a-632507.html. Accessed April 13, 2013.

81. Ibid.

82. Jesse Heath, "Ikea in Russia: Now 'Everything is Possible' . . . for a price," *oD Russia; Post Soviet world,* February 22, 2010, http://www.opendemocracy.net/od-russia/jesse-heath/ikea-in-russia-now-everything-is-possiblefor-price. Accessed April 13, 2013.

83. Oleg Nikishenkov, "Ikea Case Exposes Bribe Culture in Russia," *The Moscow News,* February 23, 2010, http://themoscownews. com/news/20100223/55414629.html. Accessed April 13, 2013.

84. Jesse Heath, "Ikea in Russia: Now 'Everything is Possible' . . . for a price," *oD Russia; Post Soviet world,* February 22, 2010,

85. Anna Molin, "IKEA Regrets Cutting Women From Saudi Ad," *The Wall Street Journal,* October 1, 2012, http://online.wsj.com/ article/SB10000872396390444592404578030274200387136.html. Accessed April 12, 2013.

86. Ibid.

87. Ibid.

88. Ibid.

89. Ibid.

90. Jennifer Preston, "Ikea Apologizes for Removing Women From Saudi Catalog," *The New York Times,* October 2, 2012, http:// thelede.blogs.nytimes.com/2012/10/02/ikea-apologizes-for-removing-women-from-saudi-catalog/. Accessed April 12, 2013.

91. Nicholas Kulish and Julia Werdigier, "Ikea Admits Forced Labor Was Used in 1980s," *The New York Times,* November 16, 2012, http://www.nytimes.com/2012/11/17/business/global/ikea-to-report-on-allegations-of-using-forced-labor-during-cold-war. html?_r=0. Accessed April 12, 2013.

92. Tiffany Hsu, "Ikea: 'We Deeply Regret' use of forced labor in East Germany," *Los Angeles Times,* November 16, 2012, http:// articles.latimes.com/2012/nov/16/business/la-fi-mo-ikea-forced-labor-germany-20121116. Accessed April 13, 2013.

93. IKEA (2013). "Investigation on IKEA Group Purchasing Practices in the Former German Democratic Republic (GDR) Completed." http://www.ikea.com/us/en/about_ikea/newsitem/fy13_wk46_ IKEA_Group_investigation_GDR. Accessed March 6, 2013.

94. Bo Edvardsson, Bo Enquist, and Michael Hay, "Values-Based Service Brands: Narratives from IKEA," *Managing Service Quality* 16, no. 3 (2006), pp. 230–246.

95. Nicholas Kulish and Julia Werdigier, "Ikea Admits Forced Labor Was Used in 1980s," *The New York Times,* November 16, 2012, http://www.nytimes.com/2012/11/17/business/global/ikea-to-report-on-allegations-of-using-forced-labor-during-cold-war. html?_r=0. Accessed April 12, 2013.

96. Anna Molin and John Stoll, "IKEA's Iconic Meatball Drawn Into Horse-Meat Scandal, February 25, 2013, http://online.wsj.com/ article/SB10001424127887323384604578325864020138732.html. Accessed April 12, 2013.

97. Ibid.

98. IKEA (2013). "IKEA US Meatball Content is Only Beef and Pork Products. IKEA US Does Not Sell Wiener Sausages." http://www.ikea.com/us/en/about_ikea/newsitem/2013_IKEA_ US_Meatballs_only_pork_beef_no_sausages. Accessed March 6, 2013.

99. Anna Molin and John Stoll, "IKEA's Iconic Meatball Drawn Into Horse-Meat Scandal," February 25, 2013, http://online.wsj.com/ article/SB10001424127887323384604578325864020138732.html. Accessed April 12, 2013.

100. Jens Hansegard, "IKEA: Chinese Officials Find Coliform Bacteria in IKEA Cakes," *The Wall Street Journal,* March 5, 2013, http://online.wsj.com/article/BT-CO-20130305-702744.html. Accessed April 13, 2013.

101. "China Finds Excessive Levels of Coliform Bacteria in IKEA Chocolate Cake," *CBS SF Bay Area,* March 6, 2013, http:// sanfrancisco.cbslocal.com/2013/03/06/china-finds-excessive-levels-of-coliform-bacteria-in-ikea-chocolate-cake/. Accessed April 13, 2013.

102. Roger Blitz, "Marriott and Ikea Team Up in Europe," *The Financial Times Limited,* March 5, 2013, http://www.ft.com/intl/ cms/s/0/c1bc8b46-85b4-11e2-9ee3-00144feabdc0.html. Accessed March 6, 2013.

103. Ibid.

104. Victoria Bryan, "Marriott Pairs with IKEA for Its First Budget Hotels," *Reuters,* March 5, 2013, http://www.reuters.com/article/2013/03/05/marriott-ikea-hotels-idUSL6N0BXBWD20130305. Accessed March 6, 2013.

105. Roger Blitz, "Marriott and Ikea Team Up in Europe," *The Financial Times Limited,* March 5, 2013, http://www.ft.com/intl/cms/s/0/c1bc8b46-85b4-11e2-9ee3-00144feabdc0.html. Accessed March 6, 2013.

106. Ibid.

107. Victoria Bryan, "Marriott Pairs with IKEA for Its First Budget Hotels," *Reuters,* March 5, 2013, http://www.reuters.com/article/2013/03/05/marriott-ikea-hotels-idUSL6N0BXBWD20130305. Accessed March 6, 2013.

108. Roger Blitz, "Marriott and Ikea Team Up in Europe," *The Financial Times Limited,* March 5, 2013, http://www.ft.com/intl/cms/s/0/c1bc8b46-85b4-11e2-9ee3-00144feabdc0.html. Accessed March 6, 2013.

109. Jenna Goudreau, "How IKEA Leveraged The Art of Listening to Global Dominance," *Forbes,* January 30, 2013, http://www.forbes.com/sites/jennagoudreau/2013/01/30/how-ikea-leveraged-the-art-of-listening-to-global-dominance/. Accessed June 19, 2013.

110. Jenna Goudreau, "How IKEA Leveraged The Art of Listening to Global Dominance," *Forbes,* January 30, 2013, http://www.forbes.com/sites/jennagoudreau/2013/01/30/how-ikea-leveraged-the-art-of-listening-to-global-dominance/. Accessed June 19, 2013.

111. Jens Hansegard and Sven Grundberg. "IKEA Chief Executive to Step Down." *WSJ.com,* September 17, 2012. http://online.wsj.com/article/SB10000872396390443816804578001922463079746.html/. Accessed July 8, 2013.

112. Ibid.

113. Ibid.

In-Depth Integrative Case 4.1

1. "China's Banking Industry; A Great Big Banking Gamble," *The Economist,* October 25, 2005.

2. "The HSBC Group: A Brief History," Hsbc.com, accessed August 10, 2006.

3. Ibid.

4. Tarun Khanna and David Lane, "HSBC Holdings," *Harvard Business School,* July 18, 2005.

5. Ibid.

6. Kerry Capell and Mark Clifford, "John Bond's HSBC," *BusinessWeek,* September 20, 1999, www.businessweek.com.

7. Carrick Mollenkamp, "HSBC Plans Push in Emerging Markets," *The Wall Street Journal,* October 24, 2005, p. B2.

8. Khanna and Lane, "HSBC Holdings."

9. Kevi Hamlin, "The Quiet Revolution at HSBC," *Institutional Investor,* January 2001, p. 54.

10. Ibid.

11. See Interbrand rankings.

12. Jon Menon, "HSBC to Raise $17.7 Billion as Subprime Cuts Profit," *Bloomberg,* March 2, 2009.

13. B. Yerak, "HSBC Plans to Close Household Financial, Beneficial Consumer Loan Units," *Chicago Tribune,* March 3, 2009, http://www.chicagotribune.com/business/chi-tue-hsbc-mar03,0,5848827.story.

14. Ibid.

15. Jon Menon, "HSBC Rues Household Deal, Halts U.S. Subprime Lending (Update1)," *Bloomberg,* March 2, 2009, http://www.bloomberg.com/apps/news?pid=newsarchive&sid=ajBfkUKrgsZY.

16. "HSBC Cuts 6,100 Jobs," CNN Money, March 2, 2009, http://money.cnn.com/2009/03/02/news/international/hsbc.reut/.

17. Jon Menon, "HSBC to Raise $17.7 Billion as Subprime Cuts Profit (Update5)," *Bloomberg,* March 2, 2009, http://www.bloomberg.com/apps/news?pid=newsarchive&sid=aGiiBHDGHLHY.

18. Ibid.

19. S. Schaefer Munoz and C. Mollenkamp, "HSBC Pulls Back as Profit Declines," *The Wall Street Journal,* March 3, 2009, http://online.wsj.com/article/SB123597285673407215.html.

20. J. Menon and P. Paulden, "HSBC Said to Pay Buyout Debt Bankers $35 Million (Update 1)," *Bloomberg,* March 2, 2009, http://www.bloomberg.com/apps/news?pid=newsarchive&sid=ardeqKgP2KUU.

21. "The HSBC Group: A Brief History."

22. "Strategy," www.hsbc.com/hsbc/investor_centre/strategy, accessed August 11, 2006.

23. Ibid.

24. John Barha, "The Thinking Banker's Thinking Banker," *LatinFinance,* September 2001, p. 10.

25. Karina Robinson, "HSBC's Killer Move," *The Banker,* October 2003, p. 24.

26. Carrick Mollenkamp, "HSBC CEO Discusses the Bank's Expansion Plans," *The Wall Street Journal,* October 23, 2005.

27. Mollenkamp, "HSBC Plans Push in Emerging Markets."

28. HSBC Global Asset Management, January 11, 2010, http://www.assetmanagement.hsbc.com/hk/attachments/weekly/market_outlook.pdf.

29. Peter S. Goodman, "China Approves Plan for Huge Bank IPO," *The Washington Post,* July 20, 2006, p. D5.

30. "China's Banking Industry; A Great Big Banking Gamble."

31. Ibid.

32. Barney Jopson, "China Struggles to Overcome Shortage of Good Accountants," *Financial Times,* June 6, 2006, p. 11.

33. Joshua Cooper Ramo, "Chinese Investors Focus on Return, but Not Risk," *Financial Times,* August 11, 2006, p. 13.

34. Brian Bremner, "Betting on China's Banks," *BusinessWeek,* October 20, 2005.

35. "China's Banking Industry; A Great Big Banking Gamble."

36. Goodman, "China Approves Plan for Huge Bank IPO."

37. Abe De Ramos, "View from Asia: Leveling the Chinese Playing Field," *CFO Magazine,* October 15, 2005.

38. "Putting China's Capital to Work: The Value of Financial System Reform," *McKinsey Global Institute,* May 2006.

39. Ibid.

40. Ibid.

41. "HSBC Doubles China Insurer Stake with $1.04b," *China Daily,* May 9, 2005.

42. Amy Or, "HSBC Has Applied for China Life Insurance License," June 28, 2007, www.marketwatch.com.

43. Sir John Bond, "China: The Re-emergence of the Middle Kingdom," Speech, July 19, 2005.

44. Stephen K. Green, "The Financial System and Economic Development: Challenges and Opportunities for China," Speech at China International Financial Services Convention and Expo, Beijing, July 1, 2004.

45. Mollenkamp, "HSBC Plans Push in Emerging Markets."

46. Bremner, "Betting on China's Banks."

47. Stephen K. Green, "Professor Sir Roland Smith Chief Executive Lecture: The Rise and Rise of Asia," *Speech,* February 14, 2005.

48. "Managing for Growth in Commercial Banking," *Fair Disclosure Wire,* Conference Call, March 21, 2006.

49. Justine Lau, "Loan Growth Boosts BoCOM," *Financial Times,* March 29, 2006, p. 18.

50. K. C. Swanson, "Buying into China's Banks," *Corporate Dealmaker,* September–October 2006, p. 18.

51. Ibid.

52. Associated Press, "ICBC Raises $19B in World's Biggest IPO," October 20, 2006, www.washingtonpost.com/wp-dyn/content/article/2006/10/20/AR2006102000207.html?nav=hcmodule.

53. Kate Linebaugh, "Morgan Stanley Expands in China with Bank Deal," *The Wall Street Journal,* October 3, 2006, p. C3.

54. David Barboza, "Rare Look at China's Burdened Banks," *The New York Times,* November 15, 2006, www.nytimes.com/2006/11/15/business/worldbusiness/15bank.html?ex=1164344400&en=94836291a17fe947&ei=5070.

55. James Areddy, "Citigroup's Risky Win in China," *The Wall Street Journal,* November 17, 2006, p. C10.

56. David Barboza, "Citigroup Is Part of Deal to Control a Bank in China," *The New York Times,* November 17, 2006, www.nytimes.com/2006/11/17/business/worldbusiness/17bank.html.

57. Barboza, "Rare Look at China's Burdened Banks."

58. Rick Carew, "China's Guangdong Development Bank Sets Five-Year Plan," www.marketwatch.com, June 13, 2007.

59. "HSBC Opens a New Sub-branch in Beijing," Media Release on September 11, 2006, www.hsbc.com.cn/cn/aboutus/press/content/06sep11a.htm, accessed on October 5, 2006.

60. HSBC Bank Malaysia, http://www.hsbc.com.my/1/2/about-hsbc/newsroom.

61. Ibid.

62. V. Guevarra, "HSBC Aims to Expand in Vietnam," *The Wall Street Journal,* January 6, 2009, http://online.wsj.com/article/SB123118518780954725.html.

63. Ibid.

64. Terrence Poon and Andrew Batson, "China Targets Inflation as Economy Runs Hot," *The Wall Street Journal,* January 22, 2010, http://online.wsj.com/article/SB10001424052748704320104575015900325556896.html.

65. "China's FDI Climbs a Seventh Month," *China Economic Net,* March 3, 2010, http://en.ce.cn/Business/Macro-economic/201003/16/t20100316_21125600.shtml.

66. Li Yanping, "Foreign Investments in China Jump for a Ninth Month (Update 1)," *Bloomberg,* May 14, 2010, http://www.bloomberg.com/apps/news?pid=20601089&sid=apq6Vvomq7rg.

67. Richard Yorke, HSBC Bank (China) Company Limited, "China Strategy," May 26, 2009, London.

68. Ibid.

69. Ibid.

70. "HSBC Bank (China) Co Expands Further in Bohai Rim," *Shanghai Daily,* July 22, 2009, http://www.china.org.cn/business/2009-07/22/content_18183627.htm.

71. Douglas Flint, Group Financial Director HSBC Holdings Plc, "HSBC: Strategy Reconfirmed in a Period of Regulatory Change," December 2, 2009.

72. Ibid.

73. Ibid.

74. Li Tao, "HSBC Eyeing Strong China, India Markets," *China Daily,* January 12, 2010, http://www.chinadaily.com.cn/hkedition/2010-01/12/content_9303109.htm.

75. Ibid.

76. Ibid.

77. Ibid.

78. Rose Yu, "HSBC Plans to Keep Expanding in China," *The Wall Street Journal,* April 9, 2010, http://online.wsj.com/article/SB10001424052702304024604575173233848501488.html.

79. Ibid.

80. Ibid.

81. Ibid.

82. Ibid.

In-Depth Integrative Case 4.2

1. "Chiquita Names New CEO," *Cincinnati Business Courier,* January 12, 2004.

2. Shanon Murray, "Chiquita's Exit Plan Jumps Big Hurdle," *The Daily Deal,* March 5, 2002, p. C3.

3. Chiquita 2006 Annual Report, www.chiquita.com.

4. Marco Were, "Implementing Corporate Responsibility—The Chiquita Case," *Journal of Business Ethics* 44, no. 2–3 (May 2003), p. 247.

5. "Trade Feud on Bananas Not as Clear as It Looks," *New York Times,* February 7, 2001, p. A5.

6. Sonja Sherwood, "Chiquita's Top Executive," *Chief Executive,* June 2002, p. 18.

7. Geert de Lombaerde, "Chiquita Outlook Improves Following EU Deal," *Cincinnati Business Courier,* April 20, 2001.

8. Nicholas Stein, "Yes, We Have No Profits," *Fortune,* November 26, 2001, pp. 182–196.

9. Ruth Mortimer, "A Strategy That's Bearing Fruit: When Is a Banana Not a Banana? When It's a Brand," *Brand Strategy,* May 26, 2003, p. 40.

10. Stein, "Yes, We Have No Profits."

11. Chiquita 2006 Annual Report. www.chiquita.com.

12. Jerome Goldstein, "Greasing the Wheels of Sustainable Business," *In Business Magazine,* March–April 2003, p. 21.

13. "Corporate Social Responsibility," www.chiquita.com.

14. Sherwood, "Chiquita's Top Executive."

15. Were, "Implementing Corporate Responsibility."

16. J. Gary Taylor and Patricia J. Scharlin, *Smart Alliance: How a Global Corporation and Environmental Activists Transformed a Tarnished Brand* (New Haven: Yale University Press, 2004), p. 10.

17. Collin Dunn. "Chiquita Cleans Up its Act." TreeHugger.com. August 10, 2006. http://www.treehugger.com/green-food/chiquita-cleans-up-its-act.html.

18. "Trade Feud on Bananas Not as Clear as It Looks."

19. Mortimer, "A Strategy That's Bearing Fruit."

20. Forest Ethics. 2012. "16 major companies (and one important us city) act to clean up their transportation footprints." http://www.forestethics.org/major-companies-act-to-clean-up-their-transportation

21. "Chiquita Earns 2004 Corporate Citizen of the Americas Award," *PR Newswire,* April 5, 2004.

22. "Chiquita Brands International Corporate Responsibility Awards/Recognition," *News from Chiquita,* www.chiquita.com.

23. Cliff Peale, "Protection Payments Ensured Safety: Chiquita Disclosure Revealed a Darker Side of Global Economy," *The Cincinnati Enquirer,* May 12, 2004.

24. Ibid.

25. Michael Mitchell, "Chiquita Statement on Agreement with U.S. Department of Justice," Chiquita Press Release, March 14, 2007, www.chiquita.com.

26. Ibid.

27. Stein, "Yes, We Have No Profits."

28. Were, "Implementing Corporate Responsibility."

29. Taylor and Scharlin, *Smart Alliance,* p. 152.

30. Ibid., p. 133.

31. Kintto Lucas, "Chiquita Brand Suffers in Banana Wars," Interpress Service: Global Information Network, November 30, 2001.

32. CERES (Coalition for Environmentally Responsible Economies) Sustainability Awards 2004, www.ceres.org/newsroom/press/rep_award_slist.htm.

33. Chiquita 2006 Annual Report: Corporate Responsibility Section, www.chiquita.com.

34. Chiquita Brands International. "Chiquita Brands International, Inc: Chiquita Reports Fourth Quarter and Full-Year 2011 Results." February 21, 2012. http://investors.chiquita.com/phoenix.zhtml?c=119836&p=irol-newsArticle&id=1663424.

35. Ibid.

Glossary

achievement culture A culture in which people are accorded status based on how well they perform their functions.

achievement motivation theory A theory which holds that individuals can have a need to get ahead, to attain success, and to reach objectives.

act of state doctrine A jurisdictional principle of international law which holds that all acts of other governments are considered to be valid by U.S. courts, even if such acts are illegal or inappropriate under U.S. law.

adaptability screening The process of evaluating how well a family is likely to stand up to the stress of overseas life.

administrative coordination Strategic formulation and implementation in which the MNC makes strategic decisions based on the merits of the individual situation rather than using a predetermined economically or politically driven strategy.

alliance Any type of cooperative relationship among different firms.

ascription culture A culture in which status is attributed based on who or what a person is.

assessment center An evaluation tool used to identify individuals with potential to be selected or promoted to higher-level positions.

authoritarian leadership The use of work-centered behavior designed to ensure task accomplishment.

balance-sheet approach An approach to developing an expatriate compensation package that ensures the expat is "made whole" and does not lose money by taking the assignment.

base of the pyramid strategy Strategy targeting low-income customers in developing countries.

bicultural group A group in which two or more members represent each of two distinct cultures, such as four Mexicans and four Taiwanese who have formed a team to investigate the possibility of investing in a venture.

biotechnology The integration of science and technology to create agricultural or medical products through industrial use and manipulation of living organisms.

born-global firms Firms that engage in significant international activities shortly after being established.

cafeteria approach An approach to developing an expatriate compensation package that entails giving the individual a series of options and letting the person decide how to spend the available funds.

centralization A management system in which important decisions are made at the top.

chaebols Very large, family-held Korean conglomerates that have considerable political and economic power.

charismatic leaders Leaders who inspire and motivate employees through their charismatic traits and abilities.

chromatics The use of color to communicate messages.

chronemics The way in which time is used in a culture.

civil or code law Law that is derived from Roman law and is found in the non-Islamic and nonsocialist countries.

codetermination A legal system that requires workers and their managers to discuss major decisions.

collectivism The political philosophy that views the needs or goals of society as a whole as more important than individual desires (Chapter 2); the tendency of people to belong to groups or collectives and to look after each other in exchange for loyalty (Chapter 4).

common law Law that derives from English law and is the foundation of legislation in the United States, Canada, and England, among other nations.

communication The process of transferring meanings from sender to receiver.

communitarianism Refers to people regarding themselves as part of a group.

conglomerate investment A type of high-risk investment in which goods or services produced are not similar to those produced at home.

content theories of motivation Theories that explain work motivation in terms of what arouses, energizes, or initiates employee behavior.

context Information that surrounds a communication and helps to convey the message.

controlling The process of evaluating results in relation to plans or objectives and deciding what action, if any, to take.

corporate governance The system by which business corporations are directed and controlled.

corporate social responsibility (CSR) The actions of a firm to benefit society beyond the requirements of the law and the direct interests of the firm.

cultural assimilator A programmed learning technique designed to expose members of one culture to some of the basic concepts, attitudes, role perceptions, customs, and values of another culture.

culture Acquired knowledge that people use to interpret experience and generate social behavior. This knowledge forms values, creates attitudes, and influences behavior.

decentralization Pushing decision making down the line and getting the lower-level personnel involved.

decision making The process of choosing a course of action among alternatives.

democracy A political system in which the government is controlled by the citizens either directly or through elections.

diffuse culture   A culture in which public space and private space are similar in size and individuals guard their public space carefully, because entry into public space affords entry into private space as well.

direct controls   The use of face-to-face or personal meetings for the purpose of monitoring operations.

distributive negotiations   Bargaining that occurs when two parties with opposing goals compete over a set value.

doctrine of comity   A jurisdictional principle of international law which holds that there must be mutual respect for the laws, institutions, and governments of other countries in the matter of jurisdiction over their own citizens.

downward communication   The transmission of information from superior to subordinate.

economic imperative   A worldwide strategy based on cost leadership, differentiation, and segmentation.

Eiffel Tower culture   A culture that is characterized by strong emphasis on hierarchy and orientation to the task.

emotional culture   A culture in which emotions are expressed openly and naturally.

empowerment   The process of giving individuals and teams the resources, information, and authority they need to develop ideas and effectively implement them.

environmental scanning   The process of providing management with accurate forecasts of trends related to external changes in geographic areas where the firm currently is doing business or is considering setting up operations.

equity theory   A process theory that focuses on how motivation is affected by people's perception of how fairly they are being treated.

esteem needs   Needs for power and status.

ethics   The study of morality and standards of conduct.

ethnocentric MNC   An MNC that stresses nationalism and often puts home-office people in charge of key international management positions.

ethnocentric predisposition   A nationalistic philosophy of management whereby the values and interests of the parent company guide strategic decisions.

ethnocentrism   The belief that one's own way of doing things is superior to that of others.

European Union   A political and economic community consisting of 27 member states.

expatriates   Managers who live and work outside their home country. They are citizens of the country where the multinational corporation is headquartered.

expectancy theory   A process theory that postulates that motivation is influenced by a person's belief that (*a*) effort will lead to performance, (*b*) performance will lead to specific outcomes, and (*c*) the outcomes will be of value to the individual.

expropriation   The seizure of businesses by a host country with little, if any, compensation to the owners.

extrinsic   A determinant of motivation by which the external environment and result of the activity are of greater importance due to competition and compensation or incentive plans.

fair trade   An organized social movement and market-based approach that aims to help producers in developing countries obtain better trading conditions and promote sustainability.

family culture   A culture that is characterized by a strong emphasis on hierarchy and orientation to the person.

femininity   A cultural characteristic in which the dominant values in society are caring for others and the quality of life.

Foreign Corrupt Practices Act (FCPA)   An act that makes it illegal to influence foreign officials through personal payment or political contributions; made into U.S. law in 1977 because of concerns over bribes in the international business arena.

foreign direct investment (FDI)   Investment in property, plant, or equipment in another country.

formalization   The use of defined structures and systems in decision making, communicating, and controlling.

franchise   A business arrangement under which one party (the franchisor) allows another (the franchisee) to operate an enterprise using its trademark, logo, product line, and methods of operation in return for a fee.

geocentric MNC   An MNC that seeks to integrate diverse regions of the world through a global approach to decision making.

geocentric predisposition   A philosophy of management whereby the company tries to integrate a global systems approach to decision making.

global area division   A structure under which global operations are organized on a geographic rather than a product basis.

global functional division   A structure that organizes worldwide operations primarily based on function and secondarily on product.

global integration   The production and distribution of products and services of a homogeneous type and quality on a worldwide basis.

globalization   The process of social, political, economic, cultural, and technological integration among countries around the world.

globalization imperative   A belief that one worldwide approach to doing business is the key to both efficiency and effectiveness.

global product division   A structural arrangement in which domestic divisions are given worldwide responsibility for product groups.

global strategy   Integrated strategy based primarily on price competition.

GLOBE (Global Leadership and Organizational Behavior Effectiveness)   A multicountry study and evaluation of cultural attributes and leadership behaviors among more than 17,000 managers from 951 organizations in 62 countries.

goal-setting theory   A process theory that focuses on how individuals go about setting goals and responding to them and the overall impact of this process on motivation.

groupthink   Social conformity and pressures on individual members of a group to conform and reach consensus.

guanxi   In Chinese, it means "good connections."

guided missile culture A culture that is characterized by strong emphasis on equality in the workplace and orientation to the task.

haptics Communicating through the use of bodily contact.

home-country nationals Expatriate managers who are citizens of the country where the multinational corporation is headquartered.

homogeneous group A group in which members have similar backgrounds and generally perceive, interpret, and evaluate events in similar ways.

honne A Japanese term that means "what one really wants to do."

horizontal investment An MNC investment in foreign operations to produce the same goods or services as those produced at home.

horizontal specialization The assignment of jobs so that individuals are given a particular function to perform and tend to stay within the confines of this area.

host-country nationals Local managers who are hired by the MNC.

hygiene factors In the two-factor motivation theory, job-context variables such as salary, interpersonal relations, technical supervision, working conditions, and company policies and administration.

incubator culture A culture that is characterized by strong emphasis on equality and orientation to the person.

indigenization laws Laws that require nationals to hold a majority interest in an operation.

indirect controls The use of reports and other written forms of communication to control operations.

individualism The political philosophy that people should be free to pursue economic and political endeavors without constraint (Chapter 2); the tendency of people to look after themselves and their immediate family only (Chapter 4).

inpatriates Individuals from a host country or third-country nationals who are assigned to work in the home country.

integrative negotiation Bargaining that involves cooperation between two groups to integrate interests, create value, and invest in the agreement.

integrative techniques Techniques that help the overseas operation become a part of the host country's infrastructure.

international division structure A structural arrangement that handles all international operations out of a division created for this purpose.

international entrepreneurship A combination of innovative, proactive, and risk-seeking behavior that crosses national boundaries and is intended to create value for organizations.

international management Process of applying management concepts and techniques in a multinational environment and adapting management practices to different economic, political, and cultural environments.

international selection criteria Factors used to choose personnel for international assignments.

international strategy Mixed strategy combining low demand for integration and responsiveness.

intimate distance Distance between people that is used for very confidential communications.

intrinsic A determinant of motivation by which an individual experiences fulfillment through carrying out an activity and helping others.

Islamic law Law that is derived from interpretation of the Qur'an and the teachings of the Prophet Muhammad and is found in most Islamic countries.

job-content factors In work motivation, those factors internally controlled, such as responsibility, achievement, and the work itself.

job-context factors In work motivation, those factors controlled by the organization, such as conditions, hours, earnings, security, benefits, and promotions.

job design A job's content, the methods that are used on the job, and the way the job relates to other jobs in the organization.

joint venture (JV) An agreement under which two or more partners own or control a business.

kaizen A Japanese term that means "continuous improvement."

karoshi A Japanese term that means "overwork" or "job burnout."

keiretsu In Japan, an organizational arrangement in which a large, often vertically integrated group of companies cooperate and work closely with each other to provide goods and services to end users; members may be bound together by cross-ownership, long-term business dealings, interlocking directorates, and social ties.

key success factor (KSF) A factor necessary for a firm to effectively compete in a market niche.

kinesics The study of communication through body movement and facial expression.

leadership The process of influencing people to direct their efforts toward the achievement of some particular goal or goals.

learning The acquisition of skills, knowledge, and abilities that result in a relatively permanent change in behavior.

license An agreement that allows one party to use an industrial property right in exchange for payment to the other party.

localization An approach to developing an expatriate compensation package that involves paying the expat a salary comparable to that of local nationals.

lump-sum method An approach to developing an expatriate compensation package that involves giving the expat a predetermined amount of money and letting the individual make his or her own decisions regarding how to spend it.

macro political risk analysis Analysis that reviews major political decisions likely to affect all enterprises in the country.

management Process of completing activities efficiently and effectively with and through other people.

maquiladora A factory, the majority of which are located in Mexican border towns, that imports materials and equipment on a duty- and tariff-free basis for assembly or manufacturing and re-export.

masculinity A cultural characteristic in which the dominant values in society are success, money, and things.

merger/acquisition   The cross-border purchase or exchange of equity involving two or more companies.

micro political risk analysis   Analysis directed toward government policies and actions that influence selected sectors of the economy or specific foreign businesses in the country.

Ministry of International Trade and Industry (MITI)   A Japanese government agency that identifies and ranks national commercial pursuits and guides the distribution of national resources to meet these goals.

mixed organization structure   A structure that is a combination of a global product, area, or functional arrangement.

MNC   A firm having operations in more than one country, international sales, and a nationality mix of managers and owners.

monochronic time schedule   A time schedule in which things are done in a linear fashion.

motivation   A psychological process through which unsatisfied wants or needs lead to drives that are aimed at goals or incentives.

motivators   In the two-factor motivation theory, job-content factors such as achievement, recognition, responsibility, advancement, and the work itself.

multicultural group   A group in which there are individuals from three or more different ethnic backgrounds, such as three U.S., three German, three Uruguayan, and three Chinese managers who are looking into mining operations in South Africa.

multi-domestic strategy   Differentiated strategy emphasizing local adaptation.

national responsiveness   The need to understand the different consumer tastes in segmented regional markets and respond to different national standards and regulations imposed by autonomous governments and agencies.

nationality principle   A jurisdictional principle of international law which holds that every country has jurisdiction over its citizens no matter where they are located.

negotiation   Bargaining with one or more parties for the purpose of arriving at a solution acceptable to all.

neutral culture   A culture in which emotions are held in check.

nongovernmental organizations (NGOs)   Private, not-for-profit organizations that seek to serve society's interests by focusing on social, political, and economic issues such as poverty, social justice, education, health, and the environment.

nonverbal communication   The transfer of meaning through means such as body language and the use of physical space.

North American Free Trade Agreement (NAFTA)   A free-trade agreement between the United States, Canada, and Mexico that has removed most barriers to trade and investment.

oculesics   The area of communication that deals with conveying messages through the use of eye contact and gaze.

offshoring   The process by which companies undertake some activities at offshore locations instead of in their countries of origin.

operational risks   Government policies and procedures that directly constrain management and performance of local operations.

organizational culture   Shared values and beliefs that enable members to understand their roles and the norms of the organization.

outsourcing   The subcontracting or contracting out of activities to endogenous organizations that had previously been performed by the firm.

ownership-control risks   Government policies or actions that inhibit ownership or control of local operations.

parochialism   The tendency to view the world through one's own eyes and perspectives.

participative leadership   The use of both work- or task-centered and people-centered approaches to leading subordinates.

particularism   The belief that circumstances dictate how ideas and practices should be applied and that something cannot be done the same everywhere.

paternalistic leadership   The use of work-centered behavior coupled with a protective employee-centered concern.

perception   A person's view of reality.

personal distance   In communicating, the physical distance used for talking with family and close friends.

physiological needs   Basic physical needs for water, food, clothing, and shelter.

political imperative   Strategic formulation and implementation utilizing strategies that are country-responsive and designed to protect local market niches.

political risk   The unanticipated likelihood that a business's foreign investment will be constrained by a host government's policy.

polycentric MNC   An MNC that places local nationals in key positions and allows these managers to appoint and develop their own people.

polycentric predisposition   A philosophy of management whereby strategic decisions are tailored to suit the cultures of the countries where the MNC operates.

polychronic time schedule   A time schedule in which people tend to do several things at the same time and place higher value on personal involvement than on getting things done on time.

positive organizational behavior (POB)   The study and application of positively oriented human resource strengths and psychological capacities that can be measured, developed, and effectively managed for performance improvement in today's workplace.

positive organizational scholarship (POS)   A method that focuses on positive outcomes, processes, and attributes of organizations and their members.

power distance   The extent to which less powerful members of institutions and organizations accept that power is distributed unequally.

principle of sovereignty   An international principle of law which holds that governments have the right to rule themselves as they see fit.

proactive political strategies   Lobbying, campaign financing, advocacy, and other political interventions designed to shape and influence the political decisions prior to their impact on the firm.

process theories of motivation   Theories that explain work motivation by how employee behavior is initiated, redirected, and halted.

profit   The amount remaining after all expenses are deducted from total revenues.

protective and defensive techniques   Techniques that discourage the host government from interfering in operations.

protective principle   A jurisdictional principle of international law which holds that every country has jurisdiction over behavior that adversely affects its national security, even if the conduct occurred outside that country.

proxemics   The study of the way people use physical space to convey messages.

public distance   In communicating, the distance used when calling across the room or giving a talk to a group.

quality control circle (QCC)   A group of workers who meet on a regular basis to discuss ways of improving the quality of work.

quality imperative   Strategic formulation and implementation utilizing strategies of total quality management to meet or exceed customers' expectations and continuously improve products or services.

regiocentric MNC   An MNC that relies on local managers from a particular geographic region to handle operations in and around that area.

regiocentric predisposition   A philosophy of management whereby the firm tries to blend its own interests with those of its subsidiaries on a regional basis.

regional system   An approach to developing an expatriate compensation package that involves setting a compensation system for all expats who are assigned to a particular region and paying everyone in accord with that system.

repatriation   The return to one's home country from an overseas management assignment.

repatriation agreements   Agreements whereby the firm tells an individual how long she or he will be posted overseas and promises to give the individual, on return, a job that is mutually acceptable.

return on investment (ROI)   Return measured by dividing profit by assets.

ringisei   A Japanese term that means "decision making by consensus."

safety needs   Desires for security, stability, and the absence of pain.

self-actualization needs   Desires to reach one's full potential, to become everything one is capable of becoming as a human being.

simplification   The process of exhibiting the same orientation toward different cultural groups.

social distance   In communicating, the distance used to handle most business transactions.

socialism   A moderate form of collectivism in which there is government ownership of institutions, and profit is not the ultimate goal.

socialist law   Law that comes from the Marxist socialist system and continues to influence regulations in countries formerly associated with the Soviet Union as well as China.

social needs   Desires to interact and affiliate with others and to feel wanted by others.

sociotechnical designs   Job designs that blend personnel and technology.

specialization   An organizational characteristic that assigns individuals to specific, well-defined tasks.

specific culture   A culture in which individuals have a large public space they readily share with others and a small private space they guard closely and share with only close friends and associates.

strategic management   The process of determining an organization's basic mission and long-term objectives, then implementing a plan of action for attaining these goals.

strategy implementation   The process of providing goods and services in accord with a plan of action.

sustainability   Development that meets humanity's needs without harming future generations.

tatemae   A Japanese term that means "doing the right thing" according to the norm.

territoriality principle   A jurisdictional principle of international law which holds that every nation has the right of jurisdiction within its legal territory.

terrorism   The use of force or violence against others to promote political or social views.

Theory X manager   A manager who believes that people are basically lazy and that coercion and threats of punishment often are necessary to get them to work.

Theory Y manager   A manager who believes that under the right conditions people not only will work hard but will seek increased responsibility and challenge.

Theory Z manager   A manager who believes that workers seek opportunities to participate in management and are motivated by teamwork and responsibility sharing.

third-country nationals (TCNs)   Managers who are citizens of countries other than the country in which the MNC is headquartered or the one in which the managers are assigned to work by the MNC.

token group   A group in which all members but one have the same background, such as a group of Japanese retailers and a British attorney.

totalitarianism   A political system in which there is only one representative party which exhibits control over every facet of political and human life.

total quality management (TQM)   An organizational strategy and the accompanying techniques that result in the delivery of high-quality products or services to customers.

training   The process of altering employee behavior and attitudes in a way that increases the probability of goal attainment.

transactional leaders   Individuals who exchange rewards for effort and performance and work on a "something for something" basis.

transfer risks   Government policies that limit the transfer of capital, payments, production, people, and technology in and out of the country.

transformational leaders   Leaders who are visionary agents with a sense of mission and who are capable of motivating their followers to accept new goals and new ways of doing things.

transition strategies   Strategies used to help smooth the adjustment from an overseas to a stateside assignment.

transnational network structure   A multinational structural arrangement that combines elements of function, product, and geographic designs, while relying on a network arrangement to link worldwide subsidiaries.

transnational strategy   Integrated strategy emphasizing both global integration and local responsiveness.

two-factor theory of motivation   A theory that identifies two sets of factors that influence job satisfaction: hygiene factors and motivators.

uncertainty avoidance   The extent to which people feel threatened by ambiguous situations and have created beliefs and institutions that try to avoid these.

universalism   The belief that ideas and practices can be applied everywhere in the world without modification.

upward communication   The transfer of meaning from subordinate to superior.

validity   The quality of being effective, of producing the desired results. A valid test or selection technique measures what it is intended to measure.

values   Basic convictions that people have regarding what is right and wrong, good and bad, important and unimportant.

variety amplification   The creation of uncertainty and the analysis of many alternatives regarding future action.

variety reduction   The limiting of uncertainty and the focusing of action on a limited number of alternatives.

vertical investment   The production of raw materials or intermediate goods that are to be processed into final products.

vertical specialization   The assignment of work to groups or departments where individuals are collectively responsible for performance.

wholly owned subsidiary   An overseas operation that is totally owned and controlled by an MNC.

work centrality   The importance of work in an individual's life relative to other areas of interest.

World Trade Organization (WTO)   The global organization of countries that oversees rules and regulations for international trade and investment.

Name Index

Note: Page numbers followed by "n" indicate materials in source notes and footnotes.

Subject Index

Note: Page numbers followed by "n" indicate materials in source notes and footnotes.